risk reasonable?, consistent with
manager's values?, responsibility to society?,
stimulate entire organization?, see
early success?.

p.140: Conformity of strategy with competitors
doesn't necessarily mean its valid.

p.141. "Luck = opportunity + preparation idea" as applied to
a business -- "preparation" is the strategy

THE COMPANY & ITS ENVIRONMENT - RELATING OPPORTUNITIES TO RESOURCES

p.247 Company's environment: external conditions (technology,
economics, society, political) that influence it.
The environment must be continuously monitored.

p.254 Opportunity identification is not enough - must have
the resources.

p.255 The process of identifying a company's strengths and
weaknesses may be more useful then the product

p.256 A company's distinctive competence is that which
it does very well.

p.257 "Opportunism without competence is a path to
fairyland".

BUSINESS POLICY
Text and cases

BOOK TWO - ~~IMPLEMENTING CORPORATE STRATEGY~~
~~THE ACCOMPLISHMENT OF~~
~~PURPOSE:~~

THE ACCOMPLISHMENT OF PURPOSE: ORGANIZATIONAL
STRUCTURE AND RELATIONSHIPS

p.593   In business, "it is not enough to have an idea
and to be able to evaluate its worth".

p.595   The organization must be structured to
implement the strategy. The purpose of
administration is implementation of corporate
strategy.

p.599   Perhaps "administration" is not enough. Also
need dynamic leadership.

p.599   Have only the minimum amount of structure necessary to
implement the strategy. Permit informal organi-
zation/structure that is consistent with
the corporate strategy.

p.602   Design an information system that provides interpretation, not just facts. And that is oriented to
management by exception.

BUSINESS POLICY

Text and cases

C. ROLAND CHRISTENSEN, D.C.S.
George Fisher Baker, Jr., Professor of
Business Administration

KENNETH R. ANDREWS, PH.D.
Donald Kirk David Professor of
Business Administration

JOSEPH L. BOWER, D.B.A.
Professor of Business Administration

All of the
Graduate School of Business Administration
Harvard University

 Fourth Edition 1978

RICHARD D. IRWIN, INC.   Homewood, Illinois   60430
Irwin-Dorsey Limited   Georgetown, Ontario   L7G 4B3

Fourth Edition

90 K 5 4 3 2 1

Case material of the Harvard Graduate School of
Business Administration is made possible by the
cooperation of business firms who may wish to remain
anonymous by having names, quantities, and other
identifying details disguised while basic relationships
are maintained. Cases are prepared as the basis for
class discussion rather than to illustrate either effective
or ineffective handling of administrative situations.

ISBN 0-256-01989-4
Library of Congress Catalog Card No. 77–79383

Printed in the United States of America

To
Edmund P. Learned
For reasons he knows well

Preface

THIS Fourth Edition of *Business Policy: Text and Cases* provides educational concepts, text, and cases for a course in business policy. Building on previous editions, the authors have incorporated a number of changes in both text and case material; we hope these modifications of our basic format will increase the usefulness of this edition to all.

We are in debt to those individuals—both practicing business people and academic instructors and students who have taken the time and effort to send us suggestions for improvement. Their continuing interest has helped us develop a policy course which can be taught effectively at the undergraduate, graduate, and executive seminar levels.

The basic administrative processes and problems with which business policy is concerned have been part of organizational life for centuries; the history of business policy as an academic field dates back less than seven decades.

This volume builds on substantial contributions made by former policy colleagues; it carries their efforts further along the way to greater understanding and applicability. The specific core idea—the concept of corporate strategy and the organizational plan used in this book—began to be developed in the early 1960s under the leadership of Kenneth R. Andrews, C. Roland Christensen, and Professor Emeritus Edmund P. Learned. Maintaining traditional course interests in a generalist-senior management orientation and in the administrative and organizational problem of the enterprise as a totality, the course concentrates on the determination of corporate strategy (Book One) and the implementation of strategy (Book Two).

Despite its incompleteness, the concept of corporate strategy provides both academic and practical usefulness. As coauthor Andrews has stated:

> This concept is far from complete. But its early development shows this framework allows all other fields to be brought to bear upon the

highest function of the general manager—supervision of the continuous process of determining the nature of the enterprise and setting, revising, and attempting to achieve its goals. So far the development of organizational behavior fits well into the framework of implementation. The sophisticated developments in quantitative analysis are not yet readily available to policy problems, but if all goes well, this will come.

The idea of corporate strategy constitutes a simple practitioner's theory, a kind of Everyman's conceptual scheme. It is nonetheless capable of including the most extensive combination of interrelated variables involved in the most important of all business decisions. It is a definition of the manager's central function, whether he is a staff specialist contributing in depth and detail to the identification of alternatives and to the predicted return on investment for each of these alternatives, or the senior executive who must finally make or complete the decision.[1]

In summarizing the relationship of strategy to the education of general managers, coauthor Christensen has noted:

> The uniqueness of a good general manager lies in his ability to lead effectively organizations whose complexities he can never fully understand, where his capacity to control directly the human and physical forces comprising that organization are severely limited, and where he must make or review and assume ultimate responsibility for present decisions which commit concretely major resources for a fluid and unknown future.
>
> These circumstances—lack of knowledge, lack of an ability to control directly, and a mixture of past, present, and *future* time dimensions in every decision—make the concept of strategy so important for the generalist, senior manager. For strategy gives the manager reasonably clear indications of what he should try to know and understand in order to direct his organization's efforts. It counsels him on what to decide, what to review, and what to ignore. It gives him guidelines as to what critical, central activities and processes to attempt to influence— or in rare occasions—to attempt to control. It encourages him to view every event and question from multiple time dimensions.
>
> Chester Barnard said that the highest managerial traits are essentially intuitive "being so complex and so rapid, often approaching the instantaneous, that they could not be analyzed by the person within whose brain they take place." If Barnard is correct, and I think that he is, how do those of us interested in management education strive to contribute to the development of future general managers? We do this first by disciplined classroom drill with the concept of strategy. Drill in the formal and analytic—what is the current strategy of the firm? What are its strengths and weaknesses? Where, in the firm's perceived industry, are profit and service opportunities? And, how can those corporate capacities and industry opportunities be effectively related? This framework of questions helps to give order to the familiar chaos of complex organizations. It provides the manager with a map relating past, present and future, industry and company, and specific decisions to wider corporate strategy.

---

[1] Kenneth R. Andrews, "The Progress of Professional Education," in Olga Craven, Alden L. Todd, Jesse H. Ziegler, eds. *Theological Education as Professional Education* (Dayton, Ohio: The Association of Theological Schools, 1969).

Moreover, this analytic classroom process focuses attention on a key administration skill—the process of selecting and ordering data so that management asks the critical questions appropriate to a particular situation. Here the choice of abstraction level is key, for the question has to be stated in a way that avoids the "specific that has no meaning and the general that has no content."

We seek also, via the classroom group discussion process, to educate in the nonlogical—that mixture of feelings and sentiment, comment and commitment, certainty and uncertainty—which goes into every decision and judgment. Such directed group discussions force attention to the human dimensions through which the analytic framework is filtered in real life. It serves further to emphasize the ongoing or process nature of the general manager's world.

It is a combination of these two forces: the analytic framework of strategic planning and the process framework emphasizing human interaction, the complexities of persons, and the difficulty of communication and persuasion that make up our business policy educational fare. It is the discipline of practicing these two processes via a case discussion countless times, that helps us to contribute to education for the future generalist.[2]

The business policy subject area continues to evolve and develop. The need for professionally trained generalists—the men who make our organized society's critical decisions—is great; our present efforts are limited. Sir Eric Ashby has put the challenge well:

But the world needs generalists as well as specialists. Indeed you have only to read your newspaper to know that the big decisions on which the fate of nations depends are in the hands of generalists. I do not think that universities, American or British, are satisfied with the education they give to the man who is to become a generalist. Some believe he should have a rigorously specialist training in some field which he then abandons for life. Others believe he should have a synoptic acquaintance with the ways of thinking of humanists, social scientists, and natural scientists. And I suppose there are still a few antique persons who cling to the view that generalists need no higher education at all. We can with some confidence prescribe the minutiae of curriculum for doctors, physicists, and lawyers. The unpalatable fact is that we have no such confidence in prescribing curricula for men who will become presidents of industries, newspaper editors, senior civil servants, or Congressmen.[3]

We believe that the challenge will be met, at least in part, by all of us who work in the policy area, both in academic and practical pursuits, throughout this country and the world. And we hope this book will be of some help in meeting that challenge.

December 1977   C. Roland Christensen
                                  Kenneth R. Andrews
                                  Joseph L. Bower

---

[2] C. Roland Christensen, "Education for the General Manager," unpublished Working Paper, Harvard Business School.

[3] Sir Eric Ashby, Master, Clare College, Cambridge, "Centennial Convocation Address," delivered at the 100th anniversary of the granting of the charter to Cornell University, October 9, 1964.

Acknowledgments

THE HISTORY of the Business Policy course at the Harvard Business School began in 1911, when a small group of instructors first developed a course outline and materials for a pioneering venture in education for senior management. Those of us who currently teach and do research in the business policy area are in debt to those pioneers who provided the academic platform on which current efforts rest. We wish to especially recognize and thank the past efforts of A. W. Shaw, the first policy professor at the Harvard Business School and M. T. Copeland, George Albert Smith, Jr., and Edmund P. Learned who provided almost 40 years of dedicated leadership to course ideals and development. We are in their debt, as we are to those colleagues who worked under their leadership and who assisted in past course development.

Many members of the Harvard Business School faculty have contributed to the constant developments of our field. We appreciate the help of the present members of the business policy teaching group: Francis J. Aguilar, Norman A. Berg, Richard Hamermesh, Patrick Liles, Michael Lovdal, Hassell McClellan, John B. Matthews, Michael Porter, and Michael Yoshino, and we also appreciate the contributions of our associates Raymond Bauer, John W. Rosenbloom, Malcolm S. Salter, Bruce R. Scott, Audrey T. Sproat, Dan R. Thomas, Hugo E. Uyterhoeven, and Abraham Zaleznik.

Our sincere appreciation goes to the supervisors and authors of the cases included in this edition. To the following our thanks: Robert W. Ackerman for the Xerox Corporation case; Alexander Bergmann for Air, Inc.; Robert F. Bruner for The Real Paper; Ram Charan for his case, Hawaii Best Company; Paul Cook who wrote Strategy Revisited or Strategy with a Grain of Salt; Jeanne Deschamps Stanton for Textile Corporation of America; Linda Elmer for Charles River Breeding Laboratories; John J. Gabarro for the Robert F. Kennedy High School case; James Garrison who wrote Crown Cork and Seal and the Note on the Metal Container Industry; Richard Hamermesh for Federated Department Stores; Christine Harris for Marks & Spencer; Michael Hunt (assisted by John McMullen) for the Note on the Major Home Appliance Industry, Sears, Roebuck and Company: Appliances, Design and Manufacturing Corporation, and the Tappan case.

We are also indebted to Edmund P. Learned for his development of The Rose Company case; Molly Lovelock for the Fernald Workshops; Hassell H. McClellan for Air Products and Chemicals, Inc.; John Priedeman (assisted by Robert C. K. Voltz) for the Rugby Portland Cement Company (A) and (B) series; Elisabeth Lyman Rachel for the Note on the Mechanical Writing Instrument Industry, Bic Corporation, and Scripto, Inc.; John W. Rosenblum for Basic Industries and Industrial Products, Inc.; Bruce R. Scott for American Motors; Howard H. Stevenson for the Head Ski Company, Inc., case and Blow Mold Packers, Inc.; C. L. Suzman for The Polaroid Experiment in South Africa; H. Edward Wrapp (assisted by L. A. Guthart) for Texas Instruments; and finally Abraham Zaleznik (assisted by John M. Wynne) for The Saturday Evening Post case.

We continue to be indebted to Kenneth R. Andrews for all of the text material found in this book. His capacity to articulate course concepts and principles for a practitioner is demonstrated not only in this book but in his pioneering volume, *The Concept of Corporate Strategy*.[1]

We owe special thanks to M. Liotard-Vogt, Chairman of Nestlé Alimentana, and Chairman of the Board of Trustees of IMEDE and to M. Jacques Paternot, General Manager of Marketing of Nestlé Alimentana, member of the Harvard Business School Visiting Committee and a member of the Board of Trustees of IMEDE and finally to Dean Luigi Dusmet, Director of IMEDE, for his willingness to let us include IMEDE cases in this edition. IMEDE remains the leader in business education for international and European firms.

Edmund P. Learned, a "great" in the development of the business policy field of study, continues to enjoy a well-deserved retirement. We again dedicate this book to him. All who have been touched by his teaching and research efforts realize his major contributions to private and public administration. He was our teacher, counseler, and friend.

Former Dean Donald K. David, the late Dean Stanley F. Teele, and Dean George P. Baker provided the steady encouragement and support which was so essential for the development of the policy area. Dean Lawrence E. Fouraker and Associate Dean Walter Salmon encouraged us in the development of this revised edition; we appreciate their interest and assistance.

Juliet Muenchen took the management task of producing this Fourth Edition of *Business Policy: Text and Cases* and carried out this assignment with efficiency and good humor. We owe her special thanks.

Richard Rosenbloom, Associate Dean for Research and Course Development and Charles N. Gebhard, Director of Case Development

[1] Kenneth R. Andrews, *The Concept of Corporate Strategy*, (Homewood, Ill.: Dow Jones-Irwin, Inc., 1971).

and Distribution and Director of the Intercollegiate Case Clearing House have been helpful in administrative matters.

We hope this book, in which the efforts of so many good people is compressed, will contribute to constructive concern for corporate purposes and accomplishments and to the continuing and effective study and practice of business policy, in private and semiprivate and public organizations.

C. R. C.
K. R. A.
J. L. B.

Contents

INTRODUCTION

Business Policy as a field of study: *The presidential point of view. Relevance of Policy to all organization members.* Objectives in knowledge: *Knowledge of concepts. Knowledge of situations. The literature of Policy.* Objectives in attitudes: *The generalist orientation. The practitioner orientation. The professional. The innovator.* Objectives in skills: *Analytical ability. Strategic analysis. Making analysis effective. General management skills. Universal need for Policy skills.* The nature of the text and cases.

What general management is. Roles of the president. Complexity of general management tasks. The president as organization leader. The president as personal leader. The president as architect of organization purpose. Enormity of the task. Need for a concept.

CASES

BOOK ONE (Determining Corporate Strategy)

What strategy is. Summary statements of strategy. Reasons for not articulating strategy. Deducing strategy from behavior. Formulation of strategy. The implementation of strategy. Kinds of strategies. Kinds of companies. Criteria for evaluation. Problems in evaluation. Application to cases.

CASES

X **The company and its environment: Relating opportunities to resources**   247

The nature of the company's environment. Tracking the changing environment. Identification of opportunities and risks. Opportunity as a determinant of strategy. Identifying corporate competence and resources. Application to cases.

The company and its strategists: Relating corporate strategy to personal values   448

Strategy as projection of preference. The inevitability of values. Reconciling divergent values. Modification of values. Awareness of values.

The company and its responsibilities to society: Relating corporate strategy to ethical values   524

The moral component of corporate strategy. Categories of concern: *Review of management concerns for responsibility. Impact of control systems on ethical performance. The individual and the corporation. The range of concerns.* Choice of strategic alternatives for social action. Determination of strategy.

BOOK TWO (Implementing Corporate Strategy)

X **The accomplishment of purpose: Organizational structure and relationships**   593

Interdependence of formulation and implementation. Strategy and organizational structure. Subdivision of task responsibility. Coordination of dividend responsibility. Effective design of information systems.

The accomplishment of purpose: Organizational processes and behavior   661

Establishment of standards and measurement of performance: *Fallacy of the single criterion. Need for multiple criteria. Effective evaluation of performance.* Motivation and incentive systems: *Executive compensation. Role of incentive pay. Nonmonetary incentives.* Systems of restraint and control: *Formal control. Integrating formal social control. Enforcing ethical standards.* Recruitment and development of management: *Advanced recruitment. Continuing education. Management development and corporate purpose.*

Managing the strategic process   758

Strategy as a process. Managing the process.

Index of Cases   845

Introduction

Introduction

BUSINESS POLICY AS A FIELD OF STUDY

THIS BOOK is an instrument for the study of Business Policy. As a field in business administration, Policy is *the study of the functions and responsibilities of senior management,* the *crucial problems* that affect success in the total enterprise, and *the decisions* that determine the direction of the organization and shape its future. The problems of policy in business, like those of policy in public affairs, have to do with the choice of purposes, the molding of organizational identity and character, the continuous definition of what needs to be done, and the mobilization of resources for the attainment of goals in the face of competition or adverse circumstance.

The presidential point of view

In Business Policy, the problems considered and the point of view assumed in analyzing and dealing with them are those of the chief executive or general manager, whose primary responsibility is the enterprise as a whole. But while the study of Business Policy (under whatever name it may be called) is considered the capstone of professional business education, its usefulness goes far beyond the direct preparation of future general managers and chief executives for the responsibilities of office. In an age of increasing complexity and advancing specialization, and in companies where no person knows how to do what every other person does, it becomes important that the functional specialists—controller, computer scientist, financial analyst, market researcher, purchasing agent—acquire a unique nontechnical capacity. This essential qualification is the ability to recognize corporate purpose, to recommend its clarification, development, or change and to shape their own contributions, not by the canons of specializations, but by their perception of what a cost-effective purposeful organization re-

3

quires of them. The special needs of individuals and the technical requirements of specialized groups and disciplines inevitably exhibit expensive points of view that ultimately come into conflict with one another and with the central purposes of the organization they serve. The specialists who are able to exercise control over this tendency in organizations and to keep their loyalty to the conventions of their own specialty subordinate to the needs of their company become free to make creative contributions to its progress and growth. To be thus effective in their organization, they must have a sense of its mission, of its character, and of its importance. If they do not know the purposes they serve, they can hardly serve them well. Most users of this book will neither be nor become corporate chief executive officers. But virtually all can benefit from the detachment implicit in the impartial, functionally unbiased, results-oriented attitude we will call the presidential point of view.

Relevance of Policy to all organization members

The purposes of organized effort in business as elsewhere are usually somewhat unclear, apparently contradictory, and constantly changing. Except in abstract language they cannot be communicated once and for all to the variety of persons whose effort and commitment are demanded. It is not enough, therefore, for senior executives to issue statements of policy and for junior managers to salute and go about their business. In each subunit of an organization and in each individual, corporate purpose must become meaningful in ways that announcement cannot accomplish. It must be brought into balance with individual and departmental needs, satisfactions, and noneconomic aspirations. But if corporate purpose is to be reconciled with (rather than subordinated to) individual and departmental purposes, then there must be widespread knowledge of the considerations on which corporate policy is based and understanding of the risks by which it is threatened. In addition, the adaptation of corporate purpose to changing circumstances, to tactical countermoves by competitors, or to newly identified opportunities, is assisted if there can be *informed* participation in policy thinking by subordinate managers from different ranks and groups. This advantage, however, can be realized only if these subordinates are capable of looking beyond the narrow limits of their own professionalization. Thus the study of Policy is not as remote from the immediate concern of apprentice managers or students of business as it first appears. In fact whenever people are challenged—in business or out—by the problem of establishing goals for *themselves* that will shape productive and satisfying lives, they will find the study of the process of determining institutional purpose of central relevance. It is helpful to personal as well as to corporate decision. It permits discovery of the individual's own powers and the purposes to which they might well be devoted.

The study of Business Policy provides therefore a direct if distant preparation for performance as a general manager and a less direct but more immediate broadening of the perspective of the technician. In addition, it may be viewed as resulting in certain *knowledge, attitudes,* and *skills*. Some of these are unique to Policy studies. Others may have germinated in other activities in learning. But the latter are brought to fruition by examination of the most fundamental issues and problems that confront the professional manager in the course of a business career. It may prove useful to characterize briefly the expected outcomes.

OBJECTIVES IN KNOWLEDGE

The choice of objectives and the *formulation* of policy to guide action in the *attainment* of objectives depend upon many variables unique to a given organization and situation. It is not possible to make useful generalizations about the nature of these variables or to classify their possible combinations in all situations. Knowledge of what, *in general*, Policy is and should be is incomplete and inconclusive. The knowledge to be gained from Policy studies is therefore primarily a familiarity with an approach to the policy problems of business and public affairs which makes it possible, in conjunction with attitudes and skills to be discussed later, to combine these variables into a pattern *valid for one organization*. This pattern may then be examined against accepted criteria and tested for its quality. Policy must first be a study of situations.

Knowledge of concepts

The basic concept that students of Policy will in time come to understand is the concept of *strategy*, since the design and implementation of strategy provide the intellectual substance of this study. What is meant by *strategy* and, more important, how this concept may be usefully employed in the choice and accomplishment of purpose is the subject of the rest of this book. Strategy will be the idea unifying the discussions in which students will engage. These discussions will involve cerebral activities more important than simply acquiring information.

Knowledge of situations

An abundance of information about business practice is, nonetheless, a by-product of the study of Business Policy and other cases. In their deliberately planned variety, the cases in this book encompass many industries, companies, and business situations. Although the information contained in these cases is provided mainly to permit consideration of policy issues, the importance of this incidental knowledge should not be underestimated. Breadth of exposure to the conventions, points of view, and practices of many industries is inoculation against the assumption that all industries are basically the same or that all men and women in business share the same values and beliefs. Thus consideration of the policy problems of a number of different industries guards against distraction by the particular in seeking out the nature of the universal.

For this reason it is hoped that students—although they may be, or plan to be, engineers in a utility or vice presidents of a railroad—will not resent learning about the economics of the cement industry of England or the racial problems of South Africa. Knowledge of the environment and problems of other industries and companies is something that students may never consciously use. It will nevertheless widen the perspective which they bring to their own problems. It may stimulate the imagination they put to work in introducing innovation into the obsolescent practices of their own industry. It should provide a broader base for their powers of generalization.

The study of strategy as a concept will be relatively systematic. The acquisition of information about the management problems of the many firms and industries whose strategic problems are presented in this book will be less orderly. Both are important. In particular the time spent in mastering the detail of the cases will ultimately seem to be of greater value than at first appears. Graduates of a demanding Policy course feel at home in any management situation and know at once how to begin to understand it.

The literature of Policy

A considerable body of literature purporting to make general statements about policy making is in existence. It generally reflects either the unsystematically reported evidence of individuals or the logical projection to general management of concepts taken from engineering, economics, psychology, sociology, or mathematics. Neither suffices. What people wise in practice have to say is often instructive, but intuitive skill cannot be changed into conscious skill by exposition alone. The disciplines cited have much to do with business, but their purposes are not ours. Knowledge generated for one set of ends is not readily applicable to another. Besides reported experience and borrowed concepts, the literature of the field also includes the first fruits of independent research in Business Policy, guided by designs derived from the idea of strategy. Such research has been for sometime under way and begins to make a claim on our attention. We shall often allude to the expository literature of Business Policy. The most useful literature for our purposes, however, is not that of general statements, but case studies.[1] These present, not illustrations of principle, but data from which generalizations may to a limited degree be derived and to which the idea of strategy may be usefully applied. The footnotes of the text portions of this book constitute a useful bibliography for further reading. It comprises a relevant but incidental source of knowledge. You will get to know it in order to learn not information or theory but skills in using both.

OBJECTIVES IN ATTITUDES

Knowledge of either concepts or cases is less the objective of the study of Policy than certain attitudes and skills. What managers know by way

---

[1] In addition to the cases in this book, the reader is referred to such volumes as: C. Roland Christensen, Norman A. Berg, and Malcolm S. Salter, *Policy Formulation and Administration*, 7th ed. (Homewood, Ill.: Richard D. Irwin, Inc., 1976); and H. E. R. Uyterhoeven, R. W. Ackerman, and J. W. Rosenblum, *Strategy and Organization: Text and Cases in General Management*, rev. ed. (Homewood, Ill.: Richard D. Irwin, Inc., 1977). Many other cases from a variety of sources are listed in the bibliographies of the Intercollegiate Case Clearing House, Soldiers Field, Boston, Mass. 02163.

of verifiable fact about management appears to us less important than the attitudes, aspirations, and values they bring to their tasks. Instructors in Policy do not have a dogma which they force upon their students, but most of them, like their students, appear to be influenced in their analysis and conclusions by characteristic assumptions. Thus indoctrination is implicit in the study of ideas and cases included in this book. This indoctrination—tempered by the authors' exhortation to students to think for themselves—is comprised of some important beliefs of which you should be aware.

The generalist orientation

The attitudes appropriate to the resolution of policy problems are several. First, the frame of mind which you will be encouraged to adopt and which will influence the outcome of your thinking is that of the *generalist* rather than the specialist. Breadth, it follows, takes precedence over depth. Since attitudes appropriate for the generalist are not always appropriate for the specialist, the two will sometimes come into conflict. Efforts to resolve this conflict in practice should help to prove that breadth which is shallow is no more satisfactory than depth which is narrow.

The practitioner orientation

A second outlook encountered in the study of Business Policy is the point of view of the *practitioner* as opposed to that of the researcher or scientist. A willingness to act in the face of incomplete information and to run the risk of being proved wrong by subsequent events will be developed in the classroom as pressure is brought to bear on students to make decisions on the problems before them and to determine what they, as the managers responsible, would do about them. Despite the explosion of knowledge and the advance of electronic data processing, it is still true that decisions affecting the business firm as a whole must almost always be made in the face of incomplete information. Uncertainty is the lot of all thoughtful leaders who must act, whether they are in government, education, or business. Acceptance of the priority of risk-taking and problem-resolution over completeness of information is sometimes hard for students of science and engineering to achieve. Though natural and understandable, hesitation in the face of managerial imperative to make decisions will impede the study of Policy. At the same time, rashness, overconfidence, and the impulse to act without analysis will be discouraged.

The professional

The third set of attitudes to be developed is the orientation of the professional manager as distinct from the self-seeking contriver of deals and of the honest person rather than the artist in deception. The energetic opportunist sometimes has motives inconsistent with the approach to policy embodied in this book. This is not to say that quick response to opportunity and entrepreneurial energy are not qualities to be admired. Our assumption will be that the role of the business manager *includes but goes beyond* the entrepreneurial function. We shall examine what we acknowledge to be the obligations of the business community to the rest of society. We shall be concerned with the *quality* as well as the *clarity* of the alternative purposes we consider and of our final choice. Maximum short-run profit is not what we mean when we consider the purpose of business enterprise. At the same time it is assumed that profit is desirable and indispensable. It is one of the necessary *results* of business activity.

The innovator

A fourth set of attitudes to be evoked is one that attaches more value to creativity and innovation than to maintenance of the status quo. We have grown accustomed to innovation stemming from new inventions and advancing technology. But suiting policy to changing circumstances includes also the application of a firm's long-established strengths to unexplored segments of the market via innovations in price, service, distribution, or merchandising.

In any course of study that has as its object enabling practitioners to learn more from subsequent experience than they otherwise might, the attitudes appropriate to the professional activity being taught are as important as knowledge. It is therefore expected that students will take time to determine for themselves the particular point of view, the values, and the morality they feel are appropriate to the effective exercise of general management skills. Much more could be said about the frame of mind and qualities of temperament that are most appropriate to business leadership, but we will expect these to exhibit themselves in the discussion of case problems.

OBJECTIVES IN SKILLS

Extensive knowledge and positive attitudes, desirable as both are, come to nothing if not applied. The skills that a course in Business Policy seeks to develop and mature are at once analytical and administrative. Since even with a variety of stimulation and the use of case situations drawn from life, the reality of responsibility can only be approximated in a professional school, we may look to make most progress now in analytical power and to use it later in actual experience to develop executive ability.

Analytical ability

The study of Policy cases, unlike, for example, the effort to comprehend these expository notes, requires the students to develop and broaden the analytical ability brought to the task from other studies. The policy problems of the total enterprise are not labeled as accounting, finance, marketing, production, or human problems. Students are not forewarned of the kind of problem they can expect and of which tool kit they should have with them. They must now consider problems in relation to one another, distinguish the more from the less important, and consider the impact of their approach to one problem upon all the others.

They will bring to the cases their knowledge and abilities in special fields but they will be asked to diagnose first the total situation and to persist in seeking out central problems through all the distraction presented by manifest symptoms.

The study of Policy, besides having its own jurisdiction, has an integrative function. It asks the analyst to view a company as an organic entity comprising a system in itself, but one related also to the larger systems of its environment. In each diagnostic situation, you are asked to pull together the separate concepts learned in functional and basic discipline courses and adapt them to a less structured set of problems. The strategic analyst must be able to see and to devise patterns of information, activities, and relationships. The facts given or the problems observed, if dealt with one at a time, are soon overwhelming.

Strategic analysis

Besides extending to the company as a multifaceted whole the knowledge and analytic skills developed in less comprehensive studies, students of Policy must acquire some additional abilities. These are particularly needed to deal with the concept of strategy. Under the heading of thinking about strategy, you will be asked to examine the economic environment of the company, to determine the essential characteristics of the industry, to note its development and trends, and to estimate future opportunity and risks for firms of varying resources and competence. You will appraise the strengths and weaknesses of the particular firm you are studying when viewed against the background of its competition and its environment. You will be asked to estimate its capacity to *alter* as well as to *adapt* to the forces affecting it. Finally you will be expected to make a decision putting market opportunity and corporate capability together into a suitable entrepreneurial combination.

At this point you will realize the full measure of the new skill required. The strategic decision is the one that helps determine the nature of the business in which a company is to engage and the kind of company it is to be. It is effective for a long time. It has wide ramifications. It is the most important kind of decision to be made for the company. It requires the best judgment and analysis that can be brought to it. Practice in making this decision while still safe from most of the consequences of error is one of the most important advantages offered by an education for business.

Making analysis effective

But the analysis is not the whole of the task implied by the concept of strategy. Once the entrepreneurial decision has been determined, the resources of the organization must be mobilized to make it effective. Devising organizational relationships appropriate to the tasks to be performed, determining the specialized talents required, and assisting and providing for the development of individuals and subgroups are essential tasks of strategy and policy implementation. These tasks, together with prescribing a system of incentives and controls appropriate to the performance required, and determining the impetus that can be given to achievement by the general manager's personal style of leadership, demand that you bring to the discussion of Policy everything previously learned about administrative processes.

Administrative skills can be approached, though not captured, in the classroom. Patterns of action will be judged as consistent or inconsistent with the strategy selected according to criteria which must be developed. Students approach the study of Business Policy with skills nurtured in studies like accounting and control, personnel and human relations, financial management, manufacturing, and marketing. The balanced application of these skills to the accomplishment of chosen purpose in a unique organizational situation is the best test of their power. Any failure to see the impact on the program as a whole of a decision based on the tenets of a special discipline will be sharply called to its proponent's attention by the defenders of other points of view.

General management skills

General management skills center intellectually upon relating the firm to its environment and administratively upon coordinating departmental specialties and points of view. Some students of business and even some students of Policy believe that these skills cannot be taught. General management is indeed an art to be learned only through years of responsible experience. And even through experience it can be learned only by those with the necessary native qualities: intelligence, a sense of responsibility, and administrative ability.

But if education means anything at all, students with the requisite native qualities can learn more readily and more certainly from experience and can more readily identify the kinds of experience to seek if they have at their disposal a conceptual framework with which to comprehend the analytical and administrative skills they will require and the nature of the situations in which they will find themselves. If, in addition, they have had practice in making and debating the merits of policy decisions, they will be more likely to grow in qualification for senior management responsibility than if they are submerged in operational detail and preoccupied by intricacies of technique.

This book is not a manual for policy makers or a how-to-do-it checklist for corporate planners. In fact it virtually ignores the mechanisms of planning on the grounds that, detached from strategy, they miss their mark. The authors do not believe that the conceptual framework described here can take the place of informed judgment. All the knowledge, professional attitudes, and analytical and administrative skills in the world cannot fully replace the intuitive genius of some of the natural entrepreneurs you will encounter in this book. Native powers cannot be counterfeited by reading textbooks.

We do not propose the acquisition of knowledge in the usual sense. We plan instead to give men and women with latent imagination the opportunity to exercise it in a disciplined way under critical observation. We expect to prepare people for the assumption of responsibility by exposing them, for example, to the temptation of expediency. We plan to press for clarification of personal purposes and to challenge shoddy or ill-considered values. We expect to affect permanently analytical habits of mind in a way that will permit assimilation of all, rather than part, of experience. The ideas, attitudes, and skills here discussed are adequate for a lifetime of study of one of the most vitally important of all human activities—leadership in organizations. Education is the prelude to true learning, which often does not take place without it.

Universal need for Policy skills

The need for general management ability is far too acute to be left to chance. The ideas, attitudes, and skills that comprise this study are much in demand not only throughout our own economy but also—in this age of rapid economic development abroad—throughout the world. In addition to their utility, these ideas are their own reward. For those who wish to lead an active life, or to provide for themselves and their families the material comfort and education that make culture possible, or to make substantial contributions to human welfare, the acquisition of policy skills is essential. Not all who turn to business are called to leadership, to be sure, but all are affected by it. No one suffers from study of its place in business.

THE NATURE OF THE TEXT AND CASES

The vehicles here provided for making progress toward these objectives are the text and cases that follow. All the cases are drawn from real life; none is selected to prove a point or draw a moral. Accuracy has been attested to by the sources from which information was taken; disguise has not been allowed to alter essential issues.

The text is designed to assist in the development of an effective approach to the cases. Its content is important only if it helps students make their analyses, choose and defend their conclusions, and decide what ought to be done and how it can be accomplished.

The text is dispersed throughout the book so as to permit a step-by-step consideration of what is involved in corporate strategy and in the subactivities required for its formulation and implementation. The order of cases is only partially determined by the sequence of ideas in the text. Each case should be approached without preconceptions as to what is to come. To make conceptual progress without predetermining the students' analysis of the problem or the nature of their recommendations, the cases focus initially on problems in strategy formulation and later on problems of building the organization and leading it to the accomplishment of the tasks assigned. As the course unfolds, considerations pertinent to previous cases are included in new cases. Students should not feel constrained in their analysis by the position of the case in the book; they are free to decide that an apparent problem of strategy implementation is actually a problem of strategy choice. However, the increasing complexity of the material provided will enable most students to feel a natural and organic evolution of subject matter, in keeping with their own evolving understanding, perspective, and skill.

The text suggests only that order is possible in approaching the enormous purview of Policy. The concept of strategy is an idea that experience has shown to be useful to researchers and practitioners alike in developing a comprehension of, and an approach to, policy problems. It is not a "theory" attended in the traditional sense by elegance and rigor. It is not really a "model," for the relationships designated by the concept are not quantifiable. But in lieu of a better theory or a more precise model, it will serve as an informing idea to which we can return again and again with increasing understanding after dealing with one unique case situation after another. The idea is intended to sharpen the analytical skills developed in the process of case discussion, and to serve as the basis for identifying uniformities and generalizations that will be useful later on, in practice. Our energies should be spent not so much on perfecting the definition of the concept as on using it in preparing to discuss the cases and in coming to conclusions about their issues. Students will not really learn how to distinguish effective from ineffective recommendations and good from bad judgment by study of these words or any others, but rather by active argument with their classmates. Such discussion should always end in the clarification of their own standards and criteria. The cases, we know from experience, provide stimulating opportunity for productive differences of opinion.

The chief executive's job: Roles and responsibilities

WHAT GENERAL MANAGEMENT IS

WE POINTED OUT in the introduction to this book that Business Policy is essentially the study of the knowledge, skills, and attitudes constituting general management. *Management* we regard as leadership in the informed, planned, purposeful conduct of complex organized activity. *General* management is in its simplest form the management of a total enterprise. Before we examine some cases presenting the range of decision issues we will consider more thoroughly later on, we should look at the position of the general manager. The senior general manager in any organization is its chief executive officer, who for the purposes of simplicity we will often call the *president*. As we said earlier, the role of the chief executive in examining the situation of a company may be initially an uncomfortable assignment for students of some modesty who think themselves insufficiently prepared for such high responsibility. It is nonetheless the best vantage point from which to view the processes involved in (1) the conception of organization purpose, (2) the decision to commit an organization to deliberately chosen purposes, and (3) the effort required to achieve purposes decided upon.

ROLES OF THE PRESIDENT

We will therefore begin by considering the *roles* which presidents must play. We will examine the *functions* or characteristic and natural actions, which they perform in the roles they assume. We will try to identify *skills* or abilities to put one's perceptions, judgment, and knowledge to effective use in executive performance. As we look at presidential *roles, functions,* and *skills,* we may be able to define more clearly aspects of the *point of view* which provides the most suitable perspective for high-level executive judgment.

13

Many attempts to characterize executive roles and functions come to very little. Henri Fayol, originator of the classical school of management theory, identified the roles of planner, organizer, coordinator, and controller, initiating the construction by others of a later vocabulary of remarkable variety. Present-day students reject these categories as vague or abstract and indicative only of the objectives of some executive activity. Henry Mintzberg, who among other researchers has observed managers at work, identifies three sets of behavior—interpersonal, informational, and decisional. The interpersonal roles he designates as *figurehead* (for ceremonial duties), *leader* (of the work of his organization or unit), and *liaison* agent (for contacts outside his unit). Information roles can be designated as *monitor* (of information), *disseminator* (internally), and *spokesman* (externally). Decisional roles are called *entrepreneur, disturbance handler, resource allocator,* and *negotiator.*[1]

Empirical studies of what managers do are corrective of theory but not necessarily instructive in educating good managers. That most unprepared managers act intuitively rather than systematically in response to unanticipated pressures does not mean that the most effective do so to the same extent. If in fact the harried, improvisatory, overworked performers of ten roles do not really know *what* they are doing or have any priorities besides degree of urgency, then we are not likely to find out what more effective management is from categorizing their activities. On the other hand it is futile to offer unrealistic exhortations about long-range planning and organizing to real-life victims of forced expediency.

The simplification which will serve our approach to policy best will leave aside important but easily understood activities. The executive may make speeches, pick the silver pattern for the executive lunchroom, negotiate personally with important customers, and do many things human beings have to do for many reasons. Roles we may study in order to do a better job of general management can be viewed as those of *organization leader, personal leader,* and *chief architect of organization purpose.* As leader of persons grouped in a hierarchy of suborganizations, the president must be taskmaster, mediator, motivator, and organization designer. Since these roles do not have useful job descriptions saying what to do, one might better estimate the nature of the overlapping responsibility of the head of an organization than to draw theoretical distinctions between categories. The personal influence of leaders becomes evident as they play the roles of communicator, exemplar, or focus for respect or affection. When we examine finally the president's role as architect of organization purpose, we may see entrepreneurial or improvisatory behavior if the organization is just being born. If the company is long since established, the part played may be more accurately designated as manager of the purpose-determining process or chief strategist.

---

[1] See Henry Mintzberg, "The Manager's Job: Folklore and Fact," *Harvard Business Review,* July–August 1975, pp. 49–61; and for more detail *The Nature of Managerial Work* (New York: Harper and Row, Publishers, 1973).

COMPLEXITY OF GENERAL MANAGEMENT TASKS

The point of this nontechnical classification of role is not its universality, exactness of definition, or inclusiveness. We seek only to establish that general managers face such an array of functions and must exercise so various a set of skills as to require a protean versatility as performing executives. When you see Howard Head invent and perfect the metal ski, set up his company, devise a merchandising and distribution program of a very special kind, you see him in a role different from his arranging for the future of his business, his maintaining year-round production in a cyclical industry in order to meet the needs of his work force, his withdrawal from supervision of the company, and his selection of a successor. We make no claim to definitiveness in distinguishing executive roles as just attempted. It is essential to note, however, that the job of the general manager demands successful action in a *variety* of roles, which differ according to the nature of the problem observed or decision pending, the needs of the organization, or the personality and style of the president. The simpleminded adherence to one role— one personality-determined, for example—will leave presidents miscast much of the time as the human drama they preside over unfolds.

We are in great need of a simple way to comprehend the total responsibility of chief executives. To multiply the list of tasks they must perform and the personal qualities they would do well to have would put general management capability beyond that of reasonably well-endowed human beings. Corporate presidents are accountable for everything that goes on in their organizations. They must preside over a total enterprise made up often of the technical specialties in which they cannot possibly have personal expertness. They must know their company's markets and the ways in which they are changing. They must lead private lives as citizens in their communities and as family members, as individuals with their own needs and aspirations. Except for rare earlier experience, perhaps as general managers of a profit center in their own organizations, they have found no opportunity to practice being president before undertaking the office. Only the brief study of Policy for which this book is intended to be the basis, has been available as the academic preparation for general management. New presidents are obliged to put behind them the specialized apparatus their education and functional experience have provided them. Engineers, for example, who continue to run their companies strictly as engineers will soon encounter financial and marketing problems, among others, that may force their removal.

This book, together with the directed series of case discussions which will bring its substance alive, is intended to provide a way for the observer to comprehend the complexity of the president's job and for the president to put past experience in a new perspective and comprehend the world of which he or she has been put in charge. We will elaborate briefly the functions, skills, and points of view which give force and substance to the major roles we have just designated. This may lay a foundation for later discussion of the performance of presidents in the cases that follow. In due course we will have an organizing perspective to reduce to practicable order the otherwise impossible agenda of the president.

THE PRESIDENT AS ORGANIZATION LEADER

Chief executives are first and probably least pleasantly persons who are responsible for results attained in the present as designated by plans made previously. Nothing that we will say shortly about their concern for the people in their organizations or later about their responsibility to society can gainsay this immediate truth. Achieving acceptable results against expectations of increased earnings per share and return on the stockholder's investment requires the president to be continually informed and ready to intervene when results fall below what had been expected. Changing circumstances and competition produce emergencies upsetting well-laid plans. Resourcefulness in responding to crisis is a skill which most successful presidents develop early.

But the organizational consequences of the critical taskmaster role require presidents to go beyond insistence upon achievement of planned results. They must see as their second principal function the creative maintenance and development of the organized capability that makes achievement possible. This activity leads to a third principle—the integration of the specialist functions which enable their organizations to perform the technical tasks in marketing, research and development, manufacturing, finance, control, and personnel, which proliferate as technology develops and tend to lead the company in all directions.[2] If this coordination is successful in harmonizing special staff activities, presidents will probably have performed the task of getting organizations to accept and order priorities in accordance with the companies' objectives. Securing commitment to purpose is a central function of the president as organization leader.

The skills required by these functions reveal presidents not solely as taskmasters, but as mediators and motivators as well. They need ability in the education and motivation of people and the evaluation of their performance, two functions which tend to work against one another. The former requires understanding of individual needs, which persist no matter what the economic purpose of the organization. The latter requires objective assessment of the technical requirements of the task assigned. The capability required here is also that required in the integration of functions and the mediation of the conflict bound to arise out of technical specialism. The integrating capacity of the chief executive extends to meshing the economic, technical, human, and moral dimensions of corporate activity and to relating the company to its immediate and more distant communities. It will show itself in the formal organization designs which are put into effect as the blueprint of the required structured cooperation.

---

[2] See P. R. Lawrence and J. W. Lorsch, *Organization and Environment: Managing Differentiation and Integration* (Boston: Harvard University Graduate School of Business Administration, 1967), for a study of the process of specialization and coordination.

The perspective demanded of successful organization leaders embraces both the primacy of organization goals and the validity of individual goals. Besides this dual appreciation, they exhibit an impartiality toward the specialized functions and have criteria enabling them to allocate organization resources against documented needs. The point of view of the leader of an organization almost by definition requires an overview of its relations not only to its internal constituencies but to the relevant institutions and forces of its external environment. We will come soon to a conceptual solution of the problems encountered in the role of organizational leader.

THE PRESIDENT AS PERSONAL LEADER

The functions, skills, and relevant point of view of chief executives hold true no matter who they are or who makes up their organizations. The functions that accompany presidential performance of their role as communicator of purpose and policy, as exemplar, as the focal point for the respect or affection of subordinates vary much more according to personal energy, style, character, and integrity. Presidents contribute as persons to the quality of life and performance in their organizations. This is true whether they are dynamic or colorless. By example they educate junior executives to seek to emulate them or simply to learn from their behavior what they really expect. They have the opportunity to infuse organized effort with flair or distinction if they have the skill to dramatize the relationship between their own activities and the goals of corporate effort.

All persons in leadership position have or attain power which in sophisticated organizations they invoke as humanely and reasonably as possible in order to avoid the stultifying effects of dictatorship, dominance, or even markedly superior capacity. Formally announced policy, backed by the authority of the chief executive can be made effective to some degree by clarity of direction, intensity of supervision, and the exercise of sanctions in enforcement. But in areas of judgment where policy cannot be specified without becoming absurdly overdetailed, chief executives establish in their own demeanor even more than in policy statements the moral and ethical level of performance expected. At the national level of executive behavior, even presidents reveal in their deportment their real regard for the highest levels of ethical conduct. The results are traceable in the administrations of Presidents Kennedy, Johnson, Nixon, and Carter. Failure of personal leadership in the White House leads to demoralization different only in scale and influence from corporate analogies.

Formal correctness of structure and policy is not enough to inspire an organization. Enthusiasm for meeting ethical problems head on and avoiding shoddy solutions comes not so much from a system of rewards and punishments as from the sentiments of loyalty or courage stimulated by the personal deportment of the chief executive. By the persons they are, as much as by what they say and do, presidents influence their organizations, affect the development of individuals and the level of organized performance. At this moment in the history of American business enterprise, conscious attention to the essential integrity of the chief executive becomes an important requirement if confidence in the corporate institutions of a democratic society is to be restored.

The skills of the effective personal leader are those of persuasion and articulation made possible by having something worth saying and by understanding the sentiments and points of view being addressed. Leaders cultivate and embody relationships between themselves and their subordinates appropriate to the style of leadership they have chosen or fallen into. Some of the qualities lending distinction to this leadership cannot be deliberately contrived, even by an artful schemer. The maintenance of personal poise in adversity or emergency and the capacity for development as an emotionally mature person are essential innate and developed capabilities. It is probably true that some personal preeminence in technical or social functions is either helpful or essential in demonstrating leadership related to the president's personal contribution. Credibility and cooperation depend upon demonstrated capacity of a kind more tangible and attractive, than, for example, the noiseless coordination of staff activity.

The relevant aspects of the presidential point of view brought to mind by activities in the role of personal leader are probably acknowledgement of one's personal needs and integrity as a person, and acceptance of the importance to others of their own points of view, behavior, and feelings. Self-awareness will acquaint leaders with their own personal strengths and weaknesses and keep them mindful of the inevitable unevenness of their own preparation for the functions of general management. These qualities may be more important in the selection of a general manager than in the study of general management. But students of the cases that follow will quickly see the personal contributions of George Romney to the survival of American Motors, the values of John Connelly in Crown Cork and Seal, and Sir Halford Reddish in Rugby Portland Cement, and Joseph C. Wilson of the Xerox Corporation.

Michael Maccoby, author of *The Gamesman* [3] has conducted a provocative inquiry into executive character types. Using some terms of dubious usefulness, he designates these as the Craftsman, the Jungle Fighter, the Company Man, and the Gamesman. The craftsman is dedicated to quality but unable to lead changing organizations. The jungle fighter is the anti-hero who after rising rapidly is destroyed by those he has used. The company man is committed to corporate integrity and success but is said to lack the daring required to lead innovative organizations. The gamesman is the dominant type—able and enthusiastic, a team leader whose main goal is the exhilaration of victory. His main defect is said to be that his work has developed his intellectual but not his emotional gifts. Despite the disclaimer that each person is a combination of types, these attention-getting labels produce caricature in the

---

[3] Michael Maccoby, *The Gamesman.* (New York: Simon and Schuster, Inc., 1976). For a brief summary see "The Corporate Climber Has to Find His Heart," *Fortune*, December 1975, pp. 98–108.

effort to distinguish overlapping or coexisting traits. Similarly labels applied to roles suggest distance between them.

Despite the shortcomings of such classification, the work of psychoanalysts like Maccoby and Zaleznik brings support to the thesis developed here that such qualities as generosity, idealism, and courage should accompany the gifts of the persons devoted to their company and its objectives. If Maccoby is right in saying that the gamesman (by which he seems to mean quarterback or captain) is the representative type in leading American corporations today, then we have come a long way from the Carnegies, Rockefellers and Astors of the 19th century. We would still have a long way to go. The route passes directly through the pages that follow.

The prototype of the chief executives we are developing is, in short, the able victory-seeking organizational leader who is making sure in what is done and the changes pioneered in purpose and practice that the game is worth playing, the victory worth seeking, and life and career worth living. If the stature of corporation presidents as professional persons is not manifest in their concern for their organizations, they will not perform effectively over time either in the role of organization or personal leader. If we concede that the gamesman should be concerned with what the game is for, we are ready to consider the role of the president in the choice of corporate objectives. That choice determines what the contest is about.

THE PRESIDENT AS ARCHITECT OF ORGANIZATION PURPOSE

To go beyond the organizational and personal roles of leadership, we enter the sphere of organization purpose, where we may find the atmosphere somewhat rare and the going less easy. We think students of the companies described in these cases will note, as they see president after president cope or fail to cope with problems of various economic, political, social, or technical elements, that the contribution presidents make to their companies goes far beyond the apparently superficial activities that clutter their days.

Their attention to organization needs must extend beyond answering letters of complaint from spouses of aggrieved employees to appraisal (for example) of the impact of their companies' information, incentive, and control systems upon individual behavior. Their personal contribution to their company goes far beyond easily understood attention to key customers and speeches to the Economic Club to the more subtle influence their own probity and character have on subordinates. We must turn now to activities even further out—away from immediate everday decisions and emergencies. Some part of what a president does is oriented toward maintaining the development of a company over time and preparing for a future more distant than the time horizon appropriate to the roles and functions identified thus far.

The most difficult role—and the one we will concentrate on henceforth—of the chief executive of any organization is the one in which he serves as custodian of corporate objectives. The entrepreneurs who create a company know at the outset what they are up to. Their objectives are intensely personal, if not exclusively economic, and their passions may be patent protection and finance. If they succeed, like Howard Head, in passing successfully through the phase of personal entrepreneurship, where they or their bankers or families are likely to be the only members of the organization concerned with purpose, they find themselves in the role of planner, managing the process by which ideas for the future course of the company are conceived, evaluated, fought over, and accepted or rejected.

The presidential functions involved include establishing or presiding over the goal-setting and resource-allocation processes of the company, making or ratifying choice among strategic alternatives, and clarifying and defending the goals of the company against external attack or internal erosion. The installation of purpose in place of improvisation and the substitution of planned progress in place of drifting are probably the most demanding functions of the president. Successful organization leadership requires great human skill, sensitivity, and administrative ability. Personal leadership is built upon personality and character. The capacity for determining and monitoring the adequacy of the organization's continuing purposes implies as well analytic intelligence of a high order. The president we are talking about is not a two-dimensional poster or television portrait.

The crucial skill of the president concerned with corporate purpose includes the creative generation or recognition of strategic alternatives made valid by developments in the marketplace and the capability and resources of the company. Along with this, in a combination not easily come by, runs the critical capacity to analyze the strengths and weaknesses of documented proposals. The ability to perceive with some objectivity corporate strengths and weaknesses is essential to sensible choice of goals, for the most attractive goal is not attainable without the strength to open the way to it through inertia and intense opposition, with all else that lies between.

Probably the skill most nearly unique to general management, as opposed to the management of functional or technical specialties, is the intellectual capacity to conceptualize corporate purpose and the dramatic skill to invest it with some degree of magnetism. As we will see, the skill can be exercised in industries less romantic than space, electronics, or environmental reclamation. John Connelly did it with tin cans, Sir Halford Reddish with cement. Ralph Hart of Heublein, Inc. thought he could do it with beer because he did do it with Smirnoff vodka. No sooner is a distinctive set of corporate objectives vividly delineated than the temptation to go beyond it sets in. Under some circumstances it is the president's function to defend properly focused purpose against superficially attractive diversification or corporate growth that glitters like fool's gold. Because defense of proper strategy can be interpreted as mindless conservatism, wholly appropriate defense of a still valid strategy requires courage, supported by detailed documentation.

Continuous monitoring, in any event, of the quality and continued suitability of corporate purpose is over time the most sophisticated and essential of all the functions of general management alluded to here. Because of its difficulty and vulnerability to current emergency, this function may not be present in some of the companies the student will encounter in the pages that follow. Because of its low visibility, this activity may not be noticed at first in cases where it is properly present. The perspective which sustains this function is the kind of creative discontent which prevents complacency even in good times and seeks continuous advancement of corporate and individual capacity and performance. It requires also constant attention to the future, as if the present did not offer problems and opportunities enough.

ENORMITY OF THE TASK

Even so sketchy a record of what a president is called upon to do is likely to seem an academic idealization, given the disparity between the complexity of role and function and the modest qualifications of those impressed into the office. Like the Molière character who discovered that for 40 years he had been speaking prose without knowing it, many managers have been programmed by instinct and experience to the kind of performance which we have attempted to decipher here. For the inexperienced, the catalog may seem impossibly long.

Essentially, however, we have looked at only three major roles and four sets of responsibilities. The roles deal with the requirements for organizational and personal leadership and for conscious attention to the formulation and promulgation of purpose. The four groups of functions encompass (1) securing the attainment of planned results in the present, (2) developing an organization capable of producing both technical achievement and human satisfactions, (3) making a distinctive personal contribution, and (4) planning and executing policy decisions affecting future results.

Even thus simplified, how to apply this identification of presidential role and function to the incomparably detailed confusion of a national company situation cannot possibly be made clear in the process of generalization. Students using this text will wish to develop their own overview of the general manager's task, stressing those aspects most compatible with their own insight and sense of what to do. No modifications of the deliberately nontechnical language of this summary should slight the central importance of purpose. The theory presented here begins with the assumption that in the life of every organization (corporate or otherwise), every subunit of organization, every human group and individual should be guided by an evolving set of purposes or goals which permit forward movement in a chosen direction and prevent drifting in undesired directions.

NEED FOR A CONCEPT

The complexity of the president's job and the desirability of raising intuitive competence to the level of verifiable, conscious, and systematic analysis suggest the need, as indicated earlier, for a unitary concept as useful to the generalist as the canons of technical functions are to the specialist. We will propose shortly a simple practitioner's theory which we hope will reduce the four-faceted responsibility of the company president to more reasonable proportions, make it susceptible to objective research and systematic evaluation, and bring to more well-qualified people the skills it requires. The central concept we call "corporate strategy." It will be required to embrace the entire corporation, to take shape in the terms and conditions in which its business is conducted. It will be constructed from the points of view described so far. Central to this Olympian vantage point is impartiality with respect to the value of individual specialties, including the one through which the president rose to generalist responsibilities. It will insist upon the values of the special functions in proportion to their contribution to corporate purpose and ruthlessly dispense with those not crucially related to the objectives sought. It necessarily will define the president's role in such a way as to allow delegation of much of the general management responsibility described here without loss of clarity. After students have examined and discussed the roles, functions, and skills evident or missing from the cases that immediately follow these comments, we will present the concept of corporate strategy itself. Our hope will be to make challenging but practicable the connection between the highest priority for goal setting and a durable but flexible definition of a company's goals and major company-determining policies. How to define, decide, put into effect, and defend a conscious strategy appropriate to emerging market opportunity and company capability will then take precedence over and lend order to the fourfold functions of general management here presented.

Despite a shift in emphasis toward the anatomy of a concept and the development of an analytical approach to the achievement of valid corporate strategy, we will not forget the chief executive's special role in contributing quality to purpose through standards exercised in the choice of what to do and the way in which it is to be done and through the projection of *quality* as a person. It will remain true, after we have taken apart analytically the process by which strategy is conceived, that executing it at a high professional level will depend upon the depth and durability of the president's personal values, standards of quality, and clarity of character. We will return in a final comment on the management of the strategic process to the truth that the president's function above all is to be the exemplar of a permanent human aspiration—the determination to devote one's powers to jobs worth doing. Conscious attention to corporate strategy will be wasted if it does not elevate the quality of corporate purpose and achievement.

Head Ski Company, Inc.

THE HEAD SKI COMPANY, INC., of Timonium, Maryland, was formed in 1950 to sell metal skis which had been developed by Howard Head during three years of research. In the first year six employees turned out 300 pairs of skis. By the 1954–55 skiing season, output reached 8,000 pairs, and by 1965 it passed 133,000. Growth in dollar sales and profits was equally spectacular. When Head went public in 1960, sales were just over $2 million and profits just under $59,000. By 1965 sales were up to $8.6 million and profits to $393,713. In the next two years, volume continued upward, though growth was less dramatic. In the 53 weeks ended April 30, 1966, sales were $9.1 million and profits $264,389. For a like period ending April 29, 1967, sales were $11.0 million and profits $401,482. (For financial data, see Exhibit 1.)

THE INDUSTRY

Head was an enthusiastic participant in the growing market generated by leisure-time activities, of which skiing was one of the most dynamic segments. The industry association, Ski Industries America (SIA), estimated that skiing expenditures—including clothing, equipment, footwear, accessories, lift tickets, travel, entertainment, food and lodging—rose from $280 million in 1960 to $750 million in 1966–67. Gross sales were expected to reach $1.14 billion by 1969–70. This growth was attributed to both the rising number of skiers and greater per capita expenditures. In 1947 it was estimated that there were fewer than 10,000 active skiers in the United States. SIA estimated that there were 1.6 million in 1960, 3.5 million in 1966–67 and predicted 5 million for 1970. Another industry source estimated that the number of skiers was increasing by 20% a year.

As of 1966–67 the $750 million retail expenditures on skiing were estimated to be divided into $200 million going for ski equipment and

Exhibit 1

HEAD SKI COMPANY, INC.

Consolidated Balance Sheet, 1965–67

ASSETS

	As of April 24, 1965	As of April 30, 1966	As of April 29, 1967
Current assets			
Cash	$ 162,646	$ 233,330	$ 263,896
Short-term commercial paper receivable	1,200,000	800,000	1,200,000
Notes and accounts receivable—less reserve	334,503	174,127	242,632
Inventories—valued at lower of cost or market	2,815,042	3,522,235	3,102,069
Prepayments and miscellaneous receivables	207,279	223,864	402,879
Total current assets	$4,719,470	$4,953,556	$5,211,476
Fixed assets, at cost			
Building—pledged under mortgage	$1,014,738	$1,012,085	$1,010,149
Machinery and equipment	847,974	1,059,274	1,540,707
Other	147,336	213,692	715,089
	$2,010,048	$2,285,051	$3,265,945
Less accumulated depreciation	822,255	892,153	1,123,203
Total fixed assets	$1,187,793	$1,392,898	$2,142,742
Other assets			
Unamortized bond discount and expenses	$ 277,636	$ 263,564	$ 252,004
Cash surrender value of life insurance	103,117	120,589	133,568
Other	28,583	22,364	70,194
Total other assets	$ 409,336	$ 406,517	$ 455,766
Total assets	$6,316,599	$6,752,971	$7,809,984

LIABILITIES AND STOCKHOLDERS' EQUITY

	As of April 24, 1965	As of April 30, 1966	As of April 29, 1967
Current liabilities			
Accounts payable	$ 521,031	$ 299,040	$ 829,826
Current portion of long-term debt	20,600	21,000	23,100
Accrued expenses	451,062	413,865	549,720
Income taxes payable	39,102	299,452	333,514
Other	94,899	91,271	51,120
Total current liabilities	$1,126,694	$1,124,628	$1,787,280
Long-term debt			
Mortgage on building—5¾%, payable to 1978	$ 396,646	$ 376,036	$ 331,115
Convertible subordinated debentures	2,125,000	2,125,000	2,125,000
	$2,521,646	$2,501,036	$2,456,115
Less current portion	20,600	21,000	....
Total long-term debt	$2,501,046	$2,480,036	$2,456,115
Commitments and contingent liabilities, stockholders' equity			
Common stock—par value 50¢ per share (authorized 2,000,000 shares; outstanding 1966, 915,202 shares; 1965, 882,840 shares adjusted for 2-for-1 stock split-up effective September 15, 1965)	$ 220,710	$ 457,601	$ 459,401
Paid-in capital	1,820,323	1,679,700	1,694,700
Retained earnings	647,826	1,011,006	1,412,488
Total stockholders' equity	$2,688,859	$3,148,307	$3,566,589
Total liabilities and stockholders' equity	$6,316,599	$6,752,971	$7,809,984

Consolidated Statement of Earnings

	52 Weeks ended* April 25, 1964	52 Weeks ended* April 24, 1965	53 Weeks ended* April 30, 1966	52 Weeks ended April 29, 1967
Net sales	$6,018,779	$8,600,392	$9,080,223	$11,048,072
Cost of sales	4,033,576	5,799,868	6,357,169	7,213,188
Gross profit	$1,985,203	$2,800,524	$2,723,054	$ 3,834,884
Expenses:				
Selling, administrative and general	$1,169,392	$1,697,659	$2,029,531	$ 2,756,939
Research and engineering	102,358	303,884	239,851	327,857
Total expenses	$1,271,750	$2,001,543	$2,269,382	$ 3,084,796
Income before income taxes and nonrecurring charges	$ 713,453	$ 798,981	$ 453,672	$ 750,088
Federal and state income taxes	367,542	392,515	221,034	348,606
Income before nonrecurring charges	$ 345,911	$ 406,466	$ 232,638	$ 401,482
Nonrecurring debt expense—after giving effect to income taxes		$ 63,678	......	......
Net earnings	$ 345,911	$ 342,788	$ 232,638	$ 401,482
Net earnings as restated	$ 376,788	$ 393,713	$ 264,389	$ 401,482
Earnings per share before nonrecurring charges	$ 0.40	$ 0.51	$ 0.26	$ 0.44
Earnings per share after nonrecurring charges	$ 0.40	$ 0.43	$ 0.26	$ 0.44
Earnings per share as restated	$ 0.48	$ 0.49	$ 0.29	$ 0.44

Earnings per share are based on average shares outstanding of 904,237 in 1966 and 801,196 in 1965 after giving effect to the 2-for-1 stock split-up effective September 15, 1965, and the 3-for-1 stock split on July 7, 1964.

* Earnings restated April 29, 1967, to give effect to an adjustment in the lives of depreciable assets for federal income tax purposes.

(Statement is continued on next page.)

Exhibit 1—Continued

	52 Weeks ended April 27, 1963	52 Weeks ended April 25, 1964	52 Weeks ended April 24, 1965	53 Weeks ended April 30, 1966	52 Weeks ended April 29, 1967
Net sales.	$4,124,445	$6,018,779	$8,600,392	$9,080,223	$11,048,072
Net earnings.	$ 191,511	$ 376,788	$ 393,713	$ 264,389	$ 401,482
Expenditures for plant and equipment.	$ 272,154	$ 513,130	$ 558,865	$ 304,102	$ 1,027,854
Depreciation.	$ 79,719	$ 132,497	$ 211,683	$ 238,161	$ 249,961
Working capital.	$ 654,676	$1,525,015	$3,542,857	$3,828,928	$ 3,424,196
Plant and equipment and other assets, net.	$ 701,875	$1,187,246	$1,745,839	$1,799,415	$ 2,598,508
Long-term debt.	$ 287,245	$1,176,647	$2,501,046	$2,480,036	$ 2,456,115
Shareholders' equity.	$1,069,306	$1,535,614	$2,787,650	$3,148,307	$ 3,566,589
Earnings per share.	$ 0.25	$ 0.48	$ 0.49	$ 0.29	$ 0.44
Average shares outstanding.	777,600	777,600	801,196	904,237	916,542

Average shares outstanding reflect the 2-for-1 stock split-up effective September 15, 1965, and 3-for-1 stock split on July 7, 1964.
Statistical data for the years 1963 to 1966, inclusive, have been adjusted to reflect retroactive adjustments.
Source: Company records.

ski wear, and $550 million going to the 1,200 ski areas and the transportation companies carrying skiers to their destinations. Ninety-eight manufacturers belonged to the SIA. *Skiing International Yearbook* for 1967 listed 85 brands of wooden skis available in 260 models, 49 brands of metal skis in 101 models, and 53 brands of fiberglass skis in 116 models. For each model there could be as many as 15 sizes. Many manufacturers made all three types of skis and some had multiple brands, but even so the industry was divided into many competing units.

The table which follows illustrates the division of the market by price and type:

Type	Number of brands of skis by price range		
	$0–$49.99	$50–$99.99	$100 and up
Wood.......................... 69	69	27	3
(85 brands)			
Metal........................ 0	0	22	28
(49 brands)		(28 models)	(73 models)
Fiberglass.................... 0	0	24	39
(53 brands)		(35 models)	(81 models)

Source: *Skiing International Yearbook, 1967*, pp. 90–91. Copyright by Ziff-Davis Publishing Co.

Ski Business summed up an analysis of industry trends as follows:

> Imports of low-priced adult wood skis into the United States are skidding sharply.
>
> U.S. metal skis are gaining faster than any other category.
>
> The ski equipment and apparel market is experiencing an unusually broad and pronounced price and quality uptrend.
>
> Ski specialty shop business appears to be gaining faster than that of the much publicized department stores and general sporting goods outlets.
>
> The growth in the national skier population is probably decelerating and may already have reached a plateau.[1]

Supporting these statements of trends, *Ski Business* made some other observations.

> Foreign skis clearly lost in 1966 at the gain of domestic manufacturers. (The total of imported and domestic skis sold in the United States is believed to be running at over 900,000 pairs annually.) By conservative estimate, U.S. metal ski production in 1966 (for shipment to retail shops for the 1966–67 selling season) was up by at least 40,000 pairs from 1965. . . .
>
> But far more important than the domestic American ski gain (which will continue now that American fiberglass ski makers are entering the market) is the remarkable upward price shift. Thus while 10 per per cent fewer foreign skis entered the United States in 1966, the dollar value of all the skis imported actually rose by more than 10 per cent or $700,000. . . . Here was the real measure of growth of the ski market; it was not in numbers, but in dollars.

[1] John Fry, *Ski Business*, May–June 1967, p. 25.

The principal beneficiary of this remarkable upward shift in consumer preference for higher product quality is, of course, the ski specialty shop. The skier bent on purchasing $140 skis and $80 boots will tend to put his confidence in the experienced specialist retailer. The ski specialist shops themselves are almost overwhelmed by what is happening. Here's one retailer's comment: "Just two or three years ago, we were selling a complete binding for $15. Now skiers come into our shop and think nothing of spending $40 for a binding. . . ."

. . . Most of the department store chains and sporting goods shops contacted by *Ski Business* were also able to report increased business in 1966–67, but somehow the exuberant, expansionist talk seems to have evaporated among nonspecialty ski dealers. Montgomery Ward, for instance, says that ski equipment sales have not come up to company expectations. Ward's has specialized in low end merchandise for beginning and intermediate skiers. . . . Significantly, department stores or sporting goods shops which reported the largest sales increases tended to be those which strive hardest to cast their image in the ski specialist mold. . . .[2]

Ski imports for 1966 served both the low-priced and high-priced market. More than half the Japanese imports of 530,000 pairs of skis were thought to be children's skis which helped to explain the low valuation of the Japanese skis. This value of $6.84 a pair was the f.o.b. price at the door of the Japanese ski factory and does not include shipping, duty, importer's or retailer's margins.[3] *Ski Business* reported imports into the United States as follows:

1966 SKI IMPORTS INTO THE UNITED STATES
(by country of origin)

Country of origin	No. of pairs	Change: 1966 vs. 1965	$ Value	Average $* value per pair 1965	Average $* value per pair 1966
Canada.............	7,091	+6,350	149,961	23	21.14
Sweden.............	2,767	+1,131	22,386	9	8.09
Norway.............	1,125	−698	18,221	6	16.20
Finland.............	10,184	+5,411	98,275	9	9.65
Belgium.............	129	+129	6,327	. . .	49.05
France.............	5,257	+2,828	265,018	49	50.41
West Germany.......	44,736	+9,959	1,010,354	18	22.58
Austria.............	72,536	−20,872	1,511,563	21	20.84
Switzerland........	2,835	+1,155	124,068	39	43.76
Italy...............	7,494	+351	195,723	14	26.12
Yugoslavia.........	22,540	+5,122	254,962	11	11.31
Japan.............	529,732	−89,632	3,625,639	5.54	6.84
Australia...........	2,307	+2,307	114,091	. . .	49.45
1965 total..........	785,746	. . .	$6,692,451	. . .	$8.52
1966 total..........	708,733	−77,013	$7,396,588	$8.52	$10.44

* The average value per pair of skis represents an f.o.b. plant price and does not include charges for shipping and handling, tariff, excise tax, or profit for trading company or wholesaler. Tariff on skis was 16⅔%.

Source: *Ski Business*, May–June 1967, p. 31.

2 Ibid.

3 Ibid.

In the high-price market segment, where skis retailed at $100 or more, the annual market was estimated by industry sources to be approximately 250,000 pairs of skis. Here estimates of the leading contenders according to these industry sources were:

Brand	Type	Estimated sales	Price range
Head (United States).............	Metal	125,000 pairs	$115.00–$175.00
Hart (United States).............	Metal	44,000 pairs	$ 99.50–$175.00
Kniessl (Austria)................	Epoxy	20,000 pairs	$150.00–$200.00
Yamaha (Japan)................	Epoxy	13,000 pairs	$ 79.00–$169.00
Fischer (Austria)................	Wood ⎫ Metal ⎬ Epoxy ⎭	13,000 pairs	$112.00–$189.00

Source: *Skiing International Yearbook, 1967*, pp. 90–91. Copyright by Ziff-Davis Publishing Co.

Fischer was believed to have $15–$18 million sales worldwide. Kniessl was believed to be about the same size as Head worldwide, but only about one-tenth Head's size in the United States. In addition Voit, the recreational products division of AMF, was entering the market with a fiberglass ski. Voit also manufactured water skis, a wide variety of aquatic equipment, and rubber products. AMF's total 1966 sales were $357 million. Recreational equipment accounted for approximately 20%, not including bowling equipment which accounted for an additional 22% of sales.

The skier's skill level was one determining factor in his choice of skis. (For those unfamiliar with the differences among skis designed for each group, a discussion of ski construction is included as Appendix A.) Of the 3.5 million active skiers, 17,000 were regarded as racers, another 75,000 were considered to be experts, and another 100,000 were classed as sufficiently skillful to be strong recreational skiers.

THE MARKET

Skiing was considered to be a sport which attracted the moderately well-to-do and those on the way up. This conception was borne out by the following market data:

A statistical study released early this year [1965] by the Department of Commerce disclosed that the American skier has a median age of 26.2 and a median annual income of $11,115. Moreover, it showed that about two-thirds of all skiers are college graduates.

How do these young, affluent and intelligent men and women spend their skiing dollars? At a typical resort, a person might spend each day $10 for accommodations, $10 for food, $5.00 for a lift ticket and $10 for renting everything needed to attack the slopes from pants and parka to skis, boots, poles and bindings. . . .

The initial purchases of a person determined to have his or her own good equipment and to look well while skiing could easily be about $200. For this amount, a skier could buy everything from winter underwear to goggles and perhaps even have a bit left over for a rum toddy in the ski lodge the first night of his trip.

For instance, ski boots cost from $20 to $150 and average $50 a pair. Skis range from $30 to $200 and poles from $5 to $35.

When it comes to apparel, costs vary considerably. Snow jackets or parkas might cost as little as $20 or as much as $1,000 for those made with fur. Many jackets are available, though, at about $30.

Stretch pants have an average price of about $20. Other apparel requirements for skiing include sweaters which retail from $10 to $50, winter underwear which costs about $5, and ski hats and caps which sell for $3 and up.[4]

There was an apparent fashionability to skiing. Fashion consciousness was apparent in the design of ski equipment, ski wear, and the influx of a new type of skier. Under the headline "The Nonskiers: They Flock to Ski Resorts For The Indoor Sports," *The Wall Street Journal* reported as follows:

Want to take up a rugged, outdoor sport?
Cross skiing off your list.
The sport has gone soft. Ski resorts now have all the comforts of home—if your home happens to have a plush bar, a heated swimming pool, a padded chair lift, boutiques and a built in baby sitter. . . . Skiing, in fact, has become almost an incidental activity at some ski resorts; indeed, some of the most enthusiastic patrons here at Squaw Valley and other resorts don't even know how to ski. They rarely venture outdoors.

So why do they come here? "Men, M-E-N. They're here in bunches, and so am I, baby," answers slinky, sloe-eyed Betty Reames as she selects a couch strategically placed midway between the fireplace and the bar. . . .

Squaw Valley houses half a dozen bars and restaurants and often has three different bands and a folksinger entertaining at the same time. Aspen, in Colorado, throws a mid-winter Mardi Gras. Sun Valley, in Idaho, has a shopping village that includes a two-floor bookstore and boutique selling miniskirts.

Life has also been made softer for those skiers who ski. . . . Also some resorts are making their chair lifts more comfortable by adding foam padding. But even that isn't enough for some softies. "What? Me ride the chair lift? Are you crazy? I'd freeze to death out in the open like that," says blond Wanda Peterson as she waits to ride up the mountain in an enclosed gondola car. She doesn't stand alone. The line of the gondola is 200 strong; the nearby chair lift, meanwhile, is all but empty. . . .

. . . for beginning skiers most resorts offer gentle, meticulously groomed inclines that make it almost impossible to fall. "We try to make it so that the person who has no muscle tone and little experience can't be fooled, can't make a mistake," says one resort operator. "Then we've got him. He's a new customer as well as a happy man."

Once he gets the hang of it—whether he's any good or not—the happy man starts spending lots of money, and that's what the resorts love.[5]

---

[4] *The New York Times*, December 12, 1965. © 1965 by The New York Times Company. Reprinted by permission.

[5] *The Wall Street Journal*, February 1967.

In line with the concern for style, some manufacturers of skiwear and ski equipment developed new colors and annual model changes to inspire annual obsolescence and fad purchases.

HEAD COMPANY HISTORY

Howard Head, chairman and founder of the company bearing his name, was the man responsible for the development of the first successful metal ski. Combining the experience of an aircraft designer with dedication to a sport which he enjoyed, he spent more than three years developing a ski which would not break, turned easily, and tracked correctly without shimmying and chattering. Others had tried to produce metal skis, but Head succeeded almost five years before his nearest competitors, Hart and Harry Holmberg, introduced the Hart metal skis. *Ski Magazine* described the reason behind Howard Head's success:

> . . . He was obsessed, to be sure, and being relatively unencumbered by stockholders, high overhead and strong yearnings for luxurious living, he was well braced for the long haul. . . .
> "I made changes only where I had to make them," he has said of the days when his skis were undergoing trial by fire. "When they broke, I made them stronger only where they broke. . . ."[6]

In 1960 Howard Head described the early years of his enterprise and the trials which surrounded it as follows:

> Twelve years ago I took six pairs of handmade metal skis to Stowe, Vermont, and asked the pros there to try them out. It had taken about a year to make those six pairs of skis. The design, based on engineering principles of aircraft construction, was radically different from any ever tried before. I thought it was sound but the pros weren't a bit surprised when all six pairs promptly broke to pieces. After all, others before me had tried to make metal skis and all they had proved was what everyone knew anyway—a ski had to be made of wood.
> That was in January 1948. Today about 60% of all high-grade skis sold in the United States are metal skis. The reasons for this revolution in ski manufacturing industry are simple. People like the way metal skis ski, they like their durability, and they like their easy maintenance. . . .
> Many small refinements and changes in design have been introduced through the years because of our continued testing and development program and to meet the advances in technique and changes in skiing conditions. But the basic structural design hasn't changed, which speaks well for the original concept.[7]

Mr. Head further indicated that his personal interest in technical problems played a major part in leading him to create his business:

> When I started out, I was a mechanical design engineer—the whole origin of the business was the feeling that it should be possible to build a better ski. What started as an engineering puzzle ended as a business.
> I distinctly remember wondering at that time whether we would ever grow to the point where we would be making 5,000 pairs of skis a year.

---

[6] *Ski Magazine*, January 1964.
[7] "On Metal Skis" (manuscript by Howard Head, 1960).

Price-volume considerations exerted small influence over initial marketing policy. Mr. Head priced his first metal skis at $75 in spite of the fact that most skiers were using war surplus skis that cost $20, including bindings. Mr. Head discussed his early ideas on quality, costs, and prices as follows:

> The great disadvantage of all metal skis is simply their high price. This became apparent to us when we were pioneering the original metal ski and found it was going to cost a good bit more than a wood ski. We didn't let that stop us because we believed the striking advantages of a metal ski more than compensated for its high price. As it turned out, even with a higher initial price, Head Skis proved to cost less in the long run because they are so durable. . . .
>
> In the early days people had no way of knowing the skis would last so long that they actually ended up costing less than cheaper skis. They simply liked them enough to go ahead and buy them in spite of the price.[8]

Mr. Head found a market which was quite unexpected. In spite of the high price, Head skis appealed more to the average beginner or slightly better skier than to racers. Among skiers, Heads became known as "cheaters." This designation grew out of the skis' ability to make almost anyone look good. "They practically turned themselves." Soon the black plastic top of the Head ski became a ubiquitous status symbol on the slopes.

PRODUCT POLICY

The keynote of Mr. Head's product policy was quality. His fundamental belief was that the consumer should get all he pays for and pay for all he gets. The 17-year history of the company had seen considerable upgrading of the products. Several times in the past the company had called in particular models or production runs of skis which had been found to be defective. One executive commented that this had been done without hesitation, even when the company was in precarious financial condition.

Asked what set Head apart from its competition, Mr. Head replied as follows:

> I believe that it is a tradition of attention to detail which grew out of its entrepreneurial history. In every aspect we attempt to follow through. Service, dealer relations, product quality, style, advertising are all important and must be done in the best way we know how.
>
> We stress continued emphasis on quality of product and quality of operating philosophy. We pay meticulous attention to the individual relationships with dealers and the public.
>
> I have attempted to make creativity, imagination, and standards of perfection apply across the board. This was always our desire, and we only failed to live up to it when the business got too big for the existing staff. The philosophy remained constant, and now we have the people to live up to it.

---

[8] Ibid.

We get a return on this attention to detail. The feedback from success allows us to maintain the necessary staff to insure continuation of this philosophy.

We allow no sloppiness.

Head skis came in one color—black. There was no special trim to designate the model, only a modification in the color of the name "Head" embossed on the top of the ski and a change in the color of the case: red for some models, yellow or black for others. Although at one time a chrome top was considered, it was rejected because of the glare, and because it was difficult to see against the snow. In addition to these factors, one executive described black as being a conservative color which would go with anything. Howard Head explained that he "did not want to complicate the consumer's choice."

> I deeply believe in sticking to function and letting style take care of itself. We have stuck so rigorously to our black color because it is honest and functional that it has become almost a trademark. While we constantly make minor improvements, we never make an important model change unless there is a performance reason for it. In other words, we skipped the principle of forced obsolescence, and we will continue to skip it.

This policy had been consciously chosen and maintained, in spite of competition which had introduced six or eight different colors and yearly color changes to keep up with fashion.

Apart from color and style, skis had to perform well on the slopes. There were three fundamental things which a ski had to do. It had to "track,"[9] "traverse,"[10] and "turn."[11] The need to perform these functions imposed certain constraints on ski design, and the necessity to both track and turn required some compromises in design. *Ski Magazine* listed some of the characteristics which this balancing involved:

1. The tip must be pointed and turned up in a gradual curve to permit the ski to climb over obstacles without changing directions, to prevent it from diving beneath soft snow, and to help prevent the skis from crossing. (Splay)
2. The bottom should be flat and perfectly flush with its steel edges, except for a narrow groove extending the length of the ski which increases tracking stability.
3. The skis must be straight without warp or twist, each side must have the same curve to it, and the groove must be straight and in the middle.
4. The bottom surface must be slippery so that it will run smoothly.

---

[9] Track: If you point a ski down a slope and allow it to run freely, it should hold a straight course—over bumps and through hollows and on every type of snow surface.

[10] Traverse: A ski should be able to hold a straight line while moving diagonally across a slope over obstacles and various snow conditions.

[11] Turn: When a skier releases the edges of his skis, the skis must be capable of slipping sideways, and, when edged, they must bite into the snow evenly. (A skiing turn is nothing more than a slideslip carved into an arc by the controlled bite of the edges.)

5. To distribute the skier's weight over the length of the ski, a cambered or arched shape is necessary.
6. A ski must be flexible.
7. The shape or "sidecut" of the ski must be correlated to the flexibility of the ski and the torsional rigidity of the material used. A flexible ski will have difficulty holding if the sidecut is too straight, for the ends will barely touch the snow. Only a correct sidecut will tolerate a momentary twist of the skis, reducing the effect of edges just enough to allow smooth passage over bumps yet not enough to pull the ski out of line.
8. A sharp edge is needed to hold on hard surfaces.
9. For maximum stability, the skier must choose the proper length ski.[12]

Mr. Head found a proper combination of these elements for the recreation skier in his earliest metal ski. Designated the "Standard," this model underwent substantial improvement over its 17-year history. Until 1960, however, the goal of providing the best ski for experts eluded Head and other metal ski makers. Mr. Head said of this period, "During the early years at Head Ski, we were too busy making the best ski we could for the general public to spend much time developing a competition ski."

For experts, the basic complaint against metal skis was that they were too "soft" and tended to vibrate badly at racing speeds. This problem was substantially solved in 1960, when Head introduced its "Vector" model, to be followed in 1962 (and later entirely replaced) by the "Competition." In these skis, an imbedded layer of neoprene dampened vibrations and considerably improved performance. Whereas in 1960 most competitors in the Squaw Valley Olympics had stuck to their wooden skis, by the end of 1962 Head skis were in wide use, and they had carried 77 racers out of 141 to positions among the top six contenders at races conducted by the International Professional Ski Race Association in Canada and the United States. Also about half the skis used in the U.S. National Junior and Senior Championships that year were Heads.

By 1966 Head had established itself as an important factor in the ski racing world. Two Americans had set the world speed record—106.527 m.p.h.—on Head skis. In major international competition in 1966, one-third of all finishers in the top ten places at all events were on Head skis, and Head was the outstanding single manufacturer on the circuit with 18 gold medals, 15 silver medals, and 15 bronze medals.

The 1968 Head line included a ski for every type of skier from the unskilled beginner to the top professional racer. The line was described in Head's *Ski Handbook* as follows:

> . . . the most important design consideration is you—the type of skier you are and where you ski. That's why your dealer was able to offer you nine different models of Head Skis to choose from. You can be sure the model he helped you select was the optimum—for you.
> STANDARD—THE MOST FORGIVING SKI: For beginners of average size and athletic ability up to intermediates learning stem christies.

---

[12] *Skiing International Yearbook 1967*, pp. 62–63. Copyright by Ziff-Davis Publishing Co.

Also for the better, occasional skier who prefers an easy-going, lively, light-weight ski that practically turns for him.

The *Standard* is medium soft in flex overall for easy turning and responsiveness. Engineered side camber and relative overall width contribute to ease and slow-speed stability. Its light weight and torsional rigidity make traversing and other basic maneuvers simple. Thin taper in the tip allows the *Standard* to cut easily through the heaviest snow instead of ploughing.

Standard. $115. Thirteen sizes from 140 to 215 cm. Black top, sidewalls and bottom; white engraving.

MASTER—MORE OF A CHALLENGE: For the skier who has mastered the basic techniques and wants to begin driving the skis and attacking the slope. As lively as the *Standard,* this is also the ski for the heavier, more athletic beginner who wants more "beef" underfoot.

The *Master* is like the Standard in basic shape but thicker and heavier. The tip radius is longer for extra shock absorption. Slightly stiffer flex overall acts as a heavy-duty shock absorber over bumps.

Master. $135. Nine sizes from 175 through 215 cm. Black top and sidewalls; blue base and engraving.

THE FABULOUS 360—THE MOST VERSATILE SKI: Finest all-around ski ever made—for the skier beginning stem christies on through the expert class. Remarkable for its ease of turning as well as its steadiness and precision, the 360 is the serious skier's ski for attack or enjoyment on the slope, under any condition of snow or terrain.

With its smooth-arcing flex pattern, the 360 has the supple forebody of the other recreational skis, but is slightly stiffer at the tail. Its side camber is similar to that of the *Giant Slalom.* Narrower overall than the *Standard* or *Master.* Rubber damping in the lightweight top-skin unit makes the 360 a very responsive ski, allowing the expert to control his turns beautifully and set his edges precisely. Tip splay is designed to give easiest entrance through snow and to provide excellent shock absorption, particularly in heavily moguled areas.

The Fabulous 360. $155. Eleven sizes from 170 to 220 cm. Black top and sidewalls; yellow base and engraving.

SLALOM—THE HOT DOG: For the expert skier who likes to stay in the fall-line, slashing through quick short-radius turns on the steepest, iciest, slopes. The *Slalom* has been totally redesigned this year to fit the special needs of the expert recreational skier, who wants the lightest, fastest-reacting, and best ice-holding ski possible.

Slalom is Head's narrowest ski overall. And, thanks to the lightweight top-skin unit and core, it is also one of Head's lightest skis. Lightness and narrowness allow for carved or pivoted turns, reflex-fast changes in direction. Special engineered side camber and relative softness at the thin waist give the ultimate in "feel" and control on ice. Neoprene rubber gives the damping and torque necessary for a top-performance ice ski.

Slalom. $160. Five sizes from 190 to 210 cm. Black top and sidewalls. Racing red base and engraving.

DOWNHILL—BOMB!: Widest and heaviest Head ski, the *Downhill* is for the advanced skier—recreational or competitor—who wants to blast straight down the slope. It offers the ultimate in high-speed performance, tracking ability, and stability over bumps and moguls.

The long tip splay and supple forebody is the secret of the *Down-*

hill's exceptional speed advantage. It virtually planes over the surface of the slope. With its firm midsection and tail acting like the rudder of a hydroplane, the *Downhill* affords the skier utmost control coupled with great turning ability at slower speeds. Heavy duty topskin unit and added rubber damping contribute to the stability and high-speed "quietness" of the *Downhill*. This is the elite international-class racing ski, and experts have found it an excellent powder ski as well.

Downhill. $175. Seven sizes from 195 to 225 cm. Black top and side-walls. Yellow base and engraving.

GIANT SLALOM—GRACE PLUS SPEED: The *"GS"* incorporates the best features of the *Downhill* and *Slalom* models. It offers the expert skier—recreational and/or competitor—the optimum in stable all-out speed skiing, combined with precise carving and holding ability in high-speed turns. It is another favorite on the international racing circuit.

The *Giant Slalom's* stability and precision come from a unique combination of sidecut and relatively stiff flex. The *"GS"* is similar to the *360* in overall dimensions, but has a stiffer flex pattern than the *360*, particularly underfoot. This gives the *"GS"* the versatility of the *360* but with greater control at high speeds. Tip splay is designed for maximum shock absorption and easy riding.

Giant Slalom. $165. Nine sizes from 175 to 215 cm. Black top and sidewalls. Yellow base and engraving.

YOUNGSTER'S COMPETITION—JUNIOR HOT DOG: Carrying the *Giant Slalom* engraving, this ski is designed for expert youngsters who want, and can handle, a faster, more demanding ski than the small size *Standard*. Similar in cut and performance characteristics to the *Giant Slalom*, but without the *"GS's"* neoprene damping, to provide the junior racer with easier turning ability.

Youngster's Competition. $120. Two sizes, 160 and 170 cm. Black top and sidewalls; yellow bottom and engraving.

SHORTSKI—FUN WITHOUT EFFORT: Not just a sawed-off *Standard*, but a totally different ski with totally different proportions. Very wide for its length, quite stiff overall, the *Shortski* is the only ski of its kind with an engineered side camber. Ideal for quick learning of the fundamentals of skiing. Also for the older or more casual skier who enjoys being on the slopes and wants the easiest-possible tracking and turning ski ever built.

Shortski. $115. Four sizes from 150 to 190 cm. Black top, sidewalls and bottom. White engraving.

DEEP POWDER—SHEER BUOYANCY ON THE SLOPES: Super soft flexibility and buggy-whip suppleness allow this specialized ski to float in powder, while maintaining easy turning plus full control and tracking ability on packed slopes.

The *Deep Powder* is very wide and soft overall, with a "hinge-like" effect in the forebody that enables it to glide through the deepest powder.

Deep Powder. $115. Five sizes from 195 to 215 cm. Black top, side-walls and bottom. White engraving.

Head was constantly experimenting with new designs and introducing minor modifications to improve the performance and durability of its product. When asked about a major change in product construction, such as to the fiber-reinforced plastic type ski, Mr. Head gave the following reply:

We think that the metal sandwich construction is the best material. We do not see this situation changing in the foreseeable future. Certainly now the other exotic materials are not gaining ground. They lack the versatility of application of the metal sandwich ski. The epoxy or fiber reinforced plastic have low durability and don't have the wide performance range of our skis.

We believe that the advantage of the metal ski is that you can build in any performance characteristic which you desire. Naturally, we have a research department investigating other materials, but until a major improvement is found, we should stick to our basic material. We can always build the best ski for beginners, and we can adapt that ski to get the performance required by experts.

MARKETING POLICIES

Head's emphasis on quality extended beyond the product to the dealer and service network. The company sold through only a limited number of franchised dealers, who had satisfied management that "they know something about skis and skiing." Ten district sales managers were employed, who sold to about 900 dealers throughout the United States. Of these about 85% were ski specialty shops, 12% were large full-line sporting goods stores, and the remainder were full-line department stores (see Exhibit 2). Head skis were distributed in Europe through an exclusive distributor, Walter Haensli of Klosters, Switzerland. In 1964 he sold 19% of Head's output. This figure appeared to be declining gradually.

Exhibit 2

HEAD SKI COMPANY, INC.

Dealer Organization, 1962–67
(franchised dealers)

Year	Number at beginning	Newly franchised	Terminated or not renewed	Number at end
1962	390	105	41	454
1963	454	136	30	560
1964	560	167	57	670
1965	670	96	39	727
1966	727 (est.)	N.A.	N.A.	900
1967	900 (est.)	30	N.A.	—

N.A.—Not available.
Note: In addition the franchised dealers had approximately 300 branches which are not included in the above figures.
Source: Company records.

Head believed that a Head franchise was valuable to a dealer. Many large stores had wanted to sell Heads, but had been turned down. Saks Fifth Avenue had waited eight years before it was given a franchise. Mr. Head commented on dealer selection as follows:

Getting Saks Fifth Avenue as a dealer is consistent with our operating philosophy of expecting the same quality from our dealers as from ourselves.

Once they become a dealer, however, we get to know the people involved and work closely with them. Increasingly, we are recognizing the business value of providing more assistance and leadership to our dealers in helping them to do a better job for their customers.

Even a large, well-managed department store or sporting goods store may need help in the specialized area of skis. They may need help in display stock selection, or even personnel selection. We are increasingly concerned about the type of personnel who sell skis. There is a high degree of dependence on the salesman. He must be a good skier himself.

We have seen instances of two department stores of essentially identical quality in the same area where one store could sell eight pairs of skis a year and the other three hundred simply because of a different degree of commitment to getting the right man to sell. Skis can only be sold by a floor salesman who can ski and who can sell from personal experience.

The company was committed to the belief that selling skis was an exacting business. The ski size had to be matched to the individual's height and body weight, flexibility had to be chosen correctly depending on use, and bindings had to be mounted properly.

Following up on the initial sale, Head offered extensive customer service. Dealers were expected to have service facilities for minor repairs and the factory had facilities for sharpening edges, rebuilding the plastic portion of the ski, and matching a single ski if the mate had been broken beyond repair. Even in the busiest part of the season, service time was kept under three weeks.

In March 1967, Mr. Harold Seigle, the newly appointed president and chief operating officer of Head, sent out a "management news bulletin" outlining Head's marketing philosophy:

Marketing Philosophy

1. Our current selective dealer organization is one of Head Ski Company's most valuable assets, next to the product itself.
2. Our continued sales growth will be based on a market-by-market approach aimed at increasing the effectiveness of our present dealers and by the very selective addition of new dealers wherever present dealers prove to be inadequate rather than by mass distribution and merchandising techniques.
3. Our future marketing efforts, particularly personal selling, advertising, merchandising, and sales promotion, will be geared to the specific needs of our dealers to sell all Head Ski products.
4. We want and will have the finest sales forces in the industry . . . who rely upon personal integrity, service, and hard work to do a professional selling job rather than inside deals and short cuts.
5. We feel that, next to quality products, strong personal selling at the manufacturer's level and the retail level is paramount to our continued success and tends to transcend other facets of marketing that contribute to the sale of merchandise.

Advertising was done on a selective basis. An outside source reported as follows:

The company invests about 2% of gross sales in advertising, split between the skiing magazines (50%) and *Sports Illustrated*, *The New Yorker*, and *Yachting*—"the same kind of people like to sail."

The most effective promotion, however, is probably the ski itself. Head is delighted at the growing demand for his skis in the rental market. "We sold 10,000 pairs—almost 10% of our business—for rental last year," he points out, "and everyone who rents those skis becomes a prospect."[13]

To aid in placing rental skis, Head gave an additional 12%–15% discount on skis which a dealer purchased for rental. Ski rental was seen as the best way to introduce a customer to the ease of skiing on Heads.

The Head Ski Company approach was a "soft sell." Unlike many sporting goods companies, Head did not rely on personal endorsements of famous skiers. According to one executive, it was impossible under American Amateur rules even to have posters featuring an amateur skier. Professional endorsements were probably ineffective anyway, since so many other sporting goods companies used them, and most of the public knew that such endorsements could be bought. Head tried to get actual news pictures of famous skiers or racers using Head skis and winning. To make certain that top skiers would use Head skis, the company did lend skis to racers for one year. Even this practice was expensive and had to be tightly controlled. A good skier might need upwards of nine pairs of skis a year, which would represent an expenditure of nearly $1,000. Head did feel this type of promotion yielded a secondary benefit of product development information which could not be overlooked.

Head had received many requests for a promotional film made in conjunction with United Airlines showing famous ski slopes. Head was mentioned in the title, at the end, and in a few identifiable spots in the body of the show. This film was used by ski clubs and other organizations to promote interest in the sport.

Other Head promotion came as a result of skiwear and resort advertisements. As *Sales Management* put it:

> So great is the worldwide prestige of Head skis that although Howard Head claims he makes no promotional tie-in deals, the ski buff can hadly miss seeing the familiar black skis in ads for anything from parkas to ski resorts. They're status symbols.[14]

PRODUCTION

Head skis were produced in three steps. The Detail Department made up the various components which were to go into the assembly, including the core, the nose piece, the tail piece, the top plastic, the top and bottom skins, the running surface, and the edges. The separate pieces were then taken to the Cavity Department, where they were assembled. Here, too, the various layers were laid into a mold and heated and bonded under controlled time, temperature, and pressure. At this point

---

[13] *Sales Management*, February 5, 1965.
[14] Ibid.

the skis were roughed out on a band saw. From that time on, all work was done on the skis as a pair. In the Finishing Department, the skis were ground to final form, buffed, polished, and engraved.

Manufacture involved a great deal of handwork, of which 70% was characterized as requiring a high degree of skill. The basic nature of the assembly process meant that operations did not lend themselves to mass production techniques.

In May 1967, Head completed the fifth addition to the plant since its construction in 1959. Prior to the new addition, the plant contained 105,668 square feet, of which 93,040 was devoted to manufacturing and warehouse facilities, and 12,628 to office space. Included were a cafeteria, locker rooms, and shower areas for the workers.

Howard Head commented on the difficulty of the manufacturing process and on the relationship between costs and price:

> [There are] approximately 250 different operations, involving a great number of specially developed machines, tools, and processes. None of the processes is standard. It all had to be developed more or less from scratch.
>
> Some of the special-purpose machines involved are those for routing the groove in the bottom aluminum, for attaching the steel edges, and for profiling the ski after it comes out of the presses. Also there are the bonding procedures which require an unusual degree of control of heat and pressure cycles.
>
> Supplementing all the special-purpose machines, we have learned to make rather unusual use of band saws. A good example of a demanding band-saw operation is the profiling of the plywood and plastic core elements. Since the stiffness of a ski at any point goes up as the square of the spacing between the top and bottom sheets—i.e., the core thickness—a normal band-saw tolerance of about 0.010″ would grossly affect our flexibility pattern and would be out of the question. However, by special adapters and guides, we are actually able to band saw these parts in high production at about ten seconds apiece to a tolerance of plus or minus 0.002″ over the entire contour.
>
> An example of effective but low cost equipment in our factory is the press used to laminate 3′ x 10′ sheets of plywood core material to their corresponding sheets of sidewall plastic. This operation requires a total load of some 90,000 pounds. By using a roof beam as the reaction point, the floor for a base, and three screw jacks for pressure, we are able to produce enough material for 600 pairs of skis at one shot with equipment costing a total of about $250.
>
> It's been our policy from the start to put absolute emphasis on quality of product. We never compromise on old material, nor reject a new one on the basis of cost. In principle, if better skis could be made out of sheet platinum, I suspect we would wind up with it. In other words it is our policy to make the best product we can regardless of cost and then price it accordingly to the trade.

Production at Head was on a three-shift basis throughout the year, with skis being made for inventory during the slow months. There were over 600 employees.

Six attempts had been made to unionize the plant, but all had been rejected, several times by three-to-one majorities. One warehouse employee with 12 years' seniority said, "It's a nice place to work. We don't need a union. If you have a problem, Mr. Head will listen to you."

All employees received automatic step raises based on seniority, as well as merit reviews and raises. In addition there was a profit-sharing trust plan which in the past had generally added 6%–7% to the employees' salaries. These funds became fully vested after three years.

Another important benefit in which exempt salaried employees participated was the year-end bonus plan. Under this plan, three groups received different bonus rates. For the lowest paid group, the rate was 3% if pretax profits on sales were under 2%, but 10%–11% if profits were 8%–12%. For the middle group, no bonus was paid if profits were 2% or below, but the rate was 20%–22% if profits ranged between 8% and 12%. For the top group rates were not disclosed, but it was indicated that their bonus plan was even more steeply peaked. For most of the past several years, the payoffs had been at or near the upper range.

FINANCE

The initial financing of Head Ski Company was $6,000 from Howard Head's personal funds. In 1953 Mr. Head sold 40% of the stock in the company for $60,000. This, together with retained earnings and normal bank debt, financed expansion until 1960 when common stock was issued. Additional financing was required to continue the rapid expansion, and in January 1965 a $3,527,500 package was sold, made up of 5½% convertible subordinated debentures in face amount of $2,125,-000, and 42,500 shares of common stock. Until the stock issue of 1965, Howard Head had owned 42.4% of the common stock, and the other directors and officers had owned 46.1%. At no time had there been any question about the commanding role of Howard Head when important decisions were made. Full conversion of the new issue would represent 17.1% ownership.

Expansion was viewed by many in the company as a defensive tactic. The belief was expressed that "if you do not grow as fast as the market will allow you to, you are taking substantial risk that someone else will come in and take that market away from you." In addition, the new funds provided capital for two diversifications started in 1966: The Head Ski and Sportswear Co., and the Head plastics division.

In spite of the drop in earnings growth, the stock market continued to evaluate Head's prospects at 29 to 60 times previous years' earnings. During the period January 1966 to July 1967, its stock sold in the range from 9⅜ to 17¾. As late as January 1965, however, the stock had sold at 22¾.

ORGANIZATION

As of June 1967, the Head Ski Company was organized along functional lines. Reporting to the president were the vice president for operations, the treasurer, and the directors of marketing, quality control, and the director of personnel. This organization pattern had been

introduced by Mr. Harold Seigle when he was named chief operating
officer on January 16, 1967 (see Exhibit 3).

Of the 26 men shown on the organization chart, 12 had been with
Head one year or less. When asked about the potential difficulties of that
situation, Mr. Head responded,

> I would only say that if you are to have a lot of new people, you
> must have one man in command who is an experienced and gifted
> professional at utilizing people. My job is to support and use that man.

Mr. Head reviewed the history of the organization which had led to
the current structure as follows:

> I think that this is typical of the kind of business that starts solely
> from an entrepreneurial product basis, with no interest or skills in
> management or business in the original package. Such a business
> never stops to plan. The consuming interest is to build something new
> and to get acceptance. The entrepreneur has to pick up the rudiments
> of finance and organizational practices as he goes along. Any thought
> of planning comes later. Initially he is solely concerned with the prob-
> lems of surviving and building. Also, if the business is at all success-
> ful, it is so successful that there is no real motivation to stop and ob-
> tain the sophisticated planning and people-management techniques.
> Such a business is fantastically efficient as long as it can survive. One
> man can make all of the important decisions. There is no pyramidal
> team structure.
>
> In our case this approach worked quite successfully until about
> 1955 when we sold 10,000 pairs of skis and reached the $500,000 sales
> level. The next five years from 1955 to 1960 saw a number of dis-
> organized attempts to acquire and use a more conventional pyramidal
> organizational system. To put it succinctly, what was efficient at the
> $500,000 level was increasingly inefficient as we reached $1 million,
> then $2 million in sales. One man just couldn't handle it. I made too
> many mistakes. It was like trying to run an army with only a general
> and some sergeants. There were just no officers, to say nothing of an
> orderly chain of command.
>
> In 1960 came the first successful breakthrough, where I finally
> developed the ability to take on a general manager who later became
> an executive vice president. It was hard for me to learn to operate
> under this framework. The most striking thing missing from this
> period was a concept of people-management. I spent five years grad-
> ually learning not to either over- or under-delegate.
>
> Let me interject that the final motivation necessary to make a com-
> plete transition to an orderly company came because the company got
> into trouble in 1965–66. Even five years after the beginning of a team
> system, the company got into trouble, and this was the final prod which
> pushed me to go all the way. It is interesting that it took 12 years. Up
> until 1960 the company was totally under my direction. From 1960 to
> 1965 we stuttered between too much of my direction and not enough.
>
> The chief difficulty for me was to learn to lay down a statement of
> the results required and then stay out of details. The weakness was in
> finding a formula of specifying objectives, then giving freedom as long
> as the objectives were met.
>
> The appointment of Hal Seigle as president brought us a thoroughly
> sophisticated individual who can bring us the beginning of big business

Exhibit 3

HEAD SKI COMPANY, INC.
Organization Chart
(June 1967)

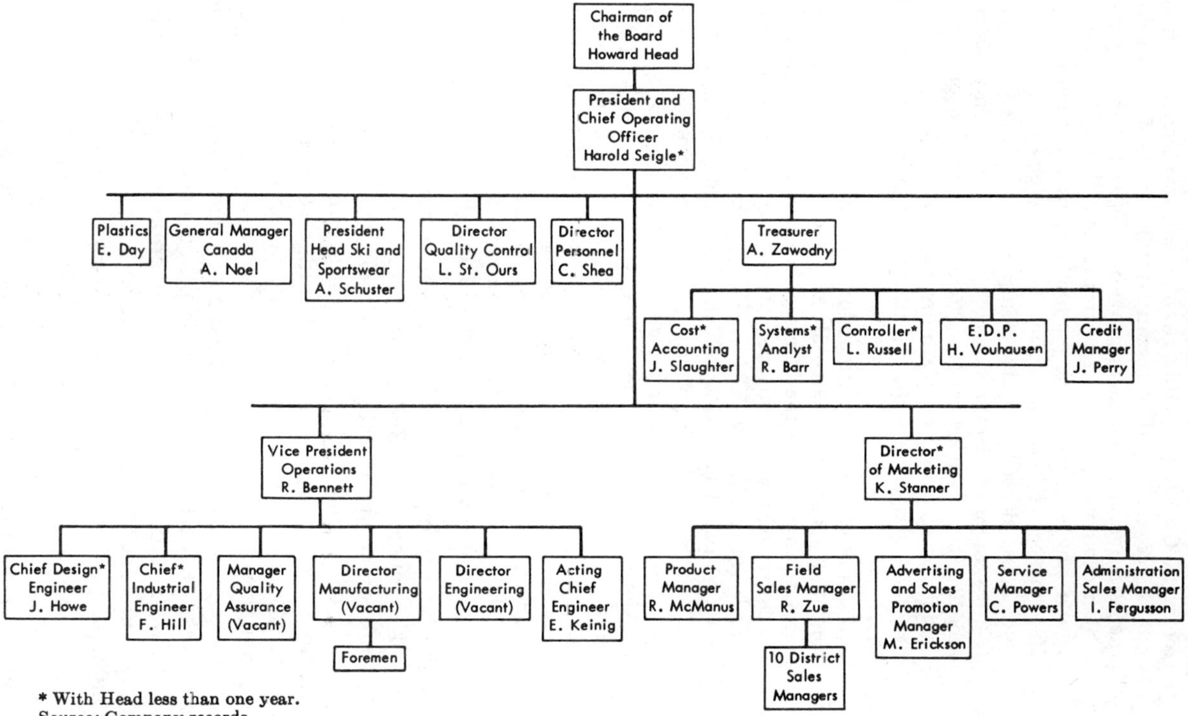

Chairman of the Board
Howard Head

President and Chief Operating Officer
Harold Seigle*

Plastics
E. Day

General Manager Canada
A. Noel

President Head Ski and Sportswear
A. Schuster

Director Quality Control
L. St. Ours

Director Personnel
C. Shea

Treasurer
A. Zawodny

Cost* Accounting
J. Slaughter

Systems* Analyst
R. Barr

Controller*
L. Russell

E.D.P.
H. Vouhausen

Credit Manager
J. Perry

Director* of Marketing
K. Stanner

Vice President Operations
R. Bennett

Chief Design* Engineer
J. Howe

Chief* Industrial Engineer
F. Hill

Manager Quality Assurance
(Vacant)

Director Manufacturing
(Vacant)

Foremen

Director Engineering
(Vacant)

Acting Chief Engineer
E. Keinig

Product Manager
R. McManus

Field Sales Manager
R. Zue

10 District Sales Managers

Advertising and Sales Promotion Manager
M. Erickson

Service Manager
C. Powers

Administration Sales Manager
I. Fergusson

* With Head less than one year.
Source: Company records.

methods. On my part, this change has involved two things: first, my finally recognizing that I wanted this kind of organization; second, the selection of a man with proven professional management skills.

Unfortunately, with an entrepreneur, there are only two courses which can be taken if the company is to grow beyond a certain size. He can get the·hell out, or he can really change his method of operation. I am pleased that this company has made the transition.

Now more than ever the company is using my special skills and abilities, but I am no longer interfering with an orderly and sophisticated management and planning system. We have given the company new tools to operate with, and I have not pulled the rug out from under them.

I am reserving my energies for two things. First, there is a continuation of my creative input—almost like a consultant to the company. Second, I have taken the more conventional role of chairman and chief executive officer. In this role I devote my efforts to planning and longer range strategy.

I feel that I can serve in both capacities. I can only be successful in the role of creative input if I can be solely a consultant without authority. It has to be made clear in this role that anything said is for consideration only. It has been demonstrated that this role is consultative, since some of my suggestions have been rejected. I like this role because I like the freedom. I can think freer, knowing that my suggestions will be carefully reviewed.

Of course, in areas of real importance like new product lines such as binding or boot, adding new models to the ski line, or acquisitions, etc., I must exert authority, channeled through the president.

Prior to coming to Head, Mr. Seigle had been vice president and general manager of a $50 million consumer electronics division of a $150 million company. His appointment was viewed as "contributing to a more professional company operating philosophy." He hoped to introduce more formalized methods of budget control and to "preside over the transition from a 'one man' organization to a traditionally conceived functional pattern."

Mr. Seigle introduced a budgeting system broken down into 13 periods each year. Reports were to be prepared every four weeks comparing target with actual for each of the revenue or expense centers, such as marketing, operations, the staff functions, and the three subsidiaries. The hope was eventually to tie the bonus to performance against budget. Previously statements had been prepared every four weeks, but only to compare actual results against previous years' results.

Being new to the company, Mr. Seigle found that much of his time was being spent on operating problems. He believed, however, that as the budget system became completely accepted and operational, he would be able to devote more of his time to looking ahead and worrying about longer term projects. He said: "Ideally, I like to be working six to eighteen months ahead of the organization. As a project gets within six months of actual operation, I will turn it over to the operating managers." He had hired a manager for corporate planning with whom he worked closely.

Under the previous organization from March 1966 until Mr. Seigle's appointment, Howard Head had presided directly over the various departments and marketing functions. There was no overall marketing director at that time. Even in the period from 1960 to 1966 when there was an executive vice president, Mr. Head indicated that he had concerned himself with the operating details of the business.

A VIEW TOWARD THE FUTURE

Head's first diversification was to ski poles. These were relatively simple to manufacture and were sold through existing channels. As with the skis, Head maintained the highest standards of quality and style. The poles were distinguished from competition by their black color and adoption of the tapered shape and extra light weight which at the time were unavailable on other high-priced, quality ski poles. Head's prices were well toward the upper end of the spectrum: $24.50, as compared with as little as $5 for some brands. Success in selling poles encouraged the company to look at other products it might add.

Two further steps taken were toward diversification in late 1966 when Head formed a plastics division and established a subsidiary, Head Ski and Sportswear, Inc.

The plastic division's activity centered on high molecular weight plastics. In March 1967 a press release was issued concerning this activity:

> Head Ski Co., Inc., has signed a license agreement with Phillips Petroleum Company . . . to use a new method developed by Phillips for extruding ultra-high molecular weight high density polyethylene into finished products. . . .
>
> Developmental equipment has been installed at the Head plant here and limited quantities of sheet have been extruded and tested in the running surface of Head skis with excellent results. . . . Production of ski base material is scheduled for this Spring. . . .
>
> In addition to its own running surface material, the Head plastics division has been developing special ultra-high molecular weight high density polyethylene compound to serve a variety of industrial applications. . . .
>
> Ultra-high molecular weight high density polyethylene is an extremely tough abrasion-resistant thermoplastic capable of replacing metal and metal alloys in many industrial areas. Compared with regular high density resins, the ultra-high molecular weight material has better stress-cracking resistance, better long-term stress life and less notch sensitivity.

The diversification into skiwear was considered by company executives to be the more important move. Howard Head talked about the logic of this new venture as follows:

> Skiwear is "equipment" first and fashion second. We are satisfied that our line of skiwear is better than anything done before. It represents the same degree of attention to detail which has characterized our hardware line.

The president of the new subsidiary, Alex Schuster, said:

> Many people thought that Head should stay in hardware such as poles, bindings, and wax. As I see it, however, by going into skiwear we are taking advantage of ready-made distribution and reputation.

There is no reason why the good will developed through the years can't be related to our endeavor.

This new market offers a greater potential and reward than the more hardware oriented areas. Any entry into a new market has difficulties. These can only be solved by doing things right and by measuring up to the Head standards. Having a Head label commits us to a standard of excellence.

Assuming that we live up to those standards, we shall be able to develop into a supplier in a small market but with formidable potential. We are creating a skill base for further diversification.

Our products are engineered, not designed. We are concerned with the engineered relationship among fabric, function, and fit. The engineering details are not always obvious, but they are related to functional demands. Emphasis is placed on function over fashion, yet there is definite beauty created out of concern for function. We are definitely in tune with fashion trends.

[See Exhibit 4 for examples of the new products.]

We will provide a complete skiing outfit—pants, parkas, sweaters, accessories, sox, and gloves. We will offer a total coordinated look.

Along with the design innovations, we shall offer innovations in packaging, display and promotion. We have to go beyond simply preparing the proper apparel.

Head Ski and Sportswear did both manufacturing and subcontracting. The products which had the highest engineering content were made in the Head plant. Sweaters, with less engineering, were contract-made to Head specifications by one of Europe's leading sweater manufacturers.

The collection was first shown to dealers in April 1967 and was scheduled for public release for the 1967–68 skiing season. Initial response by dealers and by the fashion press had been extremely encouraging. *Ski Business* reported:

HEAD'S UP.

. . . way up, in fact 194% ahead of planned volume on its premier line of skiwear.

Anyone who expected Howard Head's entry into the world of fashion to be presented in basic black was in for a surprise. Ironically the skiwear collection that blasted off with the hottest colors in the market is offered by a man who is totally color blind. . . .

On pants: The $55 pant was the big surprise. It was our top seller—way beyond expectations—and the basic $45 pant came in second in sales. Another surprise was the $70 foam waisted pant for which we only projected limited sales—it's a winner. . . .

On orders: Way beyond expectations. Ninety per cent of the orders are with ski shops and 10% with the department stores. Naturally we are committed to selling Head Ski dealers but it definitely is not obligatory.[15]

The sportswear subsidiary had been set up in a separate plant five miles from Head's Timonium headquarters. It was an autonomous operation with a separate sales force and profit responsibility. The initial premise was that the sportswear should be distributed through current

---

[15] *Ski Business,* May–June, 1967.

Exhibit 4

SAMPLES OF THE NEW HEAD SKIWEAR

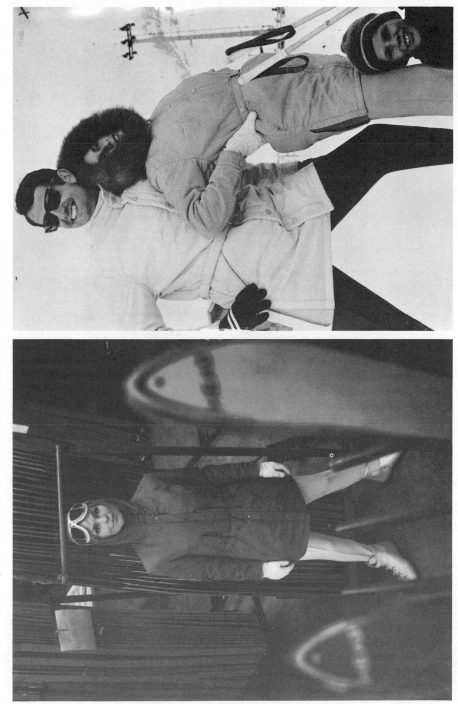

Exhibit 4—Continued
SAMPLES OF THE NEW HEAD SKIWEAR

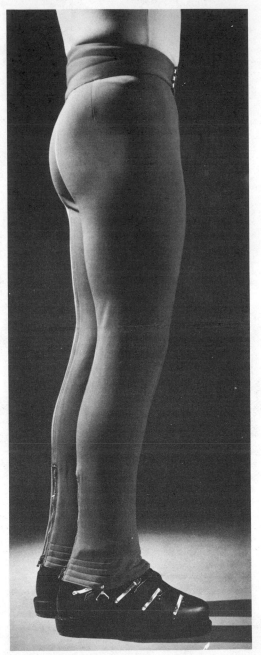

Head dealers, although according to Mr. Seigle the marketing decisions of the sportswear division would be made independently of decisions in the ski division. Although Head dealers were offered the Head sportswear line, it was not sold on an exclusive basis. Distribution would be directly from factory salesmen to the dealer. Within the company, the necessity for a separated and different type of sales force was acknowledged. As one executive phrased it, "I can't imagine our ski salesmen trying to push soft goods. Our salesmen got into the business first and foremost because they were excellent skiers." As with skis and poles, the product line was to be maintained at the high end of the spectrum in both quality and price.

When asked about future growth potential, Mr. Seigle replied that he believed Head would continue to grow rapidly in the future. He saw the potential of doubling the ski business in the next five years. Although he characterized the sportswear business as a "good calculated risk," he believed it offered the potential of expanding to $5 to $8 million per year. Beyond that he felt that Head might go in three possible directions. First, he believed that Head should once again explore the opportunities and risks of moving into the other price segments of the ski market, either under another brand or with a nonmetallic ski. Although he believed that by selling in a lower price range Head could sell 50,000 or more pairs of skis, the risks were also high. Second, he felt that Head should explore the opportunity in other related ski products, such as boots or bindings. Third, he felt that eventually Head should expand into other specialty sporting goods, preferably of a contraseasonal nature.

In looking to these new areas, Mr. Seigle had formulated a two-part product philosophy as follows:

Any new product which Head will consider should:
1. Be consistent with the quality and prestige image of Head Skis.
2. Should entail one or more of the following characteristics:
    a) High innovative content.
    b) High engineering content.
    c) High style appeal.
    d) Be patentable.

We will consider getting into new products through any of the normal methods such as internal product development, product acquisition, or corporate acquisition. If we are to move into a new area we definitely want to have a product edge. For example, if we were to manufacture a boot, we would want to be different. We would only seriously consider it if we had a definite product advantage such as if we were to develop a high quality plastic boot.

Howard Head, in speaking of the future, voiced the following hopes:

I would like to see Head grow in an orderly fashion sufficient to maintain its present youth and resiliency. That would mean at least 20%–25% per year. This statement does not preclude the possibility that we might grow faster. We believe the ski business alone will grow 20%–25% per year. As our staff capabilities grow, we will probably branch into other areas.

As to our objectives for the next five years, I would say that the first corporate objective is to maintain healthy growth in the basic ski business. It is the taproot of all that is good in Head. Second, we must be certain that any new activity is carefully selected for a reasonable probability of developing a good profit and an image platform consistent with the past activity of Head.

APPENDIX A*

TYPES OF SKIS

ELEMENTS OF A WELL-DESIGNED SKI

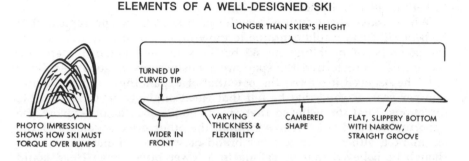

LONGER THAN SKIER'S HEIGHT

TURNED UP
CURVED TIP

PHOTO IMPRESSION
SHOWS HOW SKI MUST
TORQUE OVER BUMPS

WIDER IN
FRONT

VARYING
THICKNESS &
FLEXIBILITY

CAMBERED
SHAPE

FLAT, SLIPPERY BOTTOM
WITH NARROW,
STRAIGHT GROOVE

Wood skis

If you are on a tight budget, well-designed wood skis at low prices are available from domestic and foreign manufacturers. Wood is a bundle of tubular cellulose cells bound together in an elastic medium called lignin. The internal slippage of wood skis not only lets them torque over the bumps in traverse, but damps any tendency to vibrate or chatter on hard rough surfaces. There are wood skis for any snow, any speed, and they are fun to ski on. Their only problem is a lack of durability. Wood skis are fragile. Besides, as wood skis are used, the internal slippage of the fibers increases, and they lose their life.

In choosing a wood ski, it is probably wise to pay more than the minimum price. Multiple laminations of hickory or ash, a soft flex pattern, interlocking edges, polyethylene base, plastic top and sidewalls, tip and tail protectors are some of the features a beginner or intermedi-

WOOD SKI CROSS-SECTION

PROTECTIVE TOP EDGES

PROTECTIVE PLASTIC TOP

PLASTIC
SIDEWALL

STEEL EDGES   PLASTIC SOLE   MULTI-LAMINATED
WOOD CORE

---

* Source: *Skiing International Yearbook,* 1967, pp. 63–68. Copyright by Ziff-Davis Publishing Co.

ate should look for in a better wood ski. When you get past the $40 to $70 range, your own dealer's recommendations will be your best guarantee of value.

FRP skis

A few years ago there were only a handful of "epoxy" skis on the market, and skiers were eyeing them with mixed interest and distrust. Now the available models have multiplied almost unbelievably. New companies have been formed, and many of the established manufacturers have now brought out versions of their own. The plastic skis are still new enough for most skiers to be confused about their true nature —and with good reason, since there are so many types.

The word epoxy is part of the confusion. The true family resemblance of all the skis that are currently being lumped under that designation is the use of glass fibers locked into a plastic medium to create layers of great strength. The plastics engineers use the term fiber-reinforced plastic (FRP) to designate this type of structural solution. It is very strong.

The reinforcing layers used in these new designs derive their strength from the combined strength of millions of fine glass fibers or threads locked in the plastic layer. The potential strengths of materials in this family of structural plastics can exceed those of aluminum or steel. Unfortunately, there is no simple way to evaluate them or describe the materials actually in use. The wide variety of glass fibers, resins, and systems of molding and curing the fiber-reinforced layer produces a wide range of results. These can be evaluated only by laboratory tests or, finally, by actual in-service results.

FRP materials are being used for all sorts of sporting goods, industrial, and space-age applications. The strength-to-weight ratio is attractively high, and the possibility of creating new reinforced shapes by means of molding operations has proved to be attractive enough to encourage a great deal of experimentation. Skis seem to adapt to this structural technique.

Metal skis

In the search for more durable skis, the metal skis took over the quality market about a decade ago, and are widely accepted as ideal for both recreational skier and expert. Except for specialized racing uses, the wooden skis have been largely outmoded in the better ski market. Today, the fiber-reinforced plastic designs are the only challengers to the primacy of the metals.

Metal skis obtain their strength from aluminum sheets that are light in weight but very strong. The structure of a metal ski is somewhat like an "I" beam; when the ski is bent, the bottom sheet is stretched and the top sheet is compressed. The core material serves as the web—the vertical portion of the "I"—and must be attached to the top and bottom metal sheets securely enough to resist the shearing stress that occurs when the ski is bent.

Service potential of metal skis

The possibility of rebuilding and refinishing metal skis has been one of the key sales attractions of the metal ski in this country. So long as bonding remains intact, only the effects of wear and tear—rocks, skis banging together, rough treatment in transportation, etc.—limit the life of the skis. The possibility of having the plastic surfaces and edges, or even the structural members themselves, replaced has strong appeal for the skier investing well over $100 in his skis. The rebuilding potential also tends to keep the trade-in and used resale value of the skis higher, making it less expensive for the skier to move to higher performance or more recent models as his skiing ability—or his desire for something new—dictates. The American companies were the first to develop rebuilding techniques, but more recently European factories have been establishing service centers in the U.S.

METAL SKI CROSS-SECTIONS

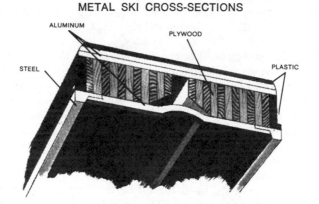

Northland Golden Jet—Cross-laminated fir plywood core with no filler in center, full-length bonded steel edge, aluminum sheets on both the top and the bottom.

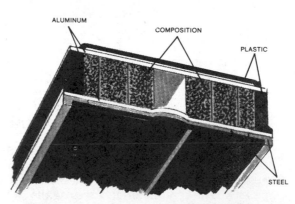

Hart Javelin—Grainless core of pressed particles, continuous full-length steel L edge welded to steel sheet, revealed aluminum top edge, phenolic plastic top.

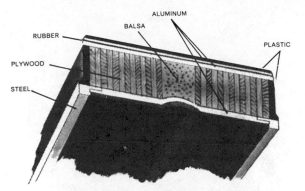

Head Competition—Cross-laminated fir plywood core, rubber damping layer on top of structure, full-length bonded steel L edge, high-density plastic base.

FRP CROSS-SECTIONS

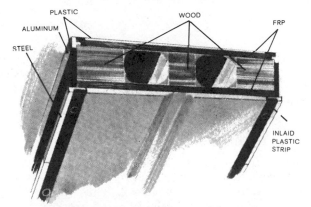

Kneissl White Star—Epoxy sandwich with interrupted wood core for lightness, sectional steel L edge screwed-in, aluminum top edge, two-color inlaid base.

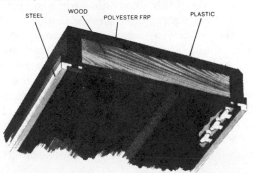

A&T K2—Vestigial core of pine, full wrap-around construction, bonded full-length L edge. ABS plastic top sheet. Bonded edges have tab construction for strength.

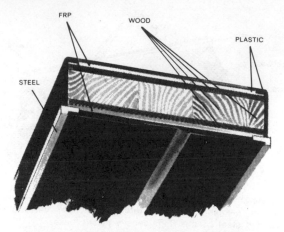

Yamaha Hi-Flex—FRP sandwich, hardwood core with grain running lengthwise, full-length bonded stainless steel L edges on bottom, with top edges of celluloid.

There are three basic elements of FRP construction: the plastic material or resin; the glass fibers themselves; and the method of combining, curing, and shaping the composite reinforcing layer. Variation of any of these three elements affects the characteristics of the end product.

Service potential of FRP skis

One of the problems facing the manufacturers of fiber-reinforced plastic skis has been how to service and rebuild them—once the normal wear and tear of skiing has taken its toll. Only the metal skis, it has seemed, could be refinished and rebuilt.

Though it is true that you cannot heat up an FRP ski, melt the glue, resand, recoat, and reconstruct it quite as easily as you can a metal ski, progress has been made in this direction during the past season. Several manufacturers have set up regional service centers.

What these various service centers can accomplish is considerable. They are replacing bases and edges. They are renewing and refinishing top surfaces. In some cases, the structural fiberglass members can be separated from the wood core and replaced, producing in effect a brand-new ski. The sum of all this is real benefit to the average skier, who is unwilling to discard a pair of skis every season or so. The gap between metal and FRP skis, as far as service potential is concerned, is being narrowed. You will find that the costs range over approximately the same spread as the metal skis and that guarantee provisions are similar.

The Real Paper, Inc. (A)

THE *Real Paper* (*T.R.P.*) and its "give-away" school edition counterpart, the *Free Paper*, were organized in July of 1972 by a group of former staff members of the *Cambridge Phoenix* for the purpose of publishing "metropolitan Boston's weekly journal of news, opinion and arts."

All of *T.R.P.*'s founders were former members of the Phoenix Employees Union. Their decision to form the *Real Paper* came after a bitter dispute with the ownership of the *Cambridge Phoenix*, which featured strikes, lockouts, picketing, fistfights, and legal action. Central to the organizing group's concept, The *Real Paper*'s operations and ownership were to be on a "community" basis. Staff members owned equal shares of T.R.P., Inc., and elected its board of directors. Paula Childs, a member of the editorial staff described the *Real Paper* as "a staff-owned, capitalistic enterprise. It's a group of people who came together so that they could have control—complete control—over their own business and at the same time make money doing it."

Starting without facilities, operating funds or an established circulation organization, *T.R.P.* achieved revenues of $462,000, profit before tax of $53,000, and a circulation of approximately 30,000 paid and 40,000 free in its first eight months of operations. Comparable data for fiscal 1974 were $998,000, $73,000, and approximately 40,000 paid and 50,000 free circulation.

Substantial achievements, however, had not left the staff of the *Real Paper* without uncertainties. Bob Rotner, publisher of *T.R.P.*, commented, "The *Real Paper* is making money but we're still not out of the woods. We are subject to too many ups and downs." Jeff Albertson, associate publisher, noted "the personality of this paper is hard to talk about. It has been a problem and we have had an identity crisis starting from day one. No one knows what 'it' is, and 'it' suffers from this lack of clearly defined purpose." And Paula Childs reflected:

The *Real Paper* was founded on the theory that most cooperatives are formed on—you know—everyone shares equally and things are fair, just, and good—and all that kind of stuff. But I think, and a lot of people who came to the paper since its founding with those same thoughts about it, have since been disillusioned. Within the *Real Paper* there's a definite hierarchy, there's a definite kind of bureaucracy. It's —it's a real—I mean it's—in some ways just like any other business.

THE MILIEU

Leaving the Harvard Business School with its carefully pruned plantings, manicured lawns, and freshly painted doorways, the researcher walked across the Larz Anderson bridge into Cambridge, past the Georgian-styled undergraduate living halls guarded by their high iron fences, and headed for the Lampoon Castle (home of Harvard's humor magazine). The Castle, itself a parody on Harvard's red brick and ivy style, served as a rough marker dividing University Cambridge from its more egalitarian neighborhood, Central Square.

Walking down Mount Auburn Street, the researcher dodged plastic bags of refuse awaiting collection, as he passed a potpourri of small shops featuring services ranging from "Chinese Laundry" and "Tim's Lunch" to the "Mules Mirage" (a boutique) and "Bowl and Board" (an expensive furniture store). The *Real Paper* offices were located at 10–B Mount Auburn on two floors of a yellow, wood frame building nestled between the Cambridgeport Problem Center ("Free counselling, non-hassling assistance for legal, psychological, social and family problems") and a row of triple-decker rooming houses. Ten–A housed a hairworks salon ("haircuts for men and women") and a school of dance whose students seemed to continue their lessons as they walked out of the building onto the sidewalk at the end of the class. Across the street other converted triple-deckers housed a number of research and professional offices.

The lamppost in front of the *Real Paper*'s office tolled a counterculture zeitgeist:

> Boycott Grapes: March! East–West Foundation Seminars in Spiritual Development. Meditations: Yin Meditations, Yang Meditations.—Meditations of Light, Nectar, Inner Sound, Love and Inner and Outer Infinity.—Declaration of Godhood; Basic techniques of Palm and Spiritual Healing; Stop Outrages in Psychiatry; Old Cambridge Common Pet Parade; Save the Cambridge Common Concerts; Filmmakers—workshops; Boycott Lettuce; Our rights we will defend with our lives if need be!

Mt. Auburn was a busy Cambridge street. Mixed with a heavy flow of commercial traffic were bicyclists, motorcyclists, and hordes of small foreign cars jousting with an infrequent standard size model as traffic inched its way forward to Central Square. Joggers were there, too, but in a minority position. And the pedestrian flow was heavy. Almost universally young, the passersby walked with a bounce that often sent long hair flying in the wind. Legs and faces tended to be unshaven.

Exhibit 1

THE REAL PAPER, INC.
Statement of Income for the Year
Ended April 26, 1974, and the Eight Months
Ended April 27, 1973

	1974	1973
Net sales	$995,793	$462,557
Other income	2,675	269
	$998,468	$462,826
Costs and Expenses		
Cost of publication	$618,802	$273,468
Selling, general and administrative expenses	304,674	135,738
Interest expense	372	124
Total costs and expenses	$923,848	$409,330
Net income from operations, before provision for federal income tax	$ 74,620	$ 53,496
Provision for federal income tax	1,092	2,100
Net Income	$ 73,528	$ 51,396
Retained earnings, beginning of period	51,396	—
Retained earnings, end of period	$124,924	$ 51,396
Net income per common share, based on the weighted average number of shares outstanding at the end of the year, which was 2,800 shares in 1974 and 3,300 shares in 1973	$ 26.26	$ 15.57

Clothing was simple: smocks, or T-shirts, army surplus rucksacks, colorful headbands or hats of Humphrey Bogart fame, blue jeans and sandals or hiking boots were the order of the day. The researcher was reminded that the metropolitan Boston area was a youth center heavily influenced by large numbers of young people who studied or worked there, or who merely drifted in and out.[1]

A loud exhaust backfire from a blue Porsche—a student with patched jeans of bright and varied hue—provided the last insight to the Mt. Auburn Street scene. "Porsche and Patches" mused the researcher as he turned and entered the door marked "The Real Paper." Coming into the ground-floor area, his first impression was that the area was too small for the ten desks and numerous people working there. The main room was often a maelstrom of phone calls, shouts, advertising personnel walking back and forth, and a steady stream of visitors coming to place classified advertisements with Ellen Paul, the staff person in charge of that activity.

On one side of the main door a bicycle was stored; on the left wall a bulletin board hosted a series of announcements: a lost cat, flea market

[1] At a later date, the researcher obtained some population data on two- and four-year colleges, degree granting technical-trade institutes and universities located in the New England area. There were over 35 of these institutions in metropolitan Boston, with approximately 130,000 students; approximately 120 schools in Massachusetts, with approximately 320,000 students; and 250 in New England, with approximately 600,000 students (of which 2,262 were primarily students of religion). He was intrigued with the academic program for one of the schools: "The Institute of Anatomy, Sanitary Science and Embalming."

Exhibit 2

THE REAL PAPER, INC.
Balance Sheet
April 26, 1974, and April 27, 1973

ASSETS

Current assets.................................	$161,812	$88,812
Fixed assets...................................	6,220	2,223
Other assets..................................	7,606	1,407
Total assets..........................	$175,638	$92,442

LIABILITIES AND STOCKHOLDERS' EQUITY

Current liabilities.............................	$ 48,507	$37,320
Stockholders' equity..........................	127,131	55,122
Total Liabilities and Stockholders' Equity..........................	$175,638	$92,442

sales, advertisements for the City Dance Theater, numerous plays, and The 100 Flowers Bookstore. Ellen's dog, Martha, padded around the room seeking attention, occasionally barking but never committing any grave social errors. To the left was the receptionist Cyndi Robbins, wearing a flannel shirt, blue jeans, and sandals. Social pleasantries completed, she commented, "It is a hassling job with the phone and so many visitors, but I like it here—the people, the experience, and the atmosphere."

Looking to the back of the room, the researcher noticed a man (later identified as the comptroller, Howard Garsh) sweeping the floor and stacking telephone reminder slips in a cabinet. Cyndi's directions to the publisher's office sent the researcher to the back of the main room, where the publisher and the advertising sales director shared a small office, furnished in the same spartan manner as the remainder of the office.

In a brief meeting the researcher explained his general interest in the alternative newspaper industry and his specific interest in the *Real Paper*. Both Rob Rotner and the researcher agreed there were opportunities for learning in the development of a case history on the *Real Paper*. Later, after consultation with other staff members, Bob welcomed the researcher to the group and agreed to collaborate on the project. (See Exhibits 1, 2, and 3.)

Exhibit 3

COST BREAKDOWN
(provided by Howard Garsh)

	Cost	Percent
Printing, composition, trucking, and circulation........	$368,515	37%
Salaries—editorial, circulation, art, free-lance editorial (including bonus).................................	217,147	22
Salaries—sales, accounting, and clerical...............	125,613	12
Selling, general, and administrative expenses...........	212,001	21
Net profit before tax (note: bonus totaled 4%).........	74,620	8

HISTORY OF THE *REAL PAPER* AND ITS COMPETITION

Early interviews with staff members highlighted the need to study the intertwined history of the *Real Paper* and its primary local competitor, the *Boston Phoenix*.

The story seemed to begin in September 1965, when *Boston After Dark* (*B.A.D.*) was born, in a spirit of entrepreneurialism, as a special centerfold supplement to the *Harbus,* the Harvard Business School student paper. *Boston After Dark* was meant to be a student's guide to Greater Boston's arts and entertainment world. As a "freebie" its distribution soon expanded to other Boston campus locations. In 1970, Stephen Mindich, a Boston University graduate and former art critic and advertising salesman for *B.A.D.*, purchased the paper. His early and major innovation was to add politically oriented news to *B.A.D.*'s coverage of arts and entertainment.

The second critical historical event was the founding, in October of 1969, of the *Cambridge Phoenix* by a 26-year-old Vietnam veteran as an "alternative" newspaper for the Boston area. The *Phoenix* statement of purpose indicated that it "was conceived with the discovery that Boston, the intellectual, artistic, and economic center of New England was a journalistic vacuum." Within a year, the undercapitalized *Phoenix* was bought by Richard Missner, a 26-year-old M.B.A. Throughout 1970 and 1971, brisk competition developed between the *Phoenix* and *B.A.D.*

Fusion magazine, commenting on the competitive situation noted:

> . . . local college students had a twin forum in which to see their revolutionary outrage expressed. . . . Horror stories of government murder and graft ran alongside reviews and advertisements for films and rock performances that created for viewers a fantasy world of glamorous sex and violence. . . . Needless to say, both writers and readers were college-educated, white and middle class, reveling in self-righteousness as they defended people they rarely met, attacking the economic system while enjoying some of the most extravagant luxuries it could provide. Boston's weeklies provided access to the many valuable varieties of this lifestyle, as well as the impression that it was profound.

The *Phoenix,* however, soon began to develop major operating and financial problems. Its financial backer withdrew and the staff of the *Phoenix* became increasingly disgruntled with Missner, his leadership style, and his vision of what the paper should be. Once, holding up a copy of the *Wall Street Journal*, Missner indicated editorial changes he wanted made.

On May 2, 1972, the *Phoenix* staff agreed to form a union in support of a popular, just-fired editor-in-chief, whom Missner had planned to replace with a former advertising executive. A strike, a series of confrontations and negotiations ensued. By the end of the month, compromises were effected and the union was officially recognized. Chuck Fager, one of the union leaders and a current member of the *Real Paper* staff commented on the strike and the effect it had:

> It was really a surprise that we unionized. Sort of WHAM! There it was. People in every department had gripes of their own. . . . So we

went out. As a result of the strike, we went through a proletarianiza-
tion. For instance, we noticed the mailman. Well, he saw our picket
signs and he refused to cross the line. Management had to go down to
the post office to get their mail. We hadn't seen things from this perspective. . . . But once we were out, our jobs were on the line; we
stood to lose everything. . . . But it was fun too. We were working
together in a way that we had not worked before—making signs, picketing, and cooking food.

T.R.P. was "born" on July 31, 1972. The *Boston Globe*[2] reported this
event as follows:

> On July 27, in a 2 P.M. memo, he [Missner] informs all Phoenix
> staffers to get out by 5 o'clock. The paper, it seems, has been sold to
> none other than B.A.D.'s Stephen Mindich for a figure Mindich claims
> to be $320,000. Outraged at Missner's move, they met outside their
> locked offices and decided to publish their own newspaper by working
> without pay. It hits the streets on July 31, and it is called The Real
> Paper. On the same day, the new Boston Phoenix, with a second section
> called Boston After Dark, appears.

Born into a field of competitive entrepreneurs, yet itself a creature of
communal militance, the *Real Paper's* trials were not yet over. For the
first four weeks investors were sought, but to no avail. Chuck Fager
said, "The most serious was the *New York Magazine*, but they weren't
certain as to how willing we would be to respond to management policy.
They were quite right to question that."

Walter Harrison[3] recalled some of the sacrifices of that period:

> We worked virtually 24 hours a day. The financial sacrifices were
> great. We all started collecting unemployment compensation. People
> donated phones and office space. We had meetings virtually every
> night. For the first two weeks with donations and sales we just broke
> even.

Then, by the fourth week, having found no backers, but having established the viability of their new enterprise, Fager said, "A decision
was reached. We had a meeting. Everyone wrote down on little cards
what they had to have in order to keep going. Rotner presented a
financial statement. And we found that we could cover salaries. Suddenly we had the option of independence and almost everyone was
willing to take it. Why have a backer if you don't need one?"

One hundred shares of stock were issued to each employee in lieu of
back pay. Corporate and administrative positions were filled by elections. According to Fager, "We had the equivalent of $50,000 to $100,-
000 of capital in our momentum, i.e., free press coverage, willing advertisers, and hawker and reader willingness to buy."

The early months of the new association were rewarding, if not in a
financial, certainly in a communal sense.

The biggest change, some of the staff members say, has been the new
atmosphere. Paul Solman, the *Real Paper's* editor, says: "Having our

---

[2] *Boston Globe—Globe Supplement*, June 9, 1974, p. 11.
[3] Assistant to the publisher.

paper shot out from under us may have been the best thing that ever happened. Coming over here and starting a new paper and running it ourselves, we've set a real precedent. Before this, 'democracy in the newsroom' has always had the clinker that one guy owns the paper, and you can't really tell the people what to do with their own money. But we've gotten rid of the clinker now."

Joe Klein, another writer, says that there is a greater feeling of participation at the paper by all of its staff. "I've never felt as close to the whole process of something I've worked on. I've never been so interested in the business side of the paper. . . . Everybody talks about how much like a family it is here."[4]

In the intervening year and one-half, staff attention was turned to consolidating and expanding T.R.P.'s position. Advertisers and readers gained confidence in the Real Paper as evidenced by its substantial growth in revenues and circulation. And, as would be expected, operational policies and practices were modified and personnel came and left. In 1974, the Real Paper was a well-recognized Cambridge phenomenon.

THE ALTERNATIVE NEWSPAPER INDUSTRY

Various members of its staff characterized the Real Paper as an alternative newspaper. Local newspaper columnists had, on occasion, described the Real Paper and the Boston Phoenix as "underground press" or "counterculture" papers. Some news distributors interviewed referred to them as "radical sheets" or "sex papers for freaks."

With circulation in the tens of thousands and distribution via hundreds of news outlets, the term "underground" seemed inappropriate to the researcher. If the Real Paper and the Boston Phoenix were alternative papers, alternative to what? What were the key, current developments? A survey of literature available in libraries and observations by industry members provided some limited information and insight.

Although the alternative weekly was often referred to as "a paper," the genre suited more a magazine than a newspaper model. It assumed a readership that obtained its basic news from other sources, such as daily newspapers, radio, or television. The alternative press typically serviced one or two specialized segments of a larger reader market, for example, a politically liberal or youth subcommunity. Most of the large and thriving alternative papers were located in large cities or near large college campuses.

In 1972, the Underground Press Syndicate estimated that there were 300 regularly published "underground papers" in the United States, with a combined readership of 20 million. The UPS also estimated that one in three persons in the 15-to-30 age bracket were regularly exposed to underground publications.

The model for the alternative newspaper was judged by many observers to be the Los Angeles Free Press. That paper, founded in 1964, was described by the Underground Press Syndicate as:

---

[4] Nation, April 23, 1973, p. 531.

. . . in basic ways demonstrably different from all predecessors. First, the Los Angeles Free Press was specifically designed for a mass, though specialized, audience; second, it was in a format inexpensive to produce, simple to learn, yet with high readability, creativity, general appeal and possibilities for development and refinement; third, it was economically self-supporting and self-spreading—it was successful; fourth, it was both hip and radical (the same thing, as we now know); and fifth, it was part of a people's movement and remained a part because it was, in general, operated in a communistic style.

Paul Solman, editor of *T.R.P.*, commenting on the history of the industry and current trends noted:

. . . the rise of the underground press in the 1960s was concurrent with the rise of "The Movement" in this country. They were not so much businesses as they were political organizations. The relative inexpensiveness of offset printing enabled these organizations to turn to printed media. There was little stability and a great deal of manpower turnover within these organizations. Then as The Movement began to wane, these enterprises waned. The inheritor of these underground publications is the contemporary Alternative Press. It features the same format—offset tabloid—and many of the same people. But there was a dramatic transition in becoming a stable Alternative Press. This involved a commitment to becoming an ongoing business institution. It meant accepting responsibility, getting away from drug cartoons and sex stuff, avoiding the utter tripe we used to get, and making a transition from being purely political—and using language like "pig" and "Amerikka"—to doing something more than just indulging your political biases.

Change and evolution appeared to be very much a part not only of the alternative but also of the wider newspaper industry scene. That industry was the tenth largest American industry in terms of revenues ($5.5 billion in 1972) and the fifth largest employer (380,500 in 1972). Some 75 percent of that revenue came from advertising—local retail, classified, and national; the latter category appeared to be diminishing somewhat in terms of importance.

Economically the industry had to bear the cost of high capital investment characteristic of many manufacturing operations, as well as the relatively high labor cost of many service organizations. Efforts to improve profits, described as marginal by some investment houses, depended on the newspapers' abilities to deal with distribution problems, antiquated production facilities, and a continuing rise in the cost of newsprint. The latter item has habitually made up 25–30 percent of the revenue dollar. Cost of Canadian newsprint had gone up 20 percent in 1973 and further major increases, as well as shortages, were expected to occur in 1974. Some papers had adopted a strategy of diversification into related communication areas as a "solution" to these problems.

THE *REAL PAPER* AND THE *FREE PAPER*

The *Real Paper* "book," as it was referred to by its staff, was an unstapled and folded collection of newsprint pages, typically 50 to 60 in number, in tabloid format. The front page usually featured *T.R.P.*'s logo as well as a multicolored graphic design, which related to one of the feature articles in that issue. Titles or references to other stories were also highlighted on the front page.

In describing the paper's content, *T.R.P.*'s editorial department distinguished between "the front of the book" and "the back of the book." The front of the book section accounted for the first 20 to 25 pages. It typically included several long feature articles, human-interest articles —for example, an attempt by girls to enter the all-male Boston Little League baseball competition—and a number of shorter news or political items. In addition, there were four regular features: Letters to the Editor; "Short Takes," a news column; a political cartoon; and Burt Solomon's "Cambridge Report," a column covering the political and cultural life of Cambridge.

Paul Solman, the editor, indicated that two to three "compelling" front of the book feature articles were the key to his editorial composition of the paper. A random sampling of some of these articles, from the spring of 1974 issues, follows: "The Great Commuter Race. Bikes Beat Cars and MBTA by a Wheel"; "TV Guide to Impeachment"; "The Behavior Mod Squad. Clockwork prisons: Brainwashing Saga Continues"; "A Shopper's Guide to Confession. What You Have to Know to Get the Best Deal on Penance"; "Have You Been Swindled? Nuclear Disaster Strikes Plymouth: A Shocking Scenario for the Future"; "The Death and Resurrection of the Black Panthers"; "The Strange CIA Past of Deputy Mayor Robert Kiley"; and "Prostitutes in Boston." It was evident, from a review of the titles listed on the front cover of these same editions, that feature and news articles ranged from local and national to international topics and touched on a variety of cultural and political topics.

Letters to the Editor made interesting reading in their own right and often created a dialogue between readers and staff that gave continuity to the weekly issues of *T.R.P.* The letters printed were usually only a fraction of those received. A random survey indicated letters from a variety of well-known personalities (Daniel Ellsberg) to unknown readers; from Boston College and MIT professors to AWOL American soldiers living in Sweden. Most of the letters printed appeared to be from students, or the young in age or spirit living in the metropolitan Boston area. Correspondents' addresses, however, indicated readers in each of the New England states.

The second regular front of the book item, "Short Takes," in the words of its compiler Craig Unger, "tries to get six or seven news items which I think are most interesting, amusing, and politically significant that get the least media play. It has very broad limits ranging from local news to international news. About two-thirds to three-quarters are of a political nature, and the rest are amusing."

The back of the book section accounted for approximately 60 percent of *T.R.P.*'s pages. It featured a number of regular departments, such as commentary and reviews on theater, cinema, music, and art; and "Local Color" by Henry Armetta, a column about the metropolitan Boston's entertainment field; plus a back page calendar for the upcoming week, which listed events of artistic interest in the Cambridge–Boston area. The staff of *T.R.P.* believes that its coverage of arts and entertainment, particularly the music field, was excellent and customers interviewed by the researchers tended to support that conclusion.

A substantial section of the back of the book was devoted to listings and classified advertisements. The researcher's random sample of approximately 100 purchasers of *T.R.P.* indicated that the Listings and Classified sections were extremely popular. Listings provided an accurate and thorough calendar of well-known artistic events, as well as information on a host of lesser publicized activities, many of which were available at no or minimum cost. The film rating service gave staff evaluations of each film on a scale of worthless to masterpieces.

The classified pages' popularity was readily understandable to the researcher. They seemed to be an open-door communicating device among the many subgroup cultures in the community. This section had its own language system—the researcher was a WM–24–Stu (can you translate?). The advertisements or notices were a potpourri of every known youth interest or need. There were advertisements for jobs, apartments, and where to get advice about drugs, pregnancy, V.D., and low-blood-sugar problems; Personals—"Sarah from Newton—why did you walk out on me?"; leads on where to buy a wide range of products, inquiries for pen pals—often from prisoners; and a variety of travel and educational opportunities were presented (see Table 1).

And if the reader wanted new relationships, they came offered in group packages from "encounter" to "philosophic" discussion meetings. If one wanted individual companionship it came in a variety of formats: male–female, male–male and female–female.

Bob Williams, *T.R.P.*'s advertising manager commented on the importance of the listing and classified sections in an interview with a *Nation* writer.[5]

> The real reasons our paper or *B.A.D.* are essential to the lives of the people who read them are the classified ads and the listings. Around here, people move around a lot, a couple of times a year at least. Things change hands all the time. Apartments, stereos, TVs, cars, sex. There has to be a way for the things and the people to get together. Let's face it, Boston is one big party, with 350,000 kids looking for something to do. So the film listings, and the listings in general, are a big selling point. These things are the spine of the paper—the writers give it a competitive edge.

The *Free Paper* edition of *T.R.P.* was similar to *T.R.P.* in most respects. In any given week there were some differences in editorial content because of a post office ruling that price preferences given one reader over another must be accompanied by a minimum 20 percent content difference. The post office also required that a certain percentage of a paper's circulation must be paid to obtain second-class mailing

---

[5] *Nation*, April 23, p. 533.

Table 1

REPRESENTATIVE CLASSIFIED ADVERTISEMENTS

WARM, sincere attractive WJM. Pisces, 29, dislikes dating bars and phony people, would like to meet warm, sincere, affectionate, cuddly slightly mesugah WJF 18–30, short and pretty, with long hair, for lasting relationship. White CF, PO Box _____ Framingham, Mass. 01701

WHITE Male 25 Walpole Prisoner wants letters & visits from young women I'm 6′ tall weigh 160 blond hair blue eyes. Real Box 749

TALL dark and sane. Are you still out there? Sorry didn't get in touch. Please send phone number or suggest meetings. Let's get it together this time. Patricia Box 750

I'm a young woman planning to bring former hillside farm in Western Mass. to long lost fullness. Educated, intelligent, willful, crazy, occasionally impossible, but often spontaneous, loving, energetic, able, funny, practical. Smoke insanely and visions a joy to me. Physically attractive, but so what? Want to feel the isness of things but that takes time and living. Want to make a home for friends to visit when in need of love, slowness, wholeness, rest, healing. Box 728.

WM 27 grad student, warm, aware, seeks female to enjoy the intoxication of spring with. I like tennis, books, nature, hiking, beautiful sex, politics, playing guitar. Let's get together. Real Paper Box 752.

ONE well-adjusted woman wanted to share sunny spacious, furnished 2-bedroom apartment in North End for summer. $100/month rent. Please call Joan at _____

privileges. Circulation of the *Free Paper*, since it was distributed to school living and dining halls, varied with the local student population, dropping during vacation periods.

Supplements to *T.R.P.* and the *Free Paper* were added to the regular editions about once each month. Jeff Albertson, newly assigned supplements editor, felt that the frequency of supplements would increase in the fall of 1974. Supplements were similar to the regular book in format and design. However, each was typically organized around one theme, such as buying guides to high-fidelity equipment, camping equipment, etc. Articles on the theme were prepared and advertisers with a particular interest in that field were sought.

The Metropolitan Boston competitive situation

In addition to several dozen weekly suburban newspapers covering their local scenes, three standard daily and two major weekly alternative newspapers were published in Boston. The daily newspapers included the *Christian Science Monitor*, whose masthead declared it to be "An

International Daily Newspaper," and whose principal circulation was outside of metropolitan Boston.

The second paper, the *Boston Herald-American,* owned by the Hearst Corporation, was a recent merger of the *Herald-Traveler,* which had circulation strength in the suburbs, and the *Record-American* with "blue collar" readership in Boston. An industry observer described it as an "independent, conservative, Republican paper. It's probably losing a lot of money. There is a rumor that Mr. Mindich is considering launching a major Boston daily, contingent upon future plans of the *Boston Herald-American.*"

The *Boston Globe* was the largest of the three standard papers in circulation and was financially the most successful (net income of $3 million on $90 million in revenues in 1972). Local journalists conceded the *Globe*'s competitive aggressiveness, citing its use of specialists covering such topics as urban renewal, mental health, affairs of the elderly, and the women's movement. One observer described the *Globe* as a paper "which serves the liberal educational community well and the City of Boston with less enthusiasm. The *Globe* espouses its liberal causes stridently and rarely hesitates to show a bias in its reporting."

In attempting to gain information about the alternative newspaper competitive situation, the researcher visited a dozen newsstands in the Greater Boston area. Clearly the leaders in this race were *T.R.P.* and the *Boston Phoenix.* But the customer had a variety of papers from which to make a selection depending upon his or her particular mix of reading interests. Larger newsstands typically carried, as a minimum, three other nonlocal alternative papers: the *Village Voice,* the *Free Press,* and *Rolling Stone.* The *Village Voice* (weekly price 35 cents, 125 pages, over 150,000 circulation) was owned by *New York Magazine;* its masthead stated that it was "The Weekly Newspaper of New York." The *Voice* had an East Coast and national distribution pattern. Its content was focused on a wide range of local New York and national political issues and personalities; it had major, in-depth coverage of art, music, and the theater. As a member of the Audit Bureau of Circulation its advertisers included prominent local and national firms.

The *Los Angeles Free Press* (weekly, 35 cents, about 40 pages, circulation 150,000) also had achieved regional and national distribution. Its coverage included politics, the arts, and a 20-page classified "sex" insert —literally a cornucopia of erotica. In contrast to the more academic style of the *Voice* (an interview with three African female jurists and an analysis of Shakespearean Theater), the *Freep*'s editorial style seemed to the researcher to be sensational and its word system and headlines were strident in character.

The *Rolling Stone*'s (biweekly, 75 cents, over 100 pages, circulation 300,000) content was heavily built around popular music and the entertainment world, with some political coverage, e.g., an interview with Jane Fonda on her latest visit to North Vietnam. While both the *Voice* and *Rolling Stone* carried classified advertisements, these tended to down play sex themes and products.

A Boston newsdealer mentioned the *Texas Monthly* as a prototype of recent entries in the field. *Newsweek* magazine reported that it sold for $1, "has taken provocative looks at the inner workings of the state's highway lobby, banks, law firms and daily newspapers, dismissing the latter 'as strikingly weak and ineffectual.' The *Texas Monthly* received the prestigious 1974 National Magazine Award for Specialized Journalism."[6] "*Ramparts*, of course," the newsdealer said, "has been around a long time and there are a batch of others of the same cast."

In metropolitan Boston, *T.R.P.*'s primary competitor was the *Boston Phoenix*. Both papers were similar in format and price, both were published weekly, both used the same distribution methods—although with different emphasis—and both had free school editions.

Differences were also apparent to the researcher. The *Phoenix* was a larger book—often over 80 pages compared with *T.R.P.*'s 50- to 60-page editions. The larger *Phoenix* was divided into two distinct subparts: the *Phoenix* and its insert, *Boston After Dark*—the Arts and Entertainment section. The *Phoenix* enjoyed a larger circulation; industry estimates ranged from 80,000 to 110,000, with approximately 40,000 being the free edition. The *Phoenix* appeared to the researcher to enjoy a wider range of local and national advertisers than did *T.R.P.* In terms of visual appearance, the *Phoenix* appeared to be more crowded and less willing to use open space to lead the reader's eye around a page than did *T.R.P.*

The researcher wanted to obtain data on why a customer purchased *T.R.P.* versus the *Phoenix* and what was the market for these two papers. A random survey of purchasers by the researcher obtained limited information. Most could not make explicit their preference for one paper over the other. *T.R.P.* customers often mentioned "better Cambridge coverage," "more liberal," "easier to read," while *Phoenix* purchasers stressed "red hot classifieds" and "*B.A.D.* is the best guide." (See Exhibit 4.)

In reviewing this competitive situation between the *Real Paper* and the *Phoenix,* a *Boston Globe* writer commented:[7]

> The two papers continue in the image of advocacy journalism planted firmly left of center and sprinkled with occasional muckraking. But while in days past they overlapped on stories, they almost never do today. In fact, except for arts coverage—particularly music —you can browse through two issues of the same week and not see two pieces about the same thing. What you will find is that the *Phoenix,* reflecting its publisher's little-subdued dream to become a force in the community, concerns itself more with the news of the day, dealing with many of the same subjects and events as the city's dailies. "We've made a shift to respond to news happenings," says Miller. "We want to be topical." The *Real Paper,* on the other hand, seems to be moving more and more towards becoming a weekly magazine, opting for stylized features and columns rather than news reporting. Part of the reason for this is undoubtedly the *Real Paper's* constituency, which is more Cambridge-oriented than that of the *Phoenix. . . .*

6 *Newsweek,* June 17, 1974, p. 29.

7 *Boston Globe—Sunday Supplement,* June 9, 1974, p. 7.

Exhibit 4

COMPARISON OF ARTICLE CONTENT OF THE *REAL PAPER* VERSUS THE *BOSTON PHOENIX*

	Real Paper		*Boston Phoenix*	
Category	*Number of articles*	*Percent*	*Number of articles*	*Percent*
International events or politics..........	2	1.7	5	2.8
Art, movies, books, TV, dance..........	32	26.7	59	33.0
Exposés.............................	5	4.2	1	0.5
Rock music, other types of music, album review columns.....................	15	12.5	32	17.9
Local events/politics..................	21	17.5	34	19.0
Counterculture, e.g., communes, drugs, etc..........................	1	0.8	2	1.1
National events/politics...............	9	7.5	20	11.2
Movements, including prison reform, women's, and gay..................	9	7.5	4	2.3
Sports..............................	2	1.7	14	7.8
Miscellaneous, including food, "Local Color," travel, tax information.......	24	20.0	8	4.5
Totals.......................	120	100.1	179	100.1

Source: These data were prepared by Kim Panushka of *T.R.P.* staff. She surveyed eight issues of each paper for the months of March and April 1974. The total number of major feature articles for *T.R.P.* was 120; for the *Boston Phoenix*, 179. Excluded were regular columns from staff writers.

What was the market for the two publications? Bob Williams, advertising manager for *T.R.P.*, gave one specific definition.[8]

In Boston you have 350,000 young people, under 30, within 2.5 square miles of space. You don't find a concentration like that anywhere in the country except Boston. It's a unique market. These kids spend around $40 million or $50 million a year.

Dennis Hale, staff writer for the *Nation* magazine, gave a more general comment.

So the New Journalism is not much "new" as it is specific in its choice of audience. For the most part that audience consists of young, white, relatively affluent college students, graduates and dropouts. Like newspaper readers everywhere, these people have a set of opinions, of whose truth they are fairly certain, and they do not enjoy seeing these opinions challenged in print. At least, not too often. And the editors of "underground" and "alternative" papers are as sensitive as editors everywhere to the outer limits of their readers' tolerance.

Over a period of months, the researcher observed *T.R.P.*'s operations and interviewed a substantial number of its staff. Early in his research, he studied the production process, the financial and accounting systems, the circulation department, and the advertising sales activity. As the research progressed he then worked with the editorial area. A summary of this information follows.

[8] "Prospects for the Alternative Press," *Nation*, April 23, 1973, p. 533.

Production

Getting the "book" out each week was a central activity at *T.R.P.* As in any daily or weekly publishing operation, this activity was characterized by speed, deadlines, coordination of a host of detail and people, and the ever-present last-minute changes.

The production of *T.R.P.* basically involved the laying out and printing of five types of copy within the time constraint of weekly publication, and the size constraint of how large a paper could be profitably published. This process could be summarized around six stages of production.

First, the various "copy traffic controllers" accumulated the five kinds of copy: editorial, advertising, art, classified, and listings. Each controller determined the space required for his or her copy and relayed that information to the layout editor.

Second, on Thursday, as the accumulation of copy was drawing to a close, the comptroller, managing editor, and advertising sales director met to determine the number of pages in the book. The comptroller would project the week's profit and loss statement under varying assumptions about advertising, density, and number of pages in the book.

Third, the layout editor was informed as to the number of pages to be published as well as about additions or deletions to copy. He then proceeded to allocate sections of each page of the book to various kinds of copy. This involved the use of a "paste-up board," a full-scale representation of a page.

Fourth, the paste-up boards were transferred to the composition shop. Here copy, which had been typed in even columns, was physically pasted onto the paste-up boards, which were photographed and the resulting negatives developed. These negatives, along with the negatives of copy photographs—called "halftones"—were combined by taping them together.

Fifth, the final negatives were taken to the printing plant where printing plates were made and the paper was printed on a webb offset press. It took about three hours to print an edition of 50,000 papers.

Sixth, on Saturday morning the newsstand distributors picked up papers from the printing plant for distribution to newsstands on Sunday. The hawker edition was distributed at 5:30 A.M. Monday mornings to hawkers. Subscription copies were addressed and mailed on Saturday for delivery to the post office on Monday.

Production of the *Free Paper* followed on Monday, when editorial people altered the layout boards and changed the front page design to conform to the required 20 percent content difference regulation. The paper was printed that same day and delivered to college campuses on Tuesday.

Neither composition nor printing facilities were owned by *T.R.P.*, and that work was subcontracted to local, independent firms. "Both of those operations would require substantial capital investments in equipment," Howard Garsh explained.

Control

The comptroller's office consisted of two people, Howard Garsh, the comptroller, and Stanley Korytko, the bookkeeper.

One day, while walking into 10–B Mt. Auburn with the researcher, Howard said, "I don't see how you can do this study without some reference to the figures. Let's talk for a few minutes?" The researcher and Garsh walked upstairs, through a small office and into a connecting closet that served as Garsh's "cubbyhole," as offices were referred to at T.R.P. Garsh proceeded to search for papers in his files and in the clutter on his desk.

A lot of what I do here deals with keeping track of the company's financial status, either projected or actual. Accordingly, there are several tools I use, the weekly P & L projection according to various book size assumptions, the monthly profit and loss statement, and the semi-annual cash and operating budget projections. These budgets tend to be conservative, pessimistic, and possibly just a little extreme. That is, we overestimate expenses and underestimate income just so we don't get cocky and overextend ourselves.

Our auditor says he's never seen such beautiful papers. That's partly because we don't just make broad assumptions of percentage increases, but instead get down to the real arithmetic of it. For instance, the budget is based on Bob Williams' projection of revenue from display[9] advertising since that's the source of about 80 percent of our revenue. We ask for the most reasonable, honest estimate that doesn't pull the figures out of the air. He talks to the salesmen, looks at the economy, and maybe talks to some advertisers. And his estimate is usually conservative. As you can see from this. Remember, his projections were made one year ago.

April 5, 1974   Budgeted $12,000   April 19, 1974   Budgeted $12,000
                 Billed   14,500   Billed   14,000
     (including a $2,000 ad insert)   (including a $2,000 ad insert)

April 12, 1974   Budgeted $12,000   April 26, 1974   Budgeted $12,000
                 Billed   12,500   Billed   15,000

Our bread and butter is accounts receivable. We stay right on top of them. Our credit allowances are 30 days net. And we allocate 4 percent of revenue to bad debt although experience shows at 1 percent is sufficient.

And we virtually have no accounts payable. Other than salaries, our major expenses are printing, composition, subscriber service, mailing, trucking, and editorial free-lance payments. We've never been in a position to keep any of them waiting. Certainly every account is paid within 30 days. There are reasons for this: first, we want a top Dun and Bradstreet rating, a reputation of being a good company to do business with, a company that pays its bills. Right now our D&B rating is two. D&B told us that all it would take to get

---

[9] Regular advertisements from commercial customers, as opposed to classified advertising, e.g., notices of apartments for rent.

a number one is for us to be in business a little longer. Second, we have the money so why not pay it, so we try to help them out by paying on the spot.

The main reason why you'll find differences between actual and projected is in the economics of each week's book, that is the number of pages and ad density. In order to consider those very issues in our weekly business planning, I project the weekly P&L based on assumptions about number of pages and ad density. We like to see about a $2,000 profit and not more than 55 percent ad density. Within those parameters we come to a decision about the number of pages in the book and transmit that decision to the layout editor, who plans the book accordingly.

The economics of our operation greatly affect our performance. For instance, profitability increases very rapidly with an increase in ad density. As past weekly projections have shown, most of our costs are fixed, e.g., mailing, trucking, sales expense, art expense. The only variable costs we have are composition, which really varies only slightly, editorial free-lance, which varies because nonstaff articles are used as editorial copy if we opt for a larger book. Printing costs, which increase by about $1,500 for every eight-page increase we make, and salesmen's commissions (10 percent of collections), which vary with billing but not by size of paper.

For instance, assuming a 56-page paper is average, we will probably spend a total of $20,000, most of which will be on fixed type costs. Typically we will get $2,800 from circulation revenue, and $3,000 from classified advertising, and that means we'd need about $14,000 from display advertising to break even. Usually the salesmen can bring in some last-minute advertising if we think we're running low. But there's a danger in thinking you can cram a lot of advertising into a book, because too much doesn't look good. So it can cause a problem: At what ad density do you decide you have to increase the size of the paper? And is increasing the size of the paper economically profitable? Anything over that $14,000 is gravy until we have to increase the book size. And increases come only in jumps of eight pages. Because each jump costs about $1,500, only one full page of ads (worth about $640) never justifies a book increase of eight pages. But what is the cutoff? I don't know.

The special supplements are pure gravy. The profit margin varies between 20 percent and 50 percent because the regular kinds of expenses are charged against the regular edition, and so that supplement must only cover its incidental printing, composition, editorial free-lance, artwork, and mailing expenses.

Garsh's responsibilities also included relationships with the First National Bank of Boston. That bank, since T.R.P.'s founding, had financed all major capital needs of the organization.

Circulation Department

Kevin Dawkins, who had joined T.R.P. in January of 1973, had just been put in charge of circulation activities.

T.R.P. was distributed through four channels: newsstands, hawkers, subscription, and controlled circulation—i.e., free distribution. The percentage breakdown of distribution channels in 1974 was newsstands 30 percent, hawkers 14 percent, subscription 4 percent, and controlled 52 percent. In 1972, Kevin pointed out, the newsstand and hawker percentages had been reversed with hawkers selling over 30 percent and newsstands roughly 15 percent of *T.R.P.* circulation.

Controlled circulation of the *Free Paper* goes to "every conceivable college from here to Worcester, Mass." A formula of one copy per four students was used, and never were more than 50,000 copies distributed. Dawkins commented, "It's gravy. It boosts our circulation which entitles us to boost our advertising rates. Besides, the audience is captive. This edition builds reading habits which can extend to higher newsstand sales. In college towns, though, if we miss delivery to the school for some reason, newsstand sales stay about the same. Sometimes I think the markets are separate."

As for newsstand circulation, two-thirds occurred within Route 128 (metropolitan Boston), and one-third beyond. *T.R.P.* worked through one distributor, Greater Boston Distributors, Inc., within the Route 128 area. Greater Boston had over 800 outlets including the Union News outlets in subways, railroad stations, and Logan Airport.

T.R.P. was sold at 75 percent of these newsstands. Money was paid only for copies sold. The price to the distributor was 12 cents; he sold it to the independent newsstand operators for 19 cents, and the newsstand price was 25 cents. Greater Boston handled between 1,500 and 2,000 titles, among which were the most profitable in the country. Dawkins felt that *T.R.P.* should be at more newsstands, and be featured more prominently.

Newsstand relationships beyond Route 128 were handled through independent distributors. The newsstand circulation area extended as far to the west as Holyoke–Springfield, Massachusetts, as far east as Portland, Maine, and as far south as Providence, Rhode Island. The objective here was to penetrate outlying markets by first reaching college communities and communal areas.

Hawker relationships were one of Kevin's responsibilities. Hawkers were independent operators who bought a paper for 5 cents and sold it for 25 cents on busy street corners throughout Greater Boston.

> In 1970, 200 hawkers used to sell almost 40,000 copies of the *Old Cambridge Phoenix;* now we have 100 hawkers selling 15,000 copies of *T.R.P.* We used to have 75 hawkers in Boston alone—now there are only 45. There is a very high turnover here but we have a hard core of about 50 old-timers.
>
> The papers are trucked to a number of distribution points in Boston and Cambridge. The hawkers buy the papers for cash, but if someone is in a rough way we will front him or her for ten or 20 copies. They can turn unsold copies in the next week for new papers. All hawkers sell both our paper and the *Phoenix.*
>
> The typical hawker is the kind of person you would see at a rock and roll concert: long hair, T-shirt, blue jeans, and sandals. They are street people and they keep us anchored to that community.
>
> They do pretty well. Richie on the Boston University Bridge must make $80 from *T.R.P.* and the same from the *Phoenix* in a couple of days. Other hawkers can make $100 in two days and some people

living in a group setup can clear $25–$30 in two days and they can live on that.

And they have their codes too: the oldest one in seniority gets to take the best corner, although the old-timers have the territory well staked out. We don't even know some of their real names. One of them calls himself King Kong. They don't want to have any tax records.

I'm trying to push hawker sales. We are advertising in *T.R.P.* and I'm preparing posters to put up around the city. Hawkers are great publicity for us, standing at each street corner and practically putting the paper through your car window. Everyone can see that front page, whereas on the newsstands we are buried. I'm trying to extend hawking to the suburbs by promoting hawking through guidance counselors.

They are street people—that community is important to us. And I don't think the *Phoenix* really wants to use them; they aren't sophisticated enough. The *Phoenix,* you know, has hired two former *Herald-American* pros for their circulation department.

Subscriptions had been an increasingly expensive channel of distribution to service. The paper was physically distributed by Hub Mail, Inc. The cost per paper per subscription was about 22 cents, making it the least economic of all channels. Since the mailing service refused to operate on weekends, a mailed paper arrives at its earliest on Tuesday, whereas *T.R.P.* was delivered to newsstands on Sundays. The one redeeming feature about subscription sales, Kevin noted, was that *T.R.P.* gets "the money up front." Kevin intended to eliminate the discount that subscribers get by subscribing (raising the price from $10 to $13 per year) in an attempt to cover cost increases, and he hoped to negotiate a new mailing agreement which would have the paper in the mail on Saturday and delivered by Monday.

Kevin had growth in *T.R.P.* circulation as one of his primary goals. He was assisted in this program by a "road man" who visited newsstand owners to "sell" them on the advantages of carrying *T.R.P.*

We are one of Greater Boston's top ten best selling accounts. They formerly had sort of a monopoly and weren't aggressive. Terrible things happen to people when they have power. But they are getting competition now and that helps us. We are considering selling papers via machines located in grocery stores.

Our toughest competition is the *Phoenix.* They are supposed to have 110,000 circulation and their revenues are twice ours—they up their ad density and charge higher advertising rates than we do. But we will catch up with them! Within one year we will be bigger! I get excited about this! Walter Harrison (the former circulation director) has suggested to me that we experiment with a home delivery system.

In the spring of 1974 Bob Williams began to advocate broadcast media promotion as a means of building *T.R.P.*'s visibility and consumer demand. Except for development costs, it was anticipated that the program would operate largely through reciprocal advertising, with commercial radio and television broadcasters.

Kevin concluded:

I want us to get recognition; we put out the best paper in the country and I know because I am in touch with lots of them. Our problem is we just aren't taken as seriously as we should be. We want to be an important part of the Cambridge–Boston community in the near future. We want people to use T.R.P. as more than just reading material. We want to serve as "the reference" for what goes on here. We want it to be an important part of their lives.

Advertising Sales Department

The advertising sales department was concerned with selling display and classified advertising, and comprised five display salespeople, one classified salesperson, Linda Martin (the advertising traffic controller), and Bob Williams, the department director. Advertising sales accounted for approximately 80 percent of the revenue of T.R.P.

Talking about T.R.P.'s advertising market, Williams said:

> There are basically two levels of advertisers we're concerned with. The first group is people who have clubs, restaurants, concert tours, Army–Navy stores, clothing, bookstores, record stores—all the people who sell mainly to college students. These people came in right away. They really had to. They need papers like ours as much as we need them. The second level is the larger companies—GM, stereo companies, Jordan Marsh, and the other big clothing stores, which don't have an immediate relation between advertising money spent and dollars earned. With these people, it's only a matter of time.[10]

There was no formal system of account assignment, since Williams believed that a strict delineation of "turf" was not healthy. Nevertheless, each salesperson seemed to have specialized in one way or another. For example, one salesman, Steve Cummings, concentrated in cameras, symphony, sex, and religion, e.g., Boston Symphony Orchestra, adult bookstores, Indian Gurus, and meditation movements. The four most important industries for advertising revenue were stereo components, liquor, phonograph records, and cameras.

The approach each salesman used was individualized. Price bargaining was allowed which "makes selling tougher," Bob commented. "Otherwise, it is just stating standard rates." A sense of flexibility, of tailoring to the advertiser's needs, seemed to the researcher to be a dominant theme in the advertising efforts of T.R.P. In two instances, the researcher observed that Williams was willing to bend contractual agreements or trade advertising for the specific products of the business. "It's those little guys we've got to help. They're where our future lies." T.R.P.'s advertisers were primarily Boston firms but about 15 percent of display advertisements were placed by national firms.

It seemed to Bob Williams that the T.R.P. advertising staff sold access to a special kind of consumer—a youthful, liberal, student market. But "hard" and reliable data was limited. A 1974 company-financed survey of approximately 300 purchasers of T.R.P. (Free Paper customers were not canvassed) provided the following profile: Average age 23.7:

---

[10] *Nation*, April 23, 1973, p. 533.

sex 55 percent male and 45 percent female; 87 percent had some college education and 47 percent were college graduates; 24 percent were professional-technical personnel, 23 percent full-time students, 12 percent unemployed, 11 percent clerical, 10 percent blue collar, 5 percent sales, 4 percent managerial, 1 percent housewives, and 10 percent miscellaneous. Thirty-six percent of the papers were sold in Boston, 32 percent in Cambridge, 5 percent in Brookline, 3 percent in Newton, 3 percent in Somerville, and the remainder scattered in other Boston suburbs.

T.R.P.'s advertising charges were geared to its circulation rate base of 90,000 copies per week. Rates for display advertisements were $14 per column inch, or $1,120 for a full page. Discounts were given for continuity of placement: 13 weeks—10 percent, 26 weeks—15 percent, and 52 weeks—20 percent. Classified advertisements were $1.90 per line.

> In terms of rates we want to get between $11.00 and $11.50 per thousand readers and stay about 50¢ per thousand under the *Phoenix*. The more specialized your market is, the higher you can charge. Publication get $2 to $3 per thousand for a very general audience, to $5 to $6 for a somewhat specialized audience, up to $30 to $40 for a very specialized group.
>
> We don't cut our stated rates in the summer even though with school vacations, our free circulation drops, but we do make deals. Many of our advertisers are on yearly contract (a total of two-thirds of T.R.P. advertisers were on some kind of contractual basis)—they get more power in the fall and winter than in the summer but it balances out. In this business, one-half your customers don't even know what your circulation is; they are only interested in how much response the advertisement gets, and we have a very loyal readership.
>
> With free copies, we don't go above 52 percent at the top; Bob Rotner makes that decision. Free circulation is good but it makes things a bit more fluffy—particularly for A.B.C.[11] counts. It makes it harder for you to really prove your circulation.

Some of the problems Williams noted were the business community's lack of respect for T.R.P. and the staff's prohibition of certain kinds of advertising. With regard to the former, Williams noted that some advertisers regularly abuse credit terms, and said, "People don't respect us the first time around. They think we're just a weak underground paper. Meanwhile, the staff prohibits cigarette advertising because it felt that it was detrimental to the paper's image, but that means a loss of revenue."

As for the future, Williams doubted that T.R.P. should follow the *Phoenix* to pursue suburban advertisers. He noted that the *Phoenix* was his roughest competition.

> I don't think the future is necessarily there. There is a 50 percent bad-debt ratio on advertising beyond Route 128,[12] mostly motorcycle

---

[11] Audit Bureau of Circulation, an agency which attested to the circulation figures of newspapers and magazines.

[12] A belt highway, approximately 12 miles west of the central city. Route 128 tended to be a dividing line between the more developed suburbs of Boston and the less developed, higher status suburbs of the city.

places, bars, and so on. The people who read *T.R.P.* and shop are here in town. We sell our circulation and a kind of readership. It would be foolish not to exploit it here. The *Phoenix* is entering the suburbs and doesn't have the circulation to back it up. That will hurt alternative weeklies in general. Furthermore, we're still thrashing around editorially. It would have been unwise to move until we get that straightened out. Finally, we are best sold to small and medium-sized businesses; and they are most cencentrated here in town.

The trick is to get local advertisers to transfer ad money from radio to print and more particularly, *T.R.P.* There are about 50 stations in this area, and ten of them program directly for the youth market. We do some reciprocal advertising with them now.

I love music and have a hi-fi set. The reality of Boston is that there is an important radio market here. If the company were interested, and it isn't, we could go into partnership with one of these stations. It would provide a great new combination for us. Bob Rotner once thought we should go into the newsstand distribution business.

By 1975–76, if my plans work out, we should be in a position to enter the suburbs. I am shooting for advertising sales this year of $1.5 million.

Editorial

Editorial offices were located on the second floor at 10–B Mt. Auburn Street. The physical layout consisted of a main room (about one-fourth the size of the first floor) and two closet-size offices at the far end; one of the latter also served as a hallway to the back porch. Paul Solman (editor) and Tim Friedman (managing editor) were technically assigned this space, but all members of the department seemed to participate in its use. Jeff Albertson's (the associate publisher) desk was next to Tom's office.

The main room contained five desks, two tables, filing cabinets, and all of the usual paraphernalia of an editorial operation. A chair, with one of its casters off, occupied the center of the room. "We bought all of this equipment secondhand," Paula Childs noted. "We sure scrimp around here. Howard buys us discard, advertising promotion pencils but no pens. But we are getting more space in the basement here—that should help a lot."

The researcher agreed that space was needed. Even in a summer lull period, editorial personnel flowed in and out and often there were not enough available desks and chairs. The room had a used and noncleaned look with papers on the floor and boxes of editorial supplies stacked in every conceivable place. A number of bulletin boards seemed to be a part of the communication system, telling Peter to get a photo at 10:30 and noting that a free-lance writer wanted his check right away—"He is flat broke." Office decor consisted of wall-sized pictures of Katherine Hepburn, et al., and advertisements for concerts and artistic events; a somewhat tired and dehydrated plant provided the final touch.

The researcher sought to capture the office tone. Clearly busyness was the order of the day, with editorial personnel constantly using the multiple phones and the limited desk space. Friendliness was another factor. Martha, the receptionist, seemed unflappable despite the constant barrage of questions and calls with which she was confronted. There was an air of informality. Standard dress seemed to be T-shirts, shorts, and sandals; it made the first floor look almost "Establishment."

Editorial proved to be a complex part of *T.R.P.* scene to "paint" for the reader. After several abortive attempts the researcher finally decided to look first at "who was in the area and what did they do," next at the "organization and leadership of the work," and finally at *T.R.P.*'s "editorial posture."

T.R.P.'s masthead (July) carried the names of 54 individuals, 32 of whom were listed under "Editorial." Of those names, Paul Solman commented, "14 are full-time personnel, eight are part-time members who regularly contribute, and ten are free-lance or irregular contributors to the book."

The editorial staff tended to specialize by function. On the "support" side, Paul and Tom were assisted by Jan Freeman (copy editor) and Paula Childs (listings and general editorial person), and general assistance to the entire group was given by Peter Southwick (photos) and recently "on board" Bruce Weinberg (production manager).

On the "creative" side the situation was more complicated since most staffers handled multiple assignments. The largest number worked primarily on "back of the book" material—the arts and entertainment section and, in addition, contributed regular columns used throughout the entire paper. The smallest number of full-time masthead personnel were involved with the development of feature stories. "When we came over from the *Phoenix* we had six full-time feature writers," Paul said. "Until recently we had four, but Joe Klein just left to go with *Rolling Stone* at twice what we could pay, and Ed Zuckerman is going back to journalism school. We need to hire another two writers; we're short-handed."

In addition to back of the book and feature writers there were a number of individuals (often part-timers) who specialized in writing a political or news column or, as in the case of Omar White, created a political cartoon. In addition to masthead personnel, there was a pool of free-lance writers who, on occasion, submitted articles to *T.R.P.* Boston seemed to attract a large number of writers, many of whom could not find, or did not want, a regular organizational relationship.

The editorial group was responsible for the creation and processing of copy with copy coming from staff columnists, staff feature writers, solicited manuscripts from free-lancers, and unsolicited manuscripts. This editorial activity, Tom commented, was organized along the back and front of the book lines.

> Jim Miller is our music editor and Stuart Byron is our film editor. They, along with Art Friedman, our regular theater columnist, and Kay Larson, our art columnist, hand me back of the book material each week. The back of the book tends to run itself, but Paul is looking for a back of the book editor. Both of us are front of the book oriented, and a good deal more of the budget goes into the front than the back of the book.

Exhibit 5

MASTHEAD—JULY 17, 1974

EDITORIAL
PAUL SOLMAN, EDITOR
TOM FRIEDMAN, MANAGING EDITOR
HENRY ARMETTA
HARPER BARNES
BO BURLINGHAM
STUART BYRON
PAULA CHILDS
STEPHEN DAVIS
CHUCK FAGER
JAN FREEMAN
ARTHUR FRIEDMAN
RUSSELL GERSTEN
ANITA HARRIS
JOE HUNT
JAMES ISAACS
JOE KLEIN, NEWS EDITOR
ANDREW KOPKIND
CHUCK KRAEMER
JON LANDAU
KAY LARSON
JON LIPSKY
DAVE MARSH
JIM MILLER
LILITH MOON
ARNIE REISMAN
LAURA SHAPIRO
BURT SOLOMON
PETER SOUTHWICK, PHOTOGRAPHER
CRAIG UNGER
BRUCE WEINBERG, PRODUCTION
DAVID OMAR WHITE
ED ZUCKERMAN

ADVERTISING
ROBERT WILLIAMS, DIRECTOR
JONATHAN BANNER
STEVE CUMMINGS
MIKE FORMAN
LINDA MARTIN
DONALD MONACK
ELLEN PAUL
RICHARD REITMAN
DICK YOUSOUFIAN

ART
RONN CAMPISI, DIRECTOR
DAVID BROWN
PAT MEARS
REBECCA WELZ

CIRCULATION
KEVIN DAWKINS, DIRECTOR
DON CUMMINGS
CYNDI ROBBINS
MIKE ZEGEL

BUSINESS
HOWARD GARSH, COMPTROLLER
STANLEY KORYTKO
WALTER HARRISON, ASST. TO THE
PUBLISHER
JEFF ALBERTSON, ASSOC. PUBLISHER
ROBERT ROTNER, PUBLISHER

Metropolitan Boston's Weekly Journal of News, Opinion and the
Arts. Address all correspondence to the Real Paper, 10B Mt
Auburn St., Cambridge, Mass. 02138. Telephones Editorial and
Art, 492-8101; Advertising, Circulation and Business, 492-1650
Second-class postage paid at Boston, Mass. Published weekly by
The Real Paper, 10B Mt. Auburn St., Cambridge, Mass. 02138
  Copyright © 1974 by The Real Paper. All rights reserved.
Reproduction by any method whatsoever without permission of
staff is prohibited.
  Unsolicited manuscripts should be addressed to Jan Freeman
and must be accompanied by stamped self-addressed envelope
Photographs should be submitted to Jeff Albertson, Photo Editor
  Subscription rates 1 year, $10.00; 2 years, $18.00

Printing by Arlington Offset

JULY 17, 1974   Vol. 3, No. 29

All staff members, with whom the researcher spoke, indicated that Paul was the central person in the process of generating or reviewing story concepts, interesting and assigning writers to develop those stories, and finally nurturing and reviewing the resultant manuscript as it evolved. It seemed to the researcher that this was an extremely personal and intuitive process, difficult for all involved to articulate and yet critical for *T.R.P.*'s success.

At a regular Friday morning meeting the editorial staffers gathered with Paul in an informal session to review the copy program. Story ideas were reviewed, modified, or discarded in a free-flowing meeting with staffers sitting on the floor and Paul, his chair tilted against the wall, leading the discussion.

Paul's primary operating pattern, however, seemed to be on an individual-to-individual basis. He often began the process of copy creation by talking with a writer about an idea. "At any given time I expect I am working on 50 story ideas of which five may actually come to print. I work at home two days a week because I can concentrate better there and handle the writers more effectively by telephone."

The researcher appreciated the latter comment since Paul's office routine could be described as frenetic. He was constantly on the phone, answering questions, reviewing edit problems with Tom or working with a writer. Paul's informal style and personal warmth made it easy for all to approach him and he seemed always to be "in conference" outside the office building, on the stairs, or even walking through the office. "When do you get time to reflect?" the researcher asked. Paul smiled, "It's tough."

With full-time, front of the book personnel, Paul's primary function seemed to be reviewing story ideas that they brought to him. With part-time and free-lance writers, Paul seemed to play a more active role in initiating concepts, but he also reviewed their suggestions and manuscripts. He had a wide acquaintanceship in the Boston community and seemed to the researcher to have knowledge about and interest in a wide range of topics and institutions.

> I handle all of the free-lance work. It is a shifting group of people. Some work for other outfits, some are teachers, some have a cause, most need money—it's hard to make a living free-lancing. We pay them $75 for a short thousand-word story, $250 for a feature article or part thereof. Once in the judge and court system story, where a lot of research work was needed, we paid $600. But we negotiate with each; the budget puts on real limits.

Jan Freeman in commenting on copy development said:

> Paul's job is to think up ideas and then assign them to either regular or free-lance writers, although usually the regular staff generates their own ideas. It is a very difficult job and I suspect the ratio of ideas to finished stories is about 15 to one. The process depends a lot upon who is available and whether or not they are interested.
>
> A lot of what Paul wants to do this fall is to make the paper more useful. Tom would probably want more news stories of a political

bent. Everyone's ideal would be to do more apartment rental agency stories. Did you read that? They are a real rip-off and take money under false circumstances. We did a lot of research on them. It was both an exposé and a news story.

I want us to do more stories like that or the one in this week's issue on airline safety—more consumer-oriented pieces—but they take lots of time. We should do more local investigatives, like the article on the coroner's office in Boston's City Hall. We should do stories that make a real difference—a protest that demands a response.

And we need more middle of the book material—material between the arts and listings and the political and news and feature stories at the front. We need think pieces, like the story in the *New York Times Magazine* section. A woman in an apartment house was robbed—bound and gagged. What was it like? What were her fears? Did she behave bravely enough? This was a special story and a woman wrote it from a woman's point of view. We need more material on ideas and people. I suggested to Paul that we do an article on people living together— roommates or lovers—or whatever. It should be funny and yet factual. These aren't news stories—they are people and idea combinations. And we should do more on scientists and science articles—the article in the *New York Times* on "black holes" in space is a good example.

Tom, who had joined *T.R.P.* in November of 1973, had as his prime objective introducing more organization into the editorial process. He felt progress had been made in this area and, by July, lead feature articles had been planned and were in process for the next five months.

It was in my own self-interest to get some planning going—things were frantic here when I first came. I wish we had more full-time feature writers; we need at least three now. It would make my job easier. You get to know the regulars and how to work with them; they have to produce. But it isn't as cost effective. People don't have story ideas regularly every week, and so there are bound to be slow times when we won't get stories.

Both Paul and Tom spoke highly of the caliber of *T.R.P.*'s editorial staff, and conversations with other Boston journalists confirmed that evaluation. Some staffers had achieved awards, national publicity, and peer recognition from the wider journalistic field.

In trying to pin down *T.R.P.*'s current editorial style and format, the researcher talked with various members of the staff. Tom Friedman reflected, "Partially it's form—longer paragraphs and in-depth analysis. Partially it's an emphasis on the human dimension. We just don't feed them information; we create an ambience whereby the reader can relate to the event. We give them more than historical background, we give them more than information—we get to the basic reasons."

Joe Klein, who had received several journalist awards, contrasted *T.R.P.*'s and the *Phoenix*'s editorial style.

Our style strives for both a sense of immediacy and perspective. Our copy is written more dramatically. We're also much more careful. We want to write the definitive story on the subject. Paul and I talk it out and decide what the story should be; it has to have a larger focus than just what happened last week; we take specific incidents and show

how they reflect on institutions. I don't see that happening with any other publication in town.

Paul Solman commented:

> Our major articles, in contrast to the *Phoenix*, are long—we do in-depth reporting. Our feature article on selling the Encyclopaedia Britannica was a good example. The writer actually sold Britannicas. We want to be able to help people see why they behave as they do. Why does a blue collar making $14,000 spend 800 bucks on a set of encyclopaedias? Or our article on the hearing aid racket is another good example. We want to be at the cutting edge—what is really going on in that business. We want to answer questions. We want the truth. But the budget limits us; we are small and they are larger. We can't compete with them in terms of coverage.

> The development of a pool of feature article ideas is fairly random, he continued. A lot depends on what I read or hear from friends. We get lots of suggestions from people outside the staff. And one of my critical inputs is to gather staff who can contribute ideas. I have a sense of balance for the make-up of the paper but I don't have a specific formula for a certain amount of political, or human interest, or exposé material in any issue or any month.

Chuck Fager, one of the original staffers, reflected, "We have an ephemeral editorial policy now. Writers just stream in and out. The *Phoenix* does a better job of covering Boston and the State House than we do. But any differences between the *Phoenix* and us now is more individual writer style than editorial strategy."

An evolving editorial posture

In the summer of 1974, the researcher noted, the topic of future editorial direction was the object of considerable discussion, not only within the editorial staff but within the paper at large. Paula Childs commented:

> We're not covering events enough—issues that deal with people's daily lives. We're not covering what's happening with rent control, what's happening in the ecology movement, what's happening in the neighborhoods—that kind of stuff. Also, I think we're too Cambridge-oriented. Our strongest following is Cambridge. We cover Cambridge things to a much greater extent than Boston. And I think that that's one of the reasons why people on the other side of the river continue to pick up the *Phoenix* instead of *T.R.P.*

Howard Garsh believed "more hard investigative reporting should be our first priority now." Walter Harrison wanted more emphasis on quality editorial work. Tom Friedman commented feelingly, "I want to have more impact on people's lives. My basic attitude is deep distrust of the people who run our country and our businesses. Some staffers want more emphasis on entertainment; some just want more people to buy it. I want the people to get the information they wouldn't get otherwise. I want more investigations. I want to work on an investigative paper, not just a successful operation. I'm trying to hold on to my sense of moral outrage."

Bob Rotner, from his perspective, saw two approaches to future editorial direction. "The edit people want witty headlines. The business people want headlines that sell. The edit people feel the paper ought to be political, serve the left. The business people see it as the ultimate guide to Boston, serving the consumer element. I want it to do more investigative reporting."

Paul Solman reflected not only on near-term and future editorial direction, but plans to get there, noting:

> We are planning some minor modifications for the fall. We will have two long feature stories and a larger number of shorter stories that will provide more information in readable form. And we will expand the number of vignettes from New York City and Washington events. One of the latter might be an interview with the aide of a congressman.
>
> And we're trying to figure out what we want the paper to be. The paper is essentially a reflection of the people here and they are not homogeneous. But in the longer run, we're working toward a personality for this paper that is intelligent, political, which I mean to say politically progressive, interesting to people, compelling, and well written.
>
> We're not real close now, but we're making progress. Our effort now is oriented to four activities. First, we simply want to get more copy available for our use. Copy can always be edited and rewritten. So getting the basic fund is important. This means asking more of our staff people, as well as really pursuing the free-lance sources. This also means we will have to pay higher rates than competitors, pay for research, and make appeals to the really good people based on prestige, personal ties, and even convenience.
>
> Second, we want to tie down regular contributors—good writers who may not be on the staff but can be relied on for quality stuff. We want to create a circle of regular free-lancers.
>
> Third, we have to fight the tendency to diffuse our efforts. Accordingly, we created the position of managing editor which will free me from the day-to-day operational problems.
>
> Fourth, we want to run two or three solid articles per week in the front page of the book that are smart and fascinating.
>
> Success for most people is to be big and powerful. I don't have a specific vision of T.R.P. and success, but I want it to be something that serves the people. I want us to be a wing of society—out there after the bad gals and guys. Yet I want it to be entertaining too, for literate people. And I want it to be instructive to the public.

LOOKING AHEAD

The former *Cambridge Phoenix* and T.R.P. had been organized and had their early operating years during a period of major societal and youth unrest. Campus stories headlined strikes, riots, and "take-overs," while on the wider scene, the counter-culture movement was in full bloom.

Reporters of the mid-70s youth movement indicated that much of the past turbulence seemed to have disappeared. While the president of Ohio University did resign in June of 1974, citing "the mindless destructive events of the past week," most college campuses seemed quiet and the counter-culture movement had, in many observers judgments, "plateaued."

The transition from activism to a more restrained protest pattern was captured for the researcher in Sara Davidson's article on the Symbionese Liberation Army. She interviewed Dan Siegel, a well-known participant in the 1969 Berkeley disturbances about his changing career and life style.

> Siegel is 18, an attractive, modest-looking young man in a sports shirt and slacks. In 1969, when he was student-body president at Berkeley, he gave a speech that sent thousands surging down Telegraph Avenue to reclaim People's Park. Bob Dylan was singing from speaker vans: "You can have your cake and eat it, too."
>
> Siegel says he no longer had "the illusion that revolution will be easy or that a few gallant people can do it. Winning the hearts and minds of tens of thousands of people—that's what making revolution is about." He walks toward the courthouse where he is preparing a test case in which the community is suing the district attorney, and he says that it's funny but in some ways, he feels old.[13]

Given these changes, as well as major developments in the wider environment, the researcher wondered what, if any, impact these forces would have on the future plans of *T.R.P.* He raised the question of future direction with Paula Childs. She commented:

> I'd like to see this paper eventually be able to own its own composition shop as well as its own printing company. I'd like to see this company own its own other media resources, like its own radio station. And I'd like to see the paper get to a large enough size that we can be covering the things we should be covering. You know. Right now we're in a tug-of-war between whether to be more like a magazine, or whether to be more like a newspaper. Right now, we're much more like a magazine than a newspaper.

Joe Klein, a former staff member, added:

> From here I'd like to see us grow in several ways. First, I want us to develop a broader base of readers and not be read by just street people and hippies. This would mean expanding into older neighborhoods and suburbs, as well as becoming more and more frequently read downtown. I want it to have impact. Furthermore, and I guess this is a second point, I want us to expand beyond Boston to a regional and even national scope. I want us to have as many readers outside of Boston as the *Village Voice* has outside New York. And third, I want us to become an alternative for top-notch daily journalists.

Bo Burlingham, another staff writer, asked:

> Have we reached the end of our growth with this format? It has worked so well. And the answer is so important because it affects so many things. Who do we hire? Young kids just out of college and ask them for a full-time commitment? Or, do we hire older more experi-

---

13 *New York Times Magazine*, June 2, 1974, p. 44.

enced part-timers who can work here—and write the book they always really wanted to create?

It raises questions as to who our audience is—is it Cambridge, Boston, New England, or ——? How we work with that influences Howard's financing plans and Bob Williams' advertising programs. And questions, too, need to be asked editorially. Should we go on primarily with feature stories about current causes or events or institutions? There are lots of reasons why we should. They take less resources and time and are less risky. Or do we become an investigative journal? That's really rough. It takes lots of money and time to do well and it's risky.

Jan Freeman reminisced:

So much of what we are, is what we were—a collection of people who grew up in the late 60s and who, by luck, got into an organization that we like and where we can do what we want.

Our audience is like us—it's growing up! It's no longer the 60s. Our audience isn't clear any more—it is a mixture. Paul knows this. We know we can't just do what we do best. We never have been a doctrinaire leftist paper—we have sort of been, as I told you—a newspaper-magazine. But what's next?

A *Boston Globe* reporter, Nathan Cobb, raised the question of future direction with various members of *T.R.P.* and the *Phoenix* staff. He commented:

Times change. *T.R.P.*, having achieved financial success, wonders where to go. "It's much less clear now what we should be doing than it used to be," says Paul Solman. "It used to be automatic. You didn't have to think about what you did because there was a counter-culture not being covered by anyone else. Now we're asking what kinds of things we can provide that no one else can."

*   *   *   *   *

One suspects, though, that the two papers really are still viewed as a legitimate journalistic alternative by the fading remnants of the "youth culture." But out in the great beyond, out in those suburbs where folks are easing into their 30s and 40s, each may indeed be viewed as just another newspaper. "The dailies are getting more like us and we're getting more like the dailies," says Joe Klein of *T.R.P.*, an experienced and professional newsperson. "And that's all right with me. I'd like to see *T.R.P.* on every doorstep."

Bob Rotner, publisher, in talking with the researcher about his job and responsibilities as publisher, noted:

But to plan the future of the paper, and to make sure that just because the paper is successful now, it doesn't mean that it's going to be successful in a year or two, and there are certain things happening in the city and the country which need to be understood. We're not making ourselves obsolete. . . . What I hope I can do now is to make the decisions about the future by going to the appropriate places and finding out what is going to happen in the future, and then to make sure that *T.R.P.* is going in the direction it needs to go, so that it doesn't have to worry about the future.

Charles River Breeding Laboratories

DESCRIBED by a competitor as the General Motors of the laboratory animal industry, the Charles River Breeding Laboratories of Wilmington, Massachusetts had achieved major corporate success both in terms of financial results as well as in technical reputation. Company sales were $25,000 in 1950 with operating net profit of $1,400; comparable 1975 fiscal year data were $15,405,100 and $1,565,600. The company's technical publication *The Charles River Digest*, unique to the industry, circulated quarterly to 13,000 members of the international research community.

Charles River specialized in the production of scientifically bred, high-quality laboratory animals for pharmaceutical and chemical companies, commercial testing laboratories, hospitals and universities. Other firms in the industry manufactured cages and scientific equipment, feed and bedding supplies, animal by-products for use in research, and operated independent testing laboratories.

Charles River's first and still primary products were laboratory rats and mice; in 1976, sales of these animals comprised over 90 percent of the company's sales revenues. The company had been the leader in the breeding and introduction of disease-free rats and mice. Beginning in 1955, Charles River commercialized a process known as COBS®, allowing the company to produce disease-free animals which enabled researchers to conduct more effective experimental research. In 1976 this process had been adopted widely by breeders throughout the world.

The executive group of Charles River had been relatively stable over the past decade with company policy being to promote from within whenever possible. Executives described Charles River as a "family firm" and took pride in the Foster family's public generosity in giving Brandeis University a bio-medical research laboratory building and the furnishing of a contemporary gallery at the Boston Museum of Fine Arts.

In reviewing his company's current situation, Dr. Henry L. Foster, D.V.M., president and chief executive, commented, "So far it has been great. We just do what is necessary to produce the best and the results follow. When we went public, we announced a 15 percent–20 percent per year growth goal in both sales and earnings and we are sticking to that target. Once you become a public company, you enter a race and are always out of breath.

"Observers and investors are now asking—what next? We have to deal with that question *now* since the action lead time is a long one. Of course we will continue to grow in our basic animal product lines—but that is not enough. We are going to have to expand into new areas and there are lots of opportunities.

"Where do we go now? How does a manager answer that question? And, how do I organize to get these decisions made? We want internal growth, new product additions and acquisitions. But how do we do this without getting a case of corporate indigestion? We don't want to eat *too* much but we want a good meal."

LABORATORY ANIMAL USE

Laboratory animals, primarily rats and mice, were the basis for product safety testing, drug development and human health research, especially cancer treatment research. Most pharmaceuticals, cosmetics, toiletries, and food additives were tested on animals for toxic side effects before the FDA would approve their sale. Lab animals were used to measure side effects of environmental pollutants and industrial and agricultural chemicals. Medical research on the causes and treatment of cancer, heart disease, nutritional deficiencies and birth defects also relied on experiments with laboratory animals. Studies using lab animals took place at drug companies, independent testing laboratories, universities, hospitals, and a variety of government agencies. The largest governmental users were the National Institutes of Health, the Food and Drug Administration, and the Environmental Protection Agency.

There were two important distinctions to be made about laboratory animals. One refers to the genetic makeup of the animals: whether they were inbred or outbred. The second concerns the method of raising the animals and their consequent state of health: "conventional" breeding methods versus various "pathogen-free" or "disease-free" methods.

Inbred versus outbred lab animals

Although any animal may be inbred or outbred, these terms usually referred to genetic and physical characteristics of the various rodent species[1] which accounted for over 98 percent of all lab animals used in

---

[1] Laboratory animals were distinguished by *species* and *strains*. As defined by the National Academy of Sciences in *Animals for Research*, a *species* is all animals of the same kind that can (actually or potentially) mate together and produce fertile offspring. Examples of common species names are cats, dogs, mice, hamsters, etc. A *strain* is a subset of a species comprised of a group of animals of known ancestry maintained by a deliberate mating system, generally with some distinguishing characteristics.

the United States. The most common rodents were: mice, rats, guinea pigs, and hamsters.

Inbred animals were brother-sister mated for a minimum of 20 generations to produce specific heritable characteristics, such as susceptibility or immunity to a particular disease. For example, the C-3H inbred mouse strain carried a virus which can develop breast cancer in its young, while the SHR (spontaneous hypertensive) rat consistently exhibited blood pressure above 180°. These and hundreds of other inbred rodent strains were used to understand the effects of diseases and to develop drugs and other treatment methods. The largest user of inbred animals was the National Cancer Institute, but medical and drug researchers in universities, hospitals, pharmaceutical firms, and contract testing laboratories also required inbred animals. Inbred strains were more expensive than outbred because of the additional labor and record keeping required by brother x sister mating.

Breeders produced outbred animals by consistently avoiding brother-sister mating in order to produce a heterogeneous population. Heterogeneous populations were made up of animals with a variety of characteristics, much like the human population. These animals were used to test overall product safety and effectiveness. Many more outbred animals were used than inbred, and the largest consumer groups for outbreds were pharmaceutical companies and independent testing labs.

"Conventional" versus "disease-free" animals

"Conventional" methods of lab animal breeding involved putting animals in an enclosed pen or cage, and feeding, watering, and cleaning them. The breeder then waited for the animals to mate and sold the offspring as soon as they were weaned.

Until the mid-1950s, the "conventional" method was the principal way commercial breeders raised lab animals. It was a high-risk, labor-intensive business with many small-scale participants. Risk came from the frequent outbreaks of disease which could rapidly destroy a breeder's entire animal inventory. Commercial breeding businesses were small-scale operations because they were part-time endeavors and few breeders would risk the capital necessary to support larger scale breeding. Animals properly housed and cared for under small-scale conventional methods could sometimes perform as well as animals reared under the more elaborate "disease-free" methods described below. All animal species and both inbred and outbred strains could be raised in a "conventional" manner.

In 1955 Charles River introduced the first of various disease-free animal breeding methods to commercial lab rodent breeding. Disease-free breeding techniques improved animal health, reduced the risk of losing animals from disease, but required special breeding facilities and processes. By the mid-1970s almost half of all lab rodents were raised using one or more of the following "disease-free" techniques.

Specific pathogen-free (SPF) animals were free of specific parasites, and microorganisms which could impair their health, for example, salmonellosis.[2] The specific pathogens eliminated depended both on the species and on the breeder supplying the animal. The process required obtaining a healthy animal through selection or through chemotherapy to eliminate one or more specific pathogens and then following strict quarantine procedures to keep the animals from outside contamination.

Cesarean derivation was a technique which prevented diseases and parasites from being transferred from mother to her young, and resulted in healthier longer living, more vigorous animals. The process is termed a hysterectomy, because the mother's entire uterus containing the pups is removed shortly before normal birth would occur. The uterus is then introduced, using sterile techniques, into a germ-free plastic bubble where the pups are surgically removed and then nurtured by a germ-free foster mother or hand-fed sterile milk. The animals could then remain in a germ-free environment or be placed in a barrier system (see below).

Germ-free animals were cesarean-derived in a germ-free environment, as described above, and were continuously maintained in a germ-free isolator. They were completely free of all identifiable bacteria, viruses, fungi, protozoa, or other parasites (collectively called flora). The most common type of isolator was a two foot by five foot completely sealed clear plastic chamber. All water, feed, and bedding were sterilized, and researchers handled the animals through rubber gloved sleeves which protruded into the isolator. Animals could die within 12 to 24 hours if removed from their germ-free bubble. The advantage of using germ-free animals was that a researcher could be more certain that any animal abnormalities were directly related to a research procedure rather than due to an environmentally induced disease.

Cesarean-derived-barrier-reared (or barrier-sustained) animals began as germ-free pups delivered by hysterectomy. Specific flora were then associated with the animals so that they developed normal digestive and immunological systems, enabling them to survive outside of the germ-free isolators. The animals were housed in barrier buildings which were equipped with filtered air systems, temperature and humidity controls, autoclaves to sterilize feed and bedding, and controlled personnel access in order to prevent contamination.

Barrier facilities and germ-free equipment required substantial capital investment. A plastic germ-free bubble, for example, to house 50 mice cost $400 in 1976. (Prior to the development of plastic isolators in the mid-50s, a steel isolator cost $5,000–$10,000.) There were different degrees of barrier systems and each company employed a unique combination of barrier styles. The simplest method provided a number of separate rooms for animals and controlled the direction of air flow and personnel from "clean" to "dirty" areas. The most sophisticated facilities involved the construction of many small breeding rooms and corridors with extensive air conditioning and filtration systems, sterilizing facilities for equipment, feed and bedding, and elaborate personnel

---

[2] Salmonellosis, in man, is a type of "food poisoning" which can cause severe dehydration.

locks. One industry source estimated the minimum, initial investment for an acceptable small-scale barrier facility to be at least $500,000.

Scope of animal-based research and testing

The majority of laboratory animals were used in human health-related research, drug development, and drug testing. According to the National Institues of Health (NIH), U.S. government expenditures for research and treatment development totaled $1.5 billion in 1975.[3] U.S. pharmaceutical firms spent $930 million on research and development in 1974, according to the Pharmaceutical Manufacturers' Association. Pharmaceutical companies accounted for about 50 percent of the dollar volume of animals purchased, and government-funded research purchases accounted for over 20 percent.

The cost of the compound tested, physical facilities, and salary costs for Ph.D.s, M.D.s and technicians were the major research budget expense items. One industry source estimated that, of the $930 million pharmaceutical companies spent to screen 700,000 new compounds in 1974, lab animal purchases accounted for 5 percent of the total and lab animal maintenance accounted for an additional 5 percent of R&D expenditures.

Animal usage by species

Rats and mice were the most widely used laboratory animals because they were small, readily available, and inexpensive. Hundreds of strains of mice and rats had been developed to be hosts for specific human cancer tumors or to exhibit signs of a specific disease such as arthritis. However, each species and strain had characteristics which were preferred for different types of research, and consequently there was limited substitutability among species and strains.

Dr. Joseph Mayo, director of the Animal Breeding Program at the National Cancer Institute (NCI) and a former researcher, explained why mice were widely used to evaluate cancer treatment drugs.

> First of all, through careful genetic control, mice can be bred to develop a susceptibility to a particular tumor. Secondly, mice are small and easy to handle, so the expense of housing and feeding the animals is minimized. More importantly, it means that the dosage level can be low. Vincristine, a compound we are testing now, interfered with cell division and costs $100,000 a gram.

U.S. research used 41.7 million animals each year and a comparable number, Dr. Foster estimated, were used annually in Europe. Rats and mice accounted for 96 percent of all laboratory animals used in the

---

[3] Of the total $1.5 billion NIH budget, $1.1 billion was allocated to research conducted by various agencies of the NIH itself (e.g., $30 million for the National Cancer Institute's Division of Cancer Treatment), or to researchers in universities, hospitals, and medical schools. Four hundred million dollars was allocated to contract research and testing by independent commercial testing laboratories such as Arthur D. Little or Hazelton, by universities, and by pharmaceutical firms. Much of this $400 million allocation supported animal-based research.

United States, with rabbits, guinea pigs, hamsters, dogs, cats, and monkeys also popular research subjects. Table 1 shows the number of animals used yearly for U.S. research by species. "Wild animals," a heterogeneous category of animals collected from nature, includes amoebas, frogs, marine animals, cattle, poultry, lions and elephants, most of which were used in agricultural and veterinary research.

Table 1

U.S. LABORATORY ANIMAL USAGE
BY SPECIES, 1974

Species	Number
Mice	30,000,000
Rats	10,000,000
Guinea pigs	430,400
Hamsters	430,800
Rabbits	425,600
Dogs	199,200
Cats	74,000
Primates	51,300
Wild animals	81,021
Total	41,692,321

Source: Mice and rats estimates by Charles River Breeding Laboratories and the Institute for Laboratory Animal Resources. Other species data from *Animal Welfare Enforcement 1974*, Report of the Secretary of Agriculture, U.S. Department of Agriculture.

Lab animal performance requirements

Lab animal users considered animal performance and availability more important than price. One industry observer noted:

> Time pressures on researchers are great. Pharmaceutical companies are under pressure to meet market introduction dates and academic research grants usually have a calendar year limit. Therefore any delay in receiving the right number of animals at the right time, or receiving animals that die before the experiment is concluded, has cost the researcher both time and money far beyond the mere cost of the animals.

Lab animal performance during an experiment depended on the animal's state of health when it arrived at the researchers' facility. Breeding the animals in a healthy environment and minimizing transportation stress were the most important determinants of animal health. A breeder's ability to supply a healthy animal depended on obtaining a clean animal to start his breeding colony and then on maintaining production processes and facilities adequate to prevent disease introduction. The division leader of Arthur D. Little's Tumor Screening Program for the National Cancer Institute, Mr. Wodinsky, discussed the importance of familiarity with a breeder's operations in ascertaining animal quality.

> Most suppliers now offer cesarean-derived animals, so the basic animals do not differ much among breeders. The difference is facilities and

production colony management that keeps the animals separate and healthy. It is the people working for them that are the critical factor in controlling contamination. I know the actual setup of all the breeders who supply us.

Dr. Henry Agersborg, associate director of research for Wyeth Laboratories, elaborated on the problem:

> A rat can lose 20% of its body weight in a day and will die of starvation in 5 to 7 days. Loss of weight during transport is a shock to the animal's system. It may regain weight rapidly, but it might be permanently weakened and break down part way into an experiment. That is why transport stress can be a potential problem and why we prefer a breeder who can guarantee same day delivery. A local breeder only has an advantage if he does not use a public carrier. REA can take three days to transport animals 12 miles.

Almost half of the animals used in laboratory research were transported by air freight. Airborne, an air freight forwarder specializing in lab animals, confirmed the problems of timely delivery and promoted its services which monitored the location and status of shipments.

Product availability and reliable delivery were important to researchers in three ways. First was obtaining the specific strain and species required among the several hundred varieties raised. Second was securing enough animals of the specific age, sex, and weight required to meet the needs of several hundred to several thousand animals per program per week. Finally, delivery reliability was very important because research procedures were frequently standardized on a particular breeder's animals.

INDUSTRY TRENDS

An industry observer identified four trends which were having a major impact on the laboratory animal breeding industry in the mid-1970s. These included slower market growth, more sophisticated uses of lab animals, rising quality standards for animals and facilities, and consolidation among breeders.

Slower market growth

Between the late 1940s and early 1970s, the demand for laboratory animals had grown from a few million mice and rats to approximately 42 million animals of many species. The most rapid growth in demand had occurred between 1965 and 1970 when volume doubled. The rapid growth in the mid-60s was spurred by a large influx of funds into government-sponsored research on cancer and viral diseases in combination with stricter Food and Drug Administration test data requirements on the efficacy and safety of new drugs. In the early 70s a cutback in federal funding for health research had slowed the growth of lab animal use for basic research, but pharmaceutical and chemical company use of lab animals for testing continued to expand at a rate of 7 percent—

12 percent per year. By 1974, government-sponsored research expenditures had resumed a growth rate of 5 percent to 10 percent per year. Table 2 shows U.S. drug company research and development expenditures from 1950 to 1974.

Table 2

U.S. DRUG INDUSTRY
RESEARCH AND DEVELOPMENT
EXPENDITURES,
1950–1974 (in thousands)

Year	Expenditures
1950	$ 39,000
1955	91,000
1960	212,000
1965	351,000
1970	619,000
1974	930,000

Source: Pharmaceutical Manufacturers Association, *Annual Survey Report 1973–74* and *1968–69*.

More sophisticated uses of lab animals

Continuing from the late 1960s was a long-term trend toward increased use of "life-span" studies of animals in both research and drug testing. In research, long-term studies were spurred by the desire for more information about the long-term effects of environmental and industrial pollutants and by intensified study of long-term health problems such as cancer and cardiovascular diseases. In drug testing long-term studies had become more common as a result of increasingly stringent requirements by the FDA to identify and disclose long-term effects of drugs. One pharmaceutical industry spokesman stated that 1975 R&D budgets had risen to twice 1970 budgets in order to get the same number of new drugs approved by the FDA. In addition to increasingly longer studies, experiments using lab animals had become increasingly complex, frequently investigating the interactions of two or three drugs in a living organism. Both of these trends pointed to an increasing demand for well-defined,[4] healthy animals which would survive the rigors of longer experiments.

Rising quality standards

The increasing demand for healthier, well-defined animals was responsible for the growing proportion of cesarean-derived-barrier-reared (CDBR) and specific pathogen-free (SPF) animals sold by the larger commercial breeders since the mid-1960s. CDBR and SPF rodents lived longer and were more vigorous than the conventional animals breeders had traditionally raised. Although CDBR and SPF animal breeding re-

---

[4] The "definition" of a laboratory animal included, among other things, information about its "normal" heart rate, blood count, respiratory rate, blood chemistry, and intestinal flora.

quired a substantial capital investment in facilities and equipment, the improved facilities allowed breeders to raise more animals per square foot and to better control infectious diseases within production colonies. The larger breeders' ability to supply SPF and CDBR animals in large volume at a cost only slightly above that of conventional animals was credited with further increasing demand for these improved lab animals.

Longer term and increasingly complex research and testing procedures continued to stimulate increasing demand for higher quality animals in the mid-1970s. Dr. Albert Jonas, director of Laboratory Animal Services at the Yale Medical School, was among a growing group of users imposing higher standards. Quality control screening procedures for animals brought in from the outside involved detailed pathology tests, bacteriology tests, and veterinary exams. Quality control standards were high both to screen out substandard animals and to ensure a stable and consistent data base for experiments.

Dr. Jonas commented:

> Quality in lab animals is becoming increasingly important because of the trend toward long-term studies, especially in carcinogenesis and in long-term effects of pharmaceuticals.

Dr. Mayo agreed that users would be increasingly critical of animal quality, commenting:

> There will be big changes in animal breeding in the next five years. Users will demand more uniformity, in terms of health and, for inbred animals, in genetic control. Researchers will be saying, "My results are different from yours. What animals did you use?" Few breeders will be able to supply the higher quality animals. Few are in a financial position to make the heavy investment in buildings and equipment.

Breeder consolidation

The decade between 1955 and 1965 had brought the transfer of most laboratory animal breeding from users' in-house facilities to commercial breeders. At the same time, many new breeders entered the industry and established breeders prospered. Even "backyard breeders" who raised animals in garages or sheds were successful in the early years. With the recent increase in quality demands and attendant capital investment requirements, few new companies entered into rat and mouse production after the late 60s. Smaller companies went out of business each year or were acquired by larger breeders, and by 1975 "backyard breeders" of rats and mice had largely disappeared.

In the new environment more than financial strength was needed to be a successful laboratory animal breeder. The failure of two large corporations who attempted to enter the industry in the 1960s, Ralston-Purina and Becton, Dickinson & Company, attested to the difficulties of breeding.

Ralston-Purina, which supplied over 50 percent of the lab animal diet market, attempted to establish a breeding facility in Puerto Rico. One industry observer commented that the original product had been good but transportation to major market areas was difficult because of the remote location. In addition to its production and distribution problems, Ralston-Purina encountered marketing problems. Their animal diet sales force was not effective in selling animals since the purchasing agents who bought animal diets could not control a researcher's lab animal purchase patterns. Finally, minimum management attention was given to the endeavor because the $1.5 million facilities investment was such a small part of Ralston-Purina's overall capital budget. Dr. Foster commented that the purchase was like Ralston-Purina's buying another water cooler.

In 1964 Becton, Dickinson & Company, a large manufacturer of medical and laboratory supplies, acquired the Carworth Company, at that time the largest commercial breeder of mice in the industry. The company prospered for a few years after its acquisition, but began a downward spiral that continued until the division's sale in 1974 to Charles River. Between 1968 and 1973 Carworth's fiscal year sales declined from $3.4 million to $2.9 million and gross margins declined from 38 percent of sales to 7 percent of sales. During the same period net income after tax went from a profit of $110,000 to a loss of $471,-000.

THE MARKET FOR LABORATORY ANIMALS

The $78.5 million market for laboratory animals was fragmented and regionalized. In addition to government agencies, pharmaceutical com-

Table 3

ESTIMATED LABORATORY
ANIMAL SALES BY SPECIES, 1975
(in thousands)

Species	Sales
Mice	$25,000
Rats	20,000
Rabbits	3,000
Hamsters	1,000
Guinea pigs	3,500
Primates	10,300
Other species*	11,500
	$74,300

* Includes dogs, cats, gerbils, sheep, poultry, and a wide variety of animals from nature such as fish and frogs.
Source: Researcher estimates.

panies and universities, food manufacturers, and cosmetic and toiletries firms were steady users of lab animals. The total number of lab animal purchasers was well over 2,000 with a multitude of departments and project groups purchasing animals at each company or institution. Most users of lab animals were located along the eastern seaboard between Washington, D.C. and Boston, or in the Great Lakes region between Chicago and Cleveland. California and Texas were the other sizable market areas.

Mice and rats were the most widely used species, accounting for 96 percent of the unit volume of sales and close to 50 percent of dollar volume. Most customers for laboratory animals used some hamsters, guinea pigs, and rabbits in addition to mice and rats. Markets for primates and animals from nature were significantly different from the market for smaller animals. Primates were used almost exclusively by the National Institutes of Health and by contract testing laboratories. Universities and government agencies were the primary users of animals from nature.

Table 4 shows the number of registered users and number of animals

Table 4

REGISTERED USERS AND NUMBER OF
ANIMALS USED, BY STATE, 1974

	Number	
		Animals
State	Users	Used
California	85	156,400
Illinois	63	122,800
Indiana	20	75,500
Massachusetts	46	69,500
Michigan	13	72,500
New Jersey	42	126,100
New York	102	227,100
Ohio	69	68,800
Pennsylvania	57	69,000
Texas	31	142,700
Total	518	1,130,400
Total U.S.	867	1,692,500

Source: U.S. Department of Agriculture, Report of the Secretary of Agriculture, *Animal Welfare Enforcement 1974.*

employed in research for the United States as a whole and for the ten largest user states. Table 4 includes data only for species controlled under the Animal Welfare Enforcement Act.[5] Mice and rats were uncontrolled species, so comparable data were not available.

Laboratory animal markets outside the United States

Outside the United States, the majority of medical research and pharmaceutical testing using laboratory animals was conducted in Japan and western Europe. Most users maintained in-house breeding

---

[5] "The Laboratory Animal Welfare Act of 1966, as amended by the Animal Welfare Act of 1970 (referred to as the Animal Welfare Act), empowers the Secretary of Agriculture to establish standards to regulate the transportation, purchase, sale, housing, care, handling and treatment of animals intended for use for research or experimental purposes or for exhibition purposes or for use as pets." *Animal Welfare Enforcement 1974,* Report of the Secretary of Agriculture, U.S. Department of Agriculture.

facilities and commercial breeding activities were limited, although conditions varied widely among countries. Pharmaceutical and chemical companies comprised the largest user group as they did in the United States, and mice and rats were the most commonly used animals.

There was little data available on the dollar size of lab animal markets outside the United States or on the number of animals used, but Dr. Foster estimated the annual market at $60 million–$80 million, of which Europe accounted for $40 million–$60 million. The researcher estimated that of that total, $6 million was spent on laboratory animals by United States companies in their overseas facilities in 1974.[6] Table 5 presents the researcher's estimates of the market available to commer-

Table 5

ESTIMATED LAB ANIMAL SALES
(dollar equivalents)

	Sales
France	$10,000,000
England	7,500,000
Italy	3,200,000
Japan	10,000,000
Canada	7,500,000

cial breeders in France, England, Italy, Japan, and Canada based on Charles River data.

LABORATORY ANIMAL BREEDERS

The laboratory animal breeding industry was specialized and localized, with most breeders clustered around customer concentrations on the Atlantic seaboard, and in the Midwest. Although the Institute of Laboratory Animal Resources cited 113 sources of laboratory animals in 1975, 27 firms produced over 98 percent of the animals used, and only 5 firms had annual sales of $2 million or more. Some firms participated in allied industries serving the health research community, such as lab animal cage, feed and bedding supply, and the operation of commercial testing and research laboratories.

Within the laboratory animal breeding industry there were three major types of businesses, which were distinguished by the species of animals raised and by their production methods: (1) large-scale breeding of cesarean-derived-barrier-maintained and germ-free rodents; (2) small-scale breeding of conventional animals; and (3) primate importing and breeding.

Large-scale rodent breeding

The five large-scale breeding businesses with annual sales over $2 million were primarily producers of mice and rats, and accounted for

---

[6] Based on an allocation for lab animals of 5 percent of total overseas R&D expenditures of $124.5 million in 1974, as reported by the Pharmaceutical Manufacturers Association, *Annual Survey Report 1973–74.*

approximately 50 percent of total industry rodent sales (in dollars). Most of their sales were in cesarean-derived-barrier-maintained and germ-free animals. Twenty-two small local breeders competed for the remaining 50 percent of the rodent market and raised animals in "conventional" or simple barrier facilities.

Charles River and the four other large-scale breeders carried a wide variety of rodent strains, and severeal of the firms raised additional species, such as hamsters, guinea pigs, or primates. Each company had a strong market position in its immediate geographic area as well as selling to major users across the United States. Charles River and ARS/Sprague-Dawley were the only public firms in the group, and the only firms to operate multisite facilities.

> *Jackson Laboratories*, Bar Harbor, Maine.   A nonprofit genetic research foundation, Jackson laboratories had started the large-scale production of inbred mice in the United States in the 1930s. It raised over 75 strains of mice bred for specific research needs and had a quality reputation. The company commercially marketed 50 percent of its animals, the balance of which were internally for its own research. It offered animals raised by germ-free and conventional methods.

> *ARS/Sprague-Dawley*, Madison, Wisconsin.   With approximately $3 million in annual sales, ARS/Sprague-Dawley was the second largest commercial breeder in the United States. It was a division of the Mogul Corporation (1972 sales $32 million). Sprague-Dawley was a brand name so widely recognized that it had become a generic term for laboratory rats in the same way Kleenex had for facial tissues. A significant proportion of the company's business involved raising animals under government contract.

> *Harlan Industries*, Indianapolis, Indiana.   Harlan was the second largest breeder in the Midwest and had a substantial customer base among pharmaceutical companies. The firm was relatively young and was highly respected for the quality of its animals.

> *Simonsen Laboratories*, Gilroy, California.   Simonsen was the only significant supplier of animals on the West Coast. Company products included mice and rats, and guinea pigs. No information on company sales was available.

Small-scale commercial breeding

Traditionally, the laboratory animal breeding industry had been composed of small-scale, family-operated businesses which specialized in a single species delivered to a limited number of local customers. In 1975, these small-scale breeders still accounted for approximately 55 percent of lab animals sold and close to 30 percent of industry dollar volume. They produced about half of the rats and mice available in the United States, as well as almost all hamsters, guinea pigs, rabbits, cats, and dogs. Small breeders raised animals by "conventional" methods or with simple "barrier" systems where the direction of airflow and personnel access were controlled from "clean" to "dirty" areas. Except for mice and rats, the animals were neither specific pathogen-free nor cesarean-derived.

The operations of the Murphy Breeding Laboratory, Inc., were representative of a successful small-scale breeder. The company, founded in 1968, was the largest producer of quality guinea pigs in the United States and also raised mice for the National Cancer Institute. Company revenues were approximately $300,000 in 1975. As it was for many small breeders, the National Cancer Institute contract was crucial to the company's financial stability. It was one of the few companies to successfully enter the lab animal breeding business in recent years.

Jobber, satellite, or "backyard" breeding described the method used to raise most guinea pigs and rabbits. It differed from small-scale breeding businesses in that demand for these animals was erratic and few producers engaged in the business year-round. Under a satellite breeding system, the jobber or main breeder maintained a small conventional breeding colony at his own facility and subcontracted additional production demands to part-time breeders who kept under a hundred animals in a garage or backyard pen.

Primate importing and breeding

After mice and rats, primates accounted for the largest dollar volume of sales in the United States lab animal industry: approximately $10.3 million in 1975. This represented the sale of approximately 48,000 animals, including gorillas, baboons, and a wide variety of monkeys. Another 1,500 primates were raised each year by the National Institutes of Health in their Regional Primate Centers.

Most primates available commercially in the United States were trapped abroad. Primate importers purchased animals from trappers in the host country, arranged for transportation and quarantine, and treated any obvious diseases at their U.S. holding facilities before offering the animals for sale. Two major companies engaged in primate importing: Prime Labs, and Primate Imports Corporation, which was 50 percent owned by Charles River Breeding.[7]

The market for primates was split equally between two user groups. Universities and government agencies comprised the first group and used a wide variety of primates in medical, psychological, and sociological studies. Commercial testing laboratories and pharmaceutical companies comprised the second group and used the smaller rhesus monkeys for drug screening and for testing cosmetics. About half of all primates used in research were rhesus monkeys.

The major sources of supply for primates were the Indian subcontinent (the rhesus' only natural habitat), Africa, South America, and Indonesia. Rhesus prices had almost doubled since 1973, when the government of India had declared the monkeys an endangered species and reduced exports from 50,000 to 20,000 per year. Further regulations

---

[7] In August 1973, Charles River acquired 50 percent of the stock of Primate Imports Corporation for $268,400 and an option to acquire the remaining 50 percent prior to October 1976. In early 1976 Charles River indicated its intention to exercise that option at a price not to exceed $375,000.

were imposed in subsequent years. Both the export quotas and regulations were expected to be permanent.

The researcher estimated that commercial primate breeders in the United States produced fewer than 1,500 animals a year. In addition to Charles River, only three companies engaged in domestic primate breeding, and it represented a small part of their total annual sales. Litton Bionetics was primarily a supplier of biological and scientific equipment, while Gulf South was one of the largest commercial testing laboratories and used most of the primates it raised on its own research activities. Hazelton Laboratories, a company newly organized in 1969, was a rapidly growing diversified enterprise. (See the Appendix.)

CHARLES RIVER BREEDING LABORATORIES

Company history

From a warehouse loft with a $1,200 investment in used rat cages in 1947, Henry Foster built Charles River Breeding Laboratories into the industry's dominant producer of rats and mice with 1975 sales of $15.4 million, net assets of $16.9 million, and an OTC stock whose price-earnings ratio fluctuated between 20 and 60. (See Exhibits 1 and 2 for company financial information.)

Dr. Henry Foster commented:

> In 1947 I graduated from Middlesex Veterinary School in Waltham and wanted to establish a practice near Alexandria, Virginia. I couldn't find a location I could afford, but in my search I bumped into an abandoned rat farm in Clinton, Md. They sold me their old rat cages for $1,200 and showed me their records and customer lists.
>
> I had the cages shipped to Boston and started looking for a location. It was hard to find a landlord who would take a bunch of smelly rats, but I finally got the loft of an old warehouse on Leverett Street, behind Beacon Hill near the Charles River.
>
> I really didn't have a product to sell. No other veterinarian was in the field of animal breeding. Ventilation control in the loft consisted of opening and closing the window. I didn't really know what I was doing. There was no formal training in lab animals sciences available but the one thing I had was my veterinary degree. I could create an image of professionalism, and "Dr. Foster" gave me access to researchers. I didn't get left in the waiting room with the other salesmen.

When Charles River first went public in 1968, the company was still regarded as specializing in rats and was the largest commercial breeder with sales close to $4 million. Between 1969 and 1975 Charles River sales grew 400 percent from both internal growth and acquisitions.

Still, in 1976 COBS® (cesarean-originated, barrier-sustained) rats and mice accounted for 90 percent of sales, and Henry Foster attributed much of the company's success to its pioneering commercialization of the COBS® technique for breeding *rats* in 1955. Dr. Foster described the COBS® introduction.

I was aware of a germ-free derivation technique developed at Notre Dame. Building upon this technique we developed colonies of disease-free animals that could survive experiments without succumbing to an endemic disease and would not cloud results with the side effects of those diseases. Germ-free animals were not in abundant supply because they were so expensive to maintain in a germ-free state. What we did was to develop a technology that started with clean, germ-free animals, then introduced flora which would allow them to live outside of isolators. The barrier facility we built kept them from being recontaminated by germs in the environment.

In order to build the new facility, I took out a $100,000 loan. With this we were able to construct a building with three separate units. We equipped it with the first steam and gas autoclave in New England for sterilizing feed, bedding and cages. This was far in advance of the equipment anyone else had. We also installed a mechanized feed and bedding transport system.

All that investment and innovation appeared to be an unjustifiable capital expenditure, but it gave us some life insurance. With three separate areas we'd still have animals to sell even if an entire room were wiped out. Once you started to work with an institution and they developed baseline data on your animals, they wouldn't dump you unless you fell on your face and failed to supply them with quality animals on a continuing basis.

Not everyone could have gotten into the COBS® business. Notre Dame was willing to give me three or four germ-free animals to start only because I had a veterinary degree. I put myself completely in hock with the SBA loan. At the same time that our new facilities went up, I began to publish in scientific journals about developing techniques for large-scale animal breeding. This commitment to raise cesarean-derived animals was an indication of professionalism and gave us recognition. Harvard Medical School and Smith, Kline and French discovered we could teach them something.

I started out with a handicap because the veterinary college I attended was not accredited. That made me work harder. It pushed me to do things I wouldn't have done otherwise.

The year 1955 also heralded a major shift in Charles River Breeding Laboratories' (CRBL) marketing efforts. From supplying mainly universities, medical schools, and hospitals, Dr. Foster set out to break into the large lab animal market at pharmaceutical and chemical companies. Not only did this provide a new outlet for CRBL's increased production, but it smoothed demand for animals throughout the year.

Charles River Breeding Laboratories grew steadily and profitably between 1955 and 1965. At the urging of their now substantial pharmaceutical company customers, Charles River entered into the production of cesarean-derived *mice* in 1959. New breeding facilities went up in Wilmington and new rat strains were added. In 1964 the company built its first overseas COBS® facility in Elbeuf, France. By 1965 all facilities at Wilmington were upgraded to guarantee that Charles River was the only commercial breeder all of whose rodents were cesarean-derived, barrier-sustained [COBS®]. Other breeders began to adopt similar techniques to remain competitive.

Exhibit 1

CHARLES RIVER BREEDING LABORATORIES
Consolidated Balance Sheets
October 31, 1968–1975
(in thousands)

ASSETS	1968	1969	1970	1971	1972	1973	1974	1975
Current assets:								
Cash	$ 320	$ 203	$ 340	$ 202	$ 352	$ 284	$ 373	$ 316
Certificates of deposit	105	100	100	208	200	633	492	388
Marketable securities	949	712	150	646	—	1,009	577	452
Accounts receivable	585	761	808	1,284	1,357	1,775	2,495	2,635
Inventories and supplies	256	262	366	508	657	886	1,445	1,618
Other current assets	44	132	117	91	114	140	142	134
Total current assets	$2,259	$2,170	$1,881	$2,939	$ 2,680	$ 4,727	$ 5,524	$ 5,543
Property and equipment, at cost:								
Land	173	183	262	306	626	683	1,139	1,143
Buildings and improvements	1,643	2,277	2,707	3,135	4,284	5,462	7,078	7,519
Equipment	1,217	1,559	1,908	2,387	3,427	3,870	4,843	5,851
Motor vehicles	75	121	200	248	272	325	374	454
Construction in progress	187	47	571	1,579	1,491	1,120	520	1,390
	$3,295	$4,187	$5,648	$7,655	$10,100	$11,460	$13,954	$16,357
Less—accumulated depreciation	(912)	(1,179)	(1,543)	(1,975)	(2,355)	(2,823)	(3,437)	(4,215)
	$2,383	$3,008	$4,105	$5,680	$ 7,745	$ 8,637	$10,517	$12,142
Investments and other assets:								
Investment in Primate Imports Corporation	—	—	—	—	—	284	378	535
Cost of purchased businesses in excess of net assets	—	—	—	108	104	102	97	91
Investment in Japanese joint venture, at cost	—	—	—	—	106	114	—	—
Cash surrender value of insurance on lives of officers and key employees	25	29	37	44	51	140	208	645
Other assets	44	69	63	105	266	257	211	188
	$ 69	$ 98	$ 100	$ 257	$ 527	$ 897	$ 894	$ 1,459
	$4,711	$5,276	$6,086	$8,876	$10,952	$14,261	$16,935	$19,144

LIABILITIES AND STOCKHOLDERS INVESTMENT

	1968	1969	1970	1971	1972	1973	1974	1975
Current liabilities:								
Loans payable	$ —	$ —	$ —	$ 185	$ 322	$ 445	$ 365	$ 410
Current installments of long-term debt	268	298	163	113	121	13	154	388
Accounts payable	203	279	370	465	460	718	842	974
Accrued payroll	—	—	—	—	—	106	147	217
Accrued expenses and taxes	183	213	212	286	369	437	741	885
Accrued federal and foreign income taxes	254	255	228	340	147	338	321	360
Total current liabilities	$ 908	$1,045	$ 973	$1,389	$ 1,419	$ 2,057	$ 2,570	$ 3,234
Long-term debt	1,611	1,573	1,504	1,978	3,138	723	1,771	1,893
Less—current installments included above	(268)	(298)	(163)	(113)	(122)	(12)	(154)	(388)
	$1,343	$1,275	$1,341	$1,865	$ 3,016	$ 711	$ 1,617	$ (1,505)
Deferred income taxes	8	31	203	218	285	331	337	475
Stockholders' investment:								
Common stock outstanding, $1 par value	686	686	690	752	1,414	1,531	1,531	1,534
Capital in excess of par value	1,063	1,056	1,132	2,246	1,632	5,442	5,451	5,478
Retained earnings	703	1,183	1,747	2,406	3,186	4,189	5,429	6,918
	$2,452	$2,925	$3,569	$5,404	$ 6,232	$11,162	$12,411	$13,930
	$4,711	$5,276	$6,086	$8,876	$10,952	$14,261	$16,935	$19,144

Source: Charles River Breeding Laboratories, Inc., *Annual Reports 1968–1975*.

Low- and High-Bid Prices for Charles River
Common Stock Calendar Year 1975

1975	Low Bid	High Bid
First quarter	19	24½
Second quarter	22	28
Third quarter	15	25½
Fourth quarter	17	24

Source: Adams, Harkness and Hill.

Exhibit 2

CHARLES RIVER BREEDING LABORATORIES
Consolidated Statements of Income
For the Years Ended October 31, 1968–1975
(in thousands)

	1968	1969	1970	1971	1972	1973	1974	1975
Net sales	$4,243	$4,717	$5,505	$6,469	$7,993	$9,875	$12,574	$15,405
Cost and expenses:								
Cost of sales	2,535	2,678	3,185	3,791	4,781	6,091	7,768	9,921
Selling and administrative expenses	925	1,042	1,213	1,350	1,683	1,824	2,406	2,595
	$3,460	$3,720	$4,398	$5,141	$6,464	$7,915	$10,174	$12,516
Income from operations	783	997	1,107	1,328	1,529	1,960	2,400	2,889
Other income (expenses):								
Equity in net income of affiliate, less amortization of goodwill	—	—	—	—	—	16	94	157
Interest income	—	—	—	—	—	94	88	87
Interest expense	(56)	(75)	(75)	(85)	(119)	(116)	(179)	(200)
Income before income taxes	$ 727	$ 922	$1,032	$1,243	$1,410	$1,954	$ 2,403	$ 2,933
Provision for income taxes:								
Current	354	441	416	547	519	951	1,163	1,367
Deferred	—	—	52	37	111	—	—	—
	$ 354	$ 441	$ 468	$ 584	$ 630	$ 951	$ 1,163	$ 1,367
Net income	$ 373	$ 481	$ 564	$ 659	$ 780	$1,003	$ 1,240	$ 1,566
Earnings per share	$ 0.59	$ 0.70	$ 0.82	$ 0.48	$ 0.55	$ 0.67	$ 0.81	$ 1.02
Average number of shares of common stock outstanding (000s)	631	686	689	1,376	1,412	1,493	1,531	1,534

Source: Charles River Breeding Laboratories, Inc., *Annual Reports 1968–1975.*

After going public in 1968, CRBL entered a period of rapid expansion. Between 1969 and 1971 Charles River acquired five companies including facilities in Canada, England, and Italy. It entered into a joint venture with Ajinomoto to form Charles River Japan in October 1972,[8] a 50 percent interest in Primate Imports Corporation in October 1973. More strains of rats and mice were added to the Charles River product line, as well as four new species, including hamsters, rabbits, guinea pigs, and rhesus monkeys.

Product line

Fourteen strains of COBS and germ-free mice and rats accounted for 90 percent of Charles River Breeding Laboratories fiscal 1975 sales of $15.4 million, with COBS® guinea pigs, COBS rabbits, and conventional hamsters rounding out the company's broad line of small lab animals.

Table 6

SALES BY SPECIES, FISCAL 1975

(000s)

Species	Sales
Rats	$ 8,500
Mice	3,500
Guinea pigs	200
Hamsters	500
Direct government business	2,500
Rabbits	—
Key Lois primates	—
Primate imports (income share only)	160
Other (e.g., preserved specimens)	$15,400

Source: Researcher estimates.

A 50 percent-owned Charles River subsidiary, Primate Imports, Inc., sold a wide variety of imported primates accounting for approximately a third of all U.S. primate sales. A new Florida production facility on company-owned Key Lois Island was to sell its first domestically bred, rhesus monkeys in 1976. Table 6 shows Charles River estimates sales by species for 1975.

Charles River production facilities

Almost half of Charles River's productive capacity was located at company headquarters in Wilmington, Massachusetts, 14 miles outside of Boston, where COBS® mice, rats, guinea pigs, and rabbits were raised; all administrative and research and development facilities were also located there. Other Charles River Breeding Laboratories production facilities were located at four sites in the United States, as well as over-

---

[8] During fiscal 1974, the joint venture was converted to a percentage of sales licensing agreement which provided for the use of the Charles River name and a continuing transfer of technical know-how.

Table 7

PRODUCTION CAPACITY

Location	Products	Hour a day capacity number of animals per year*	General information
Wilmington, Mass.........	Rats, mice, rabbits, and guinea pigs	6,000,000	
Newfield, N.J.............	Hamsters (not COBS®)	400,000	
Stoneridge, N.Y...........	Rats, mice	3,000,000	
Portage, Mich.† (beginning 1976)........	Rats, mice	2,500,000	
Port Washington, N.Y.....	Primate conditioning (imports)	24,000	
Key Lois, Florida.........	Primate breeding	1,500	
Elbeuf, France............	Rats	1,000,000	
	Mice	2,000,000	
St. Constant, Quebec......	Mice	1,000,000	Also non-COBS
	Rats	520,000	rabbits and guinea pigs.
Margate, England........	Mice	600,000	Flexible space
	Rats	300,000 +	for 156,000
	Guinea pigs	20,000	rats or 488,000 mice.
Milan, Italy..............	Mice	900,000	
	Rats	300,000	
Atsugi, Japan............	Rats and mice	1,000,000 (1976/77)	Licensing agreement only.

* Except for Stoneridge, Portage, Margate, Atsugi, and Key Lois, all facilities operated at close to 100 percent of capacity.
† Acquired as part of 1974 Carworth purchase. In 1975, $1.7 million was invested in upgrading and expanding capacity to serve the Midwest market.
Source: 1972 Annual Report and 10-K.

seas. Table 7 shows Charles River locations, products produced at each site, and production capacity.

The barrier system

The barrier rooms and their associated environmental control systems formed the core of the Wilmington production facilities and accounted for the capital intensity of Charles River's business. A barrier room was a sealed room about 40 feet by 50 feet by 10 feet high. Animals were housed in metal or plastic cages stacked in tiers five to ten cages high and arranged in neat rows. Each separate breeding area had its own feed and bedding holding tanks. Sterilized feed and bedding were delivered to the breeding areas through an extensive pneumatic pipe system. A separate vacuum system removed waste to a central silo in the Charles River compound.

Personnel "entry locks" or cubicles prevented the people caring for the animals from bringing any contaminants into the barrier. In the first cubicle, the employee undressed and left all of his or her street clothes in a locker. Then in the second lock, the employee showered and washed his hair. In the third lock, the employee put on a complete sterile surgical style uniform maintained in the unit. Even the employees' lunch containers were sterilized before being passed into the unit.

Charles River took extensive precautions to maintain contaminant-free breeding areas. All air entering the areas was filtered to exclude particles larger than 0.3 microns and each area was kept at a higher pressure than the external atmosphere in order to prevent air leaks. Room controls were checked hourly to monitor room pressures and maintain temperatures between 72° and 74° F. A IBM System 7 computer automatically regulated energy use and monitored temperature, pressure, and energy alarm systems. The company also maintained six emergency generators.

Additionally, Charles River supported its own in-house maintenance team. Bill Keough, CRBL's treasurer and financial vice president, explained why.

> We have an environmental control oriented facility that allows us to raise twice as many animals per square foot as any other breeder. Preventive maintenance on this system is high, and emergency repair is crucial. We can lose animals or a whole barrier facility if the system is down for long. Maintenance workers must be familiar with the system so that they can repair it rapidly and their work must be perfect. Our own people know how to do it, will work overtime to get it done, and respond immediately. It's our insurance policy. These people are also a good technical resource when we build or renovate purchased facilities. We're better at building and equipping facilities than anyone else in the business.

Charles River labor force

Laboratory animal breeding was a labor-intensive as well as a capital-intensive enterprise. Production employees, called animal technicians, were needed to feed, water, and clean the animals; weigh, select, and pack animals for shipment. Tasks were routine but exacting and the work pace was fast. Two hundred of Charles River's Wilmington employees were directly involved in production. Their wages and fringe benefits accounted for close to 25 percent of total costs. Three shifts of technicians worked 24 hours a day, seven days a week, operating the sterilization equipment while animal technicians worked one shift, seven days a week caring for the animals. Bud Otis, vice president of Operations and officer of the corporation, described the work force and the difficulty of managing the production operation at Charles River.

> It is crucial that the entire work force follows entry and exit procedures exactly in order to preserve the integrity of the barrier. People are the greatest source of potential contamination. Someone may have a sick cat at home.
> It takes about twenty minutes for a technician to pass through the three lock barriers entry system, so employees do not leave the breeding

rooms during their shift. People remain in a 40' by 50' room for 8 or 9 hours a day with only 2 or 3 other people. Personalities play a big part in maintaining morale.

This is an unskilled job. Most of the animal technicians are men and women between 18 and 24 who are just out of high school. Average tenure is about 18 months.

The real strength of our production areas is our supervisory personnel. We always promote from within and we have a good supervisory training program. Supervisors are mainly policemen, although they are also responsible for setting the pace and meeting production deadlines.

Mr. Otis, who had begun working for Charles River 13 years ago as an animal technician, showed the researcher the Wilmington facility. They stood in the spotlessly clean shipping area outside one of the 46 breeding rooms, looking in through a plate glass window. Inside the breeding room three animal technicians and a group leader were working. They were all wearing one piece white and green jumpsuits with soft boots that overlapped the jumpsuits and tied above the ankle. White surgical caps covered their hair and all wore surgical masks. Every hour a buzzer went off and they replaced their masks and prepowdered disposable surgical gloves with fresh ones. A public address system piped in popular music. One technician was rapidly weighing animals and sorting them into weight groups. Two other technicians were moving back and forth along the banks of cages replacing water bottles. The group leader was checking the sex and weights marked on the exterior of cages of animals set aside for standing orders. Three animal technicians could pack 10,000 animals in a day, but would have to handle 20,000 in order to achieve customer weight tolerances.

Marketing

Sumner Foster, CRBL's executive vice president, described to the researcher the marketing policies which he had designed and implemented. He attributed the company's 40 percent share of the East Coast rat and mouse markets to its ability to provide a reliable source of quality animals. CRBL's award winning advertising program stressed quality and reliability, while extensive customer relations activity and efficient order processing supported the company's high-quality, high-service position. Charles River animals commanded a 10 percent price premium. Dr. Foster elaborated on the meaning of quality:

> We have credibility. Our animals perform well because our product is consistent and people know that our quality control is good. We bring our customers here to show them our innovative facilities and production processes. Our best sales tools are our animals and facilities wherever they are.

Sumner Foster emphasized the importance of a reputation for reliability when seeking new customers.

> We are a sure source of supply and guarantee delivery on standing orders. This is something few other breeders are able to do. When we go after a new customer who is standardized on another breeder's strain,

we compete on the basis of superior quality and reliability of supply. Our size is important here because we can bring in animals from our subsidiaries to cover peak periods.

Animals were sold FOB at the production facility and customers paid all freight charges. Charles River transported 60 percent of its animals in the company's climate controlled delivery vans. The remaining animals were shipped air freight.

Advertising

Charles River's advertising activities included regular paid advertisements in scientific journals, plus the publication of a quarterly newsletter, *The Charles River Digest*, and a research bibliography. Mr. Foster explained that these activities were designed to project an image of quality, reliability, and scientific innovation. No other breeder engaged in such an extensive program.

Magazine advertisements were placed in a variety of specialty scientific journals, such as the *Journal of Toxicology* and the *Journal of Endocrinology*, in order to reach the researchers who were the primary decision makers for lab animal purchases. Other breeders advertised only in the *Journal of Laboratory Animal Science*, which targeted a less specific audience. Annual advertising expenditures were approximately $200,000.

The Charles River Digest was an informational quarterly with articles of general interest to the research community which reported all major projects using Charles River animals. It was received by over 13,000 researchers and scientific libraries. Every two years, the company also published an extensive bibliography of all scholarly articles and research reports mentioning Charles River animals. Mr. Foster stated that this extensive literature on Charles River animals was one of the major reasons for their wide acceptability.

Customer relations

Mr. Foster explained that the company's focus was on personal customer contact by top management at Charles River. "Top management has to be the visible part of the company. Users want to talk to someone responsible." Charles River engaged in three customer relations activities which he said emphasized CRBL's position as the only commercial breeder with in-house laboratory support, quality control, and research ability. These activities included management attendance at trade shows associated with national scientific conferences, participation in scholarly symposia, and consultation on lab animal health.

Gil Slater, director of Marketing and operating head of Lakeview Hamster Colony, attended all regional and national scientific conferences and called directly on customers. Dr. Foster and Dr. George Pucak, director of Veterinary Services, attended and made presentations at symposia in the United States and abroad.

Since joining the company three years ago, Dr. Pucak had gradually assumed Dr. Foster's former role in consulting with customers and other researchers on lab animal health problems. Dr. Pucak spent close to

50 percent of his time with correspondence and user telephone calls in response to customer problems. He diagnosed and recommended treatments for diseases, as well as answering more general questions about research procedures and animal health problems.

Selling and order processing

Sumner Foster explained that most orders for small laboratory animals were placed over the phone for delivery in three to five days and were very specific as to strain, age, sex, and weight within tolerances of a few grams. Consequently, up-to-date inventory systems and rapid order processing were important to Charles River in meeting the wide, short-term fluctuations in demand. All U.S. order processing was centralized in Wilmington. This allowed the company to maintain a computerized order processing system which provided a daily updated stock list of animal inventories in all U.S. and overseas facilities, with data supplied by remote access terminals in all subsidiary locations. Charles River sold a high percentage of animals raised and produced at close to 100 percent of capacity. Sumner Foster commented that the effective use of the computer for order processing and customer sales analysis was one of the company's major advantages over the rest of the industry.

Pricing

According to Mr. Foster, the greatest volume of Charles River animals were outbred rats and mice sold in the lower price ranges, but there was

Table 8

Species	Price range (per animal)
Mice	$ 0.46–$ 3.30
Hamsters	1.20– 5.50
Rats	1.35– 8.75
Guinea pigs	3.90– 50.00
Rabbits	3.50– 60.00
Primates	50.00–500.00

steady demand for other species and for the more expensive inbred strains. Aged animals, pregnant and lactating females, and surgically altered animals also commanded higher prices. Table 8 shows price ranges by species for Charles River animals.

Bill Keough explained the company's position of price leadership in the industry.

Charles River Breeding Laboratories is the industry price leader in every product. Our goal is to achieve an overall corporate margin of 10% after tax and we are usually able to achieve price levels which cover costs and meet margin goals. Others in the industry follow our prices, at a level about 5%–10% lower. However, our new COBS® rabbits, which are more expensive to produce, sell at two to three times current prices for conventional rabbits, but we initially only want the premium quality segment on the market.

Dr. Foster explained his view of the company's pricing strategy.

> We are lucky in our industry because it is price flexible, but sometimes I wonder how we operate so profitably when Charles River charges only $1.35 for a rat and competitors get as much as $1.28. Maybe a wise manager would say that you should get everything you can, but I don't want to lose credibility by being a pirate. I think there are ethics and morals and we can practice them because we deal with ethical and moral people.

Charles River customers

Mr. Foster said that Charles River Breeding Laboratories now sold to over 2,000 customers in every segment of the laboratory animal market. Its preferred customers were the large East Coast pharmaceutical companies because they regularly purchased large quantities of animals. A good customer could place orders amounting to $167,000 per year. Table 9 shows the percentage of 1974 dollar sales accounted for by each customer segment.

Table 9

Customer type	Percentage of CRBL's 1974 dollar volume
Pharmaceutical and chemical companies	54%
Governmental agencies	17
Universities	16
Commercial testing labs and hospitals	13
	100%

Dr. Foster was pleased with this customer mix:

> We have a broad market base and no single customer accounts for more than 5% of sales. No one customer could dramatically cripple us or chip away at our margins if they stopped buying animals for 8 to 10 weeks. Smaller breeders are very vulnerable to interrupted purchases and something like that could put a small breeder out of business.

RESEARCH AND DEVELOPMENT

Charles River Breeding Laboratories was the only commercial breeder in the industry to maintain its own professional research staff and laboratory which was responsible for production quality control and for new product development. Sumner Foster commented that the Research Department gave Charles River a competitive advantage by providing a uniquely healthy product and an advantage in adding new species and strains.

The research staff at Charles River included Dr. George Pucak, a veterinarian who was a specialist in laboratory animal medicine; Dr. Roger Orcutt, a microbiologist specializing in intestinal flora; and a staff of ten full-time laboratory technicians. The Research Department operated from a fully equipped laboratory and animal quarantine facilities located at company headquarters in Wilmington.

Every eight weeks 25 animals were selected from each breeding colony. Tissue samples, cultures, and blood samples were taken from and tested for each animal. Technicians also inspected animals for parasites. Diagnostic technicians working in a separate necropsy, microbiological, and pathology lab examined all the animals which died in production colonies to determine cause of death. Also, randomly selected healthy animals were sacrificed for extensive testing to establish baseline data on bacteriology, serum chemistry, and tissue values which helped researchers to improve the efficiency of their experiments.

These extensive quality control procedures and in-house laboratory capability, management stated, were unique to Charles River. Dr. Foster explained the rationale behind these expenditures which amounted to $175,000 in 1974:

> We have imposed standards on ourselves by learning what kind of infections will cloud a researcher's results. We learned how to improve the environment and microbiologically define the animals. If you learn of something to give you a better product, you do it because you know it's all right, and later the benefits will be there.

New product development

New product introductions had contributed 30 percent of Charles River's growth in sales between 1970 and 1975, and were expected to contribute to the company's growth over the next five years. There were three separate new product development activities at Charles River: (1) adding new mice and rat strains, (2) developing new COBS® species, such as guinea pigs and rabbits, and (3) entering new lines of business, such as primate breeding.

The National Institutes of Health's genetic center supplied samples of newly developed strains of breeding animals to lab animal breeding companies. This has enabled Charles River to introduce two new rat strains and three mouse strains into commercial production in the last three years. Sumner Foster described the process.

> The whole process for introducing new rodent strains is rather routine because it's little different from starting foundation and breeding colonies for animals already in production. It takes about one year from the first cesarean to volume production of 10,000 to 20,000 animals per week. I can't even tell you how much it costs to start a new strain of small rodents because it is a normal part of our production activity. Any problems encountered are usually surgical and might take time, but are not expensive.

COBS ® development

The development of COBS® animals in new species, such as guinea pigs and rabbits, was initiated as part of the company's growth plans after going public in 1968. Charles River saw the development of COBS® rabbit and guinea pig products as a way to enter new markets with a domestic sales potential of $4 million a year. The company would introduce a unique product which no other commercial breeder had either the R&D expertise to develop or the production economies of scale to produce competively. It would also enable Charles River to maintain its reputation for scientific innovation in commercial breeding techniques. The market risk inherent in the traditionally erratic demand patterns for these animals also made the necessary facilities investment very difficult for a less securely financed company.

Research efforts for COBS® rabbits and guinea pigs focused on developing the correct feed formulas and the correct intestinal flora to introduce to the germ-free animals so that they could be raised in barrier rooms on a large scale similar to the rat and mouse operations. Guinea pig development took six years, but by late 1975 Sumner Foster considered their 10 percent market share reasonable in light of their price level which was initially double that of conventional guinea pigs.[9] Rabbits had been a more difficult task and were just coming into production in early 1976. Sumner Foster related the problems encountered in developing the COBS® rabbit that had cost the company close to $500,000 in expenses and committed facilities during its eight-year development period.

> We started to work on a COBS® rabbit in 1968 and thought we could get it into production in a year as we did with new rodent strains. But, unlike rats and mice, nothing was known about the animal before we started and it involved a much bigger R&D effort. We had no foster mother for the germ-free young and had to hand-feed them every hour, which is very expensive. We lost a lot of animals trying to develop the correct milk formula for hand-feeding. Also the rabbit was a special problem in association from the germ-free to a COBS® state.

Primate breeding

Charles River began plans to engage in rhesus monkey breeding in 1971 with the goals of entering a growing new market and of continuing to develop its reputation for improved laboratory animals. By breeding animals under controlled conditions in the United States, the company hoped to eliminate major health problems that made rhesus difficult to use in research. Rhesus trapped in the wild had an unknown medical history and frequently carried tuberculosis, a Herpes B virus which was lethal to man, and other diseases, communicable to humans. The animals also frequently suffered from Salmonella and Shigella, bacterial diseases which could weaken or kill the animals through severe dehydration.

Charles River's rhesus breeding program began with trapping the animals themselves in remote areas of northern India in order to select the healthiest animals and to bypass the usual quarantine compounds in India and the United States. The company by 1976 had developed an expertise in testing, diagnosing, and curing rhesus diseases and designed innovative feeding, trapping, and quality control procedures for production colonies.

---

[9] Due to a tight supply situation, breeders of conventional guinea pigs quickly followed with price increases of their own.

By early 1976 there were 1,500 healthy, thoroughly tested rhesus on Key Lois, which comprised a breeding stock expected to eventually produce 900 marketable animals annually. Rhesus dollar sales were expected to grow to $500,000 by 1978 from $50,000 in 1976. At the end of 1975 total development costs to date amounted to $700,000, of which the federal government had cost shared approximately $300,000 for noncapital expenditures.

Overseas operations

Charles River operations in Canada, England, France, and Italy accounted for a third of total company sales and net income in 1975. COBS® rats and mice were each division's main product, but competitive situations, product lines, profitability, and growth potential varied substantially among the divisions. Lab animals bearing the Charles River name were first produced in Japan in 1976 under a licensing and royalty agreement with the Ajinomoto Company.

Table 10

Division and product lines	Approximate 1975 sales (dollar equivalents: in millions)	Net profit after tax as a percent of sales	Estimated market share (commercial breeders only)	Additional sales potential by 1980 (in millions)
Canada				
Rats				
Mice				
Rabbits	$1.5	8%	n.a.	n.a.
Guinea pigs				
France				
Rats				
Mice	$2.5	11–16	44%+	$1.5
England				
Rats				
Mice	$1	10	25	$2
Guinea pigs				
Italy				
Rats				
Mice	$1+	10	33+	$1+

n.a.—not available.
Source: Researcher estimates.

Dr. Foster stated that his overseas expansion strategy required establishing an independent operating division in each country where a large market share was desired. Each division was managed by a national of the country where the facilities were located, although the parent corporation supplied assistance in facilities construction, production management techniques, quality control, and pricing decisions. All of Charles River's overseas divisions, except for France, had been acquired between 1969 and 1971 and substantial investments had been made in upgrading facilities and training production personnel. Serving multinational markets from a single facility was difficult due to language barriers, currency exchange problems, customs clearance, tariffs, and tax structures. Charles River was currently investigating acquisition candidates in Germany.

Charles River France was constructed in 1965 with the aid of Rhone Poulenc, S.A., one of France's largest chemical and pharmaceutical firms. Their agreement included a 15-year contract for Charles River to supply Rhone Poulenc's lab animals at a reduced price, in return for their assistance in local financing, engineering, land acquisition, and zoning problems. One eighth of Charles River France's current production was sold under contract to Rhone Poulenc. CRBL's initial cash investment was low, and as a result the French division's ROI was substantially higher than the ROI for the company as a whole.

Financial policies

Charles River's vice president of Finance, Bill Keough, characterized the company's capital structure as very conservative because of a heavy internal cash flow and a highly successful common stock issue in 1973. In that year Charles River had issued 110,000 common shares, raising close to $3.9 million, $2.3 million of which was used to retire a long-term debt. Mr. Keough described the issue as an attempt to get a more widely held stock and to take advantage of an inexpensive source of capital. He commented:

> As a result, we have no problem getting money. I could pick up the phone and borrow $2 million within the next few hours. Our total unused debt capacity is between $5 million and $6 million. Right now we're not more leveraged because we can't use it.

Since becoming public, the company had been gradually revising its performance goals. Mr. Keough explained the situation.

> We were previously getting a 10 percent ROI with a dollar of annual sales per dollar of facilities investment. Because we were willing to accept that 10 percent ROI, and because our operations were more efficient—no one else's sales margins are as good as ours—the marginal guy has gone out of business and we've discouraged others from entering. The financial community has been insisting that the return was too low, so now we're looking for 15 percent.[10]

Charles River declared its first dividend in 1975 in an attempt to broaden the company's base of stockholders[11] and to stabilize its stock price which fluctuated between 20 and 60 times earnings. The company was investigating the possibility of becoming listed on a major stock exchange during 1976, and Bill Keough described the type of investor he hoped these actions would attract:

---

[10] Part of that increase was expected to come from increased sales yield per square foot of plant and equipment costs achieved by changing male/female rodent production ratios to more closely approximate demand. This change had already contributed 1 percent to after-tax margins in fiscal 75 and was expected to produce an additional 1 percent in fiscal 76.

[11] In mid-1976 Charles River Breeding Laboratories had 1,007 shareholders. Dr. Foster, held approximately 40 percent of the company's stock and his brother, Sumner Foster, held approximately 2 percent.

We don't want to become a speculative stock, we're just trying for steady growth. We want a loyal investor who believes in us and plans to be with us for the long haul.

Planning and management systems

Formal planning and reporting systems at Charles River were kept as simple as possible in order to minimize the company's administrative overhead. All company officers reported directly to Sumner Foster as executive vice president, who in turn reported to Dr. Foster. The primary management planning document was an annual business plan and budget, reviewed monthly in conjunction with computer-produced financial statements comparing budgeted to actual results. The only other regular financial reporting documents were weekly reports of the number of animals produced and shipped and a weekly payroll and overtime report. Mr Keough commented:

> It's a conscious effort to keep things simple. The company is basically run by four people: the Fosters, Bud Otis and myself. We all wear a lot of hats so that we're not burdened with staffing and can stay flexible, adapt quickly to change. We don't want the expense of having all the answers, so we just control the key areas, labor and sales. You can't run this business with a bureaucracy.

Although Mr. Otis, Mr. Keough, Sumner Foster, and Dr. Foster held a formal meeting every Friday morning and reviewed major management control documents weekly, the main communications channels in the company were personal and informal. Executives were in and out of each other's offices several times a day. Mr. Keough kept in his office closet a large refrigerator well-stocked with beer, affectionately referred to as "Duffy's." Everybody from delivery truck drivers to Dr. Foster dropped by after five o'clock.

Dr. Pucak described the atmosphere that contributed to such a high degree of internal cooperation at Charles River.

> Everybody is involved with everything around here. The atmosphere is open and any idea you come up with, no matter how far out, is going to be discussed. We can all speak our minds. Dr. Foster creates a tremendous sense of pride. He works hard and sets the tone, yet we all feel we have contributed to the success of the company and share in its financial rewards.

Meeting strategic goals

In June of 1976, Dr. Foster spoke with the researcher about his company's future plans.

> Come on in. What do you think of our new conference table? We put it to good use every Friday when the four of us get together. Sometimes when we meet we have an agenda—specific questions; other times we just review our general situation.

Dr. Foster's office was a large, zebra-wood paneled room with a crisp, modern decor. A small marble conference table occupied one end of the room; at the other was a massive desk and chair. On the desk was an intercom system which allowed Dr. Foster to speak immediately with any of his officers or staff members. Behind the desk was a large digital clock and a hi-fi system capable of programmed output. The walls were decorated with abstract art, pictures of wife and family, replicas of the plaques honoring the Henry and Lois Foster gifts to Brandeis University and The Museum of Fine Arts, and a dozen or so framed organizational honorary awards and memberships in distinguished technical, industrial, and service (Rotary) institutions.

Dr. Foster continued:

> We have a real challenge ahead of us in meeting our growth goals of 15 percent in both sales and earnings. Because of our current dominance in the industry, we cannot acquire additional laboratory animal breeding firms. We can, however, expect continued growth from our existing lines. But that won't be enough; we will never get to a hundred million that way! We are going to have to add some new products and do some acquisitions. In five years we must be in other areas.
>
> I'm only interested in ideas related to the general area of biomedical research. There is, for example, the whole area of potential uses of invertebrates for teaching rather than research purposes, and we should get involved. There is a San Diego business that collects marine specimens, but it is 3,000 miles away and too much of a management drain for sales of $200,000 a year.
>
> What Charles River can bring to an acquired company is capital and management expertise. We need to get into a growing market with an already profitable company. We don't want any more businesses that needs a dollar of facilities investment to produce a dollar of sales, and we can't absorb losses of $100,000 to $300,000 a year like our early Japanese joint venture experience.
>
> We would want the principal to stay on for at least two or three years to provide operating expertise. We can't rebuild an organization or train a whole new team of people.

Biologicals

> A natural area of interest would be the production of biologicals.[12] We could use our retired breeders[13] and substandard animals, our entry would be essentially in the animal parts by-product business. We already have generated $100,000 in preserved organ sales as a by-product of our monkey importing business with only a couple of people working on it. One of the problems though is that the market is so unorganized, and we don't have a marketing organization that sells to one of the key markets—schools and universities.
>
> There is a possible, fine acquisition here—it's Quality Biologicals.[14] They are one of the largest in the business—I think about 20 million

---

[12] The production of biologicals was a $30 million a year business in 1975, company officers estimated. The products included monkey kidney cell cultures which were used as a growing media for producing Salk polio vaccine, rodent liver powder used as a filter in separating portions of cells, and animal organs such as rodent lungs, brains, or eyes for special experiments. This estimate did not include school sales of related products, for example, slides, models, or laboratory specimens for dissecting purposes.

[13] Retired breeders were one year or older female rodents which had produced many litters of young in the production colonies.

[14] Disguised name.

in sales, and a superior profit record. Let's look at their Dun and Brad-street!

After studying it, Dr. Foster continued. "Guess they are only 5 or 6 million in sales and about 2 million in assets. It's a private family firm and their management is getting old. They sell things such as one-celled animal slides, plastic models of specimens, and the general biologicals line to schools plus universities and wholesale suppliers in the United States and 30 different countries.

Contract testing and research

"Another area we might consider is what some people call contract testing and research—I prefer to call that type of business an industrial toxicology laboratory. Its purpose would be to help get new products through the constantly changing testing regulations required by the Food and Drug Administration before human clinical trial tests can be done. Firms in this field are growing at 10 to 20 percent per year.[15] We were offered a $20 million diversified biomedical company, which had an industrial toxicology lab, several years ago, but we couldn't swallow it at the time. We would have to enter this field through an acquisition."

People like Revlon [cosmetics], Gillette [personal health care products] and Du Pont [paint]—all are customers, all are now doing industrial toxicology work. Some of their tests are long—two years or so—and they can't do everything themselves so they subcontract. We have a natural interest in this field.

At our March meeting of the Society of Toxicology Dr. Russell Peterson, chairman of the Council on Environmental Quality talked about the proposed Toxic Substances Act. If that is passed every drug will have to be tested for long-term cancer-inducing possibilities. That will be good for our basic business. And, since they can't do all that long-term testing work themselves, they will have to use outside firms for some of this testing work.

To enter the field it takes good physical space and environmental controls (costing in total about $80–$100 a square foot), the technical competence to maintain large animal colonies over long time periods, good management, and superior toxicology competence. We would have to hire the latter and it would have to be good. The risk would be that you have contamination when you are 18 months into a test or that your toxicologist misinterprets the data. That happened with a large midwestern drug company recently, and it really gave that company a black eye. In our case that "black eye" might damage our basic business reputation and that would be serious. I worry about that.

A middle ground would be to subcontract the use of our facilities; we have some excess space in upstate New York. We could set up the colony, feed and care for the animals per their instructions, sacrifice animals per their schedule, and send the specimens to the main company.

On another occasion, Sumner Foster commented on some of the drawbacks of establishing a large-scale contract testing business. "With

---

[15] The Pharmaceutical Manufacturers Association estimated that U.S. pharmaceutical companies alone purchased $106 million worth of supplementary R&D services in 1974.

a general contract testing business, Charles River would be directly competing with some of our largest lab animal customers. Testing is very people dependent. The principals must be well known, respected in their field, and have personal contacts at the FDA. It is very easy for a principal to go off and start his own testing business."

The director of product testing for a large cosmetic and personal care products company commented on contract testing noting that, beginning in 1974, many of the firms in his industry had brought this work back "in-house." "There are few capable companies in the field. Many do tests, but they are not reliable enough to keep you out of the courts. The 'in-house testing' trend may be because of this lack of reliability and short supply of competent firms. We went in-house out of necessity. We have 30,000 very expensive square feet of facilities; the best air-handling units in the country. We don't have as extensive facilities as CRBL and we are not as automated as they are nor do we use COBS ® or pathogen-free animals for our work."

Clinical testing

Dr. Foster continued, "You know we were once in the clinical testing field—that's different from contract testing. You analyze throat cultures, blood samples or human tissue for your local doctor or hospital. We built up a $0.5 million business and then quit. We were early in the game too and an innovator. But the little lab down the street would cut the price on a test a nickel or a dime and kill you. The only way to bring needed quality to this important field is to move away from human to instrumental analysis. You ought to talk with Bill on this."

Bill Keough in a later interview emphasized that much of the company's success had resulted from staying out of areas about which the company didn't know anything. He cited, as an example, Charles River's venture into the clinical testing business between 1968 and 1970. "Charles River was one of the first New England businesses in clinical testing, and now successful companies have sales of a $100 million a year. But we got out of it because it took too much management time for its profitability. The technology was changing so fast, each year you'd need a new machine, and price competition was more important than quality."

Cage manufacturing

"We were offered a chance again recently to buy a cage company in Maryland. It was a good company with a good record—there is money to be made there—but, we don't have expertise in that area," Dr. Foster said.

Charles River, the researcher learned later, had had an opportunity to enter the lab animal cage manufacturing business when the company purchased Carworth from the Becton, Dickinson & Company, but had chosen to sell Carworth's cage manufacturing division. The total market for both metal and plastic lab animal cages, company officers estimated, was between $7 million and $10 million a year. Hazelton Laboratories had recently acquired several leading metal cage producing companies, and one New Jersey Company accounted for nearly $4 million in annual sales of plastic cages. Plastic cage manufacturing was a simple technology and only required a $50,000 to $60,000 capital investment. Lab animal cages were a durable commodity product. Company officers believed there had been little recent design innovation and that patent protection was not available. The business was price competitive and relied on a substantial sales organization. Marketing costs alone were estimated to amount to 50 percent of sales.

Animal colony management and consulting services

"We are now performing lab animal colony management services for our licensee in Japan," commented Dr. Foster. "We have an administrator there who was trained here at Wilmington and who reports to us weekly by phone.

"But animal colony management for a drug firm or institution holding test animals is different from our production-oriented process at Charles River. I'm concerned about offering other expertise to our current customers. If anything went wrong, we could lose the total relationship. However, we could consult on facilities design. That's an area where we have expertise and most people are not qualified.

Making the strategic choice

"How do I choose? It's terribly difficult to get started and there is risk. What is my 'vehicle' to get involved? There are so many possibilities open to us.

"How do we go about this choice? Do I set up a prestigious scientific biomedical committee, like the committees of the Academy of Science, to discuss where we should be going, where we should be looking? They should be paid a fine honorarium, and we could meet in Bermuda.

"I have to get staff assistance to give me the time to work on this. We missed a company in Canada, and I ought to go down and see the owners of Quality Biologicals. We need to start now. But I don't really know what button to push. What is the right button?"

APPENDIX

INFORMATION ON FIRMS INVOLVED IN THE BIOMEDICAL INDUSTRY*

INTERNATIONAL RESEARCH AND DEVELOPMENT COMPANY—1972[1]

. . . let me state that International Research and Development is an independent research laboratory engaged primarily in safety evaluation of chemical compounds. . . . Much of our business is in the areas of toxicology [the study of possible harmful effects of substances] and pharmacology [the science of drugs]. Other major areas of involvement include environmental health studies, pathology and chemistry; and more specific areas such as carcinogenesis, mutagenesis, and microbiology.

---

* Information abstracted from latest annual report available in Charles River Breeding's files on firms involved in the biomedical industry.

[1] 1972 President's report by Dr. F. X. Wazeter, Ph.D. In 1972 company revenues were $2,134,377 with net earnings of $324,098, and 1972 revenues were $3,601,343 with net earnings of $384,391. Stockholders' equity in 1972 was $4,370,660.

In addition to this research work, we provide all clients with computerized statistical analysis; preparation of all types of material to be filed with governmental regulatory agencies; and overall counsel on research needs. In short, IRDC serves as a totally self-contained, safety evaluation research arm for big business and small . . . for private industries of all types, government and institutions . . . and for locations here and in other countries.

NATIONAL LABORATORIES, INC.[2]

The company's product

The company's products can be conveniently grouped as living cells, chemical media, animal sera, diagnostics, laboratory animals, and specialty laboratory equipment.

A changing market

. . . Cancer research and treatment has been a high priority of the health industry over the past several years with the budget for the National Cancer Institute rising sharply each year. There are signs that the general budget tightening within the National Institutes of Health is now extending to the Cancer Institute, which is an imporant source of funding for the company's services and products. Spending in research appears to be shifting away from the large "goal-oriented problems" into more modest beasic research programs. . . .

News release[3]

CAMBRIDGE, Mass.—National Laboratories, Inc. announced today that Dr. Arthur S. Sterling, Senior Vice President, has resigned effective March 1, 1976. Dr. Sterling has been with the company since 1965 and during that time has been instrumental in enabling the company to carry on a continuing cancer research program funded by contracts with the National Cancer Institute. His departure is likely to affect the company's ability to retain these contracts, the loss of which would have an adverse effect on the company's earnings.

HAZELTON LABORATORIES CORPORATION

As Hazelton Laboratories Corporation completes its sixth most successful year, it is appropriate at this time that we reflect on our past

[2] Disguised name. This material abstracted from the company's 1975 annual report. In 1975 National sales were $14,109,000 and net income was $576,000. Comparable results in 1974 were $11,763,000 and $432,000. Stockholders' equity in 1975 was $4,090,070; 1974—$3,513,796.

[3] This material contained in a company news release published November 26, 1975.

[4] Information abstracted from 1975 annual report. Hazelton revenues in 1974 were $11,306,892 with net earnings of $231,900 while revenues in 1975 were $15,961,946 with net earnings of $425,600. Contract revenue and costs were, respectively $7,709,601 and $5,987,390 in 1974, and $11,152,951 and $8,421,459 in 1975. Net stockholders equity was $3,832,232 in 1974 and $4,077,426 in 1975. Hazelton Laboratories division and Hazelton Laboratories employed approximately 600 scientific and technical personnel. Company officers stated that Hazelton was the largest independent biological contract research organization in the world.

accomplishments, present growth and future potential. Hazelton today is the result of a corporate growth program initiated in 1969. At that time it appeared that the life science industry offered unlimited growth potential. Subsequent analysis of this industry proved it to be in an embryonic state, highly fragmented in terms of specialized resources, and lacking a single company responsive to the increasingly integrated demands of the industry on a broad scale. Plans were formulated to amalgamate several of the leading companies of this industry into one large, well-financed company. This strategy was followed and the company today is the culmination of 11 acquisitions.

The businesses of Hazelton all relate to the life science industry, and as originally projected in 1969, the industry continues to grow at a rate at least double that of the overall economy. The demand for safety and efficacy testing is increasing at an accelerating rate as industry and government develop new compounds and evaluate old ones. Demand is further increased by new government regulations requiring additional evaluation of well-established and widely used compounds and products.

Services provided: Testing of products and chemical compounds; consultation on regulatory affairs; laboratory facilities design; laboratory animal colony management. *Products evaluated:* agricultural, industrial and household chemicals; drugs; food and color additives; cosmetics; medical devices. *Products manufactured:* animal housing systems; metabolism units; germ free environmental equipment; veterinarian surgical instruments and hospital equipment; intensive care oxygen units; pathological waste disposal systems. *Laboratory animal breeding:* primate colony management; canine breeding; primate breeding.

BOOK ONE

*Determining
corporate strategy*

The concept of corporate strategy

WHEN we were looking at the chief executive's job, we promised that a simple central concept called "corporate strategy" would be developed here. It would be offered, we said, as a means to reduce the general management function to manageable proportions and enable technical specialists to understand the proper relationship between their departmental objectives and the goals of their companies. We come now to the central idea of this course and this book. We will look at what strategy is, what form it takes in different kinds of companies, what tests of validity may be applied to it, and what it is good for. If you think back to your discussions of Head Ski, *The Real Paper*, and Charles River Breeding, you may already be able to see or imagine what does or can happen to this idea in living organizations and sense both its inherent difficulties and its power.

WHAT STRATEGY IS

As the outcome of the decision process we will later analyze in detail, corporate strategy is the pattern of decisions in a company that (1) shapes and reveals its objectives, purposes, or goals, (2) produces the principal policies and plans for achieving these goals, and (3) defines the business the company intends to be in and the kind of economic and human organization it intends to be.

The strategic decision contributing to this pattern is one that is effective over long periods of time, affects the company in many different ways, and focuses and commits a significant portion of its resources to expected outcomes. The pattern resulting from a series of such decisions will probably define the central character and image of a company, the individuality it has for its members and various publics, and the position it will occupy in its industry and markets. It will permit the specification of particular objectives to be attained through a timed sequence of investment and implementation decisions and will govern directly the deployment or redeployment of resources to make these decisions effective.

Some aspects of such a pattern of decision may be in an established corporation unchanging over long periods of time, like a commitment to quality, or high technology, or certain raw materials, or good labor relations. Other aspects of a strategy must change as or before the world changes, such as product line, manufacturing process, or merchandising and styling practices. The basic determinants of company character, if purposefully institutionalized, are likely to persist through and shape the nature of substantial changes in the allocation of resources and of product policy. It would be possible to extend the definition of strategy for a given company to separate a central character and the core of its special accomplishment from the manifestations of such characteristics in changing product lines, markets, and policies designed to make activities profitable from year to year.

The New York Times, after many years of being shaped by the values of its owners and staff, is now so self-conscious and respected an institution that its nature is likely to remain unchanged, even if the services it offers are altered drastically in the direction of other outlets for its news-processing capacity. It is important not to take the idea of strategy apart—to separate goals from the policies designed to achieve those goals, or even to overdo the difference between the formulation of strategy and its implementation. The interdependence of purposes, policies, and organized action is crucial to the particularity of an individual strategy. It is the unity, coherence, and internal consistency of a company's strategic decisions that gives the firm its identity and individuality and its power to mobilize its strengths and its likelihood of success in the marketplace. Refinements like Richard Vancil's distinction between goals and objectives are useful.[1] At present, however, we should get on to understanding the need for strategic decision and for determining the most satisfactory pattern of goals in concrete instances. Refinement of definition can wait, for you will wish to develop definition in practice in directions useful to you.

SUMMARY STATEMENTS OF STRATEGY

Before we proceed to clarification of this concept by application, we should specify the terms in which strategy is usually expressed. A summary statement of strategy will characterize the product line and

---

[1] Richard F. Vancil, "Strategy Formulation in Complex Organizations," *Sloan Management Review*, Winter 1976. Vancil designates an objective as "an aspiration to be worked toward in the future" and a goal as "an achievement to be attained at some future date." Pursuing this distinction, his definition of strategy is as follows: "the strategy of an organization *or* of a subunit of a larger organization, is a conceptualization *expressed or implied by the organization's leader*, of (1) the long-term objectives or purposes of the organization, (2) the broad constraints and policies, *either self-imposed by the leader or accepted by him from his superiors* that *currently* restrict the scope of the organization's activities, and (3) the *current* set of plans and near-term goals that are adopted in the expectation of contributing to the organization's objectives." (Italics in the original.)

services offered or planned by the company, the markets and market segments for which products and services are now or will be designed, and the channels through which these markets will be reached. The means by which the operation is to be financed will be specified, as will the profit objectives and the emphasis to be placed on the safety of capital versus level of return. Major policy in central functions such as marketing, manufacturing, procurement, research and development, labor relations, and personnel, would be stated where they distinguish the company from others, and usually the intended size, form, and climate of the organization would be included.

For Head Ski, a statement of Howard Head's intuitive or consciously designed strategy, some of these categories would be missing (profit objectives, for example) but others stressed (for example, quality of product). Each company, if it were to construct a summary strategy from what it understands itself to be aiming at, would have a different statement with different categories of decision emphasized to indicate what it wanted to be or do.

To indicate the nature of such a statement, a student of the Heublein case[2] deduced this statement from the account of the company when it was much smaller and less diversified than it is now and was about to acquire Hamm's Brewery:

> Heublein aims to market in the U.S. and via franchise overseas a wide variety of high margin, high quality consumer products concentrated in the liquor and food business, especially bottled cocktails, vodka, and other special-use and distinctive beverages and specialty convenience foods, addressed to a relatively prosperous, young-adult market and returning over 15 percent of equity after taxes. With emphasis on the techniques of consumer goods marketing [brand promotion, wide distribution, product representation in more than one price segment, and very substantial off-beat advertising directed closely to its growing audience] Heublein intends to make Smirnoff the number one liquor brand worldwide via internal growth [and franchise] or acquisitions or both. Its manufacturing policy rather than full integration is in liquor to redistill only to bring purchased spirits up to high quality standards. It aims to finance its internal growth through the use of debt and its considerable cash flow and to use its favorable price earnings ratio for acquisitions. Both its liquor and food distribution are intended to secure distributor support through advertising and concern for the distributor's profit.[3]

Although it might be argued that the statement was not clearly in the chief executive's mind when he contemplated purchasing Hamm's Brewery and therefore did not help him refrain from that decision, it was in his experience and in the pattern of the company's past strategic decisions—at least as reported in the case.

---

[2] The Heublein case may be found in earlier editions of this book or obtained from the Intercollegiate Case Clearing House.

[3] Kenneth R. Andrews, *The Concept of Corporate Strategy*, (Homewood, Ill.: Dow Jones-Irwin, Inc., 1971), p. 34.

REASONS FOR NOT ARTICULATING STRATEGY

For a number of reasons companies seldom formulate and publish as complete a statement as we have just illustrated. Conscious planning of the long-term development of companies has been until recently less common than individual executive responses to environmental pressure, competitive threat, or entrepreneurial opportunity. In the latter mode of development, the unity or coherence of corporate effort is unplanned, natural, intuitive, or even nonexistent. Incrementalism in practice sometimes gives the appearance of consciously formulated strategy, but may be the natural result of compromise among coalitions backing contrary policy proposals or skillful improvisatory adaptation to external forces.[4] Practicing managers who prefer muddling through to the strategic process at the heart of Business Policy would never commit themselves to an articulate strategy.

Other reasons for the scarcity of concrete statements of strategy include the desirability of keeping strategic plans confidential for security reasons and ambiguous to avoid internal conflict or even final decision. Skillful incrementalists may have plans in their heads which they do not reveal to avoid resistance and other trouble in their own organization. A company with a large division in an obsolescent business which it intends to drain of cash until operations are discontinued could not expect high morale and cooperation to follow publication of this intent. Finally, since in any dynamic company, strategy is continually evolving, the official statement of strategy, unless it were couched in very general terms, would be as hard to keep up to date as an organization chart. Finally, a firm that has internalized its strategy does not feel the need to keep saying what it is, valuable as that information might be to new members.

DEDUCING STRATEGY FROM BEHAVIOR

The cases in this book enable students of Policy to do what the managements of the companies usually have not done. In the absence of explicit statements, we may deduce from decisions observed what the pattern is and what the company's goals and policies are, on the assumption that some perhaps unspoken consensus lies behind them. Careful examination of the behavior described in the cases will reveal what the strategy must be. At the same time we should not mistake apparent strategy visible in a pattern of past incremental decisions for conscious planning for the future. What will pass as the current strategy of a company may almost always be deduced from its behavior, but a strategy for a future of changed circumstance may not always be distinguishable from performance in the present. For all of Howard Head's skill in integrating a series of product development, distribution, merchandising, service, manufacturing, and research and development de-

---

[4] For an extended account of incrementalism, see David Braybrooke and Charles E. Lindblom, *A Strategy of Decision*, (New York: The Free Press, 1963).

cisions around the metal ski, was he as well prepared as he might have been for the advent of the fiberglass ski?

FORMULATION OF STRATEGY

Corporate strategy is an organization process, in many ways inseparable from the structure, behavior, and culture of the company in which it takes place. Nevertheless, we may abstract from the process two important aspects, interrelated in real life but separable for the purposes of analysis. The first of these we may call *formulation*, the second *implementation*. Deciding what strategy should be may be approached as a rational undertaking, even if in real life emotional attachments (as to metal skis or investigative reporting) may complicate choice among future alternatives (for ski manufacturers or alternative newspapers). The principal subactivities of strategy formulation as a logical activity include identifying opportunities and threats in the company's environment and attaching some estimate or risk to the discernible alternatives. Before a choice can be made, the company's strengths and weaknesses should be appraised together with the resources on hand and available. Its actual or potential capacity to take advantage of perceived market needs or to cope with attendant risks should be estimated as objectively as possible. The strategic alternative which results from matching opportunity and corporate capability at an acceptable level of risk is what we may call an *economic strategy*.

The process described thus far assumes that strategists are analytically objective in estimating the relative capacity of their company and the opportunity they see or anticipate in developing markets. The extent to which they wish to undertake low or high risk presumably depends on their profit objectives. The higher they set the latter, the more willing they must be to assume a correspondingly high risk that the market opportunity they see will not develop or that the corporate competence required to excel competition will not be forthcoming.

So far we have described the intellectual processes of ascertaining what a company *might do* in terms of environmental opportunity, of deciding what it *can do* in terms of ability and power, and of bringing these two considerations together in optimal equilibrium. The determination of strategy also requires consideration of what alternatives are preferred by the chief executive and perhaps by his or her immediate associates as well, quite apart from economic considerations. Personal values, aspirations, and ideals do, and in our judgment quite properly should, influence the final choice of purposes. Thus what the executives of a company *want to do* must be brought into the strategic decision.

Finally strategic choice has an ethical aspect—a fact much more dramatically illustrated in some industries than in others. Just as alternatives may be ordered in terms of the degree of risk that they entail, so may they be examined against the standards of responsiveness to the expectations of society that the strategist elects. Some alternatives may seem to the executive considering them more attractive than others when the public good or service to society is considered. What a company *should do* thus appears as a fourth element of the strategic decision.

The ability to identify the four components of strategy—(1) market opportunity, (2) corporate competence and resources, (3) personal values and aspirations, and (4) acknowledged obligations to segments of society other than stockholders—is nothing compared to the art of reconciling their implications in a final choice of purpose. Taken by itself each consideration might lead in a different direction.

If you put the various aspirations of individuals in *The Real Paper* against this statement you will see what we mean. Even in a single mind contradictory aspirations can survive a long time before the need to calculate trade-offs and integrate divergent inclinations becomes clear. Growth opportunity attracted many companies to the computer business after World War II. The decision to diversify out of typewriters and calculators was encouraged by growth opportunity and excitement. But the financial, technical, and marketing requirements of this business exceeded the capacity of most of the competitors of IBM. The magnet of opportunity and the incentive of desire obscured the calculations of what resources and competence were required to succeed. Most crucially, where corporate capability leads, executives do not always want to go. Of all the components of strategic choice, the combination of resources and competence is most crucial to success.

THE IMPLEMENTATION OF STRATEGY

Since effective implementation can make a sound strategic decision ineffective or a debatable choice successful, it is as important to examine the processes of implementation as to weigh the advantages of available strategic alternatives. The implementation of strategy is comprised of a series of subactivities which are primarily administrative. If purpose is determined, then the resources of a company can be mobilized to accomplish it. An organizational structure appropriate for the efficient performance of the required tasks must be made effective by information systems and relationships permitting coordination of subdivided activities. The organizational processes of performance measurement, compensation, management development—all of them enmeshed in systems of incentives and controls—must be directed toward the kind of behavior required by organizational purpose. The role of personal leadership is important and sometimes decisive in the accomplishment of strategy. Although we know that organization structure and processes of compensation, incentives, control, and management development influence and constrain the formulation of strategy, we should look first at the logical proposition that structure should follow strategy in order to cope with the organizational reality that strategy also follows structure. When we have examined both tendencies, we will understand and to some extent be prepared to deal with the interdependence of the formulation and implementation of corporate purpose. Figure 1 may be useful in understanding the analysis of strategy as a pattern of interrelated decisions.

Figure 1

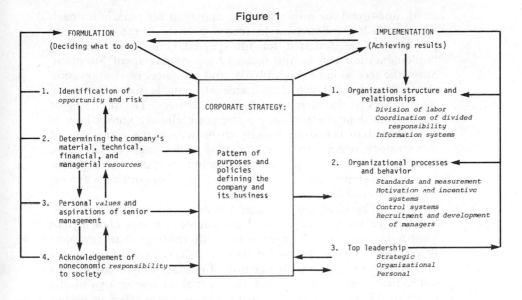

KINDS OF STRATEGIES

The most important characteristic of a corporate pattern of decision that may properly be called strategic is its uniqueness. A creative reconciliation of alternatives for future development is made unique by the special characteristics of an organization, its central competence, history, financial and technical resources, and the aspirations and sense of responsibility of its leaders. The environment—market opportunity and risk—is more nearly the same for major companies operating in the same geographical regions than are the resources, values, and responsibility components of strategy. For the company unequipped to dominate the full range of opportunity, the quest for a profitable segment of, or niche in, a market is, if successful, also likely to distinguish one company from another. In fact in an industry where all companies seem to have the same strategy, we will find trouble for all but the leaders—as at various times American Motors, Chrysler, and Ford have had different degrees of difficulty following General Motors, which got where it is by *not* following the previous industry leader, Henry Ford.[5]

Nonetheless it is useful to have in mind the full range of possible strategies when the question is posed whether the present strategy is the best possible. When you begin to consider other possibilities, the generation of alternatives will take place within the following common-sense range of possibilities.

Low-growth strategies

1. *No change.*   The strategy properly identified and checked out against the tests of validity outlined below can be closely moni-

---

[5] For a basic study in strategy formulation, see Alfred P. Sloan, *My Years at General Motors* (Garden City, N.Y.: Doubleday & Co. Inc., 1964).

tored, fine-tuned for minor defects, managed for maximum cash flows, with low investment in forced growth. Defensive contingencies will be designed for unexpected change and efficient implementation will be the focus of top management attention. Since the recession of the mid-70s, and the onset of conservation and environmental protection, this strategy is more attractive than it was in the heyday of "more is better." The profit to be made from doing better what a company already knows how to do rather than investing heavily in growth is the attraction of this strategy, which can be protected by achievement of low costs. Its disadvantage is the possibility of being overtaken or displaced by new developments and the restriction of opportunity for organization members.

2. *Retreat.* The possibility of liquidation is not to be sought out but may be for companies in deep trouble a better choice than continuing the struggle. Less drastic alternatives than complete liquidation include discontinuance or divestment of marginal operations or merging with a ceding of management control. This alternative may come to mind as you look at one or two of the cases in this book. It would have come up more often in earlier editions around cases from the farm equipment, typewriter, and sewing machine businesses.

3. *Focus on limited special opportunity.* A more constructive course of contraction is concentration on a profitable specialty product or a limited by significant market niche, as if Head had elected to concentrate on high-priced, high-quality skis without diversification into ski wear and other equipment. Success in a narrow line almost always tempts a company to broaden its line, but the McIlhenny strategy (Tabasco sauce only) may not be totally obsolete. If the proper focus is chosen, the limits may relax and growth may come in any case. Once the risk of limited life is accepted, the advantages of the no-change strategy can be sought.

Forced-growth strategies

1. *Acquisition of competitors.* In the early states of its development, a company with a successful strategy and proven record of successful execution can acquire small competitors in the same business to expand its market. (See, for example, Blow-Mold Packers' acquisitions of its present divisions, below.) Eventually antitrust regulation will put an end to this practice, unless the prospective acquisition is very small or on the edge of bankruptcy. Such acquisitions are usually followed by an adaptation of strategy either by the parent or acquired company to keep the total company a single business or one dominated by its original product-market specialization.

2. *Vertical integration.* A conservative growth strategy, keeping a company close to its core competence and experience in its industry, consists of moving backward via acquisition or internal

development to sources of supply and forward toward the ultimate customer. When a newspaper buys a pulp and paper mill and forest lands or news agencies for distribution, it is extending its strategy but not changing materially the nature of its business. Increasing the stages of integration provides a greater number of options to be developed or closed out as, for example, the making of fine paper and the distribution of magazines.

3. *Geographical expansion.* Enlargement of territory can be accomplished by building new plants and enlarging marketing organizations or by acquisition of competitors. For a sizable company the opportunity to enlarge international operations, by export, establishments of plants and marketing activities overseas, with or without foreign partners, may protect against contraction forced by domestic competition. You could have considered the possibility of Head Ski's seeking growth overseas, where 19 percent of its sales were accomplished by a single agent about whom almost nothing is said in the case.

4. *Diversification.* The avenue to growth which presents the most difficult strategic choices is diversification. Diversification can range from minor additions to basic product line to completely unrelated businesses. It can be sought through internal research and development, the purchase of new product ideas or technology, and the acquisition of companies.

5. New classes/types of clients.

KINDS OF COMPANIES

The process of strategic decision differs in complexity depending upon the diversity of the company in question. Just as having the range of strategy from liquidation to multinational diversification in mind will stimulate the generation of strategic alternatives, so a simple way of differentiating kinds of companies will help us see why different kinds of companies have different kinds of problems in making their activities coherent and effective and in setting a course for the future.

Bruce Scott has developed a model of stages of corporate development in which each stage is characterized by the way a firm is managed and the scope of strategic choice available to it.[6] *Stage I* is a single product (or line of products) company with little or no formal structure run by the owner who personally performs most of the managerial functions, uses subjective and unsystematic measures of performance and reward and control systems. The strategy of this firm is what the owner-manager wants it to be.

Stage II is the single product firm grown so large that functional specialization has become imperative. A degree of integration has developed between raw materials, production processes, distribution, and sales. The search for product or process improvement is institutionalized in research and development, and performance management and control

---

[6] See Bruce R. Scott, "Stages of Corporate Development, Parts I and II" (unpublished paper, Harvard Business School, 1970).

and compensation systems become systematic with the formulation of policy to guide delegation of operating decisions. The strategic choice is still under top control and centers upon the degree of integration, size of market share, and breadth of product line.

Stage III is a company with multiple product lines and channels of distribution with an organization based on product-market relationships rather than function. Its businesses are not to a significant degree integrated; they have their own markets. Its research and development is oriented to new products rather than improvements and its measurement and control systems are increasingly systematic and oriented to results. Strategic alternatives are phrased in terms of entry into and exit from industries and allocation of resources by industry and rate of growth.

If a company grows it may pass from Stage I to Stage III, although it can be very large in Stage II. Its strategic decisions will grow in complexity. The stages of development model has proved productive in relating different kinds of strategies to kinds of companies and has led other researchers into productive classification. Leonard Wrigley and Richard P. Rumelt[7] have carried Scott's work forward to develop suggestive ways of categorizing companies and comparing their strategies.

First, of course, is the *single business* firm (Stages I and II firms) with 95 percent or more of its revenues arising from a single business —an oil company or flour-milling company, for example, to say nothing of Crown Cork and Seal.

Second is the *dominant business* consisting of firms diversified to some extent but still obtaining most of their revenues from a single business. The diversification may arise from end products of integration, with products stemming from strengths of the firm or minor unrelated activities. A large oil company in the petrochemical and fertilizer business would fall in this category.

Third is the *related business* comprising diversified firms in which the diversification has been principally accomplished by relating new activities to old—General Electric and Westinghouse, for example.

Fourth is the *unrelated business.* These firms have diversified primarily without regard to relationships between new businesses and current activities. The conglomerate companies fall in this category.

Each of these categories have subdivisions devised by Rumelt which you may wish to examine at a more advanced stage of Policy studies. In the meantime it is interesting to note that Rumelt has found significantly superior performance in the related businesses, suggesting that the strategy of diversifying from the original business to a significant degree has been the most successful strategic pattern among the *Fortune 500* under conditions prevailing in recent years.

The range of strategy and the kinds of company which different

---

[7] Leonard Wrigley, "Division Autonomy and Diversification" (unpublished doctoral dissertation, Harvard Business School, 1970) and Richard P. Rumelt, *Strategy Structure and Economic Performance* (Division of Research, Harvard Business School, 1974). Malcolm Salter has added a refinement to Stage III in "Stages of Corporate Development," *Journal of Business Policy,* vol. 1, no. 1 (1970), pp. 40–51.

growth strategies have produced suggests, in short, that the process of defining the business of a company will vary greatly depending on the degree of diversification under way in the company. The product-market choices are crystal clear in Crown Cork and Seal and a single business oil company; they could not even be exhaustibly listed for General Electric. That top management decides product-market questions in such a company, except in such instances as entry into nuclear energy, is conceivable only as an oversimplification.

As diversification increases, the definition of the total business turns away from literal description of products and markets (which become the business of the separate product divisions) toward general statements of financial results expected and corporate principle in other areas. A conglomerate firm made up of many different businesses will have many different strategies, related or not depending upon the desire for synergy in the strategic direction of the total enterprise. The overall strategy of a highly diversified firm may be only the total of its divisional strategies. That it should be more than that is a matter for argument. To make it so puts heavy demands on the ability to conceptualize corporate purpose.

The task of identifying the coherence and unity of a conglomerate is, of course, much greater than that of even a multidivision related business. Students should be prepared, then, to adapt the beginning definition offered here to the complexity of the business they are examining. Since the trend over time is product diversity in growing firms and evolution from Stage I to Stage III, it is well to have this complication in mind now.

For as Norman Berg makes clear in "Strategic Planning in Conglomerate Companies,"[8] strategic choice is not merely the function of the chief executive office. It is of necessity a multilevel activity, with each unit concerned with its own environment and its own objectives. The process will reflect the noneconomic goals of people at the level at which proposals are made. In a conglomerate of unrelated businesses the corporate staff is small, the divisions relatively autonomous, and the locus of strategic planning is in the divisions. This makes supervision of the strategic planning process and allocation of resources, depending upon the evaluation of strategies submitted, the strategic role of the corporate senior managers.

The differences in the application of a concept of strategy to a modest single business on the one hand and to a multinational conglomerate on the other—although important—mean that the ability to conceive of a business in strategic terms must be distributed throughout the organization in a complex company. The problems of choosing among strategic alternatives and making the choice effective over time, together with the problems of ensuring that such organization processes as performance measurement do not impede the choice, must be part of the management ability of many people besides the general managers. All

---

[8] Norman Berg, "Strategic Planning in Conglomerate Companies," *Harvard Business Review*, May–June 1965, pp. 79–92. See also his "What's Different about Conglomerate Management?" *Harvard Business Review*, November–December 1969.

those involved in the strategic process, it follows, are vitally concerned with how a strategy can be evaluated so that it may be continued, amended, or abandoned as appropriate. Operating level managers who make a strategic proposal should be able to test its validity against corporate norms if for no other reason than their own survival. Those who must approve and allocate funds to such proposals should have a criterion to evaluate their worth going beyond a general confidence (or lack of it) in the ability of the proponents.

CRITERIA FOR EVALUATION

How is the actual or proposed strategy to be judged? How are we to know that one strategy is better than another? A number of important questions can regularly be asked. As is already evident, no infallible indicators are available. With practice they will lead to reliable intuitive discriminations.

1. *Is the strategy identifiable and has it been made clear either in words or practice?*

The degree to which attention has been given to the strategic alternatives available to a company is likely to be basic to the soundness of its strategic decision. To cover in empty phrases ("Our policy is planned profitable growth in any market we can serve well") an absence of analysis of opportunity or actual determination of corporate strength is worse than to remain silent, for it conveys the illusion of a commitment when none has been made. The unstated strategy cannot be tested or contested and is likely therefore to be weak. If it is implicit in the intuition of a strong leader, the organization is likely to be weak and the demands the strategy makes upon it are likely to remain unmet. A strategy must be explicit to be effective and specific enough to require some action and exclude others.

2. *Does the strategy exploit fully domestic and international environmental opportunity?*

An unqualified yes answer is likely to be rare even in the instance of global giants such as General Motors. But the present and future dimensions of markets can be analyzed without forgetting the limited resources of the planning company in order to outline the requirements of balanced growth and the need for environmental information. The relation between market opportunity and organizational development is a critical one in the design of future plans. Unless growth is incompatible with the resources of an organization or the aspirations of its management, it is likely that a strategy that does not purport to make full use of market opportunity will be weak also in other aspects. Vulnerability to competition is increased by lack of interest in market share.

3. *Is the strategy consistent with corporate competence and resources, both present and projected?*

Although additional resources, both financial and managerial, are available to companies with genuine opportunity, the availability of each must be finally determined and programmed along a practicable time scale. This may be the most difficult question in this series. The key factor which is usually left out is the availability of management for effective implementation or the opportunity cost implicit in the assignment of management to any task.

4. *Are the major provisions of the strategy and the program of major policies of which it is comprised internally consistent?*

A foolish consistency, Emerson said, is the hobgoblin of little minds, and consistency of any kind is certainly not the first qualification of successful corporation presidents. Nonetheless, one advantage of making as specific a statement of strategy as is practicable is the resultant availability of a careful check on fit, unity, coherence, compatibility, and synergy—the state in which the whole of anything can be viewed as greater than the sum of its parts. For example, a manufacturer of chocolate candy who depends for two thirds of his business upon wholesalers should not follow a policy of ignoring them or of dropping all support of their activities and all attention to their complaints. Similarly, two engineers who found a new firm expressly to do development work should not follow a policy of accepting orders that, though highly profitable, in effect turn their company into a large job shop, with the result that unanticipated financial and production problems take all the time that might have gone into development. An examination of any substantial firm will reveal at least some details in which policies pursued by different departments tend to go in different directions. Where inconsistency threatens concerted effort to achieve budgeted results within a planned time period, then consistency becomes a vital rather than merely an esthetic problem.

5. *Is the chosen level of risk feasible in economic and personal terms?*

Strategies vary in the degree of risk willingly undertaken by their designers. For example, a small food company in pursuit of its marketing strategy, deliberately courted disaster in production slowdowns and in erratic behavior of cocoa futures. But the choice was made knowingly and the return was likely to be correspondingly great. The president was temperamentally able to live under this pressure and presumably had recourse if disaster struck. At the other extreme, another company had such modest growth aspirations that the junior members of its management were unhappy. They would have preferred a more aggressive and ambitious company. Although risk cannot always be known for sure, the level at which it is estimated is, within limits, optional. The riskiness of any future plan should be compatible with the economic resources of the organization and the temperament of the managers concerned.

6. *Is the strategy appropriate to the personal values and aspirations of the key managers?*

Until we consider the relationship of personal values to the choice of strategy, it is not useful to dwell long upon this criterion. But, to cite an extreme case, the deliberate falsification of warehouse receipts to conceal the absence of soybean oil from the tanks which are supposed to contain it would not be an element of competitive strategy to which most of us would like to be committed. A strong personal attraction of leisure, to cite a less extreme example, is inconsistent with a strategy requiring all-out effort from the senior members of a company. Or if, for example, a new president abhors conflict and competition, then it can be predicted that the hard-driven firm of an earlier day will have to change its strategy. Conflict between personal preferences, aspirations, and goals of the key members of an organization and the plan for its future is a sign of danger and a harbinger of mediocre performance or failure.

7. *Is the strategy appropriate to the desired level of contribution to society?*

Closely allied to the value is the ethical criterion. As the professional obligations of business are acknowledged by an increasing number of senior managers, it grows more and more appropriate to ask whether the current strategy of a firm is as socially responsible as it might be. Although it can be argued that filling any economic need contributes to the social good, it is clear that manufacturers of cigarettes might well consider diversification on grounds other than their fear of future legislation. That the strategy should not require violations of law or ethical practice to be effective has become abundantly clear with the revelation in the mid-70s of widespread bribery and questionable payments, particularly in overseas activities. Honesty and integrity may seem exclusively questions of implementation, but if the strategy is not distinctive, making it effective in competition may tempt managers to unethical practice. Thus a drug manufacturer who emphasizes the production of amphetamines at a level beyond total established medical need is inevitably compelling corruption. The meeting of sales quotas at the distribution level necessitates distribution of the drug as "speed" with or without the cooperation of prescribing physicians. To the extent that the chosen economic opportunity of the firm has social costs, such as air or water pollution, a statement of intention to deal with these is desirable and prudent. Ways to ask and answer this question will be considered in the section on the company and its responsibilities to society.

8. *Does the strategy constitute a clear stimulus to organizational effort and commitment?*

For organizations which aspire not merely to survive but to lead and to generate productive performance in a climate that will encourage the development of competence and the satisfaction of individual needs, the strategy selected should be examined for its inherent attractiveness to the organization. Some undertakings are inherently more likely to gain the commitment of able men of goodwill than others. Given the variety of human preferences, it is risky to illustrate this difference briefly. But currently a company that is vigorously expanding its overseas operations finds that several of its socially conscious young people exhibit more zeal in connection with its work in developing countries than in Europe. Generally speaking, the bolder the choice of goals and the wider range of human needs they reflect, the more successfully they will appeal to the capable membership of a healthy and energetic organization.

9. *Are there early indications of the responsiveness of markets and market segments to the strategy?*

Results, no matter how long postponed by necessary preparations, are, of course, the most telling indicators of soundness, so long as they are read correctly at the proper time. A strategy may pass with flying colors all the tests so far proposed, and may be in internal consistency

and uniqueness an admirable work of art. But if within a time period made reasonable by the company's resources and the original plan the strategy does not work, then it must be weak in some way that has escaped attention. Bad luck, faulty implementation, and competitive countermoves may be more to blame for unsatisfactory results than flaws in design, but the possibility of the latter should not be unduly discounted. Conceiving a strategy that will win the company a unique place in the business community, that will give it an enduring concept of itself, that will harmonize its diverse activities, and that will provide a fit between environmental opportunity and present or potential company strength is an extremely complicated task.

We cannot expect simple tests of soundness to tell the whole story. But an analytical examination of any company's strategy against the several criteria here suggested will nonetheless give anyone concerned with making, proving, or contributing to corporate planning a good deal to think about.

PROBLEMS IN EVALUATION

The evaluation of strategy is as much an act of judgment as is the original conception, and may be as subject to error. The most common source of difficulty is the misevaluation of current results. When results are unsatisfactory, as we have just pointed out, a reexamination of strategy is called for. At the same time, outstandingly good current results are not necessarily evidence that the strategy is sound. Abnormal upward surges in demand may deceive marginal producers that all is well within their current strategy, until expansion of more efficient competitors wipes out their market share. Extrapolation of present performance into the future, overoptimism and complacence, and underestimation of competitive response and of the time required to accommodate to changes in demand are often by-products of success. Unusually high profits may blind the unwary manager to impending environmental change. His concern for the future can under no circumstances be safely suspended. Conversely, a high-risk strategy that has failed was not necessarily a mistake, so long as the risk was anticipated and the consequences of failure carefully calculated. In fact, a planning problem confronting a number of diversified companies today is how to encourage their divisions to undertake projects where failure can be afforded but where success, if it comes, will be attended by high profits not available in run-of-the-mill, low-risk activities.

Although the possibility of misinterpreting results is by far the commonest obstacle to accurate evaluation of strategy, the criteria previously outlined suggest immediately some additional difficulties. It is as easy to misevaluate corporate resources and the financial requirements of a new move as to misread the environment for future opportunities. To be overresponsive to industry trends may be as dangerous as to ignore them. The correspondence of the company's strategy with current environmental developments and an overreadiness to adapt may obscure the opportunity for a larger share of a declining market or for growth in profits without a parallel growth in total sales. The decision

of American Motors not to follow trends toward big cars in the middle 1950s provides us with an opportunity to examine the strategic alternatives of adapting to, or running counter to, massive current trends in demand.

The intrinsic difficulty of determining and choosing among strategic alternatives leads many companies to do what the rest of the industry is doing rather than to make an independent determination of opportunity and resources. Sometimes the companies of an industry run like sheep all in one direction. The similarity among the strategies, at least in some periods of history, of insurance companies, banks, railroads, and airplane manufacturers may lead one to wonder whether strategic decisions were based upon industry convention or upon independent analysis. Whether the similarity of timing, decision, and reaction to competition constitutes independent appraisals of each company's situation, or whether imitation took the place of independent decision is the basis of some wonder. At any rate, the similarity of one company's strategy to that of its competitors does not constitute the assurance of soundness which it might at first suggest.

A strategy may manifest an all-too-clear correspondence with the personal values of the founder, owner, or chief executive. Like a correspondence with dominant trends and the strategic decisions of competitors, this may also be deceptive and unproductive. For example, a personal preference for growth beyond all reasonable expectations may be given undue weight. It should be only one factor among several in any balanced consideration of what is involved in designing strategy. Too little attention to a corporation's actual competence for growth or diversification is the commonest error of all.

It is entirely possible that a strategy may reflect in an exaggerated fashion the values rather than the reasoned decisions of the responsible manager or managers and that imbalance may go undetected. That this may be the case is a reflection of the fact that the entire business community may be dominated by certain beliefs of which one should be wary. A critic of strategy must be at heart enough of a nonconformist to raise questions about generally accepted modes of thought and the conventional thinking which serves as a substitute for original analysis. The timid may not find it prudent to challenge publicly some of the ritual of policy formulation. But even for them it will serve the purposes of criticism to inquire privately into such sacred propositions as the one proclaiming that a company must grow or die or that national planning for energy needs is anathema.

Another canon of management that may engender questionable strategies is the idea that cash funds in excess of reasonable dividend requirements should be reinvested whether in revitalization of a company's traditional activities or in mergers and acquisitions that will diversify products and services. Successful operations, a heretic might observe, sometimes bring riches to a company which lacks the capacity to reemploy them. Yet a decision to return to the owners substantial amounts of capital which the company does not have the competence or desire to put to work is an almost unheard of development. It is

therefore appropriate, particularly in the instance of very successful companies in older and stable industries, to inquire how far strategy reflects a simple desire to put all resources to work rather than a more valid appraisal of investment opportunity in relation to unique corporate strengths. We should not forget to consider an unfashionable, even if ultimately also an untenable, alternative—namely, that to keep an already large worldwide corporation within reasonable bounds, a portion of the assets might well be returned to stockholders for investment in other enterprises.

The identification of opportunity and choice of purpose are such challenging intellectual activities that we should not be surprised to find that persistent problems attend the proper evaluation of strategy. But just as the criteria for evaluation are useful, even if not precise, so the dangers of misevaluation are less menacing if they are recognized. We have noted some inexactness in the concept of strategy, the problems of making resolute determinations in the face of uncertainty, the necessity for judgment in the evaluation of soundness of strategy, and the misevaluation into which human error may lead us. None of these alters the fact that a business enterprise guided by a clear sense of purpose rationally arrived at and emotionally ratified by commitment is more likely to have a successful outcome, in terms of profit and social good, than a company whose future is left to guesswork and chance. Conscious strategy does not preclude brilliance of improvisation or the welcome consequences of good fortune. Its cost is principally thought and work for which it is hard but not impossible to find time.

APPLICATION TO CASES

As you attempt to apply the concept of strategy to the analysis of cases, try to keep in mind three questions:

1. What is the strategy of the company?
2. In the light of (*a*) the characteristics of its industry and developments in its environment, and (*b*) its own strengths and weaknesses, is the strategy sound?
3. What recommendations for changed strategy might advantageously be made to the president?

Whatever other questions you may be asked or may ask yourself, you will wish constantly to order your study and structure your analysis of case information according to the need to *identify, evaluate,* and *recommend.*

By now you have an idea of strategy, which discussion of the cases will greatly clarify. You know how it is derived and some of its uses and limitations. You have been given some criteria for evaluating the strategies you identify and those you propose. And you have been properly warned about errors of judgment which await the unwary.

The cases which immediately follow will permit you to consider what contributions if any the concept of strategy (if mostly missing as a conscious formulation) would have made to these companies. What strategic alternatives can be detected in the changing circumstances affecting their fortunes? Which ones would you choose if you were responsible or asked to advise? By the time these cases have been examined, you will be ready to turn from the nature and uses of strategy to a study in sequence of its principal components—environmental opportunity, corporate capability, personal aspirations, and moral responsibility.

American Motors Corporation I

AMERICAN MOTORS was formed on May 1, 1954, through the merger of two faltering automobile companies, Nash-Kelvinator Corporation and the Hudson Motor Car Company. Combined sales for the fiscal year ended September 30, 1954, showed unit sales off 42% from the preceeding year of separate operations, and the combined statement of earnings showed a net loss of slightly more than $11,000,000 after receipt of a tax loss credit of $11,500,000, i.e., a total operating loss of more than $22,000,000 (see Exhibits 1 and 2).

In the three succeeding years sales volume declined about 25% and market share fell to less than 2%. Successive operating losses of $15,257,000; $32,362,000; and $11,035,000 forced the company to borrow heavily from various banks in order to maintain minimal working capital balances. Near the nadir of its fortunes, sometime financier Louis E. Wolfson began buying shares, and by early 1958 was believed to be within easy reach of a controlling interest in the company. In July 1957 one of his nominees joined the board of directors, and another in February 1958.

Then as the columnists began writing obituaries for the company, AMC made a spectacular comeback. By the end of 1960 unit sales had risen about 300% from their low, market share had more than tripled, the company had an operating profit of $105 million, and all bank indebtedness had been repaid. With its "compact" cars the company had become a leader in the low-price field, and the "Big Three" were taking preliminary steps toward following AMC's lead in making cars with a "unitized" body.

Commenting on the company's comeback, and on the public acceptance of compact cars, George Romney, AMC's chairman and president since 1954, noted that there was a long lead time between the development of a new basic concept, the acceptance of this concept by the organization, and finally its acceptance by the public.

143

Exhibit 1

AMERICAN MOTORS CORPORATION I

Consolidated Statements of Profit and Loss

(in thousands)

	1954		1955		1956		1957	
Sales.............		$416,845		$468,773		$429,074		$383,175
Less: Excise taxes...		16,502		27,646		20,666		20,941
Net sales.........		$400,343		$441,127		$408,407		$362,234
Other income:								
Dividends from subsidiaries*....	$ 1,043		$ 2,900		$ 202		$ 133	
Interest on securities......	120							
Sundry income...	1,748	2,912	2,801	5,701	2,099	2,302	2,104	2,327
		$403,255		$446,828		$410,709		$364,472
Costs and expenses:								
Cost of product sold..........	$363,437		$395,950		$377,102		$323,009	
Depreciation (Plant), (Tools & dies)	6,342		5,307		5,033		5,088	
Cost of pensions..	4,267		5,278		6,272		3,127	
Selling, advertising & administration	48,339		54,100		50,508		41,004	
Refrigerator warranties.....	586		187		182		370	
Interest.........	2,202		2,119		2,502		1,842	
Sundry expenses..	740	425,913	541	462,085	969	442,571	973	375,507
Net profit or loss on operations.....		$ (22,658)		$ (15,257)		$ (32,362)		$ (11,035)
Credits on income tax...........		11,590		9,700		1,453		502
Nonrecurring income or (loss)......		....		....		10,662		(1,300)
Income tax........		....		....		....		
Net Income after Tax..........		$ (11,071)		$ (6,956)		$ (19,746)		$ (11,833)

* Changed in 1960 to reflect equity in subsidiaries rather than dividends received.
Note: Failure of figures to add is due to rounding.
Source: Annual Reports.

. . . it seems to require about seven years for a good idea to really catch on. It took seven years to develop the Rambler idea internally (1943–50)—and it wasn't sold internally at the end of seven years. Only three men in top management believed in the Rambler at that point.

It was just seven years—(1950–1957)—before the Rambler took hold publicly. It was in the Spring of 1957, just seven years after it was introduced, that Rambler's sales began to move up.[1]

Mr. Romney noted on other occasions that confidence in the Rambler had been anything but universal in the company up through 1956, thirteen years after the original experiments on a lightweight, compact car were begun. During this period, a handful of members of top management had built a strategy around this new idea, had merged two companies, closed factories, retired a number of key executives who were "big car minded," and borrowed to the limit of the company's capacity in order to put over this new concept. Perhaps most important of all, the company had discontinued its Nash and Hudson lines, and

[1] Report to Stockholders, February 7, 1962.

1958		1959		1960		1961		1962	
$502,788		$935,738		$1,139,508		$938,599		$1,135,190	
32,439		65,888		81,791		62,876		78,795	
$470,349		$869,849		$1,057,716		$875,723		$1,056,395	
$ 1,163		$ 1,567		$ 2,858		$ 1,009		$ 2,568	
2,413	3,577	5,040	6,607	5,574	8,433	3,556	4,565	6,475	8,944
	$473,926		$876,458		$1,066,849		$880,290		$1,065,439
$391,188		$684,198		$862,899		$726,529		$870,701	
4,787		4,717		7,239		10,608		9,744	
		11,933		10,892		18,041		19,876	
5,893		6,852		6,738		7,420		10,144	
42,896		62,543		72,003		67,101		81,731	
647		......		......		......		......	
993		390		300		210		120	
350	446,756	379	771,017	631	960,706	......	829,911	......	992,299
	$ 27,170		$105,441		$ 105,443		$ 50,378		$ 73,140
	515		......		......		......		......
	(1,600)		......		......		......		......
			45,100		57,200		26,800		38,900
	$ 26,085		$ 60,341		$ 48,243		$ 23,578		$ 34,240

[handwritten: ← 11.2% of gross sales] *[handwritten: 6.4% of gross sales]*

had concentrated all its efforts on the remaining line, the Rambler. By 1957 the company had bet all of its chips on the next roll, the 1958 models, and Mr. Romney conceded to members of his organization that if they didn't bring the company into the black in 1958 the game was up.

As the company's fortunes improved during 1958, the strategy shifted to one of expansion in the compact field. But despite its rapidly increasing output, the company was unable to meet the total demand for its cars for almost a year. Then as the Big Three brought out directly competitive cars, company strategy shifted once again, as AMC sought to hold its share of market.

Mr. Romney frequently described AMC's strategy in terms of this seesaw between offense and defense, likening it to a sequence of "campaigns" where a campaign was a program of action stretching over a period of years. On one occasion he reviewed the campaigns following the founding of the company as follows:

> On many occasions I have discussed our program in terms of campaigns. Between 1954 and 1957 we won our "campaign for survival." Between 1957 and 1958 we won our "campaign opportunity" and since

Exhibit 2

AMERICAN MOTORS CORPORATION I

Consolidated Balance Sheets

(in thousands)

ASSETS	1954		1955		1956		1957	
Current Assets:								
Cash and government securities............	$ 45,402		$37,859		$26,517		$22,600	
Accounts receivable (net)...............	19,996		20,925		23,624		23,788	
Due from subsidiaries...	1,949		2,589		3,101		351	
Income tax refund due...	16,853		9,683		......		......	
Inventories (net)........	80,616		89,553		83,980		67,965	
Miscellaneous items.....	5,023	$169,841	4,078	$164,690	3,504	$140,728	3,300	$118,006
Investments in subsidiaries...........		13,957		12,888		7,355		8,563
Miscellaneous assets.......		774		6,741		3,524		3,467
Property, plant and equipment (net)......		82,138		75,960		73,297		65,934
Total Assets.......		$266,711		$260,281		$224,905		$195,972
LIABILITIES AND NET WORTH								
Current Liabilities:								
Bank notes, and amount due on long-term debt.	$ 31,200		$38,500		$36,000		$28,569	
Accounts payable.......	48,834		56,338		43,795		37,072	
Accrued expenses......	2,212		2,251		2,172		2,731	
Warranties on refrigerators..........	4,729		4,096		3,491		2,886	
Income tax.............	......		......		......		......	
Miscellaneous..........	781	$ 87,756	1,097	$102,283	624	$ 86,084	504	$ 71,768
Long-term debt...........		16,000		14,000		14,569		13,000
Stockholders' Investment:								
Common stock.........	$ 28,352		$28,352		$28,352		$27,939	
Additional paid-in capital...............	27,136		27,136		27,136		26,334	
Retained earnings......	107,465	162,954	88,509	143,998	68,763	124,251	56,930	111,204
Total Liabilities and Net Worth.......		$266,711		$260,281		$224,905		$195,972

Source: Annual Reports.

1959, as our competitors imitated Rambler, we have successfully faced their "campaign counterattack." We have shown those financial advisors and those who said we could not compete successfully with the Big Three head-on that they were wrong. We have demonstrated this by our success in competing with them head-on. We expect conclusively to win in this year [1962] by selling the largest number of Ramblers in our history despite all-out compact car competition. Next year we expect to resume the offensive with "campaign leadership." In the years ahead, we can expect to begin a long-range battle for the number one brand name position in the automobile industry in this country.

This case describes the automotive strategy of American Motors in relation to market conditions and the strategies of its major competitors in the American market. It omits the appliance business, in which AMC's Kelvinator division was a participant, and it also omits all but the briefest consideration of the foreign markets for automobiles. The case focuses on the seven-year period following the formation of American Motors, i.e., from 1954 to 1961. In particular, the case describes the competitive position of AMC at three points in time (1954, 1957,

1958		1959		1960		1961		1962	
$44,553		$ 60,041		$ 43,762		$ 69,752		$ 87,058	
28,757		33,177		38,856		36,239		45,579	
2,352		1,633		1,688		3,968		4,815	
......		......		......		......		......	
59,931		98,070		115,569		93,254		96,078	
3,010	$138,586	2,938	$195,861	3,938	$203,815	3,697	$206,913	3,916	$237,448
	10,603		24,428		33,416		34,635		40,946
	5,509		5,546		6,367		5,676		7,891
	51,484		58,617		94,792		85,731		88,789
	$206,184		$284,453		$338,392		$332,957		$375,076
$ 3,000		$ 3,000		$ 3,000		$ 4,000		0	
50,367		73,243		78,314		67,805		$ 86,998	
2,125		2,725		21,609		24,069		28,207	
2,669		2,570		......		......		......	
......		4,102		4,735		7,888		5,761	
508	$ 58,670	990	$ 86,631	3,442	$111,102	3,507	$107,207	4,654	$125,522
	10,000		7,000		4,000		......		......
$28,068		$ 29,694		$ 29,981		$ 30,096		$ 31,199	
26,429		34,052		34,518		34,866		44,772	
83,015	137,514	127,074	190,821	158,790	223,290	160,724	225,687	173,482	249,454
	$206,184		$284,453		$338,392		$332,957		$375,076

and 1961), and the AMC "campaign" strategy for dealing with each situation. In conclusion, it describes the situation in 1962 and poses the question of what "campaign leadership" might mean.

THE SITUATION IN 1954

As the postwar seller's market in automobiles changed to a buyer's market in 1953, the independents (Packard, Studebaker, Kaiser-Willys, Hudson, and Nash) began merger talks. Amid the varying combinations and deals, several considerations stood out.

First, the independents were producing too many body styles relative to the volume of cars for their unit costs to remain competitive with the big three. Packard, Nash, and Hudson together marketed only eight series of cars, yet required five basic body styles. In contrast, Ford made seven series from two basic body shells, while Chrysler made eleven series from four shells, and GM made fourteen from only four shells.[2] The difference in tooling costs thus gave the Big Three a sizable ad-

[2] Tom Mahoney, *The Story of George Romney* (New York: Harper & Bros., 1960).

vantage with each model change-over, and the greater volume of each model allowed the Big Three to spread the tooling costs over more cars. The advantage was thus twofold, and in a style-conscious market it was a compelling one.

Second, and less tangible, none of the independents could count on generating enough sales volume for their dealer organizations to keep the dealers profitable and strong. Declining dealer strength would lead to reduced service as well as reduced sales, and might sooner or later spell disaster. As a real buyer's market developed, and price wars developed, this would hasten the plight of the weak, "off-brand" dealer.

Thus the independents knew the days of "independent" operations were numbered. While various proposals were tried, the results were a merger between Hudson and Nash, and later a belated merger between Packard and Studebaker. In the aftermath of these mergers, three of the famous names in American automotive history disappeared. Nash and Hudson cars succumbed to the American Motors Rambler, and the Packard disappeared in favor of the Studebaker.

While the independents were working on their tooling and dealer problems, GM had returned to its strategy of the 1930's. It marketed progressively longer, lower, more powerful cars. Unlike the earlier era, however, Ford and Chrysler now followed suit. And as the 1954 model year got under way, Ford and Chevy were once more running neck and neck for leadership in total new car registrations.

In 1958 Mr. Romney, in discussing the background of these competitive developments, reviewed the industry's history as follows:[3]

> I think as further background we might review some of the basic changes that have taken place in the automobile market since the start of the industry. At the beginning, of course, a lot of companies went into the business. Then Ford emerged as the dominant factor as Henry Ford developed the concept of building a dependable piece of transportation within the reach of the mass market. He succeeded by 1921—his peak year—in securing 62% of total industry sales. In that year there were 88 companies manufacturing automobiles. At that time the Ford was a 100-inch wheelbase vehicle—in wheelbase, the same size as this Rambler American we have which is at the top end of the small-car field. From 100 inches, other makes went as high as 145 inches in wheelbase, 10 inches beyond anything on the market today. There was an assortment of vehicles in terms of size and engines and various components, and so on, of a very widespread character indeed.
>
> With the growth in American prosperity and with the growth that the Ford success helped to bring about, American car buyers began to indicate a desire for more than just bare transportation. General Motors excelled in its recognition of the change that was taking place in consumer preference. The result was that by 1927 they had succeeded in capturing about a third of the market, and Ford at that time still had a third. But a third of the market was not enough to permit Ford to operate profitably; so he shut down to convert over to the Model A in an effort to meet this new-type consumer demand.

___
[3] Tobé and Associates, *The Tobé Lectures in Retail Distribution, 1958–1959* (Boston, Mass.: Harvard Graduate School of Business Administration).

General Motors continued and adopted the basic philosophy that has dominated the automobile industry in the United States, from a product standpoint, until the last few years. As a matter of fact, you'd almost have to say it still dominates in terms of current product volume. But General Motors adopted the policy—clearly stated by their technical people and policy people—of building cars each year a little bit bigger, a little bit more stylish, for the purpose of progressive, dynamic obsolescence. That product philosophy, coupled with other contributions they made—because General Motors has made many very substantial and significant contributions to the concepts of large industrial management—made General Motors the largest industrial corporation in the world.

Ford never quite came back. Under Henry Ford, Sr., the company never really adopted the product philosophy of General Motors. But following World War II the new management, in an effort to recapture first place, literally jumped onto the General Motors bandwagon, and basically adopted the General Motors product philosophy.

Then five years ago, when there was a change in the Chrysler management, [1953–54] Chrysler did the same thing. By 1954, therefore, at the time of the formation of American Motors, you had the three dominant factors in the automobile industry all going down substantially the identical product road.

As a result of this philosophy of making their cars a little bigger and more powerful each year, they kept moving them up in size and reducing the degree of variation and distinction. The result was that they created a vacuum back of them in the market and they created a concentration of competition as between their own models, with effects that we're beginning to see.

American Motors set out to fill this vacuum. But it took several years to produce a car to fill the need, and still longer to convince the mass market that there was indeed something "below" the low-priced three. While working to develop the product and the market, the company very nearly succumbed to competitive pressures. Its strategy was one of fighting for survival.

CAMPAIGN SURVIVAL: 1954–57

American Motors' long-run objectives were to become a leading competitor in the automotive field. To accomplish this, the company was relying primarily on (1) its conception of the unfilled need in the American market, the need for a car between the big cars of the big three and the small cars imported from Europe; and (2) its belief that its concept of a "compact" car filled this need.

The evidence of need was supported by a survey of transportation habits which showed "that 85% of all [automobile] trips in the United States were 13 miles or less in length, and that the bulk of them were for essential purposes."[4] The automobile was not primarily a vehicle of transcontinental travel, nor one of pleasure cruising. It was becoming a part of everyday urban and suburban living. From this knowledge

---

[4] Mahoney, *The Story of George Romney*, p. 197.

sprang the conviction that there was a real market for a comfortable car with improved economy and maintenance which could be maneuvered easily, parked easily, and for which styling changes for change's sake might be avoided. It was this conception which lay behind the experimental development of the compact car.

In the design itself, the principles of aircraft engineering had been successfully applied by Nash-Kelvinator for almost a decade, permitting the company to make the car strong but light while at the same time preserving the riding comfort of which Americans are so fond. The resulting development was called a unitized or a single unit body, where the parts were welded together rather than being bolted to a strong, heavy frame, as was the universal practice in the United States at the time.

With this conception of a need and of a product to fill the need, American Motors faced the formidable task of devising a strategy which could (1) get the idea of this need across to the public, (2) gain the commitment of the organization to the product concept, and (3) keep the company from going under while management tried to get the first two steps accomplished. American Motors strategy in 1954–1957 was called a campaign for survival, since the short-run problems were so acute that long-range goals had to be tempered if the company was to survive. The strategy included the following major steps.

Product line. Effective with the consolidation of 1955 model production at Nash's Wisconsin facilities in December 1954, the product line was made up of three basic elements: the standard automobiles (with approximately a 116-inch wheelbase), the Rambler (some with 108-inch and some with 100-inch wheelbase), and the Metropolitan (with an 85-inch wheelbase). There were four models of the standard autos, two sold under the Hudson name (Hornet and Wasp) and two under the Nash name (Ambassador and Statesman). The Ramblers were sold under both brand names, giving the two surviving dealer organizations identical products to sell under different brand names. Sales of standard automobiles and Ramblers developed opposite trends over the first three years, as indicated by the following figures:

Year	Unit Total Sales	Hudson and Nash Standard	Hudson and Nash Rambler	Rambler as % of Total
1954	99,774	61,995	37,779	38%
1955	194,175	110,323	83,852	43
1956	104,189	25,023	79,166	77

Even more significant, however, was the fact that by 1955 sales of the 108-inch Ramblers were running four to one over the 100-inch model. It was on this basis that management decided to discontinue the 100-inch Rambler for 1956, and to concentrate on the larger model. But the problem of defining a clear product policy remained. The Hudson and Nash cars were just "above" the low-priced three in retail price,

while the Ramblers were intended to be just below the low-priced—
even though they were only slightly lower in price at this point. At any
rate, the company did not market a car which was directly competitive
in size and price with the low-priced three, but rather it straddled this
market segment by being on both flanks. Was AMC going to compete
with the low-priced three directly, or be above and below them, or just
below them, or what?

Mr. Romney spoke on this question in September 1956, in a speech
entitled "In League with the Future" at a meeting introducing the 1957
models:

> Sales of compact cars will continue to grow, but more big cars than
> compact cars will be sold during the transition period. For that reason
> American Motors has no plans to drop its big car program.
>
> American Motors is wedded to the program of supplying its dealers
> cars for each major segment of the future car market. For 1957 you
> have a big Nash or Hudson, the compact Rambler, and the small and
> increasingly popular Metropolitan. In 1958, Nash dealers will have an
> all new big car with the Nash name to sell and the Hudson dealers
> will have an all new big car with the Hudson name to sell.
>
> Our 1958 cars will be the first ones resulting from combined Nash
> and Hudson engineering. Our 1958 program will be the first one to
> basically reflect the new management's product philosophy.

Product styling. In a speech to the dealer organization, Mr. Romney
pointed out that company policy on automobile styling was being
changed:

> We have changed the company's previous styling policy. Under the
> old policy, styling distinction was sought to the point of production
> designs with high controversial and sometimes unacceptable features.
> Looking ahead, American Motors cars will be styled in the basic ad-
> vanced patterns of future cars with elements of distinction that are not
> so extreme as to be controversial. We should avoid styling controversy
> or pioneering because our cars themselves are basically advanced, dis-
> tinct, and superior.

Marketing. The marketing program faced the twofold task of selling
the organization as well as the public:

> The biggest difficulty we had in the early marketing and merchandis-
> ing of the Rambler concept was internal, not external. The biggest prob-
> lem was to change the attitude of our own vice president in charge of
> sales and of our sales organization and of our dealers. As late as the
> spring of 1954, just following the merger—at a meeting of all the Nash
> zone managers—I asked how many of them thought the Rambler would
> ever become a bread-and-butter car for American Motors. There were
> only two out of twenty-three zone managers who thought that was even
> a remote possibility. Our vice president in charge of sales was insisting
> internally that what we had to have was a car directly competitive with
> the Chevrolet, Ford, and Plymouth. And our biggest dealers were taking
> the same position.
>
> *   *   *   *   *
>
> The first thing that happened after I succeeded to the presidency
> (in October of 1954) of the company was that I brought in a new man

(Roy Abernethy, now president of the corporation) to head up our sales effort who believed in this product approach. The second thing we did was to use the new model announcement meetings in the fall of 1954 to stress this theme with our dealers. The theme of my talk to our dealers across the country was "Get your sights up on the Rambler."

*   *   *   *   *

As a result of a lot of effort, we succeeded in convincing our dealer body that this product concept had merit in the market place. What convinced them as much as anything else that first year was that in the spring of 1954, the resale value of used Ramblers moved ahead of the resale value of Chevrolet, Ford, and Plymouth models. And it has remained above ever since. That was conclusive evidence that in one vital aspect of automotive marketing—namely, what the buyer can expect when he takes his car back in to buy a new car—we had a competitive advantage.

We also had public attitudes to deal with, as well as the internal attitudes. We were faced with a difficult public attitude created by the failure of all independent companies except two. And in the fall of 1954 somebody was giving us a mock burial almost every day in the press.

*   *   *   *   *

There was also a frozen big-car mentality in this country that had been built up almost from the beginning of the automobile industry, but particularly as the new product philosophy took over in the late 1920's.

Now how did we [try to] change that public attitude? Well, we went to work to tell the basic product advantage story of Rambler, and to tell it not only in terms of calling attention to the product specifically, but also by way of comparison. At that point people were not inclined to pay any attention to us. So we had to be dramatic, and we had to make people stop, look, and listen. And probably the biggest break we had was one day when I happened to read an article by an automotive editor, who talked about dinosaurs. And I said, "That's it, we're competing against gas-guzzling dinosaurs." And that stuck.[5]

Later Mr. Romney took to giving speeches where he used scale model dinosaurs as props. At a meeting of the National Parking Association in 1957 he led off as follows:

This fellow is called a Brontosaurus. He was about seventy feet long. . . . He weighed a good many tons. His fuel consumption was tremendous. His mouth was relatively so small that he had to spend all of his waking hours eating. This streamlined fellow here was called Dimetrodon and is considered a predecessor of the modern horse. One of his problems was he began developing a fin on his back to a point where it became larger and larger and finally upset his equilibrium.

This handsome model was known as Stegosaurus. He perhaps represented the highest development of the dinosaur in terms of useless, nonfunctional decorative treatment.[6]

*   *   *   *   *

---

[5] Tobé, *The Tobé Lectures in Retail Distribution, 1958–1959*, pp. 30, 34.
[6] Mahoney, *The Story of George Romney*, p. 21.

While moving with this concept of the competitors' "dinosaurs," American Motors also moved to change the way its own products were advertised and promoted. Mr. Romney pointed out that—

> We . . . changed our advertising policy, and that was a tough one. Boy, Madison Avenue has got fixed ideas. . . . It took us three years to get our advertising agency not only to agree that our policy should be different on advertising, but also to reach the point where they could reflect accurately our product story in ads that would command the attention of the American people.[7]

He went on to stress that American Motors advertising must henceforward meet standards such as the following:

> 1. American Motors copy must be as simple, informational, and factual as possible. Banish the superlatives . . . rule out conventional advertising language [and], use new language to the greatest extent possible.
> 2. Every advertisement must be centered on a dominant idea that is validated by a quality or feature in the product.[8]

Dealer organization. American Motors had a combined total of 2,800 Nash and Hudson dealers in 1954. In less than two years this had declined to 1,900, largely through dealer resignations. While the downward trend was reversed following the consolidation of the Nash and Hudson franchises, a weak distribution organization remained a key problem for the company. In 1956, with unit sales slipping almost 50% from the previous year, the company instituted a dealer bonus plan which credited the dealer with from $30 to $50 extra per car on all domestic sales. Over a two-year period, the plan cost the company more than $7 million, but it was credited with being instrumental in keeping the dealer organization together during these lean years.

Finance and control. At the time of the merger the company was losing about $2 million a month. On the one hand this called for drastic cost cutting, and on the other it called for a campaign to turn nonessential resources into cash so the company could carry forward long enough to give its compact car concept a chance to prove itself in the marketplace. Backing up this move meant betting the company's last chips on automobiles, just at a time when some of the most vocal stockholders were recommending the company bow out of the automotive field altogether.

In addition to securing a loan from an insurance company and increased credit from a group of banks, the company sold its Hudson body plant, its West Coast assembly plant, and its 60% interest in Ranco, Inc., a highly successful manufacturer of thermostatic controls for appliances. The three sales gave the company an additional $15 million in "chips" to put behind Rambler. Part of these funds was used to tool the company's own V-8 engine (introduced in March 1957) to replace the very expensive V-8 engine and transmission bought from Packard and used in the 1955 and 1956 models. Still, as 1956 progressed, it be-

[7] Tobé, *The Tobé Lectures in Retail Distribution, 1958–1959*, p. 34.
[8] Ibid.

came clear that more drastic measures were required. With working capital down almost 50% in two years, and only a few million dollars above the minimum required by bank loans, heroic cost cutting measures were taken.

In the management echelons, it meant selling the company airplanes, a new policy urging managers to take more modest hotel accommodations when traveling, and an "end to the two-hour lunches." The company resigned from the NAM, went through a systematic curtailment of magazine subscriptions, and to bring the point home to all concerned, Mr. Romney and other top executives took "voluntary" salary reductions up to 40%.

At lower levels, the company advertising agency was required to pay rent for its office space at the company headquarters. Company garages stopped giving free gas and service to executive cars.

> At one point, offices were cleaned only every other day, for a saving of forty thousand dollars a year. Another forty thousand dollars a year was deferred by delaying the customary gifts of watches or clocks to employees with thirty years of service. . . . Offices went unpainted, and sheet toilet paper replaced rolls.[9]

CONSOLIDATION

Besides the consolidation of production into the Nash plants and the sale of the Hudson facilities, American Motors was able to effect economies from utilizing common tooling for the 1955 models, and from running all of the 1956 models on the same assembly lines. Following consolidation, disposal of the surplus plants, and write-downs of $12 million of other Hudson facilities, the company entered the 1957 model year with an estimated break-even point at below 150,000 units. The 1956 annual report noted: "The primary automotive objective since the merger has been to reduce the automotive break-even point, and simultaneously, to develop new lines of cars needed to increase sales to profitable levels."

The significance of the consolidation is easily seen by comparing performance from 1955 through 1958:

Year	Unit Sales	Pretax Earnings
1955	194,000	$(16,700,000)
1956	104,000	(30,000,000)
1957	119,000	(11,000,000)
1958	189,000	26,000,000

By 1958 the break-even had been reduced to a point where a volume smaller than the one achieved in 1955 was adequate to generate a sizable pretax profit (American Motors Corporation was not able to fill all of its orders in 1958), and this even though 1955 had been a good year

---

[9] Mahoney, *The Story of George Romney*, p. 191.

in the industry, whereas 1958 was one of the worst in the postwar period. Survival was to be based in large measure on keeping the break-even low, and the low break-even was to be maintained by manufacturing only the bare essentials (motors, bodies, transmissions, and a few other items), by purchasing the remaining items from outside suppliers, and by maintaining a single assembly center. By the end of 1957 American Motors had become the least integrated manufacturer in the business, and had thereby helped prepare a flexible base from which to operate in the ups and downs of the auto business. So much for "campaign survival."

THE SITUATION IN THE FALL OF 1957

While American Motors was retrenching and proceeding largely unnoticed by others in the industry, a battle was shaping up in the medium-priced cars between General Motors and Ford. The battle came to a climax with the introduction of the 1958 models in the fall of 1957. As reported by *Fortune*,[10] the giants prepared for the clash in the following manner:

> The Big Three were caught off base in the shifting markets of 1956 and 1957 because of some decision making back in 1954. That year, G.M.'s President Harlow Curtice and the high command at Chevrolet were disturbed by reports that Ford was planning to attack Chevrolet with a car "as big as Buick." It was to be ready for introduction in 1957.
>
> Indeed, G.M. heard that Ford was committing itself to big cars in all its brands. Ford's Edsel division was being set up to swing across all price lines except at the very bottom and top of the market. This was as wide a market as Buick had carved out. The G.M. high command also knew that Ford was designing a bigger body shell for Mercury which would interchange with the larger Edsels, and that smaller Edsels would interchange with the big Ford.
>
> What had happened was this: Ford had tested the lower end of the medium-price market with luxury-model Fords. It had found no resistance and raked in some nice profits. With this experience, and with the knowledge that consumer income was up sharply, Ford had every reason to believe that the markets of the future would favor the medium-price entries at the expense of the low-price cars. Also, Ford division officials were worried by the tremendous sales surge of Buick, which had recently pushed Plymouth out of third place. They believed that if the market continued to demand big cars, Buick might push the Ford for second place.
>
> It seemed apparent to the bosses at Ford that the medium-price Mercury was no match for Buick. This meant that far too much of the burgeoning medium-price market would be captured by G.M., which had not only Buick in that arena but Pontiac, Olds, and the top end of Chevrolet. What to do? Fight Buick with Ford. How? By making Ford as big as a 1954 Buick.
>
> By early 1955, G.M. knew that Ford had definitely committed itself to this strategy. Curtice and his officers also learned that Chrysler, with

---

[10] "Detroit Shoots the Works," *Fortune*, June 1959. Reproduced by permission.

no one division capable of achieving the savings that accrue to a factory that can make and sell a million units, had committed itself to one line of body shells for all of its cars. Watching their own labor costs mounting, G.M. officials reflected that one body shell for all their brands would save scores of millions of dollars. Late in 1955, G.M. decided on one big body shell for all its brands by 1958. It had to be big so that Chevrolet could meet the threat the big Ford would pose. And to hedge the bet on bigness, G.M. shortly put into motion plans for the compact Chevrolet that will be introduced this fall [1959], as related above, and Ford and Chrysler felt obliged to follow.

(While it takes eighteen months' to two years' lead time to make a major model change on a current car, it takes three years for a complete re-engineering job.)

Work had hardly been started on the big Chevrolet before G.M. statisticians pointed out that something odd was happening to Buick and Olds. Both had broken their records in 1955 (738,000 for Buick and 590,000 for Olds), but sales in the metropolitan areas had not kept pace with total sales. What could this mean? The big cities were normally the principal volume markets for these luxurious cars, for no other markets had enough upper-middle incomes. Evidently buyers outside the big cities had used three-year credit, which was widely available in 1955, to trade themselves up to Buicks and Oldsmobiles. This was apparently the reason for the 1955 increase in sales for these brands, for they were unable to hold their gains.

By the end of the first half of 1956, Buick and Olds were limping. Was the move to suburbia bad for Buick because more people needed two cars and couldn't afford two Buicks? Surveys showed that this might be one factor. Another factor might be the size of the new Buicks and Olds, which made them awkward to park in the cities. G.M. concluded that size and high prices were in some way at the root of Buick's and Olds' problem, so the company also put compact models for these two cars in work. And again Ford and Chrysler followed.

The figures show how radically the market changed between 1956 and 1957.

In 1956, 61 per cent of domestic sales were in the $1,800 to $2,300 range; the medium-price markets, which spread from $2,300 to $4,000, took about 35 per cent of the business; 4 per cent went to high-price cars. Buick had dropped back nearly 210,000 units to 529,000; and Olds, at 438,000, was off more than 150,000. This was the reverse of the sales pattern Ford had predicted for Buick—a fact that gave Ford, with the medium-priced Edsel poised for introduction the next year, something to ponder.

In 1957, when Ford began its fight against G.M. with big Fords, low-price cars tobogganed down from 61 per cent to a little under 20 per cent of the market. (The larger Fords were classed as medium-priced automobiles.) High-price cars went up to almost 6 per cent. Buick slid still further, to 395,000 units, Olds to 372,000, while the medium-price market soared to an astonishing 75 per cent. Imports more than doubled, to nearly 200,000 units—a figure that looked impressive for the first time. Ford trounced Chevrolet for the first time in a generation. Chrysler, which since 1953 had been on a feast-or-famine diet, did nicely with the Plymouth and its other lines. [See Exhibit 3.]

The sobering fact of the 1957 market was that the invasion of the

Exhibit 3

PER CENT OF INDUSTRY NEW CAR REGISTRATIONS BY MAKES
CALENDAR YEARS 1954–62

	1954	1955	1956	1957	1958	1959	1960	1961	1962
Chevrolet..........	25.6	22.9	26.3	24.3	26.6	23.5	25.8	27.2	29.9
Pontiac............	6.5	7.4	6.0	5.4	4.9	6.3	6.1	6.4	7.6
Oldsmobile........	7.3	8.2	7.4	6.2	6.6	6.0	5.4	5.6	6.4
Buick.............	9.3	10.3	8.9	6.6	5.7	4.1	4.1	5.0	5.8
Cadillac..........	2.0	2.0	2.2	2.4	2.6	2.2	2.2	2.4	2.2
GM...............	50.7	50.8	50.8	44.9	46.4	42.1	43.6	46.6	51.9
Ford.............	25.3	21.9	23.1	25.0	22.1	24.4	21.6	22.7	21.2
Edsel.............	...	...	...	0.4	0.8	0.7	...	...	...
Mercury..........	4.9	5.2	4.6	4.4	2.9	2.6	4.7	5.3	4.6
Lincoln...........	0.7	0.5	0.7	0.6	0.6	0.5	0.3	0.5	0.5
Ford Motor Co.....	30.9	27.6	28.4	30.4	26.4	28.2	26.6	28.5	26.3
Plymouth..........	6.9	9.0	8.1	10.0	8.4	6.4	6.8	5.1	4.4
Dodge............	2.8	4.0	3.7	4.3	2.9	2.8	5.4	3.9	3.4
De Soto...........	1.4	1.6	1.7	1.7	1.0	0.7	0.4	...	...
Chrysler..........	1.8	2.0	1.8	1.8	1.3	1.1	1.2	1.6	1.6
Imperial..........	...	0.2	0.2	0.5	0.3	0.3	0.2	0.2	0.2
Chrysler Corp......	12.9	16.8	15.5	18.3	13.9	11.3	14.0	10.8	9.6
Hudson............	0.6	0.3	0.2	0.1	...	...	...	...	...
Nash.............	0.9	0.6	0.5	0.2	...	...	...	...	...
Rambler..........	0.6	1.0	1.2	1.5	4.0	6.0	6.4	6.3	6.1
AM*.............	2.1	1.9	1.9	2.0	4.3	6.0	6.4	6.3	6.1
Studebaker........	1.7	1.4	1.3	1.0	1.0	2.2	1.6	1.2	1.1
Packard..........	0.7	0.7	0.5	0.1	0.1	...	...	...	...
S-P..............	2.4	2.1	1.8	1.1	1.1	2.2	1.6	1.2	1.1
Crosley...........	...	...	...	...	...	...	...	...	...
Frazer............	...	...	...	...	...	...	...	...	...
Henry J...........	...	...	...	...	...	...	...	...	...
Kaiser............	0.4	0.2	...	...	...	...	...	...	...
Willys............	0.3	0.1	...	...	...	...	...	...	...
Others............	0.3	0.6	1.6	3.3	7.9	10.2	7.8	6.6	5.0
Industry..........	100.0	100.0	100.0	100.0	100.0	100.0	100.0	100.0	100.0

* Includes imported Metropolitan 1958 and prior years, but not 1959–62.
Source: *Ward's Automotive Yearbook, 1963*, p. 145. Reproduced by permission.

medium-price field by the former low-price three had murdered the old-timers in that market. Buick will never forget the slaughter of 1957, and neither will Ford, for in the process the big new 1957 Mercury lost business, and the brand-new Edsel fizzled in the market that wasn't there.

When 1958 and recession rolled around, G.M. offered a Chevrolet bigger than a Ford, as big, in fact, as a Cadillac.

It was the Cadillac-sized Chevrolet pitted against the almost as large Ford and Chrysler models which gave American Motors its opening for "campaign opportunity."

CAMPAIGN OPPORTUNITY

American Motors faced its crucial test just at the time when the medium-priced cars were being squeezed the hardest. Sales of Buick and Olds were declining, Edsel was unable to get rolling, and the medium-priced cars of American Motors—the Nash and Hudson lines —were declining sharply. Thus it was that in early 1957 a decision was made to stop production and to withdraw these lines from the market. American Motors made a historic decision to bet all of its chips on the Rambler, believing that the "Rambler concept" was the key to an opportunity. To back up its bet, the company took the following steps:

Product line.   The Nash and Hudson lines were dropped after a stormy meeting of the board of directors, and two names of long-standing tradition disappeared from the market. The company made special allowances to dealers to help them move the last of these cars off the showroom floors.

Instead of introducing new Nash and Hudson models, as previously planned, the company introduced a 117-inch Ambassador by Rambler. By design this model used the same body shell as the 108-inch Rambler American, using largely the same dies and tooling as when the car had been discontinued in 1955.

When asked why American Motors had discontinued the 100-inch Rambler for almost three years and then revived it, Mr. Romney pointed out that the company had tried both the two-door 100-inch model and the four-door 108-inch model, and found that the latter had outsold the "more compact" model about four to one. He went on to point out that he believed there was a very good reason why the larger model had achieved greater acceptance:

> I think there's a very logical reason for that having happened. I once read that if you ever wanted to start a revolution—and after all, that's what we were trying to start in products—you should sell the basic idea with the least possible departure from existing forms. Now the 108-inch model was a smaller departure from the big-car concept in this country than the 100-inch model. And our figures indicated you could probably sell that size car, and break through the big-car mentality, quicker than you could with a 100-inch.
>
> Later the American public was not only accepting the compact car idea but also accepting the small car idea; and therefore we not only decided to have our Metropolitan model, which is an 85-inch small model, but also decided to bring back the 100-inch model because we were convinced that the small car idea had taken hold well enough to do that. And we brought it back in February of this year [1958], just the two-door model, and that two-door model is now second only to the Volkswagen in small car sales in America.[11]

Later that same day, asked why the 1958 Rambler had tail fins, Mr. Romney returned to the same theme, answering to the effect that "it's the basic idea that counts. If we have to use tail fins to get people to try compact cars, we'll use tail fins. Later on we will certainly be able

---

[11] Tobé, *The Tobé Lectures in Retail Distribution, 1958–1959,* p. 43.

to do away with them, and to build clean, simple, uncluttered cars."

Marketing. With the reintroduction of the 100-inch car, and with a restyled 108-inch car, 1958 was the "do or die" year for American Motors. In the fall of 1957:

> Romney felt constrained . . . to tell his deficit ridden [organization] that if the new year didn't see the corporation in the black, there could be a change in management. In consequence, 1958 [began] with Romney and every other executive who could grab a lapel, seize an ear, or clamber on a rostrum, hammering home the points that this was American Motors' year, this time the Big Three had gone too far, this was the moment when common sense in car buying could stretch the recession's "skimpy pay-checks."
>
> We resorted to something akin to shock treatment [one executive recalled], in an effort to shatter the prevailing myth that the greatest car values were to be found in products built by the Big Three.[12]

Not only did top executives take to the road selling and promoting,

> Celebrated cartoonists like William Steig, Whitney Darrow, and Chon Day were put to work on full page American Motors ads featuring . . . "Siegfried Slays the Dragon . . . Again" (he'd stabbed his fire breathing monster in the gas tank, after finding it unparkable and ungarageable). . . .[13]

With the "dinosaurs of the driveway" larger and longer than ever, the lampooning spread, and numerous cartoons appeared in magazines and newspapers all over the country. The spontaneous cartoons, plus the success of the Volkswagen, plus the persistent drumfire of American Motors, finally turned the tide.

> In March, Consumer Reports, a monthly buyer's guide, hit the stands with the news it had selected the Rambler Ambassador V-8 as the "consultant's choice," the one U.S. car that year which could "serve as the foundation for a hypothetical but eminently desirable automobile."
>
> In June, Ford became so alarmed over the success of American Motors propaganda that it devoted an entire advertising campaign to counter "talk about gas-guzzling monsters . . . claims of big car room with small car economy."
>
> In September, with . . . 26 million [in] profit (for the fiscal year just ended) George Romney announced he expected to sell 300,000 of his 1959 Ramblers, and to get 6 per cent [of the] market (vs. 4.4 per cent of 1958's).
>
> In October . . . sales were nearly triple those of October 1957.
>
> In December, the corporation started a $10 million expansion program that would permit an increase in Rambler capacity to 450,000 units by the end of 1959.[14] [See Exhibit 4.]

Dealer organization. Beginning early in 1957 the company was able to turn the tide in its dealer organization. Having slipped from 2,700 to about 1,900, the company lost 368 more, but was able to sign 741

---

[12] "Will Success Spoil American Motors?" *Fortune*, January 1959, p. 98. Reproduced by permission.

[13] Ibid.

[14] Ibid.

Exhibit 4

MARKET SHARES: 1953–62

Year	Imports	Independents	Big three
1953	0.5	9.0	90.5
1954	0.6	5.0	94.4
1955	0.8	4.0	95.2
1956	1.7	3.6	94.7
1957	3.4	3.0	93.6
1958	8.1	5.1	86.8
1959	10.2	8.3	81.5
1960	7.6	8.1	84.3
1961	6.5	7.7	85.8
1962	4.9	7.3	87.8

Source: *Ward's Automotive Yearbook, 1963*, p. 145. Reproduced by permission.

new ones to finish the year with 2,300. By September 1958 the number had reached 2,636. From this point on the effort was to upgrade the quality of the dealerships, and to see that the dealers earned enough to provide both the working capital and the incentives needed to provide good service for the cars being sold.

Finance and control. The first fruits of operating in the black went for the repayment of bank debt. By September, the bank debt had been completely repaid, and working capital rose from less than $50 million the preceding year to $80 million. It was under these circumstances that the company appropriated $10 million to make provisions for a 50% increase in auto capacity, the $10 million going primarily for expanded assembly facilities. The company had reduced its break-even point to an estimated 125,000 units, and was in no mood to add the bricks and mortar necessary for a full-blown expansion of facilities. In addition, management could feel some satisfaction in the fact that though volume exceeded 1954, the number of salaried employees was only 50% as large as when the company had been formed.

THE SITUATION IN 1961

Strategies for 1959 differed little from those of 1958, as the Big Three played out their biggest, longest, most expensive models, appropriately adorned with the high watermark in fins and ornamentation. The serious business of new strategy formulation began to show up that fall, as four compacts were introduced in the 1960 product lines. The real punch came in the fall of 1960, however, as four more compacts were introduced in the 1961 lines, thus giving GM four and Chrysler and Ford two each. The competitive pressure generated by the proliferation of new models was particularly acute because the automobile market had, according to some estimates, settled down to being largely a replacement market, a market which fluctuated with purchasing power and grew with the population rather than one which expanded in reflection of rising living standards. The significance of this development was that if the overall market was no longer basically a growth market, then the flood of new models was competing for shares of a relatively stable pie. One could get a bigger share only if someone else got a smaller share. As *Fortune* remarked,[15]

> When the pie was getting bigger all the time, a manufacturer could accept a smaller slice and still come out ahead. Today, however, quite a different situation prevails. Automobile manufacturing in the U.S. has become primarily a replacement industry. The ratio of cars per person has changed only slightly since 1955; the car population itself stands at a whopping 61 million. Last year there was roughly one automobile for every three Americans, compared to one for five in 1945 and one for every seven in the middle Twenties. This does not mean thin pickings for Detroit from now on, but it does mean that in an average annual market of even 6,750,000 units between 1961 and 1965, a relatively small number will represent absolute growth. Some of the long-range forecasts: General Motors, most bullish of the Big Three, foresees a 3 per cent annual increase in new car sales, the trend line passing the seven-million mark in 1965. Ford's forecast is for a 2.8 per cent increase, a difference of some 80,000 cars in a seven-million car market.
>
> Those estimates show that the automobile manufacturer of 1961 has virtually given up the push for the bigger pie. Not very much can be done today about the total size of the market, summed up a Big Three economist this November. We measure success by per cent of penetration. Thus American Motors, Studebaker-Packard, and the imports are out to maintain, or better, their 17.4 per cent of the market (September registrations), three-fourths of which was wrung from G.M., Ford, and Chrysler between 1955 and 1960. As for the major manufacturers, G.M. with 42.7 per cent of the market is pressing to regain the 50.8 per cent it had in 1955; Ford at 26.9 per cent has set its sights on the 30.4 per cent of 1957; Chrysler's hope is to move its percentage from 12.9 to 20.

As far as Big Three strategies were concerned, *Fortune* had the following to say:

> The briefest summary of future strategies is this: Ford and Chrysler place prime emphasis on a generally lower-priced market, which includes the compacts, and Ford is strongly impressed by the "segmented" character of the over-all market. General Motors appears much less committed to the new emphasis on the bottom of the price range. It seems to be pulling for the standard-sized machine, and a rejuvenation of the middle-price brackets, with the compacts a fringe or supplemental market. With those very broad strategic patterns in mind, we can look more closely at the thinking of each company.
>
> At Ford, the central element is its concept of the new U.S. market. "The most important thing to remember about selling automobiles today," said the company's new president, Robert S. McNamara, in early December, "is that this isn't a single or homogeneous market. Ford's product strategy is based on a segmented market where different groups of consumers want different types of cars. We believe the general-pur-

---

[15] "Detroit Is Flying by the Seat of Its Pants," *Fortune*, January 1961. Reproduced by permission.

pose car will become a thing of the past; the expanding need is for specialized vehicles designed to fill a particular requirement."

In putting this concept into operation, Ford has undergone perhaps the most extensive transformation within the Big Three. The number of models it offered in the medium and high-price field was sharply cut, the Edsel being discontinued in 1960 and Lincoln's twelve models reduced to two for the 1961 market. At the same time Mercury was given six new models, raising its total to nineteen. These were heavily concentrated in the low-priced area; indeed, one of them was simply the Ford Galaxie, wearing the Mercury name plate and a slightly higher price tag. [See Exhibits 5 and 6.]

*   *   *   *   *

Ford's strategic posture, though committed to the compacts and to Mercury's new positioning in the low-price field, nevertheless preserves considerable flexibility. The company is acutely aware of the squeeze on profits that would occur should the proportion of compacts to standard-sized machines move from its present one-to-three ratio to parity or better. Any switch in public preference back to standard-sized machines, such as some of its executives now discern, will find Ford more than ready. What won't be altered is the impetus given interchangeability and cost control by a public in search of better but cheaper cars. Body stampings of the Continental and the Thunderbird are already interchangeable. So are those of the Falcon and the Comet, the latter being fundamentally a "stretched"—i.e., pieced-out amidships—version of the Falcon. Further economies of interchangeability can be expected to follow the centralizing of all car production under one manager, announced last November. Eventually there may be consolidations between the lines themselves.

. . . and as the two grand divisions come more and more to duplicate each other's products, their own consolidation into a single division may follow. Interestingly enough, where the divisions have in a sense been combined, with one dealer offering both the Falcon and the Comet, sales of each compact have showed marked improvement— a point that would gain force if the compacts took over more of the car market.

General Motors' over-all strategy, like that of Ford, recognizes the concept of a segmented market. This year in particular the variety of its 119 models—it was the only Big Three company to raise rather than lower the total—is the gauge of its efforts to offer something to virtually every segment. At the same time there are important differences in outlook and situation that differentiate G.M.'s strategy from Ford's, indeed from that of any other automobile manufacturer. To begin with, G.M.'s drop in total share of the market from 50.8 per cent in calendar 1955 to 42.1 per cent in 1959 came fundamentally from a decline of its middle-price makes. Chevrolet managed to do a little better than hold its own at 23 to 24 per cent, in part because G.M. permitted it to push up into the middle-priced market. But Buick declined steadily from 10.3 in 1955 to 4.1 in 1959, Oldsmobile slid from 8.2 to 6, Pontiac from 7.4 to 6.3. The actual unit volumes tell an even sadder story, Buick falling from 738,000 units to 246,000. On the other hand, Buick-Oldsmobile-Pontiac commanded 16.4 per cent of the 1959 market even after their slump and this made their representation in the middle-priced class five times more important than Ford's, more than triple Chrysler's. Thus the prime strategic question facing General

Exhibit 5

1961 MODEL PRICES

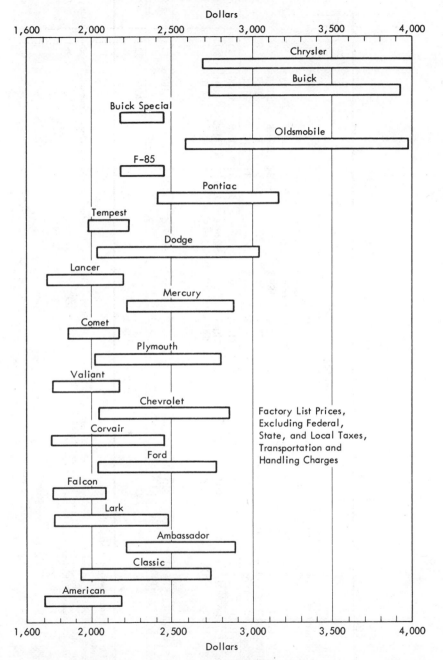

Ford and Chrysler, as the chart above reveals, are committed to the compacts and a generally lower-priced market; General Motors seems to be trying to husband its strength in Chevrolet, revitalize the middle-priced bracket, and give little play to the compacts.

Source: *Fortune*, January 1961. Reproduced with permission.

Exhibit 6

A.M.A. SPECIFICATION COMPARISON FOR 1961 AUTOMOBILES

	Compact cars											Low-priced standard-size cars		
	Rambler American	Studebaker Lark	Chevrolet Corvair	Ford Falcon	Plymouth Valiant	Olds F-85	Buick Special	Dodge Lancer	Pontiac Tempest	Rambler Classic	M-L Comet	Chevrolet Biscayne	Plymouth Savoy	Ford Fairlane
Overall length	173.1	175.0	180.0	181.2	183.7	188.2	188.4	188.8	189.3	189.8	194.8	209.3	209.5	209.9
width	70.0	71.4	67.0	70.6	70.4	71.5	71.3	72.3	72.2	72.4	70.4	78.4	80.0	79.9
height	56.2	56.5	51.5	54.5	53.3	52.6	52.5	53.3	53.5	57.3	54.5	55.5	54.4	55.0
Wheelbase	100.0	108.5	108.0	109.5	106.5	112.0	112.0	106.5	112.0	108.0	114.0	119.0	118.0	119.0
Engine type	LHD-6	OHV-6	Flat-6	OHV-6	Slant-6	Alum V/8	Alum V/8	Slant-6	Slant-4	OHV-6	OHV-6	Inline 135 (6)	Slant 145 (6)	Inline 135 (6)
horsepower	90	112	80	85	101	155	155	101	110	127	85	170 (V/8)	230 (V/8)	175 (V/8)
Price*	$1,730 1,809	$1,822 1,961	$1,800 1,860	$1,803 1,875	$1,838 1,927			$1,889 1,968	$1,975†	$1,918 2,071	$1,880 1,961	$2,106	$2,106	$2,105
Price: V/8 engine		$1,940 2,079				$2,175 2,300	$2,175 2,300			$2,038 2,191		$2,206	$2,169	$2,213

* Factory list price: four-door sedan, six-cylinder engine.
† Four-cylinder.

The Compacts have sharpened many old questions such as whether a car's interior dimensions would have to be reduced when overall length was cut. The above table provides answers to some of these, plus comparisons with the "low-priced three," Ford, Plymouth, and Chevrolet.

Source: *Fortune,* January 1961. Reproduced by permission.

Motors was how the company could move with the current trend toward cheaper, smaller cars at the least possible sacrifice of its B-O-P strength and profitability.

A partial answer was provided in the 1960 model year with the introduction of the Corvair by the Chevrolet Division. Nobody could reasonably conceive of Corvair's being a threat to B-O-P or to Chevrolet, either. For one thing, the car's rear engine—most radical engineering innovation since the Cord of 1934—made it an automotive novelty. Production of 250,000 did go higher than one might have expected of a novel machine making its way against no-nonsense competition in the economy field, but it merely emphasized the probability that G.M.'s strategy had been to get token participation in the compact-car market without injury to Chevrolet sales. Competitive figures tend to support this view. Ford Division production was off 1.6 per cent in the 1960 model year, while its Falcon volume reached a whopping 436,000 cars; conversely Chevrolet Division sales were up 11.7 per cent, with Corvair volume at only 250,000.

The complete tip-off on G.M.'s strategy came, however, with the introduction of its new small B-O-P cars in 1960. The Buick Special and the Olds F-85 extended B-O-P lines further down toward the low-price field, but a good $100 short of the most expensive Falcon, $17 short of the highest-priced Comet. Pontiac's Tempest alone touched the top of the Falcon range. Moreover, the term "compact" was sedulously avoided in describing them; they were billed as smaller versions of B-O-P cars. G.M.'s strategy, in essence, was to give the public what it wanted (i.e., smaller, cheaper, more economical cars) while at the same time trying to lead the buyers back to the standard-sized, middle-priced market, where G.M. still possessed so much competitive strength. Pointedly, G.M. refused to follow Ford's formula of concentrating on the lower-priced segments of the market with compacts and middle-priced cars at sharply reduced price tags. The G.M. strategy of going only part of the way down with the market was based on the hope that the "man who had always wanted an Oldsmobile" (or Buick or Pontiac) would buy one of the new less expensive models and eventually trade up in the line, to the rejuvenation of the middle-priced market. Chevrolet, in the meantime, would be expected to hold the fort in its own area. [See Exhibit 7.]

*   *   *   *   *

General Motors' power to implement its strategy is, of course, immense and it can be expected to use that power to the fullest. No fear of antitrust prosecution is likely to inhibit G.M.'s efforts to push its market percentages as high as they will go. Nor is it likely to pay much attention to the recent outcry against "planned obsolescence" in automobiles. For G.M. the cost of model changes is minimal: old body dies would wear out anyway after a couple of years' production at the huge volumes attained by G.M.; new dies with new designs can be had for little more than the cost of replacing the worn-out ones. Thus G.M. is attracted naturally to a two-year model cycle. By talking of such a cycle it may compel its competitors, most of whom would prefer a three-year cycle, to follow suit, even though a two-year cycle would often force them to discard dies that have not worn out simply because they lack G.M.'s high levels of production. G.M. initiative, in consequence, may force its competitors to bear model-change costs that G.M. itself will not bear.

Exhibit 7

MOTORS A LA MODE: THE STYLING RACE PICKS UP SPEED

Model Years		1949	1950	1951	1952	1953	1954	1955	1956	1957	1958	1959	1960	1961	1962	1963
	Chevrolet	B	M			B		B	M	M	B	B	M	B	M	B
	Corvette						C							M		M
	Corvair												C	M	M	C
	?															B
	Pontiac	B				B		B	M	M	B	B	M	B	M	B
	Tempest													C	C	C
	?															C
GENERAL	Oldsmobile 88	B		B		M	B	M	M	B	B	B	M	B	M	B
MOTORS	Super 88	B		B	B	M	B	M	M	B	B	M	M	B	M	M
CORPORATION	98		B			M	B	M	M	B	B	M	M	B	M	M
	F-85												C	C	M	B
	?															C
	Buick Special Century		B	B		M	B	M	M	B	B	M	B	B	M	B
	Super Roadmaster	B	B	B		M	B	M	M	B	B	M	M	C	M	M
	Special											C	C	C	M	B
	?															C
	Cadillac	M	B				B	M	M	B	M	M	B	B	M	B
	?	B			B			B		B	M	B	B	B	C	B
FORD	Ford	B			B			B	B	B	B	B	B	B	C	B
MOTOR	Thunderbird							C		M	B		C	B	M	
COMPANY	Falcon									M						C
	?															
	Mercury	B		M	B			B	M	B	M	M	M	B	M	M
	Comet				B									B	M	M
	Lincoln	B			B					M	B	B	M	B		
	Continental Mk. II								B							
	Edsel								C		C	B	B			
	Plymouth	B	M	M		B		B	M	B	M	M	B	M	B	M
CHRYSLER	Valiant												C	C	B	M
CORPORATION	Dodge	B	M	M		B		B	M	B	M	M	B	M	B	M
	Lancer												C	C		M
	De Soto	B	M	M		B		B	M	B	M	M	B	M		
	Chrysler	B	M	M		B		B	M	B	M	M	M	M	M	B
	Imperial			M		B		B		B			M	B	M	
AMERICAN	American						M				C					
MOTORS	Rambler	B	C		B			B	B					B	B	M
STUDEBAKER	Nash	B	M	M	M	B		M		M		C	M			M

NEW CAR—C   NEW BODY—B   MAJOR CHANGE—M

While the horsepower race has petered out and the size race appears to be running backward, it is clear from the chart at right that the style race is hotter than ever. More models were offered by Detroit for 1961 than at any time in automotive history. G.M. alone spent $480 million for new tooling. Next year (1962) the pace is expected to slacken somewhat as the industry waits for its second wind. Ford will probably bring out a new standard-sized machine, to fit in between the Fairlane and the Comet. Chevrolet may follow suit with a smaller Chevy. Chrysler will likely strengthen its all-important low-price divisions with a new body for Plymouth and one for Dodge. But another big push for the industry is expected for 1963. Probabilities then are for three new G.M. cars (assigned to the Buick, Oldsmobile and Pontiac divisions and intended to compete against the Thunderbird) and a new Ford, a "subcompact" approximating the Volkswagen in size. Should Ford go ahead on its subcompact, G.M. stands ready to turn out a competitive car, built at its West German Opel plant. However some of the other companies might yearn for a three-year cycle, nobody can chance one so long as General Motors sticks to its two-year push.

Source: *Fortune*, 1961. Reproduced by permission.

The strategy of the remaining member of the Big Three, Chrysler, is focused on one overriding objective: remaining a member of the Big Three rather than joining American Motors and Studebaker-Packard in a Little Three. In calendar 1959, Chrysler's percentage of the market (in registrations) dropped to 11.3 per cent, the lowest level since 1930. Last year the company managed a significant gain; its percentage of the market rose to 14.4 for the first nine months, and it even turned in a third-quarter profit of $1,400,000, the first in that period since 1957.

The strategy employed was much like Ford's. Chrysler moved an increasing number of its entries down into the low-priced sector of the market, and put its main emphasis there. The Plymouth Division got a new compact, the Valiant. The Dodge Division models were concentrated in the lower-price areas, leaving only a single series of cars in the upper brackets. Then the destructive competition between Dodge dealers (who also handled Plymouth) and the Plymouth dealers themselves was mitigated by taking the Plymouth out of the Dodge agencies and replacing it with the new Dart, essentially a Plymouth under another name. With the Dart going very well indeed, Chrysler further strengthened Dodge dealership by giving them a new compact, the Lancer. This car was really a Valiant with slightly better upholstery, five inches added to trunk space, and a few dollars to the price tags, but it gave Chrysler two compacts to push. And push them it has. By mid-November, 34 per cent of Chrysler's 1961 model production was devoted to Valiant and Lancer. This performance was topped by the 39 per cent of Ford output going to its compacts, but way ahead of the 19 per cent of. G.M.'s smaller car volume. With its share of the market (registrations) rising, Chrysler had grounds for hoping that by the first quarter of this year it would be back to 15 per cent.

What Chrysler's strategy will be from here on out is not too difficult to foresee. It estimates that the compacts of all companies will take 33.4 per cent of the whole 1961 market, and that this figure will rise only slightly (34.7 per cent) in 1962. At the same time the company expects the Plymouth-Ford-Chevrolet-Dart sector to rise to 46 per cent this year and hold that percentage in 1962. Best bet is that Chrysler will make only minor changes in its compacts this coming September. With DeSoto discontinued, its fighting money will likely go into new bodies for Dodge and Plymouth, and even greater emphasis on the low end of the market.[16]

In summary, the counterattack by the Big Three included the following major steps. First, they reversed the trend toward longer, lower, more ornamented automobiles throughout their entire line. Second, they offered a greater variety of sizes, styles, and horsepower ratings, giving the public a much wider range of choice, particularly in the low-priced ranges. Third, they brought out eight new automobiles aimed specifically at the "compact" car market, the market where American Motors had been largely unopposed in 1958–59. Beyond this, their strategies appeared to diverge, with Ford and Chrysler appearing to bet that compacts were here to stay, while GM appeared to be betting that it could lead the public back up to larger cars in due time through its

---

[16] *Fortune,* January 1961.

Exhibit 8

1962 MODEL YEAR U.S. CAR PRODUCTION BY $100 PRICE GROUPS*

(entire model year)

$100 Price groups	Chevrolet	Chevy II	Corvair	Pontiac	Tempest	Olds-mobile	F-85	Buick	Special	Ford Galaxie	Fair-lane	Falcon
$1,601–$1,700	.....	.....	.....	.....	.....	.....	.....	.....	.....	.....	.....	.....
1,701– 1,800	.....	11,457	16,245	.....	.....	.....	.....	.....	.....	.....	.....	.....
1,801– 1,900	.....	63,479	53,842	.....	.....	.....	.....	.....	.....	.....	.....	64,266
1,901– 2,000	.....	168,044	.....	.....	52,903	.....	.....	.....	.....	.....	23,511	173,866
2,001– 2,100	135,692	1,663	199,797	.....	51,981	.....	.....	.....	42,384	.....	65,282	31,559
2,101– 2,200	72,195	40,467	3,716	.....	.....	.....	15,983	.....	.....	26,114	91,550	62,416
2,201– 2,300	174,591	41,497	18,931	.....	38,309	.....	18,736	.....	40,202	66,810	99,804	55,256
2,301– 2,400	226,104	.....	.....	14,263	.....	.....	32,461	.....	7,382	93,178	17,969	22,624
2,401– 2,500	430,298	.....	13,491	68,620	.....	.....	6,864	.....	36,874	288,126	.....	4,295
2,501– 2,600	197,469	.....	.....	76,275	.....	.....	6,861	7,418	18,712	55,548	.....	.....
2,601– 2,700	138,607	.....	.....	.....	.....	108,143	9,898	56,783	8,913	47,217	.....	.....
2,701– 2,800	38,707	.....	.....	27,760	.....	53,438	3,765	62,997	.....	70,802	.....	.....
2,801– 2,900	10,345	.....	.....	50,158	.....	24,125	.....	.....	.....	15,385	.....	.....
2,901– 3,000	.....	.....	.....	42,345	.....	12,212	.....	13,471	.....	28,412	.....	.....
3,001– 3,100	.....	.....	.....	44,015	.....	38,712	.....	20,698	.....	.....	.....	.....
3,101– 3,200	.....	.....	.....	51,777	.....	6,417	.....	9,131	.....	13,183	.....	.....
3,201– 3,300	.....	.....	.....	4,527	.....	.....	.....	12,717	.....	.....	.....	.....
3,301– 3,400	.....	.....	.....	.....	.....	3,837	.....	.....	.....	.....	.....	.....
3,401– 3,500	.....	.....	.....	.....	.....	.....	.....	.....	.....	.....	.....	.....
3,501– 3,600	.....	.....	.....	.....	.....	7,653	.....	22,445	.....	.....	.....	.....
3,601– 3,700	14,531	.....	.....	.....	.....	47,006	.....	16,734	.....	.....	.....	.....
3,701– 3,800	.....	.....	.....	.....	.....	40,641	.....	.....	.....	.....	.....	.....
3,801– 3,900	.....	.....	.....	.....	.....	.....	.....	7,894	.....	.....	.....	.....
3,901– 4,000	.....	.....	.....	.....	.....	3,691	.....	15,395	.....	.....	.....	.....
4,001– 4,100	.....	.....	.....	.....	.....	.....	.....	.....	.....	.....	.....	.....
4,101– 4,200	.....	.....	.....	.....	.....	.....	.....	.....	.....	.....	.....	.....
4,201– 4,300	.....	.....	.....	.....	.....	7,149	.....	.....	.....	.....	.....	.....
4,301– 4,400	.....	.....	.....	.....	.....	.....	.....	.....	.....	.....	.....	.....
4,401 & Over	.....	.....	.....	.....	.....	.....	.....	.....	.....	.....	.....	.....
Totals	1,438,539	326,607	306,022	378,740	143,193	353,024	94,568	245,683	154,467	704,775	298,116	414,282

* Based on suggested factory list prices before excise tax, dealer handling charges and optional equipment installations. 1962 model prices include deduction of heater prices for General Motors Corp. and Ford Motor Co. car lines to put industry-wide prices on an equal basis with entire 1961 model year. Source: Ward's Statistical Dept.
Source: *Ward's Automotive Yearbook, 1963,* p. 22. Reproduced by permission.

"B-O-P" compacts, on the one hand, and through keeping its Corvair out of the styling race and thereby de-emphasizing it. Taken together, these strategies put the squeeze on American Motors, though at the same time they involved a significant change in industry competition. While attacking AMC (and each other) with their compacts, the Big Three were now playing on AMC's home ground, and they were advertising the values of compactness, economy, and durability—long the bywords at American Motors. The counterattack stood to help as well as hurt AMC.

FACING UP TO THE COUNTERATTACK: 1959–62

During the years 1959–62, American Motors reached and maintained about a 6% share of the market (Exhibit 8). Pretax profits reached a high of $105 million in 1959 and 1960, and then tapered off, owing in part to the rigors of immediate competition and in part to increasing outlays for automotive styling changes, including a significant redesign of the Rambler American for 1961. In facing the counterattack, then,

Thun-derbird	Mercury Mon-terey	Meteor	Comet	Plym-outh	Valiant	Dodge	Lancer	Chrysler	Cadillac Lincoln Imperial	Rambler	Stude-baker	Units	% of Total
.....	.....	.....	.....	.....	.....	.....	.....	.....	.....	29,948	.....	29,948	0.45
.....	.....	.....	.....	.....	21,803	.....	7,327	.....	.....	44,352	15,793	181,243	2.71
.....	.....	.....	62,491	.....	32,413	.....	16,775	.....	.....	62,071	23,897	512,345	7.66
.....	.....	.....	60,701	.....	47,967	.....	19,024	.....	.....	106,816	14,277	566,573	8.47
.....	.....	11,230	.....	47,682	34,303	35,457	14,140	.....	.....	5,521	3,115	736,931	11.02
.....	.....	30,603	29,128	27,885	8,867	13,648	2,699	.....	.....	76,793	9,599	512,757	7.67
.....	.....	21,524	10,667	21,344	.....	8,753	4,306	.....	.....	61,482	9,811	554,932	8.30
.....	641	5,695	.....	13,083	.....	19,138	.....	.....	.....	21,893	5,393	461,855	6.91
.....	5,328	.....	2,318	29,090	.....	27,743	.....	.....	.....	21,281	2,861	937,189	14.01
.....	26,435	.....	.....	14,115	.....	12,907	.....	.....	.....	4,379	1,149	420,268	6.28
.....	46,501	.....	.....	12,566	.....	21,963	.....	50,832	.....	6,401	.....	507,824	7.59
.....	8,932	.....	.....	2,410	.....	15,862	.....	10,313	.....	1,289	320	296,595	4.43
.....	15,085	.....	.....	3,959	.....	5,564	.....	7,705	.....	.....	8,467	140,793	2.11
.....	.....	.....	.....	.....	.....	3,933	.....	.....	.....	.....	.....	100,373	1.50
.....	.....	.....	.....	.....	.....	.....	.....	21,337	.....	.....	.....	124,762	1.87
.....	2,772	.....	.....	.....	.....	893	.....	3,319	.....	.....	.....	87,492	1.31
.....	.....	.....	.....	.....	.....	.....	.....	2,371	.....	.....	.....	19,615	0.29
.....	1,315	.....	.....	.....	.....	.....	.....	.....	.....	.....	.....	5,152	0.08
.....	.....	.....	.....	.....	.....	.....	.....	.....	.....	.....	.....	.....	...
.....	.....	.....	.....	.....	.....	.....	.....	1,786	.....	.....	.....	31,884	0.48
.....	.....	.....	.....	.....	.....	.....	.....	.....	.....	.....	.....	78,271	1.17
.....	.....	.....	.....	.....	.....	.....	.....	12,083	.....	.....	.....	52,724	0.79
57,845	.....	.....	.....	.....	.....	.....	.....	6,638	.....	.....	.....	72,377	1.08
10,282	.....	.....	.....	.....	.....	.....	.....	.....	.....	.....	.....	29,368	0.44
.....	.....	.....	.....	.....	.....	.....	.....	.....	.....	.....	.....	.....	...
.....	.....	.....	.....	.....	.....	.....	.....	.....	.....	.....	.....	7,149	0.11
8,457	.....	.....	.....	.....	.....	.....	.....	781	.....	.....	.....	9,238	0.14
1,427	.....	.....	.....	.....	.....	.....	.....	1,374	206,238	.....	.....	209,039	3.13
78,011	107,009	69,052	165,305	172,134	145,353	165,861	64,271	118,539	206,238	442,226	94,682	6,686,697	100.0

the company had a profitable operation with a relatively stable market share, i.e., a much stronger position than in the days of the "campaign for survival."

Product line. The American Motors product line consisted of the 117-inch Ambassador, the 108-inch Rambler Classic, the 100-inch Rambler American, and the 85-inch Metropolitan, with the two larger models accounting for approximately 70% of sales, the American about 20%, and the Metropolitan about 5%.

Forbes,[17] in discussing the product line, made the following observations:

> The product that American sends to compete in the market place shows interesting similarities to the facilities that bore it. As a car, the Rambler could be described as a sound whole made up of frequently improvised parts. Most Ramblers, for example, are powered with a basically old-fashioned six-cylinder engine first designed in the 1930's. (There is also a quite modern V-8 that is used on one Rambler

---

[17] "Can George Do It Again?" *Forbes*, August 1, 1961. Reproduced by permission.

Classic line and on the larger Rambler Ambassador.) However, in typical Rambler fashion this engine was converted in 1956 from L-head to valve-in-head design for use on most Ramblers, and in addition is now being offered with an ultra-modern aluminum cylinder block.

Nevertheless, management believed that continued successful participation in "economy runs" by this engine contributed significantly to Rambler's reputation for economy and quality.

To continue with *Forbes*:

> Yet the Rambler has consistently had elements of solid and often unique worth. Its unit-body-and-frame construction is miles ahead of the traditional technique followed on U.S. cars, although all the new compacts have come over to Rambler's side. Its ceramic-coated muffler promises to remedy at last an almost scandalous piece of automotive misdesign; its dip-coating of the entire body shows how to prevent the moth-eaten appearance around the bottom that marks so many five-year-olds and up among U.S. cars; and Rambler bodies now get the benefit of a water spray test that should at least keep them from leaking when brand new, as many U.S. cars do.

Given this combination of homemade improvisations plus specific technological leads over major competitors, American Motors' timing of introducing new models was of particular interest. On several occasions the company employed what has been called a "Notre Dame" strategy, a strategy of introducing major model changes one year after its competitors. *Forbes* illustrated this in the case of the Rambler Classic, the company's bread-and-butter model:

> This quiet, almost sedate vehicle plays a crucial part in American Motors strategy. The company feels that to date it has had practically no direct competition for its major product, the 108-inch wheelbase Rambler Classic that Romney describes as a "family-sized compact." For the two leading competitive compacts are nearer in size to the 100-inch wheelbase Rambler American (an "economy compact," in Romney lingo). But within the next few months (fall 1961) both Ford and Chevy will introduce brand new lines, slightly larger than the Falcon and Corvair, that will meet the Rambler Classic head-on.
>
> Romney expects to take on this new competition with only slightly face-lifted versions of the present Ramblers, praying that the car's general reputation will carry it through. Meantime, however, he is preparing new 1963 models whose tooling alone will cost considerably more than this year's entire $20 million–$25 million capital outlay for tooling, expansion, plant modernization and whatnot. American's future will hinge on how much ground (if any) it must give in the fiscal year just ahead, and how much it gains back as a result of its 1963 counterattack.
>
> Thus Romney displays a strategy of timing not unlike that Notre

Dame once used in football, namely, employing the second team to take the initial shock before putting the first team in.

The second team was aided, however, by across-the-board price cuts. Thus the company advertised that every single model had been reduced in price for 1962. The following fall, when the new Classic and Ambassador models were introduced, prices were raised some $30 to $50 per car. Meanwhile, American Motors was able to maintain its market share in 1962, choosing to do this at the expense of substantially lowered profits for that year. As the 1963 models were introduced and the price increases became effective, profits improved sharply, up 30% from the preceding year.

Mr. Romney explained this strategy to the AMC shareholders in the following way: ". . . we sharply increased product value without a corresponding increase in prices in 1962 models. This was a very calculated decision because we thought it was more important to increase our penetration of the market—more important in terms of the interests of stockholders and others associated with this company—than to make maximum current profits our primary objective."[18]

Marketing. With acceptance of the compact car idea, AMC advertising and promotion focused increasingly on specific product features, such as the unit-body construction, deep-dip rust prevention, and the ceramic muffler. The company also took the lead in extending the warranty on its automobiles, a move which spread rapidly, and led competitors to extend 90-day warranties up to five years in some cases. Longevity had become a selling point—a development which would have seemed unthinkable only a few years previously.

Dealer organization. Having rebuilt its dealer organization during the previous campaign adroitly captained by the aggressive Roy Abernethy, who succeeded George Romney in 1962 as president of the corporation, the company now attempted to maintain existing numbers and to strengthen individual dealerships. To implement this, the company once again resorted to granting extra discounts to dealers when the going got tough. Thus as the United States slid into a recession in 1961, the company sales and profits slipped, but at the same time dealer discounts were increased $30–$40 per car, causing corporate profits to slide still more. By paying an extra $6 to $8 million in dealer commissions (while operating profits dropped from 105 to 50 millions), the company was able to report a net loss in dealers of 1.3% in the first six months of 1961 while its competitors reported losses as follows:[19]

G.M.	1.0%
Ford	1.7
Chrysler	4.3
Studebaker-Packard	7.9

[18] Report to Stockholders, February 7, 1962.
[19] *Forbes,* August 1, 1961, p. 17.

This left the company's dealer strength relatively unimpaired, though AMC's dealer organization was still weaker than those of its major competitors. *Forbes* noted that AMC's dealers

> were outnumbered six-to-one by G.M.'s dealers and nearly three-to-one by Ford's and Chrysler's. But old sales boss Abernethy has some factors working for him, too. The rapidly increasing number of Ramblers on the road—now close to 2 million—means an equally rapid increase in the parts-and-service business that provides the dealer's bread and butter. And Rambler leads all U.S. cars except Cadillac in owner loyalty, as measured by the percentage of Rambler owners who become repeat buyers. The latest score: 67%. Thus American has the distinction of being the only carmaker that is increasing its dealer corps, though its map is not still without blank spots.

Finance and control.   In 1961 the company became the only U.S. automobile manufacturer to be completely free of long-term debt. The company maintained, however, a standing line of credit of approximately $50 million which it could call upon in an emergency.

The company's elimination of all debt had been accompanied by an expansion of capacity to an estimated 600,000 cars per year. To accomplish the debt reduction and the expansion of output at the same time, the company had maintained its policy of not integrating its operation to include any but the essential elements. Thus, capacity was doubled from 300,000 to 600,000 at an estimated investment of about $30 million, mere peanuts compared to the outlay for a comparable expansion of an integrated operation.

> That American could get so much additional capacity at this relatively small cost is partly because of the company's style of play and partly because of a fortunate break. The style of play refers to American's preference for making maximum use of its suppliers' investment r ither than pouring its own money into integrated facilities. If G.M. were given an index number of 100 on an "integration scale," then Ford would rank perhaps a little above 100 (with its steel and glass plants more than offsetting certain other components that Ford does not make) and American Motors probably at about 70. Thus new capacity will obviously cost American less per unit (the degree of integration remaining unchanged) than its two biggest competitors.
>
> The lucky break was the sudden availability in Kenosha, Wisconsin cheek by jowl with American's main plant, of a 2-million square-foot plant where Simmons once made metal beds. The Simmons plant was quite capable of being converted into the building of Rambler bodies, one of American's worst bottlenecks. Precisely this was done, at an annual rental cost (with options to buy) of only $450,000. And while it took nearly $15 million to equip it for production, the company still

got by with a fraction of the capital cost it would have taken to build a new facility from scratch.[20]

Corresponding to this lack of integration, the company was estimated to have a smaller profit margin per car than GM or Ford, but a higher return on the capital invested, as below:

1960 RESULTS*

	Pretax Profits		Capital Employed per Vehicle Produced	Return on Capital before Income Taxes
	Per Vehicle Produced	As a % of Auto Sales		
General Motors............	$400	16%	$1,000	40%
Ford.....................	240	15	825	29
American.................	200	11	400	50

* In American's case the fiscal year ends September 30; for the other two it ends December 31.

All figures are *Forbes'* estimates. In each case they represent earnings and capital employed in the auto business on a worldwide basis. Non-automotive activities have been screened out. In GM's case, GMAC earnings and capital are included in automotive results.[21]

With this approach, the company was able to maintain a low break-even point even with its sharply expanded scale of operations. Thus *Forbes* estimated the break-even in 1961 to be 150,000 units, up only slightly from 1959 despite the increase in productive capacity from 300,000 to 600,000 units. On the other hand, one American Motors executive noted that with this approach the company was not able to attain significant economies of scale in the 400,000–600,000-car range. Unit costs were about the same over the entire range. Strategy remained essentially unchanged, then, with the company placing heavy emphasis on safety (via a low break-even) at the expense of the opportunities for rising profits per unit from integrated operations (with their attendant fixed costs).

Production.   As for the strength of American's production sinews, the company's car output takes place in two Kenosha, Wis., plants and a third in Milwaukee, 40-odd miles away. Little about any of the plants represents a production man's dream of efficiency. For example, the very thought of trucking Rambler bodies from the Milwaukee body plant to Kenosha for assembly, at a $5 cost per car, would flabbergast the average factory boss. But American's production heads are hardened to the practice. They insist that in view of the huge capital

[20] Ibid., p. 16.
[21] Ibid.

costs that would be involved it would not prove economical to move the Milwaukee operation to Kenosha. They take much the same view toward the frequent multi-story sections in America's plants: conveyor belts simply run upstairs and down, in fine disregard of auto industry dogma that only single-story plants make sense.

All of American's auto production operations have an air of artful and thrifty improvisation, as though new equipment is added only when absolutely essential, or when it is a leadpipe cinch to pay back its cost in a matter of months. Thus, fine, new automated tools operate side by side with virtual clunkers—a practice perhaps necessary for a company in American's spot, but one that always carries the danger of falling too far behind.

American also contravenes industry—or at least Big Three—practice by crowding all its auto output into one Wisconsin area, instead of seeking a calculated scatter of component and assembly plants across the country. In fact, measured in unit output American's Kenosha assembly plant is the industry's largest, outranking even Ford's River Rouge.

Romney explains: "In 1948, we made a study which showed that a volume of 200,000 cars assembled on the West Coast yielded a saving of $60 per unit, which justified the use of east and west coast plants. However, a 1958 study, assuming a volume of 400,000 cars, showed that freight rates on components vs. completed vehicles had changed so much in the meantime that a West Coast assembly plant meant a penalty of $59 per car." American is, therefore, quite content with its current concentration—though its executives readily grant that it might not pay other companies to change their own established patterns.[22]

Labor relations.   In keeping with its strategy of maintaining a low break-even for safety in bad years at the expense of possible economies and profits in good years, the company negotiated an unusual labor contract in 1961. Called a "progress sharing" agreement, the contract provided for profit sharing in lieu of a certain portion of the straight hourly increase granted by the Big Three.

Mr. Romney explained the concepts involved in the 1961 agreement as follows:

> While much has been written about this historic Progress Sharing labor agreement, which we negotiated with the UAW last summer, we find continuing public interest in this subject. Since my written report to you on the agreement, all of our nonrepresented salaried employees also are now participating in this program.
>
> The management of your company is convinced that the progress sharing approach—founded on the principle of sharing progress equitably among employees, stockholders, consumers, dealers and suppliers—will make it possible to expand our sales, increase our earnings and substantially benefit our stockholders. If you had been

---

[22] Ibid.

familiar with the internal operation of the company, you would realize that this dedication to progress sharing has been as fundamental in this company's growth as has the pioneering of the compact Rambler.

Let me tell you why this contract with the union is important:

First, in the initial paragraph of our new union contract, it is recognized by the union as well as the management that for employees to enjoy high wages and good working conditions, they must make progress *and it must be shared with customers.* In other words, our contract repudiates the idea that you can turn over to workers, or workers and stockholders, *all* of the progress—and still make progress. It's premised on the concept that if you're going to make progress, you must share that progress with the customer. This is sound. Without progress sharing, the American economy would not be what it is today. But this was a unique principle to write into our labor contract in face of national policies that are of an opposite character.

Second, our unique contract with the UAW is designed specifically to meet the needs and opportunities of American Motors. It is not a pattern settlement imposed on us—it was our idea—nor a pattern settlement to be imposed on others. We weren't trying to say what others ought to have. Flexibility and freedom of action and choice are great principles. It is based on the opportunities of American Motors and the needs of American Motors.

Third, the fixed-cost increases are *lower* for American Motors than for any other automobile company. In other words, while the employee benefit increases which all the companies have provided for in their labor contracts are generally similar, their method of financing is not the same. All the benefit increases granted by the Big Three represent fixed-cost increases. Virtually all the increased benefits granted under our contract will come out of profits, and therefore our fixed-cost increases are *lower* than those of our major competitors. And "if there ain't no profits, there ain't no sharing." It's just that simple.

Fourth, a large share of our cost increases is placed on a variable basis—subject to actual earnings. This is a distinct advantage to us because the determinations are to be made after the facts instead of before the facts are known. This permits more realistic forecasting, sounder fiscal approaches and greater mutuality of interest in progress.

While the "Progress Sharing Agreement" has been described previously as "unusual," consideration of this plan must include the entire 1961 labor agreement of which the plan was only a portion. Additional considerations in the contract affecting such matters as paid time not worked, seniority benefits, and production standards resulted in tangible savings of several millions per year, and intangible, but nonetheless significant benefits, which have improved the company's competitive position.

THE SITUATION AT THE END OF 1962

In its 1962 Annual Report, American Motors described its competitive position in part as follows:

Setting a new Rambler world-wide record, wholesale sales of Rambler cars in the U.S. and foreign markets increased to 478,132 units. This was a 24.2% gain over the 1961 fiscal period.

With several new entries attracted to the compact car segment of the U.S. car market in 1962, Rambler experienced the most vigorous onslaught to date on its domestic market position [see table]. Our strengthened distribution and dealer organization, however, demonstrated full capability for meeting the competitive challenge. Rambler U.S. wholesale sales increased 18.5% over the previous fiscal year.

Year	U.S. only	Outside U.S.	Total
1961.................	366,384	18,445	384,829
1962.................	434,486	43,646	478,132

Rambler's percentage of U.S. industry registration was 6.7%, virtually unchanged from the previous year.

*   *   *   *   *

Advertising and selling expense increased during the fiscal year as Rambler made a successful bid for larger volume. Additional customer benefits were provided by the extension of warranty terms.

The building of a stronger distribution system to meet the requirements of a growing business is a continuing activity. To provide better service to dealers and retail customers, we added a new automotive zone office in Newark, N.J., and a new parts warehouse at Queens, L.I., during the fiscal year. Additional parts warehouses have since been opened in Houston and San Francisco. We also expanded our financial program of assisting the development of Rambler franchises in important markets.

A net of ninety-six new Rambler dealers was franchised in the U.S. during the fiscal year, bringing our total automotive dealer count as of September 30 to 3,076 dealers.

Increased strength · of our Rambler dealers is reflected in their aggregate net worth of $216,714,000 currently which compares to $100,877,000 in 1957.

*   *   *   *   *

In line with our policy of making changes only when they truly benefit the customer, American Motors introduced major engineering and structural improvements in the 1963 Classic and Ambassador models which permitted wholly restyled cars.

An advanced method of unit construction, which contributes greater strength, solidity, precision and quality to Rambler bodies, made feasible the attractive new styling of the 1963 models. The new Rambler car body was designed to use curved glass side windows with doors that curve into the roof. This feature is available only on a few expensive U.S. cars. Combined with these exterior appearance changes is a new development in power transfer—the Tri-Poised engine mount —which provides a quieter Rambler ride at all speeds.

The Rambler American line has been broadened and enhanced with the addition of new hardtop models. A new Twin-Stick floor shift transmission with overdrive is available as optional equipment on the top line of all series. U.S. prices were maintained at the same level as a year ago on fifteen of the 1963 models, were reduced on two models and increased modestly on 12 models.

Rambler remains the leader in the segment of the U.S. market that continues to be the fastest growing. We believe the compact car will take an ever greater share of total car sales in the 1963 calendar year. The factors that have contributed to Rambler's rapid growth are accelerating: the dispersal of population to suburban areas, the dependence of more and more people upon the motor car for personal mobility, and the traffic congestion, parking problems and other trends arising from increasing urbanization.

Cars that are more practical and convenient to use, while equally comfortable and attractive, are in the ascendency in the American market. Rambler's present and future product programs are well timed and ideally adapted to those strong trends in customer preference.

American Motors also launched major moves overseas during 1962. The annual report noted, for instance, that the company's overseas investment increased fivefold during the year. Continuing, the report had this to say about AMC's international operations:

More Rambler cars are appearing throughout the world.

American Motors now accounts for 18% of shipments of new cars from the United States. Sales of these cars, plus Ramblers produced by foreign plants, increased 136% over unit sales in the prior year.

American Motors of Canada is developing a firm position in the Canadian market. The subsidiary recorded a 75% gain in sales, reaching a level of 19,000 units, and substantially increased its percentage of industry registrations over the previous year. Our Canadian automobile manufacturing plant has under construction at Brampton, Ontario a new addition which will enlarge its work space by two-thirds. The new building is scheduled to be completed in the March quarter. The cost of this expansion will be paid for out of the subsidiary's earnings.

Rambler is now the best selling car of American origin in Latin America. Production of Rambler cars has been under way since January 1962 in Argentina. Despite political unrest in that nation, the output of our cars by Industries Kaiser Argentina S.A. is at a highly satisfactory rate. Rambler is now taking 40% of U.S. car sales in that country.

Rambler assembly for distribution in Common Market countries commenced in March 1962 in the Renault plant at Haren, Belgium. Since then a steady monthly step-up in Rambler output has been achieved, and further growth is indicated as Rambler gains the benefit of added distribution through Renault's wide network of dealers.

In sum, then, American Motors was maintaining its domestic position and expanding abroad. With the introduction of restyled Ambassadors and Classics for 1963, it was hoping to move ahead in the domestic market as well.

Reviewing these events in February 1962, Mr. Romney noted that the company had successfully weathered "campaign counterattack." Looking to 1963, he stated that "next year we expect to resume the offensive with 'campaign leadership.' In the years ahead, we expect to begin a long-range battle for the number-one brand-name position in the automobile industry in this country."

Crown Cork and Seal Company and the Metal Container Industry

IN 1963, the Crown Cork and Seal Company, a major producer of metal cans and crowns with sales of $205 million, had experienced the largest growth in sales and profitability since 1958 of any company in the metal container industry. Unlike most other can manufacturers, Crown had not diversified into packaging fields outside of metal containers in response to increasing competitive pressures. Instead it narrowed its product line, concentrating upon supplying the fast-growing aerosol market and the expanding market for canned beer. Crown had also invested extensively in international facilities, particularly in underdeveloped countries, anticipating a tremendous growth in the overseas demand for metal containers.

Company executives believed the international markets, as living standards increased, would be the major source of future expansion. According to Mr. John F. Connelly, President and Chairman of Crown Cork and Seal, "We have been moving as fast as we can into the international field, building plants in all underdeveloped countries. Presently we are only producing crowns in most of these facilities as nobody is canning in these areas as yet. But when they do start canning, we need only to add a body-maker and a seamer in order to produce cans."

Mr. Connelly planned for Crown's domestic operations to be the stable base from which the company would expand internationally. Connelly's approach to doing business represented a considerable contrast both to the policies of his predecessors at Crown and to the strategies adopted by his principal competitors. The problem he faced in 1963 is still perplexing today, how to develop a base of stable domestic earnings in a highly competitive mature industry.

The following pages describe the nature and structure of the metal container industry, the crisis facing Connelly in 1957, the pattern of operations and strategy that evolved from this crisis, the outlook for the future, and the situation as of February 1964.

THE METAL CONTAINER INDUSTRY

The metal container industry produced metal cans, crowns (bottle caps) and closures (screw caps, bottle lids) for over 135 industries that use these products to hold or seal an almost endless variety of consumer and industrial goods. During the 1950s a number of metal container manufacturers experienced declining profit margins and loss of market share because of increasing competitive and technical pressures from within and outside the industry.

In 1963, two firms dominated the metal container industry: the American Can Company and the Continental Can Company. Of the 48 billion cans produced in 1963, 34 billion were manufactured by these giant corporations. Another 5 billion cans were manufactured by the Crown Cork and Seal Company and the National Can Company, both companies having an annual sales volume of over $100 million. In 1963, Crown Cork and the Bond Division of the Continental Can Company also produced approximately 70% of the 313 million gross of crowns used. In all, there are about 100 companies in the industry.

The 48 billion cans produced in 1963 had an estimated shipment value of $2.3 billion. The primary users of metal containers have been the food and beer industries, the two industries utilizing almost 80% of all metal cans produced (see Exhibit 1A). In the five years from 1960 to 1964 the soft-drink bottler also became an important user. In addition to consuming annually approximately 70% of all metal crowns produced, bottlers used over 2 billion cans in 1963, an increase of 500% from 1958.

Despite the over-all growth, however, the industry faced a number of challenging problems. This industry description focuses on: (1) new competitive pressures that have confronted the industry from 1955–1964; (2) the effect of these pressures on the industry; and (3) the strategic responses of the major companies in the industry to these pressures. Additional information as to economic and technological characteristics of the industry is provided in an Appendix.

New pressures

While industry executives were confident that the "tin can is not on its way out," major strategic questions arose during the 1953–1963 decade that stemmed from efforts to assess the long-term effects on the industry of:

1. changes in the basic concept of a container—termed by many the "packaging revolution."
2. the rapid acceleration in packaging technology.
3. the increased threat of self-manufacture.

The "packaging revolution"

Perhaps the trend of greatest long-run significance to the industry is the increasing number of functions the "container" is being asked to perform. Originally the container was designed solely to hold, protect, and preserve its contents. Then someone decided that a container,

Exhibit 1

CROWN CORK AND SEAL COMPANY

A. Shipments of Metal Cans by Product Packed Expressed in Terms of Thousands of Base Boxes* of Metal Consumed in Their Manufacture

	1955	1956	1957	1958	1959	1960	1961	1962	1963
Total shipments	98,024	105,107	101,702	103,818	108,162	105,166	109,358	114,956	109,707
For sale	85,477	89,928	87,667	89,180	93,993	89,917	89,656	93,764	88,739
For own use	12,547	15,179	14,035	14,638	14,169	15,249	19,702	21,192	21,192
Type of metal									
Steel							n.a.	112,714	107,350
Aluminum							n.a.	1,792	2,356
Food cans, total	61,773	66,884	62,046	64,054	65,060	65,073	66,164	68,618	
Fruits & vegetables (including juice)	31,764	34,899	31,980	34,236	33,684	32,984	34,805	37,081	
Evaporated/and condensed/milk	6,138	6,150	5,425	5,175	5,085	4,883	4,737	4,393	
Other dairy products	1,034	1,083	889	728	636	510	519	582	
Fish and seafood	2,535	2,588	2,636	2,843	2,657	2,850	2,898	3,082	
Lard and shortening	2,580	2,394	2,248	2,383	2,324	1,986	2,256	2,356	
Meat (including poultry)	2,919	3,825	3,047	2,951	3,190	3,203	3,460	3,483	
Coffee	4,000	4,213	4,286	4,452	4,707	4,567	4,846	4,846	
All other food cans	10,803	11,732	11,584	11,286	12,777	14,090	12,643	12,795	
Nonfood cans, total	36,251	38,223	38,278	39,764	43,102	40,093	43,194	45,888	
Oil, open top—1 qt. and 5 qt.	6,778	6,778	6,230	6,338	6,811	5,715	6,026	6,304	
Beer cans	14,919	15,806	16,305	16,902	18,563	17,776	17,522	18,150	
Pet food	3,485	4,034	4,154	4,154	4,332	4,486	4,475	4,654	
All other nonfood cans	11,069	11,605	12,370	12,370	13,386	12,116	15,171	16,780	

* A base box is a measure of metal use.

B. Comparative Growth of Population, Gross National Product, and Can Shipments (1953 = 100)

	1953	1954	1955	1956	1957	1958	1959	1960	1961	1962
Population (millions)	100.0	101.8	102.9	103.9	105.0	106.1	107.22	108.36	109.5	110.7
Gross national product (billions)	100.0	99.5	108.7	114.2	120.9	121.1	131.9	137.4	141.9	151.8
Can shipments (000's of base boxes)	100.0	100.1	110.0	117.8	112.0	112.9	121.8	117.6	122.0	128.2

Source: U.S. Department of Commerce—Bureau of the Census.

imaginatively labelled, could also provide a strong point-of-purchase reminder of the consumer's need for the "product inside." So the container was redesigned to add more utility and appeal to the product by means of devices ranging from recipes printed on the outside to easy-dispensing spouts. The result has been that during the 10 years from 1954–1963, this redesigning in combination with advances in methods of product preservation and packaging technology, has reduced the importance of the preservation function of the container relative to its sales function. The container, or rather the "package," and the "product inside" have become increasingly one unit in their selective appeal to the consumer, and, to a lesser extent, in creating primary demand, e.g., aerosol dispensed whipped cream.

Some authorities have attributed the preoccupation with packaging in the United States to radical changes in merchandising patterns. The package now functions as the salesman. Also, with the rapid advances in manufacturing technology, products tend to be of increasingly high quality and often little product differentiation can be achieved by "just more quality." In addition, there has been a rapid growth in the use of private labels, and this has tended to make brand names a somewhat less important influence on sales. All these factors, packaging experts argue, put a burden on products to speak for themselves. As one authority concluded:

> These days you had better have an easier-to-open beer can [and] an easier-opening cereal carton or you are out of business.[1]

"Extras" on consumer goods have taken many forms, for example, plastic bottles for hair preparations, aerosol containers which spurt products ranging from mustard to touch-up paint, miniature beer kegs that provide tap beer in the family refrigerator, and self-opening or "pop-top" metal cans. Extras on industrial packages have been added to increase the usability and convenience of handling, both for the distributor and the ultimate customer, e.g., color coded packages to facilitate inventory maintenance and the use of polystyrene foam instead of shredded paper as packing material to obtain lighter and more compact containers.

The tremendous growth in the sale of packaging materials since 1940 reflects, in part, the increasing recognition given by manufacturers to the role of packaging in selling their products. In 1940, shipments of packaging materials totaled slightly over $2 billion. By 1958, these shipments had growth to about $10 billion. In 1963, shipments of packaging materials amounted to $13 billion (55% of the total expenditure for packaging activity), an increase of 650% since 1940. During the same period two general economic indicators, Gross National Product and Consumer Expenditures for Nondurables, increased 550% and 234%, respectively.

A major reason behind the growth of the packaging industry has

---

[1] Carmon M. Elliot, Jr., Manager of Package Design, Eastman Kodak Co., as quoted in Leon Morse, "The Swing to Service," *Dun's Review & Modern Industry,* November 1963, p. 133.

been the shift to packaging for products previously sold in "containers." For example, starch in the aerosol dispensing form was introduced in 1960 and in 1963 accounted for over 25% of consumer starch purchases. Similar shifts were experienced with other household products such as room deodorants, car waxes, and furniture polishes. Estimated to be increasing at an annual rate of over 12%, sales of nonfood aerosol units in 1963 were over 1 billion units—18 times the number sold in the first year after the commercial aerosol container was introduced in 1948. Recent technological developments have also introduced food items to aerosol dispensing.

The aluminum top easy-opening can was heralded as the first significant innovation in the beer industry since the introduction of the can. This was quickly followed by the "pull-tab" top developed by Alcoa, providing still another example of the impact of imaginative packaging. Pull-top cans, introduced in the spring of 1963, accounted for 40% of the beer cans sold in 1963. Beer company executives predicted this figure would climb to 75% by the fall of 1964.

The evolution of the packaging concept has posed major, strategic issues for the metal container industry. This is an industry that grew up converting steel into shapes designed to achieve a high level of product preservation (over 55% of the cans produced in 1963 packaged food) and one which has had little or no contact with the ultimate buyer generating and responding to the new trends.

The rapid acceleration in packaging technology

The original characteristics that promoted the use of the tin can and the crown in the early 1900's still make them well suited to certain food and beverage packaging jobs. These qualities are: (1) immunity to handling abuse, (2) ability to resist great heat and pressure, allowing pasteurization in the package, (3) preservation of a sterile condition for long periods, (4) lightness compared to the contents, (5) amenability to fabrication into differing sizes, and (6) low cost, allowing destruction after use. However, recent advances in packaging technology have challenged the future competitive strength of these characteristics.

The integration of packaging into the production process. As the distinction between the product and its container has become increasingly blurred, product manufacturers, pushed by the machinery companies who design custom packaging systems, have moved toward carrying out a greater number of container conversion functions in their own plants. The development "that may ultimately prove to have the most far-reaching impact on the [package-supplying] industry is the production of the container by the customer himself, with only the basic packaging material being supplied by the 'container manufacturer.' Packaging Corporation of America has a system which allows carton making as well as filling by frozen food packers all at once; the company only delivers the rolled stock to the customer rather than the finished container as is the usual case now."[2]

---

[2] "Container Makers Grow with the Economy," *Financial World,* May 29, 1963, p. 7.

Reduced container requirements. The technical requirements of the can and crown have been, for the most part, a function of high-speed manufacturing and the *need* for a perfect seal to preserve (1) sanitation, (2) container strength and (3) the flavoring or coloring of the contents. But for some products, these characteristics have been relatively unimportant, e.g., a container for wrapped candy in contrast to aerosol dispensed whipped cream. The packaging of the candy, termed an easy application by trade experts, has not required a coated or sealed container nor one able to withstand pressure, all in contrast to the whipped cream dispenser.

Packagers who have made heavy use of tin cans have been experimenting with new production processes and product designs that, among other things, reduce the structural demands placed on the container. The beer industry is a prime example of this trend. Brewers, who used 20% of the cans produced in 1963, have been experimenting with changes in the basic pasteurizing process. Traditionally, beer has been pasteurized in the bottle or can. But lately, brewers have been experimenting with pasteurization in bulk. If successful, the techniques would reduce the need for strong containers.

New methods of food preservation. The development of better methods of product preservation has been a major goal of food processors. Since the early 1950's, despite the short shelf-life of frozen foods, their relatively high cost due to slow processing methods, and the sometimes poor quality, the fastest growth in food consumption has been in foods preserved by freezing rather than by canning (see Exhibit 2).

Exhibit 2

CROWN CORK AND SEAL COMPANY

Consumption of Fruits and Vegetables in Pounds Per Capita, (1953–1962)

	Vegetables			*Fruit*		
	Fresh	*Canned*	*Frozen*	*Fresh*	*Canned*	*Frozen*
1962............	99.4	45.0	10.5	90.9	35.2	10.9
1961............	104.3	44.6	10.0	92.1	35.3	8.9
1960............	106.0	44.5	9.8	97.5	34.5	9.1
1959............	102.9	44.8	8.9	100.9	33.9	8.8
1957............	104.6	43.9	7.5	99.5	35.6	9.0
1955............	104.6	43.5	6.6	101.6	35.5	8.7
1953............	108.6	43.3	5.4	111.3	34.0	7.1

Source: U.S. Department of Commerce.

To overcome the problems of quality, shelf-life, and production time, a technique called freeze drying has been developed. Products processed by this method can be stored at room temperature for long periods. Reportedly the technique has been improved to the point where food quality closely approximates that of fresh items.

Although the commercial use of freeze drying has thus far been limited, trade experts anticipate that the improved quality combined with handling and transportation economies (in contrast to canned foods) will greatly increase the number of applications.

New packaging materials. Expenditures for packaging materials (excluding value added by filling, labelling, and sealing) accounted for almost 35% of total U.S. expenditures for packaging during 1963. Of the estimated $13 billion spent on materials, $2.6 billion was spent on metal materials, 80% of which was used in the fabrication of metal cans. Steel has been virtually the sole metallic raw material used by the metal container industry. Next to automobiles and construction, the industry has been the third largest consumer of steel in the country. During the last decade, however, aluminum, and to a lesser extent fibre-foil and plastic, have increasingly entered traditional tinplate markets.

Discussing the growing competitive strength of aluminum, one author stated:[3]

> Steel has been the master of the can makers' fate for so long that both American and Continental seemed to find it [the competitive strength of aluminum] hard to recognize when it came along. In discussing aluminum, too many can executives had been tending to talk problems, not potential. Aluminum was commonly more costly than steel; it could not resist the same pressures. Changes would have to be made in production lines before aluminum could be run through. . . . The aluminum industry, led by Reynolds Steel Co., claims it had to shoulder its way directly to the can buyer to overcome can company inertia.

Although still a relatively small factor in the metal container field in 1963 (see Exhibit 1A) aluminum has made sizeable inroads in the container market for motor oil and frozen concentrates, products that are shipped long distances and are not packed under pressure. Reflecting these inroads, the use of tinplate containers in 1963 dropped 5% from 1962, while the use of aluminum containers rose 20% despite a curtailed demand for citrus containers.

The use of aluminum for beer can ends, spurred by the introduction of the self-opening top developed by Alcoa, has become another major market for this metal. Both Reynolds and Alcoa, furthermore, have built can plants to hasten the acceptance of an all-aluminum container in the beer industry. Reynolds also has built plants in Florida to supply aluminum cans to the citrus packers.

The principal appeal of aluminum has been its light weight, particularly when transportation costs have been an important factor in total cost. Aluminum experts argue, however, that the aluminum can is also (1) a better looking container than its tin counterpart, (2) cheaper to lithograph as the brushed aluminum plate serves as a base color, and (3) capable of sharper lithographing. In addition they point out that brewers have long agreed that aluminum is "more friendly to beer," reducing the problem of flavoring, a major concern of both the brewing and soft drink industries. If the aluminum executives' confidence that the beer industry can be converted to use of aluminum is

---

[3] "The Fight for 9/10 of a Cent," *Fortune* magazine, April 1961, p. 157.

Exhibit 3

CROWN CORK AND SEAL COMPANY

The Aluminum Can Market

	Total potential annual market (millions of cans)	Aluminum cans produced (millions of cans)			Penetration % of total		
		1961	1962	1963*	1961	1962	e-1963
Frozen Juice Concentrate..........	1,750	900	1,000	1,400	51	57	80
Motor Oil..............	1,700	300	350†	800†	18	21	47
Aerosol................	1,000	25	30	45	2	3	5
Beer Cans..............	9,000	40	60	120	0.5	0.7	1
Beer Lids (on tinplate beer cans) .	9,000	25	600	3,000	0.3	7	40

* Estimated.
† Includes fibre-foil cans.
Source: Reynolds Metals Company as quoted in *Standard and Poor's Industry Survey*.

confirmed, domestic brewers would be the aluminum industry's biggest market. Exhibit 3 gives one company's estimate of the potential market for the aluminum can.

Aluminum has made further inroads in traditional tinplate markets as a component of the new fibre-foil containers. Packaging experts point to the fibre-foil container as an example of the great potential of composite materials. Developed jointly by the R. C. Can Company and Anaconda Aluminum in 1962 for the motor oil market, the composite can accounted for an estimated 55% of the 2 billion motor oil cans sold in 1963 and 10% of total can production.

> Cans made of fibre-foil are also making a strong bid for other metal container markets. Citrus juice may be next. Coca-Cola's Minute Maid Division reportedly has converted already to fibre-foil. . . . If, as it is believed, the can can be made strong enough for beer and vacuum packaged coffee, for example, their potential market may be as large as 15 billion units, or a third of the 45 billion cans currently sold. . . .
>
> The potential of the new type container is deemed so great that other major companies have invaded the market. These include Container Corporation, Crown Zellerbach, Seal-Right-Oswego Falls and Stone Container. . . .[4]

A strong appeal of the composite can, as with the aluminum can, has been its low weight. Generally the composite has run about 20% lighter than its "thin-tin" counterparts but slightly heavier than the all-aluminum container. But in addition to the advantages accruing from lighter weight, the composite can reportedly costs about 15% less to manufacture than either type of all-metal can.

Despite these advantages, many industry experts expect some of the recent gains of the composite can to be of short duration. The motor oil market is a case in point. In late 1963, blow-molded plastic containers, following developments that gave them significant econo-

---

[4] *Financial World*, May 29, 1963, p. 7.

mies over the metal and composite containers available, were introduced in one-quart sizes by major oil companies. In the last few years
blow-molded plastic containers also packaged the major portion of
liquid detergent sold, which as late as 1958 had been packaged solely
in glass or metal. A recent article in *Printer's Ink* magazine reported
that blow-molded plastic containers strong enough to serve as aerosol
dispensers had been developed. While the plastic aerosol is more expensive than its metal aerosol counterpart, its proponents point out that
the plastic aerosol can be fabricated into a variety of hitherto "impossible" can shapes.[5]

Perhaps the greatest long-term significance of the influx of new
materials will be that can companies will have to contend with the
research and marketing strength of such giant, integrated companies
as Du Pont, Dow Chemical, Weyerhaeuser Timber, Reynolds, and Alcoa.
The forward integration of major material suppliers into the metal
container industry has economic repercussions for the can manufacturer. In late 1963, for instance, Reynolds & Alcoa announced price
increases in the sheet aluminum stock sold to can makers, but neither
were reported to have increased the price of their own aluminum cans.

The threat of self-manufacture

The threat of customers manufacturing containers for their own use
has hung over the metal container industry since World War II. For
years the Campbell Soup Company has been the third largest manufacturer of cans in the country.

While only one large user of metal containers, Libby, McNeil & Libby,
has converted to manufacturing its own cans since 1955, other packagers, smaller than the giant food packers but users of billions of cans
annually, have been giving serious consideration to self-manufacture.

Effects of pressures on the metal container industry

The primary effects on the industry during the 1950s of the three
principal pressures described in the first section of this note were the
loss of minor market shares, and the narrowing of profit margins in
traditional product lines.

Loss of market share

In 1957, the president of American Can estimated that his company
was losing over $70 million annually in sales because of self-manu-
facture.

Department of Commerce figures indicate that from 1950 to 1960,
self-manufacturers increased their share of the metal container market
from 11% to 15%.

During the same period, packagers of motor oil and citrus concentrates, users of 4 billion cans a year moved rapidly away from the tin
can, switching first to aluminum and then to fibre-foil containers. By
1960, the tin can's share of these markets had declined 50%.

While statistics on the packaging industry are characterized by many

---

[5] *Printer's Ink*, April 24, 1964, p. 19.

Exhibit 4

CROWN CORK AND SEAL COMPANY

Growth in the Production of Plastic and Metal Containers 1953–1962

(1957–1959 = 100)

	1953	1954	1955	1956	1957	1958	1959	1960	1961	1962	1965*	1970*	1975*
Plastic.....	50.1	49.0	64.6	74.4	82.9	91.9	125.8	134.7	156.0	189.5	263	437	720
Metal......	100.3	90.2	98.3	98.8	101.5	92.9	105.3	107.6	106.5	117.1	128	150	175

* Projected.

Source: Federal Reserve Board Index of Industrial Production. Projections adapted from forecast of *Printer's Ink* magazine, August 30, 1963, p. 315.

gaps, Exhibit 4 illustrates the decline in the growth rate of tin cans in contrast to "newer" packaging materials.

Narrowing of profit margins in traditional product lines

From 1956 to 1960, the average net income (before nonrecurring items) of the major producers of metal containers fell from 4.7% of net sales to 3.3%. One contributing factor was that steelmakers since 1954 had raised their prices five times, totaling a 15.2% increase. During this same period can makers raised their prices six times for a 19% increase, but in 1959 on the initiative of American Can the industry reduced its prices by 8%. In 1960, price increases had not offset rising raw material costs to the can makers, let alone increases in labor costs.

Reflecting the pressure of rising material and labor costs and the threat of self-manufacture, the margin on the typical packer's can (65% of independent can sales in 1960 were packer cans) declined to the point where in 1960 on a price of 2½¢ per can approximately 1.6¢ went to the tinplate producer. The remainder had to cover fabrication costs, the cost of coating and sealing compounds, and the cost of packing and shipping the can.

An executive of one can company, in summarizing his feelings about the difficulties his company was experiencing in adjusting to declining margins throughout the industry, commented: "Sometimes I think the only way out of this is to sell out to U.S. Steel, or to buy General Foods."[6]

The response of the metal container industry

In responding to the events of the 1950s, the four major companies reacted in one or more of the following ways: product diversification, increased customer service, heavy investment in research, closer cooperation with the steel industry, movement abroad, and product specialization. Exhibit 5 provides data on the four major competitors.

Product diversification

During the last decade three of the four major companies in the industry have adopted some form of diversification. In each case the move to diversify was an effort to (1) gain opportunities in packaging

[6] As quoted in *Fortune* magazine, "The Fight for 9⁄10 of a Cent," April 1957.

Exhibit 5

CROWN CORK AND SEAL COMPANY

Summary Financial Figures—Four Major Can Manufacturers
(in millions)

	1954	1955	1956	1957	1958	1959	1960	1961	1962	1963
American Can										
Sales	652.4	714.8	771.6	1,000.6	1,037.0	1,107.4	1,059.0	1,093.3	1,180.5	1,149.4
Profit Margin*	11.5	12.2	11.7	12.7	12.9	11.8	11.8	13.6	13.0	12.3
Continental Can										
Sales	616.2	666.3	1,010.3	1,046.3	1,080.4	1,146.5	1,117.0	1,153.3	1,182.9	1,154.0
Profit Margin*	8.4	9.5	11.4	10.5	10.7	9.8	8.7	10.6	11.4	11.5
Crown Cork and Seal										
Sales	111.4	113.0	115.1	114.9	116.3	123.2	121.2	177.0†	190.2	205.4
Profit Margin*	6.1	5.7	3.5	3.7	5.5	6.7	8.1	12.8	13.4	13.2
National Can										
Sales	41.1	70.9	81.5	88.4	100.7	101.8	109.5	114.8	121.8	126.6
Profit Margin*	4.4	6.7	9.1	7.2	6.9	5.0	5.6	7.5	7.1	7.6

* Operating profit margin before interest, taxes and depreciation.
† Crown Cork & Seal merged with International subsidiary.
Source: Adapted from reports by the *Value Line.*

areas growing more rapidly than the metal containers sector, and (2) to reduce vulnerability to competition from new packaging materials.

The American Can Company and the Continental Can Company moved from being can manufacturers to become "diversified suppliers of packaging."[7] Both companies manufacture products to supply almost any form of packaging desired. Whereas metal containers used to account for over 75% of Continental's volume, they comprised only 50% in 1963. American's reliance on metal can sales dropped from 80% in 1955 to slightly over 60% in 1963.

"These two firms have diversified to the point where they are important factors in papers, plastics, and glass products. . . . With their integrated paper-making facilities, they are in a good position to serve the needs of any customer who prefers foil-fibre containers. . . ."[8]

National Can, the third largest producer of metal containers, moved into the production of plastic containers, purchasing a small plastic firm in 1963. The company also invested heavily in fibre-foil machinery.

Increased customer service

As competition from new material suppliers and the interest of packagers in self-manufacture intensified, all four companies moved to expand the services they offered their customers. American Can, for example, provided customers with market studies of pet food consumption, and of seasonal and demographic influences on the consumption of citrus fruits, beer, and frozen bakery goods. Another service increasingly offered by the four companies has been help in new product planning and development, material handling advice, and assistance in production layout and design. American Can and Continental Can and to a lesser extent Crown Cork and National Can have established special service organizations to work with manufacturers on a large variety of technical and marketing problems. By broadening the scope of the peripheral services offered to their customers, the companies hoped to increase the economic reliance of the packager upon the industry.

Heavy investment in research

It is estimated that during the early 60s, packaging suppliers were spending over $150 million annually on research to upgrade materials and machinery.[9] Both Continental Can and American Can spent an estimated 1.5% of their annual gross sales on research.

In 1963, the Continental Technical Research Center in Chicago occupied several buildings, employed over 1,000 people, and was reported to be the largest and most comprehensive packaging research and development center in the United States. A principal focus of the center's efforts has been the testing and evaluation of all types of materials and production processes for the creation of new packages. In

---

[7] "Price Trends Favor Can Makers," *Financial World,* August 22, 1962, p. 14.

[8] "Container Makers Grow with Economy," *Financial World,* May 29, 1963, p. 7.

[9] "The Packaging Push, Aerosols to Flip Tops," *The Wall Street Journal,* April 9, 1963, p. 23.

1962, Continental reported that it had budgeted over $20 million for research during the 1963 fiscal year.

In 1963, American announced the start of construction on a research center at Princeton, New Jersey. The company's annual report of that year stated that the center would give major attention to "basic research in such areas as solid state physics and electro-chemical phenomena, as a potential source of new products."

In addition to searching for new applications for existing containers and competitive uses of new materials, the can companies also have concentrated upon cutting their manufacturing costs. One way was to increase the speed at which cans were manufactured. As recently as 1958, typical production speeds rarely exceeded 400 cans/minute. In 1963 the most modern machinery produced certain types of cans as fast as 1,500/minute.

New methods of decorating the can have also appeared. "Electrostatic printing," a process designed to improve printing on irregular surfaces, is expected to make feasible the use of containers with more unusual shapes and surfaces. These types of containers have had limited use because of labeling difficulties. The process, unlike present methods, requires no contact with the material to be printed.[10]

Closer cooperation with the steel industry

Because the metal container industry has bought over $2 billion a year in tinplate, the threat of the technological obsolescence of the tin can created a strong response from the steel industry. One such development has been a new lighter weight "skinny" tinplate, resulting from double rolling the conventional gauge of tinplate.

> Until they [steelmakers] were faced with aluminum's claim based on lightness, the steelmakers had traditionally solved canners' problems by sheer bulk with heavier cans than need be. But . . . by cold-working the metal by a second pass through the rolling mill . . . they could cut the cost of freight for the material, the can, and the ultimate product.
>
> . . . With all their new special equipment, tinplate makers can continue reducing the gauge of their material as far as can makers find it safe and convenient to go. . . .[11]

The economic stake of the steel industry in the future of the can companies, many can company executives believed, would be a significant factor in the ability, particularly of the non-giants, to adjust effectively to new competitive pressures. As an executive of one of the smaller companies put it: "A week doesn't go by that we are not working with some steel company on a new development . . . we won't lose this market to the aluminum and paper companies as they [the steel companies] have the resources to do fantastic things with steel."

Recently the United States Steel Corporation announced the introduction of a new steel foil designed to be used with composite con-

---

[10] "American Can Acquires Rights to New Process for Printing on Packages," *The Wall Street Journal*, November 7, 1963.

[11] "Thin Tin Gets Rolling," *Business Week*, May 11, 1963.

tainers. Steel manufacturers have also been testing an assortment of cans to be used as cooking utensils and serving dishes.

> U.S. Steel [has] tested bulk cheese in a decorated reclosable tin can, which doubles both as an original container and as a table server. The company has no plans to enter the consumer packaging field; it devised the new containers as a stimulus for tinplate, a company spokesman says.[12]

Movement abroad

As margins in traditional markets narrowed in the United States under the increasing competitive pressures, some can companies established manufacturing facilities overseas, not only in Europe but also in Latin America, Africa, and the Far East. The purpose was to get into a position to profit from the rising standard of living of overseas countries. There was a need for inexpensive food preservation in many countries and needed demand for convenient food packaging was increasing in the more advanced foreign countries. Crown Cork and Seal, for example, established or expanded plants in 17 foreign countries from 1958 to 1964, becoming the largest potential overseas producer of tin cans in the short space of six years.

Product specialization

The Crown Cork and Seal Company, nearly bankrupt in 1957, in large measure because of poor operating procedures, had not expanded outside the metal container field by the end of 1963. Instead, it specialized in the aerosol field, becoming the largest producer of steel aerosol containers. Following the strategy of concentrating upon the development of this container, while downgrading product lines (such as packer cans) most vulnerable to self-manufacture, Crown Cork enjoyed the highest profit margins of the four leaders in the industry. The remainder of this case focuses on the development of Crown strategy.

CROWN CORK AND SEAL COMPANY

The crisis

In 1956, Crown reported earnings of $381,000 on domestic sales of $115 million, not enough to cover payment of $550,000 in preferred dividends. The steady downward trend in operating profits during the early 1950s, in part a result of the elaborate line and staff organization and the increasingly costly research and development programs maintained, also stemmed from the company's very large and geographically concentrated production facilities (see Exhibits 6 and 7). For example, in 1954 Crown had built a plant in Leeds, Alabama, transferring a major portion of its crown production there in order to be near the Birmingham steel mills. In Philadelphia the company operated one of the largest can plants in the world, concentrating over 80% of its can production under one roof on 55 can lines. (Although industry execu-

---

[12] "The Packaging Push, Aerosols to Flip Tops," *The Wall Street Journal*, April 9, 1963, p. 23.

Exhibit 6

CROWN CORK AND SEAL COMPANY
Organization
(February 1957)

Division	Plant locations
Crown & Closure.....................	Baltimore, Maryland
	Detroit, Michigan
	Leeds, Alabama
	St. Louis, Missouri
Can.............................	Philadelphia, Pennsylvania
	Erie Avenue Plant
	Ashton Road Plant
	Baltimore, Maryland
	Chicago, Illinois
	Bartow, Florida
	Orlando, Florida
Machinery........................	Baltimore, Maryland
Western..........................	San Francisco, California
	Los Angeles, California

tives did not agree on the optimum number of lines for a can plant, most concluded that anything over 20 lines tended to be unwieldy and uneconomical.) In both cases the plants were located hundreds of miles from the markets needed to utilize the huge capacity of these facilities.

Except for the investment in the new Leeds plant in 1954, less than $1 million was invested in updating and replacing the machinery used in all locations between 1950 and 1957.

In the spring of 1957 after Crown reported a loss of $600,000 in its first quarter of operations, the Bankers Trust Company of New York withdrew its line of credit and asked for repayment of the $2½ million currently being extended. At a special meeting of the board of directors, Mr. John F. Connelly, Chairman and a substantial stockholder of the company (estimated at 24% in 1964) was named president.

Domestic operations since 1957

When Mr. Connelly assumed the presidency of Crown Cork, the company was on the verge of bankruptcy. In addition to the $2½ million loan called by Bankers Trust, there were $4½ million of short-term notes due by the end of 1957. In his first annual message to the stockholders, Mr. Connelly described his task as "halting, reversing and rebuilding [the company's] status with the stockholder and customer alike," a task he saw as "appalling" in the spring of 1957.

> Management was extremely discouraged. Sales were diminishing as reports were freely circulated among our customers that we were in difficulty. The complaints of stockholders were numerous and violent. . . . Six and one-half million dollars were owed to the banks and it was thought that an additional $7 million would be needed to get us through the seasonal peak of our business.

Exhibit 7

CROWN CORK & SEAL COMPANY

Manufacturing Facilities
Domestic Plants

1955

Location	*Products*
Baltimore, Maryland	Machinery, crowns, closures, cans
Bartow, Florida	Cans
Chicago, Illinois	Cans
Leeds, Alabama	Crowns and cans
Los Angeles, California	Cans
Orlando, Florida	Cans
Philadelphia	Cans
San Francisco, California	Cans
St. Louis, Missouri	Crowns, closures

1962

Atlanta, Georgia	Cans, crowns and closures
Baltimore, Maryland	Machinery, crowns, closures
Bartow, Florida	Cans
Chicago, Illinois	Crowns and cans
Dallas, Texas	Cans
Ft. Worth, Texas	Cans
Orlando, Florida	Cans and crowns
Philadelphia	Cans and crowns
San Francisco, California	Cans, crowns and closures
Spartanburg, North Carolina	Cans and crowns
St. Louis, Missouri	Cans, crowns and closures
Winchester, Virginia	Cans and closures

Foreign plants

Antwerp, Belgium	Crowns, closures and machinery
Rio de Janeiro, Brazil	Crowns
Sao Paulo, Brazil	Crowns
Toronto, Canada	Cans and crowns
Montreal, Canada	Crowns
London, England	Crowns
Paris, France	Crowns
Tredegar, Wales	Crowns
Milan, Italy	Crowns
Mexico City, Mexico	Crowns
Casablanca, Morocco	Crowns
Rotterdam, The Netherlands	Crowns
Lima, Peru	Crowns
Lisbon, Portugal	Cork rods, discs, etc.
Salisbury, Southern Rhodesia	Crowns
Johannesburg, South Africa	Crowns
Port Elizabeth, South Africa	Crowns

As a result of these conditions, Mr. Connelly instituted severe changes in the company's pattern of operations in an effort to survive the crisis of 1957 and rebuild the company into a stronger long-term competitor. These changes, initiated over a period of two or three years were:

1. An extensive reorganization of the management and financial structures.

2. The modernization and geographical diversification of product facilities.
3. Product specialization.
4. Emphasis on customer service.

The management reorganization. Shortly after he became president, Mr. Connelly moved the company's headquarters from Baltimore to Philadelphia and started to eliminate the complicated divisional structure, an outgrowth of the previous management's efforts to improve the company's earnings position. The old structure had consisted of four major operating divisions: the Crown and Closure Division, the Can Division, the Machinery Division, and the Western Division (see Exhibit 6). A fifth division had existed, but in December of 1955 this [the Specialty] division, whose main plant was in St. Louis, was merged with the Crown and Closure Division "in the interests of economy."

The 1955 Annual Report had commented on the rationale behind the institution of the divisional organization and the increased overhead it brought about:

> In 1953 the company began to adapt a headquarters and operating division type of organization such as has been employed successfully by a larger number of American industrial corporations. The three former principal subsidiaries became divisions of the company and the Baltimore operations were established as two separate divisions in addition to the headquarters staff.

From 1957 to 1959, Mr. Connelly consolidated the management structure, reducing sharply the overhead. By 1959, Crown's employment had been reduced by 1,647 people or 24% of its labor force. As one executive carefully put it: "We also lost the services of 11 or so vice presidents." In addition, the central research and development facility was disbanded. Within two years, overhead was reduced from over $11 million to $5 million. In the 1957 and 1958 Annual Reports, Mr. Connelly described these changes:

> A few years ago, the company introduced an elaborate and costly line and staff type of organization. Aside from its cost and other disadvantages, it was incompatible with the size of our business. This type of organization has been largely eliminated and changed to one of greater simplicity, flexibility, and effectiveness. We consolidated three independent divisional product selling groups into one integrated sales organization. [In addition] a careful review of all classes of personnel accomplished by year end [1957] a reduction of 968 employees. These reductions were unrelated to business activity in that they largely comprised excess and nonessential personnel. In headquarters alone, which in the past has been severely criticized, there was a reduction of 80 people to approximately one-half of its original size. . . .
> Elimination of this divisional staff-type of organization and the institution of straight-line operating management in our various manufacturing plants [has given] us better and more direct control over our operations.

While the company did not maintain an organization chart in 1963 ("we would spend all our time just trying to keep it up-to-date"), Exhibit 8 reflects how one might have looked.

Exhibit 8

CROWN CORK AND SEAL COMPANY
Organization
(February 1964)

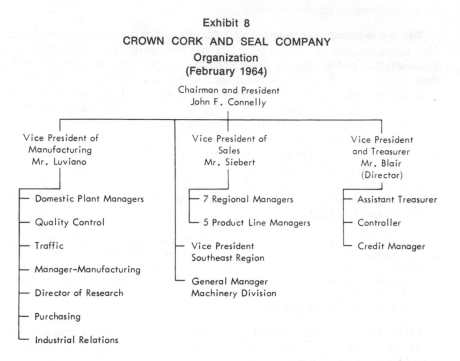

In addition to the drastic reorganization and reduction of executive positions undergone since 1957, Crown also experienced a considerable turnover in top-level personnel. Mr. Siebert, Mr. Luviano, and the controller had been in their present positions less than two months as of February 1964. These gentlemen were the third group of executives to occupy these positions since 1958. The rapid turnover of top-level personnel reflected, in part, Mr. Connelly's strong belief as to (1) the importance of an immediate and measurable contribution from his subordinates and (2) the company not being a "training ground or retirement home" for executives.

As part of the company's reorganization, Mr. Connelly discarded divisional accounting practices at the same time he eliminated the divisional line and staff concept. Except for one accountant maintained at each plant location, all accounting and cost control was performed at the corporate level, the corporate accounting section occupying one-half the space used by the headquarters group.

According to Mr. Connelly, "When we took over this place, it was completely demoralized. So we started talking profits, a $10,000 saving would improve earnings 1 cent a share, a $1,000 saving ¹⁄₁₀ and so forth. We went to all our plants and did this, stressing that the company's future and that of the individual manager would depend solely on his profit performance not on whether he was related to someone at corporate headquarters."

Whereas in 1956 each plant manager had had his own accounting-control section and was responsible for all costs controllable at the plant level, in 1963 the control function was centralized; also, each plant manager had been made totally responsible for plant profitability, including any allocated costs (all company overhead, estimated at 5% of sales, was allocated to the plant level). As explained by Mr. Blair, Vice President and Treasurer, the cost and profit consciousness of the plant managers had expanded to all aspects of company operations when they were made responsible for al costs. "The manager is even responsible for the profits on each product manufactured in his plant." The plant manager's compensation was not tied directly to profit performance. But as Mr. Blair pointed out, "He is certainly rewarded on the basis of that figure."

Financial reorganization.   Reductions in personnel and inventory levels moved Crown past the 1957 crisis with the banks. Since that time the company had reduced the cash drain of its capital structure by purchasing or redeeming a major portion of the outstanding preferred and preference stock. By so doing, the company reduced required dividend payments by over $600,000. Crown also purchased and retired about 1.2 million shares of common stock (after giving effect to a four to one stock split in 1963). The company also repurchased its plants, which had been sold on a leaseback arrangement during the late 1940s.

In 1963, Crown, through the sale of 400,000 shares of common stock and the issuance of $30 million in convertible debentures, raised $42 million. It used this to refund all existing long-term indebtedness, substantially reducing its interest expense. Mr. Blair believed this last change in the company's capital structure had corrected all the financial errors that had carried over from the pre-1958 period (see Exhibits 9 and 10).

Modernization and diversification of facilities.   In 1957, the bulk of the company's products were produced in three locations (Baltimore, Leeds, and Philadelphia). Because of this concentration, high transportation costs had, in effect, eliminated Crown as a factor in many market areas. An additional limitation had been imposed by the fact that the company's 13 plants typically produced only one classification of products (see Exhibit 7). Consequently, the new management sought to introduce greater "flexibility" to their production capacity by expanding the number of geographical areas that could be served profitably. Crown, from 1958 to 1963, spent almost $82 million in relocation expenses and on new facilities, a sum representing over one-half its total plant investment as of 1963.

In Baltimore, the company's crown and closure manufacturing facilities, occupying over 50 multistoried buildings, were vacated, much of the obsolete equipment being sold. New facilities occupying three

Exhibit 9

CROWN CORK AND SEAL COMPANY

Comparative Statement of Profit and Loss for the Fiscal Years
1954–1963, 1961–1963 Consolidated

	1963		1962		1961*		1960	
Sales								
Products sold.	$205,396	100.0%	$190,178	100.0%	$176,992	100.0%	$121,211	100.0%
Interest, royalties and other income...	908	0.4	505	0.3	874	0.5	804	0.6
Dividend from Crown International...							700	0.6
	$206,304	100.4%	$190,683	100.3%	$177,866	100.5%	$122,715	101.2%
Costs and expenses								
Costs of products sold excluding depreciation.	163,033	79.3	150,093	78.9	139,071	78.6	101,931	84.1
Selling and administration.	15,033	7.4	14,694	7.7	15,311	8.7	9,488	7.8
Depreciation.	6,039	3.0	4,908	2.6	4,627	2.6	2,513	2.1
Interest.	2,636	1.2	1,579	0.8	1,252	0.7	1,225	1.0
Nonrecurring expense covering relocation of operating facilities, etc...	1,505	0.7	1,820	1.0	2,517	1.4	1,826	1.5
	$188,246	91.6	$173,094	91.0	$162,778	92.0	$116,983	96.5
Profits from operations.	$ 18,058	8.8	$ 17,589	9.3	$ 15,088	8.5	$ 5,732	4.7
Estimated taxes on income.	7,250	3.5	8,081	4.3	7,625	4.3	2,325	1.9
Net profits.	$ 10,808	5.3	$ 9,508	5.0	$ 7,463	4.2	$ 3,407	2.8
Pro forms combined summary of earnings reflecting terms of 1961 merger								
Net sales.							$168,866	100.0%
Cost of product sold excluding depreciation.							135,276	80.2
Depreciation.							3,828	2.3
Selling and administrative expenses...							15,972	0.5
Interest.							1,298	0.9
Income tax.							5,491	3.2
Net income.							$ 6,392	3.8

single-storied buildings replaced the former ones. The company's
electrolytic tin mill in Baltimore also was sold, in 1958.

The company's gigantic can plant in Philadelphia was vacated and
set up as rental property. Its can lines were relocated to existing plants
in order to expand their capacity and to convert them from single to
multiproduct facilities. In 1959, the Leeds, Alabama, plant was vacated,
its crown lines being transferred to a new plant constructed in Atlanta.
In 1960, a plant was opened in Winchester, Virginia, to manufacture
packer cans for the apple packing industry in the Shenandoah Valley
region. A plant to manufacture cans and crowns was purchased in
Dallas. This plant was to be a temporary facility until a new plant
could be constructed in Texas. Crown manufacturing equipment was
added to the Chicago can plant. Can lines were installed in the St.
Louis crown and closure plant. In 1963, the company was constructing
can plants in Fort Worth, Texas, and Spartanburg, South Carolina.
Aerosol can lines were installed in the Atlanta, Chicago, and San
Francisco plants and aerosol capacity was being expanded in Philadelphia and Baltimore.

Crown management believed that, because of this extensive investment in new facilities, its domestic equipment was the most technically
advanced in the industry. Mr. Blair thought it was unlikely that any
other major can producer could claim 60% of its total investment as

1959		1958		1957		1956		1955		1954	
$123,191	100.0%	$116,348	100.0%	$115,923	100.0%	$115,098	100.0%	$112,954	100.0%	$110.064	100.0%
339	0.3	559	0.5	237	0.2	188	0.1	499	0.4	190	6.2
600	0.5	500	0.4	500	0.4	400	0.4	400	0.4	400	0.4
$124,130	100.8%	$117,407	100.9%	$116,660	100.6%	$115,736	100.5%	$113,583	100.8%	$110.654	106.6%
104,251	84.6	96,922	83.3	98,278	84.8	95,803	83.3	92,430	81.8	90,449	82.2
10,636	8.6	13,074	11.2	13,337	11.5	15,280	13.3	14,042	12.4	13,598	12.4
2,087	1.7	2,381	2.1	2,494	2.1	2,577	2.2	2,672	2.4	2,723	2.5
955	0.8	677	0.6	894	0.8	1,150	1.0	1,030	0.9	1,160	1.0
2,033	1.7	1,203	1.0	637	0.5	440	0.4	448	0.4	112	0.1
$119,962	97.4	$114,257	98.2	$115,640	99.7	$115,250	100.1	$110,622	97.9	$108,042	98.2
$ 4,168	3.4	$ 3,150	2.7	$ 1,020	0.9	$ 486	0.4	$ 3,230	2.9	$ 2,612	2.4
1,525	1.2	1,213	1.0	266	0.2	105	0.1	1,406	1.3	1,196	1.1
$ 2,643	2.2	$ 1,937	1.7	$ 754	0.7	$ 381	0.3	$ 1,824	1.6	$ 1,416	1.3
$171,012	100.0%	$161,733	100.0%	$158,668	100.0	$153,578	100.0%	n.a.		n.a.	
137,162	80.4	130,183	80.6	129,260	81.5	123,541	80.4				
3,395	2.2	3,706	2.4	3,787	2.4	3,669	2.4				
16,745	9.8	17,694	10.9	17,597	11.2	19,001	12.3				
1,104	0.8	896	0.7	1,115	0.7	1,342	0.9				
5,076	3.2	3,801	2.5	3,165	2.1	3,024	2.0				
$ 5,831	3.6	$ 4,739	2.9	$ 3,232		$ 3,173	2.0	n.a.		n.a.	

* Crown Cork and Seal merged with Crown International in 1961.

being new within the last five years. To this factor, Mr. Blair attributed much of Crown's recent ability to maintain the highest operating margins in the industry.

In November 1963, Crown announced the purchase of the Mundet Corporation, a producer of polystyrene and specialty cork insulation materials and gaskets made of composition cork and rubber. The company also produced metal bottle caps and had a small plastics operation. By early 1964, Crown had sold the insulation and plastics portions of the business, recovering almost its entire initial investment. Crown also discontinued the manufacture of insulating materials. As explained by Mr. Connelly, "We are primarily interested in obtaining the Mundet crown plant which is ideally located to service the New York Metropolitan Area. The plant is being expanded to include can-forming lines." Previously, New York customers had been serviced from the Philadelphia plant at a substantial transportation expense to the company. Mr. Connelly estimated that savings in trucking expense alone would exceed $300,000 a year.

Product specialization. In 1963 Crown derived about 50% of its sales from the production of cans and metal containers, about 43% from crowns, and the balance from bottling and packaging machinery. Domestically, cans accounted for over 65% of the total volume and almost 40% of profits. Although the profit margin on crowns was

Exhibit 10

CROWN CORK AND SEAL COMPANY

Balance Sheets for Fiscal Years 1954–1963, 1961–1963 Consolidated
(dollars in thousands)

	1963	1962	1961	1960	1959	1958	1957	1956	1955*	1954*
Current assets										
Cash	$ 6,235	$ 5,831	$ 5,343	$ 2,204	$ 2,587	$ 1,905	$ 1,677	$ 3,030	$ 2,786	$ 4,064
Government securities	1,735	913	527				2,179†			
Receivables	30,199	25,387	23,729	15,775	15,286	15,781	14,962	12,919	11,743	9,705
Inventories										
Finished goods	33,349	27,206	25,011	16,251	16,013	13,417	16,582	19,319	17,845	17,625
Work-in-process	14,168	11,644	10,275	3,416	6,039	10,068	10,062	14,133	14,036	13,384
Prepaid expenses	3,539	2,397	1,463	513	593	479	610	817	776	771
	$ 89,225	$ 73,378	$ 66,348	$38,159	$40,518	$41,650	$46,072	$50,218	$49,318†	$45,676†
Current liabilities										
Notes payable	$ 31,344	$ 21,635	$ 5,190	$ 1,875	$10,000	$ 8,205	$ 8,005	$ 7,700	$ 3,200	$ 5,700
Accounts payable	21,017	20,597	14,956	8,887	10,620		7,494	7,575	4,644	
Customer deposits				213	291	160	268	212	213	180
Provision for income tax	2,722	2,926	4,679	2,056	1,529	2,038	749	172	1,280	1,211
	$ 55,083	$ 45,158	$ 24,825	$13,031	$22,440	$10,403	$ 9,022	$15,578	$12,268	$11,736
Working capital	$ 34,142	$ 28,220	$ 41,523	$25,128	$18,078	$31,247	$37,050	$34,640	$35,050	$33,940
Investment in Crown International Corporation	750	750	13,215							
Investment in Crown Financial Corporation				1,460	1,460	1,460	1,460	1,460	1,460	1,460

Plant and Equipment

Buildings	51,889	42,005	35,119	17,834	14,310	12,231	16,924	16,875	16,751	16,724
Machinery equipment	95,666	77,486	65,621	49,158	40,675	36,030	44,855	45,490	45,018	45,994
Construction in progress	7,667	5,102	3,387	1,446	7,372	3,744	1,007	1,111	1,306	1,543
Loss: Depreciation	(59,899)	(48,719)	(45,004)	(26,339)	(24,717)	(24,258)	(32,464)	(31,167)	(29,468)	(28,899)
Land	4,563	4,000	3,131	1,694	1,383	1,706	1,615	1,720	1,744	1,515
Patents, less amortization	332	382	616	312	329	350	368	536§	393	382
	$100,218	$ 80,256	$ 62,870	$44,105	$39,352	$29,803	$32,305	$34,582	$35,744	$37,258
Total assets less current liabilities	$135,110	$109,226	$104,393	$82,448	$58,890	$62,510	$70,815	$70,682	$72,293	$72,702
Preferred stock	$ 5,007	$ 5,624	$ 6,279	$ 7,269	$ 7,269	$ 7,875	$11,475	$12,375	$12,375	$12,375
Convertible stock			9,917							
Common stock	11,527	10,642	2,699	2,448	2,423	2,655	3,019	3,019	3,019	3,019
Paid-in surplus	11,274		2,036	9,793	9,656	10,420	11,059	10,705	10,705	10,705
Earned surplus	61,157	54,724	55,609	40,717	25,878	25,702	25,936	24,383	24,794	24,003
	$ 88,965	$ 70,990	$ 77,540	$60,229	$45,226	$46,652	$51,489	$50,482	$50,893	$50,102
Minority shareholders' equity in subsidiaries	8,320	7,871	7,639							
Long-term debt	30,676	25,454	17,654	21,125	13,000	15,400	19,000	20,200	21,400	22,600
Deferred income taxes	7,149	4,911	1,560	1,094	664	458	326			
	$135,110	$109,226	$104,393	$82,448	$58,890	$62,510	$70,815	$70,682	$72,293	$72,702

* Discrepancies in total figures due to rounding.
† Claims for prior years' federal income and excess profits taxes.
‡ Adjusted to reflect cash surrender value of life insurance, $132,000 and $126,000, respectively.
§ Listed as Other Assets in 1956 Annual Report.
‖ Since January of 1963.

typically higher than those on cans and closures the percentages were also generally representative of the importance of any one product group to net earnings.

The breakdown of total volume by the individual product groups had remained relatively constant since 1960. Within the container group, however, Crown had concentrated upon producing cans for "hard-to-hold" products such as beer, soft drinks, and whipped cream that needed high strength or sensitivity protection from their containers and/or utilized convenience features such as aerosol dispensing or a "tear-top" lid. Specializing in these types of high-margin applications, the company had dropped over $20 million in low margin or breakeven applications since 1957; the percentage of "packer" cans in Crown's total volume declined greatly relative to the other three major manufacturers.

According to Mr. Siebert, Sales Vice President, the specialization in difficult applications, particularly beer and aerosol containers, had reduced the threat of self-manufacture to the company. Part of the reasoning behind the decision not to produce the fibre-foil container for the oil industry was a case in point. Despite its several million-dollar stake in the motor oil can business, Crown having captured 50% of this market by introducing the first aluminum one-quart oil can in 1958, management had decided not to produce the composite can. Their reasoning was:

1. There is a better and quicker return in the beer and carbonated beverage industries.
2. That the economies of the paper can are such as to give the paper companies a significant cost advantage.
3. That because (a) the technology is simple, and (b) the petroleum industry is very standardized, the paper can lends itself to self-manufacture, nor could the price be low enough to prevent it.
4. If necessary, the company could always make the container as they already made spiral paper tubing in which to ship can ends. In addition, the "Dacro" bottle cap utilizes a paper-foil composite material.
5. Finally, the composite can appeared to be only a stage as some oil companies were already experimenting with plastic containers.

By the end of 1963, the company had lost over $8 million in sales to the composite oil can.

One manager described the concentration on producing cans of high ability as:

> A result of the way we think the industry is going. Easy applications are already taken care of. To expand the use of the can, and particularly the aerosol, greater demands are being made of the "can as a package."

One measure of the reliance upon difficult and demanding can applications was that aerosol sales, in 1963, accounted for 20% of total company sales, and sales to the beer industry 50% of total volume. The emphasis on the beer can was also in part an outgrowth of a belief that the crown market was stagnating as beverages were being packed increasingly in cans.

Strong customer service. Believing that (1) there was little technical difference in product quality throughout the industry, all manufacturers having the ability to produce a high-quality can; and (2) the company with the strategically located and available line capacity would have a competitive advantage; Crown executives viewed their greatest competitive strength and challenge to be the provision of a very high level of customer service. Mr. Connelly and Mr. Blair believed this to be the advantage of "operating the company as a small business —we are only as big as our local plant." Messrs. Connelly, Luviano, and Siebert estimated they spent at least half of their time traveling in order "to stay close to the business and informed." Mr. Connelly explained that he gave a major portion of his time to sales, and handling accounts. "I insist on personally hearing about all complaints and problems. I may not know the answer but I will show concern and see that an answer is obtained very quickly." The deep involvement of the top corporate officers in the operations of the company reflected, according to Mr. Blair, "the key aspects of the can industry: the fact that nobody stores cans, and customers want them in a hurry and on time. As far as we are concerned, fast answers get customers."

As part of the policy of providing the fastest possible service, Crown tried to avoid the necessity of changeovers on its lines preferring to invest in additional equipment. As explained by one manager:

> Our thinking has been to have the equipment and then go out and sell it. We believe the cost of 90% machine utilization and warehousing to be prohibitive. Also changing machine setups is a slow and inefficient process. Therefore we have had a heavy investment in additional lines which are maintained in a setup condition and can be gotten rolling in 15 or 20 minutes.

A major objective of the reorganization in 1957–1959 had been to increase the service capacity of the sales force by consolidating the sales organization. Dividing the sales force geographically rather than by product, each salesman was given account responsibility for all products. This consolidation was thought to provide customers with a service unique in the industry, a single contact for crowns, cans, closures and machinery.

According to company executives, however, the most important aspect of Crown's emphasis on service was not its ability to deliver quickly, but rather the ability of the Crown sales force and its technical department to solve customer problems. For example, to the bottler this often meant a complete study of his markets, their growth potential, his distribution methods; for the food packer, a study of his most effective plant layout or technical help on a sanitation problem; for the aerosol packager, the redesign of a dust cap, or help with a production problem resulting from faulty valve mechanisms; and so forth.

Both the manufacturing engineering group and the research and development section devoted a large portion of their time to customer's production process and product development problems, respectively. Dr. Cliffcorn, Director of Crown Research, estimated that over 60% of his section's time was spent on test-packing new products.

A heavy service orientation was reflected in all aspects of the company's research program. As explained by Dr. Cliffcorn:

> Our problem isn't basic research. Our research activities are directed primarily to technical problems. For example, the greatest problem facing the packaging industry is the determination of the true requirement of the container. We are using materials today that five years ago everybody said wouldn't do. We just get more out of it, but also we re-evaluate the true demands placed upon the container.
>
> Basically, we are looking for new uses for cans and new uses for existing shapes. For instance, I have been trying to interest the sales department in the extruded metal can—perhaps for dog food—so I have had some made up and sent to interested friends. As soon as we learn what they want we will make 1,000 of them within a week—timing is crucial around here.

Mr. Luviano, Vice President of Manufacturing, believed there was often a great deal of value in being second to implement a new idea thereby learning from the mistakes of the first.

> There is a tremendous asset inherent in being second, especially in the face of the ever-changing state of flux you find in this industry. You try to let others take the risks and make the mistakes as the big discoveries often flop initially due to something unforeseen in the original analysis. But somebody else, learning from the innovator's heartaches, prospers by refinement. For example, the "spot" insert used in a beer crown is 0.0018 inches thick. Now what determined that? Not brains, nobody envisioned that a 0.0018 inch thickness would be just what was needed, but rather experience; the trial and error of building upon, and learning from, your own and other people's mistakes and problems.

Mr. Blair felt that Crown's lack of interest in not "becoming enamored with all the frills of an R&D section of high class, ivory towered scientists getting little use out of such expenses," was a significant factor behind its recent success.

> Certainly in the electronics industry high class research is needed but this is a much different "being" than the can industry. Too many people have been sucked in on this and have lost a great deal of money. In fact, at one time even Crown made this mistake but we have recovered from these errors.

According to Mr. Connelly, Crown limited its pioneering.

> We are not truly pioneers. Our philosophy is not to spend a great deal of money for basic research. However, we do have tremendous skills in die forming and metal fabrication, and we can move to adapt to the customer's needs faster than anyone else in the industry.

Mr. Luviano believed that Crown's introduction of the tear-top lid reflected another aspect of the company's service policy. "When we developed our first tear-top lids we made them available to all our customers at the same time rather than committing ourselves to giving preferential treatment to one of the large national brewers as did Continental."

With the exception of Mr. Blair, Mr. Connelly and all of his vice presidents were ex-sales executives. Mr. Connelly said this was indicative of the importance he attached to an "aggressive sales-minded" organization. Aggressiveness was emphasized by Mr. Siebert. While he admitted that personal relationships were important selling factors in the industry, Crown salesmen were evaluated on the basis of new business produced, all of the company's products being sold directly to customers by 100 technically-trained salesmen.

In addition to the direct-line sales organization, five product sales managers also reported to Mr. Siebert. Their primary responsibility was the development of new product applications and the maintenance of customer service within their respective product lines or industries. These industries and lines were: (1) the brewing industry, (2) the soft drink industry, (3) fabricated aerosol cans, (4) drawn aerosol cans, and (5) packer and general-line cans. The manager of fabricated aerosol containers described his job as:

> A combination of titles—sales and product development. On the development side—new applications, and ideas. The problem is to put more and different products into the can. If I see a future in any idea, I work it out with R&D and quality control to test its feasibility. If there is enough volume to justify tooling costs, I will go to the supplier and develop his interests. We don't do basic development, but we will work with supplier to provide specs and answer technical questions. The basic thing is to sell him on an idea to increase his market and then to work with him to develop it.

To the soft drink industry and to a lesser extent with the brewing industry, Crown Cork was the only company in the country which could supply all of the packager's needs from the filling equipment to the cans and/or the crowns needed to seal the bottles. The machinery division supplied 60% of all the filling equipment used in the soft drink industry and 90% in the brewing industry. The company's ability to offer a unique range of services, i.e., cans, crowns, machinery, to major beverage packers, had often provided an entryway for new crown and can business.

March 1962

In his stockholder message of March 1962, Mr. Connelly concluded that the rebuilding and sharpening of Crown Cork's domestic operations had been more than accomplished.

> In 1957, your present management accepted the challenge to rebuild your company. At that time we planned a very ambitious five-year program, the goal of which was to produce additional profits of $1 per share each year.
> We have exceeded this goal so it is only natural to ask about the future.

We still feel that we have hardly scratched the surface of our potential. We have built a splendid organization full of enthusiasm—one that is now ready to take on a new challenge. We are confidently planning for the years 1962–1967, expecting equal or even more dramatic performance than the past five years.

Admittedly long-range prognostication is risky but the groundwork has been laid so solidly that again we are setting goals to add a minimum of $1.00[13] per share profit in each of these years. We consider this goal very realistic and will determinedly do everything within our power to accomplish this objective.

The expansion of production capacity and its breaking up into smaller and more dispersed units, along with a strong service orientation, all introduced to correct conditions which had helped to precipitate the 1957 crisis, had become, according to company executives, the "solid groundwork" on which the effort to accomplish this objective would be based. International expansion was to be the principal means.

International expansion

Following its policy of selling in selected geographical markets, and locating plant facilities as near as possible to large customers, Crown, in 1960, had established a program to build plants in overseas locations. The objective was to be closer to what was anticipated would be the major growth areas for metal cans in the next 20 years. In 1928, Mr. McManus had organized an International Company as a subsidiary to manage the production and sale of crowns overseas. In 1961, the two companies were merged. The merger's proxy statement listed four primary objectives:

1. Corporate structure will be a simplified and a single management will be able to better coordinate and integrate the operation of the domestic and international business.
2. The foreign subsidiaries will become more closely identified with Seal and with each other by working directly with Seal rather than through an intermediary company.
3. Seal and International presently hope to eliminate the risk inherent in the substantial reliance of International's subsidiaries on a single product (crowns) by adding new products when market conditions are suitable in certain countries. The merger will simplify efforts to this end by enabling Seal to provide directly to the subsidiaries the necessary experience and management.
4. The merger will result in a reduction of administrative expense.

By the end of 1963, Crown was operating 21 plants outside the United States: seven in Europe, five in South America, two in Canada, one in Mexico, one in the Far East and five in Africa. Several additional building sites had been selected in Africa for construction within the next five years.

Crown's policy was to create a wholly owned subsidiary operated by

---

[13] In 1963 this goal was restated to read $0.25 per share due to a 4 to 1 stock split.

the nationals in each country. The corporate headquarters assisted but did not get directly involved in the development of the organization, nor the production facilities. For instance, in Nigeria, the British subsidiary had played the major role in developing the facilities because they had a long-standing understanding of the key social, political and educational aspects involved. "Then we don't get involved in the personnel problems of family moving, fringe benefits, local tax problems, tax laws, and so forth."

In the 1963 Annual Report, Mr. Connelly commented on the development of the international side of the business.

> Our associate companies are very well established locally and well guided by experienced, competent managements, nearly all being nationals of the countries where we are located.
>
> It is impossible to place a value on our international business since the rights we have to operate in these countries, some on a pioneer basis, could not be obtained today.
>
> Our profits and sales in the United States will continue to grow each year and growth in the international market is unlimited.

According to Mr. Blair, the company did not worry about expropriation as "our country diversification greatly reduces this risk. In addition, if we didn't believe in the people and their basic goodwill, we would not have any business being there at all."

The outlook for the future

Assessing the probable effect new materials would have on the company, both Mr. Luviano and Mr. Siebert stated that the company had no present plans to become involved in composite containers or to expand its use of aluminum beyond its current commitment to aluminum ends for beverage cans and the production of aluminum cans for citrus packers at its Bartow, Florida plant. As to plastics both executives pointed out that the company was familiar with the technical problems of plastic fabrication, having been one of two developers of the plastic-lined crown, which in 1963 accounted for 20% of the industry's domestic crown sales. In addition Crown recently had acquired two small plastic moulding companies in England. Both men believed the company would probably become involved with new materials as their acceptance became "a fact." In the meantime Crown didn't plan "to pioneer."

Mr. Luviano questioned the wisdom of investing huge sums of money in a container "that next year may be obsolete. Our belief is that the aluminum and paper composite is still an interim package—one which just holds the product and costs less. We can't afford to work on the same thing. Ideally, we would like to anticipate our competitors, but if you're caught off guard you try to come up with something better."

Commenting on the possibility of further integration by major suppliers and customers, Mr. Siebert, Vice President of Sales, thought the steel industry would not become involved in can manufacturing as "we (can manufacturers) are their biggest single profit factor right now."

As to the possibility of major breweries producing their own cans, Mr. Siebert believed the beer can was "so far too technical" for self-manufacture to be a meaningful threat.

Mr. Blair, Vice President and Treasurer, believed that Crown's future sources of growth would be twofold: that which would come from (1) an increase in the general consumption of cans as consumer income rose, particularly in overseas markets; and (2) attacking the 75% market share held by Continental and American.

> I think the basic tin can has been put to nearly every use there is so I don't feel new uses offer our greatest potential. Rather, if we can get 20% to 40% of all new (geographic) areas we enter, we have a great growth potential in contrast to American and Continental. This is where better service comes in and if you're a customer with a gripe you will always be able to immediately reach John Connelly. (Crown maintained an open-phone policy for all its executives.)

According to Mr. Connelly the important dimension of the company's future growth would be international development.

> Right now we are premature but this has been necessary in order for Crown to become established in these areas. In 20 years, I hope whoever is running this company will look back and comment on the vision of an early decision to introduce can-making in underdeveloped countries.

February of 1964. In 1963, Crown's operating margins declined for the second year in a row. In late 1963 and early 1964, Mr. Connelly made major personnel changes in the operations area of the company replacing (1) the manager of the company's largest can plant ($50 million in annual sales), and (2) the vice president of operations, the latter's job being filled by Mr. Luviano, the new vice president of manufacturing.

According to Mr. Connelly, the ex-vice president of operations' inability to control operating variances had brought about his replacement. Mr. Luviano's predecessor had sought to control manufacturing operations by maintaining strong functional responsibility at the corporate level. Discussing the changes he planned to institute Mr. Luviano stated:

> I'm a great believer in responsibility at the plant level. Consequently I plan to remove all authority from the corporate level people, making their function that of giving assistance to the plant managers. Then if the plant managers can't do the job—we will get someone who can.

As to the objective established in 1962 of adding $0.25 per share per year in earnings, 1963 fell short of this goal. In his 1963 message to the stockholders, Mr. Connelly commented:

> While 1963 produced the highest sales and profits of our history, we in management are far from being satisfied with these results for we feel we could and should have done better.

Mr. Connelly, however, was able to report earnings of $2.03 per share compared with 1962's figure of $1.83, the latter being computed on the basis of 400,000 fewer shares of stock outstanding.

APPENDIX

A BRIEF DISCUSSION OF THE ECONOMICS AND HISTORY OF THE METAL CONTAINER INDUSTRY

The problem for the can companies of responding profitably to environmental change has historically been influenced by two major industry characteristics:

1. The high capital investment required for a manufacturing facility, and
2. Marketing and distribution practices.

The evolution of the structure of the metal container industry represents the efforts of companies and the federal regulatory agencies to cope with these two phenomena.

The production of metal containers is a highly mechanized and expensive operation in which direct labor represents a small part of the final price. (See Exhibit A1.)

The capital costs of installing a "line" (the equipment required for making cans) have been extensive. For example, a line to run beer cans costs from $750,000 to $1 million. The basic machinery or body forming equipment costs approximately $500,000 per can line and lithography and coating equipment require an additional $300,000 and $225,000, respectively. One lithography and coating line typically feeds three or four forming lines, most can plants having a minimum of 12 to 15 forming lines. A complete line for beer might cost $1.5 million. It might have the capacity to produce more than 100 million cans in a year.

The large capital investment coupled with high cost of changeover has placed can plants in the difficult position of trying to maintain a high level of line utilization while minimizing setup costs. Consequently, volume discounts are often given for quantities in excess of 700,000 cans in order to obtain long runs.

Because of the high level of facility investment, it has been natural for can manufacturers to seek customers with large volumes. The standardized needs of brewers and packers were ideal. In fact a single large packet might easily absorb the output of more than one plant. Brewers and food packers have been the major can industry customers taking over 75% of annual can production.

Because certain customers were so desirable, and because idle plant was so expensive, competition had a tendency to be severe. Efforts to avoid this competition led to two of the most important antitrust cases in United States history. The American Can Company was a classic trust formed to eliminate cut-throat competition among can manufacturers through merger. Prosecuted in 1913 under the Sherman Act and

Exhibit A1

CROWN CORK AND SEAL COMPANY

1962 Value Added by Manufacture

	No. employees	Production workers	Man-hours (in millions)	Wages (in millions)	Value added (in millions)	Cost of materials (in millions)	Value of shipments (in millions)
All manufacturing establishments	16,777,734	12,138,758	24,306.0	$59,176.0	$179,322	$221,404	$399,327
Fabricated metal product	1,085,000	834,090	1,724.0	4,287.0	11,115	11,217	22,298
Metal cans	53,069	46,018	99.0	305.4	772	1,339	2,112
Rubber and plastics	397,958	313,590	636.0	1,585.0	4,313	4,255	8,516
Stone, clay, glass	573,926	464,619	944.0	2,281.0	6,600	6,600	11,537

convicted in 1916, the public spirited behavior commended by the judge in his decision not to dismember American, provided the quiet climate in which Continental was able to grow.

During the 1920s and 30s, both American and Continental used their resources to develop faster closing machinery for their cans. This machinery, covered by patents, was only made available to customers who would buy American or Continental cans as well on five- and ten-year contracts. Thus through patent protected positions in closing machinery, American and Continental continued to dominate the container business. The Justice Department's suit begun in 1946 and concluded in 1956, brought such "tie-in" contracts under the scope of the antitrust laws.

Pricing and distribution practices

Pricing.   Where the manufacturers have been unable to respond to market conditions with new or differentiated products, price competition has been severe. For example, in the fall of 1963, Continental Can announced plans to raise prices on aluminum beer can ends, motor oil can ends, citrus cans, and miscellaneous other products. The company gave recent increases by aluminum companies in the price of aluminum sheet as the reason for the increases in keeping with its "policy of adjusting can prices to reflect changes in plate costs."[1] Because other can manufacturers, particularly American, did not announce similar increases, Continental was unable to maintain the new prices. Customers sometimes "punish" such attempts at increasing prices by reducing the offender's share of the business.

The competitive situation has also been aggravated by the trends noted in the earlier description of the industry. Also, faced with rising costs, the can manufacturers have not wanted to provide, by raising prices, further inducement for large can users to set up their own can plants. Also, rising prices would weaken the competitive position of tin cans in relation to plastics, aluminum, and glass containers.

Distribution.   Because cans are relatively bulky items, transportation costs have been a major consideration in setting distribution policies. Various estimates have placed the radius of economical distribution for a plant at between 150 and 300 miles, depending upon the size and weight of the cans.

A critical determinant of transportation costs is the weight/volume relationship, the cost climbing rapidly with an increase in can size and/ or weight. A major advantage of aluminum and composite cans has been their low weight/volume ratio relative to the standard tinplate can.

The high cost of transportation has led can companies to operate many plants (American and Continental manufacture cans in over 100 domestic locations). Usually a plant is located next door to or down the street from its major customer. Because of this, the manufacturer who has lost a large account has been in a difficult position.

---

[1] "Continental Can Planning Some Increases," *The Wall Street Journal,* October 17, 1963, p. 26.

Air Products and Chemicals, Inc.

IN EARLY 1975, Mr. Edward Donley, president and chief executive officer, was reviewing a pending major plant investment. The project had the potential to establish Air Products and Chemicals, Inc. as the number one producer of toluene diamine (TDA), which was an intermediate chemical for the production of polyurethane foams. The plant design was based on the latest technology and as the largest plant in the industry, it would give Air Products the lowest cost position. Although this market was not unfamiliar to Air Products, the company was a relative newcomer to the chemical industry. In Mr. Donley's mind, many of the elements of Air Products' overall strategy, which had worked well in the industrial gas business, were present in this opportunity to establish a strong competitive position in the polyurethane intermediates market.

Air Products and Chemicals, Inc. was founded in 1940 to manufacture and sell air separation equipment. By 1974, Air Products had become the third largest supplier of industrial gases and also had become an important supplier of a number of chemical products. Sales of $562.6 million in 1974 and earnings of $39.7 million placed the company on *Fortune*'s list of the top 500 manufacturing concerns in the United States.[1] The year 1974 marked the 14th consecutive year of earnings growth for the company. As a result of this performance the company was highly regarded and this was reflected in the performance of its stock, which traded at a P/E (price/earnings) multiple above the average of chemical companies on the NYSE.

The company had gradually shifted its marketing emphasis from government to civilian sales, and in the 1950s it had been instrumental in expanding the primary demand for oxygen, nitrogen, and other gases

---

[1] In 1974, the company ranked 308th, up from 360th in 1973. *Fortune*, May 1975.

for use in chemical and metallurgical processes; e.g., steelmaking. The company's continued success was reflected in the 18 percent annual increase in sales for the six-year period ending in 1974; this rate of growth far surpassed the total growth of the chemical industry which had grown at a compound rate approximately 7 percent for the same period.[2]

Industrial gases and related equipment still accounted for over 59 percent of total corporate revenues; however, chemical sales had become a more significant part of Air Products' activities. From 13 percent in 1965, chemical sales had expanded to over 39 percent of corporate sales in 1974. This increase was largely due to diversification efforts initiated in 1961. By early 1975, Air Products had made three major chemical acquisitions with the intent of acquiring proprietary chemical products and/or processes and bringing to bear its management and technical expertise to develop a viable position in chemical manufacturing.

The growth of Air Products had resulted largely from a strategy that focused on the exploitation of technology and economies of scale in both industrial gases and chemicals. James Dempsey, vice president of corporate planning commented:

> Our strategy has been to serve markets in which we could achieve technological and market leadership. We have successfully applied this strategy to the industrial gas business and have achieved a pre-eminent position in process and applications technology. Our cost position is as good as anybody's in the industry. We have attempted to use the same strategy in specific segments of the chemical industry as well. The TDA project is a natural extension of this strategy.

THE INDUSTRIAL GAS INDUSTRY

Industrial gases

Industrial gases were produced by a variety of methods. Oxygen, nitrogen, and argon were manufactured by the liquefaction and subsequent separation of air by cryogenic (ultra-low temperature) technology. Helium was extracted from natural gas, while acetylene and carbon dioxide were made by chemical methods.

Argon and helium were inert elements produced and utilized for their lack of reactivity and other physical properties. Nitrogen and carbon dioxide were also nonreactive under normal conditions. Oxygen and acetylene, on the other hand, were used in processes where their high reactivity was important.

Oxygen was the most important industrial gas, and in 1973 accounted for an estimated 39 percent or $240 million of total industry sales.[3] (See Exhibit 1.) Oxygen found extensive use in steel manufacture, chemical processing, ceramics manufacture, and in the medical field.

---

[2] Source: Industry data.

[3] C. H. Kline, *Guide to the Chemical Industry* and industry data.

Exhibit 1

U.S. PRODUCTION AND SHIPMENTS OF INDUSTRIAL GASES—1963–1973

	Oxygen, high-purity*	Nitrogen, high-purity*	Acetylene†	Carbon dioxide‡	Hydrogen§	Argon, high-purity	Other	Total
Shipments (in millions)‖								
1963........	$136	$ 40	$ 95	$49	$26	$18	$30	$394
1964........	157	48	100	52	36	20	51	464
1965........	172	69	98	53	38	23	60	513
1966........	174	81	97	50	43	27	60	532
1967........	209	100	87	47	39	25	65	572
1968........	225	115	89	42	38	33	66	608
1969........	229	119	99	41	38	39	65	630
1970........	238	123	99	37	35	39	62	633
1971........	226	128	103	39	32	29	52	609
1972........	217	130	95	39	30	33	55	599
1973#......	240	150	70	35	32	36	57	620
Production (billion cubic feet)**								
1963........	129	51	15	977	—	1	—	—
1964........	158	57	16	1,007	—	1	—	—
1965........	182	72	17	1,086	—	1	—	—
1966........	213	90	17	1,082	—	2	—	—
1967........	225	104	14	1,089	—	2	—	—
1968........	248	119	15	1,058	—	2	—	—
1969........	276	133	16	1,167	65	3	—	—
1970........	284	151	15	1,135	60	3	—	—
1971........	319	168	12	1,344	56	3	—	—
1972........	353	194	12	1,481	59	4	—	—
1973#......	390	225	9	1,365	62	4	—	—

* Excludes amounts produced for synthetic ammonia and derivatives.
† Excludes acetylene made from hydrocarbons and by small establishments for captive use.
‡ Excludes quantities produced and consumed in plants making soda ash and urea.
§ Excludes hydrogen produced and consumed for synthetic ammonia, methanol, and petroleum refining.
‖ Shipments include interplant transfers, but exclude production consumed in producing plants.
Estimates.
** Sources: *Current Industrial Reports*, M28C; and estimates by C. H. Kline & Co.

The substitution of oxygen for air in combustion processes often enabled firms to increase reaction and production rates or decrease the amount of waste from the process.

Nitrogen was the second most important industrial gas, with total shipments of $150 million in 1973.[4] Used primarily for its chemical inertness and low temperature, nitrogen enjoyed wide acceptance to freeze foods, prevent oxidative deterioration, and cool products during transport. Of the total nitrogen produced, about 66 percent was in gaseous form, with the balance, 34 percent, produced in a liquid state.[5]

Acetylene, with 1973 shipments of $70 million, was the third largest gas in terms of usage.[6] These $70 million shipments did not include

[4] Ibid.
[5] Ibid.
[6] Ibid.

the acetylene produced from hydrocarbons and used as feedstocks for the synthesis of chemicals such as vinyl chloride and neoprene. Almost all of the acetylene reported in statistics on industrial gases was used by metal fabricators for welding and cutting. Minor amounts were used in marine illumination and emergency lighting. Production declined in recent years as the largest market, gas welding, was being supplanted by electric welding.

The fourth largest industrial gas in dollar volume was carbon dioxide. Between 1963 to 1970, production grew only by 2.2 percent per year as the market for solid carbon dioxide (dry ice) declined. It has, however, achieved substantial recent use in freezing meats, poultry, and frozen foods. In 1973, it experienced increased competition from nitrogen in

Exhibit 2

INDEXES OF AVERAGE MANUFACTURERS' PRICES
OF INDUSTRIAL GASES—1963–1972
(1967 = 100)

	Oxygen, high-purity	Nitrogen, high-purity	Acety-lene	Carbon dioxide	Hydro-gen	Argon, high-purity	Total*
1963.........	121.1	83.9	99.9	114.1	91.2	140.1	124.4
1964.........	112.3	86.5	99.6	117.4	107.6	145.8	118.1
1965.........	105.8	97.8	94.8	111.1	104.5	133.0	111.1
1966.........	90.8	94.5	95.8	108.6	99.2	117.2	99.5
1967.........	100.0	100.0	100.0	100.0	100.0	100.0	100.0
1968.........	99.7	100.5	102.4	90.8	94.7	117.5	99.5
1969.........	91.5	92.5	98.6	77.0	105.9	111.5	94.7
1970.........	91.9	84.1	104.0	74.0	119.5	107.0	92.3
1971.........	89.0	76.8	124.7	64.8	128.4	71.8	87.4
1972.........	75.9	68.1	122.5	58.6	119.4	65.2	75.8

* Excludes carbon dioxide.
Source: Calculated from data of *Current Industrial Reports*, M28C, C. H. Kline & Co.

this application and production declined. About 50 percent of all carbon dioxide was used for food refrigeration.

Most hydrogen was produced captively by manufacturers of ammonia, methanol and refiners of petroleum. Data for these uses were excluded from Exhibit 2. In 1973, more than 60 billion cubic feet or $32 million was produced for such uses as hydrogenating vegetable and animal oils, fats and fatty acids, manufacturing hydrochloric acid, annealing and other metalworking, and as a rocket fuel with oxygen or fluorine.

Industry structure

Although sales approximated $620 million, the industrial gas industry consisted of only a few national scale producers and several large regional producers. (See Table 1.) Relatively concentrated, the industry's top six companies accounted for slightly more than 80 percent of sales, while the top ten producers accounted for almost 95 percent of the total industry shipments.[7] Union Carbide's Linde Division was the industry leader, with an estimated 30 percent of the market, followed by AIRCO, Inc., and Air Products and Chemicals with approximately 18 percent and 16 percent, respectively.[8] The companies producing industrial gases also had substantial sales of related equipment and systems for handling industrial gases.

Although considered a part of the chemical industry, industrial gas producers exhibited significantly different cost structures from the rest of the industry. For example, in 1971, production and payroll-related costs constituted 27.4 percent and 11.8 percent of shipments, respec-

Table 1

MAJOR U.S. PRODUCERS OF INDUSTRIAL GASES—1972

Company	Industrial gas revenues (in millions)
Union Carbide	$175
AIRCO	110
Air Products and Chemicals	95
Chemetron	60
Houston Natural Gas (Liquid Carbonic)	50
Big Three Industries	30
Liquid Air	15
Burdett Oxygen	15
Cities Service	10
Puritan-Bennett	10
Other	30
Total	$600

Source: Estimates by C. H. Kline & Co.

tively, compared to 46 percent and 15.5 percent for the industry as a whole.[9]

Industry trends

Over the period 1963 to 1973, total dollar shipments of industrial gases had grown at an annual rate of 4.6 percent per year, expanding from only $394 million in 1963 to $620 million in 1973.[10] Overshadowing this growth trend, physical unit production of industrial gases had increased at an annual rate of 11.7 percent for the same ten-year period. With the exception of synthetic fibers, this represented the fastest growth of any segment of the chemical industry.[11]

The rapid growth of the largest volume industrial gas, oxygen, had occurred largely because oxygen had replaced air in many important applications in steel manufacturing, chemical processing, ceramics, and

---

[7] Ibid.
[8] Estimates by Mitchell, Hutchins, Inc.
[9] Kline, *Guide to the Chemical Industry*.
[10] Ibid.
[11] Ibid.

the medical field. Almost 55 percent of all oxygen used in 1973 (down from 69 percent in 1970) had been used in steelmaking in the basic oxygen furnace (BOF). First introduced in the United States in the late 1940s, the BOF process had gradually replaced the open-hearth furnace (OHF) and generated a dramatic increase in demand for oxygen. Unlike the OHF, which utilized air, the BOF process required oxygen to provide the oxidant for heating purposes; the BOF process had lower capital and operating costs than the OHF process as pure oxygen eliminated the need for other fuels and provided a faster heat of steel.[12] Although the conversion from OHFs to BOFs required substantial capital investments on the part of the steel industry, the 1960s was a period of changeover for most steel companies. Between 1963 and 1969, the tonnage of U.S. steel produced by BOFs rose from 8.5 million tons to 60.2 million tons and from 7.8 percent to 42.6 percent of total raw steel produced.[13] The impact of this trend on oxygen prices was described by Mr. Harry Dimopoulos, manager of strategic planning at Air Products, as follows:

> The explosive growth of the steel industry oxygen requirements during the sixties created a very favorable environment for companies able to demonstrate competence in industrial gas technology. It was common practice for a qualified supplier to receive a firm oxygen purchase contract from a steel producer and then use that contract as collateral for loan funds to construct the oxygen plant. Funds were thus available to suppliers in the industry with basic technical competence. As in most commercial situations where a vast new market was opening up, competition was intense. This competitive atmosphere unfortunately resulted in declining prices as the companies in the industry tried to gain market share.

In addition to steel production, oxygen was utilized in numerous chemical processes. Substantial quantities of oxygen had also been consumed in nonchemical uses; these included utilization as oxidants for aerospace fuels, in cutting and welding of metals, and in medical applications.

In terms of dollar volume, industrial gas sales had been depressed by widespread price attrition, particularly between 1969 and 1972. Between 1963 and 1969, average prices had fallen at a rate of only 4.5 percent per year, while total dollar sales had increased an average of 8.2 percent per year. This trend was reversed for the period 1969–1972 as average prices declined about 7.2 percent annually and dollar shipments remained level through 1973.[14] (See Table 2 and Exhibit 2.)

Although price declines had been severe and were typical of the chemical industry, price attrition in industrial gases had been both offset and caused by lower costs gained through technological improve-

---

[12] The cost of oxygen constituted only about 0.5 percent of the selling price of steel.

[13] Industry data.

[14] C. H. Kline, *Marketing Guide.*

Table 2

INDEX OF AVERAGE
MANUFACTURERS' PRICES
FOR INDUSTRIAL GASES
(1967 = 100)

Year	Average Price
1963	124.4
1964	118.1
1965	111.1
1966	99.5
1967	100.0
1968	99.5
1969	94.7
1970	92.3
1971	87.4
1972	75.8

Source: C. H. Kline, *Marketing Guide.*

ments. Elimination of the distribution costs of high-purity oxygen and other gases by the construction of on-site air separation plants and a system of pipelines for large users had been instrumental in expanding the demand for industrial gases.

Exhibit 3 shows the method of distribution for oxygen and nitrogen, the two major industrial gases. As can be seen, both gases were principally shipped in the gaseous state, via pipeline, which was the most economical way to deliver product to such continuous and large volume users as steel mills and chemical plants. These were the on-site users. Merchant users on the other hand received product either as gas in cylinders, or as liquid in tank trucks or rail tank cars. The liquid was subsequently gasified at the user's premises, for all but cryogenic applications.

Exhibit 3

U.S. SHIPMENTS OF OXYGEN AND NITROGEN
BY METHOD OF DISTRIBUTION, 1972
(percentage of total cubic feet)

	Oxygen	Nitrogen
Shipped as gas		
Pipeline	69.9%	58.0%
Cylinder and bulk delivery	0.2	0.4
	70.1%	58.4%
Shipped as liquid		
Cylinder and bulk delivery	12.4	30.5
For pipelines or other air-separation plants	2.9	2.6
	15.3%	33.1%
Consumed in producing plant	14.6	8.5
TOTAL	100.0%	100.0%

Source: C. H. Kline & Co., *Current Industrial Reports.*

Future

Physical production of industrial gases was expected to rise since there were several potentially large markets to be developed. This included wastewater treatment, coal gasification, food freezing, solid waste disposal, and new applications in chemical processes. In Virginia, for example, the Chesapeake Corporation had successfully used oxygen to replace chlorination as a first stage bleaching process in the production of Kraft pulp. Results had shown that when used in the first stage, oxygen bleaching produced pulp of higher brightness and reduced consumption of chlorine in subsequent stages. The aluminum industry had also begun to use oxygen in firing smelt furnaces. The glass industry had also utilized a similar oxy-fuel process. Oxygen was being used as a replacement for air in the treatment of wastewater in order to increase microbial action. Oxygen was also being used to dispose of solid waste by incineration in a closed cycle. Industry researchers felt that this latter approach would achieve both more complete incineration and reduce air pollution. Oxygen utilization was also being studied as a means of converting coal to gas and/or liquid fuels. Industry executives generally thought that these opportunities held considerable potential for on-site consumption of industrial gases.

Future price attrition was also expected to be much less as the major companies consolidated the industry and market shares became more stable. Emphasis was expected to be on finding new market applications rather than seeking increased market share through price reductions. Shipments of industrial gases, in constant dollars, were projected to reach $950 million in 1980 and $1,250 million in 1985.[15]

HISTORY OF AIR PRODUCTS AND CHEMICALS, INC.

Beginnings

In 1939, a district manager for the Compressed Industrial Gases Company, Mr. Leonard Pool, combined with a young engineer, Mr. Frank Pavlis, to build a small oxygen generator in the garage of Mr. Pool's brother in Detroit, Michigan. Based on 12 years of experience as an oxygen salesman, Mr. Pool was convinced that a major opportunity existed in the oxygen and industrial gas business. Mr. Pool felt that the key to exploiting this opportunity was technology and the fact that the "cost of transportation of oxygen was more expensive than the gas itself."

At that point in time, the standard industrywide method of supplying industrial gases was expensive. First a company built a large volume gas production plant, and then supplied customers via railroad tank cars, tube trailers, or over-the-road hauling of cylinders weighing far more than the gas they contained.[16] In 1940, the price of oxygen was approximately $1 per hundred cubic feet in cylinders and $0.30 per

---

[15] Department of Commerce, and Paine, Webber, Jackson and Curtis estimates.

[16] Tube trailers were truck trailers used to haul gases in bulk over highways.

hundred cubic feet in large tank-car lots.[17] Mr. Pool was convinced that if the high cost of transportation and handling could be reduced, the demand and markets for oxygen would expand. As oxygen was produced from air, Mr. Pool's solution was fairly straightforward: since there was just as much air over the plant using the oxygen, why not build generating facilities on the premises of the users?

Although the solution seemed fairly simple, the problem Mr. Pool faced was the lack of gas-producing equipment to be placed on-site. This period in the company's history was described by Mr. Pool:

> In the late 1930's, the industrial gas business was dominated by Union Carbide, which had an extensive network of tube trailers and cylinder supply. All gas production equipment, except for Union Carbide's, was imported, primarily from Germany. With the outbreak of the war, there developed a need for a domestic supply of equipment and generators.
>
> After we had initially developed a working model of our generator, our intentions were to manufacture, lease and/or sell the small generators to commercial customers. I tried to interest my old company, Compressed Industrial Gases Company, in them, but they refused. I then showed our generators to other companies such as Ford; while they expressed an interest they demonstrated little inclination to purchase. Then the war came along.
>
> At the beginning of the war, Union Carbide and others were reluctant to make and sell gas equipment to the government. Instead, they tried to move tank cars all over the country to supply the government requirements. We, however, moved to Chattanooga, Tennessee, and devoted all of our efforts to making oxygen generators for the military. Had the war not come along, I don't think the company would have been successful.

During this period, the company grew and developed a reputation for its technical skills and ability to perform. Mr. Frank Pavlis, a vice president and director, indicated that Mr. Pool was instrumental in pushing the company for superior performance during this period:

> Leonard was always pushing us and forcing us to stretch out. He even took one order for generators to be used on ships, although we had never built them before. Our competitors thought the task was impossible as oxygen generators had to remain level; a rolling ship therefore presented problems. Leonard simply told Clarence Schilling, the head engineer, that he had an order and needed designs in a week. Needless to say, Clarence came up with a solution which made it possible to place generators on ships. Our generators were used throughout the war.

Postwar years

By the end of World War II, Air Products had built 240 oxygen and nitrogen generators for the military. Reflecting the company's growth during this period, sales had expanded from $8,295 for fiscal 1941 to $5,224,856 in fiscal 1945. Net earnings in 1945 also reached a record

---

[17] Estimates provided by Air Products' management.

$96,759, compared to a loss of $33,466 in 1941.[18] However, with the end of the war, the company's military business declined dramatically. Lacking a commercial customer base, the company faced a serious crisis. According to Mr. Pool:

> After the war, we didn't have one penny's worth of commercial business; thus, everyone with a white shirt imediately became a salesman. During this time, we called on everyone and anybody we thought might be a prospect. However, we were practically unknown in the civilian market and we were in a location far removed from the country's principal markets for our product. Then we got our first break with Weirton Steel Company in 1945. Weirton was somewhat of a maverick in the steel industry and decided to try our new on-site oxygen generators. On Halloween, they agreed to take two plants if we would meet a January 1 deadline. There was no way these plants could have been built and put in operation in that short period of time, but I agreed anyway. It just so happened that we had two large generating plants in process for the Lend-Lease Program which the government was going to ship to Russia. I went to Washington and persuaded them to cancel the contract. Then Len Volland took over and got the plants ready for Weirton. On Christmas Eve, they went into operation at Weirton. That was our first.

Despite this initial success, the company still faced serious problems. The rest of the steel industry was reluctant to buy Air Products' new concept, and the industrial gas business was still dominated by Union Carbide (Linde Division) and Air Reduction Co. (AIRCO), both of whom had extensive delivery systems of cylinders and tube trailers. Mr. Pool, however, remained committed to his concept.

In early 1946, Air Products decided to move from its Chattanooga plant. To raise money to purchase a new facility in Emmaus, Pennsylvania, and generate operating capital to develop its on-site concept, Air Products went public in May of 1946. Despite a prospectus which read: "The company . . . has no background in prewar civilian business . . . proposes to compete by a new method of distribution in a well-established field against experienced competitors who have much greater financial resources . . . expects to operate at a loss following completion of its government contracts," the company encountered little trouble in selling $300,000 in shares and moved to Pennsylvania.

In 1947, Air Products again struck a responsive chord with pioneering Weirton Steel. Weirton Steel had decided to utilize low purity oxygen for blast furnace use. This represented a technological advancement in steelmaking which had not been accepted in the United States because of the unavailability of low-cost tonnage quantities of oxygen. When Weirton decided to use oxygen, they requested that Air Products provide a facility capable of producing up to 400,000 cubic feet of oxygen per hour. Mr. Pool described this period in the company's history:

> Weirton had an obsession that oxygen could improve its steelmaking process and wanted an oxygen producing facility capable of

---

[18] Air Products, annual reports.

producing 400 tons per day. We tried to get that order, along with Linde, AIRCO, and Kellogg. A major problem was how to build the heat exchanger for such a large plant. We didn't know how, but on a train ride to Weirton, Clarence Schilling stayed up all night and figured out how to do it. After we had solved the heat exchanger problem, we found we couldn't finance the project, so we did it on a cost basis. We got the order, built, and operated the plant.

Mark Halsted, vice president—Europe, commented on the significance of this plant to Air Products:

> The Weirton plant put us in a new league. This plant was 100 times the size of anything we had ever built. Further, it was about 50 times the size anything anyone else had built. This plant alone produced one-third of the total oxygen produced in the United States. It was a major technological breakthrough. After this plant, others became convinced that we could build large plants. In all fairness, we had made a mistake on our exchangers, but our competitors didn't know how to make them either.

Mr. Pool also commented on another significant development during this period:

> About this time, we had decided to build big plants and take revenues over time. At our own expense, we decided to build plants on or adjacent to the customer's property and supply oxygen via pipelines. The customer, in turn, agreed to purchase given quantities of oxygen during a contract period. I felt it was better to sell milk instead of the cow!
>
> Our directors were bitterly opposed to this concept and wanted us to make one-time killings by selling the plants and equipment. We told them we wouldn't do it. They held a meeting and tried to get rid of management. They failed, however, and we continued to develop the on-site concept.

Expansion of the on-site concept

After the Weirton plant, Air Products' business entered a period of substantial growth. With the outbreak of the Korean War, government contracts again became an important part of Air Products' business. Several new factors, however, were to spur the company's growth during this period.

Seeking new markets, Air Products approached chemical companies and sold a number of oxygen and hydrogen plants for the processing of hydrocarbons, ammonia, and other chemicals. The U.S. Missile and Space Program also created a huge demand for liquid oxygen and hydrogen for rocket fuel. Beating the competition, Mr. Pool actively cultivated this market and obtained many government contracts for liquid plants, including the first tonnage liquid hydrogen plant. Located in Florida, this plant was to eventually supply the total product demands of the U.S. Defense and Space Program. The company's aggressive posture during this period was described by Mark Halsted:

> In 1954 when the Missile Program was just starting up, Union Carbide told the government that there was plenty of oxygen for the

Titan Program. This was about the time the world realized the Russians were moving ahead in the space race. Leonard told the government that there is no way they had enough oxygen capacity for our program. Although the Pentagon hesitated, Leonard came back and told us to begin work on plants and programs even before they decided to use us. When they decided, we were ready and able to deliver long before any of our competitors. We then sold the government 13 oxygen plants which produced more oxygen than had previously been available in the United States.

Complementing the Missile Program, Air Products continued to generate customers in steel and other industries. As the competitive advantages of the BOF process became more apparent, steel companies began to demand tonnage oxygen capabilities. With its ability to supply oxygen on-site at a price of about 5 cents per hundred cubic feet versus 30 cents per hundred cubic feet in tank-car lots, Air Products had a significant market advantage over other gas companies, including Union Carbide, still supplying gas in cylinders and tube trailers. By the mid- and late 1950s, Air Products was supplying oxygen to not only Weirton and Jones and Laughlin Steel Co., but also to Acme Steel, U.S. Steel, Bethlehem Steel, and Ford Motor Co. Air Products continued its policy of taking revenues over time by building, financing, operating, and retaining ownership of the on-site plants. Oxygen and other gases were supplied to those companies under long-term, "take-or-pay"[19] contracts. Typically, the period of the contract equaled the depreciable life of the on-site plant (about 15 years).[20] By 1960, Air Products' earnings totaled $1,914,000 on revenues of $48,561,000. Cash flow approximated $4,000,000.[21]

Also during this period, the company further refined and developed its marketing and production strategy. Management was aware that small volume users of industrial gases (merchant customers) constituted a large share of the total market for industrial gases. Because of the high cost of distribution to merchant customers, this market had been dominated by independent regional gas producers and merchandisers, and Union Carbide with its large network of distributors and tank cars. Acquiring several regional gas distributors, and adding a new production concept, "piggy-backing," Air Products developed a significant merchant market customer base for oxygen, nitrogen, argon, and other gases. Under the "piggy-back" concept, new large on-site plants were designed with sufficient production capacity to satisfy the base-load (primary) customers by pipeline and in addition provide incremental product for merchant customers served by road or rail transport. The charges to the primary (pipeline) customers were generally adequate to cover the amortization and operating costs of the

---

[19] Under "take-or-pay" contracts, the customer is guaranteed, during the contract period, a minimum level of revenues to Air Products, regardless of the volume of products taken from the plant. Any volume over the agreed minimum was priced on a variable price basis. Cost escalator provisions were borne by the customer.

[20] Company sources.

[21] Net income plus depreciation.

plant and provide a reasonable return on the investment. Thus, Air Products' incremental capital and operating costs to service merchant customers were significantly less than the costs encountered by small, regional producers. The rationale for this strategy was explained by Frank Pavlis:

> Piggy-backing became extremely important in merchant markets principally because it enabled us to geographically dominate a market. Increased piggy-back capacity and acquisition of smaller regional companies allowed us to get merchant customers and increased market share.

To finance the continued building and operation of its $5 million to $20 million plants, Air Products utilized the credit worthiness of its customers. Using the guaranteed long-term revenues from customers like Bethlehem Steel as collateral, Air Products was able to borrow cash to finance the plants. According to Mr. Pool and Mr. Halsted, this technique was instrumental in the success of the company. Mr. Halsted reflected:

> At the beginning we were just a composite of human beings. If we had depended on our own balance sheet and financial statements, we would never had made it, but it was all part of Leonard's strategy. From the outset Leonard built a team consisting of the best technical people in the oxygen business which included Carl Anderson and Clarence Schilling and Len Volland, who were widely respected in the industry. Along with the financing strategy, I guess our major strength was in our ability to expand the use of existing knowledge without having to push back and develop basic technology.

Mr. Pool emphasized the "quality of people" aspect even further:

> The success of our company was naturally based on a number of factors. At the top of the list, I suppose I would have to put the people. We have had, and continue to have, a long-term quest for people with ability, particularly young people who bring into the company a surge of fresh ideas and who are encouraged to express differing views through dialogue with management at all levels. I believe this has been an important component in our success and we would like to continue to search for people of extraordinary promise.

Mr. Donley elaborated further on the technical capabilities of Air Products during this period of time:

> A turning point in the company's history came in the middle 50s. We recognized that the technologies with which the company was dealing were becoming increasingly complex. A concerted effort to advance the "professionalism" of both the engineering function and the research function occurred. We employed the services of outside professional consultants; we also brought into the company nationally recognized professional experts to either head up or play important technological and engineering roles in our engineering and research functions. These steps made it possible to attract, on a continuing basis, professionally trained graduates in these technical disciplines; through this mechanism, we were able to produce increased professional capabilities.

Expansion and diversification

From its initial base, Air Products expanded its activities both domestically and abroad. In 1952, a license arrangement was made with the Butterley Company of England concerning the use of Air Products' patents in the British Commonwealth and some European countries. Late in 1957, an agreement was made which resulted in Air Products owning 51 percent of the newly created company, Air Products (Great Britain) Ltd. This company took over the manufacturing facilities and assets of Hughes & Lancaster. In July 1961, Air Products purchased the remaining 49 percent interest. In 1963, Air Products Limited acquired Saturn Industrial Gases Ltd., a manufacturer and distributor of industrial gases and welding equipment and supplies, constructed two major on-site plants in the United Kingdom, sold three large tonnage plants to the Italian steel industry, and was on its way to becoming a major competitor in the United Kingdom industrial gas industry.

In 1964, a 60 percent-owned subsidiary was formed in the Benelux countries with Société Générale de Belgique, an important European financial and industrial holding company. The venture received a long-term contract from Sidmar Steel to provide tonnage quantities of oxygen by pipeline to their new steel works at Ghent, Belgium.

At about the same time, a new wholly owned subsidiary was formed in Germany to provide tonnage quantities of oxygen and nitrogen to Rheinstahl, a major steel company near Essen, West Germany, on a long-term, take-or-pay basis. Both of these activities were precursors of an expanded European industrial gas production and marketing program. The company subsequently developed into an important merchant industrial gas supplier in Europe.

In the U.S., Air Products also benefited from the federal helium conservation program which developed in the 1950s and 1960s. As helium was a minor component in some U.S. natural gas fields and was lost to the atmosphere when the gas was burned, Congress decided to finance a conservation program to separate helium from natural gas and store it underground. Air Products won contracts to build several helium stripping plants.

The liquefaction and storage of natural gas in the summer for use during peak demand periods in the winter was another area which the company had moved to explore.[22] Air Products had entered into a long-term contract with the Alabama Gas Corporation to furnish and operate a liquefaction facility. The LNG area had also proved to be a profitable international market.[23] Air Products won contracts to supply the cryogenic equipment for a large Libyan natural gas liquefaction plant, to provide LNG for export to Europe. Heat exchangers were also manufactured and sold to international oil companies. The helium and natural gas technologies were expected to provide a good base for Air Products' response to the market created by the energy crisis.

Penetration of these and other markets had enabled Air Products to

---

[22] This technique was commonly known as "peak-shaving."
[23] LNG is the abbreviation for liquid natural gas.

expand revenues and profits dramatically. Over the period 1961 to 1969, revenues increased at a compound annual rate of 11.1 percent and reached $221.5 million in 1969. Earnings in 1969 totaled $13.6 million or 11.8 percent of revenue. Cash flow in 1969 (earnings plus depreciation) approximated $32.3 million.

Diversification into chemicals

The company's first effort in noncryogenic chemical activities was a joint venture with the Tidewater Oil Co. in 1961. This venture called for conversion of certain refinery by-products into oxo-alcohols for use as plasticizers. In order to further increase its capabilities in chemicals, Air Products in 1962 acquired the Houdry Process Company in Philadelphia, together with its subsidiary, the Catalytic Construction Company.

The Houdry Process Company had established an international reputation in process licensing and in the production and sale of catalysts and organic chemicals. These catalysts and processes were especially useful in the production of high octane gasoline and aromatics, butadiene, and isoprene. Another of the company's products was used commercially as a catalyst in the production of polyurethane foams.

The Catalytic Construction Company was well known in the contract engineering and construction field and had pioneered in the contract maintenance of chemical and petroleum plants for the aerospace, petroleum, and chemical industries.

Mr. Frank Ryan, president of Industrial Chemicals Division, explained the rationale for the company's move into chemicals:

> Initially, we got into the chemical business because we realized that we were in an abnormal growth period in the industrial gas business. We had expanded rapidly due to the increased use of the BOF process, but we knew this would eventually taper off. We believed our skills of management, production, engineering and research would be transferable to industrial chemicals.

Mr. Pool also commented:

> We started out in the industrial gas business and moved into chemicals in the early 60s. We said in the 50s that we possessed a lot of in-house ability, technical knowledge and marketing expertise that was applicable to chemicals. We began to look for the right company. Houdry was offered to us in 1961. It had been a joint venture of Sun Oil and Mobil and was highly regarded; among other things Houdry had developed moving bed catalysts for cracking petroleum. We had a good idea of what we wanted to do in chemicals, and decided that Houdry was a good opportunity.

Air Products later made two additional acquisitions which rapidly expanded their base in the chemical industry. The first of these was the acquisition of Escambia Chemical Corporation in Florida from Ebasco Industries for $19.5 million in cash in April of 1969. At that time, Escambia's sales approximated $38 million and were evenly divided among three areas: industrial chemicals, polyvinyl chloride resins

(PVC), and fertilizers. Escambia had been marginally profitable and had reported a loss for its last year under previous management. Its agricultural business was particularly unprofitable and according to Air Products' management, "beyond hope." Therefore in December of 1969, Air Products sold the retail portion of its agricultural business for $9 million to $10 million in cash and receivables. Air Products was then left with a company with $32 million of annual sales, more than $1 million in after-tax profits and what management considered excellent growth potential, all for a net cost of $10 million.

In January of 1971, Air Products made its third major chemical acquisition, purchasing the chemical business of AIRCO, Inc. In this diversification effort, Air Products bought certain facilities for $3 million in cash, and existing inventory for about $6.5 million. The additional plant facilities, located at Calvert City, Kentucky, were leased from AIRCO over an eight-year period for approximately $1.5 million per year. Air Products also received a purchase option exercisable for about $3.5 million at the end of that time. At the time of purchase, these acquired properties had sales approaching $40 million annually, divided as follows: acetylenic chemicals, $3 million; PVC resins, $10 million; polyvinyl acetate emulsions, $23 million; and fabricated plastics, $4 million. Although losing money when bought by Air Products, this operation was in the black within 30 days after purchase by Air Products. Air Products' actions during this period were explained by Mr. Pool:

> Escambia was not a profitable company. In fact it was losing money. Its owners once wanted to buy us but I told them I'd buy Escambia from them when they got tired of it. Finally, they decided to sell and we bought the assets at a good price. This deal was a quantum leap for us; we obtained the technology that moved us into urethane intermediates.
>
> The AIRCO acquisition has also worked out well. AIRCO had gotten into chemicals, principally polyvinyl acetate emulsions and PVC, and then decided to get out. We bought it at a good price and the timing was perfect. The PVC market had turned down while AIRCO owned the business, but turned up shortly after we purchased it.

Reflecting on the history of Air Products' expansion and diversification strategy, Mr. James Dempsey commented:

> We don't want to leave the impression that everything worked out well for us during this period of time. We have had our share of failures. Happily, these were not significant enough to affect our growth trends. For example, early in our history, we acquired KG, which was a manufacturer of gas welding equipment. KG had low market share, inadequate distribution, and a technology which in the 50s and 60s was obsoleted by other technologies. That company didn't grow to meet our expectations.
>
> More recently, in the mid-60s, we acquired Adkins-Phelps, a formulator of pesticides. At the time, they had an exclusive arrangement to distribute Treflan®, an important herbicide which was a very successful product with rapid growth and was profitable. Air Products also

Exhibit 4

AIR PRODUCTS AND CHEMICALS, INC.
Condensed Income Statements
(in thousands)

	9/30/69	9/30/70	9/30/71	9/30/72	9/30/73	9/30/74
Net Sales and Income:						
Net sales..........	$221,510	$261,366	$307,697	$351,167	$398,901	$562,574
Other income........	2,393	1,120	991	445	2,778	5,897
Gross income........	$223,903	$262,486	$308,688	$351,612	$401,679	$568,471
Cost of sales........	106,024	128,826	156,768	184,385	207,853	307,673
Gross profit........	$117,879	$133,660	$151,920	$167,227	$193,826	$260,798
Expenses:						
Selling, distribution, administration, research and development.	$ 66,164	$ 76,644	$ 88,990	$ 91,903	$102,779	$127,041
Depreciation........	18,730	22,211	25,512	32,555	37,484	45,841
Interest expense.......	7,336	8,963	9,499	10,499	11,497	14,545
	$ 92,230	$107,818	$124,001	$134,957	$151,760	$187,427
Income before taxes.....	$ 25,649	$ 25,842	$ 27,919	$ 32,270	$ 42,066	$ 73,371
Provision for income taxes	$ 12,030	$ 10,830	$ 11,650	$ 13,936	$ 18,007	$ 33,649
Net income..........	$ 13,619	$ 15,012	$ 16,269	$ 18,334	$ 24,059	$ 39,722
Net income per share.......	$ 1.06	$ 1.16	$ 1.25	$ 1.40	$ 1.83	$ 3.01
Income Statement Breakdown:						
Items as a percent of sales:						
Cost of sales........	47.9%	49.3%	50.9%	52.5%	52.1%	54.7%
Selling, distribution, administration, and research and development....	29.9	29.3	28.9	26.2	25.8	22.6
Income before taxes.....	11.6	9.9	9.1	9.2	10.5	13.0
Net income..........	6.1	5.7	5.3	5.2	6.0	7.1

Sources: Company reports and researcher's analysis.

had an R&D program on pesticides and we felt Adkins-Phelps would give us a vehicle to move our new pesticides. Well, the R&D program never developed successful products, and simultaneously the manufacture of Treflan cancelled Adkins-Phelps' exclusive distribution arrangement. Without Treflan and without the new products, there was no viable business: we partly liquidated it and ultimately sold off the remainder.

Needless to say, we have learned from such experiences. Our acquisition program is now primarily focused on complementing the strategies of our existing businesses, and to establish us in new businesses where we can become an important competitive factor.

AIR PRODUCTS IN 1975

By 1975, Air Products and Chemicals, Inc. was an acknowledged leader in the manufacture of industrial gases and related equipment, and an increasingly important competitor in selected chemical products. Revenues which had totaled $107 million in 1963 had grown to $563 million for fiscal 1974. Earnings had increased at a faster rate during the same period and totaled a record $39.7 million for 1974. Assets totaled $659 million (see Exhibits 4, 5, and 6).

The company's principal products in 1975 were industrial and specialty gases, cryogenic equipment for the production and liquefaction of gases, other low temperature, special-purpose equipment, medical gases and health products, agricultural and industrial chemicals, welding equipment and related products, engineering and construction services, contract management and maintenance, licensing of process technology, and contract research. While some products were sold throughout most of the world, the company's largest markets were in North America and Western Europe.

Research and development

R&D was an integral part of Air Products' activities. In 1975, approximately 350 employees were engaged in research and development activities at the company's laboratories in Allentown, Pennsylvania; Linwood, Pennsylvania; and Middlesex, New Jersey. The laboratories in Allentown were devoted to applied cryogenic R&D, including process improvements and customer applications. The labs in Linwood and Middlesex were devoted to chemical research. Research expenses were charged to income as incurred and totaled $11,219,000 in 1974, equal to 2 percent of sales.

The operating divisions each had their own research staff and capability which focused on research related specifically to their business. For example, the Cryogenic Systems Division emphasized research aimed at developing and improving cryogenic processes and plants; the Industrial Gas Division's research efforts were oriented toward finding new applications for industrial gases and the development of systems and equipment to utilize them.

Chemical research activities had been consolidated after the acquisition of AIRCO and Escambia. Current research efforts in this area

Exhibit 5

SUMMARY OF OPERATIONS BY OPERATING GROUPS

		1962	1963	1964	1965
U.S. Gas and	Sales (in millions)	$ 90.0	$ 92.0	$ 86.8	$ 96.6
Equipment..........	Income*	11.6	12.0	10.9	13.2
	Margin (%)	12.9	13.0	12.5	13.7
Foreign Gas and	Sales (in millions)	$ 3.7	$ 8.0	$ 16.5	$ 17.0
Equipment..........	Income*	.3	1.4	2.6	2.6
	Margin (%)	8.1	17.5	15.8	15.3
Chemicals..............	Sales (in millions)	$ 14.5	$ 14.8	$ 16.9	$ 17.6
	Income*	1.3	.8	1.6	1.2
	Margin (%)	9.0	5.4	9.5	6.8
Catalytic..............	Sales (in millions)	$ 5.6	$ 2.6	$ 3.2	$ 5.3
	Income†	1.8	.5	.8	2.9
	Margin (%)	32.1	19.2	25.0	54.7
Total.................	Sales (in millions)	$113.8	$117.4	$123.4	$136.5
	Income†	12.6	11.8	11.8	15.6
	Margin (%)	11.1	10.1	9.6	11.4
Sales as percent of Total:					
U.S. Gas and Equipment (%).....		79.1%	78.4%	70.3%	70.7%
Foreign Gas and Equipment........		3.3	6.8	13.4	12.5
Chemicals...........		12.7	12.6	13.7	12.9
Catalytic............		4.9	2.2	2.6	3.9
		100.0%	100.0%	100.0%	100.0%

* Profit before interest and taxes.
† Profit before taxes.
Source: Company annual reports.

were devoted to process development and improved products for specific applications; in addition, a significant amount of work was carried out to develop new products, plastics, resins, and processes which the chemical group could offer for licensing.

Air Products also had a Corporate Research activity. Mr. Donley described its function:

> Corporate R&D is a relatively small group whose efforts are directed at new technologies. Its efforts are not related to problems of existing divisional business. We are highly product oriented and once it becomes clear that a project of corporate R&D is related to a particular division or product group, it is transferred to that particular area.

Finance

The financial area was considered by management to be a key area of the company and integrally related to its overall strategy. The company's high capital investment required that debt levels of the company

1966	1967	1968	1969	1970	1971	1972	1973	1974
$111.9	$118.0	$131.5	$120.0	$138.6	$157.3	$172.0	$180.5	$218.4
13.8	16.4	15.9	16.0	14.8	19.5	24.4	26.3	28.5
12.3	13.9	12.1	13.3	10.7	12.4	14.2	14.6	13.5
$ 20.5	$ 29.9	$ 31.0	$ 38.3	$ 48.2	$ 52.3	$ 67.1	$ 78.5	$113.0
2.1	3.1	5.4	7.1	9.6	9.1	8.2	9.8	11.9
10.2	10.4	17.4	18.5	19.9	17.4	12.2	12.5	10.5
$ 27.9	$ 32.6	$ 33.0	$ 51.3	$ 62.7	$ 86.9	$102.6	$128.8	$216.5
6.2	4.8	3.0	4.0	5.6	5.8	7.0	12.1	39.3
22.2	14.7	9.0	7.8	8.9	6.7	6.8	9.4	18.2
$ 5.6	$ 7.8	$ 11.7	$ 11.9	$ 11.9	$ 11.2	$ 9.5	$ 11.1	$ 14.7
2.9	3.2	6.4	6.4	5.7	4.3	3.2	5.4	8.2
51.8	41.0	54.7	53.8	47.9	38.4	33.7	48.6	55.8
$165.9	$188.3	$207.2	$221.5	$261.4	$307.7	$351.2	$398.9	$562.6
19.5	21.2	23.6	26.2	26.7	29.2	32.3	42.1	73.4
11.7	11.2	11.4	11.8	10.2	9.5	9.2	10.5	13.0
67.5%	62.7%	63.5%	54.2%	53.0%	51.1%	49.0%	45.2%	38.8%
12.3	15.9	15.0	17.2	18.4	17.1	19.1	19.7	20.1
16.8	17.3	15.9	23.2	24.0	28.2	29.2	32.3	38.5
3.4	4.1	5.6	5.4	4.6	3.6	2.7	2.8	2.6
100.0%	100.0%	100.0%	100.0%	100.0%	100.0%	100.0%	100.0%	100.0%

be substantial. By the end of 1974, long-term debt was $163 million, equal to 65 percent of net worth; of this amount, 56 percent was secured by long-term customer contracts. Capital expenditures in 1974 had approximated $110 million, while earnings and depreciation had totaled $86 million. (See Exhibit 7.) For 1975, it was estimated that Air Products might spend as much as $170 million on capital expenditures, most of which would be covered by internally generated funds. The importance of the financial area was underscored by the vice president—finance Mr. John Mountain:

Historically Air Products did its financing essentially on a project-by-project basis. Since investments were dependent upon contracts with a single customer, they were either go or no-go situations which made long-term capital planning extremely difficult.

Over the last five years, our business mix has changed markedly. Our on-site revenues as a percentage of total revenues has been declining. We are becoming more and more a merchant-oriented company serving a variety of industries and customers. You can detect two trends on our balance sheet. First, the portion of our total debt, secured by long-term customer contracts, as a percentage of total debt has been

Exhibit 6

AIR PRODUCTS AND CHEMICALS, INC.
Condensed Balance Sheets

ASSETS*	9/30/68	9/30/69	9/30/70	9/30/71	9/30/72	9/30/73	9/30/74
Current Assets:							
Cash and securities	$ 15,550	$ 9,213	$ 14,931	$ 13,108	$ 10,402	$ 13,143	$ 45,820
Receivables (less reserve)	48,453	61,768	72,072	75,616	78,923	93,413	117,178
Inventories†	20,218	30,678	35,835	33,035	33,843	32,701	55,127
Prepaid expenses	2,603	2,617	3,560	4,623	4,711	4,840	4,875
Total Current	$ 86,824	$104,276	$126,398	$126,382	$127,879	$144,132	$223,000
Investment (joint ventures)	$ 4,807	$ 8,874	$ 7,870	$ 8,557	$ 11,101	$ 10,692	$ 10,635
Plant and Equipment:							
Land	$ 4,470	$ 5,160	$ 5,162	$ 4,964	$ 6,865	$ 6,933	$ 8,610
Buildings	22,476	25,017	27,137	29,200	29,896	30,530	36,781
Generating facilities (installed under long-term contracts pledged to lenders)	154,241	153,569	165,620	220,214	239,632	242,312	240,099
Other operating facilities, machinery and equipment	95,012	129,374	168,664	164,774	181,627	216,068	301,916
Other construction in progress	22,836	22,574	8,125	13,208	12,849	30,167	48,621
	$299,035	$335,694	$374,708	$432,360	$470,869	$526,010	$636,027
Less Depreciation	78,515	90,901	108,670	121,863	151,529	169,224	220,392
	$220,520	$244,793	$266,038	$310,497	$319,340	$356,786	$415,635
Other Assets	3,207	3,207	7,944	8,009	8,065	8,062	9,875
Total	$315,358	$361,150	$408,950	$452,845	$466,376	$519,633	$659,145

Current Liabilities:							
Bank and notes payable	$ 1,059	$ 3,869	$ 7,722	$ 4,074	$ 7,065	$ 3,277	$ 3,967
Accounts payable and customer adv.	26,895	30,625	36,751	35,116	37,628	54,741	86,259
Accrued liabilities	10,386	13,355	16,205	18,737	18,965	24,165	37,482
Accrued U.S. and foreign income taxes	4,233	3,498	3,596	7,799	2,387	5,337	11,042
Current portion of long-term debt	11,901	15,688	12,154	15,355	13,967	18,099	22,914
Total Current	$ 54,474	$ 67,035	$ 76,428	$ 81,081	$ 80,012	$105,619	$161,664
Long-Term Debt:							
Secured by long-term customer revenues	$ 95,326	$ 84,562	$ 77,765	$ 98,277	$103,052	$102,297	$ 90,892
Unsecured	5,044	28,048	52,345	49,107	29,867	23,838	25,887
	$100,370	$112,610	$130,110	$147,384	$132,919	$126,135	$162,595
Deferred income	$ 3,986	$ 4,712	$ 5,322	$ 7,771	$ 7,406	$ 10,515	$ 10,842
Deferred taxes	24,244	30,405	36,301	41,144	48,980	55,152	61,508
Deferred investment credit	5,058	7,095	7,819	6,864	7,550	8,351	10,570
Other liabilities	0	0	0	0	3,313	3,111	3,515
Shareholders' Equity:							
Preferred stock	$ 242	242	$ 242	$ 42	0	0	0
Common stock	5,075	5,200	5,342	6,019	6,292	12,903	13,192
Capital in excess of par value	66,497	71,594	76,232	82,211	91,264	95,411	107,865
Retained earnings	55,412	62,257	71,154	80,326	89,640	104,436	127,394
Total Shareholders' Equity	$127,226	$139,293	$152,970	$168,598	$187,196	$212,750	$248,451
Total	$315,358	$361,150	$408,950	$452,842	$467,016	$519,653	$659,145

* All figures are rounded to thousands ($000s).
† Inventories are shown less progress billings.
Source: Company reports.

Exhibit 7

STATISTICAL SUMMARY
(all dollars in millions except data per common share)

	Summary of changes in financial position					
	Source		Disposition			
Fiscal year	Internal funds generated	Additional long-term debt and stock issued	Additions		Reduction of long-term debt	Investments and cash dividends
			Plant and equipment	Working capital		
1974	$96.7	$62.7	$109.8	$22.9	$22.3	$4.4
1973	73.3	6.1	63.9	(9.4)	23.4	1.5
1972	62.8	16.3	41.7	3.2	30.4	3.8
1971	49.7	45.1	67.5	(5.3)	30.0	2.6
1970	46.3	25.5	45.7	12.8	7.5	5.8
1969	42.6	27.3	43.6	4.8	15.2	6.3
1968	38.9	1.0	37.4	1.4	11.1	(10.0)
1967	33.5	28.3	38.8	1.2	12.6	9.2
1966	29.5	36.6	45.0	2.4	10.9	7.8
1965	24.7	30.2	45.2	1.8	7.0	.9

Note: Retroactive restatements have been made for those businesses which were acquired for stock and accounted for on a pooling of interests basis. Businesses acquired for cash have been accounted for from rate of acquisition.
Source: Annual report.

declining and second our debt/equity ratio is not as high as it used to be in the 60s. We must now have a more flexible financing capability which focuses on the long term and recognizes the changing mix of our business.

Mr. Donley also commented on the relationship of finance to the company's future needs:

We need to find investments which are larger than those we have been dealing with previously. We have to be interested in large magnitude projects in order to utilize our cash flow and leverage. The financial advantages of this are significant. For example, on the average, $75 million of a $100 million project would be debt and $25 million would be internally generated. We would get back almost $35 million in the first year due to the investment tax credit and depreciation.

Organization

In 1975, Air Products was organized into three main operating groups: Gases and Equipment Group (59 percent of sales), Chemicals Group (38 percent of sales), and Catalytic, Inc. (3 percent of sales). Within each group the company managed its businesses and/or product lines through divisional profit centers. (See Exhibit 8.)

Gases and Equipment Group. The Gases and Equipment Group manufactured and sold industrial and medical gases and related equipment. Group sales in 1974 were approximately $331 million. Group revenues were principally derived from the sale of industrial gases, metallurgical systems and equipment, cryogenic equipment, and medical products such as gas piping and disposable products. Operations were divided into five divisions, four of which were organized on a product line basis, and a fifth on a geographical basis. These five di-

Capitalization			Resources			Data per common share			
Long-term debt	Share-holders' equity	Number of share-holders at year-end	Plant and equipment (net)	Work-ing capital	Number of em-ployees at year-end	Fully diluted earnings	Market price range	Cash divi-dends	Return on average shareholders equity
$162.6	$248.5	9,800	$415.6	$61.3	13,000	$3.01	$58–38	$.20	17.3%
126.1	210.8	9,400	356.8	38.5	10,300	1.83	53–33	.15	12.1
131.9	187.2	9,300	319.3	47.9	9,000	1.40	36–25	.10	10.5
147.4	168.6	9,900	310.5	44.7	9,200	1.25	28–20	.09	10.1
130.1	153.0	10,800	266.7	50.0	9,100	1.16	23–15	.09	10.3
112.6	139.3	11,000	244.8	37.2	8,700	1.06	21–14	.09	10.2
100.4	127.2	10,900	220.5	32.4	8,200	.95	22–13	.09	10.0
115.2	114.4	10,700	203.7	31.0	8,500	.90	21–13	.09	10.4
100.0	105.0	10,100	182.4	29.8	8,300	.90	19– 9	.06	11.8
94.4	75.4	8,700	151.9	27.4	7,900	.74	17–10	.04	11.8

visions were: Cryogenic Systems Division, Industrial Gas Division, Medical Products Division, Metallurgical Systems Divsion, and Air Products—Europe.

1. *Cryogenic Systems Division (CSD).* This division was responsible for designing, constructing and operating all the cryogenic process plants of Air Products including some chemical process plants as well. They had a very strong process engineering orientation. In 1974, approximately 85 percent of their revenues were generated by the supply of gaseous oxygen and nitrogen to on-site customers. In addition, CSD derived revenues from the outright sale of manufactured process equipment for the liquefaction of natural gas, OASES® systems for wastewater treatment and advanced cryogenic products for other industrial and military uses.

2. *Industrial Gas Division (IGD).* This division was responsible for marketing merchant industrial gases and related equipment in the western hemisphere. Until recently, its market focus had been the United States; but lately it entered the South American and Canadian markets as well. Gas sales accounted for about 85 percent of the division's revenues, with the bulk of those being attributable to liquid products such as liquid oxygen, nitrogen, and argon.

3. *Medical Products Division (MPD).* This division was responsible for serving the needs of the medical community, particularly anesthesiology and respiratory care, with medical gases, hospital equipment, anesthesia machines, laryngoscopes, nebulizers, and so on. The division was established in 1969 and expanded with the acquisition of Foregger, a well-known manufacturer of anesthesia equipment. In the gas area, there still existed a close cooperation between IGD and MPD.

4. *Metallurgical Systems Division (MSD).* This, too, was one of the newer divisions of Air Products, composed of four subsidiary operations—Arcair, Exomet, TekTran, and Gases and Equipment Depart-

Exhibit 8

AIR PRODUCTS AND CHEMICALS, INC.
Organization chart

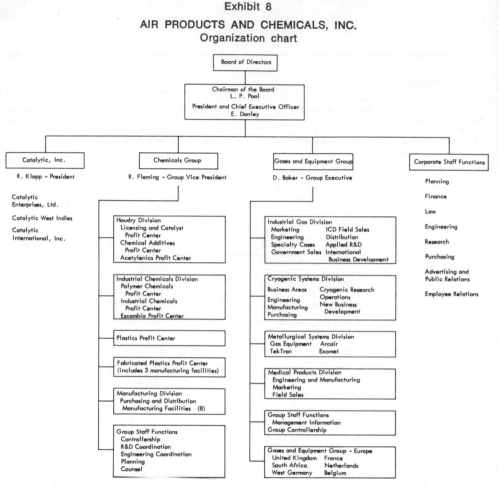

Source: Company records.

ment (GED). The division sold torches, electrodes, gas regulators, power sources, and heat treating and nondestructive testing equipment. In addition, the division had metallurgical recovery operations where valuable metals were recovered from scrap.

5. *Air Products—Europe.* Headquartered in London, Air Products —Europe manufactured and sold industrial and medical gases and equipment in Europe. Sales for 1974 were $113 million, 20 percent of total corporate revenues.

The two largest divisions were IGD and CSD. Although engaged in similar businesses, these two divisions had different orientations in several respects. For example, IGD was much more market oriented than the Cryogenic Systems Division. Mr. Alexander Dyer, president of the Industrial Gas Division, indicated:

> The Industrial Gas Division serves the merchant industrial gas requirements of a multitude of customers in almost every industry. By

merchant gas requirements we mean any quantity from a cylinder to a truck or railroad tank-car quantity as differentiated from an on-site pipeline supply which would be handled by the Cryogenic Systems Division. IGD's entire orientation is toward the creation of new uses or applications and thus new markets for our industrial gas products, plus optimizing the growth, service and profitability of existing business. Consequently, we are investing large sums of money in applied research and development and long-term development encompassing potential applications of our products. By actually working with present and potential customers on these new applications, we find that we can reduce the competitive element and maintain a growth rate far in excess of the traditional rate for our industry. The potential applications for many of our products are almost limitless. Some of our customers grow from cylinder delivery to bulk delivery and subsequently to the point where they are served by an on-site facility. In the latter case the account is then transferred from IGD to CSD.

The difference in the two divisions was also reflected in the staffing of the respective divisions. As noted by Mr. Harry Dimopoulos, manager of strategic planning:

> Approximately 70 percent of the personnel in the Industrial Gas Division are involved with marketing, selling and delivering the products. On the other hand, roughly 90 percent of the personnel in the Cryogenic Systems Division are in operations, engineering, and manufacturing.

More so than any other area, the Cryogenic Systems Division reflected the company's basic overall strategy. The division operated and built the on-site plants, which supplied gas by pipeline under a long-term contract. A typical contract was for 15 years on a "take-or-pay" basis at a fixed price with escalator provisions to provide for increases in the cost of electricity and labor. This provision guaranteed a certain level of profits on the plant for the 15-year period.

Opportunities for the Gases and Equipment Group.   Air Products' executives and the planning staff believed that the Gases and Equipment Group would continue to grow rapidly despite a tapering off in business from the steel industry. In addition to more on-site business from other industries, the company was beginning to develop several completely new areas that would utilize both existing and new technologies. Mr. Donley described the nature of these opportunities:

> The energy crisis provided some new opportunities for us in the gas business. We're working on processes for coal gasification, liquefaction of natural gas [LNG], and the development of synthetic natural gas [SNG]. These promise to be areas of tremendous potential for us. Already we are making and selling heat exchangers which are a critical part of LNG plants. We're involved in the first project to bring LNG to the United States from the Middle East, and we've provided exchangers for a large LNG facility in Borneo. The oxygen requirements of coal gasification and SNG plants could dwarf the size of the BOF market.

Mr. Pool also commented on the opportunities for the company:

> There are some real opportunities for us in clean air and anti-pollution efforts. We hope and think our wastewater treatment plants, desulphurization of stack gas, and coal gasification will lead to more on-site business. These will be leveraged projects with real cash throw-off, which we will of course reinvest.

The company expected primary competition to come from the Linde Division of Union Carbide. Linde had already marketed processes using oxygen for the secondary treatment of sewage and had the major share of that market. Along with Air Products, Linde was also believed to be one of a few companies fully integrated and able to compete domestically for the installation of new on-site cryogenic facilities.

Catalytic, Inc.   The Catalytic Group was engaged principally in the engineering and construction of process plants for the chemical, petroleum, and metallurgical industries. It also provided technical services on a contractual basis, which included design and feasibility studies for waste treatment and disposal plants, and the expansion of atomic power plants. Management believed that Catalytic, Inc., was the largest process plant maintenance contractor in the western hemisphere, maintaining over 40 individual chemical, petroleum, aerospace, and industrial plants in the United States. While the contract maintenance served to soften the cyclical effects, the group's construction and engineering business tended to fluctuate with industry and economic conditions.

Chemicals Group.   The Chemicals Group, with 1974 sales of $217 million, was organized along product lines. The group was divided into the Houdry Division, Industrial Chemicals Division, Plastics Profit Center, and the Fabricated Plastics Profit Center. These were supported by a manufacturing division and group staff functions.

Houdry Division.   The Houdry Division consisted of process licensing and catalysts, chemical additives, and the acetylenic chemicals profit center, the latter having been acquired from AIRCO. Houdry had commercialized the first catalytic cracking process for high octane gasoline in 1931. The division's various catalysts were used to make a variety of chemicals, gasoline, polyurethane foam, and in numerous other industrial processes. Houdry had also developed a catalyst for the catalytic converter used by General Motors on its 1975 cars.

Industrial Chemicals Division.   The Industrial Chemicals Division consisted of the industrial chemical business acquired from Escambia and AIRCO, and a joint venture with Getty Oil. The division's products included methanol, alkyl amines, dinitrotoluene, toluene diamine, ammonium nitrate, ammonia, polyvinyl acetate emulsions, and polyvinyl alcohol. The Industrial Chemicals Division accounted for slightly more than 50 percent of the Chemicals Group revenues. It had shown significant growth over the past five years and now faced major investment opportunities. The division was the sponsor of the TDA project.

Plastics Profit Center.   Air Products' plastics business consisted of the company's polyvinyl chloride (PVC) operations. Most of the company's PVC was of a commodity type. The division, however, had devoted considerable effort to developing specialty products with superior flame retardancy, flow properties, and/or low costs. One proprietary product, STA-Flow, had enjoyed a measure of success as a specialty product to the extrusion and injection molding industry.

Fabricated Plastics Profit Center.   The Fabricated Plastics Profit Center was based on special expertise in the molding of flexible and rigid vinyls. Products included handlebar grips, and a variety of hoses for vacuum service, recreational vehicles, industrial ducting, and swimming pools.

Since products sold by the different divisions within the Chemicals Group were produced in the same plants, the company treated manufacturing as an independent cost center. This allowed centralized planning and control of manufacturing, although the marketing and development activities were independent.

Exhibit 9

AIR PRODUCTS POSITION IN PETROCHEMICALS

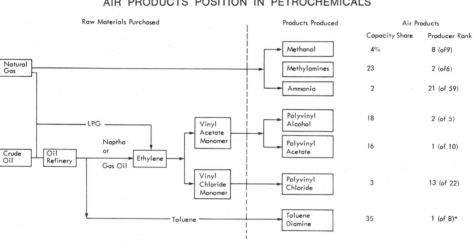

Products Produced	Air Products Capacity Share	Producer Rank
Methanol	4%	8 (of 9)
Methylamines	23	2 (of 6)
Ammonia	2	21 (of 59)
Polyvinyl Alcohol	18	2 (of 5)
Polyvinyl Acetate	16	1 (of 10)
Polyvinyl Chloride	3	13 (of 22)
Toluene Diamine	35	1 (of 8)*

* Potential, if project approved.
Source: Company records.

Opportunities in chemicals.   In 1975, Air Products had a significant market share in five of its product lines: polyvinyl acetate emulsions, polyvinyl alcohol, DNT, toluene diamine, and alkyl amines. (See Exhibit 9.) All these product lines were expected to grow at a rate in excess of the growth rate of the economy or of the chemical industry as a whole, thereby creating major investment opportunities for Air Products. In addition, considerable progress was being made in developing specialty chemical products in a number of product lines.

As a result of these opportunities, management thought a goal might soon be reached to "make chemicals account for at least 50 percent of the company's business." Chemicals currently accounted for 38 percent of the revenues, and sales had grown at a 25 percent average annual rate between 1969 and 1974, compared to a growth rate of 15 percent for industrial gases.

Despite the rapid growth of chemical revenues, the implementation of an effective chemical strategy was perceived by management to be one of its most pressing tasks. Mr. Donley commented:

> As we look at various potential opportunities, both in gases and chemicals, we will continue to follow the overall strategy that has made us successful; that means we must have economies of scale greater than competition's, have products that have dominant positions in growth markets, have process technologies that are better than the competition, and have long-term commitments from buyers that permit debt. We basically want to be the leader in the specific business segments in which we compete. We are content to have the lowest costs, not necessarily the largest market share. This means making and exploiting products cheaper than others can produce them. We also want businesses to generate high cash flows and be capital intensive for investment purposes; this again implies our involvement in commodities and large volumes of products and utilization of our engineering skills.

Mr. Donley also realized that the industrial chemical business implied market confrontations with larger chemical firms, whose abilities and research efforts to develop new products were far more established. Mr. Donley continued:

> Although chemicals require considerable R&D, we can be extremely competitive in some areas. For example, we are as big in merchant polyvinyl alcohol (PVA) and amines as Du Pont, which is a $4.6 billion company. We can do this since we try to focus our research budget on specific areas. Also we are more engineering oriented than most companies. When we develop a product, we try to tie engineering features to the properties of the product which will give us an advantage in production.

Mr. Donley elaborated on the strategic implications of Air Products' engineering orientation:

> We visualize that in the 1970s and 1980s comparable opportunities exist for those companies who are wise enough and lucky enough to create new technologies which will respond to a society which will have less crude oil at higher cost, an insistence on a clean environment, and an abundance, in the United States at least, of low cost coal. If we are to maintain acceptable levels of chemical industry profit growth, we will need to not only master new technologies but also we will need to achieve maximum efficiency overall, and we will need to do it not just as individual companies or countries, but as an overall chemical system. As Adam Smith told us two centuries ago, maximum efficiency is achieved by maximum degree of specialization.
>
> The development of interlocking chemical complexes, such as we see for example in places like Houston, Rotterdam, and elsewhere, will contributed to overall efficiency.
>
> One company will sell raw materials to several others. Another company will produce intermediates for several others, and yet other companies will provide final chemical end products to producers of final manufactured consumer goods. The most efficient company and most efficient overall chemical system will be characterized by the

linking of specialists both horizontally and vertically rather than by one company both backward and forward integrating over a wide span of specialized operations.

Overall benefits will flow from this system because a company engaged in a specialized area will have a single-minded incentive to develop the most advanced process technologies in its particular field.

The users get the benefit of lower unit cost since the large feasible scale of operation is used to produce enough of a given intermediate to furnish the needs of several end users.

In discussing the outlook and strategy for Air Products' chemical business, Mr. Frank Ryan, president of the Industrial Chemicals Division remarked:

> Assurance of low cost supply over the long term has become a critical element in the chemical industry. The on-site concept is very consistent with this trend. What we are attempting to do is to identify high growth segments of the chemical industry like TDA, where we can exploit our old on-site strategy and put ourselves in a position to dominate those market segments. TDA is growing at 12 percent to 15 percent per year and I am confident we can obtain 50 percent of the market. What we also need is the right technical, marketing and research teams who would identify those opportunities and put such projects together. The growth of the Chemicals Group has been so outstanding that we haven't been able to add to our staff at the rate we would like to. We are working to correct this.

The Toluene Diamine Project.[24]   In the spring of 1975, at the top of Air Products' capital expenditures agenda was a proposed $90 million investment in facilities to manufacture toluene diamine (TDA), an important intermediate chemical for the polyurethane foam industry. (See Exhibit 10 for the structure of the polyurethane foam industry.)

Toluene diamine was used for the production of toluene di-isocyanate (TDI), which in turn was utilized to manufacture flexible and semi-flexible polyurethane foam products. Typical end uses for these products were automobile seats and padding, furniture and bedding such as mattresses, and cushions.

Toluene diamine was manufactured from toluene, sulfuric and nitric acids and hydrogen. The intermediate product, prior to the hydrogenation, was dinitrotoluene (DNT), which Air Products already manufactured at Pace, Florida.

Sulfuric acid was a large volume commodity chemical available from numerous suppliers while nitric acid was made from ammonia. Significantly, Air Products already produced nitric acid and had a large ammonia plant at New Orleans with secure raw material supply. Air Products also produced hydrogen both at New Orleans and LaPorte, Texas.

Air Products' initial entry into DNT manufacturing had begun with the acquisition of Escambia. After signing a base-load requirements contract in 1965 with one of the nonintegrated producers of TDI, Escambia

---

[24] Investment, capacity, and market-related information has been disguised for proprietary reasons. The relationships, however, remain unaltered.

Exhibit 10

THE STRUCTURE OF THE POLYURETHANE INDUSTRY

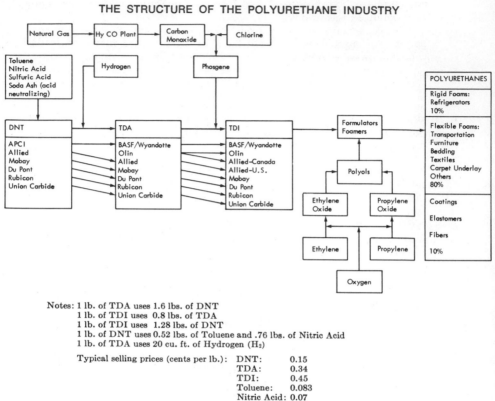

Notes: 1 lb. of TDA uses 1.6 lbs. of DNT
1 lb. of TDI uses 0.8 lbs. of TDA
1 lb. of TDI uses 1.28 lbs. of DNT
1 lb. of DNT uses 0.52 lbs. of Toluene and .76 lbs. of Nitric Acid
1 lb. of TDA uses 20 cu. ft. of Hydrogen (H₂)

Typical selling prices (cents per lb.):

DNT:	0.15
TDA:	0.34
TDI:	0.45
Toluene:	0.083
Nitric Acid:	0.07

Source: Air Products records and estimates.

had built a 20-million pounds per year plant and had disposed of the spent sulfuric acid in their agricultural products business area. Through small investments coupled with a variety of operational changes, the company subsequently expanded this plant's capacity to 50-million pounds per year. Additional DNT customers were obtained and the plant was essentially in a sold-out position. Almost all of the plant's production went to companies in the polyurethane industry. Mr. Dimopoulos commented:

> The polyurethane industry is one in which a limited number of chemical companies sell the chemical components of foam to a large number of formulators and foamers, who then make foam and foam products. The industry is highly integrated; for example, the manufacturers of TDI generally also produce DNT and TDA. Until 1973, Air Products had no experience in TDA production, but we had begun an investigation of TDA technology, and have recently licensed it from a French company.

Mr. Howard Harwell, general manager of the Industrial Chemicals Profit Center, expanded on this subject:

We had developed a sound nitration technology at Escambia which opened to us a number of business opportunities; when combined with Air Products' traditional business strategy and engineering skills, these opportunities make very good sense. Additionally, we'll be able to enter the TDA business because we're not a TDI producer and therefore not in competition with our potential customers. Historically, TDI producers had to make TDA themselves or else buy it from competition; naturally, they preferred the former.

As described by Air Products' management, a key factor in favor of the project was the expected demand for TDI. In 1974, the world market for TDI was estimated to be around 745 million pounds, having grown at a rate of 15 percent to 20 percent over the preceding decade. In the ensuing decade, management anticipated a 12 percent to 15 percent growth rate. At the 12 percent rate, demand would be about 2,170 million pounds in 1984. (See Exhibit 11.) In the past, U.S. capacity had exceeded demand with resultant strong competition and price declines. In 1974, industry production in the United States was running at about its effective capacity including the exports.

Based on this projected growth in polyurethane demand, Air Prod-

Exhibit 11

WORLDWIDE TDI DEMAND AND CAPACITY
(in millions of pounds)

	Demand			Capacity	
		Projected		Projected 1979	
	1974	1979	1984	Name plate	85% on-stream
United States..............	270	473	800	540	450
Western Europe............	275	490	770	828	700
Japan.....................	80	130	205	128	110
Other.....................	120	250	395	40	34
Subtotal............	745	1,343	2,170	1,536	1,294

NAME PLATE CAPACITIES IN THE UNITED STATES*
(millions of pounds—1974)

	DNT		TDA		TDI
Company	Capacity	Captive	Capacity	Captive	Capacity
Allied Chemical.............	60	60	40	40	50
Du Pont....................	130	85	50	50	105
Mobay.....................	120	120	75	75	100
Olin.......................	—	—	40	40	40
Rubicon...................	35	35	40	40	50
Union Carbide.............	70	70	45	45	55
BASF-Wyandotte..........	—	—	25	25	40
Air Products...............	50	—	—	—	—
Total...............	465	370	315	315	440

* Actual productive capacity was believed to be about 85 percent of name plate capacity.
Source: Disguised estimates by Air Products' corporate planning staff.

ucts' management was aware that a number of TDI producers were considering plant expansions in 1975–76. Management also believed that a major chemical company planned to enter the TDI industry. Air Products had held discussions with several TDI producers in the Gulf Coast area to explore the possibility of building a large TDA facility to satisfy their combined TDA requirements; through superior engineering technology and economies of scale, Air Products' Chemicals Group executives felt TDA could be produced more economically than each of the users could produce it individually. In addition, the company contemplating entering the TDI industry had expressed an interest in having Air Products provide the TDA for its TDI needs. The Chemicals Group's management therefore believed that an opportunity

Exhibit 12

TOLUENE

(data in 1,000 metric tons)

| Year | | United States and Puerto Rico | | | |
	Production	Sales	Imports	Exports	Consumption
1965	1,805	1,067	44	154	1,695
1966	1,920	1,189	96	167	1,849
1967	2,117	1,265	101	81	2,137
1968	2,287	1,454	106	119	2,274
1969	2,498	1,374	188	104	2,582
1970	2,729	1,416	307	74	2,962
1971	2,882	1,592	329	48	3,163
1972	2,707	—	489	85	3,111

Production: Data include both coal- and petroleum- derived toluene. Data are probably understated in most years due to the fact that some companies have not reported the production of that portion of their toluene that was fed to hydrodealkylation. In 1972, reported production of petroleum-derived toluene was 5,864,000 metric tons.

Exports: Data are the sums of reported quantities of "pure or commercially pure" toluene and "crude" toluene.

Consumption: Data are calculated as Production + Imports − Exports (data are therefore probably understated: see "Production" footnote above). Data for toluene consumption for 1966 and 1971 follow:

	1966	1971
Benzene	1,099	431
Solvent	444	477
Toluene di-isocyanate	56	99
Benzyl chloride	26	26
Phenol	23	30
Benzoic acid	16	33
Other nonfuel uses	82	214
Motor and aviation gas	103	1,853
Total	1,849	3,163

Sources: A. U.S. Tariff Commission, *Synthetic Organic Chemicals, U.S. Production and Sales* (production and sales data for 1965–1972). B. U.S. Department of Commerce, Bureau of the Census, *U.S. Imports for Consumption and General Imports*, Report FT 246 (imports data for 1965–1972). C. U.S. Department of Commerce, Bureau of the Census, *U.S. Exports, FT 410* (exports data for 1965–1972). D. Stanford Research Institute, *Chemical Economics Handbook*. E. Air Products and Chemicals, Inc.

existed for Air Products to build a TDA plant in the Gulf Coast area with about 200 million pounds per year of capacity at a cost of about $90 million to serve the needs of three or four customers, with the investment financed through long-term, take-or-pay contracts. Contract customers had, in fact, already been lined up. Access to the basic raw material for TDA, toluene, had been firmed up through contracts, although they were only for three to five years with cost escalation clauses. Toluene was widely available from refiners who normally used toluene to upgrade the octane rating of gasoline. (See Exhibit 12.) The central role played by toluene and its availability, however, were major management considerations in the TDA investment decision. Reflecting on this factor, Mr. Dempsey observed:

> In the past, the problem was just running out the learning curve on technology. This worked extremely well in industrial gases. As we move into chemicals, we have to see if we can continue to do so, since basic raw material positions are crucial. Our ability to successfully do projects like TDA will hinge on our access to hydrocarbon feedstocks.

CHEMICAL INDUSTRY CHARACTERISTICS

An examination of the chemical industry indicates that the industry is composed of a variety of chemical producers participating at various stages of the "process chain." Because of the number of competitors, industry prices and the strategies adopted by various firms.

It is important to note that company strategies are related to either product differentiation (Du Pont), preferred raw material positions in commodities (Dow), dominant market positions in specific product or geographic segments (Big Three, Air Products), or some combination (Monsanto, Union Carbide). The economics of each of these strategies vary with implications for profitability and resource requirements of the respective firms.

For companies pursuing a differentiated or specialty product strategy, a strong R&D and technological capability is a prerequisite. Investment *product* research is seen as a basic part of business. In some instances, product distinctions are achieved through development of patented and/or brand name products. Du Pont's strategy is an example of this approach. This strategy often insulates the company from price competition which allows the firm to enjoy significant profit advantages. The potential weakness of this strategy lies in its reliance on other companies for its basic raw materials and intermediate chemicals; resources and skills tend to be oriented toward marketing and research.

The preferred raw material position and/or commodity chemical strategy has significantly different requirements. Sales of these products, such as chlorine and PVC, are based on having the lowest costs and dominant market share. Economies of scale in plants are crucial; the result is continuing investment in larger and larger plants. The focus of research efforts tends to be on "process" technology or ways to obtain the lowest cost of production. Capital spending on plants tends to be very substantial for companies pursuing this approach. One weakness of this strategy is that because the products are basically the same from producer to producer, price competition is severe.

In the specific product or geographic strategy, the requirement for success is based upon having a dominant market share. The products sold may be either differentiated or commodity type items, with profitable marketing due to low transportation costs, service, reliability, or competitive advantage in a specific class of product (industrial gases, carbon). For these companies, a key element of success is being able to supply the product with an edge on competition due to engineering features, technical capabilities, or service features. Many of these companies produce intermediate chemicals, rather than end-use consumer products.

In general, chemical industry processing costs are a major portion of total costs. Value added can be high, which accounts for the profitability enjoyed by the chemical industry, which in turn has allowed the large investments in R&D and plants.

The company and its environment: Relating opportunities to resources

DETERMINATION of a suitable strategy for a company begins in identifying the opportunities and risks in its environment. This chapter is concerned with the identification of a range of strategic alternatives, the narrowing of this range by recognizing the constraints imposed by corporate capability, and the determination of one or more economic strategies at acceptable levels of risk. We shall examine the complexity and variety of the environmental forces which must be considered and the problems in accurately assessing company strengths and weaknesses. Economic strategy will be seen as *the match between qualification and opportunity that positions a firm in its environment*. We shall attempt in passing to categorize the kinds of economic strategies that can result from the combination of internal capability and external market needs, and to relate these categories to the normal course of corporate development.

THE NATURE OF THE COMPANY'S ENVIRONMENT

The environment of an organization in business, like that of any other organic entity, is the pattern of all the external conditions and influences that affect its life and development. The environmental influences relevant to strategic decision operate in a company's industry, the total business community, its city, its country, and the world. They are technological, economic, social, and political in kind. The corporate strategist is usually at least intuitively aware of these features of the current environment. But in all these categories change is taking place at varying rates—fastest in technology, less rapidly in politics. Change in the environment of business necessitates continuous monitoring of a company's definition of its business, lest it falter, blur, or become obsolete. Since by definition the formulation of strategy is performed with the future in mind, executives who take part in the strategic planning process must be aware of those aspects of their company's environment especially susceptible to the kind of change that will affect their company's future.

Technology. From the point of view of the corporate strategist, technological developments are not only the fastest unfolding but the most far-reaching in extending or contracting opportunity for an established company. They include the discoveries of science, the impact of related product development, the less dramatic machinery and process improvements, and the progress of automation and data processing. We see in technical advance an accelerating rate of change—with new developments arriving before the implications of yesterday's changes can be assimilated. Industries hitherto protected from obsolescence by stable technologies or by the need for huge initial capital investment become more vulnerable more quickly than before to new processes or to cross-industry competition. Science gives the impetus to change not only in technology but also in all the other aspects of business activity.

Major areas of technical advance foreseen by students of the management of technology include increased mastery of energy, its conservation and more efficient use, the reorganization of transportation, technical solutions to problems of product life, safety, and serviceability; the further mechanization of logistical functions and the processing of information, alteration in the characteristics of physical and biological materials, and radical developments in controlling air, water, and noise pollution. The primary impact upon established strategies will be increased competition and more rapid obsolescence. The risks dramatized by these technical trends are offset by new business opportunities opened up for companies that are aggressive innovators or adept at technical hitchhiking. The need intensifies for any company either to engage in technical development or to maintain a technical intelligence capability enabling it to follow quickly new developments pioneered by others.

Economics. Because business is more accustomed to monitoring economic trends than those in other spheres, it is less likely to be taken by surprise by such massive developments as the internationalization of competition, the return of China and Russia to trade with the West, the slower than projected development of the Third World countries, the Americanization of demand and culture in the developing countries and the resulting backlash of nationalism, the increased importance of the large multinational corporations and the consequences of the host country hostility, the recurrence of recession, and the persistence of inflation in all phases of the business cycle. The consequences of world economic trends need to be monitored in more detail for an industry or company.

Society. Social developments of which strategists keep aware include such influential forces as the quest for equality for minority groups, the demand of women for opportunity and recognition, the changing patterns of work and leisure, the effects of urbanization upon the individual, family, and neighborhood, the rise of crime, the decline of conventional morality, and the changing composition of world population.

Politics. The political forces important to the business firm are similarly extensive and complex—the changing relations between communist and noncommunist countries (East and West) and between the prosperous and poor countries (North and South), the relation between private enterprise and government, between workers and management, the impact of national planning on corporate planning, and the rise of what George Lodge calls the communitarian ideology.[1]

Although it is not possible to know or spell out here the significance of such technical, economic, social, and political trends, and possibilities for the strategist of a given business or company, some simple things are clear. Changing values will lead to different expectations of the role business should perform. Business will be expected to perform its mission not only with economy in the use of energy but with sensitivity to the ecological environment. Organizations in all walks of life will be called upon to be more explicit about their goals and to meet the needs and aspirations (for example, for education) of their membership.

In any case, change threatens all established strategies. We know that a thriving company—itself a living system—is bound up in a variety of interrelationships with larger systems comprising its technological, economic, social, and political environment. If environmental developments are destroying and creating business opportunities, advance notice of specific instances relevant to a single company is essential to intelligent planning. Risk and opportunity in the last quarter of the 20th century requires of executives a keen interest in what is going on outside their companies. More than that, a practical means of tracking developments promising good or ill, and profit or loss, needs to be devised.

TRACKING THE CHANGING ENVIRONMENT

Unfortunately the development of knowledge in a flourishing business civilization has produced no easy methodology for continuous surveillance of the trends in the environment of central importance to a firm of ordinary capabilities. Predictive theories of special disciplines such as economics, sociology, psychology, and anthropology do not produce comprehensive appraisal readily applicable to long-range corporate strategic decision. At the same time many techniques do exist to deal with parts of the problem—economic and technological forecasting, detailed demographic projections, geological estimates of raw material reserves, national and international statistics in which trends may be discerned. More information about the environment is available than is commonly used.

John D. Glover has developed an approach to the total environment

---

[1] George C. Lodge, *The New American Ideology* (New York: Alfred A. Knopf, Inc., 1975).

of a business firm as an ecological system.[2] His framework consists of
four subsystems (the immediate total community of a company, the
culture in which it operates, the flow of goods and services being produced or consumed, the natural and manmade physical setting). For
each of these categories an enormous amount of data is available, with
projections of future movement. Schemes such as Glover's provide
the means for planning staffs to reduce to rational analysis what
is now practicing managers' intuitive and fragmentary vision of the
developing forces offering opportunity to their firms and taking it
away.

Further study of the problem of strategic information will take you
to Aguilar's research in how managers in the chemical industry obtained strategic information about environmental change.[3] Aguilar
found that even in this technically sensitive industry, few firms attempted any systematic means for gathering and evaluating such information. Publications provided only about 20 percent of the information from all sources, with current market and competitive information from personal sources dominating the total input of information.
Internally generated information comprised only 9 percent of the total,
and more information received was unsolicited than solicited. (Interestingly enough, very few people in subordinate positions felt they were
getting useful strategic information from their superiors.)

Aguilar's findings were corroborated by Robert Collings' study of investment firms.[4] The obvious moral of these studies is that the process
of obtaining strategic information is far from being systematic, complete, or even really informative about anything except current developments, at least in these industries. These researchers show that it is
possible to organize better the gathering and integrating of environmental data through such means as bringing miscellaneous scanning
activities together and communicating available information internally.

Certain large companies organize this function. General Electric has
maintained for years a Business Environment Section at its corporate
headquarters and prepares reports on predicted changes for use by its
divisions. Consulting firms, future-oriented research organizations, and
associations of planners provide guidance for looking ahead. The sense
of futility experienced by executives in the face of complexity is reduced when they begin the task by defining their strategy and the most
likely strategic alternatives they will be debating in the foreseeable future. Decision on direction spotlights the relevant environment. You
cannot know everything, but if you are thinking of going into the furniture business in Nebraska, you will not be immoderately concerned

---

[2] Most of this work is unpublished, but Glover's approach is summarized in
"Strategic Decision-Making: Planning, Manning, Organization," in John D. Glover
and Gerald A. Simon, *Chief Executives' Handbook* (Homewood, Ill.: Dow Jones-
Irwin, Inc., 1976), pp. 423–41.

[3] Frank J. Aguilar, *Scanning the Business Environment* (New York: The Mac-
millan Company, 1967).

[4] Robert Collings, "Scanning the Environment for Strategic Information" (unpublished doctoral thesis, Harvard Business School).

about the rate of family formation in Japan. Clarification of present strategy and the few new alternatives it suggests narrows sharply the range of necessary information and destroys the excuse that there is too much to know.

IDENTIFICATION OF OPPORTUNITIES AND RISKS

For the firm that has not determined what its strategy dictates it needs to know or has not embarked upon the systematic surveillance of environmental change, a few simple questions kept constantly in mind will highlight changing opportunity and risk. For the student of cases, conveniently presented with the most important information needing interpretation, these questions should lead in short order to an estimate of opportunity and danger in the present and predicted company setting.

1. *What are the essential economic and technical characteristics of the industry in which the company participates?*

Whether these are in flux or not, they may define the restrictions and opportunities confronting the individual company, and will certainly suggest strategy for it. For example, knowledge that the cement industry requires high investment in plant, proximity to a certain combination of raw materials, a relatively small labor force, and enormous fuel and transportation costs suggests where to look for new plant sites and what will constitute competitive advantage and disadvantage. The nature of this product may suggest for a given company the wisdom of developing efficient pipeline and truck transportation and cheap energy sources rather than engaging in extensive research to achieve product differentiation or aggressive price competition to increase market share.

2. *What trends suggesting future change in economic and technical characteristics are apparent?*

Changes in demand for the product of one industry in competition with the products of another, and changes in the product itself, occurring as a result of research and development, affect the chance for growth. For example, the glass container industry's development years ago of strong, light, disposable bottles and more recently combinations of glass and plastic recouped part of the market lost by glass to the metal container. The need for the glass industry to engage in this development effort was made apparent by the observable success of the metal beer can. Similarly the easy-opening metal container suggested the need for an easily removable bottle cap. The physical characteristics of any product can be examined against the master trend toward simplicity, convenience, and serviceability in consumer goods and against competitive innovations. Both the glass bottle and the metal container face increasingly formal attack by environmentalists, who constitute a noneconomic and nontechnical force to be reckoned with.

3. *What is the nature of competition both within the industry and across industries?*

A small rubber company, in an industry led by Uniroyal, Goodyear, Goodrich, and Firestone, will not, under the economic condition of overcapacity, elect to provide the automobile business with original tires for new cars. The structure of competition, quite apart from the resources of the firm, may suggest that a relatively small firm should seek out a niche of relatively small attraction to the majors, and concentrate its powers on that limited segment of the market.

Present and developing competition usually extends, of course, beyond the industry in which a company finds itself. For example, the competition for the cement industry from producers of asphalt road-building materials is as important as that from other cement producers.

4. *What are the requirements for success in competition in the company's industry?*

In every industry some critical tasks must be performed particularly well to ensure survival. In the ladies' belt and handbag business style and design are critical, but so (less obviously) are relationships with department store buyers. In the computer business, a sales force able to diagnose customer requirements for information systems, to design a suitable system, and to equip a customer to use it is more important than the circuitry of hardware.

Although the question of what tasks are most critical may be chiefly useful as a means of identifying risks or possible causes of failure, it may also suggest opportunity. Imagination in perceiving new requirements for success under changing conditions, when production-oriented competitors have not done so, can give a company leadership position. For example, opportunity for a local radio station and the strategy it needed to follow changed sharply with the rise of television, and those who first diagnosed the new requirements paid much less for stations than was later necessary.

5. *Given the technical, economic, social, and political developments that most directly apply, what is the range of strategy available to any company in this industry?*

The force of this question is obvious in the drug industry. The speed and direction of pharmaceutical research, the structure of the industry, the characteristics of worldwide demand, the different and changing ideas about how adequate medical care should be made available to the world's population, the concern about price, and the nature of government regulation suggest constraints within which a range of opportunity is still vividly clear. Similarly, in a more stable industry, there is always a choice. To determine its limits, an examination of environmental characteristics and developments is essential.

OPPORTUNITY AS A DETERMINANT OF STRATEGY

Awareness of the environment is not a special project to be undertaken only when warning of change becomes deafening; it is a continuing requirement for informed choice of purpose. Planned exploitation of changing opportunity ordinarily follows a predictable course which provides increasing awareness of areas to which a company's capabilities may be profitably extended. A useful way to perceive the normal course of development is to use Bruce Scott's stages referred to briefly above.

The manufacturer of a single product (Stage I) sold within a clearly defined geographical area to meet a known demand finds it relatively easy to identify opportunity and risk. As an enterprise develops a degree of complexity requiring functional division of management decision, it encounters as an integrated Stage II company a number of strategic alternatives in its market environments which the Stage I proprietor is too hard pressed to notice and almost too overcommitted to consider. Finally, Stage III companies, deployed along the full range of diversification, find even a greater number of possibilities for serving a market profitably than the resources they possess or have in sight will support. The more one finds out what might be done, the harder it is to make the final choice.

The diversified Stage III company has another problem different from that of trying to make the best choice among many. If it has divisionalized its operations and strategies, as sooner or later in the course of diversification it must, then divisional opportunities come into competition with each other.

The corporate management will wish to invest profits not distributed to stockholders in those opportunities that will produce the greatest return to the corporation. If need be, corporate management will be willing to let an individual division decline if its future looks less attractive than that of others. The division on the other hand will wish to protect its own market position, ward off adverse developments, prolong its own existence, and provide for its growth. The division manager, who is not rewarded for failures, may program projects of safe but usually not dramatic prospects. The claims regarding projected return on investment, which are submitted in all honesty as the divisional estimate of future opportunity, can be assumed to be biased by the division's regard for its own interest and the manager's awareness of measurement.

The corporate management cannot be expected to be able to make independent judgments about all the proposals for growth which are submitted by all the divisions. On the other hand, all divisions cannot be given their heads, if the corporation's needs for present profit are to be met and if funds for reinvestment are limited. In any case, the greatest knowledge about the opportunities for a given technology and set of markets should be found at the divisional level.[5]

The strategic dilemma of a conglomerate world enterprise is the most complex in the full range of policy decisions. When the variety of what must be known cannot be reduced by a sharply focused strategy to the capacity of a single mind and when the range of a company's activities spans many industries and technologies, the problems of formulating a coherent strategy begin to get out of hand. Here strategy must become a managed process rather than the decision of the chief executive officer and his immediate associates. Bower and Prahalad[6] have shown in important research how the context of decision can be con-

[5] See Norman Berg, "Strategic Planning in Conglomerate Companies," *Harvard Business Review*, May–June 1965.

[6] Joseph L. Bower, *Managing the Resource Allocation Process* (Boston: Division of Research, Harvard Business School, 1970); and C. K. Prahalad, "The Strategic Process in a Multinational Corporation" (unpublished doctoral thesis, Harvard Business School 1975), partially summarized in "Strategic Choices in Diversified MNCs," *Harvard Business Review*, July–August 1976, pp. 67–78.

trolled by the top management group and how power can be distributed through a hierarchy to influence the kind of strategic decision that will survive in the system. The process of strategic decision can, like complex operations, be organized in such a way as to provide appropriate complementary roles for decentralization and control.

To conceive of a new development in response to market information and prediction of the future is a creative act. To commit resources to it only on the basis of projected return and the estimate of probability constituting risk of failure is foolhardy. More than economic analysis of potential return is required for decision, for economic opportunity abounds, far beyond the ability to capture it. That much money might be made in a new field or growth industry does not mean that a company with abilities developed in a different field is going to make it. We turn now to the critical factors that for an individual company make one opportunity better than another.

But, do we have the horses?

IDENTIFYING CORPORATE COMPETENCE AND RESOURCES

The first step in validating a tentative choice among several opportunities is to determine whether the organization has the capacity to prosecute it successfully. The capability of an organization is its demonstrated and potential ability to accomplish, against the opposition of circumstance or competition, whatever it sets out to do. Every organization has actual and potential strengths and weaknesses. Since it is prudent in formulating strategy to extend or maximize the one and contain or minimize the other, it is important to try to determine what they are and to distinguish one from the other.

It is just as possible, though if anything more difficult, for a company to know its own strengths and limitations as it is to maintain a workable surveillance of its changing environment. Subjectivity, lack of confidence, and unwillingness to face reality may make it hard for organizations as well as for individuals to know themselves. But just as it is essential, though difficult, that a maturing person achieve reasonable self-awareness, so an organization can identify approximately its central strength and critical vulnerability.

Howard H. Stevenson has made the first formal study of management practice in defining corporate strengths and weaknesses as part of the strategic planning process.[7] He looked at five aspects of the process: (1) the attributes of the company which its managers examined, (2) the organizational scope of the strengths and weaknesses identified, (3) the measurement employed in the process of definition, (4) the criteria for telling a strength from a weakness, and (5) the sources of relevant information. As might be expected, the process Stevenson was looking at was imperfectly and variously practiced in the half dozen companies he studied. He found that the problems of

---

[7] Howard H. Stevenson, "Defining Corporate Strengths and Weaknesses: An Exploratory Study" (an unpublished doctoral thesis deposited in Baker Library, Harvard Business School, 1969). For a published summary article of the same title, see *Sloan Management Review,* Spring 1976.

definition of corporate strengths and weaknesses, very different from those of other planning processes, center mostly upon a general lack of agreement on suitable definition, criteria, and information. For an art that has hardly made a beginning, Stevenson offers a prescriptive model for integrating the considerations affecting definition of strength or weakness. Indicative of the primitive stage of some of our concepts for general management, Stevenson's most important conclusion is that the attempt to define strengths and weaknesses is more useful than the usual final product of the process.

Stevenson's exploratory study in no way diminishes the importance of appraising organization capability. It protects us against oversimplification. The absence of criteria and measures, the disinclination for appraising competence except in relation to specific problems, the uncertainty about what is meant by "strength" and "weakness," and the reluctance to imply criticism of individuals or organizational subunits —all these hampered his study but illuminated the problem. Much of what is intuitive in this process is yet to be identified.

To make an effective contribution to strategic planning, the key attributes to be appraised should be identified and consistent criteria established for judging them. If attention is directed to strategies, policy commitments, and past practices in the context of discrepancy between organization goals and attainment, an outcome useful to an individual manager's strategic planning is possible. The assessment of strengths and weaknesses associated with the attainment of specific objectives becomes in Stevenson's words a "key link in a feedback loop" which allows managers to learn from the success or failures of the policies they institute.

Although this study does not find or establish a systematic way of developing or using such knowledge, members of organizations develop judgments about what the company can do particularly well—its core of competence. If consensus can be reached about this capability, no matter how subjectively arrived at, its application to identified opportunity can be estimated.

Sources of capabilities. The powers of a company constituting a resource for growth and diversification accrue primarily from experience in making and marketing a product line. They inhere as well in (1) the developing strengths and weaknesses of the individuals comprising the organization, (2) the degree to which individual capability is effectively applied to the common task, and (3) the quality of coordination of individual and group effort.

The experience gained through successful execution of a strategy centered upon one goal may unexpectedly develop capabilities which could be applied to different ends. Whether they should be so applied is another question. For example, a manufacturer of salt can strengthen his competitive position by offering his customers salt-dispensing equipment. If, in the course of making engineering improvements in this equipment, a new solenoid principle is perfected that has application to many industrial switching problems, should this patentable and marketable innovation be exploited? The answer would turn not only on whether economic analysis of the opportunity shows this to be a durable and profitable possibility, but also on whether the organization can muster the financial, manufacturing, and marketing strength to exploit the discovery. The former question is likely to have a more positive answer than the latter. In this connection, it seems important to remember that individual and unsupported flashes of strength are not as dependable as the gradually accumulated product- and market-related fruits of experience.

Even where competence to exploit an opportunity is nurtured by experience in related fields, the level of that competence may be too low for any great reliance to be placed upon it. Thus a chain of children's clothing stores might well acquire the administrative, merchandising, buying, and selling skills that would permit it to add departments in women's wear. Similarly, a sales force effective in distributing typewriters may gain proficiency in selling office machinery and supplies. But even here it would be well to ask what distinctive ability these companies could bring to the retailing of soft goods or office equipment to attract customers away from a plethora of competitors.

Identifying strengths. The distinctive competence of an organization is more than what it can do; it is what it can do particularly well. To identify the less obvious or by-product strengths of an organization that may well be transferable to some more profitable new opportunity, one might well begin by examining the organization's current product line and by defining the functions it serves in its markets. Almost any important consumer product has functions which are related to others into which a qualified company might move. The typewriter, for example, is more than the simple machine for mechanizing handwriting that it once appeared to be when looked at only from the point of view of its designer and manufacturer. Closely analyzed from the point of view of the potential user, the typewriter is found to contribute to a broad range of information processing functions. Any one of these might have suggested an area to be exploited by a typewriter manufacturer. Tacitly defining a typewriter as a replacement for a fountain pen as a writing instrument rather than as an input-output device for word processing is the explanation provided by hindsight for the failure of the old-line typewriter companies to develop the electric typewriter and the computer-related input-output devices it made possible before IBM did. The definition of product which would lead to identification of transferable skills must be expressed in terms of the market needs it may fill rather than the engineering specifications to which it conforms.

Besides looking at the uses or functions to which present products contribute, the would-be diversifier might profitably identify the skills that underlie whatever success has been achieved. The qualifications of an organization efficient at performing its long-accustomed tasks come to be taken for granted and considered humdrum, like the steady provision of first-class service. The insight required to identify the essential strength justifying new ventures does not come naturally. Its cultivation can probably be helped by recognition of the need for analysis. In any case, we should look beyond the company's capacity to invent new products. Product leadership is not possible for a majority of companies, so it is fortunate that patentable new products are not the only major highway to new opportunities. Other avenues include new marketing services, new methods of distribution, new values in quality-price combinations, and creative merchandising. The effort to find or to create a competence that is truly distinctive may hold the real key to a company's success or even to its future development. For example, the ability of a cement manufacturer to run a truck fleet more effectively than its competitors may constitute one of its principal competitive strengths in selling an undifferentiated product.

Matching opportunity and competence.   The way to narrow the range of alternatives, made extensive by imaginative identification of new possibilities, is to match opportunity to competence, once each has been accurately identified and its future significance estimated. It is this combination which establishes a company's economic mission and its position in its environment. The combination is designed to minimize organizational weakness and to maximize strength. In every case, risk attends it. And when opportunity seems to outrun present distinctive competence, the willingness to gamble that the latter can be built up to the required level is almost indispensable to a strategy that challenges the organization and the people in it. Figure 2 diagrams the matching of opportunity and resources that results in an economic strategy.

Before we leave the creative act of putting together a company's unique internal capability and evolving opportunity in the external world, we should note that—aside from distinctive competence—the principal resources found in any company are money and people—technical and managerial people. At this stage of economic development, money seems less a problem than technical competence, and the latter much less critical than managerial ability. In reading the cases that follow, by all means look carefully at the financial records of each company and take note of its success and its problems. Look also at the apparent managerial capacity and, without underestimating it, do not assume that it can rise to any occasion. The diversification of American industry is marked by hundreds of instances in which a company strong in one endeavor lacked the ability to manage an enterprise requiring different skills. The right to make handsome profits over a long period must be earned. Opportunism without competence is a path to fairyland.

Besides equating an appraisal of market opportunity and organizational capability, the decision to make and market a particular product or service should be accompanied by an identification of the nature of the business and the kind of company its management desires. Such a guiding concept is a product of many considerations, including the managers' personal values. As such, this concept will change more slowly than other aspects of the organization, and it will give coherence to all the variety of company activities. For example, a president who is determined to make his or her firm into a worldwide producer and fabricator of a basic metal, through policies differentiating it from the industry leader, will not be distracted by excess capacity in developed markets, low metal prices, and cutthroat competition in certain markets.

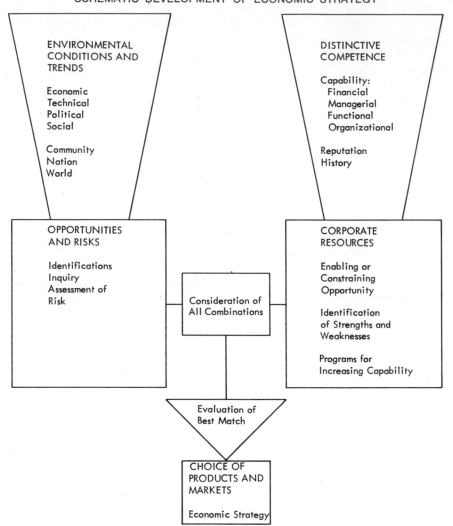

Figure 2

SCHEMATIC DEVELOPMENT OF ECONOMIC STRATEGY

Such a firm would not be sidetracked into acquiring, for example, the Pepsi-Cola franchise in Africa, even if this business promised to yield a good profit. (That such a firm should have an experimental division exploring offshoot technology is, however, entirely appropriate.)

Uniqueness of strategy. In each company, the way in which distinctive competence, organizational resources, and organizational values are combined is or should be unique. Differences among companies are as numerous as differences among individuals. The combinations of opportunity to which distinctive competences, resources, and values may be applied are equally extensive. Generalizing about how to make an effective match is less rewarding than working at it. The effort is a highly stimulating and challenging exercise. The outcome will be unique for each case and each situation, but each achievement of a viable economic strategy will leave the student of strategy better prepared to take part in real-life strategic decisions.

APPLICATION TO CASES

Students could profitably bring to the cases they study not only the questions suggested earlier, but the following as well:

> What really is our product? What functions does it serve? To what additional functions might it be extended or adapted?
>
> What is happening to the market for our products? Is it expanding or contracting? Why?
>
> What are our company's major strengths and weaknesses? From what sources do these arise?
>
> Do we have a distinctive or core competence? If so, to what new activities can it be applied?
>
> What are our principal competitors' major strengths and weaknesses? Are they imitating us or we them? What comparative advantage over our competitors can we exploit?
>
> What is our strategy? Is the combination of product and market an optimum economic strategy? Is the central nature of our business clear enough to provide us with a criterion for product diversification?
>
> What, if any, better combinations of market opportunities and distinctive competence can our company effect, within a range of reasonable risk?

These questions will prove helpful throughout the course in the task of designing an economic strategy. However, they are never wholly sufficient, for the strategic decision is never wholly economic in character.

Note on the Mechanical Writing Instrument Industry

> Competition in this industry is fierce. Materials and labor costs keep rising, and prices keep falling. The situation is a terrible headache, but new companies keep appearing because it's a high-growth market. They're willing to take the risk. As long as there is one firm making it, they think they can, too.
>
> *Frank King**

THE mechanical writing instrument industry involved the manufacture and sale of four basic product types: fountain pens, ball-point pens, soft tip pens,[1] and mechanical pencils; and their component parts.[2] Each product was introduced in the marketplace to meet a new and specific writing need, rather than to replace an existing product. The fountain pen, for example, was traditionally used in signing documents and letters, while the ball-point pen was used in making carbon copies, the soft tip pen in marking and underlining, and the mechanical pencils in working with figures.

In 1973, approximately 200 companies were engaged in the manufacture and sale of mechanical writing instruments, of which 131 made refillable ball-point pens, 102 nonrefillable ball-point pens, 22 ordinary fountain pens, 16 cartridge-filled fountain pens, 78 thick line markers, 99 fine line porous pens, and 85 mechanical pencils. It was uncommon for firms to manufacture all of the four basic product types. Most firms competed selectively in the industry on the basis of: (1) product type: fountain pen, ball-point pen, soft tip pen, and mechanical pencil; (2) price range: low (<$0.50), medium ($0.50–$1.00), and high (>$1.00); and (3) market: retail, commercial, advertising/specialty, premium, export, government, and military.

---

* Executive Vice President, Writing Instrument Manufacturers Association.

[1] *Soft tip pens* were defined as broad line felt tip markers and fine line porous point pens.

[2] Wooden pencils were customarily considered as a separate industry, the non-mechanical writing instrument industry. The 1973 annual growth rate in manufacturers' dollar sales was 2 percent.

HISTORY OF MECHANICAL WRITING INSTRUMENTS

Product evolution

The first writing instruments had their origins lost in antiquity, but could be traced through drawings and crude messages smeared with natural colored ore by a finger or scratched by a sharpened stone fragment onto cave walls. The first known instrument, the stylus, appeared around 340 B.C., and was used to make impressions on wax and clay tablets. About 300 B.C., the Egyptians invented papyrus, the forerunner of modern paper and the standard medium for carrying the written word, which marked the beginning of the development of more sophisticated writing tools. Graphite, the main ingredient in the modern-day pencil, was introduced around 1400 A.D., the first fountain pen around 1650 A.D., and the mechanical pencil at the turn of the 20th century. The ball-point pen was introduced in 1945, the soft tip pen in the mid-1960s, and the combination pen[3] in 1969. Proposed future writing instrument products are presented in the Appendix.

Product life cycle

Mechanical writing instrument product types tended to follow similar life cycle patterns in the marketplace:

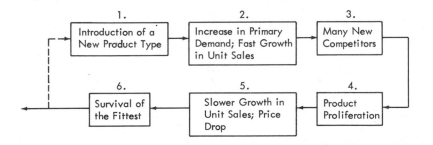

The one exception to this pattern was the fountain pen, whose average price increased relative to a decline in unit sales. As industry prices began to polarize into the high and low price ranges, the low price/high volume manufacturers tended to drop their fountain pen lines, which left only the high price/low volume manufacturers competing in that market.

Exhibits 1–4 present information on manufacturers' dollar sales, unit sales, and average prices by product from 1954 through 1973. During that period, total dollar sales increased from $117.1 million to $353.3 million; total unit sales from 261.7 million to 2,342.4 million, and the average writing instrument price decreased from $0.45 to $0.15.

---

[3] The combination pen had a rotating carbide ball point, which wrote with the flow of a marker using water-based ink, had the hard feel and carbon-making feature of a ball-point pen, and the overall feel and writing effect of a fountain pen.

Exhibit 1
MANUFACTURERS' SALES IN DOLLARS—BY PRODUCT

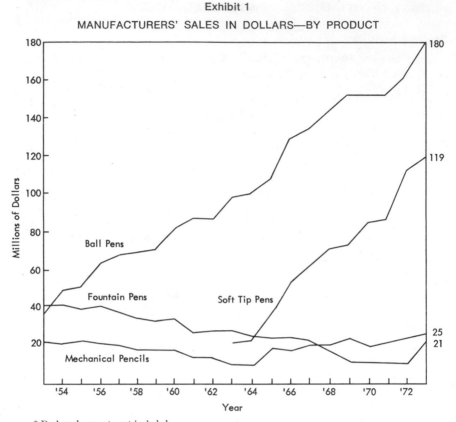

* Desk and pen sets not included.
Source: Writing Instrument Manufacturers Association.

The price war

The price war in the mechanical writing instrument industry began
in the early 1960s with the overwhelming success of the BIC 19 cent
stick pen. It was BIC Pen Corporation's objective "to place a generic
name (BIC) on all the cheap 'no-name'[4] ball-point pens in the industry." Using heavy advertising, BIC created the concept of the "disposable pen" as well as quantity selling in multipacks. By stimulating
primary demand, BIC encouraged many other firms to enter the low-
priced ball-point pen market, which represented the fastest growing
segment of the mechanical writing instrument industry at the time.
Several well-established writing instrument manufacturers, namely
A. T. Cross, Sheaffer, and Parker, chose not to follow suit and continued
to position their products in the high-price segment, where margins
rather than sheer volume could be relied upon to produce profits.

[4] No-name products were those which were not advertised and were marketed
at retail prices far below the comparable, inexpensive, nationally advertised products.

Exhibit 2

UNIT SALES—BY PRODUCT

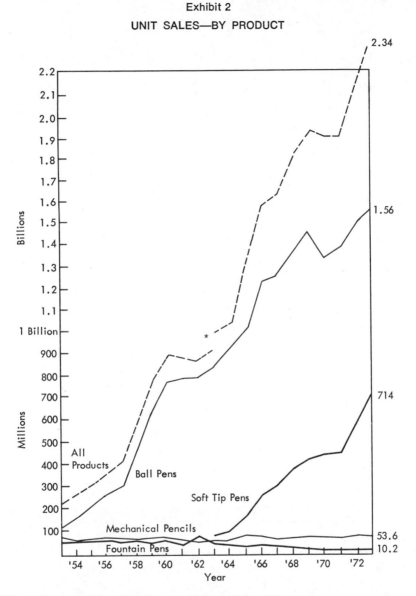

* Unit sales line for "All Products" adjusted in 1963 to include soft tip pens.
Source: Writing Instrument Manufacturers Association.

The price war history repeated itself with soft tip pens in the early 1970s. By 1973, industry officials believed that ball-point pen prices had fallen as far as they would go, although soft tip pen prices were still dropping. The price wars were thought to be manufacturer imposed, particularly by high volume producers such as BIC, rather than con-

Exhibit 3

AVERAGE PRICE—BY PRODUCT

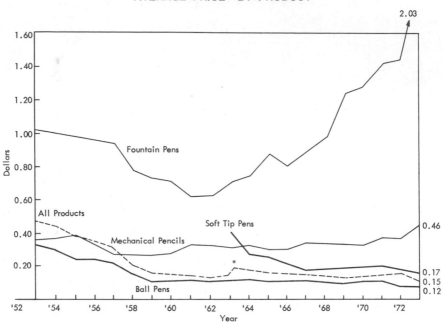

* All-product line adjusted in 1963 to include calculation for soft tip pens.
Source: Writing Instrument Manufacturers Association.

sumer influenced, which accounted for the fact that prices in the low price market segment were never raised despite inflation. Almost all porous point pens and 93 percent of all ball-point pens retailed for less than $1 each in 1973.

The competition

No single manufacturer dominated the mechanical writing instrument industry in 1973. Rather, individual manufacturers dominated specific industry segments, which were identified by product type, price range, and market. In most cases, purchases were made on the basis of individual products, rather than on the basis of a manufacturer's complete product line.

Industry market shares were subject to wide fluctuation. Those innovative firms which had made an early entry into newly discovered markets, and had subsequently supported their new products with heavy national advertising, tended to become the dominant forces in those markets. BIC Pen, for example, dominated all markets in low-priced ball-point pens, as did Gillette in fine line porous point pens. Exhibit 5 presents the 1973 primary corporate focus of major writing instrument competitors, with respect to product line, market, product price range, advertising program, and new products.

Table 1
ANNUAL GROWTH RATE (percent)

Product line	1969	1970	1971	1972	1973	5-Year average	1973* Unit sales	1973* $ sales	1973* Average price
Fountain pens	(29.8)%	(17.8)%	(0.6)%	(3.1)%	4.7%	(9.3)%	0.4%	6.2%	$2.03
Mechanical pencils	17.2	11.8	(3.6)	6.8	(9.9)	(0.3)	2.3	7.2	0.46
Ball-point pens	7.3	(4.3)	0.3	7.1	4.7	3.8	66.7	52.3	0.12
Refillables	5.0	(10.0)	(2.2)	8.9	1.2	1.0	31.5	32.0	0.15
Nonrefillables	10.0	2.0	2.9	5.5	8.1	6.8	35.2	20.3	0.09
Soft tip pens	11.7	4.5	1.6	33.5	19.7	14.2	30.6	34.3	0.17
Broad line markers	(5.4)	(10.0)	(2.7)	17.7	74.0	14.7	9.0	9.8	0.16
Porous point pens	20.0	10.0	3.0	38.1	6.0	15.4	21.6	24.5	0.17
Total industry	10.8%	(2.7)%	1.0%	13.3%	8.4%	6.2%	100.0%	100.0%	$0.15

* Excludes desk and dip pen sets.
Source: Writing Instrument Manufacturers Association.

Exhibit 4

MECHANICAL WRITING INSTRUMENT INDUSTRY STATISTICS
(dollars and units in millions)

	1954		1955		1956		1957		1958	
	Estimated number of units shipped	Estimated total $ value at factory prices (exclusive of tax)	Estimated number of units shipped	Estimated total $ value at factory prices (exclusive of tax)	Estimated number of units shipped	Estimated total $ value at factory prices (exclusive of tax)	Estimated number of units shipped	Estimated total $ value at factory prices (exclusive of tax)	Estimated number of units shipped	Estimated total $ value at factory prices (exclusive of tax)
Fountain pens...........	40.3	$ 41.7	40.8	$ 40.2	42.8	$ 41.5	40.9	$ 38.2	44.9	$ 35.0
Ball-point pens.........	162.0	48.9	210.7	50.6	265.9	63.5	300.5	67.7	485.6	65.0
Mechanical pencils......	57.6	22.0	55.8	22.5	64.0	21.8	67.8	20.7	64.6	18.9
Desk and dip pen sets....	1.8	4.5	2.3	4.8	3.2	6.2	2.9	6.5	2.5	4.1
	261.7	$117.1	309.6	$118.1	375.9	$133.0	412.1	$133.1	597.6	$123.0

	1959		1960		1961		1962		1963	
	Estimated number of units shipped	Estimated total $ value at factory prices (exclusive of tax)	Estimated number of units shipped	Estimated total $ value at factory prices (exclusive of tax)	Estimated number of units shipped	Estimated total $ value at factory prices (exclusive of tax)	Estimated number of units shipped	Estimated total $ value at factory prices (exclusive of tax)	Estimated number of units shipped	Estimated total $ value at factory prices (exclusive of tax)
Fountain pens...........	44.3	$ 33.5	48.7	$ 35.1	43.9	$ 28.1	46.4	$ 29.6	37.7	$ 27.8
Ball-point pens.........	657.2	71.0	761.9	81.6	775.2	86.1	779.3	85.7	846.2	97.8
Soft tip pens*..........									55.0	21.7
Mechanical pencils......	63.8	18.8	60.1	18.7	45.1	15.1	45.1	15.0	50.7	15.5
Desk and dip pen sets....	8.1	5.0	4.1	3.7	3.2	2.6	2.9	3.0	1.3	2.8
	773.5	$128.3	874.8	$139.1	867.4	$131.9	873.7	$133.3	990.9	$165.6

	1964		1965		1966		1967		1968	
Fountain pens	33.1	$ 25.4	27.8	$ 24.2	29.7	$ 24.2	25.7	$ 22.9	17.6	$ 17.4
Ball-point pens†	914.7	100.7	1,051.5	106.8	1,217.2	126.4				
Refillable							662.2	80.6	725.0	89.6
Nonrefillable							577.4	52.0	623.6	53.4
Soft tip pens*	6.5	22.8								
Markers (thick line)			75.2	22.1	79.6	24.2	103.0	26.2	123.5	28.8
Porous point pens			82.5	15.2	169.6	28.8	195.0	34.9	253.4	41.9
Mechanical pencils	47.2	16.0	64.0	18.9	61.4	18.2	56.4	20.4	55.9	20.1
Desk and dip pen sets	2.2	3.3	10.7	5.0	3.0	4.6	3.3	4.4	6.1	9.7
	1,083.7	$168.2	1,311.7	$192.2	1,560.5	$226.4	1,623.0	$241.4	1,805.1	$260.9

	1969		1970		1971		1972		1973	
Fountain pens	12.3	$ 16.0	10.2	$ 15.2	10.1	$ 14.7	9.8	$ 15.3	10.2	$ 20.8
Ball-point pens†										
Refillable	761.3	94.1	685.5	92.7	670.3	90.9	729.8	99.2	738.6	110.5
Nonrefillable	686.3	58.7	700.3	59.8	720.4	61.4	760.3	64.6	821.8	69.8
Markers (thick line)	116.8	26.8	105.1	25.4	102.2	25.0	120.3	29.5	209.4	33.7
Porous point pens	304.1	50.3	334.5	58.9	344.5	60.7	475.9	80.8	504.5	85.7
Mechanical pencils	65.5	22.3	57.8	20.1	55.7	21.5	59.5	22.9	53.6	24.9
Desk and dip pen sets	7.2	10.3	5.6	7.0	3.7	6.5	4.1	7.1	4.3	7.9
	1,953.5	$278.5	1,899.0	$279.1	1,906.9	$280.7	2,159.7	$319.4	2,342.4	$353.3

* No sales breakdown until 1965.
† No sales breakdown until 1967.
Source: Annual estimates compiled by Writing Instrument Manufacturers Association.

Exhibit 5

1973 PRIMARY CORPORATE FOCUS

Writing instrument firms	Product line	Market	Price range	Ad program	Newest product
BIC	bp, pp	All	Low	Consumer (TV)	Disposable lighter
Berol	wp, bp	Commercial	Middle, low	Trade	Combination pen
Cross (A.T.)	mp, bp	Retail	High	Consumer (mag's)	Luxury pp
Gillette	bp, pp	All	High, low	75%–consumer (TV) 25%–trade	Disposable lighter
Lindy	bp	Retail	Low	Consumer (mag's); formerly trade	Disposable lighter
Magic Marker	bp, pp, bm	All	Low	Consumer (all media) trade	pp
Pentel	pp, bm	All	Low, middle	Consumer (TV); formerly trade	Combination pen
Parker	fp	Retail	High	Consumer (mag's)	Luxury pp
Scripto	mp, bp, pp	Retail, ad/ specialty	Low	Consumer (TV, mag's); formerly trade	Disposable lighter
Sheaffer	fp	Retail	High	Consumer (mag's)	Luxury pp
Venus Esterbrook	Full line	All	Low, Middle	60%–trade 40%–consumer (mag's)	Technical drafting products

Abbreviations:
bp = ball-point pens.
bm = broad tip markers.
fp = fountain pens.
mp = mechanical pencils.
pp = fine line porous point pens.
wp = wooden pencils.
Source: Case researcher's interviews with the corporate marketing personnel.

Manufacturers felt that success depended heavily upon the strength of their financial resources, which was reflected in their marketing and distribution programs as well as upon their ability to be innovative. Advertising, packaging, and distribution costs combined were estimated to average close to 100 percent of the manufacturer's unit cost of low-priced products. Manufacturers unable to sustain those costs in all markets tended either to position their products in the retail market as no-name brands or to concentrate the bulk of their resources in specific market segments.

INDUSTRY STRUCTURE

Manufacturers

There were two types of writing instrument firms: assemblers (70 percent) and producers (30 percent).

The *assemblers* were typically small, privately held, product specialists which sold their products by direct mail on a special order basis to the three most price-sensitive markets: commercial, advertising/specialty, and premium. To become an assembler required very little capital investment, manufacturing expertise, or marketing know-how, which accounted for the large number of assemblers and the fact that they tended to come and go. Assemblers bought writing instrument components from suppliers which were then assembled and packaged for sale. Competition was based heavily on price, and product promotions were common.

Producers tended to be larger firms, some publicly held, which sold their products to all markets with special emphasis on the retail. Competition centered around the strength of their distribution networks (number of outlets reached and distributor loyalties) and national advertising programs. Producers manufactured most of their own component parts before assembling and packaging products. Their operations were characterized as capital-intensive and precision-oriented. It was not uncommon for some producers to manufacture certain products and to import others.

Distribution

Company sales forces. A typical producer used three types of sales forces: regular, specialized, and detail (optional).

The *regular sales force* made direct sales to large retail chains and discount houses, and indirect sales through specialized distributors to smaller retail stores and commercial supply outlets.

The *specialized sales force* made direct sales to the government, military, export, and premium markets, and indirect sales through advertising/specialty distributors to the ad/specialty market.

Some firms added a *detail sales force* to work at the retail level, taking orders and arranging displays. Smaller firms relied more heavily on indirect selling than did the larger firms, which could afford to cover the cost of direct selling to large accounts.

Specialized distributors. Specialized distributors (wholesalers) first appeared in the writing instrument industry when manufacturers came to realize that they could no longer handle an enormous number of accounts on their own. They carried a multitude of products, and were not captive to any one manufacturer. Their sales function was one of showing promotional items and order taking, for which they received a 15 percent margin off the retail price. In most cases, they assumed ownership of inventories. Along with the percentage markup, their own sales forces often received promotional monies ("p.m.s"), which were tied to major manufacturers' promotions at the retail level.

Distributors assisted dealers and retailers by providing an inventory management service, which guaranteed replacement of faulty merchandise, better product selection, and faster inventory turnover.[5] "A better return on investment" became their key selling tool, which was supported by fair and attractive margins (40 percent off retail price) and frequent sales calls.

The late 1960s marked the beginning of an industry shift in distribution patterns in the retail market (largest market)—away from indirect selling via specialized distributors to small, independent retail outlets, towards direct selling to large national chains and discount houses. The turn sparked embitterment on the part of distributors, who felt that they were not only being abandoned by the very firms which had influenced their creation, but were also being victimized by manufacturers' price-cutting actions affecting margins on the business which they still had. By 1973, approximately 60 percent of the dollar volume in the retail market represented direct sales from the manufacturers to mass-merchandise outlets.

Markets

In 1973, manufacturers' dollar shipments by market segment were estimated by industry sources to be: retail (50 percent), commercial (20 percent), ad/specialty (16 percent), export (9 percent), premium (4 percent), and military and government (1 percent).

Retail market. The retail market represented by far the highest concentration of manufacturers' dollar sales (50 percent) in the mechanical writing instrument industry in 1973. The only instrument which was selling better in another market was the fountain pen, of which 63.6 percent of its dollar volume was sold overseas. Drug stores were the highest volume retail outlet for writing instruments, capturing over 33 percent of the industry's total dollar retail sales, and one out of every two ball-point pen sales. Grocery stores were the smallest with 3 percent of the retail sales. Specialized distributors (tobacco, drug, and sundries) sold products to small chains and independent stores, while large chains and discount houses bought writing instruments direct from manufacturers.

Retailers selected product lines based primarily on product quality and reputation of the manufacturer. National advertising support was

---

[5] Dealers were office products stationers in the commercial market. Retailers were over-the-counter marketers in the retail market.

believed to be important for boosting retail sales, particularly in the low-priced items.

A survey of retail customers conducted by the researcher indicated the following consumer purchase priorities: (1) function, (2) quality, (3) price, (4) style, and (5) packaging. It was generally felt that:

Products were selected for specific purposes.

Low-priced items tended to be impulse purchases often bought in quantities, while higher priced instruments were planned purchases bought individually.

Prices which varied (a few cents in the low-price range) among fairly undifferentiated products *did not* sway selection of a preferred brand.

Consumers associated generic names with particular products which had been heavily advertised: such as Flair for porous point pens, and Cross for mechanical pencils.

Commercial market. The commercial market represented 20 percent of the total manufacturers' dollar shipments in 1973. Manufacturers' sales were made primarily through office supply distributors to dealers (commercial stationers), whose customers were corporate purchasing agents and students. Distributor/dealer loyalties were common in the commercial market, and were built up over the years on the basis of good account service, good quality merchandise, and attractive product offerings (at least one type at each price point). Commercial sales were heavily concentrated in the low-price range (<$0.50).

As in the retail market, quality was considered the most important factor affecting a purchase decision by the dealer in the commercial market. However, price was more critical to the dealer than to the retailer, because companies were interested in obtaining cost savings through bulk buying, whereas retail customers took personal pride in selecting their merchandise and were often willing to pay a premium for the products of their choice.

Advertising/specialty market. Sales in the advertising/specialty market represented 16 percent of manufacturers' dollar shipments in 1973. Purchasers tended to be organizations requesting inexpensive products on which to stamp advertisements. Price was the most important factor affecting a purchase decision. Orders were placed through ad/specialty distributors and filled by a specialized company sales force. Approximately 70 percent of the 200 writing instrument firms were engaged in the ad/specialty business, many of whom were assemblers.

Premium market. The premium market represented approximately 4 percent of manufacturers' total sales in 1973. Competitors included nonwriting instrument firms, as well as writing instrument companies, which: (1) could meet the price objectives of the purchaser, and (2) could offer products acceptable as give-away promotional items for other products.

Other markets. In 1973, export sales represented 9 percent of the total manufacturers' sales. The rising trend in export sales was attributed to: (1) the lowering of tariffs on imported products in foreign countries, and (2) the increased activities of firms which held licenses or ran operations abroad. The average prices of writing instruments sold abroad were markedly lower than the average retail prices in the United States since so much of the cost in the domestic market was tied up in distribution, advertising, and packaging. Heavy U.S. import taxes (about 2 cents per unit) on writing instruments continued to bar entry of low-priced foreign-made products into the United States on a large scale.

The military and government markets combined represented only 1 percent of manufacturers' unit sales in 1973.

CIGARETTE LIGHTERS

By 1973, many mechanical writing instrument companies had entered the cigarette lighter business as a means of product line diversification and yet another way to capitalize on their production expertise and market contacts. Although the two classes of products were functionally unrelated, their manufacturing processes, distribution patterns, and product life cycles bore striking similarities. The only major differences centered around market appeal, susceptibility to government regulation, and import trends.

Lighter/writer similarities

Product life cycle. Cigarette lighter product and price patterns almost exactly paralleled those of mechanical writing instruments—only a decade later. Until the late 1960s, competition among dominant cigarette lighter companies was concentrated almost exclusively in regular refillable lighter products selling in the middle price range ($2–$12). Following the introduction of an inexpensive disposable lighter by Garrity Industries in 1967, and an expensive electronic lighter by Maruman in 1970, sales of cigarette lighters began to polarize by price and product: disposables at <$2 and electronics at >$12, leaving the backbone of the business, regular refillable lighters, in a vulnerable position with respect to sales prospects.

Distribution patterns. Cigarette lighters were sold direct from the manufacturer, or indirect through specialized distributors, to writing instrument markets. In 1973, there were 175,000 retail outlets in the United States marketing cigarette lighters. Grocery stores represented the largest number (45 percent–50 percent) of lighter sales. Of all cigarette lighters retailed, 75 percent–80 percent were for less than $6.95. Like writing instruments, lighter sales were slightly seasonal, with the heaviest concentration occurring around the holidays. Distributors' margins off retail price generally ran between 15 percent–25 percent, increasing proportionately with the price of the product. Retailer margins were 40 percent off retail price.

Manufacturing process. Cigarette lighter production required the same basic technology as that of mechanical writing instruments: plastics injection molding of parts, followed by a precision assembly process. The average mechanical writing instrument consisted of seven parts and could be produced in a matter of minutes, whereas the average lighter had 21 parts and required a three-day production schedule because of "cure time" (a 24-hour wait between lamination of the subassemblies and filling the fuel reservoir).

The porous point pen and liquid fuel lighter operated on the same basic principle: The tank of the porous point pen held ink; the tank of the lighter held lighter fluid. The nib of the porous point pen was analogous to the wick of the lighter. Both drew the fluid out of their respective tanks by capillary action.

Lighter/writer differences

Import trends.   Unlike mechanical writing instruments, many cigarette lighters, particularly the disposables (70 percent), were imported into the United States for sale by domestic firms, which felt that the 25 percent duty fee on a foreign manufacturer's product was less than the additional amount required for direct labor costs in the United States. An added attraction was the quick access gained to a fast-growth market opportunity. In 1972, 45 percent of the lighters sold in the United States represented foreign imports, versus 36 percent in 1965. Japan was by far the largest supplier in every class of imported lighters (54.5 percent overall), with the exception of disposable butane lighters, 71 percent of which were imported by France.

Government regulation.   Until 1973, most cigarette lighter regulation related to the transportation of lighters containing flammable fuel. However, in 1973 the Consumer Products Safety Commission was given the authority to evaluate the quality of consumer products and enforce stringent safety standards. Cigarette lighters, particularly the inexpensive imports, were likely to be subject to CPSC attack if they lacked a flame adjuster (controlled height) or constant flame length regulator (controlled duration).[6] Although they were ranked 38th on the CPSC list in terms of severity of accidents, mechanical writing instruments were considered less hazardous. They were represented in Washington, D.C., by an industry trade association, the Writing Instrument Manufacturers Association, while lighters were not.

Market appeal.   Writing instruments appealed to a much broader consumer base than cigarette lighters did. All persons of all age groups were considered potential users of writing instruments, whereas cigarette lighter users were mostly smokers or campers.

Industry trends

Cigarette smoking.   During 1972, domestic consumption of cigarettes rose slightly from the previous year's level, which had reversed a four-year downtrend. Americans, including those at home and those abroad in the armed forces, consumed 565 billion cigarettes, or 2 percent above the prior year's level. Annual consumption per adult of 4,040

---

[6] The $1.29 disposable lighter by Rogers was the first disposable lighter to be recalled because of a flame adjuster problem (fall 1973).

cigarettes (202 packs) remained about the same, which was 7 percent below the 1963 peak.

There were three principal reasons for the rise in cigarette consumption in 1972:

> Increased concentration of the American population in the heaviest smokers' age group (25–39), which was 18.4 percent in 1972 and forecast to be 20 percent by 1975 and 22.9 percent by 1980.
>
> Minimal cigarette price boosts, which had not affected the demand for cigarettes.
>
> A decrease in the influence of anti-smoking campaigns after medical research evidence linking cigarette smoking to serious disease was termed inconclusive.

Cigarette lighter sales.   Cigarette lighter dollar sales in the United States were estimated to be $153 million in 1973. Compared to a 5.1 percent drop in per capita cigarette consumption, lighter sales had nearly doubled since 1965. Industry sources attributed the sudden sales surge to: (1) the advent of disposable lighters, and (2) an increased consumer awareness of cigarette lighters as the result of new and vigorous advertising campaigns.

Table 2

CIGARETTE LIGHTER RETAIL
DOLLAR SALES
(dollars in millions)

Year	Sales
1965	$ 72.6
1966	85.9
1967	90.2
1968	94.3
1969	94.9
1970	98.1
1971	106.9
1972	115.0
1973 (est.)	153.0

Source: Case researcher's estimates based on trade and company interviews and unpublished figures from the *Drug Topics* magazine research group (1972).

Product types

There were three basic lighter product types: (1) disposable, (2) regular refillable, and (3) electronic. These types could be further differentiated by: (1) price range: low (<$2), medium ($2–$12) and high (>$12); (2) style: compact, pocket, or table; (3) fuel type: butane gas or naphtha liquid fuel; (4) consumer purpose: refillable or disposable; and (5) starter mechanism: wick, flint, quartz crystals, or battery.

Disposable lighters.   Disposable butane lighters represented the faster growing segment in the cigarette lighter industry, accounting for 35 percent of total lighter unit sales in 1973.

Table 3

CIGARETTE LIGHTER DIFFERENTIATION

Product type	Price range	Starter mechanism	Fuel	Style	Consumer purpose
Disposable.......	> $2	Flint	Butane gas	Compact	Disposable
Regular refillable.......	Mostly $2–$12	Flint	Butane gas (90%)	Compact Table Pocket	Refillable
	Some > $12	Wick	Naphtha (10%)		
Electronic.......	> $12	Quartz crystals Battery	Butane gas	Pocket Table	Refillable

Disposable lighters were introduced in the United States in 1967 by Garrity Industries, Inc. They earned immediate consumer acceptance due to their low price and no reflint/no refill feature. They appealed for the most part to match users, an untapped end-user market within the lighter industry, and to regular refillable lighter users who were tired of losing personal lighters and wished to trade down to the inexpensive line. Like inexpensive mechanical writing instruments, disposable lighters were considered impulse purchase items, which had to be backed with heavy consumer advertising support and sold in mass-merchandise channels.

The success of the disposable lighter in the American market caused a chain reaction among mechanical writing instrument firms which had been seeking to diversify into related product lines. Most firms entered the cigarette lighter business as distributors of foreign-made models. Some intended to eventually set up domestic manufacturing operations of their own.

In 1973, there were three clear contenders for industry dominance in the disposable butane lighter business: Gillette, BIC, and Garrity Industries, with Scripto running a distant fourth. Gillette introduced a $1.49 French-made product called "Cricket," in 1972, through mass merchandise channels, and used heavy consumer advertising. It planned to manufacture lighters domestically by 1973. BIC followed a similar plan one year hence with its $1.49 "BIC Butane." Garrity Industries distributed its $1.49 "Dispoz-a-lite" in smoke shops, hotel stands, and drug stores, and used trade advertising. Scripto introduced its 98 cents

Table 4

DISPOSABLE LIGHTER RETAIL SALES
(dollars in millions)

	1971	1972	1973	1975 (est.)
Dollar sales.............	$18	$36	$50	$120
Unit sales.............	13	21	40	100

Source: Trade estimates.

Japanese-made "Catch 98" in 1973 through independent retailers and used no consumer advertising. It planned to introduce a family of disposable lighters in 1974.

Regular refillable lighters. By 1973, cigarette lighter sales had grown rapidly at the inexpensive and luxury price ends of the market. Victimized by this trend was the regular refillable lighter, the mainstay of the lighter business, 95 percent of whose sales were concentrated in the middle price range. Industry sources attributed the slow decay of the middle price segment to three factors.[7]

1. Style changes in lighters, which reflected the growing consumer interest in either more decoration (luxury lighters) or more functionally (disposables).
2. A trade-down to disposable lighters by the former purchaser of the refillable butane lighter, who became tired of losing refillable lighters.
3. The trend towards distribution through mass merchandise outlets, where profitability depended upon high volume turnover of inexpensive products away from independent retail outlets, where most regular refillable lighters were sold.

For years three companies had dominated the regular refillable lighter market: Ronson, Zippo, and Scripto. Together they produced two thirds of the 1973 sales in that product segment. Industry sources believed that, of the three, Zippo would be the least affected by the product/price polarization trend, as Zippo had developed long-time customer loyalties with its high quality product, which held a life-time guarantee. Ronson had lost market share by moving to higher-priced regular refillable lighters and decreasing its advertising support of its products. Scripto lacked the advertising and marketing strength necessary to support its lower-priced regular refillable lighters against the competition from disposable lighters.

Electronic lighters. Electronic lighters represented less than 2 percent of the total cigarette lighter unit sales in 1973. They required no flint or wick, as their flames were produced, electronically, by the striking together of ceramic quartz crystals, or with a battery. As luxury gift items, they were sold exclusively in department and jewelry stores and were priced above $12. Electronic lighters were new to the American market in 1973, and had not yet earned wide consumer acceptance— due in part to a lack of consumer awareness of their existence, and in part to the fact that consumers had traditionally thought of lighters as functional, rather than as highly decorative jewel-like products.

The leading distributors of electronic lighters in 1973 were Maruman, Dunhill, Colibri, Crown, and Consul. All electronic lighters were imported either from Europe or from the Far East. As was the case with

---

[7] Industry sources believed that sales patterns for regular refillables would have been much worse, had it not been for the support of the ad/specialty market in the middle-price range.

disposables, a number of companies, such as Scripto and Ronson, had introduced electronic lighters in order to expand their product lines and to take advantage of sales opportunities in a high growth segment of the cigarette lighter market.

APPENDIX

THE MECHANICAL WRITING INSTRUMENT INDUSTRY

Mechanical writing instruments of the future

Multicolor blending. A pen that will provide many colors, shades, and hues with a simple push of a button or twist of the cap to blend inks. Colors can be darkened, lightened, changed by interaction of inks —an artist's palette within a pen barrel.

Variable tip marker. For the Jekyll and Hyde writer who must switch from the fine lines used for underlining to the bold strokes of a package address, he will have to go no further than this soft tip pen. Three point sizes—fine, medium, broad—can be included in the barrel and are as easily interchangeable as a push on the cap top.

Computerized writing. Enables the most modern businesses to keep the personal touch alive in the computer age. Personalized notes will be produced on a large scale by programming individual handwriting into the memory. It will write any message fed into the computer in exact duplication of the handwriting.

Dictating pen. "What you say is what you get." A pen that is able to translate spoken messages into your own style of handwriting.

The permanent writer. Pen carries its own 100-year ink supply and never needs replacement.

Multitip pen. A ball-point, soft tip, marker, and fountain pen—all in the same writing instrument. For the worker with four jobs at once, and no time to hunt up or change his writing instrument.

Multipointed mechanical pencil. Soft, medium, and hard pencil points all encased in one unit for ease in switching from one job to another— without searching through pencil boxes or desk drawers.

Self-destruct ink. For keeping those hush-hush secrets really secret. This ink disappears after 48 hours, leaving no trace of important information that is written "For Your Eyes Only."

Radio transmitting writing instruments. Write down your message at one location and it is transmitted to another miles away and written down—without connection.

Homing device. This device will transmit a short sound beam so that you can keep tabs on your mislaid writing instruments. Great for big offices with absent-minded "borrowers."

Power writing. The conversion of atomic power into a writing ink. Lines will be burned into paper by converting light, neutrons, or other power sources in the barrel of the writing instrument.

Source: *Office Products*, May 22, 1972.

Scripto, Inc.

IN JANUARY OF 1974, Mr. Herbert "Bo" Sams, president of Scripto, Inc., an Atlanta-based mechanical writing instrument and cigarette lighter company, was reviewing the performance of the Atlanta Division which accounted for 64 percent of the firm's total revenues in 1973. Mr. Sams was conducting his review with an awareness of his decision made in 1971 to rebuild Scripto's writing instrument business. Regarding that decision, he had stated:

> Sometimes I wake up at three o'clock in the morning wondering if that was the right decision. Would it have been better to get out of the writing instrument business and consolidate the cigarette lighter operation? All the numbers said to get out of writing instruments, and we were certainly more profitable in lighters. But people had always thought of us as a writing instrument company. They associated the Scripto name with pens and mechanical pencils. Our name was our biggest strength. So we decided to reestablish Scripto as a meaningful factor in the mechanical writing instrument industry.

This case study traces the history of Scripto, Inc., by presidential era from its inception in 1923 through 1973. It focuses on the operations and decision problems of the Atlanta Division which manufactured and/or distributed mechanical pencils, fine line porous point pens, ballpoint pens, and three types of cigarette lighters, disposable, regular refillable, and electronic, in the domestic and foreign markets. Exhibits 1 and 2 present the consolidated financial statements by presidential era from 1963 to 1973.

CORPORATE HISTORY BY PRESIDENTIAL ERAS

Harold Hirsch (1923–39)

Scripto, Inc. was established as a manufacturer of mechanical pencils in Atlanta, Georgia, in 1923. The idea for Scripto was conceived by the then only independent pencil lead manufacturer in the United States, Mr. Monie Ferst, who wanted to prevent the Germans from recapturing the U.S. lead and eraser market which they had held before World War I. Rather than seek government aid to restrict German imports, Mr. Ferst decided to create his own market for leads and erasers by mass producing a quality mechanical pencil which would sell for 25 cents or less and thus appeal to the American mass market.[1] The product earned immediate market acceptance and industry dominance in its product class, although thousands of pencils had to be given away to distributors and retailers initially to overcome the disbelief that a quality mechanical pencil could be produced and sold so inexpensively. Under the leadership of its first president, Mr. Harold Hirsch, Scripto reached its breakeven point in sales in 1930, whereupon the price of the mechanical pencil was dropped from 25 cents to 10 cents and maintained at that level through the war.

Eugene Stern and E. P. Rogers (1940–46)

During World War II, two interim presidents, Mr. Eugene Stern and Mr. E. P. Rogers, managed the firm. Scripto remained a one-product firm relying heavily upon M. A. Ferst, Ltd., Mr. Ferst's company, for its lead and eraser supply. The manufacture of mechanical pencils was halted only temporarily during the war when Scripto adapted its precision manufacturing operation to the production of ordnance materials for the U.S. government.

James Carmichael (1947–63)

In 1947, Mr. Jimmy Carmichael, following an unsuccessful bid for the Georgia governorship against Mr. Eugene Talmadge, was selected by Mr. Ferst as the new president of Scripto, Inc. His stated objectives were twofold: (1) to develop Scripto into a full-line mechanical writing instrument manufacturing firm, and (2) to make Scripto the largest manufacturer of mechanical writing instruments in the world. Over his 17 years as president, Scripto in fact achieved the first objective, but not the second.

A full line of mechanical writing instruments. Mr. Carmichael's principal objective was to expand the Scripto product line by adding other mechanical writing instruments. His first step was to take advantage of the demand in the U.S. market for the new ball-point pen which had been introduced by Reynolds in 1946 at a retail price of $15. As it had successfully done with the mechanical pencil, Scripto set out to prove that a quality ball-point pen could be produced and sold inexpensively. The ball-point pen was introduced on the market in 1947 at a retail price of 25 cents and, like the mechanical pencil, earned immediate market acceptance.

By 1952, Scripto was known as a full-line writing instrument manufacturer in the low-price market. Fountain pens had been introduced at

---

[1] Mechanical pencils on the market at the time were only of fair quality and were sold exclusively as gift items priced well over $1.

Exhibit 1

SCRIPTO, INC.

Consolidated Balance Sheets by Presidential Eras

	Carmichael		Singer	
	1963	1964	1965	1966
Net Sales:				
Dollars..................................	$26,344,306	$25,237,265	$36,664,054	$33,494,076
Percent................................	100.0%	100.0%	100.0%	100.0%
Cost of goods sold.........................	54.4	58.8	63.8	57.7
Gross profit..............................	45.6	41.2	36.2	42.3
Expenses:				
Selling and administrative.................	32.3	34.4	28.0	30.4
Interest (net)..........................	0.4	0.4	0.7	0.4
Others (net)...........................	0.9	0.6	0.2	0.8
Profit before tax.........................	12.0	5.8	7.3	10.7
Provision for income tax....................	6.2	2.7	3.1	4.9
Net income (loss) before				
extraordinary item......................	5.8	3.1	4.2	5.8
Extraordinary item.......................	—	—	—	(2.4)*
Net income.......................	5.8%	3.1%	4.2%	3.4%
Ratio Analysis:				
Net sales/total assets.....................	1.5	1.5	1.5	1.5
Net income (before extraordinary				
items)/total assets.....................	8.7	5.7	6.9	8.6
Net income (before extraordinary				
items)/net worth.......................	12.4	6.5	12.6	14.3
Depreciation/net sales.....................	3.7	3.4	3.3	2.9
Dividend payout..........................	51.2	98.0	48.3	41.8
Investment in plant and				
equipment/net sales....................	3.7	5.2	5.7	8.7

* $793,000 lost on discontinued carpet operations.

† Losses: (1) start-up costs for Canadian subsidiary ($264,000); (2) losses on product lines, abandonment of properties.

Gains: (1) reevaluation of currencies ($55,000); (2) sale of properties ($730,000); (3) tax-loss carryforward credit ($170,000).

‡ Losses: Sale of product lines, abandonment of properties ($105,000).

Gains: (1) sale of properties ($105,000; (2) tax-loss carryforward credit ($60,000).

§ Gains: Tax-loss carryforward ($89,000).

Source: Scripto, Inc., annual reports.

retail prices of $1 and $3.50; the ball-point pen line was expanded to include models retailing at $0.29, $0.39, and $1; a $1 mechanical pencil was added, as well as a matching fountain pen and pencil set retailing for $5. All products were supported by heavy consumer advertising and dealer promotion programs.

Cigarette lighters: A new business. In 1957, Scripto introduced its first nonwriting instrument product, a naphtha fuel lighter called the "Vu-lighter" which derived its name from the fact that its liquid fuel supply was visible. Although it was well known that Mr. Ferst, founder of Scripto and then chairman of the board, had always wanted to add a cigarette lighter to the product line, Scripto had not been consciously seeking product line diversification into nonwriting instruments. Rather, it came across an available opportunity in 1954 to rescue a small cigarette lighter firm in Missouri which was experiencing production and quality control problems. At the time, Scripto was selling its writing instrument products exclusively to the retail and ad/specialty markets, both of which were well suited for the distribution of the Vu-lighter because the same sales force and distributors could be used. The company was purchased in 1954 for a nominal price. The lighter was subse-

	Ferst		Harris		Sams	
1967	*1968*	*1969*	*1970*	*1971*	*1972*	*1973*
$30,462,424	$30,914,857	$31,229,304	$31,928,975	$30,979,108	$28,378,819	$31,154,608
100.0%	100.0%	100.0%	100.0%	100.0%	100.0%	100.0%
60.7	65.9	72.1	71.0	72.8	71.2	70.6
39.3	34.1	27.9	29.0	27.2	28.8	29.4
34.0	31.7	32.9	31.9	25.4	25.4	23.1
0.6	0.6	0.8	1.3	1.3	0.9	1.0
0.3	1.3	0.2	—	0.4	0.4	1.4
4.4	0.5	(6.0)	(4.2)	0.1	2.1	3.9
2.1	1.1	(2.2)	(0.8)	1.5	1.5	2.5
2.3	(0.6)	(3.8)	(3.4)	(1.4)	0.6	1.4
—	—	—	—	1.5†	0.2‡	0.3§
2.3%	(0.6)%	(3.8%)	(3.4%)	0.1%	0.8%	1.7%
1.4	1.5	1.3	1.3	1.4	1.5	1.4
3.2	(0.8)	(5.0)	(4.2)	(3.1)	1.0	2.0
5.3	(1.3)	(9.7)	(9.6)	(6.2)	1.6	3.6
3.0	3.0	3.5	2.9	3.1	2.3	2.2
114.0	—	—	—	—	—	—
4.7	3.2	3.1	3.9	2.7	3.2	2.7

quently redesigned at an investment of $1 million and then reintroduced on the market in 1957 selling at $3.95 for the regular size; and in 1960, $4.50 and $5 for the compact models.

International expansion. Mr. Carmichael's second objective was to develop Scripto, Inc., into the largest mechanical writing instrument manufacturing firm in the world. In the early 1950s, he felt that the growth of Scripto's business outside of the United States was being curtailed by high tariffs imposed on U.S.-made products and a shortage of dollars abroad. He concluded, therefore, that owning and operating manufacturing subsidiaries abroad was more desirable than exporting American-made products to foreign countries. In 1957, Scripto was reorganized into a corporate group, which managed all domestic and foreign subsidiaries, and a domestic group, which managed the Atlantic operation. By the time that Mr. Carmichael resigned for health reasons in 1963, Scripto had either established or purchased foreign operations in Canada (1950), the United Kingdom (1955), Southern Rhodesia (1955), Australia (1957), Mexico (1959), New Zealand (1959), and Colombia (1959). All were 100 percent–owned by Scripto with the exception of Colombia, which became a licensing agreement. The purchases and operation of the foreign subsidiaries were funded in three ways: through internally generated funds, long-term debt, and a $2.5 million common stock issue in 1956 at $7 per share.

Scripto's response to a changing market. In 1957, domestic sales began to slip for the first time in Scripto's history. Mr. Carmichael attributed the performance setback to two factors: (1) an oncoming re-

Exhibit 2

SCRIPTO, INC.

Consolidated Balance Sheets by Presidential Eras

	Carmichael		Singer	
	1963	1964	1965	1966
Total assets ($)...........................	$17,570,967	$17,168,506	$24,155,764	$22,700,251
Assets (%)...............................	100.0%	100.0%	100.0%	100.0%
Current assets:				
Cash....................................	5.5	6.0	4.3	5.3
Accounts receivable.....................	32.8	29.4	30.0	32.6
Inventory...............................	27.9	27.6	34.3	26.3
Total Current Assets.................	66.2	63.0	68.6	64.2
Property, plant, and equipment				
(net)...................................	31.1	34.4	29.4	30.0
Investments in affiliates.................	—	—	—	4.2*
Prepaid expenses.........................				0.8
Other assets.............................	2.7	2.6	2.0	0.8
Liabilities (%)...........................	100.0%	100.0%	100.0%	100.0%
Current liabilities:				
Notes payable..........................	1.7	1.5	8.3	2.2
Accounts payable........................	4.5	6.5	7.5	6.4
Accrued taxes...........................	4.0	3.4	3.3	2.7
Accrued liabilities......................	6.0	4.8	4.7	5.6
Total Current Liabilities..............	16.2	16.2	23.8	16.9
Long-term debt...........................	13.2	11.3	20.8	22.2
Deferred income taxes....................	—	—	0.9	1.2
Minority interest........................	—	—	—	—
Stockholders' equity:				
Common stock...........................	7.5	7.6	5.7	6.1
Paid-in surplus.........................	18.3	18.7	14.4	15.3
Retained earnings.......................	44.8	46.0	36.2	40.0
(Treasury stock)........................	—	—	(1.8)	(1.7

* Acquisition of Modern Carpet Industries, pooling of interests.
† 7½ cumulative preferred stock issued by the Irish subsidiary to a bank ($316,000).
‡ Joint ventures between: (1) Wilkinson Sword and Scripto, Inc., in Scripto (Eng), Ltd., and Scripto Industries (Shannon, Ireland), Ltd.; and (2) Scripto, Inc., and Scripto de Mexico.
Source: Scripto, Inc., annual reports.

cession in the United States, and (2) the gradual shift from an over-demand to an oversupply of products in the mechanical writing instrument market. From that year on to the end of his presidential term (1963), Mr. Carmichael responded to the squeeze on Scripto's profit margins by:

1. Implementing a stringent across-the-board cost-cutting program.
2. Upgrading the Scripto product line to higher-priced writing instruments (>$1) with the objective of eventual dominance in the higher priced gift item field. (Ball pens retailing at $1.98 and $2.95 were added plus an innovative Tilt-tip pen ($1.95) which featured accurate performance when held at any angle).
3. Acquiring three domestic subsidiaries (Burnham Products Corporation, Broadway Pen Corporation, and Austin Metal Products, Inc.) in 1959 in order to strengthen Scripto's position in the advertising/specialty market where very inexpensive, unbranded pens were sold.
4. Revamping the foreign manufacturing operations, particularly in the United Kingdom, with the objective of improving Scripto's competitive position in the Common Market countries where the price war had become even more severe than in the United States.

	Ferst		Harris		Sams	
1967	*1968*	*1969*	*1970*	*1971*	*1972*	*1973*
$22,556,707	$21,180,588	$23,428,666	$25,210,155	$22,295,681	$18,946,674	$21,705,004
100.0%	100.0%	100.0%	100.0%	100.0%	100.0%	100.0%
5.5	6.4	4.3	8.6	5.7	5.0	2.0
26.7	27.1	31.5	27.6	30.7	31.2	30.9
30.6	28.3	31.3	31.5	29.1	28.8	37.8
62.8	61.8	67.1	67.7	65.5	65.0	70.7
31.4	31.4	27.1	25.8	24.5	22.9	22.0
3.2	5.5	4.2	4.1	4.4	8.5‡	5.5
1.5	0.7	0.7	1.1	1.2	1.0	1.4
1.1	0.6	0.9	1.3	4.4	2.6	0.4
100.0%	100.0%	100.0%	100.0%	100.0%	100.0%	100.0%
5.5	2.8	14.8	23.4	15.0	16.1	23.7
6.0	6.6	8.3	9.2	8.3	3.9	7.6
1.9	1.0	} 6.3	} 7.2	} 9.7	} 9.8	8.0
4.7	5.0					
18.1	15.4	29.4	39.8	33.0	29.8	39.3
20.7	20.2	16.9	14.0	14.1	8.3	4.5
1.5	1.7	1.5	0.3	1.0	1.2	0.8
—	—	—	1.2†	1.4	—	—
6.1	6.5	6.1	5.6	6.5	7.6	6.7
15.4	16.4	15.3	14.2	16.6	19.2	17.0
39.9	41.6	32.6	26.0	29.5	36.0	33.8
(1.7)	(1.8)	(1.8)	(1.1)	(2.1)	(2.1)	(2.1)

5. Making heavy expenditures in the research and development of new markets and products.

During Mr. Carmichael's final six years at Scripto, the firm's market share in writing instruments slipped from 16 percent (ranked second to Paper Mate) to less than 10 percent (ranked fifth behind Paper Mate, Waterman–BIC, Parker Pen, and Sheaffer). Performance results were:

Table 1

FINANCIAL PERFORMANCE (1958–1963)

(dollars in thousands)

	1958	*1959*	*1960*	*1961*	*1962*	*1963*
Consolidated net sales.......	$22,369	$23,106	$21,001	$21,156	$25,750	$26,344
Consolidated PAT..........	1,433	1,080	653	1,150	1,706	1,536
PAT/sales (%).............	6.5%	4.7%	3.1%	5.4%	6.6%	5.8%

Source: Scripto, Inc., annual reports, 1958–63.

Mr. Carmichael retired in 1963. Despite his own assessment of the factors affecting Scripto's performance during his final years, some company officials believed that those factors were not entirely of external origin. Both Mr. Ferst and Mr. Carmichael had had serious health problems. Mr. Carmichael had been seriously injured in a car accident in his early teens and had been on crutches or in a wheelchair ever since. Scripto had assumed the cost of his medical expenses. In addition to his disability, Mr. Carmichael had held many civic obligations which kept him away from the day-to-day operation of the company. In an article appearing in *Business Week* magazine, one company executive re-marked:

> The most dangerous time in a company's existence is when things are going well. Lax habits and bad decision-making are hidden by the success of the moment. Jimmy (Carmichael) was paternalistic, so that jobs that were poorly done and decisions that were poorly made tended to be overlooked and condoned. What happened was that an organiza-tion was allowed to build up over a period of years that was lax in work habits and in accepting the necessity of getting the job done.[2]

Carl Singer (September 1964–July 1967)

In September of 1964, Mr. Carl Singer, former president of the Chi-cago-based Sealy Mattress Company, became president of Scripto, Inc. Found by an executive search firm and representing the first top man-agement change at Scripto in 17 years, Mr. Singer was described by his colleagues as "a man of action from a marketing background who saw Scripto's problems with a sense of urgency." Assessing the morale at Scripto as very low, Mr. Singer described his task as one of "complete changeover and repositioning," which he planned to carry out in two stages: Stage I was to focus on cost-cutting measures to improve profit margins which had been Mr. Carmichael's objective; and Stage II was to focus on revenue-generating activities, primarily in foreign markets.

Stage I: Cost-cutting (1964–66). Mr. Singer felt that Scripto's most immediate problem was the inadequacy of its production facilities. The decline in profit margins, he felt, underscored the need to trim costs by modernizing manufacturing facilities, both in Atlanta and overseas. Scripto's Atlanta plant had fallen into a state of disrepair. A plan was developed to rehabilitate the existing manufacturing facilities (a group of three-story buildings near downtown Atlanta) as well as to build a new plant on newly acquired land outside of Atlanta which would double production capacity. Production improvements were also made on existing facilities in Mexico, Canada, and the United Kingdom, as it was Mr. Singer's objective to continue the worldwide expansion en-visioned by Mr. Ferst, Scripto's founder, who had died in 1965.

In 1965, $2.1 million was spent on plant and equipment improve-ments, and in 1966, another $2.9 million. To finance the improvements and to provide additional working capital, Mr. Singer negotiated a $5 million, 15-year loan at 5.45 percent interest with the Metropolitan Life Insurance Company. A portion of the proceeds was used to retire a $2.3 million balance in previous long-term Metropolitan loans. The new agreement allowed Scripto to take revolving short-term bank loans, pro-

---

[2] "Rewriting the Script for Scripto," *Business Week*, December 17, 1966, p. 171.

viding the total did not exceed $2 million in any 60-day period each year.

A second problem which Mr. Singer faced was how to deal with the low morale of Scripto's employees. He increased the size of the total employee work force from 2,500 to 2,900 to prepare for the expected increase in unit production in Atlanta; he drew the control of subsidiary operations more closely to management in the Atlanta Division; and he made substantial reassignments and redefined responsibilities at the top-management level. As the result of a six-week labor dispute, factory workers became unionized (International Chemical Workers Union), much to the opposition of a number of Scripto's managers, some of whom subsequently resigned or were replaced.

In keeping with his "repositioning" theme, Mr. Singer took steps during Stage I to move Scripto in two product directions: (1) to higher priced writing instruments, and (2) to wholly new product areas unrelated to writing instruments. This objective was to increase profit margins and to lessen the risk of concentration in one or two industries. At the time when Mr. Singer became president of Scripto, the company was in the process of installing highly automated equipment in its manufacturing facilities, which would enable high volume production of low-priced products. Mr. Singer reversed that process in the belief that "low margin products were uneconomical to produce and sell." He began phasing out products such as inexpensive ball-point pens and fountain pens. Two "dramatically new" product lines were introduced: (1) butane (gas) lighters retailing at $4.95, and (2) fiber tip pens retailing at $0.39.

Aside from the move to higher priced writing instruments and lighters, Mr. Singer set in gear a large-scale product diversification program which he carried out either through internally generated research and development or through company acquisitions. Three new products were under internal development: a thermo-fax copier machine, a wide-angle lens camera, and a special butane lighter ("Vu-tane"). The copier machine was intended to gain a better foothold in the commercial (office supply) market where Scripto's sales had been practically nonexistent. The copier made transparencies to be used as audio-visual aids and was to be marketed at a retail price of $250 by a separate sales force through a separate distribution network (A. B. Dick and Heyer Corporation). The wide-angle lens camera was a personal research interest of a long-time Scripto employee, for which he had received between $1–$1.5 million in R&D funds. While no suitable direct application had been found during the lengthy time of its development, management believed that the camera would be of interest to the U.S. military in reconnaissance missions or for underwater photography. The Vu-tane lighter was to become Scripto's first entry into the plastic-encased butane lighter field at a price point of well under $5.

Two acquisitions were made during Stage I. In 1965, Scripto issued 143,000 shares of its stock in exchange for all of the stock of Modern Carpet Industries, a leading privately owned carpet manufacturing firm.

The carpet line was compatible with Mr. Singer's background in home furnishings, and he was attracted by "its outstanding organization and position in the fast-growing tufted carpet industry, which was considered to be the most volatile segment of the multibillion home furnishings field." Following the acquisition, management devoted a great deal of time and money to enlarging, modernizing, and adding equipment to MCI. The second acquisition was Florence Ceramics Company, a Pasadena-based firm which produced imprinted ceramic products, such as ash trays. Mr. Singer described the ceramic products "as naturals for Scripto's retail outlets and ad/specialty activities."

Stage II: Revenue generation (1966–67). Mr. Singer's master "repositioning" plan proved a little too grandiose, and Stage II, which dealt with his long-range objective of revenue growth, hardly met with implementation before his departure from Scripto in July of 1967. During his final months with the firm, Mr. Singer continued to introduce higher priced writing instruments ($1 and $1.95 ball point pens and a $1 refillable fiber tip pen) as he had intended, but his visions for the production area and his favorite project, Modern Carpet Industries, fell flat. Construction was delayed on the new Atlanta plant "for economic reasons." MCI was sold in 1966 because "it no longer fit into the redefined long-range growth projections for Scripto."[3] The employee base was reduced in number from 2,900 to 2,700.

Robert H. Ferst (August 1967–March 1968)

In August of 1967, Mr. Robert Ferst, president of M. A. Ferst, Scripto's graphite and eraser subsidiary, replaced Mr. Singer as an interim president of Scripto, Inc. Company sales revenues had slumped to $30.46 million by the end of that year, returning $716,000 in net profits. Mr. Ferst attributed the poor performance to necessary write-offs of obsolete and excess inventories which had accumulated because of major product changeovers, as well as to currency devaluations on foreign markets.

While only at the helm for eight months, Mr. Ferst saw his mission as twofold: (1) to continue the cost-cutting program which dated back to the Carmichael days, and (2) to focus his attention on marketing the Scripto products aggressively, with specific aim at consumer acceptance, an area which he felt had been neglected over the years. New systems of inventory controls were implemented. Drastic cost-control measures were enforced. Dividend payments were halted for the first time since Scripto's public offering in 1956, in order to conserve working capital for development and promotion of new and diversified products. Plans to proceed on the construction of a new Atlanta plant were again postponed. Higher priced butane lighters ($7.95–$16.95) were added to the cigarette lighter product line to follow the continuing emphasis on higher priced products with sizable profit margins. Independent design consultants were employed to restyle all products as an attempt to at-

---

[3] Scripto retained a 35 percent investment in the acquiring company, Modern Carpet Mills, Inc. The sale represented a $793,000 loss to Scripto, Inc.

tract new consumers, particularly the younger generation and the adult gift buyers. Mr. Ferst resigned in March of 1968.

Arthur Harris (April 1968–March 1971)

In April of 1968, Mr. Arthur Harris signed a five-year contract to become president of Scripto, Inc., with the option to terminate after three years. Mr. Harris came to Scripto from the Mead Paper Company where he had been head of its packaging division for many years. He was a fellow Atlantan and personal friend of the Ferst family who owned approximately 43 percent of the Scripto stock and controlled the executive committee of Scripto's board of directors.

Mr. Harris' three-year term as head of Scripto was characterized by change on all fronts: in organizational structure, international activities, marketing and sales programs, and product policies, with the overall objective "to reposition Scripto at the point-of-sale." One Scripto executive described Mr. Harris as "brilliant, strong-willed, and even dictatorial" in his attempt to turn the company around.

1968: Corporate overhaul. In 1968, Mr. Harris introduced substantial changes in the areas of: (1) corporate organization, (2) marketing programs, and (3) product policies. His first step involved a complete overhaul of both domestic and foreign organizations. In Atlanta, he reassigned existing personnel and added new personnel to develop second echelon depth. Attempts were made to revitalize foreign subsidiaries: in Mexico, new top management was added; in Canada, top management was also changed as well as the entire organizational structure; and in the United Kingdom, plans were made to relocate the plant in Ireland. A second step was to revamp marketing and sales programs which involved:

Complete realignment of sales territories in the United States.

Implementation of a new incentive method of compensation.

Installation of a sophisticated electronic data system for market research and forecasting.

Introduction of a new advertising scheme to tie merchandising more closely to point-of-purchase displays.

Addition of a special detail sales force at the retail level.

Development of an entirely new approach to marketing for the subsidiaries in South Africa, Rhodesia, New Zealand, and Modern Carpet Mills, Inc.

The third step was to "reevaluate all Scripto products." Many old products reappeared in new designs and colors. Three new products: the thermal copier, wide-angle lens camera, and Vu-tane lighter, all of which had been under development since 1964, were given deadlines for launching. A network of distributors and dealers was formed to sell the copier, an appropriate market for the wide-angle lens camera was still being sought, and the Vu-tane lighter was scheduled to be introduced on the market in 1969.

Despite his efforts, Scripto reported a net loss of $173,000 in 1968 based on net sales of $30.915 million. Mr. Harris summed up the performance results by calling the year one of "evaluation and appraisal." He attributed the losses to tax-loss carrybacks which could no longer be applied for tax purposes against foreign losses ($364,000 in 1968) as well as to inventory write-offs.[4]

1969: A wave of new products. Mr. Harris looked to 1969 as a year to "capitalize on conclusions drawn in 1968 and to continue to reposition Scripto at the point-of-sale." However, despite an increase in sales revenues to $31.2 million, Scripto reported an even greater net loss ($1.183 million) than the year before. Management attributed the losses to the costs and expenses related to the introduction of new products and the elimination of other products, all of which exceeded $1.6 million before tax credits. In that year, the Vu-tane lighter ($3.95), Scripto-fax copier ($250), a thin line mechanical pencil ($0.49) and fiber tip ink crayons (in England), along with many new packages, particularly blister cards,[5] were introduced. In a letter to stockholders, Mr. Harris emphasized the importance of "keeping Scripto's identity as the only nationally advertised company with a *complete* line of writing instruments to meet almost any writing need in price ranges to fit anyone's budget."

Scripto acquired the Butane Match Corporation of America in 1969, which added a $0.98 refillable butane lighter ("Butane Match") to its product line. The net assets of BMC were acquired in a pooling of interests transaction for an exchange of 66,000 shares of restricted Scripto stock at $1.23 per share for accounting purposes, and an additional 62,500 shares contingent upon BMC's future earnings.

In contrast to his predecessors, Mr. Harris began to shift the corporate focus in 1969 from international activities to those centered around the U.S. operation. The Mexican operation, upon its reorganization in 1968, was turned into a joint venture with Novaro, publishers of *Time* magazine in Mexico. The South African and Rhodesian operations were turned into licensing agreements, and the English plant was moved to Ireland where its operations would be free from British taxation.

1970: Demise of a vision. Mr. Harris' third and final year at Scripto, Inc., again produced a substantial earnings loss ($1.075 million) due to the condition of the economy and to heavy advertising and promotion commitments. Sales of the Scripto copier were minimal, and Florence Ceramics once again proved unprofitable. Renewed plans to relocate the Atlanta facilities were again termed financially infeasible and were finally abandoned. Scripto exchanged its 35 percent common stock investment and all previous advances to Modern Carpet Mills, Inc., for convertible preferred stock ($436,000 liquidation preference) in a newly formed parent company, Modern Holdings, Inc., and for an unsecured note receivable ($464,000) payable over five years. The New Zealand subsidiary was turned into a licensing arrangement.

Mr. Harris resigned in March of 1971. In his statement to stockhold-

---

[4] Inventories were reduced by approximately $900,000 during that year.

[5] Blister cards were product packages which could be hung on a peg board for display purposes, and were designed to protect the retailer against pilferage.

ers, he remarked that he had met his principal objectives—"to form an aggressive and capable management team, eliminate unnecessary costs, and streamline operations in general." His future intention was to reside in Europe and spend a portion of his time as a special consultant to Scripto on the sale of Scripto products in the Common Market countries and on new product development.

Herbert "Bo" Sams (April 1971–   )

On April 1, 1971, Mr. Herbert "Bo" Sams was elevated to the presidency of Scripto, Inc., from the position of vice president and general manager of the Atlanta Division which he had held since 1969. A veteran of Scripto for 35 years, most time of which was spent in the manufacturing area, Mr. Sams had known Scripto in its heyday as well as at the depths of poor performance.[6] It was at the latter point that he found himself in 1971. With that recognition, he set out to rebuild a company which had digressed far from its original business at the expense of an overall declining market share in writing instruments and fluctuating operating results.

Mr. Sams envisioned his mission as twofold: (1) to stop the company-wide losses which implied a "disciplined" approach to cost cutting in the European, Atlanta, and Canadian operations, and (2) to develop a long-range plan for the Atlanta division which would clearly define the corporate business and eliminate those products and activities which were not consistent with that plan. It was the latter decision which, in part, was unclear to "Bo" Sams. He considered two courses of action: (1) to abandon the writing instrument business altogether, and rebuild Scripto-Atlanta solely as a cigarette lighter company, or (2) to reestablish Scripto-Atlanta as a viable competitor in the U.S. writing instrument business, as well as to continue in cigarette lighters. He chose the latter.

Stage I: A short-range profitability plan. In the 1970 annual report, Mr. Sams named profitability as his immediate goal, with special attention to be given to the three greatest loss-producing areas: the Atlanta Division and the Canadian and English subsidiaries.

Atlanta Division. When Mr. Sams became general manager of the Atlanta Division in 1969, the division had reported a net loss of $1.5– $2.0 million for that year.[7] Mr. John Tucker, vice president of finance,[8] assessed the problems in Atlanta:

> Scripto's performance in the early 1970s could not be blamed upon current decisions because it had its roots a decade before. The company had felt that the writing instrument market was locked up in the United States so we had decided to look elsewhere. We had illusions of grandeur which marked the beginning of problems because the U.S. market had not been developed properly. BIC came along and Scripto's

---

[6] Mr. Sams had worked at Scripto, Inc., during his college days and had joined the firm upon his graduation from Georgia Institute of Technology in textile engineering in 1936.

[7] The Atlanta Division reported a $404,925 before-tax loss in 1972.

[8] Mr. Tucker was described by a colleague as "Mr. Sams' right-hand man. He adds front office continuity to the team."

attitude was to laugh. Whoever thought that people would buy such a cheap and ugly stick pen? So we chose to go international and later learned that we were not powerful enough. All that time, the Atlanta Division was neglected. The company grew fat with people, and sales did not justify the advertising dollars spent. We didn't have the marketing capability to see if our products were right. And it seemed that every time there were problems, we cut out our research effort and capital expenditures program.

To eliminate the losses in Atlanta, Mr. Sams outlined a six-point program aimed at creating "a leaner organization with a new disciplined approach to marketing." His objectives were:

To build an aggressive, sound, and talented management team (see Exhibit 5).

To eliminate several unprofitable product variations.

To place a new emphasis on accurate sales forecasting.

To orient Scripto's market research toward better identification of consumer needs.

To improve the computerized accounting procedures to give faster, more accurate accounting and better inventory control.

To reduce costs by lowering overhead and streamlining the manufacturing process.

Canada and the United Kingdom. Aside from the Atlanta Division, the Canadian and British operations represented the major sources of losses to Scripto in the late 1960s. Over the five-year period 1966–71, the Canadian operation produced roughly $500,000 in cumulative net losses. In 1972, Scripto entered a business partnership with the John A. Huston Company in Canada, in which the latter contracted to manufacture and market Scripto products while Scripto, Inc., supplied component parts and the Scripto name. The Canadian operation broke even in 1972 on revenues of $600,000 and was expected to break even again in 1973.

The British operation faced a crunch in 1970. Scripto sold its rundown English plant and moved its facilities to Ireland where income from operations was tax free and government grants were readily available for equipment purchases. Despite those benefits, however, the English skilled labor refused to move to Ireland. The subsidiary reported a $1 million net loss in 1971. In 1972, Scripto, Inc., sold 55 percent of its equity in Scripto Pens, Ltd. (England), and Scripto Industries (Shannon), Ltd., to Wilkinson Sword, Ltd., for which it received $1.1 million and the option to return to a 50–50 deal after five years. Scripto, Inc., continued to supervise the British manufacturing operation while Wilkinson assumed the marketing responsibility. By year's end, the British operation had cut its net losses to $0.5 million; in 1973, to $175,000, and a small profit was predicted for 1974.

Butane Match Corporation of America. In 1972, Scripto, Inc., arranged to sell the business of its wholly owned subsidiary, Butane Match Corporation of America, and certain related patent rights. Contrary to

Exhibit 3

SCRIPTO, INC.
Consolidated Income Statement

	1973	1972
Income:		
Net sales	$31,154,608	$28,378,819
Costs and Expenses:		
Cost of sales	22,006,870	20,192,819
Selling and administrative expenses	7,202,628	7,004,770
Interest expense, net	301,075	241,562
Equity in loss of foreign companies	192,267	157,971
Provision for losses on investments and long-term notes receivable	219,751	200,000
Other (income) expense, net	19,441	(18,943)
	$29,942,032	$27,778,179
Income before income taxes and extraordinary items	$ 1,212,576	$ 601,160
Provision for income taxes	779,000	420,000
Income before extraordinary items	$ 433,576	$ 181,160
Extraordinary items, net of applicable income taxes	89,648	58,301
Net income	$ 523,224	$ 239,461
Per Share:		
Income before extraordinary items	$0.15	$0.06
Extraordinary items	0.03	0.02
Net Income	$0.18	$0.08

Source: Scripto, Inc., annual report, 1973.

management's expectations, sales of the 98 cents refillable butane lighter ($644,000 in 1972) had been minimal. Due to the buyer's subsequent inability to meet the financial requirements of the sale, Scripto chose to reacquire Butane Match in September of 1973.

Atlanta property. During 1971, the holder of the 5.45 percent long-term note agreed to purchase Scripto's undeveloped property in Atlanta for a specified amount, subject to a third party's option to acquire the property at a higher price. The sale was recorded in 1971, and an extraordinary gain of $407,000, net of applicable income taxes, was included. In 1972 the third party exercised its option to purchase the property; an additional $104,768 net gain was included in the 1972 extraordinary item.

Further eliminations. In 1971, Scripto sold its ceramic products firm, the French operation, and the thermal copier product rights, whose combined contribution to profits had been only marginal. The decline of $1 million in sales revenues for that year was attributed to the elimination of those three revenue-generating activities, as well as to limited production at the new Irish plant facility.

Stage II: A return to the basic business in Atlanta. Management shifted its attention and allocation of resources in 1972 to the task of achieving its long-range objective: the realization of prominence by Scripto in the U.S. mechanical writing instrument industry. Over the previous 15 years and five presidential terms, profitability achieved through cost reduction, particularly in the manufacturing operation, had been the primary concern. The new focus in 1972 became the generation of revenues through the use of aggressive marketing programs, and product line positioning, in the fastest-growth segments of the writing instrument and lighter industries.

Product line. In 1973, management described Scripto, Inc., as "a full-line manufacturing company in mechanical writing instruments and cigarette lighters." The company reported 0.62 percent of the industry's dollar sales in ball point pens, 0.34 percent in markers, 13.2 percent in mechanical pencils, 2.4 percent in porous point pens, and 10.7 percent in cigarette lighters. Table 2 presents the major consumer products which were manufactured and/or distributed by the Atlanta Division from 1965–1973. Exhibit 4 presents a sales breakdown by product line in the Atlanta Division from 1965–1973.

Mechanical writing instruments. In 1972, Scripto introduced two inexpensive writing instruments: the 19-cent "Superpen" (a stick model ball-point pen), and the "19-center" (a disposable fiber tip pen). It was management's hope that the Superpen would provide a reentry point for Scripto in the commercial market and that the "19-center," as a price competitor and quality instrument, would revitalize Scripto's overall position in the mechanical writing instrument industry. Scripto's competitive action was explained in an article appearing in *Distribution Executive,* as follows:[9]

Table 2

ATLANTA DIVISION
1973 Major Consumer Product Line*

	Price	No. of models	Production location	Production capacity (millions of units/year)	1973 Production rate (percent capacity)
Writing instruments					
Ball-point pens					
Retractable	$0.39, $0.98	2	Atlanta	15	28
Nonretractable (nonrefillables)	0.19, 0.25	2	Burnham	>50	60–70
Porous point pens	0.19, 0.49	6	Atlanta	40–50	About 100%
Mechanical pencils					
Regular	0.39, 0.49, 1.29	5	Atlanta	25	75
Marking	0.49	2	Atlanta	15–20	75
Cigarette lighters					
Disposables (butane)	0.98	1	Japan	Purchased	—
Regular refillables					
Butane	0.98	1	Butane Match	4.5	50
	3.95–14.95	10	Atlanta	6	90
Naphtha	4.95, 5.95	2	Atlanta	6–7	100
Electronic	17.95–29.95	10	Japan	Purchased	—

* Ball point pen refills, leads, erasers, lighter fuel, and no-name brand pens were manufactured and distributed by other U.S. subsidiaries.

---

[9] "Scripto Taking on the Giants," *Distribution Executive,* March 1972, p. 12.

Exhibit 4

SCRIPTO, INC.
Consolidated Balance Sheet

ASSETS	1973	1972
Current Assets:		
Cash..	$ 432,354	$ 941,659
Receivables, less reserves of $545,963 in 1973 and		
$418,649 in 1972..............................	6,704,883	5,902,845
Inventories:		
Raw materials and supplies........................	3,585,031	2,029,475
Work in process..................................	3,720,943	2,627,531
Finished goods...................................	895,120	791,571
	8,201,094	5,448,577
Prepaid expenses.................................	318,633	184,554
Total current assets...........................	15,656,964	12,477,635
Property, plant, and equipment, at cost:		
Land..	633,220	633,220
Buildings..	2,246,016	2,216,530
Machinery and equipment.........................	9,972,760	8,995,502
	12,851,996	11,845,252
Less accumulated depreciation......................	8,086,531	7,511,753
	4,765,465	4,333,499
Investments:		
Equity in net assets of and advances to jointly-owned		
foreign companies..............................	1,199,666	1,408,247
Modern Holdings, Inc.:		
Investment in preferred stock less reserve of $436,000...	—	—
Notes receivable................................	—	200,000
	1,199,666	1,608,247
Other assets.......................................	82,909	527,293
	$21,705,004	$18,946,674

LIABILITIES AND STOCKHOLDERS' INVESTMENT	1973	1972
Current Liabilities:		
Notes payable....................................	$ 4,520,000	$ 2,447,154
Accounts payable.................................	1,659,834	734,555
Accrued liabilities................................	1,613,978	1,534,213
Income taxes payable.............................	131,934	331,659
Long-term debt due within one year..................	611,776	605,440
Total current liabilities........................	8,537,522	5,653,021
Long-term debt due after one year:		
5.45% term loan.................................	965,620	1,565,620
Other...	9,485	10,880
	975,105	1,576,500
Deferred income taxes..............................	179,000	227,000
Commitments and contingent liabilities		
Stockholders' investment		
Common stock, 50¢ par value; authorized 5,000,000 shares,		
issued 2,891,200 shares........................	1,445,600	1,445,600
Paid-in surplus...................................	3,693,459	3,693,459
Retained earnings.................................	7,342,453	6,819,229
	12,481,512	11,958,288
Less:		
Treasury stock, at cost (42,520 shares)...............	320,935	320,935
Notes receivable from officers and employees for		
stock issued...................................	147,200	147,200
	468,135	468,135
Total Stockholders' Investment.................	12,013,377	11,490,153
	$21,705,004	$18,946,674

Source: 1973 Scripto, Inc., annual report.

Scripto, Inc., back in the black last year after three years in the red, is taking an aggressive new posture in writing instruments to increase its profitability.

The Atlanta-based manufacturer, always a factor in writing instruments, has for some time given primary emphasis to its cigarette lighters.

"With the growth of our lighter business, which is substantial, we tended to neglect our writing instruments somewhat," says Marketing Vice President George L. Curran. "It was an easy thing to do. We were making money on lighters and the company in general was profiting. Then we suddenly awakened to the fact that, though we had both a name and adequate production facilities for writing instruments, we had not been active in this field for a long time."

To regain its former position of prominence in writing instruments, Scripto is going after BIC's market with its new 19¢ Superpen and it's challenging Paper Mate's 49¢ Flair with a new 19¢ fiber tip pen.

Scripto, though it has had entries in both these markets, hasn't been a real contender in either. Of the two, the one it's most interested in developing is the fiber tip. In fact, its objective seems to be to become to the fiber tip business what BIC has become to the ball point business.

"Basically," says Curran, "the fiber tip has been a 49¢ market. What we're doing is positioning ourselves as the BIC of the fiber tip line."

In explaining why Scripto is marketing a fiber tip that's 30¢ lower than the popular price level, Curran mentions that the growth of the ball point market coincided with the gradual price reduction from the initial $12.50 to the present 19¢. The market, which had been a few hundred thousand units in the early Fifties, is now something like 1.8 billion units.

"As late as ten years ago," he says, "everybody felt that $1.00 was the popular pen and 49¢ was the inexpensive pen. Then BIC proved that 19¢ was a lot more popular.

"So, we're trying to repeat this phenomenon in fiber tips. We're bringing the fiber tip into line for more purchases, for an ultimately higher volume of sales.". . .

. . . "Frankly," Sams says, "we're challenging our major competition head on.". . .

At the end of 1973, the three competitors, BIC, Gillette, and Scripto, held the following retail market shares:

Table 3

1973 COMPARATIVE RETAIL MARKET SHARES
(units)

	Gillette	BIC	Scripto
19¢ nonretractable ball point			
pen Price ($).............	$0.19	$0.19	$0.19
Market share (%)........	5%	31%	<1%
Fine line porous pens			
Price ($)...............	$0.29, $0.49	$0.29	$0.19, $0.49
Market share (%)........	35%	22%	3%
All ball-point pens			
Price ($)...............	$0.19–$0.98	$0.19–$1.00	$0.19–$0.98
Market share (%).......	15%	66%	2%

Source: Corporate records.

During 1962–73, the three firms made the following consumer advertising expenditures on writing instruments:

Table 4

CONSUMER ADVERTISING EXPENDITURES ON WRITING INSTRUMENTS
(dollars in thousands)

	BIC	Gillette	Scripto		BIC	Gillette	Scripto
1962......	$ —	$ 146	$ 634	1968......	$4,194	$3,346	$ 209
1963......	132	165	736	1969......	3,626	1,900	56
1964......	285	126	413	1970......	3,968	4,033	153
1965......	654	61	536	1971......	5,000	6,000	1,800
1966......	943	61	1,449	1972......	6,900	8,500	650
1967......	3,071	2,720	766	1973......	7,000	9,000	545

* Network TV, spot TV, consumer magazines.
Source: Corporate records.

Cigarette lighters. For years, three companies: Ronson, Scripto, and Zippo, dominated the regular refillable lighter market, which represented two thirds of the total industry sales in lighters in 1973.

In 1973 cigarette lighter sales were rapidly increasing in the disposable (<$2) and electronic (>$12) lighter market segments. Sales in the regular refillable ($2–$12) segment had begun to level off. Industry sources believed that Zippo would be the least affected by the polarization trend. Zippo had built up long-time customer loyalties based on the high quality of its metal lighters, which held a life-time guarantee. Ronson had lost market share to Scripto and Zippo when it moved to higher priced regular refillable lighters in the early 1970s and simultaneously cut back on its advertising support. It was felt that Scripto lacked advertising and marketing strength, and its lower priced regular refillable lighters faced keen competition from the inexpensive disposable lighters which were new to the marketplace. Additions to its regular refillable product line were largely responsible for its dramatic growth (32 percent) in lighter sales in 1972.

Table 5

1973 REGULAR REFILLABLE LIGHTER RETAIL SALES
(dollars in thousands)

	Estimated lighter sales	Percent of share	Estimated fuel and accessory sales	Percent of share	Estimated total sales	Percent of share
Ronson...............	$ 16,672	16.5%	$26,676	78.0%	$ 43,348	32.1%
Scripto...............	18,339	18.2	3,335	9.7	21,674	16.1
Zippo................	31,678	31.4	1,667	4.9	33,345	24.7
Estimated Total market........	$100,809	100%	$34,235	100%	$135,044	100%

Source: Corporate records.

Scripto became a full-line cigarette lighter firm during 1973 upon the introduction of its "Catch 98" disposable lighter and its series of "Piezo" electronic lighters. The Japanese-made Catch 98 retailed at 98 cents. Management stated that the Catch 98 had captured a 10 percent share of the disposable lighter market and represented 24 percent of Scripto's dollar sales in cigarette lighters in 1973. A tobacco distributor commented on the Catch 98:

> Disposable lighters are not a perfect product yet. In the expansion stage of the market, lighters of questionable quality can be sold when they can't be sold in later stages. The Catch 98 is not the same quality as the Cricket, BIC Butane, or Dispoz-a-lite, which sell at $1.49. It has a smaller fuel reservoir and no pressure wick.

The Japanese-made Piezo series lighters ranged between $17.95–$29.95 in retail price and were sold in jewelry outlets. Their sales were minimal in 1973.

Table 6

CONSUMER ADVERTISING EXPENDITURES ON CIGARETTE LIGHTERS
(dollars in thousands)

	Ronson	Scripto	Zippo		Ronson	Scripto	Zippo
1966	$432.7	$ 8.6	$729.0	1970	$378.0	$1,006.0	$692.7
1967	634.8	533.3	799.6	1971	164.0	175.3	409.8
1968	554.0	312.0	804.7	1972	419.2	8.2	470.9
1969	422.8	317.3	709.6	1973	261.7	0.0	480.5

Source: Leading National Advertisers, Inc.

Problems facing Scripto. In an interview with the case researcher in October of 1973, Mr. Sams stated that there were four major problems facing Scripto at that time:

1. Potential embitterment on the part of independent distributors who felt that Scripto was going to abandon them in favor of direct selling to mass-merchandise outlets.
2. Uncertainty as to the availability and price of plastic because of the current worldwide energy shortage.
3. Limitation of financial resources due in part to loan covenant restrictions placed on future borrowing and, in part, to a shortage of internally generated cash.
4. Rising vocalism and absenteeism among the labor force in the Atlanta plant.

Disgruntled distributors. Management's intention to emphasize direct selling to mass-merchandise outlets added to the frustrations of distributors who had relied heavily on the Scripto business over the years and who had already become disenchanted with the firm's marketing and sales programs in recent years. In a survey conducted by Scripto in 1971, distributors complained that the company salesmen were un-aggressive and made infrequent sales calls, that deals and promotions were unattractive because they required high minimum orders to get full discounts, that the product line was too broad, and that the products received very little advertising support. Generally, they felt that Scripto was a me-too company which had concentrated too long on cigarette lighters and had neglected its writing instrument business.[10]

In 1973, approximately 58 percent of Scripto's dollar sales in writing instruments and 81 percent in lighters were concentrated in the retail market, 16 percent and 1 percent, respectively, in the commercial market, and 10 percent and 7 percent, respectively, in the ad/specialty market. The remaining sales were distributed among the firm's minor markets. Despite the direct selling trend, Scripto had continued to rely on indirect selling through its distributors.

Table 7

ATLANTA DIVISION
Dollar Shipments (percentages)

	Writing instruments		Cigarette lighters	
	1972	1973	1972	1973
Regular sales*				
Direct.................	11%	15%	21%	26%
Indirect...............	60	71	66	66
Specialized sales†				
Direct.................	12	5	5	2
Indirect...............	17	9	8	6
Total sales..........	100%	100%	100%	100%

* Retail and commercial sales.
† Ad/specialty, premium, government sales, etc.
Source: Corporate records.

Mr. Sams commented on Scripto's position:

> Scripto had been devoted to the drug and tobacco distributors for many years and did not change as the market did because we were protecting those distributors. Now we must change, and the specialized distributors whose businesses are rapidly declining feel that they may be jilted.

The increasing price of plastic. Due to a serious worldwide fuel shortage in 1973, industries which relied heavily on oil-based supplies were predicting a rise in the price of plastics in 1974 and possible production cutbacks in the event of plastics shortages. Cigarette lighter and writing instrument firms, which used metal rather than plastic as their primary raw material, owned their own refineries, or imported products

---

[10] One manager stated that the salesmen were responsible for the shift to lighters because the sales commissions were more attractive on cigarette lighters than on writing instruments in years past.

from countries that were looked upon with favor by the Arabs, were likely to be less directly affected by the energy crisis. Scripto, whose products were made primarily from plastic, was predicting at worst a 20 percent production cutback in its Atlanta plant.

Financial limitations. At the end of 1973, approximately $1.6 million remained outstanding on the original 5.45 percent long-term loan of $5 million negotiated in 1965 with Metropolitan Life Insurance Company. The loan agreement, amended in 1972, required a $600,000 principal plus interest payment at the end of 1974 and 1975 with a balloon payment of $366,000 in 1976. Provisions under the loan agreement required the U.S. and Canadian companies to maintain a minimum net working capital balance of $6.5 million, limited short-term borrowings to $3 million until April of 1974, and prevented dividend payments to stockholders or additional advances to foreign subsidiaries. During 1972, Scripto applied $959,380 from the sale of certain properties to payment of loan principal.

In 1973, there were approximately 2.8 million shares of Scripto common stock outstanding of which 43 percent was controlled by the Ferst family. No dividends had been paid on outstanding stock since 1967.

Work force attitudes. In 1973, the absenteeism rate of plant workers ran as high as 7 percent. Mr. Sams had said, "Morale is improving. It was at ground zero in 1971." Absenteeism had never forced an operations shutdown, but production efficiency was always severely damaged.

Management attributed the labor problems primarily to a "change in social attitudes in the United States" but also to the available work force pool within Atlanta itself. About 60 percent of the work force had been with Scripto for over ten years, and it was felt that those workers felt a sense of loyalty to the company and to their jobs. Absenteeism problems prevailed among the remaining 40 percent who in management's judgment tended to be the younger workers, many of whom were hired from the small group of unemployed persons (2.8 percent of the total work force) in Atlanta in 1973.

The work force was composed primarily of black women. About 60 percent–70 percent of the male workers were black. Management stated that racial tension existed among black assembly line workers and white foremen, but tension was greater between black foremen and black assembly-line workers who resented the foremen for their professional advancement. Base salaries ranged from $2.25–$2.60 per hour (unskilled work) to $4 (skilled work).

Factory conditions were felt by some managers to contribute to worker dissatisfaction on the job. The plant facility consisted of a group of old three-story buildings five minutes from downtown Atlanta. The manufacturing areas were noisy (workers were supplied with ear plugs and eye glasses for protection against noise levels above 85 decibels, flying debris, and sparks), dirty and hot (no air conditioning). Production rates were machine-paced. The work was seasonal and layoffs were a common occurrence.

MR. SAMS LOOKS TO THE FUTURE

Mr. Sams viewed his role as that of a major policy maker. Consistent with that view, he had great faith in the capabilities of his management team to oversee the day-to-day operation of the business and to implement his decisions. As president, he felt that he had made three key decisions: (1) to cut the losses in Atlanta, Canada, and Britain; (2) to reemphasize the writing instrument business; and (3) to introduce such products as the 19-center porous point pen and the Catch 98 disposable lighter, which would compete in the high-growth areas of the market.

Management outlined the 1974 sales objectives for the Atlanta Division:

To increase dollar sales in writing instruments by 10 percent and cigarette lighters by 5 percent using proven promotions and programs.

To increase distribution of the basic product line with current chain customers, and to develop new chain customers, with special emphasis placed on writing instruments.

To concentrate sales attention on the products with the greatest potential, that is, disposable lighters, broad tip markers, and porous point pens.

Sales objectives. Plans to achieve the 1974 sales growth objectives for writing instruments and cigarette lighters centered around a reorganization of the sales organization in the Atlanta Division. Specifically, the commercial stationery division was to become a specialized sales operation in which all sales would be handled through 11 manufacturer's representatives in lieu of the 2,000 distributors which it had used in the past. Direct retail sales would be handled by a national accounts manager working with 75–100 large chain accounts, and by 17 company salesmen and 14 manufacturer's representatives working with the 150 small chain accounts in the northeast, central, southern and western divisions. Indirect retail sales would be made through 4,500 specialized retail distributors and 40 food brokers. Scripto would use its five specialized company salesmen to sell to the 1,344 ad/specialty distributors and would sell direct to the other markets. A detail force of 35 women would be used at the retail level. Exhibit 5 presents the new organizational chart.

Chain store expansion. In 1973, Scripto sold 15 percent of its writing instruments and 26 percent of its cigarette lighters direct to chain store accounts. Management hoped to increase chain store sales by at least 10 percent and 5 percent, respectively, in 1974, by assigning district managers and detail salespersons to handle all national and regional chain accounts and divisional sales managers to coordinate those activities.

New products. Management planned to concentrate on rapidly growing segments of the writing instrument and cigarette lighter markets in 1974. A family of disposable lighters selling at retail prices of $1.19, $1.39, and $1.69 would be introduced. The $1.69 lighter would be manu-

Exhibit 5

1973 TOP MANAGEMENT—ATLANTA DIVISION

Name	Title	Years at Scripto	Job(s) prior to Scripto	Expertise
"Bo" Sams..............	President	37	—	Manufacturing
John Tucker............	Executive vice president	4	Controller (Kelsey–Hayes Tools); accountant, Touche Ross	Accounting
Jack Bozarth...........	Vice president, marketing	½	Marketing manager, consumer Products division of Gulf & Western	Marketing
Morton Chaber.........	Vice president, manufacturing	4	Vice president of manufacturing at Ronson; vice president of manufacturing at Revlon	Manufacturing
George Dinnerman......	Vice president, sales	3	Vice president of marketing at Ronson	Sales
Bill Black.............	Vice president, national accounts	8	Sales director at Timex	Sales
Roberta Haynes........	Assistant vice president, sales and marketing	10	Army Services	Administration
John Dolan............	Controller	1	Accountant at Price Waterhouse	Accounting

factured at full capacity (10 million units per year) in the Atlanta plant. The $1.39 lighter would be imported from Japan. The $1.19 product was the former Catch 98 at 98 cents. The 19-center porous point pen would be repositioned at the point-of-sale to "provoke greater impulse purchases." The 49 cent porous point pen would be aggressively marketed in the commercial market. Scripto was testing a finer point porous pen with a harder tip which would write through carbons. Scripto planned to introduce a "better canister marker" in 1974, which management claimed could be differentiated from competitors' products.

An allocation of $1.6 million was planned for the 1974 advertising program which was to cover all products at the trade and consumer levels. Scripto intended to use two themes: (1) Scripto (products) works; and (2) Scripto (company) is alive and well.

Mr. Jack Bozarth, vice president of marketing and sales, summed up Scripto's position in 1974:

> Scripto is in a different position than anyone else in the industry. We're the only full-line writing instrument supplier left. Whether they know it or not, BIC is the stick, Paper Mate is the Flair, Magic Marker is the canister marker.
>
> For the first time, Scripto is going with the industry. We're competing in the growth areas but are protected by our full line. Right or wrong, it will be interesting to see how the industry goes.

Exhibit 6

ATLANTA DIVISION SALES, 1965–1973

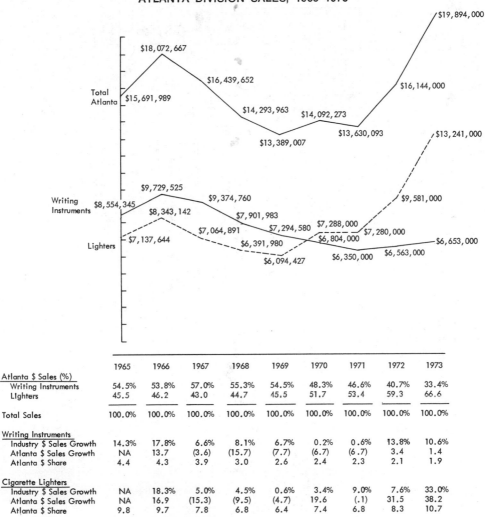

	1965	1966	1967	1968	1969	1970	1971	1972	1973
Atlanta $ Sales (%)									
Writing Instruments	54.5%	53.8%	57.0%	55.3%	54.5%	48.3%	46.6%	40.7%	33.4%
Lighters	45.5	46.2	43.0	44.7	45.5	51.7	53.4	59.3	66.6
Total Sales	100.0%	100.0%	100.0%	100.0%	100.0%	100.0%	100.0%	100.0%	100.0%
Writing Instruments									
Industry $ Sales Growth	14.3%	17.8%	6.6%	8.1%	6.7%	0.2%	0.6%	13.8%	10.6%
Atlanta $ Sales Growth	NA	13.7	(3.6)	(15.7)	(7.7)	(6.7)	(6.7)	3.4	1.4
Atlanta $ Share	4.4	4.3	3.9	3.0	2.6	2.4	2.3	2.1	1.9
Cigarette Lighters									
Industry $ Sales Growth	NA	18.3%	5.0%	4.5%	0.6%	3.4%	9.0%	7.6%	33.0%
Atlanta $ Sales Growth	NA	16.9	(15.3)	(9.5)	(4.7)	19.6	(.1)	31.5	38.2
Atlanta $ Share	9.8	9.7	7.8	6.8	6.4	7.4	6.8	8.3	10.7

Source: Scripto, Inc., annual reports, and Writing Instrument Manufacturers Association.

Exhibit 7
SCRIPTO, INC.
1974 Organizational Chart—Atlanta Division

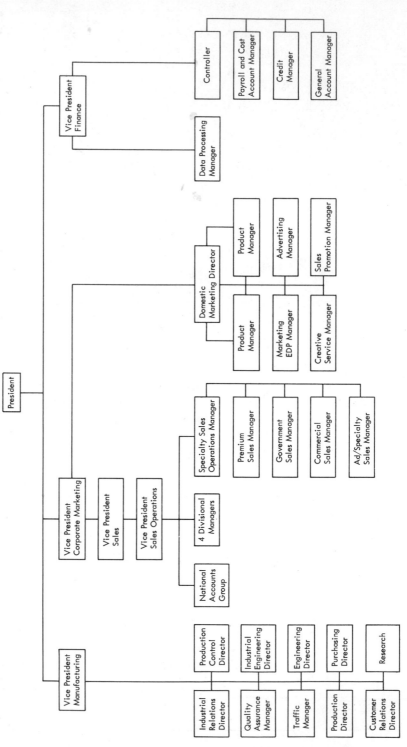

Source: Company records.

BIC Pen Corporation (A)

DESCRIBED by an economic observer as "one of the classic success stories in American business," the BIC Pen Corporation was widely acknowledged as a leader in the mechanical writing instrument industry in 1973. "The success was dramatic," the observer had said, "because it was achieved from the residue of a deficit-ridden predecessor company, over a short period . . . , in the extremely competitive, low-price sector of the industry. 'BIC' had become a generic name for inexpensive ball-point pens."

Mr. Robert Adler, president of BIC, was extremely proud of the firm's success, which he attributed to "numerous and good management decisions based 40 percent on science and 60 percent on intuition." BIC had reported its first profit in 1964 based on net sales of $6.2 million. Over the following nine years, net sales increased at a compounded rate of 28.2 percent and the weighted average after-tax profit as a percentage of net sales was 13.2 percent. (See Exhibits 1–3 for a summary of financial data from 1964–73).

Until 1972, BIC concentrated exclusively on the design, manufacture, and distribution of a complete line of inexpensive ball-point pen products. The most successful pen was the 19-cent Crystal, which accounted for over 40 percent of BIC's unit sales in ball point pens and about 15 percent of industry unit sales in ball-point pens in 1972. That same year, BIC expanded its writing instrument product line to include a fine line porous point pen. In 1973, it added a disposable cigarette lighter.

COMPANY HISTORY

The name "Waterman" meant a writing instrument since Mr. Louis Waterman invented the first practical fountain pen in 1875. For many years, the Waterman Pen Company led the world in the manufacture of fountain pens. But in the late 1950s, when the shift to ball-point pens

303

Exhibit 1

FINANCIAL HIGHLIGHTS 1964–73

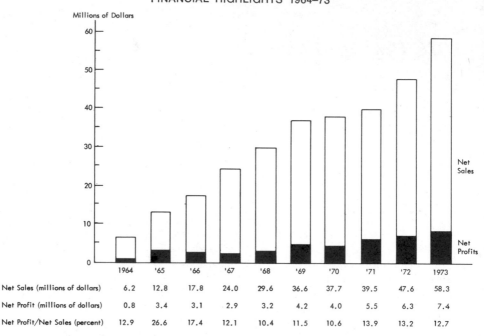

	1964	'65	'66	'67	'68	'69	'70	'71	'72	1973
Net Sales (millions of dollars)	6.2	12.8	17.8	24.0	29.6	36.6	37.7	39.5	47.6	58.3
Net Profit (millions of dollars)	0.8	3.4	3.1	2.9	3.2	4.2	4.0	5.5	6.3	7.4
Net Profit/Net Sales (percent)	12.9	26.6	17.4	12.1	10.4	11.5	10.6	13.9	13.2	12.7

Source: BIC Pen Corporation annual report, 1973.

swept the United States, the Waterman Company continued to concentrate on its fountain pen line, and its performance slipped substantially.

In 1958, M. Marcel Bich, a French businessman well established as a leading European pen maker, bought the facilities, trademark, and patent rights of the ailing Waterman Company, which then became the Waterman-BIC Pen Company. Believing strongly that the ball-point pen was the writing instrument of the future, M. Bich established the objective of becoming the leading firm in the low-price disposable ball-point pen industry. To obtain that position, management proposed the use of forceful consumer advertising and mass distribution policies.

At the time of M. Bich's purchase of Waterman, ball-point pens constituted only 8 percent of Waterman's unit sales. By 1964, however, all fountain pen and ink products had been eliminated, and most sales came from the 19-cent stick-type ball-point pen. The conversion process was costly, as reflected in the five years of deficits (1959–63). BIC reached its turning point in 1964, marked by the national success of its Crystal pen.

From 1964 through 1973, the company expanded its ball-point pen line to include 12 models of retractable and nonretractable pens offered in varying point sizes, ink colors, and barrel colors at retail prices be-

Exhibit 2

BIC PEN CORPORATION
Consolidated Financial Statements
For the years ended December 31, 1973 and 1972
(in $1,000)

Consolidated Statement of Income

	1973	1972
Net sales	$58,326	$47,571
Cost of goods sold	26,564	19,892
Gross Profit	31,762	27,679
Selling, advertising, and general and administrative expenses	17,191	15,248
Profit from operations	14,571	12,431
Other income	589	269
Total	15,160	12,700
Other deductions	327	196
Income before income taxes	14,787	12,504
Provision for income taxes	7,357	6,240
Net income	$ 7,430	$ 6,264
Earnings per share	$ 1.15	$ 1.00

Consolidated Statement of Retained Earnings

	1973	1972
Balance—beginning of year	$11,683	$10,262
Net Income	7,430	6,264
Total	19,113	16,526
Dividends:		
Cash:		
Common shares	1,750	1,603
Preferred shares		
Total Cash	1,750	1,603
Common shares		3,240
Total Dividends	1,750	4,843
Balance—end of year	$17,363	$11,683

Source: BIC Pen Corporation annual report, 1973.

tween 19 cents and $1. A 29-cent fine line porous point pen was added in 1972 and a $1.49 disposable butane cigarette lighter in 1973. In addition to product line expansion, BIC established a 100 percent-owned operation in Canada (1967), joint ventures in Japan (1972) and Mexico (1973), and a distributor arrangement with a firm in Panama (1973).

On May 1, 1971, the company changed its name to the BIC Pen Corporation. The Waterman trademark was subsequently sold to a Zurich firm, and BIC went public with an offering of 655,000 shares of common stock listed at $25 per share on the American Stock Exchange. In 1973, BIC's parent company, Société Bic, S.A., held 62 percent of the BIC stock.

Exhibit 3

BIC PEN CORPORATION
Consolidated Financial Statement
December 31, 1973 and 1972
(in $1,000)

Consolidated Balance Sheet

	1973	*1972*
ASSETS		
Current Assets:		
Cash	$ 683	$ 919
Certificates of deposit and short-term investments—at cost, which approximates market	8,955	10,000
Receivables—trade and other (net of allowance for doubtful accounts, 1973—$143,000, 1972—$102,000)	9,445	8,042
Inventories	9,787	6,299
Deposits and prepaid expenses	644	633
Total current assets	29,514	25,893
Property, Plant, and Equipment—at cost (net of accumulated depreciation, 1973—$9,687,000, 1972—$7,091,000)	15,156	9,687
Investments and other assets	1,790	1,329
Total	$46,460	$36,909
LIABILITIES AND SHAREHOLDERS' EQUITY		
Current Liabilities:		
Notes payable—banks	21	—
Construction loan payable (due March 21, 1974)	560	—
Accounts payable—trade	3,872	$ 1,245
Mortgage payable	62	58
Accrued liabilities:		
Federal and state income taxes	1,231	815
Pension plan	306	265
Other	488	402
Total Current Liabilities	6,540	2,785
Deferred liabilities	361	275
Mortgage payable	459	520
Minority interest*	91	—
Shareholders' equity:		
Common shares	6,480	6,480
Capital surplus	15,166	15,166
Retained earnings	17,363	11,683
Total Shareholders' Equity	39,009	33,329
Total	$46,460	$36,909

* Mexican subsidiary is 80 percent-owned.
Source: BIC Pen Corporation annual report, 1973.

MEN OF INFLUENCE

M. Marcel Bich

M. Marcel Bich has been described as having done for ball-point pens what Henry Ford did for cars: produce a cheap but serviceable model.

> In 1945, Bich and his friend Edouard Buffard pooled their wealth—all of $1,000—and started making ball point refills in an old factory near Paris. Soon it occurred to Bich that a disposable pen that needed no refills would be more to the point. What his country needed, as Bich saw it, was a good 10¢ pen. Today the cheapest throwaway BIC sells for close to that in France—about 7¢. In the United States the same pen retails for 19¢, and it is the biggest seller on the market. . . .
>
> Marcel Bich is a stubborn, opinionated entrepreneur who inherited his title from his forebears in the predominantly French-speaking Val D'Aoste region of northern Italy. He abhors technocrats, computers, and borrowing money. At 58, he attributes his business successes to his refusal to listen to almost anyone's advice but his own. Bich says that his philosophy has been to "concentrate on one product, used by everyone every day." Now, however, he is moving toward diversification. A disposable BIC cigarette lighter that gives 3,000 lights is being test marketed in Sweden; if it proves out, Bich plans to sell it for less than 90¢. . . .
>
> In the United States, Bich is best known for his fiasco in the 1970 America's Cup Race: His sloop *France*, which he captained, got lost in the fog off Newport. He speaks in aquatic terms even when describing his company: "We just try to stick close to reality, like a surfer to his board. We don't lean forward or backward too far or too fast. We ride the wave at the right moment."[1]

Société BIC, S.A., was known as a "one-man empire" which in 1972 accounted for a third of the ball-point pen sales worldwide and included full operations in 19 countries. M. Bich's personal holdings were estimated to be worth about $200 million. "The only way he could control his empire," BIC's treasurer Mr. Alexander Alexiades had said, "was to have certain rules and guidelines. All Société Bic companies were quite autonomous once they had become consistent with his philosophies."

BIC Pen Corporation had been characterized as the "jewel in M. Bich's crown." In the firm's early years, M. Bich had provided much of the machinery, production techniques, and supplies from the French parent company. By 1973, the only substantial business exchange which still remained between the two firms was in research and development. One of the few visible signs of the American company's European heritage was the Renaissance artwork which M. Bich had hung in BIC's reception and board rooms.

Mr. Robert Adler

In 1955, the day after Connecticut's Naugatuck River raged out of control and flooded the countryside, Mr. Adler reported to work at the

---

[1] "Going Bananas over BIC," *Time,* December 18, 1972, p. 93.

old Waterman Pen Company as a newly hired junior accountant fresh out of Pennsylvania's Wharton School of Finance. Instead of being shown to his desk and calculating machine, he was handed a shovel and ordered to help clean out the mud which had collected in the plant during the flood. Nine years later, at the age of 31, he became president of the Waterman-BIC Pen Corporation, which under his leadership became the largest ball-point pen manufacturer and distributor in North America.

Mr. Adler was described by a business associate as "a president who liked to be totally familiar with and completely immersed in every area of his company's operations, one who felt that he should never quash his instincts with an over-dependency on numbers and facts alone . . . a shirt-sleeved president who made it his personal concern to know intimately every facet of the BIC marketing and manufacturing process, including highly technical matters involving complex moulding equipment, advanced production techniques, merchandising, advertising, and sales . . . a do-it-yourself investigator-president who regularly made the rounds of the plant, keeping himself available at all times."

Mr. Adler had stated that he personally selected his colleagues on the basis that they demonstrated aggressiveness and an unswerving belief and conviction that they were serving a company that produced the world's finest writing instruments—products of exceptional quality and value. "A businessman is born, not made," he said, "and education can only enhance and refine what already exists." He attributed much of BIC's success to the fact that in the firm's early years he had consciously hired persons who were unfamiliar with the industry and who therefore did not question BIC's ability to succeed by selling an inexpensive ball point pen via extensive advertising. He emphasized the importance of his own role in determining BIC's performance by stating:

> A lot of decisions are easy because there is only one way to go. Sometimes you're lucky and sometimes, no matter what, you'll get the same outcome. A president gets paid to make decisions. That's his big job. What's important is once a decision is made is to make sure that it comes out right. The decision is not so important; it's the outcome. A president must say to himself: "I will now make my decision successful."

WRITING INSTRUMENT PRODUCT LINE

The BIC Pen Corporation manufactured and sold inexpensive writing instruments in a variety of shapes: stick or pocket pen; ink colors, 1–10; point sizes, medium or fine; and retail prices, $0.19–$1. All retractable pens were produced in a pocket pen shape; all nonretractables in a stick shape.

The most successful product, the Crystal, accounted for over 40 percent of all ball-point pen units sold in North America. Its sister product, the $0.25 Fine Point Pen, which differed from the Crystal only in point size, accounted for over 15 percent of all ball-point pen units sold.

In 1973, writing instruments accounted for approximately 90 percent of BIC's consolidated net sales. Nonretractable pens accounted for 80 percent of the writing instrument unit sales, retractable pens for 6 percent, fine line porous point pens for 12 percent, and refills for 2 percent. Table 1 presents the 1973 BIC writing instrument product line.

Table 1

1973 WRITING INSTRUMENT PRODUCT LINE

Product name	Ink colors	Point sizes	Retail price
Ball-Point Pens			
Nonretractable/nonrefillable:			
Crystal.	4	m	$0.19
Fine point.	4	f	.25
Reproduction.	4	m	.25
Eraser.	4	m,f	.25
Deluxe eraser.	4	m,f	.29
Deluxe.	4	m	.39
Accountant.	4	f	.49
Retractable/refillable:			
Clic.	4	m,f	0.49
2-color pen.	2	m,f	.69
4-color pen.	4	m,f	.98
Citation.	1	m	1.00
Retractable/nonrefillable:			
Pocket pen.	3	m	0.29
Fine Line Porous Point Pen			
BIC Banana.	10	m,f	0.29

Source: Corporate records.

Nonretractable ball point pens

The Crystal, a nonretractable/nonrefillable ball point pen, was introduced on the market in 1959 at a retail price of $0.29. As the first product of the newly formed Waterman-BIC Corporation, the BIC Crystal was intended to become a "brand name replacement for all no-name,[2] disposable pens in a market where no dominant competitor existed." Its retail price was dropped to $0.19 in 1961. In commenting on the success of the Crystal, Mr. Jack Paige, vice president of marketing, remarked:

> We built this company on the 19¢ pen. In 1961 it was selling for 19¢, and in 1973 it is still 19¢. One-third of all retail sales are from the 19¢ stick. It's a highly profitable business. We've found ways to become more efficient and still maintain our profitability.

Between 1961 and 1968, BIC expanded its nonretractable ball-point pen line to include six other models of varying point sizes, ink colors, and usages. Nonretractables were priced from $0.19 to $0.49.

---

[2] No-name products were those which were not advertised and were marketed at retail prices far below the comparable, inexpensive, nationally advertised products.

Retractable ball-point pens

In 1968, BIC introduced its first retractable/refillable ball-point pen, the 49-cent Clic.[3] Management felt that the Clic would (1) improve the overall corporate profit margin, (2) enable the company to sell merchandise in multipacks (quantity selling in one package), such as for school specials, and (3) increase distribution—as some retail outlets, particularly those not dependent on BIC for their profits—had been reluctant to sell the 19-cent and 25-cent pens.

Following the Clic, four other retractable ball-point pens were added to the BIC product line. Three imported French pens: the 98-cent 4-Color Pen (1971), the 69-cent 2-Color Pen (1972), and $1 Citation Pen (1973) were introduced to "upgrade ball-point pen sales." The 29-cent Pocket Pen, the only nonrefillable pen in the retractable line, was added to "expand primary demand for ball-point pens."[4]

Fine line porous point pens

In April of 1972, BIC introduced its first nonball-point pen product, the 29 cent BIC Banana, which was a fine line porous point pen produced in a stick shape. Mr. Paige commented on the Banana decision:

> The development of the concept of entering the porous point pen market was not a sudden decision. Our philosophy was simply that as soon as we had a porous point pen that would reflect BIC quality and could be mass marketed at a popular price that anybody could afford, we would then move into that business.
>
> For openers, we were faced with a couple of major problems. First we were a late entry and the market was dominated by a 49¢ strong brand name of good quality that had a 50% market share. Maybe for some companies that stark statistic would have been enough not to enter. However, at BIC there is an aggressive attitude about marketing. That attitude manifested itself a year and one-half ago when we began plotting our sales course for the introduction of this new product. (BIC spent $3 million on advertising the BIC Banana in 1972.) We took the attitude that we weren't going to be squeezed into that remaining 50% share that the leading brand left for the rest of the field. Our plan was to expand the consumer market for this type of writing instrument—to make it grow. In a larger market, we felt we would have the opportunity to build a franchise that would give us a substantial share.

In reviewing the same product decision, Mr. Alexiades said:

> In 1966 we saw the product opportunity for the soft tip pen, but Marcel Bich owned 90% of the company, and we had a difficult time convincing him that this was the right approach. He thought that the soft tip pen was a passing thing and that it was impractical because it wouldn't write through carbon. But we're in a carbon society and

---

[3] In retractable pens, industry sales volume in dollars was concentrated in the high-priced products and in units in the no-name brands.

[4] Despite a major introductory campaign ($1.5 million spent on advertising), sales in the Pocket Pen were "disappointing," according to one company spokesman. He attributed the poor results to styling problems and a lack of room for new products in a market with a declining sales growth rate.

there's no logical explanation for the consumer. However, M. Bich's philosophy changed. Years ago, he only wanted to sell ball point pens. He's now interested in inexpensive, disposable, mass-produced items. He has the marketing know-how, the distribution, the name.

We saw that the porous point pen was not a fad so we got in, perhaps a little late, but at least we entered an expanding portion of the market. The growth rate of ball point pen sales had leveled off. If we didn't enter the porous pen market, it would have been difficult to grow since we're so dominant in the industry. We knew that the only way to grow was through product line diversification or acquisition.

Our objective is to become the largest producer of fine line porous point pens. We are in ball point pens. It might be difficult because Gillette's Flair has been there for five years. Papermate brand is not a no-name brand with no resources like those which we initially attacked in the ball point pen market.

A competitor commented on the market entry of the BIC Banana:

Many people associated BIC with the ball point pen. BIC had a difficult time because people thought that the Banana was a ball point. It's a stick shape and looks like a ball point. They don't have that problem with the lighter (1973) because it is a different looking product altogether. BIC hasn't done well with the Banana against the Flair. After all, who could enter the stick pen market now and do well against BIC? But at least BIC broke the price point (49¢) with its 29¢ point which softened the retail and commercial markets. Maybe they'll get smart and get out.

THE MARKETS

Mr. Adler's philosophy had always been "to sell BIC products wherever there was a doorknob." Consistent with that view, marketing efforts had been focused on all writing instrument markets, with special emphasis placed on the "four key sales volume opportunities": the retail, commercial, ad/specialty, and premium markets, which represented about 90 percent of the dollar sales volume in the writing instrument industry in 1973. The other three markets, government, military, and export, accounted for the remaining 10 percent. In 1973, the Writing Instrument Manufacturers Association estimated total industry sales at $353.3 million.

Retail market

The retail market, or over-the-counter market, was the largest mechanical writing instrument market, accounting for over 50 percent, or $176.6 million, of the total industry dollar sales in 1973. Of significance in the retail market was the growing trend away from indirect selling through retail distributors to independent stores towards direct selling from the manufacturers to mass merchandise outlets.

Since the national success of the 19-cent Crystal pen in 1964, BIC had completely dominated the ball point pen segment of the retail market. By the end of 1973, BIC held a 66 percent share of that segment, followed by Gillette with 15 percent and Lindy with 5 percent. In fine line porous point pens, Gillette was the front runner with a 35 percent share followed by BIC with 22 percent, Magic Marker with 8 percent, and Pentel with 5 percent.

Management attributed BIC's successful penetration of the retail market to its aggressive marketing and distribution policies, as well as to the low price and high quality of its products.

Commercial market

The commercial market, or office supply market, was the second largest mechanical writing instrument market, accounting for about 20 percent, or $70.6 million, of total industry sales in 1973. Selling in the commercial market was primarily handled through commercial distributors, who channeled products from the manufacturers to office supply dealers, who in turn sold to commercial customers. Large office supply dealers bought directly from manufacturers and used distributors to fill in inventory gaps.

At the end of 1973, management estimated that the leading market shareholders in ball-point pens in the commercial market were BIC with 50 percent, followed by Berol with 18 percent, and Gillette with 5 percent. In fine line porous point pens, it was estimated that Gillette held a 40 percent share, Berol 25 percent, Pentel 10 percent, and BIC 4.5 percent.

In commenting on BIC's 4.5 percent market share in fine line porous point pens, Mr. Adler said:

> We have had difficulty in the commercial market because that market is conditioned to something like the Flair, Pentel, or Berol porous pens which sell for 49¢ and allow good margins to the distributors. The model which BIC manufactures does not compete head on with is the Flair. Ours is a stick model; theirs is a pocket model. Because of the design of the product, it's difficult to get a certain percentage of the market. The Flair product costs twice as much to manufacture (has a clip, etc.). The 29¢ Write-Brothers also has a clip. For us, we're a long way from being Number 1. To get into the porous pen business, we had to use the stick model. Our problem is that the distributors do not want to push the Banana because they have a 49¢ market. Naturally, they make less on a 29¢ model. It will take time.

Advertising/specialty and premium markets

The ad/specialty and premium markets together accounted for approximately 20 percent or $70.6 million of the total industry dollar sales volume in 1973.

Ad/specialty sales referred to special orders made through specialized distributors for products imprinted with a slogan or organization name. Competition in the ad/specialty market was based heavily on price which accounted for the strength of the no-name brands in that market. BIC held close to a 5 percent share in the ad/specialty market in 1973.

A "premium" was defined as a free promotional item which was attached to another product in order to promote the sale of that product. Premium sales were made through distributors or direct from the manufacturer to customer. As in the ad/specialty market, competition was based upon price. Unlike in that market, it was also based upon brand recognition and included a broader base of product types, not just writing instruments. Although it was a small market, management considered BIC's participation in the premium market as important in "reinforcing the firm's dominant position in the pen business." BIC held close to a 100 percent market share among writing instrument firms in the premium market in 1973.

THE COMPETITION

In 1973, approximately 200 firms were engaged in the manufacture and sale of mechanical writing instruments in the United States. Most firms competed selectively in the industry on the basis of (1) product type: fountain pen, mechanical pencil, ball-point pen, or soft tip pen; (2) price range: high (>$1), medium ($0.50–$1.00), and low (<$0.50); and (3) market: retail, commercial, ad/specialty, premium, military, government, and export. Strong advertising programs and mass-distribution networks were considered critical for national success.

In management's view, BIC had four major writing instrument competitors: Berol, Gillette, Lindy, and Pentel.[5] The five firms competed at the following price points with similar products.

Table 2

1973 SELECTED PRODUCT LINES

Product type	BIC	Berol	Gillette Paper Mate	Gillette Write-Bros.	Lindy	Pentel
Ball-Point Pens						
Retractable:						
Refillable..........	$0.49	$0.29	$0.98	$ —	$1.00	$2.98
	0.69	0.39	1.50			5.00
	0.98	0.49	1.98			7.00
	1.00	0.59	3.95			8.50
		1.49	5.00			
			5.95			
Nonrefillable.......	0.29			0.39		0.79
Nonretractable.......	0.19	0.19		0.19	0.19—	
	0.25	0.25			0.59	
		0.29			(0.20)	
		0.39				
Fine Line						
Porous point pens.....	0.29	0.29	0.49	0.29	0.59	0.29
		0.49	0.98			0.35
			1.95			0.49

Source: Corporate records.

[5] The Magic Marker Corporation was considered a strong competitor in fine line porous point pens with four models selling from $0.19–0.49 and comprising an estimated 8 percent share of the retail market. However, Magic Marker was best known for its broad tip markers (ten models, from $0.39 to $1.29). Its ball point pen products were sold strictly as no-name brands.

The Berol, Lindy, and Pentel corporations were well known for product innovation. In 1973, the Berol Corporation, best known for its drafting products, particularly for its Eagle brand pencils, was the second firm to introduce the rolling writer combination pen, a pen which performed like a regular fountain pen, yet could write through carbons. Lindy Pen Corporation had earned its reputation as an early entrant into new markets, yet lacked the advertising strength to back the sale of its new products. Lindy introduced a 39-cent stick pen prior to the introduction of the BIC Crystal in 1959, a fine line porous point pen in 1969, and a disposable lighter in 1970. Pentel Corporation had earned the reputation of "revolutionizing the U.S. mechanical writing instrument industry" with the introduction of the soft tip in 1964 and the rolling writer combination pen in 1969. Like Lindy, it lacked the resources to support heavy advertising and mass distribution programs.

Gillette

The Gillette Company was considered BIC's major competitor in all writing instrument products. The comparative performance in writing instruments for the two firms from 1968–73 is shown in Table 3.

Table 3

COMPARATIVE PERFORMANCE IN WRITING INSTRUMENTS
(consolidated statements)

	1968	1969	1970	1971	1972	1973
BIC						
Net sales ($ millions)	$29.6	$36.6	$37.7	$39.5	$47.6	$52.4
Net income ($ millions)	3.2	4.3	4.0	5.5	6.3	7.3 (est.)
Net income/sales	10.8%	11.7%	10.6%	13.9%	13.2%	14.0% (est.)
Net sales/total assets*	—	—	1.6	1.4	1.3	1.3
Total Assets/Total Equity†	—	—	1.3	1.2	1.1	1.2
Gillette (Paper Mate Division)						
Net sales ($ millions)	$33.2	$36.5	$47.0	$51.1	$60.9	$74.5
Net income ($ millions)	2.5	3.3	3.3	2.5	3.0	4.3
Net income/sales	4.5%	9.0%	7.0%	4.9%	4.9%	5.8%
Net sales/total assets*	1.4	1.4	1.3	1.3	1.3	1.3
Total Assets/Total Equity†	1.8	1.8	1.8	1.9	2.0	2.1

* Estimated total assets allocated to writing instruments.
† Total corporate assets and equity.
Source: Corporate 10-K reports.

In 1973, Gillette competed in the high-price market with its Paper Mate products and in the low-price market with its Write-Brothers products. The Paper Mate ball-point pens had been the mainstay of its writing instrument business since the early 1950s. In the late 1960s, management at Gillette "recognized the potential of Pentel's new soft tip pens." Backed by a large research and development capability, a well-known corporate name, and advertising and distribution strength, Gillette set out to capture that market with a fine line porous point pen

Table 4

BI-MONTHLY RETAIL MARKET SHARE PATTERNS
(units)

	JF'72	MA	MJ	JA	SO	ND	JF'73	MA	MJ	JA	SO	ND
Ball-Point Pens												
Total BIC	66%	67%	65%	65%	66%	65%	67%	66%	65%	66%	68%	66%
$0.19 Crystal	36	35	34	33	31	31	32	32	31	31	31	31
0.25 Fine Point	12	14	13	13	11	13	13	12	13	13	11	12
0.29 Pocket Pen	—	1	2	2	3	3	3	3	3	2	2	2
0.49 Accountant	8	7	7	8	9	7	8	8	7	8	10	9
0.49 Clic	8	8	7	7	9	8	8	8	8	8	9	7
Other	2	2	2	2	3	3	3	4	3	4	5	5
Total Gillette	8	8	9	13	13	13	13	15	15	14	14	15
$0.19 W-B	—	—	—	3	3	3	4	6	5	5	5	5
0.39 W-B	—	—	1	2	2	2	2	2	2	2	2	2
0.98 Retractable	4	4	4	4	4	4	4	4	4	4	4	4
Other	4	4	4	4	6	4	3	3	4	3	3	4
Lindy	7	7	8	7	6	7	6	6	6	5	5	5
Other	19	18	18	15	15	15	14	13	14	15	13	14
Total	100%	100%	100%	100%	100%	100%	100%	100%	100%	100%	100%	100%
Fine Line Porous Point Pens												
BIC	—	—	5	11	15	16	16	19	19	20	23	22
Total Gillette	49	46	45	43	43	40	39	37	36	37	35	35
$0.49 Flair	45	43	41	36	34	33	32	30	30	30	28	29
0.49 Hotliner	2	2	1	1	1	1	1	1	1	1	1	1
0.29 W-B	—	—	2	5	7	5	5	5	5	5	5	4
Other	2	1	1	1	1	1	1	1	—	1	1	1
Lindy	5	5	4	4	4	4	3	3	2	2	2	2
Magic Marker	—	—	—	—	—	—	6	6	7	8	9	8
Pentel	9	9	9	7	7	7	7	6	6	5	4	5
Other	37	40	37	35	31	33	29	29	30	28	27	28
Total	100%	100%	100%	100%	100%	100%	100%	100%	100%	100%	100%	100%

Source: Corporate records.

called "Flair," which retailed in three models from $0.40 to $1.95. In 1972 Gillette created the Write-Brothers products: a 39-cent retractable ball-point pen, a 29-cent fine line porous point pen, and a 19-cent non-retractable ball-point pen, in order "to take advantage of growth opportunities in the low-price end of the mechanical writing instrument market." The Write-Brothers name was selected to prevent confusion on the part of consumers who had associated the Paper Mate name with high-priced ball-point pen products and middle- to high-priced Flair products.

Retail market share patterns for BIC and Gillette are shown in Table 4. (The BIC Banana was introduced in May of 1972 and the Write-Brothers products in July of 1972.)

Over the five-year period 1969–73, BIC and Gillette made the following advertising expenditures on writing instruments:

Table 5

WRITING INSTRUMENT ADVERTISING BUDGET ESTIMATES
(dollars in millions)

	1969	1970	1971	1972	1973
Gillette...............	$1.9	$4.0	$6.0	$8.5	$9.0
BIC.................	3.6	4.0	4.3	7.0	6.8

Source: Case researcher's estimates derived from corporate records, interviews with company officials, and journal articles.

In commenting on advertising programs and the BIC/Gillette competition in general, Mr. David Furman, advertising director at BIC, said:

> Our strategy has been to emphasize profit, and therefore look for the mass market. Gillette has said: "Let's make the most money and not worry about the size of the market." Gillette had a nice profitable business with Flair. It kept Papermate alive. But they can't stay alive with one-dollar-plus pens. We expanded the market so now their unit sales are up. The philosophy of Gillette has been to spend heavily to develop the product, then let the products decay and spend on new product development. Their unit sales continue to go up but their loss of market share is considerable.

COMPANY POLICIES AND STRUCTURE

Mr. Adler had sometimes described his company as a car with four equally important wheels: sales, manufacturing, finance, and advertising, all of which had to be synchronized in order for the car to accelerate and sustain itself at high speed. That car, he claimed, had equal responsibility to its stockholders, employees, and customers. It followed, therefore, that management's attention should be focused on achieving a good return on investment, which Mr. Adler felt was derived by improving: (1) productivity (unit production per hour), (2) efficiency in production (cost savings methods), and (3) quality control standards and checks.

Finance

In the spring of 1971, BIC Pen effected a recapitalization which resulted in an aggregate number of 3.03 million outstanding common shares, 87 percent of which were owned by Société Bic, S.A., 3 percent by M. Bich, 9 percent by Mr. Adler, and 1 percent by other officers and directors (stock bonuses).[6] On September 15 of that year, 655,000 of those common shares were offered to the public at $25 per share, resulting in a new capital structure of 67 percent of the shares owned by Société Bic, S.A., 3 percent by M. Bich, 7 percent by Mr. Adler, 1 percent by other officers, and 22 percent by the public. Proceeds from the public offering after underwriting discounts and commissions amounted to $15.4 million. On July 27, 1972, M. Bich exercised his warrants for the purchase of 210,000 shares of common stock at $25 per share, totaling $5.25 million, which BIC received in cash. That same day, the company declared a 2-for-1 share split in the form of a 100 percent share dividend of 3.24 million shares, $1 par value, which resulted in the transference of $3.24 million from retained earnings to common stock. At the end of 1972, 6.48 million shares were outstanding of the 10 million shares authorized in June of 1972; none of the 1 million authorized shares of preferred stock had been issued.

Since 1967, the company paid the following cash dividends:

Table 6

BIC PEN CORPORATION DIVIDEND PAYMENT HISTORY

	1967	1968	1969	1970	1971	1972	1973
Consolidated net income (dollars in millions)	$2.862	$3.231	$4.233	$4.033	$5.546	$6.264	$7.430
Dividends (dollars in millions)	2.591	—	1.175	1.166	1.319	1.603	1.750
Adjusted net dividend/ share*	0.43	—	0.19	0.19	0.22	0.26	0.27
Stock price range*	—	—	—	—	12¼–18	16¼–37	11⅝–32½

* After giving retroactive effect to a 2-for-1 share split in 1972.
Source: BIC Pen Corporation annual report, 1973.

Regarding dividend policy, Mr. Alexiades said:

When we were a private firm, there was no dividend policy. Dividends were only given when declared by M. Bich. In 1969 when we knew that we would be going public, we tried to establish a policy, to find the proper relationship between earnings and dividends. 20%–25% of earnings seemed like a good target policy. Now we're having trouble increasing our dividends, due to government guidelines, although we would like to increase the payout in accordance with our rise in earnings.

[6] Four million common shares were authorized.

The purchase of the original BIC plant from the Norden Company in 1963 was financed with a 5¾ percent mortgage loan from Connecticut General, payable in monthly installments of $7,749 (principal and interest) until January 1, 1981.[7] The three plant expansions—$1 million for 110,000 square feet in 1965, $1.8 million for 100,000 square feet in 1969, and $5–$6 million for 275,000 square feet in 1973—were financed through short-term loans and cash on hand. Regarding the 1973 expansion, Mr. Alexiades said: "We decided to use our own cash so that if something develops in 1974 or 1975, such as an acquisition or new product opportunity, we can always fall back on our credit rating."[8]

In keeping with BIC's informal organizational structure, management used no formalized budgets. "We use goals, not budgets. We just keep surprising ourselves with our performance," said Mr. Alexiades, "although perhaps as we mature, we will need a more structured arrangement."

BIC was known in the New Haven area for its attractive compensation plan. It was Mr. Adler's belief that good people would be attracted by good pay. Plant workers received the highest hourly rates in the area ($4.53 base rate for the average grade level of work). All employees were invited to participate in a stock purchase plan whereby up to 10 percent of their salaries could be used to purchase stock at a 10 percent discount from the market price, with BIC assuming the brokerage commission cost. Executives participated in a bonus plan which Mr. Adler described as follows:

> We have a unique bonus system which I'm sure the Harvard Business School would think is crazy. Each year I take a percentage of profits before tax and give 40% to sales, 40% to manufacturing, and 20% to the treasurer to be divided up among executives in each area. Each department head keeps some for himself and gives the rest away. We never want bonuses to be thought of as salaries because they would lose their effect. So we change the bonus day each year so that it always comes as a pleasant surprise, something to look forward to.

Manufacturing

Manufacturing had emphasized the development over the years of a totally integrated, highly automated production process capable of mass producing high-quality units at a very low cost. Except for the metal clips, rings, and plungers, all components—even the ink—were produced in the Milford plant. Société Bic had supplied the basic production technology, machinery, and research and development.[9] Some raw materials, particularly the brass, were still imported from France.

The U.S. energy crisis posed a major threat to BIC in 1973. Poly-

---

[7] The loan had not been paid off by 1973, because of its low interest rate.

[8] BIC borrowed on a seasonal basis to meet working capital needs, using bank lines of credit ($15.5 million available; maximum borrowed was $10.6 million in 1970).

[9] BIC Pen Corporation spent $30,368, $15,254, and $128,553 on R&D in 1971, 1972, and 1973, respectively.

styrene, the key raw material used in making pens, was a petroleum-derivative. Mr. Adler commented on the shortage of plastic:

> We've reached a point in our economy where it's become more difficult to produce than sell. I mean I have this big new plant out there [pointing to the new $5–$6 million addition] and I may not be able to produce any products. I have to worry about the overhead. I'm reluctant to substitute materials.
>
> I predict that in 1974 polystyrene will cost more than double what it costs in 1973, which is 15 cents per pound. It represents about 10 percent of the manufacturing cost of the ball point stick pen.

The production process consisted of three stages: (1) manufacture of parts, (2) assembly of parts, and (3) packaging. Porous pens (4 parts) were the simplest instrument to manufacture followed by ball-point pens (7 parts) and lighters (21 parts). Some parts, such as non-retractable pen barrels, were interchangeable, which built flexibility into the production process. Production rates were steady throughout the year, while inventory build-ups were seasonal. In mid-1973, BIC was producing on average about 2.5 million ball-point pen units per day and 0.5 million porous pens per day, which was close to plant capacity.

Management felt that production costs were substantially controlled by the strict enforcement of a quality control system. One fourth of the plant's employees participated in quality control checks at each stage of the production process, which was precision-oriented, involving tolerances as close as 0.0002±. Mr. Charles Matjouranis, director of manufacturing. had stated that it was his job to search for cost-savings programs which would protect profit margins on products. He said:

> We are in the automation business. Because of our large volume, one-tenth of one cent in savings turns out to be enormous. Labor and raw materials costs keep increasing, but we buy supplies in volume and manufacture products in volume. One advantage of the high volume business is that you can get the best equipment and amortize it entirely over a short period of time (four to five months). I'm always looking for new equipment. If I see a cost-savings machine, I can buy it. I'm not constrained by money.

In 1973, there were 700 persons working at BIC in Milford, of which 625 were production personnel represented by the United Rubber Workers Union under a three-year contract. Management considered its relations with employees as excellent and maintained that BIC offered the best hourly rates, fringe benefits, and work environment in the area. Weekly meetings between supervisors and factory workers were held to air grievances. Workers were treated on a first-name basis, and were encouraged to develop pride in their jobs by understanding production technicalities and participating in the quality control program and production shift competition. Most assembly-line workers were women. At least 40 percent of the factory workers had been with BIC for over ten years, and 60 percent–65 percent for over five years. Despite increased automation, very few layoffs had occurred because workers were able to be retained for other positions to compensate for the increase in production unit volume. Over 50 percent of the workers had performed more than one job.

Marketing and sales

In admiring his BIC ring studded with six diamonds, each representing an achieved sales goal, Mr. Ron Shaw, national sales manager, remarked:

> It's almost a dream story here. When I started with the company in 1961 as an assistant zone manager, we were selling 8 million units a year. We now sell 2.5 million units a day. Everyone said that: One, we couldn't sell 5,000 feet of writing in one unit and succeed; two, we couldn't have the biggest sales force in the writing instrument industry and make money; and three, we couldn't advertise a 19-cent pen on TV and make money. Well, we did and we're Number One!

Distribution. The BIC products were sold in the retail and commercial markets by 120 company salesmen who called on approximately 10,000 accounts. Those accounts represented large retailers, such as chains, as well as wholesale distributors. Through those 10,000 accounts, BIC achieved distribution for its products in approximately 200,000 retail outlets, of which 12,000 were commercial supply stores. In addition, the salesmen called on 20,000 independent retail accounts which were considered important in the marketplace. In the case of those accounts, the BIC salesmen merely filled orders for the distributors. A specialized BIC sales force sold ad/specialty orders to ad/specialty distributors and most premium orders directly to corporate customers.

The backbone of BIC's customer business had originally been the mom and pop stores. They had initially resisted selling BIC pens, but were later forced to trade up from the no-name products once BIC had become a popular selling brand. As product distribution patterns moved away from indirect selling toward more direct selling to large chains and discount houses, the mass merchandisers became eager to carry BIC products, which had earned a reputation for fast turnover, heavy advertising support, and brand recognition. In 1973, BIC did 60 percent of its sales volume through distributors and 40 percent through direct sales channels.

Pricing policy. BIC had never raised the original retail prices of any of its products. Management, therefore, placed a great deal of importance on retail price selection and product cost management. Advertising expenses generally ran 15 percent of the manufacturer's selling price; the combined costs of packaging and distribution approximated 20 percent–30 percent of the manufacturer's selling price. The distributor's profit margin was 15 percent off the listed retail price; the indirect retail buyer's was 40 percent; and the direct retail buyer's was 55 percent. Regarding pricing policy, Mr. Adler said:

> If I increase my price, I help my competition. The marketplace, not ourselves, dictates the price. We must see what people are willing to pay. You must sell as cheaply as possible to get the volume.

Customary marketing tools. In a speech made before the Dallas Athletic Club in September of 1972, Mr. Paige remarked: "We're in the *idea* business. Selling is an idea. Many people have products but we have ideas."

BIC used four basic marketing tools to sell its "ideas": (1) advertising, (2) point-of-purchase displays, (3) packaging forms, and (4) trade and consumer promotions. Management felt that the only way to enter a new market was to be innovative either by: (1) introducing a new product, (2) creating a new market segment, or (3) using unique merchandising techniques designed specifically for that market. The BIC salesmen were known to be aggressive.[10] Products were always introduced on a regional roll-out basis with the entry into each new region attempted only after market saturation had been achieved successfully in the prior region.

Advertising was considered the most important element of the BIC marketing program. Company research had shown that seven out of ten writing instruments sold were impulse purchase items. With that knowledge, management felt that widespread distribution of a generic name product line was essential for success. It was further felt that retailers and commercial stationers preferred to carry nationally advertised brands.

BIC used TV advertising, "the cheapest medium when counting heads," almost exclusively. In 1973, BIC added advertising in *T.V. Guide* and the Sunday supplements "in order to reach more women, the biggest purchasers of writing instruments."

In keeping with the belief that merchandising techniques should be designed differently for each product and market, BIC varied its TV commercials substantially, depending upon the intended product usage, time of entry into the market, and demographic interest. Each advertising message was designed to be simple and to communicate *one* idea at a time. Exhibit 4 presents examples of four different themes: (1) BIC has a lighter (BIC Butane); (2) BIC's products are durable (Crystal); (3) BIC has coloring instruments for children (Ink Crayons[11]); and (4) BIC offers a "new and fun way to write" (BIC Banana).

Another marketing tool was the *point-of-purchase display.* Mr. Paige remarked:

> Merchandise well displayed is half sold, particularly on a low consumer interest item. Displays must be designed to fit every retail requirement because, for example, what's good for Woolworth's may not be good for the corner drug store.

Packaging was considered another form of advertising. "We want to make the 19-cent pen look like a one-dollar pen," Mr. Paige had said. BIC was one of the first firms to use the concept of multipacks. Packag-

---

[10] On average, assistant zone managers earned $12,000 and zone managers earned $22,000 a year. Compensation consisted of a base salary plus commission.

[11] Ink Crayons consisted of multipack of BIC Banana pens in an array of ink colors.

Exhibit 4

TELEVISION ADVERTISING THEMES

Source: BIC Pen Corporation annual report, 1972.

ing forms were changed as much as six times a year. Regarding packaging and *promotions*, Mr. Alexiades commented:

> We've created a demand for constant innovation, excitement in the marketplace. Many people say that's the reason for BIC's success. We change the manner in which we sell (blister packs,[12] multipacks, gift

------
[12] Blister packs were product packages which were designed to be displayed on peg boards.

packages), which makes our merchandise turn and keeps our name in front of the wholesaler and retailer all of the time. The consumer remembers us because we offer a true value. The retailer and dealer remember us because they receive special incentive offers, free merchandise, and promotional monies, plus their merchandise turns.

Exhibit 5

BIC PEN CORPORATION
1973 Internal Organizational Chart

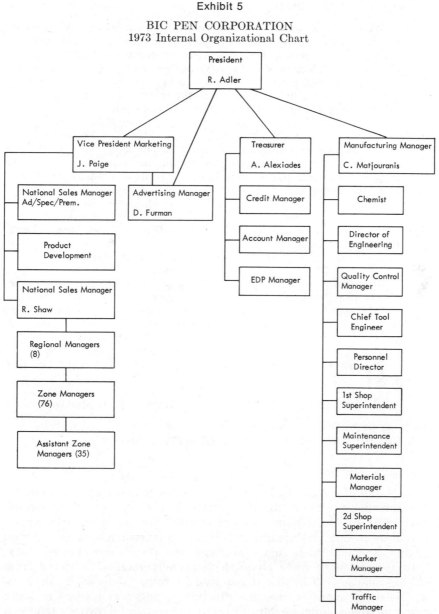

Source: Corporate records.

Organizational structure

Throughout its 15-year history, the BIC organizational structure had remained small and simple. (See Exhibit 5 for the 1973 organizational chart.) In 1973, the average tenure (since 1958) of the six key executive officers was 13 years. At least 40 percent of the factory workers had been at BIC for over ten years. Several of the managers commented on the BIC environment:

> We try to run this company as a family organization. We don't try to run it as a General Motors. We've been very successful with this concept. It's a closely knit management group—very informal. Decisions are made immediately. A young guy comes here. He sees that we [management] exist. We understand him. He gets his decisions immediately. We try to get him to join the family. Inside of two to three years, if he's not in the family, he won't work out.
>
> Mr. Robert Adler
President
>
> Part of the success of management is our ability to communicate with one another. We're trying to remain the same. It's one of the regrets that growth has to bring in departments and department heads, but we're trying to maintain a minimum.
>
> Mr. Alexander Alexiades,
Treasurer
>
> We have few managers, but the best. One real good one is better than two average.
>
> Mr. Charles Matjouranis,
Manufacturing Director
>
> This company does not believe in assistants. Philosophically, we try to stay away from any bureaucracy. There are no politics involved here, no knifing, no backbiting. Part is a function of size. Everybody knows his place and area of responsibility. We don't want to break from that.
>
> Mr. David Furman,
Advertising Director
>
> We promote from within. We recognize the abilities of our own people.
>
> Mr. Ron Shaw,
National Sales Manager

THE BIC BUTANE DISPOSABLE CIGARETTE LIGHTER

The lighter decision

In March of 1973, BIC Pen Corporation introduced its first nonwriting instrument product, the BIC Butane disposable lighter, at a retail price of $1.49. Management viewed the BIC Butane as a logical extension of its current product line as it was inexpensive, disposable, of high quality, and able to be mass-produced and distributed through most writing instrument trade channels, especially retail. It differed from writing instruments in that it required 21 rather than the basic 7 assembly parts, more precise manufacturing, and was subject to strict governmental standards. Mr. Furman made the following statement regarding BIC's decision to enter the disposable lighter business:

For years we were in the high-level, profitability trap. We had had it as far as that market would go. The Banana was the first break out from the trap and now the lighter. We utilize our strengths, but we're no longer a writing instrument company. We're in the expansion stage where writing instruments are a base from which we are expanding. We're using the skills we've gained and are applying them to any kind of mass-produced product.

Introductory campaign

The decision to sell a disposable lighter dated back to 1971 when M. Marcel Bich purchased Flaminaire, a French lighter company, with the objective of marketing a substitute for matches in Europe. Matches had never been free in Europe, and for that reason disposable lighter sales had been very successful there far before they caught on in the United States. The BIC Butane was imported from Flaminaire, but was scheduled to be produced at the Milford plant on a highly automated production line by March of 1974.

The BIC Butane was introduced first in the Southwest, where management claimed it had captured a 32 percent retail market share by year's end. Management expected its national retail market share of 16 percent to rise to 25 percent when the product reached full national distribution in February of 1974. The regional roll-out was backed with a $1 million advertising campaign. A $3 million campaign was planned for 1974. Lighter sales approximated 10 percent of BIC's consolidated net sales in 1973. An industry source estimated their pretax margin at 15 percent–21 percent.

The cigarette lighter industry

Lighters were categorized in three basic product classes: disposables, regular refillables, and electronics. Disposable lighters contained butane gas; electronic lighters contained butane gas or a battery; regular refillable lighters contained either butane gas (90 percent) or liquid fuel (10 percent). There were three basic price categories: <$2 (all disposables), $2–$12 (most regular refillables), and >$12 (all electronics and fancy regular refillables). It was estimated that 75 percent–80 percent of all cigarette lighters sold in 1972 were priced below $6.95 at retail.

Table 7

U.S. CIGARETTE LIGHTER RETAIL SALES
(dollars and units in millions)

	1969	1970	1971	1972	1973 (est.)
Total lighters ($)	$94.9	$98.1	$106.9	$115.0	153.0
Disposables ($)	n.a.	8.5	18.0	36.0	50.0
Units (no.)	—	—	13	21	40

Note: n.a. - not available.
Source: Case researcher's estimates based on trade and company interviews and unpublished figures from the *Drug Topics* magazine research group (1972).

Cigarette lighter sales in the middle price range had begun to fall off in the early 1970s. As a replacement for matches, disposable lighters had expanded the primary demand for lighters and represented the major growth opportunity in the U.S. lighter industry.

Major competitors

By 1973 many firms, particularly manufacturers of writing instruments, had entered the disposable lighter business. Most firms served as distributors of foreign-made products, many of which were reputed by trade sources to be of questionable quality. As with writing instruments, BIC's management believed that industry success was heavily dependent on the strength of a firm's advertising program and distribution network, although most firms did well initially due to the excessive demand for disposable lighters relative to the available supply.

There were three clear contenders for industry dominance in the disposable lighter business: Gillette, Garrity Industries, and BIC, with Scripto a distant fourth. Gillette's Cricket lighter was the leading market shareholder, accounting for one-third of all disposable lighter sales in 1973.

Table 8
1973 MAJOR COMPETITORS IN DISPOSABLE LIGHTERS

	BIC	*Gillette*	*Garrity*	*Scripto**
Market entry (year).......	1973	1972	1967	1972
Product..................	BIC Butane	Cricket	Dispoz-a-lite	Catch 98
Price....................	$1.49	$1.49	$1.49	$0.98
Product produced in.......	France (→'73); U.S. (after)	France (→'73); Puerto Rico (after)	France	Japan
Ad $ strategy (1973).......	Consumer	Consumer (¾) Trade (¼)	Trade	None
Distribution emphasis*.....	Mass/chains	Mass/chains	Smoke shops, hotel stands, drug stores	Independent retailers

* In 1974, Scripto planned to raise the price of the Catch 98 to $1.19, add another Japanese disposable lighter at the $1.39 price point, and produce a $1.69 disposable lighter in its Atlanta plant.
Source: Casewriter's interviews with corporate marketing managers.

In speculating on the future of the BIC Butane lighter, Mr. Paige stated:

> We think that the disposable butane will cannibalize every low-priced lighter. BIC, Dispoz-a-lite and Cricket will do 90 percent of the business in 1973. Cricket advertises extensively. BIC will compete with Cricket at the $1.49 price point. BIC and Cricket will dominate the industry in the future. The cheaper disposables of lesser quality will only sustain themselves.

BIC Pen Corporation (B)

News release: January 11, 1974

BIC Pen Corporation, which has specialized successfully in mass marketing consumer products, soon will introduce a new product which it will distribute in the $1.3 billion retail pantyhose market, Robert P. Adler, president, disclosed today.

"The sale of pantyhose is for BIC a further expansion into other mass-produced disposable consumer products," Mr. Adler said. "Because of BIC's strong reputation for value, and our ability to merchandise successfully to the consumer through more than 200,000 retail outlets, we believe our new pantyhose product will be well received in this marketplace."

THE WOMEN'S HOSIERY INDUSTRY

Hosiery had always been the most rapidly consumable apparel item in a woman's wardrobe. For years the women's hosiery industry had been stable in unit sales and repetitive in product offerings. Many low-profile brands were sold in a wide range of sizes and typical colors. The business "kicked up its heels" in the late 60s with the advent of the convenience product pantyhose and miniskirts. Hosiery became a fashion item, costing as much as $10 a pair, depending upon style, texture, color, and brand name. Prosperity did not last, however, and by 1973 the $2 billion women's hosiery business was characterized as "having to run faster to stay in the same place." The market had become plagued by an uncertainty in consumer demand, sagging profits, price battles, distribution changes, and the rising fashion trend of women's pants. Hosiery makers claimed that women had begun to go without hose or to wear ripped stockings under pants.

327

Exhibit 1

U.S. WOMEN'S HOSIERY INDUSTRY TRENDS

	1964	1965	1966	1967	1968	1969	1970	1971	1972	1973
Numbers of:										
Companies..........	645	609	576	579	574	530	502	471	457	390
Plants.............	828	782	750	746	741	734	699	665	604	521
Annual per capita consumption:										
Pantyhose........	—	—	—	—	2.3	9.0	13.3	11.0	12.7	11.7
Stockings........	1.48	15.7	17.3	19.5	18.1	12.7	6.3	4.2	3.1	2.5
Knee-highs, Anklets..........	0.1	0.1	0.1	0.1	0.1	0.1	0.1	0.3	0.6	1.2
Total Consumption	14.9	15.8	17.4	19.6	20.5	21.8	19.7	15.5	16.4	15.5

Source: National Association of Hosiery Manufacturers.

The pantyhose market

As an attempt to interject some life into the stable pantyhose market, the three big hosiery makers: Hanes Corporation, Kayser-Roth Corporation, and Burlington Industries, launched an unprecedented $33 million promotional campaign in 1973. They cast aside their established merchandising techniques and began pushing new, low-priced pantyhose in supermarkets. The firms adopted catchy brand names and used dramatic advertising campaigns centering around "trendy" packaging. Their assumption was that women would buy more pantyhose if the products were cheaper, more accessible, and more attractively displayed than before. No longer were branded products available exclusively in department or specialty stores at $3 a pair; rather they could be purchased at every corner market for 99¢ to $1.39. As a result, pantyhose sales in food outlets rose from 5 percent in 1968 to 28 percent of the industry pantyhose sales in 1973, with analysts predicting a 50 percent share by 1975. Despite the surge in supermarket buying, sales of pantyhose declined by 7 percent in 1973.

The private label business represented 50 percent of the hosiery sales in food stores in 1973, with some labels selling as low as 39 cents a pair. The supermarket invasion by known brands—"L'eggs" by Hanes, "Activ" by Burlington, and "No-Nonsense" by Kayser-Roth—resulted in a general upgrading in the quality of the private label brands, and an expansion of the branded lines to cover additional market segments, such as pantyhose in large sizes for heavier women, and pantyhose for less than $1 for price-conscious women.

In describing pantyhose purchase behavior, one industry source said:

> Generally, all women are interested in quality, price, fit, and availability, but purchasers do tend to fall into three basic categories: (1) women who think that all hosiery is the same and therefore look for the lowest price; (2) women who feel that an extremely low price implies inferior quality; and (3) women who switch off between high and low prices, depending upon their needs.

L'eggs was the largest selling brand name in 1973 with a 9 percent dollar volume share of the total hosiery market. The idea for L'eggs was born out of the recognition that no high-quality name brand dominated the highly fractionated pantyhose market; nor was one available at a reasonable price (<$2) at convenience locations (supermarkets). The L'eggs integrated marketing program centered around the theme, "Our L'eggs fit your legs," and the distinctive egg-shaped package. The L'eggs direct selling approach leaned heavily on a platoon of 1,000 young delivery women clad in hot pants and traveling their appointed routes in distinctive white vans. Their task was to restock flashy "L'eggs Boutiques" in supermarkets and drug chains. L'eggs retail sales rose from $9 million in 1970 to $110 million in 1973. Hanes spent $20 million on their promotion in 1972 and $13 million in 1973.

Activ and No-Nonsense pantyhose were priced at 99 cents a pair, in contrast with L'eggs at $1.39.[1] Both brands were backed by $10 million promotional campaigns in 1973. The "Activ Girls" competed with the "L'eggs Ladies." Similarly clad and driving red vans, they also sold products on consignment. Besides supermarkets, Activ pantyhose appeared in outlets serviced by tobacco distributors, thus supporting Burlington's motto: "Activs are everywhere." Kayser-Roth shunned the distribution system favored by the other two hosiery makers and delivered its No-Nonsense brand-name pantyhose to food brokers at supermarket warehouses. The No-Nonsense approach—without vans, hot pants, and comely delivery women—allowed the retailers a 45 percent profit margin, compared with the 35 percent return guaranteed by Hanes and Burlington.

THE PANTYHOSE DECISION

Mr. David Furman, advertising director, commented on BIC's entry into the pantyhose business:

> The hosiery industry used to be dominated by manufacturing, not marketing, companies. L'eggs was the first attempt to change that. The success of L'eggs and other industry leaders has depended on an extremely expensive direct selling distribution system which is good for large volume outlets but is not feasible for smaller stores or local advertising. BIC intends to use its usual jobbers and make it profitable for them to act as middlemen and garner the independent stores.
>
> Nearly all companies deal primarily with pantyhose as a fashion item. The market is moving away from the fashion emphasis, which cannot be successful in food stores. BIC will address the fit problem by using the slogan: "It fits there, it fits everywhere"; hence the name —Fannyhose. Ours is a utility story as it was with ball point pens.

In introducing Fannyhose to the trade, management used the theme of "taking a simple idea and making it pay off." The quality product was priced at $1.39, came in two sizes and three colors, and was packaged in a compact little can with a see-through top. The advertising

---

[1] Hanes introduced First-to-Last pantyhose at 99 cents a pair to counter the price competition from Activ and No-Nonsense pantyhose.

program centered around the "better fit" concept, as was illustrated in animated television commercials and Sunday supplements. Product promotions included cents-off coupons and free samples.

In contrast with its major competitors, BIC planned to act as a distributor of pantyhose, rather than as a manufacturer/distributor, and to establish a specialized sales force to sell the product direct or through distributors to its wide variety of writing instrument retail accounts. BIC's supplier was DIM, S.A., one of France's largest hosiery makers ($100 million in sales), which M. Bich bought control of in 1973. Mr. Furman called the BIC plan "a brilliant stroke around L'eggs. Theirs is a fixed system—low profits, no risk, fixed price. We add promotional profits by passing on to the trade the money we've saved by avoiding the need for our own service crews."

BIC's investors react

An article appearing in the February 4, 1974, edition of the *Wall Street Journal* described the reaction of the investment community to BIC's entry into the pantyhose business. One analyst cited several obstacles which BIC faced in its new venture, namely: (1) the limited pricing flexibility which BIC would have because of import duty costs[2]; and (2) the fact that BIC had not been particularly strong in supermarkets. Another analyst took a more positive view, citing the recent market price decline in the BIC stock to "investors' questions over the competitive nature of the pantyhose business without understanding the philosophy of BIC: to produce inexpensive disposable consumer products once there is an established market for them and to use its widespread marketing system to become a powerful force in the industry." A third analyst predicted a bright future for BIC in the pantyhose business because of its "access to materials through Société Bic, its reputation for high-quality products, its well-developed distribution system, and its commitment to marketing, rather than manufacturing, pantyhose."

---

[2] Duty fees averaged 33 percent per unit. One analyst speculated that the pre-tax margin on Fannyhose was 15 percent.

The Fernald Workshops

I'm concerned! We have some sticky problems here at the workshops now and some major questions about what the future holds and where we should be going.

Ms. Sue Sankar, coordinator of the Fernald Workshops in Waltham, Massachusetts, was talking about the situation confronting that institution and its staff.

Our immediate headache is subcontracts for the workshops. We employ over 160 mentally retarded residents of the Fernald School on a variety of production work. But the amount of available work has dropped substantially in recent months. We just lost a major contract for assembling and packing plastic flower pots; and there have been others. The recession hit us hard. If we don't get subcontracts, the shops can't run. All of us here are spending a good bit of our time trying to find ways to increase that activity. We did grow very rapidly in 1974, but there are still a *great* many residents of the school on waiting lists to get into workshops.

Some of us wonder whether we should try to expand our business in prime products—items we design, manufacture and sell ourselves. We already make and sell hand-made greeting cards and we assemble inexpensive ballpoint pens.

But there are other questions too. There are lots of developments going on now in our field. The Commonwealth of Massachusetts is actively pursuing a policy of deinstitutionalization for its major institutions—youth reformatories, prisons and mental hospitals. Its objective is to have fewer people living in large-scale state institutions and devote more resources to helping those people in their local communities. If you talk with Jim Spartichino [Contract Procurement], Bob Zevin [START Workshop], Rick Fentin [FLOW] or Steve Santis [head of Vocational Training], you will see that there is a wide variety of future roads for us to travel. They range from doing more of what we are doing now, or starting up workshops in private companies outside the Fernald grounds, to a host of in-between combinations. And we have competition too!

CASE ORGANIZATION

The Fernald case history begins with historical data on the School and an overview of the sheltered workshop phenomena. A "tour" of the Fernald Workshops hopefully will give the reader a partial picture of the workshops; this will be followed by staff members' comments about rehabilitation and the workshops. Next will be data about production work in the shops, "getting contracts," finance, organization, and control. The final section will summarize staff views on possible future directions for the workshops.

FERNALD HISTORY

The Walter E. Fernald State School was the oldest institution for the retarded in the country, and the extensive "campus" dated from 1891, when Dr. Fernald and 61 retarded clients moved from the original location in South Boston. At the time, "feeblemindedness" and "excessive sexuality" were thought to be related. Complete segregation from the community was considered the only way to curb retardation and deviance. The School was located in Waltham on some 200 acres beyond the end of the Waverley Street railway lines, at that time suitably distant from Boston. Dr. Fernald saw, "the shady groves and grassy lawns" as an appropriate setting for "patient and continued habit-training, and daily and hourly lessons in decency and behavior."

An employee at the School for 27 years recently wrote about the past:

> The boys were segregated from the girls both inside and outside the building. At the dances even, the boys danced with the boys and the girls with the girls. When a new person was admitted to residency, his or her parents or friends could not visit for two months. All visitors came on "company day." The Ward B dayroom would be tidied up for the guests. A rug was placed on the floor, curtains were hung, and rocking chairs and fancy pillows were added. We, the attendants, were not permitted to talk to the visitors.

Until relatively recent years, physical conditions had been similarly Victorian, staff members reported: all wards had been locked, hazards such as open radiators were frequent, and the smell excruciating. Fernald buildings were institutional looking, and many of them dated from the turn of the century.

In the past children had often been sent to Fernald simply for being problems and because there was a lack of available community resources and alternatives. Typically they spent the rest of their lives at Fernald, becoming totally institutionalized.

In recent years, however, both the composition and size of Fernald underwent major changes. Beginning about 1971 fewer new clients entered Fernald and those that did enter usually had multiple problems, such as medical needs or family difficulties as well as being retarded. In addition, motivated by the new state policy of deinstitutionalization,

Exhibit 1

ORGANIZATIONAL CHART OF THE FERNALD SCHOOL AND VOCATIONAL TRAINING DIVISION

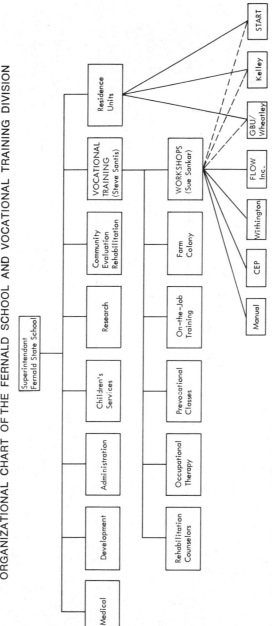

Source: Researcher's interviews with Fernald staff members.

Exhibit 2

STATISTICS ON WORKSHOPS

Workshop	Number of clients	Principal activity	Purpose	Staff
FLOW	23	Subcontracting	Preparation for community competitive employment in factory (light assembly, packaging, stock) work and porter work and preparation for community sheltered workshops.	3 vocational instructors *1 part-time truck driver *1 part-time bookkeeper/secretary *1 part-time rehabilitation counselor *1 special needs worker (teaches money, travel, and grooming skills)
Manual	40	Subcontracting	Majority are in Manual as an extended placement. 5–8 are being prepared to move to FLOW for more realistic, more demanding work training.	*1 senior vocational instructor 1 vocational instructor 2 attendants *1 part-time bookkeeper/secretary *1 part-time vocational instructor
Withington	25	Subcontracting produce cards	Part- and full-time also includes four-week vocational evaluation clients. Withington mostly serves wheelchair clients and clients with emotional problems. Prepares some people for FLOW although most clients will continue to be extended sheltered workshop employees.	2 occupational therapists 1 senior vocational instructor ½ occupational therapy aide *1 part-time card cutter *1 part-time bookkeeper

CEP (Community Experience Program)	9	Produce cards	Part-time (afternoons) all clients in morning participate in Community Experience Program learning travel and money skills. Clients are being prepared for FLOW.	2 teachers (teach ½ time in CEP program)
Green Blind Unit/ Wheatley (GPU)	16	Subcontracting	Prevocational workshop. Introduction to work skills. Five clients are blind.	1 teacher 1 attendant
START	16	Subcontracting Produce ball-point pens	Clients with psychiatric problems. Several "crisis" spots for clients returning from placement in workshops in the community or other programs, who need temporary placement or further training. Preparing for FLOW.	2 attendants
Kelley	25	Subcontracting Produce ceramic products	Most on part-time basis, introduction to work training, emphasis on teaching of work skills: fine and gross motor coordination, sitting, concentration, appropriate work behavior.	1 vocational instructor 1 attendant ½ attendant

* Indicates salary paid totally by workshops.
Source: Researcher's interviews with Fernald staff members.

many long-time Fernald residents who could either get jobs, or were able to live in a less structured community residence, were moving out of the School. As a result, Fernald's population had dropped from 2,800 to 1,700 of which 1,100 were living on the School grounds. The future size of Fernald's population was uncertain but the researcher believed further declines might be expected depending on the extent of deinstitutionalization and the transfer of state funds to local communities.

In the past, such teaching as there was, tended to concentrate on the 3Rs. Staff members indicated that, for many retarded people, such training was often frustrating and resulted in the barest minimum of achievement. The School, however, had recently been expanding its vocational training efforts. Vocational Training had been separated from the Educational Division and given separate organizational status, recognizing the increased importance of the programs it operated. These included rehabilitation counseling and occupational therapy, a farm colony for 300 men in Templeton, Mass., on-the-job training at Fernald for about 70 residents in kitchens, and other areas of the school, and prevocational classes teaching skills such as counting and color recognition.

The Fernald Workshops began operations in 1969, with the incorporation of FLOW (Fernald League Opportunity Workshop). In 1975 there were seven separate workshops, each employing between 9 and 40 people. The total current volume of business for all workshops was approximately $130,000 per year.

Operationally, the workshops were substantially autonomous. The FLOW, for example, trained residents of the School who might hope to go out and work competitively in the local community. Others, Manual Workshop, for example, worked with less capable residents of the School. Although it was unlikely that Manual residents would ever be able to hold a job in the outside community, they did achieve substantial gains. Staff members listed these as significant improvement in skills and behavior, a chance to meet and work with other residents and staff, and an opportunity to earn their own money.

All workshop members were paid on a piece-rate basis; the average wage in most workshops was 50 cents an hour. All members lived at the School and most had been there since they were children. All workshops had long waiting lists of Fernald residents. Staff members also asserted there were never enough job openings outside the School for work trained residents.

Each workshop was staffed by several supervisors, most of whom had professional degrees and training in rehabilitation work. These supervisors, responsible for workshop operations, were assisted by a small full-time executive staff comprising Sue Sankar (general coordination) and Jim Spartichino (contract procurement).

In terms of formal organization, the workshops in general came under the Vocational Training Division of the School although the exact formal arrangement was not consistent among shops. (Exhibit 1 gives an organizational chart of the School and the workshops, while Exhibit 2 has statistics about the seven shops. Exhibit 3 contains information on staff supervisors.) Space for the shops and most staff salaries were provided by the state. A number of expenses, salaries of the workers, and some contribution to staff salaries came from subcontracting revenue. Exhibit 4 gives sample monthly financial data.

As a result of growth in workshop size and the increasing complexity

Exhibit 3
STAFF INVOLVED IN THE FERNALD WORKSHOPS

Staff

Steve Santis
Director of Vocational Education and Training
10 years at Fernald
7 years as rehabilitation counselor
M.A. in rehabilitation counseling

Arthur Leventhal
Rehabilitation counselor position
1 year at Fernald
Worked at Wrentham State School in Workshop
M.A. in Rehabilitation Administration

Sue Sankar
Coordinator of Workshops
1½ years FLOW
1 year coordinator of Workshops
B.A.

Jim Spartichino
Contract procurement person
10 years at Fernald working with residents
2 years selling home improvements.

Workshop Directors

FLOW
Rick Fentin
3 years director
  FLOW
2 years attendant
M.A. Rehabilitation
  Administration

START
Bob Zevin
1 year START
6 months as director
M.A. in Psychology

Manual
Peggy Beck
1¼ years Manual
  Workshop
9 months—director
Attendant experience
Teaching certificate

Withington
Mary Lou Kollach
Occupational therapist
2 years Withington
  Workshop
M.A. in occupational
  therapy

GBU/Wheatley
Steve Robichard
  (acting head)
1½ years Workshop
B.A.

Kelley
Phil McGee
1½ years director of
  Shop Attendant experience, B.A.

CEP
Becky Woodecock—
  teacher (teaching
  certificate)
Steve Draft—B.A.

Exhibit 4

SAMPLE MONTHLY FINANCIAL DATA FOR SEVERAL WORKSHOPS
(February statements)

Manual Workshop

Contract income		
McHutchinson Pots		
(canceled)	$	369.00
Barry		145.00
Math Shop (canceled)		105.00
West Vaco		33.70
Teaching Resources		150.00
	$	802.70
Expenses		
Office	$	48.25
Postage		33.00
Mileage		41.00
Client wages		915.00
Bookkeeper (half-time		
supervision)		349.00
		$1,386.25
Cash in bank		1,855.75

Withington Workshop

Contract income		
Western Electric	$	694.11
Greeting cards		46.30
	$	740.41
Outstanding contract income		
West Vaco (not steady)	$	161.00
Western Electric		1,140.00
Hendrix (canceled end of		
February)		171.00
Expenses (monthly)		
Manufacturing (card		
supplies)	$	94.21
Mileage		41.50
Client wages		565.31
Bookkeeper		75.00
Card cutter (approxi-		
mately 20 hours per		
month)		50.00
Petty cash		20.00
	$	846.02
Loaned to other workshops		25.00
In bank		3,109.00

FLOW Workshop

Contract income	
Polaroid	$3,505.31
Other	386.16
	$3,891.47
Expenses	
Client wages	$1,900.56
Makeup wages	26.23
Stock-work wages	52.76
Job training	38.90
	$2,018.45
Staff salary (state staff	
subsidy, part-time reha-	
bilitation counselor, truck	
driver, special needs per-	
son, accountant/	
secretary)	$1,505.66
Miscellaneous	
Office	$ 74.22
Lunches	20.00
Job training	12.00
Coffee	8.00
Chair covers	61.73
Loans to new programs	92.00
Advertisements	9.80
	$ 277.75
Other	$ 180.45
Total expenses	$3,980.31

START Workshop

Income		
Western Electric	$	822.00
West Vaco		140.00
Pots		132.00
Hendrix		78.00
		$1,172.00
Monthly expenses		
Subsidy of staff wages	$	75.00
Tape, jugs, coffee, etc.		25.00
Every six weeks to Jim		
Spartichino		10.00
Average monthly payroll		560.00
	$	670.00
Owed		
For pots		$2,000.00
Savings		$1,500.00

of the operation, Sue Sankar, who had worked for a year and a half as a supervisor in FLOW, became coordinator of the workshops. Although the workshops continued to be run each as their own separate business, with no central budget, as coordinator Ms. Sankar distributed any production jobs that came into the central office, participated in the screening process for new clients wanting to enter the workshops, consulted with all the shops on ways to improve operations and services, and made any decisions, through the Vocational Division, that would affect all the shops.

Members of a workshop group, all of whom were Fernald residents, were generally referred to as "clients." Sue Sankar noted that clients in the workshops comprised a range of skills and capabilities. For instance, a client might lack reading and counting skills or have a speech impediment, but still be capable of being trained for competitive employment. Abilities to do abstract thinking and make independent judgments differed widely among clients in the different workshops. Less capable clients needed more supervision in order to attend to a task. More capable clients could deal with less structure and had greater independent motivation. The qualities less capable and more capable, she said, were rather intangible, but were clearly evident in the workshops.

SHELTERED WORKSHOPS

Several thousand facilities, commonly referred to as sheltered workshops and located throughout the United States, offered jobs and rehabilitation for people unable to be competitively employed. The researcher found that, although individual workshops were aware of the existence of other shops, they had little knowledge about other such activities. Sue Sankar commented:

> I realize that we don't really have a sense of what's been tried in other places. We really approach things pretty blindly. We don't go and read different articles or research about things that have been tried in sheltered workshops. And we're not—at least I'm not—attached to any professional organizations, which I imagine at their best could provide that sort of information. I guess Fernald is just so overwhelming that I always felt that to join one of those organizations and to spend a day and $12 at the Marriott Motel going to a conference was always a waste of time.

Certainly, the researcher found government and library sources to be of limited assistance in understanding either present dimensions or future trends affecting these operations. Some general information was available. A 1973 article by an employee of the Rehabilitation Services Administration of the Department of Health, Education, and Welfare (HEW) estimated that there were between 1,500 and 1,800 workshops in the country serving not only retarded people, but also other individuals not capable of competitive employment. Workshops had expanded rapidly since the 1950s, particularly those employing mentally retarded people.

In Massachusetts there were currently about 6,000 mentally retarded people in state institutions like Fernald. Others lived in private homes or community residences. No precise figures were available on the number of retarded people in the state, although 3 percent of the population was the generally accepted estimate. A 1971 study determined that about 4,000 workshop positions were needed in Massachusetts, mainly for retarded people, but also for example, for the blind and alcoholics. At that time, there were only 775 positions in workshops.

The Massachusetts Rehabilitation Commission, a state agency involved in workshops, published a list of about 100 workshops in the state. Just to talk about numbers, however, misses the fact that the term "workshops" included both long-established, major facilities, and small, short-term activity centers. In addition, workshops performed a variety of work, varying from subcontracting, salvage (Goodwill Industries, for example), to manufacturing and selling prime products. In Massachusetts, there were only a few large and established workshops. The researcher visited two of those located in the Boston area.

Community Workshop, the oldest workshop in the country, was founded in the late 1880s. Located on the seventh floor of a building in Boston's garment district, it seemed to the researcher to be "business" oriented. Community had originally manufactured hospital gowns, but by 1975 the 120 clients worked on subcontracts in a range of shops from electronics to kitchen work to typing pools. Most of the supervisors had experience as foremen in industry, rather than professional social service experience. Community's orientation was toward production work to meet specific customer needs and not toward counseling. The administration consisted of the director, a full-time contract procurer with extensive workshop experience, and a production manager.

Another, the Jewish Vocational Service's workshop in Boston, served 150 clients on a nonsectarian basis. JVS had a nationwide system of 17 workshops, the largest of which served 650 clients. Originally started in 1938 to aid refugees and assist unemployed Jewish workers, JVS also provided services such as school counseling and skill training as well as the sheltered workshop. Here clients were assigned a counselor who worked out an individual program, often with different jobs every day. Shop supervisors typically had industrial experience. There were two professional contract procurement persons at JVS in Boston. Although JVS was experimenting with nationwide contract procurement, the workshops were basically locally oriented and independent, although occasionally a large job might be shared among all JVS shops.

One important characteristic of JVS and Community was that they served "more capable" clients. A number of workers in both these and other workshops were there temporarily in preparation for later work in competitive jobs. Programs such as Community or JVS did not deal with clients with very low skill levels, such as might work in some of the shops at Fernald. State funding, available to organizations providing rehabilitation, was an important source of revenue for JVS, Community and many other workshops in the state.

Other workshops might be a peripheral activity, operated by a mental hospital, a drug rehabilitation program or a community residence for the retarded. These organizations would obtain a small subcontract and use the work in lieu of arts or crafts or other rehabilitation activities. Such workshops operated very informally and did not have contract procurers, factory equipment, or even in some cases, space specifically devoted to the workshop.

Workshops were also being organized to serve a far greater range of handicapped people than traditionally had been the case. For instance, Sage Workshop in Cambridge employed normal, elderly people on a half-day basis and provided them with a chance to get out and be with people and to earn a little money. Sage was an independent organization supported totally by subcontracting. Veteran organizations also ran a number of workshops. Some workshop directors spoke unfavorably of veterans shops, saying that their quality of work was sometimes poor and that they often underbid.

All workshops, except those employing veterans, fell under U.S. Department of Labor regulations. Because the common characteristic of most workshop employees was that they were not able to achieve normal work productivity, special exemptions were granted from governmental minimum wage requirements. There were five different types of certificates depending on workshop purposes, physical and mental characteristics of individual clients, and methods of payment. A workshop using more capable clients might have several different types of certificates, each requiring fairly extensive record-keeping. Because of the regulations, most workshops employed a piece-rate compensation system. In addition, careful time studies were required on bidding for any job to determine the rate a typical company would have to pay. At least 50 percent had to be added for overhead to ensure that workshops did not compete "unfairly" with private industry.

Workshops also tended to specialize by type of contract. The majority of shops did subcontracting, although prime products were significant in some cases (e.g., household products by Industries for the Blind) and salvage for others. A 1966 Cornell University study of 123 sheltered workshops in New York, New Jersey, and Pennsylvania indicated the breakdown of work as:

	New York	New Jersey	Pennsylvania
Prime manufacturing	16.3%	1.7%	24.5%
Subcontracting	73.9	82.8	52.1
Salvage	3.6	11.1	6.2
Other	6.3	4.4	17.2
Total	100.0%	100.0%	100.0%

One interesting study of prime products was done in the late 1960s by the Federal Manpower Administration and HEW. "Product Earning Power" was designed to see if successful prime products might be developed by workshops. The study noted that volunteers in marketing, production, and design worked with permanent staff of several workshops in the Los Angeles area and elsewhere to develop a number of prime products, for example, a set of giftware. However, this effort failed to develop into a successful operation.

One reason, observers reported, why workshop personnel tended to have little sense of what was happening in other sheltered workshops was that shops were all working on a great variety of different products, whether subcontracting or prime products. Their contacts, moreover, were not primarily in the final marketplace but rather with suppliers of subcontracts. The expanding number of workshops in the Boston area, however, had made each more aware of other competitors. Often one workshop lost a job, finding out later that it had been picked up by another shop. The poor economic situation in early 1975 seemed to have caused a drop-off in work for workshops in general, and reputedly even the large workshops in downtown Boston had to occasionally close down or temporarily lay off workers.

A TOUR OF FERNALD WORKSHOPS

The tour began with a visit to Manual Workshop. This was a typical, institutional brick building, built around 1900, which currently housed a workshop and the office of the Vocational Training Division. The office was a large, open second-story room, with a number of tables and old desks, and an abundance of plants.

Downstairs in the Manual Workshop, workers were sitting at long tables putting together plastic hanging flower pots. It was obvious that some of the workers were quite retarded, some had physical disabilities and some combined both of these problems. The "job" had been broken down into a series of small, sequential steps which allowed each client to take one part and fit it into the assembly process. One worker inserted the first hanging string into the pot, another client the next, someone else a loop; each passing the product on to the next person. Several other clients packaged the item. The researcher observed another resident working on a special jig learning a specific, simple task so she could enter the "line" at a later date. Workers were eager to demonstrate their particular job—and skill—to the researcher, or point out with evident pride the number of pieces they had completed.

In the next room, other clients were assembling an educational toy. One man slowly and carefully placed large red beads into a wooden jig with five indentations. When it was full, he painstakingly removed the beads and placed them in the toy package. Even though he could not count, the job had been set up by using a special jig so that he always packaged the right number of beads, and giving him assistance in performing what was, for the client, a major task.

A few buildings away in Withington Workshop, several workers lined up to collect their money and go for coffee and donuts at a stand run by residents of that building. Here physically handicapped workers in wheelchairs were sorting phone cords—by color, serial number, and style—for a Western Electric subcontract. The main Withington activity, though, was hand-made greeting cards, which Fernald designed, produced and sold. At one table, one client stamped three yellow fish, the next client imprinted a blue fish, and the final person in the assembly line stamped the water. Nearby, several workers slowly wrapped groups of cards in plastic wrap and put them through a shrink-wrap machine for final packaging.

About a half-mile away from the Manual and Withington buildings, the tour continued in FLOW. FLOW seemed to the researcher to replicate, in measure, an assembly shop in a small craft-oriented factory. In the background the noise of a radio and a time clock was much in evidence. The primary task was a packaging job for Polaroid, but other small subcontracts were also being completed. Some clients worked on their own; three others worked on a small moving assembly line. One man checked a part with a micrometer supplied by a company. A woman operated a small drill press used to make a part which was later incorporated into a larger product assembly at the company's main plant. Rick Fentin, head supervisor at FLOW, pointed out the charts giving each individual's daily production, as well as comments on behavior, such as work habits, neatness, and promptness.

A visit to all of the workshops made evident the major differences between the mission and population of each shop; the contrast between FLOW and a shop like Manual, for example, was most striking. FLOW clients were less obviously retarded, and some of them appeared to be like people you might see every day on the subway. At FLOW, jobs were more independent and clients were working at many different types of jobs, working at their own pace, and getting parts for their own use from supply areas. Less obvious was the fact that pay at FLOW averaged $1.05 an hour compared to $0.25 in a lower level shop. Since bids by Fernald Workshops included 100 percent of wages to cover overhead costs, the overhead earned by FLOW was similarly higher.

A special grant from the Massachusetts Department of Education, Division of Occupational Education, helped FLOW workers learn how to use banking facilities, order meals in restaurants, tell time, and take public transportation. FLOW had other special programs, such as porter training, where clients were paid to get additional specific job skills. Another significant characteristic of FLOW operations was the method of pay; all Fernald clients were paid once a week. In other workshops, clients were paid in cash, normally $1 bills and change rather than larger bills, to emphasize how much they had earned. At FLOW clients were paid by check.

THE STAFF TALKS ABOUT CLIENTS AND THE WORKSHOPS

Supervisors in the workshops and members of the Vocational Training Division were, in the researcher's judgment, highly committed to the importance of their career work, to the potentialities of their clients, and to the benefits of production work for Fernald residents. Mary Lou Kollach, director of Withington Workshop, and an OTR (registered occupational therapist), commented:

> One of the biggest things I meet when I talk to people is they say, "Oh, the children at Fernald made those." And I say, "Actually, most of the people at Fernald are adults. There are only a few hundred children out of the 1,100 residents. Children grow up, and they are

adults." I don't think people realize, or maybe they avoid realizing, that there are a lot of adults who get dubbed with the name mentally retarded who really aren't that bad off and who can do a lot of good work. That's one of the biggest barriers we meet in people's minds. They think of someone being retarded, and they only think of a child. They don't think of the fact that they're adults, with adult feelings and adult reactions. They may not be able to read and write or they might have physical handicaps, but they're still adult human beings. Every adult wants to work or wants somehow to make their living and somehow experience the kind of independence that earning money gets you.

Steve Santis, head of the Vocational Training Division also commented on workshop mission and contribution:

> What our workshops really do is give clients a chance to assume more adult and normal roles. Workshops have come about because we have not made places in the mainstream of society for people who fall below or outside certain limits, either physically, mentally or emotionally, and as a result we have all these people who are in institutions.
>
> It's the basis for rehabilitation. We believe that the gains people make through work extend to many other areas of their personality. They have more self-esteem. They can buy things through money they earn. They can become more adult in the sense that they earn their money, rather than being given money like a child is given an allowance.
>
> I've always had the feeling that even if we didn't pay, people would come to work. And that in fact took place at a workshop in England. It's an opportunity for them to be more normal. A lot of the time what retarded people learn in school is that they're stupid or that they can't learn, or that they don't learn in the same way. And those are really very negative things. No matter how we accept those things, to call someone stupid is devastating.
>
> To be able to work makes one more normal; the work we provide is the kind of work that most people can do. They can be successful at it. And they can be successful at it all day long. So what may be repetitious to us gives them perhaps many opportunities to be successful. And for people who are accustomed to doing things wrong, and have been criticized for a good part of their lives, that's a very pleasant situation. Then there's the whole social kind of thing about work. I think they find work rewarding for the same reasons, whatever they are, that we find work rewarding.
>
> Most all of the staff work here because they like it. Most of the people are fairly young—it's a very meaningful kind of work. You just see—you can dramatically change somebody's life by providing this kind of program. We've had people that never talked—they just sat in the building all day long—that never had any money, that never went off the grounds, that now can earn money, buy their own clothes, go to a restaurant, go to a movie, that have begun to talk and become more social.

Bob Zevin, supervisor in START,[1] a psychiatrically oriented workshop, highlighted what he felt made the workshops so special:

---

[1] This was simply the name of the workshop rather than a true acronym.

From what I gather, the shops here are the best in the state. It seems to me that retarded people are *people* here. Period! And that isn't always the case. All right, you figure emotionally, retarded people are children at least in part. To that extent, some very balanced and careful mothering is necessary for somebody to grow. FLOW's got it without it being overt.

Finally, Rick Fentin, supervisor in FLOW, commented on the mission of FLOW in particular, and what he saw as exciting in his job:

Our "mission" is to train people for competitive jobs, and that's pretty much what the end product is anyway. To do that involves a lot of different things; mainly because our people have never worked before.

What we're trying to train them in is job flexibility. We're not training for a particular skill, but we want people to develop work habits. At some time in the future—maybe three, four, five years from now— not as many people will be going into competitive jobs from the School. This program has been running for about five years and a good many people have been placed in jobs and I think that more of the people in the School four or five years to come will be more severely retarded than we have here now. At that time, the goal may be just employment for the day.

The exciting thing is when someone gets a job. Most people, when I tell them what I do, say "That must really require patience." Well, it requires some patience, but what it requires more is judging progress in a different way: breaking it down into smaller kinds of things: if someone starts to work a little faster, if someone starts to come in at the right time—little things like that are really exciting. The *most* exciting thing is when someone is placed, and is doing well and seems happy. But it doesn't happen every day. So, in a way, you kind of have to lower expectations.

Fernald staff felt that they badly needed a larger number of extended positions for workshop clients. When FLOW had first been started in 1969, most of its clients had only spent about six months in the workshop before getting competitive jobs in the community. Present FLOW clients, however, were less capable. They tended to stay longer—perhaps two to three years—and were more likely to move out subsequently into another, outside workshop rather than take a competitive job. In mid-1975, there were about 20 Fernald School residents on the wait-list for FLOW vacancies. Manual Workshop had a waiting list of about 40 Fernald residents and openings were few since most of this workshop's existing clients were there on extended job placement.

PRODUCTION WORK AND THE WORKSHOPS

Production operations and capacities seemed to the researcher to be critical to an understanding of the Fernald Workshops. Interviews with workshop supervisors seemed to indicate that the characteristics of *how* the "job" was to be performed were more important than the end product. It was apparent that they considered rehabilitation as much a product of Fernald as the goods and services produced by the workshops.

Fernald had the most limited of simple factory equipment and facilities. Occasionally a company might furnish a machine on loan for a particular job. The workshop staff, according to one production observer, had developed exceptional skills in designing jigs and fixtures to hold pieces so that clients with a wide variety of physical and mental limitations might do the job. For example, they modified standard production practices so that operations could be performed by clients in wheelchairs. Considerable attention was given, with ingenious results, to breaking larger complicated tasks into smaller, more easily learned, subtasks, or to taking simple operations and making them "supersimple."

Job requirements, of course, differed by workshop, from FLOW, which dealt with more capable clients, to Manual, which worked with less capable clients. Jobs requiring complicated counting and reading, complex procedures, or working with somewhat dangerous materials or tools required a high degree of a scarce resource—supervision—and were limited to clients with certain skills. Some clients found jobs requiring fine motor skills to be too difficult. But simple, repetitive jobs, such as putting items in a package, punching a few holes or collating, could be done even by less capable clients at Manual.

The clients at FLOW had a higher skill level and could perform tasks requiring counting or more complex procedures, and sometimes became bored if the jobs were too repetitive. Rick Fentin, though, commented on his view of appropriate work:

> The kind of work you do depends a lot on the supervision you have. Most of the people in FLOW could do more complicated tasks, but whether or not there could be enough supervision supplied to teach them the complicated tasks and stay with them is a question. One of the reasons we are able to operate the way we do now is that we have a lot of jobs that are sort of easy. They don't take a lot of training or skill for the people and they don't require a lot of staff supervision, so all the other things involved with rehabilitation—the meetings, the plans, the coordination, the looking for contracts—can be done.
>
> This easy work would also be good for long-term clients. We would not *want* to have too many supervisors in the shop. It's sort of a balance: on the one hand, we want to keep a real factory setting so that there are not ten supervisors around, one per person. On the other hand, we do like to have more complicated jobs too, and we do bring in some. Usually we have some printed circuit board assembly or jobs using a micrometer, different kinds of tools that are more complicated. You need a base of easy work, like simple packaging-assembly, sorting, folding jobs, that kind of thing. It's a real break for Fernald to get that kind of job.

Sue Sankar explained her views on production:

> The biggest problem is not having enough work. We're really oriented to having people come in and do production work, and base our rehabilitation treatment plans for our people around the fact that

they're going to be busy during the day and we can use work as a medium to relate to them. In a lot of cases, we're not really concerned with the amount a person is producing, but rather, we are concerned with a resident's ability to attend to a task for a given period of time, listen to directions, and interact with peers and supervisors.

I think not having enough jobs affects staff morale. It can really bustle like a factory when there is lots of work coming in. When there is nothing coming in, and what we're basically doing is taking work we've already done, taking it apart, and doing it over again, it's very depressing for the staff. The residents don't always pick us up on it, but some of them do. It's also bad financially on us. We continue to pay people at the rate that they would be paid at if they were actually doing the work for the first time, so it definitely dips into our budget.

Bob Zevin, supervisor in START, emphasized that in dealing with clients who also had emotional problems, consistency of work was crucial:

What's bad is that, except for FLOW, which has some great, steady contracts of their own, we haven't gotten any consistent work in since we had the flower pot job a long time ago. If you get a new job, and take a couple days to train people, then you can take time to observe everyone. Then you can really do some therapy. There is a lot of talent in here, and when people are not being crazy, they are *excellent* workers. What happens now is, we get a job, and if it's an easy job, they learn it in a half a day and finish it the next day. If it's a hard job, they learn it in a whole day and finish it two days later. And it's all real vocational supervision. Which doesn't hurt them, but if we could get a decent contract, we could do *so* much more, attitude- and behavior-wise.

GETTING SUBCONTRACT WORK

For most of the workshops, getting and negotiating contracts was done by the central workshop office. The process was informal, and differed from company to company. First a lead would come in, either through Jim Spartichino, or by word of mouth; e.g., response to a mailing. Then either Sue Sankar or Arthur Leventhal, a rehabilitation counselor in the Vocational Training Division, would go to the company, talk over the job, and bring back a sample. One of the workshops would experiment with the job to ascertain that it was do-able, and then the workshop staff would get together and make a time study of a normal person doing the job. This information provided data for a bid, based on minimum wage requirements plus 100 percent overhead. Even if the bid was accepted, sometimes a company might initially send only a small first shipment until they were certain of quality control and logistics.

The workshops operated with several different types of contract. A few were long term and provided work on a consistent basis. FLOW had had such contracts with Polaroid and Teaching Resources (a subsidiary of *The New York Times*) for several years. Withington's telephone cord job was similar, although there had been a shortage of work during the winter. The hanging flower pot contract originally had been large and consistent enough to employ several workshops full time; its withdrawal because of loss of sales had, therefore, seriously affected the workshops. Another fairly steady contract for Cambridge Plating generally supplied work for 20 people about two days a week.

Over the past year, the Fernald Workshops had five intermittent contracts. For example, one company had a particular part that Fernald worked on about once every eight weeks. The job would last for five days and employ about 30 people. Two of these "steady-intermittent" contracts had been discontinued, in one case because the company had stopped making the product. The workshops also had eight short-term contracts lasting one to three weeks during the past year, which ended either at the completion of the needed work or because of customer dissatisfaction.

Motivation for customer use of a workshop was difficult to ascertain. An informal survey by the researcher of a dozen companies doing business with the Fernald Workshops was somewhat informative. In almost all cases, the quality of Fernald work was cited as a crucial determinant for a contract award. Reasonable costs were also given as a key reason by a majority of companies. A response by a company often was: "We like to help out, but we wouldn't do it if their quality wasn't good and their costs low."

Virtually all companies contacted said that the particular job "suited" workshops: that it was relatively simple, probably did not involve the need for rush work, and, in a few cases, was monotonous work not enjoyed by their own employees. In some cases, too, the location of Fernald was a factor (for instance, being near suppliers), or the workshops' storage and delivery facilities. Several companies used Fernald for peak load situations, thereby being able to avoid subsequent layoffs of extra employees or having to invest in extra space.

No company gave "rehabilitation" or "helping the retarded" as the sole reason for subcontracting with Fernald; however, in the researcher's judgment, this was clearly a factor. Almost all the companies had previous experience with workshops, or were currently using other workshops in addition to Fernald. In one case, the company had been alerted to the idea of workshop use by an employee with a retarded child. Several of the long-term users particularly emphasized their favorable impression of the staff at Fernald, along with liking the idea of supporting a workshop. As one company spokesman remarked: "When we went out there, we melted like butter."

Jim Spartichino had developed the contract procurer's job at Fernald. He described his pattern of contract development as "informal." When first hired, in August 1973, he "cold-called" a number of companies in the Boston area, particularly those geographically close to Fernald. He then revisited likely prospects on a fairly regular basis, relying on intuition, memory, and rough notes to provide leads. He talked about some of the problems in getting contracts:

At the onset the problem is that the immediate feeling I get from the signals from the businessman, whether it's the production man or the president of the company, is that I'm asking for charity. In fact, I've been a little rough and sometimes I've said, "I am *not* asking for charity, and if you're going to continue, I've got to leave. I don't want your charity, I'm going to save you a dollar if you give me a chance to bid." They want to put $50 in your hand, to give you something to get rid of you.

I do know this, many, many people don't want a retarded person around. They'll take a convict more than a retarded person. Outside, I mean. Most people would say "The retarded plus social workers and psychologists—how can they run anything efficiently. They'll foul it all up. I'll lose money." Without having experience in a workshop, they'll still think that way. It is wrong, the questions people have about the institutional-type employee and the institutional-type client. It is wrong. There is so much competence here.

Many of the employees that got us jobs were just low-level production people that talked to their boss. It was their local boss that did it. At times it was Purchasing. Very few times it was Personnel. Don't use the charity issue; the individual will do it themselves.

Arthur Leventhal, a rehabilitation counselor, worked closely with the workshops on developing new business. One approach that had been tried was a mailing to some 900 companies in the Boston area. Letters and accompanying brochures were addressed simply to "manager." There were about 70 generally polite responses, but only about 10 to 15 of these thought they might ever have appropriate work.

Mr. Leventhal had also investigated speaking to various business groups, and had succeeded in addressing a Rotary Club group. A small job which he felt was perhaps just a token, developed. From his experience in working on company contracts, Arthur Leventhal commented:

About 80 percent of the companies we talk to don't consider us as a business. They want to keep our letter in their files so they can count it in for companies they've contacted related to affirmative action. Sometimes they'll have their equal employment personnel officer talk to us. Mostly, it's talk, tokenism. Very few companies see us as a legitimate business, with legitimate services.

We basically talk to them as a business person talking to another business person, but mention that the people are handicapped. Just a simple declarative statement; they are handicapped, but these are the services we provide for a company. We talk about how a contract with the Fernald Workshops being not a one-way street and give them a list of a half-dozen benefits to their company from doing business with us —not just directly saving money with the contract, because of our low overheads.

One area which we don't know how to attack is making ourselves known to the independent entrepreneur, or the company that does seasonal work, where they have to hire 10, 15, 20 more people for a season and lay them off and where they'll have high workmen's compensation. A private entrepreneur that has an idea, wants to market it, wants to develop the market themselves, but needs someone to put together the product—assembly, packaging, shipping—and doesn't have any floor space, and needs a short-term labor force on a semi-skilled job. We're just ideal for them, because they can use us and drop us.

The frustrating thing is that there is so much work of an unskilled nature being performed by normal people, that bores them and doesn't bore handicapped people. And people are probably being paid more than the minimum wage. I think for some companies, it's a nuisance, it requires time and effort by some supervisor to organize it, to get it shipped out and have it come back. And they're not sure it's going to be done adequately because it's not in their own physical plant. That's a problem, too. There's a reluctance for that, which is a legitimate reluctance, even with all our guarantees, quality controls, inspections.

In some cases, the individual workshops went out and found their own subcontracts, or customers approached a particular shop. The only workshop which used this approach to any extent was FLOW. Because it had been organized before there was a substantial central administrative function, FLOW had developed skill at working directly with companies. It operated very much more independently than other shops, and currently supplied other shops with about 40 percent of their work. Rick Fentin commented on the FLOW contracts:

Most of the work—maybe 80 percent—is long-standing, but it's a matter of keeping up on what is long-standing. Finding the contracts is very difficult. Keeping the contract is another thing, too; keeping the kinds of relationships with the business, making sure they're serviced in the right way. Keeping your prices down, if possible, and raising your prices when you have to, all are really key things.

PRIME PRODUCTS

Because of the frustration of dealing with companies as a subcontractor, Fernald was seriously investigating "prime products"—products which the workshops would develop, manufacture and distribute. The most important prime product to date was cards. Mary Lou Kollasch of Withington commented:

Prime products are what carries us through when we don't have subcontracts. We've put more into that recently, especially when we've had fewer subcontracts from the community. We tend to stop making cards, stop the production when we have a whole lot of subcontract work and move back to the prime product when we don't have any subcontract work.

We hope people buy the cards because they're good cards. We've been trying to place them in settings where they wouldn't be purchased just because they're made by the handicapped or retarded, although we do put a leaflet in the back saying that they are made by multiple-handicapped people at the Fernald School. We want people to know that, too.

The Christmas sales are different here, too, in that we've only sold Christmas cards out of the workshop itself. And that might actually attract more of a charity appeal. You have to be interested in the retarded or you're not going to come to a school for the retarded to buy a product made by them. Or you know someone here, or heard about the product.

We tried showing cards around to companies to distribute, the contract procurement person showed them around, but at that time we were afraid of big orders. If they said "OK, we'll take 3,000 packets tomorrow and distribute them in all our stores," well, that would be the end.

Another product was ceramic beads and pots. These had been developed by the Kelley Workshop. One of the supervisors was a potter, and had some experience making and selling such products. Profitability, however, was fairly marginal, sales being only through one craft store in Cambridge and occasional craft fairs.

START Workshop had experimented with a more production-oriented prime product, assembling inexpensive ball-point pens, but had not yet had much success in selling them.

The workshops were considering hiring a person to work full-time on developing prime products. They had seriously talked with someone trained in industrial design who would research, design, and help them market some new prime products. When asked about possible products where Fernald might have an edge, Sue Sankar commented:

I think maybe what we can look into is something that can be handcrafted by our people here but can be mass produced. For instance, the Protestant Guild for the Blind is selling holders for hanging plants and I imagine in selling that part of the appeal is that it looks slightly rustic or resembles a hand-crafted item. Yet they've worked out a system to make them where it can be, not automated, but assembled by clients in a very efficient way. So I think maybe we can look into some products like that.

Maybe we could do something with games or toys. I think that might be a saturated market, but it seems right now there are a lot of wooden toys around and perhaps we could work something out with jigs where people could use drill presses and different sorts of jig-saws and be able to make the pieces and then have another workshop assemble the toys. This is an idea we have, but we don't really have the staff to devote full time to looking into something like this.

ORGANIZATION, CONTROL, AND FINANCE

The Fernald Workshops were in a somewhat unusual position being both part of a state school and a separate independent institution. Staff salaries were paid primarily by the state. On the other hand, each workshop had its own income, derived from sales and subcontracts, which was used to pay for supplies and equipment and also to hire additional staff such as part-time bookkeepers. This independence was most pronounced in the case of FLOW, which was actually incorporated as a nonprofit business. Half of the salaries of FLOW staff members were paid from workshop funds, including both some part-time people and supplements to the modest wages paid by the state for some of the full-time staff. The salary paid by the state to most workshop staff was about $7,000 per person a year.

Workshop staff came under normal state employment policies, although state job descriptions often had little relationship to the actual workshop jobs. If a job became available, it had to be publicly "posted" and any Fernald School staff member meeting the job specifications had first consideration. The hiring was done by the overall school promotions committee on the basis of seniority. If hiring was from external candidates, Sue Sankar had primary authority. In either case significant inputs came from supervisors of the individual workshops.

Staff turnover in the workshops was fairly high, most supervisors' average length of service was about a year and a half. Although it took a number of months for someone to really break into the job, most felt the turnover was reasonable given the demands of the job, need for change, and low pay. Most workshop supervisors were young and college educated, and frequently had worked previously as attendants at Fernald, and might well move on from the workshop job to other positions at the School.

The head of Vocational Training, Steve Santis, commented on the general situation of operating workshops in a state institution:

> The frustrating part for me is dealing with all the paper work of the state bureaucracy, not having the right positions to recruit or put people in. The state works on having certain titles for positions—e.g., teacher, social worker, that kind of thing. We don't have a title for workshop director, we have no title for somebody to go out and get contracts and we don't have a title for a person to design products that we could manufacture here. Everything is somewhat improvised. For example, to fill our new contract procurement position, that person is listed under an attendant's position title. You have to sort of manipulate the system. You can't advertise for somebody who is really good at selling. What you have to do is post the opening for the institution as an attendant opening, and you have to deal with people who apply and think that way, "Well, I could go out and do that," but have no experience.

State funding was an acute problem in Massachusetts in 1975, as newly elected Governor Michael S. Dukakis was working on a program of major budget cuts. Whenever someone quit a job there was uncertainty as to whether that position would be funded in the future.

When asked about the possibility of other types of fund raising, Sue Sankar commented:

> I don't know who we could appeal to for money, being part of a state institution. I couldn't imagine community groups wanting to support us, given that institutions like Fernald are seen by some as a thing of the past.

The central workshop office, although it handled part of contract procurement, allocation of work, and generally coordinated the activities of the shops, had no operating budget of its own and did not have any full-time clerical staff. All books were kept by the individual workshops, who handled all details such as paying clients. In most cases, arrangements with companies such as invoicing or pickup and delivery were also handled by the actual shop doing the work. Sue Sankar gave her views of the independent nature of the workshops:

> I think it's good in terms of the kind of commitment a staff develops. It's so unique on the Fernald grounds, and in almost any kind

of work situation. Where can you have three staff members working and pretty much making a lot of their own decisions about their money, and how they're going to work with clients? There is a lot of autonomy there just in terms of what you're going to do with your day: how you're going to structure your day, when does work start for the people, when does it end and how are you going to be working with this or that resident. I think that kind of autonomy has really made this a very different kind of place to work. And it's why we've had a lot of good people in the workshops.

Most of our workshops tend to be pretty conservative in their spending. Sometimes workshop staff have a hard time figuring out what money should be spent on: is this the time to subsidize someone's salary or is this the time to buy a time clock? Making those kinds of decisions is difficult for people. Also having everybody control their own money makes it difficult for us to work as a department—the workshops as a group. Some one has to be making decisions that affect all the workshops, and if you're making those decisions that require money, you have to have some money behind you to make the decisions.

I think one of the changes we'll see is some kind of central budget. I would like to see the basic bank accounts kept separate for each workshop, but have some sort of central fund. We've been haggling for a year over how this might be set up. Is it 10 percent of overhead, or 10 percent of overhead minus fixed costs, whatever. FLOW feels like they do put a lot in and have for several years—and they do. They have a truck driver, and give us a lot of Teaching Resources work. Other places feel that because of the level of their clients, they'll never generate much overhead. So they don't feel it's fair to have a certain amount taken from them. So it's a very, very touchy issue—I think that's true whenever money's a question.

If we had a general fund, we'd probably have some kind of committee—probably made up of workshop directors—that maybe would review decisions for money being spent.

Regarding who should manage company contacts, she continued:

It's a hard thing to figure out what is most efficient. In some cases, the individual workshop do mess up. It's because they have a thousand other things going on. Supervisors are obviously oriented more toward the rehabilitation of the residents; for instance, there could be some crisis that day, and they forget to call the company and say we need more such and such to finish this job by the required date. Sometimes people have a hard time with our system. But in a lot of ways it's more efficient having the workshop that's doing the work be the contact point, for instance, that's the way FLOW works. FLOW does all the contact work with Polaroid. Polaroid can come out and take a look at what's going on anytime. They can call Rick Fentin and talk about the shipments, and Rick knows about the shipments. Whereas anybody who is not right in the workshop, probably wouldn't know about the shipments.

THE FUTURE OF THE WORKSHOPS

The primary immediate concern of the workshop personnel was trying to obtain new subcontract work. A new contract procurement person was to be recruited to replace Jim Spartichino who was leaving to re-enter industry. The idea of hiring a person to develop prime products was also being very seriously considered. For the longer run, the staff was considering a variety of changes in workshop direction.

The workshops, with the exception of FLOW, which was already incorporated, were considering the possibilities of becoming a nonprofit corporation. Sue Sankar, though, saw this as a move having little actual operating effect, but which might make it easier to get a tax-exempt number for paying staff salaries or perhaps receiving certain types of outside funds. She hoped, too, that the board of directors might provide useful inputs.

Bob Zevin commented about the future of the workshops:

> Ideally, this workshop [START] should be physically off the grounds, but I don't think it should be very far away from the school. This is a workshop for people who maybe have vocational skills, but if you stuck them with a competitive employer, they could not survive. I would like it to be near a place like FLOW—I think that has really helped a lot. If there are more than 16 people, you start a new workshop. Each workshop should have people who are sophisticated in the psychological end of rehabilitation. And I think, any sort of community experience type of program such as learning to ride the bus or eat in a restaurant should be associated with a person's job at the workshop so that they would see the relationship between earning the money and putting the money to use.

Rick Fentin described one upcoming plan for the workshops, the idea of having a work station in industry:

> I don't think I want this particular workshop to grow in size. Mainly because of the types of things we do here that require a really in-depth knowledge of clients. I've seen shops of 40–50 people, and they're much better for extended employment[2] where the clients don't need as much input. What could happen instead is that there would be extensions of FLOW outside the school.
>
> We're hopefully starting a project at a company in Waltham, that will be part of FLOW, where we will set up a workshop right in their factory. We have a new staff position approved for it and I think it's going to happen. We're thinking of starting with six people and one supervisor. If it works out, what I envision at some point is a whole program there, maybe 25 people. Using their equipment, doing some different jobs of theirs, being able to bring in jobs of our own if we want some variety. That's what I would picture as a finishing place for people who are at FLOW but who deserve the opportunity to get off the grounds, to mingle with new people, and come back at night.
>
> If it works out, this kind of program will be, to begin with, a separate area of the company, not an enclosed area, but a separate space. But people will be punching in with the company employees in the morning, having coffee break and lunch with them. It will be a good integration. They're the only company that we've approached on it. I think that they're unusual; I'm not sure what their motives are, though. I don't think their motives are all that humanitarian.

---

[2] Where clients stay in the workshop rather than moving on to other jobs.

Steve Santis saw the future direction for workshops as servicing an increasingly wide range of clients:

> We probably will expand present workshop efforts, assuming the economy improves, to a number of people like those in Manual that we don't have room for now. Then we have people who will not really be competitive, but do benefit from going to work every day on a higher level. We have a number of people here for whom we haven't tried the workshops and I think we'll expand there. We keep finding that people are more capable than you think.
>
> The school accepts very few people now. We used to joke around and say it was harder to get in here than into Harvard.
>
> Or if our clients want to live in a group home in the community they could. We could offer work either to retarded people or people maybe with other disabilities. Then our people would gradually become more a part of the community—the community would come in here, they wouldn't perhaps be so frightened.
>
> For instance, we started the first "group home" by going out and renting a house. People were talking about it for 15 years before I got here, and then I just had so many people who were out in rented rooms, at a fairly high price, that I realized if we put them together we'd have enough money to rent a house. So we did. That's not the way the state likes to do things, but if you can do it, and demonstrate it, sometimes things just evolve like that. Current plans do not include what I'm talking about, in terms of the workshops and the community, but sometimes you have to work around that and go ahead and do things.
>
> I could see us as a resource center for this region. I would see us as probably being more capable of assuming this kind of role than a small group could. We have helped people start workshops. We have an awful lot of expertise—I don't know how many years, five years— of running six workshops of having people staff them, of having bookkeeping systems, teaching people how to time-study contracts, how to go out and get their own. Perhaps if we develop some capacity in manufacturing prime products, we could actually subcontract some of that. The primary responsibility is providing programs for everybody here.
>
> Right now we have a few people coming in from outside the school to work here. If we have people coming from the community into our workshops, the local groups who are looking for help are going to be pleased. We could offer work for either retarded people or people with other disabilities. Then our people would gradually become more a part of the community and the community would come in here and they perhaps wouldn't be so frightened.

Finally, Sue Sankar commented about possible new assignments involving Fernald's present population.

> We're going to have to try new things given that our present population has no vocational experience—we don't have as many people with competitive employment potential as we had, say, five years ago. The workshops will have some actual production, but also will be teaching people just the basics that are needed for work—learning how to count, sort, and color discrimination. These aren't always necessary in every job, but certainly if there is a job where that's

needed, and someone lacks that skill, it's a hindrance. And also help-ing people with behavior—learning to sit for a longer time, or to take directions. We're talking about a population that has a very difficult time doing that.

I guess what I'd like to see happen, and I think it is going to hap-pen, is for us to get more business-oriented, with a contract coordi-nator and with a prime products person.

I think the state would provide for additional teaching type posi-tions. Where we've had problems is getting the kind of support that a workshop needs for production-oriented tasks.

We've been looking into getting money from the Massachusetts Re-habilitation Commission, and they may be interested in funding some of our people to develop the work station idea in industry or to bring in outside clients to FLOW type shops.

I also think that the workshops here are really good, but at some point we might be caught in a transition as the institution gets phased out. But one thing we have talked about is keeping this as a regional training center and de-emphasizing the residential part for people that can live outside, but to keep the facility here for the workshops. The state is going to be putting $70,000 into West Building to make it a viable workshop, putting in a real loading dock, making the doors wide enough.

In the researcher's judgment all of those alternatives had to be evalu-ated in light of a critical but almost impossible to predict variable—de-institutionalization. Although state and federal authorities were "push-ing for" deinstitutionalization, at the time of the case there seemed to be no information as to precisely what this meant. The only public planning document on deinstitutionalization in Massachusetts was dated from the late 1960s. It emphasized having a variety of programs rather than one agency or department, and suggested that residence schools branch out into more community-oriented services or become regional centers.

Because of federal funding requirements and other pressures, the population of institutions like Fernald would probably drop. A major unsettled issue, though, was whether alternative facilities in the com-munity could be provided for all Fernald residents. For instance, at the time of the case, no community residences and other facilities existed for residents in wheelchairs and other multiple handicapped people. Although more capable clients would continue to leave Fernald, it seemed likely that the institution would continue to be needed for mul-tiple handicapped and less capable clients.

Although institutions such as Fernald still received the bulk of state resources, there was continuing pressure to put more money into com-munity programs. For instance, a representative from the Massachusetts Association for Retarded Citizens (MARC), a group made up of rela-tives and other concerned individuals, commented on the generally questionable image of institutions such as Fernald and stressed the need for more varied training in workshops, and teaching of living skills and socialization as opposed to workshops as a "babysitting" enterprise.

Note on the Major Home Appliance Industry

In 1970, the major home appliance industry, including refrigerators, freezers, ranges, disposals, dishwashers, clothes washers and dryers, and room air conditioners, shipped 28.2 million units with a retail value slightly in excess of $6 billion. This represented an 82% increase in units and a 62% increase in dollar sales over 1961. It was believed that the 1970s promised even greater growth.

These shipments in 1970 represented a unit volume over three times as great as the automobile industry though less than one fifth the dollar value. Compared to the four automobile manufacturers, there were more than 60 appliance manufacturers. But seven of these firms accounted for 75% of the volume. (See Exhibits 1 and 2.)

While during the decade of the 1960s, the automobile industry suffered increasing public criticism for its failure to produce a better and less expensive product to meet consumer needs, the appliance industry (often referred to as the white goods industry)[1] produced greatly improved appliances whose average price declined 10% in the span of the same decade. (See Exhibits 4, 5, and 6.)

Prior to World War II, most appliance manufacturers produced a limited line of appliances developed from the original products of their companies. General Electric started a refrigerator business, Maytag made washers, and Hotpoint produced electric ranges. The lines broadened but not until after World War II did manufacturers recognize the demand for a full line of products. Expansion continued in the decade following the war.

After 1955, however, the industry experienced overcapacity, concentration through mergers and acquisitions among the manufacturers (see Exhibit 7), and a proliferation of brands, both national and pri-

---

[1] The term white goods stemmed from the original color of these products and was used to distinguish them from other appliances like televisions, stereos, and radios which were referred to as brown goods.

vate. There was some feeling in the industry that home appliances were destined to become commodities sold on price alone and that then the Japanese might well become a dominant industry force. Others felt that certain peculiar industry forces, such as the giant vertically integrated retailers (e.g., Sears, Roebuck), would lead to the development of a unique structure. Finally, there were those who felt that entirely new products and revolutionary changes in existing products would drastically alter the industry.

If the structure of the industry was changing, so was the business competed for (see Exhibits 4 and 5). Several products experienced very high rates of growth during the 1960s. For example, room air conditioner sales almost quadrupled, dishwasher sales more than tripled and clothes dryers sales more than doubled. Even products in highly saturated markets like refrigerators and ranges (99% of wired homes had refrigerators and ranges) were selling about 50% more units by 1970. At the same time, the individual products themselves were changing. New features were added and the capacity of appliances increased (witness the trend toward larger refrigerators and air conditioners). Product reliability also increased.

With this brief scanning of industry history and trends as background, the remainder of this note examines white goods and their manufacturers, major industry trends, and industry performance, and considers possible future trends.

THE INDUSTRY: ITS PRODUCTS AND ECONOMICS

In 1970, there were two basic ways to classify the products of the appliance industry—by customer use and by technology. Looking first at customer use, appliances were sold for the kitchen—refrigerators, freezers, ranges, dishwashers, and disposals; for the home laundry—washers and dryers; and for room air conditioning. Technologically, appliances could be categorized as: water bearing—dishwashers, disposals, clothes washers, and some dryers; refrigerating—refrigerators, freezers, and room air conditioners; and heating—ranges. A number of part-line producers had diversified by filling out a line of products along one or both of these classifications (see Exhibit 1).

Appliances were manufactured on specialized high capacity assembly lines. Typically, a single factory would produce several models of a single product (e.g., side-by-side and top mount refrigerators) or for some companies a product category. The assembly lines in these factories were not generally convertible for use in manufacturing other product categories. An efficient plant's capacity would range from 100,000 air conditioners a year to 500,000 ranges, refrigerators, and dishwashers. One engineer estimated that production costs for refrigerators, ranges, and dishwashers might be 10% higher for a plant half the optimal size and 20%–40% higher for a plant a fifth the optimal size (see Exhibit 8).

The cost of a production facility that operated at minimum efficient scale (MES) for a full product line was estimated by an industry source to be around $500 million. The cost of a single-product plant at MES for dishwashers was estimated to be $50 million, while the cost of a single-product plant for refrigerators, freezers, clothes washers, clothes dryers, or ranges was estimated to be somewhat more than $50 million.

Even with capacity of the minimum efficient size, a firm might refrain from totally integrated manufacturing. Indeed, appliance companies often chose to buy components such as compressors and motors since these could be purchased from a number of large and efficient competing firms. Having a plant larger than the minimum efficient size resulted in economies in maintenance, quality control, inventory, and management. These had to be weighed against the increased transportation costs associated with the larger geographic area necessary to support the larger plant.

Economic analysis helps in understanding the manufacturer's problem. The industry in 1971 comprised a number of stages—product design, manufacturing, sales, distribution, and post-sale service. There were economies of scale at each stage. The significant economies of scale affecting the choice of plant size were in manufacturing and distribution (i.e., shipping). It was generally recognized in the industry that a manufacturer could reduce his transportation costs an estimated 8% to 10% by shipping full carloads. A full-line producer could fill a carload with a number of kinds of appliances, and hence could ship full carloads to those retailers who would never buy a full carload of one appliance. By placing all his production facilities in one location the full-line producer could exploit these economies of scale in shipping.

On the other hand, a single production location increased the total shipping distance in comparison with shipping distances expected for geographically dispersed production facilities. Hence, the manufacturer faced a dilemma. It appeared to the casewriter that economies of scale in production were more important than the cost savings from geographical diversity. G.E., for example, did not build at a new location until they felt that they could no longer lower costs by expanding a given facility.

Turning to sales cost, other economies of scale could be realized in selling the full line. Most appliance purchasers—both retail and contract— bought more than one type of appliance. Hence the additional time it took a salesman to sell more than one appliance was small in comparison with the time he spent traveling and waiting to see a buyer. Estimating the magnitude of this economy of scale is difficult. Tappan, a part-line manufacturer with dollar sales one eighth of G.E.'s, estimated that its sales costs per unit were twice those of G.E. Hence, this economy appears to be significant.

Economies of scale also existed in product development. Volume supported a higher R&D budget at lower unit cost. Since the materials technology was similar for the various white goods there were also economies of scale in being a multiple-product producer. But, R&D could be contracted from firms outside the industry. Firms in the industry tended to view economies of scale in R&D as the least important in terms of gaining a competitive advantage.

There were economies of scale, as well, in providing service once the appliance was sold and installed in the home. Large full-time manufacturers like G.E. and national retailers like Sears sold a sufficient number of appliances in most areas to allow them to provide their own service. Since servicemen serviced all white goods there were economies of scale to be derived from a full line as well as from high volume of any single product. Other firms in the industry that did not have as great a volume as Sears and G.E. relied heavily on franchised service agents who serviced several brands. Industry sources believed that owning the service facility did not reduce cost significantly, but did allow a greater control over service quality, which could in the long run improve the owner's brand image.

Finally, there was a different kind of economic power which had proved important: buying clout. High-volume national retailers (e.g., Sears, Penneys) were able to exact price concessions from manufacturers, which tended to shift cost savings derived from scale economies of production and shipping from the manufacturer to the retailer. Retail muscle, then, could operate to deny to the manufacturer some of the advantage of scale economies.

MANUFACTURERS' LINES AND SOURCING

There were seven full-line manufacturers in 1971. However, many of the specialist producers (e.g., Tappan) would "source"—buy from another manufacturer—appliances that they did not manufacture, in order to broaden their lines. Even a full-line producer like G.E. sourced certain products during a period when it was considering whether to mass-produce them. Examples include gas ranges or small apartment-sized washers and dryers. At the retail level, some national chain retailers sourced their entire line and sold under their own brand name. Sears led in this practice, buying most of its appliances from Whirlpool, Design and Manufacturing, and Roper. Other national chain retailers were moving in this direction. In 1966 Penneys introduced its Penncrest appliances made by G.E.

APPLIANCE BRANDS

Brands such as Kenmore, Coldspot, Penncrest, etc., were national brands but they were *retail* national brands as opposed to *manufacturers'* national brands. They were the only brand carried by a given chain of stores. Still other retailers sourced a product for use as "bottom-of-the-line" brands to be sold primarily on a low-price basis. Jordan Marsh's (Allied Stores) Ambassador washer and dryer, produced by Westinghouse, was an example of this practice. These private brands were not available nationally and were carried along with other brands. The retailer carrying private brands usually did not advertise them heavily or require that they be designed to their specifications. Some appliance manufacturers, e.g., White Consolidated, specialized in producing for this market segment, and most manufacturers were engaged in it to some extent. (See Exhibit 9.)

These three types of brands—manufacturers, retail, and private— also differed significantly in feature content. A feature is an extra, added to the basic appliance unit. The self-cleaning oven, the microwave oven, and thermostatic controlled burner were features available on the basic range. Traditionally, new features were introduced at the "top-of-the-line" with a high price. Then, over time, as other new features were added and competitors copied them, the price on older features fell until eventually they became standard equipment. In fact, the product line of a manufacturer was defined in terms of feature content, the appliances with more and newer features being higher in the line. All national manufacturers followed this policy. Sears, however, made no attempt to introduce new features, but instead copied the last year's "top-of-the-line" features and sold them at "middle-of-the-line" prices. Private brands had low feature content and hence usually were competitive with the "bottom-of-the-line" of the national brands.

MARKET SHARE

In terms of market share, the industry leaders were in the full-line national brand category. By 1969, the four leading brand groups—Sears (Kenmore-Coldspot), G.E. (G.E.-Hotpoint), Whirlpool, and Frigidaire —enjoyed 71% of the washer market, 65% of the dryer market, 42% of the range market, 63% of the refrigerator market, and 65% of the dishwasher market. (See Exhibits 2 and 3 for market shares.) Sears was the leader in most product categories. Since Whirlpool produced many products for Sears, Whirlpool was by far the largest manufacturer after G.E. In spite of the impressive production capacity of G.E. and Whirlpool, even essentially single-product manufacturers like Maytag, Hobart (KitchenAid), and Tappan had increased their market share during the 1960s.

Of all the major producers, only Frigidaire was losing market share in 1971. Frigidaire, one of the oldest and most identifiable brands, had a unique problem. Being a division of GM its labor contract was negotiated by the UAW at the corporate level even though the division had an IUE union. Other manufacturers in the industry had IUE contracts set at considerably lower hourly wages. (The difference was in excess of $1 per hour lower.) The result was a cost disadvantage that severely threatened Frigidaire's future. (See Exhibit 10.)

APPROACHES OF COMPETITORS

Competitors in the appliance industry followed a variety of basic approaches, the diversity of which was unusual for American industry. More unusual still is the fact that firms as different in basic approach as Sears, Tappan, and G.E. were all successful. This section describes in some detail the approaches followed by a selected group of competitors in the white goods industry. General Electric, Westinghouse, and

General Motors represent the full-line manufacturers; D&M and Tappan, the part-line producers; Sears and Penneys, the large national retailers; and Raytheon, the high technology approach to appliance manufacturing.

General Electric (G.E.). G.E. entered the appliance field in 1918 with the acquisition of Hotpoint. Hotpoint, which produced and marketed irons and ranges, operated as a separate division and constituted G.E.'s sole effort at that time in the appliance field. Hotpoint's business grew rapidly through the 1920s. In the 1930s, with the advent of the electric refrigerator, G.E. introduced its own appliance brand. Gradually during the 1930s and after the war, the G.E. and Hotpoint lines expanded independently and began to compete with one another. Independent development continued through the 1950s under G.E.'s decentralized organization structure, although the two appliance divisions were formally merged in 1952.

In the 1950s, G.E. adopted a policy of building capacity ahead of demand. Construction of the vast Louisville manufacturing facility was the result. The goal seemed to be to achieve high market share and attendant scale manufacturing economies. Low unit production costs thus attained later gave G.E. a distinct competitive advantage in the increasingly price-sensitive appliance industry. This advantage was not shared as fully by the Hotpoint line which maintained separate and more modest production facilities into the 1960s.

In the 1960s, development of the appliance business took a back seat at G.E. to three new capital-intensive businesses: computers, breeder reactors, and heavy jet aircraft engines. The 1960s did, however, see the merger of Hotpoint and G.E. production facilities in 1965.

As G.E. entered the 1970s, the appliance business again moved to the forefront as a potential money maker in the wake of disappointments and even some outright failures in the three glamour businesses of the 1960s. Organizationally, G.E. integrated Hotpoint and G.E. appliance lines into one centrally coordinated appliance group. This merely gave official recognition to the informal working arrangements which had been followed since the merger of production facilities in 1965. In 1973, the company was considering another large investment in production capacity to maintain its cost advantage and protect its market share in the appliance field.

In the 1970s, G.E.'s basic approach appeared to be aimed at achieving high-volume, low-cost production coupled with extensive retail marketing coverage through multiple branding. The G.E. brand was marketed primarily through traditional, higher margin channels. Hotpoint also penetrated the national retail brand market (and increased production volume) by manufacturing appliances for Penneys' Penncrest line.

In addition, G.E. pursued a regular program of product innovation and placed engineering emphasis on product reliability. Since these two qualities were associated in the customers' eyes with technical competence and quality, G.E.'s approach here was designed to establish and maintain a favorable brand image.

The other major thrust of G.E.'s appliance strategy was in the new construction segment of the appliance market. Here the G.E. brand and reputation for innovation were a tremendous asset in competition for the business of home builders. Manufacturing and distribution muscle also helped in fighting for share in this highly price-sensitive market. With no competition from Sears both the G.E. and Hotpoint brands achieved important market positions.

Westinghouse.   Westinghouse entered the appliance field in the 1920s and like G.E. gradually became a national full-line appliance manufacturer. From World War II through the better part of the 1960s, Westinghouse held its own as a full-line producer and marketer of home appliances. However, Westinghouse did not achieve the same low level of production costs as G.E. and signs of discontent appeared in Westinghouse's appliance business. For one thing, the Consumer Products Division lost money in 1971—a record year for Westinghouse as a whole. As a result, management adopted an attitude of retrenchment toward its traditional business. Cost cutting became the watchword.

Westinghouse seemed to be coasting with the traditional appliance business while it shifted emphasis to new concepts. The theme of the new approach was Homecology—improving the quality of life in the home. To this end, Westinghouse created new appliance products (e.g., the room air cleaner, the tap water purifier) and introduced new appliance systems to replace, in time, part of the market for the older appliance units. Examples of the new systems were home security systems and interior subsystems for industrial housing—including prepackaged kitchens, bathrooms, and central air conditioning apparatus. To gain better control of the flow of systems containing appliances to the ultimate buyer, Westinghouse constructed the first of what might become a series of plants for factory production of modular housing units.

Design and Manufacturing (D&M).   In the late 1950s, D&M management perceived that the major dishwasher producers (G.E. and Hobart) were not willing to supply the national retailers with dishwashers. D&M elected to fill this market niche by producing only dishwashers for the private brand market of the national retailers—especially Sears. By restricting production to dishwashers in a market segment with just two other producers, D&M was able to develop sufficient volume to manufacture efficiently and at very competitive cost. Low cost, in turn, enabled D&M to supply Sears and thus build volume. At the same time, D&M was able to establish attractive profit margins on sales to those customers who could be made to pay higher prices than Sears could negotiate. Thus D&M was very successful in the market niche in which it operates.

Tappan.   Tappan has been in the stove business since the 1880s, first with wood and coal burning stoves and later with gas fueled ranges. By 1946, Tappan was a leading producer of gas ranges with 8% of a market with 140 competitors.

Though Tappan continued to grow in the decades of the 1950s and 1960s, it found itself with problems to surmount in the seventies. It was at a cost disadvantage with respect to full-line producers and at a disadvantage in penetrating retail channels because large retailers preferred to carry a full line of a given brand. To deal with these problems, Tappan introduced major feature innovations to induce large retailers to carry its line, and went after private brand and mobile home business to build volume and thereby lower production costs.

For the longer term, Tappan was also developing major new products (e.g., unit kitchen, gas air conditioners) as well as a new channel of distribution—the Tappan Home Center, to sell the unit kitchen concept.

Sears. Founded in 1895 as a catalog operation, it was not until 1925 that Sears began to move into direct retail selling. From the beginning, home appliances were a mainstay of Sears' retail operations. These operations expanded through the 1920s and 1930s. But it was after the war that Sears' current approach began to take shape. In the late 1940s, Sears dropped the idea—which it had toyed with since the 1920s—of integrating backward into appliance production. Instead, Sears began to use its rapidly expanding retail volume to advantage in negotiating low-cost production arrangements with appliance manufacturers.

At the same time, Sears began to adopt distinctive brand names under which to sell its appliances nationally (e.g., "Coldspot" and "Kenmore"), thereby creating the concept of a retail national brand.

Since the late 1940s, Sears had attempted to establish the fullest possible control over retail sales. Sears continued to use the buying clout derived from its high volume of retail sales to exact near-cost selling prices from manufacturers. Volume buying permitted Sears' suppliers to produce appliances at a price to Sears less than the production cost of all but the most efficient manufacturers. Thus Sears had firm control over the cost of appliances it retails.

Sears took advantage of low cost in two ways. First, in advertising it played up the low prices of the lower end-of-the-line products. This attracted customers to Sears stores. Then, Sears used its sales force—also fully within Sears' control—to trade customers up to the higher price models on which Sears realized handsome profit margins, especially handsome in view of Sears' low unit cost throughout the range of appliance models.

Sears tailored its product line to the trade-up strategy by positioning products at convenient price increments throughout the possible range of sales prices. Indeed, Sears was first to establish and exploit the idea of a retail price point spectrum.

Penneys. Since 1963 Penneys had adopted a policy of head-on competition. Penneys added large ticket items, especially appliances, to new full-time stores. It followed an aggressive building program, matching Sears store for store. In 1970, Penneys was the second largest national retailer with 240 stores carrying appliances compared with Sears' 827.

On the supply side, Penneys, like Sears, was having its private brand appliances manufactured outside the company umbrella. G.E. manufactured the Penncrest appliance line, an arrangement that enabled Penneys and G.E. to cooperate in competing with Sears.

Raytheon. Though founded in 1928, Raytheon did not enter the appliance field until 1965, when it acquired Amana, an old-line refrigerator and air-conditioning manufacturer. Raytheon followed that acquisition with another in 1967 when it acquired Caloric Corporation, a manufacturer of gas ranges and other kitchen appliances.

Raytheon was an example of a high technology company which, by expanding into the appliance field, began to introduce radically new technologies to the industry. For example, by 1971 Raytheon had gained a significant share of the new microwave oven market—a market which it pioneered.

Other new products in the offing included a home trash compactor (introduced in 1971), compact refrigerators and freezers made possible by improved insulation technology, quiet air conditioners which took advantage of the noise engineering competence which Raytheon had gained from the defense industry, and an electric ignition gas range which eliminated the pilot light.

Raytheon's approach to the appliance business was designed to create new markets or capture a share of existing markets by catching current manufacturers off guard with new technology.

THE MARKET FOR WHITE GOODS

The diversity of the markets for which these very different firms competed was just as great as the variations, unusual for industry, in the firms themselves. This section examines the characteristics of the market segments in which white goods were sold in 1970 and estimates the possibilities for future growth in these segments.

White goods were sold to two entirely different sets of buyers—retail merchants and construction firms of various types for installation in dwelling units prior to purchase. The former is called the "retail market" segment, while the latter is referred to as the "contract market" segment. Since the basic characteristics of these two market segments, as well as their growth rates in the past and projections for the future, were quite different, they will be considered separately.

The contract market. The contract segment of the market had grown in importance since World War II. It accounted for over 70% of the unit sales of built-in ranges, under counter dishwashers, and disposals. In total, contract sales accounted for around 28% of all appliance unit sales in 1970 according to study. The future of contract sales appeared even brighter.

Contract sales were related directly to new housing starts.[2] In the 1960s housing starts held at a low level, but in the 1970s they were expected to rise dramatically in the wake of a sharp expected rise in the rate of new family starts. Housing starts during 1966–71 had totaled 8,000,000. The 1971–75 projection of 12,000,000 represented a 50% increase. If this jump actually occurred, and assuming an average of three appliances installed in a new home prior to purchase, the contract market segment was expected to capture 34% of total appliance unit

[2] These forecasts are from a study made by one appliance manufacturer, as is the data on housing starts. Other companies differed somewhat in their estimates.

sales. According to econometric projections of retail demand growth (based on the age configuration of present appliances in 1971 and projections of disposable income), this growth in contract sales represented 50% of forecast growth in total appliance unit sales. Growth in total unit sales of appliances for 1971–75 was forecast at 30%. Looking at the decade to 1980, G.E. forecast a 91% increase in industry dollar sales on an increase of 74% in units shipped. Given these projections, and assuming the same average dollar price per unit in both the retail and contract segments,[3] contract dollar sales would account for 60% of the growth in total appliance dollar sales and have 42% of the total dollar market by 1980. Other estimates forecast contract sales to be as high as 50% of the total dollar market by 1980.

The nature of new housing starts was also undergoing a fundamental change. In 1963, apartments accounted for approximately 25% of total new starts.[4] By early 1971, apartments were accounting for approximately 50% of housing starts. Because many young families wanted to live in or near a large city and because the cost of home ownership was rising, many in the industry believed that the apartment share of the market would continue to increase. The impact of this trend was twofold. The number and types of appliances furnished in single-family dwelling units, apartments and mobile homes, were different in each case. (See Exhibit 11.) The differences were greatest in refrigerators, clothes washers and dryers, and perhaps, unit air conditioners (though here no data are available). With refrigerators and unit air conditioners, the trend toward apartment living implied increased sales for the contract segment since these were provided in many apartments but few homes. With home laundry, the impact of the trend was harder to anticipate. If coin-operated laundromat equipment, often placed in the basement by the builder, gained acceptance, it could mean slower growth since one machine would serve several families. On the other hand, if mini-washers and dryers, designed to fit into small apartments, gained consumer acceptance, rapid growth could result. These, however, were sold through retail channels.

The second impact of the trend toward apartment living was to increase the average number of appliances purchased by a given builder since each apartment would require appliances. With this larger volume, more builders would buy directly from the manufacturer.

Manufacturers sold appliances to the contract segment both directly to the large builders and indirectly through local builder suppliers. Direct sales to construction firms and mobile home manufacturers were made by corporate salesmen for most of the full-line companies and to a limited extent by independent distributors for the smaller manufacturers. These direct sales accounted for 80% of the contract sales and it was thought that the trend toward apartment living could increase their importance.[5] To understand the approaches various manufactur-

---

[3] The implications of this assumption are explored later in the subsection entitled "The Retail Market."

[4] See footnote 2.

[5] Industry estimate.

ers took to these direct sales, the needs of the builder must be considered.

Appliances were crucial in selling homes even though they made up a small percentage of total home costs (10% or less). In the industry it was generally believed that the consumer did not have the knowledge to evaluate objectively the quality of the dwelling unit. On the other hand, it was thought that he did have opinions as to the quality of various brands of appliances and that he associated this judgment with the quality of the dwelling unit. It was believed, therefore, that appliance brand image was crucial in selling to builders. In fact, because of the perceived importance of brand image, builders seldom bought private brands.

Builders, however, were very cost conscious. They typically bought the middle and lower end of the product line. By buying all the appliances from one manufacturer they could save on transportation costs and also establish the leverage to demand and obtain a lower price. Finally, when a dwelling unit was ready for the appliance, it was crucial that the appliance be there. If it was not, the builder had to hold the completed dwelling in inventory. The interest cost could be substantial. By maintaining a relationship with one manufacturer, the builder could put on pressure for timely delivery.

The major companies in the contract market segment in 1970 were G.E. (G.E. and Hotpoint brands), Whirlpool, Frigidaire, Tappan (sourcing products not manufactured) and Westinghouse.[6] Whether Sears could compete in this market was one of the most interesting questions facing the industry. Sears had yet to make any significant inroad, though it appeared to be planning an attack. Many in the industry thought that Sears' brand image and lack of experience in the contract market would preclude the success it experienced in the retail market segment. Yet given the past success of Sears, few were willing to deny the significance of the Sears threat. By 1973, there were clear indications that Sears would attempt to enter this market segment.

All of the major companies active in the contract market sold full lines. Some manufacturers provided kitchen designing services to large builders and all were able to advise builders how to match the quality of the appliance to the price and quality of the dwelling unit. The market traditionally was highly price competitive because each builder could play the manufacturers off against one another. The larger construction firms—with substantial buying power—were able to negotiate lower prices on the same principle that Sears used at the retail level.

For selling the finished unit it was crucial to have highly trained salesmen who could convince the builder of the merits of the particular brand. Delivery also was important, and the major manufacturers gave close attention to logistics.

The major manufacturers differed only slightly in their approach to the market—Westinghouse favored large-scale land and community

---

[6] No data were available on market share in the contract segment as opposed to the retail segment. In general, these five companies were viewed by industry experts as enjoying the bulk of the contract market.

developments; Tappan sold cabinets as well as appliances. Hotpoint had its own home centers in markets where there were no builder suppliers. G.E. and Westinghouse enjoyed one advantage over other manufacturers in the contract segment. Having a diverse product line of electrical goods, certain divisions frequently received builder contracts for wiring, for heavy electrical equipment, and so on. This gave other areas of the company, like the appliance group, early information as to future construction. It also gave G.E. and Westinghouse a chance to sell a larger package of goods to the builders. But this was not a great advantage. Price, brand image, and delivery were believed to be the three dominant factors in the contract market segment.

There were, however, some signs that the basic nature of the contract market might change. Two of the most likely changes were the evolution of the "core-kitchen" and the development of a systematic kitchen remodeling business. The core-kitchen was a prefabricated kitchen including all kitchen appliances, cabinets, and counters. It could be installed as a single unit in the home. The core-kitchen reduced the amount of relatively expensive on-site craft labor. In 1970, Tappan already had begun to produce these core-kitchens on an experimental basis. Two factors inhibited the growth of the core-kitchen: labor union resistance and the need to ship more "kitchen-cores" than most builders could use, in order to reduce transportation costs.

While the development of the core-kitchen would not change the traditional channels of distribution in the contract market since it would still be sold to builders, the development of the remodeling business might well bring substantial change. One industry expert estimated that there were 5 million kitchens in existence that needed complete remodeling—new appliances, cabinets, and counters. Traditionally small builders and, to a lesser extent, Sears had serviced this market. Most manufacturers agreed that lack of a major marketing effort and generally poor service had limited the exploitation of this market segment. By 1973, however, Sears had begun to consider the remodeling market more seriously. Its most recent catalog featured several pages on the home center concept. Tappan was exploring another more comprehensive approach to this market segment. This was based on setting up Tappan home centers that displayed six or more model kitchens, provided a kitchen design service, and installed the new kitchen. This approach was predicated on the assumption that customers needed to see what could be done by remodeling and also needed a guarantee that the job could be done in a few days. Tappan felt that most small builders could supply neither of these services and hence new channels had to be developed.

The retail market.   While total dollar sales were expected to increase 91% by 1980 and retail dollar sales were expected to increase 52% during the same period, retail as a share of total dollar sales was expected to drop from 72% in 1970 to 58% by 1980.[7] The faster growth of the contract market meant that the absolute growth of the retail segment represented a declining share of the total market.

---

[7] Industry estimate.

The conclusion was a tentative one, however, for two reasons. First, since total unit sales were expected to increase only 74% by 1980 (compared with 91% for dollar sales), the analysis reflected a belief that average prices per unit would rise over the decade of the 1970s. This could happen in one of two ways: (1) The average price per unit could increase, or (2) customers could be traded up more frequently to expensive products. The first of these possibilities contradicted the 1960s experience of declining average appliance prices. The second possibility was plausible only for customers in the retail segment because of the extreme price sensitivity of builders in the contract segment. However, prices in the contract segment had tended to be lower on the average than in the retail segment. There was, therefore, uncertainty surrounding the forecasted price increase.

WHOLESALE DISTRIBUTION CHANNELS

Retail sales in 1970 were made through distributors, either company-owned or independent. National retailers, like Sears, had complete control over distribution since they bought directly from manufacturers and did the retailing themselves. Manufacturers sold their products to retailers through both independent and owned distributors. G.E. led in sales through owned distribution. All of Hotpoint's sales and 90% to 95% of G.E.'s brand sales were made through company-owned distribution.[8] Frigidaire was second, with roughly 60% through owned distribution in 1970, down from 80% in the mid-1960s.

Most large full-line manufacturers had sufficient sales in large metropolitan areas to operate their own distribution network efficiently. Except for the very largest manufacturers, it was not efficient to own distribution in low-volume areas. Most part-line and single-product manufacturers were at an absolute disadvantage since they could not utilize their salesmen efficiently or ship full truckloads of their products to retailers. Hence, they were forced into accepting higher distribution costs or using private distributors. They were forced, as well, to accept higher sales costs.

Ownership of distribution channels was important to both manufacturers and retailers because whoever owned the distribution channels would have substantial influence over the retailer. Three degrees of control were observed, depending on who owned the distribution channels.

National retail brands like Sears had complete control since manufacturers sold directly to Sears and Sears controlled wholesale distribution as well as retail selling. They could set retail price and control sales presentations and advertising. They could also control inventory directly.

Single-product manufacturers like Maytag and Hobart exemplified a second degree of control. They sold and shipped directly to carefully selected retailers (often exclusively franchised) and maintained close communication with these retailers. Their retail strategy was one of

---

[8] Industry estimate.

intensive coverage. Though they could not set retail price or inventory levels, they did have considerable influence over both. These manufacturers concentrated on the high-price/high-quality end of the line. The choice of retailers to maintain or enhance this image was believed to be crucial. The effort they placed on dealer relationships was of key importance.

A third degree of control was obtained by manufacturers which owned distribution. This allowed the manufacturer to choose his retailers, set the wholesale price and determine advertising allowances. For the large multiproduct manufacturers, however, the close relationship with individual retailers obtained by Maytag and Hobart was impossible. They not only sold to a much larger number of retailers, but they also sold to retailers that carried several brands of each product. Direct shipment from the factory to many retailers was impossible because of their strategy of extensive coverage. They did, however, ship direct to very large retailers.

The most indirect control was obtained through selling to independent distributors. This method of selling precluded direct control by the manufacturer over wholesale price and choice of retail outlets. Private distributors posed a threat to national brand manufacturers since they could sell anywhere to anyone and had strong incentives to do so. For example, independent distributors could sell to builders and hence could create problems in the contract market segment for companies that sold to this segment directly.

RETAIL MARKETING STRATEGIES

The choice of the desired degree of control depended to a large extent on the choice of marketing strategy. Though all the firms in the industry were selling very similar products, there was considerable difference in their marketing approach. One way of distinguishing between these approaches was to classify their marketing strategies as "pull" or "push."

A pull strategy was characterized by national advertising, leadership in product innovation (i.e., introducing more and better new features than any other manufacturer), selective choice of local dealers with the best reputations, and development of a very good service network. Pull brands such as G.E., Frigidaire, Westinghouse, Maytag, Hobart, Caloric, and Amana followed various mixtures of these methods. The full-line producers tended to depend more on national advertising and less on careful dealer choice and close dealer relationship than did the single-product manufacturers. On the other hand, the full-line producers owned as much of their distribution as possible. Product innovation was important not only because it temporarily differentiated the manufacturer's product from the others, but also because consumers associated continued innovation with high quality.[9] Studies at G.E. had shown that innovation was directly related to brand image. The pur-

---

[9] Industry experience had been that new product features were usually copied by other manufacturers in 12 to 18 months.

pose of the pull strategy was to get the customer to make the decision as to the brand he would buy before he entered the store. Hence, "switching" him to another brand in the store would be difficult for a salesman.

A push strategy attempted to encourage switching in the store. Here, it was important to have a unique product—a brand not readily available elsewhere or a feature or model no other store in the area carried. To encourage switching, push brands usually had higher retail margins and higher local advertising allowances. Private brands fell into this category. Carried by selected stores in a single retail area, they were low price but not necessarily low margin. Leading push brands were Philco-Ford, Fedders-Norge, Hotpoint, and White Consolidated.

The national retail brands like Sears were neither push nor pull but rather a hybrid. Sears pulled customers into the store with its store name and heavily advertised sales on low-price/low-feature items. Sears' salesmen then attempted to "sell the customers up" to higher featured, higher priced products. The service contract offered by Sears was used to distinguish it from other brands, as was the fact that only Sears stores carried the brand. Sears could pursue this strategy because it controlled retail price, sold only through its own stores, and trained and motivated its salesmen to "sell up" with strong commission incentives.

BRAND LOYALTY

Each of these strategies was designed to get sales volume in an industry with high brand loyalty. One survey showed that 70% of appliance owners would strongly consider buying the same brand that they now owned. (See Exhibit 12.) Yet, this brand loyalty did not appear to be the result of heavy advertising. For example, in 1971 G.E. spent $3,300,000 on national advertising, Tappan spent $106,000, and Maytag spent $562,000.[10] This is less than 1% of sales for each of these companies. All companies did, however, give retailers an advertising allowance based on sales, which was to be spent on local newspaper advertising.

Firms in the industry had different views on the causes of brand loyalty. Some firms thought it resulted from their continuing production of a reliable product over a long period of time, others felt that it was the result of leadership in product innovation, while still others indicated that loyalty was decreasing as consumers had more experience with the product and as the products in general became more reliable. No executive interviewed suggested that national advertising was a major factor in generating brand loyalty.

RETAIL CHANNELS OF DISTRIBUTION

The various approaches to marketing and distributing appliances must be considered in light of the changes in channels of distribution.

---

[10] Leading National Advertiser, Inc., *National Advertising Investment.*

The channels of distribution were changing rapidly during the 1960s. The small appliance retailer carrying a limited number of brands and models of appliances lost volume relative to the large chain appliance dealers and discount stores. (See Exhibit 13.) Sears, Penneys, Montgomery Ward, and other national chains grew in importance. These stores carried predominantly retail national brands.

Also, large regional chain stores specializing in appliances developed during the 1960s—Lechmere in Massachusetts and Polk Brothers in Illinois, for example. In the early 1960s, these regional chain stores sold national manufacturers' brands as well as private brands. According to one industry executive, the strategy of some of these stores was to switch customers to their private brands and eventually develop their own retail brand. Such stores found, however, that to induce such a switch they had to price their private brands so low as to make little money. They soon discovered that their strength lay in generating traffic and underselling competition on the basis of the operating efficiencies gained from high volume. These lessons learned, by the end of the 1960s virtually all of the mass merchandisers were concentrating on national manufacturers' brands, and these stores were rapidly gaining strength as the primary outlet for national manufacturers' brands. The "discounters" attempted to limit the number of brands and models that they carried in order to reduce inventory and gain maximum savings from volume buying. Hence, they tended to buy predominantly from full-line manufacturers.

The growth of the giant discounters did not affect all appliance products in the same way. Room air conditioners were more often sold through department stores and other small outlets like radio and TV shops than were kitchen and home laundry appliances. Room air conditioners (RAC) were referred to as impulse goods in the industry. On the first hot day of summer sales skyrocketed. Consumers tended to go to the closest store to buy air conditioners since they wanted their house cooled immediately. In aggregate data, such as that shown in Exhibit 13, the rapid growth in RAC sales during the 1960s tended to mask the trend toward chain and discount stores as preferred channels for retail sales of the rest of the appliances.

FOREIGN COMPETITION

Along with changing markets and channels of distribution, another problem facing manufacturers of white goods was the threat of foreign competition. In 1966, 309,000 refrigerators were imported. By 1970, refrigerator imports had tripled in volume to 935,000 with a retail value of $58 million.[11] Though refrigerator imports were primarily small units often used for home bars, offices, or recreational vehicles the increase was still significant. It represented slightly less than 20% of the units sold in 1970 but, because of the lower price, less than 5% of dollar sales. Foreign competition also was making inroads on other

_____
[11] *Merchandising Week*, February 22, 1971, p. 34.

appliances—again primarily with small-sized units like counter top microwave ovens. Most imports were small-sized appliances because these were the type typically used abroad. Exports to the U.S. market represented incremental volume for Japanese and Italian manufacturers. As per capita income rose, especially in Japan, it was thought that larger appliances might become more common. In that event the United States could expect a similar influx of larger appliances in the future.

The role of the United States as an incremental market stemmed from the need for economies of scale in production. Industry experts considered it doubtful that a foreign competitor could gain a large enough market share in the United States to justify producing for the United States alone. If, however, he could sell the goods in his own country as well, he could gain the size to compete in the United States.

PATTERNS OF INDUSTRY PERFORMANCE

Price and growth. The white goods industry had been characterized by high growth in unit volume, price erosion in a time of general inflation and rapid product innovation. The 82% increase in units shipped during the 1960s was matched by only a 62% rise in dollar sales. But to truly appreciate the 10% drop in retail prices during the 1960s, one has to consider that average product size increased. Feature content and reliability also improved. (See Exhibit 16.) At the same time as wholesale and retail prices were falling, production costs were increasing by up to 40% for labor, metalworking, machinery, and non-ferrous metal. (See Exhibit 6.) This price-cost squeeze put tremendous pressure on the manufacturers not only to produce existing products more efficiently, but also to redesign the products to achieve lower manufacturing costs. Since the price of an average service call according to G.E. was rising dramatically toward $20,[12] manufacturers were also under continual pressure to improve reliability while cutting costs. This pressure came because appliances carried a one-year warranty period. One result of this effort to produce a more reliable product was that service calls made during the warranty period had fallen 60% on dryers and 75% on washers during the decade of the 1960s. (See Exhibit 14.)

Innovations. As noted, the price-cost squeeze had not suppressed innovation in the industry. To the contrary, Exhibit 15 shows that many innovations took place in the highly saturated products—in particular washers, ranges, and refrigerators. A major innovation on one of these highly saturated products tended to differentiate the product from that of the competitors and speed up replacement demand—i.e., innovation induced consumers to buy a new appliance before the old one was worn out (see Exhibit 16). A successful innovation could expand total market size as well as market share. For less saturated products experiencing high growth, the impact of innovations on the growth of total sales was less significant.

---

[12] Service calls were labor intensive and hence the cost tended to rise faster than in appliances where capital could be substituted for labor.

Innovations came from several sources. A number originated from changes in contiguous industries such as food processing or synthetic fabrics. For example, the side-by-side refrigerator had its origin in the growing use of frozen food and the resulting need for more freezer space. The mini-basket on washers was designed to handle small loads of delicate synthetic fabrics previously requiring hand washing.

Other innovations resulted from attempts to cut manufacturing cost. For example "foamed-in-place" insulation was cheaper than regular insulation and equally effective, but it dramatically reduced the wall width of refrigerators as well. The plastic case developed for room air conditioners was less expensive and lighter than metal, and did not rust. But, the bulk of major innovations listed in Exhibit 15 were the result of an explicit effort to fit the appliance better to the needs of the consumer. For example, the self-cleaning oven was developed because consumers disliked the messy job of cleaning the oven. An ice dispenser on the outside of the refrigerator door made it easier to get ice and eliminated the primary reason for opening the freezer door.

Profits. Financial performance varied considerably for the firms involved in the industry. One industry expert estimated that return on assets averaged 6% to 8% for the industry as a whole. Though it was impossible to obtain financial data on most of the major competitors, Exhibits 17 and 18 give financial data on a number of firms in the industry. Maytag was generally accepted as the industry leader in terms of return on assets and sales. In sharp contrast Admiral Corporation was only one tenth as profitable In commenting on the industry leaders, one executive stated that G.E. and Sears were well above the industry average in terms of profitability while Frigidaire and Westinghouse were below average.

SOME CONJECTURES AS TO THE FUTURE

Speculation as to the future of any industry is difficult at best, but there were several threats to the industry in 1971 that warrant consideration. If the industry doubled in volume during the 1970s, as suggested by the predictions previously discussed, there would need to be a marked increase in capacity. But the primary source of growth would be new family formation. If the population growth rate stabilized, the decade of the 1980s and 1990s could see substantial overcapacity. In an industry where price stability had been an ongoing problem, the results of this overcapacity could be disastrous.

Another threat to the industry was continuation of the price-cost squeeze. This squeeze could result in elimination of the new product development effort and turn the industry into a commodity industry. Becoming a commodity industry not only would adversely affect the consumer, but would also increase the threat of foreign competition since production efficiency would be the major ingredient of success.

The industry was also susceptible to revolutionary new technologies. There was little to guarantee that the majority of traditional competitors would be able to adapt to such radical changes. Raytheon entered the industry in the mid-1960s through the acquisition of Amana and Caloric in order to apply the technologies they had developed for the aerospace and other high technology industries. By 1971, Raytheon had gained a significant share of the microwave oven market. Corning had also entered the market to utilize its superior knowledge of glass and had introduced the glass surface range. The threat of such companies could not be ignored, especially in light of the rising pressure on high technology firms to diversify out of the aerospace and defense industries.

Finally, increasing control of the industry by a few large manufacturers coupled with a rising tide of consumerism enhanced the possibility of government intervention. Government intervention might take the form of legal action to limit the market share of large firms or, as was more likely, it could take the form of a bar on future acquisitions. Finally, there was the possibility that legislation similar to the Automotive Safety Act might be passed for appliances.

Exhibit 1

NOTE ON THE MAJOR HOME APPLIANCE INDUSTRY
Product Lines of Appliance Producers
(January 1, 1971)

Name	Dishwashers	Disposals	Air conditioners (unit)	Ranges	Refrigerators	Home laundry
Full-Line Producers						
Fedders Corp.	x		x	x	x	x
General Electric (G.E. & Hotpoint)	x	x	x	x	x	x
General Motors (Frigidaire Division)	x	x	x	x	x	x
Westinghouse	x	x	x	x	x	x
Whirlpool	x	x	x	x	x	x
White Consolidated (Gibson, Hupp, Franklin, and Kelvinator Div.)	x	x	x	x	x	x
Raytheon (Amana, Caloric Division)	x	x	x	x	x	x
Part-Line Producers						
Admiral Corp.			x	x	x	
Malleable Iron Range Co.	x			x	x	
Modern Maid, Inc.	x			x		
Mullins Mfg.	x	x		x		
Norris Industries, Inc.	x			x		
Ford (Philco Division)			x	x	x	x
Rangaire Co.	x		x	x	x	
Tappan Co.	x	x		x		
Waste King Corp.	x	x		x		
King Refo Co.			x		x	
Maytag Co.	x	x				x
Hobart Mfg.	x	x				
Republic Co.	x		x	x		
Single-Product Producers						
Athens Stove Works				x		
Autocrat Co.				x		
Boston Stove Co.				x		
Brown Stove Works, Inc.				x		
Columbus Stove Co.				x		
Cory Corp.				x		
Crown Stove Works				x		
Eagle Range Mfg.				x		
Gray and Dudley				x		
Hardwick Stove Co.				x		
Hedges Mfg.				x		
Hill Shaw Co.				x		
Knox Stove Works				x		
Magic Chef				x		
Peerless Enamel Products				x		
Corning Co.				x		
Phillips and Buttorf Co.				x		
Prizer Painter Stove Works, Inc.				x		
Roper Co. (Sears Subsidiary)				x		

Exhibit 1—Continued

Name	Dishwashers	Disposals	Air conditioners (unit)	Ranges	Refrigerators	Home laundry
Sunral Stove Co. (Division of Glenwood Range Co.)...				x		
Wolf Range Co.....................				x		
Hager, Inc.........................					x	
Herrick Refrigerator Co.............. (Division of Diebold, Inc.)..........					x	
Nor-Lake, Inc......................					x	
Victory Metal Mfg. Co..............					x	
Blackstone Corp....................						x
Centrex Corp......................						x
Ero Industries, Inc.................						x
Hoover...........................						x
Midwest Metal Stamping Co.........						x
Design & Manufacture, Inc..........	x					
Day and Night Mfg. Co..............			x			
National Union Electronics Corp.......			x			
Addison Products Co................			x			
Albion Division (McGraw-Edison).....			x			
Carrier Corp......................			x			
Heat Controler, Inc.................			x			
International Heater Co..............			x			
York (Division of Borg-Warner).......			x			
Residential Air Conditioning (Division of American Standard)....			x			
Emerson Radio and Phonograph Co....			x			
Tran Co...........................			x			

Source: *Standard and Poor's Directory, Moody's Industrial Manual.*

Exhibit 2

NOTE ON THE MAJOR HOME APPLIANCE INDUSTRY
Market Share, Percentage of Units Shipped
Home Laundry

	Automatic washers		
	1954	*1964*	*1969*
Sears...	8%	18%	34%
G.E...	8	11	13
Maytag......................................	8	11	10
Whirlpool...................................	10	9	12
Frigidaire...................................	8	8	9
Westinghouse.............................	n.a.	n.a.	3
Hotpoint....................................	n.a.	n.a.	3
All other....................................	58	43	16
Total..	100%	100%	100%

	Dryers		
	1954	*1964*	*1969*
Sears...	17%	35%	33%
G.E...	6	8	11
Whirlpool...................................	9	8	12
Maytag......................................	2	9	9
Frigidaire...................................	9	8	6
Hotpoint....................................	n.a.	n.a.	3
Westinghouse.............................	n.a.	n.a.	3
All other....................................	57	32	23
Total..	100%	100%	100%

Kitchen Appliances

	Ranges—gas and electric		
	1954	*1964*	*1969*
Sears...	9%	18%	17%
G.E...	7	9	11
Magic Chef.................................	5	6	13
Tappan......................................	7	6	12
Frigidaire...................................	7	9	8
Westinghouse.............................	n.a.	n.a.	3
Whirlpool...................................	n.a.	2	2
Roper..	n.a.	n.a.	2
Hotpoint....................................	5	4	4
All other....................................	60	46	25
Total..	100%	100%	100%

Exhibit 2—Continued

	Refrigerators		
	1954	*1964*	*1969*
Sears...............................	8%	18%	20%
G.E.................................	19	15	15
Frigidaire...........................	19	18	15
Hotpoint............................	7	6	6
Whirlpool...........................	n.a.	6	7
Admiral.............................	n.a.	n.a.	5
Kelvinator..........................	n.a.	n.a.	5
Westinghouse.......................	n.a.	n.a.	7
All other............................	47	37	20
Total...............................	100%	100%	100%

	Home freezers	
	1954	*1964*
Sears................................	13%	27%
G.E.................................	7	6
Frigidaire...........................	5	5
Whirlpool...........................	n.a.	4
Montgomery Ward...................	n.a.	7
All other............................	75	51
Total...............................	100%	100%

	Dishwashers		
	1954	*1964*	*1969*
Sears................................	8%	18%	21%
G.E.................................	38	30	23
Hobart..............................	11	10	20
Whirlpool...........................	n.a.	10	5
Frigidaire...........................	12	7	10
Hotpoint............................	n.a.	n.a.	6
Westinghouse.......................	n.a.	n.a.	5
All other............................	31	25	8
Total...............................	100%	100%	100%

	Room air conditioners	
	1954	*1964*
Sears................................	6%	19%
Frigidaire...........................	10	4
G.E.................................	8	12
Whirlpool...........................	4	6
Fedders.............................	4	11
All other............................	68	48
Total...............................	100%	100%

Source: Estimates by casewriter based on industry research.

Exhibit 3

NOTE ON THE MAJOR HOME APPLIANCE INDUSTRY
Summary of Exhibit 2 for the Year 1969

	Share of market (percent) in 1969							
Company	*Dish-washers*	*Dis-posals*	*Freezers*	*Room A.C.*	*Ranges*	*Refrig-erators*	*Washers*	*Dryers*
Sears............	21	↑	27	↑	17	20	34	33
G.E.............	23	1969 Data not Avail-able	6	1969 Data not Avail-able	11	15	13	11
Hotpoint.........	6		?		4	6	3	3
Frigidaire........	10		5		8	15	9	6
Whirlpool........	5		4		3	7	12	12
Tappan..........	?		?		12	?	?	?
Westinghouse.....	5		?		8	7	3	8
Maytag..........	—	↓	—	↓	—	—	10	9
Total Market in Units for 1970 (000,000).......	2.1	2.0	1.4	5.9	4.5	5.3	4.1	3.0

Source: Derived from Exhibits 1, 2, and 4.

Exhibit 4

NOTE ON THE MAJOR HOME APPLIANCE INDUSTRY
Sales, Price, and Growth Data, 1961–1970
Home Laundry

	Clothes washers					
	(1)	*(2)*	*(3)*	*(4)*	*(5)*	*(6)*
	Total washer sales units (000)	*Total washer sales dollars (000)*	*Average price (2) ÷ (1)*	*Average growth in units (%)*	*Auto-matic units as % of total units*	*Satura-tion* (%)*
1961..............	3,444	$ 881,585	$256		79%	85.4%
1962..............	3,795	887,675	234	10%	80	85.7
1963..............	4,030	936,632	233	6	88	86.2
1964..............	4,190	981,006	234	4	85	86.5
1965..............	4,430	1,013,885	229	6	85	86.9
1966..............	4,446	1,018,134	235	—	88	87.4
1967..............	4,323	1,016,860	235	(3)	90	88.2
1968..............	4,482	1,074,296	240	4	92	89.3
1969..............	4,379	1,045,823	239	(2)	93	90.8
1970..............	4,094	957,316	237	(6)	95	91.9

Average life span, 10 years
Replacement sales as percent of total, 50%–75%

* As a percentage of wired living units as of January 1 of each year.

Exhibit 4—Continued

Clothes dryers

	Total dryer sales units (000)	Total dryer sales dollars (000)	Average price gas dryer	Average price electric dryer	Gas units as % of total units	Growth in total units	Saturation (%)
1961	1,236	$245,278	$215	$189	36%		19.6%
1962	1,420	275,745	212	185	34	15%	21.1
1963	1,599	303,972	208	181	34	13	22.9
1964	1,826	319,900	185	170	35	14	23.5
1965	2,098	366,600	184	170	34	15	24.2
1966	2,360	422,440	190	174	32	12	26.4
1967	2,648	474,523	195	172	31	12	30.5
1968	2,862	520,122	197	175	31	8	34.6
1969	3,022	547,241	200	173	30	6	38.8
1970	2,981	525,089	194	169	29	(1)	40.3

Average product life, 12 years
Replacement sales as percent of total sales, 30%–44%

Kitchen Appliances

Refrigerators

	Unit sales (000)	Dollar sales (000)	Average price	Growth in units (%)	Saturation (%)
1961	3,480	$1,026,600	$295		98.2%
1962	3,775	1,083,425	283	8%	98.3
1963	4,125	1,146,750	274	9	99.0
1964	4,545	1,172,610	258	10	99.1
1965	4,430	1,281,800	260	8	99.3
1966	4,974	1,328,058	267	1	99.5
1967	4,713	1,286,649	273	(5)	99.6
1968	5,151	1,442,280	280	9	99.7
1969	5,296	1,466,992	277	3	99.8
1970	5,286	1,448,364	274	—	99.8

Average product life, 15 years
Replacement sales as percent of total, 67%–70%

Exhibit 4—Continued

Dishwashers

	Total sales units (000)	Total sales dollars (000)	Price of portable dish-washers	Price of under-counter dish-washers	Portable units as % of total units (%)	Average growth in total units (%)	Satura-tion (%)
1961...........	620	$155,000	$236	$259	39%		7.1%
1962...........	720	174,260	212	259	36	16%	7.9
1963...........	880	211,285	212	255	35	22	8.9
1964...........	1,050	231,600	180	240	32	19	9.0
1965...........	1,260	276,060	188	236	35	20	11.8
1966...........	1,528	330,048	184	234	36	21	13.5
1967...........	1,585	337,640	185	230	38	4	15.7
1968...........	1,961	432,432	195	234	35	24	18.1
1969...........	2,118	474,646	193	239	32	8	20.8
1970...........	2,116	465,904	191	234	32	—	23.7

Average product life, 10 years
Replacement sales as percent of total, 24%–29%

Ranges

	Total sales units (000)	Total sales dollars (000)	Aver-age price gas	Aver-age price electric	Gas units as % of total units (%)	Growth in units (%)	Gas satura-tion (%)	Electric satura-tion (%)
1961...........	3,360	$ 680,275	$150	$266	54%		62.5%	37.3%
1962...........	3,656	746,311	158	259	54	9%	61.3	38.5
1963...........	3,942	866,531	187	256	53	8	60.8	39.0
1964...........	4,135	831,839	186	218	52	5	59.8	40.1
1965...........	4,331	880,772	192	216	52	5	58.4	41.4
1966...........	4,192	867,820	193	222	52	(3)	57.4	42.4
1967...........	4,033	836,745	195	221	53	(4)	54.3	44.6
1968...........	4,592	1,001,863	207	230	50	14	52.8	47.0
1969...........	4,814	1,071,716	215	230	51	5	49.9	49.9
1970...........	4,519	1,005,528	216	229	48	(6)	47.2	52.7

Average product life, 16 years
Replacement sales as percent of total, 61%–70%

Exhibit 4—Continued

Disposals

	Disposal sales units (000)	Disposal sales dollars (000)	Average price	Average growth in units (%)	Satura-tion (%)
1961...............	800	$ 63,960	$80		10.5%
1962...............	890	66,750	75	11%	11.5
1963...............	1,090	79,570	73	22	12.5
1964...............	1,300	78,000	60	19	13.4
1965...............	1,360	81,600	60	5	13.5
1966...............	1,410	84,600	60	4	13.6
1967...............	1,357	81,420	60	(4)	15.9
1968...............	1,738	104,280	60	28	18.0
1969...............	1,943	126,295	65	12	20.5
1970...............	1,976	128,440	65	2	22.9

Average product life, 9 years
Replacement sales as percent of total, 24%–29%

Freezers

	Total sales units (000)	Total sales dollars (000)	Average price	Average growth in units (%)	Satura-tion (%)
1961...............	1,050	$293.205	$279		23.4%
1962...............	1,670	283,790	265	2%	24.7
1963...............	1,090	277,320	254	2	25.6
1964...............	1,110	261,525	236	2	26.4
1965...............	1,160	271,485	234	5	26.7
1966...............	1,100	255,658	232	(6)	27.2
1967...............	1,100	256,290	233	—	27.5
1968...............	1,125	262,677	234	2	27.7
1969...............	1,195	272,450	228	6	28.5
1970...............	1,359	302,173	222	14	29.6

Average product life, 18 years
Replacement sales as percent of total, 45%

Exhibit 4—Concluded

	Room air conditioners				
	Total sales units (000)	Total sales dollars (000)	Average price	Average growth in units (%)	Saturation (%)
1961.............	1,500	$ 388,500	$251		15.1%
1962.............	1,580	410,000	260	5%	17.0
1963.............	1,580	490,140	252	23	18.8
1964.............	2,755	592,325	215	42	19.4
1965.............	2,945	624,390	212	14	20.2
1966.............	3,345	699,105	209	14	24.2
1967.............	4,129	867,090	210	23	27.9
1968.............	4,026	845,460	210	(2)	30.7
1969.............	5,459	1,119,095	205	36	33.5
1970.............	5,887	1,206,835	205	8	31.7

Average product life, Not Available
Replacement sales as percent of total, Not Available

Source: *Merchandising Week*, February 22, 1971. Reproduced with permission.

Exhibit 5

NOTE ON THE MAJOR HOME APPLIANCE INDUSTRY
Summary of Exhibit 4 for 1961 and 1970

	1970		1961	
Item	Units (000)	Dollars (000)	Units (000)	Dollars (000)
Washers...................	4,049	$ 957,316	3,444	$ 881,585
Dryers....................	2,981	525,089	1,236	245,278
Refrigerators...............	5,286	1,448,364	3,480	1,026,600
Dishwashers...............	2,116	469,904	620	155,000
Ranges...................	4,519	1,005,528	3,360	680,275
Disposals..................	1,976	128,440	800	63,960
Freezers...................	1,359	302,173	1,050	293,205
Room Air Conditioners.......	5,887	1,206,835	1,500	388,500
Total....................	28,173	$6,043,649	15,490	$3,734,403

Source: Derived from Exhibit 4.

Exhibit 6

NOTE ON THE MAJOR HOME APPLIANCE INDUSTRY
Major Appliance Price Index and
Significant Cost Indices (1957–1959 = 100)

	Major appliance	Paint	Steel	Nonferrous metal	Metalwork machinery	Straight hourly wages*
1960............	94.2	100.7	102.0	103.6	105.5	107.9
1961............	93.1	103.6	101.8	100.9	107.0	110.0
1962............	89.0	103.8	101.8	97.7	110.0	114.7
1963............	87.8	105.1	103.8	101.0	110.0	116.8
1964............	82.0	104.8	103.4	113.4	114.2	116.3
1965............	82.0	105.9	103.3	117.2	118.9	118.8
1966............	83.0	108.0	104.3	121.0	126.3	120.7
1967............	83.0	112.2	107.0	123.7	125.8	129.5
1968............	84.7	115.9	109.1	123.5	130.5	135.6
1969............	83.0	120.3	116.4	150.1	138.0	145.8
1970............	82.5	123.3	123.5	141.1	142.5	—

* At a major appliance manufacturer.
Source: U.S. Department of Labor (except column 1, which was derived from Exhibit 4).

Exhibit 7

NOTE ON THE MAJOR HOME APPLIANCE INDUSTRY

Industry Mergers and Acquisitions

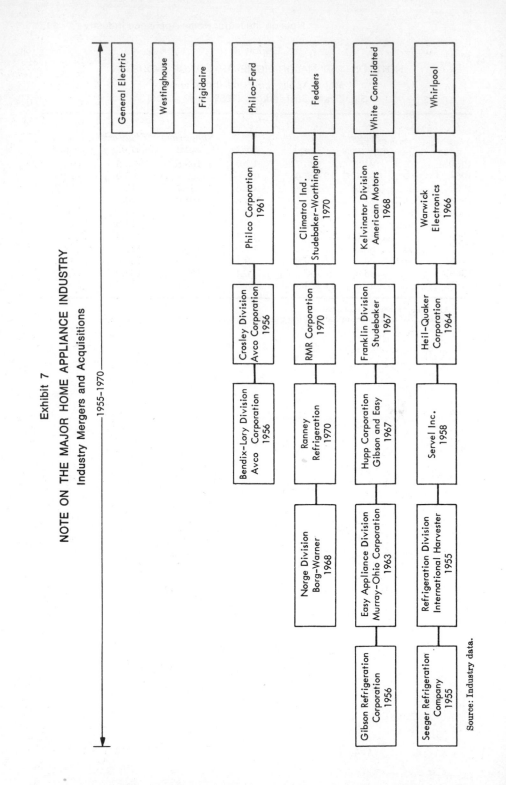

Source: Industry data.

Exhibit 8

NOTE ON THE MAJOR HOME APPLIANCE INDUSTRY
Average Variable Cost Curve for Dishwashers, Home Laundry,
Ranges, and Refrigerators

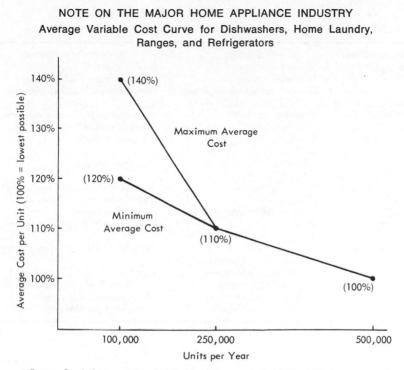

Source: One industry engineer's estimate. (Please note that this exhibit is a very rough estimate of the kind of variable cost relationship that might be expected. It is offered to illustrate the form this relationship could take and is in no way intended to represent a definite consensus of industry experience.)

Exhibit 9

NOTE ON THE MAJOR HOME APPLIANCE INDUSTRY
Selected Manufacturers and Retailers of Private Brand Appliances

Manufacturer	*Product*	*Retailer (brand name)*
Westinghouse.....	Washers, dryers	B. F. Goodrich (Goodrich)
	Washers, dryers	Allied Stores (Ambassador)
	Ranges, refrigerators, freezers	Montgomery Ward (Signature)
Kelvinator (White Cons.)...	Washers, dryers	E. J. Korvette (Leonard-Korvain)
Whirlpool........	Refrigerators, freezers	Sears (Coldspot)
	Washers, dryers	Sears (Kenmore)
G.E.............	Refrigerators, freezers, ranges, dishwashers, dryers	Penneys' (Penncrest)
Borg-Warner (Fedders-Norge).	Washers, dryers	Montgomery Ward (Signature)
Magic Chef.......	Ranges	Gamble-Skogmo (Coranado)
Roper...........	Ranges, dishwashers	Sears (Kenmore)
Tappan..........	Ranges	Montgomery Ward (Signature)
Franklin Div. (White Cons.)...	Washers	Associated Merchandising Corp.
"	Refrigerators, freezers, washers, dishwashers	Gamble-Skogmo (Coranado)
"	Refrigerators, freezers	B. F. Goodrich (Whiteking)
"	Refrigerators, freezers	W. T. Grant (Bradford)
"	Refrigerators, freezers	Western Auto (Wizard)

Source: Industry data.

Exhibit 10

NOTE ON THE MAJOR HOME APPLIANCE INDUSTRY

GM's Frigidaire Slates Layoff of 1,152 Workers In Dayton Area Friday

By a WALL STREET JOURNAL *Staff Reporter*

DAYTON, Ohio—The Frigidaire division of General Motors Corp. said it plans to lay off 1,152 employes on Friday, and Harold W. Campbell, a GM vice president and general manager of the division, said "our competitive problem is very serious, and we have been hard at work to find a solution."

Mr. Campbell issued the statement after a series of "state of the company" meetings with employes, which have been conducted for several weeks.

The division has undergone a series of layoffs in recent months. It had about 11,400 union workers prior to the most recent layoff announcement, down from around 15,000 in early 1970.

In seeking to solve the division's problems, Mr. Campbell said, "We have investigated having another manufacturer build our appliances. We have investigated the possibility of plants located in areas outside of Dayton. We have talked with one of the largest manufacturers in Japan, concerning the possibility of building our appliances. These investigations haven't been resolved at this time and no decisions have been made."

He said Frigidaire is "restructuring our organization in many areas to meet this challenge. Also, we are working to eliminate certain of our practices in the plants, and we are working to increase our productivity."

In explaining the company's situation, Mr. Campbell said "Frigidaire has been disadvantaged for some time because it's hourly-rate employes in the appliance end of the business are receiving the much higher rates paid in the automotive industry as compared to employes in the appliance business generally."

Mr. Campbell's statement said Edward Cole, GM's president, during a recent trip to Dayton, had "reflected the confidence General Motors has in the future growth of the appliances business. The appliance business, industry wide, is good. The projected growth is very good." Other competitors, Mr. Campbell said, appear to be expanding facilities and employment.

Source: *The Wall Street Journal*, June 15, 1971. Reproduced with permission.

Exhibit 11

NOTE ON THE MAJOR HOME APPLIANCE INDUSTRY
Appliances in New Housing
(1970)

	Percent of Units Containing Appliance on Occupancy			
	Single family (homes)	5-Family and over (apart- ments)	Mobile homes	Percent of product sold to new housing*
Ranges	96	99	100	38
Refrigerators	15	96	100	21
Dishwashers	60	58	6	42
Disposals	65	65	1	53
Clothes washers	3	3	20	3
Clothes dryers	3	3	15	3
Commercial washers (coin-operated)	—	10	—	n.a.
Commercial dryers (coin-operated)	—	5	—	n.a.

* Includes homes and apartments but not mobile homes. Mobile homes have thus far represented a negligible percentage of the appliance market.
Source: *The Major Appliance Industry*, Oppenheimer & Co., 1971, N.Y.

Exhibit 12

NOTE ON THE MAJOR HOME APPLIANCE INDUSTRY
Survey of Appliance Owners' Brand Loyalty
Question: If you were going to get a new appliance, do you think it would be the same brand or a different brand, or don't you know?

Appliance	Would buy same brand again	Would not	Don't know
Electric refrigerator	67.4%	14.8%	17.8%
Electric range	63.1	17.9	19.0
Gas range	51.3	23.7	25.0
Dishwasher	81.3	5.1	13.6
Clothes washer	74.3	12.3	13.4
Electric clothes dryer	75.4	12.1	12.5
Gas clothes dryer	81.1	9.0	9.9
Room air conditioner	70.6	8.7	20.7
Disposal	67.1	19.2	13.7
Average for all appliances	70.1	13.6	16.3

Source: *Look, National Appliance Survey, 1963.*

Exhibit 13

NOTE ON THE MAJOR HOME APPLIANCE INDUSTRY
Channels of Distribution
Retail Outlets

	1967			1963		
	Number of outlets	*Sales (millions)*	*Market share*	*Number of outlets*	*Sales (millions)*	*Market share*
Total..................	22,872	$3,529.4	100.0%	19,522	$2,300.8	100.0%
Appliance dealers..........	15,044	1,747.5	49.5	13,663	1,245.3	54.1
Department stores, chain stores, and discount stores..................	3,877	1,496.4	42.4	2,444	935.3	40.7
Radio and TV stores........	3,951	285.5	8.1	3,415	120.2	5.2

Appliance Dealers

	1967		1963	
Number of stores	*% of stores*	*% of sales*	*% of stores*	*% of sales*
Single stores..............	73.0	63.9	75.7	67.1
Chains				
2–5 stores..............	5.8	12.3	7.5	12.2
6–25 stores.............	4.1	8.6	4.3	8.9
25+ stores.............	17.1	15.2	14.7	11.8

Source: *Home Furnishing Daily.*

Exhibit 14

NOTE ON THE MAJOR HOME APPLIANCE INDUSTRY

Index of Trends in Service Requirements of
Home Laundry Equipment
(based on number of valid warranty service calls per year)

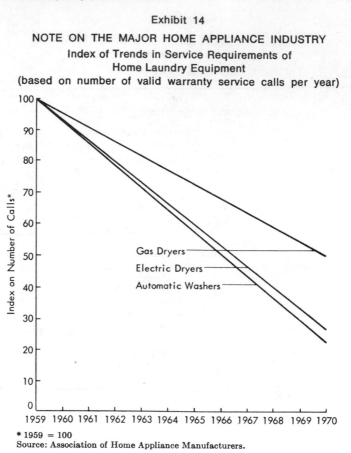

* 1959 = 100
Source: Association of Home Appliance Manufacturers.

Exhibit 15

NOTE ON THE MAJOR HOME APPLIANCE INDUSTRY
Appliance Industry Innovations
(1960–1970)

1. WASHERS:
   Mini-basket—washer within a washer—G.E.
   Large capacity—increased from 8–10 lbs. to 18–20 lbs.
   Solid state controls—Hotpoint
   Mini-washer and mini-dryer—Maytag
   Over/under "skinny mini" washer and dryer—Frigidaire

2. RANGES:
   Self-cleaning pyrolytic oven—G.E.
   Double oven over/under configuration—G.E. Americana
   Electronic oven—Tappan
   Countertop electronic oven—Amana "Radarange"
   Self-cleaning combinal electronic/conventional oven—G.E.
   Catalytic oven cleaning—Norge
   Glass-top surface unit—Corning

3. DISHWASHERS:
   Convertible dishwasher (free standing or built in)

4. DISPOSERS:
   Stainless steel disposer with lifetime warranty on water bearing parts—G.E.

5. REFRIGERATORS:
   36″ SXS refrigerator—Admiral
   Foamed-in-place insulation—G.E.
   Custom ice and water dispenser—G.E.
   Compact refrigerators and freezers (Ignis/Delmonico—Italy)

6. ROOM AIR CONDITIONERS:
   "Portable" air conditioner—Westinghouse
   Zoneline—40″ air conditioner—G.E.
   Non-rusting lexan plastic case—G.E.
   Carry-Cool portable air conditioner—G.E.

7. NEW PRODUCTS:
   Waste compactor—Whirlpool

Note: Precise dates on which these innovations were introduced were not readily available in trade publications nor had they been documented by the industry.
   Source: Industry data.

Exhibit 16

NOTE ON THE MAJOR HOME APPLIANCE INDUSTRY

Refrigerator Models, 1952 and 1969

1952   1969

Comparably priced (about $299 at retail) refrigerators of 1952 (left) and 1969 (right) demonstrate product engineering concentration on consumer value. Differences include 8.2 versus 16.6 cu.ft. capacity, one door versus separate freezer and refrigerator doors, manual versus automatic defrosting, white versus improved styling in a choice of three colors or white. Newer model also provides easier access to foods including the door storage shelves and more specialized storage drawers and compartments. Individual temperature controls, versus one in the 1952 model, provide independent compartment control. The 1969 freezer compartment can maintain zero, which the 1952 compartment could not achieve. An automatic icemaker can be installed, before or after refrigerator purchase, as an option on the 1969 unit. The back of the new appliance is free of coils for cleanliness, flush-to-wall installation. Roll-out wheels provide for cleaning beneath the 1969 unit. Some added benefits: more efficient and higher-capacity compressor; acrylic finish for increased corrosion protection and longer-lasting beauty.

Source: *Appliance*, January 1970.

Exhibit 17

NOTE ON THE MAJOR HOME APPLIANCE INDUSTRY

Financial Data for Selected Corporations

	1970	1969	1968	1967	1966	1965	1964	1963	1962	1961
Whirlpool*										
Sales ($)	1,196,845,000	1,153,530,000	1,019,408,000	773,717,000	704,816,000	630,745,000	590,777,000	538,704,000	465,257,000	436,865,000
Profits (A.T.) ($)	35,619,000	45,943,000	36,223,000	33,272,000	36,219,000	35,860,000	29,327,000	24,294,000	18,643,000	13,500,000
Assets ($)	549,794,000	573,929,000	499,599,000	401,196,000	343,816,000	282,711,000	252,669,000	199,695,000	212,309,000	222,683,000
Return on assets (%)	6.5	8.0	8.0	8.3	10.5	12.7	11.6	11.4	8.8	6.1
Profits as a percentage of sales (%)	3.0	4.0	4.0	4.3	5.2	5.7	5.0	4.5	4.0	3.1
Ten-year average return on assets (%)	9.1									
Ten-year average profits/sales (%)	4.2									
Maytag										
Sales ($)	173,685,326	166,302,646	157,335,028	139,873,132	131,285,920	120,769,510	124,399,018	117,249,231	111,150,457	107,405,254
Profits (A.T.) ($)	22,713,675	21,614,231	22,600,000	17,275,000	16,044,974	15,157,350	16,185,379	14,007,100	12,731,516	12,092,821
Assets ($)	106,389,969	99,909,888	89,681,961	88,386,561	85,701,356	81,147,454	80,263,290	76,272,971	71,770,922	69,189,968
Return on assets (%)	21.4	21.6	25.2	19.5	18.7	18.7	20.2	18.4	17.7	17.5
Profits as a percentage of sales (%)	13.1	13.0	14.4	12.4	12.2	12.6	13.0	12.0	11.4	11.3
Ten-year average return on assets (%)	19.9									
Ten-year average profits/sales (%)	12.5									
Admiral†										
Sales ($)	368,532,957	354,393,567	377,013,813	380,941,526	414,644,696	306,903,967	238,014,520	216,146,661	201,505,441	193,548,438
Profits (A.T.) ($)	(16,103,313)	1,492,449	494,430	(3,770,061)	10,016,963	653,146	4,042,474	3,024,532	1,965,501	2,915,265
Assets ($)	228,879,013	200,197,798	262,883,820	214,140,762	201,613,083	144,276,516	120,251,473	115,252,878	113,819,757	110,649,688
Return on assets (%)	(7.0)	.8	2.4	(1.8)	5.0	.5	3.4	2.6	1.7	2.6
Profits as a percentage of sales (%)	(4.4)	.4	1.3	(1.0)	2.4	.2	1.7	1.4	1.0	1.5
Ten-year average return on assets (%)	1.7									
Ten-year average profits/sales (%)	.4									
Fedders										
Sales ($)	295,812,000	264,341,000	134,964,000‡	88,872,000	62,345,000	63,685,000§	56,827,000	51,165,000	60,550,526	59,316,003
Profits (A.T.) ($)	15,561,000	12,080,000	6,345,000‡	4,342,000	1,182,000	3,395,000§	3,150,000	1,689,000	2,511,344	3,508,221
Assets ($)	194,488,000	161,503,000	129,050,000‡	61,477,000	57,614,000	58,268,000§	46,367,000	49,271,000	49,528,421	38,943,867
Return on assets (%)	8.0	7.5	4.9	7.1	2.0	5.8	6.8	3.4	5.1	9.0
Profits as a percentage of sales (%)	5.3	4.6	4.7	4.9	1.9	5.3	5.5	3.3	4.2	5.9
Ten-year average return on assets (%)	6.0									
Ten-year average profits/sales (%)	4.6									
Hobart Corp.										
Sales ($)	212,022,000	201,016,000	172,305,000	156,031,000	142,101,000	123,055,000	104,208,000	92,829,000	85,050,000	77,006,000
Profits (A.T.) ($)	11,389,000	13,102,000	11,684,000	11,678,000	12,290,000	10,334,000	7,386,000	6,527,000	6,665,000	5,752,000
Assets ($)	175,224,000	162,328,000	141,110,000	121,904,000	105,463,000	83,715,000	73,478,000	68,352,000	63,238,000	58,290,000
Return on assets (%)	6.5	8.1	8.3	9.6	11.7	12.3	10.0	9.6	10.5	9.8
Profits as a percentage of sales (%)	5.4	6.5	6.8	7.5	8.6	8.4	7.1	7.0	7.8	7.5
Ten-year average return on assets (%)	9.6									
Ten-year average profits/sales (%)	7.3									
Tappan Company										
Sales ($)	313,892,000	133,878,000	124,209,000	95,746,000	97,175,000	93,755,000	85,775,000	76,975,000	72,994,000	71,465,000
Profits (A.T.) ($)	2,231,000	3,441,000	3,970,000	1,005,000	1,105,000	2,640,000	2,860,000	2,845,000	2,803,000	5,019,000
Assets ($)	80,129,000	76,833,000	60,340,000	52,376,000	50,626,000	48,047,000	41,098,000	36,090,000	33,286,000	30,456,000
Return on assets (%)	2.8	4.5	5.3	1.9	2.8	8.3	8.1	8.1	8.4	8.6
Profits as a percentage of sales (%)	1.7	2.6	2.6	1.0	1.5	3.6	3.9	3.8	3.8	3.7
Ten-year average return on assets (%)	5.9									
Ten-year average profits/sales (%)	2.8									

* Sales include nonwhite goods (estimated less than 10 percent of sales).
† Includes brown goods.
‡ Purchased Norge.
§ Diversified into other white goods besides room air conditioners.
Source: Corporate Financial Reports.

Exhibit 18. NOTE ON THE MAJOR HOME APPLIANCE INDUSTRY

Financial Data on Corporations*

(dollars in millions)

	1970	1969	1968	1967	1966	1965	1964	1963	1962	1961
Sears										
Sales ($)	9,262.0	8,863.0	8,198.0	7,330.0	6,805.0	6,390.0	5,740.0	5,116.0	4,603.0	4,268.0
Profits (A.T.) ($)	464.0	441.0	418.0	382.0	377.0	354.0	330.0	282.0	253.0	243.0
Assets (approx.) ($)	5,000.0	4,600.0	4,300.0	3,900.0	3,800.0	2,400.0	3,000.0	2,500.0	2,200.0	2,000.0
Return on assets (%)	9.3	9.6	9.7	9.8	9.9	10.4	11.0	11.3	11.5	12.1
Profits as % of sales	5.0	5.0	5.1	5.2	5.5	5.5	5.7	5.5	5.5	5.7
Ten yr. avg. ROA (%)	10.5									
Ten yr. avg. profits/sales (%)	5.4									
G.E.										
Sales ($)	8,726.7	8,448.0	8,381.6	7,741.2	7,177.3	6,213.6	5,319.2	5,177.0	4,986.1	4,666.6
Profits (A.T.) ($)	328.5	278.0	357.1	361.4	338.9	355.1	219.6	272.2	256.5	238.4
Assets (approx.) ($)	3,000.0	2,800.0	2,400.0	2,100.0	1,850.0	1,500.0	1,300.0	1,200.0	1,350.0	1,250.0
Return on assets (%)	11.0	10.0	14.8	17.2	18.3	23.6	16.8	22.6	19.0	19.0
Profits as % of sales	3.8	3.3	4.3	4.7	4.7	5.7	4.1	5.3	5.1	5.1
Ten yr. avg. ROA (%)	17.2									
Ten yr. avg. profits/sales (%)	4.6									
Penneys										
Sales ($)	4,150.9	3,828.5	3,379.2	2,927.0	2,702.8	2,407.9	2,155.1	1,834.3	1,701.3	1,553.5
Profits (A.T.) ($)	114.1	114.3	111.5	94.3	82.4	80.7	69.2	55.3	54.8	51.7
Assets (approx.) ($)	1,627.1	1,394.5	1,207.3	953.9	847.0	744.8	667.4	611.0	537.0	447.0
Return on assets (%)	7.0	8.2	9.2	9.8	9.7	10.8	10.4	9.0	10.2	10.8
Profits as % of sales	2.7	3.0	3.3	3.2	3.0	3.4	3.2	3.0	3.2	3.3
Ten yr. avg. ROA (%)	9.5									
Ten yr. avg. profits/sales (%)	3.1									
Montgomery Ward† (MARCOR Inc.)										
Sales ($)	2,227.0	2,155.0	1,986.0	1,879.0	1,894.0	1,748.0	1,697.0	1,500.0	1,425.0	1,326.0
Profits (A.T.) ($)	35.2	43.8	23.3	17.4	16.5	24.0	21.9	21.0	20.4	15.9
Assets (approx.) ($)	893.0	833.0	Not Reported	1,187.0	1,177.0	1,147.0	986.0	790.0	624.0	572.0
Return on assets (%)	3.9	5.3	"	1.4	1.4	2.1	2.2	2.7	3.3	2.8
Profits as % of sales	1.5	2.2	1.7	0.9	0.87	1.3	1.3	1.4	1.4	1.2
Ten-year ROA (%)	2.8									
Ten-average profits/sales (%)	1.4									

* These four companies include three major retailers and one diversified industrial company. The data reported is for the full product line of each company, not just their appliance sales.

† After 1967, data is just for Montgomery Ward Division of MARCOR.

Source: Corporate Financial Reports.

Sears, Roebuck and Company: Appliances*

BEGINNING after World War II, Sears, Roebuck and Company had steadily expanded its share of the White Goods market. (See Exhibits 1 and 2.) In 1970 more appliances were sold carrying the Sears brands of Kenmore and Coldspot than any other brand. Sears' 827 retail stores were well positioned to exploit the pre-1970 appliance markets. The decade of the 1970s, however, brought with it the first major threats to Sears' supremacy in the White Goods industry. A fat 72% of appliance sales in the United States were in the retail segment of the market. In contrast, the bulk of the growth in the appliance industry was expected to be in the contract segment.[1] In fact, contract sales were forecast to account for roughly 50% of the market by 1980.[2]

The growth of contract sales was one of two significant phenomena Sears would have to contend with over the decade of the 1970s. The other is the growing threat of meaningful direct competition from J. C. Penney, among others at the retail level.

Currently, Sears' share of the appliance market was due almost entirely to retail sales. And Sears' appliance strategy had thus far been directed to the retail segment. But if Sears was to maintain its appliance market share over the next decade without entering the contract market, it would have to increase its share of the retail segment by about 14 share percentage points during that time (see Exhibit 3).[3] Given grow-

---

* This case is based entirely on published information and statements about Sears made to the casewriter by individuals knowledgeable in the field. Sears in no way participated in its preparation.

[1] The term "contract segment" is shorthand for sales to construction firms for installation in dwelling units prior to occupancy.

[2] The casewriter could find no detailed information on contract sales or projections in either public or private sources. It should be noted, however, that other estimates of the share of the market in 1980 which would be accounted for by contract sales ranged as low as 42% (see *Note on Major Home Appliance Industry,* p. 357).

[3] This represents a rate of increase of 1.4 share percentage points per year, but a rate of increase over Sears' existing share of 4% per year (44% over 10 years).

ing retail competition from Penneys and others (including energetic competition for appliance sales), many industry experts believed this could be difficult even for Sears. By this line of thought, Sears would have to consider making a major effort in the contract segment to maintain or expand its share of the appliance market. Alternatively, Sears could opt to compensate for declining appliance share by putting strategic emphasis on other areas of its business which held out greater promise of growth. In any event, the changes occurring in the appliance business raise serious questions about Sears' current appliance strategy.

This case briefly examines Sears' history, including the evolution of Sears' retail strategy and organization. Next, it focuses on what appears to have been Sears' appliance strategy; it examines Sears' various functional policies and their relationship to Sears' appliance strategy. Then the case describes recent changes in the nature of Sears' competition. Finally, it explores the implications for Sears of its changing environment.

SEARS' HISTORY

Richard Warren Sears entered the mail-order business in 1886 with the founding of the Sears Watch Company. The watch industry at this time was engaged in a fierce attempt to maintain price. By buying discontinued lines (often encouraging the company to continue production of them) and by buying the stock of bankrupt companies, Sears put itself in a position to undercut prices. This advantage, enhanced by the low overhead of a mail-order business relative to the small retail jewelers, and high volume, allowed Sears to sell profitably for just slightly more than the retail jewelers' costs.

In 1895 Richard Sears, then in partnership with Alvah Roebuck, a watch repairman, was joined by Julius Rosenwald and Aaron E. Nusbaum. These two men brought with them the capital and executive ability necessary for the profitable exploitation of the rural American market. "In his semiannual catalogue, Sears offered the American farmer a wide variety of goods and, because he purchased in large quantities and often directly from the manufacturer, offered them at a lower price than did the local merchants and storekeepers."[4]

Between 1895 and 1925 the Sears company grew at a very rapid rate. A highly centralized, functional operation was developed in Chicago to handle purchasing, sales promotion, and distribution. This centralized organization allowed the company to take advantage of the economies of mass purchasing and also allowed for tighter inventory control.

"In 1925, Sears initiated a strategy that quickly put an excessive strain on Sears' top management."[5] The new component of strategy was entry into direct retail selling. General Robert E. Wood, the president of Sears and an avid reader of the *Statistical Abstract of the United States,*

---

[4] Alfred D. Chandler, *Strategy and Structure* (Cambridge, Mass.: The M.I.T. Press, 1962), p. 226.

[5] Ibid., p. 233.

had identified the trend toward urbanization in the United States. General Wood thought that the shifting market required direct retail selling if Sears was to continue to grow.

Wood approached the retail market with a three-pronged attack based (1) on store location (locating on the fringes of urban areas with populations over 100,000), (2) on the character of the stores (concentrating on hard goods like hardware, guns, tools, and consumer durables like major home appliances), and (3) on mass purchasing and limited backward integration into the production of these goods. The importance of durables in this strategy led Sears toward "basic buying." "The merchandising departments [at Sears] began to design their own products, determine the best location for production in relation to the market and supplies, and then to go to a manufacturer in a given area with these specifications and negotiate a contract."[6] To guarantee supply Sears also purchased common shares (often a controlling interest) of its suppliers of these "big ticket items."

Sears' new strategy placed increasing pressure on its centralized organization. Throughout the 1920s and 1930s a new form of organization developed (see Exhibit 4). The merchandising functions (e.g., purchasing, designing, and advertising) were controlled at the corporate level. While the retail operations were each organized into profit-center territories, each store manager had considerable autonomy as to his actions. If he wanted, he could even do his own purchasing. He had available to him, however, the merchandising support of the home office. Needless to say, almost all stores took complete advantage of these services.

The three-pronged strategy developed by General Wood and the organization that evolved to implement that strategy continued to serve Sears up to 1970. It is important to note that sales of appliances played an important role in this strategy. By 1965, $1 billion of Sears' $6 billion revenues were White and Brown Goods.[7] Two major strategic changes did occur at Sears between 1945 and 1970 that directly affected appliance sales, and these are discussed below.

Brand name

Sears had since its very beginning sold its products (including White Goods) under a variety of names. As the number of products Sears carried increased, the number of names escalated. Also, with the advent of Fair Trade Laws, Sears' ability to set its own prices appeared to be in question. In order to avoid fair trade difficulties, in 1945 Sears reduced the list of its brands to less than 50 and stressed the importance of having a unique product. Dating from this move are "Coldspot" refrigerators and freezers, and "Kenmore" washing machines and ranges. These two brands replace more than 15 names associated with various lines and models of appliances.

---

[6] Ibid., p. 236.

[7] *Mart Magazine*, July 11, 1965, p. 95.

The growth of Sears' appliance business made the two brands widely known. Still, by 1970 Sears' appliances were carrying the phrase "by Sears" in addition to the Kenmore or Coldspot label. Industry observers suggested that Sears was strongly considering dropping the Kenmore and Coldspot and selling under the single brand name of "Sears."

THE DECLINE OF VERTICAL INTEGRATION

A second major change in strategy during the postwar period was the move away from factory ownership. At the outset in 1925 the appliance industry was highly fragmented with many regional privately owned producers. To guarantee a steady source of supply, part ownership was important to Sears—especially since Sears could often increase the efficiency of the controlled operation. But with the growing concentration of the appliance industry after World War II, the increasing complexity of the product and production process, and Sears' rapidly increasing retail volume, backward integration became less attractive. The investment and management required were a distraction. Moreover, others were doing the manufacturing job well.

To understand the decreasing attractiveness of backward integration for Sears, it is important to look at Sears' relationship with its suppliers. With the scale required for economic production rising to 500,000 units for many White Goods, Sears could not purchase from small regional companies and remain cost competitive. Forced into buying from national manufacturers, Sears faced a critical problem because the large, efficient national producers viewed Sears as a competitor. Even so for any given product, Sears' volume was so large that it permitted any one of the smaller national producers to achieve the economies of scale in production.

Furthermore, it was to Sears' advantage to have its suppliers sell their own national brand because it forced the manufacturer to keep up on new product development. Though Sears could design its own products, it did not have the engineering capability necessary for continual development of new features or imitation of competitors. Since Sears needed a product with competitive features, it was essential that Sears' suppliers have strong product development capability. Finally, in this postwar environment Sears no longer had the production expertise to improve the efficiency of its large, sophisticated suppliers.

Sears' response was to develop strong ties with Whirlpool (home laundry and refrigerator/freezers), Design and Manufacture (dishwashers), and Roper (ranges) but to avoid ownership. Of these three companies, Sears had a controlling interest only in Roper and this position was reduced from 76% to 59% by the sale of 300,000 shares of Roper stock in 1965. One observer commented that "The mutual dependency between these suppliers and Sears allows Sears to buy at a low price while allowing the suppliers a fair profit, especially when the cost savings on their other sales are considered. And then," he said, "the [Sears] organization takes over."

SEARS' APPLIANCE ORGANIZATION

Two segments of the Sears' organization were of crucial importance to its appliance business—the retail merchandising office at the corporate level and the department managers' office at the store level. This section of the case examines these two activities in detail.

Merchandising office (corporate level)

In their study of Sears, Corey and Star noted that "The largest Parent Department was the Merchandising Department, which was responsible for the development, procurement, and promotion of all merchandise sold in Sears' stores or catalogs."[8] Reporting to the merchandising vice president were 51 national merchandising managers, each with responsibility for a given group of products. In appliances, four national merchandisers were responsible for, respectively, home laundry; freezers, air conditioners, and dehumidifiers; refrigerators; and kitchens (including ranges, disposers, and dishwashers).

"Reporting to each National Merchandiser Manager was a Retail Sales Manager, a Catalog Sales Manager, a Merchandise Controller and from six to 25 buyers."[9] Since catalog sales were not significant for major appliances, the two key positions were the buyer and retail sales manager. The buyer was responsible for everything having to do with his product. He determined the source of the product, the purchase price, product design, product research and development, retail pricing, service and, most important of all, sales and profit. The retail merchandising office was responsible for advertising, promotion, placement within the store, and so on.

The merchandising manager and his staff, however, had no power to compel the retail stores to make use of any of their services or, for that matter, even their products. In fact, the stores typically followed the policies set by the buyers. In these circumstances one of the prime functions of the retail merchandising office was to keep in close touch with the stores to make sure that friction did not develop between store operations and the buyer.

Sears was organized so that each buyer was a profit center, with responsibility for the sales and profits of his products in all of the retail stores and the catalog. He took this responsibility very seriously and was encouraged to do so by an aggressive reward system. One industry observer in close contact with Sears described the buyer compensation scheme as follows:

> Each buyer receives a bonus that can work out to be greater than his salary. It is based entirely on his annual sales and margin growth. Buyers can become very wealthy, *if* they can keep growth up along both of these dimensions. The last thing a buyer wants is to get

---

[8] E. Raymond Corey and Steven H. Star, *Organization Strategy* (Boston: Division of Research, Graduate School of Business Administration, Harvard University, 1971).

[9] Ibid., p. 301.

stuck with a lot of inventory at the end of the year since getting rid of this inventory would reduce his profit margin. That could kill his bonus and endanger his job.

Department manager's office (store level)

At the retail end of the chain, each retail store in the Sears operation was also a profit center. Reporting to the store manager were department heads responsible for various product groups within the store. These department heads, with the store manager's approval, had the power to set product policy for that store. Usually they followed the buyers' guidelines. As the buyers were evaluated on the basis of the profits these divisions earned, it was reasonable to conclude that they had strong incentives to develop a product policy that would maximize the division head's profits and bonus. Indeed, it is not surprising that there was a good deal of cooperation between department heads and buyers.

These evaluations were reflected in compensation. At the retail store level, from the manager down to the salesman, a bonus based on profits was a large part of total compensation. Many in the industry felt that the heavy bonuses available to Sears' salesmen were crucial to Sears' success in the appliance field.

SEARS' APPLIANCE STRATEGY

Because of the overall importance of big ticket items as traffic builders, Sears' *appliance* strategy cannot be separated from Sears' *corporate* strategy. In turn, the facts that Sears had entered the retail market early, had located its stores in what would rapidly become prime shopping areas, and not least of all, that the name "Sears" was associated with low price and high quality by many consumers, certainly affected Sears' strategy. Sears' appliance strategy was characterized as a focused approach to retailing through merchandising. In order to get the sales and profit growth expected from appliances, Sears' buyers concentrated on two things—generating traffic, that is, getting customers into their stores, and selling the middle and top of their line. Sears got traffic by heavily advertising their low-priced/low-featured appliances, by maintaining consistent quality and providing good service, and by taking advantage of the natural traffic a Sears store generates. However, once the customer was in the store, every effort was made to sell him up the line. Salesmen were trained and heavily rewarded for doing this, and individual product lines were designed and priced to make it easier.

The Sears strategy was based on volume. The higher the volume, the lower the price Sears could get from its suppliers and the lower Sears' distribution costs. The latter cost reduction was based on the savings achieved from shipping full carloads both to regional warehouses and to the larger Sears stores. This saving could be as much as 8% to 10% of the freight cost. In fact, volume was important to Sears' entire appliance strategy. Volume determined *cost* and margins. The higher Sears' volume, the stronger the competitive position Sears achieved vis-à-vis its competitors—particularly "the National-Full-Line-Manufacturers."

To achieve such volume, Sears placed emphasis on product development, pricing, advertising, sales training, and service. These policies will be described in detail below.

Product development

A Sears National Merchandising Manager for home laundry described product development as follows:[10]

> In structuring our product line we pay close attention to the selling strategy used in the stores. We begin with the top-of-the-line, the very best product we can make with all the most advanced features. We then build a low-priced machine, of the same quality as the top-of-the-line but with fewer features.

One industry expert with considerable knowledge as to Sears' operations elaborated on this statement:

> To understand Sears' product development policy you have to understand the dilemma facing the buyer. To stay competitive Sears needs to have the really hot new features. But every time the buyer changes the line he increases the production costs. Production costs fall the longer a given model is produced—partly because efficiency increases and partly because fixed costs associated with the line can be written off against a larger volume.
>
> The buyer could keep adding models to the top-of-the-line, but this hurts him in two ways. The more the volume is spread across a larger number of models, the higher the cost for each model. Second, the larger the number of models, the higher the inventory costs.
>
> Given this environment, you can bet that buyers want to make as few changes as possible. By and large Sears doesn't introduce any major new features—the risk is too great. They copy the really hot new features (i.e., those that sold well) of their competitors and that is about all they do.

The above observation that Sears' top-of-the-line products had fewer features than some national manufacturers' brands seemed to be true in 1972. For example, the GE Americana series range had features such as burners with thermostatic controls and ovens thermostatically controlled by a meat thermometer. These features were not available on the Sears' top-of-the-line. Sears had, however, followed GE by introducing a self-cleaning oven, Tappan by introducing an "over-under" range, and Admiral by introducing an automatic ice maker. These features were viewed by the industry as crucial selling points on ranges and refrigerators.

Sears' pricing policy

In describing Sears' pricing policy, the National Merchandising Manager for Home Laundry stated:[11]

---

[10] Ibid., p. 302.

[11] Ibid.

After we have established the top-of-the-line and the bottom-of-the-line (our opening price point) we ask, "How many models do we need to fill the gap?" On the one hand, each price point must give the consumer real benefits as compared to the price point below it. On the other hand, the jump between price points must not be so great that the consumer will not be willing to move up. And we do not want to have too many price points, since every increase in stock-keeping units increases inventories. On automatic washing machines we have six basic retail price points: $119, $149, $169, $189, $219, and $239. Approximately 60% of our sales are between $189 and $219.

There were two key aspects to the pricing policy described above. First, the "bottom-of-the-line" price was set to be as low or lower than any of Sears' competitors. This was important for attracting the customer into the store. The second crucial aspect was the use of a limited number of carefully spaced "pricing points"—each point associated with a separate feature. This was necessary to facilitate the trade-up.

In talking about Sears' pricing policy, one expert on Sears stated, "The beauty of the pricing policy is that it makes selling up a cinch. Given that margins on Sears' appliances rise faster than price, selling up is crucial to Sears' financial success."

Sears' advertising policy

"Our advertising covers various models but usually emphasizes the lower price machines," stated the National Merchandising Manager for Home Laundry.[12] Besides heavily advertising the bottom-of-the-line, Sears frequently ran heavily advertised sales. A study done by an appliance dealer in Chattanooga, Tennessee, showed that in one year Sears ran 18 sales on their low-priced freezer, 10 sales on their low-priced electric range, 7 sales on their low-priced washer and 6 sales on their low-priced refrigerator.[13] The vast majority of Sears' regular and sale advertisements for appliances were full-page ads in local newspapers. Sears ran at least one full-page ad a week in each area and often one a day during sales.[14]

Given that the bulk of Sears' sales were not in these low-priced range appliances (e.g., as stated before 60% of washer sales were in the $189–$219 range), there could be little doubt that the rationale for Sears' advertising was to get customers into the stores so that they could be traded up to more expensive models by the salesman.

Sales training

The appliance strategy and each of the functional policies described above were predicated on the Sears' salesman's ability to sell the customer up. Because the "sell-up" was crucial to Sears' success, Sears made a strong effort to train its salesmen in "the art of selling up."

The cornerstone of this training was the Sears' salesman's handbook. This document explained why selling up was important and how the

---

[12] Ibid.

[13] *Mart Magazine,* July 11, 1965, p. 59.

[14] *The Story of Sears* (Fairchild Publications, Inc., N.Y., 1961), p. 61.

salesman should go about doing it. (See Exhibit 5 for examples of training material.) Each Sears' salesman was required to read this book and pass an examination on its contents. One of the key jobs of a department supervisor was to work continually with his salesmen to develop this skill.

Beyond education, Sears structured its commissions and other incentive programs to reward salesmen for selling up. Finally, since department supervisors were rewarded heavily on the basis of department profits, they had strong incentives to work with the salesmen to develop this selling-up skill.

Sears' service policy

Prior to the late 1960s, service represented Sears' clearest competitive advantage—only Sears offered a service contract backed up by its own servicemen. While other manufacturers were forced to rely on franchised service operations, Sears could undertake its own service because of its high volume, especially in home laundry (the highest service call product). Just as important, the ability to locate service facilities in or near its stores allowed Sears' store managers to supervise the service operation. Finally, Sears had always serviced its own products, and this extensive experience permitted Sears to develop a superior service capability early in the development of the appliance industry.

Sears' suppliers, however, were responsible for breakdowns during the warranty period. This motivated Sears' suppliers to design as reliable a product as possible as well as one that was easily serviceable. This policy also led Sears' suppliers to train Sears' servicemen so as to minimize the cost of service during the warranty period.

The competitive advantage Sears derived from providing its own service was beginning to erode by 1970. GE was developing factory service outlets in most metropolitan areas with a population over 100,000. Even a part-line producer like Tappan was beginning to supply its own service in major metropolitan areas. Still, only a high-volume, full-line manufacturer like GE had sufficient service volume to compete effectively with Sears.

COMPETITION

While in the past Montgomery Ward had been thought of as Sears' closest retail competition, a new and much more energetic competitor began to emerge in the 1960s. That competitor was J. C. Penney, which by 1970 had become the second largest retailer in the United States.

Exhibit 6 shows that Penneys has been growing more rapidly than Sears in both sales and profits over the past 10 years.

Exhibit 7, which compares retail store construction for Sears and Penneys, gives part of the reason why. Since 1963 Penneys has been committed to a "full-line department store"[15] strategy. All of its new stores since then have been full line. And Penneys has been growing, store for

---

[15] Full-line stores carry hard goods like appliances while the older soft-line stores did not.

store, with Sears during that time. Indeed, in the last two years reported, Penneys had actually been adding substantially more stores than Sears.

Thus, since 1963 Pennys has apparently been implementing a new strategy of head-on retail competition with Sears. Exhibit 6 shows that this new strategy has been very effective for Penneys. It is clear that Sears must worry not only about Penneys in the future, but also about other large retailers (e.g., Montgomery Ward), who may well be tempted by Penneys' success to take on the giant themselves.

And if this were not enough, Penneys is tied in with GE, Sears' largest competitor in the appliance market. GE has contracted to sell appliances to Penneys for resale under the Penneys name. This alliance between the largest national full-line appliance manufacturer and the second largest retailer could be a source of trouble for Sears' appliance business in the future. At the least, such an arrangement will help both GE and Penneys make inroads on Sears' current volume advantage.

THE FUTURE

As the 1970s unfolded two clear threats to Sears' appliance strategy began to emerge from the changing environment of the appliance industry.

First, since Sears' strategy now emphasized retail sales, the growing importance of builder (i.e., nonretail) sales meant that Sears could lose market share to its competitors who were better positioned to exploit the contract segment. A loss of market share to major competitors could erode Sears' relative cost advantage—which was volume sensitive.

This threat was especially great if Sears' suppliers were unable to attack the builder market successfully—because then suppliers' volume would drop and with the decline would come loss of scale economies. On the other hand, if Sears' suppliers did penetrate this market segment, Sears' business would not be as important to them. Hence, Sears would lose some of its buying power.

The second threat took the form of strong and growing competition to Sears at the retail merchandising level. Strong competition from retailers like J. C. Penney meant it was unlikely that Sears could count on dramatic increases in retail market share to make up for the declining magnitude of this segment in the total appliance market. Indeed, the competition might even make headway into Sears' current share of the retail segment. In either event, Sears would have to plan to move into the contract business to hedge the growing threats to its retail share.

Loss of market share would not only put pressure on Sears' cost advantage, it might also result in the loss of Sears' service advantage. GE was already establishing factory service outlets in major metropolitan areas. If other competitors grew to GE's size (in appliance sales share), they could also start their own service operations.

Despite these changes in the environment, Sears' management did not appear to be directing a large part of its attention to the appliance business. Indications were that the primary changes in Sears' strategy went in the opposite direction—placing heavier relative emphasis on soft goods. Indeed, a *Business Week* article[16] tended to confirm this conclusion. It indicated Sears had a new strategy to maintain growth despite bigness. The strategy called for broadening Sears' entire market and diversifying its growth. To accomplish this as the company approaches saturation of its traditional middle-class market, Sears planned to aim for the low- and high-income segments of the market which it previously eschewed. Soft goods, especially clothing, were expected to lead the way.

There were signs, however, that Sears had also begun to consider the contract appliance market. In fact, the 1972 Sears catalog featured several pages on the home center concept. This concept could attract business from the rehabilitation market but without further elaboration was unlikely to attract the business of builders of new dwelling units who, for example, expected volume discounts.

In this environment, Sears faced the future. The final strategy its management adopted vis-à-vis the contract market would clearly have far-reaching effects for Sears as well as for the industry.

---

[16] "How Giant Sears Grows and Grows," *Business Week*, December 16, 1972.

Exhibit 1
SEARS, ROEBUCK AND COMPANY: APPLIANCES
Results for the Year (all products)

	1961	1962	1963	1964	1965	1966	1967	1968	1969	1970
Net sales (millions)	$4,268	$4,603	$5,116	$5,740	$6,390	$6,805	$7,330	$8,198	$8,863	$9,262
Net income (millions)	243	253	282	330	354	377	382	418	441	464
Long-term debt (millions)	475	475	475	451	439	427	403	483	455	630
Shareholders' equity at year end (book value) (millions)	1,860	1,994	2,152	2,339	2,531	2,732	2,939	3,173	3,440	3,708
Return on average shareholder's equity (percent)	13.6	13.1	13.6	14.7	14.5	14.3	13.5	13.7	13.3	13.1
Earnings per share (dollars)	1.61	1.67	1.86	2.17	2.32	2.47	2.50	2.73	2.87	3.01
Retail stores (excluding foreign stores):										
Number of	747	748	761	777	786	801	809	818	826	827
Store space (gross sq. ft. in millions)	52	53	56	61	65	71	76	80	83	86
Catalog, retail and telephone sales offices and independent catalog merchants	994	1,009	1,112	1,216	1,449	1,653	1,731	1,934	2,131	2,310

Source: 1971 *Corporate Annual Report.*

Exhibit 2

SEARS, ROEBUCK AND COMPANY: APPLIANCES

(unit sales in thousands)

	1964	*1969*
Clothes washers..............	745	1,420
Clothes dryers...............	639	997
Refrigerators................	818	1,059
Ranges.....................	744	818
Dishwashers.................	189	445
Room air conditioners........	523	1,037*
Total units..................	3,658	5,776
Sears growth 60%		
Industry growth 35%		

* Assuming same market share in 1969 as 1964.
Source: Exhibits 2 and 4 in the *Note on the Major Home Appliance Industry.*

SEARS, ROEBUCK AND COMPANY: APPLIANCES
Market Segment Analysis for Sears
U.S. Appliance Sales

	Retail	Contract
1970..........	72%	28%
1980 (est.)......	50%	50%

Sears' Share of Market—1969 Data

	Dishwashers	Freezers	Ranges	Refrigerators	Washers	Dryers	Air conditioners
Percentage of units..........	21	27*	17	20	34	33	19*
No. of units (000)........	445	322	818	1,059	1,420	997	1,037
Average dollar value per unit†........	220 (est.)	228	222	277	239	190 (est.)	205
Estimated dollar sales ($000)........	93,500	73,500	182,000	294,000	348,000	190,000	213,000

Calculation of Sears' 1969 Share of Total Appliance Market

	Sears	Total	Sears %
Unit sales (000).........	6,098	26,283	23.3
Dollar sales (000,000)......	1,394†	5,998	23.3†

Analysis of Sears' Appliance Market Share for 1980

Question: Assuming Sears' appliance sales in 1969 were all retail sales, and assuming the changing mix in retail and contract segments by 1980, what percentage of retail sales will Sears need in 1980 to keep its 23.3 percent share of the total market?

x = Total appliance market
y = Sears' percent of retail segment

1969

$.233\,x = y(.72)x$
$y = 32.3\%$

1980

$.233\,x = y(.5)x$
$y = 46.5\%$

Conclusions:

Sears will need to increase its share of the retail market by 44 percent (14.2 share points) over the decade to 1980 to retain the same 23.3 percent share of the total appliance market solely with retail sales. This represents a compounded growth rate of about 4 percent per year.

* 1964 S.O.M.
† Sears probably sold greater than the average dollar amount per unit, given its trade-up policy, so these numbers are undoubtedly low.
Source: Basic data from Exhibits 2 and 4 of the *Note on the Major Home Appliance Industry.*

Exhibit 4

SEARS, ROEBUCK AND COMPANY: APPLIANCES

Corporate Organization Chart, 1967

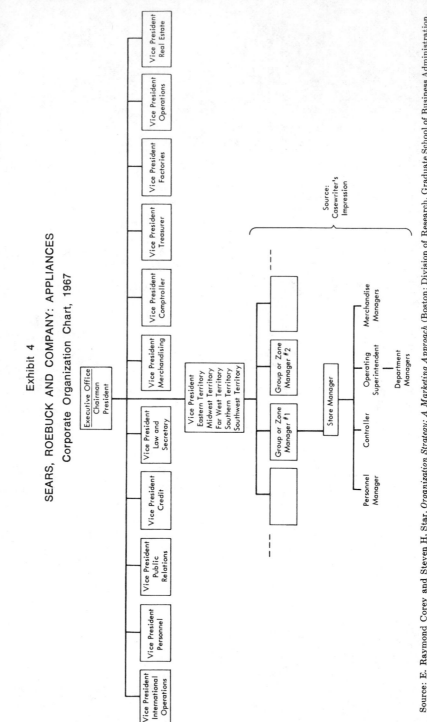

Source: E. Raymond Corey and Steven H. Star, *Organization Strategy: A Marketing Approach* (Boston: Division of Research, Graduate School of Business Administration, Harvard University, 1971), p. 319.

Exhibit 5

SEARS, ROEBUCK AND COMPANY: APPLIANCES
A Page from *Sears Sales Handbook*

Platoon System for Division 26

Division 26 has four lines of merchandise: automatic washers, automatic dryers, and the Kenmore Combination automatic washer and dryer, complete in a single unit, and wringer washers.

All the division's merchandise is divided into three "platoons," or selling groups, based on the price and quality of the items.

Although the 1st, 2nd, and 3rd platoons correspond roughly to Sears' "good-better-best" classifications, the platoon system goes further than just grouping. For example, the function of Platoon 1 is to advertise; of Platoon 2, to trade up to and through; of Platoon 3, to sell in depth. It's important to note that each platoon includes a complete assortment. Platoon 1 has a good representation of each item in the division for the customer who buys strictly on price. So Sears can state honestly in their advertising that we will not be undersold by any legitimate competition, including discount houses.

Platoon 2 merchandise satisfies the needs of the customer who is willing to pay a little more to get more features or better quality. More important, Platoon 2 is the logical place to begin trading up to Sears' top-quality lines, the third platoon.

Platoon 3 is the top of each of the division's lines. It's the group that offers the most in quality and features. And it makes the most profit for you and Sears. Merchandise in the third platoon is responsible for the tremendous success of the Kenmore home-laundry lines. Although this de luxe, top-quality line is usually sold successfully through the use of the first two platoons, many customers who are attracted by Platoon 1 prices can be traded up directly to Platoon 3. Some may be sold Platoon 3 merchandise without trading up at all.

The system should be regarded as flexible, and its most effective use is largely a matter of the skill and judgment of the salesman. In order to develop this skill and judgment, the salesman must know his merchandise.

Kenmore Automatic Washers

The automatic washer line, the largest in Division 26, accounts for about 64 percent of national sales. The line offers a dependable washer that is durable, completely automatic, and will add style and beauty to the basement, laundry, or kitchen. Twelve-pound automatic washer cabinets are available in acrylic or all-over porcelain. All models come in white although the Lady Kenmore models are also available in pink, yellow, shaded copper and aqua. The 24-inch models are available in white acrylic finish only. All Kenmore automatic washers (except 24-inch models) are available with Suds-Saver. Washers offer 2-speed washing, self-cleaning filters, water temperature selections, porcelain tops, lighted dials, plus many other work-and-time saving features.

Source: A page from the *Sears Sales Handbook* as it appeared in *Mart Magazine*, July 11, 1965, p. 48.

Exhibit 6

SEARS, ROEBUCK AND COMPANY: APPLIANCES

Comparison of Selected Retail Competitors
($000,000)

	1970	1969	1968	1967	1966	1965	1964	1963	1962	1961
Sears										
Sales............................	9,262	8,863	8,198	7,330	6,805	6,390	5,740	5,116	4,603	4,268
Profits (A.T.)...................	464	441	418	382	377	354	330	282	253	243
Assets (approx.)................	5,000	4,600	4,300	3,900	3,800	3,400	3,000	2,500	2,200	2,000
Return on assets (%)............	9.3	9.6	9.7	9.8	9.9	10.4	11.0	11.3	11.5	12.1
Profits as % of sales...........	5.0	5.0	5.1	5.2	5.5	5.5	5.7	5.5	5.5	5.7
Ten-year ROA (%)................	10.5									
Ten-year average profits/sales (%)	5.4									
Penneys										
Sales............................	4,150.9	3,828.5	3,379.2	2,927.0	2,702.8	2,407.9	2,155.1	1,834.3	1,701.3	1,553.5
Profits (A.T.)...................	114.1	114.3	111.5	94.3	82.4	80.7	69.2	55.3	54.8	51.7
Assets (as reported)............	1,627.1	1,394.5	1,207.3	953.9	847.0	744.8	667.4	61.1	53.7	47.7
Return on assets (%)............	7.0	8.2	9.2	9.8	9.7	10.8	10.4	9.0	10.2	10.8
Profit as % of sales...........	2.7	3.0	3.3	3.2	3.0	3.4	3.2	3.0	3.2	3.3
Ten-year ROA (%)................	9.5									
Ten-year average profits/sales (%)	3.1									
Montgomery Ward* (MARCOR Inc.)										
Sales............................	2,227.0	2,155.0	1,986.0	1,879.0	1,894.0	1,748.0	1,697.0	1,500.0	1,425.0	1,326.0
Profits (A.T.)...................	35.2	43.8	34.3	17.4	16.5	24.0	21.9	21.0	20.4	15.9
Assets (approx.)................	893.0	833.0	†	1,187.0	1,177.0	1,147.0	986.0	790.0	624.0	572.0
Return on assets (%)............	3.9	5.3	†	1.4	1.4	2.1	2.2	2.7	3.3	2.8
Profit as % of sales...........	1.5	2.2	1.7	0.9	0.87	1.3	1.3	1.4	1.4	1.2
Ten-year ROA (%)................	2.8									
Ten-year average profits/sales (%)	1.4									

* After 1967, data are for Montgomery Ward Division of MARCOR.
† Not reported.
Source: Annual Reports for each company.

Exhibit 7

SEARS, ROEBUCK AND COMPANY: APPLIANCES

Competitive Analysis: Sears and J. C. Penney

A. Store Data

	Total stores		Millions of sq. ft. (gross)		Total stores carrying appliances*		New stores carrying appliances†		Old stores dropped	
	Sears	Penneys	Sears	Penneys	Sears	Penneys	Sears	Penneys	Sears‡	Penneys§
1970	827	1,647	86	70.0	827	240	24	32	6	31
1969	826	1,646	83	64.9	826	208	27	32	5	36
1968	818	1,652	80	60.8	818	176	32	32	8	41
1967	809	1,658	76	55.5	809	141	32	34	11	31
1966	801	1,656	71	50.3	801	108	46	24	11	34
1965	786	1,664	65	46.5	786	82	38	32	9	37
1964	777	1,671	61	43.4	777	52	41	16	7	23
1963	761	1,678	56	41.4	761	36	25	8	1	—

B. Investment in New and Improved Facilities‖ (millions)

	Sears	Penneys
1970	$292	$267
1969	235	214
1968	169	214
1967	186	173
1966	224	122

* Generally these are full-line or hard-line stores.
† Includes new markets as well as relocations of old stores (new additions for both Sears and Penneys are full-line stores).
‡ Smaller hard line.
§ Soft line.
‖ Includes amounts invested by landlords in improvements.
Source: Annual reports for each company.

Design and Manufacturing Corporation

"My biggest problem is to develop the management capability of Design and Manufacturing Corporation (D&M) so that we can continue to fashion a better product at a lower cost," stated Mr. Samuel Regenstrief, president of D&M. "Our success over the last twelve years has been based on accomplishing these two tasks and I see no reason for any change in the future."

This case will examine the history of D&M and its present strategy. It will then describe D&M's organization and functional policies. Finally, it will explore the threats and opportunities D&M's management see in the future.

HISTORY OF THE DESIGN AND MANUFACTURING CORPORATION

In the late 1950s Mr. Samuel Regenstrief undertook a study of the dishwasher market. The study concluded:

1. The dishwasher market had high growth potential.
2. The industry was dominated by GE, which sold a very high-priced dishwasher.
3. No manufacturer existed with the capacity to supply the national retail brand companies (like Sears) and manufacturers of other appliances with dishwashers to be sold under their brands.

Mr. Regenstrief was committed to the report. In commenting on it he stated:

> It was clear to me that the dishwasher market was going to take off. The dishwasher accomplished a chore most families disliked and gave the housewife more free time. It also was beneficial from a health standpoint since very hot water could be used.
>
> I also felt that the national retailers offered a very attractive market. Originally manufacturers were creating the need for a specific brand of appliance. The "Frigidaire refrigeration" and "G.E. range"

were examples of this. But as consumers came into closer contact with a wider range of appliances and appliances became more uniform in quality, the need that was being created was the need for the appliance. Value became key. National retailers gave the most value per dollar. In my opinion their success will continue because they are catering to the needs of today's consumers—the need for value.

There was another more philosophical reason for my interest in dishwashers. Home appliances like dishwashers improve the quality of life. I feel that the social problems that face this country arise from the great divergence in the quality of life. In the late 1950s dishwashers were too expensive to be purchased by any but the rich. This in my opinion contributed to the divergence in the quality of life.

Yet the only measure of performance available to a businessman is profits. The dishwasher business offered a unique opportunity. By going into it with the intention of mass producing appliances and selling to national retailers and other manufacturers, I would make a profit only by continually lowering my production costs. Dishwasher prices would fall and dishwashers would quickly become available to any consumer that wanted one. Hence, by concentrating on profits I could make a positive contribution to society.

In 1959 Mr. Regenstrief left an executive position at Philco and purchased the Appliance Division of Avco located in Connersville, Indiana. A former Avco executive described this Avco Division and its problems as follows:

> The Appliance Division of Avco in 1959 was producing dishwashers, other major appliances, sinks, and cabinets. After World War II, like most major manufacturers of appliances, it had broadened its line. However, the division was having trouble getting retail distribution because of the extreme competition within the industry. It was furthermore in direct competition with other divisions of Avco also manufacturing and selling their own brands of appliances.
>
> With regard to dishwashers the Avco Division had a quality product. In the middle 1940s we began work on the dishwasher. By 1959 we had a competitive product and the capacity to be a major competitor in the market. "All" we lacked was sales!
>
> By 1958 the Appliance Division was incurring substantial and consistent losses. We had considerable excess capacity. For example we made only 50,000 dishwashers and we could have made several times that with the existing plant and equipment. Given the drain other Avco divisions were placing on Avco's resources and management, Avco decided to sell the division.

A D&M executive described the purchase of the Avco Division as follows:

> The Avco Division had a good production facility and a good dishwasher. What it lacked was a viable approach to the market. In simple terms, it lacked management.
>
> The Avco Division was precisely what Sam was looking for. Its book value was low because the plant was almost fully written off. It was also incurring heavy losses. Hence, Sam could afford to buy it and Avco could afford to sell it. Sam had the management capability to turn it around and turn it around he did.

In commenting on the past 12 years Mr. Regenstrief stated:

> When I acquired the Avco Division it had a core of good engineering and production talent as well as the physical plant. With this as a base, we got rid of everything but the dishwasher, sink, and cabinet business. The latter two we kept until the mid-sixties before dropping them because of their contribution to overhead. This contribution helped in the early days.
>
> Starting with less than 100 employees and sales of 60,000 units we have grown to a position of being the largest producer of dishwashers in the world with over 25% of the U.S. market. Our sales go to a leading national retailer and to 12 manufacturers. We now have in excess of 1,600 employees.
>
> Prices have fallen over the last 12 years. We have, however, at the same time reduced costs considerably, but our margin has also decreased. [See Exhibit 1 for financial data.] Total profits have definitely increased.

An executive employed by a competitor, in commenting on D&M's performance, said, "D&M is privately held so I don't have any numbers, but based on what I do know I can safely state D&M's financial and growth performance is exceptional for this or any other industry."

D&M'S STRATEGY

In commenting on D&M's strategy Mr. Regenstrief stated:

> Our basic approach hasn't really changed over the last 12 years. We are in business to make as high profits as possible by fashioning and manufacturing a quality dishwasher and selling it to national retailers and other manufacturers. To succeed we have to have a product of competitive quality and a low cost position in the industry.
>
> The reason that the low cost position is crucial is that we can succeed only if we can sell a product for less than our customer can make it or buy it elsewhere. Our maximum margin is determined entirely by our production efficiency relative to our customers, our present competitors and our future competitors.
>
> Given the importance of cost to this approach, I have been concerned with getting volume up and costs down since day one. We needed volume to have the operating efficiencies necessary for low cost. But we also need the most efficient product facility possible. As a result, we often scrap a piece of machinery a year or two after we buy it, if we can replace it with a better machine.
>
> The whole reason for starting D&M was that I felt that we could get the volume to make the strategy work. G.E. was skimming the cream off the market and no one was around to do what I wanted to do. The market had obvious growth potential. By getting it first and getting the volume, we could have a natural advantage.
>
> Things have changed in the last 12 years. G.E., for example, is now willing to slug it out on a cost basis where volume is involved. But we have the volume and the efficiency now to play this game profitably. No one can match our production costs today.

In summarizing D&M's strategy, one executive said: "Sam knew precisely what segment of the market he was going after; he hit it at exactly the right time; and he has set up a tightly run organization to take full advantage of these opportunities."

D&M'S ORGANIZATION

In describing the organization he had developed at D&M, Mr. Regenstrief stated:

> I could draw you an organization chart with vice presidents in charge of production, engineering, new product development, etc., on it, but it would be meaningless. We have a very informal operation here. Each of my executives has a general area of responsibility but there are no empires here. If I see that production costs are out of line for a given day, I don't call up Bud Kaufman, my production vice president. I call the foreman responsible and find out why. If his explanation doesn't suit me or it happens again, then I talk to Bud.
>
> When I or any of my executives see a problem, they deal with it. We can't afford the time or the money to go through formal channels. Everyone knows that's the way things work around here and accepts it.
>
> My general approach is to keep the corporate overhead as low as possible. I want the best possible managers, but as few as possible. The same is true with our data collection. I want to know exactly what is going on in as few numbers as possible.
>
> Red tape would kill this organization. It would raise our costs and slow us down. We have to be ready to turn on a dime and this takes a lean, flexible organization not a fat, rigid one.

In discussing compensation, Mr. Regenstrief stated:

> Our executives are rewarded heavily on the basis of corporate performance. Bonuses in a good year may be greater than salary. We carry this philosophy down to the worker level. A worker may earn 25% of his salary in bonus during a good year. Since our basic wage is competitive with other manufacturers, this means that we are among the highest paying firms in the industry.
>
> We do this not out of a sense of altruism but rather to guarantee that we get maximum effort out of everyone.

In talking about D&M, Mr. Glenn "Bud" Kaufman, vice president in charge of production, made the following comments.

> There is no "red tape" at D&M. We each deal with the problems we see. This goes all the way down to the worker. If he is going to run out of parts it is his responsibility to get them—not just tell his foreman.
>
> I guess this is what I like about D&M. The hours are long. I get here at 6:15 A.M. and leave after 6:00 P.M. Last year there might have been three Saturdays I didn't work. But the pay is good and I can see the results of the work I do. I couldn't stand to work in a big company where everything has to get approved by five different people.

Throughout the company, the casewriter observed a strong commitment to getting cost down and volume up by whatever means were necessary. Cutting across functional lines in this endeavor appeared to be the rule rather than the exception.

FUNCTIONAL POLICIES

D&M's strategy was predicated on strengths in several key functional areas—particularly production, sales, finance, new product development, and quality control and service. This section will look at D&M's policies in each of these key areas.

Production policy

Bud Kaufman commented on D&M's production policy as follows:

> Our approach to production is based on two concepts—simplicity and standardization. We want to produce the least complicated product possible because it will be cheaper to make and more reliable. At the same time we strive to get as many standardized parts as possible for each model. Since we sell several different models to 13 different customers, it is crucial that we get as much standardization as possible in the parts. This allows us longer production runs and lower costs.
>
> We are continually installing new, more efficient equipment. The age of the equipment we replace is not important. We are continually looking for the best way to make the product. We have a subsidiary company that specializes in machinery and equipment and automation with the aim in mind of reducing material usage, improving the quality, and offering the latest in automation. I feel this is a tribute to our production leadership.
>
> Another factor that contributes to our efficiency is ingenuity. For example, what is now our main plant used to be made up of several buildings. We realized that we could speed the flow up if we had all these operations in one building. But we couldn't afford to shut down to build a new plant. Sam and an architect figured out the solution—build the new plant over the existing buildings and then tear them out. They got the plant we needed without slowing production.

Throughout the company the casewriter observed a strong concern with daily volume and cost in relation to schedule. Meeting or bettering this schedule was the prime concern of almost everyone at D&M.

Sales policy

In commenting on sales Mr. Regenstrief said:

> I handle sales. The crucial three factors in each contract are price, volume, and design specification. These are obviously related.
>
> In setting the price I start with a margin I am trying to achieve for our total sales. But with regard to each of 13 companies I set the price based on what they could produce it for and/or what it will take to keep them in business. Hence, I have to consider the companies' volume and their marketing and distribution costs. I want to supply as many companies as possible but only if each of them can give me the volume I need.
>
> With regard to design I give more leeway to the companies with higher volume. I occasionally will give a new company more leeway than their volume deserves to get them established in the market. But if the volume doesn't come I won't carry them. In the long run custom designing for a customer has to be justified by volume. If I didn't follow this philosophy our costs would go sky-high.

In support of this approach to sales all inventory was carried at direct cost. Mr. Regenstrief explained the reason as follows: "Given our approach to the industry what I need to know is the direct cost. The product doesn't make us any money until it is sold regardless of what we inventory it at."

Financial policy

D&M was privately held with 97% of the stock owned by members of the company. Mr. Regenstrief owned the vast majority of this stock. One D&M director described the effect of this as follows:

> Since the company is privately held, Sam doesn't have to worry about earnings per share. The result of this is that he can scrap equipment and take a capital loss without worrying about the short-term impact on profits. In my opinion this freedom has contributed strongly to D&M's present strong position.

D&M had no substantial long-term debt at the time of the case. The rapid expansion in output, and hence plant and equipment, throughout the 1960s was financed almost entirely out of current profits. As one D&M executive described it, "After the first couple of years, the capital needed for expansion didn't really make much of a dent in current profits."

New product development

"Our basic philosophy in this area is to maintain D&M's position in the industry by helping our customers maintain theirs," said Dr. Harold DeGroff, vice president of new product development and professor of business policy at Purdue University. "We basically work in three areas—new features, environmental acceptance (e.g., noise and safety), and new processes. The first area is handled by our engineering staff at Connersville while the second two areas are handled at a facility we built in Lafayette, Indiana, near Purdue University.

In commenting on the feature aspect of product development, Dr. DeGroff stated:

> To understand our approach you have to understand the needs of our customers. The large national retailer we sell to needs a product of competitive quality that he can sell at a low price. He is particularly concerned with having unique features, and he also needs to have those successful features that his competitors have.
>
> With the rest of our customers, dishwashers serve the purpose of broadening their product line. They need the dishwasher especially for the builder market, and this market is highly competitive.

In commenting on the environmental acceptance and process segments of the operation Dr. DeGroff stated:

> These two operations are located in Lafayette because they draw heavily on Purdue for part-time consultants. We work in these two areas to protect ourselves. In areas like noise and safety we are continually faced with the threat of new standards or tightening of old standards. We have to be ready to respond.

In the area of new processes, we are faced with the threat of a whole new way to clean dishes. We are periodically working on ultrasonics and other approaches to protect ourselves from being out of business should one of these new technologies come to market.

The reason for using part-time help is not because it is cheaper— I am not entirely sure that it is. Rather we can get people with highly specialized skills to deal with each problem. These people are experts in their respective area and hence minimize the chance that we will overlook something.

It was generally agreed at D&M that the chief thrust of their product development was defensive. However, having a good defense resulted in occasional innovations. Finally, D&M occasionally introduced a new feature or product (e.g., the counter top dishwasher) where they felt that there could be considerable demand and being first would be a strong advantage.

Service and quality control

Though D&M did not service the appliances they sold, they were responsible for service incurred during the warranty period. As a result of this responsibility D&M was greatly concerned with quality control.

D&M's approach to quality control was twofold. First, they were continually concerned with designing as simple a product as possible. They felt that a simple product would be less likely to break down and would be cheaper to service if it did. Second, they had a rigid inspection system throughout the production operation, and they are continually going through a "customer acceptance" check where the product is thoroughly tested to assure that the day's production meets the rigid quality necessary.

Since D&M was responsible for repairs incurred during warranty, they also engaged in training their customers' service personnel. The rationale for this was to minimize the service expense for any given breakdown by improving the efficiency of the customers' field service staff.

In commenting on the problem of quality control, Mr. Lee Burke, executive vice president, stated:

> We are becoming more and more concerned about improving the reliability of our product. The reason for this increasing concern is that repair costs are rising very rapidly. This rise in cost stems from the fact that repair work is highly labor intensive and labor costs are rising quickly. Hence, it is cheaper to handle as much as possible of the problem in the factory.

D&M'S FUTURE

In commenting on the future Mr. Regenstrief stated:

> The future looks good. Only 25% of the U.S. homes have dishwashers. This means that there is considerable growth potential for the product. If anything, the market share of national retailers will

expand because they offer the greatest value. Hence, I see no reason to expect our growth to slow.

Of course I am concerned about competition. A lot of companies would like to take our business away from us. To do that they would need our volume. The only way they could get it is if they introduced a significantly better product and could match our costs. Since we are continually improving our product I doubt if anyone could do this. But it is certainly something we are always looking at. It is one reason we stay lean and flexible. We must be able to move quickly to match any major changes in the product.

Another D&M executive described what he viewed as D&M's biggest threat as follows:

I doubt if any company could take our market away from us. What I see as the biggest problem is making sure that someone in our organization will be able to carry on as a replacement for Sam. Sam is in his early 60s. He is without a doubt the most creative, energetic, dynamic person I have ever known. He built D&M and runs it with superb skill.

It was in this environment that D&M faced the future. The plans for 1972 showed no decrease in D&M's sales or profit growth.

Exhibit 1

DESIGN AND MANUFACTURING CORPORATION
Unit Volume, Dollar Sales, and Margin Growth
(1961 = 100%)

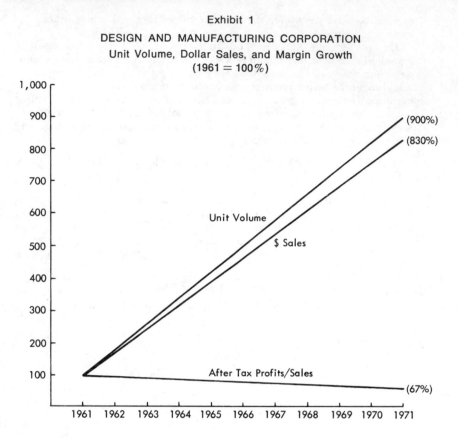

Tappan Company (A)

"My biggest problem is the competition, especially the giants like GE, Frigidaire, and Whirlpool," commented Mr. W. "Dick" Tappan, president of the Tappan Co. "The appliance industry is a numbers game and we're a pretty small number. The critical problems facing me as president are how do we survive now, and how do we get to a big number in the future. Certainly one option is to sell out, but frankly I, and most of our executives, wouldn't like the loss of freedom. Hence, we want to make it and make it as an independent."

HISTORY

The Eclipse Stove Co. was founded in 1881 as a partnership by W. J. Tappan, W. A. Gorby, and H. M. Lewis. They produced and sold cast-iron ranges both coal and wood burning. When Mr. Tappan married the "favorite" niece of Mr. Gorby who had provided the financial backing, Mr. Lewis was bought out and the name was changed in 1921 to the Tappan Stove Co. Its location was in Mansfield, Ohio, and W. J. Tappan was president. The name was changed again in 1957 to the Tappan Co. The presidency of Tappan Co. has continued to be filled by Tappans with W. R. Tappan assuming the presidency in 1962 upon the retirement of his uncle, Alan P. Tappan.

The twentieth century saw the Tappan Co. move from wood and coal burning ranges to gas-fueled ranges. Tappan built the first porcelain enamel range and the first insulated range. By 1946, out of 140 competitors Tappan was a leading producer of gas ranges with about 8% of the market.

Since 1946, the company has continued to grow. Two major sources have been increased market share in the growing range market and new products deriving primarily from acquisitions. Though the rationale for diversification was the low growth potential of the highly saturated range market and the marketing advantages arising from offering a broader range of kitchen products, development of the gas range business, and Tappan's diversification will be described separately.

RANGE BUSINESS

Between 1946 and 1950, three major decisions were made concerning the Tappan range business. First, realizing the growing importance of electric ranges (see Exhibit 1), Tappan designed and produced its first electric range. Also during this time Tappan began experimentation with microwave cooking, obtaining a license for the basic technology from Raytheon. The rationale for entry into microwave cooking was twofold. First, Tappan felt that this quick cooking method would eventually revolutionize the range industry. Second, Tappan was still thought of by consumers and more importantly by retailers as a gas range company. By having the most advanced product on the market it was hoped that Tappan's credibility as a producer of electric ranges would be improved. Tappan introduced the first electronic range in 1954. Though Tappan continued its efforts in microwave cooking, it did not become the success envisioned and efforts were slowed in 1970.

The second major decision was to build a large modern gas range plant in Murray, Kentucky. This 285,000-square-foot plant was designed to be one of the most efficient facilities in the country. It was located near the population center of the United States and in a region that appeared to have low labor costs. Labor trouble developed almost from the start, however, and the construction of a federal atomic energy plant nearby accentuated the problem. Plagued by strikes, the plant was almost closed down at one point and not until the mid-1950s did it become profitable. By 1970, however, the plant, now expanded, had capacity to produce 340,000 ranges per year and was Tappan's most efficient range plant. (See Exhibit 2.)

The third major decision was to acquire O'Keefe and Merrit, a leading West Coast manufacturer of branded gas ranges. (See Exhibit 3 for financial data.) Dick Tappan described the reasons for the move:

> The West Coast at this time [late 1940s] was a different market. Ranges sold on the West Coast had more chrome and different features, like built-in griddles, from those sold elsewhere. Also there was a substantial freight disadvantage for eastern manufacturers competing with local companies. We felt the fastest and best way to get into this market was by acquiring one of the best producers of gas ranges on the West Coast. O'Keefe and Merrit (O&M) fit this plan well.
>
> Unfortunately, 1950, the year we acquired O&M was their best year ever. Since we have maintained the O&M brand, O&M has also posed a management problem to us. They often find themselves in direct competition with the Tappan brand and since O&M is a separate profit center, friction has often developed between the Tappan and O&M divisions.

By 1970 the O&M division had the capacity to produce 200,000 ranges per year.

Though these three decisions increased the breadth of the range line and production capacity, the basic strategy for competing in the range market remained unchanged from that followed prior to 1946. One Tappan executive described this strategy as follows:

> We sold a high quality range with the newest features to retailers and contractors under the Tappan and O'Keefe and Merrit brands.

Basic changes in the appliance industry, however, led to a reexamination of this strategy by the mid-1960s.

"The growing power of large full-line manufacturers with the retailers,[1] the increasing sales of private and national retail brands, and the increasing importance of electric range sales where we were still at a disadvantage because of our late entry led us to consider new markets for ranges," stated Mr. Dick Tappan. Tappan chose to enter the private brand market by selling to Montgomery Ward on a contractual basis and selling ranges to Admiral from whom Tappan purchased refrigerators.[2] Tappan also went after the mobile home market, which was primarily gas. By 1970, these new markets (private brand and mobile home) accounted for 30% of the Tappan division sales and more than one third of Tappan's ranges went to these markets. The basic strategy for Tappan brand products in the traditional markets remained unchanged.

HISTORY OF DIVERSIFICATION

In 1956, Tappan sold only ranges. By 1970, about 35% of the Tappan corporate sales were outside the range market. The first move toward product diversification came with the introduction of the Tappan dishwasher in 1957. Tappan manufactured this dishwasher with reversing spray arms[3] at its Mansfield plant. According to Mr. Dick Tappan, "The rationale for entering the dishwasher business was simple. We were selling a lot of gas ranges to builders. Up until 1957, the range was just about all that was built in by the builder. But with the increasing popularity of the dishwasher more and more of these were being built in. Selling dishwashers strengthened our position in the builder market and was profitable in and of itself."

The next major move toward product diversification came with the acquisition of the Crystal Disposal Co. (1963) and the Whirl-a-way (Disposer Co. (1964) both producers of electric food waste disposers. (See

---

[1] Large retailers relied more heavily on the full-line manufacturers—partly because these full-line manufacturers could reduce shipping and inventory costs and partly because to get the volume necessary to run a high-volume retail outlet the retailers had to carry the major brands. Single product producers found it increasingly difficult during the 1960s to get retail floor space.

[2] In 1971, the company's largest single customer, Montgomery Ward, accounted for approximately 10% of sales. A majority of Ward's gas and electric range sales were supplied by Tappan under an agreement that extended to December 31, 1973. The company also sold trash compactors and portable electronic air cleaners to Montgomery Ward.

[3] By developing spray arms that reversed, Tappan increased the cleaning performance of their dishwashers in comparison with the existing machines on the market at that time.

Exhibit 3 for Tappan's expenditures on each of its acquisitions.) These two acquisitions were merged into the Anaheim Manufacturing Co. and a new 52,000-square-foot facility was built to house it. Anaheim produced disposers to be sold under the Tappan, O'Keefe and Merrit, Whirlaway, and private brands. Anaheim set a pattern of multiple branding that was followed in future acquisitions. The Tappan and O'Keefe and Merrit brand disposers were transferred at the market price to the respective range divisions to be distributed. The Whirlaway brand was sold by Anaheim salesmen as were the private brands.

The Anaheim division pioneered in private brand selling of disposers by designing a disposer that could be assembled on one assembly line with the individual features any private brand wanted. This flexibility in production made Anaheim the low-cost producer of disposers in the country. Anaheim had capacity to make 1,000,000 disposers a year.

The next step in the diversification program was Tappan's acquisition in 1964 of Nautilus Industries of Freeland, Pennsylvania. Nautilus was the nation's largest producer of nonduct ventilating fans and hoods for bathrooms and kitchens. As with Anaheim, Nautilus sold under the Nautilus brand and also produced Tappan brand products sold through the Tappan division. Transfer pricing was not as easy for Nautilus products as there was not a readily usable market price. The Nautilus products were transferred at standard cost plus a markup.

Tappan acquired Kemper Brothers Cabinet in 1965 and in 1969 acquired Quaker Maid, the "Cadillac" of the kitchen cabinet industry. Tappan also built a 150,000-square-foot cabinet plant in Williamsport, Pa., to make Kemper and Tappan cabinets. The rationale for going into kitchen and bathroom cabinets was stated by Mr. Dick Tappan, as follows:

> Kitchen cabinets are the single most expensive item in a kitchen. Traditionally they have been made by carpenters in small shops. The market is still highly fragmented and is wide open for economies arising from mass production. Plants, however, will have to be limited in size because the market is regional in nature due to the high cost of shipping cabinets. Shipping boxes by air a long distance is prohibitively expensive.
>
> By getting into the market early and by growing rapidly to become the industry leader, we hope to establish Tappan in this industry. We now have a full range of cabinets in terms of price levels and sell under the Kemper, Quaker Maid, and Tappan brands.

Unlike the Anaheim and Nautilus divisions, the cabinet division, though selling cabinets under the Tappan brand, sold only through their own division's salesmen. Commenting on this Mr. Dick Tappan said, "Appliance salesmen just don't know how to sell cabinets. We tried getting them to sell Tappan cabinets and it was a failure."

Tappan had made various efforts to expand internationally during the 1950s and 1960s. Two major efforts had been made by setting up a Canadian subsidiary and a joint venture with Singer in Europe. Both of these had failed. Though it still had small international investments, by 1970 Tappan relied on licensing agreements as its primary source of income from foreign markets.

ORGANIZATIONAL HISTORY

Tappan had been functionally organized up until 1950. Later each of the acquired divisions was set up as an independent operating unit with the president of Tappan Co. also president of the Tappan division. By 1965, severe problems with this form of organization were developing. Mr. Dick Tappan commented as follows:

> I was trying to run the company while I was head of the Tappan division. I just couldn't do both as we got to be larger. Inventory was getting out of hand across the whole company and profits were dismal. In 1966 we set up a small corporate staff with division presidents reporting to it.

By 1970, the formal organization was as shown in Exhibit 4. Each division was a profit center. Division presidents received a bonus based half on their division's profits and half on corporate profits. This bonus might range as high as equal to their salary.

Besides the change in formal organization, other fundamental changes in the Tappan organization were initiated during the 1960s to improve corporate performance. Two areas where these changes were most dramatic were in corporate planning and inventory control.

"In 1963 Tappan was a marketing company," commented Mr. Walter Gummere, executive vice president. "Major decisions such as product design and wholesale price were made on the basis of the sales that would be generated." The result of this approach was a proliferation of models as each regional sales manager pushed for the design and price that would fit his needs. Salesmen also tended to order large numbers of potential "hot items" in order to be able to guarantee delivery. The result was a rapid increase in inventory.

Along with the change in formal organization, Tappan implemented a formal planning system—called Blueprint Planning. Mr. Gummere described this change as follows.

> We didn't change overnight. We worked steadily to get our division executives to think in terms of profits—first in terms of total division profits and eventually down to profit for each model. The planning system allows us to communicate with the divisions. They tell us what we can expect one year out and in general for the next five years. We tell them what we need. Then we work out a detailed plan for the next year for each division.

By 1970, formal planning was in full operation at Tappan.

In the mid-1960s Tappan also hired an outside consulting firm to do a large systems analysis of the Tappan Co. with a view toward gaining a tighter control over inventory. By 1970, a new inventory control system and production scheduling system were under way. During 1971, inventory was reduced by $5 million in the face of more than a 10 percent increase in sales. Complaints as to late delivery also dropped drastically. The results of these two programs were described by Mr. Gummere as follows, "Tappan is still a marketing-oriented company, but we have moved so as to take advantage of our marketing skills rather than being led by them."

PERFORMANCE

The 1960s saw Tappan's sales almost double, rising from $71.5 million to $131.9 million. But during 1966–1970 return on assets and on equity fell considerably from the 1961–65 level. (See Exhibit 5.) Commenting on the low profits, Mr. Dick Tappan noted:

> There were several reasons for this downturn. First, the company was getting out of control. Second, about half of our sales go to builders. The last half of the 1960s was very bad for the construction industry—especially 1967. In 1967 we bought market share by cutting our prices and profits fell off. The reorganization and other steps to get the company back under control didn't take effect until 1968. They did improve overall operations, but 1970 was another bad year for housing starts.

The upturn in the economy in 1971 led to record third-quarter profits for Tappan.

Tappan was still primarily a range producer in 1970. In 1969, 67% of corporate sales were ranges, 12% were cabinets, 5% were hoods and fans, 5% were disposers, 6% were dishwashers, 3% were refrigerators, and 2% were from foreign operations and other sources. The bulk of profits, however, came from ranges and disposers. The casewriter estimated that these two products contributed 90% of total corporate profits. Cabinets (Kemper and Quaker Maid), dishwashers, and refrigerators were estimated to contribute 10%. The Williamsport cabinet facility ran at a loss, as did the Nautilus division.

Tappan had increased its market share in the range industry steadily through the decades of the 1930s, 1940s, and 1950s up to about 10% of the total market. From 1960 through 1968, Tappan's market share fluctuated but drifted downward. Then the addition of private brand business and gas ranges for mobile homes reversed the trend, as Tappan's market share rose dramatically to 13% of the total market.[4] Tappan Co. had about 17% of the gas market and 9% of the electric market in 1970 as compared with 10% and 6%, respectively in 1965.[5] The casewriter estimated that Tappan had about 15% of the disposal market and about 4% of the dishwasher market in 1970.

PRODUCT-MARKET STRATEGY—1971

The two major problems facing the Tappan Company as described earlier by Mr. Dick Tappan—short-run survival and long-run success—provide a basis for analyzing Tappan's history and its present strategy. One Tappan executive explained the reason for dual strategies as follows:

---

[4] According to industry sources, mobile home production in 1971 was 491,700 units, up from 217,300 in 1966. Tappan's share of the market increased from approximately 11% to 40% and represented 19% of total net sales of ranges.

[5] Tappan's profitable growth occurred during a period of rapid increase in concentration—especially in the gas range market. In 1946, there were 140 producers of gas ranges as compared with about a dozen in 1970.

We can't beat the GEs at their own game. If we followed the traditional approach to the industry we would either be driven out of business or become a supplier of private brand goods. We would lose our key resource—the Tappan name. Hence, the key is to come up with new products and new approaches to existing products. But this takes time and hence we have to concentrate on profitable survival in the short-run as well as long-run success.

In this section the short-run and long-run product-market strategies of Tappan will be described. The next section will look at the key functional policies of Tappan. The last section will look at the internal and external threats to the success of these strategies.

The short-run strategy

Mr. Tappan commented:

> One of the biggest problems we face is keeping our products on the retail floor. Full-line producers use the power of their line and sales incentives like "trips"[6] to push us off the floor. The loss of retail floor space means not only lost retail sales but less opportunity to build brand image. Brand image is built at the retail level, but is crucial to the builder market.
>
> A second major disadvantage when compared to the full-line producers is higher sales costs and somewhat higher production costs. A GE salesman might sell $1 million worth of appliances compared with less than half that for a Tappan salesman. On the production side the Mansfield and O'Keefe and Merrit facilities are higher cost plants than some of the newer plants in the industry.

Tappan's short-run strategy was designed to attempt to offset these weaknesses. "To get into the retail outlets we have to have a product with unique features," stated Mr. Tappan. "We have to give the retailer something no one else has—something he can sell."

Some of the recent examples of these features for Tappan were the "Pan-O-Matic" (see Exhibit 6), the smooth top range (one that did not require special utensils), and the gallery warming shelf.

On the cost reduction side Tappan made several efforts to improve its cost competitiveness. Mr. Tappan commented, "The private brand business and mobile home business are low margin business but high turnover. They not only are profitable because of the high turnover and low sales costs, but absorb a large chunk of overhead that helps reduce the cost of other Tappan ranges." Tappan had also attempted to reduce the number of models and standardize the chassis for ranges to reduce production costs. The latter effort had been highly successful.

"By selling unique highly featured products we have been able to command a retail price premium that has more than compensated for our cost disadvantage," stated Mr. Tappan. "The builder market is easier for us since the big companies like GE didn't sell gas ranges until

---

[6] Many appliance firms, especially full-line producers, gave retail salesmen bonuses like trips to Europe or Mexico in return for selling more than a certain number of various types of their appliances.

very recently. We have been able to get a lot of business because of our high brand image and selling both gas and electric ranges."

Dishwashers presented a different short-run problem. Tappan had developed a dishwasher in 1957 that was unique. It gained considerable acceptance in the builder trade and sold 60,000 units in 1970. But these were all undercounter units. To get production costs down to make dishwashers meet the corporate objectives for profitability Tappan had to increase volume drastically. Tappan couldn't source dishwashers because of their unique design.

To get the volume needed for production economies Tappan had to go after the portable dishwasher market dominated by Sears, GE, and Hobart. The problem was that the existing product even if produced in higher volume would be too expensive to sell in the portable market. A good competitively priced portable dishwasher would strengthen Tappan's position in the retail market as well as increase dollar sales per salesman. A new dishwasher design was needed and much of Tappan's short-run success in this market would be based on its design.

Another problem that faced Tappan Co. was the strong tendency of its divisions—especially the Tappan and O&M divisions—to concentrate sales efforts on the products they produced because they could make higher division profits. The divisions often gave their salesmen a higher percent commission on their own products. Added to this was the desire of the O&M division to not make Tappan ranges even though they could set longer production runs and lower costs. Here the reason was that they would have to give up to the Tappan division the production of the higher price/higher featured ranges. It was felt by many corporate executives that an integral part of the survival strategy would be a new form of organization and control system that would solve these problems.

One final short-run problem facing Tappan was improving the profitability of current nonrange operations. This was especially urgent for the Williamsport cabinet plant and the Nautilus division. It was felt that the Williamsport plant would improve as Tappan developed a more efficient marketing operation for cabinets. At the time of the case Williamsport was operating well below 50% of its capacity and hence costs were well above the break-even point. The Nautilus division, however, posed a more serious problem because its Nautilus brand image was poor. This was compounded by the fact that the Tappan division was not as interested in selling Nautilus products under the Tappan brand. The hope for Nautilus rested with the development of new products which will be discussed later and cost reduction from tighter management.

In terms of the long-run cost reduction the systems study undertaken in the late 1960s was felt to offer great promise in reducing inventory and lengthening production runs. A new plant under construction in Ontario, Ohio, near Mansfield with eventual capacity for 500,000 ranges was described by one manufacturing executive "as guaranteeing our long-term cost position." The plant was being built in stages starting with a 300,000-square-foot distribution center already completed.

Then the assembly, paint, and metal fabrication sections would be built in that order. This method would allow the subcontracting of the incompleted sections to outside firms as well as other Tappan plants. In this way the plant could upon completion operate at full capacity of 250,000 units. Then it could be expanded to 500,000 units. Another advantage of this method was that if demand for ranges fell off, the plant construction could be slowed down.

The long-run success strategy

If the short-run survival strategy was to be based on improving Tappan's operations and profitability in traditional markets, "the long-run success strategy was," as Mr. Tappan described it, "based on new approaches to the appliance industry and new products while continuing to hold Tappan's position in traditional markets." The rationale for this strategy was the limited growth potential in the traditional appliance market where GE and other large manufacturers were dominant and would remain so even if Tappan's short-run strategy was a success.

Though Tappan was interested in new products and approaches, it limited its search to the "core of the home"—the kitchen, the heating/air-conditioning system, and bathroom. Mr. Tappan explained the rationale for this as follows:

> The core of the home makes up about 35% of the construction cost of a home or apartment. We feel that concentrating on this core offers the best chance for long-run success for several reasons.
>
> First, a home that is heated and cooled by electricity is unlikely to be hooked up for gas. With the advent of electric air-conditioning peak demand for electricity moved from the winter to the summer in many areas. Given that electric utilities are highly capital intensive, they responded by lowering their rates in the winter, making electric heat more attractive than gas. The result was that an incremental number of new homes are heated by electricity and hence not hooked up for gas.
>
> This phenomenon has been partially responsible for the decline in gas cooking. If we could develop an efficient gas air-conditioner we could get gas into more homes. This development not only offers a large market for heating/air-conditioning units but it would increase the sale of gas ranges where we are still the strongest.
>
> A second reason for considering the core of the home as our market is that it presents the opportunity for new approaches to the industry. By viewing the kitchen as our product rather than individual appliances we pioneered in developing the kitchen wall [see Exhibit 7]. The kitchen wall contains all the kitchen appliances and cabinets. It can be assembled in the factory and shipped completed to the builder. This means that much relatively expensive construction labor can be eliminated.
>
> There are two major problems with the kitchen wall. First, the construction unions are opposed to it. However, the need for lower cost housing is so great that the unions in many areas are already giving in. The second disadvantage is that to get the cost down these units have to be shipped nine to the truckload. Not many builders com-

plete nine units at a time. This means that the unit must be kept in inventory. This is not only expensive, but increases the probability that they will be damaged.

But if we build a bathroom on the back of the wall and put in a heating and air-conditioning unit we can put two into a truckload rather than nine. There are a lot of builders that finish two units at a time.

A third advantage to viewing the core unit as our market stems from the remodeling business. There are 40 million dwelling units that need a new core. With the rising cost of housing many people will turn to remodeling rather than buying a new house. But the remodeling business is highly fragmented and no one does a very good job of meeting the customer needs.

We are approaching this market segment with the Tappan Home Center [see Exhibit 8]. The Home Center will have six to thirteen model kitchens and several model bathrooms in it. It will have the facilities to custom design a kitchen, install it via reliable subcontractors, and finance it through channels we have set up.

The Home Center will be set up as a franchise limiting our capital commitment to it. It will display and sell our full line of cabinets and appliances. It will pay its subcontractors a premium over the going price in return for a guarantee that they will meet all scheduled commitments. Hence, a kitchen will have to be torn up for only a couple of days rather than several weeks as often happens now.

The problem with the Home Centers to date has been finding and training people to run them. It is important that a Home Center should develop a good reputation in its area, which means that it has to be run well. We are moving slowly opening up a few a year for the time being. People trained in one then can go out and start new ones. We hope to be able to expand more rapidly in the future.

We are also moving into new products for the home. We have designed and are ready to market what we feel is the best compactor on the market. We have a new electrostatic air cleaner and are working on many other new products. [See Exhibit 9.] But again these pertain to the core of the home.

Though the above describes the basis for much of Tappan's growth in the future, it was agreed by most Tappan executives that the existing business would contribute to the success and that businesses like Montgomery Ward and mobile homes would someday provide a substantial market for these new products just as they did now for traditional appliances.

Mr. Tappan commented on research and development possibilities:

We don't have the money or the talent to undertake research and development on a lot of these sophisticated products. We really scramble a lot to get the money and the talent. For example, we made a presentation to the American Gas Association and explained why it would benefit them to fund our research on a low-cost gas air-conditioning/heating unit. We got a substantial sum from them to do this research. We often go directly to companies that are doing research that we might be able to use. We went to Thermo-Electron when we heard about their work in heating and cooling. We worked out an agreement with them so that we got the rights to the commercial applications of their research. We exchanged some of our stock for 5% of their stock which in and of itself turned out to be a pretty good deal.

Tappan was engaged in joint projects with a large number of companies and organizations like Thermo-Electron, AGA, Rheem, Owens-Illinois, Pittsburgh Plate Glass, Honeywell, Philco-Ford, and others (see Exhibit 9). One Tappan executive commenting on this stated, "Dick Tappan's greatest contribution in the long run may well be his ability to get other companies to develop new products for us often while also providing the money."

FUNCTIONAL POLICIES

The short- and long-run product strategies described in the preceding section were dependent for their success on the various functional policies—particularly finance, new product development, manufacturing, and sales and service. In this section each of these policies will be discussed and the next section will consider the potential threat from the environment.

Financial Policy

"The financial criteria for investment are that they make 5%, net of tax, on sales and 15% return on gross investment," said Mr. Lorin Ellison, vice president and controller. "These are what we view as reasonable corporate goals and not the result of an elaborate financial analysis. Acquisitions are judged on their short-term impact on earnings per share and how the product fits in."

Commenting on capital budgeting and control, Mr. Ellison stated:

> We don't go in for highly sophisticated financial analysis of investment projects. We look at whether they meet the objectives and at the pay back. Until recently we approved almost all the requests. But, the capital spending of $9 million in 1969 and 1970 created a cash drain. Hence we placed a $2.5 million year limit on capital expenditures for 1971. However, the expenditures for 1972 and beyond will be substantially greater. This may mean that we have to consider individual expenditures more closely.
>
> Big expenditures that relate to the long-run success of the company are occasionally made on the basis of "gut feel." We won't undertake them if they are considerably below our stated corporate objectives for investments or acquisitions, but they don't necessarily have to meet our short-run financial objectives.

Mr. Walter Gummere explained the reason for this "gut feel" approach:

> Often you just don't have time to do an elaborate analysis—especially in acquisitions where other firms are interested. It is also true that in some situations where the long-run success of the company is at stake short-run profitability may be outweighed by the long-term impact.

It was generally felt by Tappan executives that the flexibility allowed by this "gut feel" approach was crucial to Tappan's success.

In further commenting on the nature of capital budgeting, Mr. Ellison stated:

> We have become slightly more sophisticated over the last several years. We track investment projects via an internal audit so that we can judge whether they meet the estimates. We also have developed a more formalized planning system.
>
> The impetus for these changes has come partly from our rapid growth and diversification which requires more formal control. The impetus has also come partly from new members on the board who want this information.
>
> We will become more formal in the future as we need to be, but this change will be an evolutionary one, not a revolutionary one.

New product development policy

New product development and product innovation were of crucial importance to both Tappan's short- and long-run strategies. Mr. Chuck Lair, corporate manager of product development, described Tappan's activities as follows:

> For a long time we were a pretty small company. Most of our innovations came internally. The "Fabulous 400," the first over-under double oven range was developed internally in the late 1950s. That one innovation nearly doubled our sales in one year. It was copied by Frigidaire about a year later and we lost a legal suit protecting our design. Most innovations follow this pattern of being copied within a year or two.
>
> Most product innovations still come internally. We read all the scientific literature, our salesmen make suggestions, our design engineers make suggestions, and we get 600 to 700 calls a year from independent inventors. I circulate a letter periodically to the divisions listing potential new products and innovations. Often divisions don't have the man-hours to undertake development of these suggestions, but sometimes they do.
>
> For example, after Whirlpool introduced the compactor, I asked our divisions if any of them would be interested in developing one. Anaheim had two engineers with some free time. In six months they designed and tested a compactor that was more efficient and easier to use than Whirlpool's. We got it on the market in less than one year after we first thought about it. One of our largest competitors with a huge engineering staff wants to license it.
>
> Of course, we often don't have the man-hours to undertake major innovations. Here we go to independent design outfits to get the work done. For example, Ford has a lot of design engineers that are idle because Ford has cut back in its automobile design efforts. We approached Ford with a proposal to design a new product for us. It was in their interest to keep their men employed. We got some of their best men working on it—talent we couldn't afford to keep.
>
> Where innovations require basic research, we work almost entirely through our suppliers and outside companies. We can't afford basic research. But by not doing it ourselves we often can get a number of firms to do the development and, what's more, pick up the bill for it.

We get a lot of opinions and get to choose from a lot of different ideas. If we did it ourselves we would get locked in to one idea early in the development process. We have used this approach for projects like the smooth-top ranges and self-cleaning oven. In both cases we feel we have developed a better product than the introducer of the innovation. [Corning and GE, respectively.]

For entirely new products like the new gas heater and air-conditioner and others, we work entirely through outsiders. But here again they pick up a large chunk of the bill as do agencies like AGA.

Our total R&D budget runs between $1 million and $2 million a year. In addition we get half this much typically from outside sources —like our suppliers, AGA, and many others. You have to sell a lot of ranges to net over half a million dollars. Not only that but by using our approach we avoid a lot of overhead in high-priced talent.

Commenting on the disadvantages of using outside design and research, Mr. Lair stated:

There are some disadvantages. Occasionally you get locked into a project that limits you elsewhere. When working on the smooth-top range we guaranteed one firm that in return for their design we would introduce a gas smooth-top before an electric. It took us two years to get to the point that we could cost out their design and find that it was too expensive. That hurt us.

Suppliers occasionally make promises they can't keep because it turns out that they can't develop a product they thought they could. If we had our own talent we would be in a better position to judge their problems and evaluate their statements.

But I feel that the flexibility we get by shopping around offsets these disadvantages even ignoring the money we save.

Describing his job, Mr. Lair remarked:

I guess to be good at my job you have to be a carnival man—you have got to be able to sell dreams both outside and inside the organization. On the other hand you have to be pragmatic because you are dealing with engineers. If an engineer had been in charge of producing the first wheel he would still be trying to make it rounder and we would still be walking. You have to be able to say it's good enough, let's make it.

One football fan made the following statement that summarized Tappan's product development strategy as follows, "If you can't afford the best front line in football, it pays to have a quarterback who can scramble."

Manufacturing policy

One Tappan manufacturing manager said:

Marketing is the tail that wags the dog at Tappan. However, things have changed somewhat in the last few years. The company has limited the number of models and given us longer guaranteed orders (eight weeks instead of four). Because of this we have been able to standardize the chassis for the range and have cut production costs. Also, the longer orders allow longer production runs again reducing costs.

Commenting on the potential for future cost reduction one manufacturing executive said:

> The biggest opportunity for cost reduction will come from the new plant. It will have longer production lines which will reduce handling. It will have newer equipment in some areas. But most important it will give us the space to build a lot of components we are now sourcing. I think that we can make 20% to 30% return on investment by making some of these.

Commenting on the practice of redesigning products so as to cut cost, Mr. Lair stated:

> We don't do much of this in general—especially for ranges where we have a lot of volume. Where we do this is with something like the dishwasher. To go into the portable market we have to cut costs. We told our design engineers—design a dishwasher such that if we double our volume its costs will be let's say 75% of present cost.

Other ideas of cost cutting came from the production engineers, foremen and workers. When driving out to the Mansfield plant, the casewriter noted another car was parked in Mr. Dick Tappan's space. Mr. Tappan explained that each month one employee was given this for his cost-cutting suggestion. Other competitions of this nature netted cost reductions of about $1 million per year.

The location, size, and age of the company's principal facilities are set forth in Exhibit 2.

Sales distribution and service policy

Tappan had about 200 salesmen with about 120 of these in the Tappan division. These salesmen sold to retailers, large builders, and independent builder distributors. Until 1970, these salesmen were paid on straight commission and averaged about $14,000 per year. As was stated earlier in the case, commissions were often higher for products their divisions produced. One major change being undertaken at the time of the case was to switch salesmen to a base salary, plus commission and a bonus. The commission structure would not favor any division's products. The bonus would be based on whether the salesman sold the mix of products and models set out by the company. It was hoped that this method would get salesmen to sell products and particular models of these products that were most profitable to the company.

Tappan did no national television advertising because it was prohibitively expensive. But Tappan did provide prizes for give-away shows like "Queen for a Day." "This provides us with a lot of cheap publicity," stated Mr. Tappan. "It also gets to a large segment of our potential customers. Each show stresses the Tappan name and one feature. We get more out of this than magazine and co-op newspaper advertising where we spend a lot."

Distribution was also changing. Tappan had originally shipped to 60 private warehouses. The systems study suggested that Tappan set up its own central and regional warehouses. Tappan was in the process of implementing this suggestion, having completed construction of a central warehouse and planning of a dozen regional warehouses. "We still don't know what is in some of those old warehouses. With our new system we can get a computer printout that will tell us where everything is at any point in time," commented Mr. Tappan.

Tappan had factory service outlets in six cities. "We just don't have the volume to support factory service in any but the largest cities. We do, however, train in our factory the servicemen that we franchise. We are at a disadvantage here when compared with the giants. But we work on getting our franchised agents to do a good job."

THREATS FOR FUTURE SUCCESS

Mr. Dick Tappan commented on possible threats to success:

> Certainly one threat would be that none of our new products come to fruition, but given the number of projects and talent of people working on them as well as the need for them this is highly unlikely.
>
> The Japanese are a big threat. As appliances become more sophisticated and higher value in terms of physical volume the Japanese will be in a better position. They already have come out with a countertop microwave oven for $100 less than the American model. But the best way to prevent the Japanese from taking over the market is to develop more and better new products. If you stand still, you're dead. We have, also, sent a number of our men to Japan to look for opportunities for sourcing components and get a feel for what they are doing.

"Labor troubles could be a problem," Mr. Tappan said. "My dad was great with our employees, but I am more interested in new products. I could get us into trouble."

The casewriter noted, however, while walking through the plant at Mansfield that Mr. Tappan knew and was known by most of the employees. One worker stopped him and showed him a part that Tappan made in Mansfield and shipped to O&M where it was reworked and then shipped back to Mansfield. Later in the day, this situation was corrected. Another worker had a short discussion with him about the possibility of acquiring a favorite bird dog of Dick's. (The offer was refused.) Throughout the plant and the company first names were used and a very informal atmosphere prevailed.

Mr. Tappan summarized his problem as follows:

> The Tappan Co. is changing rapidly—it is growing and moving into new markets. These changes present managerial problems in terms of organization and other types. But to succeed we have to keep flexible and be ready to move. We can't become inflexible by over-reacting to our problems. We have to steer a delicate middle course if we are to become a big number in this numbers game.

Exhibit 1

TAPPAN COMPANY
Ratio of Gas to Electric Ranges Sales,
1934–67

Year	Ratio of gas ranges to electric ranges manufactured
1934	6.9
1935	5.1
1936	4.6
1937	3.5
1938	3.6
1939	4.5
1940	3.4
1941	3.1
1942	n.a.*
1943	n.a.*
1944	n.a.*
1945	n.a.*
1946	3.9
1947	2.0
1948	1.9
1949	1.9
1950	1.6
1951	1.6
1952	2.0
1953	1.7
1954	1.5
1955	1.4
1956	1.4
1957	1.4
1958	1.4
1959	1.2
1960	1.2
1961	1.2
1962	1.2
1963	1.1
1964	1.1
1965	1.0
1966	1.0
1967	1.1

* War year.
Source: Tappan Company records.

Exhibit 2

TAPPAN COMPANY

Property

The following table sets forth the location, size and age of the Company's principal facilities (all of which are owned by the Company), and the principal products or use of each:

Location	Approximate square feet (000) floor space	Original construction	Last major addition	Principal products or use
Mansfield, Ohio............	414	1875	1971	Gas, electric and electronic ranges, dishwashers
Ontario, Ohio..............	365	1970	1972	Warehouse for appliance products and data processing center
Elyria, Ohio..............	895	1900	1970	Air conditioning and heating products
Cleveland, Ohio............	70	1928	1954	Engineering laboratory for air conditioning division
Murray, Kentucky...........	420	1946	1970	Gas and electric ranges
Los Angeles, California.......	416	1933	1971	Gas and electric ranges, dishwashers
Richmond, Indiana..........	500	1909	1957	Kitchen cabinets and bathroom vanities
Anaheim, California..........	60	1970	1970	Food waste disposers
Leesport, Pennsylvania.......	200	1961	1968	Kitchen cabinets
Williamsport, Pennsylvania...	150	1969	1969	Kitchen cabinets

In addition, the company leases a 160,000-square-foot plant in Freeland, Pennsylvania, which presently is operated by the Nautilus Division.

Source: Prospectus, the Tappan Company, June 6, 1972.

Exhibit 3

TAPPAN COMPANY

Acquisitions

Name	Year acquired	Method of payment	Value ($)	Accounting treatment
O'Keefe & Merrit	1950	a) Cash b) 2-year notes c) Stock	a) $3,044,437 b) 200,000 c) 2,025,024* Total $5,269,461	Purchase
Tappan-Gurney†	1954–1968	Cash	1,609,000	Purchase
Crystal	1963	Stock	100,000*	Purchase
Hedland (Whirl-a-way).......	1964	Cash	2.556,000	Purchase
Nautilus............	1965	Stock	1,400,000*	Pooling
Kemper.............	1965	Stock	5,039,663*	Pooling
Quaker Maid........	1969	a) Stock b) Cash	a) $5,825,000* b) 200,000 Total $6,025,000	Pooling/ Purchase

* Estimated value of stock at time of acquisition.
† Canadian operation.

Exhibit 4

TAPPAN COMPANY

Organization Chart, March 1, 1971

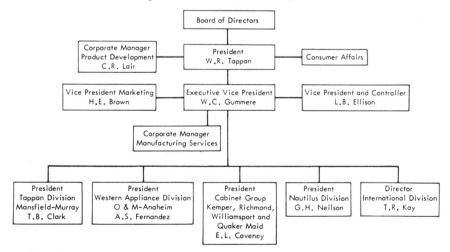

Source: Tappan Company, *Annual Report*, 1970.

Exhibit 5

TAPPAN COMPANY
Financial Data, 1961–70
(000s omitted)

	1970	1969	1968	1967	1966	1965	1964	1963	1962	1961
Financial results										
Sales............................	$131,892	$133,878	$124,209	$95,746	$97,175	$93,755	$85,775	$76,975	$72,994	$71,465
Earnings before federal income taxes.......................	4,306	7,041	7,154	1,984	2,547	6,046	6,190	5,770	5,453	5,019
Federal income taxes..............	2,075	3,600	3,970	1,005	1,105	2,640	2,860	2,845	2,650	2,405
Net earnings....................	2,231	3,441	3,184	979	1,442	3,406	3,330	2,925	2,803	2,614
Depreciation provisions...........	1,688	1,266	1,058	1,104	1,176	1,134	1,066	975	922	987
Capital expenditures, net of disposals......................	4,833	4,531	1,235	755	1,156	1,461	1,384	1,703	78	1,039
Common stock*										
Average number of shares outstanding..................	2,477,434	2,457,610	2,448,208	2,427,883	2,415,908	2,421,063	2,417,639	2,411,790	2,399,477	2,375,557
Earnings per share:										
Primary......................	$ 0.90	$ 1.40	$ 1.30	$ 0.40	$ 0.60	$ 1.41	$ 1.38	$ 1.21	$ 1.17	$ 1.10
Fully diluted.................	$ 0.89	$ 1.31	—	—	—	—	—	—	—	—
Dividends per share...........	$ 0.40	$ 0.40	$ 0.40	$ 0.475	$ 0.70	$ 0.85	$ 0.80	$ 0.75	$ 0.75	$ 0.75
Book value per share...........	$14.81	$14.31	$13.29	$12.33	$12.40	$12.42	$11.80	$11.00	$10.33	$ 9.34
Financial condition										
Working capital................	$ 42,635	$ 45,259	$ 32,631	$ 23,006	$ 24,458	$ 24,938	$ 18,159	$ 18,422	$ 17,090	$ 14,019
Current ratio...................	3.31	3.81	3.04	2.39	2.53	2.93	2.44	2.95	3.03	2.54
Net plant......................	13,938	10,730	7,464	7,862	8,190	8,210	7,883	7,564	6,819	7,663
Total assets....................	80,129	76,833	60,340	52,376	50,626	48,047	41,098	36,090	33,286	30,456
Long-term debt.................	24,991	25,319	11,668	4,500	4,750	5,000	—	—	—	—
Shareholders' equity...........	36,694	35,435	32,639	30,183	29,864	30,107	28,503	26,599	24,846	22,341
Return on assets†..............	2.8%	4.5%	5.3%	1.9%	2.8%	8.3%	8.1%	8.1%	8.4%	8.6%
Return on equity†..............	6.1%	9.7%	12.2%	3.2%	4.8%	11.3%	11.7%	11.0%	11.3%	11.7%
Debt/equity ratio†..............	0.68	0.71	0.36	0.15	0.16	0.17	0	0	0	0
Profit/sales ratio†..............	1.7	2.6	2.6	1.0	1.5	3.6	3.9	3.8	3.8	3.7

* Prior years have been restated for a two-for-one stock split in 1969 and a 2 percent stock dividend in 1963.
† Computed from above data.
Source: Tappan Company, *Annual Report*, 1970.

Exhibit 6
TAPPAN COMPANY
Pan-O-Matic Range

Source: *Appliance Manufacturer*, December 1970.

Exhibit 7. TAPPAN COMPANY
Kitchen Wall

Integral Kitchen Satisfies Industrialized Building Needs

Tappan's innovative ability is vividly exemplified in the "kitchen wall module" which it developed for the Dept. of Housing and Urban Development's "Operation Breakthrough" program. Designed to cut on-site kitchen installation costs, the module combines the kitchen wall, appliances, cabinets, electrical wiring and plumbing into a single, factory-assembled unit. The concept allows two men to install a complete kitchen in less than an hour.

Practically everything needed for the module is made by Tappan's divisions. If the concept is broadly accepted by builders, the module could become Tappan's most profitable product in the future.

Two HUD contract winners —Aluminum Co. of America and Republic Steel Corp.—are planning to use the modules in their industrialized building concepts. A number of other HUD selectees are also working with Tappan on the use of the modules.

"The Government wants to build homes as fast and as economically as possible," Robert M. Lamb, Jr., kitchen systems administrator, explains. "Pre-fab construction may be the answer because it eliminates expensive on-site labor and the weather factor. It will also assure better uniformity of construction.

"Before the concept can move, however, the Government must resolve certain issues on building codes. Some plan will also have to be created to integrate the building trade unions and builders into the program, rather than eliminate them."

To date, about 50 of the kitchen modules have been made at the Mansfield plant for evaluation by various builders. The modules will be assembled at the Ontario plant when it is completed.

"If there is a big demand for kitchen walls, we will probably have to assemble them at various locations throughout the country because of the shipping problems," Lamb concludes. "We could wind up making them at our distribution centers."

The factory-built "kitchen module" is trucked to a home site and hoisted in place. The unit is supported by a stress wall of 1⅛-in.-thick sheets of U.S. Plywood's "Novoply" compressed particle board. To this wall are attached the kitchen storage cabinets, range, sink, dishwasher, refrigerator and other appliances, along with the necessary water piping and electrical wiring.

Source: *Appliance Manufacturer*, December 1970.

Exhibit 8

TAPPAN COMPANY
Tappan Home Center

HOME CENTERS—
Showcase for
Remodelers

A nationwide network of franchised remodeling centers is being set up by Tappan. Primary purpose of the Home Centers is to provide a permanent location for remodelers and homeowners to obtain professional assistance in planning remodeling projects.

Illustrated on this page is the Mansfield, Ohio, Tappan Home Center which the Tappan Div. will use as a training center for other home center franchisees. The Mansfield unit will also function as a remodeling center locally.

Within the Home Center are a number of "designer kitchens" which are intended to serve as a guide for remodeling jobs. Naturally Tappan appliances and cabinets are used throughout.

Adjacent to the Mansfield Home Center is a home furnishings store. This retail outlet is intended to serve as a source of supply for items not showcased within the Home Center itself.

The company is not planning to expand the Home Center concept too quickly, since a great amount of investigation and training will be involved before Home Center franchisees are selected.

Source: *Appliance Manufacturer*, December 1970.

Exhibit 9

TAPPAN COMPANY
New Products under Development

'Firsts' for the Future

COMPACT HEAT EXCHANGER. An improved gas warm air furnace that is only one-third the size of conventional furnaces. The unit is based on a modular design. Each module has an output of 40,000 btuh. The furnace, which can be made in upflow, downflow or counterflow models, was developed by Thermo-Electron under the sponsorship of Tappan, Rheem and the American Gas Assn.

TOTAL GAS COMFORT SYSTEM. The unique system combines a Freon vapor generator with a Rankine cycle engine that drives the compressor of a mechanical refrigeration system. The generator provides high-pressure vapor for the engine in the cooling mode and also serves as the heat source. Thermo Electron is researching the system under the joint sponsorship of Tappan, Rheem and A.G.A.

SMOOTH-TOP RANGE. Four infra-red burners will heat cooking areas of a thermo-resistant glass top to over 1000 F for direct radiant heating of utensils. Tooling for the range is complete, and it will go into production shortly. The unit was developed by Tappan. The glass top was developed by Owens-Illinois and will be made by Pittsburgh Plate Glass.

SAFETY CONTROL PANEL. Designed to increase home safety, the panel could combine solid-state devices that sense odors to turn on and off an air purification system; signal when air filters are clogged; detect gas leaks and electrical failures; and combine burglar and fire alarms. Research on the panel has been completed by Honeywell. Tappan plans to use it on future range lines.

THERMIONIC GENERATOR. A method of generating electricity from heat with no moving parts. The generator could be placed in a furnace exhaust duct to make electricity to power the blower drive motor. The concept is being vigorously pursued by Thermo Electron, but no real breakthrough has yet been made.

FURNACE/WATER HEATER COMBINATION. A low-cost unit that will be compact enough for use in mobile homes. It has just one burner which is sized to provide instantaneous hot water and heat. Thermo Electron is developing the unique boiler under a program sponsored by Tappan, Rheem and A.G.A.

AIR PURIFIER. A low-cost unit which could be portable or added to a furnace, air conditioner or range hood to effi-ciently remove dirt and smoke from the air. Tappan has funded money for research on electrostatic air purification to Honeywell, Gourdine, Thermo Electron and its own engineers.

"COOL" OVEN. Heat from a gas burner will be forced through the oven. The heat movement is expected to cut cooking time in half and greatly reduce oven temperatures. The cool operation may permit the use of plastic for the range side panels. Tappan is researching this forced-convection oven itself.

"MINI" DISPOSER. About half the size of conventional disposers, the unit provides more storage space under the sink. The product, which has been under development at the Anaheim division for three years, also mounts flush against the sink drain to eliminate mounting ring and collar.

Source: *Appliance Manufacturer*, December 1970.

The company and its strategists: Relating corporate strategy to personal values

Up to this point we have argued that a concept of purpose and a sense of direction strengthen a company's ability to survive in changing circumstances. We have seen, to be sure, the difficulties of understanding clearly both a company's circumstances and its strengths and weaknesses. The action implied by these difficulties has been an objective and alert surveillance of the environment for threats and opportunities and a detached appraisal of organizational characteristics in order to identify distinctive competence. We have considered the suitable combination of a company's strengths and its opportunities to be a logical exercise characterized by perhaps not precise but reasoned, well-informed choices of alternatives assuring the highest possible profit. We have been examining the changing relationship of company and environment almost as if a purely economic strategy, uncontaminated by the personality or goals of the decision maker, were possible.

STRATEGY AS PROJECTION OF PREFERENCE

We must acknowledge at this point that there is no way to divorce the decision determining the most sensible economic strategy for a company from the personal values of those who make the choice. Executives in charge of company destinies do not look exclusively at what a company might do and can do. In apparent disregard of the second of these considerations, they sometimes seem heavily influenced by what they personally *want* to do.

We are ourselves not aware of how much desire affects our own choice of alternatives, but we can see it in others. Note, for example, George Romney's dramatic promotion of economic sensible transportation and the small car in the early days of American Motors and his subsequent repayment of all debt, in place of investment through research in the development of variations in the small car which might

448

have retained leadership in an important segment of the market. Almost certainly we see reflected here the higher value Romney placed on economy than on consumer preferences, on liquidity over debt, and other values derived more from his character and upbringing than from an objective monitoring of the best course for American Motors to follow.

Frank Farwell came from IBM to the presidency of Underwood in 1955, it has been said, saying that he would be damned if he would spend his life peddling adding machines and typewriters. This aversion may explain why Underwood plunged into the computer business without the technical, financial, or marketing resources necessary to succeed in it. Similarly, when Adriano Olivetti purchased control of Underwood after three days of hurried negotiations, he may well have been moved by his childhood memory of visiting Hartford and by the respect for once the world's leading manufacturer of typewriters that led his father to erect in Ivrea a replica of the red-brick, five-story Hartford plant.[1] That he wanted to purchase Underwood so badly may explain why he and his associates did not find out how dangerously it had decayed and how near bankruptcy it had been brought.

The three presidents of J. I. Case in the years 1953 to 1963 seem to have been displaying their own temperaments as they wracked the company with alternatives of expansionism and contraction far beyond the needs of response to a cyclical industry environment.[2] In all these cases, the actions taken can be rationalized so as not to seem quite so personal as I have suggested they are.

THE INEVITABILITY OF VALUES

We will be able to understand the strategic decision better if we admit rather than resist the dimension of preference. If we think back over the discussions of earlier cases in this book, the strategies we recommended for the companies probably reflected what *we* would have wanted to do had we been in charge of those companies. We told ourselves or assumed that our personal inclinations harmonized with the optimum combination of economic opportunity and company capability. The professional manager in a large company, drilled in analytical technique and the use of staff trained to subordinate value-laden assumptions to tables of numbers, may often prefer the optimal economic strategy because of its very suitability. Certain entrepreneurs, whose energy and personal drives far outweigh their formal training and self-awareness, set their course in directions not necessarily supported by logical appraisal. Such disparity appears most frequently in small privately held concerns, or in companies built by successful and self-

---

[1] See "Underwood-Olivetti (AR)," Edmund P. Learned, C. Roland Christensen, Kenneth R. Andrews, and William D. Guth, *Business Policy: Text and Cases*, original edition (Homewood, Ill.: Richard D. Irwin, Inc., 1965), p. 212. This case is also in the Intercollegiate Case Clearing House, No. 9–312–017.

[2] "J. I. Case Company," Learned et al., *Business Policy*, pp. 82–102. This case is also in the Intercollegiate Case Clearing House, No. 9–309–270.

confident owner-managers. The phenomenon we are discussing, however, may appear in any company, especially if it is large, in its divisions.

Our problem now can be very simply stated. In examining the alternatives available to a company, we must henceforth take into consideration the preferences of the chief executive. Furthermore, we must also be concerned with the values of other key managers who must either contribute to or assent to the strategy if it is to be effective. We therefore have two kinds of reconciliation to consider—first, the divergence between the chief executive's preference and the strategic choice which seems most economically defensible and, second, the conflict among several sets of managerial personal values which must be reconciled not only with an economic strategy but with each other.

Thus, when Mr. Edgar Villchur, inventor of the acoustic suspension loudspeaker, founded Acoustic Research, Inc.[3] in 1954, he institutionalized a desire to bring high fidelity sound to the mass market at the lowest possible cost. He licensed his competitors freely and finally gave up his original patent rights altogether. He kept not only his prices but his dealer margins low, maintained for a considerable time a primitive production facility and an organization of friends rather than managers, and went to great lengths to make the company a good place to work, sharing with employees the company's success. The company was dominated by Mr. Villchur's desire to have a small organization characterized by academic, scientific, and intellectual rather than "commercial" values. Product development was driven by some of these values away from the acoustical technology which Mr. Villchur's personal competence would have suggested into development of record players, amplifiers, and tuners which were to offer less in superiority over competitive products than did his speakers. Again, these were priced far below what might have been possible.

Mr. Abraham Hoffman, for years vice president and treasurer, had the task of trying to overcome his superior's reluctance to advertise, to admit the validity of the marketing function, and of maintaining the business as a profitable enterprise. That the company had succeeded in at long last developing and producing a music system of great value in relation to its cost and in winning the respect of the high fidelity listener market does not alter the fact that the first determination of strategy came more from Mr. Villchur's antibusiness values than from an analytical balancing of opportunity and distinctive competence. The latter would have led, with perhaps much greater growth and profitability, into acoustical systems, public address equipment, long-distance communications, hearing aids, noise suppression, and the like—all areas in which technical improvement in the quality of available sound is much needed.

We must remember, however, that it is out of Mr. Villchur's determination and goals that his company came into being in the first place.

---

[3] "Acoustic Research, Inc.," Learned et al., *Business Policy*, pp. 466–519. This case is in the Intercollegiate Case Clearing House, No. 9–312–020.

The extraordinary accomplishments of an antimarketing company in the marketplace are directly traceable to the determination to innovate in quality and price. The reconciliation between Mr. Villchur's values and Mr. Hoffman's more business-oriented determination to manage the company's growth more objectively occurred only when the company was sold to Teledyne, Mr. Villchur retired to his laboratory, and Mr. Hoffman became president. The quality achievements of this firm have been rewarded, but the economic potential of its strategy was for years unrealized.

We should in all realism admit that the personal desires, aspirations, and needs of the senior managers of a company actually *do* play an influential role in the determination of strategy. Against those who are offended by this idea either for its departure from the stereotype of single-minded economic man or for its implicit violation of responsibilities to the shareholder, we would argue that we must accept not only the inevitability but the desirability of this intervention. If we begin by saying that all strategic decisions must fall within the very broad limits of the manager's fiduciary responsibility to the owners of the business and perhaps to others in the management group, then we may proceed legitimately to the idea that what a manager wants to do is not out of order. The conflict which often arises between what general managers want to do and what the dictates of economic strategy suggest they ought to do is best not denied or condemned. It should be accepted as a matter of course. In the study of organization behavior, we have long since concluded that the personal needs of the hourly worker must be taken seriously and at least partially satisfied as a means of securing the productive effort for which wages are paid. It should, then, come as no surprise to us that the president of the corporation also arrives at his work with his own needs and values, to say nothing of his relatively greater power to see that they are taken into account.

RECONCILING DIVERGENT VALUES

If we accept the inevitability of personal values in the strategic decision governing the character and course of a corporation, then we must turn to the skills required to reconcile the optimal economic strategy with the personal preferences of the executives of the company. There is no reason why a better balance could not have been struck in Acoustic Research, without sacrifice to the genius of the founder or the quality of life in his company. It is first necessary to penetrate conventional rationalization and reticence to determine what these preferences are. For without this revelation, strategic proposals stemming from different unstated values come into conflict. This conflict cannot be reconciled by talking in terms of environmental data and corporate resources. The hidden agenda of corporate policy debates makes them endless and explains why so many companies do not have explicit, forthright, and usefully focused strategies.

To many caught up in the unresolved strategic questions in their own organizations, it seems futile even to attempt to reconcile a strategic alternative dictated by personal preference with other alternatives oriented toward capitalizing on opportunity to the greatest possible extent. In actuality, however, this additional complication poses fewer difficulties than at first appear. The analysis of opportunity and the appraisal of resources themselves often lead in different directions. To compose three, rather than two, divergent sets of considerations into a single pattern may increase the complexity of the task, but the integrating process is still the same. We can look for the dominant consideration and treat the others as constraints; we can probe the elements in conflict for the possibilities of reinterpretation or adjustment. We are not building a wall of irregular stone so much as balancing a mobile of elements, the motion of which is adjustable to the motion of the entire mobile.

As we have seen, external developments can be affected by company action and company resources, and internal competence can be developed. If worst comes to worst, it is better for a person to separate from a management whose values he or she does not share than to pretend agreement or to wonder why others think as they do. Howard Head, whose passionate dedication to the metal ski not only produced a most successful business, but delayed unnecessarily its entry into plastic skis, has realistically retired from his now diversified business and has sold his holdings. It is not necessary, however, for all members of management to think alike or to have the same personal values, so long as strategic decision is not delayed or rendered ineffective by these known and accepted differences. Large gains are possible simply by raising the strategic issues for discussion by top management, by admitting the legitimacy of different preferences, and by explaining how superficial or fundamental the differences are.

MODIFICATION OF VALUES

The question whether values can actually be changed during the reconciliation process is somewhat less clear. A value is a view of life and a judgment of what is desirable that is very much a part of a person's personality and a group's morale. From parents, teachers, and peers, we are told by psychologists, we acquire basic values, which change somewhat with acquired knowledge, analytical ability, and self-awareness, but remain a stable feature of personality.[4] Nonetheless the preference attached to goals in concrete circumstances is not beyond influence. The physicist who leaves the university to work in a profit-making company because of a combined fondness for his work and material comfort, may ask to continue to do pure rather than applied research, but he presumably does not want his company to go bankrupt. The conflict in values is to some degree negotiable, once the reluctance to expose hidden agendas is overcome. Retaining the value orientation of the scientist, the ambivalent physicist might assent to a strategic al-

---

[4] See for example W. D. Guth and Renato Tagiuri: "Personal Values and Corporate Strategy," *Harvard Business Review*, September–October 1965, pp. 123–32.

ternative stressing product development rather than original investigation, at least for a specified time until the attainment of adequate profit made longer range research feasible.

AWARENESS OF VALUES

Our interest in the role of personal values in strategic formulations should not be confined to assessing the influence of other people's values. Despite the well-known problems of introspection, we can probably do more to understand the relation of our own values to our choice of purpose than we can to change the values of others. Awareness that our own preference for an alternative opposed by another stems from values as much as from rational estimates of economic opportunity may have important consequences. First, it may make us more tolerant and less indignant when we perceive this relationship between recommendations and values in the formulations of others. Second, it will force us to consider how important it really is to us to maintain a particular value in making a particular decision. Third, it may give us insight with which to identify our biases and thus pave the way for a more objective assessment of all the strategic alternatives that are available. These consequences of self-examination will not end conflict, but they will at least prevent its unnecessary prolongation.

The object of this self-examination is not necessarily to endow us with the ability to persuade others to accept the strategic recommendations we consider best: it is to acquire insight into the problems of determining purpose and skill in the process of resolving them. Individuals inquiring into their own values for the purpose of understanding their own positions in policy debates can continue to assess their own personal opportunities, strengths and weaknesses, and basic values by means of the procedures outlined here. For a personal strategy, analytically considered and consciously developed, may be as useful to an individual as a corporate strategy is to a business institution. The effort, conducted by each individual, to formulate personal purpose might well accompany his or her contributions to organizational purpose. If the encounter leads to a clarification of the purposes one seeks, the values one holds, and the alternatives available, the attempt to make personal use of the concept of strategy will prove extremely worthwhile.

Introducing personal preference forces us to deal with the possibility that the strategic decision we prefer (identified after the most nearly objective analysis of opportunity and resources we are capable of) is not acceptable to other executives with different values. Their acceptance of the strategy is necessary to its successful implementation. In diagnosing this conflict, we try to identify the values implicit in our own choice. As we look at the gap between the strategy which follows from our own values and that which would be appropriate to the values of our associates, we look to see whether the difference is fundamental or superficial. Then we look to see how the strategy we believe best matches opportunity and resources can be adapted to accommodate the values of those who will implement it. Reconciliation of the three princi-

pal determinants of strategy which we have so far considered is often
made possible by adjustment of any or all of the determinants.

The role of self-examination in coming to terms with a conflict in
values over an important strategic determination is not to turn all strategic decisions into outcomes of consensus. Some organizations—you
can see them in this book—are run by persons who are leaders in the
sense that they have power and are not afraid to use it. It is true that
business leaders, in Zaleznik's words "commit themselves to a career in
which they have to work on themselves as a condition for effective
working and working with other people."[5] At the same time, a leader
must recognize that "the essence of leadership is choice, a singularly
individualistic act in which a [person] assumes responsibility for a
commitment to direct an organization along a particular path. . . . As
much as a leader wishes to trust others, he has to judge the soundness
and validity of his subordinates' positions. Otherwise, the leader may become a prisoner of the emotional commitments of his subordinates, frequently at the expense of making correct judgments about policies and
strategies."[6]

When a management group is locked in disagreement, the presence
of power and the need for its exercise conditions the dialogue. There are
circumstances when the exercise of leadership must transcend disagreement that cannot be resolved by discussion. Subordinates, making the
best of the inevitable, must accept a follower role. When leadership becomes irresponsible and dominates subordinate participation without
reason, it is usually ineffective or is deposed. Participants in strategic
disagreements must not only know their own needs and power but those
of the chief executive. Strategic planning, in the sense that power attached to values plays a role in it, is a political process.[7]

You should not warp your recommended strategy to the detriment of
the company's future in order to adjust it to the personal values you
hold or observe. On the other hand, you should not expect to be able to
impose without risk and without expectation of eventual vindication
and agreement, an unwelcome pattern of purposes and policies on the
people in charge of a corporation or responsible for achieving results.
Strategy is a human construction; it must in the long run be responsive
to human needs. It must ultimately inspire commitment. It must stir
an organization to successful striving against competition. Some people
have to have their hearts in it.

---

[5] Abraham Zaleznik and Manfred F. R. Kets de Vries, *Power and the Corporate
Mind* (Boston: Houghton Mifflin, 1975), p. 207.

[6] Ibid., p. 209.

[7] See Abraham Zaleznik: "Managers and Leaders: Are They Different?" *Harvard
Business Review*, May–June 1977, pp. 67–78.

The Saturday Evening Post (R)

> The real history is going to have to be written by a psychiatrist.[1]
> —Cary Bok, grandson of the founder of Curtis Publishing Company.

ON THE AFTERNOON of January 9, 1969, standing before the glaring television lights at the Overseas Press Club in New York City, Martin Ackerman, Curtis Publishing Company's fourth president in six years, calmly read, "This is one of the saddest days of my life, a sad one for me, for our employees, officers, and directors; indeed, it is sad for the American public. Apparently there is just not the need for our product in today's scheme of living."[2] With Ackerman's announcement, Curtis officially ceased publication of The Saturday Evening Post.

The Post, which had been suffering from increasing costs and decreasing revenues for the past decade, had once been the most profitable magazine in the United States, considered both the pulse and maker of American opinion. The death of the Post had been predicted by denizens of Wall Street and Madison Avenue since its first financial troubles in the early 1960s. It is impossible, though, to isolate the plight of the Post from the plight of Curtis, a company whose assets included not only such national magazines as the Post, Ladies' Home Journal, and Holiday, but also paper mills in Pennsylvania, a sprawling printing plant outside Philadelphia (where every copy of every Curtis publication was printed), a circulation company, and extensive timberlands. During the years 1960–1969 inclusive, Curtis' operating revenues (net of commissions) declined from $192.8 million to $32.0 million, and the company sustained a cumulative loss of $67.6 million (Exhibit 1).

---

[1] Joseph Goulden, The Curtis Caper (New York: G. P. Putnam's Sons, 1965), p. 11.

[2] Otto Friedrich, Decline and Fall (New York: Harper and Row, 1970), p. 449.

HISTORY: 1897–1962

In 1897, Cyrus Curtis, the founder of Curtis Publishing Company, purchased a struggling journal put together for ten dollars a week by a newspaper man in his spare time. The journal, which Curtis bought for $1,000, consisted of a mailing list of 2,231 names, a wagon-load of battered type fonts, and a name, *The Saturday Evening Post*. At the time, Curtis was the publisher of the leading women's magazine in the nation, the *Ladies' Home Journal*, which he and his wife had built from scratch up to a circulation of 446,000 during the six-year period between 1883 and 1889. Referring to the *Post*, *Printers' Ink*, the printing trade journal, commented that the *Ladies' Home Journal* was a "wonderful property" but that Curtis was "blowing his profits on an impossible venture" with the purchase of this latest magazine.[3]

Curtis was undaunted, for he felt that just as the *Journal* had become a success by dealing with what was most important to the American woman, her home, the *Post* would become a success by dealing with what was important to men, "their fight for livelihood in the business world."[4]

The Lorimer *Post:* 1899–1936

For the first year under Curtis, the *Post* was edited by William Jordan, but Curtis soon became dissatisfied, and the editorship passed to George Horace Lorimer. The son of a famous Boston minister, Lorimer was considered one of the best newspaper men in Boston.

Lorimer immediately proceeded to alter the *Post*, changing it from a weekly newspaper into a magazine, and cutting the price from ten cents to five, thus making it less expensive than any competitive periodical. He also instituted a new procedure in American publishing, that of paying authors at the time their material was accepted for publication rather than when it was actually published.

> Lorimer knew exactly what he wanted to make out of the *Post*. It was to be a magazine without class, clique, or sectional editing, but intended for every adult in America's seventy-five million population. He meant to edit it for the whole United States. He set out to interpret America to itself, always readably, but constructively.
>
> As he settled into the job of interpretation, Lorimer sensed accurately the mood of the country at the beginning of the new century. People were weary of reading about problems, politics, radicalism, war, and even uplift. They wanted to read historical novels and dwell in the past, and Lorimer gave them covers showing Ben Franklin, Washington, and Independence Hall in appropriate poses, while inside he displayed the romances of the Rev. Cyrus Townsend Brady and Robert W. Chambers.
>
> Always the accent was heaviest on business. Charles R. Flint praised the benefits of the business combination; the mayors of San Francisco and Baltimore wrote jointly on the need for better business methods in

---

[3] Goulden, *The Curtis Caper*, p. 22.
[4] Ibid., p. 22.

civic administration; and Harvard's director of physical culture advised the businessman on home gymnastics.[5]

Lorimer himself contributed several articles related to business, which appeared in the *Post* as an unsigned serial entitled "Letters from a Self-made Merchant to His Son." An immediate success, this series was later published in book form and translated into "a dozen" foreign languages.

Lorimer must have hit some chord in the heart of the country, for the *Post's* circulation increased from 33,000 in 1898 to 97,000 in the following year, and then to 182,000 in the year after that. Circulation reached half a million in 1903, a million in 1909, two million in 1913, and three million in 1927.

A propitious environment.   During the early 1900s fundamental changes were occurring in America. Mass production, transportation, and distribution were making America a nation rather than a collection of geographically contiguous regions. Curtis anticipated the need for a national magazine and adroitly applied the evolving principles of mass production and distribution to his publications.

Advertising revenue for the *Post* increased from $8,000 in 1898 to $160,000 in 1899 and then to more than $1 million in 1905, $3 million in 1909, and $5 million in 1910. By the end of the 1920s, advertising revenue was over $50 million and the *Post* collected almost 30 cents of every advertising dollar spent in magazines in the United States.

> The vehicle that the *Post* rode to tremendous financial success was the automobile. The *Post* carried its first auto ad, about a W. E. Roach horseless buggy, in an issue in March 1900. For the next two decades auto advertising expanded as rapidly as the industry; at one point it made up 25 per cent of the total volume.[6]

The zenith of this period of the *Post's* history was the issue of December 1929, a virtual "paper monument" to Curtis and Lorimer.

> It contained 272 pages and weighed almost two pounds. Sixty forty-five ton presses rolled around the clock for three weeks to produce it, consuming 6,000,000 pounds of paper and 120,000 pounds of ink. The reading fare was enough to keep the average adult busy for more than 20 hours, *Post* editors estimated. And the issue—largest of any magazine in Curtis' history—put $1,512,000 from 214 national advertisers into Cyrus Curtis' money box. This grandiose effort was so mammoth in bulk that scrap dealers eagerly paid five cents to newstands for the paper alone.[7]

A series of blows.   With the end of the prosperity of the 1920s, *Post* advertising revenues decreased substantially. By 1932, issues of only 60 pages, a quarter of them filled with advertising, were commonplace.

Cyrus Curtis died in 1933 at the age of 83, leaving his daughter and two grandsons effective control of the company with 32% of the stock. Lorimer, retaining his position as editor of the *Post*, assumed the presidency. During the period between 1933 and 1936, the year of his re-

---

[5] John Tebbel, *George Horace Lorimer and The Saturday Evening Post* (New York: Doubleday and Company, Inc., 1948), pp. 23–26.

[6] Goulden, *The Curtis Caper*, pp. 25–26.

[7] Ibid., p. 32.

tirement, Lorimer increased advertising revenue from an $18 million low in 1933 to $26 million in 1936 in spite of the severe economic conditions and increased competition from Henry Luce's *Time* and *Life*. During this same period, Lorimer placed the editorial power of the *Post* behind an attempt to defeat Franklin D. Roosevelt in his reelection bid in 1936.

> Lorimer called the New Deal "a discredited European ideology"; he railed against "undesirable and unassimilable aliens"; and the *Post* declared: "We might just as well say that the world failed as the American business leadership failed."[8]

The election landslide for Roosevelt and his New Deal in 1936 was a humiliating blow to Lorimer and indicated "a fundamental, distinct shift of the *Post's* role in American life. It would be accepted as entertainment, but not as a guide to life."[9]

Hand-picked successors: 1936–1962

Following Lorimer's retirement in 1936, Walter D. Fuller, Lorimer's hand-picked successor, was named chief executive officer of Curtis. Fuller, a man more conservative politically than Lorimer, had worked his way up in the organization from the accounting department as successively controller, corporate secretary, first vice president, and president, all while under the guidance of Curtis and Lorimer.

Fuller became chairman of the board for 1950–1957, and his protégé, Robert MacNeal, took over the position of president and chief executive officer. MacNeal had first attracted management attention during the 1920s by designing a folding machine that enabled the *Post* to print more than 200 pages, the previous limit.

> Even when he became president he would go into the machine shops and, at the risk of soiled white cuffs, talk about and help solve mechanical problems. In his coat pocket was a little leatherbound black notebook crammed with facts and statistics about Curtis and its multitude of subsidiary companies. The information—even including the names and addresses of directors—was typed on a "miniature Gothic" typewriter so more characters would fit onto a page. Why the notebook? MacNeal's superior in the scheduling division had carried a similar book way back in the 1920s. "He was the fount of all knowledge, so we had to have one, too," MacNeal explained.[10]

Corporate strategy. The corporate strategy under the guidance of Fuller and MacNeal was to build Curtis into a fully integrated magazine publishing company which grew its own trees, made its own paper, printed every issue of every magazine, and distributed the magazines through a circulation subsidiary. This was an arrangement that other publishers looked upon unfavorably, inasmuch as it. tended to accentuate corporate losses in periods of economic decline, served as a

---

[8] Friedrich, *Decline and Fall,* p. 10.
[9] Goulden, *The Curtis Caper,* p. 45.
[10] Ibid., pp. 71–72.

drain on funds available for diversification, and tended to increase the size and complexity of corporate management.

Otto Friedrich, in *Decline and Fall,* discussed the Fuller and Mac-Neal years as follows:

> Fuller's presidency began during the difficult days of the Depression, when Curtis and many other companies tottered near bankruptcy, and the value of ideas may well have seemed less obvious than it does to-day. And then, during World War II, the shortage of supplies convinced many an executive of the value of hoarding and stockpiling. What-ever his reasons, Fuller held to his empire-building philosophy with an exceptional singleness of purpose. He could have bought the entire Columbia Broadcasting System for $3 million, but he declined the offer; a few years later, he declined a similar opportunity to buy the American Broadcasting Corporation. Television, radio, the growth in book publishing, the so-called "paperback revolution," the rise of suburban newspapers, the increasing need for school texts—Walter Deane Fuller had not been blessed with a gift for prophesying such developments. Instead, just after World War II, he bought a 108-acre site on the outskirts of Philadelphia, shipped in twenty new printing presses, and constructed the gigantic Sharon Hill printing plant. It was, in its day, the largest and best-equipped printing plant in the world. And as late as 1950, when Fuller finally passed on the presi-dency to his protégé, Robert A. MacNeal, Curtis reaffirmed its dedica-tion to machinery by investing $20 million to become full owner of a paper company in which it already held a controlling interest.[11]

By 1960, the number of individuals actually employed in creating the Curtis magazines was minuscule compared to the number engaged in its manufacture:

> The editorial staff of the *Post* numbered about 125 people; the em-ployees in the printing division numbered 2,600; the employees of the whole corporation numbered about 11,000. And in surveying the cor-porate assets, Curtis executives liked to boast that the company owned not just a few magazines but a $40 million printing plant, three large paper mills, 262,000 acres of timberland, and a circulation company that distributed 50-odd magazines through 100,000 outlets.[12]

Editorial strategy. In 1936, Lorimer's successor as editor of the *Post* was Wesley W. Stout. Like Fuller and MacNeal, Stout was hand-picked by Lorimer and was a conservative politically:

> In editorial outlook, Stout was every bit as conservative as Lorimer; the popular support given the New Deal by voters in 1936 goaded the *Post* into increasingly vicious attacks on the Administration. President Roosevelt never answered directly, but he showed several visitors a large envelope containing what he termed the "dirtiest" attacks pub-lished against the government. The bulk of them were from the *Post.* The magazine's editorials were a cacophony of ridicule directed against organized labor, social reform programs, social security, the Tennessee

---

[11] Friedrich, *Decline and Fall,* p. 15.
[12] Ibid., p. 15.

Valley Administration—in sum, just about anything attempted by FDR.[13]

Advertising revenue dropped $4 million during Stout's first year as editor, and at a stockholders' meeting in 1941 minority stockholders "denounced management's isolationism and called for the opening of *Post* pages to opposing points of view."[14] Stout's editorship of the *Post* came to an end in 1942 with what has been called "the biggest misunderstanding in Curtis editorial history."[15] Stout had published a three-article series on the American Jew, the last article of which was entitled "The Case Against the Jew." A furor erupted with cancellations of subscriptions and advertising, threats of a boycott, and destruction of *Posts* at newsstands. In May of 1942, the *Post* ran an editorial apologizing for the article, saying that Stout had believed

> . . . "a frank airing of the whole question would serve to clear the atmosphere in this country and perhaps help prevent anti-Semitism from gaining a foothold here." The *Post* expressed regret that the article had been "misunderstood."[16]

Discord between Editor Stout and President Fuller had been rumored for some time, and the controversy over the article and the *Post*'s operating loss for the first quarter of 1942 precipitated Stout's resignation. The editorship of the *Post* then went to Ben Hibbs, a native of Kansas, who had been the editor of another Curtis magazine, *Country Gentleman*. Hibbs immediately began making major changes in the *Post*. He found the *Post*'s editorial content resting on the same "glamour of business" product that Lorimer had developed decades earlier. Feeling that this product was dated, Hibbs broadened the *Post* by stressing that he considered to be the more enduring part of America— namely, life in country towns. But Hibbs also looked beyond middle America and recognized the Second World War as "the greatest news story of our time. Things were happening more exciting than what fiction writers could dream up."

> Hibbs and his lanky young managing editor, Bob Fuoss, reduced the emphasis on fiction and set out to cover World War II. The *Post* then had only one war correspondent, who was home on leave in New York. Hibbs recruited MacKinlay Kantor, Samuel Lubell, Edgar Snow, Richard Tregaskis, Demaree Bess. C. S. Forester wrote about the sinking of the *Scharnhorst*, Ambassador Joseph E. Davies wrote from Moscow about the Russian front, and Norman Rockwell painted his version of Roosevelt's slogan, the Four Freedoms. In this silver age, the money came and went at an unprecedented rate. Hibbs spent $175,000, a record for extravagance at that time, for *My Three Years with Eisenhower,* by the general's naval aide, Captain Harry C. Butcher. He spent another $125,000 for the memoirs of Casey Stengel, and $100,000 for a biography of General Douglas MacArthur. The last of these, which had been commissioned without any safeguard as to its quality, was

---

[13] Goulden, *The Curtis Caper,* p. 48.

[14] Ibid., p. 49.

[15] Ibid., p. 51.

[16] Ibid.

never published, and Hibbs referred to it, in a private office memorandum, as "my worst mistake in twenty years." At the same time, Hibbs willingly led the *Post* into a circulation war against *Life* and *Look*, and the *Post* bought its way up from 3.3 million to more than 6.5 million during his twenty-year regime. Advertising revenue rose just as spectacularly, from $23 million to $104 million a year.[17]

Losing the postwar race with competition.   Under the continued guidance of Fuller as chairman, MacNeal as president, and Hibbs as editor of the *Post*, the 1950s proved to be difficult years. Although *Post* advertising revenue increased over the decade, the number of advertising pages per issue decreased. The circulation battles of the late 1950s between the *Post*, *Life*, and *Look* were a mixed blessing for Curtis. A two-year subscription to the *Post* cost the subscriber $7.95 and represented a liability to the *Post* of $20, the production and delivery costs. The larger circulation figures led to increased advertising rates, but these made it impossible for many of the small manufacturers, on whom the *Post* had depended for a substantial amount of its advertising revenue, to continue advertising in the magazine. At the same time the *Post* was losing large corporation advertising to television, which in the years since World War II had built up advertising revenues twice those of magazines.

Market research studies continually eroded the effectiveness of the *Post* as an advertising medium. For example, *Life* underwrote a study which showed that each of its issues had a readership of 5.2 persons and that readership multiplied by circulation brought *Life* equal with radio and television in the numbers-game of media reach—a claim that the *Post* could not equal. *Life* then underwrote another study which indicated that the *Post* was a magazine bought for reading and not for looking; *Life* immediately turned this fact to its advantage by stressing to advertisers that the busy young housewife would not have time to read *Post* articles, so advertising in the *Post* would be less effective than in a magazine bought for looking, such as *Life*.

Madison Avenue wanted to cover the younger segment of the consumer market (base age of 35, with the extra dollars to give discretionary buying power). In the late fifties, *Life*'s circulation included twice as many families in this category as the *Post*'s. Madison Avenue began to feel that the *Post* was not reaching the market "where the action was."

Life was also active during the 1950s building a power base with merchants. *Life* persuaded merchants to tag goods "as advertised in *Life*," with the implication that *Life* put its editorial integrity behind the product.

> The retailers also received low-cost promotional material which a skilled young man would help convert into an attractive display, free of charge. The merchants, in turn, made their warm feelings toward *Life* felt all the way up the distribution line to top management at the manufacturer.[18]

---

[17] Friedrich, *Decline and Fall*, p. 12.
[18] Goulden, *The Curtis Caper*, p. 85.

The business recession of 1961 caused the number of advertising pages per *Post* issue to plummet even more. As the advertising pages decreased, the *Post* became thinner and thinner, and the professionals on Madison Avenue started placing even fewer ads in the *Post* as a result:

> "We're a bunch of sheep," David Ogilvy, of Ogilvy, Benson and Mather, said candidly. "One agency leaves a magazine, we all wonder why and follow. The magazine thins again, and more of us leave. Suddenly there's nothing left. No one wants his copy in a thin book."[19]

Curtis' profits declined during the 1950s from $6.2 million in 1950 to only $1.6 million in 1960. Although gross advertising revenue (including commissions) increased from $98.6 million to $151.8 million during the 10-year period, advertising pages decreased. Production and distribution expenses rose substantially over the same time, while selling and administrative expenses more than doubled, going from $27.7 million to $61.2 million.

The "new *Post*."   Late in 1960, an administrative decision was made under President MacNeal that a "new *Post*" should be created with a "fashionable look" that would appeal to Madison Avenue, increase *Post* advertising revenue, and thus increase corporate profits. Editor Hibbs, on the other hand, felt that the *Post* was already hitting the American market:

> The *Post* was widely considered to be old and stodgy, edited by the old and stodgy to be read by the old and stodgy, and Ben Hibbs couldn't accept it. "The ad people were always hollering in my last year about the Norman Rockwell covers, that they were old-fashioned," he protested. "Heck, those were the *Post*'s most popular feature." And the books he kept buying kept becoming best sellers. "Dammit. We were hitting the American market," said Hibbs. "We had to be with that kind of record." And did someone say that *Post* fiction was unreal? "After all, the world is not entirely composed of hydrogen bombs, juvenile delinquency, race riots, mental institutions, heart disease and cancer," said Hibbs. "I can remember the time when people thought it was *fun to read*."[20]

The "new *Post*" was developed during 1961 and first appeared in September of that year. Six million dollars in advertising was sold for this issue, and its 148 pages created the thickest *Post* in years. Described as a "peculiar mixture of new and old,"[21] it featured a Norman Rockwell cover depicting the artist puzzling out a new *Post* cover; a new column entitled "Speaking Out," different print and layout styles; and articles ranging from the memoirs of Casey Stengel to an account of an American doctor in the jungles of Haiti. The response to the "new *Post*" was immediate.

> The look of the "new" *Post* infuriated its readers, and they wrote in to protest at a rate of ten thousand letters a week. "Idiotic . . . please

---

[19] Ibid., p. 95.
[20] Friedrich, *Decline and Fall*, p. 13.
[21] Ibid., p. 17.

change it back . . . Cancel my subscription. . . . I have been be-
trayed—and many others with me." As for Madison Avenue, for which
the "new *Post*" had been created, it responded as it usually does to
such efforts—with a shrug. "The mistake was," in the words of one
cynical old *Post* editor, "that you forced them to read the magazine."
Basically, the *Post* had announced change and then attempted to
counterfeit change, and the increased advertising didn't last a month.
Over the whole year, in fact, advertising plummeted from $104 million
to $86 million. The *Post* consequently went into the red by $3 million,
and Curtis by $4 million.[22]

Challenge and change: 1962

On March 29, 1962, President MacNeal announced Curtis' $4 mil-
lion loss for the previous fiscal year, the first corporate loss since the
company's inception in 1891. Apparently the loss would have been
nearly $9 million except for a tax credit of $1 million and a nonrecurring profit of $3.5 million from the sale of securities.

Ten days earlier, the *Gallagher Report*, a Madison Avenue newsletter, had suggested that a major shake-up in Curtis' corporate leadership might be in the cards:

> THE CURTIS CRISIS. Major changes in Curtis Publishing manage-
> ment and ownership expected shortly. Financier Peter G. Treves has
> been quietly buying Curtis stock for more than a year. Has acquired
> sizable holdings.[23]

Apparently Curtis was an attractive target for corporate raiders.
For one thing, the corporate assets were understated: 250,000 acres of
timberland, for example, were valued at between $10–$15 per acre,
while they were carried on the books at $3 per acre. Moreover, the
company's stock was underpriced by the market, with the two issues of
Curtis preferred selling well below their liquidation values.

In 1962, when Treves was buying into the company, effective operating control was in the hands of Curtis' heirs. A trust, to continue
through the life of Curtis' daughter and her two sons, controlled 17.3%
of the outstanding stock, and the Curtis heirs themselves owned 14.6%.
With 32% of the Curtis stock, the heirs over the years had placed family
friends and management sympathetic to the wishes of the family on
the board of directors.

True, a minor change had occurred in the late 1950s, when minority
stockholders complained that common stock dividends were too low
($.00 for 1933–1950 and $.20 from 1951–1956), and threatened a
stockholder suit. As a result, President MacNeal had increased the
size of the board and had dropped from it those Curtis executives who
held ex-officio seats. The newly opened board seats went to investment
and insurance interests. At the same time, however, effective working
control of the company became vested in a newly created executive
committee which included the same editors and executives who had

[22] Ibid., pp. 17–18.
[23] Matthew Culligan, *The Curtis Culligan Story* (New York: Crown Publishers, Inc., 1970), p. 30.

been removed from the board. Moreover, the men filling the newly opened board seats were sympathetic to the wishes of the heirs and thus were considered "family members" of the board.

In April 1962, Treves and Co. and J. R. Williston and Beane, the firms which had been purchasing Curtis stock, sent an emissary to the Curtis Building. This was Milton Gould, a Philadelphia lawyer, who was to play a major role in Curtis' subsequent history. On this occasion, Gould requested an immediate appointment with MacNeal, and stated that the interests he represented wanted two seats on the Curtis board. Not knowing the extent of Treves' and Williston and Beane's ownership, the board agreed to enlarge the number of seats from 11 to 13, with the two new seats going to Gould and R. McLean Stewart, an investment banker. Asked why the directors did not fight the intrusion, Cary Bok, grandson of Cyrus Curtis and member of the board, replied as follows:

> "There are many reasons," Bok said one winter morning in 1964, during a rambling interview at his seaside home in Maine.
>
> "First of all, you never are assured of absolute control unless you have 51 per cent. We have only 32 per cent; we were unsure of what other people had.
>
> "Second, the Curtis board is elected with cumulative voting. The others could have pooled their votes and elected one director for sure; probably two, and possibly three."
>
> Third, Bok said, the company didn't relish the idea of a public proxy fight during a time of internal stress. First-quarter losses that year had already touched $4 million—more red ink than went on the books during all of 1961. Curtis management had more important things to do than scurry around the countryside soliciting proxies from widows and small-time investors. The Wall Street groups, on the other hand, specialized in just this type of scurrying. Had Curtis chosen to fight, there was at least a 50–50 chance that Curtis would have been licked. Management and the heirs feared this, because they didn't know any more about the investors' long-range intentions than they did of the investors' holdings.
>
> Additionally, Curtis by this time was so desperate for cash that it was ready to befriend anyone who came along and offered new ideas and fresh leadership. That spring it was forced to peddle two of its strongest sidelines to raise operating cash. Curtis sold part of its holdings in Bantam Books, Inc., and Treasure Books, Inc., to Grosset & Dunlap, Inc., for a $4.8 million profit. Both companies were returning a profit. But the need for immediate cash was overpowering and the book subsidiaries were something that could be conveniently cut from the empire.[24]

In an interview given shortly after he joined the Curtis board, Gould said that he had sought a directorship because the brokerage houses that had taken a substantial financial position in Curtis had become alarmed by the accelerated operating losses and by Curtis' inability to adapt to changing markets. "New and energetic management is

[24] Goulden, *The Curtis Caper,* pp. 123–124.

needed," he added.[25] (For a list of major changes in Curtis' direction during the 1960s, see Exhibit 2.)

"UNDER NEW MANAGEMENT": 1962–1969

In the early summer of 1962, MacNeal left for a trip to Europe, and during his absence, spurred by Gould, the board voted him out as president. Although it was decided to withhold the news from the press until his return, the news was leaked to *The Wall Street Journal* three hours after the meeting ended. An executive committee was formed to run the company until a new president could be found. Gould was named legal counsel to the executive committee.

The Culligan years: 1962–1968

Gould's personal choice for the presidency of Curtis was Matthew Culligan, an executive at Interpublic, an advertising conglomerate headed by Marion Harper. Previous to his employment at Interpublic, Culligan had been an executive vice president at NBC, where he had been credited with turning around the failing NBC Radio Network. Gould arranged a meeting between Culligan and the Curtis executive committee, which Culligan later described as follows:

> Gould conditioned the executive committee on my behalf, warning them that I was just about the final hope and softening them up for my salary demands and fringe benefits. He actually assigned one of his associates to write my contract for me![26]

Shortly after its meeting with Culligan, the executive committee named him president of Curtis. Culligan described his first week at the company as frantic. He raced between the editorial and sales offices in New York City and the corporate offices and the circulation, manufacturing, and paper companies in Pennsylvania. Marion Harper, Culligan's boss at Interpublic, got together the best "media brains" in his organization "to contribute the best cerebration and intuition to the problems at Curtis"[27] in order to help Culligan in his new position. Culligan described the resulting suggestions as follows:

> When the report was finished, Harper invited me to his office and gave me the benefit of the accumulated experience and judgment of a dozen of his best people. The report was fascinating. In essence, it said that Curtis could not survive in the form in which I had inherited it—with the same magazines, same circulations, same frequencies—under the economic conditions then prevailing at Curtis. The task force recommended that the *Post* go biweekly; that *Holiday* be sold to generate working capital; that *American Home* be folded into the *Ladies' Home Journal*, saving millions in subscription costs. The final recommendation was to get Curtis out of the paper and manufacturing business. I accepted the Harper report with overflowing gratitude and rushed back to Curtis as though I'd found the

---

[25] Ibid., p. 125.
[26] Culligan, *The Curtis Culligan Story*, p. 35.
[27] Ibid., p. 60.

Holy Grail. Calling in my inherited key men—Bob Gibbon, secretary of the executive board; Ford Robinson, head of Operations; Leon Marks, head of Manufacturing; G. B. McCombs, number two man in Circulation—I discussed the report with them. My soaring spirits plummeted as each of the Harper recommendations was shot down in flames, not because the ideas were faulty, but because of artificial, legal, or financial strictures that appeared to block every turn.[28]

Immediate tasks.   After assuming the presidency of Curtis, Culligan was faced with several immediate tasks. Curtis owed $22 million to four creditor banks that were expressing concern over Curtis' financial position. Culligan promised an extensive cost-reduction program, and the banks agreed to a 12-month extension of the loan with a commitment for an additional $4 million in working capital. One additional stipulation added to the agreement was that Culligan would attempt to remove a debt restriction from the Curtis bylaws, which required a two-thirds vote of the preferred stockholders before management could pledge any collateral for loans. This provision protected the preferred stockholders in the case of liquidation, but it also barred long-term loans. Up to this point in time, all Curtis debt had been short-term at higher interest rates. Culligan proposed the removal of the restriction to the preferred stockholders, who eventually voted down the change.

During the period he was negotiating with the banks, Culligan also busied himself with two other major problems at Curtis: the need for cost reductions, and the increasing loss of advertising. In a move that was to have serious repercussions, Culligan called in a former colleague, J. M. Clifford, who was suffering from political infighting at NBC, and made him executive vice president of finance and operations. Clifford ordered an immediate 20% cut throughout the entire Curtis structure:

> By mid-1963 enough rank and file deadwood was chopped out of Curtis—3,500 jobs in all—to lower the annual payroll by $13 million. Printing operations were streamlined; workmen disassembled the huge mechanical innards of the Curtis building and packed the presses off to Sharon Hill. Fixed expenses dropped by $15 to $18 million annually, meaning the *Post* and the other magazines had a lower break-even per issue. According to Curtis annual reports, selling, general, and administrative expenses in 1961 were $62.6 million; this was down to $58.2 million in 1962 and $44.9 million in 1963. Production and delivery expenses dropped from $116.3 million to $106.5 and $103.2 million in the same stages.[29]

With the internal organization left to Clifford, Culligan set out to do what he knew best, selling.

> Curtis was bleeding to death. Too much unnecessary expense and not enough advertising income would bury Curtis by January 1963, unless . . . .
>
> I was the "unless"; no one else was in a position to deliver. This statement is not intended to be boastful—the burden was actually on

---

[28] Ibid., pp. 60–61.
[29] Friedrich, *Decline and Fall*, p. 64.

my shoulders. No amount of promotion, advertising, or sales calls by others would suffice. So I followed my instinct and decided on an unprecedented personal sales effort. I determined to do what no other executive in United States business had ever done—call personally on the heads of America's two hundred leading corporations within six months.[30]

Culligan, noted for his travels by helicopter, and described as a "rambunctious figure whose black eye patch had become a trade-mark,"[31] began selling the presidents of the nation's largest companies on the *Post:*

> The new president set out on an orgy of salesmanship, with press agents keeping track of every move. It was said that he traveled 3,500 miles a week to sell ads. It was said that he flew to Detroit and made presentations to General Motors, Chrysler, and Lincoln-Mercury all in one day. It was said that he signed $30 million in new ads within his first month. "From late fall of 1962 through the spring of 1963," said Culligan, "I ran Curtis almost entirely by telephone, memo and crash personal meetings at airports, in cars roaring along turnpikes, in the Curtis plane (a sturdy old twin Beech), and even a helicopter, which I leased, to cut down the time wasted getting from New York to Philadelphia." He expressed his philosophy by saying, "I had two choices. I could have stayed in Philadelphia and listened to everybody's problems, or I could go out and start selling, and let the problems take care of themselves."[32]

Despite Culligan's selling efforts, advertising revenue of the *Post* continued to decrease, from $86 million in 1961 to $66 million in 1962 to $60 million in 1963. Curtis' losses, which had been $4 million in 1961, soared to $18.9 million in 1962, then decreased to $3.4 million in 1963, the first year for which Culligan was fully responsible. But part of the improvement was of an accounting nature. At the time of Culligan's takeover, Price Waterhouse, attempting to get Curtis' business, had suggested that Curtis change its accounting policies and handle subscription liabilities in the same manner as most other publishing firms. Following this advice, Curtis spread its subscription liabilities over the life of the subscriptions and thus decreased its losses for 1963 from $10 million to $3.4 million.

By mid-1963, Culligan was again faced with the problem of the short-term bank loans coming due. Assistance came in the form of Serge Semenenko, vice president of the First National Bank of Boston. Russian-born Semenenko was considered one of the "mystery men" of U.S. finance. His loans from the First for the period 1920–1950 "practically supported the United States film industry,"[33] and his list of corporate "saves" included Fairbanks, Whitney; The International Paper Company; the Hearst publishing empire, and the Kindall Company.

By August 17, which was the deadline on the short-term loans to

---

[30] Culligan, *The Curtis Culligan Story*, pp. 78–79.
[31] Friedrich, *Decline and Fall*, p. 4.
[32] Ibid., p. 64.
[33] Goulden, *The Curtis Caper*, p. 157.

Curtis in 1963, Culligan and Semenenko had agreed on a $35 million loan from six banks.

> Semenenko doesn't sign blank checks, however, and especially when they are for $35 million. From Curtis he elicited a pledge that all management decisions be "reasonably satisfactory" to him, as the designated agent of the banking syndicate. As a service fee Semenenko's bank got ¼ of one per cent of the loan ($87,500)—plus, of course, its interest, one per cent above the prime rate on its share of the total loan.
>
> There is conflicting testimony on just how active a role Semenenko took for himself in the day-to-day conduct of Curtis' affairs. One former executive maintains that Culligan "wouldn't push the elevator button without calling Serge." This is disputed, however, by Cary W. Bok. "All he asks is that he be kept informed of what's going on," Bok said recently. "So long as he is given complete information on what management is doing, he's satisfied." Bok had unconcealed admiration for Semenenko.
>
> "Were it not for Semenenko," he said, "Curtis would have been dead. . . . He is a quiet little genius who inspires confidence in everything he touches."[34]

Corporate infighting. Although it appeared in early 1964, with the bank loans refinanced and a modest first-quarter profit for Curtis, that Culligan's major problems were over, internal problems were about to erupt that he had not anticipated. These problems were precipitated by Clay Blair, Jr., a Curtis executive who had aspired to Culligan's job, or, failing that, at least to the job which Culligan had given to Clifford.

Blair had come to Curtis in 1959 as assistant managing editor of the *Post* under managing editor Bill Sherrod, Blair's one-time supervisor at the Pentagon, when both had worked for *Time-Life*. When Fuoss, who had replaced Hibbs as editor in December 1961, resigned after four months, Sherrod became editor of the *Post*, with Blair moving up to managing editor. Back in 1962 Blair had been aware that Curtis was in financial trouble, that MacNeal would go, and that the result would be a void into which he might be able to move. In bidding for the presidency, Blair had hoped to gain some leverage from the fact that he was a personal friend of Admiral Lewis Strauss, formerly chairman of the Atomic Energy Commission, but currently a member of the New York brokerage firm which was providing the stimulus behind merger talks between Curtis and Doubleday & Company, book publishers. The Blair-Strauss friendship dated back to a time when Blair and his *Time-Life* colleague, James Shepley, had written a book praising Strauss' role in the development of the hydrogen bomb. What made the friendship relevant to Blair's ambitions was its implied ability to influence Doubleday.

At the same board meeting during which MacNeal had been fired, Blair had been elected vice president with unspecified responsibilities in the editorial offices of Curtis magazines. Asked by Gould what he

---

[34] Ibid., p. 163.

would do if elected president of Curtis, Blair had responded with a written report entitled "Tomorrow Morning Plan":

> Blair's recommendations were Draconian. For one, he recommended the liquidation of the *Ladies' Home Journal* and *American Home* which were losing several million dollars a year. He recommended selling the Curtis Building in Philadelphia, getting rid of the paper mills, tightening the Curtis Circulation Company, moving everything except printing and distribution to New York. For the *Post* he recommended a deliberate reduction in circulation from 6.5 to 5 million.[35]

Blair recounted that his "Tomorrow Morning Plan" had upset ex-president Fuller, who was still a power at Curtis as a member of the board and of its executive committee. Blair attributed his inability to attain the presidency of Curtis to Fuller's opposition:

> "Walter Fuller invited me privately to his office, a gloomy, oak-paneled room with a fireplace, on the fourth floor of the Curtis Building," Blair recalled. "It was Fuller who had integrated Curtis, bought the paper companies, built the Sharon Hill printing plant. Now he seemed disturbed that I wanted to divest them."[36]

After Culligan was chosen as president, Blair was placed in the newly created position of editorial director of all Curtis magazines, a position above that of his old boss and mentor, Sherrod. Blair related a conversation between Gould, Culligan, and himself on the day of Culligan's takeover:

> "Culligan," Gould said, "you're Mr. Outside." Then turning to me: "Blair," he said, "you're Mr. Inside." He paced the floor and puffed on a huge cigar. "Culligan, you bring in the advertising and straighten out the image of this company. Blair, you keep the books, fix the products, and deal with manufacturing and the rest of it." It was an eloquent proposition, and when he finished, Culligan and I took the deal, with Culligan pledging then that "no one will ever come between us." We shook hands all around.[37]

If Blair had believed that he would be "Mr. Inside," he was quickly disappointed, for Culligan in effect turned this position over to Clifford.

> The conflict between Clifford and Blair came quickly and inevitably. They fought over every one of the technical and financial problems that lie at the heart of corporate power. "During 1963, Clifford got a throttle hold on the company," Blair said later. "He took over circulation, manufacturing, and paper mills, then accounting, personnel, and legal. He brought in three obnoxious lieutenants: Maurice Poppei, controller; Gloria Swett, legal; Sidney Natkin, personnel. By summer, Clifford's control of money and people was so complete that nobody, including me, could hire or fire or give a raise or sign a check without his specific approval."[38]

[35] Friedrich, *Decline and Fall*, p. 32.
[36] Ibid., p. 33.
[37] Ibid., pp. 33–34.
[38] Ibid., p. 50.

By January 1964, Blair was refusing to permit any of Clifford's staff on the editorial floors of the Curtis Building in New York. Clifford retaliated by refusing any cooperation of the corporate operations and finance areas that he controlled. The conflict grew to include not only Blair, but most of the Curtis editors. Recognizing that action had to be taken, Culligan gave Clifford a $20,000 raise and removed him from his position as executive vice president of finance and operations. Culligan temporarily took over the duties of operations, which consisted mainly of manufacturing, and gave the financial responsibilities to Maurice Poppei, then treasurer.

Changing editorial policy.   At the same time he was fighting Clifford, Blair was also solidifying his control over the editorial pages of the Curtis magazines. Two months after becoming editorial director, Blair announced that he was taking over the editorship of the *Post* and that Sherrod would go to India to produce a story on Nehru with Norman Rockwell, the *Post* cover artist. Blair asserted his control over the other magazines by immediately firing the editor of the *Ladies' Home Journal* and three members of the *Journal*'s art department.

As editor of the *Post*, Blair set out to change the magazine:

> Blair really needed only a few weeks, all in all, to change the entire magazine—not just what it published, photographic covers, investigations and exposés, fiction by celebrities, and raucous editorials, but the way it operated. Instead of letting editors putter along in their departmental specialties, he insisted on getting everyone involved in the continuous uproar. And at the end of these first few weeks, in January of 1963, he sent us all a memorandum: ". . . You are putting out one hell of a fine magazine. The articles are timely, full of significance and exclusivity. The . . . visual aspects have improved tremendously. . . . [Fiction] could be one of the great breakthroughs in magazine publishing. The final yardstick: We have about six lawsuits pending, meaning we are hitting them where it hurts, with solid, meaningful journalism."[39]

One of the lawsuits was to cost the Curtis Publishing Company over $1 million. The *Post* had published an exposé of an alleged football fix between the coaches Butts of Georgia and Bryant of Alabama. Even though Georgia's Attorney General concluded that the evidence "indicates that vital and important information was given about the Georgia team, and that it could have affected the outcome of the game and the margin of points scored,"[40] Butts won his libel suit, and the *Post* settled with Bryant out of court.

Building coalitions against Culligan.   During the days of corporate infighting and changing editorial policy, Blair was busy building coalitions against Culligan. He formed an Editorial Board consisting of the editors of the major Curtis magazines, with the idea "that it might serve as a political tool to offset the tremendous corporate political drives of Culligan and Clifford."[41] Blair also formed an alliance with

[39] Ibid., p. 40.
[40] Ibid., p. 461.
[41] Ibid., p. 50.

Marvin Kantor, a former member of Williston and Beane, the brokerage firm that had helped to put Gould and Stewart on the Curtis board in 1962 (and, incidentally, a firm in which Culligan's father-in-law had once been a managing partner). Kantor had joined Curtis early in 1963 as a member of the board of directors and he had become chief executive assistant to Culligan in January 1964. Kantor stepped into the power vacuum created by the fight between Blair and Clifford:

> Within three months of his arrival at Curtis, Kantor had taken charge of editorial, advertising sales, manufacturing, and just about everything else that interested him. At this point, Culligan was doing his best to portray Curtis as a company that had been saved, a company that had already moved from paralyzing losses into a state of profit by the end of 1963. Once Kantor got access to the ledgers, however, he began expressing suspicions of Culligan's optimistic predictions. In March, Curtis neared the limits of its bank credit, and Kantor brought in some new cash by selling Curtis' one, halfhearted venture in book publishing, a one-third interest in Bantam Books, for $1.9 million. Culligan got the board to agree to new investments in Curtis' printing and paper plants, but Kantor, after looking into the plants, began arguing that they should be sold, just as Blair's group had said two years earlier. And when Kantor checked Culligan's advertising forecasts for the *Post*, he decided that they were going not up but down (in actual fact, *Post* ad revenues for the first six months of 1964 eventually proved to be 17 per cent lower than similar revenues for 1963). All in all, Kantor told Blair, Joe Culligan was leading Curtis not to salvation but to ruin. The company would again lose heavily during 1964, Kantor said—perhaps another $10 million. Blair was appalled.[42]

Blair and Kantor joined forces early in 1964 in an attempt to gain the presidency and control of Curtis. They presented findings of mismanagement to individual members of the board and rallied the editorial departments behind their bid. At one time, Blair and Kantor invited a dozen of the company's leading editors and publishing executives to Manero's steak house in Greenwich, Connecticut, to plot Culligan's overthrow. Largely at Kantor's insistence, Blair was elevated to the Curtis board in February 1964 replacing Stewart.

Culligan received a temporary reprieve from the Blair and Kantor onslaught in April 1964, when it was announced that Texas Gulf Sulphur had discovered major deposits of copper, zinc, and silver, valued at up to $2 billion, just 300 feet from 110,000 acres owned by a Canadian subsidiary of Curtis, the T. S. Woollings Company. Immediately Curtis stock rose from $6 to $19.25 per share.

Although the ore find promised a degree of financial solvency for Curtis, by Labor Day 1964 Curtis' losses for the year were predicted to be $7 million, and, in actuality, would reach $14 million. The company's working capital position was also dangerously close to the $27.5 million minimum level set by the banks. Given the discrepancy between Culligan's "turn around" predictions earlier in the year and the

---

[42] Ibid., p. 76.

company's actual financial position, Blair and Kantor made their move, armed with a proposal for saving the company and with a letter signed by most of the editors asking that Culligan be stripped of his executive power.

Confrontation—An "ancient tribunal."   A confrontation took place between Blair, Kantor, and Culligan at an ensuing board meeting. Otto Friedrich, in *Decline and Fall,* discussed the composition of this tribunal at this time (Exhibit 3):

> Who, then, controlled the Curtis board of directors? Unlike many boards, which are acquiescent allies of the reigning management, the Curtis directors were divided into a number of factions, which not only were hostile to one another but scarcely even comprehended one another. The chairman was Joe Culligan, who counted on the support of his own appointees—Clifford and Poppei—but their loyalties were less than certain. Clifford, having been demoted from the Number Two position by Culligan, apparently believed that he himself would be a more efficient president than Culligan. Poppei's loyalties seemed to belong partly to Culligan, partly to Clifford, partly to the discipline of the accountant's profession. On the insurgent side, Blair spoke only for himself and the editors. Kantor had made himself an ally of Blair's but still had ties to the stock interests that had brought him to the board in the first place. The most ambiguous of all these new directors was Milton Gould, once the attorney for Kantor, once the discoverer of Culligan. Gould was also a partner in the law firm of Gallop, Climenko & Gould, and since the *Post* alone paid him more than $600,000 a year for legal expenses, Gould had a natural interest in this aspect of Curtis.
>
> Since none of the main antagonists could create a majority, their conflicts served as a kind of ballet staged for the amusement of the old board members, who represented a plurality of the stock, and who retained a veto over any attempts to save the corporation. Of these old board members, the basic group was known as "the family," which owned 32 per cent of all common stock and officially consisted of two people: Mary Louise Curtis Bok Zimbalist, then aged eighty-eight, the daughter of Cyrus H. K. Curtis, who occasionally was wheeled into critical board meetings by her Negro servants; and her son, Cary W. Bok, aged fifty-nine, who was in rather poor health but periodically came to Philadelphia, dressed in the old Khakis that he liked to wear at his country place in Maine. (There was another son, Curtis Bok, who might have helped to save the company, but that was not to be. Lorimer had denounced him a generation earlier as "that damned Bolshevik," and things were arranged so that Curtis Bok would never have a voice in the operation of the Curtis magazines. He went on to become a distinguished judge, and his son was recently made dean of the Harvard Law School.) As for Mrs. Zimbalist, let us remember her by a story told by a retired executive. Once a year, according to this chronicler, Mrs. Zimbalist would engage in exactly the same colloquy with Walter Deane Fuller, who was then president of the corporation. "She would very respectfully ask Mr. Fuller that her salary as a director be doubled. Very gravely he would reply that economic conditions were such that this could not be done. She would thank him and

sit down. Of course, her salary was only one dollar. But she and Mr. Fuller seemed to enjoy the byplay."

The rest of the old directors tended to support "the family," to the extent that they could determine what the family wanted, but Mrs. Zimbalist and her son rarely attended board meetings during these declining years—refusing either to sell the stocks they had held all their lives or to exercise the authority that these stocks gave them. The old directors were thus left to decide matters for themselves, and for this, they were of an age and distinction that would have done credit to the United States Senate. The most senior of them, of course, was Walter Deane Fuller, the tiny, bald gentleman of eighty-two, who had joined the accounting department of Curtis in 1908 and worked his way up to be president and board chairman for more than twenty-five years. Next came M. Albert Linton, seventy-seven, retired president of the Provident Life Insurance Company of Philadelphia and now chairman of the board's executive committee, assigned to deal with the accusations. Then there was Walter S. Franklin, aged eighty, retired president of the Pennsylvania Railroad; and Ellsworth Bunker, aged seventy, former president of the United Sugar Company, former U.S. Ambassador to India, former president of the American Red Cross; Moreau D. Brown, aged sixty-one, partner in the private banking firm of Brown Brothers, Harriman; Harry C. Mills, aged sixty-three, retired vice president of J. C. Penney; and Curtis Barkes, aged fifty-eight, executive vice president of United Air Lines.

Once the managerial civil war had broken out, it soon became apparent that this board, this ultimate court of appeals, knew relatively little about the Curtis Publishing Company and was quite bewildered by the problems that were being placed before it. More than half the directors were over sixty—"Why," someone asked Clemenceau, "are the presidents of France always octogenarians?" And Clemenceau replied: "Because we have run out of nonagenarians"—and most of them, except for the actual combatants, were weary of combat. Thus, when Blair and Culligan wanted to accuse each other of guilt for Curtis' condition, they had to carry their case before this ancient tribunal, which, in consenting to hear the arguments, denied that the ultimate guilt was its own.[43]

The result of the confrontation was the immediate dismissal of Blair and Kantor on October 30, 1964, and the eventual removal of Culligan from the presidency. Culligan's removal was announced after a meeting of several of the directors at Bok's apartment in Philadelphia. Culligan, not allowed to attend, found out a year later that Clifford and Poppei had threatened to resign if Culligan remained as president.

Rumors began to circulate as to who the next president of Curtis would be. Reportedly the job had been offered to Newton Minow, chairman of the FCC under Kennedy and to Ed Miller, publisher of *McCall's*, both of whom turned the position down. Miller commented on his reasons for rejecting the presidency of Curtis:

---

[43] Ibid., pp. 125–127. Reprinted from *Decline and Fall* by permission of Harper and Row. © 1969–1970 Otto Friedrich.

I came in ready to sign a contract that morning. The amount of money was almost embarrassing—$150,000 a year. But I had other conditions. One was that the banks guarantee a period of grace of twenty-four months, without anybody blowing the whistle, because no miracle would work in less than twenty-four months. Then the other element was John Kluge, the head of Metromedia. We talked to him about taking over the financial responsibilities, and Kluge loved the idea, but his bankers didn't see it in the same light. So that morning, I learned that neither of these conditions would be met, and I said, "To hell with it," and walked out.[44]

The Clifford presidency: 1964–1968

Apparently the board's difficulty in finding a new chief executive and the banks' increasing concern over Curtis' financial position created a situation into which Clifford could move. Clifford, supported by the second most senior board member, Linton, made a bid for the presidency and was accepted in December 1964.

Once in power, Clifford fired several editors, demanded that the magazines cut their budgets by 40%, appointed acting editor William Emerson editor of the Post, and changed the Post into a bi-weekly publication.

Worried about the $37.3 million that Curtis owed the banks, Clifford sold a paper mill in Pennsylvania for $10.3 million and used $8 million for debt reduction. He also negotiated $24 million in cash from Texas Gulf Sulphur for mining rights on Curtis' Canadian timberlands and utilized the money to pay off bank debts. During 1965, Curtis' assets decreased from $112.6 to $86.9 million with liabilities decreasing from $103 to $68.4 million. Curtis lost $3.4 million in 1965 and showed an operating profit of $347,000 in 1966, the first profit of the decade. Otto Friedrich described the method by which Clifford produced this profit:

The technique was simple. The conscientious employees worked hard at their jobs, because that was their nature, and then the supreme command ordered everyone to cut costs until the year's activities came out even on the balance sheets. This was not simply a matter of operating expenses. It was a philosophy of life. It was a perfect example, however, of the cost accountants' system of doing business—to cut, shrink, tighten, until we reached the theoretical goal of not producing anything at all. Or, as Emerson put it, "It's like being nibbled to death by ducks."[45]

The nibbling apparently would not save Curtis. The company recorded a loss of $4.8 million for 1967, which Clifford blamed on an advertising decline "due primarily to softened national economic conditions and costly strikes in key industries."[46] The company's cash position during this period became dangerously low:

As of the end of the year, current assets had declined by more than $6 million, liabilities had increased by more than $1 million, and

---

[44] Ibid., p. 172.
[45] Ibid., p. 270.
[46] Ibid., p. 307.

actual cash in hand had dropped from $10,102,000 at the start of 1967 to $425,000 at the start of 1968. Obviously, for a company that was operating on a budget of almost $130 million a year, a cash supply of $425,000 was virtually no cash at all.[47]

The low cash position necessitated a quick cash inflow. Clifford attempted to sell the old Curtis building in Philadelphia and offered CBS Curtis' magazines for $15 million provided CBS gave Curtis a printing and distribution contract. CBS reportedly was amazed, since they had just done a study on Curtis which indicated that the magazines alone would earn $10 million a year without the other Curtis overhead.

Ackerman takes over

Into this precarious financial position, with the banks reportedly pushing for a management change, stepped Martin Ackerman, who was quickly pressed into service as Curtis' next president. Aged 36, Ackerman, a former lawyer, was currently head of Perfect Film & Chemical Corporation, a conglomerate he had pushed from sales of $20 million in 1962 to $100 million in 1964 through a series of acquisitions.

Ackerman has related the origin of his interest in Curtis and also the events of a special meeting of the Curtis board in April 1968 that led to his entry into Curtis management:

> J. M. Clifford, then president of Curtis, reported a proposal which I had made under which Perfect Film & Chemical Corporation, which I headed, would arrange for a $5 million loan to Curtis. This loan was to be secured and guaranteed, and would give Perfect Film a chance to see whether the combinations of the activities of the two corporations made any sense. The proposal was discussed at length, along with a number of alternate proposals for obtaining the immediate capital needed by the company. Later in the afternoon, Milton Gould, a director, told the Board that I had informed him that the Perfect proposal was subject to withdrawal if not accepted then and there at the meeting. Accompanied by former governor Alfred Driscoll, another director, I was invited to attend the board meeting for about twenty minutes.
>
> After further discussion, my proposal was approved and I was elected a regular director, along with Eugene Mason, Perfect's attorney. Clifford was voted out of the presidency of Curtis and elected chairman of the Board of Directors. I was made president in his place.[48]

Ackerman began his presidency in April 1968 by arranging a two-month extension of all overdue bank loans and outlining a plan to save the *Post*. Ackerman announced that the *Post*'s circulation would be cut from 6.8 million to 3 million and that the *Post* would be promoted "as a magazine of class, not mass."[49]

In August 1968, Ackerman issued a report on the financial position at Curtis for the first half of 1968. A loss of $7 million on revenues of

---

[47] Ibid., pp. 307–308.

[48] Martin Ackerman, *The Curtis Affair* (Los Angeles: Nash Publishing, 1970), pp. 8–9.

[49] Friedrich, *Decline and Fall*, p. 328.

$58 million was reported, compared to a loss of $370,000 on revenues of $63 million for the first half of the previous year. He also disclosed that Curtis' bank loans of $13.2 million had been taken over by Perfect Film from the Semenenko group at an interest rate of one per cent above the prime rate with maturity on demand.

During his first six months at Curtis, while liquidating part of the Curtis empire, Ackerman also worked incessantly at the *Post* offices in New York, developing schemes to save the magazine, and attempting to write editorials and a column for it (much to the dismay of the editors). But with increased losses for 1968 becoming more evident, Ackerman moved out of the Curtis offices into a town house he had purchased. Friedrich describes the changes that ensued:

> An environment not only expresses a man's ambitions; it also changes his perspectives. The Ackerman who sat enthroned in the town house was not the same man who bustled in and out of offices on our editorial floor. Now, he received us only by appointment, negotiated through one of his two secretaries, and we appeared not as the managers of our own domain but as emissaries to his castle. And in the act of physical withdrawal from the Curtis building, he inevitably withdrew, to some extent, from his intense physical involvement in the day-to-day problems of the *Post*. This was quite understandable, too, for in six months of hard labor, his involvement had really accomplished relatively little. And so, as all executives like to fall back on the specialties that originally brought them their success, Ackerman in his town house began to revert to what he had been before he ever came to Curtis, a financier, a maneuverer of stocks and corporations, an expert at mergers and acquisitions, a banker and millionaire.[50]

As a financier and maneuverer of stocks and corporations, Ackerman reportedly was a master. For example, ostensibly to raise cash for Curtis, he sold the *Ladies' Home Journal* and *American Home* to Downe Communications, Inc., for 100,000 shares of Downe stock valued at $5.4 million, a price low enough to "evoke the image of a fire sale."[51] He later had Curtis turn the Downe stock over to Perfect Film for a $4.5 million reduction in the Curtis loans and then sold the stock privately through a Wall Street firm for $5 million.

> The same day that his sale of the Downe shares was disclosed, it was announced that Perfect Film was spending $9 million to buy from Gulf & Western two Desilu film studios in Culver City, California, the fourteen-acre Culver Studio and the twenty-nine-acre Culver Backlot, both of which were being used by Paramount and various television producers.[52]

But for all Ackerman's financial wizardry, by early 1969 he apparently had neither the ability nor the desire to save the *Post*. The predicted losses for the *Post* for 1969 were between $3.7 and $7 million, based on the trend of decreasing advertising revenue.

Utilizing this financial data as justification, Ackerman, who six

---

[50] Ibid., p. 416.
[51] Ibid., p. 417.
[52] Ibid.

months before had stated that as long as he was at Curtis "there would not be a last issue of the *Post*,"[53] announced the end:

> No other decision is possible in view of the sizable predicted losses which continued publication would have generated. Quite simply, this is an example of a new management which could not reduce expenses nor generate sales and income fast enough to halt mounting losses. . . . Having refinanced the Saturday Evening Post Company with $15 million in new capital, I assured directors and stockholders of the company that regardless of my own personal feelings, if we could not return a profit we would have to shut down the *Post*.[54]

The reaction from the stockholders was immediate. Philip Kalodner, a young Philadelphia lawyer and representative of minority stockholders, filed suit against Ackerman for alleged illegal, oppressive, and fraudulent action that had wasted and misapplied more than $45 million of Curtis assets. The trustees of the Cyrus Curtis estate also began an assault against Ackerman:

> They, too, accused Ackerman of dissipating the Curtis assets, and they publicly demanded that he resign from the presidency by noon on the coming Saturday, February 8. They also demanded the resignations of his closest allies on the board of directors. The trustees were vague in their accusations, citing only "conflict of interest," but Cary Bok told a reporter who telephoned his home in Camden, Maine: "That company is in such a damn mess that it's time we got into it—don't you think?"[55]

POSTSCRIPT

At the next board meeting (March 1969), Ackerman resigned as president in favor of G. B. McCombs, who had recently been promoted to senior vice president, after being with Curtis since 1930. Kalodner, who held only 100 shares of stock, was named vice president, director, and a member of the executive committee "in return for agreement not to press his lawsuit against the company."[56]

McCombs lasted five weeks as president; the position then went to Kalodner after some stormy meetings of the board:

> The board itself, depleted by the latest resignations of Ackerman, Gould, and McCombs, now consisted of only six members (one of whom was serving as U.S. Ambassador to Saigon). Three of these had been allies of the departed Milton Gould, and they all favored a petition of bankruptcy. "But I spoke up against them," Kalodner said. "In fact, I filibustered against them." The board meeting went on for five hours, and then ended inconclusively. And the day after the crisis, Kalodner simply decreed himself to be, if not the president of Curtis, then "chief executive officer." Once again, Curtis was without a president.
> The deadlock lasted through most of April, and then, on April 24,

[53] *Newsweek*, May 20, 1968, p. 70.
[54] Friedrich, *Decline and Fall*, p. 449.
[55] Ibid., p. 466.
[56] Ibid., p. 469.

it was broken long enough for Kalodner, like yet another Roman emperor, to become president. In that capacity, he offered repeated invitations to the unhappy trustees to "join" him in salvaging the wreckage of the company, but the trustees had no intention of collaborating in Kalodner's presidency. Kalodner alone, therefore, had the responsibility of announcing that the Curtis operating loss during the Ackerman year of 1968 had been $18.3 million. He also had to admit that the Curtis contract to print the *Ladies' Home Journal* and *American Home* for Downe Communications would run out at the end of June. "The contract," said *The Wall Street Journal*, "is practically the only ongoing venture Curtis has left."[57]

Kalodner and the trustees spent the early weeks of May 1969 mailing rival proxy statements to the stockholders in anticipation of the May 21 stockholders' meeting. At the meeting the trustees won nine seats on the board of directors, and a representative of the trustees, Arthur Murphy, past president of *McCall's*, took over as president and chairman of the board. A short time later, Murphy dropped the presidency, and W. J. MacIntosh, a lawyer for the board, took over as acting chief executive officer.

In May of 1970, the trustees sold the 700,000 shares of Curtis stock they had controlled since 1933 to Beurt SerVaas, a self-made millionaire from the Mid-West, who took over control as president and principal stockholder of Curtis. SerVaas related his initial actions as head of the company as follows:

> "I came into this company to preside over its death, but instead I decided I could save it," he said. "I'm the first person since Cyrus Curtis himself who's been both the chief executive and the chief stockholder, and so I've had the kind of authority you have to have in order to make vital decisions."
>
> Throughout the summer and fall Mr. SerVaas proceeded to make a series of "vital decisions." He sold all the manufacturing companies that Curtis owned, including a printing plant and a paper mill, decreased the over-all size of its staff from 9,000 people to 100, and "reduced its voluminous debts to zero."
>
> It was the burden of these financial responsibilities that prevented the company from reaping profits, Mr. SerVaas explained.
>
> "Now we're no longer in manufacturing and real estate," he added, "we're just a little publishing company that puts out magazines, and for the first time in years we're no longer in the red."[58]

SerVaas has decided that the *Post* will return to publication as a "200 page quarterly directed toward the 'middle American.' "

> "Toward the end the *Post* became worldly and sophisticated and hard-nosed in an attempt to rejuvenate itself," Mr. SerVaas said, "but it failed, and what we intend to do now should make everyone happy. We're not going to print any more exposés or muckraking articles; we're going to concentrate on writing about those institutions and mores in contemporary America that are good for America."[59]

---

[57] Ibid., pp. 472–473.

[58] *The New York Times,* November 6, 1970.

[59] Ibid.

Exhibit 1

FINANCIAL HIGHLIGHTS: 1960–1969

(dollars in millions)

Year	Operating revenues[a]	Operating profit[b]	Net profit	Stockholders' equity[c]	Current assets	Current liabilities	Total assets
1960	$192.8 (restated)	$ 3.5	$ 1.6	$ 49.7	$60.7	$23.3	$133.5
1961	178.4	(8.7)	(4.2)[d]	46.8[e]	56.7	24.5	135.5
1962	149.3	(21.0)	(18.9)[f]	27.9	55.6	41.9	127.8
1963	152.0	(1.4)	(3.4)	24.5	53.8	19.0	123.0
1964	139.4	(13.0)	(13.9)[g]	9.5	46.7	18.5	112.7
1965	122.7	(0.7)	(3.4)	20.5[h]	39.9	22.6	88.9
1966	128.8	2.0	0.3	21.5	44.4	24.6	94.6
1967	124.6	(3.2)	(4.8)	16.7	38.3	25.9	91.5
1968	98.7	(15.2)	(20.9)[i]	2.0[j]	16.7	19.8	43.6
1969	32.0	(10.7)	(19.4)[k]	(14.7)[l]	10.1	15.4	20.3

Note: Parentheses indicate deficit figures.

a Reflects advertising and circulation revenue (net of commissions), paper sales, and miscellaneous operations.

b After production and delivery expense, SGA, and depreciation, but before interest (ranging between $1.2 million and $2.7 million 1960–1968) and miscellaneous income and expenses.

c Includes prior preferred ($16.7 million), preferred ($2.4 million), common ($3.6 million), capital surplus (under $1 million) and undivided profits. As of December 31, 1969, arrears on preferred were $8.9 million.

d Reflects $3.5 million gain on sale of securities and $1.3 million tax credit.

e Reflects $1.7 million transferred to surplus from reserves.

f Reflects $3.8 million tax credit.

g Reflects $1.8 million profit on sale of securities.

h Reflects $14.3 million profit on sale of properties.

i Reflects $1.6 million loss on Saturday Evening Post, and $2.6 million net extraordinary charges (after $20 million provision for plant obsolescence and $1.5 million for future loss on home-office lease, partly offset by gains of $1.1 million on sale of property, $3.4 million on sale of circulation and subscription companies, $13.7 million on sale of Ladies' Home Journal and American Home, and $.7 million gain from reduction in Post circulation).

j Reflects $6.1 million recovery of pension plan funding.

k Reflects $8.3 million in net extraordinary charges associated with curtailment of operations.

l Reflects $2.7 million additional recovery of pension plan funding.

Sources: Curtis Publishing Company, Annual Reports, and Moody's Industrial Manual.

Exhibit 2
THE POWER STRUGGLE AT CURTIS—HOW THEY ROSE AND FELL

	1961	1962	1963	1964	1965	1966	1967	1968	1969
CHAIRMAN OF THE BOARD	Vacant since 1957			Mathew Culligan		Vacant			Vacant / Thos Moses / Arthur Murphy
PRESIDENT	Robert MacNeal (since 1950)		Mathew Culligan			John Clifford		Martin Ackerman	Arthur Murphy
HEAD OF MAGAZINE DIVISION			Created in April 1963 / John Veronis	Marvin Kantor	Vacant		G. B. McCombs		
POST EDITOR	Ben Hibbs (since 1942)	Robert Sherrod	Clay Blair		Vacant	William Emerson			
NO. 2 POST EDITOR	Robert Fuoss (since 1942)	Clay Blair	Davis Thomas*l	Don Schanche*	William Emerson	Otto Friedrich			
NO. 3 POST EDITOR	Robert Sherrod (since 1955)	Vacant	Don Schanche*	William Emerson	Otto Friedrich	Don McKinney*			
TOP POST ADVERTISING EXECUTIVE	Peter Schruth* (since 1957)		C.L. MacNelly*	Vacant		Jess Ballew*		Stephen Kelly*	
MAIN EVENTS IN THE DECLINE AND FALL OF CURTIS	September 1961 Disastrous revamping of Post. December 1961 Curtis loses money for the first time.	July 1962 Blair hires new editors. September 1962 Post moves to New York.	March 1963 Butts article brings libel suits for $20 million. September 1963 Semenenko loans Curtis $35 million.	April 1964 Copper found under Curtis land. September 1964 Blair's rebels meet at Manero's. October 1964 Blair-Kantor dismissal.	January 1965 Post becomes a biweekly. October 1965 Clifford sells copper land for $24 million.	December 1966 Curtis manages a "mini-profit."	March 1967 Clifford purges Schanche. July 1967 Clifford purges Ballew.	April 1968 Ackerman arrives with $5 million.	January 1969 Ackerman kills Post. February 1969 Ackerman is sued. March 1969 Ackerman resigns.
FINANCIAL POSITION	LOSS $4 Million	LOSS $19 Million	LOSS $3.5 Million	LOSS $14 Million	LOSS $3.5 Million	PROFIT $347 Thousand	LOSS $5 Million	LOSS $18 Million	IN AUDIT

DEATH OF THE POST

* Not mentioned in text.
Source: Otto Friedrich, Decline and Fall (New York, Harper & Row, Publishers, 1969), end papers.

Exhibit 3
THE CURTIS BOARD, 1964

(clockwise from Blair, nearest camera): John Clifford, Marvin Kantor, Walter Franklin, Harry Mills, M. Albert Linton, Mary Curtis Bok Zimbalist, Matthew Culligan, Gloria Swett, Cary Bok, Walter Fuller, Moreau Brown, Curtis Barkes, and Milton Gould.

Marks and Spencer, Ltd (A)

THE PRINCIPLES on which the business was founded do not change. The original ideas have been expanded to conform to the changing requirements of a more knowledgeable and discerning public—a public which has broadened to include wider strata of the community.

In the course of the years, we have built up three great assets:

The goodwill and confidence of the public.

The loyalty and devotion of management and staff throughout the system.

The confidence and cooperation of our suppliers.

The principles upon which the business is built are:

1. To offer our customers a selective range of high-quality, well-designed and attractive merchandise at reasonable prices.
2. To encourage our suppliers to use the most modern and efficient techniques of production and quality control dictated by the latest discoveries in science and technology.
3. With the cooperation of our suppliers, to enforce the highest standard of quality control.
4. To plan the expansion of our stores for the better display of a widening range of goods and for the convenience of our customers.
5. To foster good human relations with customers, suppliers, and staff.

These ideas were expressed in the Notes of Lord Marks of Broughton, chairman of Marks and Spencer, from 1916 to 1964. Operating on these principles, Marks and Spencer (M and S) had become, in the winter of 1974, the largest retail organization in the United Kingdom. The range of merchandise sold by the company included 3,000 items of textiles and other nonfoods and 700 food items. Its store on Marble Arch, London, took in more money ($1,000 per square foot) for every foot of floor space than any shop or store of any kind in the world. It owned no factories, but all products were sold under its exclusive brand name, "St. Michael." The company accounted for 12 percent of national consumer expenditures for clothing and footwear in the United Kingdom and had over a third of the market in women's briefs, slips, bras, and men's underwear.

M and S ordered approximately $25 million worth of goods every week. In Great Britain, over 13 million customers made purchases from the company's 251 stores every week. Sales per selling square foot averaged $260 (compared to the $180 average of Britain's top retailers). The annual stockturn in textiles was 8, in food, 60.

The company was managed from its head office in London, where the buying, merchandising, distribution, quality control, and finance functions were centralized. Led by a board of 22 executives, the company was enjoying record prosperity.

In 1974, sales were $1,422,109,000, up 16 percent over 1973, with a pretax profit of $180,538,000, 10 percent over 1973 pretax profit dollars. Textiles accounted for 71 percent of the total sales, while food accounted for 27 percent, and exports 2 percent. (Exhibit 1 shows the 1974 profit and loss account, balance sheet, and ten-year statement.)

Despite these results, management was concerned. The base of M and S business was England, and England was floundering as perhaps never before. National income had declined 2 percent; unemployment was 2.6 percent; and inflation was running at a rate of 15 percent— 18 percent annually. A Labour government under Harold Wilson occasionally seemed to challenge the legitimacy and morality of a free enterprise within a mixed economy. In his 1974 account statement, Sir Marcus Sieff, chairman of M and S, commented on the situation.

> We believe that if we guard the standards of our goods, improve our systems and look after both our staff and our customers, we shall continue to grow and to make profits.
>
> We need profits, after paying taxes:
>
> 1. To improve the pay and working conditions of our staff and to take care of them during retirement. The high morale and productivity of our staff owes much to these factors; most of them take pride in working for a successful business which is quality-oriented;
> 2. To have funds for investment in the develoment of the business, which is clearly desired by our many customers;
> 3. To pay a proper dividend to our 240,000 shareholders, which include many small savers, individual pensioners and pension funds.
>
> Marks and Spencer has over the years, under a private enterprise system, made a significant contribution to the economic life of the country and has helped to raise the standard of living. We doubt whether we could have achieved this under any other system.
>
> The statutory controls under which we have been operating throughout the year have taken much time to interpret and implement. They have diverted effort from the real issues of the business and have created additional elements of uncertainty. They have, and will increasingly distort our ability to meet the real needs of our customers.

Yet despite these challenges, 1975 saw M and S management embarking on some of the biggest undertakings in its history. On top of the addition of new lines of merchandise, M and S had crossed the Atlantic to open stores in Canada and was planning the opening of two French stores and one Belgian store in the spring.

HISTORY

The origins

In 1975, the descendants of M and S's founders spoke of themselves as "shopkeepers." To understand what they meant and how it influenced their strategy, it is necessary to begin with the penny bazaar of Michael Marks.

Beginning in the open market at Leeds in 1884, Michael Marks, a Polish Jew, traveled the north of England, setting up stalls in town markets. He classified his merchandise according to price—"Don't Ask the Price—It's a Penny." The slogan proved so popular that he adopted the principle of the fixed price in all his stalls [bazaars]. This method was convenient for him as well as the customer. He kept no accounts and the adoption of the fixed price simplified his calculations considerably. This policy also had another result. It meant that he had to search for as wide a variety and as high a quality of goods as could be sold for a penny. Consequently, he had to accept very low profit margins and make up for them by achieving the largest turnover (sales volume) possible.

The business flourished, and, in 1894, he took into partnership Thomas Spencer, who came from one of Marks' wholesale suppliers. By 1903, the number of branches had increased to 40. In addition, M and S moved its headquarters to Manchester, which had a very pleasant Jewish society.

It was in Manchester that the Marks formed their lifelong affiliation with their future partners, the Sieffs. Ephraim Sieff had built a business in textile wholesaling. The friendship of Simon Marks (son of Michael and later chairman of the board) and Israel Sieff (chairman of the board after Simon Marks) began in Manchester Grammar School. Later Simon married Miriam Sieff, and Israel, Becky Marks.

In 1903, Marks and Spencer, Ltd. was formed, with control entirely in Marks and Spencer family hands. In that same year, Spencer retired (and subsequently died in 1905). The period between 1908 and 1914, following the death of Michael Marks, was the only time when control of the company was not in the family hands. Nonetheless, the business continued to prosper. At the end of 1914, there were 140 branches, of which 10 percent were in market halls. Though M and S was now a fully developed chain organized on a national basis, they still preserved features characteristic of the market—open display, easy accessibility to goods, and self-selection.

By this time, another M and S characteristic had emerged. The staff was provided for as well as the customer. Every store had a heated room in which the staff ate their meals and made tea or cocoa. Since the management of the store was vital to the success of the business, a store manageress was put in charge of management training for the operation. Management tried to make work in the stores an enjoyable experience.

During World War I, the influence of Chaim Weizmann had a remarkable effect on both Simon Marks and Israel Sieff, as well as on the future policies of the firm. Weizmann was a great scientist and statesman. He drew both Marks and Sieff into the Zionist movement and encouraged their commitment to the benefits and applications of technology. Wiezmann also stimulated in them a sense of social responsibility so that they came to see, through their business, a means of creating a social service for the customer and the employee. These ideas became the cornerstones of the modern M and S.

Marks learned from other sources. A visit to America in 1924 had a profound impact on the growth of his business. In the States, Marks studied the growth and operations of the major variety chains and returned to England determined to transfer the business into a chain of "super stores." This idea implied, for him, a continuous flow of merchandise and a central organization that would be acutely sensitive to what the public wanted. These ideas gradually transformed the character of the business.

The company had become a public company in 1926. By the middle of the 1930s, M and S was represented in every town of significant size throughout the country and the geographical pattern of its development had become basically what it is today. The chain developed a character all its own and in 1928 the brand name, "St. Michael," was registered. The company was the first general store operation in the United Kingdom to pursue an exclusively "own brand" policy.

The growth of the company's staff created new responsibilities with regard to their welfare and training. Amenities for the staff included a well-appointed staff dining room, excellent meals served at very low prices, a comfortable rest room and a staff training room. Medical and dental services were also introduced into the stores. These services were directed by the welfare department, which was established in 1933. Also during that year, chiropody services at the store began. Apart from laying down a welfare policy which implemented the views and wishes of the directors, the department undertook the training of the staff manageresses, who were primarily responsible for the well-being of the staff in the stores and coordinating the welfare services available to them. In 1936 the pension plan was introduced.

Technological advances in materials and production processes in the 1930s led M and S to increasingly close cooperation with their suppliers. M and S eventually took over the wholesaler's function (a violent break in British tradition) and further promoted the brand name of St. Michael.

Textiles were not the only area in which modern technological advances were applied. Efforts to develop the food business were successful, and, by 1939, food accounted for one fifth of the company's sales.

Post-World War II development

In the 1950s, as M and S's growth escalated, the company's image changed from being a leading retailer to that of a national institution. Between 1946 and 1955, sales increased 450 percent, while pretax profits increased 351 percent. The St. Michael label gradually emerged on all products—it was a certificate of good quality and good value. The great rise in sales led to further concentration on a very limited range of goods, giving M and S a dominant position in the textile market. By 1960, textile sales were £123 million. The market share in some lines was over 33 percent. The confidence in the St. Michael label trade name carried over into its foods, where consistently high standards of hygiene were developed.

Sales growth required new storage space. The company developed a building policy that became one of continuous modernization and extension of its stores, so that at no one moment could the process ever be said to be complete. When postwar building controls were abolished in the 1950s, the rate of growth accelerated:

	Sales*	Profits	Stores	Space (average square feet)
1946..............	£ 19,693	£ 2,027	224	1,407
1955..............	108,375	9,168	234	2,461
1968..............	282,308	33,871	241	3,929
1974..............	571,650	76,825	251	5,489

* Including exports.

Simplification

Despite management's intention, the business after the war became increasingly complex. Primarily by becoming so involved in production without really manufacturing, M and S had made its business more complicated than many other retailers. And its belief in simplicity got further away from reality until February 16, 1956. Presented with a spending budget, millions in excess of the previous years, Simon Marks (Lord Marks) blew his top and began to throw out paper. Working up enthusiasm as he went along, Lord Marks began exposing every procedure and sacred routine in his empire to scrutiny. Instead of trying to improve parts of the existing system, the system itself was questioned. He said to his brother-in-law, "Israel, it's not a law of business growth that administrative costs continue to increase. Anyway, if things go on like this, we shan't be able to sell women's blouses for less than ten pounds a piece."

The goal of all the changes was to permit the store staff and management as well as *all* supporting services to focus on one task—increase of sales measured in pounds sterling. Profitability was a complexity delegated to a limited group of senior executives who determined the initial markup target applied to *all* goods. In fact, this resulted in a single initial markup target for all food items, and a single target for textiles. With margins standardized the problem for the selectors was to find quality goods that would sell at an acceptably high turnover, while for the stores the problem was to utilize space and help customers so that a maximum of goods would sell.

The general principles accepted and followed for Operation Simplification were:

1. Sensible approximation—the price of perfection is prohibitive. Where it is costly to account precisely, an approximation is likely to do just as well with considerable economies.
2. Reporting by exception—it is assumed that events will occur as arranged or anticipated.
3. Manuals—no attempt is made to legislate for every contingency and every eventuality. Before simplification there were 13 instruction manuals, now there are basically 2 small booklets: *Guide to Staff Management* and *Store Regulations*.
4. Decategorization—people have been removed from watertight compartments and placed in general categories.
5. Most people can be trusted—now this principle is accepted. In short, checks and nonchecks can be eliminated. This, in turn, saves time, staff and money and leads to increased self-confidence and a sense of responsibility among staff. Management control can be effectively exercised by selective and occasional spot checks, which are usually more satisfactory and productive and certainly less costly than a whole series of permanent control systems and continuous routine checks.

At the head office, managers of departments or groups were responsible for the efficiency of the activities under their control, including the improvement of methods, procedures and forms (or their abolition). One of the significant benefits resulting from the operation was that senior officers were not constantly tied to their desks or bogged down with paper work; they were able to become personally involved and concerned in the efficient management of the activities under their charge.

The savings included 26 million pieces of paper per year representing 120 tons in weight. (There was a symbolic bonfire of old records.) A total staff of 32,000 was at one point reduced to 22,000 and the head office establishment was pruned by a third. The reduction in staff resulted from nonreplacement of personnel who left, not termination.

But there was more to the drive for simplicity than savings on paper. The central theme was that paper came between management and the people who had the knowledge to run the business. In 1969 Lord Sieff wrote to his management:

> Both the executives and the merchandisers of the departments should *probe* into the goods in the stores *with seeing eyes and a critical mind.* The departmental supervisor and the sales girl are his best sources of

information. To depend on statistics is to asphyxiate the dynamic spirit of the business.

As the administrative process placed more emphasis on people, M and S improved the amenities provided to its staff. In 1956 a social and recreational center was established at the head office, and various social clubs were established at individual stores. Weekly visits of chiropractors to the stores were added to the list of amenities. The pension plan was also improved.

In 1964, Lord Simon Marks died in his office. His brother-in-law, Lord Israel Sieff, Lord Marks' associate in business and Zionism since 1909, brought to M and S a broad and humanistic view of what the object of business should be. He believed that the purposes of M and S were "to make a profit and serve the community."

> M and S started with people. We [Lord Marks and I] both felt that making people happy was the great thing in life. So, when we got into the stores, we automatically thought in these lines. For instance, we found that the girls were going without lunch when they were broke or busy. So we put in lunchrooms and saw to it that they got time to eat their meals.

In addition to expansion within the United Kingdom, M and S had built up the export of St. Michael goods. The company developed a close relationship with retailers abroad, exporting to 159 retailers in 41 countries, who operated "St. Michael" shops in departments stocked exclusively with M and S merchandise. In July 1972, a company was formed jointly with People's Department Stores Limited of Canada, under the name of St. Michael Shops of Canada Limited.

Nineteen hundred and seventy-two marked another successful transition year in the management of M and S. The chairmanship passed from J. Edward Sieff to his nephew, Sir Marcus Sieff (Lord Sieff's son). Michael Sacher and Michael Sieff became vice chairmen.[1]

The philosophy under Sir Marcus continued to develop from the social philosophy summed up by his father, Lord Sieff:

> The main purpose of building up a great business should not be merely to make money. A company has its responsibilities, not only to the shareholders, but also to the staff, the customer, and the whole community in which it trades. Unless it gives satisfaction, and even happiness to all concerned, it will fail in its aims in the long run. . . . Long-term success calls for a simple, human approach.

In order to understand the sources of M and S's success, the researchers observed the work of the management board, its senior executives, and in addition, the operating departments and stores. They quickly concluded that the comment of Mr. Brian Howard was apt. "Management at M and S," he said, "is concerned with a flow that begins with the manufacturers of synthetic fibers or the import of raw goods and ends with what we hope is a steady movement of merchandise across store counters."

---

[1] Michael Sacher's father had married a second daughter of Michael Marks.

The remainder of this case study reflects the M and S organization for handling this flow beginning with the marketing philosophy and then following the flow from manufacturers on to the work of the stores. The concluding sections are concerned with the top management: the process and style with which the organization was managed. Exhibit 2 is an organizational chart.

The marketing philosophy

The essence of M and S's approach to marketing was summarized by the late Lord Sieff:

> The future of the business depends on quick imaginative study of what the people need—not of what the public can be persuaded to buy; but of what the people really need. Only in supplying real needs will a business flourish in the long term. Only by giving the people what on reflection they continue to want will a business earn the respect of the customer, which is essential to anything more durable than a cheap-jack's overnight success. So long as Marks and Spencer continues to study what the people need, and efficiently produce it by means of a staff humanely organized, we can meet any economic trend and any economic challenge. Efficient and humane adaptation to the needs of the people is the first and last principle of Marks and Spencer. It is, in my view, the goal of all really enterprising concerns.

The company believed in, and practiced, offering quality for value. Although the prices were in the middle range, rather than being low, the quality of the product added considerable value to the purchase. It was this combination of quality and price that encouraged consumers to associate M and S with "value for your money."

The range of offering was selected, as was the range of initial markups. M and S believed in offering only those items that would produce rapid turnover. In order to accomplish this objective, it streamlined its merchandise offering. In Lord Sieff's words, "In each section there are a few lines which do a large percentage of the business and, generally speaking, it is these items, the development of which merit our first consideration. It is no use wasting time on articles which can have no future."

The 3,000-item range of textile products included: ladies' blouses, pants, skirts, dresses, suits, coats, dressing gowns, beachwear, knitted sweaters, tops, hosiery and underwear; men's ties and accessories, socks, suits, dressing gowns, knitwear, underwear, shirts, leisurewear, trousers and jeans, and jackets; boys' shirts, pajamas, underwear, trousers and jeans, and tops; children's dresses, coats, separates, knitwear, hosiery, slumberwear, underwear, tops and beachwear; foundations—slips, girdles, brassieres; footwear—ladies', men's, children's; domestic textiles—bedding, towels, bathroom sets, kitchen and table accessories; furnishings and floor coverings—curtains, bedspreads and rugs; accessories—handbags, luggage, umbrellas, scarves, belts and hats; toiletries—bath, hair care, makeup, skin care, and antiperspirants.

The 700-item food range included cake; bread; biscuits; savory/snacks; confectionery; produce—salads, vegetables, fruit; poultry;

dairy; pies—cold, hot, pastries; delicatessen—meats, poultry, pates, salads; groceries; meat products—meat, bacon, sausage; beverages—tea, coffee, fruit juices, wines and beer; frozen foods—fish, recipe dishes, sandwiches, pies, vegetables and specialties (ice cream, etc.).

Throughout its history, the company had attempted to maintain a policy of one markup percentage for all merchandise. Over the years, however, the range of markups had been expanding. Target markups were 23 percent for food, with a range of 18 percent to 24 percent; and 30 percent for textiles, with a range of 26 percent to 33 percent.

Merchandise was only reduced for clearance purposes and sales were never held at any of the stores. M and S did little advertising (approximately 0.3 percent of sales, compared to 2 percent and 3 percent in the United States) and what advertising was done was solely for the purpose of information (i.e., new product line, new store, and so on). The company believed that their products sold themselves and that word of mouth was sufficient to tell their story.

All sales within the store were on cash terms only. Although the customer did have the convenience of being able to centralize purchases for the purpose of check writing, no credit cards were accepted. The executives believed that credit only increased costs.

The company provided no fitting rooms, but maintained a liberal refund policy. M and S accepted virtually all refunds on face value. The customer feared no difficulty in this regard.

J. Edward Sieff, president, summed up the philosophy by identifying two principles the company followed:

1.   We do what's best for our suppliers, staff and customers.
2.   We get better at it all the time.

Specification buying and technological research

"It is easy enough to test goods when they are made. What is more important is to be sure they will be well made from the start. What we want to have is process control and testing at the point of production." (Lord Marks, 1960)

M and S did not own or control any manufacturing capacity, although it often was responsible for 75 percent to 90 percent of a firm's output. The company worked in close cooperation with approximately 175 food and 400 nonfood suppliers—independent companies that provided "St. Michael" merchandise to the company's specifications. Many of the suppliers had worked with the company for 30 or 40 years, sharing the M and S expansion and growing from small firms into large organizations.

As a general principle, however, no supplier "sold" M and S anything. Instead, M and S decided what it wanted and ordered it made up. This was true in both food and textiles. They didn't ask for a good product—they specified. In other words, M and S bought production, not goods. Responsibility for this specification lay with the company's group of technologists who conceived and designed goods in consultation with suppliers. In 1975, the Baker Street offices of M and S included more than 250 scientists, technologists, and supporting staff who worked with the merchandising departments, in the laboratories and production engineering (a part of M and S's industrial management group).

The textile technology departments were one of a number of services available to the buying departments and had a dual role—helping their own merchandise groups and guiding and helping suppliers. Each textile-buying group had a number of technical specialists working with it. These technicians were responsible for developing the raw material products within their groups and for monitoring the quality.

Foods were as carefully ordered and tested as clothing. A separate technological staff was completely integrated within the food group. There were separate technical groups for each of the food groups (e.g., bakery, confectionery, produce, and so on) located in the merchandise group offices, each of which reported to the senior food technologist. It was their responsibility to safeguard quality, specify standards, act as a liaison between suppliers and M and S, and keep abreast of technical developments in their fields. In essence, this responsibility paralleled those of the textile technologists.

The merchandise team

"Management at M and S is concerned with a flow that begins with the manufacture of synthetic fibers or the import of raw goods and ends with what we hope is a steady movement of merchandise across store counters."[2]

Goods were manufactured in accordance with a planned production program and were held by the supplier until instructed by M and S to deliver them to specified stores. M and S accepted title to the goods at the time of release by the supplier.

Textiles

Responsibility for managing this flow from yarn to counter was in the hands of merchandise teams. There were two corporate directors responsible for the textile groups. One director guided men's and boys' clothing, home furnishings, footwear, accessories, and new products while the other directed all women's and girls' wear. This organizational structure represented a recent shift from a production-oriented structure to customer-oriented buying groups.

The team included a variety of members. Directly responsible for the procurement of the merchandise were the merchandisers, selectors, and merchandise executives within individual merchandise lines. The chart below depicts one division—men's wear. The selectors on an individual merchandise team were responsible for developing a range of merchandise suitable for the department in style and fashion. The merchandiser, on the other hand, was responsible for the estimation of sales, actual production, packaging, and distribution of a range of merchandise.

The merchandising process always started with an estimate of sales for the coming season. These sales estimates were prepared semian-

---

[2] Quoted from Mr. Brian Howard, director of Foods.

nually, January–July and August–December, and included budgets for sales, stock (store and manufacturer, including on-order), and planned production. Merchandisers, selectors, and merchandise departmental executives were responsible for developing the estimates. The board of directors decided upon the total estimate for the company and each major division, and then reviewed the final breakdown. All estimates were expressed in pounds (sterling) and never in units of stock.

Sales performance of merchandise among departments was monitored by senior executives, with basic items continually reappraised. It was the belief of most merchandise executives that the basics needed to be watched while the fashion items would take care of themselves. Overall performance was measured internally, with the senior manage-

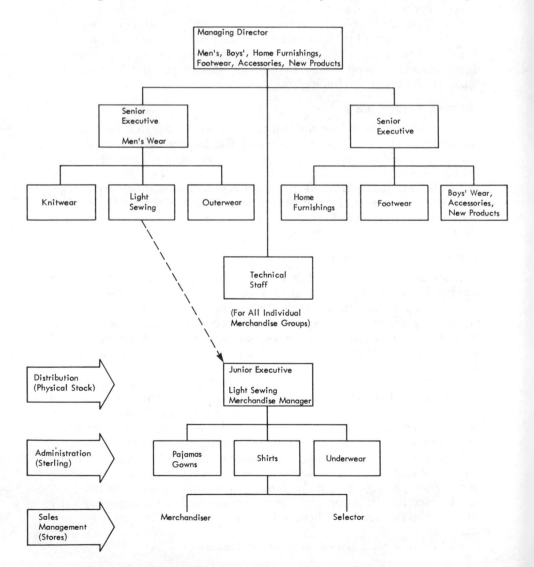

ment very reluctant to accept external conditions as the reason for sub-standard performance. Generally, if a department's sales weren't satisfactory, all internal procedures were scrutinized before evaluating outside influences. This philosophy of controlled performance was also reflected by the fact that senior management constantly monitored a department when its performance was running smoothly and eased up when the department was facing difficult problems. The reasoning was that it was too easy for a good performance to become uncontrolled if not continually pressured.

In order to witness departmental relationship between suppliers and departments, the researchers accompanied a merchandise executive on a trip to a supplier to investigate his factory production. The supplier had long been associated with M and S and three of his British factories were producing only St. Michael goods. He attributed much of his success to M and S's business and believed that it was a result of "years of dedication to the principles of the M and S business—it's what we believe and what we want to give. It's a question of being on the same mental wave length."

M and S management believed that another of M and S's major suppliers described this totally unique relationship best when he said, "We [the suppliers] are retailers without shops and they [M and S] are manufacturers without factories."

The food division followed the same basic philosophies and procedures, but there were some important differences. The division was more centralized than textiles and, because of the product shelf life, operations were frequently conducted within a shorter time span.

Store operations

In 1974, M and S had 251 stores, divided into 11 divisions, operated under a corporate director with responsibility for store operations, building and equipment, transport and packaging, and real estate. The chart below shows organizational relationships.

The divisional executive was responsible for all store operations. He actually was the company's representative in the field. Reporting to the divisional executive was the divisional staff supervisor and the divisional administrator. The divisional staff supervisor also reported to the personnel department and was the bridge between the store staff manageresses and the personnel department. It was her responsibility to be the field representative and deal with all staff welfare and problems within the stores. The divisional administrator also reported to the administration department and was responsible for operational procedures and administrative problems within the stores.

Within the individual stores, there was a dual management hierarchy. The store manager was responsible for the commercial management of the store while the staff manageress was responsible for the welfare of the staff and all personnel functions. Although the majority of store managers were men, some women had recently been promoted to that position while the staff manager positions were filled entirely by women.

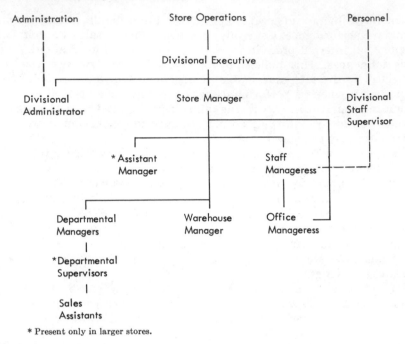

* Present only in larger stores.

The store manager was primarily responsible for sales. He had no knowledge of individual margins and was not in any way responsible for a profit margin. His entire job was to increase volume and control expenses. According to Mr. Scheinholtz, manager of the Pantheon store: "We are not interested in high margin—we're interested in high turnover. We would rather sell lower margin goods with a high turnover." It was his duty to monitor continually the movement of the merchandise, making sure there was adequate stock of the fast-moving items and eliminating the poor items, called "counter cloggers."

One of the most important positions in the company was that of the sales assistant. They were assigned to specific departments and wore identical uniforms. Their responsibility included monitoring the quality of the goods, keeping the stock plentiful and neat, taking care of the cash register (till) at which they were seated (both food and textiles), and helping customers. The sales assistant had the authority to replenish her own stock and reject goods, if she felt they were of poor quality or inappropriate for the department (although rejection of a range was seldom exercised). The company had adopted a policy of "assisted self-selection"—customers were left alone to select their goods, but sales assistants consistently covered the floor to provide assistance when desired.

The staff manager was responsible for the welfare of the staff, including all amenities. She was to take care of all staff problems to keep the staff happy and contented. Reporting to her were the office manageresses, with responsibility for those persons employed in office functions, and assistant staff manageresses. The ratio of the staff manageresses to store staff was approximately 1:60. Their prime function was dealing with people and they frequently handled the nonbusiness problems of the staff, as well as those problems within the sphere of store operations.

The dual authority structure in the stores was designed to correspond to the presence of a family entity. In each store it was considered very important that a family spirit develop quickly. In effect, the store was run by a "father" and "mother." The company tried very hard to maintain the family feeling throughout all of their stores and consequently, when a new store opened, it was policy for the manager to have had prior experience as an M and S store manager and the staff manageress to have functioned previously in that role. A "family" spirit was expected to be achieved in six months. The manager and manageress were complementary roles and each had to be very aware of the other's environment. When the store manager was not in the store, it was not uncommon to have the staff manageress in charge (in the absence of an assistant manager).

All store personnel were expected to know what was happening within the store and their department and be able to answer quickly and directly any question posed to them. The senior executives of the company frequently visited the stores (many of them visited favorite stores at least once a week) and it was not uncommon for them to ask a supervisor or sales assistant what was moving, and what was their assessment of the quality of the merchandise. In addition to being able to talk about the developments within their department, store department heads prepared periodic reports that were sent directly to the board of directors as well as other executives. For example, in the food division, four stores sent in weekly reports, prepared by the supervisors, that included information concerning sales (compared to last year) for the different food groups, points of interest regarding special lines or fast moving items, comments regarding goods or information from the merchandise departments, waste and reductions (food past the expiration date or leftover perishables), weather, and the effect of lowered or increased prices.

Reports were also sent to the stores from the various merchandise groups—both food and textiles. These reports covered a variety of topics including estimated sales for the coming period, new lines, quality control, what should be featured, and any information the merchandise groups felt that the stores should know.

The researchers had the opportunity to tour extensively one of the downtown London stores with the store manager. The tour began in the stock and receiving area. The overwhelming impression was cleanliness. Nothing was on the floors. Everything seemed neat and tidy. Merchandise was received into the store via conveyor belts to minimize stock handling. It was then spot counted and immediately put into stock. A large area was used for food stock and storage, including freezers, cold storage rooms and refrigeration—all of which were spotless. An example of the food stock handling efficiency could be seen in the unique baskets they had designed that enable stacking to ensure that the food products would not be damaged and that were nestable when empty. Whenever possible, all stock was transported on mobile units for storage within the store and movement to the sales floor.

There were a variety of amenities provided for the staff. Separate areas were provided for: a medical room staff continuously with a nurse and periodically visited by doctors (a general physician, dentist, and chiropodist) for personal appointments; a one-room infirmary with several beds for staff not feeling well (including an emergency buzzer which rang in the medical room); a hairdressing salon (charge 30 pence or 75 cents) where women were able to eat their lunch under the dryer; individual cloakroom with security lockers, shower and bathroom facilities, and a refrigerator for food storage; a recreational room with ping-pong table, etc.; and a staff dining room.[3] The dining room provided lunches for the employees, as well as coffee and afternoon tea breaks. The charge for all three was 10 pence (25 cents per day. The staff handling the food were not allowed to have pockets in their uniforms, were required to wear hairnets and used all disposable toweling and Kleenex. Exhibits 3 and 4 show pictures of a hairdressing salon and a dining room.

All of the service areas reserved for employees were spotlessly clean, tastefully decorated, cheery and well attended. The food compared favorably with what was served in the executive dining rooms. The entire amenity operation instilled a "belonged" spirit and the knowledge that someone was looking after you.

The sales floor was divided into major areas; e.g., children's, ladies' (skirts, blouses, pants), lingerie, men's wear, boys' wear, and so on. The groupings were in the process of being rearranged to reflect shopping behavior rather than production process, i.e.; knitwear was separated into men's, women's, and children's rather than combined. The sales floor was quite spartan in appearance. Except for needed area identification signs, there were no graphics or displays. The walls were painted off-white. The merchandise was displayed horizontally on tables and on garment racks. One or two items were displayed out of the package above the tables for identification.

The food department had separate checkout facilities, although there were no barriers to the department store. All of the food was packaged in see-through containers. Unlike textiles, however, the shelves were not always full. In fact, to the researchers' amazement, many shelves were completely empty. The store manager explained that it was M and S's philosophy to order only what was needed for the day plus a minimum stock for the next day. Some perishable food, such as bread, was delivered and sold on the same day. When shelf life expired, those goods which were not sold were available to the staff at half price or less. What remained was called waste and discarded. According to them, the

---

[3] Whereas the medical facilities were in all stores, the shower facilities and recreation rooms were provided only in the larger stores.

practice ensured freshness and quality. Exhibit 6 is a picture of a typical food department.

The movement of both textiles and foods was continuously monitored by the store manager. The store manager who conducted the tour remarked that "by 12:00 noon I know what's the fastest moving item in the store. It's my job to move that merchandise and make sure we get enough of it. The major problem I face is if I can't get what I know to be the best style, what will I settle for as the next best?"

Personnel

The philosophy behind the most famous area of M and S policy was captured by Lord Sieff:

> The guiding light of business enterprise is attention to human relations within the business. Firms, like our own, which study human relations—labor relations, and industrial relations, they are called in some places—are often asked to supply people to lecture on the subject. It is very difficult. How can you tell people to do things which you know they are not doing because they are the way they are? You cannot get the good will of the people who work for you by changing words such as "canteen" into "dining room," "navvy" to "worker," "office boy" to "junior clerk," and so on, or even just by paying higher wages. In the last analysis, good labor relations come from workers approving the kind of people they believe their employers to be.

This philosophy was reflected in comments of Sir Marcus Sieff:

> Good human relations, can only develop if top management believes in its importance and then sees that such a philosophy is dynamically implemented. Management must have the right mental attitude, which must be based on a sincere regard for the individual. They must come in a sensible way which we have found brings in response with few exceptions from all grades of staff. This response expresses itself in loyalty to the firm's cooperation with management, greater labor stability and a willing acceptance of new and more modern methods. The majority of workers under such conditions take pride in doing a good job. All this results in greater productivity and higher profits. This enables management to provide all those facilities which make for contented and hard-working staff, and to pay better wages based on genuinely increased productivity. So it is of benefit to the individual, the firm and the national effort.[4]

Management of personnel activities was in the hands of a corporate director. Reporting to him were executives in charge of stores personnel, head office personnel, pensions and welfare, and joint personnel services. The stores personnel executive had responsibility for four areas. The Commercial Management personnel group worked with all of the store managers and the commercial staff within the stores. The Staff Management personnel group was responsible for the training and duties of the divisional staff supervisors and staff manageresses. Store

---

[4] From a speech given by Sir Marcus Sieff at Royal Albert Hall, 1969.

Staff and Administration handled all store personnel, except Commercial and Staff Management, with responsibility for training and movement. And the Overseas group coordinated all store personnel functions in both the Canadian and the Continental operations.

The head office personnel executive had basically the same responsibilities as the stores personnel executive except that he dealt solely with personnel at the corporate headquarters in Michael House on Baker Street, London. His operation, however, was less structured and encountered different problems. For example, because of the working relationships between the executives and the staff at the head office, top management at the head office were more directly involved in promotions and appointments than was the case in the field.

The Pension and Welfare executive had responsibility for administering the pension plan. Although the plan had long been noncontributory, a recent revision had increased the coverage to all employees, part-time and full-time, and improved the benefits. Basically, the employee received 1/50th of his leaving salary for each year of service. Thus, a person with ten years would get 20 percent of his salary as a pension. In addition to providing funds, however, the group looked after pensioners, who remained attached to a particular store after retirement. In accordance with the company's human relations philosophy, pensioners were treated as retired members of the staff. The staff manageress was responsible for keeping track of pensioners and making sure they knew of the services available to them. They were entitled to a free group medical plan, chiropody services, and luncheon meals. Also, at periodic intervals there were official pensioner lunches, a Christmas lunch, and an additional hamper of food at Christmas. In 1974, there were approximately 2,500 pensioners attached to various M and S stores.

Another key to understanding the M and S organization was the operation of its employee benefit program. It was taken very seriously and when questioned about use of the term "welfare," Sir Marcus replied:

> The word *welfare* has an old-fashioned sound reminiscent of the Victorian era, but I do not know a better one to replace it. People do have troubles and it is a fundamental part of a good staff policy to be able to unobtrusively and above all speedily to give help and advice when needed.

In addition to the health and recreational facilities, M and S provided a variety of free activities, including a River Thames boat trip with a buffet bar and dancing; table tennis and bowling tourneys, and concert tickets. Sir Marcus had said of the amenities:

> They should be of such a nature that executives are pleased to take advantage of them. . . . If the facilities are not good enough for top management, then they are not good enough for staff whatever the grade.[5]

The amenity program was available at the head office as well as in the stores. On all top management store visits, the trip included inspection

---

[5] From a speech in Royal Albert Hall, 1969.

of all facilities—including, to the constant embarrassment of all, the women's rest rooms.

The provision of these amenities and commitment to staff matters was formally represented by a nine-strong senior management Welfare Committee which had met weekly at the head office since 1934 without a break. The committee debated problems of individual stores and gave judgments on cases not dealt with locally and where a "common handwriting" was needed. The decisions were *never* questioned by the board. Exhibit 7 shows selected cases considered.

The provisions of these welfare services and amenities were not, however, without cost to the company. Exhibit 8 provides a sample of an analysis of the welfare costs.

Finance

According to John Samuel, Financial Officer of M and S, the financial policy of the company was to make enough money for the company to provide for:

1.   Capital development.
2.   Retained earnings.
3.   Dividends.

The specific funds necessary for the above commitments were determined by the board. A general pretax profit goal of 10.5 percent and an expense level of approximately 12 percent determined a gross profit margin of approximately 25 percent, as discussed above.

Gross margin did not, however, preoccupy the thoughts of the senior management. They were most interested in the balance of food and clothing sales as related to margins and the volume itself. They believed fully in the pursuit of high sales and were not unaccustomed to reducing prices in order to increase sales.

Although actual sterling figures on the operating statements have changed substantially, the percentage relationships have stayed level. For example, the percentage of expenses has remained between 11 percent and 12 percent since 1970. According to John Samuel, M and S's size minimized the effect of change and violent shifts never occurred.

All store developments were planned and expansion had been dynamic since the mid-1960s. The company's debt ratio had been consistently minimized, as every attempt had been made to finance growth internally. Although the dividend pay-out was high, there had been a "massive scaling down of proportions paid out to the shareholders in order to finance continued growth."

M and S was planning major developments for Canada, France, and Belgium. The Canadian operation was equally owned and financed jointly by M and S and People's Department Stores of Canada. The European operation, however, required some local borrowing. Nevertheless, for both operations retained earnings constituted the major source of investment funds.

Recent events affecting the financial position of the company included:

1. The 1974 corporate tax was increased to 52 percent as compared with 40 percent in 1973.
2. Restrictions were made on the maximum dividend allowed under the provisions of the Counter-Inflation Act of 1973, whereby the gross equivalent of the ordinary dividends which were declared in 1973 could not exceed those declared in the previous year by more than 5 percent.
3. In spring 1974, the government forced all retailers to reduce their gross margins by 10 percent.

The effect that the M and S financial policy has had on the people, according to John Samuel, has been to disassociate profit from selling. Only the senior members of the board were aware of the profitability of the company and only they dealt with the direction it would take. The rest of the company was totally immersed in sales.

Exhibit 9 shows the organizational interrelationships within M and S.

The Marks and Spencer style

A week at M and S began with the daily 8:30 A.M. meeting, in the chairman's office, of certain members of the board. There were no members elected to the board from outside M and S. Generally eight or nine of the senior members met daily with the chairman, who was the chief operational director of the firm. The members most frequently in attendance included the president, J. Edward Sieff; the vice chairmen, and joint managing directors, M. Sacher and Michael Sieff (seated on either side of the chairman); joint managing directors, Henry Lewis and Sir Derek Rayner; and directors, R. Greenbury, W. B. Howard, and G. D. Sacher.

At 8:00 A.M., Monday before the meeting began, sales and stock figures for the previous week were available and given to all members as they entered the chairman's office. The chairman generally started the meeting by relating a particular incident he had observed during the previous several days. He frequently spoke for several minutes on one or two particular problems and how they related to the business on a whole. General comments by all members present were then interchanged. After the chairman had raised his issues, he went around the room and asked each director if he had anything he wished to discuss, starting with the vice chairman, Michael Sacher. The following excerpts are from one of these meetings the researchers attended on January 15, 1975.

SIR MARCUS: We are not taking our markdowns fast enough or sharp enough.

HENRY LEWIS: That's related to some problems we discussed yesterday. The production cutoff date is not in adequate control. We must be able to learn from production sheets so we don't make mistakes. Production changes and cutoffs should be noted for reference next year.

SIR MARCUS: If you go away from the principle, it costs you more than you gain 9 times out of 10.

BRIAN HOWARD: We are moving further into computers in food. From July 1975 to November 1975, stores will be converted from a daily indent [order] system to a weekly system. The computer then translates the weekly ordering into daily projections. It reduces paper work and by 1976, the stores probably won't be ordering at all. It's going to take a lot of training to get people to think in total terms. The one system will, however, simplify the store's life.

J. EDWARD SIEFF: I want to make a plea for self-restraint in cloth buying on price points. There's no point in buying more expensive fabrics. We are only interested in the desirability of the article. Once we see the retail price in print, it qualifies the cost price, which doesn't necessarily represent value. We should ask ourselves, "Is it better, of more value, and better quality?"

SIR MARCUS: I think the president is absolutely right. It's a matter of self-restraint. Anything else, Teddy [J. Edward]?

J. EDWARD SIEFF: I ran across a fabric yesterday, 5–8. I think it's inferior. I hear our people saying it's lousy. It may be an achievement for technology but not for women. And ICI [major fabric supplier] is pushing it.

SIR MARCUS: Are we telling them?

MICHAEL SACHER: We have a meeting Thursday.

SIR MARCUS: We must be frank with our suppliers.

J. EDWARD SIEFF: We must be frank with ourselves.

SIR DEREK RAYNER: I've been trying to work our priority stores for 1975. Over two-thirds of the sales will come from 95 stores. We need good stock composition of basic merchandise. Can we carry both basic merchandise in all stores and specialized lines in selected stores?

*   *   *   *   *

MICHAEL SACHER: I'm concerned about two operations in the stores—training of the cashiers and methods of filling up the displays. For £45 million of goods, we handle £180 million at Marble Arch. We accept too much of this and take too many things for granted. We handle everything four times before it gets to the customer.

R. GREENBURY: I have set up a team to look at the handling of bread and crisps [potato chips].

J. EDWARD SIEFF: Anything to learn from Safeway or Migros [grocery chains]?

SIR MARCUS: Let's ask them. Or Sainsbury. They'll tell us. No need to invent everything ourselves.

R. GREENBURY: I've asked them.

SIR MARCUS: O.K., but let's *do* something. I don't want to see the perfect solution.

*   *   *   *   *

On Mondays only, after the 8:30 meeting, those meeting with the chairman proceeded to a conference room for the 10:00 A.M. meeting of all directors and senior executives. A total of approximately 25–30 men gathered around a long table. On each side of the table, in the middle, were six distinguished chairs in which sat the chairman, vice chairmen, and joint managing directors. The accompanying sketch details the positioning:

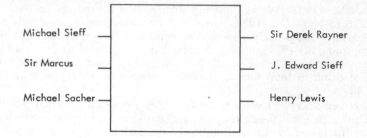

Michael Sieff ⸺   ⸺ Sir Derek Rayner

Sir Marcus ⸺   ⸺ J. Edward Sieff

Michael Sacher ⸺   ·   ⸺ Henry Lewis

The other directors and senior executives occupied the remaining chairs
and maintained the same relative position at each meeting.

The meeting was conducted in the same manner as the 8:30 A.M.
meeting. The chairman began with several points and each executive
present was called on to contribute observations or problems. The following are excerpts of the January 30 meeting:

SIR MARCUS: Henry Lewis and I visited 9 of Nottingham Manufacturing
factories [the largest M and S supplier]. They are an outstanding operation
but they have failed to innovate in the design area. However, they had no
criticism of our criterion in this respect. Also, they were making a line of
ladies nylons, 3 in a package, for 75p that was not making enough money
for them. They asked us if we really wanted them to make lines at a substantial loss. We said "certainly not" and we cancelled the line.

My second point is that we brought back goods that were of appalling
quality—not poor in make, but in conception. Are we sufficiently self-critical
—are our standards high enough—do we probe enough in our eating and
wearing?[6] You must see that it applies to you—we've got to be critical.

Another point concerns customers' criticism and complaints. Ninety-four
percent of them are replied to by me within a maximum of 48 hours. This
procedure should apply around this table. It is a job for the senior members
—not the subordinate member. "A soft answer turneth away wrath."

*   *   *   *   *

J. EDWARD SIEFF: I've heard complaints about hosiery that doesn't stay
up. We must look at the technicians' role. We are not calling on our technicians' role. We are not calling on our technicians sufficiently. Secondly, I'd
like to talk about our taste, which should be one of classic simplicity. We
give too much credibility to gimmicks that we see in foreign fairs. I know
the young people want the showy goods, but we must draw the balance.
What are the parameters of taste?

SIR MARCUS: Decent taste, reasonably up-to-date taste. (Later, Michael?)

*   *   *   *   *

MICHAEL SIEFF: The opening of Paris—we have very poor stock conditions. The outstanding orders aren't being filled. I want to know what's
happening? Next, markdowns. The trial reports and evaluations are important. We must be cautious to avoid markdowns.

Thirdly, price increases. Some of our margins have been increased to
32 percent–33 percent, which makes up for the budget line of 24 percent.

─────────
[6] It was the practice of the directors to eat M and S foods and wear the clothing.

To talk to the stores about margin is difficult. Should we bring in margin? It may not be wise.

MICHAEL SACHER: Their job is to sell whatever they've got at whatever price, including the reduced items. I don't think they shoud be told.

* * * * *

SIR DEREK RAYNER: We must take action to clear. Down to half price. Also, the spring goods, we are short of sizes and have stockouts. We should study checking lists for balance.

* * * * *

HENRY LEWIS: Some stores still have an October range. Merchandise and garment development must be worked on.

* * * * *

JOHN LEVY (Senior executive—transport and packaging): Our packaging for dark colored clothes is inadequate. People can't see the color. We are working on a flip-top package to expose half the garment in order for the customer to handle it.

* * * * *

SIR MARCUS: I received a letter from the Wolverhamptom store about our plan for extension there. As you know, we cancelled plans to extend the operation. The letter was written by departmental supervisors asking for an extension of their store. It's a very well written letter. Let me read it to you [reads the letter]. I think we should look into the situation again.[7]

At the conclusion of the general meeting, many of the directors and senior executives met with their respective groups. It was not uncommon to have the senior board members walk in during these meetings. At one of the food meetings attended by a researcher, approximately 5 minutes after the meeting began, one of the vice chairmen came in and threw a package of rhubarb crumble on the table. He scathingly commented on the poor taste and consistency of the dish.

> This is the most disgusting thing I have ever had the pleasure of serving to guests. The rhubarb was unripe and overcooked—it was inedible. Also, the product is overpackaged. We should take a closer look at our packaging policies.

These individual meetings were often conducted in the same manner as those at the senior level—with each participating member present, asked for his comments and problems.

Meetings were not, however, the only method of communication. In fact, as informal as M and S was (for a British firm) the meetings were the most formal aspects of the M and S style. Throughout the course of a day and week at M and S's head office, there was a constant parade of people going in and out of offices. The standard procedure was to knock and immediately enter, without waiting for a response. The object was to project an open-door policy and often the visitor would ask one question, get an answer and leave. Outside of each door, however,

---

[7] At an interview in March 1975, Sir Marcus noted that the supervisor's letter had led to an investment of over £1 million.

was an "engaged" sign that could be lit from the occupant's desk when he didn't want to be disturbed.

Executives out of their offices also were constantly available to anyone who wanted to work with them. Several devices made this possible. First of all, in each office, and in the halls, was a light with four colors (much like a traffic light). Each board member and senior executive was assigned a combination of lights. These lights were flashed whenever an executive was not in his office but needed to be reached. As a result of this practice, it was not uncommon for executives, when visiting other offices, to constantly refer to the blinking lights.

Second, those who weren't assigned a light combination carried pocket "bleepers" that signaled when someone was trying to reach them.

Third, two phones were located in most executives' offices. One phone had a full dial and could be used for any purpose. The other phone automatically connected the executive to the operator. The executive told her whom he was looking for, hung up, and was called back when (or if) the party was located.

The entire communication network was designed for informal, frequent contact between all staff at Baker Street. When working with the executives, we received the feeling that all of them were tied to and responding to the same umbilical cord. No executive, unless off the premises, was out of reach of anyone who wanted to see or talk with him.

Meetings and the communication network were, however, only two unique aspects of the executives' style. In addition, the executive was expected to investigate constantly and thoroughly his or her entire operation as well as the overall company. In the words of many of the executives "M and S's greatest critic is M and S." The management team was expected to be expert about M and S and not technicians in their field. This concept of continual appraisal of every detail was identified as "probing." Lord Sieff defined probing as "the method whereby the interested and inquiring mind of the executive and his colleagues penetrates beneath the surface of things and discover the facts." It was not unusual to hear probing mentioned at meetings or in discussions among executives. The word characterized the company philosophy.

Probing was not only conducted at the head office—but also, *especially*, it was carried through at the stores. All of the senior executives of the firm believed that the stores had to be frequented as often as possible. In fact, many of them stopped at neighborhood stores on their way home. Of the 251 stores, in 1974, only 10 did not have a visit from a senior board member.

Before the end of each week, each director was given a hamper of M and S food to use over the weekend. In addition, he was expected to wear M and S clothes. The purpose of both was to monitor quality and performance.

Saturday was one of the most important days of the week for the M and S executives—for it was the day when each of the board members and senior executives visited two or three stores. On these tours, the executive spent a good deal of time talking with the employees of the store. The following is an excerpt of a store tour (January 5) conducted by Sir Marcus and Brian Howard and accompanied by one of the researchers.

Staines was a small store of 10,000 sq. ft. but did £40,000 per week. We arrived around 9:15 and were greeted by one of the supervisors. The store traffic seemed brisk but the staff manageress thought it a little below normal.

A very young food department supervisor was asked to take us around. She was flustered but did her best to answer questions. It was easy to see what was meant by the necessity at M and S of being able to give straight, clear answers. Brian Howard expected her to know her numbers and her situation. There were problems of short produce deliveries and he wanted them described. He also offered comments on store layout.

Later the staff manageress took us around upstairs. The warehouse space floor was spotless. The atmosphere was one of easy-going efficiency and competence.

Leaving Staines, Mr. Howard drove on to the Reading store to meet Sir Marcus Sieff. Sir Marcus led his party around the store. All that he was wearing that day, except his shoes—slacks, shirt, sweater in blue, and blue and white houndstooth jacket—were available on the racks in the store. His questions dealt entirely with merchandise and people. What was moving? The store manager answered from memory with current sales numbers representing percentage comparison with previous weeks and years. Department managers added comments.

The discussion was candid. Of a shirt, "Here's one of our mistakes. Have you reduced this?"

"Yes, but it still isn't moving. We'll have to take it down another pound."

"Why isn't there a price notice?" to a young sales supervisor.

"We just got these this morning, Chairman, and the sign is being made."

"We buy this from Burlington. We've ordered 2 million yards of this fabric so far. It's moving very well."

Looking at a child's snowsuit jacket at £6.25 (approximately $15.00). "Is that our price? We've *got* to get a less expensive range. Our customers can't afford that." Everyone had his pad from the chairman down and all took their own notes.

"Did your boss come in to work today?" To a warehouse foreman whose wife worked as a sales clerk. "Yes, Chairman." "How is Mary?" "She's well, thank you."

On our tour of the lunchroom and offices, he asked for the hairdresser by name. "She's the queen of Reading," and gave numerous directives—"I want 'switch the lights out please' signs near the doors whenever the switches aren't near the door. They have to learn we have a balance of payments problem. When do our window lights go off?" "6:30." "When do we close?" "6:30." "I want them off at 6."

Driving to his home for lunch, Sir Marcus commented on what he had learned.

"Some lines we like don't move—like this jacket. We have to find out why. We have a problem on having enough stock for the period after New Year's without carrying too much inventory. And that store has some good people. They're doing a good job."

While touring a store on Saturday, one frequently saw several other executives in the store. For example, in a tour of the new Uxbridge store, one of the researchers accompanied Brian Howard. Over coffee we assembled a textile sales manager, a junior executive in textiles, a junior executive in food, a food technologist and the store manager. There was continual interchange. All were dressed in suits, and all were headed for other stores. As one of the head office employees remarked about the directors, "They work 60 hours during the week, they visit stores on Saturday and they talk about it on Sunday. They live, eat and breathe M and S.

Being a paternalistic, very centralized operation, M and S was not without its house rules. As recited at the request of one of the researchers, they included:

1. The first thing to remember is that it is a *family* business. Because we're a family business, we care for people. It's a paternal business. How does that affect the professional? You have to receive your inoculation. If you get a violent reaction, you'd better go. And then you grow with the business. It comes back to a recruitment policy. We have to get them young and train them ourselves.
2. You can't be a loner. You have to be part of the team.
3. You have to spread your decisions around. Some in-house decisions are "I don't like it." You learn to accept a decision and wait your time to come back with it.
4. You have to learn how to handle people in an ordinary, decent way.
5. Nobody succeeds who can't talk clearly and simply to the management.

Some concerns of the directors

The management of M and S were figures of some considerable public importance. They were well known in the business community. Asked about the future, Sir Marcus, the chairman, spoke of his concern for the economic future of Britain. He was particularly upset with the inept interventions of the government with business. When asked what these conditions would mean to his basic strategy of expansion in Britain, he commented:

> First we have to be concerned with our liquidity. We will not spend our reserves. The result is whereas we were going to spend £40 million/year to upgrade our stores we're now going to spend £20 million. We have to preserve our position.
>
> The consequences will not be important in the short term. But as a pattern they will hurt Britain severely in three to four years' time.

A particularly clear expression of Sir Marcus' views was made in the October 8, 1974 corporate statement (two days before the 1974 Parliamentary elections).

> Retailing performs a major role in the chain of production and distribution. We cooperate with whatever Government is in office, but

some Ministers and their advisers do not seem to appreciate the significant contribution which a healthy and competitive retail industry can make in stemming the rise in the cost of living. We are not helped in this task by misguided interference.

Corporation tax takes more than half our profits. The Government criticizes the private sector for its failure to invest but it omits to explain that much investment is financed out of profits. If our profits are subject to politically motivated restrictions and massively reduced, confidence is eroded and investment on which the maintenance of employment and the future prosperity of the country depends slows down.

The remaining profit (after tax and dividends) is retained in the business to finance its future growth. Present Government policy has substantially reduced the money available for such development in the immediate future.

The chairman's statement and his response to questions at a press conference announcing 1974's results made headlines in all Britain's major papers.

Michael Sacher, vice chairman, commented on some of the internal issues and problems facing M and S.

What has always astonished me is how few people have learned the simple principles on which we operate. I think we have carved a market out here which is quality goods at lower prices. As long as we stick to that we'll be okay, as long as the younger people learn the principles of the business. You have to have a clear policy where you upgrade areas in which you are weak and stay out of the caviar business. The board can help here but there are so many things distracting us from being shopkeepers, bombs, the government and so on. But we implement by generalizing from the particular. That is how you teach young people.

I always try to pick out one thing and then work on it. Take frozen canneloni; it's a new line that I think will move very well. People like canneloni and it's hard to make. Someone else suggested spaghetti. The housewife can make perfectly good spaghetti with ease, why should we? It just requires a bit of common sense. It's no good developing a slip department if everyone's wearing pants.

RESEARCHERS: Isn't it inevitable that you sell the spaghetti as well?

MICHAEL SACHER: No, I don't think so. We don't believe in a high degree of specialization and it has always been our practice to move selectors around the business. So much of selection is taste, feel, and common sense.

I was going to say something else, also immodest, and it's true of other senior colleagues. You have to become expert in a wide variety of activities: selecting goods, feel for merchandise, know what's coming, principles of building, and rudimentary technological questions.

I heard a lecture in Israel about tomatoes, so I know something about them. I've been shown cell sections of frozen material, so I can ask why our beans and sprouts have such lassitude. I've acquired enough garbage to ask technological questions that they can't throw out.

In the end, the decision has to be taken by mangement, not the experts. And you have to be humble. I just try to take a jolly good look at everything that's been here a long time in the same place. Repotting is healthy managerially if not horticulturally.

I do see problems: you can't help but lean on the strengths that you have. Take Teddy. He has an astronomic knowledge of textiles and he applies himself. His taste is not perfect, but he knows what an M and S range should be. He's done a wonderful job in his new role.

The family is a binding force in another way. Members of the family can talk to each other in a candid way that I find extremely difficult to discover with professional managers. It happens with some, but it takes time.

RESEARCHER: How much does great wealth have to do with it?

MICHAEL SACHER: Well, there is something to that. We know what good taste is. We see fashion as it emerges and whether it lasts. I once suggested that we send our selectors to the Caribbean for the winter holiday to see what is being worn.

Another problem is that most of our executives have joined us straight from the university. It compels you to have a series of graded courses outside the university. Not so much what they learn, but they can test themselves against peers. My generation had the war in which to measure themselves.

The senior members of the M and S board all agreed that the major question facing M and S concerned the proper rate of expansion in Britain, movement into the Common Market and the move into Canada. The reasons for the moves were best expressed by Sir Marcus:

> First, as an opportunity for more profit. Given the deteriorating situation in Britain we think Canada can become very important for us. Second, as a chance to expand British exports. And finally, should things be really bad, it's a life line for us abroad.

APPENDIX

MARKS AND SPENCER, LTD. (A)

Britain's situation in 1975[1]

In 1975, Britain's economic growth had been slowing down for a period of several years. The future looked difficult at best. Evidence of recession was growing—the outlook for living standards was particularly uncertain. This was evident from the range of official forecasts, with the government looking for a rise in consumer expenditures for the year as a whole, while other forecasters were suggesting a fall in consumer expenditures (approximately 0.5 percent to 1.5 percent).

According to a British securities exchange report, the major problem was in assessing the likelihood of incomes keeping pace with price rises and the effect on incomes of a downturn arising from differing levels of economic activity. Of importance in this respect were: the rate of in-

---

[1] Sources used for section included: *Britain 1975: An Official Handbook* (London: Her Majesty's Stationery Office, 1975); *Retail Trade Developments in Great Britain, 1973–1974* (London: Gower Economic Publications, 1973); *Retail Review —Stores, December 1974* Chapel-Crue Myers, London: 1974; "Worldwide Marketing: Marketing in the United Kingdom" (P.J.S. Law, London Business School, unpublished, 1972).

flation (forecasted for the 20 percent–25 percent range), the depth of the recession, and government economic policy (especially determination to maintain real incomes). Britain's gross national product, had increased 22 percent between the years of 1963 and 1973. The expanding groups were (in relation to the economy as a whole) most of the services, particularly insurance, banking and finance, public administration, and educational services. The distribution trades, however, had made a declining contribution, from 11.7 percent of the GNP in 1963 to 9.8 percent in 1973. With the creation of the Welfare State (including, for example, the National Health Service) and with the nationalization of important industries such as gas and electricity supply, coal and the railways by the post-war Labour government, the scale of government intervention in the economy increased dramatically. In what was now characterized as a mixed economy, some 27 percent of the GNP was accounted for by the public sector. Labour politician Anthony Wedgwood Benn railed against depreciation deductions as a form of hidden profit and called for nationalization of important sectors of the industry.

Although personal incomes had achieved a compound growth rate of 9 percent a year since 1963, the proportion of persons in the lower and middle income ranges had increased. The increase in consumer expenditure at constant prices had, however, been just under 3 percent per year. According to government sources, the difference was accounted for mainly by rising prices and to a lesser extent by a higher incidence of direct taxation and increased personal savings.

Significant shifts in consumer expenditures had occurred over the past several years. The proportion of expenditure devoted to food, tobacco, clothing, and footwear had fallen, while the proportion spent on housing and automobiles had risen.

Retail trade in the 65–75 decade had been characterized by upward trends in sales, downward movements in the number of establishments and virtually static numbers of persons engaged in the industry. In relation to the economy, the retail cycle had been out of phase recently with that of most other sectors of industry; profits went ahead sharply in 1972–73 but had since remained on a plateau, due to the effect of government margin controls and competitive pressures associated with a massive turnaround in stock levels.

Retail businesses in Britain were classified under three headings: independents, shops with less than ten outlets; multiples, shops with ten or more outlets; and cooperatives, voluntary organizations controlled by their members. The majority of retail sales were still attributable to independents, but the trend was declining. The following table shows trends in market share.

	1961	1966	1971
Independents	59.9%	56.4%	52.9%
Multiples	29.2	34.5	39.8
Cooperatives	10.9	9.1	7.2

Source: Provisional results of the British Census of Distribution, 1971.

Food retailing had been characterized by a steadily decreasing number of stores and an expansion of food sales. Large grocery operations were increasing their market share. With the advent of the superstore or hyper market, futher substantial reduction of store numbers in this category were expected in the next few years. This decline in numbers of shops was equally evident for clothing and footwear. In the previous 20 years, the number of these shops had declined by nearly 20 percent, while in the past 5 years, sales had increased by 30.7 percent. Increasing competition from multiple traders had been curtailing the expansion of specialized clothing outlets.

Retailing in the United Kingdom had been plagued with rising prices. Although clothing and footwear had traditionally experienced well below average price increases, in recent years the trend had been reversed. Durable goods, on the other hand, recorded increases well below the average.

Over the previous 20 years, a number of important trends had been discernible in the pattern of retailing. The most important of these were:

1.   The increase in size of shops and number of store units.
2.   The growth of self-service and self-selection.
3.   Planning in-town and out-of-town centers.

Of these trends, the mall shopping center development was most significant. Almost all of the shopping centers built were inside urban areas. Between 1965 and 1975 some form of shopping center would have been built in nearly every major city in Britain. Many forecasters believed that the further development of "out-of-town" centers in the United Kingdom was essential. Out-of-town centers had been one of the most controversial subjects in British retailing and was not going to easily be resolved. Many of its opponents objected to the use of valuable green space and were extremely interested in the preservation of England's "green environment."

The competition for Marks and Spencer

An overview of the English retailing scene provides a picture of contrasts. First, in contrast to other retailers in the Common Market, the United Kingdom had the largest percentage share of the multiple shop organizations in 1971, 29.1 percent. Second, England was characterized by the central location of fashion in the London area. The London market was composed of several very large department stores (such as Harrod's, carrying everything from designer fashion to sausage, cheese, and fish from all over the world, and Fortnum and Mason, known for its fine selection of specialty foods) and large numbers of high fashion specialty shops (such as those located on Bond and Regent Streets). If the English consumer was purchasing a fashion item, it was almost certain that the purchase was made in London. The consequences of this latter characteristic was that the establishments throughout the rest of Great Britain concentrated on basic, staple merchandise with a limited fashion selection.

The center of the small English towns was called the "high street" and generally was comprised of small, independent merchants and some multiple shop organizations. As a result, the majority of M and S locations were on these "high streets."

Although any general merchandise chain experienced competition from a large number of sources, M and S identified four major competitors for the food and textile business. In foods, J. Sainsbury Limited was one of the largest multiple grocers in the United Kingdom. The bulk of the outlets were supermarkets concentrated in Southern England with total sales nearly double that of M and S's food operation (although the variety of items cannot be compared). Market share had been more than maintained by establishing a quality image with low prices. Sainsbury was developing larger stores, with the average size in 1975 being about 16,000 square feet. Other food competitors included specialty food operations such as Fortnum and Mason and Harrod's, two unique department store operations.

In textiles, M and S faced three equivalent competitors: British Home Stores, Littlewood's and C&A. British Home Stores were one of the principal variety chain stores in the United Kingdom, with 95 outlets. The company sold the same types of merchandise as M and S—textiles and food. Nearly all of the goods were sold under their own label, "Prova," although the quality was generally considered less than equivalent to M and S. In addition, they had recently changed their food department to over-the-counter service—with separately displayed goods available in any quantity, including butchery. In an attempt to upgrade in textiles, an extensive range of quality fashion wear had recently been made available.

Littlewood's carried the same textile lines as M and S plus a food range, although the Oxford Street branch did not run foods. In an obvious attempt to copy M and S, their display of goods and store layout were identical. Although the price ranges were slightly lower, the quality of the goods was far below that of M and S. It was a small operation, with individual store sales far below that of M and S.

C&A had the appearance of a typical American department store in layout, fixturing and offering. Although they had a greater fashion orientation and variety, much of their clothing in the medium-price range (equivalent to M and S) was manufactured in Hong Kong and of medium quality.

Exhibit 1

MARKS AND SPENCER, LTD. (A)
Profit and Loss Account for the Years Ended March 31, 1973–1975
(£000)

	1975	1974	1973
Gross store sales.....................	£745,869	£591,570	£511,934
Export sales........................	21,439	13,583	10,370
Net sales...........................	£767,308	£605,153	£522,304
Operating profit.....................	81,857	76,825	70,036
Taxation............................	42,500	39,900	24,900
Profit after taxation.................	£ 39,357	£ 36,925	£ 45,136
Extraordinary item— Surplus on disposal of fixed assets.......................	49	2,383	176
	£ 39,406	£ 39,308	£ 45,312
Dividends..........................	21,052	19,008	21,388
Undistributed surplus.................	£ 18,354	£ 20,300	£ 23,924
Earnings per share..................	12.2 p	11.4 p	13.9 p

Balance Sheet as of March 31, 1974
(£000)

	1975	1974	1973
ASSETS			
Current Assets:			
Inventory.........................		£ 31,472	£ 29,638
Cash and short-term deposits........		18,400	44,612
Debtors and prepayments...........		10,502	8,150
Tax reserve certificates..............		—	4,000
Total Current Assets...........		60,374	£ 86,400
Fixed assets			
Properties........................		221,895	182,710
Fixtures and equipment.............		19,825	15,668
Total Assets...................		£302,094	£284,778
LIABILITIES			
Current Liabilities:			
Creditors and accrued charges.......		£ 28,055	£ 29,971
Corporation tax....................		28,237	23,359
Dividends (interim payable and final proposed...................		12,255	21,283
Total Current Liabilities........		£ 68,547	£ 74,613
Long-Term Liability:			
Deferred taxation..................		18,400	13,100
Debenture stock...................		45,000	45,000
Total.......................		£ 63,400	£ 58,100
Net Worth			
Shareholders' interest...............		172,417	152,117
Total Liabilities................		£304,364	£284,830

Exhibit 1—Continued

10-Year Statement—Year Ended March 31
(£000)

	1965*	1966	1967	1968	1969	1970	1971*	1972	1973	1974	1975
Turnover†	208,636	226,135	242,954	268,607	299,672	338,843	390,915	438,600	522,304	605,153	
Operating profit	27,506	29,618	30,659	33,871	38,123	43,705	50,115	53,766	70,036	76,825	
Profit after taxation	12,706	18,268	18,959	20,121	21,773	26,005	31,215	34,416	45,136	36,925	
Corporation tax rate	n.c.	40%	40%	42.5%	45%	42.5%	40%	40%	40%	52%	
Earnings per share	n.c.	5.6p	5.8p	6.2p	6.7p	8.0p	9.6p	10.6p	13.9p	11.4p‡	
Dividend payments to shareholders	9,258	9,928	9,950	10,266	10,609	11,928	13,904	15,528	17,826	19,008	
Retained profit	3,246	4,322	2,461	2,536	3,667	5,747	8,220§	9,132	23,924	17,917§	
Depreciation	1,844	1,993	2,177	2,488	2,987	3,534	4,177	4,620	5,055	5,464	
Ordinary share capital and reserves	105,468	109,790	112,251	114,788	118,455	123,152	127,711	136,843	150,767	171,067	
Total sales area (square feet—000)	3,337	3,471	3,635	3,929	4,214	4,408	4,708	4,944	5,059	5,489	

n.c. = Not comparable.

* 53 weeks.

† Turnover for the year ended March 31, 1974, is shown after deduction of V.A.T. For the purpose of comparison, turnover figures for previous years have been shown after deduction of purchase tax.

‡ Earnings per share are not comparable by reason of the change in basis of taxation.

§ Excluding surplus on disposal of assets: 1971—£2,393,000, 1974—£2,383,000.

Exhibit 2

MARKS AND SPENCER, LTD. (A)
Organization Chart

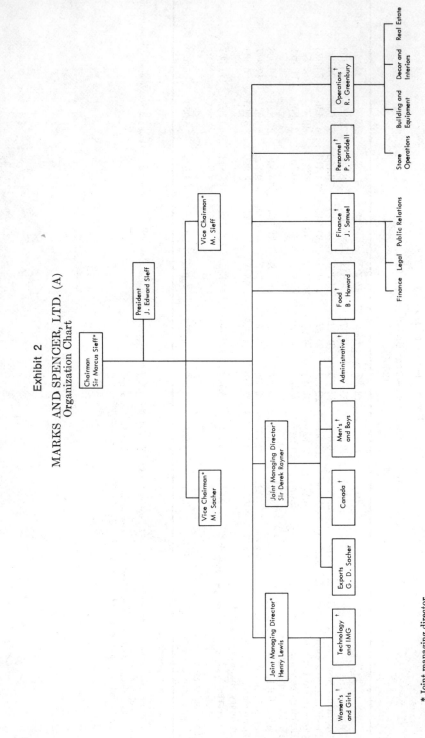

* Joint managing director.
† There were 22 directors all together.
Source: Constructed from researcher's notes.

Exhibit 3
STORE HAIRDRESSING SALON

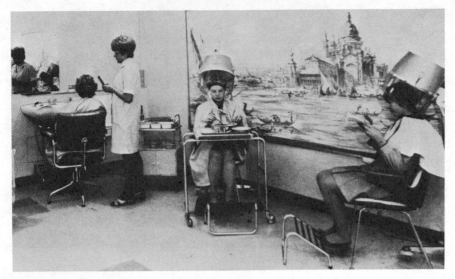

Exhibit 4

STORE DINING FACILITIES

Exhibit 5

TEXTILE AREA WITHOUT CUSTOMERS

Exhibit 6

FOOD AREA WITHOUT CUSTOMERS

Exhibit 7

SELECTED WELFARE COMMITTEE CASES FROM A WEEKLY MEETING

Mrs. L. Graves
Age: 59 years   Sales Assistant
Service: 21 years, 4 months   Cardiff
Married   £26.00

Mrs. Graves suffered from an arthritic knee which made standing all day painful for her. She was receiving treatment, but there was no cure for the condition. The Sessional Doctor had recommended that Mrs. Graves should reduce her hours to five mornings per week, this arrangement to continue until she retired in May 1975. The store recommended payment of the full-time salary.

This was agreed.

Miss M. Morell
Age: 20 years   Sales Assistant
Service: 4 years, 8 months   Bromley
Single   £25.50

Miss Morell had a very poor absence record, mainly due to migraine. As this condition did not seem to be following the usual pattern, arrangements were made for Miss Morell to have very extensive investigations, but no abnormality was found. The Sessional Doctor had come to the conclusion that Miss Morell was, to some extent, malingering. She had worked for only 24 days since April 1 and the store suggested there might be a case for not paying the full Christmas bonus.

It was calculated that Miss Morell had been absent unpaid for nine full weeks (not consecutive weeks) during the year and the committee considered it would be reasonable, therefore, that one sixth of the net Christmas bonus should be deducted. The question of Miss Morell's continued employment with the company would be discussed in the New Year.

Mrs. C. Schultz
Age: 61 years   Part-time Cleaner
Service: 15 years, 6 months   Watford
Married   £17.00 (25 at 68p)

The store reported that Mrs. Schultz died of cancer on November 27 after a short illness. She left a husband who suffered from a heart condition but was at present employed as a fire officer at a local factory, and one married daughter.

The committee agreed to make Mr. Schultz an ex-gratia gift of £900.

Mr. B. Harris
Age: 25 years   Warehouseman
Service: 3 years, 11 months   Croydon
Single   £27.50 (last salary paid)

Mr. Harris had been absent since November 3, 1972, suffering from a condition which affected the brain cells. He had been unpaid since the end of July 1973, although contact with him had been maintained. The store now reported that Mr. Harris died on November 27 from pneumonia. He had lived with his parents and his father was in regular employment.

The committee did not feel that this was a case where any payment should be made to the family, but they decided that the company would pay the funeral expenses.

Exhibit 8

ANALYSIS OF WELFARE COSTS
Year Ended March 31, 1972
(in pounds sterling)

	This Year		Last Year		1969/1970	
Headquarters:						
Head office						
Salaries	£ 63,000		£ 52,000		£ 40,000	
Traveling expenses	17,439		15,000		12,000	
		£ 80,439		£ 67,000		£ 52,000
Staff Catering:						
Salaries						
Head office	£175,000		£160,000		£145,650	
Stores	832,500		754,000		663,000	
Subsidies						
Head office	125,728		107,245		95,347	
Stores	731,571		568,107		471,881	
Gas and electricity	60,000		52,000		52,000	
		£1,924,799		£1,641,352		£1,427,878
Health Services:						
Convalescent homes	£ 4,799		£ 5,618		£ 4,649	
Chiropody	31,063		29,547		25,384	
Dental	24,557		20,201		20,252	
Medical costs	188,561		154,147		128,599	
Welfare costs	24,498		9,803		13,889	
		£ 273,478		£ 219,316		£ 192,773

Grants and Subsidies:					
Grants in aid	£ 5,711		£ 3,894		£ 2,108	
Sports and social grants	120,223		97,245		86,153	
		£ 125,934		£ 101,139		£ 88,261
Sickness salaries						
Stores	£440,000		£406,000		£380,688	
Head office	74,000		70,160		52,050	
	514,000		476,160		432,738	
		£2,918,650		£2,504,967		£2,193,650
Total per Accounts						
Additional Staff Benefits:						
Group life and pensions fund	£674,612		£601,086		£542,982	
Allocation to benevolent trust	606,000		530,000		441,000	
Staff discount	327,000		171,318		152,026	
	£1,607,612		£1,302,404		1,136,008	
Total		£4,526,262		£3,807,371		£3,329,658

Exhibit 9

MARKS AND SPENCER, LIMITED (A)
Organizational interrelationships

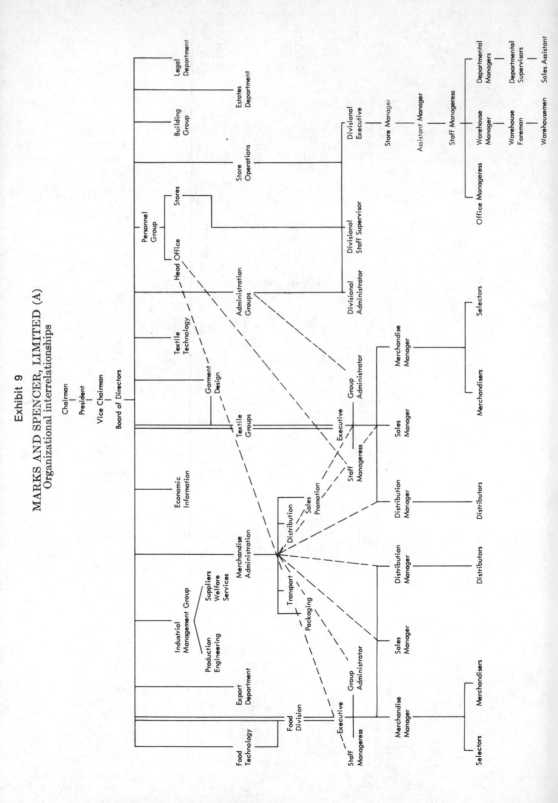

Exhibit 10

SELECTED INFORMATION ON COMPETITIVE STORES

John Lewis Partnership

A group of 17 department stores, 2 specialty stores, and 50 supermarkets, operating under a variety of names, including John Lewis, Peter Jones, Bon Marche, and Waitrose Supermarkets.

1973/74

Sales:	STG 138,982,000—Department stores
	STG 66,459,000—Supermarkets
Profit (B.T.):	STG 14,612,000
Stocks:	STG 24,693,000 (at 30/3/74)

Sainsbury

A group of 154 supermarkets, 27 self-service grocery stores, and 17 counter-service grocery stores. Total sales area is 1,617,000 square feet with the average store size (of newest stores) 16,276 square feet.

1973/74

Sales:	STG 332,623,000—Supermarkets
	STG 21,433,000—Self-service
	STG 8,081,000—Counter-service
Profit (B.T.):	STG 13,624,000
Stocks:	STG 28,206,000 (at 9/3/74)
Sales area:	1,617,000 sq.ft.—Supermarkets

British Home Stores

A group of 97 retail variety stores, carrying apparel, domestics, and food products (recently converting to counter food service).

1973/74

Sales:	STG 121,021,000
Profit (B.T.):	STG 15,464,000
Stocks:	STG 15,488,000 (at 30/3/74)
Sales area:	2,250,000 sq.ft. (estimated)

Tesco

A group of supermarkets, superstores (carrying goods for the home and wearing apparel), neighborhood grocery stores, and furniture stores. The store sizes are as follows:

Size	Number of Stores
Less than 2,000 sq.ft.	222
2,000 to 5,000 sq.ft.	250
5,000 to 10,000 sq.ft.	179
10,000 to 20,000 sq.ft.	96
Over 20,000 sq.ft.	26
	773

1973/74 Sales	£433,767,000
1974/74 Profit (B.T.)	24,538,000

The company and its responsibilities to society: Relating corporate strategy to ethical values

WE COME at last to the fourth component of strategy formulation—the moral and social implications of what once was considered a purely economic choice. In our consideration of strategic alternatives, we have come from what strategists *might* and *can* do to what they *want* to do. We now move to what they *ought* to do—from the viewpoint of various leaders and segments of society and their standards of right and wrong.

Ethics, like preference, may be considered a product of values. To some the suggestion that an orderly and analytical process of strategy determination should include the discussion of highly controversial ethical issues, about which honest differences of opinion are common and self-deceiving rationalization endless, is repugnant. This body of opinion is led by an immovable and doughty band of economic isolationists, of which Milton Friedman is the leader. They argue that business should be required only to live up to its legal obligations and that consideration of strategic alternatives should be exclusively economic.[1] A larger group of business leaders remain silent, probably suspecting the rhetorical virtue in public statements of corporate intent. A host of small business people are too busy at surviving adversity to dwell much on this subject.

THE MORAL COMPONENT OF CORPORATE STRATEGY

The emerging view in the liberal-professional leadership of our most prominent corporations is that determining future strategy must take into account—as part of its social environment—steadily rising moral and ethical standards. Reconciling the conflict in responsibility which occurs when maximum profit and social contribution appear on the

[1] The classic statement of this position, which is hardly subject to modernization, is still Milton Friedman, *Capitalism and Freedom* (Chicago: The University of Chicago Press, 1962).

same agenda adds to the complexity of strategy formulation and its already clear demands for creativity. Coming to terms with the morality of choice may be the most strenuous undertaking in strategic decision.

Attention is compelled to the noneconomic consequences of corporate power and activity by a combination of forces constituting the environment of business. Most dramatic is the decline in public confidence in public and private institutions accompanying the prosecution of the Vietnam War, Watergate, and the forced resignation of a vice president and president of the United States. Distrust of business flared with the revelation by the Watergate Special Prosecutor of illegal political contributions. The Securities and Exchange Commission's probe of other illegal and questionable payments has publicized the illegal or questionable behavior of scores of well-known companies. The deposition of the top leadership of such companies as the Gulf Oil Corporation and the Lockheed Aircraft Company was a blow to the supposition that our respected companies were abiding by the law and professional standards of ethical conduct. The quick confessions of other companies to avoid prosecution were given wide publicity.

The absence of disavowal by competitors of such practices left the impression with the public that this illegality was characteristic of all business. Successive Harris polls reported that 55 percent of the public in 1966 had felt great confidence in the chief executives of large corporations, that 21 percent felt that way in 1974, and only 15 percent in 1975. A Gallup poll in July 1975 showed big business scored lowest in confidence (34 percent) compared to organized labor (38 percent), Congress (40 percent), the Supreme Court (49 percent), the Executive branch (52 percent), the military (58 percent), education (67 percent), and organized religion (68 percent).[2]

Discussions of the responsibility of business have usually until now taken individual personal integrity for granted or have assumed that the courts were adequate discipline to ensure compliance with the law. The obvious necessity for explicit company policy now makes it necessary for decision to be made about at least how compliance with the law can be ensured. The first step is a stated policy that illegality will not be condoned and enforcement provisions will begin with corporate action rather than waiting for the law and the courts.

Since political contributions and bribery are neither illegal nor even unusual in other parts of the world, explicit policy must be made with respect to other marginal, technically legal, but in American eyes, improper kinds of payments. Once embarked on this path, companies are forced to include policy decisions about other corporate and personal ethical behavior in their strategies. Presumably, except possibly for such policy as proscribing political contributions where they are legally permitted, the economic isolationists would not object to the new necessity to articulate and enforce the unspoken strategic assumption that the company would pursue its economic objectives within the law.

---

[2] Leonard Silk and David Vogel, *Ethics and Profit: The Crisis of Confidence in American Business* (New York: Simon & Schuster, Inc., 1976), pp. 21–22.

As many a corporation that has regarded itself as socially responsible is finding out, specifying and securing ethical behavior is not easy in a company with responsibility delegated through many levels of authority and degrees of autonomy. The morality of personal behavior is not the only concern. Arguments for the active participation in public affairs and the exercise of concern for the impact of economic activity upon society are gaining ground for a number of reasons.

First, corporate executives of the caliber, integrity, intelligence, and humanity capable of coping with the problems of personal morality just cited are not happy to be tarred with the brush of bribery and corruption. They are not likely to turn their backs on other problems involving corporate behavior of the middle and late 70s. The mid-decade recession, the developing energy crisis, the growing sensitivity to environmental damage by industrial and community operations, the protection of the consumer from intended or unwitting exploitation or deception, the extension of social justice, as exemplified by the demands of minority populations and women for opportunity and recognition, the general concern for the limits of growth and the so-called quality of life —all these cannot be ignored. The need is widely acknowledged to respond as a matter of conscience as well as a matter of law.

Second, it is increasingly clear that government regulation is not a good substitute for knowledgeable self-restraint. As expectations for the protection and well-being of the environment, of customers, and of employees grow more insistent, it is clear that if corporate power is to be regulated more by public law than by private conscience, much of our national energy will have to be spent keeping watch over corporate behavior, ferreting out problems, designing and revising detailed laws to deal with them, and enforcing these laws even as they become obsolete.

Executives assuming top management responsibility today may be more sensitive on the average than their predecessors to the upgrading of our goals as a society and more responsive to the opportunity to relate corporate and public purposes. But if not, they can be sure that new regulation will force this concern upon their strategic processes. Extending the reach of strategic decision to encompass public concerns is either a voluntary response permitting latitude in choice or acquiescence to law which may involve none. New forms of regulation or effective enforcement come late to the problem without regard for feasibility or cost. The strategist can consider much earlier whether the problem is susceptible to effective and economically satisfactory solution.

CATEGORIES OF CONCERN

If you elect to admit responsiveness to society's concern about corporate power and activities to your definition of strategy, you come face to face with two major questions. What is the range of corporate involvement available to a company? What considerations should guide its choice of opportunity?

The world. The problems affecting the quality of life in the society to which the company belongs may usefully be thought of as extending through a set of densely populated spheres from the firm itself to the world community. The multinational firm, to take world society first, would find (within its economic contribution to industrialization in the developing countries) the need to measure what it takes out before it could judge its participation responsible. The willingness to undertake joint ventures rather than insist on full ownership, to share management and profits in terms not immediately related to the actual contributions of other partners, to cooperate otherwise with governments looking for alternatives to capitalism, to train nationals for skilled jobs and management positions, to reconcile different codes of ethical practice in matters of taxes and bribery—all illustrate the opportunity for combining entrepreneurship with responsibility and the terms in which strategy might be expressed.

The nation. Within the United States, for a firm of national scope, problems susceptible to constructive attention from business occur in virtually every walk of life. To narrow too wide a choice, a company would most naturally begin with the environmental consequences of its manufacturing processes or the impact of its products upon the public. Presumably a company would first put its own house in order or embark upon a long program to make it so. Then it might take interest in other problems, either through tax-deductible philanthropic contributions or through business ventures seeking economic opportunity in social need —for example, trash disposal or health care. Education, the arts, race relations, equal opportunity for women, or even such large issues as the impact upon society of technological change compete for attention. Our agenda of national problems is extensive. It is not hard to find opportunities. The question, as in product-market possibilities, is which ones to choose.

The local community. Closer home are the problems of the communities in which the company operates. These constitute the urban manifestations of the national problems already referred to—inadequate housing, unemployment in the poverty culture, substandard medical care, and the like. The city, special focus of national decay and vulnerable to fiscal and other mismanagement, is an attractive object of social strategy because of its nearness and compactness. The near community allows the development of mutually beneficial corporate projects such as vocational training. Business cannot remain healthy in a sick community.

Industry. Moving from world to country to city takes us through the full range of social and political issues which engage the attention of corporate strategists who wish to factor social responsibility into their planning. Two other less obvious but even more relevant avenues of action should be considered—the industry or industries in which the company operates and the quality of life within the company itself. Every industry, like every profession, has problems which arise from a legacy of indifference, stresses of competition, the real or imagined impossibility of interfirm cooperation under the antitrust laws. Every industry has chronic problems of its own, such as safety, product quality, pricing, and pollution in which only cooperative action can effectively pick up where regulation leaves off or makes further regulation unnecessary.

The company. Within the firm itself, a company has open opportunity for satisfying its aspirations to responsibility. The quality of any company's present strategy, for example, is probably always subject to improvement, as new technology and higher aspirations work together. But besides such important tangible matters as the quality of goods and services being offered to the public and the maintenance and improvement of ordinary craftsmanship, there are three other areas which in the future will become much more important than they seem now. The first of these is the review process set up to estimate the quality of top-management decision. The second is the impact upon individuals of the control systems and other organization processes installed to secure results. The third is a recognition of the role of the individual in the corporation.

Review of management concerns for responsibility

The everyday pressures bearing on decisions about what to do and how to get it done make almost impossible the kind of detached self-criticism which is essential to the perpetuation of responsible freedom. The opportunity to provide for systematic review sessions becomes more explicit and self-conscious. At any rate, as a category of concern, how a management can maintain sufficient detachment to estimate without self-deception the quality of its management performance is as important as any other. The proper role of the board of directors in performing this function—long since lost sight of—requires revitalization.

The caliber and strategic usefulness of a board of directors will nonetheless remain the option of the chief executive who usually determines its function. How much he uses his board for the purposes of improving the quality of corporate strategy and planning turns, as usual, on the sincerity of his interest and his skill. Recent research has illuminated the irresponsibility of inaction in the face of problems requiring the perspective available only to properly constituted boards. This organization resource is available to general managers who recognize dormancy as waste and seek counsel in cases of conflicting responsibility. A number of large corporations, including General Motors, have established Public Responsibility Committees of the board to focus attention on social issues.

The effective provision by a board of responsible surveillance of the moral quality of a management's strategic decisions means that current stirrings of concern about conflicts of interest will soon result in the withdrawal from boards of bankers representing institutions performing services to the company, of lawyers (in some instances) representing a firm retained by the company, and other suppliers or customers, as well as more scrupulous attention to present regulations about interlocking interests. As much attention will soon be given to avoiding the possibility of imputing conflict of interest to a director as to avoiding the actual occurrence. Stronger restrictions on conflict of interest will also affect employees of the firm, including the involvement of individuals with social-action organizations attacking the firm.

Impact of control systems on ethical performance

Second, the ethical and economic quality of an organization's performance is vitally affected by its control system, which inevitably leads people, if it is effective at all, to do what will make them look good in the terms of the system rather than what their opportunities and problems, which the system may not take cognizance of, actually require. We will examine the unintended consequences of control and measurement systems when we come to the implementation of corporate strategy; in the meantime we should note that unanticipated pressures to act irresponsibly may be applied by top management who would deplore this consequence if they knew of it. The process of promotion by which persons are moved from place to place so fast that they do not develop concern for the problems of the community in which they live or effective relationships within which to accomplish anything unintentionally weakens the participation of executives in community affairs. The tendency to measure executives in divisionalized companies on this year's profits reduces sharply their motivation to invest in social action with returns over longer times. Lifelong habits of neutrality and non-involvement eventually deprive the community, in a subtle weakening of its human resources, of executive experience and judgment. Executive cadres are in turn deprived of real-life experience with political and social systems which they ultimately much need.

The individual and the corporation

The actual quality of life in a business organization turns most crucially on how much freedom is accorded to the individual. Certainly most firms consider responsibility to their members a category of concern as important as external constituencies. It is as much a matter of enlightened self-interest as of responsibility to provide conditions encouraging the convergence of the individual's aspirations with those of the corporation, to provide conditions for effective productivity, and to reward employees for extraordinary performance.

With the entry of the corporation into controversial areas comes greater interest on the part of organization members to take part in public debate. It becomes possible for individuals to make comments on social problems that could be embarrassing to the corporation. It is at best difficult to balance the freedom of individuals and the consequences of their participation in public affairs against the interests of the corporation. The difficulty is increased if the attitudes of management, which are instinctively overprotective of the corporation, are harsh and restrictive. Short-run embarrassments and limited criticism from offended groups—even perhaps a threatened boycott—may be a small price to pay for the continued productivity within the corporation of people whose interests are deep and broad enough to cause them to take stands on public issues. The degree to which an organization is efficient, productive, creative, and capable of development is dependent in large part on the maintenance of a climate in which the individual does not feel suppressed, and in which a kind of freedom (analogous to that which the corporation enjoys in a free enterprise society) is permitted as a matter of course. Overregulation of the individual by corporate policy is no more appropriate internally than overregulation of the corporation by government. On the other hand, personal responsibility is as appropriate to individual liberty as corporate responsibility is to corporate freedom.

The range of concerns

What corporate strategists have to be concerned with, then, ranges from the most global of the problems of world society to the uses of freedom by a single person in the firm. The problems of their country, community, and industry lying between these extremes make opportunity for social contribution exactly coextensive with the range of economic opportunity before them. The problem of choice may be met in the area of responsibility in much the same way as in product-market combinations and in developing a program for growth and diversification.

The business firm, as an organic entity intricately affected by and affecting its environment, is as appropriately adaptive, our concept of corporate strategy suggests, to demands for responsible behavior as for economic service. Special satisfactions and prestige, if not economic rewards, are available for companies that are not merely adaptive but take the lead in shaping the moral and ethical environment within which their primary economic function is performed. Such firms are more persuasive than others, moreover, in convincing the public of the inherent impossibility of satisfying completely all the conflicting claims made upon business.

CHOICE OF STRATEGIC ALTERNATIVES FOR SOCIAL ACTION

The choice of avenues in which to participate will, of course, be influenced by the personal values of the managers making the decision. In the absence of powerful predispositions, the inner coherence of the corporate strategy would be extended by choosing issues most closely related to the economic strategy of the company, to the expansion of its markets, to the health of its immediate environment, and to its own industry and internal problems. The extent of appropriate involvement depends importantly on the resources available. Because the competence of the average corporation outside its economic functions is severely limited, it follows that a company should not venture into good works that are not strategically related to its present and prospective economic functions.

As in the case of personal values and individual idiosyncracy, a company may be found making decisions erratically related to nonstrategic motives. However noble these may be, they are not made strategic and thus defensible and valid by good intentions alone. Rather than make large contributions to X University because its president is a graduate, it might better develop a pattern of educational support that blends the company's involvement in the whole educational system, its acknowledged debt for the contributions of technical or managerial education to the company, and its other contributions to its communities. What makes participation in public affairs strategic rather than improvisatory is (as we have seen in conceiving economic strategy) a definition of objectives taking all other objectives into account and a plan that reflects the company's definition of itself not only as a purveyor of goods and services but as a responsible institution in its society.

The strategically directed company then will have a strategy for support of community institutions as explicit as its economic strategy and as its decisions about the kind of organization it intends to be and the kind of people it intends to attract to its membership. It is easy and proper, when margins allow it, to make full use of tax deductibility, through contributions, from which it expects no direct return. The choice of worthy causes, however, should relate to the company's concept of itself and thus directly to its economic mission. It should enter into new social service fields with the same questions about its resources and competence that new product-market combinations inspire. In good works as in new markets, opportunity without the competence to develop it is illusory. Deliberate concentration on limited objectives is preferable to scattered short-lived enthusiasm across a community's total need.

Policy for ethical and moral personal behavior, once the level of integrity has been decided, is not complicated by a wide range of choice. The nature of the company's operations defines the areas of vulnerability—purchasing, rebates, price-fixing, fee-splitting, customs facilitation, bribery, dubious agents' fees, conflict of interest, theft, or falsification of records. Where problems appear or danger is sensed specific rules can be issued. As in the case of government regulation of the firm, these should not be overdetailed or mechanical, for there is no hope of anticipating the ingenuity of the willful evader. Uncompromising penalties for violations of policy intent or the rarely specified rule will do more to clarify strategy in this area than thousands of words beforehand. The complexity of elevating individual behavior is thus a matter of implementation of strategy more properly discussed in the context of organization processes such as motivation and control.

DETERMINATION OF STRATEGY

We have now before us the major determinants of strategy. The cases studied so far have required consideration of what the strategy of the firm is and what, in your judgment, it ought to be. Concerned so far with the problem of formulating a proper strategy rather than implementing it, you have become familiar with the principal aspects of formulation—namely, (1) appraisal of present and foreseeable opportunity and risk in the company's environment, (2) assessment of the firm's unique combination of present and potential corporate resources or competences, (3) determination of the noneconomic personal and organizational preferences to be satisfied, and (4) identification and acceptance of the social responsibilities of the firm. The strategic decision is one that can be reached only after all these factors have been considered and the action implications of each assessed.

In your efforts to analyze the cases, you have experienced much more of the problem of the strategist than can be described on paper. When you have relinquished your original idea as to what a company's strategy should be in favor of a more imaginative one, you have seen that the formulation process has an essential creative aspect. In your effort to differentiate your thinking about an individual firm from the conventional thinking of its industry, you have looked for new opportunities and for new applications of corporate competence. You have learned how to define a product in terms of its present and potential functions rather than of its physical properties. You have probably learned a good deal about how to assess the special competence of a firm from its past accomplishments, and how to identify management's values and aspirations. You may have gained some ability to rank preferences in order of their strength—your own among others.

The problem implicit in striking a balance between the company's apparent opportunity and its evident competence, between your own personal values and concepts of responsibility and those of the company's actual management is not an easy one. The concepts we have been discussing should help you make a decision, but they will not determine your decision for you. Whenever choice is compounded of rational analysis which can have more than one outcome, of aspiration and desire which can run the whole range of human ambition, and a sense of responsibility which changes the appeal of alternatives, it cannot be reduced to quantitative approaches or to the exactness which management science can apply to narrower questions. Managers contemplating strategic decisions must be willing to make them without the guidance of decision rules, with confidence in their own judgment, which will have been seasoned by repeated analyses of similar questions. They must be aware that more than one decision is possible and that they are not seeking the single right answer. They can take encouragement from the fact that the manner in which an organization implements the chosen program can help to validate the original decision.

Some of the most difficult choices confronting a company are those which must be made among several alternatives that appear equally attractive and also equally desirable. Once the analysis of opportunity has produced an inconveniently large number of possibilities, any firm has difficulty in deciding what it wants to do and how the new activities will be related to the old.

In situations where opportunity is approximately equal and economic promise is offered by a wide range of activities, the problem of making a choice can be reduced by reference to the essential character of the company and to the kind of company the executives wish to run. The study of alternatives from this point of view will sooner or later reveal the greater attractiveness of some choices over others. Economic analysis and calculations of return on investment, though of course essential, may not crucially determine the outcome. Rather, the logjam of decision can only be broken by a frank exploration of executive aspirations regarding future development, including perhaps the president's own wishes with respect to the kind of institution he or she prefers to head, carried on as part of a free and untrammeled investigation of what human needs the organization would find satisfaction in serving. That return on investment alone will point the way ignores the values implicit in the calculations and the contribution which an enthusiastic commitment to new projects can make. The rational examination of alternatives and the determination of purpose are among the most important and most neglected of all human activities. The final decision, which should be made as deliberately as possible after a detailed consideration of the issues we have attempted to separate, is an act of will and desire as much as of intellect.

Xerox Corporation

On September 8, 1971, Mr. C. Peter McColough, then president and chief executive officer of the Xerox Corporation, announced an experimental Social Service Leave Program to begin in January 1972. The program provided an opportunity for approximately 20 Xerox employees in the United States to take up to a one-year leave of absence, with full pay and benefits, and devote the time to working with a social service organization of their choice. They were also guaranteed the same or an equivalent job with the same pay, responsibilities, status and opportunity for advancement upon return to the company.

In announcing the program to Xerox employees, Mr. McColough spoke of corporate and individual commitment and what the program represented for each:

> Xerox has always had a basic philosophy that we should be involved as a corporation in the problems of our society. We've encouraged our people to be involved. Social Service Leave is a logical extension of our commitment. We are determined to put something back into society.
>
> Many of our people share our commitment. But on a part-time basis, there is only so much they can do. A lot of them would like to really sink their teeth into a problem full time. We'll give them a chance to do this during the prime of their working careers, when they're best able to do it. They won't have to wait until they retire.
>
> Many of our best people would not be here today if Xerox stood only for profits.
>
> In the future, our conduct as corporate citizens will be even more important—if that's possible—as we try to recruit the best young people available. As a result of programs like the Social Service Leave, we think that the bright young people will be more apt to join us than some other big company.

By January, Mr. McColough and others in top management were beginning to evaluate the program to determine whether it ought to be continued and, if so, whether the scope, policies and procedures underlying it were appropriate. As far as they could determine, it had been favorably received both inside and outside the company. Several overseas affiliates had evidenced an interest in a program of their own, usually to be operated under somewhat different policies. Moreover, it had so far been implemented according to plan and without serious mishap. On the other hand, a number of unforeseen organizational problems had already been encountered and the difficult tasks of responding to the needs of the men and women on leave and replacing them in equivalent career opportunities remained ahead.

The evaluation was accompanied by a degree of urgency. There was a general feeling among those closely involved in planning the program that the best time from the employees' standpoint to begin a social leave was in September, which, if adopted, would advance the announcement of a 1972–73 program to April or May.

XEROX HISTORY

In 1971 Xerox had sales of $1.94 billion and profits of $212.6 million, placing it among the largest fifty-five industrial corporations in the *Fortune* 500. Growth had been spectacular since 1959 when sales were $33.3 million and profits $2.1 million. In fact, from 1960 to 1970, earnings per share increased at a compound rate of 47.3% per year, highest on the *Fortune* list.

The primary source of growth for Xerox had come through the commercial development of an electrostatic-photographic copying process later known as xerography. Formed in 1906 in Rochester, New York, as the Haloid Corporation by Joseph R. Wilson and three associates to process and sell sensitized photographic paper, the company had struggled through the depression and emerged from the war years with sales in 1946 of $6,750,000 and profits of $101,000. That year Joseph C. Wilson succeeded his father as president. Confronted by increasing competition and decreasing margins in traditional product lines, the younger Mr. Wilson was eager to develop new products but lacked the resources to support a significant research effort. At this time the Battelle Institute, a non-profit research organization, had been seeking industrial support for the development of a copying process patented by Chester Carlson in 1940 and since 1944 supported by the Institute. Although numerous corporations, including Kodak, IBM and RCA, had turned the invitation down, Mr. Wilson in 1947 agreed to acquire from Battelle certain licensing rights in return for future royalty payments and an annual contribution of $25,000. A short time later Xerox renegotiated the arrangement and became the sole licensing agency for all patents in the xerography field.

Xerox invested heavily in research during the next years, greatly expanding its patent position, and yielding a series of specialized applications for xerography which by the mid-1950s contributed over half of the company's revenues. From 1953 to 1960 over $70 million was poured into research, slightly more than half of it contributed by outside debt and equity financing. It was not, however, until 1960 and the introduction of the 914, the first fully automatic dry copier in the office equipment industry, that this investment really began to pay off.

On the strength of the 914, sales nearly tripled from 1960 to 1962 as Xerox became the leader in the copier field. The company sought to expand that position by aggressively broadening its product line to include desk top copiers and high-speed machines with expanded reproduction capabilities. As machine speeds increased and reproduction quality improved, the traditional distinction between the copying and duplicating fields became blurred. The pace of development and marketing efforts in office copiers and duplicators was intense as the partial list of product introductions below suggests:

Year	Product	Feature
1960	914	Basic console model (400 copies per hour)
1963	813	Desk top model (330 copies per hour)
1965	2400	Copier-duplicator (2,400 copies per hour)
1966	720	Expanded version of 914 (720 copies per hour)
1967	660	Expanded version of 813 (660 copies per hour)
1968	3600	Expanded version of 2400 (3,600 copies per hour)
1969	7000	Duplicator, expanded capabilities (3,600 copies per hour)
1971	4000	Small console, expanded capabilities (2,000 copies per hour)

By 1971, Xerox was estimated in the business press to have 65% to 80% of the office copier market in the United States. The company's record had encouraged competition from such large firms as Eastman Kodak, Minnesota Mining, Litton, Singer, and Sperry Rand and a variety of smaller ones. A recent entrant was IBM which in April 1970 introduced a machine having much in common with the Xerox model 720. *Financial World,*[1] noting that some 70% of commercial and government establishments already contained a copier, was among those predicting increasing competition in the future. Nevertheless, Xerox 1971 revenues from copiers and rentals in the United States increased 12% over the previous year, with steady improvement relative to 1970 throughout the year.

In 1956, Xerox formed a joint venture with the Rank organization of London to manufacture and sell xerographic products in world markets, a relationship which in 1961 also led to the formation of a second joint venture between Rank-Xerox and Fuji Photo Film Co., Fuji-Xerox, directed specifically at markets in the Far East. Revenues overseas also increased dramatically after the introduction of the 914. Then in 1969 Xerox purchased the 51st percent of Rank-Xerox and renegotiated certain royalty provisions in exchange for stock valued at $20 million.

During the 1970s, Xerox sought participation in several new fields. First, in 1963 Electro Optical Systems (EOS), an aerospace company involved in laser technology, solar power conversion and space reconnaissance, was acquired to gain entry into the high technology, government financed, R & D business. Then, beginning in 1964 and con-

---

[1] "Copiers: Competition Heating Up," *Financial World,* May 6, 1970, p. 6 ff.

cluding in 1968 with the acquisition of a prominent textbook publisher, Ginn & Co., Xerox assembled an education group producing a wide range of materials and information services. Finally, in 1969 in exchange for approximately $1 billion in stock, the company acquired Scientific Data Systems, a mainframe computer manufacturer with revenues of $100 million, about 70% of it derived from scientific and engineering applications.

These new ventures had not, as yet, produced a record approaching that in office copiers. Cutbacks and reallocations in government programs had seriously affected the aerospace business and dampened the growth in spending for education. The computer group, renamed Xerox Data Systems (XDS) had been subject to similar pressures and, in part due to more conservative accounting policies, had been operating at a loss. Revenues from computer products were off about 20% in 1971 and management indicated that losses were expected to continue through 1973.

A breakdown of revenues by product line was reported as follows:

	1969	1970	1971
Business products	56%	58%	56%
International operations	27	30	34
Computer products	8	5	3
Educational materials and information services	6	6	6
Government sponsored research and military products	3	1	1
	100%	100%	100%

Profits after taxes from international operations were $72 million in 1970 and $92 million in 1971 or 38% and 43%, respectively, of the corporate total. A financial summary is provided in Exhibit 1.

Xerox had a publicly stated goal of achieving continuing growth of 20% per year in earnings per share with a return on stockholder investment of 20%. This target was generally perceived in the organization to be a very demanding one. In 1971 Mr. McColough indicated that growth would be guided by two broad policies, the first directed toward industry leadership in the information industry and the second toward becoming a "great multinational company."

> We think that our field of interest is the business of supplying knowledge and information on a worldwide basis. It seems to me that this will be the fastest growing business in the world in the 1970s. The demand for knowledge and information in every country of the world is increasing geometrically each year. There seems to be no limit to where we can go in that field if we apply ourselves to it in the right way. . . . I think in the middle 70s, you will see us bring [computer and imaging capabilities] together in combination to offer new services that will be very important to our business worldwide.
>
> * * * * *
>
> One of our major objectives for the 1970s clearly has to be to make Xerox a great multinational company. Multinational. Not inter-

national. In the 1960s, as we spread our wings from the United States into the rest of the world through various partnerships we became an international company in the sense that we operated in many parts of the world.

But in the 1970s we must become a multinational company. Among other things a multinational company must provide opportunities for all its people regardless of what country they come from. The young person who joins the company today—whether in Milan or Sao Paulo or New York City—should have an equal opportunity to take my job in the future.

* * * * *

We must also put great emphasis in the 1970s on having manufacturing operations in many locations. We have to realize that if we are going to be large in the major countries of the world, we are going to have to contribute to those countries. We can't simply go in with products manufactured somewhere else; we must put something back in.

ORGANIZATIONAL STRUCTURE

Managing the company's growth constituted a formidable challenge for the Xerox organization. The number of employees grew from 9,000 in 1960 to 63,000 in 1971, about 25,000 of them overseas. Moreover, by the late 1970s this total was expected to more than double again. The average employee in the United States was estimated to be less than 30 years old and about a third of them had been with the company less than three years. Xerox had entered the 1960s with a functional organization but over the next decade changes at all levels were frequent as the company moved toward a divisionalized structure. The consequences of growth for individual managers were described by one personnel executive in the Business Products Group (BPG), which alone had 33,000 employees:

> Xerox has the ability to make organization changes quickly. In BPG going from $100 million to $1.2 billion in ten years has meant that just by staying in the same job, a manager's responsibilities increase dramatically. One of the rewards of my work is seeing people literally grow. Of course, some don't and we have had to move them down or aside. We no longer have employment contracts with our top managers but instead give them a six-month turnaround time should we decide to part ways.

Rapid growth had also prompted the company to seek managers for high-level positions from outside the company. Mr. Archie McCardell (45), president, who joined Xerox in 1966 from Ford[2] where he had held various jobs in the finance and control area, commented:

> We have grown so fast that there has not been time for enough managers to come up through the ranks. We have brought in a num-

---
[2] Other senior executives coming to Xerox from other companies since 1967 included Dr. Jacob Goldman (Sr. V.P., R & D) and Mr. James O'Neill (Gr. V.P., BPG) from Ford, Mr. Joseph Flavin (Ex. V.P.) and Mr. William Glavin (Gr. V.P. XDS) from IBM, and Mr. Robert Haigh (Gr. V.P., Education Group) from Standard Oil (Ohio).

ber of outsiders at high levels and will probably continue to do so for another two or three years. With the pressures on our organization, getting sufficient attention devoted to management development has been a continuing source of concern for us.

In 1969, Xerox announced plans to relocate the corporate offices in Connecticut. On an interim basis, pending construction of a new office building in Greenwich, headquarters were moved to the neighboring town of Stamford, Connecticut.

In December 1971, a major rearrangement at the corporate level was announced to align the organization with the company's strategy for the 1970s. The announcement, although planned for some time, took place several weeks after the unexpected death of Mr. Wilson. Mr. McColough, who came to Xerox in 1954, rose through sales to executive vice president in 1962, president in 1966, and chief executive officer in 1968, became chairman. Mr. McCardell, executive vice president since 1968, became president and chief operating officer. All U.S. operations in computers, copying/duplicating, education and aerospace were assigned to Mr. Raymond Hay (43), who formerly was responsible for BPG and for a short time overseas activities as well. Mr. Joseph Flavin (43), formerly senior vice president for planning and finance and then briefly in charge of XDS, was made responsible for international operations. The new organization is shown in Exhibit 2.

CORPORATE RESPONSIBILITY

Xerox management believed that the company was a social as well as an economic institution and had responsibilities to society beyond economic performance. Mr. Wilson articulated this attitude in a 1964 speech:

> The corporation cannot refuse to take a stand on public issues of major concern; failure to act is to throw its weight on the side of the status quo, and the public interprets it that way.
> Inevitably the corporation is involved in economic, social and political dynamics whether it wills or not, and to ignore the noneconomic consequences of business decisions is to invite outside intervention. . . .

There was a general feeling in the company that Mr. McColough's commitment to this point of view was also very strong.

The company had been involved in a number of programs which related to this social concern. In 1968 Xerox participated with local community organizations in Rochester in the founding of FIGHTON, Inc., a manufacturing company owned and managed by Blacks in the inner city, and continued to be a major customer for its products and a consultant to its management. Investments and deposits had also been made in minority-owned banks. Internally Xerox had instituted a minority hiring and development program that had substantially increased the number of minority employees. A pollution abatement control committee had also been formed to monitor the company's activities in that area.

The company had been active in sharing sponsorship of TV events of educational or cultural significance, among the recent programs being the "Civilisation" series and Sesame Street. In addition, charitable contributions of about $5.0 million were made during 1971, up from $4.4 million in 1970 and $3.7 million in 1969. The majority of the funds went to educational institutions; other recipients included Community Chests and United Funds in locations having Xerox facilities and a wide variety of civic, legal, health and urban affairs organizations. Asked in 1969 whether contributions should be cut back, 90.2% of the stockholders, representing 96.9% of the shares, voted "no."

THE SOCIAL SERVICE LEAVE PROGRAM— CONCEPTION AND DESIGN

In August 1970, Mr. McCardell and Mr. James Wainger took the night flight from New York to Los Angeles. Mr. Wainger, who originally joined Xerox in 1960 but left the company from 1966 to 1969 to teach and write plays, had been made director of personnel two months earlier.[3] The conversation turned to how Xerox might be more responsive to social and employee needs in the 1970s. Mr. McCardell suggested that the company consider making some of its people available to work on problems of their choosing. By the time the wheels touched in Los Angeles, a leave program had been outlined in some detail.

Upon his return, Mr. Wainger discussed the idea briefly with Mr. Sanford Kaplan, his immediate superior at the time, and Mr. McColough, receiving in each case enthusiastic support. He then described the program in a memorandum sent to corporate executives (see Exhibit 3).

Mr. McColough suggested one modification almost immediately: that the evaluation committee be composed of lower level Xerox employees rather than a prestigious outside board. He commented:

> Xerox is a very young company. Our average age is less than 30 and we will be hiring tens of thousands of young people in the next few years. Large corporations inevitably tend to be dictatorial which runs counter to the needs of many young people. They would like to have a voice in policy and not have to wait until late in their careers. This committee is the first of a number of things that will involve our employees in either decision or advisory roles.
>
> I also believe that such a committee can do a better job of evaluating projects. Its members are probably more in tune with the needs that those applying for leave are hoping to satisfy. This procedure will erase any tinge that the committee is there to serve our [top management's] interests.

While the remainder of the top management group was positive about the leave program, there was some feeling that the fall of 1970 was not the appropriate time to initiate it. A soft economy in the latter

---

[3] Mr. Wainger recalled that his assignment had come as a surprise; "I told Peter [McColough] I had no experience in personnel, but he said what he was looking for was someone with a sense for the company in a society in evolution." He was elected vice president in 1971.

half of the year was putting pressure on operating budgets which in turn was forcing "modest" layoffs at headquarters and in Rochester. As one manager put it, "the psychology didn't set right—to be laying off and at the same time doing this." Mr. McColough decided to delay the announcement of the program.

Mr. Wainger began to reactivate the program the following spring. It was June, however, before the interview with Mr. McColough which was to appear in the brochure describing it could be arranged. Then with summer vacations approaching and the desire to "do the brochure right," the announcement date was put off until September.

In the meantime, Mr. Wainger set in motion a procedure for selecting members of the Evaluation Committee. He first contacted the top personnel executive in each division and asked them to identify people in their units who were relatively young, had some background in social service activities, possessed an "intellectual and emotional affinity for social issues," and were not members of top management. He then reviewed the list with Mr. Robert Schneider, assistant to the president and formerly manager of corporate contributions, and selected from it those that appeared most appropriate, keeping in mind the desire for a representative group in terms of operating unit, race, background and sex. The two men, individually, then visited these people in the field. Offers to join the committee were extended to and accepted on the spot by the first five interviewed. Messrs. Wainger and Schneider, as the two "old men," rounded out the committee shown in Exhibit 4.

The final ground rules for administering the program were also worked out for inclusion in the brochure. Xerox employees in the United States with three or more years of service were to be eligible for leave. No restrictions were to be placed on the type of projects acceptable except that they be legal, nonpartisan and under the sponsorship of an existing nonprofit organization of some kind. In addition to describing how they proposed to spend their time, applicants were to have the written acceptance of the sponsoring agency. It was Mr. McCardell's original idea that to help insure the commitment of applicants to projects, the company should play no part in matching people and opportunities.

Applications were to be submitted directly to the Evaluation Committee; employee names, however, were not to be available to the committee during their deliberations. Employees would not be asked to seek permission to apply nor were their superiors to be consulted at any time in the selection process. The brochure also noted that, "It's possible that in a rare case a person selected may be so essential in his work at Xerox that he cannot be released. If that should happen, the burden of proof will be on the manager and the final decision will be made by Peter McColough."

Mr. McColough commented on the reasons behind avoiding an "up the line" approval procedure:

> I do not want Social Service Leave to be looked upon in the organization as a reward for good performance. Nor do I want it, speaking pragmatically, to be a device for managers to get rid of people they

don't want. There are other ways of doing these things, and this program should not be used as a substitute. I also do not want managers to be able to block someone from seeking leave. I would say O.K. to a manager who is emphatic about not losing a subordinate, but I could not do it lightly. Finally, putting the decision in the hands of an independent committee removes the inference that we have our own pet projects. I am able to tell agencies who call me directly that the choice is not mine.

Mr. Wainger added some further thoughts on the organization of the program:

Having a multi-level approval process—God, doesn't that sound like jargon!—would dilute the corporate commitment to the project. This is *Xerox* doing something and not the units themselves, and the judgments should be those of the corporation. I favor functionalizing not decentralizing responsibility for an activity such as this.

A bottoms-up approach, I'm afraid, would introduce a lot of extraneous judgments in this case which would cut the heart out of the program. Worst of all, approval would be based on their [operation managers] view of the value of a project. That view could be influenced by administrative convenience—can't let a good subordinate go and so forth. That's especially serious when it comes to salesmen because so often those skills are what are most needed by social service agencies. We've gone to great lengths to involve on the committee the right people with right values to judge applications.

While the employees were on leave, their salaries, including a normal increase, were to be paid from a corporate account and not charged to the operating units. The aggregate cost was estimated at about $600,000.

ANNOUNCEMENT AND REACTION

On September 9, every Xerox employee in the United States was mailed a letter from Mr. McColough, the illustrated brochure and an application form (reproduced as Exhibit 5) which together described the program, the Evaluation Committee and the procedures for applying. Thus, everyone in the company, with the exception of those few corporate executives who had been directly involved, was apprised of the program at the same time. Although he did not like the idea of a press release, Mr. Wainger had one issued to avoid the confusion and conflicting stories that he felt might reach the media from such a large mailing.

The outside reaction was "overwhelming." Newspapers all over the country carried stories about the Social Service Leave, a television network inquired if a special feature might be made of it, and numerous radio stations and magazine reporters called for interviews. Mr. Wainger spoke for many in the corporation when he said:

I felt embarrassed about the attention this has received and did what I could to draw back from it. After all, the program is a very modest, experimental expression of our concern. Naturally, the publicity is good for our image, but that's not the reason we did it.

Several hundred social agencies have also called and we have had to send them a letter saying it's up to the employees, not us.

Within the organization, the response was described by one manager as that of "quiet admiration—a feeling that the company is really putting money and people behind its words."

From his vantage point, Mr. McColough said:

> The response I have had from the organization has all been favorable. In this case, that should not be surprising, of course, since it was clearly my decision and had already been done. I am sure, on the other hand, that had the expense gone into the operating budgets, there would have been some opposition.

There being no further policy matters to attend to, for the time being, Mr. Wainger's office settled down to wait until November 1, the deadline for applications.

APPLICATIONS

There was little conversation in the organization during September and October about social leave. Mr. Douglas Reid, manager of personnel operations at BPG, received a few phone calls from applicants in need of information which he referred to Mr. Wainger's office and on one occasion from a manager in support of a subordinate's project. However, the period was an active one for those assembling proposals. Mrs. Frayda Cooper, an editor at Ginn and eventually among those selected for leave, recalled her experience:

> I had lunch with Mr. Baker's[4] secretary on September 9 and she told me about the Social Leave Program. It perked my interest. For some time I have wanted to work with the aged. That night I talked about it with my son who encouraged me to try. When the brochure came a few days later I had mixed reactions; the committee didn't look very old—would they be interested in a program for the elderly? On the other hand, this field wasn't mentioned among the examples it provided —maybe if the committee tried to pick people in different areas, others wouldn't have thought of this one. Anyway, I decided to go ahead.
>
> I didn't talk about my plans in the company. The executive editor knew I was applying because I borrowed his brochure to write the proposal, having given mine away and being unable to find another one. Of course, out of courtesy, I had earlier told my immediate superior. I didn't have the sense that a lot of people around me were applying but with 25,000 people eligible, there were bound to be a lot.

In the next three weeks, Mrs. Cooper talked during lunch hours and Saturdays with a variety of people in government and social agencies and at Brandeis University about the problems of the elderly and her interests and background. These discussions resulted in a letter of support, including a budget of $17,000 for various expenses, and a four-page work plan from the Massachusetts Department of Community Affairs, which Mrs. Cooper appended to her handwritten application form. Since a manuscript had recently been accepted by Ginn con-

---

[4] Mr. Baker was president of Ginn.

ditional upon her availability to edit it, she advanced the starting date in the leave proposal to April 1972.

Another successful applicant was Mr. Irving Bell, a salesman with Xerox Graphic Services. Referring to these weeks he said:

> I found out about the program by reading the AP story in the newspaper. I was interested—said to myself, "Now that's a good idea!" I have a few rich friends and they never get a year to do their thing. I started to think about my background and where I'd fit; I wanted to contribute more than the ordinary person working at night.
>
> This was right after Attica.[5] I have some friends who talked with me about the prisons in Massachusetts and that got me thinking. A few years ago I had taught at a technical school, but unfortunately teaching was a luxury I couldn't afford then. Nevertheless, it was very gratifying. It seemed to me that someone who wanted to teach in penal institutions could give a little dignity and a pride of accomplishment to some people who really need it.
>
> It was a lonely time, but working on this was such a personal thing. I thought my program was pretty good—I used to dream about it. I brought my plans up a little at home, but never mentioned them to my boss. Maybe I was hedging my risk—in case I didn't get it. I figured there would be an application from everyone who was eligible.

A few applications were received in Mr. Wainger's office in the first two weeks, but then the flow virtually stopped. By mid-October only 30 were in hand. However, the number began to increase rapidly during the last week; the total rose to 96 by Friday, October 28 and to 197 by November 1, including all those postmarked before midnight. Another 20 or so were postmarked after the deadline and were regretfully disqualified. Each application was given a quick review by the legal department to assess whether the project and agency involved was politically nonpartisan and legal. None was eliminated.

EVALUATION AND SELECTION

On November 1 the Evaluation Committee was convened at Xerox headquarters in Stamford. Since, with the exception of the two corporate managers, the committee members did not know one another, Mr. Wainger invited them to his house for dinner the night before to help them become acquainted with one another. The next morning, the group met with Mr. McCardell who told them that the corporation was not going to give them instructions on who or what should be selected and that it was their responsibility to set standards to govern their choices.

The committee then read a dozen proposals and with this common background set about developing the evaluation process. After considerable discussion seven criteria evolved:

1. Social impact
2. Ability (of applicant to fulfill proposal)
3. Commitments (of both individual and agency)

---

[5] There had been a violent end to a prison revolt at Attica State Prison in New York State in September 1971.

4. Innovativeness
5. Multiplier effect
6. Continuity of program (after volunteer leaves)
7. Realism

An eighth one—favorable or unfavorable impact on the corporation—was explicitly raised and set aside as not in the spirit of the Social Leave Program. The committee then agreed that each member should study each proposal and grade it high, medium, or low. After a batch of 25 or 30 had been read, the committee would then stop and compare notes before going on.

Mr. Wainger described the tenor of the ensuing deliberations in these terms:

> The discussions were very democratic. There was surprisingly little ego involved. Although I acted as chairman to keep the book,[6] I consciously avoided dominating the discussion. In most cases there was a consensus on the low end. If there was wide disagreement, we would stop and talk it through, which often led to changes in opinions. As a result, some applications went quickly while others occupied us for two hours.
>
> After we had been through most of the proposals, it became clear that some of them were bubbling up as clear winners—seven in fact. We listed these by area of concern. Then someone said that they were all similar in that they exhibited a high intellectual content and were global in scope—proposals to set up programs or work on an institutional level. On the other hand, many of those we had given low evaluations to were one-on-one type projects. Someone else noted that all the pictures in the brochure showed people helping people in a very direct way. Was narrow bad? Was that what we had encouraged? The debate lasted a while and eventually resulted in a decision to go back and re-evaluate some of those we had rated poorly.

The committee labored with an increasing sense of cohesiveness from 9:00 A.M. until dinnertime from Monday to Thursday and concluded in the midafternoon Friday. As the week progressed, the committee identified 38 proposals in 17 areas of social concern to be given special attention. A conscious attempt was made to spread the final choices across these areas of concern (15 were eventually included). In addition, a less explicit effort was made to use the salary information requested on the application to insure that a balanced cross-section of levels in the organization was represented.

Ultimately 21 employees were selected, 2 of them requesting six-month leaves. Included in the group were three women and eighteen men. Their ages ranged from 26 to 60 and lengths of service at Xerox from 3 to 10 years. Four had monthly salaries of less than $850 while one had a monthly salary in excess of $4,000. Thirteen were employed in BPG with the remainder spread among other line and staff groups. People and projects are described in Exhibit 6. Another five employees were named as alternates, with any substitutions to be made in the

---

[6] The only record of the meeting was kept on a flip chart; one page devoted to criteria, two more to areas of social concern and employee proposals and two to an analysis of those selected by age, salary level and operating unit.

same field if possible. The alternates were not to be notified and remained identified by number only.

Before the committee adjourned, Mr. McCardell met with them again. He asked the group, "If you had another 10 places, could you recommend individuals to fill them with equal enthusiasm?" The group said, "No." He then asked, "Are there five among the ones you have selected that you consider marginal?" Again the group said, "No."

That afternoon registered, special delivery letters of acceptance were sent to each of the winners. With the letter was a plane ticket and an invitation to attend a meeting at the Westchester Country Club near Stamford the following Friday and Saturday morning. The purposes of the meeting were to provide the participants with an opportunity to understand the policies to govern them while on leave, to share backgrounds, to meet members of the Evaluation Committee and to receive some advance counseling on the stresses and frustrations many of them were likely to encounter as they left the structured life of a large corporation. They were told to keep their selection in confidence until after the meeting, though it was anticipated that they might have to tell their managers in order to explain their two-day absence.

All 21 attended the meeting. Mr. McColough and Mr. McCardell mingled with the group and addressed them briefly on Friday. In addition to a considerable amount of time for informal conversation, the schedule included group meetings in which each participant described his program, and others in which an industrial psychologist and a "down to earth" urban consultant discussed potential problems. Company public relations officials also discussed how to handle press inquiries.

Mr. Wainger commented later on the relationship between Xerox and those on leave that he had stressed with them.

> I could have thought of a long list of dos and don'ts but didn't want to get into that. Basically I told them that they were still Xerox employees and we wanted them back and that we would try to help them personally if they needed it. While they are away no reports will be required or evaluations made. Members of the Evaluation Committee will visit each person at least twice to see how the program is working and we have asked for a report from the volunteer at the end of the year.
>
> There are bound to be situations we haven't anticipated. For instance, what happens if one of our people gets into legal difficulties in the course of his work? It's the agency's responsibility to back him up, but we'll do all we can to help. Or the Massachusetts Correctional Agency asks our man teaching in their prisons if Xerox will interview inmates for jobs when they are released. In such cases I told them to call me. The relationship between Xerox and the agency is a corporate matter. My suspicion is that we won't start lots of little programs to suit agencies. We have several major on-going ones initiated from the corporate level and new ones will come in the same way.

By Saturday noon, the mood was described by one man as "euphoric." Another said, "It was beautiful—the most moving experience of my life." Still another remarked, "I could sense a sigh of relief from the committee after they had been with us for a little while. By the end, we had been transformed from a bunch of individuals into a group with common bonds and a sense of purpose."

SEPARATION

Prior to the meeting at the Westchester Country Club, Mr. Wainger reviewed the list for anyone he felt might be considered indispensable, Although Mr. John Teem, Director of the Technical Staff in R & D would be difficult to replace and Mr. William Gable was a senior executive at XDS, he anticipated no major problems securing their release. Then on November 18 he sent a letter to each manager having a subordinate chosen for leave, formally announcing the selection and forcefully reminding the manager of Mr. McColough's guarantee of the same or an equivalent job for the employee after the leave. One of these letters is reproduced in Exhibit 7.

The employees were greeted with applause and admiration, although as one account representative related, it was not always universal:

> It's funny how people react. The first thing my boss said when I told him I was going to Stamford for two days was, "Who's going to look after your accounts?" Perhaps I'm expecting too much. After all, he has needs and losing his best producer won't help.
>
> And the other night one of those who wasn't selected called me at 11 o'clock and said that he understood the Evaluation Committee had a tough job, but he couldn't see why they had picked my project rather than his. He had been with Xerox a lot longer than me and had really gone to a lot of work in putting his proposal together; it even included a letter from the governor.
>
> But the response I've gotten from others, especially my clients, has more than made up for it. They have a lot of respect for Xerox. It makes me glad I'm working here.

While Mr. McColough received no petitions claiming indispensability, a number of situations were uncovered during the next several weeks which reflected the complexity of administering the Social Service Leave Program and foreshadowed the problems to be encountered reinstating those on leave in the organization.

In one instance, a manager was to have received a substantial increase in the scope of his job two days after he was notified of his selection by the Evaluation Committee. He had not known about the impending promotion prior to accepting the leave.

In another case, one of the people chosen was to have been laid off. He was a specialist, very well thought of in his division, for whom no work was available because of government spending cutbacks. The company had tried for some time to relocate him in some other unit but had been unsuccessful. In fact, while the Evaluation Committee was meeting, the lay-off request was waiting on Mr. Wainger's desk for his approval.[7] Along with the others, however, he had been guaranteed an equivalent career opportunity when he returned.

A more difficult variation of the above situation also arose. A rela-

---

[7] Xerox maintained the policy that before an employee with eight or more years of service could be released, permission had to be granted by either Mr. McColough or Mr. Wainger.

tively senior man selected for leave was in the process of being terminated because his performance did not measure up to the standards set by the manager of his department, and other departments were reluctant to pick him up. He had accepted this fact and informally agreed during the fall to use the next six months to relocate. The department manager indicated that he was not aware of the social leave application until about the time the news broke.

A final case was described by Mr. Reid:

> I got a call one day in December from a branch manager. That was unusual in itself since he was calling three or four levels up the line. He said one of his area sales managers had been selected for leave. He didn't have a replacement and regional management told him that with the budgets cut to the bone there wasn't $5,000 to cover the relocation costs associated with moving somene else in. They then suggested that he put the sales planning manager into the ASM slot. The branch manager said that meant he would end up covering for the sales planning manager.
>
> I didn't like the sound of it so I called the regional personnel manager. It finally came out that they were interested in getting the branch manager more involved in sales planning and saw this as a good way of doing it. I told him that wasn't in the spirit of the program and some way of getting a replacement had to be found.
>
> A later discussion with the branch manager revealed that there was a good salesman there who could be made ASM. The branch manager was reluctant to do this because it would mean demoting him when the old ASM returned. I suggested that he could be moved to an ASM job elsewhere, but apparently he can't move for personal reasons for two years.

Mr. Wainger indicated that he had been informed that non-budgeted relocation expense might be involved. Rather than providing the money from corporate funds, however, he decided to leave it as a proper operating unit responsibility.

CONSIDERATIONS FOR THE FUTURE

In addition to worrying through the problems of specific individuals, corporate executives were concerned about how to measure the success of the Social Service Leave Program. Mr. McCardell noted four conditions he felt were important:

1. The careers of people who have gone on leave do not suffer,
2. They have a sense of accomplishment in their year away,
3. They have a broadened perspective on the job and outside, and
4. The social agencies say their efforts have been useful.

Difficulties which he and others quickly acknowledged with such evaluation criteria were the lack of clear factual evidence and the long time span over which benefits were likely to occur.

Of more immediate concern were the number who returned to Xerox and the company's ability to reinstate them satisfactorily. A loss rate of 50% was generally viewed at corporate headquarters as "disappointing" and highly unlikely; 20% was thought by several to be "an acceptable price to pay" though again higher than expected. Mr. McCardell commented on reinstatement:

> This is probably the biggest problem we face, but with only 20 we can take a personal interest. That's why Peter's name was on the letters to the employees' supervisors. Of course, letters have been written before which have gone unheeded. A chief executive can't rule by fiat. We'll have to wait and see.

Aside from evaluation, several policy questions were raised at various levels in the organization. The first involved accounting for the costs; should they be allocated to the operating units or retained in a corporate account similar to that for charitable contributions? If the former were chosen, how far down in the organization should charges be allocated? Some difference of opinion existed among corporate officers though an immediate choice was not deemed necessary. Mr. Wainger indicated, however, that if the program grew, as he hoped it would, pressure would mount for doing away with a large, easily identifiable corporate budget item.

The second question related to the selection procedure. A senior manager in BPG put it this way:

> Had I been doing this, I would have put in more feedback from the organization and made it less a corporate-individual deal. That way we could have ironed out a lot of the administrative problems beforehand. A study of who goes on leave might be useful too. Are we encouraging the right type of people to work here? Are the ones who do this marginal? At this level—only 21 people—it isn't so bad, but if it gets any larger, I think we'll have some problems.

While most corporate executives favored direct employee access to the Evaluation Committee in the United States, for the reasons noted earlier, the issue was not as clear overseas. Mr. McColough described his dilemma:

> Just after the Social Service Leave Program was announced, I was in Europe talking with our people there. They were enthusiastic about it but asked why they weren't included. Aside from saying it was experimental, I told them this is the way we get into trouble. If we limit it to the United States, it's favoritism and if we spread our program worldwide, it's applying United States solutions to foreign problems. I told them if you want it, you must *ask* for it.

Inquiries had been received from a number of overseas subsidiaries including those in Holland, New Zealand and Canada. In most instances the subsidiary leaned in the direction of an "up-the-line" selection and approval process. However, in January the nature and scope of overseas participation remained undefined.

As the month drew to a close, the management group considered again the direction of the Social Service Leave Program. Mr. McColough's original charge had been expressed in the following way:

> Granting twenty people a leave isn't much for a company as large as Xerox. There are certain to be problems which can't be anticipated with precision beforehand. However, if we dwell on the problems, we will end up doing nothing. So, let's be cautious, but let's do it.

He now shared the task of interpreting that charge in light of the events of the previous four months.

Exhibit 1

XEROX CORPORATION

Ten-Year Statistical Comparisons

	1971[1]	1970[1]	1969[1]
Yardsticks of Progress			
Net Income Per Common Share	$ 2.71	$ 2.40	$ 2.08
Dividends Declared Per Share	$ .80	$ .65	$ .58⅓
Operations (Dollars in thousands)			
Total Operating Revenues	$1,961,449	$1,718,587	$1,482,895
Rentals, Service and Royalties	1,563,805	1,343,252	1,094,794
Net Sales	397,644	375,335	388,101
Payroll (Excluding Benefits)	590,744	514,172	419,888
Depreciation of Rental Equipment	245,164	200,189	183,187
Depreciation of Buildings and Equipment	38,999	36,149	29,888
Amortization[3]	20,070	21,406	17,449
Expenditures for Research and Development	104,137	97,524	83,682
Income Before Income Taxes	471,081	432,938	389,722
Income Taxes	217,600	211,800	204,500
Outside Shareholders' Interests	40,871	33,447	23,854
Equity in Net Earnings of Rank Xerox Limited	—	—	—
Net Income	212,610	187,691	161,368
Dividends Declared	62;834	50,935	43,969
Financial Position (Dollars in thousands)			
Cash and Marketable Securities	$ 197,921	$ 148,982	$ 56,836
Net Trade Receivables	347,768	326,623	311,997
Inventories	226,597	222,001	172,747
Current Assets	916,731	825,416	649,011
Rental Equipment and Related Inventories at Cost	1,633,207	1,345,303	1,104,506
Accumulated Depreciation of Rental Equipment	872,283	714,833	577,832
Land, Buildings and Equipment at Cost	541,817	431,624	352,951
Accumulated Depreciation of Buildings and Equipment	172,383	144,339	116,056
Total Assets	2,156,094	1,857,325	1,531,271
Current Liabilities	532,806	457,571	391,257
Long-Term Debt (Including Current Portion)	482,731	429,690	319,407
Shareholders' Equity	1,051,767	892,500	738,455
Additions to Rental Equipment and Related Inventories[4]	382,792	312,580	279,519
Additions to Land, Buildings and Equipment[4]	121,498	88,869	75,890
General and Ratios			
Average Common Shares Outstanding During Year	78,533,533	78,315,911	77,445,464
Shareholders at Year End	143,554	146,534	129,944
Employees at Year End	66,728	59,862	54,882
Income Before Income Taxes to Total Operating Revenues	24.0%	25.2%	26.3%
Net Income to Average Shareholders' Equity	21.9%	23.0%	24.1%
Current Ratio	1.7	1.8	1.7
Long-Term Debt to Total Capitalization[5]	29.4%	30.5%	28.3%

	1968[1]	1967[2]	1966[2]	1965[1]	1964	1963	1962
$	1.68	$ 1.42	$ 1.20	$ .92	$ .68	$ .39	$ .24
$	.50	$ .40	$ .30¾	$ .20	$ .14¼	$ .08½	$ .04⅔
$1,224,352		$ 983,064	$752,508	$548,795	$317,840	$176,036	$115,220
896,673		673,548	477,954	327,814	184,157	114,077	65,847
327,679		309,516	274,554	220,981	133,683	61,959	49,373
336,602		289,009	223,855	160,725	93,921	55,112	36,653
175,692		135,975	97,221	69,110	37,295	20,236	12,454
26,747		23,779	18,519	12,637	7,243	4,338	3,267
12,304		8,437	6,026	5,439	3,695	3,070	1,570
59,888		50,806	53,329	38,170	24,050	14,609	8,547
309,096		226,500	182,113	138,872	86,800	50,423	30,779
164,020		108,576	86,490	68,199	44,598	27,850	16,801
16,126		11,540	8,923	4,984	–	–	–
–		–	–	–	1,523	428	(84)
128,950		106,384	86,700	65,689	43,725	23,001	13,894
34,363		28,555	21,996	14,698	10,788	4,895	2,688
$ 66,022		$ 70,670	$ 59,508	$ 26,289	$ 10,622	$ 6,933	$ 6,322
244,838		197,650	150,810	93,982	40,847	25,233	16,284
146,871		128,303	102,116	70,633	35,531	14,300	8,672
554,530		460,904	362,204	232,255	109,678	59,327	37,412
905,180		734,708	562,480	383,044	197,408	114,517	70,868
458,350		307,482	216,972	147,272	76,512	41,565	21,760
281,285		244,964	201,546	143,833	81,317	48,219	35,798
90,360		68,414	49,212	33,124	21,080	10,980	8,222
1,268,489		1,155,274	933,991	647,359	356,142	215,801	138,917
372,942		286,496	195,613	161,013	62,774	41,982	29,310
298,904		357,888	379,870	228,622	102,982	54,028	41,258
601,003		474,155	326,254	229,104	154,770	85,235	48,686
193,303		213,169	214,058	147,061	84,802	45,401	30,929
35,424		43,323	54,117	40,152	21,148	12,828	9,163
76,565,650		75,039,803	72,467,603	71,705,645	63,897,723	59,134,557	58,263,831
91,712		87,659	89,060	73,217	62,195	26,375	14,925
45,142		40,639	33,595	24,239	12,728	7,918	5,297
25.2%		23.0%	24.2%	25.3%	27.3%	28.6%	26.7%
24.0%		26.6%	31.2%	34.2%	36.4%	34.4%	33.4%
1.5		1.6	1.9	1.4	1.7	1.4	1.3
31.1%		40.8%	50.9%	47.4%	40.0%	38.8%	45.9%

[1] The data include the accounts of Xerox Data Systems and of Rank Xerox Limited for its fiscal year ended October 31.

[2] The data include the accounts of Xerox Data Systems and of Rank Xerox Limited for its fiscal year ended in June.

[3] Amortization of deferred research and development, patents, licenses and other intangible assets.

[4] Additions prior to 1969 shown net of disposals.

[5] Total capitalization defined as the sum of long-term debt (including current portion), outside shareholders' interests in net assets of subsidiaries, and shareholders' equity. Common share data adjusted to reflect change of each common share into five common shares effective December 17, 1963, and the distribution of two additional common shares for each common share held at May 16, 1969.

Exhibit 2
XEROX CORPORATION
Organization Chart

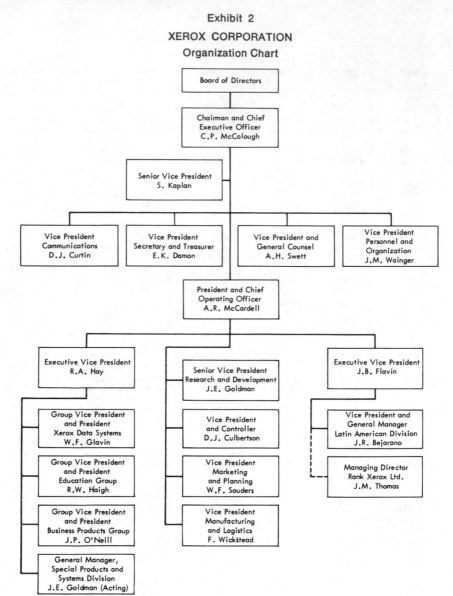

Exhibit 3

XEROX CORPORATION
Memorandum to Corporate Executives

To	See Distribution	Date	August 7, 1970
From	J. M. Wainger	Location	HR 2
Subject	Xerox Social Action	Organization	Corporate Personnel

We have decided to institute, as promptly as possible, a program for Xerox employees which we think will have substantial positive impact internally and externally, both now and for our future.

We will offer to twenty Xerox employees, regardless of level in the Corporation, (though excluding all of you) the opportunity to work for a year out of Xerox in some position that has high social value. As examples, the jobs might be with some community organization attacking urban problems, or some Federal Government agency, or a school, etc.

We plan to use the following approach. Through appropriate Xerox communications media, we will publicize the program and ask all those employees who are interested to submit a short description of the project they wish to work on and their reasons for choosing it. As part of their submission, they must include assurance that they have agreement from the prospective employer to take them on if they are freed up. We hope to receive many submissions.

All of these submissions will be screened by an impartial, outside board of prestigious men who will choose the twenty they consider to be most worthy according to the social criteria we've established.

The twenty selected employees will then be given a year to work at their chosen task. We assume they will return to Xerox at the end of that time, though no guarantee can be exacted. We will require that the projects they select be in or near their present communities. In other words, this program should not carry with it relocation subsidies for attractive long-range trips to such places as Los Angeles, Washington or Hawaii.

Xerox will maintain the employees' total compensation at the rate prevailing at the time they left Xerox by paying them the difference between whatever they receive from their outside job and their then Xerox salary.

We need to set up our outside screening board as soon as possible. I need your help. Would you please submit to me as soon as possible the names of one or more people you deem suitable to serve. The names you submit should be of people you feel fairly confident you can "deliver" if asked to contact them directly. I anticipate a board of perhaps five men, disparate in background but uniform quality.

I recognize that there are problems inherent in this program, and I'm sure you do too. However the results will more than justify taking the problems on. We will benefit and, by leading, we will influence.

You will, of course, be apprised of the details of the program as it is shaped up.

May I have your nominees for the selection board as soon as possible.

JMW/sd

Distribution:	D. J. Curtin	A. R. McCardell
	J. B. Flavin	C. P. McColough
	J. E. Goldman	J. W. Rutledge
	S. Kaplan	J. C. Wilson

EUGENE R. ALLEN, *director of international operations of the Xerox Education Group in Stamford, joined XEG in 1970 following three years as director of urban education at Litton Industries. Allen, 37, was born in Sacramento, Calif.*

ROBERT M. FLEGAL, 29, *is a scientist in the computer science laboratory at the Palo Alto Research Center. He served in the Peace Corps in Ghana for two years. He is a native of Salt Lake City, Utah. He joined Xerox in 1970.*

ERROL L. FORKNER, 29, *a commercial analyst in the product management department of Xerox Data Systems in El Segundo, is working for an MA in computer sciences at UCLA. He came to XDS in 1969 after three years with IBM.*

JANET L. KNIGHTON *is an educational and training specialist in the Business Products Group in Webster. Before joining Xerox in 1970, she had been assistant director of the adult department of the Rochester YWCA.*

ROBERT M. SCHNEIDER, *assistant to the president of Xerox in Stamford, was manager of corporate contributions for three years before assuming his present post in 1969. A native of Passaic, N.J., he is 40 years old.*

ROLAND A. STENTA, 31, *is national accounts manager of the Philadelphia branch of BPG, following work in personnel and sales. Born in Brooklyn, he joined Xerox in 1968, from the Office of Economic Opportunity in Washington.*

JAMES M. WAINGER *is corporate vice president, personnel and organization, in Stamford. He joined Xerox in 1960, but left from 1966 to 1969 to teach English in high school and write plays. He's 44, and a graduate of Harvard Law.*

Exhibit 5
XEROX CORPORATION
Application

XEROX SOCIAL SERVICE LEAVE APPLICATION

To be returned to:

Evaluation Board,
Social Service Leave Program
Xerox Corporation
Stamford, Connecticut 06904

My name: _____
          (print)   first   middle   last

Home address: _____

Phone: _____
               home   Xerox

Xerox Group/Division: _____   Location: _____

Present Position: _____   Employee Number: _____   Date Hired: _____

don't write here | Application No :

- -

don't write here | Application No :

In one sentence, what I want to do is: _____

_____

Time desired: _____   Dates desired: _____

This is the organization I'll work with: _____
                                                  name

_____
        address   department   name & function of person I would report to

Phone: _____ Acceptance Letter attached ☐   Salary, if any, I'll receive from the organization: _____

These are the details of the program I want to work on: (goals, history, scope, program, people affected, other workers involved, nature of activities, budget — *very specific description, please*, that will help us understand the project; attach any literature or reports or clippings that will help)

_____

_____

_____

_____

_____

My specific work will be: (what skill, what function, what tasks, what aims — or programmed results, if these can be stated in advance)

_____

_____

_____

_____

_____

_____

_____

Exhibit 5—Continued

I am specially qualified to do this by: (cite specific experience, training, skills, prior involvement, personal history — or just gnawing desire)

_____

_____

This is why I want to work on this project and this is what I hope to accomplish:

_____

_____

_____

_____

_____

My present monthly salary is: $ _____

Circle Highest Grade Completed:

High School	College	Graduate
9 - 10 - 11 - 12	13 - 14 - 15 - 16	17 - 18 - 19 - 20 - 21 - 22

College or University Attended	Degree Awarded	Major Subject
_____	_____	_____
_____	_____	_____
_____	_____	_____

Please use as many extra sheets as you need to answer the questions fully.

Exhibit 6

XEROX CORPORATION
1972 Recipients

Name & Xerox job	Age	Years with Xerox	Project	Agency
Joel N. Axelrod.......... Business Products Group Program Manager	39	5	Develop and implement techniques for evaluating training programs funded under the Drug Abuse Act	U.S. Office of Education
Oswaldo Aymat.......... Xerox Reproduction Center Quality Control Supervisor	35	11	Counsel and guide Puerto Rican college students with the objective of reducing the high drop-out rate	Aspira of New York
James E. Bales.......... Business Products Group Technical Representative	35	10	Manage the development of a literacy program	Greater Little Rock Literacy Council
Irving C. Bell.......... Xerox Reproduction Center Sales Representative	43	4	Teach mathematics to inmates in two prisons and instruct them in building trade skills	Massachusetts Department of Correction
Robert P. Britton.......... Business Products Group Technical Representative	29	6	Set and teach an entry level course in electro-mechanical job skills for unskilled and unemployables	Opportunities Industrialization Center
Frank V. Cliff, Jr.......... Business Products Group Account Executive	43	9	Work with minority businessmen	Economic Development Corporation of Greater Detroit
Mrs. Frayda F. Cooper.......... Ginn and Company Elementary Mathematics Editor	47	4	Organize an experimental program to provide services to the aged in a multi-town area where no such service is now available	Massachusetts Department of Community Affairs
Robert B. Cost.......... Business Products Group Account Representative	26	5	Teach and counsel in a drug rehabilitation center service high school age children from New York City	Pius XII School
Joe A. Duardo.......... Electro-Optical Systems Physicist	40	9	Counsel hard-core youth in a Mexican-American area	Abraham Lincoln High School
William Cable.......... Xerox Data Systems Vice President	43	3	Assist low-income families in black neighborhoods in achieving home ownership	Protestant Community Services
James P. Herget.......... Business Products Group A Regional Marketing Manager	27	4	As the agency's director of marketing, guide and assist minority-owned businesses in developing their marketing capability	Interracial Council for Business Opportunity of Greater Washington

Exhibit 6—Continued

Name & Xerox job	Age	Years with Xerox	Project	Agency
Robert S. Huddleston Business Products Group Technical Representative	44	9	Expand the work of an agency devoted to assisting former convicts in their return to life in their communities	The Seventh Step Foundation Topeka, Kansas
Paul S. Israel Business Products Group Area Sales Manager	38	8	Direct an effort to build a model classroom for teaching mentally retarded preschoolers	The Arizona Preschool for Retarded Children
Mrs. Esther E. Kapuschat Business Products Group Staff Nurse	60	7	Serve as director of nursing in an interdenominational crippled children's hospital	The Holy Land Christian Mission, Kansas City, Missouri
Kenneth R. Lane American Education Publications Special Education Department Editor	41	3	Establish an in-service training program leading to accreditation of house-parents in residential schools for the deaf	Conference of Executives of American Schools for the Deaf, White Plains, New York
Frederick Lightfoot Business Products Group Multiple Drill Operator	36	3	Work as a community organizer in central city area	Action for a Better Community Rochester, New York
Raymond E. Poehlein Business Products Group Development Engineering Manager	33	5	Help develop physical science curriculum and teach in a secondary school for Aglala Sioux Indians	Red Cloud Indian School
Lionel E. Reim Business Products Group A Regional Marketing Manager	28	3	Serve as business manager for an on-going coffee-house and medical clinic for youth	General Conference of Seventh Day Adventists
Michael I. Slade Corporate Research Physicist	30	5	Provide research and develop information bulletins on ecology problems (transportation and water)	Rochester Committee for Scientific Information
John M. Teem Corporate Research and Development Director of Technical Staff	46	13	Develop and teach a science curriculum in an experimental "school without walls"	Alpha Learnings Community School
Mrs. Jean G. Williams Business Products Group Programmer	26	4	Tutor and counsel minority college and pre-college students to reduce dropout rate	Project Equal Opportunity University of Colorado

Exhibit 6—Concluded

Recapitulation

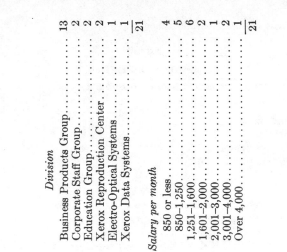

Division	
Business Products Group	13
Corporate Staff Group	2
Education Group	2
Xerox Reproduction Center	2
Electro-Optical Systems	1
Xerox Data Systems	1
	21

Salary per month	
850 or less	4
850–1,250	5
1,251–1,600	6
1,601–2,000	2
2,001–3,000	1
3,001–4,000	2
Over 4,000	1
	21

Exhibit 7

XEROX CORPORATION

Memorandum to Supervisors

November 18, 1971

Dr. J. E. Goldman
Xerox Corporation
Corporate Headquarters
Stamford, Connecticut 06904

Dear Jack:

John M. Teem, who is employed in your organization, has been selected to receive a Xerox Social Service Leave. Based on his application, he will be engaged full time away from the company for the next year on a voluntary social program of real value. Xerox is proud of the commitment of this employee, and I'm sure you share that pride.

As you know, Peter McColough has assured all employees that those who are chosen for Leaves are *guaranteed* that on their return they will return to their former job or one of equal pay, responsibility, status and opportunity for advancement. Peter and I will review each returning employee's job placement to make certain that this guarantee is fully honored.

Therefore, as you plan for the carrying on of John's work, I'm sure you'll want to keep in mind this essential provision of the Social Service Leave policy. If the job of the person going on leave is one of many jobs of the same type, I'd expect no special provisions need be made at this time.

If, however, the job is relatively unique, I suggest that you give consideration to designating any replacement as "acting." Certain jobs may even lend themselves to developmental use, permitting the rotation of several people in them during the period of the Social Service Leave.

I'm asking relevant Personnel Departments to monitor and approve the method used to fill each job vacated, and I'm requesting, too, that Personnel Departments inform me of the action taken to fill each job vacated by an employee going on Leave.

Sincerely,

James M. Wainger
Vice President
Personnel & Organization

JMW/sd
cc: C. P. McColough
    A. R. McCardell
    G. F. Wajda

The Polaroid Experiment in South Africa

THE POLAROID EMPIRE was founded on the results of a series of experiments carried out by Edwin Land, an 18-year-old Harvard student, in 1928. Land left University before graduating in order to pursue his experimentation with the polarization of light—a process of screening light beams that reduces glare more than any other diffusion process. For nine years he continued his research in the New York City Library, in a rented room, and in the Columbia University Physics Lab which he occasionally entered after hours through an unlocked window.

By 1937, Land's polarization process was perfected and he set up the Polaroid Corporation in Boston. The initial idea was to sell polarizers to the Detroit automobile manufacturers for use in the sun visors and headlights of all new cars. The plan failed, but the corporation managed to market its product idea in other forms. Polaroid nonglare glasses, which were introduced in 1927 sold well and by 1971 the company was selling over 25 million pairs of lenses annually.

Polaroid diversified its product range and grew quickly during the war years but its success story seemed to be ending after the war and in 1947 the company lost $2 million. However, Land had been working on instant photography since 1943 and the first Polaroid Land camera the "Model 95" was marketed in 1948. This camera which retailed at $89.75 proved to be an overnight success and generated large profits for the ailing company. Sales continued to grow rapidly as improvement followed improvement. In 1950, sepia toned pictures were replaced by black and white pictures and 1960 saw the introduction of 15-second pictures and an automatic exposure system. In 1963, the company marketed instant color film; in 1965, the low-priced Swinger; and in 1969 and 1971, a pair of low-priced color cameras.

The company is financially conservative and has no long-term debt. It has however enticed several big corporations to make major capital investments in its various products. By 1970, Polaroid Corporation had become one of the world's largest manufacturers of photographic and optical equipment and sales exceeded $465 million in that year. In 1971, sales increased to $504 million with a 13.8 percent profit margin on world sales. This meant that revenues had increased 400 percent over the last decade.

It is therefore not surprising that Polaroid Corporation is a glamour stock on the Wall Street market. If 1938 is used as a base year, the index value of Polaroid stock grew from 100 to a phenomenal 357,500 in 1971. If 1961 is used as a base year, the 1971 index value of the stock is 475.

In November 1970, *Fortune* magazine described Edwin Land as "Polaroid's 61-year-old founder, principal share-holder, guiding genius, president, Board Chairman and head of Research . . .". Land who controls 15 percent of the Polaroid stock seems to yield tremendous power over both employees and stockholders. To outsiders he seems to personify the company to such a degree that even rival Kodak executives usually refer to the Polaroid Corporation as "He" or "Him." Taking a close look at the hierarchical structure at Polaroid, *Fortune,* November 1970, stated the following:

> Land rules Polaroid. There is no number two man in Cambridge only a group of number threes with their aspiration submerged by Land's brilliance or by his financial control, or if necessary, by his ability to alter gently the balance of authority beneath him when one subordinate appears to have become a shade more equal than the rest.

Consequently it is not surprising that *Time* magazine summed up Polaroid's corporate image by stating in June 1972 that "Land has built Polaroid very close to his own self image—part scientist and part humanitarian philosopher."

POLAROID—THE CORPORATE CITIZEN

Polaroid is regarded by many—both employees and outsiders—as a humanistic enlightened company. The corporation enjoys a reputation for being a pace setter in both race relations policies and community relations programs.

By November 1970, almost 10 percent of the company's manpower was black. This meant that the company had just about reached its goal of employing the same ratio of blacks to whites, as existed in the population at large. This also meant that Polaroid had achieved this goal before most other companies in the United States.

Figures relating to 1969 give an idea of Polaroid's hiring practices. In that year, of the thousand people seeking employment with the company, 150 were black and of the 2,383 actually hired over 20 percent were black. In addition, 30 percent of the company's black employees completed in-company training courses in that year.

In 1968, when several other large companies were making similar moves, Polaroid opened Inner City, a wholly owned subsidiary in Roxbury—a poor black area in downtown Boston. The idea behind Inner City was to enable unemployed and underemployed people to attempt to develop work records. The purpose of this was to facilitate opportunities for them to obtain and hold permanent jobs in industry. By November 1970, 125 people from Roxbury had graduated and had obtained permanent jobs in industry. There has been an 82 percent retention rate of these graduates and in the words of Henry Morgan, Polaroid's director of human relations, this "is the highest for any black training program we know of."

The company also runs a black-oriented summer program and offers an unusually large number of fringe benefits to its own employees. These include a profit sharing plan, a full-time counselling service, education funds and education opportunities for upgrading technical skills.

Polaroid has been a pace setter in the community relations field as well. By June 1972, the company was donating either money or some other form of assistance to 143 community projects in Boston. With regard to Polaroid's community activities, the mayor of Cambridge, Barbara Ackerman, said:

> Polaroid is the only industry in this city that you can go to for land, or for some other contribution to the community. Polaroid considers itself a neighbor and actually does neighborly things.

The company's interest in and assistance to the community does not end in Boston. After the Kent State incident in 1970, some 2,220 Polaroid employees sent messages of their own choosing to President Nixon, at the company's expense. In 1972, Robert Palmer, Polaroid's director of community affairs, spent ten days at the Massachusetts State Prison mediating a prisoner revolt. Palmer also condemned a proposed I.D. card system for Massachusetts Welfare recipients as being dehumanizing. This was in spite of the fact that a Polaroid I.D. system could possibly have been used.

The company is also involved in assisting the community with regard to issues like pollution. Polaroid technicians have often gone very far in order to protect the environment and once went through an extremely costly operation in order to save trees which were situated near a chemical plant. The litter created by "instant photography" cameras has been an embarrassment to the company and to Land in particular.

Notwithstanding all the above, Donald White of the *Boston Globe* wrote in November 1970:

> Yet Polaroid itself is still dissatisfied with the progress to date, if only because though a $500,000,000 company, it is still largely a reflection of its creator, Edwin Land.

AMERICAN CORPORATE INVESTMENT IN SOUTH AFRICA

By 1969, direct foreign investment in the Republic totaled some $5,400 million; 60 percent of this total came from the United Kingdom and 14 percent (approximately $755 million) from the United States. This made the United States the second largest foreign investor in the Republic. An economic rationale for this investment was that it totaled 1.06 percent of all U.S. foreign investment, but yielded 1.6 percent of U.S. foreign earnings, with an average return 17 percent on the capital employed. During 1969, U.S. investment in the Republic increased by $56 million (8.5 percent), but of this amount $50 million (85 percent) was earnings reinvested locally and only $6 million flowed out of the United States.

By 1969, direct capital investment by the United States in South Africa constituted approximately 25 percent of the U.S. investment in Africa as a whole. It is interesting to note that with regard to U.S. investment in South Africa, Australia, and New Zealand, the one fifth of the capital which was employed in the Republic, yielded three fifths of the total earnings from these countries. By 1971, there were over 300 U.S. firms which had a substantial direct investment in South Africa. In 80.7 percent of these firms the U.S. parent held 50 percent or more of the capital investment.

The above figures are intended as a guideline only, and several sources give different figures as to the exact size of U.S. investment in South Africa. *Fortune* magazine of July 1972 states the following:

> The Republic of South Africa has always been regarded by foreign investors as a gold mine, one of those rare and refreshing places where profits are great and problems are small. Capital is not threatened by political instability or nationalization. Labor is cheap, the market booming, currency hard and convertible. Such are the market's attractions that 292 American corporations have established subsidiaries or affiliates there. Their combined direct investment is close to $900 million and their returns on that investment have been romping home at something like 19% a year, after taxes.

POLAROID IN SOUTH AFRICA

Polaroid began to sell its products in South Africa as early as 1938. Nevertheless, according to Land, the company declined a multimillion dollar deal with the South African government in 1948 on moral grounds. This was at a time when the company's sales were down and it had not yet pulled out of its postwar slump.

By 1970, Polaroid was selling about $1,500,000 worth of cameras, film and sunglass lenses in South Africa. If Polaroid's 13.8 percent worldwide profit margin applies to the Republic, the company's annual profits from South Africa exceeded $250,000 by 1970. The *Financial Mail* of January 22, 1971, estimated that Polaroid's South African profits lay between R150,000 and R200,000 per annum.[1] In 1970, the $1,500,-

---

[1] One South African Rand (R) = U.S. $1.40 in 1970, $1.46 in 1974, and $1.15 by 1977.

000 worth of sales to South Africa amounted to less than 0.5 percent of the company's annual sales and was more or less equal to its sales to a single large American department store. Note that, in 1970, Polaroid had no plant, no investments and no company in the Republic, but conducted its business through an independent distributor called Frank and Hirsch (Pty) Ltd.

In almost every other foreign situation Polaroid set up a local subsidiary when sales closed in on the $1 million mark. However, even though South African sales were greater than $1 million before 1970, no subsidiary was set up in the Republic nor had plans to do so been discussed. Donald White of the *Boston Globe* commented on this as follows:

> There seems all along to have been a subconscious effort to keep the lid on South African business. . . . Certainly Polaroid's business in South Africa could have been substantially bigger under normal circumstances.

Helmut Hirsch, the manager director of Frank and Hirsch differed from this point of view and attributed the fact that Polaroid had not set up a subsidiary in South Africa to Polaroid's respect for the distribution expertise of Frank and Hirsch. He claimed that Polaroid looked to Frank and Hirsch as an example of what an innovative company could achieve in terms of sales results in a small market. He cited one aspect of his company's ingenuity by pointing out that Frank and Hirsch had created the initative which allowed Polaroid to sell complete sunglasses (with frames) in the Republic instead of only lenses as they had done formerly. Frank and Hirsch were also one of Polaroid's largest distributors in the world.

FRANK AND HIRSCH—HISTORICAL PERSPECTIVE

Frank and Hirsch was founded in 1935. The company began by trading as a distributor of gift lines and grew steadily through the war years. In 1954, the company moved into its own building, which is situated on the periphery of the central city area of Johannesburg. This building remained the corporate headquarters and still housed the company in 1971. The company is forward looking and innovative in its approach to business. In 1964, it became the first commercial enterprise in the Republic to acquire its own computer facilities. A second computer followed in early 1970. In 1958, the photographic division—which formed 50 percent of the company's business by 1970—was made a separate division of the company. The Polaroid account constituted between 40 percent and 50 percent of this division by 1970.

The company was completely reorganized during 1968 and 1969 into six product divisions: Photographic; Sound; Watch; Sunglasses; Scientific; Stationery. This divisionalization and the changing of the corporate structure facilitated the implementation of a participative, and for a wholesale distributor, a rather unique (in South African terms) marketing strategy, which was instrumental in the company trebling its profits over the 1970/1973 period.

In 1970, Frank and Hirsch employed a staff which included a few Coloureds[2] and Indians and 155 Africans;[3] of latter, 37 were classed as unskilled. A pension fund had been initiated for the entire staff (both black and white) in 1954. Initially this fund was noncontributory for Blacks but later Blacks were given the opportunity to place 5 percent of their earnings with the fund which had the effect of doubling the benefits they could receive. In 1969, the company set up an African staff committee, which according to Mr. Hirsch, has functioned extremely well. It was still the major channel of communication between management and African staff in 1974. The owners and management of Frank and Hirsch were active in community affairs and could be considered to be "liberal, progressive" people in the community.

CONFRONTATION AT POLAROID

On October 5, 1970, Polaroid's management became aware of the existence of an in-house revolutionary movement for the first time. On this day the Polaroid Workers' Revolutionary Movement (P.W.R.M.) made their first militant proclamation about the company's involvement in South Africa. Posters reading "POLAROID IMPRISONS A BLACK SOUTH AFRICAN EVERY 60 SECONDS" appeared on company bulletin boards.

Two days later, a midday protest rally took place outside the company's Technology Square headquarters. The protesters accused Polaroid of being racist and interested in profits alone. They claimed that Polaroid's distributor in South Africa was employing "slave labor" and that the continued sale of Polaroid's products in South Africa supported and bolstered the Apartheid system. They backed this latter claim by stating the Polaroid cameras and film were being used to implement the Pass Book program—a system that was considered to be one of the keystones of the Apartheid structure. (See Appendix I for a brief résumé of the Pass laws.) The protesters who were led by Kenneth Williams, a Polaroid employee, came in the main from outside the company. They demanded an end to Polaroid's South African activities and Polaroid's investment in South Africa. They also wanted the company to publicly denounce Apartheid and use profits accrued from the company's South Africa involvement to support revolutionary movements in Southern Africa. On October 27, the P.W.R.M. called for worldwide boycott of all Polaroid products and mass demonstrations took place in Boston.

The exact size of the P.W.R.M. was unknown, but two of the identified members, Carolina Hunter and Kenneth Williams, admitted that it was not large. Polaroid management believed that there were only a handful of members. Williams whose photographic skills were considered to be extremely good resigned from the company soon after the October 7 rally.

---

[2] South Africans of mixed racial origin.

[3] The terms African or Black are used interchangeably to refer to black South Africans. There appears to have been a change in preference towards the use of the term Black with the more recent rise in black consciousness through the world.

POLAROID'S INITIAL REACTION

The company retorted quickly and sharply to the above accusations. On October 6, the company claimed that Polaroid was "unique in South Africa in its adoption of full equal employment practices for Blacks." This statement was made in spite of the fact that Polaroid itself had no direct investments in the Republic and indicates that Polaroid's management was highly upset by the events of October 5. Polaroid's management was certainly affected by the vehemence of the protest, with Dr. Land hiring a 24-hour guard for himself and his family. A memo issued soon after the protest rally substantially stated that the company had no direct investment in South Africa, that its sales were conducted by a fully independent distributor, and that its sales in South Africa amounted to less than 0.5 percent of its annual revenue. It stated also that Land had personally banned the sale of Polaroid products to the South African government as far back in 1948. Finally the memo stated that as far as anyone (including Land) knew, Polaroid equipment had not been used to enforce the Pass Book identification program.

Notwithstanding the above claims, an employee group had raised the question of whether Polaroid products were being used to enforce Apartheid in South Africa two year previously, and no action was taken by management after the employees' enquiries. The number of Polaroid executives who were aware of the use to which Polaroid products were being put is difficult to estimate: certainly some were not. However, at least one Polaroid executive admitted knowledge of the use of Polaroid products in the Pass Book program. In an interview with a *Boston Globe* reporter, Tom Wyman, Polaroid's vice president of sales and a senior member of management under Dr. Land said: "We recognized that our film, indirectly was being used in this identification program for Blacks and Whites and I think there was some discomfort about it, but the issue did not crystallize to a point where now, we wish it had."

The predominantly white top management of Polaroid was shocked by the existence of a revolutionary movement within the company. Nevertheless, the management flatly rejected their demands and stated that it would rather work within its traditional mutual problem-solving approach. Even though management decided not to succumb to outside pressure and had denied that Polaroid products were being used to help to enforce the Apartheid program, a process of double checking the role of Polaroid's products in the Apartheid system was initiated. A long distance telephone call revealed that Frank and Hirsch was the source of about 10 percent of the film for the identity pictures for the Apartheid program, although no direct sales were made to the government. As a result, Polaroid sent two of its executives to South Africa, and announced a ban on all sales to the South African government. A newsletter of early November stated:

> A number of South Africa's leading daily newspapers have carried front page stories during the past ten days announcing Polaroid's decision to halt "the sale to South Africa of its products which could be used in that country's Apartheid program." The newspaper stories have

been appearing under bold-type headlines such as "Polaroid bans 'Apartheid' sales." (*Rand Daily Mail,* Johannesburg.) Polaroid's announcement is receiving unusually heavy coverage in the South African Press because Polaroid is the first American company to take such a step in protest against the South African government's racial segregation policies. Articles have appeared in several papers, including the *Daily Mail,* on October 23 and 24 and the Johannesburg *Star* on October 23, whose headlines was, "Polaroid ban: local agent silent." Articles have also appeared in Cape Town and East London press on the Polaroid announcement.

Two of Polaroid's international marketing personnel have been in South Africa for the past ten days meeting with government officials to advise them of Polaroid's refusal to sell any identification equipment to South Africa, as well as any film which might be used to enforce the Apartheid Pass Book program.

Additionally, the two company members—Hans Jensen and Kevin Thompson—have been meeting with Polaroid's independent distributor in Johannesburg to develop procedures for the enforcement of Polaroid's ban against the sale of any products to the South African government or to individual dealers or photographers which might be used in the Apartheid program.

Jensen and Thompson have reported by telephone and cable that the corporation's decision "has made considerable impact at the governmental level, as well as the consumer and dealer levels because it is an unprecedented statement of a position by an American company."

Mr. Hirsch pointed out that he had spent a considerable amount of time with Messrs. Jensen and Thompson going over the Frank and Hirsch operation with respect to Polaroid products and had also arranged a number of meetings with government officials for them.

The effectiveness of this ban on the sale of Polaroid film for use in the Pass Book program was however questionable. While no *direct* sales took place to the government, there could clearly be no control on indirect sales, and Polaroid film could still be used by private photographers (some of whom were black) for taking Pass Book photographs. In addition, retailers were also free to supply the government with Polaroid film.

Mr. Hirsch, saw the situation very much in this way. He did however, add that in his opinion, if indirect sales were somehow stopped the government could obtain the film it required from other countries.

THE "AD HOC" COMMITTEE ON SOUTH AFRICA

During October further developments took place. William J. McCune, executive vice president of Polaroid, initiated a plan to set up a committee which would have the final say in the role Polaroid was to play in South Africa and on the engagement-disengagement decision. The committee which was constituted in late October consisted of 14 members drawn from all ranks in the company's hierarchy. The committee included both management and employees, both male and females, and consisted of seven whites and seven blacks. The committee met for the first time on Wednesday October 28 and again the following day.

THE FIRST TWO MEETINGS AND THEIR OUTCOME

At the beginning of the emotionally charged first meeting, Dr. Edwin Land, who had responded to an invitation to attend the meeting, addressed the 14 member committee for well over an hour. A synopsis of his speech as recorded in the *Polaroid Newsletter* of November 2, appears in Appendix II.

Land then joined in the six-hour discussion and urged the committee and all employees to support the ideals of dialogue and mutual problem solving on which the company was built. The committee supported Land on this issue and decided to form a united front in support of the company and against the attacks from individuals and outsiders. They concluded that a decision on the stand the company should take regarding South Africa was an internal matter and that they could not be swayed by external pressures, nor would they allow a decision to be made outside the company. Participation with management was needed to resolve the issue. Black committee members stated strongly that black employees could and should work for unity, but this had to be done "without losing their identity or their blackness." They also pointed out that as Blacks in the United States, they had had decisions made for them by people who thought they knew what Blacks needed. They stated that this should be avoided and that the affected Blacks in South Africa should be consulted.

With this underlying principle in mind and after a long discussion on the South African issue the committee made some specific recommendations. These were:

1. That a four-member fact finding group be sent to South Africa to review the feelings of blacks in South Africa at first hand. The four-man team was to report on the use of Polaroid products in South Africa, conditions of Frank and Hirsch, the use of Polaroid film in the Pass Book program, and was to give recommendations on the engagement-disengagement decision.
2. That the committee would consult outside experts in economics, African history, politics and other fields in order to assist them in making recommendations about Polaroid's future in South Africa and Polaroid's future business in "free Black Africa."

THE STUDY COMMITTEE ON SOUTH AFRICA

The result of the first meetings and the recommendations put forward by the Ad Hoc Committee was the formation of the Study Committee on South Africa. By November 12, Ester Hopkins had been appointed chairman of the committee by Dr. Land and additional members had been appointed to the committee.

The company set out to determine the feasibility and consequences of the various strategies the company could employ in South Africa. In order to accomplish this the committee had to build up a wide cross section of knowledge about South Africa. As a result, the first assignments of the members of the Study Committee were to obtain knowledge about the geography, history, and government of South Africa, the effects of embargoes on Rhodesia, and current and future Polaroid business in the rest of Africa.

The committee also sent out a questionnaire to a number of people knowledgeable on South Africa. After a brief introduction to the situation facing Polaroid, the questionnaire posed the following questions:

> If they start with the desire to effect some improvement in the situation of the black people living in South Africa, should American businesses cut off all contact with South Africa? Or should they work within the framework of their commercial activities to try and effect improvements? Are any such improvements possible in the current climate? Should we perhaps try to increase our business with South Africa? (We have not set up our own company there. Could we have a greater effect if we did?) Should we look for ways to shift our business (if such were possible) to the free black nations of Africa?

In November, the company also placed an advertisement on the South African issue in Boston newspapers headed "What Is Polaroid Doing in South Africa?" Then, during late November and December, the committee met with several specialists on South African affairs. These included: Doctors Pool and Griffith, Professors of Political Science at MIT; Emeka Eveife, Rockefeller Fellow in Economics at Harvard University; Mrs. Zanele Diamin, a black South African social worker who was then living in the United States and Dr. Nana Makomo, a black South African activist who was on a lecture tour to the United States, Europe, and the United Nations "to educate people about the [Apartheid] issue in South Africa."

Those interviewed included South Africans of several different political pursuasions and were drawn from various racial groups. One of the first questioned was a business school lecturer at the University of the Witwatersrand, who was asked his views on the consequences of withdrawal. He was amazed at just how uninformed the committee was about South Africa and felt that the committee had a great deal to learn before it could deliver a reasonable judgment. He pointed out the relatively passive role played by foreign investors in South Africa, and U.S. investors in particular, in attempting to bring about social change in South Africa. He also pointed out that several companies controlled by South African citizens were doing far more in this respect than many foreign investors.

THE TRAVEL GROUP

As a result of the committee's recommendations, Dr. Land appointed a four-man travel group to visit South Africa and obtain firsthand information. The travel group appointed by Dr. Land consisted of 2 blacks and 2 whites: Charles Jones, a black electrician; Arko Almasian, a white draftsman; Kenneth Anderson, a black engineer; and Thomas Wyman, a white vice president. The formation of this travel group was advertised in the press.

Wyman met with the U.S. State Department and officials of the South African Embassy on November 15. At first, he and the travel group were doubtful of their visas being approved, as Embassy officials had expedited the visa applications but had not committed themselves as to whether the visas would be approved. Members of the black militant P.W.R.M. rejected the concept of the travel group outright, and described the committee's action as "a sleight of hand." Even members of Polaroid's management felt that the travel group was likely to be restricted in terms of whom it talked to and what it would be allowed to see in South Africa. Nevertheless after November 15 the travel group set out to obtain all the other necessary travel documents and drew up a specific set of questions on which they would sound out opinion in South Africa. The travel group which was expecting to spend about two weeks in South Africa left on December 2 for London and after a two-day delay finally received their visas and reached South Africa where they stayed for ten days. During their stay, the travel group talked to scores of people both black and white. They met people who were in favor of the South African government and with opponents of the government (sometimes secretly). They toured plants, interviewed workers and directed their enquiries so as to assess the effects of engagement and disengagement. They were given a reasonably free hand by the South African government—certainly a far freer hand than even Polaroid management had thought likely.

THE POLAROID EXPERIMENT COMMENCES

On January 10, 1971, Robert Palmer, Polaroid's director of community affairs, announced that Polaroid would be holding a press conference the following day and would announce its decision on future involvement in South Africa. The company allowed reporters to spend an hour with the travellers and released a mimeographed statement. This statement also formed the text of an advertisement that was published on January 13 in the *Boston Globe*, the *Herald*, the *Record-American*, the *New York Times*, the *Chicago Tribune*, the *Los Angeles Times*, the *Washington Post*, the *Wall Street Journal* and 20 black weeklies, at a cost which was estimated to be over $100,000 by a *Boston Globe* reporter. (Appendix III.)

The program announced by the company had four main points:

1. Sales to the South African government were to be discontinued, but the company would not disengage from the Republic and would set up an experimental program for one year.
2. Polaroid's local distributor and his suppliers were going to improve salaries and other benefits for black employees.
3. The company's South African associates were to be obliged to start a training program for blacks so as to enable them to take up important posts.
4. A proportion of Polaroid's South African profits was to be devoted to encouraging black education.

At the press conference the travellers said that they had arrived at their conclusion after interviewing 150 persons, two thirds of whom came from South Africa. Charles (Chuck) Jones said that, "it was unanimous except for one man that the way Polaroid could help is the way spelled out in our statement." In response to a question as to what Polaroid would do if the South African government prohibited the up-grading and training program, Tom Wyman said, "Then we will have another decision to make."

SOUTH AFRICAN GOVERNMENTAL REACTION

Lourens Muller, the then South African minister of economic affairs stated that he did not object to Polaroid's proposals to increase the earnings and opportunities of "Non-Whites" in South Africa. He stated that: "We cannot object if a South African company is prepared to sub-scribe to the dictates of an American company as long as it does not contravene the law." Commenting on the fact that many people saw the Polaroid decision as a victory for anti-apartheid movements, the minister stated, "It does not seem that they have been very successful. They wanted the company to pull out of South Africa altogether." He then said that even though Polaroid had specifically stated that it abhorred Apartheid, their decision to remain suggested that they did not find conditions as bad as they had assumed them to be. Perhaps the most interesting comment the minister made, was that there was no legislation as to the maximum wage a "Non-White" could be paid. He did not mention any of the legislative and customary blocks to black advancement.

THE EFFECT ON SOUTH AFRICA

In response to its undertaking to evaluate the "Experiment" after a year, Polaroid released a report on December 30, 1971, which an-nounced the company's intention to continue doing business in South Africa. The report, partially reproduced in Appendix IV, outlined the progress that had been made in increasing black wages and making funds available to black educational organizations. The report also stated that: "Although in a year's time the visible effects on other com-panies of our experiment have been limited, the practical achievements in salaries, benefits and education have shown what can be done."

An independent report by the Institute of Race Relations' research assistants John Kane-Berman and Dudley Horner felt it was too soon to judge the results after only one year. However, they still concluded that:

> From the enquiries received during the year by the Institute of Race Relations, Frank and Hirsch and the U.S. Consulate-General it is ap-parent that many companies, whatever the nationality, are comtem-plating revision of black salary scales—some which may well involve radical improvements.
> While it is true that there is, as yet, no evidence to show that there

has been a significant improvement in the wages and working conditions of black South Africans in general, there is reason to be moderately optimistic about the effect of the Polaroid experiment as a relatively important factor in creating a new awareness among businessmen in particular, and the general public of the depressed condition of the African masses.

The effect of the experiment was also commented on in the press, and an article entitled "Move to Raise Non-Whites' Pay Is Spreading" is reproduced in Appendix V.

AN INTERVIEW WITH THE MANAGING DIRECTOR OF FRANK AND HIRSCH

In an interview in May 1974, Mr. Hirsch said that he had found the Polaroid exercise very satisfying. "It was an exciting short period that turned into a boon for Frank and Hirsch and for Polaroid as well. It also helped Blacks in South Africa and acted as a catalyst for change." Referring to the in-company results of the experiment, he said that Frank and Hirsch had been cutting down on racial discrimination long before the Polaroid experiment began, but added that

> Polaroid has given us a new awareness of what can be done. Very little racial discrimination exists at Frank and Hirsch today—blacks and whites share the same offices and the same working hours. Co-operation with white staff has improved as have black-white staff relations.
> Black staff has become more outgoing and warm in their attitude towards the company. On their initiative the Black Staff Committee co-operated with the travel group—it showed them around Soweto sometimes without permission and the necessary papers. In my December 1970 Christmas letter to the staff, I thanked every employee for their co-operation and the low incidence of friction in the heat of an hectic and trying year.
> It costs nothing to pay more. The Polaroid experiment was an experiment in human relations which resulted in the workers putting in a greater effort, more co-operation and an improved working atmosphere. Frank and Hirsch has donated a school to "TEACH" (R25,000),[4] and the African staff appreciates the company's efforts—they are able to hold their heads up high in the townships. Although there is a legal limit on Black advancement as no black man can supervise a white by law, but black supervisors are spoken to by lower white staff as you would speak to a black policeman—that is with respect and courtesy. Frank and Hirsch now employs over 340 people about 150 of whom are black. Most of these blacks work in delivery and warehousing, but there are some blacks in every department and they handle a large proportion of the clerical work done at the firm. There are no black salesmen but this is a function of white customers being unwilling to be serviced by a black man.

---

[4] Teach Every African Child: A fund to raise money to build schools in the African areas started by the Johannesburg Star.

With regard to Polaroid's efforts to aid Black education in South Africa, Mr. Hirsch referred to the annual "ASSET" reports. An extract from the 1973 report is included as Appendix VI.

Referring to the Polaroid as a catalyst for change he made the following statements as various stages of the interview:

> I am interested in South Africa and its future and American investment in South Africa. . . . Had Polaroid pulled out of South Africa, it would have affected all American companies in South Africa. . . . Polaroid was very important to Frank and Hirsch and is so today.[5] . . . Some companies are doing things quietly—perhaps they are doing more than Frank and Hirsch but the Polaroid experiment was a catalyst for change and we still get enquiries from one or two companies every week, as to how racial discrimination can be cut down to the minimum necessary under the law, and that is very little.

He added that the companies making enquiries included local companies, but were predominantly companies with overseas connections— usually local subsidiaries of overseas based companies.

Appendix VII is an editorial comment on the need to raise black wages which appeared on the cover of the *Financial Mail*, April 5.

Appendix VIII gives a selection of population and economic statistics on South Africa, and Appendix IX shows consumption expenditure and government expenditure on education by racial group.

APPENDIX I

THE AFRICAN "PASS LAWS"*

Pass laws for Africans were introduced in the early days of White settlement in South Africa. In 1952 a new system was devised, which has, since, been revised in several respects.

All Africans, men and women, who are citizens of South Africa and have attained the age of sixteen years are required to possess reference books. In these books officials enter details of where the holder is permitted to be and, if appropriate, to work, and records of employment and of the payment of general taxes. The movement of Africans is controlled by labor bureaus.

In terms of the law as amended up to 1964, an African may visit an urban area for up to 72 hours without obtaining a special permit, but may not remain there longer unless:

a. he (or she) has lived there continuously since birth;

b. he (or she) has worked there continuously with one employer for at least ten years, or has lived there lawfully and continuously for fifteen years, and has thereafter continued to live there, and has not been in employment outside area, and has not been convicted of a serious offense.

---

[5] By 1974, Frank and Hirsch had become Polaroid's biggest independent distributor in the world. Polaroid sales still accounted for 20–25 percent of Frank Hirsch's income and in 1973 amounted to more than $4 million per annum.

* Source: An extract from: Muriel Horrel, *South Africa: Basic Facts and Figures* (South African Institute of Race Relations, March 1973).

c. he (or she) is the wife, unmarried daughter, or son under the age of eighteen years of an African in one of the categories mentioned above, ordinarily resides with him, and entered the area lawfully;

d. he (or she) has been granted special permission to be in the area.

Even Africans who qualify for residential rights may be "endorsed out" (i.e. ordered out) of an urban area if they are deemed to be idle or undesirable.

[Some relaxation of the above regulations were announced between 1971 and 1973, including greater mobility between urban areas and the establishment of aid centers to help reduce the number of Africans appearing in court for purely technical offenses. At the same time, contract migrant labor regulations for rural persons wishing to seek work in urban areas, were more strictly enforced. Such contracts were for a year at a time, although they could be renewed indefinitely. Their effect, however, was to prevent the worker ever attaining permanent status under (b) above.]

APPENDIX II

DR. LAND ADDRESSES SPECIAL JOINT COMMITTEE

This is a synopsis of Dr. Land's talk last Wednesday before the joint employee-management committee studying the South African issue.

It seems to us to be a peculiar indignity for us to work together to build something wonderful, like our camera and film, work together on a basis that makes one common human family, and then see that product, our own tradition, used for the purpose of isolating a race.

We are explicitly and vigorously opposed to the apartheid program. And I can tell you that in the last two or three days, the headlines in South African newspapers say that.

When I and other members of management found out that some of our film was getting into this program, we said "we are going to stop it."

And let me make one thing clear. Our decision had nothing to do with any revolutionary worker's movement, large or small.

You can talk about situations in this company where this or that hasn't worked, but I want to call to your attention to the last two years —since Martin Luther King died—and by the way, we were the first company to close when he died because we *did* care, because we felt he was the one man who had a deep sense of how to bring one world about.

You will remember the three company meetings that took all day to hold.

What I said at those meetings was "sure, management can impose a new hiring policy, but that won't do you much good." The only thing that will do any good is to have *all* the people at Polaroid feel that the right thing to do is to expand our black population. And so our black population did expand. It went up to 900, and it went rapidly.

At every Board meeting here, and I know of no other company in the country that has done this, Bill McCune has reported on how many black people were hired, how many promoted, how many stayed and what we're going to do about it next.

Is the battle won? No, but I think it has gone a long way. There was a lot that white people have had to get used to, who had lived in the particular way they had lived. My doctrine has been for 20 or 30 years that the way to get people to begin to understand each other, the way for differences to drop away, is for them to work together.

If you leave individuals alone when they are not building together they gather into little groups that can hate each other. Not just black and white, but Catholics, Protestants, Jews, and so on. Gather them to build something together and they share in that and they come to love each other and forget the superficial differences. My life has been dedicated to that—and I want partners. I want black partners and I want white partners.

We think we are better than most other companies. But we are about one-half of what we ought to be.

Now, a couple of revolutionaries don't believe that we mean what we say. They don't believe that we will do anything to stop our film from being used for this thing in South Africa. "That's mealy mouthed," they say.

The fact is we have two men over there right now to stop it.

The fact is they have talked with the South African government about our intentions.

The fact is the South African newspapers are full of headlines about our decision. We are the first American company to make such a move.

The fact is that what no one thought could be done *will* be done.

We will stop our film from being used in this program.

Our Board of Directors has supported us solidly in our decision to stop such sales in South Africa. The passbook pictures are a malicious thing and we are going to stop our film being used for taking them.

That leaves some amateur cameras and film being sold, and the sunglass lenses. They may or may not be a useful tool toward influencing South Africa to move away from apartheid and join the family of decent nations.

Would complete withdrawal—by Polaroid or other companies—have any effect? I don't know. It didn't work in Rhodesia, which became stronger and stronger and suppressed the Blacks more and more the longer their boycott lasted.

I know one thing. If we, this moment cut off all our business in South Africa, then the newspapers will be full of a vast Polaroid revolutionary movement—a movement with its two or three people.

We would have a series of new demands, and there is no doubt that management would *not* meet them. I've never been pushed around in my life because I have ideals I live and die for.

I want to fight along with you for the things you need. I want to fight for you. I want you to fight along with me for the company and the things the company needs. I do not want to run a company that is based on demands rather than participation.

The world is watching us right now. Other companies are saying that "if Polaroid can't make the grade, none of us can."

That word—Polaroid—is known around the world. Polaroid is considered a great and generous company. Shouldn't we use that power—

the power of our great reputation—to accomplish our objectives in South Africa, or Boston, or Roxbury, or any place else? Is boycott of South Africa the right way to use that power? I don't really know. Let's examine the problem together and work together to make the decision which will prove most effective. There is a lot of hard work to be done.

You couldn't have a better management group than you have now. All of them are solid, dedicated to the idea of making this world a better place for people to live together. Their need is for the Polaroid I have dreamed of to become a reality, and that's why they stay here. They stay because they see nowhere else in the world to which they can direct their constructive energy as effectively for society as they do here.

It's that kind of participation that I want from you.

APPENDIX III

AN EXPERIMENT IN SOUTH AFRICA*

Polaroid sells its products in South Africa as do several hundred other American companies. Our sales there are small, less than one half of one percent of our worldwide business.

Recently a group has begun to demand that American business stop selling in South Africa. They say that by its presence it is supporting the government of the country and its policies of racial separation and subjugation of the Blacks. Polaroid, in spite of its small stake in the country, has received the first attention of this group.

We did not respond to their demands. But we did react to the question. We asked ourselves, "Is it right or wrong to do business in South Africa?" We have been studying the question for about ten weeks.

The committee of Polaroid employees who undertook this study included fourteen members—both black and white—from all over the company. The first conclusion was arrived at quickly and unanimously. We abhor *apartheid*, the national policy of South Africa.

The *apartheid* laws separate the races and restrict the rights, the opportunities and the movement of non-white Africans. This policy is contrary to the principles on which Polaroid was built and run. We believe in individuals. Not in "labor units" as Blacks are sometimes referred to in South Africa. We decided whatever our course should be it should oppose the course of *apartheid*.

The committee talked to more than fifty prominent South Africans both black and white, as well as many South African experts. They heard from officials in Washington. They read books, papers, testimony, documents, opinion, interpretation, statistics. They heard tapes and saw films.

They addressed themselves to a single question. What should Polaroid do in South Africa? Should we register our disapproval of *apartheid* by cutting off all contact with the country? Should we try to influence the system from within? We rejected the suggestion that we ignore the whole question and maintain the status quo.

Some of the black members of the study group expressed them-

* Source: Polaroid Corporation.

selves strongly at the outset. They did not want to impose on the black people of another country a course of action merely because *we* might feel it was correct. They felt this paternalistic attitude had prevailed too often in America when things are done "for" black people without consulting black people.

It was decided to send four of the committee members to South Africa. Since this group was to include two black and two white members, it was widely assumed they would not be granted visas. They were.

It was assumed if they ever got to South Africa they would be given a government tour. They were not.

It was assumed they would not be allowed to see the actual conditions under which many Blacks live and would be prevented from talking to any of them in private. They did see those conditions in Soweto and elsewhere. And with or without permission they met and talked to and listened to more than a hundred black people of South Africa. Factory workers, office workers, domestic servants, teachers, political leaders, people in many walks of life. They also talked to a broad spectrum of whites including members of all the major parties.

Their prime purpose in going to South Africa was to ask Africans what they thought American business should do in their country. We decided the answer that is best for the black people of South Africa would be the best answer for us.

Can you learn about a country in ten days? No. Nor in ten weeks. But our group learned one thing. What we had read and heard about *apartheid* was not exaggerated. It is every bit as repugnant as we had been led to believe.

The group returned with a unanimous recommendation.

In response to this recommendation and to the reports of the larger study committee, Polaroid will undertake an experimental program in relation to its business activities in South Africa.

For the time being we will continue our business relationships there (except for sales to the South African government, which our distributor is discontinuing), but on a new basis which Blacks there with whom we talked see as supportive to their hopes and plans for the future. In a year we will look closely to see if our experiment has had any effects.

First, we will take a number of steps with our distributor, as well as his suppliers, to improve dramatically the salaries and other benefits of their nonwhite employees. We have had indications that these companies will be willing to cooperate in this plan.

Our business associates in South Africa will also be obliged (as a condition of maintaining their relationship with Polaroid) to initiate a well-defined program to train non-white employees for important jobs within their companies.

We believe education for the Blacks, in combination with the opportunities now being afforded by the expanding economy, is a key to change in South Africa. We will commit a portion of our profits earned there to encourage black education. One avenue will be to provide funds for the permanent staff and office of the black-run Association for Education and Cultural Advancement(ASECA). A second method will be to make a gift to a foundation to underwrite educational expenses for about 500 black students at various levels of study from elementary school through university. Grants to assist teachers will also be made from this gift. In addition we will support two exchange fellowships for Blacks under the U.S.-South African Leader Exchange Program.

Polaroid has no investments in South Africa and we do not intend to change this policy at present. We are, however, investigating the possibilities of creating a black-managed company in one or more of the free black African nations.

Why have we undertaken this program? To satisfy a revolutionary group? No. They will find it far from satisfactory. They feel we should close the door on South Africa, not try to push it further open.

What can we hope to accomplish there without a factory, without a company of our own, without the economic leverage of large sales? Aren't we wasting time and money trying to have an effect on a massive problem 10,000 miles from home? The answer, our answer, is that since we are doing business in South Africa and since we have looked closely at that troubled country, we feel we can continue only by opposing the *apartheid* system. Black people there have advised us to do this by providing an opportunity for increased use of black talent, increased recognition of black dignity. Polaroid is a small economic force in South Africa, but we are well known and, because of our committee's visit there, highly visible. We hope other American companies will join us in this program. Even a small beginning of co-operative effort among American businesses can have a large effect in South Africa.

How can we presume to concern ourselves with the problems of another country? Whatever the practices elsewhere, South Africa alone articulates a policy exactly contrary to everything we feel our company stands for. We cannot participate passively in such a political system. Nor can we ignore it. That is why we have undertaken this experimental program.

APPENDIX IV

POLAROID CORPORATION
Cambridge, Massachusetts 02139

A REPORT ON SOUTH AFRICA

What specifically did we do in South Africa? Our first step was to ask the distributor and his associated companies (Polaroid has no company investments of its own in South Africa) to improve "dramatically" the salaries and benefits of their non-White employees. This has been done with diligence and some success. The principle of the same pay for the same job has been accepted and announced publicly. The average monthly salary including bonus for Black employees has increased 22 percent. Individual increases have ranged from 6 percent to 33 percent. The average is now 91 Rand (about $127 a month) up from R75. The minimum wage including bonus has been raised to R70. Whereas there were 98 black employees in the lowest salary category a year ago, there are only 39 there now. Twenty-one black employees (out of a total of 151) now make more than R130 per month (about $182). We feel that further progress is possible in this area. Wage discussions including Polaroid, our distributor and the black Employees

Committee of that company have already taken place regarding next year.

Eight black supervisors have been appointed during the course of the year in the Computer, Administration, Services and Distribution Departments. One of the first black computer operators in South Africa is one of this group. Some of these positions were formerly held by whites. The black supervisors are being paid on the same pay scale as their predecessors. In addition two men have received instruction outside the company to qualify them to run on-the-job training courses.

A pension plan with death benefits is already in operation with equal provisions for blacks and whites. Our distributor has also set up a plan that will pay the educational expenses of children of black employees as well as for vocational or scholastic training for the employees themselves. A loan service for black employees is in operation and applications are now screened and recommended by the black Employees Committee.

A second, smaller company associated with our distributor has also instituted wage increases for its black employees of from 16.5 percent to 3.33 percent. They have adopted pension and educational aid plans similar to the distributor's.

Another of the goals of our experiment was to create some mechanisms for change in the area of black education. In addition to the steps taken by our distributor and his allied company to aid the children of black employees, we have attempted three specific programs. A grant of $15,000 has been made by Polaroid to a black organized and operated institution, the Association for the Educational and Cultural Advancement of the African People of South Africa (ASSECA). This group was formed to encourage and improve black education in South Africa. The grant has provided funds for staff, transport and administration. ASSECA has embarked on several ambitious schemes in the past year including coaching classes for high school examinations, lobbying for new classrooms to be built in Johannesburg, and a million Rand fund drive to aid black students.

A second grant of $10,000 was made to the U.S.–South Africa Leader Exchange Program, a private, non-governmental organization. Under this grant two black South Africans and their wives have come to America for an extended period of travel and study. Mr. Seth Manaka, who has a Master's degree in library science, spent three months in this country. Dr. Noel Manganyi, a clinical psychologist, is currently here visiting hospitals, clinics and universities in various parts of the country.

A third grant of $50,000 (derived, as were the others, from profits earned by sales of our products in South Africa) was used to establish a foundation to underwrite educational expenses of black students and teachers in South Africa. This foundation, called ASSET (American–South African Study and Educational Trust) was organized in May 1971. Its trustees include some of the most distinguished black leaders in South Africa: Mr. M. T. Moerane, Editor of *The World;* Chief Gatsha Buthelezi, chief executive of the Zulus; Mr. R. S. Naidoo, president of the Natal Indian Teachers Association; Professor W. M. Kgware, professor of psychology, University of the North; and Mr. David Curry, a leader of the "Coloured" community. There are two white members as well, Mrs. Helen Suzman, Progressive Party member of the South African Parliament and Mr. Helmut Hirsch, managing director of Polaroid's South African distributor. ASSET has made a promising beginning. In its first nine months it has given scholarship grants to 679 students from all the major regions of South Africa. Recipients have included blacks, "coloureds," orientals and Indian students at all levels from high school through college and postgraduate study. Teacher training and vocational training have also been funded. Another 2,000 students have benefited from five special grants made for teachers' salaries in various schools. The number of applications for aid, however, has been overwhelming.

We have also participated in the formation of a black owned and operated distribution company in Nigeria (another of the goals we set for ourselves). The company has been operating out of Lagos since September.

This, then, is what the Polaroid experimental program has accomplished in the year it has been in existence. But what effects has it had? What conclusions have we drawn? What is the future of such a program?

Its effects have been quite visible in press reports from South Africa, England, Canada, and the United States. Apparently Polaroid has been the first company from any country to take a public stand against apartheid and for the improvement of black working conditions in South Africa. Literally thousands of articles and editorials have been written about the "Polaroid Program." Reactions have ranged from applause and support to thoughtful criticism to revolutionary rhetoric. In South Africa the press (which is not controlled by the government) has enthusiastically reported every detail of the program to its readers.

What have other companies done? One of the most important announcements in recent months came from the two largest international banks in South Africa, Barclay's Bank and the Standard Bank, stated that they would pay black employees the same rate for the job as white employees. About 400 black workers are affected. A major American automobile manufacturer also announced recently that they will pay equal wages for equal work, regardless of color. To date, however, whether they have instituted changes or not, most companies in South Africa have been reluctant to make any public statement of their current or future wage policies.

Polaroid has received inquiries from many American companies asking what difficulties we have encountered in South Africa and what pressures have been brought to bear on implementation of our plans. The answer is simple. We have encountered no major difficulties, have faced no pressures that would alter what we have hoped to achieve. On the contrary, we have been surprised at how much progress has been made in a relatively short time.

Two comments that have come to us in recent months have helped to crystallize our feelings on the complex subject of South Africa and our presence there. Alan Paton, novelist, poet and a leading South African liberal, spoke at the Harvard Commencement in June:

> I'm often asked the question as to whether Americans should withdraw all investments in South Africa. I know this view is strongly held by some, and I respect it, but it is not my own. If those American enterprises in South Africa—and there are not a great many—and here I am quoting from the statement of the Polaroid Corporation entitled "An Experiment in South Africa," would improve dramatically the salaries and other benefits of their non-white employees then I have no doubt that this would exert a moral pressure on South African employers to do the same. . . . Therefore I stand not for the withdrawal of American investment, but for this dramatic improvement in salaries and benefits.

The second was from a black African worker who met our four employees when they were in South Africa. He recently wrote a letter to one of the members of the group.

> The Polaroid program has brought about great ferment in this country and many people seem to be trying to do something about improving the lot of the African people. We have had the case of [a large] bank, which gave a directive to its employees to accord African people the same courtesy accorded the other racial groups. The policy makers of that institution banned the use of the appellation "boy" or "girl" when addressing adult Africans. We are to be addressed as Mr. or Mrs. now. . . . What was started by Polaroid is gaining momentum and if it goes on in this way we hope that sanity may eventually be restored to our troubled country. . . . Among the African people, the "experiment" has been applauded and . . . become the talk of the townships. This I have been able to get from people personally. . . . We would like to repeat what we said to you in December, that we are totally opposed to [your] withdrawal from South Africa. What has happened has in fact been the thin edge of the wedge, which will—we hope—lead to a breakthrough.

We share this hope also. In our opinion relatively little has happened prior to this experiment that could encourage hope for change. The alternative courses of action, after close examination, seem equally bleak to us. Although in a year's time the visible effects on other companies of our experiment have been limited, the practical achievements in salaries, benefits and education have shown what can be done. In this report the experiment has exceeded the expectations of many. Therefore, we have decided to continue our program in South Africa.

APPENDIX V

MOVE TO RAISE NON-WHITES' PAY IS SPREADING*

The "POLAROID EXPERIMENT" is starting to spread rapidly in South Africa. During the past few months a considerable number of industrial and commercial firms have been investigating ways of im-

* Source: *Sunday Times*, July 25, 1971.

proving the wages and living conditions of their non-White employees. The ripple effect of this on the country's labor pattern could be considerable.

In boardrooms in Britain, the United States and South Africa, company directors have been examining the merits of adopting the "Polaroid experiment" voluntarily before they are forced to do so by political pressure.

Significantly, those firms are not only those vulnerable to pressures for more enlightened treatment of their non-White employees, but also South African concerns which feel it is morally right and tactically wise to do so.

The South African Institute of Race Relations had received many requests from firms for information and advice on improving the conditions of non-White employees, the director of the institute, Mr. Fred van Wyk, told me this week.

The institute had seconded a senior research officer, Mr. Dudley Horner, to assist firms. He has compiled a 50-page document giving valuable information on the "Polaroid experiment," American investment in South Africa, the country's labor laws and how firms can improve conditions.

Insurance act

The document points out, for example, that Africans earning less than R10.50 a week are not covered by the Unemployment Insurance Act.

An increasing number of firms are committing themselves to pay minimum wages which will ensure that African families live above the poverty line.

The Johannesburg Municipal Non-European Affairs Department reckoned that the minimum budget for an average African family of five was R59.70 a month, and that in 1967, 68 percent of African families in Johannesburg had incomes below this breadline.

There is no statutory minimum wage in South Africa.

U.S. support

"We find that, morally, many employers accept that they must do something about their non-white workers," Mr. Horner told me. "They are sensitive to the situation, and have indicated that they would like to help their non-White workers, but are not always sure how to go about it."

The United States Government has gone so far as to support publicly the move to improve the lot of non-Whites working for American-owned firms in South Africa.

The United States Assistant Secretary of State for African Affairs told the Polaroid Corporation of Boston, which started the whole movement towards "socially responsible" action as a counter to the demand by its militant Black employees for its total withdrawal from South Africa, that the American Government "very much approves" of what it is doing in South Africa.

The United States consulate-general in South Africa has followed this up by giving tips to American firms in this country on how to meet the pressures that will be applied on them.

These tips include acceptance of equal hiring terms; equal prospects for promotion, equal pay for equal work; scholarships for workers or their dependents; pension and medical aid funds and contributions to the South African Government's National Bursaries Fund, with the proviso that the contributions should be "for non-White students."

White public opinion in South Africa favors paying Africans better wages. The churches are playing a leading part in the campaign and the Government has promised to help narrow the wide gap between White and non-White earnings.

Some firms look beyond immediate employment conditions and ask themselves what they can do to help in housing, transport and education.

The South African Government has given no indication that it resents this new attitude among employers, although it has made it clear that the promotion of non-Whites into positions of authority over Whites will not be tolerated. Firms, therefore, will have to devise some form of "parallelism" to avoid, say Black men dictating letters to White typists.

If the movement towards improvement of non-White wages and promotion chances spreads widely in South Africa this will have a ripple effect throughout the economy which could disturb the wage pattern. Enlightened firms would attract non-White workers to them like magnets. It remains to be seen what the Government would do then.

Pressures on foreign-based firms have been most evident in Britain and the United States, and the firms that have been singled out so far for attention include Barclay's Bank, Courtaulds, ICI, Rio Tinto Zinc, Plessey, Rank's Hovis McDougall, IBM, General Motors and Polaroid.

Last January Polaroid instructed their South African agents to improve "dramatically" the wages and conditions of their non-White employees. They said that if the experiment had not succeeded by January 13 next year they would pull out of South Africa altogether.

If, however, an increasing number of foreign-based firms, as well as South African-based firms with overseas connections join in the new movement, obviously the experiment will be felt to have been worthwhile and Polaroid will not pull out.

A wide range of British and the United States firms can be subjected to pressures over their treatment of non-White employees in South Africa.

Vast investment

The book value of total direct foreign investment in South Africa in 1969 was R3,502 million of which R2,403 million (60 percent) was British and R596 million American. The balance was of other foreign countries.

"The current market value of this investment is probably at least two or three times the book value," says the *Financial Mail*.

The discordant note struck by an anti-apartheid shareholder at Charter Consolidated's annual meeting in London last week can be taken as a sign of the growing campaign to put pressure on foreign-based firms with subsidiaries in South Africa to give their non-White employees better treatment.

The shareholder, Mr. Arthur Batty, complained about the wages of African workers in Cape Asbestos's South African mines (Charter owns 60 percent of Cape Asbestos), and said that asbestosis incapacitated five Black workers every week, but the sole compensation they received was a lump payment of R800.

The Department of Mines denies the allegation. It says the total number of certifications last year for asbestosis and asbestosis combined with tuberculosis was less than half the number stated by Mr. Batty.

The anti-apartheid activists who have been making the rounds of annual meetings are striking at a psychologically opportune time. Foreign-based firms which have been under pressure to withdraw altogether from South Africa are apparently eager to avoid a confrontation in this arena by acceding to the demands to give their non-White employees in South Africa a better deal.

The fact is also being accepted, abroad and in South Africa, that the case for an improvement in non-White wages and working conditions is a morally unanswerable one.

APPENDIX VI

ASSET (AMERICAN–SOUTH AFRICAN STUDY EDUCATIONAL TRUST)*

In July 1971 the first Polaroid bursaries were awarded, R35,000 having been made available for educational purposes, mainly bursaries, for the people of South Africa, by the Polaroid Company of America. A further grant of R36,500 was made for 1972, and R38,076 for 1973.

In August 1972 the first *Pepsi-Cola* bursaries were awarded, R18,500 having been made available for education by the *Pepsi-Cola* Company of America. A further grant of R35,000 was made for 1973.

In November 1972 *American Express* made a grant of R7,789 towards 1973 ASSET bursaries. Permission was given for this to be administered in conjunction with Polaroid.

The Polaroid and American Express, and the Pepsi-Cola bursaries are allocated from the funds of ASSET (American–South African Study Educational Trust), a Trust created by Polaroid, with a multi-racial board of trustees. The bursaries are collectively known as ASSET bursaries and are administered by the S.A. Institute of Race Relations. The bursaries are either ASSET Bursaries (Polaroid and American Express) or ASSET Bursaries (Pepsi-Cola), Pepsi-Cola having requested that their bursaries be administered separately.

In 1973, 612 ASSET bursaries were awarded at a cost of R61,885. In addition miscellaneous grants were given totalling R3,346.

APPENDIX VII

BLACK BELLIES AND BUSINESSMEN†

There's a time bomb ticking on every factory floor. And each day the fuse is getting shorter. African discontent is spreading as their wage packets are eaten away by inflation. Real incomes—in many cases already pitifully low—are rapidly declining again.

---

* Source: Extracted from the *Annual ASSET Report,* 1973.

† Source: *The Financial Mail,* Johannesburg. April 5, 1974. Reproduced with permission.

African living costs in Durban, for example, have already leapt a staggering 11.5% in the first quarter of 1974. At this rate, they will double by the end of the year. And for the first time, the PDL (according to Natal University) exceeds R100.

Bus-fare increases have been applied for in Durban and already operate in Johannesburg. Milk went up on April 1. Meat, rice, fruit and vegetables are expected to cost more.

Businessmen need only ask their wives to hear what inflation is doing to their housekeeping money. Africans are infinitely worse off. Not only are they perilously close to mere subsistence, their living costs have been rising twice as fast as the White consumer price index.

Industrialists were rightly conscience-stricken by the poverty wages which the Durban strikes exposed a year ago. They reacted positively. Now they must react again. Not next week, not next month. Today.

Wages should be reviewed at once, and immediate. steps taken to restore them at least to their *real* value of a year ago. So much for today.

For tomorrow, action is also urgently required. As long as prices keep rising as fast as they are, wages should be reviewed quarterly.

And by the end of this year they should be lifted at least enough to keep abreast of the rising Poverty Datum Line—and today that means a minimum of around R110 per month.

There are valid objections to the PDL. But it's the best rough and ready indicator we have of the *absolute minimum* needs of the average African family. In the absence of anything better it should be accepted as the major consideration when wage rates are determined.

Thirdly, businessmen should start looking beyond the PDL. It is no more than a survival standard, allowing nothing for doctors' and chemists' bills, savings, schoolbooks, or even the odd packet of cigarettes. To maintain any sort of decent living-standard the current Effective Minimum Level (EML) of R166 should be paid.

Businessmen should therefore set themselves a further objective: by the end of next year no employee should get less than the EML. And without hours of overtime or having to rely on the earnings of a wife or adolescent child.

What of aggravating the inflation? A fast expanding economy should allow the greater spending power to be offset by higher productivity and thus lower unit costs.

What goes for business should surely apply to Wage Board determinations, which are often used as a guideline. At the very least they should not be at figures which, on today's prices, mean near starvation.

An academically calculated PDL is, of course, no substitute for political or industrial bargaining power. But Black workers have no vote and no normal trade union rights. The PDL is an attempt to fill the gap.

White workers, with both trade unions and the vote, would never tolerate being exploited the way some Black workers are. And it would be dangerous complacency to expect Black workers to tolerate it much longer.

FACTS AT YOUR FINGERTIPS*

Unless otherwise stated, all figures include Transkei.

Area:

	Square kilometers
RSA (excl. Transkei)	1,182,329
SWA	824,269
Transkei	38,713

House of Assembly

	Total 2000 (est.)
National Party	123
United Party	36
Prog-Reform Party	12

Population	Economically active 1975	Total 1975	Total 1980 (est.)	Total 2000 (est.)
Whites	1.8	4.2	4.7	6.6
Africans	7.0	17.7	20.4	34.7
Coloureds	0.8	2.4	2.7	4.7
Asians	0.2	0.7	0.8	1.3
*Total	9.8	25.0	28.6	47.4

* Incl. Transkei, which in 1973 had a resident pop. of 1,891 m (incl. 18–700 non-Blacks).

Principal urban areas

	Pop. 1975 (000s)
Johannesburg	1,499
Durban	837
Cape Town	818
Pretoria	614
Port Elizabeth	469
Germiston	215
Benoni	178

Principal imports (Rm)

	1973	1974	1975
Machinery, electrical equipment	977.6	1,320.6	1,832.2
Transport equipment	601.5	789.4	1,084.3
Petroleum products	n/a	n/a	1,015.0
Base metals and products	244.3	507.9	573.5
Chemicals and allied products	257.3	448.3	456.4

Balance of payments (Rm)

	1973	1974	1975
Imports (including arms and oil)	−3,545	−5,734	−6,736
Exports (excluding gold)	2,510	3,137	3,563
Net gold output	1,770	2,565	2,540
Invisibles and transfers	677	−916	−1,149
Balance on current account	45	−1,032	−1,908
Capital movements	−92	885	1,897
BoP transactions (excluding adjustments)	−34	−63	115
Total reserves end of December	976	909	1,100

Gold

	1973	1974	1975
Production (metric tons)	852.2	758.5	708.1
Percent of total world production (excluding U.S.S.R.)	78.0	76.3	75.3
Average of daily London prices (Rand)	65.3	108.3	118.1
(U.S. Dollars)	91.20	159.14	161.06
Krugerrand exports (000 coins)	792.1	3,009.0	4,700.0

National accounts

	1973	1974	1975
Gross domestic product* market prices (Rm)	19,074	22,770	25,832
Percent increase over previous year	22.2	19.4	13.4
Percent increase over previous year in real terms	3.6	7.0	2.3
Gross national product† market prices (Rm)	18,444	21,874	24,669
Percent increase over previous year	22.5	18.6	12.8
Percent increase over previous year in real terms	9.5	8.5	−1.5
Per capita GNP (R)	756	871	984
Percent increase over previous year in real terms	7%	6%	−4%

* Total net output in SA.
† GDP less net payments to foreign capital and labour including changes in terms of trade.

APPENDIX VIII—Continued

Farm production

	1973/74	1974/75	1975/76	1976/77*
Maize (000 metric tons)	11,105	9,140	7,359	n/a
Sugar cane (000 metric tons)	15,454	16,895	16,814	17,400
Wool—shorn and on skins (m kg)	112.7	114.6	114.3	115.0
Deciduous fruit (controlled by DFB) (000 metric tons)	212.6	249.8	271.0	n/a
Wheat (000 metric tons)	1,871	1,596	1,780	2,030

* Estimate.

Other economic indicators

	1973	1974	1975
Retail sales (Rm)	4,329.9	5,250.9	6,146.6
Percent real increase	4.9	6.8	2.7
Consumer price index change over year (%)	9.5	11.6	13.5
Wholesale sales (Rm)	5,237.5	6,783.6	8,159.9
Percent real increase	4.3	11.5	3.0
Wholesale price index change over year (%)	13.2	18.0	17.3
Manufacturing output (1970=100)	114.4	121.2	123.7
Percent change over previous year	8.7	5.9	2.1
Cement production (000 metric tons)	6,866.0	7,302.0	7,176.0
Percent change over previous year	12.4	6.4	-1.7
Building plans passed (Rm)	1,109.2	1,167.9	1,066.3
Percent change over previous year	32.5	5.3	-8.7
Buildings completed (Rm)	620.9	836.7	806.4
Percent change over previous year	4.5	34.7	-3.6
Building society advances (Rm)	1,218.0	889.1	1,260.2
Percent change over previous year	39.8	-27.0	41.7
Commercial bank discounts and advances at year end excluding Land Bank (Rm)	2,880.0	3,414.0	3,874.0
Percent change over previous year	53.9	18.5	13.5
Commercial bank deposits at year end (Rm)	4,895.0	5,905.0	6,938.0
Percent change over previous year	22.6	20.6	17.5
Money and near-money at year end (Rm)	5,983.3	7,317.0	8,591.0
Percent change over previous year	23.0	22.3	17.4
New car sales	229,442.0	226,776.0	229,031.0
Percent change over previous year	25.4	-1.2	1.0

African homelands

	No. of blocks after consolidation	Area Km² (1973)	Pop. (000—inc. Whites) (1973)	Pop. per Km²
B'Tswana	6	37,994	988.3	26.0
KwaZulu	10	32,734	2,319.2	70.8
Lebowa	6	22,476	1,190.9	53.0
Ciskei	1	9,421	594.7	64.7
Gazankulu	3	6,331	288.8	45.6
Venda	2	6,182	291.8	47.2
Swazi	1	2,084	145.4	69.8
Qwaqwa	1	482	45.2	93.8
S Ndebele	2	202	n/a	n/a
Rest of SA (excl. Transkei—1975)		1,064,423	25,043.3	23.5

Main trading Partners: (Rm)

	1972	1973	1974	1975
U.K.				
Imports	586.8	632.4	823.1	1097.3
Exports	530.4	699.9	793.7	903.7
West Germany				
Imports	411.1	607.1	925.0	1033.9
Exports	132.6	189.7	337.2	426.8
U.S.A.				
Imports	459.9	528.3	811.5	985.0
Exports	148.0	163.7	238.1	429.7
Japan				
Imports	265.8	380.8	600.4	612.0
Exports	261.2	246.4	429.4	487.3
France				
Imports	96.7	125.3	196.9	244.8
Exports	56.7	68.9	88.3	92.6

Principal Exports (Rm)

	1973	1974	1975
Gold (in all forms)	1770.0	2565.0	2540.0
Diamonds, other precious and semiprecious stones	478.7	416.3	421.5
Krugerrands	57.3	333.2	575.1
Prepared foodstuffs: spirits; tobacco	275.8	446.4	512.7
Base metals and articles	362.4	488.8	495.6
Vegetable products	232.6	403.1	491.8

Other economic indicators

	1973	1974	1975
Electricity generated (kWh-m)	64,818.0	70,757.0	75,606.0
Percent change over previous year	9.6	9.2	6.9
Average monthly registered unemployed (non-African)	10,785.0	8,347.0	10,304.0
Percent change over previous year	−11.6	−22.6	23.4
New commercial vehicle sales	112,943.0	115,151.0	134,587.0
Percent change over previous year	2.8	2.0	16.9
Net immigration	17,615.0	28,482.0	40,209.0
Percent change over previous year	−29.2	61.7	41.2
Railway ton/km (m)	61,042.0	63,917.0	68,102.0
Percent change over previous year	3.0	4.7	6.5
Foreign tourists, inc. persons in transit	513,125.0	478,085.0	579,697.0
Percent change over previous year	10.5	−6.8	21.3

*Source: Financial Mail, Johannesburg, November 5, 1976.

APPENDIX IX

BREAKDOWN OF PRIVATE CONSUMPTION EXPENDITURE AND PER CAPITA EXPENDITURE ON SCHOOL EDUCATION BY RACE

Table 1

PRIVATE CONSUMPTION EXPENDITURE BY RACE 1970–71

	Percent	*Ratios*	
White..............	73.7		
African............	19.1	White:African	15.2:1
Asian..............	2.1	White:Asian	5.7:1
Coloured...........	5.2	White:Coloured	7.5:1
Total..............	100.0	White:Nonwhite	12.9:1

Source: Estimated by SANLAM, a large South African life assurance and pension fund group.

Table 2

PER CAPITA EXPENDITURE ON SCHOOL EDUCATION

	Year	*Primary school pupils (R)*	*Secondary and high school pupils (R)*	*General average (R)*
Whites..............	1971–72	366*	624*	461*
Asians..............	1972	112.49	155.74	124.40
Coloureds...........	1972	91.04	120.18	94.41
Blacks..............	1972	20.64*	112.71*	25.31

* Estimates

Source: *A Survey of Race Relations in South Africa* (South Africa Institute of Race Relations, 1973), p. 293.

BOOK TWO

Implementing corporate strategy

The accomplishment of purpose: Organizational structure and relationships

WE now turn our attention to the concepts and skills essential to the implementation of strategy. The life of action requires more than analytical intelligence. It is not enough to have an idea and be able to evaluate its worth. Persons with responsibility for the achievement of goals, the accomplishment of results, and the solution of problems, finally know the worth of a strategy when its power is demonstrated. Furthermore, a unique corporate strategy determined in relation to a concrete situation is never complete, even as a formulation, until it is embodied in the organizational activities which reveal its soundness and begin to affect its nature.

INTERDEPENDENCE OF FORMULATION AND IMPLEMENTATION

It is convenient from the point of view of orderly study to divide a consideration of corporate strategy, as we have divided it, into aspects of formulation and implementation and to note, for example, the requirement of the former for analytical and conceptual ability and of the latter for administrative skill. But in real life the processes of formulation and implementation are intertwined. Feedback from operations gives notice of changing environmental factors to which strategy should be adjusted. The formulation of strategy is not finished when implementation begins. A business organization is always changing in response to its own makeup and past development. Similarly, it should be changing in response to changes in the larger systems in which it moves, and in response to its success or failure in affecting its environment. For the sake of orderly presentation, we have arranged the cases so that henceforth the data will require us to focus less on what the strategy should be than on ways to make it effective in action and to alter it as required. We are taking forward with us, however, all our previous interests. We shall continue to examine each firm's strategy against the criteria we have developed in order to practice the skills we have gained and to verify the decisions made by the executives of the company.

We have already seen that the determination of strategy has four continuous subactivities; the examination of the environment for opportunity and risk, the systematic assessment of corporate strengths and weaknesses, the identification and weighting of personal values, and the clarification of social responsibility. Implementation may also be thought of as having important subactivities. In very broad terms, these are the design of organizational structure and relationships and the effective administration of organizational processes affecting behavior. The development of effective personal leadership, crucial to success in achieving planned results, has already been discussed in the first section of this text.

In deciding on strategy, general managers force their minds to range over the whole vast territory of the technological, social, economic, and political systems which provide opportunity for their company or threaten its continued existence. When they turn their attention to carrying out the strategy tentatively determined, they address themselves within the limitations of their knowledge, to all the techniques and skills of administration. To deal with so wide a range of activity, they need a simple and flexible approach to the aspects of organized activity which they must take into account. By considering the relationships between strategy and organizational structure, strategy and organizational processes, and strategy and personal leadership styles, the student should be able to span a territory crowded with ideas without losing sight of the purpose sought in crossing it.

Each of the implementing subactivities constitutes in itself a special world in which many people are doing research, developing knowledge, and asserting the importance of their work over that of other specialists. Thus the nature of organization, about which every general manager must make some assumptions, is the subject of a richly entangled array of ideas upon which one could spend a lifetime. The design of information systems—particularly at a time when the speed and capacity of the computer continue to fascinate the processors of information—appears to require long study, an esoteric language, and even rearrangement of organizational activities for the sake of information processing. Similarly, performance appraisal, motivation and incentive systems, control systems, and systems of executive recruitment and development all have their armies of theoretical and empirical proponents, each one fully equipped with manuals, code books, rules, and techniques.

It will, of course, be impossible for us to consider in detail the knowledge and theory which have been developed during the course of a half century of researches in administration. It will be assumed that your own experience has introduced you to the major schools of thought contending in the developing administrative disciplines, and that where necessary, the knowledge you have will be supplemented by further study. Just as general managers must be able to draw upon the skills of special staffs in leading their organizations, so they must be able to draw upon these special studies in effecting their own combination of organizational design and organizational practices. The simple prescription we wish to add here is that *the corporate strategy must dominate the design of organizational structure and processes*. That is, the principal criterion for all decisions on organizational structure and behavior should be their relevance to the achievement of the organizational purpose, not their conformity to the dictates of special disciplines.

Thus the theses we suggest for your consideration are first that conscious strategy can be consciously implemented through skills primarily administrative in nature. Second, the chief determinant of organizational structure and the processes by which tasks are assigned and performance motivated, rewarded, and controlled should be *the strategy of the firm*, not the history of the company, its position in its industry, the specialized background of its executives, the principles of organization as developed in textbooks, the recommendations of consultants, or the conviction that one form of organization is intrinsically better than another.

The successful implementation of strategy requires that executives shape to the peculiar needs of their strategy the formal structure of their organization, its informal relationships, and the processes of motivation and control which provide incentives and measure results. They try to bring about the commitment to organizational aims and policies of properly qualified individuals and groups to whom portions of the total task have been assigned. They must ensure not only that goals are clear and purposes are understood, but also that individuals are developing in terms of capacity and achievement and are reaping proper rewards in terms of compensation and personal satisfactions. Above all, they must do what they can to arrange that departmental interests, interdepartmental rivalries, and the machinery of measurement and evaluation do not deflect energy from organizational purpose into harmful or irrelevant activity.

To clarify our approach to the problem of adapting the concepts and findings of special disciplines to the requirements of policy, we list here a dozen aspects of implementation which may serve as a convenient map of the territory to be traversed. It should be remembered that cases you will analyze have not been researched or written to prove these propositions. The list is designed only to make it possible for you to use your own specialized knowledge and adapt it, within limits imposed by your own characteristic attitudes toward risk and responsibility, to strategic requirements.

1. Once strategy is tentatively or finally set, the key tasks to be performed and kinds of decisions required must be identified.

2. Once the size of operations exceeds the capacity of one person, responsibility for accomplishing key tasks and making decisions must be assigned to individuals or groups. The division of labor must permit efficient performance of subtasks and must be accompanied by some hierarchical allocation of authority to assure achievement.

3. Formal provisions for the coordination of activities thus separated must be made in various ways, e.g., through a hierarchy of supervision, project and committee organizations, task forces, and other *ad hoc*

units. The prescribed activities of these formally constituted bodies are not intended to preclude spontaneous voluntary coordination.

4. Information systems adequate for coordinating divided functions (i.e., for letting those performing part of the task know what they must know of the rest, and for letting those in supervisory positions know what is happening so that next steps may be taken) must be designed and installed.

5. The tasks to be performed should be arranged in a sequence comprising a program of action or a schedule of targets to be achieved at specified times. So that long-range planning may not be neglected, support for this activity should probably be entrusted to a special staff unit in larger organizations. Its influence may be enhanced by attaching it to the president's office, its usefulness by having it work in close cooperation with the line. While long-range plans may be couched in relatively general terms, operating plans will often take the form of relatively detailed budgets. These can meet the need for the establishment of standards against which future performance can be judged.

6. Actual performance, as quantitatively reported in information systems and qualitatively estimated through observation by supervisors and the judgment of customers, should be compared to budgeted performance and to standards in order to test achievement, budgeting processes, the adequacy of the standards, and the competence of individuals.

7. Individuals and groups of individuals must be recruited and assigned to essential tasks in accordance with the specialized or supervisory skills which they possess or can develop. At the same time, the assignment of tasks may well be adjusted to the nature of available skills.

8. Individual performance, evaluated both quantitatively and qualitatively, should be subjected to influences (constituting a pattern of incentives) which will help to make it effective in accomplishing organizational goals.

9. Since individual motives are complex and multiple, incentives for achievement should range from those that are universally appealing—such as adequate compensation and an organizational climate favorable to the simultaneous satisfaction of individual and organizational purposes—to specialized forms of recognition, financial or nonfinancial, designed to fit individual needs and unusual accomplishments.

10. In addition to financial and nonfinancial incentives and rewards to motivate individuals to voluntary achievement, a system of constraints, controls, and penalties must be devised to contain nonfunctional activity and to enforce standards. Controls, like incentives, are both formal and informal. Effective control requires both quantitative and nonquantitative information which must always be used together.

11. Provision for the continuing development of requisite technical and managerial skills is a high-priority requirement. The development of individuals must take place chiefly within the milieu of their assigned responsibilities. This on-the-job development should be supplemented by intermittent formal instruction and study.

12. Dynamic personal leadership is necessary for continued growth and improved achievement in any organization. Leadership may be expressed in many styles, but it must be expressed in some perceptible style. This style must be natural and also consistent with the requirements imposed upon the organization by its strategy and membership.

The general manager is principally concerned with determining and monitoring the adequacy of strategy, with adapting the firm to changes in its environment, and with securing and developing the people needed to carry out the strategy or to help with its constructive revision. Managers must also ensure that the processes which encourage and constrain individual performance and personal development are consistent with human and strategic needs. In large part, therefore, leadership consists of achieving commitments to strategy via clarification and dramatization of its requirements and value.

We shall return to each of these considerations, looking first at some general relationships between strategy and organizational structure. We shall look also at the need for specialization of tasks, coordination of divided responsibility, and design of effective information systems.

STRATEGY AND ORGANIZATIONAL STRUCTURE

It is at once apparent that the accomplishment of strategic purpose requires organization. If a consciously formulated strategy is to be effective, organizational development should be planned rather than left to evolve by itself. So long as a company is small enough for a single individual to direct both planning for the future and current operations, questions of organizational structure remain unimportant. Thus the one-man organization encounters no real organizational problem until the proprietor's quick walks through the plant, his wife's bookkeeping, and his sales agent's marketing activities are no longer adequate to growing volume. When the magnitude of operations increases, then departmentalization—usually into such clusters of activities as manufacturing, production, and finance—begins to appear. Most functional organizations ultimately encounter size problems again. With geographical dispersion, product complexity, and increased volume of sales, coordination must be accomplished somewhere else than at the top. We then find multiunit organizations with coordinating responsibility delegated to divisions, subsidiaries, profit centers, and the like. The difficulty of designing an organizational structure is directly proportionate to the *diversity* and *size* of the undertaking.

The subject of organization is the most extensive and complex of all the subtopics of implementation. It has at various times attracted the interest of economists, sociologists, psychologists, political scientists, philosophers, and, in a curiously restricted way, of creative writers as well. These have contributed to the field a variety of theoretical formulations and empirical investigations. The policy maker will probably find himself unable to subscribe wholeheartedly to the precepts of any one school of thought or to the particulars of any one model of the firm. Indeed, established theories of the firm are inadequate for general management purposes. The impact of most organizational studies, from the point of view of the eclectic practitioner looking for counsel rather than confusion, has been to undermine confidence in other studies. The activities of present-day social science have in particular badly damaged the precepts of classical scientific management. Progress in the reconciliation of divergent insights into the nature of organization, however, can be expected in due course.

Regardless of disputes about theory among scholars, the executive in, say, a company that has reached some complexity, knows three things. The tasks essential to accomplishing purpose must in some way be subdivided; they must be assigned, if possible, to individuals whose skills are appropriately specialized; and tasks that have been subdivided must ultimately be reintegrated into a unified whole. The manager knows also that once performance is out of one pair of hands, and once no one in the organization is performing the total task, information about what one group is doing must be made available to the others. Otherwise problems and risks cannot be detected and dealt with.

SUBDIVISION OF TASK RESPONSIBILITY

In every industry conventional ways of dividing task by function have developed to the extent that the training of individuals skilled in these functions perpetuates organizational arrangements. But identification of the tasks *should* be made in terms of a company's distinctive purposes and unique strategy, not by following industry convention. True, the fact that every manufacturing firm procures and processes raw materials and sells and delivers finished products means that at least production and sales and probably procurement and distribution will always be critical functional areas which must be assigned to specialized organizational units. But these basic uniformities which cut across company and industry lines provide the individual firm with little useful guidance on the issues it finds so perplexing, namely, how much weight to assign to which function, or how to adapt nearly universal structural arrangements to its own particular needs.

A manufacturer who plans to perform services for the government under cost-plus-fixed-fee contracts, to cite a very limited example, feels less need for a fully developed cost control system and cost-related incentives than one whose contracts are governed by a fixed price. To illustrate more broadly the way in which strategic choice determines the relative importance of tasks, consider the manufacturer of a line of industrial products who decides to diversify in view of declining opportunity in the original field. Product improvement and the engineering organization responsible for it become less vital than the search for new products, either internally or through acquisition. But if the latter task is not recognized as crucial, then it is unlikely to be assigned to any individual or unit, but will rather be considered as an additional duty for many. Under the latter circumstances, accomplishment may well be impaired.

Once the key tasks have been identified (or the identification customary in the industry has been ratified as proper for the individual firm), then responsibility for accomplishing these tasks must be assigned to individuals and groups. In addition to a rational principle for separating tasks from one another, the need will soon become apparent for some scale of relative importance among activities to be established.

Distribution of formal authority among those to whom tasks have been assigned is essential for the effective control of operations, the development of individual skills, the distribution of rewards, and for other organizational processes to which we shall soon give attention. The extent to which individuals, once assigned a task, need to be supervised and controlled is the subject of voluminous argument which, temporarily at least, must leave the general practitioner aware that too much control and too little are equally ineffective and that, as usual, the generalist is the person who must strike the balance.

The division of labor is thus accompanied by the specialization of task and the distribution of authority, with the relative importance of tasks as defined by strategy marked by status. The rational principle by which tasks are specialized and authority delegated may be separation by functions, by product or product lines, by geographical or regional subdivision, by customer and market, or by type of production equipment or processes. The intermixture of these principles in multiunit organizations has resulted in many hybrid types of formal structure which we need not investigate. The principal requirement is that the basis for division should be relatively consistent, easily understood, and conducive to the grouping of like activities. Above all, the formal pattern should have visible relationship to corporate purpose, should fix responsibility in such a way as not to preclude teamwork, and should provide for the solution of problems as close to the point of action as possible. Structure should not be any more restrictive than necessary of the satisfaction of individual needs or of the inevitable emergence of informal organization. The design should also allow for more complex structure as the organization grows in size.

As you consider the need to create, build, and develop an organizational structure for the firms in the cases you will study shortly, you will wish to avoid choosing a pattern of organization on the grounds that it is "typical" or "generally sound." Any preference you may have for divisional versus functional organizations, for decentralized rather than centralized decision making, for a "flat" rather than a "steep" or many-stepped hierarchy, should be set aside until you have identified the activities made essential by the strategy, the skills available for their performance, and the needs and values of the individuals involved. The plan you devise should ignore neither the history of the company nor that of its industry, for in ongoing organizations formal structure may not be abruptly changed without great cost. Any new plan that you devise for gradual implementation should be as economical as is consistent with the requirements for technical skill, proper support for principal functions, and reserve capacity for further growth. The degree of centralization and decentralization that you prescribe should not turn on your personal preference, and presumably will vary from one activity to another. Strategic requirements as well as the abilities and experience of company executives should determine the extent to which responsibility for decisions should tend toward the center or toward the field. In a consumer credit company, for example, freedom to extend credit to doubtful risks can really be allowed only to relatively experienced branch managers though company strategy may prescribe it for all.

That so little need be said about the nature of the formal organization, and so much must be determined by the particulars of each individual situation, should not be taken as evidence that formal organization does not matter. On the contrary, progress in a growing organization is impossible without substrategies for organizational development. Restructuring the organization becomes a goal in itself to be worked toward over a period of years—perhaps without the interim publication of the ultimate design.

But though it is impractical, except in cases of harsh emergency, to make sweeping organizational changes with little preparation and upon short notice, this is not to say that no major role is played by structure, by clear and logical subdivisions of task, or by an openly acknowledged hierarchy of authority, status, and prestige—all serving as the conscious embodiment of strategy and the harbinger of growth to come. As you check the relation between strategy and structure, whether in your study of cases or in your business experience, ask yourself always the policy questions: Is the strategy sound and clear? If goals are clear, have the tasks required been clearly identified and assessed for their relative importance? If key activities are known, have they been assigned to people with the requisite training, experience, and staff support they will need? The answers to these questions do not carry one very far along the road toward successful strategy implementation, but they provide a convenient starting point from which the rest of the trip can be made.

COORDINATION OF DIVIDED RESPONSIBILITY

As soon as a task is divided, some formal provision must be made for coordination. In baseball, the park outside the diamond is subdivided into left, center, and right fields, and a player is assigned to each. But if there is no procedure for handling a ball hit halfway between any two areas, the formal division of labor will help only the team at bat. Most important work in organizations requires cooperation among the departmental specialists to whom a portion of the total task has been allocated. Many forces are at work to make coordination so essential that it cannot be left to chance. For example, the flow of work from one station to another and from one administrative jurisdiction to another creates problems of scheduling and timing, of accommodating departmental needs, and of overall supervision lest departmental needs become more influential than organizational goals.

As soon as additional people join the first person in an organization, they bring with them their own goals, and these must be served, at least to a minimal degree, by the activity required of them in service to the organization. As soon as a group of such individuals, different in personal needs but similar in technical competence and point of view is established to perform a given function, then departmental goals may attract more loyalty than the overall goals of the organization. To keep individual purposes and needs as well as departmental substrategies consistent with corporate strategy is, as we have said before, a considerable undertaking. It is a major top-management responsibility in all organizations, regardless of the apparent degree of commitment and willingness to cooperate in the common cause.

The different needs of individuals and the distinctive goals of functional specialties mean that, at best, the organization's total strategy is understood differently and valued for different reasons by different parts of the organization. Some formal or informal means for resolving these differences is important. Where the climate is right, specialists will be aware of the relative validity of organizational and departmental needs and of the bias inevitable in any loyalty to expertise.

Formal organization provides for the coordination of divided responsibility through the hierarchy of supervision, through the establishment and use of committees, and through the project form of organization (which, like temporary task forces, can be superimposed upon a functional or divisional organization). The wider the sphere of any supervisor's jurisdiction, the more time is needed to bring into balance aspects of organized life which would otherwise influence performance toward the wrong goals. The true function of a committee—and were this role more widely understood and effectively played, committees would be less frequently maligned—is to bring to the exploration and solution of interdepartmental problems both the specialist and generalist abilities of its members. The need for formal committees would be largely obviated in an ideal organization, where all members were conscious of the impact of their own proposals, plans, and decisions upon the interests of others. To the extent that individual managers seek out advice and approval from those whose interests must be balanced with theirs, they perform in face-to-face encounters the essential coordination which is sometimes formalized in a committee structure.

Coordination can play a more creative role than merely composing differences. It is the quality of the way in which subdivided functions and interests are resynthesized that often distinguishes one organization from another in terms of results. The reintegration of the parts into the whole, when what is at stake is the execution of corporate strategy, is what creates a whole that is greater than the sum of its parts. Rivalry between competing subunits or individuals—if monitored to keep it *constructive* rivalry—can exhibit creative characteristics. It can be the source of a new solution to a problem, one that transcends earlier proposals that reflected only the rival unit's parochial concerns. The ability to handle the coordinating function in a way that brings about a new synthesis among competing interests, a synthesis in harmony with the special competence of the total organization, is the administrator's most subtle and creative contribution to the successful functioning of an organization.

EFFECTIVE DESIGN OF INFORMATION SYSTEMS

If corporate strategy is to be effectively implemented, there must be organizational arrangements to provide members with the information they will need to perform their tasks and relate their work to that of others. Information flows inward from the environment to all organizational levels; within the company it should move both down and up. In view of the bulk of information moving upward, it must be reduced to manageable compass as it nears the top. This condensation can be accomplished only by having data synthesized at lower levels, so that part of what moves upward is interpretation rather than fact. To achieve synthesis without introducing distortion or bias or serious omission is a formidable problem to which management must remain alert. Well handled, the information system brings to the attention of those who have authority to act not the vast mass of routine data processed by the total system, but the significant red-flag items that warn of outcomes contrary to expectations. A well-designed information system is thus the key to "management by exception." This in turn is one key to the prevailing problem of the overburdened executive.

In the gathering and transmitting of information, accounting and control departments play a major task. One obstacle to effective performance here is devotion to specialty and procedure for its own sake, as accountants look more to their forms than to larger purposes. The Internal Revenue Service, the Securities and Exchange Commission, the Census Bureau, the Environmental Protection Agency, and the Justice Department, all with requirements which must be met, impose uniformities on the ways in which information is collected and analyzed. But nothing in the conventions of accounting, the regulations of the government, or the rapidly advancing mathematical approaches to problem solving in any way prevents the generation and distribution within an organization of the kind of information management finds most useful.

Now, with the speed of the computer, data can be made available early enough to do some good. We shall have much more to say about the uses of information when we turn to the organizational processes that determine individual behavior. It is important to note that the generation of data is not an end in itself. Its function should be to permit individuals who necessarily perform only one of the many tasks required by the organizational mission to know what they need to know in order to perform their functions in balance with all others, and to gain that overview of total operations which will inform and guide the decisions they have discretion to make. Designing the flow of information is just as important as choosing a principle of subdivision in outlining organizational structure. Information is often the starting point in trying to determine how the organization should be changed. It is a way to monitor the continuing adequacy of strategy and to warn when change is necessary.

The Adams Corporation (A)

In JANUARY OF 1972, the board of directors of The Adams Corporation simultaneously announced the highest sales in the company's history, the lowest after-tax profits (as a percentage of sales) of the World War II era, and the retirement (for personal reasons) of its long-tenure president and chief executive officer.

Founded in St. Louis in 1848, the Adams Brothers Company had long been identified as a family firm both in name and operating philosophy. Writing in a business history journal, a former family senior manager comments: "My grandfather wanted to lead a business organization with ethical standards. He wanted to produce a quality product and a quality working climate for both employees and managers. He thought the Holy Bible and the concept of family stewardship provided him with all the guidelines needed to lead his company. A belief in the fundamental goodness of mankind, in the power of fair play and in the importance of personal and corporate integrity were his trademarks. Those traditions exist today in the nineteen sixties."

In the early 1950s, two significant corporate events occurred. First, the name of the firm was changed to The Adams Corporation. Second, somewhat over 50 percent of the corporation shares were sold by various family groups to the wider public. In 1970, all branches of the family owned or "influenced" less than one fifth of the outstanding shares of Adams.

The Adams Corporation was widely known and respected as a manufacturer and distributor of quality, branded, and consumer products for the American, Canadian, and European (export) markets. Adams products were processed in four regional plants located near raw material sources,[1] were stored and distributed in a series of recently constructed

---

[1] No single plant processed the full line of Adams products, but each plant processed the main items in the line.

or renovated distribution centers located in key cities throughout North America, and were sold by a company sales force to thousands of retail outlets—primarily supermarkets.

In explaining the original long-term financial success of the company, a former officer commented: "Adams led the industry in the development of unique production processes that produced a quality product at a very low cost. The company has always been production-oriented and volume-oriented and it paid off for a long time. During those decades the Adams brand was all that was needed to sell our product; we didn't do anything but a little advertising. Competition was limited and our production efficiency and raw material sources enabled us to outspace the industry in sales and profit. Our strategy was to make a quality product, distribute it and sell it cheap.

"But that has all changed in the past 20 years," he continued. "Our three major competitors have outdistanced us in net profits and market aggressiveness. One of them—a first-class marketing group—has doubled sales and profits within the past five years. Our gross sales have increased to almost $250 million but our net profits have dropped continuously during that same period. While a consumer action group just designated us as 'best value,' we have fallen behind in marketing techniques, e.g., our packaging is just out of date."

Structurally, Adams was organized into eight major divisions. Seven of these were regional sales divisions, with responsibility for distribution and sales of the company's consumer products to retail stores in their area. Each regional sales division was further divided into organizational units at the state and county and/or trading area level. Each sales division was governed by a corporate price list in the selling of company products but had some leeway to meet the local competitive price developments. Each sales division was also assigned (by the home office) a quota of salesmen it could hire and was given the salary ranges within which these men could be employed. All salesmen were on straight salary and expense reimbursement salary plan, which resulted in compensation under industry averages.

A small central accounting office accumulated sales and expense information for each of the several sales divisions on a quarterly basis, and prepared the overall company financial statements. Each sales division received, without commentary, a quarterly statement showing the number of cases processed and sold for the overall division, sales revenue per case of the overall division, and local expenses per case for the overall division.

Somewhat similar information was obtained from the manufacturing division. Manufacturing division accounting was complicated by variations in the cost of obtaining and processing the basic materials used in Adams products. These variations—particularly in procurement—were largely beyond the control of that division. The accounting office did have, however, one rough external check on manufacturing division effectiveness. A crude market price for case lot goods, sold by smaller firms to some large national chains, did exist.

Once a quarter, the seven senior sales vice presidents met with general management in St. Louis. Typically, management discussion focused on divisional sales results and expense control. The company's objective of being "number one," the largest selling line in its field, directed group attention to sales versus budget. All knew that last year's sales targets had to be exceeded—"no matter what." The manufacturing division vice president sat in on these meetings to explain the product availability situation. Because of his St. Louis office location, he frequently talked with Mr. Jerome Adams about overall manufacturing operations and specifically about large procurement decisions.

The Adams Company, Mr. Millman knew, had a trade reputation for being very conservative with its compensation program. All officers were on a straight salary program. An officer might expect a modest salary increase every two or three years; these increases tended to be in the thousand dollar range regardless of divisional performance or company profit position. Salaries among the seven sales divisional vice presidents ranged from $32,000 to $42,000, with the higher amounts going to more senior officers. Mr. Jerome Adams's salary of $48,000 was the highest in the company. There was no corporate bonus plan. A very limited stock option program was in operation, but the depressed price of Adams stock meant that few officers exercised their options.

Of considerable pride to Mr. Jerome Adams had been the corporate climate at Adams. "We take care of our family" was his oft-repeated phrase at company banquets honoring long-service employees. "We are a team and it is a team spirit that has built Adams into its leading position in this industry." No member of first line, middle or senior management could be discharged (except in cases of moral crime or dishonesty) without a personal review of his case by Mr. Adams. In matter of fact, executive turnover at Adams was very low. Executives at all levels viewed their jobs as a lifetime career. There was no compulsory retirement plan and some managers were still active in their mid–70s.

The operational extension of this organization philosophy was quite evident to employees and managers. A private family trust, for over 75 years, provided emergency assistance to all members of the Adams organization. Adams led its industry in the granting of educational scholarships, in medical insurance for employees and managers, and in the encouragement of its "members" to give corporate and personal time and effort to community problems and organizations.

Mr. Adams noted two positive aspects of this organizational philosophy. "We have a high percentage of long-term employees—Joe Girly, a guard at East St. Louis, completes 55 years with us this year, and every one of his brothers and sisters has worked here. And it is not uncommon for a vice president to retire with a blue pin—that means 40 years of service. We have led this industry in manufacturing process innovation, quality control and value for low price for decades. I am proud of our accomplishments and this pride is shown by everyone—from janitors to directors." Industry sources noted that there was no question that Adams was "number one" in terms of manufacturing and logistic efficiency.

In December of 1971, the annual Adams management conference gathered over 80 of Adams's senior management in St. Louis. Most expected the usual formal routines—the announcement of 1971 results and 1972 budgets, the award of the "Gold Flag" to the top processing plant and sales division for exceeding targets, and the award of service pins to executives. All expected the usual social good times. It was an opportunity to meet and drink with "old buddies."

After a series of task force meetings, the managers gathered in a banquet room—good naturedly referred to as the "Rib Room" since a local singer "Eve" was to provide entertainment. At the front of the room, in the usual fashion, was a dais with a long, elaborately decorated head table. Sitting at the center of that table was Mr. Jerome Adams. Following tradition, Mr. Adams's vice presidents, in order of seniority with the company, sat on his right. On his left, sat major family shareholders, corporate staff, and—a newcomer—soon to be introduced.

After awarding service pins and the "Gold Flags" of achievement, Mr. Adams announced formally what had been a corporate "secret" for several months. First, a new investing group had assumed a "control" position on the board of Adams. Second, that Mr. Price Millman would take over as president and chief executive officer of Adams.

Introducing Mr. Millman, Adams pointed out the outstanding record of the firm's new president. "Price got his MBA in 1958, spent four years in control and marketing, and then was named as the youngest divisional president in the history of the Tenny Corporation. In the past years, he has made his division the most profitable in Tenny and the industry leader in its field. We are fortunate to have him with us. Please give him your complete support."

In a later informal meeting with the divisional vice presidents, Mr. Millman spoke about his respect for past Adams's accomplishments and the pressing need to infuse Adams with "fighting spirit" and "competitiveness." "My personal and organizational philosophy are the same— the name of the game is to fight and win. I almost drowned, but I won my first swimming race at 11 years of age! That philosophy of always winning is what enabled me to build the Ajax division into Tenny's most profitable operation. We are going to do this at Adams."

In conclusion, he commented, "The new owner group wants results. They have advised me to take some time to think through a new format for Adams's operations—to get a corporate design that will improve our effectiveness. Once we get that new format, gentlemen, I have but one goal—each month must be better than the past."

Exhibit 1
THE ADAMS CORPORATION (A)
Organization Chart

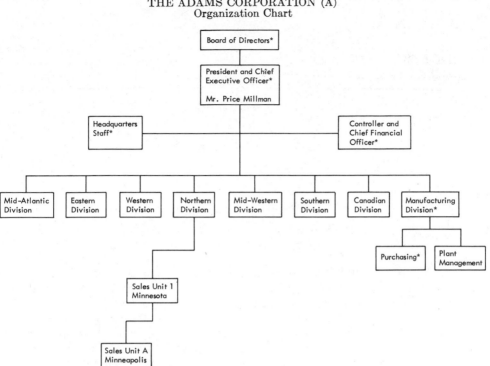

* Located in St. Louis.

Barclay, Inc. (A)

In December 1973, Mr. Robert Cannon became the new president and chief operating executive of Barclay, Inc., a firm operating in the electrical equipment field. In 1973, it was estimated, Barclay's sales were $100 million and the enterprise employed over 2,600 people.

Barclay, Inc., had recently been purchased by a group of wealthy investors. In view of their other varied business interests, the investing group planned to operate Barclay as a separate, independent company. Mr. Cannon was given complete responsibility for the direction of Barclay's affairs. He had achieved an excellent reputation among industrialists as a manager capable of dealing with difficult business problems, and the investors had agreed that he was to have a free hand to make whatever changes he thought necessary to improve the company's lackluster profit performance.

Barclay manufactured and sold electrical equipment for industrial and consumer use. Its industrial products included a wide variety of standard and specialty motors. The company had achieved an excellent reputation for engineering design work. Over the years its legal staff had built up an imposing number of patents protecting improvements created by company engineers. In the consumer products line, the firm manufactured and sold a line of small "traffic" household appliances for American markets.

In recent years company sales had increased substantially but profits had gradually declined to a point where only a very small profit was anticipated for 1973. While industrial products had been extremely profitable for many years, the competitive situation had changed substantially in the late 1960s. Consumer appliance operations varied from early losses to small profit contributions in 1970 through 1973. Barclay was encountering increasing competition for its appliances from full-line companies, e.g., Sunbeam. Despite this, Mr. Cannon believed that in the long run the consumer traffic appliance area would become the most important and profitable part of the firm's business. He hoped to add new appliance items as rapidly as production and marketing facilities permitted.

In the manufacture of these products, Barclay purchased substantial quantities of two raw materials (16 million, estimated in 1972). These raw materials were subject to substantial price fluctuations and it was important for Barclay to buy at "the right time and price."

The new owners of Barclay requested that Mr. Cannon prepare salary recommendations, for board consideration, in December 1973. His recommendations were to cover the top 20 executives in the company including himself. Knowing the backgrounds of the new owners, Mr. Cannon knew he would have to be able to defend his assignments of salary to specific jobs. He also knew that the owners had been critical of the "haphazard way" in which salary payments had been made by the former general manager.

To carry out this assignment, Mr. Cannon asked the member of the personnel department in charge of the executive payroll for the amount paid in salaries to the top 20 managers of the firm in the year 1973. This sum amounted to $860,000. He excluded individual bonus payments and incidental privileges, such as company furnished cars. Bonus payments for the Barclay management group had declined steadily during the past years and salary payments were now the important element in the firm's compensation program.

He then prepared to assign funds from this "common pool" to individual jobs in the organization. Mr. Cannon realized that, after he had determined an ideal salary structure, he would have to modify his assignments on the basis of historical precedent as well as other factors. But he believed that the process of allocating the total salary fund to individual jobs, without prejudice of past history, would help him in thinking through his problem.

Exhibit 1
BARCLAY, INC. (A)
Organization Chart

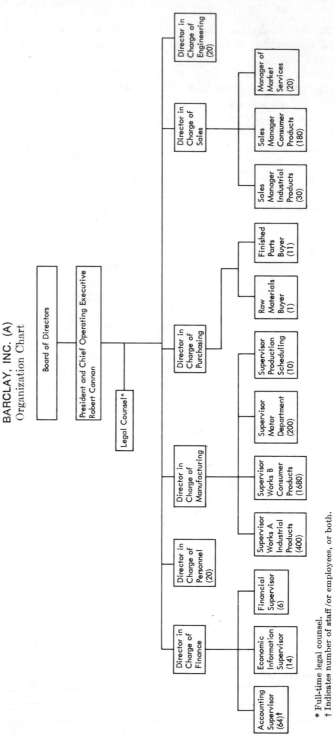

* Full-time legal counsel.
† Indicates number of staff/or employees, or both.

Texas Instruments, Incorporated (A)
(Condensed)

On April 17, 1959, Texas Instruments Incorporated (TI) of Dallas, Texas, merged with the Metals and Controls Corporation (M & C) of Attleboro, Massachusetts. One of the fastest growing large corporations in the country, TI had achieved a compound annual growth from 1946 through 1958 of 38% in sales and 42% in net income. The president had publicly predicted that volume would more than double in 1959 to a sales level near $200 million. Almost half this growth, he added, might come through mergers, with M & C contributing $42 million to $45 million. To date TI's principal business had been in electronic and electromechanical equipment and systems, semiconductors and other components, and exploration services for oil, gas, and minerals.

So highly was TI regarded by the market that in May 1960 its common was selling at about 70 times the 1959 earnings of $3.59 a share.

M & C ACTIVITIES

Itself the product of a 1932 merger and a postwar diversification, M & C had three major groups of products: clad metals, control instruments, and nuclear fuel components and instrumented cores. The company had grown steadily, and in 1959 had plants in two U.S. locations and five foreign countries. Reflecting predecessor corporation names, the clad metal lines were known as General Plate (GP) products, and the control instrument lines were known as Spencer products. Included in the former were industrial, precious, and thermostat metals; fancy wire; and wire and tubing. Included in the latter were motor protectors, circuit breakers, thermostats, and precision switches. Among these Spencer lines there were some that utilized GP products as raw materials; i.e., GP thermostat bimetals and GP clad electrical contacts.

Apart from a portion of GP's precious metal products which went to the jewelry trade (where appearance and fast delivery from stock were key considerations), most GP and Spencer products had to be designed to specific customer requirements and produced to customer order. Thus engineering know-how and close coordination between the sales and production departments on delivery dates were important. Owing to the technical nature of the products and also to their fast-changing applications, a company sales force with a high degree of engineering competence was essential. To serve its several thousand customers, many of whom purchased both Spencer and GP products, the company maintained a force of 50 men in the field, divided into Spencer and GP units.

With Spencer products facing important competition from four other firms in the $10 million to $40 million annual sales bracket, tight control of costs was important for securing the large orders generally placed by the kinds of customers to whom these products were sold. Buyers included manufacturers of fractional horsepower motors, household appliances, air conditioning, and aircraft and missiles. In contrast, GP industrial metals met no direct competition, although clad metals for industrial uses met with competition from alloys.

M & C's PREMERGER ORGANIZATION

At the time TI took over M & C, a task force of four junior executives had just completed, at the acting president's request, a critical study of M & C's organizational structure. So far its nuclear activities had been conducted by an entirely separate subsidiary, and the GP and Spencer activities had been organized as shown on Exhibit 1.

Under the acting president at the top level came a tier of predominantly functional executives (the vice presidents for marketing, engineering, and finance, the treasurer, and the controller). At the third and fourth levels of command, the structure increasingly showed a breakdown by product lines. For example, at the fourth level in manufacturing there were four separate groups corresponding to the major Spencer lines, and six separate groups corresponding to the major GP lines. Approximately the same breakdown appeared among the fourth-level product specialists in marketing. Although there was no profit responsibility at this level, the controller had been sending marketing's product specialists a monthly P & L by product line, in the hope of encouraging informal meetings among the people in marketing, engineering, and production who were working on the same lines.

Even at the second level, the predominantly functional division of responsibilities was neither complete nor unalloyed. Thus the vice president for marketing was also the vice president of Spencer Products, and in this capacity he had reporting to him the Spencer engineers. As a result, the company's vice president of engineering was, in effect, the vice president only of GP engineering, although he also served in an other-than-functional role by acting as the vice president of M & C International. (In 1958 exports and other foreign sales totaled about $2 million.)

After confidential interviews with 140 people, members of the M & C

Exhibit 1

PREMERGER METALS AND CONTROLS ORGANIZATION

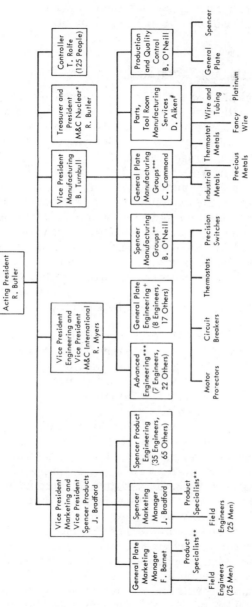

* Detail on M & C Nuclear not disclosed.
** Responsible for factory-customer coordination on specifications, prices, delivery, and new applications on different product lines (broken down about as shown in the manufacturing department).
*** Responsible for long-range product development for GP lines.
+ Worked on new applications and process designs for GP lines.
++ Principal operations in Spencer production departments were parts-making and assembly.
+++ Principal operations in GP industrial, precious, and thermostat metal departments were bonding and rolling; in GP wire and fancy wire departments, drawing; and in GP platinum department, melting and refining. Some GP facilities were shared, and roughly 5% of direct labor hours for each GP department were devoted to work for other departments.
# Reporting to Aiken were units making two GP and three Spencer parts.
Source: Interviews and company records.

task force reportedly concluded that this organizational structure was causing or contributing to a number of company problems. Accordingly the task force recommended sweeping changes, first to the acting president by whom they had been appointed, then to his successor, Mr. Edward O. Vetter, a 39-year-old TI vice president brought in following the merger.

MR. VETTER'S REVIEW AND APPRAISAL

As soon as he arrived at M & C, Mr. Vetter spent most of four days in closed meetings with task force members. At the same time he scheduled public meetings with all executives; these sessions he devoted to general discussions of his aims for the organization and to reassurances that drastic changes would not be made.

From these discussions Vetter learned that a great many people at M & C felt that the three major functional departments were not cooperating well enough in the exploitation of new product opportunities based on existing markets and skills. Although in a few isolated instances, marketing, engineering, and production personnel concerned with a particular product had formed small informal groups to work on common problems, the three departments had not been seen as working together with maximum effectiveness, particularly in new product development. To blame, besides top management's inattention and the absence of a comprehensive plan, was a lack of clear-cut responsibility and authority.

Other problems, too, provided additional evidence of the failure of functional groups to work together harmoniously and effectively. Thus there was continued squabbling between process engineers and production supervisors, with neither group being willing to accept the other's suggestions for improvements in manufacturing methods. With both groups reporting to different vice presidents, conflicts too often came up for resolution at top levels. Here many times decisions were postponed and issues left unresolved.

Vetter was also told by many members of the organization that the personal influence of marketing's product specialists played too large a role in company decisions. Formally assigned to coordinate certain aspects of factory-customer relations (see notes to Exhibit 1), these specialists were said to determine the amount of R&D time given to particular lines, with the result that some lines had grown quite strong while promising opportunities elsewhere were neglected. Similarly personal relationships between product specialists and production personnel largely determined scheduling priorities.

After becoming familiar with these problems, Mr. Vetter decided that M & C provided a golden opportunity for applying TI's philosophy of organization by what TI called "product-customer centered groups." Basically this plan involved putting a single manager in charge of sales, manufacturing, and engineering on a particular product line, and making this manager responsible for profits. This type of structure, Mr. Vetter noted, was what had been proposed by M & C's own task force on organization. According to TI's president, it offered advantages not only in managing existing lines but also in finding new opportunities for discerning and serving new customer needs.

As he was collecting information on M & C's organizational arrangements, Mr. Vetter had dictated the following set of notes for his own use:

> It appears as if natural product groups already exist here. General Plate, Spencer and Nuclear have always been separate, and International sales are set apart under Richard Myers. Within these major groupings there is also a somewhat parallel division of the manufacturing and marketing facilities along product lines. There are ten production departments that are each organized to produce a particular product line, while there is an almost parallel organization of marketing product specialists under James Bradford.
>
> Bringing together product managers and production supervisors for similar product lines would seem to be the logical implementation of TI's management philosophy. Of course, one problem would be the rearrangement of some of the production facilities in order to locate all the equipment under a product manager's control in one area. While we do have ten product-manufacturing departments, some of these share facilities and perform work for one another. In addition, the parts department performs fabrication operations for several production departments. In spite of this, there are no major pieces of equipment that would have to be physically relocated. We estimated that some duplicate equipment will have to be purchased if we go ahead with product-centered decentralization; in order to accomplish this about $1.5 million will have to be spent almost three years before it would otherwise have been committed.
>
> I believe that the "inside" product specialist—the man at the factory who lives with both the manufacturing and the marketing problems for his line—is a key man. Our products are mainly engineered to customer order and, as such, require a great deal of coordination on delivery dates, specifications, and special applications. In addition to performing this liaison, the product managers could be the men who sense ideas for new product applications from their marketing contacts and then transmit these to the product engineering personnel at the factory.
>
> These men would not be salesmen. A field sales force would still be needed to make regular calls on all of our clients and to cultivate the associations with our customers' engineering staffs. One significant question here is how to organize the sales force. These men are highly skilled and quite expensive to employ—each salesman should enter commitments of at least $1 million yearly in order to justify his expenses. Since our customers are spread all over the country, it would appear economical to assign field salesmen by geographical areas, each to sell all, or at least a number of, our products. Unfortunately, this system might take a good measure of the responsibility for the sales supervision. Our problem here is to leave sales responsibility at the product group level without having an undue duplication of field sales personnel.
>
> The filtering down of responsibility and authority would mean that we would need more "management skill" in order for the product managers to be able to manage the little companies of which each

would be in charge. The product manager must be capable of making sales, manufacturing, financial, and engineering decisions. He is no longer judged against a budget but becomes responsible for profits. We would need talented men to fill these positions—a shift in the organizational structure would undoubtedly force us to hire some new people. Nevertheless, there are tremendous benefits to be gained in terms of giving more people the chance to display their talents and in just plain better functioning of the M & C division.

The organization of engineering personnel brings up a whole hornets' nest of questions. First of all, there are two distinct engineering functions: product engineers, those concerned with current product designs and new applications for existing products; and advanced engineers, those who work on long-term product development. There is little doubt that the new applications sales effort would benefit from placing the product engineering personnel in close organizational contact with the marketers. This would mean splitting engineering up among all the product groups and would probably make for a less efficient overall operation. Decentralization of the advanced engineering groups is easily as ticklish a problem. Again, it would probably receive more marketing-oriented stimulus if it were placed under the supervision of the product manager. I wonder, however, if he might not be motivated to cut long-term development more drastically than top management normally would in times of business recession. Furthermore, I wonder if the economies of centralized advanced engineering and research in terms of combined effort and personnel selection are not so great as to make decentralization of this function an extremely poor choice. The basic question we have to answer here is to what degree should we sacrifice operating economy in order to give our engineering personnel a greater marketing orientation.

*   *   *   *   *

Scheduling has long been a bone of contention here wherever facilities are shared. Conflicts for priorities between product specialists are always occurring. If we decentralize, however, the amount of facilities that are shared will decrease substantially and this problem should be alleviated. Again we have the basic choice of retaining the centralized scheduling groups or splitting the function up among the various product groups.

In addition to the above issues, Mr. Vetter was considering the proper timing for an organizational change. He was debating whether a change should be made by gradual steps or whether the transfer in corporate ownership provided a convenient opportunity for making radical changes with a minimum of employee resentment. In general, the M & C personnel expressed some regrets because the family that had founded the company was no longer associated with it. They recognized, however, that the continual top management conflict of recent years necessitated a change and were pleased by the fact that a recognized leader in the industry had taken over the company.

Texas Instruments, Incorporated (B)

IN MAY 1960 Tom Pringle, the manager of the Industrial Metals product department at Texas Instruments' Metals & Controls division, was considering several courses of action in the face of his department's failure to meet forecasted sales and profits during the first four months of 1960. The rebuilding of inventories by M & C's customers, which had been expected as an aftermath of the settlement of the 1959 steel strike, had not materialized and shipments from Pringle's product department were running about 12% below forecast. Furthermore, incoming sales commitments during these four months were 15% below expectations. The product department's direct profit, according to preliminary statements, was 19% below plan.

In light of these adverse developments, Pringle was studying the advisability of three specific moves which would improve his profit performance: (1) eliminating his $30,000 advertising budget for the latter half of 1960, (2) postponing the addition of two engineers to his engineering group until 1961, and (3) reducing further purchases of raw materials in order to improve his department's return on assets ratio. Until now, Pringle had been reluctant to make any concessions in his department's scale of operations since there was a very strong accent on rapid growth throughout the Texas Instruments organization. This attitude toward expansion also appeared to prevail in the new top management group in the Metals & Controls division. The enthusiasm of the Texas Instruments' management had caught on at Metals & Controls with the formation of the product-centered decentralized organization.

THE 1959 REORGANIZATION

In June 1959, just three months after Metals & Controls Corporation had become a division of Texas Instruments, Incorporated, Mr. Edward

617

O. Vetter, the division vice president, instituted a product-centered organization. This decentralization was carried out in accordance with Texas Instruments' policy of placing ultimate responsibility for profitable operation at the product level. The framework that emerged was similar to that which existed elsewhere in the company.

Mr. Vetter organized four major product groups at Metals & Controls: General Plate, Spencer Controls, Nuclear Products, and International Operations. To augment these groups, six centralized staff units were organized at the division level: Research and Development, Legal, Industrial Engineering, Control, Marketing, and Personnel (Exhibit 1).

Exhibit 1

ORGANIZATION CHART, METALS & CONTROLS DIVISION

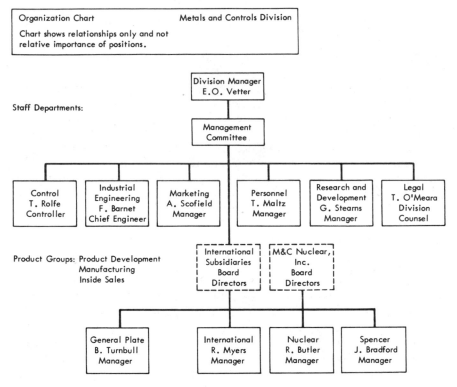

The four managers of the product groups and the six managers of these staff departments, along with Mr. Vetter, comprised the management committee for the Metals & Controls division. This committee was a sounding board for helping each responsible manager make the proper decision as required by his job responsibility. In the case of profit performance, the ultimate responsibility for the division was Vetter's.

Within each product group, several product departments were established. The General Plate products group, for example, included the Industrial Metals, Electrical Contacts, Industrial Wire, and Precious

Metals departments (Exhibit 2). The manager of each of these departments was responsible for its "profit performance." He was supported by staff units such as Industrial Engineering and Administration which reported directly to the group manager (Burt Turnbull for General Plate products). The expense of these staff units was charged to the individual product departments proportionally to the volume of activity in the various departments as measured by direct labor hours or by sales dollars less raw materials cost. The product departments were also charged with those expenses over which the manager and his supervisory group were able to exercise direct control, such as labor and materials.

Exhibit 2

ORGANIZATION CHART, GENERAL PLATE PRODUCTS GROUP

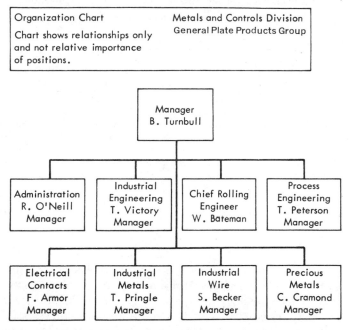

The field sales force of 50 men was centralized under the manager for marketing, Al Scofield (Exhibit 1). These men were divided about evenly into two major selling groups: one for General Plate products, and the other for Spencer products. The 25 salesmen assigned to General Plate and the 25 salesmen assigned to Spencer were shared by the four General Plate and four Spencer product departments. Each individual product department also maintained "inside" marketing personnel who performed such functions as pricing, developing marketing strategy, order follow-up and providing the field sales engineers with information on new applications, designs, and product specifications for its particular line.

The Industrial Metals department

Tom Pringle was manager of the Industrial Metals department of the General Plate products group. Sales of this department in 1959 were approximately $4 million.[1] Pringle was responsible for the profitability of two product lines: (1) industrial metals and (2) thermostat metals. His department's sales were split about evenly between these lines, although industrial metals had the greater growth potential because of the almost infinite number of possible clad metals for which an ever increasing number of applications was being found. He was in charge of the marketing, engineering, and manufacturing activities for both these lines and had six key subordinates:

INDUSTRIAL METALS DEPARTMENT

Years of Service with the Metals and Controls Organization

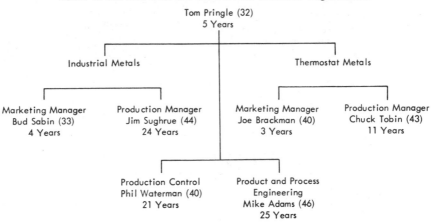

The function of the marketing managers in the Industrial Metals department (Bud Sabin and Joe Brackman) was to supervise the "inside selling units." These units were responsible for developing marketing strategy, pricing, contacting customers on special requests and factory problems, for promotional activities, and for coordinating product development and sales. In May 1960, in addition to its regular work, the Industrial Metals inside selling unit was developing a manual of special applications for its products which it hoped would improve the ability of the field sales force to envision new uses. The production managers had line responsibility for the efficient use of manufacturing facilities, for meeting delivery promises to customers, and for expenses incurred in producing the department's products. The product and process engineering group had responsibility for designing new products and devising new production processes. The production control manager formulated guidelines to aid the foremen in scheduling work through the

---

[1] All figures have been disguised.

plant, supervised the expediters and clerks who served as a clearing-house for information on delivery dates, and was responsible for ordering raw material and maintaining a balanced inventory.

In accordance with Texas Instruments' policy of placing ultimate responsibility for profitable operation at the product level, Tom Pringle's performance was measured, to a large extent, by the actual profits earned by the Industrial Metals department. The old M & C system of evaluating performance according to fixed and variable department budgets had been supplemented by the establishment of these "profit centers." Although the system passed actual profit responsibility to the product department manager level, the Texas Instruments' top management had always retained some control over the profit centers by requiring each manager to formulate a one-year plan which was subject to review by higher management. As a result, profit planning was instituted whereby each manager set forth a detailed plan for the year's operations under the direction of the management committee. His actual performance was continually being evaluated against the plan.

Formulation of the profit plan.   In October 1959, Tom Pringle began to prepare his department's profit plan for 1960. This was part of a company-wide effort in which all department managers participated. The first step in the process was to prepare a detailed estimate of expected sales for the year. These estimates were gathered from two sources: the inside selling units and the field sales force. Management felt that one would serve as a good check on the other, and, furthermore, believed that widespread participation in preparing the plan was one way to insure its effectiveness. Bud Sabin and Joe Brackman, then, began to prepare estimates of 1960 sales by product lines with the help of the individual product specialists within the inside marketing group. Sabin and Brackman were also aided by the Texas Instruments central marketing group which prepared a report which estimated normal growth for their product lines. Pringle suggested that they prepare their estimates by subdividing the market into three parts: sales resulting from normal industry growth at current levels of market penetration; increased sales resulting from further penetration of the market with existing products; and increased sales from new products detailed by specific customers. At the same time, Herb Skinner, the manager of the General Plate field sales force, asked the field engineers to predict the volume of orders that each Industrial Metals customer would place in 1960, without referring to the reports being readied by the product marketing groups. In this way, the marketing managers made forecasts by product line and the field force made forecasts by customer.

The field selling force came up with estimated thermostat metal sales of $2,350,000 for 1960, and the inside group estimated sales of $2,420,000. Pringle felt that these two estimates were in reasonably good agreement. On the other hand, Bud Sabin, the Industrial Metals marketing manager, estimated sales of $3,050,000, while Skinner's group predicted only $2,500,000. Sabin predicted that 20% of the increase would come from normal growth, 50% from increased market penetration with existing products, and 30% from new products. Sales for Sabin's group had been $1,400,000 in 1958 and $2,100,000 in 1959. Pringle felt that the disparity between the two estimates was significant and he discussed the matter with both men. All three men finally decided that the sales force had submitted a conservative estimate and agreed that Sabin's figure was the most realistic goal.

Once the sales estimate of $5,470,000 was agreed upon by Pringle and his marketing managers, the process of estimating manufacturing costs began. The manufacturing superintendents, Chuck Tobin and Jim Sughrue, were furnished the thermostat and industrial metals sales estimates and were instructed to forecast direct labor costs, supervisory salaries, and overhead expenses. These forecasts were to be made for each manufacturing area, or cost center, under their supervision. Sughrue was responsible for five cost centers and Tobin for four, each of which was directly supervised by a foreman. These expenses were to be forecast monthly and were to be used as a yardstick by which the actual expense performance of the manufacturing personnel could later be measured.

Jim Sughrue had previously calculated the hourly labor cost and the output per hour for each of his cost centers for 1959. To estimate 1960 salaries and wages, he then increased 1959 expenses proportionately to the expected sales increase. He followed the same procedure in determining 1960 overhead expenses, such as expendable tools, travel, telephone, process supplies, and general supplies. Chuck Tobin's task was somewhat simpler since the sales projection for his cost centers required a level of output that exactly matched the current production level. For salaries and wages, he merely used as his 1960 estimate the actual cost experience that had been reported on the most recent monthly income statement he received. For overhead, he applied a historical percent-of-sales ratio and then reduced his estimate by 3% to account for increased efficiency. In discussing the overhead estimate with his foremen, Tobin informed them that he had allowed for an 8% efficiency increase.

Since this was the first time any attempt at such detailed planning had been made at M & C, and since the M & C accounting system had recently been changed to match Texas Instruments', very little historical information was available. For this reason, Pringle did not completely delegate the responsibility for the various marketing and manu-. facturing estimates to his subordinates. Instead he worked in conjunction with them to develop the forecasts. He hoped that his participation in this process would insure a more accurate forecast for the year. Furthermore, he hoped to develop the ability of his supervision to plan ahead.

Pringle estimated direct materials cost and consumption factors himself. Since it was impossible to predict what all the various strip metal prices would be, he calculated the ratio of materials expense to sales for 1959 and applied it to the 1960 sales projections for each of the product lines in his department.

The marketing, administration, and engineering groups that serviced Pringle's Industrial Metals group forecast their expenses by detailing their personnel requirements and then applying historical ratios of expenses to personnel to estimate their other expenses. From these dollar figures, Pringle was able to estimate what proportions of these amounts would be charged to his department.

With the various forecasts in hand, Pringle estimated a direct profit of $1,392,000 on a sales volume of $5,470,000. Once this plan had been drawn up, it was reviewed by the division management committee in relationship to the specific profit and sales goals which it has established for the division. In reviewing the plans for each product department in terms of the specific group goals, it became obvious that the combined plans of the General Plate product departments were not sufficient to meet the overall goal, and that based on market penetration, new product developments, and other factors, the planned sales volume for Industrial Metals should be revised upward to $6,050,000 and direct profit to $1,587,000 (Exhibit 3). This was discussed among Vetter, Turnbull, Scofield, and Pringle and they agreed that it was a difficult but achievable plan.

Exhibit 3

INDUSTRIAL METALS DEPARTMENT

Initial and Revised Profit Statements for 1960*

	Initial	Revised
Sales	$5,470,000	$6,050,000
Direct labor	435,000	480,000
Direct material	1,920,000	2,115,000
Overhead	875,000	968,000
Marketing	305,000	346,000
Administration	161,000	161,000
Engineering	382,000	393,000
Direct profit	1,392,000	1,587,000

* All figures have been disguised.

Actual performance, 1960.   On May 10 Tom Pringle received a detailed statement comparing the actual performance of his department for January through April with his budget (Exhibit 4). Sales were 12% below plan, and direct profit was 19% below plan.

In addition to these figures, manufacturing expenses by cost centers were accumulated for Pringle. He passed these along to the production superintendents after he had made adjustments in the budgeted expense figures to allow for the sales decline. Pringle had devised a variable budget system whereby he applied factors to the forecast expenses to indicate what an acceptable expense performance was at sales levels other than the planned volume. Chuck Tobin and Jim Sughrue then analyzed the actual expenses and, one week later, held meetings with their foremen to discuss the causes of both favorable and unfavorable variances. The most common explanation of favorable manufacturing variances was either extremely efficient utilization of labor or close

Exhibit 4

COMPARISON OF ACTUAL AND
BUDGETED PERFORMANCE,
JANUARY–APRIL 1960*

	Budgeted	Actual
Sales	$2,020,000	$1,780,000
Direct labor	160,000	142,400
Direct material	704,000	593,000
Overhead	322,000	287,000
Marketing	100,000	116,400
Administration	54,000	55,800
Engineering	126,000	136,600
Direct profit	554,000	448,000

* All figures have been disguised.

control over overhead. Unfavorable variances most frequently resulted from machine delays which necessitated overtime labor payments.

Specific problems.   Pringle was currently faced with three specific problems. In light of his department's poor performance these past months, he was considering the effects of eliminating his $30,000 advertising budget for the remainder of 1960, postponing the addition of two new engineers to his staff for six months, and reducing raw materials purchases in order to decrease inventory and thus improve his department's return on assets performance.

He had discussed the possibility of eliminating the advertising budget with Bud Sabin and Joe Brackman but had not yet reached a conclusion. Advertising expenditures had been budgeted at $30,000 for the final six months of 1960. The Industrial Metals department ads were generally placed in trade journals read by design engineers in the electrical, automobile, and appliance industries. Pringle did not know for certain how important an aid these advertisements were to his sales force. He did know that all of his major competitors allocated about the same proportion of sales revenue for advertising expenditures and that Industrial Metals ads were occasionally mentioned by customers.

In late 1959, Pringle had made plans to increase his engineering staff from eight men to ten men in mid-1960. He felt that the two men could begin functioning productively by early 1961 and could help to revise certain processes which were yielding excessive scrap, to develop new products, and to assist the field engineers in discovering new applications for existing products. Pringle estimated that postponing the hiring of these men for six months would save $20,000 in engineering salaries and supporting expenses.

Pringle also knew that one of the important indicators of his performance was the department's ratio of direct profit to assets used. This figure had been budgeted at 40% for 1961, but actual results to date were 31%. Pringle was considering reductions in raw materials purchases in order to decrease inventories and thus improve performance. He had discussed this possibility with Phil Waterman, the production control manager for Industrial Metals. Pringle knew that significant improvements in the overall ratio could be made in this way since raw materials inventories accounted for almost 20% of total assets and were at a level of ten months' usage at present consumption ratios. He recognized, however, that this course of action required accepting a greater risk of running out. This risk was important to assess since most customers required rapid delivery and Pringle's suppliers usually required four months' lead time to manufacture the nonstandard size metals in relatively small lots required for the Industrial Metals' cladding operation.

The purpose of the profit plan.   The degree to which the plan was used as a method for evaluating performance and fixing compensation was not completely clear to Pringle. Everyone seemed to recognize that this first effort was imperfect and had errors built in because of inadequate historical data. He had never been explicitly informed of the extent to which top management desired product department decision making to be motivated by short-run effects on planned performance. Pringle stated that during the months immediately following the initiation of the plan he had concluded that short-term performance was much less significant than long-run growth and that he had preferred to concentrate on the longer run development of new products and markets.

Pringle knew that the Metals & Controls operating committee met every Monday to review the performance of each product department from preliminary reports. Customarily Burt Turnbull, the manager of the General Plate group, discussed both Pringle's incoming sales commitments and actual manufacturing expenses with him before each meeting. Pringle also knew that each manager was given a formal appraisal review every six months by his superior. It was common knowledge that the department's performance in relation to its plan was evaluated at both these sessions. Furthermore, Pringle was aware of the fact that Turnbull's performance as product group manager would be affected by his own performance with Industrial Metals. Over a period of months, Pringle had learned that the management committee utilized the comparison of actual and planned performance to pinpoint trouble spots. On occasion Vetter had called him in to explain any significant deviations from plan but normally he was represented at these meetings by Burt Turnbull. It was Pringle's impression that Vetter had been satisfied with the explanation he had given.

In their day-to-day decisions, Pringle's subordinates seemed to be influenced only in a very general way by the profit plan. They reviewed their monthly performance against plan with interest, but generally tended to bias their decisions in favor of long-run development at the expense of short-run deviations from the plan. More recently, however, Pringle realized that top management was not satisfied with his explanations of failure to meet plans. The message, though not stated explicitly, seemed to be that he was expected to take whatever remedial and alternate courses of action were needed in order to meet the one-year goals. He was certain that real pressure was building up for each department manager to meet his one-year plan.

In commenting on the use of planning at M & C, Mr. Vetter, the division vice president, stated four major purposes of the program:

> To set a par for the course. Vetter believed that performance was always improved if the manager proposed a realistic objective for his performance and was informed in advance of what was expected of him.
>
> To grow management ability. Vetter believed that the job of manager was to coordinate all the areas for which he was given responsibility. He saw the planning process as a tool for improving these managerial skills.
>
> To anticipate problems and look ahead. Vetter felt that the planning process gave the department managers a convenient tool for planning personnel requirements and sales strategy. It also set guideposts so that shifts in business conditions could be detected quickly and plans could be altered.
>
> To weld Texas Instruments into one unit. The basic goals for each division were formulated by Vetter in recognition of overall company goals as disseminated by Haggerty, the company president. These were passed down to the product department level by the product group manager at each Texas Instruments division. Profit planning was thus being carried out by the same process by every department manager in the corporation.

Vetter recognized, however, that many reasons could exist for performance being either better or worse than planned. He stated that in his experience extremely rigid profit plans often motivated managers to budget low in order to provide themselves with a safety cushion. In his view, this made the entire profit planning process worthless.

Textile Corporation of America

In 1963, the Textile Corporation of America (TEXCORP) was formed from three family-owned companies: (1) Smith-Abbott Mills, centered in Fitchburg, Mass., and directed by William Abbott; (2) North Carolina Mills, owned by the Ford family and headed by Robert Ford; (3) Carolina Cotton Company, a single large mill located in South Carolina and owned by John Rand. The three family companies had not been direct competitors. Smith-Abbott Mills produced high-grade spun rayon and wool blended fabric, North Carolina Mills specialized in fine cotton fabrics and staple synthetic fabrics, and the Carolina Cotton Company made high-quality cotton print cloth. By combining their firms' resources, Abbott, Ford, and Rand became owners of a major firm in the fine textiles industry, with sales in 1963 of $45 million.

Due to family loyalties and the strength of long-standing reporting relationships, TEXCORP existed as a single company in name only. Few functions were integrated, although accounting for all three firms was done at the corporate office in New York City. Because his North Carolina Mills represented the largest portion of the TEXCORP (1963 sales of $25 million), Robert Ford and his management team were able to dominate the company through 1966. William Abbott, the wealthy owner of Smith-Abbott Mills, avoided direct participation in TEXCORP management. He kept an office in the New York headquarters, attended board meetings, and watched the Fitchburg operations, but much of his time was spent vacationing in Europe or playing golf. In 1967, Mr. Abbott decided to spend more time in New York City.

By 1967, it was clear that the fine cotton fabric market was declining in importance in the United States. In June of 1967, representatives of the National Chemical Company were approached by TEXCORP management at the suggestion of William Abbott. National Chemical was a multinational corporation with 1967 sales of over $2 billion. They had recently begun to diversify into nonchemical markets, and several TEX-

CORP executives were personal friends of National executives. These informal relationships led to official discussions, and National Chemical purchased TEXCORP in early 1968.

In the exchange of TEXCORP stock for National Chemical stock, all of the directors of TEXCORP became wealthy men. TEXCORP's directors controlled 68 percent of the voting stock of the company when it was purchased by National Chemical. William Abbott became one of the largest individual shareholders of National Chemical common stock. Robert Ford, then 65 years old, agreed to step down as president of TEXCORP and William Abbott became the chief executive. Mr. Ford, although not entirely happy with the management arrangements, had considerable financial security in that his family's trust fund now owned over $10 million of National Chemical stock. Richard Hicks, the National Chemical vice president responsible for TEXCORP, felt that Mr. Abbott would make a better chief executive than Ford, and encouraged the management transition. Abbott made several organizational changes himself at this time. Andrew Thompson, who had been the star salesman for Smith-Abbott Mills, was promoted to vice president of sales for Smith-Abbott Mills. Walter Hogan, a former plant manager for Smith-Abbott Mills, became vice president of manufacturing.

TEXCORP's sales in 1967 had risen to $65 million. Profits had grown from 1963 through 1966, but had dipped somewhat in 1967 to $2 million. Exhibit 1 outlines the TEXCORP organization in February of 1968, and Exhibit 2 presents the background of key personnel.

JOHN MITCHELL, MBA

John Mitchell, 27, was married and had one child. He grew up in Darien, Connecticut, and graduated from Harvard College in 1963. Mitchell had chosen Harvard because it was supposed to be a very liberal school. For the first two years he remained conservative, but during his junior and senior years he committed himself as a political liberal. He took courses in religion and psychology and briefly considered being a minister. After graduation he thought about entering law school or medical school, but his father wanted him to go to Harvard Business School. After receiving his MBA in 1965, he joined a Peace Corps project in the Far East, where he taught industrial psychology.

John Mitchell liked to think of himself as good at the "gamesmanship" of life. His interest in psychology led to a certain degree of introspection and he prided himself on his ability to describe the games people played. In high school, for example, Mitchell was often called an "apple polisher" because his school work seemed to follow the particular concerns of his various teachers. He was a straight-A student. In college, he hardly ever cut classes, and was a Dean's List student for four years. He was active in athletics, and was a starting fullback for the Harvard team. John Mitchell even considered football a "psychological game." Commenting on his football experiences, he said:

> If the coach was in a mean mood, you growl and hit somebody . . .
> if not, you joke and try and have fun. Hell, the guys that were on the

field to make the big plays not only *did* the right thing in practice, but *thought* and *said* the right thing too. . . . It's all a fantastically complicated game.

Mitchell earned a varsity letter each year in college.

Mitchell's experiences overseas strengthened his political "liberalism" (labeled "radicalism" by his mother). While at the Business School, he had participated in many lengthy discussions about the businessman's social responsibilities. John Mitchell was sometimes shocked by what he considered to be the narrow-mindedness of some of his classmates, and he often wondered if the business world could offer him the satisfactions he believed he needed in life.

His interest in psychology eventually led Mitchell to a one-year research project while at the Harvard Business School, and the co-authorship of a book on psychological aspects of motivation.

In 1968, Mitchell decided to return to the United States. He did not think he had the patience to be an effective teacher, although he had been very successful as a teacher in the Peace Corps. The business world in the United States in 1968 further challenged him because of the new emphasis being placed on social responsibility. Mitchell hoped he could find a job that offered an outlet for his growing social conscience. Also, he was anxious to test himself in a real business organization:

> I wanted to see if I could compete with my classmates from HBS. But at the same time I love travel, love other cultures. But I kept wondering, if I were back in the States, would I be such a hot shot.

NATIONAL CHEMICAL COMPANY

Richard Hicks, the vice president of National Chemical and responsible for TEXCORP, heard about Mitchell through family friends. Hicks was in charge of National's nonchemical operations, and he wrote Mitchell and asked him to come to National Chemical's offices in New York to talk about the company's operations overseas. When they met, Mitchell told Hicks that the chemical industry didn't really interest him, because it was dominated by large corporations; however, after many meetings and several offers, Mitchell agreed to go to work as assistant to the president of TEXCORP, William Abbott. Mitchell would be trained for a year in the textile business and then go to a textile mill that National was planning to buy overseas. The job sounded ideal to Mitchell. He could test himself in the world of big business and also indulge his interest in travel and living abroad. The Mitchells rented a small house in Darien.

In July of 1968, Mitchell went to work at TEXCORP, which was located in an office building about ten blocks from the National Chemical headquarters in New York. William Abbott had been told very little about his new assistant, except that he was to train him for a year. Since Mitchell knew nothing about the textile business, he asked to spend two months in the mills—part of this time as a loom operator, which he did, even though this was theoretically against union regulations.

Mitchell's initial impressions about TEXCORP and TEXCORP management were very favorable. Andrew Thompson, the vice president in charge of textile products and the number 2 man at TEXCORP, was a very outgoing and personable man, and Mr. Abbott told Mitchell to see Thompson if there were any "problems" with his training. John Mitchell spent most of his time at the large Smith-Abbott Mill in Fitchburg. Although the workers believed him to be a "spy from the chemical company" at first, they soon relaxed and Mitchell developed several strong friendships. Since he was living in a motel in Fitchburg without his family, he spent 12 to 14 hours a day at the mill and got to know the personnel on both the day and the night shifts.

When he returned to New York in September, Mitchell found that there was nothing planned for him to do. Although Abbott spoke to him every day in his office for about 20 minutes in order to find out how he was getting along, Mitchell felt that no one was really interested in what he did. Consequently, he willingly accepted responsibility for helping to collect and organize the financial figures for the first TEXCORP five-year plan. (Systematic planning was one of the most well-developed management techniques at National Chemical.)

Mitchell was beginning to learn more about headquarters personnel at TEXCORP. He observed that four offices, which he called "Executive Row," were large, spacious, and thickly carpeted, while the rest of the TEXCORP offices were relatively modest. The four offices were occupied by William Abbott, Walter Hogan, John Rand, and Tom Rinehart. Mitchell was surprised to discover that Rand and Rinehart were rarely involved in the regular management meetings, and Hogan was not highly respected by many of the headquarters personnel.

Although he got along well with all the TEXCORP executives, Mitchell found that he had too little in common with them to spend much time socializing. "I was too young and unimportant. Also, I didn't play golf and I didn't drink. I had tomato juice at lunch while they were boozing it up."

Bill Berkeley, who was the "liaison man" assigned to TEXCORP by Richard Hicks, became Mitchell's closest friend, since they were the same age approximately, and the only men at TEXCORP under 40. Also, both Mitchell and Berkeley reported to Hicks:

> Bill Berkeley and I got along very well. . . . Berkeley spent half of every day over at TEXCORP talking to Abbott or one of the financial VP's about liaison work. You know, fill this form in, the appropriations meeting is next month, etc.

Mitchell was distressed at the unsophisticated level of management he found at TEXCORP, and he developed the habit of having long, one-sided conversations with his wife when he arrived home each evening:

> What a day! Discovered that I was the only—get this!—the only guy who could use a slide rule in TEXCORP, except for Kirk. . . . But he's an engineer . . . I don't know. It sure seems like some of those men

waste a lot of time and stuff trying to butter-up Bill Abbott, and there's so little real *analysis*. Hell, no!! I'm not "buttering him up" with my slide rule! You ever tried doing 20 discounted cash flows without one!?!

As October wore on, John Mitchell began to feel frustrated and bored. One day he went around the TEXCORP office asking executives if they had any jobs or projects he might help them with. He spent a day filing expense reports, and three days drawing graphs and charts showing loom utilization for the first half of 1968. He later told his wife:

It's kind of dull right now. I didn't think it would be like this. What? Sure, I've talked to Andy. He doesn't know what to do with me. Let's face it . . . none of them really know what to do with me. First I was a "spy," you know. Now I'm a "bright kid with a lot of potential." I don't want to be underfoot all the time. You can only ask a guy for work so many times, then you just have to try and make work. What a drag.

And, in early November:

Well, I finally talked to Andy today. Told him I was really going out of my mind. And I talked to Bob Cleaves. Anyway, they both told me I should lay it on the line to Abbott. "Talk to him at Oscar's" they said. [Oscar's was a large bar and restaurant often frequented by TEXCORP executives.] I'm going to ask him for more responsibility. Hell, I've got absolutely zero now. He must know how I feel . . . but he's so damn silent. No one ever knows what's on his mind. . . . Except Andy, of course. Those two are like father and son.

Because William Abbott seemed constantly preoccupied and was often out of the office, Mitchell was reluctant to speak to him about his job. ("If I catch him wrong, he'll just see me as a complainer, or, worse, an overly ambitious 'whiz kid,'" he explained to his wife.) Abbott ran TEXCORP with the help of the two executives who had come with him from Smith-Abbott Mills in Fitchburg, Andrew Thompson and Walter Hogan. Thompson and Abbott were particularly close, and virtually all company decisions were made by these two men. Abbott had also continued to direct Smith-Abbott Mills personally, and he and Thompson spent five to eight days a month in Fitchburg. Finally, in mid-December, Mitchell followed Thompson's advice and asked William Abbott if he could speak to him at Oscar's after work.

Mitchell discovered that his boss was much easier to talk to at Oscar's. Abbott liked to drink, and Mitchell found it relatively easy to ask his boss for a line position with specific responsibilities. Abbott replied that he would like to have a boy like Mitchell on his "team" and would give him a position if he would pledge to stay "with him" for three years. As the evening progressed, Mitchell observed that Abbott spoke more and more about "loyalty" and the value of a man who would "stick it out." Mitchell was reluctant to commit himself to any time period, and at 10:30, when the two left Oscar's, he remarked that he would "certainly stick it out if things went well."

During the second week of November, Mitchell had spoken to Richard Hicks. It was their first meeting since July, and Mitchell had requested it because he had heard that the National Chemical Company's plans to purchase an overseas textile firm had "fallen through." Richard Hicks' dynamic personality had been a large part of Mitchell's decision to work at TEXCORP and he enjoyed the 30 minute meeting with the National Chemical vice president. However, he learned that plans for expansion into overseas textiles had been delayed indefinitely. That night he warned his wife:

> Don't pack those bags for Europe, baby; probably will never need them. Yeah, the deal fell through . . . looks like it's TEXCORP or nothing. . . . Anyway, the glamour has worn off a little; how about you? Good, if things go well, maybe we can rent a little bigger house next year.

This change in Mitchell's original career goals forced him to examine his present situation at TEXCORP even more closely.

TEXCORP PERFORMANCE

For the next month, Mitchell continued to make work for himself. In order to keep completely busy, he fulfilled a long-time desire and signed on as a volunteer consultant for the New York Urban Coalition. Beginning in December, Mitchell spent at least two nights a week working late in New York City. He found the excitement and satisfaction of volunteer work made his late arrival home almost worthwhile. (Mitchell often skipped dinner and arrived home at midnight.) But in December, the November financial statements were released and the usual good humor in the TEXCORP offices became strained. Sales had dropped sharply, and most of the plants were losing money:

> They're all waiting for some kind of axe to fall from Hicks. Man, were the figures rotten. One of our plants was showing a 22 percent loss before taxes! I don't know what National is going to do, but I hope they do it fast. What do you mean, I should do something?! Who am I? Anyway, I think there is a project I could do.

The disappointing financial statements brought no immediate response from the Chemical company. TEXCORP managers, however, began to express their concern to Mitchell. Andrew Thompson and Walter Hogan pointed to the relatively stable performance of the Smith-Abbott plants, and at management meetings they emphasized the need to upgrade the plant efficiency at Carolina Cotton. Sam Jarvis, Carolina's plant manager, complained openly to Mitchell and other TEXCORP executives that his product mix was unprofitable because several North Carolina Mills plants were now producing what he used to produce and he was never given the money he needed to buy needed new equipment. Bill Berkeley spent two or three days each week at the TEXCORP executive offices. Berkeley and Mitchell often spoke about TEXCORP organizational problems and the need for reform. Berkeley was often asked what, if anything, the Chemical company was going to do about TEXCORP in light of the poor operating statistics, and his usual reply was one of assurance. "Calm down, fellas," Mitchell heard him say. "Just get out there and sell a little, and we'll do all right." Privately Berkeley admitted to Mitchell that he knew Hicks was concerned about the poor performance, but he didn't know if major policy changes were planned.

By the end of December, it was obvious that the year-end financial statements would also show sharp declines in sales and profitability. Although Andrew Thompson was beginning a two-week vacation in California and William Abbott was on a week's vacation in Florida, John Mitchell decided to put together a marketing research study of TEXCORP's two biggest plants. Rather than "clear" this study with the two absent executives, he approached the two plant managers involved and they responded enthusiastically to his proposed studies. For the next several weeks, Mitchell spent most of his time in Fitchburg and South Carolina (the location of the two plants he decided to study).

The poor performance reflected in the late 1968 financial reports prompted a minor TEXCORP reorganization in December. Mr. Hicks moved to create operating divisions and attempted to formally alter the old family reporting and communications channels. After close consultation with William Abbott, he announced the formation of temporary committees to run three operating divisions. Each committee would have a chairman, and the chairmanship would rotate every quarter. It was understood that this was a short-term and temporary arrangement, and that permanent division managers would be appointed as soon as possible. Andrew Thompson was made chairman of the Consumer Products Division (primarily high-grade spun rayon and wool blends), Jim White (former vice president of sales for the South Carolina Mills) was made chairman of the Industrial Products Division (fine cottons and synthetic fabrics), and the chairmanship of the Specialty Products Division was left vacant. Exhibit 3 illustrates the new organization. This chart was drawn up by Bill Berkeley, but was never identified as "official." The presence of the "unofficial reorganization chart," however, was known and accepted by TEXCORP executives.

Mitchell completed his first marketing study in mid-January. The study included an analysis of profitability by product line and by major customer, and was enthusiastically accepted by the plant manager. Mitchell sent a copy of his study to William Abbott but Mr. Abbott did not comment on it.

A REQUEST FOR PROMOTION

John Mitchell was growing increasingly impatient. He had developed a close relationship with Mary Fagan, the president's secretary, and the two often had coffee together in the cafeteria in the basement of the TEXCORP office building. Mitchell found Mary a perceptive and intelligent girl, and soon he was discussing a wide range of company problems with her:

> You know, if it weren't for Mary, I think I'd go nuts in the office. Today we talked about Kirk. She agreed with me that he's a brilliant engineer . . . but really out of sight when it comes to company poli-

tics. You know, he calls Mary from his engineering offices [located in North Carolina] just to find out what kind of a mood Abbott is in before calling him. And today he called me and asked who was meeting in the board room. He'd heard there was this big meeting and he wondered why he hadn't been invited.

The reorganization of TEXCORP into divisions had not, in Mitchell's opinion, straightened out the most serious company problems. Lines of authority were still unclear. Old, informal relationships still prevailed over the new (and as yet "unofficial") lines of communication. Abbott and Thompson continued to make most of the decisions. And overall marketing and sales objectives were left undefined. Mitchell became more and more disgusted with his situation:

> I've decided that TEXCORP reminds me of a country club. Abbott and Thompson are both top golfers. They must spend $300 a month taking customers, friends, etc., golfing. And when it comes time to make a few decisions, they do it like they might select an iron. You know, squint down the fairway, laugh a little, say "What the hell" and blast away. I'm convinced there are three or four of our top executives who ought to be retired . . . permanently . . . but Abbott could no more do that than he could give up his booze or his golf. . . . Yeah, I am depressed. . . .

Prompted by his continued frustration and the company reorganization, Mitchell decided to write Andrew Thompson a letter asking for a new job. He anticipated that Thompson would show the letter to William Abbott. It is reproduced as Exhibit 4.

Mitchell continued to work on his final marketing study. It was completed in February and focused on the declining profitability of the large Smith-Abbott Mill in Fitchburg. Using it as an excuse to talk to William Abbott, he tried to broach the subject of the unfilled position of administrative vice president. Mr. Abbott ignored Mitchell's casual inquiries, and at the end of February Mitchell's letter of January 11 still remained unanswered.

> Well, scratch one effort. I guess they couldn't have made me any Vice President. Who did I think I was. . . . Oh well, it sounded good at the time. Here I am. A guy who's supposed to be an expert in human relations. And I'm tied up in knots by a bunch of dumb playboys! I can't figure it out. One day I think I know why Hicks hasn't done anything. I see a little spark of hope for Abbott. And the next day I hear that Abbott has gone and wasted more money on a project that has no chances of success. You should hear the other executives talk about him. They're all losing confidence. And, you know, he hasn't called me into his office in almost three weeks now. Hell, he used to give me little odd jobs every day.

On February 1, 1969, Bill Berkeley resigned from the National Chemical Company. The day he left, he and John Mitchell had a long luncheon and Berkeley talked about National Chemical and Richard Hicks:

> John, I've worked for that man longer than any of his previous assistants . . . and I still don't really know him. The "in fighting" at

National is intense as hell nowadays. The President resigned last year and they still haven't filled the position. Hicks knows he's in line. I'm sure the lousy 1968 TEXCORP figures shook him up. Abbott keeps telling him "things will improve, things will improve," and I think he believes it! He won't listen to me. I've heard a lot of talk around the Chemical company about Hicks and some of the other Vice Presidents. There's the "pro-Hicks" and the "anti-Hicks" factions. . . .

Mitchell expressed his surprise at the extent of the office politics at National Chemical, but admitted that he knew Hicks must be under considerable pressure. Mitchell refrained from telling Berkeley that he preferred that Berkeley could have prevented the "communications gap" between National Chemical and TEXCORP by being more frank with his boss.

TEXCORP MANAGEMENT

Mitchell was also beginning to believe that everyone in TEXCORP and National Chemical was guilty of "playing politics." TEXCORP's plant managers operated with considerable independence. Martin Steiner, the vice president of finance, was the only home office executive who dealt with plant personnel on a continuing basis; yet, by January of 1969, he had been unable to implement a companywide cost accounting system. The controller of Smith-Abbott Mills, for example, was very "secretive" with his cost information and Steiner received only token cooperation from him. On several occasions Steiner remarked to John Mitchell that "things were sure different when old Bob Ford was running the company."

In spite of Richard Hicks' attempts to restructure the TEXCORP organization, the old company loyalties and factions continued to function. William Abbott, Walter Hogan, and Andrew Thompson directed the Smith-Abbott plants; Jim White and Martin Steiner spent most of their time dealing with the North Carolina Mills plants; and John Rand and Sam Jarvis concerned themselves with the Carolina Cotton plant. As the profitability of this latter plant declined, both Rand and Jarvis tried to "mind their own business" and avoided discussions with TEXCORP executives of overall policies and problems.

Management meetings were held once a month in the TEXCORP board room. The members of the Management Committee were: William Abbott, Andrew Thompson, Walter Hogan, John Rand, Martin Steiner, George Kirk, Sam Jarvis, Bob Cleaves, and Richard Hicks. John Mitchell was invited to attend many of the meetings. His increasing concern over the company's viability and his interest in psychology prompted him to reflect upon the "patterns of communication" that emerged among the TEXCORP executives.

When Hicks attended the meetings, a business-like atmosphere prevailed. The management meeting was almost formal, and the men seemed "on their toes." Many even took notes as the National Chemical vice president asked his pointed questions. However, Hicks was unable to attend all of the meetings. In his absence William Abbott would usually begin by smiling and saying, "Well, what'll we talk about to-day?" Mitchell noticed that these meetings often degenerated into rambling discussions of the performance of the three family companies. Members of the Management Committee were constantly being called to the phone to "put out a fire," and little seemed to get accomplished. Mitchell soon realized that it was an "unwritten rule" that nobody paid much attention to Management Committee meetings or decisions made there, for William Abbott consulted afterwards with Thompson or Hogan and decided upon the actions to be taken.

To John Mitchell, the most confusing aspect of the TEXCORP management and communications system was the lack of objectivity. No matter what subject was raised—be it a question of buying a new loom or expanding a product line—everyone seemed to have a known and fixed position. TEXCORP executives *expected* Andrew Thompson to fight for increased expenditures for blended wool fabric capacity, and everyone *expected* Sam Jarvis to say that cotton prints were the best long-term investment for the company, and Mitchell observed that they were never disappointed. Since the members of the Management Committee were already "on record" as holding certain opinions, discussions were usually routine and (Mitchell thought) uninteresting. New facts were seldom presented. The voluminous industrywide marketing statistics published by the Textile Trade Association were never cited. TEXCORP executives seemed to rely on their intuition and "gut feel" for the situation. The engineering studies of George Kirk were privately referred to as "worthless." Bob Cleaves and Martin Steiner confided to John Mitchell that on several occasions Kirk had changed his facts and figures to make the studies "come out the way Abbott wanted."

Mitchell tried to remain neutral as far as office politics were concerned, but this was often difficult:

> With a climate so politically sticky—I never pulled punches or played politics. This got me into trouble. When someone said, "How's it going?" I said, "Lousy." I was everyone's friend, and they [the execs] all wanted me for their assistant. All the division managers lacked management expertise.

Mitchell had tried to figure out why NCC was so reluctant to examine the situation at TEXCORP. He thought one reason might be the fact that the presidency of NCC had been unfilled for several months and a successor had not yet been chosen:

> Hicks may be mixed up in the hassle over who gets to be president of NCC. He wants to sweep TEXCORP under the rug because it's a bomb. They have lost at least five million in profits because of TEXCORP, and part of this is company politics. Bill Abbott is one of the largest single stockholders in NCC and he also knows Bill Scott [Board chairman of NCC]. So Abbott is formidable.

What really shocked Mitchell, however, were the day-to-day politics at TEXCORP:

> The number-one priority here is personalities. The prime commodity people fight for is Abbott's time. I'm shocked at the amount of time

spent on personalities. Eighty to eighty-five percent of people's time is spent warming up somebody or cooling off somebody or on other non-task conversation.

Another related commodity is information—facts about what's going on, who's talking to who, etc. But you can't get any data from the responsible people—the secretaries are the people to talk to if you want information. Everyone relies on rumor, and people here ask the secretaries to relate casual conversations they've overheard so they can figure out which way the wind is blowing. Mary Fagan even says that Abbott has asked her to spy on me!

Many people at TEXCORP used Mitchell as a confidant, and Mitchell felt he had to keep a delicate balance of discretion and candor. For instance, Martin Steiner would complain to Mitchell that he desperately needed a new accountant and this complaint would serve as a smoke-screen if Steiner's department got behind in its work. Mitchell felt that George Kirk, the head engineer, was almost paranoid about authority. If Abbott requested that Kirk see him in his office, Kirk would call Mitchell first to find out what Abbott wanted.

In February an incident occurred that John Mitchell found to be almost humorous. Three new looms had been installed in Bill Davis' (North Carolina Mills) plant, and William Abbott sent Walter Hogan south to "supervise the breaking-in period" at the plant. Bill Davis was not informed and was upset when Hogan walked into his plant and began asking questions. Davis placed quick calls to Jim White and John Rand protesting Hogan's presence, and finally called William Abbott. The irate plant manager said he could handle any "breaking in." Abbott explained that Hogan was just "inspecting" the new looms and said that George Kirk had suggested that Hogan be present when they started operations.

John Mitchell became involved in the controversy when he had lunch with Kirk the day following Hogan's arrival at Bill Davis' plant. Kirk was furious. He did not respect Walter Hogan and said he "didn't particularly care for Bill Davis" either. But he stated that he had never suggested that Hogan be sent to Davis' plant; "Now Jim and Marty Steiner will speak to me. They think I sicked Hogan on Davis. You should talk to them, John, and tell them what really happened. . . ." Mitchell discovered from Mary Fagan that Kirk had, in fact, written a memo about the looms to Abbott. When questioned by Abbott, the Chief Engineer had evidently agreed that Hogan might "supervise the looms for a few weeks." A few days later, Mitchell mentioned the matter to Bill Berkeley. The young National Chemical representative pointed out that George Kirk seldom disagreed with anything William Abbott suggested. The entire incident seemed ridiculous to John Mitchell, but Berkeley pointed out that such "misunderstandings" were common at TEXCORP.

A FINAL CONFRONTATION

Mitchell was becoming increasingly aware of his unique position in the TEXCORP organization. More and more often he was asked to listen to the problems of various company executives. Bob Cleaves confided in him almost daily. Cleaves' responsibilities had been reduced when TEX-CORP was reorganized, and he constantly spoke of "retiring" or quitting. Walter Hogan was also expressing personal opinions to Mitchell. Hogan's new position as "manufacturing services manager" was a clear demotion. Hogan was 62 years old and admitted to Mitchell that he knew "his days were numbered." Martin Steiner and Jim White spoke to Mitchell in January about the financial and sales deficiencies they had observed at TEXCORP. They encouraged Mitchell to "speak to someone at National Chemical" to see if Abbott could be replaced and new talent recruited. Mitchell responded by speaking to Bill Berkeley, but advised both Steiner and White that they should be the ones to approach Hicks:

> I don't know, the atmosphere is getting thick as glue around TEX-CORP nowadays. The company's going down hill. Abbott's spending more time on the links. Everyone comes to me with their problems. What am I supposed to do? Except Andy. . . . He and Abbott don't talk to me any more. I guess they know I think they're both doing a lousy job. But, hell, they're in charge. All guys like Cleaves and Jarvis and Steiner seem to be doing is bitching. . . .

During the months of February and March, Richard Hicks was out of New York City. This only added to John Mitchell's feelings of helplessness. He was now convinced, beyond doubt, that TEXCORP was being badly mismanaged. His personal future seemed to depend on the National Chemical Company: when and if it would step in and replace Abbott and his management "cronies." On March 2nd he spoke with William Abbott and told him he was "thinking of quitting." Mr. Abbott reacted very calmly and remarked that it was "too bad," but that it was his (Mitchell's) own decision:

> Hell, he just sat there. The bastard. Didn't even bat an eye. I gave him the chance to try and talk me out of it. It was half a bluff anyway. Man, now I have to find another job! Wait 'till Hicks hears this. He's going to wonder what's been going on while he was away.

The following day, Mitchell told Bob Cleaves what he had done. Cleaves reacted emotionally and told Mitchell he was a fool. "The future of TEXCORP will rest with guys like you," he exclaimed. "You're throwing away a great opportunity. You know National Chemical will have to move in soon. And when they do, you will be the one who comes out on top!" Later on that day, William Abbott called Mitchell into his office and asked if he would "reconsider" his resignation. He said he could only reconsider if "major changes" were implemented at TEXCORP, but Mitchell agreed to spell them out in writing. Abbott said he would read what Mitchell wrote and "we can talk when I get back from Augusta."

Mitchell proceeded to write a three-page description of what he saw wrong with TEXCORP and what changes might be made. Excerpts from this letter to William Abbott are reproduced as Exhibit 5. When Abbott returned to New York, he asked Mitchell to have lunch with him at the Union League Club. During the lunch, it became clear to Mitchell that writing the letter was a mistake:

> He was really upset. I mean, he had the letter with him. And he would read for a while then say, "You're right." Then he'd read on. He said he agreed with everything I said. He didn't ever argue!! He didn't question anything I said. I know now it was a mistake. I've hurt him . . . he can't ever read the words I wrote. If he *were* reading them, I know he would have disagreed with some of what I said.

After the lunch Abbott said he wanted to show the letter to Andrew Thompson. He said he would talk to Mitchell later that week.

John Mitchell was very discouraged. Word of his letter had spread around the TEXCORP offices and he spent the next several days answering questions about what he had said. His efforts to evade questions only added to the tension in the office and gave the entire incident "mysterious" overtones. Without exception, TEXCORP managers told Mitchell he was making a personal mistake to leave the company at this point in time, but they admired his "guts" and hoped his confrontation would force National Chemical into taking some action with respect to Abbott.

On March 11, Mitchell decided to speak to Hicks about TEXCORP and what he had done. Hicks was in Washington, D.C., and Mitchell flew to the capitol city and spoke with Hicks for two hours. Hicks was disturbed that Mitchell had acted so precipitously and rebuked him for not having come sooner. Mitchell showed him a copy of the letter he had written Abbott and told him that it was "impossible" for him to have come to Hicks before. "I felt I should quit first . . . before telling you all of what I know about what's going on at TEXCORP. I guess it sounds hollow and self-righteous now, but it's how I feel." After Mitchell talked for a while about TEXCORP's problems, Hicks asked him to write a more detailed analysis of the textile company's prospects for success. The National Chemical Company vice president cautioned Mitchell to be "cool" and reasonable in this report: "Tell me what my alternatives are; tell me how much it will cost to make the changes you think should be made; and tell me what the risks are."

For the next month Mitchell worked on his report for Richard Hicks. William Abbott did not ask to see him, and Mitchell decided not to renew their Union League Club luncheon discussion. On April 10, the 1969 first quarter results were published. They showed that TEXCORP had lost over $1 million after taxes during the first three months. TEXCORP executives now spoke openly of "moving to greener pastures" and the offices on Executive Row were usually empty. William Abbott took three- and four-day weekends; Walter Hogan, at Abbott's suggestion, spent all of his time at one of the large North Carolina Mills' plants in the South; Tom Rinehart seldom came into the office; and John Rand took a month's vacation.

John Mitchell, while researching and writing his report, was also actively searching for another job. He talked to his wife:

> This time I can forget about overseas work. How would you like to work in Denver? I've got a contact out there. No, I don't know if I'd stay at TEXCORP no matter what Hicks does. You never know when action might be taken. A couple of other National Vice Presidents have

been calling Steiner and asking for some financial data, so I guess the word is finally out that all is not well with their new acquisition. But I've waited too long already. The way I see it, it'll be a year before that company's alive again. Just not worth waiting around for. . . . What do you think?

On April 17, as Mitchell was putting the finishing touches on his report, Jim White stopped in his office. White announced that he had just spoken to Hicks and that he had tried to communicate to the national vice president some of the facts concerning "how bad things were at TEXCORP." White smiled and said, "John, you just can't leave now. From what Hicks told me today, I'm sure we'll see big changes very soon. Really, this time I know it will happen. You've got to stay. We'll all be better off if you do!"

Exhibit 1

TEXTILE CORPORATION OF AMERICA
TEXCORP Organization, February 1968

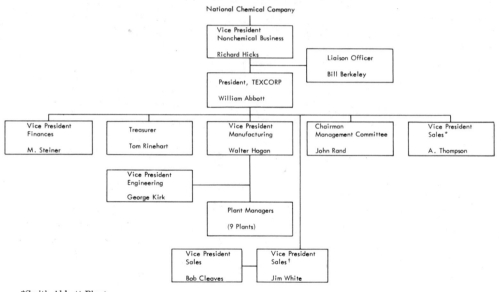

*Smith-Abbott Plant.
†North Carolina Mills.

Exhibit 2

PERSONAL BACKGROUND OF TEXCORP PERSONNEL

Name	Age	Background
William Abbott*	55	Former president of Smith-Abbott Mills, ex-All-American football player from Princeton, independently wealthy.
Andrew Thompson	41	Former salesman for Smith-Abbott Mills, former professional golfer, long-time friend of William Abbott.
Walter Hogan*	62	Former plant manager of Smith-Abbott Mills, former football coach, long-time friend of William Abbott and Mr. Abbott's father. (Founder of Smith-Abbott Mills.)
John Rand*	66	Former president of Carolina Cotton, Harvard College 25, independently wealthy.
Martin Steiner	42	Former chief financial officer for North Carolina Mills.
George Kirk	45	Hired in 1964, chief engineer for four TEXCORP engineers, offices located in North Carolina.
Sam Jarvis*	54	Plant manager of Carolina Cotton Plant, brother-in-law of John Rand.
Bob Hogan	36	Plant manager of Smith-Abbott Mills, son of Walter Hogan.
Jim White	55	Former sales manager of North Carolina Mills.
Bob Cleaves*	42	Former president of a small textile company bought out by TEXCORP in 1964, independently wealthy, a bachelor.
Tom Rinehart*	63	Treasurer of TEXCORP, former treasurer of North Carolina Mills.
Bill Davis	50	Plant manager of largest North Carolina Mills plant, appointed in 1965, son-in-law of John Rand.
Bill Berkeley	29	MBA from Berkeley, hired by National Chemical in 1967, worked for Hicks since December 1967.
Richard Hicks	50	Vice president of National Chemical, Harvard Business School class of 49, known as a "real professional" to other National Chemical executives.

* Indicates that an employment contract was in effect. (These contracts lasted through 1971 and guaranteed the men salaries ranging from $40,000–$70,000 per year.)

Exhibit 3

"UNOFFICIAL" ORGANIZATION OF TEXCORP IN DECEMBER 1968

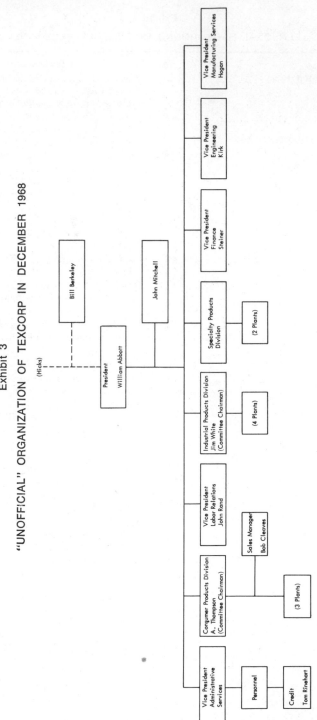

Exhibit 4

JOHN MITCHELL'S LETTER TO
ANDREW THOMPSON, DATED JANUARY 13, 1969

Dear Andy,

I hope this note will help you understand my as yet unresolved anxieties concerning my future here in TEXCORP. I am putting this in writing to save your time and to facilitate any further discussions. Let me try and describe my perspective.

First, I see a lot of work to be done at all levels of the organization. Much of this work is a matter of analysis (data collection, organization, setting priorities, etc.) Systems must be set up, studies made, programs established and monitored, etc.

Second, I see a limited number of people with the background and training to accomplish all of the analytical work that has to be done.

Third, I see myself and my own selfish goals. I have spent all of my lengthy (four year) business career doing analytical staff work. I have developed a certain facility for this kind of work. But it no longer offers the challenge I desire. I want to assume more complete responsibilities. I want to be a boss. I want to be able to look back and say, "Look, I did that . . . that's my success." When I spoke to you earlier, I hoped you might have a line position for me in your division. I have been told—and I am forced to agree—that I lack the experience to be a line manager in Sales or in Manufacturing. Those are the only two lines at the divisional level.

Given what I see around me, I conclude that from the organization's point of view, I should be in a position where I could move freely about; conduct market studies in the divisions, assist Engineering in plant relocation studies, help establish systems and procedures, etc. (As William would say, "For Chrissake, John, we have so much to do, let's just do it!") I would need some source and position of authority that everyone saw as "legitimate" so that cooperation would be maximized. I guess my present status and title of "Assistant to the President" seems best suited to these organizational needs.

From a personal point of view, however, this role is less than ideal. William, I suspect, has never quite known what to do with me. I am always a little "in the way" or "under foot." My duties too often dissolve into those of a clerk-secretary-adding machine. I bear much responsibility for this, I will admit. I haven't tried to be "pushy" and I have avoided playing too many games with too many people. And I have paid a personal price: boredom. The frustration I can handle; the boredom slowly destroys me. All of this has been changing, but the deeper I get into the problems and the personalities, the less secure any "assistant to" position becomes. As your assistant, for example, a careful (and probably not very convincing) explanation would have to go out if I were to involve myself in the Industrial Products or Specialty Divisions. I guess it comes down to the fact that I don't think being anyone's assistant will offer me the kinds of challenges I desire. (Man, this is sounding more and more presumptuous and egotistical every minute.) Anyway—from my own standpoint, I would like to be in the position of Vice President of Administrative Services. Here I would have the challenge of line responsibility and the opportunity to test myself. (Although I still wouldn't have the kind of "line" challenge and satisfaction you have when you sell a good fabric order, or a plant manager has when he reads the bottom line of his P&L statement.) In charge of Administration I would still have both the time and the authority to conduct the needed analytical studies and

Exhibit 4—Continued

services. I would be available to all departments—both informally and formally. In this position I would also be able to involve myself in those kinds of administrative tasks that do not require twenty years of experience in the textile business.

Before you laugh at my conceit, let me explain why I think it's a reasonable gamble from the organization's point of view. We all agreed some time ago that the job should be created. We knew that systems were needed and that a man was needed to supervise these tasks as well as Purchasing and Credit (neither of which involve close or imaginative supervision). Bill Berkeley can handle the job, and I've heard his name mentioned. But he has said "No" to both of us privately, and I doubt anyone will change his mind.

"NOW WAIT A MINUTE!! You really want me to say you can be VP of Administrative Services?!?!" Yes, I'm only 27 (But, just think! I'll be 28 in June!) Yes, I just started shaving last year. Yes, only six months in textiles . . . only six months in this company. I realize William is the man to talk to in the end. It's his ball game. But with your understanding and support, my feelings, expectations, and anxieties can be more carefully presented to him. Anyway, I've got enough guts to think I can do a better job there than anyone else we've got. And I don't think it's the kind of position that a new man would be able to take over. I'd be the lowest paid VP in the city, and that'll help our budgets.

I'd like to speak with you about this note and try to cover the 100 other questions that arise from my cocky, impertinent ambition before approaching William.

If and when you show this to William, remind him he once told me to stick around because "the way we are, there are plenty of opportunities to learn." Remind him he said that, and then ask him how he learned to catch a football.

John

Exhibit 5

EXCERPTS FROM MITCHELL'S LETTER TO
WILLIAM ABBOTT, DATED MARCH 3, 1969

Mr. William A. Abbott
Augusta National Golf Club
Washington Road
Augusta, Georgia

William—

I am sorry to bother your golf, but all of this is important to me and I wanted you to have time to think about it. I have not gone into personal requests. If this letter makes sense to you, we can speak about my future when you return to New York.

* * * * *

I.   Prerequisites for Success in Textiles
   1.   Must have market specialization with a well-focused sales effort. This is the only way to avoid competition based on price alone.
   2.   Must develop those services our key customer groups want (and will pay for).
   3.   Must carefully control costs. Because of the competitive situation and the large capital investments involved, incremental profits derived from cost control are often the key to success.
II. Obstacles to TEXCORP success in the Market
* * * * *

We lack almost all of the above prerequisites.

We are trying to serve too many markets. . . .

We are being forced to compete more and more on price alone . . . (cf., my Smith-Abbott study). Major product lines are declining in value and suffering heavy losses (cf., North Carolina Mills study).

We are unable or unwilling to specialize . . . our sales efforts are poorly directed . . . our cost controls are inadequate. . . . Where are our budgets?

III. Organizing to Meet the Market
   . . . must begin with the New York office.

Planning is critical . . . real planning and risk-taking depend on some very simple things: rapid, clear communication, getting the right people together to make the right decisions, collecting the right kind of data in the fastest amount of time, getting quick and decisive answers to questions that can be answered quickly.

The office of the President can set the whole "organization" in motion. . . . By demanding prompt decisions, by demanding facts (rather than feelings or opinions), and by demanding that standards be met, the office of the President can begin to make TEXCORP one company.

And this is impossible unless the example at the top is consistent with what is being asked of the rest of the organization. . . . There are many decisions that I think can be made today. . . .

While doing this housecleaning and planning, talent must be recruited. . . .

IV. Some Specific Examples
   Bring talent into the central office.

Redefine head office responsibilities. Much housecleaning is needed. . . . Have you reviewed Andy Thompson's budgets? His plans? If the

Exhibit 5—Continued

office of the President can't answer yes to these questions . . . then why not?

Reorganize the Engineering Group. . . . Create budgets for all vital functions . . . change the layout of the head office. . . . Establish a uniform cost accounting system for all of the plants . . . create a system of sales management . . . without reports and communication, how can we expect focus and direction?

If you were to consult others in TEXCORP, and if you could get honest responses, I am absolutely positive many other specific examples could be cited—examples of things that should *and can* be decided and implemented immediately. Your organization, William, will withhold information from you because they do not have confidence that the information will be used wisely.

* * * * *

In all honesty I must say that I really don't know if my leaving the company is a very good thing for TEXCORP or a very bad thing. Because, in the clutch, I guess none of the fancy degrees, and none of Harvard's "principles" count for much. And I've never been there in the clutch.

Air, Inc.[*]

In 1971, the board of directors of Air, Inc., Chicago, the oldest and one of the largest manufacturers of air filtration equipment in the world, nominated David Palma, 55, vice president as head of international operations. The International Division supervised about 50 companies throughout the world, which together generated a sales volume roughly equal to that of the U.S. operation.

David Palma, an Italian national, who had worked for Air, Inc., for 20 years, took on his new job at a moment when international operations were clearly in a bad way. During the preceding year they had netted only $50,000 profits on $300 million of sales; and although Air, Inc., was still the world leader in market share (with about 20 percent of the world market), its position was weakening.

David Palma noted the reasons for the situation to be the following:

1. Competition was cut-throat: as the industry was labor intensive, and as its products were old, without patent protection, and often custom-made, there seemed to be little advantage of size against hundreds of small local competitors.
2. Air, Inc., had made no thorough analysis of its competition, nor of the different markets it served.
3. There was no product policy; most products were developed in the United States and did not meet local needs nor local building code specifications; for lack of competitive products, Air Inc. found itself excluded from a series of growing markets; there was no product diversification.
4. Management at all levels was inadequate; it was complacent (in many cases, managers of local subsidiaries were not able to give even a gross figure on the financial performance of their unit). They

had not been asked for this information even when a company lost money for several years. There was almost no turnover in management, and no outside recruiting; there was no management development and training.

5.   Controls were inadequate; there were no performance goals and standards, no job descriptions, no performance appraisal (nor rewards for outstanding work or punishment for poor performance).

6.   Coordination between and control of the different local subsidiaries was almost nonexistent; as was any organization at division headquarters (where no one was specifically assigned to head Marketing, Production, Finance; adequate staff support was lacking in a situation where one had to turn to corporate staffs for the solution of almost every major functional problem).

David Palma, who immediately moved international headquarters to Milan, decided at once to turn the situation by taking dramatic action. He believed two major steps to be essential to realize a recovery and expansion: the introduction of a new product policy and a reorganization of structure and procedures.

As to products, one would revolutionize the industry, he believed, by trying to apply a new concept: Air, Inc. would build standardized models in a module system. This would allow for substantial economy through mass production of different standardized parts in different factories, it would allow for centralized R&D and, it would lead to better service performance. David Palma, himself an engineer, decided to focus all his attention on this strategic change in Air, Inc.'s traditional operations as well as on possibilities of diversification through mergers and acquisitions.

He decided, therefore, to leave the organizational and administrative problems to somebody else. He hired Joe Pfeffer as a director of human resources, and gave him "carte blanche" to implement these goals.

Joe Pfeffer, 38, was an American with a good record as a personnel administrator. He was the first manager to be hired from outside the company and only the third personnel administrator in the company's history. He described himself as a compulsive achiever who had struggled to advance in business ever since he was a young man. He had earned his MBA in evening courses and had written two books on management, between 10 P.M. and 3 A.M., as he said. When he moved to Milan, he left his wife and child in New York, so that he could concentrate all his energy on his new job. Work was his primary hobby. He considered business an exciting adventure and tough challenge.

He described how he approached the challenge at Air, Inc. International in the following way:

> My job was to turn this organization around from a paternalistic institution to a dynamic, successful, healthy, profitable, growing business.
>
> This meant, above all, to bring professionalism into the firm. Air, Inc. was at best 20, at worst 50 years behind in modern management techniques, with managers lacking discipline, drive, professional skills, the ability to work in teams.

Far-reaching changes were necessary. But you have to go slowly and not make mistakes. You have to establish a base from which to operate. You try to learn as much as possible. And as a human resources manager you must be as comfortable with a financial statement as a financial vice president; otherwise, nobody will listen to you.

The first thing I did, was to ask management at the operating companies controlled by Air, Inc. International to prepare action plans to improve their productivity and to reduce costs and expenses immediately. These plans were then discussed in Milan or, in the case of larger subsidiaries, at their local headquarters. If in these meetings someone came up with a watered-down budget, he was in trouble; we kicked the hell out of him. Note, however, that in a confrontation with a line man (especially one who is making money) the staff man always loses. So you have to know when to back off and wait until he makes a stupid mistake (they always do) and then sack him.

We set the objectives at headquarters—time was short; inertia had to be removed: we knew that South Africa was performing poorly and should have improved 200 percent; so we set a target of 100 percent. You have to be reasonable and practical. You can't let these people set their own goals; they'll set them too low.

I like to deal with people one by one. We had only 2 staff meetings in 3½ years. But we do have individually tailored management seminars which I conducted personally. These were really MBO sessions —very simple, basic, and completely authoritarian: We gave as an assignment to the participants to state their greatest problems at the present; we then selected from the problems mentioned a few which seemed most important and discussed possible solutions. We have come up with ideas which have saved the company millions, and I made sure that they were implemented. That is, I visited the companies frequently, giving them usually 2 months advance notice so they could shape up before my arrival.

We wanted the different companies to compete with each other. So we called, for instance, the Latin Americans together: the Mexicans were selling $11 million with 1,100 people; the Argentinians $35 million with 600—very embarrassing. . . . When I went to Australia for the first time, at 4:30 P.M. everybody was gone—no competitive spirit. Now, with my new man there, everybody works until 7:00 P.M.

As I met all these executives, I started to establish a worldwide manpower inventory. I interviewed systematically the 350 people in top positions. Interviews took typically about two hours. You give a guy the benefit of the doubt, but actually you know after 30 minutes what the man is like. In one case, I increased a man's salary by 20 percent on the spot (without even checking with his superior) and sometimes I started to look for a replacement the same day. Altogether we had to replace almost all of top management. Keeping them in their positions would really have been too costly. Either we kept them in an advisory function compatible with their technical expertise, or we just had to let them go. We hired only people from outside who had a good job; smart people . . . people who earned already $40,000, but were looking for better promotion prospects. The man on the top is decisive. I focus all the effort on him. If you have good top managers, you don't have to worry much more; they will not tolerate mediocrity down the line; you can leave them alone until they lack in performance. I have had no problems with them—I hired these guys. And none of them ever quit of his own desire.

I'll train the new men; then they'll report directly to me during the first year; and after that I maintain a heavy dotted-line relationship to them. Some may say that this is not my business—I answer that everything involving people is my business.

As to performance, I don't care what a man does (short of stealing from the company) as long as he gets results. That's why I like to hire locals as financial managers (while in many multinationals the finance men come from HQ). For they know the local conditions and how to circumvent the law, legally or illegally.

It's hard to measure the long-term impact of managers on an organization. I don't worry about the uncontrollable; there is enough of what is controllable to worry about—we measure performance; that's what counts. What happens in five years is an illusion, anyway.

After about two years, Joe Pfeffer started to (a) initiate a more formalized manpower planning system, (b) establish standard personnel policies (although he avoided having all policies down in writing—"often it is too dangerous to commit yourself"), and (c) reorganized Air, Inc. International's headquarters operations.

More specifically he developed position descriptions and performance standards for many key management positions; he introduced a uniform worldwide performance appraisal and review program (he established an incentive plan and formal annual salary reviews based on worldwide salary survey data); he encouraged on-the-job training of new managers away from their home country (while not supporting the attendance of training programs outside the company—"we can't afford to let our people go for two weeks training"); and he has made it an obligation for every manager to identify and develop high-potential young executives.

He also has worked on the (re)organization of the Milan headquarters. Operations were divided into four regional divisions: Europe, Far East, Latin America, and Other. Each of these new divisions had to be provided with sizable marketing, finance, and engineering staffs which were recruited either from the "cream" of what was available in the operating units or from outside the company. Joe Pfeffer did not create a large personal staff noting he did not have the budget to hire first-rate people and preferred to work alone rather than with second-rate people. The development of a strong group in Milan had the purpose of helping the International Division to gain more independence from Chicago (which he said lacked understanding of the international business) and at the same time of gaining control over the local operating units (which were believed to be drifting).

With all this, Air, Inc. International attained, in 1973, sales of $530 million and profits of $35 million, thus overtaking the North American operations, for the first time, both in sales volume and profitability. Employment was down 13 percent (since 1970) to 33,000.

Robert F. Kennedy High School

On July 15, 1970, David King became principal of the Robert F. Kennedy High School, the newest of the six high schools in Great Ridge, Illinois. The school had opened in the fall of 1968 amid national acclaim for being one of the first schools in the country to be designed and constructed for the "house system" concept. Kennedy High's organization was broken down into four "houses" each of which contained 300 students, a faculty of 18, and a housemaster. The Kennedy complex was especially designed so that each house was in a separate building connected to the "core facilities" and other houses by an enclosed outside passageway.[1] Each house had its own entrance, classrooms, toilets, conference rooms, and housemaster's office. (See Exhibit 1 for the layout.)

King knew that Kennedy High was not intended to be an ordinary school when it was first conceived. It had been hailed as a major innovation in inner city education and a Chicago television station had made a documentary on it in 1968. Kennedy High had opened with a carefully selected staff of teachers, many of whom were chosen from other Great Ridge Schools and at least a dozen of whom had been especially recruited from out of state. Indeed, King knew his faculty included graduates from several elite East and West Coast schools such as Stanford, Yale, and Princeton, as well as several of the very best midwestern schools. Even the racial mix of students had been carefully balanced so that blacks, whites, and Puerto Ricans each comprised a third of the student body (although King also knew—perhaps better than its planners—that Kennedy's students were drawn from the toughest and poorest areas of town). The building itself was also widely admired for its beauty and functionality and had won several national architectural awards.

---

[1] The core facilities included the cafeteria, nurses's room, guidance offices, the boys' and girls' gyms, the offices, the shops, and auditorium.

651

Exhibit 1

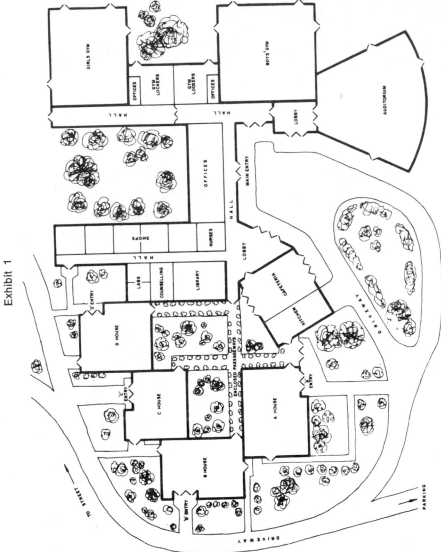

Despite these careful and elaborate preparations, Kennedy High School was in serious difficulty by July of 1970. It had been wracked by violence the preceding year, having been twice closed by student disturbances and once by a teacher walkout. It was also widely reported (although King did not know for sure), that achievement scores of its 9th and 10th grade students had actually declined during the last two years, while no significant improvement could be found in the scores of the 11th and 12th graders' tests. Thus, the Kennedy High School for which King was taking over as principal had fallen far short of its planners' hopes and expectations.

DAVID KING

David King was born and raised in Great Ridge, Illinois. His father was one of the city's first black principals and thus King was not only familiar with the city, but with its school system as well. After two years of military service, King decided to follow his father's footsteps and went to Great Ridge State Teachers College from which he received his B.Ed. in 1955 and his M.Ed. in 1960. King was certified in Elementary and Secondary School Administration, English and Physical Education. King had taught English and coached in a predominantly black middle school until 1960 when he was asked to become the school's assistant principal. He remained in that post until 1965 when he was asked to take over the George Thibeault Middle School, a large middle school of 900 pupils which at the time was reputed to be the most "difficult" middle school in the city. While at Thibeault, King gained a citywide reputation for being a gifted and popular administrator and was credited with changing Thibeault from the worst middle school in the system to one of the best. He had been very effective in building community support, recruiting new faculty, and in raising academic standards. He was also credited with turning out basketball and baseball teams which had won state and country middle school championships. King knew that he had been selected for the Kennedy job over several more senior candidates because of his ability to handle tough situations. The superintendent had made that clear when he told King why he had been selected for the job.

The superintendent had also told him that he would need every bit of skill and luck he could muster. King knew of the formidable credentials of Jack Weis, his predecessor at Kennedy High. Weis, a white, had been the superintendent of a small, local township school system before becoming Kennedy's first principal. He had also written a book on the "house system" concept, as well as a second book on inner city education. Weis had earned a Ph.D. from the University of Chicago and a divinity degree from Harvard. Yet, despite his impressive background and obvious ability, Weis had resigned in disillusionment, and was described by many as a "broken man." In fact, King remembered seeing the physical change which Weis had undergone over that two-year period. Weis' appearance had become progressively more fatigued and strained until he developed what appeared to be permanent black rings under his eyes and a perpetual stoop. King remembered how he had pitied the man and wondered how Weis could find the job worth the obvious personal toll it was taking on him.

HISTORY OF THE SCHOOL

1968–1969. The school's troubles began to manifest themselves in the school's first year of operation. Rumors of conflicts between the housemasters and the six subject area department heads were widespread throughout the system by the middle of the first year. The conflicts stemmed from differences in interpretations of curriculum policy on required learning and course content. In response to these conflicts, Dr. Weis had instituted a "free market" policy by which subject area department heads were supposed to convince headmasters of why they should offer certain courses, while headmasters were supposed to convince department heads of which teachers they wanted assigned to their houses and why they wanted those teachers. Many observers in the school system felt that this policy exacerbated the conflicts.

To add to this climate of conflict a teacher was assaulted in her classroom in February of 1969. The beating frightened many of the staff, particularly some of the older teachers. A delegation of eight teachers asked Weis to hire security guards a week after the assault. The request precipitated a debate within the faculty about the desirability of having guards in the school. One group felt that the guards would instill a sense of safety within the school, and thus promote a better learning climate, while the other group felt that the presence of guards in the school would be repressive and would destroy the sense of community and trust which was developing within the school. Dr. Weis refused the request for security guards because he believed that symbolically they would represent everything the school was trying to change. In April a second teacher was robbed and beaten in her classroom after school hours and the debate was rekindled, except that this time a group of Spanish-speaking parents threatened to boycott the school unless better security measures were instituted. Again Dr. Weis refused the request for security guards.

1969–1970. The second year of the school's existence was even more troubled than the first. Because of cutbacks ordered during the summer of 1969, Dr. Weis was not able to replace eight teachers who resigned during the summer and it was no longer possible for each house to staff all of its courses with its own faculty. Dr. Weis therefore instituted a "flexible staffing" policy whereby some teachers were asked to teach a course outside of their assigned house and students in the 11th and 12th grades were able to take some elective and required courses in other houses. During this period, Chauncey Carver, one of the housemasters, publicly attacked the move as a step toward destroying the house system. In a letter to the *Great Ridge Times,* he accused the Board of Education of trying to subvert the house concept by cutting back funds.

The debate over the flexible staffing policy was heightened when two of the other housemasters joined a group of faculty and department chairmen in opposing Chauncey Carver's criticisms. This group argued that the individual house faculties of 15 to 18 teachers could never offer their students the breadth of courses that a schoolwide faculty of 65 to 70 teachers could offer and that interhouse cross registration should be encouraged for that reason.

Further expansion of a cross registration or flexible staffing policy was halted, however, because of difficulties encountered in the scheduling of classes in the fall of 1969. Several errors were found in the master schedule which had been pre-planned during the preceding summer. Various schedule difficulties persisted until November of 1969 when the vice principal responsible for the scheduling of classes resigned. Mr. Burtram Perkins, a Kennedy housemaster who had formerly planned the schedule at Central High assumed the scheduling function in addition to his duties as housemaster. The scheduling activity took most of Perkins' time until February.

Security again became an issue when three sophomores were assaulted because they refused to give up their lunch money during a "shakedown." It was believed that the assailants were from outside of the school and were not students. Several teachers approached Dr. Weis and asked him to request security guards from the Board of Education. Again, Dr. Weis declined but he asked Bill Smith, a vice principal at the school, to secure all doors except for the entrances to each of the four houses, the main entrance to the school, and the cafeteria. This move appeared to reduce the number of outsiders in the school.

In May of 1970, a disturbance occurred in the cafeteria which appeared to grow out of a fight between two boys. The fight spread and resulted in considerable damage to the school including the breaking of classroom windows and desks. The disturbance was severe enough for Dr. Weis to close the school. A number of teachers and students reported that outsiders were involved in the fight and in damaging the classrooms. Several students were taken to the hospital for minor injuries but all were released. A similar disturbance occurred two weeks later and again the school was closed. The Board of Education then ordered a temporary detail of municipal police to the school despite Dr. Weis' advice to the contrary. In protest to the assignment of the police detail, 30 of Kennedy's 68 teachers staged a walkout which was joined by over half the student body. The police detail was removed from the school, and an agreement was worked out by an ad hoc subcommittee of the Board of Education with informal representatives of teachers who were for and against assigning a police detail. The compromise called for the temporary stationing of a police cruiser near the school.

KING'S FIRST WEEK AT KENNEDY HIGH

Mr. King arrived at Kennedy High on Monday, July 15th and spent most of his first week individually interviewing the school's key administrators (see Exhibit 2 for a listing of Kennedy's administrative staff as of July 15th). He also had a meeting with all of his adminis-

Exhibit 2

ROBERT F. KENNEDY HIGH SCHOOL
ADMINISTRATIVE ORGANIZATION

Principal: David King, 42 (black)
                                   B.Ed.; M.Ed., Great Ridge State College

Vice principal: William Smith, 44 (black)
                                   B.Ed., Breakwater State College
                                   M.Ed. (Counseling), Great Ridge State College

Vice principal: Vacant—to be filled

Housemaster, A House: Burtram Perkins, 47 (black)
                                   B.S.; M.Ed., University of Illinois

Housemaster, B House: Frank Czepak, 36 (white)
                                   B.S. University of Illinois
                                   M.Ed. Great Ridge State College

Housemaster, C House: Chauncey Carver, 32 (black)
                                   A.B. Wesleyan University
                                   B.F.A. Pratt Institute
                                   M.A.T. Yale University

Housemaster, D House: John Bonavota, 26 (white)
                                   B.Ed. Great Ridge State College
                                   M.Ed. Ohio State University

Assistant to the principal: Vacant—to be filled

Assistant to the principal: Vacant—to be filled
  (for Community Affairs)

trators and department heads on Friday of that week. Mr. King's purpose in these meetings was to familiarize himself with the school, its
problems, and its key people.

His first interview was with Bill Smith, who was one of his vice principals. Mr. Smith was black and had worked as a counselor and as a
vice principal of a middle school prior to coming to Kennedy. King knew
that Smith had a reputation for being a tough disciplinarian and was
very much disliked among many of the younger faculty and students.
However, King had also heard from several teachers, whose judgment
he respected, that Smith had been instrumental in keeping the school
from "blowing apart" the preceding year. It became clear early in the
interview that Smith felt that more stringent steps were needed to keep
outsiders from wandering the buildings. In particular Smith urged King
to consider locking all of the school's 30 doors except for the front entrance so that everyone would enter and leave through one set of doors
only. Smith also told him that many of the teachers and pupils had become fearful of living and working in the building and that "no learning will ever begin to take place until we make it so people don't have to
be afraid anymore." At the end of the interview, Smith told King that
he had been approached by a nearby school system to become its director of counselling but that he had not yet made up his mind. He
said that he was committed enough to Kennedy High that he did not

want to leave, but that his decision depended on how hopeful he felt about its future.

As King talked with others, he discovered that the "door question" was one of considerable controversy within the faculty and that feelings ran high, both in favor of the idea of locking all the doors as well as against it. Two of the housemasters in particular, Chauncey Carver, a black, and Frank Czepak, a white, were strongly against closing the house entrances. The two men felt that such an action would symbolically reduce house "autonomy" and the feeling of distinctness that was a central aspect of the house concept.

Chauncey Carver, master of "C" House, was particularly vehement on this issue as well as on the question of whether students of one house should be allowed to take classes in another house. Carver said that the flexible staffing program introduced the preceding year had nearly destroyed the house concept and that he, Carver, would resign if King intended to expand the cross-house enrollment of students. Carver also complained about what he described as "interference" from department heads in his teacher's autonomy.

Carver appeared to be an outstanding housemaster from everything that King had heard about him—even from his many enemies. Carver had an abrasive personality but seemed to have the best operating house in the school and was well liked by most of his teachers and pupils. His program also appeared to be the most innovative of all. However, it was also the program which was most frequently attacked by the department heads for lacking substance and not covering the requirements outlined in the system's curriculum guide. Even with these criticisms, King imagined how much easier it would be if he had four housemasters like Chauncey Carver.

During his interviews with the other three housemasters, King discovered that they all felt infringed upon by the department heads, but that only Carver and Czepak were strongly against "locking the doors" and that two other housemasters actively favored cross-house course enrollments. King's fourth interview was with Burtram Perkins who was also a housemaster. Perkins was a black in his late 40s who had been an assistant to the principal of Central High before coming to Kennedy. Perkins spent most of the interview discussing how schedule pressures could be relieved. Perkins was currently involved in developing the schedule for the 1970–71 school year until a vice principal was appointed to perform that job. (Kennedy High had allocations for two vice principals and two assistants in addition to the housemasters. See Exhibit 2.)

Two pieces of information concerning Perkins came to King's attention during his first week there. The first was that several teachers were circulating a letter requesting Perkins' removal as a housemaster because they felt he could not control the house or direct the faculty. This surprised King because he had heard that Perkins was widely respected within the faculty and had earned a reputation for supporting high academic standards and for working tirelessly with new teachers. However, as King inquired further he discovered that Perkins was greatly liked within the faculty but was also generally recognized as a poor housemaster. The second piece of information concerned how Perkins' house compared with the others. Although students had been randomly assigned to each house, Perkins' house had the largest absence rate and the greatest number of disciplinary problems in the school. Smith had also told him that Perkins' dropout rate for 1969–70 was three times that of any other house.

While King was in the process of interviewing his staff he was called on by Mr. David Crimmins, chairman of the History Department. Crimmins was a native of Great Ridge, white, and in his late 40s. Crimmins was scheduled for an appointment the following week, but asked King if he could see him immediately. Crimmins said he wanted to talk with King because he had heard that a letter was being circulated asking for Perkins' removal and that he wanted to present the other side of the argument. Crimmins became very emotional during the conversation, and said that Perkins was viewed by many of the teachers and department chairmen as the only housemaster who was making an effort to maintain high academic standards, and that his transfer would be seen as a blow to those concerned with quality education. He also described in detail Perkins' devotion and commitment to the school and the fact that Perkins was the only administrator with the ability to straighten out the schedule, and that he had done this in addition to all of his other duties. Crimmins departed by saying that if Perkins were transferred, that he, Crimmins, would personally write a letter to the regional accreditation council telling them how badly standards had sunk at Kennedy. King assured him that it would not be necessary to take such a drastic measure and that a cooperative resolution would be found. King was aware of the accreditation review that Kennedy High faced the following April and he did not wish to complicate the process unnecessarily in any way.

Within 20 minutes of Crimmins' departure, King was visited by a young white teacher named Tim Shea who said that he had heard that Crimmins had come in to see him. Shea said that he was one of the teachers who organized the movement to get rid of Perkins. Shea said that he liked and admired Perkins very much because of his devotion to the school but that Perkins' house was so disorganized and discipline so bad that it was nearly impossible to do any good teaching. Shea added that it was "a shame to lock the school up when stronger leadership is all that's needed."

King's impressions of his administrators generally matched what he had heard about them before arriving at the school. Carver seemed to be a very bright, innovative, and charismatic leader whose mere presence generated excitement. Czepak seemed to be a highly competent, though not very imaginative administrator, who had earned the respect of his faculty and students. Bonavota, who was only 26, seemed very bright and earnest but unseasoned and unsure of himself. King felt that with a little guidance and training Bonavota might have the greatest promise of all. At the moment, however, he appeared to be a very uncertain and somewhat confused person who had difficulty simply coping.

Perkins seemed to be a very sincere, and devoted person who had a good mind for administrative details but an almost total incapacity for leadership.

King knew that he would have the opportunity to make several administrative appointments because of the three vacancies which existed. Indeed, should Smith resign as vice principal, King would be in the position of filling both vice principalships. He knew that his recommendations for these positions would carry a great deal of weight with the central office. The only constraint that King felt in making these appointments was the need to achieve some kind of racial balance among the Kennedy administrative group. With his own appointment as principal, the number of black administrators exceeded the number of white administrators by a ratio of two to one, and as yet Kennedy did not have a single Puerto Rican administrator even though a third of its pupils had Spanish surnames.

THE FRIDAY AFTERNOON MEETING

In contrast to the individual interviews, King was surprised to find how quiet and conflict-free these same people were in the staff meeting that he called on Friday. He was amazed at how slow, polite, and friendly the conversation appeared to be among people who had so vehemently expressed negative opinions of each other in private. After about 45 minutes of discussion about the upcoming accreditation review, King broached the subject of housemaster-department head relations. The ensuing silence was finally broken by a joke which Czepak made about the uselessness of discussing that topic. King probed further by asking whether everyone was happy with the current practices. Crimmins suggested that this was a topic that might be better discussed in a smaller group. Everyone in the room seemed to agree with Crimmins except for Betsy Dula, a young white woman in her late 20s who was chairman of the English department. She said that one of the problems with the school was that no one was willing to tackle tough issues until they exploded. She said that relations between housemasters and department heads were terrible and it made her job very difficult. She then attacked Chauncey Carver for impeding her evaluation of a nontenured teacher in Carver's house. The two argued for several minutes about the teacher and the quality of the experimental Sophomore English course that the teacher was giving. Finally, Carver, who by now was quite angry, coldly warned Mrs. Dula that he would "break her neck" if she stepped into his house again. King intervened in an attempt to cool both their tempers and the meeting ended shortly thereafter.

The following morning, Mrs. Dula called King at home and told him that unless Chauncey Carver publicly apologized for his threat, she would file a grievance with the teachers' union and take it to court if necessary. King assured Mrs. Dula that he would talk with Carver on Monday. King then called Eleanor Debbs, one of the school's Math teachers whom he had known well for many years and whose judgment he respected. Mrs. Debbs was a close friend of both Carver and Mrs.

Dula and was also vice president of the city's teachers' union. He learned from her that both had been long-term adversaries but that she felt both were excellent professionals.

She also reported that Mrs. Dula would be a formidable opponent and could muster considerable support among the faculty. Mrs. Debbs, who was herself black, feared that a confrontation between Dula and Carver might create tensions along race lines within the school even though both Dula and Carver were generally quite popular with students of all races. Mrs. Debbs strongly urged King not to let the matter drop. Mrs. Debbs also told him that she had overheard Bill Smith, the vice principal, say at a party the preceding night that he felt that King didn't have either the stomach or the forcefulness necessary to survive at Kennedy. Smith further stated that the only reason he was staying was that he did not expect King to last the year. Should that prove to be the case, Smith felt that he would be appointed principal.

The accomplishment of purpose: Organizational processes and behavior

Our study of strategy has brought us to the prescription that organizational structure must follow strategy if implementation is to be effective. We have seen that structural design involves inevitably (1) a suitable specialization of task, (2) a parallel provision for coordination, and (3) information systems for meeting the requirement that specialists be well informed and their work coordinated. We have seen that a variety of structures may be suitable to a strategy so long as the performance influenced by structural characteristics is not diverted from strategic ends.

We turn now from structural considerations to other influences upon organizational behavior. A logical structure does not ensure effective organized effort any more than a high degree of technical skill in individual members insures achievement of organizational purposes. We suggest the following proposition for testing in your analysis of cases: *Organizational performance is effective to the extent that (in an atmosphere deliberately created to encourage the development of required skills and to provide the satisfactions of personal progress) individual energy is successfully directed toward organizational goals.* Convergence of energy upon purpose is made effective by individual and group commitment to purpose.

Man-made and natural organizational *systems* and *processes* are available to influence individual development and performance. In any organization the system which relates specific influences upon behavior to each other (so as to constitute an ultimate impact upon behavior) is made up of some six elements: (1) standards, (2) measures, (3) incentives, (4) rewards, (5) penalties, and (6) controls. The distinguishing characteristic of a system, of course, is the interaction of its elements. This interdependence will vary from organization to organization and from situation to situation and cannot always be observed, controlled, or completely analyzed.

The familiar processes which bear on performance are (1) measurement, (2) evaluation, (3) motivation, (4) control, and (5) individual development. The most important aspects of a process are the speed and direction of its forward motion and the nature of its side effects. So far as the uniqueness of each company situation allows, we shall look at combinations of these organizational systems and processes in the following order:

1. The establishment of standards and measurement of performance.
2. The administration of motivation and incentive systems.
3. The operation of systems of restraint and control.
4. The recruitment and development of management.

These processes have been studied in detail by specialists of several kinds. We shall not attempt to extract all the wisdom or expose all the folly which, over the years, has accumulated in the study of human relations and organizational behavior. We are now concerned, as always, with the limited but important ways in which specialized bodies of knowledge can be put to use in the implementation of strategy. The idea of strategy will dominate our approach to the internal organizational systems which animate structure, just as it dominated our discussion of the factors that determine structure itself. It may be desirable to point out that our aim is not to coerce and manipulate unwilling individuals. It is instead to support and direct individuals who are at least assenting to or, more desirably, committed to organizational goals. Commitment to purpose remains in our scheme of things the overriding necessary condition of effective accomplishment.

ESTABLISHMENT OF STANDARDS AND MEASUREMENT OF PERFORMANCE

If progress toward goals is to be supervised at all, it will have to be observed and measured. If it is to be measured, whether quantitatively or qualitatively, there must be some idea of where an organization is compared to where it ought to be. To state where an organization ought to be is to set a standard. A standard takes shape as a projection of hoped-for or budgeted performance. As time passes, positive and negative variances between budgeted and actual performance are recorded. This comparison makes possible, although it does not necessarily justify, relating incentives and controls to performance as measured against standards. For example, managers in the Hilton Hotels group prepare detailed forecasts of their anticipated revenues, costs, and operating profits, all based on past records and future projections that take growth targets into account. The reward system recognizes not only good results but accuracy of forecasting.

It is virtually impossible to make meaningful generalizations about how proper standards might be set in particular companies. It can be said, however, that in any organization the overall strategy can be translated into more or less detailed future plans (the detail becoming less predictable as the time span grows longer), which permit comparison of actual with predicted performance. Whether standards are being set at exactly the proper level is less significant than the fact that an effort is being made to raise them steadily as organizational power and resources increase. External events may, however, invalidate predictions. It must be recognized that for good reasons as well as bad, standards are not always attainable. Hence the need for skill in variable budgeting.

By far the most important problem of measurement is that increased interest in the measurement of performance against standards brings increased danger that the executive evaluation program may encourage performance which detracts from rather than supports the overall strategy.

The temptation to use measurement primarily for the purpose of judging executive performance is acute. The desire to put management responsibility in the ablest hands leads to comparing managers in terms of results. Failure to meet a standard leads naturally to the assignment of blame to persons. The general manager's most urgent duty is to see that planned results are indeed accomplished. Such pressure, unfortunately, may lead to exaggerated respect for specific measures and for the short-run results they quantify, and thus to ultimate misevaluation of performance.

Fallacy of the single criterion

The problems of measurement cluster about the fallacy of the single criterion. When any single measure like return on investment, for example, is used to determine the compensation, promotion, or reassignment of a manager, the resultant behavior will often lead to unplanned and undesired outcomes. No single measure can encompass the total contribution of an individual either to immediate and longer term results or to the efforts of others. The sensitivity of individuals to evaluation leads them to produce the performance that will measure up in terms of the criterion rather than in terms of more important purposes. Since managers respond to the measures management actually takes to reward performance, mere verbal exhortations to behave in the manner required by long-range strategy carry no weight, and cannot be relied upon to preclude undesirable actions encouraged by a poorly designed measurement and reward system.

Faith in the efficacy of a standard measure like return on investment can reach extreme proportions, especially among managers to whom the idea of strategy is apparently unfamiliar. Instances in which performance is measured in terms of just one figure or ratio are so numerous as to suggest that the pursuit of quantification and measurement as such has overshadowed the real goal of management evaluation. If we return to our original hypothesis that profit and return on investment are terms that can be usefully employed to denote the results to be sought by business, but are too general to characterize its distinctive mission or purpose, then we must say that *short-term profitability is not by itself an adequate measure of managerial performance*. Return on investment, when used alone, is another dangerous criterion, since it can lead businessmen to postpone needed product research or the modernization of facilities in the interest of keeping down the investment on the basis of which their performance is measured. Certainly we must conclude that evaluation of performance must not be focused exclusively upon the criterion of short-run profitability or any other single standard which may cause managers to act contrary to the long-range interests of the company as a whole.

Need for multiple criteria

As you discuss the cases that follow, you will be concerned with developing more adequate criteria. Our concern for strategy naturally leads us to suggest that the management evaluation system which plays so great a part in influencing management performance must employ a number of criteria, some of which are subjective and thus difficult to quantify. It is easy to argue that subjective judgments ·are unfair. But use of a harmful or irrelevant criterion just because it leads itself to quantification is a poor exchange for alleged objectivity.

Against multiple criteria, it may be argued that they restrict the freedom of the profit-center manager to produce the results required through any means he elects. This may of course be true, but the manager who does not want his methods to be subject to scrutiny does not want to be judged. Accountants, sometimes indifferent to the imperfections of their figures and the artificiality of their conventions, do not always make clear the true meaning of an annual profit figure or the extent to which a sharp rise from one year to the next may reflect a decision not to make investments needed to sustain the future of a product line.

If multiple criteria are to be used, it is not enough for top management simply to announce that short-term profitability and return on investment are only two measures among many—including responsibility to society—by which executives are going to be judged. To give subordinates freedom to exercise judgment and simultaneously to demand profitability produces an enormous pressure which cannot be effectively controlled by endless talk about tying rewards to factors other than profit.

The tragic predicament of people who, though upright in other ways, engage in bribery, "questionable payments," price fixing, and subtler forms of corruption and of their superiors who are often unaware of these practices, should dramatize one serious flaw of the profit center form of organization. Characteristically management expects this format to solve the problems of evaluation by decentralizing freedom of decision to subordinates so long as profit objectives are met. Decentralization seems sometimes to serve as a cloak for nonsupervision, except for the control implicit in the superficial measure of profitability. It would appear to preclude accurate evaluation, and the use of multiple criteria may indeed make a full measure of decentralization inappropriate.

Effective evaluation of performance

To delegate authority to profit centers and to base evaluation upon proper performance must not mean that the profit center's strategic decisions are left unsupervised. *Even under decentralization, top management must remain familiar with divisional substrategy, with the fortunes —good and bad—that attend implementation, and with the problems involved in attempting to achieve budgeted performance.* The true function of measurement is to increase perceptions of the problems limiting achievement. If an individual sees where he stands in meeting a schedule, he may be led to inquire why he is not somewhere else. If this kind of question is not asked, the answer is not proffered. An effective system of evaluation must include information which will allow top management to understand the problems faced by subordinates in achieving the results for which they are held responsible. And certainly if evaluation is to be comprehensive enough to avoid the distortions cited thus far, immediate results will not be the only object of evaluation. The effectiveness with which problems are handled along the way will be evaluated, even though this judgment, like most of the important decisions of management, must remain subjective.

The process of formulating and implementing strategy, which is supervised directly by the chief executive in a single-unit company, can be shared widely in a multiunit company. It can be the theme of the information exchanged between organization levels. Preoccupation with final results need not be so exclusive as to prevent top management from working with divisional management in establishing objectives and policies or in formulating plans to meet objectives. Such joint endeavor helps to ensure that divisional performance will not be evaluated without full knowledge of the problems encountered in implementation.

When the diversified company becomes so large that this process is impracticable, then new means must be devised. *Implicit in accurate evaluation is familiarity with performance on a basis other than through accounting figures.*

The division of corporate strategy into substrategies appropriate to each organization unit makes possible a meaningful "management by objectives" program. As superior and subordinate agree to the achievements which the subordinate will try to accomplish during the forthcoming year, priorities are dictated by strategy. The selection of objectives can be checked for the contribution they will make to the larger strategy of which they must be a part. The opportunity to discuss the relevance of a conventional objective to the total purpose of the effort undertaken can be invaluable in reconciling strategy and motivation. Quantitatively unmeasurable tasks, as well as budget items, can be included in the individual's own program of action. The concept of strategy encompassing the grand purposes of the entire firm can be brought down through each discussion to a limited strategy to guide and permit evaluation of individual effort.

A shared interest in the problems to be overcome in successfully implementing individual strategy makes possible a kind of communication, an accuracy of evaluation, and a constructive influence on behavior that cannot be approached by application of a single criterion. For one manager as for a whole company, the quality of objective and of subsequent attempts to overcome obstacles posed by circumstance and by competition is the most important aspect of a manager's performance to be evaluated.

MOTIVATION AND INCENTIVE SYSTEMS

The influences upon behavior in any organization are visible and invisible, planned and unplanned, formal and not formal. The intent to measure affects the performance which is the object of measurement; cause and effect obscure each other. The executive who refuses to leave the implementation of strategy to chance has available diverse means of encouraging behavior which advances strategy and deterring behavior which does not. The positive elements, always organized in patterns which make them influential in given situations, may be designated as motivation and incentive systems. The negative elements, similarly patterned, can be grouped as systems of restraint and control. Organization studies have led their authors variously to prefer positive or negative signals and to conclude that one or the other is preferable. The general manager will do well to conclude that each is indispensable.

Executive compensation

Whatever the necessity for and the difficulties of performance evaluation, the effort to encourage and reward takes precedence over the effort to deter and restrain. Thus, properly directed, incentives may have more positive effects than control. Certainly, general manager-strategists, whose own prior experiences are likely to have made them intensely interested in the subject of executive compensation, should welcome whatever guidance they can get from researchers or staff assistants working in the field of job evaluation and compensation. Unfortunately, here also the prevailing thinking is often oriented less toward the goals to be sought than toward the requirements of the systems adopted.

Executives, like workers, are influenced by nonmonetary as well as financial incentives. At the same time, financial rewards are very important, and much thought has been given to equitable compensation of executives.

Unfortunately for the analyst of executive performance, it is harder to describe for executives than for operators at the machine what they do and how they spend their time. The terminology of job descriptions is full of phrases like "has responsibility for," "maintains relationships with," and "supervises the operation of." The activities of planning, problem solving, and directing or administering are virtually invisible. And the activities of recruiting, training, and developing subordinates are hardly more concretely identifiable.

In any case, it is fallacious to assume that quality of performance is the only basis for the compensation of executives. Many other factors must be taken into account. The job itself has certain characteristics that help to determine the pay schedules. These include complexity of the work, the general education required, and the knowledge or technical training needed. Compensation also reflects the responsibility of job-incumbents for people and property, the nature and number of decisions they must make, and the effect of their activities and decisions upon profits.

In addition to reflecting the quality of performance and the nature of the job, an executive's compensation must also have some logical relationship to rewards paid to others in the same organization. That is, the compensation system must reflect in some way a person's position in the hierarchy. On any one ladder there must be suitable steps between levels from top to bottom, if incentive is to be provided and increased scope recognized. At the same time, adjustments must be made to reflect the varying contributions that can be expected from individuals in the hierarchy of the staff versus that of the line.

Furthermore, in a compensation system, factors pertaining to the individual are almost as important as those pertaining to performance, the job, or the structure of the organization. People's age and length of service, the state of their health, some notion of their future potential, some idea of their material needs, and some insight into their views about all of these should influence either the amount of total pay or the distribution of total pay among base salary, bonuses, stock options, and other incentive measures.

Besides the many factors already listed, still another set of influences —this time coming from the environment—ordinarily affects the level of executive compensation. Included here are regional differences in the cost of living, the increments allowed for overseas assignment, the market price of given qualifications and experience, the level of local taxation, the desire for tax avoidance or delay, and the effect of high business salaries on other professions.

Just as multiple criteria are appropriate for the evaluation of performance, so many considerations must be taken into account in the compensation of executives. The company which says it pays only for results does not know what it is doing.[1]

Role of incentive pay

In addition to the problem of deciding what factors to reward, there is the equally complex issue of deciding what forms compensation should take. We would emphasize that financial rewards are especially important in business, and no matter how great the enthusiasm of people for their work, attention to the level of executive salary is an important ingredient in the achievement of strategy. Even after the desired standard of living is attained, money is still an effective incentive. Businessmen used to the struggle for profit find satisfaction in their own growing net worth.

There is no question about the desirability of paying high salaries for work of great value. Yet until recently, it was clearly social policy in the United States, as elsewhere, that executive take-home pay be kept at a modest ceiling. As a consequence, profit sharing, executive bonuses,

---

[1] See Malcolm S. Saltor and K. R. Sririvasa Murthy, "Should CEO Pay Be Linked to Results?" *Harvard Business Review*, May–June 1975, pp. 66–73.

stock options, performance shares, stock purchase plans, deferred compensation contracts, pensions, insurance, savings plans, and other fringe benefits have multiplied enormously. They have been directed not so much toward providing incentive as toward enabling executives to avoid high taxes on current income. It is as incentives, however, that these various devices should be judged. Regarded as incentives to reward *individual* performance, many of these devices encounter two immediate objections, quite aside from the ethics of their tax-avoidance features. First, how compatible are the assumptions back of such rewards with the aspirations of the businessman to be viewed as a professional person? The student who begins to think of business as a profession will wonder what kind of executive will perform better with a profit sharing bonus than with an equivalent salary. We may ask whether doctors should be paid according to the longevity of their patients and whether surgeons would try harder if given a bonus when their patients survived an operation. Second, how feasible is it to distinguish any one individual's contribution to the total accomplishment of the company? And even if contribution could be distinguished and correctly measured, what about the implications of the fact that the funds available for added incentive payments are a function of total rather than of individual performance? In view of these considerations, it can at least be argued that incentives for individual performance reflect dubious assumptions.

If, then, incentives are ruled out as an inappropriate or impractical means of rewarding individual effort, should they be cast out altogether? We believe not. There is certainly some merit in giving stock options or performance shares to the group of executives most responsible for strategy decisions, if the purpose is to assure reward for attention to the middle and longer run future.[2] There is some rationale for giving the same group current or even deferred bonuses, the amount of which is tied to annual profit, if the purpose is to motivate better cost control— something surprisingly difficult to do in a business environment marked by inflation, booming sales, and high income taxes. Certainly, too, incentive payments to the key executive group must be condoned where needed to attract and hold the scarce managerial talent without which any strategy will suffer.

In any case, as you examine the effort made by companies to provide adequate rewards, to stimulate effective executive performance, and to inspire commitment to organizational purposes, you will wish to look closely at the relation between the incentive offered and the kind of performance needed. This observation holds as true, of course, for nonmonetary as it does for financial rewards.

Nonmonetary incentives

The area of nonmonetary incentive systems is even more difficult to traverse quickly than that of financial objectives. Executives, as human

---

[2] G. H. Foote, *Performance Shares Revitalize Stock Plans, Harvard Business Review,* November–December 1973, pp. 121–30.

as other employees, are as much affected as anyone else by pride in accomplishment, the climate for free expression, pleasure in able and honest associates, and satisfaction in work worth doing.

They are said to be moved also by status symbols like office carpets, thermos sets, or office location and size. The trappings of rank and small symbols of authority are too widely cultivated to be regarded as unimportant, but little is known of their real influence. If individual contribution to organized effort is abundantly clear, little attention is likely to be given to status symbols. For example, the R&D executive with the greatest contributions to the product line may favor the "reverse status symbol" of the lab technician's cotton jacket. This is not to say that symbols have no potentially useful role to play. Office decor, for example, can be used to symbolize strategy, as when a company introduces abstract art into its central office to help dramatize its break with the past.

Very little systematic work has been done to determine what incentives or company climate might be most conducive to executive creativity, executive commitment to forward planning, executive dedication to the training of subordinates, executive striving for personal development and growth, or commitment to high standards of personal and corporate integrity. All these are of utmost value, but their impact is long-run and in part intangible. It is well known, however, that the climate most commonly extolled by managers is one where they have freedom to experiment and apply their own ideas without unnecessary constraints. This type of positive incentive is particularly suited for use in combination with the "management-by-objectives" approach to the problem of executive evaluation. Given clear objectives and a broad consensus, then latitude can be safely granted to executives to choose their own course—so long as they do not conceal the problems they encounter. In other words, executives can be presumed to respond to the conditions likely to encourage the goal-oriented behavior expected of them.

We may not always know the influence exerted by evaluation, compensation, and advancement, but if we keep purpose clear and incentive systems simple, we may keep unintended distractions to a minimum. Above all, we should be able to see the relevance to desired outcomes of the rewards offered. The harder it is to relate achievement to motives, the more cautious we should be in proposing an incentives program.

SYSTEMS OF RESTRAINT AND CONTROL

Like the system of incentives, the system of restraints and controls should be designed with the requirements of strategy in mind, rather than the niceties of complex techniques and procedures. It is the function of penalties and controls to enforce rather than to encourage—to inhibit strategically undesirable behavior rather than to create new patterns. Motivation, as we have said, is a complex of both positive and negative influences. Working in conjunction, these induce desired performance and inhibit undesirable behavior.

The need for controls—even at the executive level—is rooted in the central facts of organization itself. The inevitable consequence of divided activity is the emergence of substrategies, which are at least slightly deflected from the true course by the needs of individuals and the concepts and procedures of specialized groups, each with its own quasi-professional precepts and ideals. We must have controls, therefore, even in healthy and competent organizations manned by people of goodwill who are aware of organization purpose.

Formal control

Like other aspects of organizational structure and processes, controls may be both formal and informal, that is, both prescribed and emergent. Both types are needed, and both are important. It is, however, in the nature of things that management is more likely to give explicit attention to the formal controls that it has itself prescribed than to the informal controls emergent within particular groups or subgroups.

Formal and informal controls differ in nature as well as in their genesis. The former have to do with data that are quantifiable, the latter with subjective values and behavior. Formal control derives from accounting; it reflects the conventions and assumptions of that discipline and implies the prior importance of what can be quantified over what cannot. Its influence arises from the responsiveness of individuals—if subject to supervision and appraisal—to information that reveals variances between what is recorded as being expected of them and what is recorded as being achieved. If the information depicts variances from strategically desirable behavior, then it tends to direct attention toward strategic goals and to support goal-oriented policy. But if, as is more often the case, the information simply focuses on those short-run results which the state of the art can measure, then it directs effort toward performance which, if not undesirable, is at least biased toward short-run objectives.

To emphasize the probable shortcomings of formal or quantifiable controls is not to assert that they have no value. Numbers do influence behavior—especially when pressures are applied to subordinates by superiors contemplating the same numbers. Numbers are essential in complex organizations, since personal acquaintance with what is being accomplished and personal surveillance over it by an owner-manager is no longer possible. As we have seen, the performance of individuals and subunits cannot be left to chance, even when acceptance and understanding of policy have been indicated and adequate competence and judgment are assured. Whether for surveillance from above or for self-control and self-guidance, numbers have a meaningful role to play, and well-selected numbers have a very meaningful role. We in no way mean to diminish the importance of figures, but only to emphasize that figures must be supplemented by informal or social controls.

Integrating formal and social control

Just as the idea of formal control is derived from accounting, the idea of informal control is derived from the inquiries of the behavioral sciences into the nature of organizational behavior. In all functioning groups, norms develop to which individuals are responsive if not obedient. These norms constitute the accepted way of doing things; they define the limits of proper behavior, and the type of action that will meet with approval from the group. In view of the way they operate, the control we have in mind is better described as *social* rather than *informal*. It is embedded in the activities, interactions, and sentiments characterizing group behavior. Sentiments take the form of likes and dislikes among people and evaluative judgments exercised upon each other. Negative sentiments, of great importance to their objects, may be activated by individual departure from a norm; such sentiments can either constitute a punishment in themselves, or can lead to some other form of punishment.

The shortcomings of formal control based on quantitative measurements of performance can be largely obviated by designing and implementing a system in which formal and social controls are integrated. For example, meetings of groups of managers to discuss control reports can facilitate inquiry into the significance of problems lying behind variances, can widen the range of solutions considered, and can bring pressure to bear from peers as well as from superiors. All these features can in turn contribute to finding a new course of action which addresses the problem rather than the figures.

Enforcing ethical standards

One of the most vexing problems in attempting to establish a functional system of formal and social controls lies in the area of ethical standards. In difficult competitive situations, the pressure for results can lead individuals into illegal and unethical practices. Instead of countering this tendency, group norms may encourage yielding to these pressures. For example, knowing that others were doing the same thing undoubtedly influenced foreign representatives of several aircraft companies to bribe government officials to secure contracts. Recurring violations of price-fixing regulations, in industries beset by overcapacity and aggressive competition, are sometimes responses to pressures to meet sales and profit expectations of a distant home office. On a lesser scale group norms can be supportive of suppliers making expensive gifts to purchasing agents, or to sales representatives offering extravagant entertainment to customers. The post-Watergate climate of the middle and late 1970s has modified sharply the general attitude toward long-established dubious practices. The environment is at least temporarily favorable to maintaining high ethical standards.

When top management refuses to condone pursuit of company goals by unethical methods, it must resort to penalties like dismissal that are severe enough to dramatize its opposition. If a division sales manager, who is caught having arranged call-girl attentions for an important customer, against both the standards of expected behavior and the policy of the company, is not penalized at all, or only mildly, because of the volume of his sales and the profit he generates, ethical standards will not long be of great importance. If he is fired, then his successor is likely to think twice about the means he employs to achieve the organizational purposes that are assigned to him. When, as happened in mid-1977, a regional vice president of a large insurance firm was fired for misappropriating $250,000 of expense money, but was retained as a consultant because he controlled several millions of revenue, mixed signals are given which may confuse the communication but call attention to the dilemmas of enforcement. In due course the Internal Revenue Service may add an unambiguous comment on this transaction.

But there are limits to the effectiveness of punishment, in companies as well as in families and in society. If violations are not detected, the fear of punishment tends to weaken. A system of inspection is therefore implicit in formal control. But besides its expense and complexity, such policing of behavior has the drawback of adversely affecting the attitudes of people toward their organizations. Their commitment to creative accomplishment is likely to be shaken, especially if they are the kind of persons who are not likely to cut corners in the performance of their duties. To undermine the motivation of the ethically inclined is a high price to pay for detection of the weak. It is the special task of the Internal Audit function and the Audit Committee of the corporate board of directors not only to make investigation more effective but to minimize its negative police-state connotations and distortions.

The student of general management is thus confronted by a dilemma: if an organization is sufficiently decentralized to permit individuals to develop new solutions to problems and new avenues to corporate achievement, then the opportunity for wrongdoing cannot be eliminated. This being so, a system of controls must be supplemented by a selective system of executive recruitment and training. No system of control, no program of rewards and penalties, no procedures of measuring and evaluating performance can take the place of the individual who has a clear idea of right and wrong, a consistent personal policy, and the strength to stand the gaff when results suffer because he or she stands firm. This kind of person is different from the human animal who grasps at every proferred reward and flinches at every punishment. His or her development is greatly assisted by the systems, standards, rewards, incentives, penalties, and controls which permit the application of qualitative criteria and avoid the oversimplification of numerical measures. It is always the way systems are administered that determines their ultimate usefulness and impact.

RECRUITMENT AND DEVELOPMENT OF MANAGEMENT

Organizational behavior, in the view we have just taken of it, is the product of interacting *systems* of measures, motives, standards, incentives, rewards, penalties, and controls. Put another way, behavior is the outcome of *processes* of measurement, evaluation, motivation, and control. These systems and processes affect and shape the development of all individuals, most crucially those in management positions. Management development is therefore an ongoing process in all organizations, whether planned or not. As you examine cases which permit a wide-angled view of organizational activities, it is appropriate to inquire into the need to plan this development, rather than to let it occur as it will.

In days gone by, before it was generally realized that relying on a consciously designated corporate strategy was far safer and more productive than simply trusting to good luck, a widely shared set of assumptions operated to inhibit the emergence of management development programs. These assumptions, which include the implication that managers are all male, have been described as follows:

1. Good management is instinct in action. A number of men are born with the qualities of energy, shrewdness of judgment, ambition, and capacity for responsibility. These men become the leaders of business.
2. A man prepares himself for advancement by performing well in his present job. The man who does best in competition with his fellows is best qualified to lead them.
3. If an organization does not happen to have adequate numbers of men with innate qualities of leadership who are equal to higher responsibilities, it may bring in such persons from other companies.
4. Men with the proper amount of ambition do not need to be "motivated" to demonstrate the personal qualities which qualify them for advancement.
5. Management cannot be taught formally—in school or anywhere else.[3]

The ideas that we have been examining here suggest that these assumptions are obsolete. People are, of course, born with different innate characteristics, but none of these precludes acquiring knowledge, attitudes, and skills which fill the gap between an identifiable personality trait and executive action. Good performance in lesser jobs is expected of persons considered for bigger jobs, but different and additional qualifications are required for higher responsibility. Thus the most scholarly professor, the most dexterous machine operator, and the most persuasive sales representative do not necessarily make a good college president, foreman, and sales manager. The abilities that make the difference can be learned from experience or to some extent from formal education. As a substitute for training and supplying the requisite experience internally, companies can import managers trained by competitors, but this approach, though sometimes unavoidable, is risky and expensive. The risk lies in the relative difficulty of appraising the quality of outsiders and estimating their ability to transfer their technical effectiveness to a new organization. The cost lies chiefly in the disruption of natural internal incentive systems.

The supply of men and women who, of their own volition, can or will arrange for their own development is smaller than required. Advances in technology, the internationalization of markets, and the progress of research on information processing and organizational behavior all

---

[3] K. R. Andrews, *The Effectiveness of University Management Development Programs* (Boston: Division of Research, the Harvard Graduate School of Business Administration, 1966), p. 232.

make it absurd to suppose that persons can learn all they will need to know from what they are currently doing. In particular, the activities of the general manager differ so much in kind from those of other management that special preparation for the top job should be considered, unless it is demonstrably impossible.

The success of company-sponsored and university management training programs is evidence that the old idea that managers are born not made has been displaced by the proposition that managers are born with capacities which can be developed. In the process of seeing to it that the company is adequately manned to implement its strategy, we can identify training requirements. In other words, strategy can be our guide to (1) the skills which will be required to perform the critical tasks; (2) the number of persons with specific skill, age, and experience characteristics who will be required in the light of planned growth and predicted attrition; and (3) the number of new individuals of requisite potential who must be recruited to ensure the availability, at the appropriate time, of skills that require years to develop.

Advanced recruitment

No matter what the outcome of these calculations, it can safely be said that every organization must actively recruit new talent if it aims to maintain its position and to grow. These recruits should have adequate ability not only for filling the junior positions to which they are initially called, but also for learning the management skills needed to advance to higher positions. Like planning of all kinds, recruiting must be done well ahead of the actual need.

Men and women with the ultimate capacity to become general managers should be sought out in their 20s, for able people today in a society in which the level of education as well as economic means is rising rapidly are looking more for careers than jobs. Companies should recruit—not meeting the needs for specific skills alone but making an investment in the caliber of executives who in 25 years will be overseeing activities not even contemplated at the time of their joining the company.

One of the principal impediments to effective execution of plans is shortage of management manpower of the breadth required at the time required. This shortage is the result of faulty planning, not of a natural scarcity of good raw material. Consider the bank that wishes to open 50 branches overseas as part of its international expansion. It will not be able to export and replace 50 branch managers unless, years earlier, deliberate attention has been given to securing and to training banker-administrators. These are not technicians who know only credit, for example; they must know how to preside over an entire if small bank, learn and speak a foreign language, establish and maintain relationships with a foreign government, and provide banking services not for an exclusively American but for a different group of individual and corporate customers.

After successful recruitment of candidates with high potential, speeding the course of management development is usually the only way to keep manpower planning in phase with the requirements of strategy. Thus the recruit should be put to work at a job which uses the abilities he has and challenges him to acquire the knowledge he lacks about the company and industry:

> For [people] educated in this generation sweeping out the stockroom or carrying samples to the quality control laboratory are inappropriate unless these activities demand their level of education or will teach them something besides humility. To introduce the school-trained men [and women] of high promise to everyday affairs may mean the devising of jobs which have not existed hitherto. Expansion of analytical sections and accounting and financial departments, projects in market research, rudimentary exploratory investigations in new products departments, process control or data processing projects are all work which will use school-taught techniques and yet require practical and essential exposure to the company and solutions to the problem of establishing working relationships with old hands.[4]

The labor force requirements imposed by commitment to a strategy of growth mean quite simply that men and women overqualified for conventional beginning assignments must be sought out and carefully cultivated thereafter. Individuals who respond well to the opportunities devised for them should be assigned to established organization positions and given responsibility as fast as capacity to absorb it is indicated. To promote rapidly is not the point so much as to maintain the initial momentum and to provide work to highly qualified individuals that is both essential and challenging.

Continuing education

The rise of professional business education and the development of advanced management programs make formal training available to men and women not only at the beginning of their careers but also at appropriate intervals thereafter. Short courses for executives are almost always stimulating and often of permanent value. But management development as such is predominantly an organizational process which must be supported, not thwarted, by the incentive and control systems to which we have already alluded. Distribution of rewards and penalties will effectively determine how much attention executives will give to the training of their subordinates. No amount of lip service will take the place of action in establishing effective management development as an important management activity. To evaluate managers in part on their effort and effectiveness in bringing along their juniors requires subjective measures and a time span longer than one fiscal year. These limitations do not seriously impede judgment, especially when both strategy and the urgency of its implications for manpower development are clearly known.

In designing on-the-job training, a focus on strategy makes possible a substantial economy of effort, in that management development and management evaluation can be carried on together. The evaluation of

---

[4] Ibid., pp. 240–41.

performance can be simultaneously administered as an instrument of development. For example, any manager could use a conference with his superiors not only to discuss variances from budgeted departmental performance, but also to discover how far his or her suggested solutions are appropriate or inappropriate and why. In all such cases, discussion of objectives proposed, problems encountered, and results obtained provide opportunities for inquiry, for instruction and counsel, for learning what needs to be done and at what level of effectiveness.

Besides providing an ideal opportunity for learning, concentration on objectives permits delegation to juniors of choice of means and other decision-making responsibilities otherwise hard to come by. Throughout the top levels of the corporation, if senior management is spending adequate time on the surveillance of the environment and on the study of strategic alternatives, then the responsibility for day-to-day operations must necessarily be delegated. Since juniors cannot learn how to bear responsibility without having it, this necessity is of itself conducive to learning. If, within limits, responsibility for the choice of means to obtain objectives is also delegated, opportunity is presented for innovation, experimentation, and creative approaches to problem solving. Where ends rather than means are the object of attention and agreement exists on what ends are and should be, means may be allowed to vary at the discretion of the developing junior manager. The clearer the company's goals, the smaller the emphasis that must be placed on uniformity, and the greater the opportunity for initiative. Freedom to make mistakes and achieve success is more productive in developing executive skills than practice in following detailed how-to-do-it instructions designed by superiors or staff specialists. Commitment to purpose rather than to procedures appears to energize initiative.

Management development and corporate purpose

A stress on purpose rather than on procedures suggests that organizational climate, though intangible, is more important to individual growth than the mechanisms of personnel administration. The development of each individual in the direction best suited both to his or her own powers and to organizational needs is most likely to take place in the company where everybody is encouraged to work at the height of his or her ability and is rewarded for doing so. Such a company must have a clear idea of what it is and what it intends to become. With this idea sufficiently institutionalized so that organization members grow committed to it, the effort required for achievement will be forthcoming without elaborate incentives and coercive controls. Purpose, especially if considered worth accomplishing, is the most powerful incentive to accomplishment. If goals are not set high enough, they must be reset— as high as developing creativity and accelerating momentum suggest.

In short, from the point of view of general management, management development is not a combination of staff activities and formal training designed to provide neophites with a common body of knowledge, or to produce a generalized good manager. Rather, development is inextricably linked to organizational purpose, which shapes to its own requirements the kind, rate, and amount of development which takes place. It is a process by which men and women are professionally equipped to be—as far as possible in advance of the need—what the evolving strategy of the firm requires them to be, at the required level of excellence.

Chief executives will have a special interest of their own in the process of management development. For standards of performance, measures for accurate evaluation, incentives, and controls will have a lower priority in their eyes than a committed organization, manned by people who know what they are supposed to do and committed to the overall ends to which their particular activities contribute. Senior managers are not blind to the needs of their subordinates to serve their own purposes as well as those of the organization. Wherever conflicting claims are made upon their attention, they require that reconciliation be found that does not obscure organizational objectives or slow down the action being taken to attain them.

*   *   *   *   *

In examining the cases that follow, try to identify the strategy of the company and the structure of relationships established to implement it. Note the standards that have been established for measurement purposes. Are they appropriate for measuring the progress of the organization toward its goals? Is the way performance is measured likely to assist or impede constructive behavior? What pattern of possible incentives encouraging appropriate behavior can be identified? Do they converge on desired outcomes? What restraints and controls discouraging inappropriate behavior are in force? What changes in measurement, incentive, and control systems would you recommend to facilitate achievement of goals? If your analysis of the company's situation suggests that strategy and structure should be changed, such recommenda tions should, of course, precede your suggested plans for effective implementation.

The Rose Company

MR. JAMES PIERCE had recently received word of his appointment as plant manager of Plant X, one of the older established units of the Rose Company. As such, Mr. Pierce was to be responsible for the management and administration at Plant X of all functions and personnel except sales.

Both top management and Mr. Pierce realized that there were several unique features about his new assignment. Mr. Pierce decided to assess his new situation and relationships before undertaking his assignment. He was personally acquainted with the home office executives, but had met few of the plant personnel. This case contains some of his reflections regarding the new assignment.

The Rose Company conducted marketing activities throughout the United States and in certain foreign countries. These activities were directed from the home office by a vice president in charge of sales.

Manufacturing operations and certain other departments were under the supervision and control of a senior vice president. These are shown in Exhibit 1. For many years the company had operated a highly centralized functional type of manufacturing organization. There was no general manager at any plant; each of the departments in a plant reported on a line basis to its functional counterpart at the home office. For instance, the industrial relations manager of a particular plant reported to the vice president in charge of industrial relations at the home office, the plant controller to the vice president and controller, and so on.

Mr. Pierce stated that in the opinion of the top management the record of Plant X had not been satisfactory for several years. The board had recently approved the erection of a new plant in a different part of the city and the use of new methods of production. Lower costs of processing and a reduced labor force requirement at the new plant were expected. Reduction of costs and improved quality of products were needed to maintain competitive leadership and gain some slight product

Exhibit 1

OLD ORGANIZATION

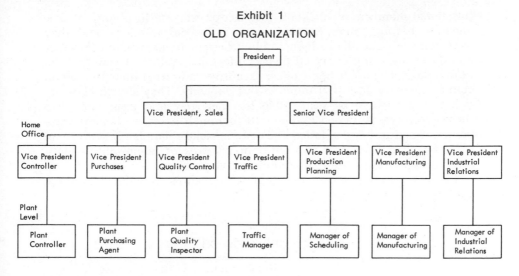

advantage. The proposed combination of methods of manufacturing and mixing materials had not been tried elsewhere in the company. Some features would be entirely new to employees.

According to Mr. Pierce the top management of the Rose Company was beginning to question the advisability of the central control of manufacturing operations. The officers decided to test the value of a decentralized operation in connection with Plant X. They apparently believed that a general management representative in Plant X was needed if the new equipment in manufacturing methods and the required rebuilding of the organization were to succeed.

Prior to the new assignment Mr. Pierce had been an accounting executive in the controller's department of the company. From independent sources the case writer learned that Mr. Pierce had demonstrated analytical ability and general administrative capacity. He was generally liked by people. From top management's point of view he had an essential toughness described as an ability to see anything important through. By some he was regarded as the company's efficiency expert. Others thought he was a perfectionist and aggressive in reaching the goals that had been set. Mr. Pierce was aware of these opinions about his personal behavior.

Mr. Pierce summarized his problem in part as follows: "I am going into a situation involving a large number of changes. I will have a new plant—new methods and processes—but most of all I will be dealing with a set of changed relationships. Heretofore all the heads of departments in the plant reported to their functional counterparts in the home office. Now they will report to me. I am a complete stranger and in addition this is my first assignment in a major 'line' job. The men will know this.

"When I was called into the senior vice president's office to be informed of my new assignment he asked me to talk with each of the

functional members of his staff. The vice presidents in charge of production planning, manufacturing, and industrial relations said they
were going to issue all headquarters instructions to me as plant manager
and they were going to cut off their connections with their counterparts
in my plant. The other home office executives admitted their functional
counterparts would report to me in line capacity. They should obey my
orders and I would be responsible for their pay and promotion. But
these executives proposed to follow the common practice of many companies of maintaining a dotted line or functional relationship with these
men. I realize that these two different patterns of home office—plant
relationships will create real administrative problems for me."

Exhibit 2 shows the organization relationships as defined in these
conferences.

Exhibit 2

NEW ORGANIZATION

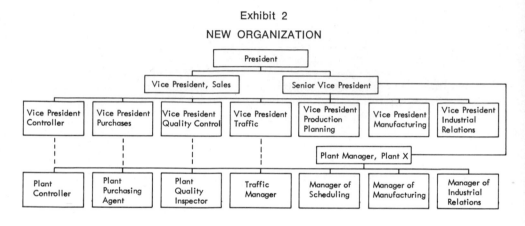

Blow-Mold Packers, Inc.

SEVEN months after taking his M.B.A. degree with distinction at Stanford University, Mr. Harold Finer, CPA, decided to quit the academic world and to accept a standing invitation to join Blow-Mold Packers, Inc. (BMP), a fast-growing firm with some $36 million sales in the blow-molded plastic container business.[1] Finer's title would be that of assistant to the president, and his assignment, staff direction of the acquisition program on which BMP had recently embarked.

In joining BMP in January 1970, Finer was entering a firm with which he already felt himself familiar. As a second-year student, he had considered writing his research report on the company and had wound up exploring a business opportunity in which BMP's president was personally interested (the sale of inexpensive teaching machines). Then, on graduation, while deciding what to do next, Finer had spent some time with BMP at the president's invitation. "I accepted his offer," Finer said, "and for a month he paid my expenses while I wandered around listening and seeing what was happening."

At this time (June 1969), BMP included four divisions in the East, Midwest, and West, all in the same line of business. The Western division, with an old plant at San Jose, California, and a new one just about to start at nearby Sunnyvale, was the original BMP; the other three divisions (Mid-America, Eastern, and Blowco) were formerly independent, smaller concerns that had been acquired in 1967 and 1968. In an industry where transportation charges were a significant element in costs, the geographic dispersal provided by these widely separated plants was believed to give BMP a cost advantage and hence also a long-term sales advantage. In 1971, two of the acquired divisions were still being run by their original managements, and all were being run on a decentralized profit-center basis. Characteristically, both the divi-

---

[1] Disguised industry.

sional and the headquarters line executives had grown up with and in the industry. (See Exhibit 1 for a profile of top management personnel.)

At headquarters, reporting to BMP's president and founder, Mr. Leo Hauptman, age 45, were a few line executives and a newly hired staff. The exact role the staff should play had not yet been decided when Finer visited the company in the summer of 1969. As his contribution to solving this problem, Finer had suggested that each staff man should define his own objectives. "I noted that the new professionals had no specific tasks, and to compound this, everyone reported to Leo," Finer

Exhibit 1

MANAGEMENT PERSONNEL DATA

Title	Name	Age	Education	Previous job experience
President..........	Leo Hauptman	45	B.S. chemistry, Reed College	Research chemist—Gigantic Chemical Co. Vice president research— National Resin Co. Founder—BMP
Executive vice president and division manager, Eastern division..........	Frank Silone	41	High school	Mechanic—Mid-America Plastics Co. Founder-president—Eastern Blow-Molding Co.
Division manager, Mid-America......	J. E. Gardner	58	B.S., M.E., University of Kansas	Salesman Vice president—Mid-America Plastics Co. President—Mid-America Plastics Co.
Division manager, Blowco..........	Frederick Winn	45	B.A., Occidental College	Treasurer and vice president—Blowco
Division manager, Western..........	Donald Ferenzi	40	B.A., CPA, City College, Los Angeles	Associate—Smith & Wesson, Certified Public Accountants Controller—BMP Treasurer—BMP
Vice president, R & D..........	Robert Quant	39	B.S. chemistry, University of Kansas	Chemist—Mid-America Packaging Vice president—Eastern-Molding Corp.
Treasurer..........	Harold Finer	30	M.B.A., Stanford University	Associate—Mitch, Lynch & Smith, Certified Public Accountants Director—Corporate Development, BMP

Source: Casewriter's interviews.

said. "We had no system of responsibility. After some discussions with me, Leo decided to get each of the corporate staff people to write up his own program of action, stating his priorities, problems, and a timetable. This led to BMP's 'red book' of goals."

While Finer saw some organizational problems during his first month's stay at BMP, looking back on this period as of April 1971, he said, "What I saw then was success!"

Past growth in sales and profits of roughly 50 percent a year from 1961 through 1969 had permitted BMP to make acquisitions through exchange of stock on a favorable basis. Although the first three companies acquired had brought dispersal rather than diversification, by 1969 BMP's president felt the time was ripe for invasion of new fields. Hence, at the time Finer joined the company, the search for acquisition

Exhibit 2

BLOW-MOLD PACKERS, INC.
Consolidated Balance Sheet as of September 20, 1970
(dollars in thousands)

ASSETS

Current:

Cash and marketable securities	$ 965.6
Accounts receivable (net)	3,817.1
Inventories at lower of cost or market	2,274.5
Other	150.9
Total Current Assets	$ 7,208.1

Fixed:

Gross fixed assets	$ 7,107.8
Less: accumulated depreciation, etc.	1,649.8
Net Fixed Assets	$ 5,458.0

Other:

Patents and copyrights (net)	6.4
Other	151.3
Total Other Assets	$ 157.7
Total Assets	$12,823.8

LIABILITIES

Current:

Accounts payable	$ 2,428.4
Accruals, including taxes payable	357.2
Current portion of long-term debt	202.6
Total Current Liabilities	$ 2,988.2
Deferred federal income taxes	55.5
Long-term debt (less current portion)	3,439.6
Contingent deferred credit	104.8
Total	$ 3,599.9

Stockholders' equity

Common stock	71.2
Capital in excess of par value and paid-in surplus	4,410.8
Retained earnings	1,753.5
Total Stockholders' Equity	$ 6,235.5
Total Liabilities and Stockholders' Equity	$12,823.8

Source: Company records.

prospects took him far away from blow molding. Examined were concerns in such diverse lines as baby foods, soap, wigs, and even plastic credit cards. Commenting on these prospects, Finer later said, "I was apprehensive of certain of the possible purchases on the grounds that there seemed little match between our company and the prospective acquisition, but it was difficult not to find Leo's enthusiasm contagious —even in the case of his most far-out ideas." As things turned out, however, none of them was purchased.

Midway through fiscal 1970, it became clear that BMP would not continue to enjoy the growth in sales and profits which had previously made financing acquisitions through exchange of stock both easy and profitable. (See Exhibits 2 and 3 for relevant financial statements.) Instead, sales appeared to be headed to a level 30 percent below budget, and profits to a level 35 percent below. Although Finer continued to look at a few prospects, he later explained, "I became unhappy selling some-

Exhibit 3

BLOW-MOLD PACKERS, INC.
Comparative Consolidated Statement of
Earnings for Years Ending September 30
(dollars in thousands)

	1970	1969	1968
Net Sales	$33,210.8	$36,640.4	$27,012.8
Cost of goods sold	30,557.0	33,432.3	24,452.4
Selling, general, and administrative expenses	1,569.1	1,437.5	1,279.5
	$32,126.1	$34,869.8	$25,731.9
Operating income	$ 1,084.7	$ 1,770.6	$ 1,280.9
Other income	39.2	28.2	55.1
	$ 1,123.9	$ 1,798.8	$ 1,336.0
Other deductions	147.8	97.0	59.6
	$ 976.1	$ 1,701.8	$ 1,276.4
Special items*	115.4	—	—
Income before federal income taxes	$ 860.7	$ 1,701.8	$ 1,276.4
Federal income taxes	235.1	764.5	585.5
Net earnings	$ 625.6	$ 937.3	$ 690.9

Percentage Breakdown

	1970	1969	1968
Net Sales	100.0%	100.0%	100.0%
Cost of goods sold	92.0	91.3	90.5
Selling, general, and administrative expenses	4.7	3.9	4.8
	96.7	95.2	95.3
Operating income	3.3	4.8	4.7
Other income	0.1	0.1	0.2
	3.4	4.9	4.9
Other deductions	0.5	0.3	0.2
	2.9	4.6	4.7
Special items*	0.3	—	—
Income before federal income taxes	2.6	4.6	4.7
Federal income taxes	0.7	2.1	2.2
Net earnings	1.9	2.5	2.5

* Start-up costs on new plant plus loss on abandonment of old equipment.
Source: Company records.

thing we didn't have. I knew we didn't have the professional management which I was trying to sell to the companies we were trying to acquire, and I was very unhappy trying to sell it. I decided that my attention should go elsewhere."

In line with this thinking, Finer began to spend his time increasingly in the treasurer's office on control problems. This was an area in which, as a CPA, Finer felt he could be of some help.

As fiscal 1970 soured, changes in organization were effected. Among the first were the creation of the post of executive vice president to coordinate manufacturing policies and the departure of the recently hired corporate sales manager, after his proposals for implementing sales centralization struck other managers as "unrealistic." As the fiscal year drew to its disappointing close in September, several additional changes were made. The corporate staff was disbanded, with 5 of 12 members leaving the company, and 5, apart from Finer and a man in R&D, moving to divisional line positions. The company's treasurer, Mr. Don Ferenzi, was reassigned to head the Western division, where shakedown problems with the new Sunnyvale plant were causing continued cost and output problems. Into the vacated treasurer's position stepped Hal Finer. "I became treasurer," he said, "because Leo asked me to step in on Don Ferenzi's departure to the Western division. I had a long-standing interest in control, so I thought I would try it."

Seven months after assuming his new post, against a backdrop of continued declines, Finer raised the issue of implementing the control proposals which he had previously put forward during his first half-year in office. In a memorandum titled, "Some Notes on BMP's Strategy and the Treasurer's Program," he drew attention to the fact that no action had yet been taken on 16 of some 40 suggestions that he and the president had made following their joint budget review of the four divisions early in fiscal 1971. Under the heading, "Taking It Seriously," Finer wrote as follows:

> A management control system cannot work unless managers take it seriously. Essentially, this means that the president and his senior colleagues must find that the management control reports are useful and that they must then use these reports and the budget reviews as an important source of information as to what is happening in the company. . . . Top management's belief in the system must be made evident if other individuals are to be motivated to act in the way intended by the system.
>
> Translating these rather philosophical observations into an actual record of our recent budget review only highlights the point at issue: viz. [the number of Presidential] requests for action as of the OCT./NOV. Budget Review in 1970 on which no action had been reported as of APRIL 1971—some six months later.[2]

In the pages that follow, data are provided regarding the environment in which Finer was trying to get his program implemented, as

---

[2] A following passage of the treasurer's "Notes" went on to summarize these neglected items. Eight were suggestions to the Western division, and are reproduced below as part of the Appendix.

well as on this program itself. These data bear on BMP's leadership and organization, company activities, industry trends, the treasurer's program and its implementation in Finer's first six months, Finer's assessment of what had been accomplished to date and why progress had not been greater, and the steps that he proposed to be taken next.

BMP's leadership and organization

After founding his company in 1959, Mr. Hauptman indicated he had run it as a one-man show for a number of years. Later, he said, he had come to see the need for a more participative leadership style:

> . . . When the company was started, it was purposely designed to function in an autocratic way. There was only one stockholder: me. There was no question about who was going to make a decision. I was answerable to no one but myself. This helped a lot during the early period. I'm sure that if someone had come and asked me why I made a particular decision, I might have thought twice and never accomplished anything.
>
> During this period, the organization was completely subservient. I was able to handle all the tasks that involved decisions. Finally, it outgrew me, and we had to bring in some heavyweights. . . . Don Ferenzi, who is now over at Western, was one of the first such men that we brought in. He had his CPA so we couldn't call him a bookkeeper, and thus was born the controller's office.
>
> From there on it has been one hell of a climb to get this group of characters to evolve into an organization. For a long time our only organization was me, meeting with someone else to solve a crisis.
>
> Finally, after I joined the YPO[3] and got some managerial ideas, we decided to have a meeting and set down some objectives and goals for the company. Twelve of us went away and formulated some goals. At the second corporate meeting we had a psychologist who helped us to discuss our two-person relationships and the problems of delegation. Soon after that meeting we went public. . . . [Pointing to his attire] That's when I got my vest.

Besides the YPO, there were other influences on the evolution of the president's role-concept and the company structure. Mr. Hauptman continued his account of these as follows:

> At the end of 1967 we started our program of acquisition, buying firms in the Midwest and East. Of course, the pattern of purchases we made gave us instant delegation of many responsibilities. But it hasn't solved many of our management problems. . . .
>
> Then, too, Du Pont, as it does with many of its smaller customers, tried to help us to set up a rational set of procedures. Du Pont's help led us to develop our "red book" of organizational problems and goals.
>
> I would say that throughout this period, our aim was to develop an organization like General Motors. That is, an organization with decentralized plants, centralized control, and creativity. General Motors's Sloan captures for me the essence of being a great manager.

---

[3] The Young Presidents' Organization, a group whose activities included conducting short-session management training programs.

*   *   *   *   *

I honestly believe Sloan had the proper approach: decentralized manufacturing, but with centralized centers for finance, research, sales, and technical services.[4]

President Hauptman went on to describe his own recent effort, in line with the General Motors model he admired, to run the several divisions of his company with the aid of a central headquarters staff. He also gave his views on why this scheme had failed:

> Finally, something happened. I got on the kick of building a centralized corporate staff. We got personnel, sales, materials management, engineering, and corporate development staff people in here. You might even say we developed "instant corporitis."
>
> What should have happened was for me to get all of those guys into a room and tell them what they were going to do. Instead, some of our old line people complained that superimposing a corporate staff would cause us to lose talent and versatility in our line divisions. The result was that we went on a decentralized basis with the staff acting as consultants.
>
> Basically, the structure which we were working toward was sound. But we had a few unfortunate things happen. First, there were a few guys on the staff who weren't congruent with corporate goals. They thought that the jungle warfare of office politics was the way to succeed. They were wrong. They are gone. Second, on top of the mismatch of people, we tried to do too much too fast. We had 14 or 15 highly paid and talented people running around without a true sense of direction. With the move to Sunnyvale and the new-plant problem there, we had to cut our goals down.

As to people in his company and his own role in relation to them, Mr. Hauptman's comments included the following:

> One of my main jobs is to protect the values of the organization.
>
> Our managers must develop the desire to learn. I think we have an interesting thing going here with our company!
>
> Our business requires creativity in sales and R&D.
>
> We have to get cross-fertilization through sharing of ideas and through crisscrossing people in the organization.
>
> Young guys have survived rather well in our organization; maybe they are more willing to listen than the older experts!
>
> Having personal help such as Hal Finer is useful. They run interference for me. They serve up material for me to make decisions.
>
> I think Hal is more concerned than I am that I get on with it and make a decision about the organization. I have to see how I think the organization should be five years hence.
>
> I think one of the terrible things about myself is my desire for involvement. I have to develop an impersonal approach eventually. I must develop a regularity and a rhythm.
>
> One of our major tasks currently is to get the right kind of information. We are developing an MIS[5] and we will get the information!

---

[4] See Alfred P. Sloan, *My Years with General Motors* (Garden City, N.Y.: Doubleday & Co., Inc., 1964).

[5] Management information system.

You ask about rewards. In my opinion, once top management understands the information they will be getting, the information itself will
be a major reward! It will be an important scorecard in the game.

Of course, we will have to come up with an incentive pay scheme.
Probably we will have to provide some form of stock incentive.

The real question is, can we both make money and make people a
little bit happier?

Managerial responses.   Interviews with management personnel
elicited many comments on BMP's organizational environment. Speaking of the president, Finer indicated that his strength lay in creativity
rather than in decision implementation through his organization.

I would say that Leo Hauptman, the president, is an intellectual who
is capable of dealing with the problems of business at a high level of
abstraction. He has a fantastic ability to conceptualize and to visualize
new products and new applications. He knows philosophically where
he wishes to go, and this is vitally important. But in some sense he
tries to wave a magic wand when it comes to implementing the detailed programs necessary to achieve his basic goals through the organization. For example, it is his policy to have a fresh flower on each
secretary's desk each Monday morning. With the same type of motion
which he makes to have this rather mundane task accomplished, he
indicates that he wants to have responsibility accounting. The intentions are often widely separated from the implementation.

There is in the company a lack of systematic relationships. Almost
all of the communications are informal and many of them obscure
completely the nominal lines of authority.

As to the corporate staff, Finer furnished the following account of
why it was hired and how:

About two years ago, Leo thought that he had the solution to some
of the problems of the growth of the company. His solution was to
"hire a corporate staff." He wanted to staff this organization with systems people. He hired these people out of a belief that the organization
would be professionalized. He hoped that the professional education of
the staff personnel would help by breathing into the organization some
systematic relationships which were desirable in the old organization,
but not obtainable.

It is interesting to note that the professionals were all interviewed
by psychologists and not by line managers. Leo is oriented toward
defining the individual rather than the problems. He doesn't want
people around whom he can't understand as people.

Reporting his own early views on the corporate staff, Finer said he
had seen it as a difficult assignment for both Leo and the professionals:

There was some question as to how professional were the professionals; there was the problem of bringing 12 staff people in on top of
an already unsystematic organization, and there was therefore the increasingly worrisome query as to whether the transition could ever be
consummated from entrepreneurial to professional. Thus the corporate
staff could not possibly learn enough about the business to cope with
the old-timers in the organization, and there was not enough of a man-

agement information system to give them the formal and numerical tools with which they could work.

Finer believed further that the effort to create a corporate staff, while not wrong in any absolute sense, could have been premature, in view of the importance of the growth and development of the line managers, whose role in the company was critical. In a memorandum drafted by Finer at the president's request and finalized and signed by the president under the title, "Ending 1970–1971 Strategy," this point was put as follows:

> The failure of the corporate staff was in my opinion not a failure of concept so much as an overly ambitious *top* management program in circumstances where the company's *middle* management had not been adequately and formally developed at the corporate and divisional level. Thus the creation of the corporate staff was fated to be a premature attempt to bring centralization into being at a time when no systematic and detailed internal procedure for sales or manufacturing financial reporting was available, and at a time when the critical manufacturing problems of efficiency and quality were largely occurring within the local plant (and even line) organization.
>
> While this experience does not diminish my belief in a long-term program to develop a corporate staff. . . . I do believe that at the present time we must emphasize internal management growth within . . . our existing corporate and divisional organization in circumstances where the facts indicate that this is where the problems are.

The idea that inexperience was a problem in the line as well as in the staff was also expressed by BMP's executive vice president, Frank Silone. This officer, who had entered the company through the recently acquired Eastern division of which he had been the founder-president, had the following to say:

> We have got to find the right people to fill the boxes on the organization chart with a minimum amount of confusion. . . . It is unfortunate, but many of the people in responsible positions just don't know their own inadequacies. For example, we have supervisors who just don't know anything about the equipment. When something breaks down, they make sure that they are nowhere around so their own ignorance will not be exposed.
>
> The managers just don't get involved. They let the decisions be left too far down in the organization. Our old corporate staff was unsuccessful because we had mechanical engineers who never had practical experience.

As to the staff, Silone believed that its members had not only been too inexperienced, they had also had a "wrong" conception of their role:

> The old staff failed, but not because the divisions were unwilling to cooperate. There has never been a hesitancy among the general managers to work together with the staff people. I have heard that there was. This is foolish. The general managers have too much to do, and they don't have enough staff people within their own groups to accomplish the tasks.

What did happen was that we got staff groups who were inexperienced, ineffective, and hired for the wrong purpose. Starting with this base, the staff people came in to work on areas that had low priority. The general managers just didn't have time to support them. Unless they were going to work in areas that were important to the line people, they should just forget it.

Staff is a supporting function. They should do the things that the line managers don't have time to do or can't do for themselves.

Another headquarters executive expressed the view that what was needed throughout BMP was better communication and direction:

Direction from a staff and from a corporate point of view has been almost negligible. In my experience, I have found that you can't have an organization without objectives, directives, reports, and instructions. There has to be communication, both up and down. The failure has been that no one person was available to monitor the organization and make sure that it was given direction.

BMP's activities

Blow molding. Blow molding was one of the most recent developments in plastic technology. Using a technique borrowed from the glass industry, the blow molders had developed a relatively inexpensive method of fabricating lightweight, inexpensive bottles, which could be lithographed directly or labeled with gummed labels. The major volume application for blow molding was initially detergent and bleach bottles, but new equipment had been developed to make possible larger products, such as automobile gasoline tanks, beer kegs, oil drums, etc. In addition, new formulations for the plastics had been developed, and these had been approved by the Food and Drug Administration (FDA) for use in food and drug containers. Other technical advances, such as the development of a clear, see-through plastic, had allowed the industry to compete successfully for some cosmetic business and other products where it was deemed desirable to have the contents visible.

The actual process of blow molding consists of blowing a thin balloon of molten thermoplastic material against the inside walls of a female mold and chilling it to a rigid solid. This technique offers extremely high production rates and low unit costs.

A typical line producing 32-ounce detergent containers could produce over 10,000 bottles per shift, with four persons employed directly in the fabrication of the bottles. Such an installation would require an investment of from $100,000 to $150,000. Industry sources indicated that additional lines could be added at a slightly lower cost owing to the overlapping of auxiliary equipment. In a completely automated operation such as BMP's, however, where all equipment was tied to a single blow molding machine, capital investment in the factory was roughly proportional to the number of lines required.

BMP was believed to be among the largest of the approximately 250 independent blow molders in the United States. In addition to this group of independents, however, there were approximately 330 blow molding plants which were integrated into the end user's operation, and another 50 blow molders which were owned by large manufacturers of resins.

The independent blow molders such as BMP were equipped to perform a variety of services for their customers. In addition to producing the package, BMP would accept contracts to fill the containers with the end product. In most cases BMP had to label the bottles produced either with paper labels, lithography, or therimage; to store the packages until needed by the marketer; and to make final shipment.

In some special cases where contamination danger was high or a particularly unusual resin was used, the customer supplied the resins employed in fabricating the bottles. In most cases, however, BMP assumed all responsibility for the purchase of raw materials. In addition, in those cases where BMP filled the bottles, it often purchased the materials for and compounded the customer's product. In either event, materials costs represented a high proportion of BMP's sales dollar, as was generally true in blow molding. On the average, BMP realized only 20 percent more sales income than it paid out in materials charges. With this breakdown of the company's sales dollar in mind, one executive stated, "We are really just a $7 million business. The other $29 million we take into sales is just dollars which we trade between our customers and our suppliers."

Product lines.   The bottles which BMP produced were originally almost all for household items, such as detergents and bleaches. Later the company had taken advantage of new formulations to develop clear plastic bottles for shampoos, etc. With the acquisition of the Blowco Company, BMP had become an important supplier to pharmaceutical houses, its lightweight containers taking over a large share of the market for aspirin and stomach-pill bottles, etc. Because some Blowco customers supplied their own resins, materials costs were not so high a portion of total costs as they were in other BMP divisions. Gross margins, too, needed to be higher than in other divisions, to compensate for higher handling costs on the very large number of very small bottles, extra quality controls, and, in some cases, filling of the containers by Blowco.

Sales.   In terms of both product applications and customers, BMP's sales were highly concentrated. Thus the five highest volume applications (bottles for like products of several customers) accounted for two-thirds of BMP's sales, with two applications alone accounting for one half. Similarly, the top ten customers accounted for 45.6 percent of sales, with the top three accounting for 24.1 percent. The loss of one important customer who had purchased his own blow molding machines had been an important factor in the profit decline of 1970.

In an attempt to mitigate the risk of losing a large account, BMP's president and division managers were actively engaged in maintaining relationships with large current customers and in seeking new ones. For fiscal 1971, BMP had developed five new accounts which were budgeted to yield 16 percent of sales.

Besides seeking to attract new customers for established applications, BMP also sought to develop new applications and find customers to adopt them. Mr. Hauptman's personal record was a particularly strong one in this area. In the past his new product-application ideas had led to some of BMP's strongest sellers. Company-developed new applications were budgeted to yield 5.6 percent of total unit sales in 1971. Thus new customers and new applications were expected to contribute almost one fifth of sales in fiscal 1971.

Purchasing and materials management.   Although materials costs were passed on, BMP had always sought to make effective use of its considerable purchasing power. Executives claimed and Finer agreed that the purchasing function was well handled, and that every possible advantage was being achieved through present procedures. Besides effective buying, BMP required effective inventory controls. From a sales standpoint it was critical for the company to have on hand materials for prompt delivery of rush orders.

Inventory and shipping requirements in turn placed a premium on efficient warehousing and materials handling. Overheads and indirect labor connected with this function were a charge on BMP and were grouped together as the materials management expense ($570,000 for the first six months of fiscal 1971).

Manufacturing.   Among its four divisions BMP had six plants. These varied from one another in terms of product lines, facilities, and machinery, and so far no effort had been made to standardize their operations. Even within a single plant, variations in the yield of finished goods from raw materials were an important factor. Different resins employed affected yields considerably. In addition, heat, air pressure, and machine speed played important roles. More manageable, but important nonetheless, were operator errors, maintenance, and mechanical downtime.

In addition to other differences, BMP's divisions in fiscal 1971 had different ratios of capacity to sales. Thus, in the first half of the year two of the divisions were looking for more volume. One was oversold. And one, Western, was in the position of having actual sales in excess of rated capacity during the first quarter, while budgeted sales for the year as a whole would be insufficient to fill up the plant—should planned improvements in efficiency actually be achieved. At the end of the second quarter, however, Western's capacity expansion program was lagging behind schedule.

Western's first-half problem with capacity was associated with a problem of high costs. Both problems were, in turn, associated with the new plant at Sunnyvale which had been opened late in 1969. As to why this plant was still having trouble, Finer laid some blame on the way its design was planned. He said:

> Leo believes in people. He let all of those who were potentially involved with the Sunnyvale plant help to design it. The result was that nobody was responsible. Many now are asking, "Who put the lines in an 'S' shape? Why did the costs jump so far?" We don't know the answers to these questions.

Although Western's cost problem at Sunnyvale attracted the most executive attention, Finer emphasized that this was not the only significant cost problem BMP had. Both direct labor and overheads were rising as a percentage of sales in other plants as well. Finer saw this upward movement as an important problem for a company performing a service function for large cost-conscious customers in an industry which, he felt, was becoming increasingly competitive.

Industry trends

BMP's analysis of industry trends as of early 1971 was expressed in a report drafted by Finer and finalized by the president as part of a policy memorandum entitled, "Ending 1970–1971 Corporate Strategy." In part, this went as follows:

> Whilst the demand for our products is increasing and whilst there is evidence for a growing acceptance of the custom molder's role, competition and consolidation amongst the various molders over the last few years have begun to rationalize a new structure for our industry in which only the most efficient will survive.

The treasurer's program

On assuming office, Finer realized that his approach to control was going to be different from that of his predecessor, Mr. Ferenzi, who was now head of the Western division. At least through the "good" year of 1969, Mr. Ferenzi had focused most of his attention on materials costs, since these were some 80 percent of the total. Mr. Ferenzi had also argued that BMP had no need for a standard cost system, or for cost records on the basis of which the relative efficiency of different line layouts and machines could be compared. Nor did Mr. Ferenzi believe it was worthwhile to try to keep track of the estimated profitability of different applications and package types and sizes. It was more important, he argued, to establish BMP in new fields as they developed than to seek to concentrate company efforts on fields with the highest current estimated payoff.

As far as imposing controls on the divisions was concerned, Mr. Ferenzi had collected reports on the basis of which, he believed, unfavorable trends could be spotted and help given. These reports were not standardized, he said, nor were divisional managers evaluated on the basis of their profit performance. Mr. Ferenzi was sure, however, that divisional managers acted like entrepreneurs and attempted to maximize profit.

In line with his belief that "only the most efficient" would survive as the blow molding industry was "rationalized," Finer had concluded that BMP's old system of controls would no longer suffice for 1971. In his previously cited "Notes," he informed the organization that these accounts "revealed very little about the performance of our factory managers" and "even less [about] our account executives." Furthermore, while the "old system was analytical to the extent that it revealed the profits by plant on a relative basis," any comparison that might be made was "subject to the obligation of the reader to exercise some judgment as to the impact of product mix on plant revenues and costs."

Finer's own program, in contrast with his predecessor's, called for measuring individual performance by a system of "responsibility accounting," for detailed budgets and budget reviews, for collection of additional data on variables "critical to the business," for an "integrated system of reports" designed to help implement the above objectives, and—as a longer-run goal—for development of standard costs, first on a product[6] and then on a process[7] basis.

Responsibility accounting. The principle of holding executives accountable for their level of performance was one that Finer wished to see applied throughout the company, at least as far down as divisional departmental managers (e.g., divisional managers for sales, production, quality control, engineering, maintenance, etc.). What responsibility accounting was and why it was important, Finer explained to other members of the organization in his previously cited "Notes" as follows:

> For management control purposes, a responsibility accounting system is nothing more or less than a way of defining the job assigned to each manager in our organization by providing him with an explicit listing of all the costs and/or revenues for which he is responsible. . . . Each individual manager then knows precisely what his boss expects of him, and, more importantly, knows that . . . superlative efforts on his part will not pass unnoticed. . . .

Holding managers accountable, Finer continued, meant measuring their performance against some yardstick. Since nothing in BMP's old system of accounts adequately served this purpose, this yardstick would at first have to be a manager's best estimate of what he could accomplish. Speaking informally of this approach, Finer said, "It's not analytical, but it seeks to record the promises which the managers make when they take over, and to see how they perform with regard to those promises." In his "Notes" he wrote, "The recommendation proposed here is . . . that a yardstick of good performance be for the time being the achievement of budgeted goals. A corollary of this policy is that managers who consistently fail to meet their promises must be replaced."

Budgets and budget reviews. As Finer envisioned his control system, the "promises" the managers made as to what they hoped to achieve would be pulled together into divisional and corporate budgets. Both the targets set and the actual performance against target would be subject to periodic review. Finer would, of course, have a role in this process, along with the president.

Collection of additional data. Besides collecting prime financial data for the operating budget and budget reviews, Finer envisioned integrating these data into statistics on critical variables. These variables Finer listed as follows:

---

[6] All costs associated with the production of a particular size and shape of container.

[7] Costs collected by type of production activity, i.e., compounding, molding, labeling, etc. These would be useful in understanding the economics of the various parts of the production process.

1. Manufacturing capacity adjusted for standard downtime versus scheduled production.
2. Standard contribution by line hour by product and plant versus overhead by line hour by plant.
3. Standard contribution by account executive, product (old/new), and customer (old/new).
4. Aged finished goods, raw material, and accounts receivable/payable statistics.

An integrated system of accounts. In line with his plans to initiate in BMP such new departures as responsibility accounting, numerical goals, and collection of more detailed data on variables critical to the business, Finer decided that one of his high-priority tasks was to prepare an integrated set of report forms on which managers would be asked to enter the kinds of information required. What would be in these reports, who would fill them out, and where they would be routed were among the issues to be decided.

Standard costs. Over the longer run, Finer knew he would not be satisfied with a budget that featured estimates based on "promises" from each manager reflecting what each "believed" he could accomplish. Finer thus looked forward to developing "analytical" standards, by which he meant standards derived from analysis of past experience. In line with this intention, standard costs would be developed in two phases, with "first priority" being given to the development of direct labor and direct material job costs, and "second priority" to process costs. To communicate to others in the company why such changes were needed in the accounting system, Finer included in his "Notes" the explanation reproduced as Exhibit 4.

Implementation of the treasurer's program

Looking back in April 1971, Finer recalled that he had first gone to work, informally and unofficially, in the treasurer's office during June of the previous year. "By September," he added, "I had a clear idea of what I wanted." Thus, when Finer became treasurer himself, he was able to move quickly to implement several parts of his program. Indeed, he had already been able, in spite of "some resistance," to get the idea of responsibility accounting accepted.

Finer's first official recommendation, made in October 1970, pertained to his goal of setting up a new integrated system of reports. Readied for presentation to the board when it convened for its December meeting was a 30-page black notebook, containing forms for the different reports that Finer saw as needed by various levels: i.e., by the board itself, by the president, by the executive vice president, by the general manager, and by the departmental managers of the divisions. Accompanying these forms was a short introduction explaining the various purposes they served, and a one-page diagram indicating where the data would be filled in and where each of the reports would be routed.

Besides for the first time introducing forms on which department

Exhibit 4

EXCERPTS FROM THE TREASURER'S "NOTES" PERTAINING TO THE NEED
FOR AN ANALYTICAL STANDARD COST SYSTEM

. . . The present policy of the treasurer's department . . . has as its
aim the establishment of an analytical system of accounting which will
yield a formal schedule of standard costs and/or standard revenues for each
of our managerial centers of responsibility and for each of our products—
and which will in this way supplement the system of responsibility accounting by adding to it such financial and statistical data as will help our
managers to analyze their performance as well as communicate it.

I. *First Priority—Job Costing:*

The earliest priority of this program is to set up an accounting system
which will determine and allocate the actual usage of raw materials and
direct labor by job and which will in this way:

1. Verify our *actual* raw material process costs on a monthly basis.
2. Refine the yardstick of good performance for 90 percent of our costs
   by:
   a. Enabling and encouraging operating improvements to be made
        (and demonstrated) on a job-by-job basis.
   b. Allowing valid comparisons of costs to be made on a product-by-
        product basis as between different plants and different time
        periods.
   c. Raising questions as to precisely where material wastage and
        poor labor utilization are occurring on particular products.
3. Refine the yardstick of good performance for all our account executives [salesmen] by creating a formal schedule of standard contribution dollars based on standard material and labor costs. In this
   way the company can break away from its overreliance on the fabricating fee concept (which in any event is contaminated with material
   price and usage variances) and instead reinforce the responsibility
   accounting concept which formalizes the separation between the
   sales (contribution) and the production (cost) functions.
4. Refine the sales strategy of the company by relating it to a formal
   monthly statement of product (as well as account executive) profitability.

II. *Second Priority—Process Costing:*

The second priority of this program is to correlate such a body of financial
and statistical data as will enable us to understand how costs behave as a
process (as opposed to a job) and how process inputs can be optimally related to process outputs. This program seeks to help our managers discover
the relationships that lie behind economic variables and, for example, seeks
to show:

1. How our "fixed" costs vary with output or investment decisions.
2. How standards of improvement can be created for our overhead cost
   centers.
3. How savings can be created *and traced* as a result of capital investment programs.
4. How the optimum use can be made of our productive capacity
   through rational sales contracts based on the financial history of
   given products and given customers.

Source: Treasurer's files.

heads in each division would record their budgeted and later their actual costs and revenues (if any), Finer made some changes in the
operating statements used internally for purposes of control by the corporation and each of its divisions. These changes reflected Finer's conviction that "fabricating fees"—especially as computed in the past (i.e.,
sales less materials at net)—had received undue attention as measures
of divisional performance. For one thing, Finer believed that divisions
should be charged with materials not at *net* but at *gross* (the reason
being that any trade discounts received were really a function of the
whole corporation's size and ability to pay). For another thing, Finer
believed that the important measure to watch was not just the fabricating fee, but the fabricating fee *minus* the direct labor costs apt to be
incurred in making up each order. To the resulting figure, which he
hoped to see used as an important measure of performance, Finer gave
the title, "contribution from sales." In essence, the changes he proposed
would affect divisional statements as follows:

Old	*New*
Sales	Sales
— Materials cost (net)	— Materials cost (gross)
= Fabricating fee	= Fabricating fee
— Direct labor costs	— Budgeted direct labor†
— Overheads	= Contribution from sales
— Corporate charges*	— Direct labor variance
= Profit before taxes	— Overheads
	= Profit before taxes

　　* No corporate charges would appear under the new setup, since cash
discounts and other income would be set against the cost of the headquarters group.
　　† Figures would reflect management's estimates until standard costs
could be developed on an analytical basis.

In addition to affecting the divisional reports by as much as $300,-
000, the proposed changes emphasized the importance of account executives by breaking out profitability by account executive as well as by
plant. As Finer put it, "Plants do not generate sales; we must control
the salesmen."

After the new report forms were devised, Finer's next major project,
carried out in October and November, was his first divisional budget
review. In company with Mr. Hauptman, he called on each general
manager to examine and discuss each division's forecast for 1971. On
returning from these trips, Finer drafted and the president finalized and
signed a letter to each manager, summarizing the conclusions reached.

Besides being sent to the officers concerned, these letters were also
bound in a black notebook for presentation to the board in December.

In each instance, these letters of review began with the assurance
that any comments made, including any that would appear "critical,"
were made "in good faith" and with the "sole intent" of helping the
manager "improve his role." There followed a review of the figures
which the manager had submitted. Here attention was directed to any

special problems which might reduce the profit below forecasted figures (e.g., inadequate sales in one division, inadequate capacity in another, the impact of downtime and quality control problems on predicted labor costs in a third). Following this analytical section, there came a section headed "Specific Actions to be Taken." Included in this were four to nine proposals per division, of which some comprised subsidiary steps. Winding up each letter was a group of exhibits. Most of these pertained to each division's problems and the actions recommended especially for it, but also included in each letter were the budgeted operating statements that had been presented by all four divisions. (Excerpts from the budget reviews of October–November 1970 are presented in the Appendix.)

The objective on which Finer indicated he had made least headway during his first six months in office was his project of developing standard job and process costs upon an analytical basis. In connection with this purpose, forms had been developed on which managers were asked to record their current cost estimates and their actual costs in detail, so that variances could be analyzed and more realistic standards developed. Managers, however, saw these forms—at least in their initial versions—as calling for more work than the information on them was worth. One divisional accountant put this point as follows:

> We are now on our third cost accounting program since Hal Finer became treasurer. We are gradually coming to an agreement and getting the program down to a level where there is a balance between the usefulness of the information and the time consumed in preparing it. Three months ago I couldn't handle all of the numbers we were supposed to be collecting. For each job we were being asked to collect far more information than we were capable of using. The detail which we were being asked to gather was far too great. No one could use it for every job. The materials quantity usage variances were not useful to me here, and no one in the factory knew how to use them. . . .

Another divisional executive, a manufacturing manager, indicated that he still believed that "feel" and a few figures were the only feasible guides to efficient operations in the kinds of business done by his plant:

> I don't find the new system particularly useful yet. As it becomes firmly entrenched and we develop some history and information, I am sure that it will be more useful to me. Right now I rely mainly on some of the numbers and estimates which I have collected to tell me how efficiently we are doing our job. I have been in the industry a long time. Experience plus a few numbers are still the best guide.
>
> The problem of this plant is that we make such a wide range of sizes that it is difficult to set numerical standards. Speed can vary all over the lot. You really have to sense the rhythm of the plant to know if things are slacking off or if they are running properly.

Lack of understanding and cooperation was also a problem, Finer indicated, in making the best use of a relatively high-cost computer ($100,000 a year) that had been installed at the beginning of 1970 in the Western division to account by skid for the actual movement of

Western's materials. Western's general manager, Mr. Ferenzi, "does not know if he wants the computer with all its detail by location and skid," Finer said. Partly for this reason, data inputs into the computer were incomplete. On material used, for example, "The fact was that 30 percent of the pallet tickets were not getting up to the data-processing center." Under these circumstances, Finer continued, Mr. Ferenzi had decided to take the computer off calculating actual material costs altogether. "Instead, the decision was made to use the computer to calculate theoretical costs based on theoretical usage per the product bill of material. Right now it is just in the process of making these unreal pro formas."

Pursuing the computer issue further in his "Notes," Finer summarized his position as follows:

> . . . viewed historically Sunnyvale has become an increasingly worrisome force for those of us who are trying to create a corporate-wide system of direct material and labor job costing.
>
> The focus of our present problem centers on Sunnyvale's computer installation, and no doubt there is currently a feeling going around that the treasurer has turned into a data addict who spends his nights kneeling before a programmed prayer wheel in his search to become the electronic-age administrator that he far from looks. Nonetheless, it is true that the computer represents the only viable way to create a job costing system at the Western division, and it is also true that as yet Western's management has been unable to collect any accurate input for this system in spite of many detailed recommendations as to how this might be done. Put as briefly as possible . . . no progress has been made in correcting inaccurate inventories, maintaining accurate inventories, or in reconciling the various skid tickets which in total make up the material handling system and which in detail can provide the basis for a real-time actual materials cost system.

Assessment of progress to date

With April 1971 came Finer's second budget review and the first review in which he could compare actual achievements for a six-month period with the budgeted promises that he had asked the division heads to make at the beginning of the current fiscal year. This time, Finer's "Treasurer's Report" assumed the form of an assessment of progress to date. Starting with a rundown on profit prospects for fiscal 1971 as a whole, the review went on to analyze where first-half cost and income factors were getting out of line, not only with the optimistic forecasts made six months before, but also with the record of past achievements. There followed a section on the revised forecasts for the second half of the year, and then a discussion of the implications of these data for BMP's sales and manufacturing policy makers.

As to profit prospects for 1971 as a whole, Finer pointed out that these now appeared headed toward being only $58,000 after taxes—a net reduction of over 90 percent from what had been expected six months earlier.

Already first-half pre-tax operating profits for the four operating divisions combined were $628,000 below budget. This variance Finer

traced to four major causes: $190,000 represented "standard contribu-
tion dollars" lost through the failure of BMP's manufacturing operations to provide capacity for budgeted volume; $152,000 represented
"failure to achieve actual output at budgeted direct labor"; $211,000
represented failure to control overhead costs; and the remaining $74,-
000 was a variance caused by "failure of BMP corporate sales to deliver
budgeted volume where manufacturing capacity was available." One of
the graphs in the back of the report (see Exhibit 5) indicated in which
divisions these four variances arose. Except in the case of inadequate
sales volume, the Western division proved the major source of unfavorable actual-to-budgeted performance, with the Mid-America division also making significant additions to variances due to lack of direct
labor and overhead controls.

Comparisons of divisional performance in 1971 with 1968 showed

Exhibit 5

FIRST-HALF VARIANCE ANALYSIS, DIVISIONAL PERFORMANCE,
SIX MONTHS ENDING MARCH 31, 1971

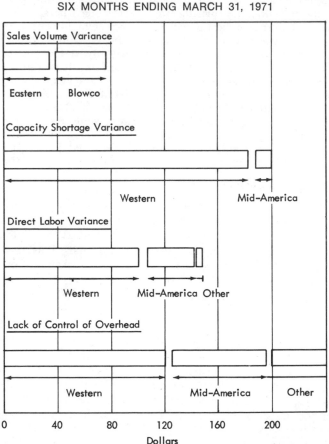

Source: Treasurer's report at the termination of the first half of fiscal 1971.

Table 1

Year	Western	Mid-America	Eastern	Blowco	Total
1968 pre-tax profit......	$ 448	$197	$259	$165	$1,069
1971 pre-tax budgeted profit (loss).........	(920)	47	44	205	(624)
Gap* 1968–71.........	($1,368)	($150)	($215)	$ 40	($1,693)

* Based on 1971 first-half actual results plus estimated second-half figures; excludes corporate income both cases.

just how far the divisions had slipped since BMP's last really good year (see Table 1).

Back of these long-term profit declines lay the same difficulties in each division that the variance analyses had shown. Rising overheads were the most at fault in Western and Mid-America, while lower contribution from sales at Eastern reflected mainly a "sales famine." (For a graph of these relationships, see Exhibit 6. For detailed divisional operating statements for the first six months of 1971, see Exhibit 7.)

Exhibit 6

HISTORICAL ANALYSIS—CONTRIBUTION AND
OVERHEAD TRENDS, 1968–1971

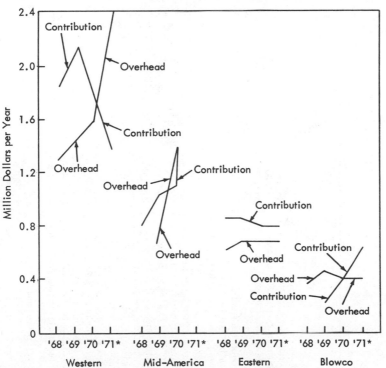

* Actual first-half plus predicted second-half figures.
Source: Treasurer's report as of the termination of the first half of fiscal 1971.

Exhibit 7

INTERNAL OPERATING DATA, FIRST HALF OF FISCAL 1971
(dollars in thousands)

	Western	Percent	Mid-America	Percent	Eastern	Percent	Blowco	Percent	Total	Percent
Sales	$5,730	100.0%	$7,150	100.0%	$3,161	100.0%	$941	100.0%	$16,982	100.0%
Materials costs (gross)	4,638	81.0	6,000	83.9	2,565	81.1	498	52.9	13,701	80.7
Fabricating fee	1,092	19.0	1,150	16.1	596	18.9	443	47.1	3,281	19.3
Standard direct labor	501	8.7	422	5.9	125	4.0	144	15.3	1,192	7.0
Sales expenses	65	1.1	52	0.7	48	1.5	21	2.2	185	1.1
Contribution from sales	526	9.2	676	9.5	423	13.4	278	29.6	1,904	11.2
Operating expenses:*										
Manufacturing (including direct labor variance)†	722	12.6	434	6.1	247	7.8	135	14.3	1,539	9.1
Materials management	256	4.5	191	2.7	94	3.0	29	3.1	570	3.3
Administrative (plant)	143	2.5	50	0.7	71	2.2	30	3.1	293	1.7
Total Operating Expense	1,121	19.6	675	9.5	412	13.0	194	20.5	2,402	14.1
Operating income (loss)	(593)	(10.4)	—	—	11	0.4	83	8.9	(498)	(2.9)
Other income (loss) (net)	—	—	2	0.03	(27)	(0.9)	5	0.5	21	0.1
Divisional income (loss)	(593)	(10.4)	2	0.03	(16)	(0.5)	88	9.4	(519)	(3.0)
Corporate income									375	2.2
Pre-tax income									(144)	(0.8)
Provision for taxes (refund)									90	0.5
Profit (loss) after tax									(54)	(0.3)

* Included in operating expense were the following costs per division:

	Western	Mid-America	Eastern	Blowco
Indirect and labor	$332	$264	$140	$77
Other manufacturing	566	169	169	82

† Total direct labor variance = $152,100.
Note: Figures fail to add due to rounding.
Source: Treasurer's report at the termination of the first half of fiscal 1971.

As to the division heads' revised forecasts for the last six months of 1971, Finer indicated he had made "an attempt to examine the validity of the operating assumptions" which lay behind the newly submitted figures. In this connection he pointed out that "Western has forecast an increase in monthly production rates exceeding, by over 50 percent, its best output performance of the current fiscal year, and at the same time has forecasted halting its long history of rapidly rising overhead costs." At Blowco, he noted, "Increases in overheads . . . are expected to halt in spite of declining excess capacity." Eastern and Mid-America, in contrast, were not at this time found to be expecting favorable reversals of past trends.

As to the implications of these data for sales and manufacturing policy makers, Finer argued that not industry trends, but BMP's own decisions seemed to be the root of the company's troubles:

> Although it is true that the packaging industry and specifically blow molding is getting more competitive, the preceding analysis shows that it is also true that BMP's deteriorating financial position is due as much to BMP's own decisions as it is to any decisions that have been made in the outside world. Thus, while on the one hand fabricating fees have generally held up, on the other hand, contribution dollars have fallen due to increased direct labor costs in the West, and pre-tax division costs have risen due to dramatic increases in Western's and Mid-America's overhead burden.

To underscore the point that the company must now take remedial actions, Finer then pointed to the break-even charts that he had prepared for the two divisions where excess overhead charges were a problem. If present cost-income assumptions were valid, Mid-America could do very little better than break even, even if it operated at 100 percent of its capacity. And Western would need to generate 40 percent more sales volume than its present contracts to achieve this same result. With expected losses at Western more than wiping out expected divisional profits elsewhere, BMP in 1971 would be dependent on its extradivisional or "corporate" income for the small profit that, overall, the company expected to show.

Impediments to progress

At about the same time as Finer wrote his midyear "Treasurer's Report," he wrote his previously quoted "Some Notes on BMP's Strategy and the Treasurer's Program." Here he posed the question why, in view of the profit decline that had started more than 12 months earlier, so little had been done to implement his past proposals for improving control.

Two answers came to mind: management's propensity for not "taking it seriously," and management's propensity to "blame it all on Sunnyvale." Finer called on top managers to set an example that would evidence its belief in controls. And he called on top managers to recognize also that BMP's problems went beyond a single plant:

> It is an easy and understandable feeling for BMP's top managers to become preoccupied with the dangers of Sunnyvale and to ascribe all

their and our difficulties to this division's lack of success. And it is certainly true that Sunnyvale represents a critical step in the development of our company and a precipitous height from which to fall should this investment become mismanaged. At the same time it must be pointed out that the disappointing financial results of the company are due to a number of factors which are quite independent of Sunnyvale's management—and which include, amongst other trends:

1. Rapidly rising overhead costs at our Mid-America division.
2. Lack of either a sales strategy or a retrenchment program for our Eastern division.
3. Insufficient emphasis on cost control at our Blowco division.
4. Rapidly falling contribution from our sales volume dollar.

The selective degree of inattention which is given to these problems is a dysfunctional force for the company and a demoralizing influence on the efforts of the treasurer's department to establish company-wide policies with regard to cost and revenue controls.

Proposed steps

Both for BMP as an organization and for himself as treasurer, Finer in his "Treasurer's Report" and his "Notes" came up with several proposals as to what should be done next.

For the corporation, Finer's "Report" prescribed as follows:

1. Controls must be more stringently created and applied to BMP's present level of overhead expenditure ($5.5 million *budgeted* in 1971 versus $3.1 million actual 1968), and in this context it is recommended that as a first step no increase in overhead expenditure should be allowed without the authorization of either the president or the treasurer.
2. A decision must be made with regard to consolidating and expanding BMP's Mid-America division, which is the fastest sales growth division in the company. The increased pre-tax operating profit potential of this division is substantial (up to $812,000 per annum at present fabricating fee rates, *if* manufacturing capacity here can be planned to equal expected sales levels).
3. Corporate sales must be given the priority responsibility of selling BMP's capacity on the East Coast. A 35 percent increase in unit sales produced by this division at current fabricating fee levels would add in excess of $312,000 to the pre-tax income of this division.
4. A definitive and integrated plan must be prepared for the president by corporate sales and Western's operating management to make some sense out of Sunnyvale.

For himself as treasurer, Finer set the following "goals for 1971":

1. To enforce the responsibility accounting system.
2. To establish direct material and labor job costing throughout the company.
3. To improve the budgetary process through the data supplied by 1 and 2.

As further elaborated in his "Notes," Finer's program of action was as follows:

It is the treasurer's belief that the president must increasingly be able to insist that the budgetary process is effectively carried out and that budgetary instructions are complied with, regardless of the rank or position of those involved. In addition it is the treasurer's position that the president will shortly have to lay down a policy with regard to the implementation of the various forms of analytical accounting that have been described in the preceding pages.

This program of action proposed by the treasurer's department is in support of these objectives and is as follows:

1. Use the May meeting to impress our managers that responsibility accounting and the budgetary process are to be taken seriously.
2. Hire a professional accountant to examine and report on monthly variances wherever and whenever they occur.
3. Use the May meeting to push for managerial programs which will aim to overcome Sunnyvale and non-Sunnyvale weaknesses alike.
4. Use James Albee . . . to implement a corporate-wide system for direct material and labor job costing *once* direction has been given by the president as to the nature of the program he requires here.
5. Conduct a financial budget review in August and September 1971, in preparation for the presentation of the fiscal 1972 budget to the president and the board of directors.

This has perhaps been yet another overelaborate attempt to state my belief that we must now set about strengthening our divisional management teams and strengthening the relationship and understanding between them and a simplified corporate organization which is geared toward financial control as the only viable prelude to greater manufacturing cost reductions, more profitable utilization of our plant capacities, and lusher incentives to those managers who can demonstrate performance excelling standard.

Though prescription is admittedly not the best method of working with others, it is the contention of this writer that we have yet to demonstrate that we can handle more complex approaches to the problem of administration.

APPENDIX

EXCERPTS FROM THE 1971 BUDGET REVIEW LETTERS OF OCTOBER AND NOVEMBER 1970

(Drafted by Harold Finer, finalized and signed by Leo Hauptman)
To Mr. Frederick Winn, General Manager, Blowco, Inc.

I. *Review of 1971 Budget Submitted by Blowco, Inc.*

1. *General Comments*
   Exhibit A, attached . . . shows that Blowco fully expects to be the Company's second most profitable division in 1971. Specifically, the Blowco budget commits your division to a 100 percent increase in unit volume . . . with . . . little or no change in indirect expense forecasted. . . . The remainder of this section is directed toward examining the credibility of what is, at first sight, a most ambitious program.

2. *Sales Forecasts*
   a. *Specific drop-outs and vulnerabilities*
     . . . detailed examination of Blowco's sales forecasts reveals certain specific weaknesses in your unit volume program:
       Of the total units forecast, some 20 percent already looked bad or doubtful.

         *   *   *   *   *

       Of the remaining units, some 32 percent are attributable to the sale of . . . a product class still subject to technical and market uncertainties.

         *   *   *   *   *

       . . . Orders for [the second most important product] have been canceled for the first quarter and . . . this whole program may yet suffer serious delay.
   b. *Lack of overall sales program*
     . . . There is in fact . . . a wide gap between Blowco's list of call priorities and what it, as a division:
       Is able to achieve with the marketing resources budgeted for it—i.e., no increase in selling expenses in spite of a 100 percent increase in volume now forecasted . . . and
       Has been able to achieve (and is forecasting) in terms of profits and production capabilities for our regular lines.
     These gaps add an atmosphere of incredibility to an already sparsely laid out framework for both future marketing strategy and individual account-call and follow-up procedures.
3. *Production*

         *   *   *   *   *

Lack of overall production program
Apart from the peaks and valleys indicated by your production plans for fiscal 1971, there seems to be a fundamental lack of production planning at Blowco—a lack of demand for systematic high levels of production at an optimum product mix.

To Mr. J. E. Gardner, General Manager, Mid-America.

  I. *Review of 1971 Budget Submitted by Mid-America*

    1. *General Comments*
      . . . Mid-America expects to be the Company's least profitable division . . . in spite of the fact that volume is forecast to increase substantially and . . . that Mid-America can truly be said to have the most favorable product mix of any division in the Company. In view of the seriousness of this fact . . . I intend to devote much of the following . . . notes to examine exactly what is amiss at your division.

         *   *   *   *   *

5. *Budgetary Practices*

*   *   *   *   *

As we discussed at the last Executive Operating Committee meeting, a budget is a commitment, and as such, it is neither optimistic nor pessimistic—rather, it is a realistic promise. . . . In this connection I was disappointed to learn that:
> Your departmental budgets were not examined by you in sufficient detail to insure that each manager involved was committed to a plan congruent with the best interests of the company.

*   *   *   *   *

> Your production capacity (which was overstated) does not in fact match with your sales program, and that quite apart from production capacity your real constraint may well prove to be warehouse space—an item which was not even referred to in your budget.

To Mr. Frank Silone, General Manager, Eastern Division.

I. *Review of 1971 Budget Submitted by Eastern*

1. *General Comments*
    . . . shows clearly that . . . Eastern is committed to improve its profit picture. . . . What . . . additionally throws credit on your shoulders are the facts that:
    > You delegated the responsibility of preparing the budget.
    > Most of the numbers in the budget clearly emanated from the departmental managers who . . . generally took an active part in the budgetary process.
    > Red-book objectives were prepared by each individual manager outlining a program of action for self and divisional improvement.
    > Your budget contained realistic assumptions; and as such, could be contrasted with the budgets of the other divisions which have all been returned for numerical adjustments.

To Mr. Donald Ferenzi, General Manager, Western Division.

DEAR DON:
Subject: Western Division—Budget Review—28–30 November 1970
This memorandum stems from the discussions which we had last week and from some of the impressions that were reported to me by Frank Silone and Hal Finer. Although some of the comments which follow may appear critical, I would like to emphasize at once that this letter is written in good faith and that, in particular, I do not hold you responsible for the present condition of the Western Division. . . .

I. *Review of 1971 Budget Submitted by the Western Division*

1. *General Comments*
    . . . the Western Division presented a budget which reflected its commitment to be the most profitable division in the company. The remainder of this section of these notes is directed towards examining the validity of this commitment.

2. *Production*
    The briefest inspection of the Sunnyvale plant highlights the
    critical production problems of your division and the impact
    that these problems are likely to have on your financial re-
    sults. Summarily, these problems may be listed as:

    a. Lack of line running time.
    b. Lack of organization.
    c. Lack of quality control effectiveness.
    d. A carryover of the San Jose housekeeping and safety
          culture.

    a. Lack of Line Running Time

    *   *   *   *   *

    . . . To be specific, in your Sunnyvale plant your current
    rate of line downtime is presently creating direct labor
    costs per thousand units of 80 percent above budget.
    In your older plant, direct labor costs are currently costing
    17 percent above budget.
    . . . The numerical impact of this situation is likely to
    add $284,000 to your direct labor costs—thereby . . .
    making your division the lowest instead of the highest
    contributor to corporate profits.

    b. Lack of Organization
    . . . During our budget review you have seriously ques-
    tioned the abilities of your

Assistant general manager	Warehouse manager
Quality control manager	M&E manager
Materials management manager	Resin manager
and your controller	

    Quite apart from whether or not your feelings are justi-
    fied, whilst these feelings exist . . . they inhibit the
    establishment of an organization to cope with your two-
    plant operation and . . . they also inhibit any rational
    attempt to analyze your indirect labor budget in terms of
    those responsible for its increase by $70,000. . . .

    c. Lack of Quality Control Effectiveness
    . . . During the course of our budget review, it became
    apparent that your division is currently suffering from an
    outbreak of quality control problems. . . . Perhaps even
    more disturbing . . . is the fact that there appears to be
    no systematic reporting procedure . . . by which you, as
    general manager, can estimate [the] physical and financial
    effects. . . .

3. *Sales*
    Of the unit sales increase forecast for the Western Division,
    150 percent of the total were contributed by account executives
    outside of the division, leaving lost ground to be accounted for.

    *   *   *   *   *

    Finally, it should be noted that this lack of marketing aggres-
    siveness arises in circumstances when 1970 was a poor year
    . . . and where our new Sunnyvale plant may well be at 56
    percent of capacity in the fourth quarter . . . with its ex-
    tremely high-cost overhead burden.

II. *Specific Action to Be Taken*

Don, as I have already indicated, I am trying to use this budget review, not as a destructive tool but as a constructive method of helping myself (and, I hope, you) to become a better manager. The following decisions are made for this reason only. . . . Specifically, I want you to see to it that:

a. You become familiar with the economic and managerial assumptions that lie behind every material figure in your budget by the time of the next budget review.

b. Frank Silone is brought into an active role in order to help you stabilize the manufacturing organization within your division.

c. You change your Sunnyvale direct labor budget figures to read their current actual rate in the first quarter, $2 less in the second, $2 less in the third, and $2 less in the fourth quarter—which will still be $2 above your present budget. Needless to say, I expect you to at least keep your manufacturing performance within these limits.*

d. You submit a written report to Frank Silone and myself by January 1st recommending the form of organization you propose to adopt at San Jose and at Sunnyvale, and justifying the $70,000 increase in indirect labor charges that your division had budgeted for the coming year.*

e. You prepare a written report to Frank Silone and myself by the end of the second quarter listing the merits and weaknesses of each key manager under your control. Each report should only be presented after discussing its contents with the individual manager concerned, and each report should be accompanied by a recommendation with regard to the manager's eligibility for future promotion and responsibility.*

At the risk of going into too much detail—but at the same time because I believe this topic is of the utmost importance—I will go further and suggest that you:

Spend between one and two hours a week with each of your key managers—using this time both to understand his point of view and to review specific situations which have arisen in his department during the course of the week.

Hold weekly staff meetings along the lines of your memorandum of November 15th.

Make no personnel changes without discussing them with Frank Silone and me.

Keep notes with regard to both the individual and the group meetings which you hold with your managers.

f. You prepare a written report to Frank Silone and myself by the end of the second quarter showing your plans for the line at San Jose and giving economic justification for either transferring it to Sunnyvale or for the dual operation which will result from leaving it at San Jose. In the meantime, please see to it that the San Jose offices and quality control laboratory are cleaned up by the end of the current calendar year.*

g. You create systematic records which account for the financial impact of ineffective quality control. In this regard, I shall want

---

* Starred entries denote actions that Finer stated were not yet implemented at the time of his second budget review during April 1971.

        to see quality control statistics on a monthly basis along the lines requested by Mark Simon in connection with his responsibility accounting program.*

h. You appoint a manager who will be responsible for housekeeping and safety procedures and who will have the authority to see that they are implemented.* In this connection, the manager appointed should:

      Study our existing safety and housekeeping rules.*

      Distribute the DuPont Safety Manual to key managers.*

      Devise some kind of competition and prize system which will encourage *all* our employees to participate fully in the program.*

j. You prepare a written report to Frank Silone and myself with regard to this up-coming Union negotiations.*

Whilst you are helping Frank Silone and me in this way, I will try to breathe some new life into our sales program. . . . In the meantime, I want to sincerely thank you for volunteering to help the company in a role which I know will mean plenty of personal anguish for you.

                With kindest personal regards,

                Leo Hauptman

Basic Industries

In May 1966, Pete Adams, plant manager of Basic Industries' Chicago plant, was worried about the new facilities proposal for toranium. His division, metal products, was asking for $1 million to build facilities which would be at full capacity in less than a year and a half (if forecasted sales were realized). Yet the divisional vice president for production seemed more interested in where the new facility was to go than in how big it should be. Adams wondered how, as plant manager, his salary and performance review would look in 1968 with the new facility short of capacity.

BASIC INDUSTRIES, METAL PRODUCTS DIVISION

Basic Industries engaged in a number of activities ranging from shipbuilding to the manufacture of electronic components. The corporation was organized into five autonomous divisions (see Exhibit 1). In 1965 these divisions had sales totaling $500 million. Of the five, the metal products division was the most profitable. In 1965, this division realized an after-tax income of $16 million on sales of $110 million and an investment of $63.7 million.

This position of profit leadership within the company had not always been held by metal products. In fact, in the early 1950s, Basic's top management had considered dropping the division. At that time, the division's market share was declining owing to a lack of manufacturing facilities, high costs, and depressed prices.

A change in divisional management resulted in a marked improvement. Between 1960 and 1965, for example, the division's sales grew at 8% a year and profits at 20% a year. The division's ROI during this period rose from 12% in 1960 to 25% in 1965.

Ronald Brewer, president of metal products division since 1955, explained how this growth had been achieved:

Exhibit 1

ORGANIZATION CHART FOR BASIC INDUSTRIES

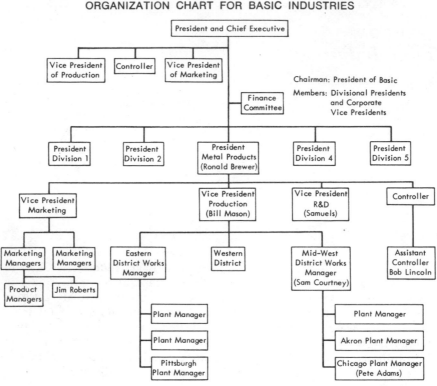

Source: Casewriter's notes.

Planning goes on in many places in the Metal Products Division, but we do go through a formal planning process to establish goals. We establish very specific goals for products and departments in every phase of the business. This formal and detailed planning is worked out on a yearly basis. We start at the end of the second quarter to begin to plan for the following year.

We plan on the basis of our expectations as to the market. If it's not there, we live a little harder. We cut back to assure ourselves of a good cash flow. Our record has been good, but it might not always be. Some of our products are 30 years old. We've just invested $5 million, which is a lot of money for our division, in expanding capacity for a 25-year-old product. But we're making money out of it and it's growing.

Along with detailed planning for the year to come, we ask for plans for years three and four. Our goal is to make sure that we can satisfy demand. Any time we approach 85% of capacity at one of our plants, our engineers get busy.

They will give the plant manager the information as to what he needs in the way of new equipment. The plant manager will then fit the engineer's recommendation into his expansion plans. The plant manager's plan then goes to our control manager. The marketing people then add their forecasts, and by that time we have built up the new facilities proposal. On the other hand, the marketing people may have spearheaded the project. Sometimes they alert the plant manager to a rapid growth in his product and he goes to the engineers. In this division, everyone is marketing minded.

*   *   *   *   *

We measure plants, and they measure their departments against plan. For example, we have a rule of thumb that a plant must meet its cost reduction goals. So if one idea doesn't work out, a plant must find another one to get costs to the planned level. We make damned sure that we make our goals as a division. Our objective is to have the best product in the market at the lowest cost. It's a simple concept, but the simpler the concept, the better it's understood.

Well, on the basis of his performance against plan, a man is looked at by his superior at least once a year, maybe more. We take a pretty hardnosed position with a guy. We tell him what we think his potential is, where he is going to go, what he is going to be able to do. We have run guys up *and* down the ladder. In this division, it's performance and fact that count. We have no formal incentive plan but we do recognize performance with salary increases and with promotions.

You know, we have divisions in this company which are volume happy. We here are profit conscious. We had to be to survive. What I'd like to see is interest allocated on a pro rata basis according to total investment. I grant you that this would hurt some of the other divisions more than us, but I think that treating interest as a corporate expense, as we do, changes your marketing philosophy and your pricing philosophy.

For example, most new facilities proposals are wrong with respect to their estimates of market size—volume attainable at a given price—and timing. You can second-guess a forecast though, in several ways, and hedge to protect yourself. There is a feeling at Basic Industries that there is a stigma attached to coming back for more money. That means that if you propose a project at the bare minimum requirement and then come back for more, some people feel that you've done something wrong. Generally, this leads to an overestimate of the amount of capital required. It turns out that if you have the money you do spend it, so that this stigma leads to overspending on capital projects. We at metal products are trying to correct this. First, we screen projects closely. We go over them with a fine tooth comb. Second, internally, we set a goal to spend less than we ask for where there is a contingency.

Also, when a project comes in at an estimated 50% return, we cut the estimate down. Everyone does. The figure might go out at 30%. But this practice works the other way too. For example, in 1958 Bill Mason [metal products' vice president of production] and I worked like hell to get a project through. Although it looked like 8% on paper, we knew that we could get the costs way down once it got going, so we put it through at 12%. We're making double that on it today. We haven't had a capital request rejected by the finance committee [see Exhibit 1] in 8 years.

Of course, every once in a while we shoot some craps, but not too often. We are committed to a specific growth rate in net income and ROI. Therefore, we are selective in what we do and how we spend our money. It's seldom that we spend $500,000 to develop something until we know it's got real market potential. You just don't send 100 samples out and then forecast a flood of orders. New products grow slowly. It takes six or seven years. And given that it takes this long, it doesn't take a lot of capital to develop and test our new ideas. Before you really invest, you've done your homework. Over the years we've done a good job in our new products, getting away from the aircraft industry. In 1945, 70% of our business was based on aircraft. Today · it's 40%. The way we do things protects us. We have to have a very strong sense of the technical idea and the scope of the market before we invest heavily.

The metal products division's main business was producing a variety of basic and rare nonferrous metals and alloys such as nickel, nickel-beryllium, and titanium in a myriad of sizes and shapes for electrical, mechanical, and structural uses in industry. One of the division's major strengths was its leadership in high-performance material technology. Through patents and a great deal of proprietary experience, metal products had a substantial technological lead on its competitors.

TORANIUM

In the late 1950s metal products decided to follow its technological knowledge and proprietary production skills into the high-performance materials market. One of metal products' most promising new materials was toranium, for which Jim Roberts was product manager (see Exhibit 1).

Roberts was 33 years old and had a Ph.D. in chemical engineering. Prior to becoming a product manager, he had worked in one of metal products' research laboratories. Roberts explained some of toranium's history:

Developing toranium was a trial-and-error process. The lab knew that the properties of the class of high performance materials to which toranium belonged were unusually flexible, and, therefore, felt such materials had to be useful. So it was an act of faith that led R.&D. to experiment with different combinations of these materials. They had no particular application in mind.

In 1957 we developed the first usable toranium. Our next problem was finding applications for it. It cost $50 a pound. However, since a chemist in the lab thought we could make it for less, we began to look for applications.

In 1962, I entered the picture.

I discovered it was an aerospace business. When the characteristics of our material were announced to the aerospace people, they committed themselves to it. Our competitors were asleep. They weren't going to the customer. I went out and called on the customers and developed sales.

In 1963, we decided to shift the pilot plant from the lab and give it to the production people at Akron. We decided that we simply were not getting a good production-oriented consideration of the process problems. The people at Akron cut the costs by two-thirds and the price stayed the same.

In 1963, I also chose to shut off R.&D. on toranium because it couldn't help in the market place. We had to learn more in the market place before we could use and direct R.&D.

I ought to mention that under the management system used by Mr. Samuels [vice president of R.&D.], the product manager, along with R.&D. and production, shares in the responsibility for monitoring and directing an R.&D. program. This arrangement is part of an attempt to keep everyone market-oriented.

From 1962 to 1965, sales of toranium increased from $250,000 a year to $1 million a year just by seeking them, and in 1965 we put R.&D. back in.

This material can't miss. It has a great combination of properties: excellent machinability, thermal shock resistance and heat insulation. Moreover, it is an excellent electrical conductor.

We can sell all that we can produce. Customers are coming to us with their needs. They have found that toranium's properties and our technical capabilities are superior to anything or anyone in the market.

Moreover, pricing has not been a factor in the development of markets to date. In fact, sales have been generated by the introduction of improved grades of toranium at premium prices. Presently, General Electric represents our only competition, but we expect that Union Carbide will be in the market place with competitive materials during the next few years. However, I don't expect anyone to be significantly competitive before 1968. Anyway, competition might actually help a little bit in expanding the market and stimulating the customers as well as in educating our own R.&D.

Now, if one assumes that no other corporation will offer significant competition to toranium until 1968, the only real uncertainty in our forecasts for toranium is related to metal products' technical and marketing abilities. R.&D. must develop the applications it is currently working on, and production will have to make them efficiently.

This production area can be a real headache. For example, R.&D. developed a toranium part for one of our fighter bombers. However, two out of three castings cracked. On the other hand, we've got the best skills in the industry with respect to high pressure casting. If we can't do it, no one can.

The final uncertainty is new demand. I've got to bring in new applications, but that shouldn't be a problem. You know, I've placed toranium samples with over 17 major customers. Can you imagine what will happen if even two or three of them pay off? As far as I'm concerned, if the forecasts for toranium are inaccurate, they're underestimates of future sales.

NEW FACILITIES PROPOSAL

Sam Courtney, district works manager (to whom the plant managers of the Chicago, Akron, and Indianapolis plants reported) explained the origin of the new toranium facilities proposal:

> The product manager makes a forecast once a year, and when it comes time to make major decisions, he makes long-range forecasts. In January 1965, we were at 35% of the toranium pilot-plant capacity. At that time we said, "We have to know beyond 1966, we need a long-range forecast. Volume is beginning to move up."
>
> The production control manager usually collects the forecasts.

Each year it is his responsibility to see where we are approaching 85% or 90% of capacity. When that is the case in some product line, he warns the production vice president. However, in this instance, toranium was a transition product and Akron (where the pilot plant was located) picked up the problem and told the manager of product forecasting that we were in trouble.

The long-range forecast that Courtney requested arrived at his office about March 1, 1965, and clearly indicated a need for new capacity. Moreover, Roberts' 1966 regular forecast, which was sent to production in October 1965, was 28% higher than the March long-range projection. It called for additional capacity by October 1966.

Courtney's first response was to request a new long-range forecast. He also authorized the Akron plant to order certain equipment on which there would be a long lead time. The district works manager explained, "It is obvious we are going to need additional capacity in a hurry, and the unique properties of toranium require special, made-to-order, equipment. We can't afford to lose sales. Producing toranium is like coining money."

At the same time, Courtney began discussions on the problem with Bill Mason, vice president of production for metal products. They decided that the Akron plant was probably the wrong location in which to expand the toranium business. Courtney commented, "There are 20 products being produced in Akron, and that plant cannot possibly give toranium the kind of attention it deserves. The business is a new one, and it needs to be cared for like a young child. They won't do that in a plant with many important large-volume products. We have decided over a period of years that Akron is too complex, and this seems like a good time to do something about it."

The two locations proposed as new sites for the toranium facilities were Pittsburgh and Chicago. Each was a one-product plant which "could use product diversification." While Pittsburgh seemed to be favored initially, Mason and Courtney were concerned that the toranium would be contaminated if it came in contact with the rather dirty products produced at Pittsburgh. Therefore, Courtney asked engineering to make studies of both locations.

The results of these initial studies were inconclusive. The Pittsburgh plant felt that the problem of contamination was not severe, and the economic differential between the locations was not substantial.

After the initial studies were completed, Roberts' new long-range forecast arrived. The following table compares this forecast with Roberts' previous long-range forecasts:

ACTUAL AND PROJECTED SALES
(dollars in millions)

Date of forecast	1965	1966	1967	1968	1969	1970	1971
March 1964	1.08	1.30	...	...	2.20	...	...
March 1965	1.17	1.40	1.60	...	...	2.80	...
March 1966	...	1.80	2.50	3.40	...	...	5.60
Actual	1.00	...	...	...	...	...	...

In response to this accelerating market situation, Courtney and Mason asked Adams (plant manager at Chicago) to make a "full-fledged study of the three locations" (Akron, Pittsburgh, and Chicago). At the same time, Mason told Brewer (president of metal products), "We're now about 90% certain that Chicago will be the choice. Associated with the newness of the material is a rapidly changing technology. . . . The metal products R.&D. center at Evanston is only ten minutes away. . . . Another important factor is Adams. Titanium honeycomb at Chicago was in real trouble. We couldn't even cover our direct costs. Adams turned it around by giving it careful attention. That's the kind of job toranium needs."

Peter Adams was 35 years old. He had worked for Basic since he graduated from college with a B.S. in engineering. After spending a year in the corporate college training program, Adams was assigned to the metal products division. There he worked as an assistant to the midwestern district manager for production. Before becoming Chicago plant manager in 1963, Adams had been the assistant manager at the same plant for two years.

In working through the financial data on the toranium project, Adams chose to compare the three sites with respect to internal rates of return. He made this comparison for the case where capacity was expanded to meet forecasted sales for 1967 ($2.5 million), the case where capacity was expanded to meet forecasted sales for 1971 ($5.6 million) and the case where capacity was expanded from $2.5 to $5.6 million. The results of Adams' analysis are summarized in the following table:

		Chicago	*Pittsburgh*	*Akron*
			(dollars in thousands)	
1.	Incremental capital investment			
	for capacity through 1967	$ 980	$1,092	$ 765
	Internal rate of return	34%	37%	45%
2.	Incremental capital investment			
	for capacity through 1971	$1,342	$1,412	$1,272
	Internal rate of return	52%	54%	55%
3.	Incremental capital investment			
	to raise capacity from $2.5 to			
	$5.6 million	$ 710	$ 735	$ 740
	Internal rate of return	45%	47%	46%

While the economics favored Akron, Adams was aware that Mason favored Chicago. This feeling resulted from conversations with Courtney about the toranium project. Courtney pointed out the importance of quality, service to customers, liaison with R.&D., and production flexibility to a new product like toranium. Furthermore, Courtney expressed the view that Chicago looked good in these respects, despite its cost disadvantage. Courtney also suggested that a proposal which asked for enough capacity to meet 1967 forecasted demand would have the best prospects for divisional acceptance.

By the end of April 1966, Adams' work had progressed far enough to permit preparation of a draft of a new facilities proposal recommending a Chicago facility. Except for the marketing story which he obtained from Roberts, he had written the entire text. On May 3, Adams brought the completed draft to New York for a discussion with Mason and Courtney. The meeting, which was quite informal, began with Adams reading his draft proposal aloud to the group. Mason and Courtney commented on the draft as he went along. Some of the more substantial comments are included in the following excerpts from the meeting.

Meeting on the draft proposal

ADAMS: We expect that production inefficiencies and quality problems will be encountered upon start-up of the new facility in Chicago. In order to prevent these problems from interfering with the growth of ·toranium, the new facilities for producing toranium powder, pressing ingots, and casting finished products will be installed in Chicago and operated until normal production efficiency is attained. At that time, existing Akron equipment will be transferred to the Chicago location. Assuming early approval of the project, Chicago will be in production in the first quarter of 1967, and joint Akron and Chicago operations will continue through September 1967. The Akron equipment will be transferred in October and November 1967, and Chicago will be in full operation in December 1967.

MASON: Wait a minute! You're not in production until the first quarter of 1967, and the forecasts say we are going to be short in 1966!

ADAMS: There is a problem in machinery order lag.

MASON: Have you ordered a press?

ADAMS: Yes, and we'll be moving by October.

MASON: Well, then, say you'll be in business in the last quarter of 1966. Look, Pete, this document has to be approved by Brewer and then the finance committee. If Chicago's our choice, we've got to *sell* Chicago. Let's put our best foot forward! The problem is to make it clear that on economics alone we would go to Akron . . . but you have to bring out the flaw in the economics: that managing 20 product lines, especially when you've got fancy products, just isn't possible.

COURTNEY: And you have a better building.

MASON: All of this should be in a table in the text. It ought to cover incremental cost, incremental investment, incremental expense, incremental ROI, and the building space. And Sam's right. Akron is a poor building; it's a warehouse. Pittsburgh is better for something like high-pressure materials. But out in Chicago you've got a multi-story building with more than enough space that is perfect for this sort of project.

COURTNEY: Pete, are we getting this compact enough for you?

MASON: Hey, why don't we put some sexy looking graphs in the thing? I don't know, but maybe we could plot incremental investment vs. incremental return for each location. See what you can do, Pete.

COURTNEY: Yes, that's a good idea.

         *   *   *   *   *

MASON: Now, Pete, one other thing. You'll have to include discounted cash flow on the other two locations. Some of those guys [division and corporate top management] are going to look at just the numbers. You'll show them they're not too different.

         *   *   *   *   *

MASON: The biggest discussion will be, "Why the hell move to Chicago?"

COURTNEY: You know, Pete, you should discuss the labor content in the product.

MASON: Good. We have to weave in the idea that it's a product with a low labor content and explain that this means the high Chicago labor cost will not hurt us.

ADAMS: One last item: Shouldn't we be asking for more capacity? Two-and-one-half million dollars only carries us through 1967.

MASON: Pete, we certainly wouldn't do this for one of our established products. Where our main business is involved, we build capacity in five- and ten-year chunks. But we have to treat toranium a little differently. The problem here is to take a position in the market. Competition isn't going to clobber us if we don't have the capacity to satisfy everyone. If the market develops, we can move quickly.

After the meeting, Courtney explained that he and Mason had been disappointed with Adams' draft and were trying to help him improve it without really "clobbering" him. "Adams' draft was weak. His numbers were incomplete and his argument sloppy. I've asked him to meet with Bob Lincoln [assistant controller for metal products] to discuss the proposal."

The result of Adams' five meetings with Lincoln was three more drafts of the toranium proposal. The numerical exhibits were revised for greater clarity. The text was revised to lessen the number of technical terms.

Adams, however, was still very much concerned with the appropriate size of the new facility. "Mason is only interested in justifying the location of the new facility!" Adams exclaimed. "We plan to sell $5.6 million worth of toranium in 1971. Yet we're asking for only $2.5 million worth of capacity. It's crazy! But, you know, I think Mason doesn't really care what capacity we propose. He just wants 'sexy looking graphs.' That's O.K. for him, because I'm the one who's going to get it in the neck in 1968. So far as I can see, Brewer has built his reputation by bringing this division from chronic under-capacity to a full-capacity, high ROI position."

The next step in the toranium facilities proposal was a formal presentation to the top management of metal products on June 2, 1966. There were two capital projects on the agenda. Brewer began the meeting by announcing that its purpose was to "discuss the proposals and decide if they were any good." He turned the meeting over to Mason, who, in turn, asked Adams to "take over and direct the meeting."

Adams proceeded by reading the draft proposal, after first asking for comments. He got halfway down the first page before Brewer interrupted.

BREWER: Let me stop you right here. You have told them [the proposal was aimed at Basic Industries' finance committee] the name, and you have told them how much money you want, but you haven't told them what the name means, and you haven't told them what the products are.

At this point a discussion began as to what the name of the project was going to be. The meeting then continued with Adams reading and people occasionally making comments on his English and on the text.

BREWER: Look, let's get this straight. What we are doing in this proposal is trying to tell them what it is we are spending their money on. That's what they want to know. Tell me about the electronic applications in that table you have there. I have to be able to explain them to the finance committee. I understand "steel" and "aerospace" but I don't understand "electronic applications" and I don't understand "electronic industry." I need some more specific words.

SAMUELS: [vice president of R.&D.]: Let me ask you a question which someone in the finance committee might ask. It's a nasty one. You forecast here that the industry sales in 1971 are going to be about $7 million, or maybe a little less. You think we are going to have 75% or 85% of this business. You also think we are going to get competition from G.E. and others. Do you think companies of that stature are going to be satisfied with sharing $1.5 million of the business? Don't you think that we may lose some of our market share?

This question was answered by Roberts and pursued by a few others. Essentially Roberts argued that the proprietary technology of the metal products division was going to be strong enough to defend its market share.

BREWER: Let me tell you about an item which is much discussed in the finance committee. They are concerned, and basically this involves other divisions, with underestimating the cost of investment projects. I think, in fact, that there was a request for additional funds on a project recently which was as large as our entire annual capital budget.[1] Second of all, as a result of the capital expenditure cutback, there was a tendency, and again it has been in other divisions, to cut back on or delay facilities. Now it's not really just the capital expenditure cutback that is the reason for their behavior. If they had been doing their planning, they should have been thinking about these expenditures five or six years ago, not two years ago. But they didn't do the estimates, or their estimates weren't correct, and now they are sold out on a lot of items and are buying products from other people and reselling them and not making any money. It's affecting the corporate earnings, so the environment in the finance committee today is very much (1) "Tell us how much you want, and tell us *all* that you want," and (2) "Give us a damned good return." Now I don't want us to get *sloppy,* but, Bill, if you need something, ask for it. And then make Pete meet his numbers.

ADAMS: Well, on this one, as I think you know, the machinery is already on order and we are sure that our market estimates are correct.

BREWER: Yes, I know that. I just mean that if you want something, then plan it right and tell them what you are going to need so you don't come back asking for more money six months later.

* * * * *

BREWER: I am going to need some words on competition. I am also going to need some words on why we are ready so soon on this project. We are asking for money now, and we say we are going to be in operation in the fourth quarter.

SAMUELS: Foresight (*followed by general laughter*).

MASON: Well, it's really quite understandable. This began last October when we thought we were going to expand at Akron. At that time, it was obvious that we needed capacity so we ordered some machines. Then as the

---

[1] Metal products division's capital budget in 1965 was $7.9 million.

thing developed, it was clear that there would be some other things we needed, and because of the timing lag we had to order them.

BREWER: OK . . . now another thing. Numerical control is hot as a firecracker in the finance committee. I am not saying that we should have it on this project, but you should be aware that the corporation is thinking a lot about it.

* * * * *

BREWER: [Much later on in the discussion.] There are really three reasons for moving. Why not state them?

1. You want to free up some space at Akron which you need.
2. There are 20 products at Akron, and toranium can't get the attention it needs.
3. You can get operating efficiencies if you move.

If you set it out, you can cut out all of this crap. You know, it would do you people some good if you read a facilities proposal[2] on something you didn't know beforehand. You really have to think about the guy who doesn't know what you're talking about. I read a proposal yesterday that was absolutely ridiculous. It had pounds per hour and tons per year and tons per month and tons per day and—except for the simplest numbers, which were in a table—all the rest were spread out through the story.

* * * * *

Adams indicated that he was disappointed with the meeting. Brewer seemed to him to be preoccupied with "words," and the topic of additional capacity never really came up. The only encouraging sign was Brewer's statement, "Tell us all that you want." But it seemed that all Mason "wanted" was $2.5 million worth of capacity.

Adams saw three possibilities open to him. First, he could ask for additional capacity.

This alternative meant that Adams would have to speak with Courtney and Mason. The Chicago plant manager viewed the prospect of such a conversation with mixed feelings. In the past, his relations with Courtney and Mason had been excellent. He had been able to deal with these men on an informal and relaxed level. However, the experience of drafting the toranium proposal left Adams a little uneasy. Courtney and Mason had been quite critical of his draft and had made him meet with Bob Lincoln in order to revise it. What would their reaction be if he were to request a reconsideration of the proposal at this late date? Moreover, what new data or arguments could he offer in support of a request for additional capacity?

On the other hand, Adams saw a formal request for additional capacity as a way of getting his feelings on the record. Even if his superiors refused his request, he would be in a better position with respect to the 1968 performance review. However, Adams wondered how his performance review would go if he formally requested and received additional capacity and the market did not develop as forecasted.

As his second alternative, Adams believed he could ask that the new facilities proposal specify that metal products would be needing more money for toranium facilities in the future.

[2] The finance committee reviewed approximately 190 capital requests in 1965.

This alternative did not pose the same problems as the first with respect to Courtney and Mason. Adams felt that saying more funds might be needed would be acceptable to Courtney and Mason, whereas asking for more might not be. However, the alternative introduced a new problem. Brewer had been quite explicit in insisting that the division ask for all that was needed so that it would not have to come back and ask for more in six months. To admit a possible need for additional funds, therefore, might jeopardize the entire project.

In spite of this problem, Adams felt that this alternative was the best one available. It was a compromise between his point of view and Mason's. If top management felt that the future of toranium was too uncertain, then why not ask for contingent funds? This would get Adams off the hook and still not actually increase metal products' real investment.

As his third alternative, Adams decided he could drop the issue and hope to be transferred or promoted before 1968.

Hawaii Best Company (A)

GRADUALLY rising from his chair in his third-floor plush office overlooking Waikiki Beach in Honolulu, James Lind, president of Hawaii Best Company (HBC), greeted Charles Carson, vice president and general manager of the company's Islands Division, and invited him to take the seat across from his desk.

"Charlie, I am sure that something has gone wrong," he said as Carson remained standing. "You have many fine qualities—I was the one who recognized them when I promoted you to vice president—but I have been reviewing your progress these past few months and . . . and the results have not met our expectations."

Carson fidgeted at the window, watching the October morning across the harbor. His face reddened, his pulse quickened, and he waited for Lind to continue.

"The costs in your division are higher than budgeted, the morale is low, and your branch managers are unhappy with your stewardship," Lind said. "And your cooperation with Gil Harris has fallen short of satisfactory."

Carson grew angrier at the mention of Harris, a young aggressive man with a master's degree from a well-known eastern business school. Harris was a latecomer to HBC, but Carson knew that everyone was pleased with his performance.

"Charles, at the country club last week, I was speaking to one of our vendors. He intimated that your dealings with him had not been entirely clean. This is what hurts me the most.

"I know you are 49, that your son is only eight, that this is a difficult time for you and your family," Lind concluded as Carson stared out the window. "You have spent almost all your life in Hawaii; . . . it would be difficult for you to move to the mainland. It will be even harder for you to find a similar position in the Honolulu community. But I must

Exhibit 1

BOARD OF DIRECTORS—1972

Name	Age, place most of life spent	Background	Current activity	Previous association in years		Number of shares represented
				Industry	Company	
Choy, Eduardo	65, Hawaii	No academic degree; financial.	Entrepreneur; corporate chairman; banker.	0	15 as director	3,000
Donahue, John	70, Hawaii	Engineer; retired.	Retired corporate executive of the company; vice president of a property management company.	40 with company	8 as director	500
Eichi, Ishi	40, Hawaii	Legal; attorney.	Practicing attorney.	0	2 as director	0
Fields, J. B.*	54, Hawaii	M.B.A. (Harvard); finance.	Executive vice president of a very large multinational company headquartered in Honolulu.	0	15 as director	2,500 + 4% owned by his company.
Fong, Charles	40, Hawaii	M.B.A. (Harvard); Finance.	Executive vice president of a real estate development and investment firm.	0	2 as director	500
Hanley, Don*	70, Hawaii	Secretary.	Retired.	19	19 as director	10,000
Johnson, T.†	48, Hawaii	Accounting	Corporate treasurer of the company.	15	2 as director	1,000
Lind, James*†	53, Mainland U.S.A.	Engineer; alumnus of Columbia Business School.	Corporate president.	28	2 as president and director	4,000

Name					
North, Roy* .... 56, Mainland and 16 years in Hawaii	Engineer; financial analyst.	16	10 as director	1,500	Executive vice president of a conglomerate headquartered in Honolulu.
Rusk, Dean* .... 52, Hawaii	Accounting and finance insurance; alumnus of Harvard Business School.	0	5 as director	0	Executive vice president of a local large company operating in insurance, sugar, real estate, and merchandising, business.
Simon, A. F.* .... 65, Hawaii	Contractor; entrepreneur.	0	20 as director	30,000	Corporate chairman and president; entrepreneur.
Vogel, Lawrence .... 63, Hawaii	Finance; fiduciary.	0	10 as director	0	Corporate president; fiduciary agent, represents a large local trust.

* Member of the board's executive committee.
† HBC employee.

ask for your resignation, and I will do my best to help you find a more suitable opportunity."

"Jim, I can't believe it," Carson finally replied. "It's just all wrong." He turned slowly from the window, his face blood-red.

"I have been with this company for ten years. I built this division. Sure, this year's results are not quite what you expect but my division is still the largest contributor to corporate profits. I'll bet your friend Gil has been telling you about the vendor deals. Well, it's a damned lie, and I won't stand for it! That boy will stop at nothing to grab power."

There was a long silence as Lind and Carson stared at opposite corners of the large office. "I will not resign," Carson suddenly declared, and he left the president's office coughing, his face flushed and his heart pounding.

Lind stood motionless as he watched the door close. He was uncertain about what to do; it never had occurred to him that Carson might refuse to resign. He decided to proceed as he had planned, but with one modification.

"Janice, please take a memo," he said to his secretary, and he dictated a note to Charles Carson informing him that his employment with HBC was terminated as of that afternoon, October 10, 1972.

After sending out a general release memo informing all division heads that Carson had resigned and that Joseph Ward, a promising young executive, presently employed as the manager of planning in the Operations Division, would assume the position of acting general manager of the Islands Division, Lind hurriedly left the office. He had less than an hour to catch the 12:30 plane, intending to visit each of the seven branch heads on the outer islands, to tell them about the change and their new acting general manager.

While Lind was having his memos sent out, Carson was trying to contact his previous boss and old friend, Roy North, past president of HBC and presently an influential member of the company's board of directors and its powerful executive committee. Carson intended to have the matter taken to the board for deliberation.

BACKGROUND

Mr. North was one of five members of the board's executive committee, which customarily approved the appointments, promotions, stock options and salary adjustments of personnel earning over $10,000. This included department heads, division managers, and vice presidents. The committee held at least one meeting a month, and these, like the regular monthly meetings of all 12 board members, were well-attended. (Exhibit 1 shows selected data about the directors).

Several of the directors were descendants or close friends of the founders of the Hawaii Best Company, but only James Lind and Thomas Johnson were HBC employees. Board members held 5 percent of outstanding stock; the rest was widely owned by the people and business concerns in Hawaii. No one outside the board represented more than 1 percent of the HBC stock.

In 1971, with $30 million in sales and an e.p.s. of $1, the Hawaii Best Company was a manufacturer and marketer of a special formula. The company was listed on the Pacific Coast stock exchange with 1 million shares outstanding which yielded a stable dividend of $1 per share over the last five years. It sold its line of special formula X to industrial, commercial, and residential customers in the state of Hawaii. Its manufacturing facilities and three sales branches were strategically located in Honolulu, and seven other sales branches were spread over the outer islands. The company usually negotiated hard for its basic raw material K, used in the manufacture of special formula X, from its only locally available long-term supplier. Imports of the raw material were deemed uneconomical for HBC and a second source of local supply did not appear on the horizon.

The company also sold special formula Y, but only in the outer island branches and not in Honolulu. It was purchased in finished packaged form from several vendors within and outside the state of Hawaii, but the company was in no way involved in its manufacture.

Over the past five years the company's sales grew at an average annual rate of 4 percent, but its market share remained constant. Relative to the competition, HBC's profit performance had declined and, according to one competitor, "it was only through some 'creative' accounting that the company barely made its dividend in 1971."

HBC had two rivals in its industry: the larger company had annual sales of $60 million, the smaller sales of $15 million a year. It was a fiercely competitive industry, and special favors or discounts, although illegal, were sometimes granted to woo customers from another company. And customers were precious; just ten clients accounted for one-quarter of HBC sales.

HBC's ORGANIZATION STRUCTURE

Exhibit 2 shows HBC's skeletal organizational structure. The president, James Lind, was responsible to the board of directors. Thomas Johnson, vice president finance and secretary, and President James Lind regularly attended the monthly board meetings, and other vice presidents were also invited frequently to keep the board informed on matters of importance in the area of their specialty. According to Andrew Simon, chairman of the board of directors, "This practice gives us an opportunity to know what we have underneath the first layer."

In addition to managing five divisions and attending to the normal duties of the president, Lind took a special interest in the negotiations involving labor contracts and purchasing of raw material K and special formula Y. The specific responsibility for negotiating labor contracts rested with the vice president of industrial relations, John Wyle. Control of the purchase of raw material K lay with the senior vice president of operations. The vice president and general manager, Islands Division, was responsible for buying special formula Y.

In all these negotiations, however, it was not uncommon for Johnson to get involved as well.

Exhibit 2

ORGANIZATION STRUCTURE 1972

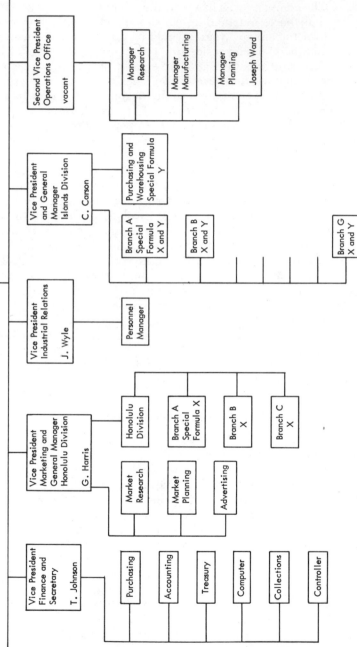
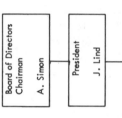

Among the corporate vice presidents in 1971, John Wyle, 51, had been the longest with the company. However, he had suffered two serious heart attacks since joining the company in 1945—one in 1959 and the other in 1968. According to the former HBC president North, "Wyle is the best industrial relations man we can find and he is a good personal friend of ours [their wives played cards together] but, frankly, his health concerns me and several of the directors."

Since joining the company in 1947 as a clerk, Thomas Johnson had risen to the position of vice president finance by 1968. In 1970 at the age of 46, he was elected to the company's board of directors at the suggestion of President Lind. Johnson had been actively under consideration for the presidency when Roy North vacated the position in December, 1969. One member of the selection committee put it this way: "Johnson is quite happy in his present position. He is a little lazy. He never wanted the top job."

Gil Harris, 33, joined the company in March, 1970 as vice president for marketing and general manager of the Honolulu Division, responsible for the conduct and performance of the three Honolulu branches and for the companywide market research, market planning, and advertising campaigns.

As vice president and general manager of the Islands Division, Charles Carson had controlled the conduct and profit performance of all the branches in the state outside Honolulu. Carson also participated in the marketing decisions, such as advertising and promotions, and his division was charged a pro-rata share of expenses on the basis of divisional sales.

The Islands Division and the Honolulu Division were created by Lind in February 1970 after the sudden death of Vice President Sales Robert Gellerman, 46. Gellerman had been responsible for the companywide sales and advertising throughout the state. Prior to the establishment of the two divisions, Lind consulted Chairman Simon, former HBC President North, and other members of the executive committee, and received their unanimous support. Also included in the restructuring were the functions of market planning and market research, which were consolidated under the new vice president for marketing and general manager, Honolulu Division.

The position of senior vice president operations had been vacant since May 1970, when Lind asked for the resignation of the man who had held that office. The three managers within the division—manufacturing, planning, and research—had since been reporting directly to Lind. They constantly vied for the attentions of the president and the corporate vice presidents in the hope that one of them could assume the vice presidency. Three key members of the board were acquainted with Donald May, the research manager, but the other two were virtually unknown to the board.

Arrival of James Lind

On January 1, 1970, James Lind replaced Roy North as president of Hawaii Best Company when the latter left the company to become an executive vice president of a multinational conglomerate headquartered in Honolulu. North, under whose control HBC had prospered for seven years, recommended Lind for the presidency after an unfruitful search for a candidate within the company and the Hawaiian community. The board of directors accepted Lind, then a top executive in a trade association in New York, and he soon proved to be a man of integrity, dedication, and charm.

Although the business community in Hawaii, according to some observers, was tight-knit and nearly impervious to outsiders, Lind was readily admitted and liked. The morale at HBC soared during the early months of his presidency, because he was a man who was both extraordinarily hardworking—he put in up to 70 hours a week—and "human." He was one of the best fund raisers for community projects in Hawaii.

Financially, however, the company was not performing well under Lind's leadership. Rising labor and material costs, and the combination of the inflationary spiral and the fierce competition put pressure on the profit margins. Lind began to make changes in key personnel in an effort to offset the problem.

In February, he promoted Charles Carson, a man who had been with the company for over eight years, to vice president and general manager of the newly created Islands Division.

Three months later he asked for the resignation of Frank Adams, senior vice president for operations. Lind felt that Adams, after 27 years at HBC was "utterly lacking in an ability to negotiate for key raw materials," and brought his grievance to the board of directors. Before Adams was asked to resign, a severance package was worked out and approved by the board. Adams, then 53, was utterly shaken. He became an estimator for a local construction firm at one-quarter of his former salary. This was the first such severance in the history of the company and as one director put it: "The event was extremely painful; it left deep scars on us and our families."

Lind's final major organizational change was to bring in an old friend of his whom he hoped could develop new marketing strategies for the entire company. Gil Harris, from the Global Chemical Company of New York, was made vice president for marketing and general manager of the newly formed Honolulu Division.

Lunch at the club

"Jason, thank you for meeting me here, and for cancelling your other engagement to see me. I'm sorry, but I had to talk to you; something has happened that I think you should know about."

Charles Carson leaned heavily on the table in the restaurant of Honolulu's only country club. The man across from him curiously fingered the stem of his martini glass. Jason Fields, the executive vice president of the third largest international company based in Hawaii, was a busy and important man. An illustrious graduate of the Harvard Business School, Fields was one of the three most influential members of the company's board and its executive committee. Fields's employer controlled 4 percent of the HBC's outstanding stock. He did not have too much time to spend with Carson, his golf buddy and a VP of one of the two companies of which Fields was a director. (The other company was a major buyer from Carson's division at HBC.)

"I'll try to be brief," Carson said. "Jim called me to his office this morning and asked me to submit my resignation. I refused. But before he left for his bloodsucking trip, he terminated my association with the company as of this afternoon."

Fields raised his eyes briefly.

"I control the company's three largest customers, you know," Carson continued. "I can easily take them to the competition. But he still has the gall to accuse me of taking a kickback, with absolutely no proof! I think Harris has put him up to it. He's been charging a substantial proportion of his division's expenses to my division. I have been arguing with him about these expenses during the last several weeks, and he finally told me he'd have my head if I went to Lind about it."

"Not even a note of thanks. Not even a mention of it to the board," Carson murmured. "I wonder how long the board will allow Lind to destroy the very people who built this company."

"I don't know what to do."

"Neither do I, Charlie," Fields answered. "I'm truly sorry to hear about this. This is strange. I had no idea this was even being considered. The executive committee met this morning and Jim, of course, was there, but this was never mentioned. I'd like to help in any way I can, Charlie. . . . All I can say is wait and see what happens at the next board meeting. It's scheduled for October 17."

"Well," said Carson, "I just hope the board takes this chance to finally straighten up the organization. Its relationship to the company, the delegation of responsibility, the criteria for employee evaluation—there are a lot of things that have remained garbled and unclear ever since Frank Adams was asked to resign. The morale of the executive staff is low. Earnings are not improving. Everyone is concerned about his own skin. Who will be axed?"

Lind's turbulent ride

Lind was deeply shaken over Carson's refusal to resign, and on the plane to Maui he tried to analyze the situation. He realized that he had made a mistake in promoting Carson a year and a half ago, although the psychological tests that he had had administered to all executives at the time pointed strongly to Carson as the man for the job. Lind remembered, too, the annual physical checkup the company executives were required to undergo, and recalled sadly the high blood pressure and excessive cholesterol level that Carson's exams revealed.

"I must stick to my guns," Lind mused. "I refuse to be blackmailed by the three powerful customers Charlie has in his pocket. I cannot let my authority be challenged, especially by a man I believe has taken kickbacks."

After a sleepless night, Lind telephoned Andrew Simon to inform him of Carson's resignation.

"Yes, Jim, Jason Fields called me yesterday to tell me," Simon relayed. "He was quite upset. And I saw Roy North at a cocktail party last night. He, too, knew about the event, and he appeared visibly disturbed. This is a sad situation. I am a little more than concerned, but you are the boss. We'll try to handle the matter appropriately at the board meeting next week."

Simon returned the receiver to the cradle thoughtfully. For the first time in his 20 years as chairman of the board, he felt that there was a conflict between the management of company affairs and the way he thought they ought to be managed.

Approaching 65, Simon was still active and healthy, and never missed a board meeting. He was once the caretaker president of HBC for one year in 1956. His deep concern for the company was reflected in the way he usually helped in its decision-making process—carefully—after long consideration and debate. He had discussed the matter of Adams' resignation privately first with Lind, then with the executive committee, and then with the entire board before Simon had been fully convinced that Adams should go. Similarly, he had spent long hours deciding on Lind's appointment, consulted extensively with several members of the board individually. Both Mr. and Mrs. Lind were interviewed thoroughly before the board selected him for the presidency.

The Rugby Portland Cement Company Limited (A)*

HISTORY, GROWTH, AND ORGANIZATION

THE RUGBY COMPANY began producing lime in the early 19th century at a works near Rugby, England. Cement manufacture under the company's "Crown Cement" trade-mark began at the works in the 1820s, and thereafter became its principal product. In 1925 the company, which hitherto had been a partnership, became a private limited company with a share capital of £100,000 owned by descendants of the previous partners. In 1929 Mr. (now Sir)[1] Halford Reddish, then a young chartered accountant with a consulting practice, joined the board, which previously had comprised only representatives of the two descendant branches of the original owners. Four years later, upon the death of the general manager, Sir Halford Reddish became managing director, and shortly afterwards, chairman.

At that time, the cement industry was in the middle of a deep depression. Prices were at a very unprofitable level. In spite of this crisis, Sir Halford decided to expand and modernize the company's production facilities. Contrary to previous industry tradition, he also decided to operate the plant 52 weeks per year, thus ensuring steady employment for the workers. Despite the depression and the difficulties of selling the increased output, a profit was realized at the end of the first year of the new management. A second manufacturing site was obtained when a nearby company went into receivership. Erection of a new factory at the second site, plus the modernization and expansion of the Rugby works, required substantial fresh capital. In 1935 the company became a public company with its shares quoted on The London Stock Exchange, and additional capital of £140,000 was introduced. Later, additional equity capital was raised by occasional "rights" issues.

---

[1] In early 1958, Her Majesty Queen Elizabeth II knighted Mr. Halford Reddish for his public services.

Rugby also acquired substantial chalk-bearing lands near Dunstable (about 48 miles to the south of its Warwickshire plants) from which high calcium carbonate chalk was railed daily to its Warwickshire plants.

By the mid-1930s Rugby was already the second largest cement company in the United Kingdom. (For an operations flow chart, see Exhibit 1.)

In 1936 Rugby acquired a third site and erected its Rochester works. In 1939 another company was purchased and its facilities were combined with those at Rochester. In 1945 Rugby acquired still another company, and, although its production facilities were closed, Rugby used its brand name and distribution organization.

Many major additions were made to these three facilities in the period after World War II, and during the 1960s Rugby made three additional acquisitions that expanded its U.K. operations, not only in cement, but also in another industry serving the building materials field.

Thus, in 1962 Rugby acquired the entire share capital of Eastwoods Cement Limited (owning three cement plants in the United Kingdom) and in 1963 the entire share capital of Chinnor Industries Limited (owning one cement plant in the United Kingdom). In 1968 Rugby acquired the entire share capital of The Rom River Company Limited, designers, fabricators and fixing subcontractors of steel reinforcement.

During the immediate postwar years, export trade was very profitable, with unit margins several times those of the home-market sales. The proportion of Rugby's deliveries accounted for by exports reached a maximum in 1951 and 1952 at about 43%. In 1961, however, Sir Halford Reddish said that in recent years export sales had become almost marginal because of the increased competition (much of it subsidized) from non-British manufacturers and the growth of cement industries in areas formerly importing cement. Rugby had itself established overseas subsidiaries, and had built manufacturing plants in Trinidad and Western Australia. The former started production in 1954, the latter in 1955. Both units were able to underprice existing imports by a substantial margin, and these facilities made useful contributions to Rugby's consolidated profits.

With a rapidly developing local market plus export trade in the Eastern Caribbean, the Trinidad factory had to be extended within less than five years of starting its operation. In 1963 the capacity of the Australian plant had to be doubled. By 1971 its capacity had been raised to one million tons per annum.

In highlighting Rugby's growth, Sir Halford spoke as follows in 1971:

> In 1946 our total share and loan capital and reserves were £1,671,-551. By 1970 they had grown to £56,220,048, and if we substituted current values in place of the book values of the assets, they would amount to at least £25 million more.
>
> In 1946 our pretax profit was £135,664; in 1970, £7,111,867.
>
> For 1946 we paid out in dividends on the Ordinary shares £40,625. For 1970 dividends on the Ordinary and Participating (non-voting) shares amounted to £2,448,000.

We now have 27,942 shareholders compared with 2,877 twenty-five years ago.

Additional capital introduced from 1st January 1933 to 31st December 1971 amounted to £60,370,867. Here is how the money has been found:

Shareholders have subscribed for shares (including premiums and loan stock)	£28,982,500
Profits have been left in the company	28,836,245
Others have contributed (by minority interests, or loans to, subsidy companies)	1,863,285
From Investment Grants	688,837
Total	£60,370,867

Net profit before taxes rose from less than £4,000 in 1933 to over £9 million in 1971. Postwar growth produced 26 years of successively record group profits, 1946–1971 (see Exhibits 2–4). By 1972 the Stock Exchange value of the company's equity capital was approximately £120 million.

In 1971 the nine company works and their annual capacities in tons were as shown in Table 1.

Table 1

COMPANY WORKS AND CAPACITIES

United Kingdom		Overseas	
Southam	540,000	Trinidad	390,000
Rochester*	400,000	Western Australia	1,000,000
Rugby	600,000	Total	1,390,000
Barrington	500,000		
Ferriby*	350,000	Grand Total	4,140,000
Lewes	80,000		
Chinnor	280,000		
Total	2,750,000		

* The Rochester and Ferriby plants were in the process of being doubled in 1972.

The company also continued to work its extensive chalk quarries near Dunstable, some 48 miles from Rugby.

At the end of 1971, Rugby had about 3,900 employees in its seven U.K. factories and subsidiaries, its overseas operations, and its headquarters at Rugby, England. The head office was organized into nine departments: engineering, production, transportation, sales (home and export), finance and accounting, legal, secretarial, property management, and computer. Above these departments was a small control and coordination group, called the administration department. This group, consisting mostly of assistants to top management, directed and coordinated the activities of the functional departments and served as the intermediate link between subsidiary companies. The subsidiaries addressed all inquiries and reports to Sir Halford Reddish, who was the chairman of each, and to the headquarters staff departments.

The board of directors comprised eight members: four "outside" (non-executive) directors, and four full-time executive directors. For over 30 years Sir Halford Reddish, as chairman and managing director, had as his deputy Mr. R. L. Evans, who passed away in 1968. Sir Halford and Mr. Evans had worked closely with each other, attempting to attain an interchangeability of talents. Sir Halford played a leading role in all major policy decisions, and was particularly concerned with financial management and public relations. Mr. Evans' background was also in accounting; as second in command, he in effect had headed the administration department.

In 1972 the executive directors were Sir Halford Reddish, chairman and chief executive; Mr. Maurice Jenkins, managing director; Mr. R. J. Morgan, and Mr. R. H. Yeatman. The last three had been with the company for many years before appointed to the board. Mr. Jenkins had moved up from assistant managing director after Mr. Evans' death. Mr. Morgan, also a chartered accountant, was particularly concerned with accounting and taxation matters and with financial administration. Mr. Yeatman, for many years general sales manager, was still primarily concerned with sales.

Sir Halford, who served on the boards of five other corporations and on a number of semi-public councils, spent the greater part of each week in London. His days in Rugby included the weekend, and he normally met with the other executive directors on Sunday morning to discuss current operations and problems, and also to engage in planning for up to "two or three balance sheets ahead."

REASONS FOR GROWTH

Sir Halford believed that the company's growth and profitability were attributable to several interrelated factors. But overriding them all, he insisted, was the human element—good human relations. These he defined simply as a recognition of the essential human dignity of the individual:

> The efficiency, the good name, the prestige, the progress of any business depend in the final analysis, not on the magnificence of its plant, not on the splendor of its offices, but on the spirit of the human beings who are working together in that business and whose lives are bound up with its success.
>
> The most valuable asset in any company's balance sheet is one written in invisible ink. It reads something like this: "The loyalty, the efficiency, the capacity for work of all employed by the company, their pride in the job and in the company's achievements, and their joy in having a part in those achievements."

Besides good human relations, Sir Halford identified five other factors as critical to his company's success:

1. *Emphasis on operating efficiency* was considered one of the most

important of these factors. Sir Halford said that the key to lower unit costs when producing with expensive, continuous-process equipment was keeping the plant operating as close to full capacity as possible and minimizing every element of operating and overhead costs. Therefore, avoiding downtime, improving efficiency of men and machines, and achieving fuel and power economies were all-important. To accomplish these ends, Rugby employed an elaborate monthly cost-reporting system which facilitated pinpointing the items of excessive costs. The factory managers were held responsible for costs under their control, and the chief engineer and production manager and their staffs were continually watching fuel and power costs and working on means of increasing machine efficiency. Excess overtime, costly repairs, stores usage, and factory staff costs were other items which attracted the attention of the central cost control department. One manager said, "We continually work on the weakest point reflected by the cost analyses."

The company's research on improvement of its manufacturing process produced several cost savings. One major outcome of such research was the development of a "wetting" agent for the slurry. Without affecting the chemical properties of the finished product, this agent produced the same "liquidity" and thus the same mixing and handling properties in a slurry containing only 35% water contrasted with 41% previously required. The smaller amount of water to vaporize meant appreciable fuel savings.

Another recent development was the installation of a pipeline from the chalk quarries near Dunstable to the two Warwickshire plants, through which a chalk slurry was pumped a total distance of some 57 miles. This became a possibility when a Pipeline Act came into force in 1962. The Rugby company received the first authorization granted under this Act.

Worker efficiency was also a matter of continuous attention. Because of the expensive equipment and the need to operate without stoppages, misconduct on the job, unexcused absences, and excessive tardiness were considered grounds for release. Such strictness was necessary because, for example, a kiln burner[2] could, through 10 minutes' neglect, permit many thousands of pounds' worth of damage to the equipment. Sir Halford said that his insistence that all employees "play the game according to the rules of the organization" was not only necessary for efficiency but was also a matter of loyalty. "But," he added, "I hold firmly to the view that loyalty should be a two-way traffic. If the head of a business expects a man to be loyal to him, then I say that that man has every right to expect that same loyalty from the head of the business. And I am sure that without discipline there can be no real happiness or success in any organization."

Finally, emphasis was placed on clerical and procedural efficiency. Sir Halford said that greater use of mechanical accounting and invoicing, and continuous analysis and improvement of office procedures, had slightly reduced the head office staff in the past few years. Periodic

---

[2] The kiln burner was the worker in charge of operating one or more kilns.

evaluation of the forms and paper-work systems was conducted to elimi-nate the unnecessary. "We have even had our competitor friends," he said, "come to look over our reporting and accounting systems. They are amazed by the fact that we get our data faster than they do with a proportionately smaller clerical staff."

2. *An effective sales organization* was said to be the second contribut-ing factor to growth and profits. Manufacturing savings effected by maintaining peak production were attainable only as long as the output could be sold. The general sales manager remarked, "Since the industry sells on a common price arrangement, you don't sell cement by selling cheaper than the next man. You sell on delivery service, good will, product quality, and on contact with the customer. We like to think that we rate very high on all these counts. Selling cement is very much of a team effort, and we have a fine organization here." Under the general sales manager were an export manager and five area sales managers. Depending upon the circumstances, each area manager controlled a number of salesmen, ranging from seven in the Midlands to three in the South West. There were in all 28 salesmen, all of whom worked from their homes. The greatest concentration of salesmen was in the London area where three were located. The salesmen were paid entirely by salary.

3. *Overseas manufacture and other subsidiary activities* were a third factor to which credit was given for much of the company's growth and its increased profits in the past few years. Rugby was continually con-ducting site investigations and negotiations in search of new overseas opportunities for expansion.

4. *"Efficient" transportation of the U.K. cement sales* was another reason given for Rugby's growth and profitability. Rugby's fleet had grown from 52 trucks in 1946 to 394 in 1971 (102 flat-bed trucks, 12 bulk tippers and 280 pressurized bulk wagons),[3] and extra trucks were hired in the peak construction season. Rugby was proud of the efficiency of its fleet, the operating costs of which remained below the transporta-tion allowance in the delivered price. At one time the fleet averaged less than 7% delays for repairs, less than 10% nonoperating idleness, and 6% on-the-job delays. The requirements of the Transport Act of 1968 had, however, increased the delays for repairs. Company officials be-lieved that their truck fleet was one of the most efficient in the industry. The major reason for this efficiency, the directors believed, was the highly centralized scheduling of truck dispatches. Each day the central transportation department, working with the sales department, prepared schedules of the following day's dispatches of all trucks from each of the works. Scheduling attempted to maximize the number of deliveries by each truck and to make as uniform as possible the work-load at the pack-ing and loading plants.

5. *A company-wide philosophy of teamwork* was seen by Sir Halford and the other directors as the most important reason for the company's

---

[3] Flat-bed trucks carried cement in bags; pressurized bulk wagons carried loose cement in large tanks which were slightly pressurized to remove the cement at the delivery site; bulk tippers were fully enclosed dump trucks which carried loose cement.

success. Teamwork had been achieved, they believed, through the chairman's human relations philosophy and through the application of profit-sharing and employee-shareholding plans. Rugby had no "personnel" department; development of teamwork was the job of managers at all levels within the firm. The impersonal term "personnel" and the word "welfare," with its connotation of charity, were banned from the Rugby vocabulary.

During the course of his career, Sir Halford had developed a philosophy of business as a team effort. A concrete expression of this philosophy was his introduction at Rugby of employee-shareholding and profit-sharing plans. Commenting on the relationship between his philosophy and these plans, he said:

> I am convinced that no scheme of profit-sharing or employee-shareholding can succeed unless it is built on a firm foundation of confidence within the business and of real *esprit de corps*—a strong feeling on the part of all employees of pride in the company and its achievements. The good will of those working together in an industrial enterprise cannot be purchased for cash—of that I am sure. A scheme which is put in with the primary object of buying good will is almost certainly doomed to failure from the start. It may indeed not only do no good but may even do positive harm by creating suspicion, however ill-founded.[4]

Teamwork, seen as commendable in any organization, was held to be doubly important in the cement industry where production in large units of continuous-process plant made it impossible to associate individual effort with specific product output. Mutual confidence was felt to be the basic ingredient of teamwork: on the part of the board, this meant confidence that all employees would put forth a fair day's work, would operate and maintain the plant intelligently, and would follow the leadership of the company; on the part of the employees, it meant confidence in the capability and integrity of the directors and a conviction that discipline "which was as fair as it was firm" would be maintained.

Leadership, in Sir Halford's view, was primarily setting an example. "You lead from in front," he said, "not from behind. It is saying, 'Come on,' not 'Go on.'"

ESPRIT DE CORPS AND COMPANY POLICIES

The following paragraphs summarize the policies singled out by Sir Halford as making the most important contribution to the sense of *esprit de corps* within Rugby.

1. *Personal contact between top executives and operating people all over the world* was relatively frequent. Sir Halford visited the Trinidad and Australia plants at least once a year, and someone from the central headquarters staff visited them, on an average, every two or three months. At home, Sir Halford not only delivered his annual message to

---

[4] Quotation from "This Is Industrial Partnership," a pamphlet written by Sir Halford in 1955 to explain his philosophy and the profit-sharing and employee-shareholding schemes of Rugby.

his "fellow-workers," but he always personally made presentations which were given to men with 25 years' service and again after 50 years' service. Such presentations were made in the presence of the recipients' colleagues, and Sir Halford usually gave a brief review of the recent progress of the company.

2. *Annual messages from Sir Halford to his "fellow employees"* described recent developments within the company, and emphasized the cooperative roles played by employees and shareholders. On these occasions, Sir Halford frequently discussed the importance of profits. The following example is from his message on operations for 1951:

> I want now to say something about profits, because a lot of nonsense has been talked about profits in the last few years, often by politicians of all parties who have never been in industry and have no practical knowledge of industry.
>
> You and I know that profits are the reward and the measure of economy and efficiency, and are essential to the maintenance and expansion of a business. They are, in fact, the real and only bulwark behind our wages and salaries, for if this company ceases to make profits it can only be a comparatively short time before you and I are out.
>
> Let us recognize that it is up to every one of us in this team to go all-out all the time, to give of our best, to maintain and increase our production with economy and efficiency, and in turn, the profits of the company: first—and note that I put this first—because it is the job we are paid to do, and it is only common honesty to our shareholders to do it; and secondly in our own interest to safeguard our jobs for the future.

3. *A "Works Committee" at each plant* functioned as another instrument of teamwork. Composed of the works manager, the works engineer, the safety officer, and five representatives elected from the factory work force, the committee met without exception each month with a senior member of the headquarters staff in attendance. The committee discussed matters of particular interest to the works concerned, and considered suggestions for operational improvements. The head office staff took this opportunity to clarify and discuss newly announced changes in policy and other company developments, such as the annual financial statements.

Toward the end of 1961, an IMEDE[5] researcher had the opportunity to attend a Works Committee meeting at the Rochester Works. The late Mr. R. L. Evans was the head-office representative in attendance. The committee chiefly discussed matters of plant safety and amenities for the workers, such as a sink and hand towels for workers at a remote plant location. The Rochester Works manager said that this meeting was typical, especially insofar as it was primarily concerned with safety and working conditions. The researcher was impressed at the free and easy manner in which the workers entered into the discussions. Mr. Evans explained in great detail some minor points of company policy

---

[5] The *Institut pour l'Etude des Méthodes de Direction de l'Entreprise,* Lausanne, Switzerland.

on tardiness and vacation time. He commented that the worker representatives occasionally brought up very minor points in the committee. "I think," he added, "that some men do this just to show that they are on their toes and doing a good job for their fellow-workers. The result is that the committee functions very well, and in a very good spirit."

4. *Layoffs, and even decisions about layoffs,* were treated as a matter of top consideration. Thus, no one but Sir Halford had the authority to release people during slack periods. He had in fact never authorized a layoff. For instance, the rail strike in 1955 almost closed the Rochester factory as coal reserves ran low.[6] As the shutdown date approached, Sir Halford announced that no one would be laid off, but that (*a*) some men would have to take their vacations during the shutdown; and (*b*) everyone would have to agree to do any job given him (at his usual pay rate) during the shutdown.

5. *Low employee turnover* had long been the rule at Rugby. One executive commented on the fact that the turnover of weekly paid workers was low, as follows:

> If we set aside employees with less than two years of service, our average worker has been here about 13 years. We do find that some new employees, especially young men, are not prepared for the demanding work in a cement plant, and such men leave, usually within 12 months. Thus, new employees should not fairly be included in our average turnover figure.
>
> Incidentally, taking total annual wages and bonuses as an indicator, the cement industry ranks in the top half-dozen British industries in terms of earnings.

6. *Early and adequate communication* was regarded as important by Sir Halford, who summarized his views on this key policy as follows:

> If there is to be a lively interest and pride in the company and its doing, then it is necessary that all employees be kept informed as far as possible about what is going on.
>
> *   *   *   *   *   *
>
> We try as far as we can to ensure that everyone has an opportunity of reading on the company's notice boards a few hours *before* it appears in the newspapers any release issued to the Press. We do not think it right that a man should learn from the newspapers something which he could quite properly have heard at first hand within the company.
>
> And all Press comments on the company are posted on all our notice boards as soon as they appear.[7]

Sir Halford held strongly to the view that, to be effective, leadership must embrace an adequate system of communication—and communication in the widest sense of the term. "Example," he said, "is in itself one facet of communication."

Besides all the above-listed means of building teamwork, other means

---

[6] Last-minute settlement of the rail strike saved Rugby Cement from its contemplated shutdown.

[7] Quotations from "This Is Industrial Partnership."

of interest to Sir Halford included well-designed profit-sharing or share-holding schemes. To be effective, Sir Halford believed these must have two necessary features. First, they must be tailored to suit the circumstances of the company and the outlook, philosophy, and intent of its leader. Second, the schemes must be simple.

THE PROFIT-SHARING SCHEME

Sir Halford said that the Rugby profit-sharing scheme, inaugurated in 1935, was designed to emphasize two things:

a) that the efforts of the employees are the efforts of a team—that we are all working to one end; and

b) the essential partnership which exists between the ordinary shareholders and the employees.[8]

In speeches to both shareholders and workers, Sir Halford referred to the partnership between capital and employees. He said that capital was nothing more than the "labor of yesterday—the production of yesterday which was surplus to the consumption of yesterday."

Fundamental to the partnership was the following bargain:

. . . the labor of today is guaranteed payment for its services and the profit is calculated only after the remuneration of that labor has been paid. Capital, therefore, takes the risk and in return takes such profit (or loss) as arises after the labor of today has been paid in full.

But to my mind this difference in the basis of their respective remuneration in no way destroys the conception of industrial enterprise as essentially a partnership between the labor of yesterday (capital) and the labor of today. Nor is it destroyed if the "bargain" is varied slightly by guaranteeing the greater part of labor's remuneration irrespective of profit or loss and by making an additional but smaller part of it dependent on the results of the enterprise as a whole.[9]

The Employees' Profit-Sharing scheme provided for an annual bonus in excess of industry-negotiated wages or contracted salary for all Rugby wage earners and staff. Basic points of the scheme are summarized below:[10]

1. To qualify for the profit-sharing bonus, an hourly or salaried employee must have completed, on December 31, 12 months' unbroken service to the satisfaction of the directors. An employee who joined the company after January 1 but not later than July 1 would for that year qualify for one-half of the bonus he would have received if he had completed one year of service.

2. For the purpose of calculating the bonus, each qualified employee was treated as if he held a certain number of Ordinary shares in the company. A staff employee's "notional shares" were related to his annual salary. An hourly worker's shares varied in proportion to his length of service up to 40 years.

---

[8] Ibid.

[9] Ibid.

[10] This explanation summarizes only the major aspects.

3. The bonus was calculated at the full rate per share of the gross dividend declared and paid to the Ordinary shareholders for the financial year in question, and was paid immediately after the annual general meeting. For example, in 1971 the Ordinary dividend declared was 3.75 pence per share. Thus a worker with five years' service holding 1,315 notional shares, would receive a bonus of (1,315 × 3.75p) or £49.31.

4. Certified sickness or compulsory National Service were ignored in calculating the number of years of unbroken service.

5. Any employee who left or was under notice to leave prior to the date of payment forfeited his bonus.

6. The scheme conferred no rights in respect of any capital distribution other than those declared as dividends on the Ordinary shares of the company out of profits.

7. The scheme was subject to modification or withdrawal at any time at the discretion of the directors.

Sir Halford emphasized that the bonus was not automatic. In a very small number of cases each year, bonuses were withheld completely or in part because service was not "to the satisfaction of the directors." If a man's record for the year was questionable, including several unexplained tardinesses, for instance, it was submitted, without name, to the Works Committee of the factory. In all cases, the directors had abided by the committee's recommendation. Sir Halford said that withholding the bonus was not so much a penalty to the slack worker as it was a necessary act of fairness to those who gave 100% service during the year. Summarizing, Sir Halford said:

> I believe that this is important: the bonus must be something that is earned—not something which becomes a right. I also feel that the link with the Ordinary shareholders' dividend is fundamental: if the dividend per share goes up, so does the bonus; if the dividend is reduced, the bonus falls too—which is as it should be.

THE "A" SHARE SCHEME[11]

After World War II, Sir Halford saw two factors that made the profit-sharing scheme inadequate for emphasizing the partnership between capital and labor. He felt that the twin virtues of hard work and thrift no longer assured a man of personal savings for his old age—*taxation* restricted savings and *inflation* devalued them. Unlike the Ordinary shareholder's income, which flowed from an asset whose market value reflected both the company's prosperity and inflationary pressures, the employee's profit-sharing bonus was not reflected in a realizable capital asset. Thus he did not have a "hedge" against inflation.

To supply this need, Sir Halford presented his "A" share plan, in late 1954, for approval by the Ordinary shareholders. He said that the scheme was designed to do three things:[12]

---

[11] In 1966 the "A" shares were re-named Participating (non-voting) shares.

[12] This explanation of the "A" share plan is summarized from "This Is Industrial Partnership."

To give practical form to the unity of interest which I have always held to exist between the Ordinary shareholders and the employees; to give a return to the Ordinary shareholders on profits "ploughed back" in the past; and to give to every full-time employee the opportunity to have in his hands a capital asset readily realizable on death or retirement. It was received enthusiastically by shareholders and employees alike.

One million "A" shares with a par value of one shilling each were created with the following conditions attached to them:

1. Starting with 1955, in any fiscal year for which (a) pretax net profits were not less than £900,000, and (b) the gross amount distributed as dividend to the Ordinary shareholders was not less than £300,000, the holders of the "A" shares would be entitled to an amount of £70,000 plus 20% of any excess of the said net profits over £900,000 (see Exhibit 5). However, (i) the amount attributable to the "A" shares would not exceed 12½% of the net profits; and (ii) in the event of the issue of additional Ordinary share capital by the company after 31st December 1954 (otherwise than by the way of a capitalization of reserves or undistributed profits), the said figure of £900,000 would be increased by a sum equal to 6% of the proceeds or other consideration received by the company.[13]

2. Any amount attributable to the "A" shares as ascertained under (1) above would be distributed as dividend or carried forward in the books of the company to the credit of the "A" shares for subsequent distribution, as the directors might decide.

3. The holders of "A" shares would have no voting rights.

4. In a winding-up, the "A" shares would participate only insofar as the amount of their paid-in capital value and the "A" share credit carried forward on the company books, but would have no further participation in assets.

5. No further "A" shares would be created without the sanction of an extraordinary resolution passed by the holders of the "A" shares.[14]

Half of the "A" shares were offered to the Ordinary shareholders at par and half to the employees.

"*All* full-time employees of the company were included: this was not a get-rich-quick exercise for the favored few," said Sir Halford.

Allocation to the employees was effected by dividing all employees into groups according to remuneration, responsibility, and status within the company; length of service was not a factor. Those in the first group (which included most factory production workers) were offered 250 shares; other groups were offered 500, 750, 1,000, 1,500, 2,000 shares, and so on. After some years, when these one shilling "A" shares were quoted at over £6 on the Stock Exchange, the allocation of shares to newcomers was proportionately reduced. Over 95% of Rugby's employees had exercised their option and purchased the "A" shares.

---

[13] Because additional equity was introduced after 1954, the "A" shares began participating at a net profit of £1,748,190 for 1972.

[14] After January 1964, the number of "A" shares was increased, however, by a "scrip" issue of five new shares for each one held. See "The 'A' Share Scrip Expansion," below.

Sir Halford was particularly concerned about two aspects of the scheme. About the first, he wrote as follows:

> I was anxious that there should be no element of a "gift" from one partner (the holders of the Ordinary shares) to the other (the employees), and that the equity owned by the Ordinary shares should be unimpaired. I was convinced that the holders of the Ordinary shares could have no legitimate cause for complaint if the profits were so substantially increased in the future and some comparatively small part of the increase went to the employees as a reward for their efforts.
>
> The "A" shares should be worth no more than was paid for them when issued, so that the employees could feel that whatever increased value accrued thereafter was due to their teamwork, with, I do not forget, nor do I allow them to forget, the capital provided by their partners in the enterprise.[15]

Both this reason and tax considerations [16] dictated that the minimum profit level at which the "A" shares would start participating (originally £900,000) should be well above the profit levels when the "A" shares were issued.

The second aspect of the scheme that was of concern to Sir Halford was that the main object would continue to be assuring employees a capital sum on death or retirement. Sir Halford foresaw that the "A" shares might have some speculative attraction to the general public, and he did not want the employees to be tempted into selling and thus depriving themselves of retirement or death benefits from the plan. He also felt that anyone leaving the firm should be required to sell his shares back at par, thus enabling newcomers to participate. To accomplish these ends, Sir Halford designated that the shares allocated to the employees were to be held on their behalf by an entity called Staff Nominees Limited. This would be accountable to the employees for dividends declared, and it would be authorized to act on their behalf in all matters relating to the "A" shares.

The following conditions applied:

1. Initially, whenever an employee moved upward to a new group, he would be given the opportunity to buy his allocation of shares at par. Failing to do so, he would not be given a subsequent opportunity.
2. "A" shares could be sold by the employee at any time at par to Staff Nominees Limited, and must be sold whenever he left the company.
3. An employee's shares could be sold at market value[17] *only* in the event of the employee's death while in the service of the company, or upon his reaching age 65 (55 for women).
4. Any dividend declared on the "A" shares would be paid immediately to the employee.

The "A" share scrip expansion. After the original "A" share distribution, 50,000 shares remained unallocated. These were held by RPC

---

[15] Quotation from "This Is Industrial Partnership."

[16] See "The Taxation Aspect," below.

[17] Market price was established by quotation on The London Stock Exchange of the "A" shares allotted originally at par to the Ordinary shareholders.

Benevolent Fund Ltd. (a company formed for the aim indicated by its title) pending their issue to newcomers. The directors felt that this block of shares, plus those which Staff Nominees Limited bought back at par from departing employees, would be sufficient to offer shares to new and promoted employees for the foreseeable future. Thus, no expansion in the number of "A" shares was originally contemplated.

In December 1963, however, the company's Articles of Association were amended, giving power to the "A" shareholders to capitalize from time to time any part of the profits allocated to the "A" shares in the past but remaining undistributed, and therefore to increase the number of "A" shares for this purpose. The "A" shareholders agreed to capitalize £250,000 of the net amount standing to the credit of the "A" shares by a scrip issue of five new shares for each one held. The effect was to amend the market price of the "A" shares, which had by then reached over £9, to around 30 shillings. By this action, the marketability of the shares was increased. In 1971 a second scrip expansion brought the par value of the "A" shares from £300,000 to £360,000.

The taxation aspect.   For the company, the profit-sharing bonus was considered a wage bonus and therefore a before-tax expense. The "A" share dividends, however, were similar to Ordinary dividends, being paid out of after-tax profits.

For the employees, the profit-sharing bonus was taxed as ordinary wage or salary income. Taxation of the employees in connection with "A" share distribution was a most difficult problem and one on which Sir Halford spent many hours in consultation with the Board of Inland Revenue.

The law held that if, at the time of issue, the value of the shares was greater than the amount the employees paid for them, the difference was taxable as a "benefit" arising from employment. The Rugby "A" share sale to its employees, however, had two characteristics which affected any ruling under this law:

1.   "A" shares were not quoted on the market until two months after issue; thus it was a matter of discussion whether at time of issue they were worth more than the par value paid for them.
2.   Employees were not free to sell their shares at market price except on retirement or death.

Final agreement with the Inland Revenue was reached, putting the assessed value of the "A" shares at the time of issue slightly above par.

Tax assessment for shares issued subsequently to newcomers or to promoted employees required a different arrangement with the Inland Revenue, since by that time a market value had been established. Final agreement resulted in considering a variable fraction of the difference between current market value and par value as taxable income. The fraction varied inversely with the length of time between the recipient's age and the date when he would reach age 65, and be able to realize the market price of the "A" shares. For instance, a 25-year-old newcomer receiving 500 "A" shares would have to consider as income, for income tax purposes, only 10% of the difference between market value and the price

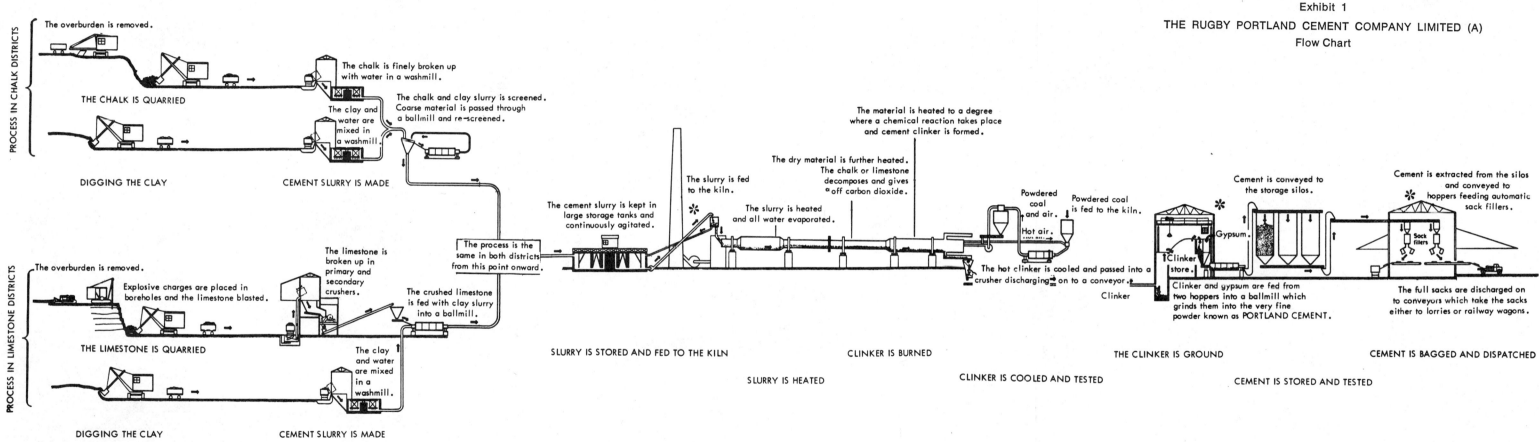

Exhibit 1

THE RUGBY PORTLAND CEMENT COMPANY LIMITED (A)

Flow Chart

paid (one shilling per share), because he could not realize the market value for 40 years. On the other hand, a 50-year-old man receiving 500 "A" shares would have to consider 42½% of the difference as taxable income, because he was much closer to realizing the gain. (All dividends received by employees on their "A" shares up to retirement age were treated, for tax purposes, as "earned" income and therefore were subject to the earned income allowance.)

Results.   In his message to his fellow-workers in the company following the 1958 operations, Sir Halford spoke about the "A" share plan as follows:

> . . . Quite often a man will say to me: "This 'A' share scheme of yours—tell me, has it increased production?" and I reply: "I haven't the slightest idea, but I shouldn't think so." So he says, "But surely that was the object. It's an incentive scheme, isn't it?" "On the contrary," I tell him, "I have always insisted that it should *not* be called an incentive scheme, because that to my mind would imply that we in Rugby Cement were not already doing our best, were not doing our duty in return for our wages and salaries. And that I will not have."
>
> What our "A" share scheme does is to give to the employees the opportunity to build up capital available on retirement or on earlier death, and to promote the feeling that we are all one team working on the same end in partnership with our shareholders. The value of the "A" shares depends in the long run on the success of our efforts in making profits. And don't overlook the fact that half the "A" shares were issued, also at par, to the holders of our Ordinary shares. They very rightly benefit too, as they have seen these one shilling shares change hands on the Stock Exchange at prices up to 42 shillings.[18]
>
> Apart from the capital aspect, the holding of "A" shares by the employees of the company, and also, of course, our "profit-sharing" schemes, give some reward for successful endeavor—which is surely right.

---

[18] In January 1964, prior to the scrip issue referred to above, the "A" shares were quoted on the Stock Exchange at up to the equivalent of 186 shillings per share.

Exhibit 2

THE RUGBY PORTLAND CEMENT COMPANY LIMITED (A)

Consolidated Balance Sheet Statements,
Selected Years, as of December 31
(in thousands of pounds)

	1946	1956	1961	1966	1967	1968	1969	1970	1971
ASSETS									
Current assets	576	4,521	8,226	14,581	17,560	22,875	27,592	30,550	31,592
Fixed assets (as valued, or at cost, less sales)	1,673	8,613	11,258	24,989	30,571	37,916	40,890	45,332	50,349
Less accumulated depreciation	436	1,969	3,930	7,589	8,876	10,328	13,119	15,064	17,129
Net fixed assets	1,237	6,644	7,328	17,400	21,695	27,588	27,771	30,268	33,217
Investment in subsidiary companies (nonconsolidated)	209	—	—	—	—	—	—	—	—
Premiums on acquisition of shares in subsidiary companies	—	—	—	4,226	4,226	7,424	7,424	7,424	7,424
Total assets	2,022	11,165	15,554	36,207	43,481	57887	62,787	68,242	72,233
LIABILITIES AND NET WORTH									
Current liabilities	367	1,759	1,328	4,138	5,134	5,898	6,073	7,945	10,410
Bank overdraft	—	—	—	2,126	4,382	961	2,490	3,085	1,343
Debt capital:									
4% debenture	420	—	—	—	—	—	—	—	751
Mortgage and unsecured loans	—	1,980	2,268	608	1,130	1,035	940	846	—
6% unsecured loan stock, 1993/98	—	—	—	—	—	12,000	12,000	12,000	12,000
7¾% unsecured loan stock, 1993/98	—	—	—	—	—	—	500	500	500
Total debt	420	1,980	2,268	608	1,130	13,035	13,440	13,346	13,251
Share capital:									
4% and 6% Preference shares*	325	825	825	1,000	1,000	1,000	—	—	—
Ordinary shares 5s. Od. par	325	1,500	2,000	10,000	12,000	13,200	13,200	13,200	15,400
"A" shares ls. Od. par†	—	50	50	300	300	300	300	300	360
Capital reserve	325	1,358	2,002	3,728	5,667	7,066	7,403	7,458	5,483

Revenue reserves:									
General reserve†	100	1,750	—	—	—	—	—	—	—
Taxation equalization account§	—	—	—	1,137	—	—	—	—	—
Investment Grants suspense account	—	—	—	—	39	413	1,001	847	689
Reserve for future taxation‖	—	320	1,373	380	594	790	1,140	1,163	1,023
Reserve for Ordinary and "A" share dividend payments¶	—	230	383	1,575	1,575	1,515	1,873	2,448	3,210
Undistributed profit	161	275	4,520	10,671	10,972	12,964	15,006	17,459	19,997
Total capital and reserves	1,236	6,308	11,153	28,791	32,147	37,248	39,923	42,875	46,117
Minority interests	—	1,117	805	544	688	745	861	991	1,112
Total liabilities and net worth	2,022	11,165	15,554	36,207	43,481	57,887	62,787	68,242	72,233
Net working capital	210	2,762	6,898	8,317	8,044	16,016	19,029	19,520	19,839
Equity debt ratio	2.9/1	3.2/1	4.9/1	47.4/1	28.4/1	2.9/1	3.0/1	3.2/1	3.5/1

Note: Some figures may fail to add because of rounding.
* Cancelled on December 31, 1969. Loan stock substituted.
† Name changed to Participating Non-Voting (PNV) shares in 1966.
‡ Merged with undistributed profit in 1958.
§ Transferred to undistributed profit in 1967.
‖ From 1966 onward, this reserve applied only to overseas taxes.
¶ Net in 1946–1961; gross for remaining years on the chart.
Source: Company records.

Exhibit 3

THE RUGBY PORTLAND CEMENT COMPANY LIMITED (A)

Consolidated Profit and Loss Account, Selected Years
(in thousands of pounds)

	1946	%	1956	%	1961	%	1966	%	1967	%	1968	%	1969	%	1970	%	1971	%
Consolidated trading profits	213		1,369		2,465		4,895		5,667		6,423		7,844		8,902		10,687	
Other income	—		65		105		103		170		157		241		284		402	
Less depreciation	79		340		550		1,070		1,276		1,415		2,166		2,074		2,083	
Net profit before taxes	134	100	1,093	100	2,020	100	3,928	100	4,561	100	5,165	100	5,919	100	7,112	100	9,006	100
Taxation—Profits tax/corporation tax			109		174		510		370		276		273		667		1,717	
Income tax/overseas tax*	39		255		602		393		733		912		1,170		1,305		1,247	
Total taxes	39	29	364	33	776	38	903	23	1,103	24	1,188	23	1,443	25	1,972	28	2,964	33
Net profit after taxes	95		729		1,244		3,025		3,458		3,977		4,476		5,140		6,042	
Minority interests	—		—		—		—		152	4	142	3	210	4	239	3	234	2
Preference dividends†	12	9	23	2	24	1	50	1	50	1	50	1	50	1	—		—	
Ordinary dividends†	22	16	194	18	306	15	1,200	31	1,200	26	1,380	27	1,650	28	1,848	26	2,310	26
"A" share dividends‡	—		36	3	77	4	375	10	375	8	413	8	525	8	600	9	900	10
Retained in business	61	46	477	44	837	42	1,400	35	1,681	37	1,992	38	2,041	34	2,453	34	2,598	29
Ordinary dividend per share (gross)	7½d		1½d		½d		7.2d		6d		6.6d		7½d		8.4d		3.75p§	
Capital distribution per share (gross)	3d		—		—		—		—		—		—		—		—	
"A" share dividend per share (gross)	—		⅓d		⅜d		1s.3d		1s.3d		1s.4½d		1s.9d		2s.0d		12.50p	
Net profit before taxes as return on total capital and reserves	10.85%		17.30%		18.11%		13.64%		14.19%		13.87%		14.83%		16.66%		19.53%	
Gross Ordinary dividend as return on capital equity employed, i.e., Ordinary shares plus disclosed reserves (less reserves credited to "A" shares)	4.36%		6.36%		5.06%		4.47%		4.00%		3.95%		4.29%		4.49%		5.22%	

* Profits tax and corporation tax were the estimated liability for the year ending with the statement. Income tax was the estimated liability for the subsequent two-year period. This procedure gave rise to the reserve for future income tax in the balance sheet. The estimated income tax for the future period was put into this reserve, and at the end of each year, the actual tax liability for the year was withdrawn from the reserve and put into current liabilities, from which the actual remittance was made.

† Net 1946–1961; gross for remaining years on chart.

‡ Changed to Participating (Non-Voting) shares in 1966.

§ After Britain went on a metric monetary system, the number of pence per pound changed from 240d to 100p.

Source: Company records.

Exhibit 4

THE RUGBY PORTLAND CEMENT COMPANY LIMITED (A)
Indices of Deliveries, Profit, and Net Worth, Selected Years
(base: 1946 = 100)

Year	Deliveries*	Capital†	Profits
1946	100	100	100
1956	307	510	816
1961	388	902	1,507
1966	729	2,329	2.931
1967	766	2,601	3,404
1968	845	3,014	3,854
1969	851	3,230	4,417
1970	859	3,469	5,307
1971	946	3,731	6,723

* These are total group deliveries, in tons, and as an index basing point.

† "Capital" here equals total equity capital, including reserves.

From 1947 through 1971, the capital account was affected by the following transactions:

Year	Amount	Transaction
1947	£1,000,000	Sale of new Common shares (£500,000) and new preference shares (£500,000).
1953	500,000	Sale of new Common shares.
1954	1,050,000	Sale of new Common shares (£1,000,000) and of "A" shares (£50,000).
1959	1,075,000	Sale of new Common shares.
1962	n. a.	Rights issue of 2 million Ordinary shares, and payments of 2 million Ordinary and 175,000 preference shares to shareholders of the acquired Eastwoods Company.
1963	—	Ordinary shares split three for two; "A" shares split five for one.
1966	—	Ordinary shares split four for three.
1967	—	Ordinary shares split six for five.
1968	n. a.	Rights issue of 4,800,000 Ordinary shares on the basis of two new for twenty old.
1971	—	"A" shares split six for five.

Source: Company records.

Exhibit 5

THE RUGBY PORTLAND CEMENT COMPANY LIMITED (A)

Summary of Earnings and Gross Dividend Payments
Selected Years
(in thousands of pounds)

	1956	1961	1963	1964	1965	1966	1967	1968	1969	1970	1971
Profit before tax........	1,093	2,020	2,656	3,311	3,664	3,928	4,561	5,165	5,919	7,112	9,006
Gross Ordinary dividend........	338	500	938	1,125	1,125	1,200	1,200	1,380	1,650	1,848	2,310
Gross payable to "A" shares........	109	252	287	414	458	491	540	613	696	836	1,074
Actual "A" share dividend........	63	125	187	300	388	375	375	413	525	600	900
Difference carried forward as "A" share credit........	46	127	100	114	120	116	165	200	171	236	174
Cumulative "A" share credit*........	91	493	316†	430	550	666	831	1,031	1,202	1,438	1,514‡

* The "A" share (later PNV share) credit was contained in the undistributed profit account in the balance sheet. The directors considered this credit as a "dividend equalization reserve" to supply "A" dividends if they were not earned according to the formula (i.e., if pretax profits were below £1,568,190 from 1964 to 1967; £1,618,846 for 1968; and £1,748,190 from 1969 onwards).
† After deducting £408,163, the gross equivalent amount of the scrip issue of £250,000.
‡ After deducting £97,959, the gross equivalent of a scrip issue of £60,000.
Source: Company records.

The Rugby Portland Cement
Company Limited (B)*

LATE IN 1961, an IMEDE research team decided to attempt to expand the Rugby Portland Cement case by adding information on the ways in which various employees of the company viewed their jobs. To this purpose, an IMEDE researcher toured each of the company's three cement works in England; he also conducted interviews with a number of hourly paid workers and with a substantial number of middle- and top-management executives. This case includes excerpts from some of these interviews, as well as some of the researcher's impressions of what he saw.

VIEWS OF SOME RUGBY WORKMEN

Rugby's management was very cooperative in helping the researcher to interview some of the workmen. Although, in theory, it would have been useful to interview a rather large number of workers selected at random, this was not practicable for certain reasons:

1. There were limitations on the research time available for these interviews.
2. There was a chance that some men, if chosen at random, might:
   a)   Not be able to articulate their views;
   b)   Be less than wholly frank;
   c)   Be unable to leave their work posts at the desired time.

Accordingly, Mr. R. L. Evans, deputy managing director, and Mr. Baker, works manager of the Rugby works, selected from the Rugby work force four workers who, they thought, would be articulate, honest, and as representative as possible of the general sentiments of the entire Rugby worker group. The researcher interviewed the four men separately, in an office at the Rugby plant; nobody else was present during the interviews. The names of the four men interviewed have been disguised.

Interview with Mr. Ryan

Mr. Evans and Mr. Baker, in arranging the interviews, mentioned that Mr. Ryan should provide a highly entertaining and useful interview, that he was outspoken and highly articulate. Mr. Ryan, who had been working for the company since 1956, was an Irishman; he appeared to be about 40 years old. He worked in the transport department of the company as a truck driver and had been a member of the Rugby works committee for some time. The researcher asked each of the four men only one question to begin: What did the man think about working for the company, what were the bad points and the good points? Mr. Ryan began:

> Well, I might tell you I'm an old union man, been a sort of union agitator all my working life. Before I came here I never held a job longer than eighteen months. I've been here almost six years now, and I can tell you this, I'm going to stay here the rest of my life. And, mind you, I got a lot less to gain by staying here than most of the men. I have no A-shares, because you know you only get one chance to buy them A-shares, and when I had to buy them, I didn't have the money because my wife just had to have an operation. So now for the rest of my life I got to work here knowing that I'll never have no A-shares, and I think this is unfair, and I keep fighting to get me shares, and maybe I will and maybe I won't, but I'll stay on here no matter what.
>
> And another thing is I'm a very bad timekeeper—sometimes it's my fault, and sometimes it was because I had to take my wife to the doctor and so I'd come in late, and so for three straight years I lost my profit-sharing bonus on account of being late so much. [Mr. Ryan had actually lost his bonus in two nonconsecutive years, management reported.] So you can see what I mean when I tell you that I got much less to gain by working here than the other men.
>
> But even though there's lots of little things could be done, this is a wonderful place to work, and that's the Lord's own truth. I'm not saying anything to you I wouldn't say right to the Chairman's face if he asked me—I'm not a man to say what he doesn't mean.
>
> You got to remember this: It's no good coming down to a cement works if you don't want to work hard. But they pay you good, and the main thing is, you always get treated fair. If you got a complaint, you can take it as high as you want, right up to the Chairman himself, but it's no good complaining unless you give 'em the facts. That's what they want to see: facts.
>
> Another thing you ought to write down is this: In this company, I'm just as good as anybody, as good as the Chairman or Mr. Evans—that's what you won't get anywhere else. We all know this here, and we know you've got to work as a team. And I'll tell you this, I know the Chairman would let me buy my A-shares if he could, but you see he's got to be fair to the other workers too. But I do think that you get punished awful hard for being late. [Mr. Ryan's profit-sharing bonus would have amounted, in those years when he lost it, to about £30. His weekly wages were about £15.]

Over in Coventry, you know [about 15 miles away], in the car and airplane factories a man can make £30 a week, while here he'll only make about £15, but we get the £15 for 52 weeks of the year, plus the profit-sharing, the A-shares, and lots of other benefits. The company buys up lots of clothes for us, so we can get them cheaper. I once compared what I earned in a year with a friend of mine who works in Coventry for £29 a week, and you know what? I came out £48 ahead of him for the year, because those fellows are always getting laid off.

And let me tell you this: You'd never get a better firm to work for, no matter where you went; there isn't another company like this, at least none I've ever heard about.

You know, when I tell you we work hard here, you've got to remember that the Chairman doesn't ask us to do anything he doesn't do himself. You know, he works 18 hours a day, and when he come down sick recently and had to have that operation, his doctors told him to take it easy, and so he did—he only worked ten hours a day.

[Mr. Ryan then gave the researcher a very detailed description of what was involved in his truck driving. He stressed that the equipment was the best obtainable, that the company paid much more attention to driver safety than to delivering a maximum daily tonnage of cement, that scrupulous care was taken, at great expense, to be certain that the customer received all the cement he had been billed for.]

You see my truck out there? That truck, it's brand new, and it cost £10,000, and they expect me to take care of it like if it was my own, and I do. [The truck in fact cost slightly over £3,500.] And I know I've got 42 hours a week guaranteed, and more hours on weekends if I want to make extra money, and that's a hell of a nice thing for a truck driver. And as soon as I've driven 11 hours in a single day, even if I didn't get home with the truck by the time my 11 hours was up, the company would send out another lorry with two drivers to drive me and my truck home, that's how careful they are about the 11-hour rule. And you see them fine overalls we drivers got, and them jackets? Mr. Reddish, I believe, bought them for us out of his own pocket. That's just the kind of man he is. [In fact he didn't; they are provided by the company.]

I told you I used to be a union man, but I tell you this, if a union came in here now, it would hurt the workers—they'd get less pay, they couldn't touch anything they weren't supposed to. That's the kind of a union man I am today.

In summing up, and this is God's own truth, I think Sir Halford Reddish ought to be England's Prime Minister, and Mr. Evans ought to be the Secretary for Foreign Affairs.

Interview with Mr. Mason

Mr. Mason was a foreman in the "raw plant," where the slurry was made. He had been working for the company about 14 years and appeared to be about 50. He began:

Well, wherever I went, I don't think I could better myself, that's what I'd say. The Chairman puts us in the picture about what's going on; he has more of a fatherly concern for us, I think. I've known the Chairman 30 years, and if he says a thing he means it. He's put in some wonderful plans for the men, he has. For example, when my father died, we got about £1,000 for his A-shares, and this was a big help, because I've got a sister who isn't very well, and this money pays for her. From the workman's point of view, if you want it, I find that they're very, very satisfied. I've got 30-odd men working for me, and I get all the points of view, so to speak, and I think I can say that they're all happy to be working here. Now, of course, there's some men as will always find something to complain about, you're going to have that anywhere, but in the main I think that the men like working here very much.

You're an American, so I'll put it in American: Damn it all, we're on to a good thing here and we know it.

I've got a brother, a son, and two brothers-in-law working here, and my father before he died. They all came to work here before I did. Now do you think they'd have come if this wasn't a good place to work?

I do believe honestly, and I'm not handing you any bull, that we couldn't better ourselves. And you've got to remember this: Sir Halford will give any of his men a proper hearing any time. And what's astonishing is that as the firm gets larger, the company seems to give us more attention, when you'd think it'd be the other way around.

Now you take your average Englishman, he's the biggest grumbler in the world, about anything at all. But you won't find much grumbling here. You'd have to kick them out to get the men here to leave.

Interview with Mr. Toot

Mr. Toot, who appeared to be about 50, had been with Rugby about seven years. The researcher received the distinct impression that Mr. Toot was temperamentally a sort of cynic who only grudgingly would admit that a workman's life could be decent, although this impression was formed on the basis of very little evidence. Mr. Toot began:

Taken all around, I should say that this is a very good place to work. A workman here knows that he can go as high as he likes, if he has the ability. You get fair treatment here. I suppose that work here is 80% satisfactory. For the other 20%, it's hard to say what the objections might be. But one thing is, when a man first came to work here, he didnt get enough participation in the bonus system [the profit-sharing scheme], but they've changed that now.

If a man's willing to do an honest day's work, he'll generally be satisfied here. I suppose I could say this: The longer a man's been here, the more he wants to stay.

Now, you get some fellows, especially young ones, come in and they can't stick the work; it's too heavy or too hard for them. They usually leave, if they're this type, in 12–18 months. If a man sticks it a year or a year and a half, he'll probably stay here until he's through working.

This is a long-term policy job, so to say. It's good if you're thinking about your old age, because the company really takes care of you after you retire. I don't suppose you know this, but all the company's pensioners [retired workers] get a ton of coal from the Chairman at Christmas. There's a Christmas party for the pensioners. And men like Mr. Evans and Mr. Baker visit the pensioners very regularly. The company doesn't just forget you when you've stopped working for them—they take care of you.

I suppose when I think of it, it's hard to say what kind of objections, you might say, a man could have to working here, if he's not just a casual laborer who doesn't care about doing an honest day's work, if he doesn't care about doing a good job. This is a good place to work.

Interview with Mr. Forster

Mr. Forster had been working for Rugby for 48 years, and he worked in the quarry. He talked rather little, much less than the previous three men.

Well, I've been working here all my life, and that's a fact. It's hard work, and no doubt about it, but it's a wonderful company to work for I was here, you know, when Sir Halford took over, and it was wonderful when he did. He promised us steady work, and we've had it ever since. Some of your casual lads, now, who come here looking for an easy day's work and high pay, they don't stay; but a real man, a man who doesn't mind work, he'll be happier here than anywhere else I've ever heard of.

RANDOM IMPRESSIONS OF THE RESEARCHER

In the course of his tour of the three different works, the researcher spent a great deal of time with Mr. R. L. Evans, who toured each plant with him, and with the works managers. The researcher was especially struck by two facts. First, Mr. Evans and the works managers appeared to know a great deal about the background of every company employee. The researcher was, while walking through the plant, introduced to one worker who had been a chef in Wyoming some years ago. Another worker was pointed out as having been (he was now 72) a good rugby player in his youth. These and similar details were forthcoming quite frequently from Mr. Evans or the works managers. Second, the workers all said "Hello" to Mr. Evans as he passed through the plant, and Mr. Evans would chat with them about their families and how things were going.

Another impression, although a difficult one to justify with explicit evidence, was that the various managers were more than superficially concerned with their workers and their lives. Words and phrases which often recurred in the four days of conversation included: "fair treatment," "decent work for a man," "take care of our men," "expect them to work as part of a team." All individuals interviewed referred to themselves as being part of a single team; they did so either implicitly or explicitly.

Managing the strategic process

THE LAST SET of cases in this book presents an opportunity to observe the range, unity, and interrelation of the concepts and subconcepts essential to the conscious formulation and implementation of a strategy governing the planned development of a total organization. The idea and its components have now been quite carefully and separately explored. It becomes appropriate at this point to reexamine corporate strategy not so much as a concept complete and still but as an organizational process forever in motion, never ending.

STRATEGY AS A PROCESS

For the purposes of analysis, as you have already noted, we have presented strategy formulation as being reasonably complete before implementation begins, as if it made sense to know where we are going before we start. Yet we know that we often move without knowing where we will end at last; the determination of purpose is in reality in dynamic interrelation with implementation. Implementation is itself a complex process including many subprocesses of thought and organization which introduce into prior resolution tentativeness and doubt and lead us to change direction.

That strategy formulation is itself a *process of organization*, rather than the masterly conception of a single mind, must become clear. The sheer difficulty of reconciling uncertain environmental opportunity, unclear corporate capabilities and limited resources, submerged personal values, and emerging aspirations to social responsibility suggests that at least in complicated organizations strategy must be an organizational achievement and may often be unfinished. Important as leadership is, the range of strategic alternatives which must be considered in a decentralized or diversified company exceeds what one person can conceive of. As technology develops, chief executives cannot usually maintain their own technical knowledge at the level necessary for accurate personal critical discriminations. As a firm extends its activities internationally, the senior person in the company cannot himself learn in detail the cultural and geographical conditions which require local adaptation of both ends and means.

As in all administrative processes, *managing the process becomes a function distinct from performing it.* The principal strategists of technically or otherwise complex organizations therefore manage a strategic decision-making process rather than make strategic decisions. When they "make" a decision approving proposals originating from appraisals of need and opportunity made by others, they are ratifying decisions emerging from lower echelons in which the earliest and most junior participants may have played importantly decisive roles.[1] The structure of the organization may predetermine the nature of subsequent changes in strategy. In this sense strategy formulation is an activity widely shared in the hierarchy of management, rather than being concentrated at its highest levels. Top management, indeed, may bear the same relationship to divisional management as an outside board of directors does to top management. Unless it meddles improperly, such a board does not itself originate or conceive of the corporate strategy it has the ultimate responsibility of approving. The chief recourse of executives or directors ratifying strategy is not to second-guess proponents of specific alternatives but to make sure that the process is working right, that the quality of judgment applied to uncertainty is good, and that the context of strategic decision is conducive to adaptations of strategy of the magnitude required by changing opportunity and risk.

Participation in strategy formulation may thus begin with the market manager who sees a new product opportunity or the analyst who first arranges the assumptions that make possible a 30 percent return on investment in a new venture. But strategy may be influenced by organization structure as much as by individuals. The strategic alternatives generated in a functionally organized integrated company will be different in kind and scope from those maturing in divisionalized and diversified companies. Autonomous corporate units inevitably compete for resources with a wide variety of unrelated new product ideas to ensure their own survival and growth. Opportunities requiring joint exploration of several of these autonomous organization units may be doomed by separation to neglect.

Similarly the cement plants in Rugby, all units in a functionally organized cost-controlled company are not going to suggest daring diversifications. We have seen that structure should follow strategy in organization design. What is important now is that in part structure *is* strategy. If, in short, the process of strategy formulation, as it must be, is distributed throughout an organization, the shape of that organization and the influences that motivate it will be reflected in the strategy it produces. The strategic decision must, of course, be made in the

---

[1] See Joseph L. Bower, *Managing the Resource Allocation Process* (Boston: Division of Research, Harvard Business School, 1970).

light of organization and human consequences. Furthermore, it must be arrived at recognizing the constraint of structure and systems derived from previous strategy which influence the generation of new alternatives. Context is both supportive and inhibiting. It may be necessary to change organization before certain strategic alternatives can be fully explored or experimentally attempted.

The subunits of an organization established to implement a given corporate purpose soon are developing divergent strategies to support their own growth and development, especially if responsibility for profit and growth has been assigned to those units. It is true, therefore, that the organization processes and measurement systems by which the functioning of the structure is evaluated will influence strategy. When an international company once tried to interest its Latin-American subsidiaries in profit rather than in the number of sewing machines sold, the country managers, inexperienced but responsive, began making ice cream, selling insurance, and manufacturing stove grates in unused plant space. These diversifications, all aimed at increasing profitability within one year, changed, at least for a time, the local strategy of this company. The structure—geographically discrete and relatively autonomous profit centers—and the incentive system—reward for short-run profitability—together could ultimately have changed the strategy of the entire company. As it happens it was the corporate intention that the company go through a transition emphasizing profitability while its future strategy, too difficult a question for anybody in a company unused to strategic planning to settle, became a problem which could be managed.

In the course of a never finished process in which corporate strategy may be changing only imperceptibly in response to changing capabilities and changing market environments, sudden opportunity or major tactical decision may intrude to distract attention from distant goals to immediate gain. Thus the opportunity for a computer firm to merge with a large finance company may seem too good to pass up, but the strategy of the company will change with the acquisition or its ability to implement its strategy will be affected. A strategy may suddenly be rationalized to mean something very different from what was originally intended because of the opportunism which at the beginning of this book we declared the conceptual enemy of strategy. The necessity to accommodate unexpected opportunity in the course of continuous strategic decision is a crucial aspect of process. Accepting or refusing specific opportunity will strengthen or weaken the capability of an organization and thus alter what is probably the most crucial determinant of strategy in an organization with already developed market power.

MANAGING THE PROCESS

Study of the cases and ideas of this book usually leads to acceptance as the basis for management action of the need for a continuous process of strategic decision. This process extends from the origin of a discrete decision to its successful completion and incorporation into subsequent decisions. With this need established in an organization, the next step is to initiate the process and secure the participation first of those in senior management positions and then of those in intermediate and junior positions. The simplest way for the chief executive of a company to begin is to put corporate objectives on the agenda of appropriate meetings of functional staff, management, or directors.

Consider, for example, a large, long-established, diversified, and increasingly unprofitable company. Its principal division was fully integrated from ownership of sources of raw materials to delivery of manufactured products to the consumer. Its president, after a day's discussion of the concept of strategy, asked his seven vice presidents, who had worked together for years, to submit to him a one-page statement expressing each officer's concept of the company's business, a summary statement of its strategy. He had in mind to go on from there, as users of this book have done in handling these cases. After identifying the strategy deducible from the company's established operations and taking advantage of their participation in resource allocation decisions, the vice presidents would be asked to evaluate apparent current strategy and make suggestions for its change and improvement. This first effort to establish a conscious process of strategic decision came to a quick recess when the president found that it took weeks to get the statements submitted and that, once collected, they read like descriptions of seven different companies.

When discussion of current strategy resumed, a number of key issues emerged from a study of a central question—why so successful a company was seeing its margins shrink and its profits decline. The communication of similar issues to those assigned responsibility to deal with the function they affect is an obvious next step. The soundness of the company's recent diversification was assigned as a question to the division managers concerned. They found themselves asked to present a strategy for a scheduled achievement of adequate return or of orderly divestment. The alternative uses of the company's enormous resources of raw material was examined for the first time. The record of the research and development department, venerable in the industry for former achievements, was suddenly seen to be of little consequence in the competition that had grown up to take away market share. Decisions long since postponed or ignored began to seem urgent. Two divisions were discontinued and expectations of improved performance began to alert the attention of division and functional managers throughout the organization to strategic issues.

Getting people who know the business to identify issues needing resolution, communicating these issues to all the managers affected, and programming action leading to resolution usually leads to the articulation of a strategy to which annual operating plans—otherwise merely numerical extrapolations of hope applied to past experience—can be successively related. It is not our purpose here, however, to present a master design for formal planning systems. This is a specialty of its own, which like all such other specialties, needs to be related to corporate strategy but not allowed to smother or substitute for it.

When formal plans are prepared and submitted as the program to which performance is compared as a basis for evaluation, managers in intermediate position are necessarily involved in initiating projects within a concept of strategy rather than proceeding ad hoc from situation to situation. Senior managers can be guided in their approval of investment decisions by a pattern more rational than their hunches, their instinct for risk, and their faith in the track record of those making proposals, important as all these are. They have a key question to ask: what impact upon present and projected strategy will this decision make?

Sustaining the strategic process requires monitoring resource allocation with awareness of its strategic—as well as operational—consequences and its social, political, as well as financial, characteristics. Seeing to it that the process works right means that the roles of the middle-level general manager be known and appropriately supported.

As Hugo Uyterhoeven has pointed out,[2] middle-level general managers occupy a role quite different from that of the senior general manager, relevant as is their experience as preparation for later advancement. With strategic language and summary corporate goals coming to them from their superiors and the language and problems of everyday operations coming to them from their subordinates, they have the responsibility of translating the operational proposals, improvisations, and piecemeal solutions of their subordinates into the strategic pattern suggested to them by their superiors.

Faced with the need to make reconciliation between short-term and long-term considerations, they must examine proposals and supervise operations with an eye to their effect on long-term development. As they transform general strategic directions into operating plans and programs, they are required to practice the overview of the general manager under the usual circumstance that their responsibility for balanced attention to short- and long-term needs and for bringing diverse everyday activities within the stream of evolving strategy far outruns their authority to require either change in strategy or to alter radically the product line of their division.

General managers at middle level, certainly in a crucial position to implement strategy in such a way as to advance it rather than depart from it, need to be protected against such distractions as performance evaluation systems overemphasizing short-term performance and to be supported continually in their duty of securing results which run beyond their authority to order certain outcomes. They need to learn how to interpret the signals they get as proposals they submit for top-management approval are accepted or turned down. Their superiors will be dependent upon their judgment as their proposals for new investment come in and will often be guided more by past performance or the desire to give them greater responsibility than by the detailed content of their proposals. Their seniors will do well then to realize the complexity

---

[2] See Hugo E. R. Uyterhoeven, "General Managers in the Middle," *Harvard Business Review,* March–April 1972, pp. 75–85.

of their juniors' position and the necessity of their being equal to the exigencies of making tactical reality subject to strategic guidance and to directing observation of operations toward appropriate amendment of strategy.

Developing the accuracy of strategic decision in a multiproduct, technically complex company requires ultimately direct attention to organization climate and individual development. The judgment required is to conduct operations against a demanding operating plan and to plan simultaneously for a changing future, to negotiate with superiors and subordinates the level of expected performance and to see, in short, the strategic implications of what is happening in the company and in its environment. The capacity of the general manager, outlined early in this book, must as part of the process of managing the strategy process be consciously cultivated, if the firm is to mature in its capacity to conduct its business and to be able to recognize in time the changes in strategy it must effect.

Executive development, viewed from the perspective of the general manager, is essentially the nurturing of the generalist capabilities referred to throughout the text portions of this book. The management of the process of strategic decision must be concerned principally with continuous surveillance of the environment and development of the internal capabilities and distinctive competence of the company. The breadth of vision and the quality of judgment brought to the application of corporate capability to environmental opportunity are crucial. The senior managers who keep their organization involved continuously in appraising its performance against its goals, appraising its goals against the company's concept of its place in its industry and in society, and debating openly and often the continued validity of its strategy will find corporate attention to strategic questions gradually proving effective in letting the organization know what it is, what its activities are about, where it is going, and why its existence and growth are worth the best contributions of its members.

The chief executive of a company has as his or her highest function the management of a continuous process of strategic decision in which a succession of corporate objectives of ever-increasing appropriateness provides the means of economic contribution, the necessary commensurate return, and the opportunity for the men and women of the organization to live and develop through productive and rewarding careers.

Sigma Consultants, Inc. (A)

EDWARD ROBSON put down the two memoranda he had been reading and wondered what conclusions he should draw about the best way to develop health care consulting at Sigma Consultants, Inc. Sigma was a large research and management consulting company with headquarters on the West Coast and offices in a number of major United States cities and various foreign countries. At the August 6, 1969, meeting of Sigma's Executive Committee, two weeks earlier, the senior management of the company had concluded that Sigma would like to support the health care field as one of its primary development areas in the near future. Edward Robson, Executive Vice President of Sigma, had been given the responsibility for determining how this development should be effected.

The main question, thought Mr. Robson, was: What should Sigma management do to encourage development of this area?

> Do we try to respond to, and encourage, individual efforts by staff members, and leave it at that? Do we try to identify the areas we think are of interest, decide what action seems indicated, and try to take it? Or do we announce our interest to the staff and then sit back and let individual efforts determine what will happen?
>
> Several issues have to be faced. First, our operating process is set up essentially to keep our existing activities going rather than to develop new ones. Second, any new development cannot depend on unilateral "management" action; it needs professional staff participation. Third, health care activities are widely scattered in Sigma at present; some like to keep an area this way—others dislike it. Finally, any proposed management action with visibility and impact is going to be met with some resistance from individual staff members and managers because of the threat to individual freedom, support of an activity the person does not understand or is not interested in, concerns over exclusion or loss of control of business, and because of the need to make choices about what to support.

BACKGROUND INFORMATION

Sigma Consultants, Inc. had annual revenues in 1969 of $50 million and was widely recognized as one of the leading organizations in its field. It provided professional services to industrial, commercial, not-for-profit, and government organizations in the United States and abroad. Its full-time professional staff of approximately 1,000 persons (a great number of whom were based on the West Coast) included specialists with training and professional experience in such varied fields as economics, engineering sciences, chemistry, physics, mathematics, biology, operations research, behavioral sciences, business management, finance, marketing, and many other areas. In addition, Sigma had contract relationships with a number of independent individual consultants, many of whom were internationally known specialists and faculty members of prominent academic institutions. Top management at Sigma believed that one of the company's major assets was the range of diverse, outstanding talents it could marshall for a client and considered the firm's capacity to attract and engage the interests of such high caliber staff to be a principal corporate strength.

The official Sigma statement of corporate goals indicated that the objective of Sigma was to operate profitably by:

1. applying our technical and managerial competence to social, economic, technical, and business issues of significance to our clients;
2. maintaining a corporate environment that will attract and develop the best people, encourage enterprise, excellence and high ethical standards;
3. operating throughout the world; and
4. achieving pre-eminence in our fields of activity.

Hierarchical organization was kept to a minimum at Sigma; hence there were very few official titles. As one observer remarked, "A lot of people at Sigma—and the lucky ones everyone agrees—are simply, uncomplicatedly, staff. Staff is rank enough." There was no official organization chart at Sigma; however the professional staff responsible for client assignments were divided into six divisions, each of which had a division head who was a Sigma vice president. (A list of the divisions, together with the names of the various persons mentioned in this case, is given in Exhibit 1.)

In the words of one division head, "The divisions are profit centers— but they are more political entities than rational groupings; and there is substantial overlap and competition between divisions." Within each division there were usually departments. "In a very rough sort of way, staff members of the same profession, or primary professional interest, tend to cluster together," said one senior professional, "but this is not stated as a requirement in principle, nor is it followed in practice. Sometimes people who can serve a particular type of client are grouped together. But, in fact, one cannot make any general statement on how these departments have come to have their current composition, except to say that personal empathy and current expediency have apparently each played a large part."

"More important than in many organizations," observed another professional, "is the need—in describing Sigma—to stress the separation and coordination of the work and administrative organizations and the individual's multiple membership in both. The most important organizational unit at Sigma is the 'project team'," he explained:

> These teams are created for each new client assignment and consist of the staff specialists required to handle the project problem. The leader of a project team need not be a designated member of the organizational hierarchy (that is, a division head, department head, etc.). In fact, some members of a project team are often more senior in some area of experience or higher in the administrative organization than the project leader; but for the purpose of that assignment, they subordinate themselves to the technical and administrative direction of the project leader. The project is the basic unit of Sigma's work; and the agreement to conduct an assignment is normally arrived at by negotiation between the project leader and the client. It is the project leader who chooses the team to work with him, often with advice from other staff members. It is company policy, however, that an individual's participation on a team is a matter of choice and agreement between himself and the project leader. A staff member is ordinarily active in two to four or more projects at any given time. The average project lasts about six months, at which time the team dissolves and the members become involved in other activities; sometimes, of course, a team member is used only in a particular aspect of a project and for a short time. Another aspect of the limited role of the formal structure is that it is expected that the members of a department will work anywhere in the organization that particular project problems require, and that most individuals will be able to generate business and lead projects with clients as soon after joining Sigma as they are reasonably integrated through experience on others' projects.

"A problem—and a strength—in the Sigma organization is that the system requires independence, initiative and self-control on the part of the staff," observed one senior executive. "The problem is general but it shows up particularly in the kind of situation the organization is currently facing. For example, in health care, one of the main issues which has to be considered is the extent to which corporate initiative and professional independence can be combined."

THE EARLY DEVELOPMENT OF HEALTH CARE CONSULTING AT SIGMA

Laboratory-based, health-related work had been a part of Sigma's activity for some years. The analysis, development and testing of drugs had been lodged primarily in the Life Sciences Division, with significant efforts in the design and evaluation of medical equipment conducted in the Engineering Division. In recent years, however, there had been another, growing set of activities in health *care* work. This was not centered in lab-based work; it included consulting on hospital organization, medical instrument marketing research, design of health care delivery systems, and so forth.

Many individuals were involved in this growing activity. Fairly typical of Sigma's entry into health care work, however, were the experiences of four particular Sigma professionals who had become active in health care. It should be noted that many other individuals became involved in health care work—to an equal or lesser degree than the four cited. However, the four persons were among the small number who were most prominently involved and their experience, since it was typical, is an illustration, and offers some understanding, of the process of entry into health care work.

Peter Dowell. After graduation from Stanford Business School in 1962, Mr. Dowell joined Sigma and began his career there in market research. In 1963, Sigma was asked to conduct a diversification study for a business firm, and in connection with this, Mr. Dowell did a study of the medical electronics market. His work in this relatively new field established Mr. Dowell as something of an expert on medical electronics and he co-authored a paper on the subject in 1964 for one of Sigma's publications. A second assignment on the subject for another client was subsequently conducted.

In 1966, a letter came to the Sigma contracting office requesting a feasibility study of a hospital merger in Oregon. The request was passed on to Mr. Dowell's division head, who asked Mr. Dowell to undertake the study. The day before the inquiry came in, Mr. Dowell had been introduced to a new staff member, Mr. Hobart; remembering their discussion and Mr. Hobart's ideas on organizational behavior, Mr. Dowell invited Mr. Hobart to work on the project with him. The $20,000 project was a success: the hospitals merged, client-relationships were good, and Mr. Dowell and Mr. Hobart were asked to make two or three presentations to their professional peers at Sigma. Mr. Dowell was "turned on" by the challenge of handling the human problems: "It blew my mind. It became obvious to me also," he said, "that health care could be a gold mine." From this point onwards, Mr. Dowell became increasingly involved in health care assignments, particularly ones which involved some aspect of organizational development or change, and he shifted the medical electronics work to another professional.

Norman Williams. Mr. Williams was a vice president without portfolio and had had a long and varied career at Sigma, which he joined after graduating from Harvard Business School in 1935. In 1940 when Sigma started its first biological research, Williams was asked to serve as a guide to the newly formed work group. Later, in 1950, Mr. Williams had taken on the task of developing Sigma's Operations Research work. During the 1950s this involved him in leading a couple of projects on the marketing of drugs for two business firms. During the 1960s other health-related work came to Mr. Williams in connection with Congressional investigations of the drug industry and government studies of the relationship between smoking and health.

In 1966, a client inquiry came to the contracting office from Western Blue Cross; it was brought to Williams who became the project leader. Williams sought out Dowell, who suggested Hobart join them; and so the three, together with three faculty members from prominent schools of Medicine and Public Health, began work on a planning study for the largest carrier of health insurance in its market. "For me," said Williams, "that project was the turning point. The work required that I learn about the trends in health care and I became convinced of the opportunities in the field and the importance of the field." After this experience, Williams became involved in further health care assignments.

Wynn Day.   Mr. Day joined Sigma's Engineering Division in 1964 with a Ph.D. in applied mathematics from Berkeley. His first years were devoted to mathematical, simulation, and systems analyses for the Air Force. After two years of full-time military-oriented cases, Day concluded he wanted to spend the major part of his time on a permanent basis in nondefense areas and he moved into a small, newly formed Systems Engineering department in the same division, which did some defense work but was making attempts to develop business outside the military sphere.

His first introduction to hospitals and health care came as a result of an acquisition study done in 1966 by Sigma for Eastex Corporation, as a result of which Eastex purchased a foreign firm which manufactured automated materials delivery systems for hospitals. After the purchase, Sigma provided some assistance in re-engineering the systems for the American market. When the engineers were faced with possible bottleneck and material shortage problems in the complicated automated system, Day suggested they might use a simulation program. As a result he ran a $19,000 case in 1967 to develop a simulation model suitable for many hospital configurations.

Although he continued doing military projects, Day was interested by hospital problems and proceeded, on his own initiative (and with the concurrence of his department head), to write proposals for studies advertised in the government's *Commerce Business Daily*. Some of this was done in his own time. The first project was for Walter Reed Hospital in Washington, D.C.; the Sigma proposal ranked seventh out of the twelve submitted and Day observed that he later saw that "it was a naïve job." A second proposal, in 1968 to the Public Health Service for a Dallas public hospital, was also unsuccessful. (Another top consultant firm got the job at two-thirds the Sigma price.) Meanwhile Mr. Day was also engaged in some engineering work on artificial heart equipment. Early in 1969, he submitted a third proposal, to the Department of Defense; in June, Sigma was awarded a large contract for a major study. of a new military hospital system.

Nicholas Vogel.   Mr. Vogel joined Sigma's Operations Research staff in 1960 after obtaining his Ph.D. in chemical engineering from the Massachusetts Institute of Technology. His early work involved him in the development and application of computer models to problems as diverse as antisubmarine warfare, the feasibility of national centralized facilities for the storage and retrieval of scientific documents, and inland waterway transportation.

In July 1963, the switchboard operator at Sigma received a call from a professor of preventive medicine at the Los Angeles College of Medicine who wanted some help from an applied mathematician. The professor, Dr. Baxter Warren, subsequently visited Sigma and talked with a couple of professionals about developing quantitative planning methods for cancer control. The Los Angeles institution had funds from the U.S. Public Health Service and planned to develop a general model for use in local health departments. Mr. Vogel was brought into the discussion because he had been trained to apply mathematical sophistication to similarly messy problems, had shown marked adaptability, and had a computer background. The result of the meeting was a $17,000 project. The relatively unplanned nature of Mr. Vogel's involvement in health care was compounded by the fact that the original team leader resigned from Sigma shortly after the contract was signed and Mr. Vogel, whose qualifications were comparable, was made team leader in his place. As a result of this project, Vogel was retained as a consultant by the Los Angeles College and a series of further projects for Sigma followed. During this period Vogel became extremely interested in epidemiology[1] and public health as a fertile area in which to pursue his general career interest in the interactions of theory and practice. As a consequence he had been engaged almost exclusively on health care assignments since 1963.

Mr. Vogel's work with the Los Angeles College of Medicine also led to Sigma's later employing Dr. Baxter Warren in 1966, when Warren decided to leave his Los Angeles post. "We were taking a risk with Baxter Warren," said the head of the division that had engaged him, "because he had a very specialized skill; but Warren brought a union card. Also, he has a very broad knowledge at a detailed level, knows who is doing what in the field and where, helps the company get jobs, knows who to call if a specialized consultant is needed, and has an ability to review and edit the output of Sigma staff to ensure that nonmedical staff do not make inadvertent errors." Since joining Sigma, Dr. Warren had worked entirely on health care projects.

In addition to the four persons discussed above, many other individuals at Sigma also entered the field and activity in health care continued to increase during the period from 1966 through 1969. Some indication of the development of health work is given in Exhibit 2, which lists some of the major projects conducted during the four-year period, and in Table 1 which summarizes the increase in the total dollar volume of business.

Table 1

HEALTH CARE AND RELATED PROJECTS SOLD ($000)

Size of project	1966	1967		1968		1969 (est.)
$1–$100...................	440	453		716		930
$100–$250...............	—	—	(3)	544	(3)	575
Subtotal................	440	453		1,260		1,505
Over $250...............	(1)* 415	—	(2)	825	(1)	835
Total.................	855	453		2,085		2,340

* Figures in parentheses represent the number of projects.
Source: Prepared by Sigma staff from company records.

---

[1] Epidemiology: a science that deals with the incidence, distribution, and control of disease in a population.

INITIAL STEPS TOWARDS THE ORGANIZATION OF
HEALTH CARE ACTIVITIES

As one member of Sigma observed, "Health-care work in the initial years involved a variety of individuals in many divisions; development was the result of individual initiatives and chance circumstance; communication and coordination was purely at the personal level." Some first steps towards formalization, however, began to be taken.

Monday lunches. In the fall of 1967, Norm Williams suggested that those interested in health care might meet informally over lunch on a regular basis. The practice of Monday lunches was launched that November. A table for seven was reserved every Monday and each week Williams' secretary would call up some of those on the list of professionals interested in health care. The group would vary from week to week and provided a convenient opportunity for colleagues to discuss common interests.

Health care brochure. During 1967, Pete Dowell had the idea for a health care brochure. From a practical standpoint a brochure was envisaged as an aid to public relations with clients. It was also described by Mr. Dowell as a tangible way of moving things along, and a way of consolidating health care activities. "This idea took a long time to move to fruition," commented Mr. Dowell; "it was 1969 before a brochure was finally produced by the Sigma Public Relations Office—and many professionals have serious reservations about the document and its usefulness. The development of a brochure, however, automatically raised other issues: practical problems, such as the development of a mailing list and the identification of a place or person in Sigma to whom potential clients should direct their inquiries."

Client Inquiry Committee. The problem of who should receive the client inquiries evoked by a brochure posed a difficulty. As one professional put it, "No one person should be selected because any individual is identified with one viewpoint and because one person should not capture the inquiries." A solution emerged one day as four professionals (Jackson, Thompson, Evans, and Dowell) discussed what to do about the problem, while walking back after one of the Monday lunches: Why not form a group to handle inquiries? Subsequently, a discussion between three men (Lewis, Hobart, Dowell) generated the notion of rotating the membership of the group. The idea was discussed at a Monday lunch, then with the head of the contracting office, then at a larger meeting of professionals convened by Mr. Dowell. Edward Robson and Stephen Bayne, the president of Sigma, were apprised that the proposal had the agreement of the contracting office and the health care people and so the Client Inquiry Committee was formed in May 1969.

At a group meeting (to which everyone working on any kind of health care task was invited) the first three committee members were selected informally: Mr. Williams for a 2-month term, Mr. Dowell for 4 months, and Mr. Lewis for 6 months. It was anticipated that subsequently a more formal voting system and, occasionally, a mail ballot would be used. At the same time, meetings for all professionals interested in health care were planned to take place every two months.

THE DECISION TO SUPPORT HEALTH CARE

During the spring of 1969, the Executive Committee of Sigma had been considering possible areas of new business which the company might develop. Management had concluded previously that a growth rate of 15% per year was a desirable corporate objective. The subject of the spring meetings was to consider, out of the vast number of alternatives, which new business areas should be selected and developed in order to achieve the company's growth objectives.

"Health care was an obvious candidate," said one executive. "Merely from one's reading of the newspapers and so forth—one knew that health care was a large market, with many problems, and ripe for change." (An example of material which bore out this executive's remarks and data on the growth of the multibillion dollar health care business are shown in Exhibits 3, 4, 5 and 6.) "In addition," he continued, "our people had been doing health care work and the opportunities for growth were apparent from their experiences. A strong factor in our thinking, too, was the fact that Sigma appeared to have a tremendous opportunity—because of its wide range of expertise in laboratory work on drugs, facilities planning, systems design and management consulting—to make a unique contribution to a field that required a broad interdisciplinary approach."

As executive vice president of Sigma, Ed Robson had specific responsibility for the planning of overall corporate development at Sigma. He had also had contacts with some of the persons involved in health care work; for example, two or three years earlier, when Robson had been head of the Management Division,[2] he had encouraged the efforts of some of his staff who were doing health care work. Later he had supported Pete Dowell's proposal for a health care brochure. In choosing health care as a field for special development, it had been agreed at the Executive Committee meeting that Mr. Robson would accept responsibility for determining how this development should be brought about. Consequently, following the Executive Committee's decision on health care, Mr. Robson decided to call a meeting of six Sigma professionals who had been active in health care work, ensuring that he had one person at least from each of the divisions with an active interest in the field.

The brief memorandum that Mr. Robson sent out to the six professionals described the reason for the meeting as follows:

> The senior management of the company, in a recent discussion, concluded that Sigma would like to support the health care field as one of its primary development areas in the near future. It seemed appropriate to take to the addressees the question of how this can best be done.
>
> In brief, I would like to discuss with you the development of a program involving financial investment, organization, recruiting, promotion, training, or whatever other steps ought to be taken to get maximum corporate thrust in the development of health care as a significant Sigma professional activity, and recognized as such in the outside world.

---

[2] In 1969, there was no longer a division of this name; the former Management Division had been split up into three units: Public Management Division, a Corporate Management Division, and a Management Sciences Division.

THE HEALTH CARE MEETING

The six persons Mr. Robson invited to the meeting in his office on August 12 were Pete Dowell, Wynn Day, Frank Jackson, Sam Lewis, Nick Vogel and Norm Williams. During the three-hour meeting, it was apparent to Mr. Robson that different members of the group held widely differing views about which would be the best way to develop health care work at Sigma. Although the discussion raised many significant issues and identified a number of alternative possible courses of action, there was no agreement about what would be the best thing to do. In light of this, it was agreed that the group should meet again in ten days' time and that meanwhile two or three members of the group would each write up draft memoranda outlining some alternatives and their relative merits. As a result, on August 19 Mr. Robson had received two memoranda from two members of the group, Frank Jackson (an urban affairs expert who had become involved in health work) and Pete Dowell. Excerpts from these memoranda are reproduced in Exhibits 7 and 8.

After Mr. Robson had carefully read these two memoranda, he wondered what conclusions he should draw from them about the development of health care—and what position he should take at the next meeting with the six professionals.

Although there were a number of points of contact between Mr. Jackson's memo and Mr. Dowell's, Mr. Robson thought that they could probably be viewed as representing two of the opposed positions that had come up in the August 12 meeting—a conflict between those who, in Mr. Jackson's phrase, favored "a centralized, organized development strategy" and those who, like Mr. Dowell, favored a more evolutionary, grass-roots effort in which "the constituency of the [health care] business development organization should be the professional staff."

ALTERNATIVE VIEWS OF THE PROBLEM

Although it was useful to examine the dichotomy represented by Mr. Jackson's memo and Mr. Dowell's, Mr. Robson realized that the viewpoints expressed by the two men represented more than the opinions of two individuals. Strong views were held by many individuals and genuine differences of opinion existed at many different points in Sigma.

One of those who favored a more organized approach was Nick Vogel. In Mr. Vogel's view, "We've been staggering along like a drunken man for five years. Maybe we've had some glimmering of the goal we wanted to reach five years down the road, but we've wandered off—been diverted by something—and could really get where we want to far more rapidly if we developed a plan. We need to decide what kinds of business we should do and which projects we should and should not accept. Of course I may be a Victorian," he said with a smile; "I think one has to consider what is of value to the corporation, not just what is of interest to myself. At a personal level I'm interested in epidemiology. But that doesn't have to be the focus of our work—epidemiology has many ramifications and I can do the same thing in a number of different areas of

health care. One thing we need, though, is a health care department—
for a whole variety of reasons."

Another aspect of the situation was mentioned by another Sigma
professional, who pointed out some of the problems of leadership in
health care:

> Leadership at Sigma is a tricky thing. For the individual, you have
> to want leadership—but you also have to know how to get it . . . and
> how to cope with the rugged independents—you know, the guys who
> will say to themselves, "If someone's going to be my boss, he's going to
> have to prove that he is suitable for the position better than I have
> done." I suspect also that some kinds of resistance, competition, call it
> what you will, have resulted in some guys' talents not being used fully
> —you know, they just weren't included in things. From management's
> standpoint too, developing leadership is difficult since there would al-
> most certainly be a rejection on the part of the staff of any unilateral
> management action to establish a leader.
>
> In the case of health care there is the added difficulty of whether
> the area needs to be headed up by somebody with professional qualifi-
> cations in the field of medicine. I guess some of the staff feel that, if
> you bring someone in on the basis of medical qualifications, he may
> hold all the old vices that we have discovered in the health care field—
> and that clients pose enough trouble on this score without having some-
> one on the staff who represents the same ingrained traditions. Of
> course it's conceivable you could find a maverick. But from our stand-
> point, which of us could judge a good maverick from a bad one?

Another perspective on the development of the health care area was
that of Nelson Hobart, a professional whose special field was human relations and organizational development. Hobart described what he
thought were some common misconceptions of how development occurs
in an organization:

> The business of asking questions about whether the firm should
> enter, or develop, health care consulting is in one sense a top manage-
> ment game! It reminds me of a situation I once heard of which arose
> in one of the large contract research organizations about twenty years
> ago. The president of the organization invited a friend (who was then
> a vice president of one of the top management consultants) to take a
> look at his organization and see whether it should go into management
> consulting. After six weeks of talking to people and analyzing the fig-
> ures, the friend returned to the president and asked him to repeat the
> first question that he had asked him to investigate. When the president
> had repeated his question about whether the organization should move
> into management consulting, his friend replied that, from his analysis
> of the figures, 37% of the work that they were doing at that time rep-
> resented what he and other management consulting firms would de-
> scribe as management consulting!
>
> When some of these questions came up at Sigma, you know, about
> whether we should enter health care, or how to develop health care, it's
> very tempting to respond, "Damn it, we are in health care. Can't you
> see? Do we have to hire tired experts before people around Sigma see
> us as legitimately in health care?"

He added:

> I know the cry goes up to "organize" health care or another area—but the development process needs to be seen as an evolutionary process . . . the process has its own logic but it is not the logic of conventional "planning." The real problem with defining the health care field, for example, lies in the risk that one may proscribe other fields and also limit the new field you are trying to get at . . . that is, your definition may be comprehensible to you but shut off other people whose perspectives might provide a richer insight into, or even a new conception of, the newly emerging area. It's one thing to buy some experts, who allow you to compete in an established field. It's another to go into a field that really doesn't exist, and in which your own behavior is necessarily a shaping force.

Mr. Hobart's colleague, Chuck Ryder, joined in on this point:

> In fact the best decision about defining a field in a case like health care may be to decide not to make a decision on definition at this time. Instead, let the process develop . . . recognize the risks of formalization . . . acknowledge the organization's possible incapacity to select the right new people until more experience has built up . . . and avoid, for example, not recognizing new things, new developments in the field, because one has focused on growing, say, through buying existing hospital consulting firms.
>
> You can't preconceive the nature of a change process. In developing a new area the real force lies in the vital juices of human beings . . . their interests and their commitments. Commitment is never in organizations—it's in people. So the way growth in an area is accelerated is by doing work in it . . . not by "establishing an organization" but by letting the organization be defined operationally by which guys are on board.

One who held a contrary view of what was required was Zach Kennedy, who had joined Sigma two months earlier, having been chief administrator for nine years of a major urban hospital with 700 physicians on its staff and an annual budget of approximately $85 million. Mr. Kennedy had originally come to know Sigma as a client when he had asked them to conduct a small study. Later, when he decided to move from his hospital post, and had been invited to join Sigma's professional staff through the initiative of Sigma staff he had met previously, Mr. Kennedy's views on health care were direct:

> The health field is really not a field at all—it needs an agglomeration of talent . . . and that is Sigma's great strength. There is no one who is good in the health field anywhere . . . and that is what helps make it such a ripe field for development. What Sigma lacks, of course, is health credibility . . . and health is a very close field; everybody knows everybody and if you make a boo-boo you're out—but if you do two or three good projects, you're in. If Sigma gets credibility one could make a killing. We're doing $2 million of health care business at present—but we could be doing $10 million—the Sigma name is gold and so are the people and talents we have here. The trouble is that all they've been doing is scratching at the market, when what is required is discipline and boldness.

Within two weeks of getting here I saw that what we needed was a small, powerful, talented group. We would have top people in the field —risk not having them chargeable for a while—and do a major project or two at cost. Maybe we'd even have to spend $350,000 or $500,000 on them. In this way we could make a name for ourselves and perhaps publish a book on our experience. But we must have quality control. The trouble is that an expert here is a guy who has done a project on a subject. But we need a core of people who know how a hospital operates, and how a board of trustees operates, and what motivates doctors. There's no mystery to these things—but it requires exposure.

A different view of the role of and need for health specialists, however, was indicated by Mr. Dowell who had noted in a memo to Mr. Robson in late 1967:

I am not at all dismayed about our lack of experience. . . . I can think of at least three cases over the past year where our lack of "hospital expertise" has been no drawback—Belvue, S. F. General, and Western Blue Cross. Current possibilities with two other potential clients carry that same flavor.

Different viewpoints about the organization of health care were also held by different division heads. Thorley Elliott, the head of Management Sciences, for instance, had read a copy of Dowell's latest memo and commented:

In reviewing Pete Dowell's memo, I find that I am disappointed with the approach taken to-date. . . . I feel it will be inadequate to do what we ought to do. The most important issue, to my mind, centers around the question of whether the overall activity requires that some small group of Sigma staff be highly specialized, dedicated, and committed to that given activity with no other real alternatives available within the Sigma framework. If this is necessary then I think the rather loose, traditional methods described in Pete's memo are far from adequate. Our normal approach simply leaves such people much too vulnerable to decision-making in which they have limited participation even though it is vital to their future; at the same time, I don't believe it establishes an adequate framework for budgeting and business development.

As far as I can see, sooner or later we will have to either form a formal core group or we will never do more than dabble in the health care field. I know this is a hard issue to face, but I don't think you can dodge it. From my point of view, incidentally, almost exactly the same needs are encountered in the fields of transportation, education and regulatory economics. In each case we have an area that sounds as though it was a market—but is really a series of separate and somewhat interrelated different markets—and in each case we have subject matter that cuts broadly across the divisional activities of Sigma.

George McDonald, head of the Public Management Division, disagreed with Elliott's view though:

Forming a department is by no means an automatic way of developing an area. In fact forming a department might insulate health care . . . tend to encourage a cloistered approach. I would prefer to see some stronger coordination—possibly a coordinator, someone with some tools, someone who could report progress in the field. But the proposal for a department is gutless; it doesn't innovate . . . or encourage a man to show how he can get round organizational obstacles. Health care is always going to require talents from all parts of the company and we can't avoid the reality of dealing with that problem by forming a health care department.

CONCLUSION

Mr. Robson smiled as he recalled a recent visitor's description of Sigma as "one of the world's most varied assortments of prima donnas." Clearly there were strong differences of opinion on what should be done —and some of these differences reflected different views of consulting (as Pete Dowell had put it once: "Who owns the problem: the client or the consultant?") and concerns for different types of health care work, as well as basically different approaches to the issue of how to develop a new business area at Sigma.

The health care market, it seemed to Robson, had great potential and Sigma's range of skills was eminently suited to it. However, it was an area, he realized, in which a number of firms were very interested. One of Sigma's staff had reported to Robson what he had heard about the efforts of one of the large systems-oriented aerospace companies to move into nondefense work:

> The Civil Systems Division is about five years old now. . . . From meagre beginnings it has grown to about 55 full-time people with various others from the organization spending occasional time on specific assignments and projects. The Department is organized on a project area basis with Transportation, Health, Pollution, Urban and Other being the five departments.
>
> The most striking difference between the activities of the people with whom I talked and our own efforts is the scale upon which they are basing their involvement as it compares with ours. Having the aerospace orientation has led them into the civilian area looking for large efforts of years' duration involving millions of dollars and many, many people and much development and proposal-writing expense (they price people differently when they are working toward an accepted proposal than they do when the proposal becomes a contract). They are not yet sure to what extent such a market exists but they have become involved in it enough to make the future look fairly bright and they have a couple of years to continue to spend considerably more than they make.
>
> Another difference is their exclusive reliance on the technical skills of physical sciences and engineering to perform the task. Their "systems" orientation up to this point includes every component but people and they are skeptical of the place into which someone with a social science orientation would fit.

Two days earlier Mr. Robson had received another indication of potential competitor activity in a memo from Norm Williams. Mr. Williams had reported that one of Sigma's senior outside medical consultants on a major current project had told Williams privately that one of the smaller top-quality management consulting groups was to announce shortly the formation of a new Institutional Consulting Subsidiary and that he and "some friends" of his had been invited to become affiliated with it and been offered stock options as an inducement.

In light of all this, thought Mr. Robson, "What direction should Sigma take?"

Exhibit 1

SIGMA CONSULTANTS, INC. (A)

List of Persons Referred to in Health Care Case

Sigma Corporate level:
Stephen Bayne, President
Edward Robson, Executive Vice President

Corporate Management Division: (5)*
Zach Kennedy
Charles Young

Engineering Division: (7)
Wynn Day
Paul Isaac
Henry Turner

Life Sciences Division: (5)
Robert Stringer (Division Head)
Samuel Lewis

Management Sciences Division: (7)
Thorley Elliott (Division Head)
Harold Satterlee
Nicholas Vogel
Baxter Warren
Norman Williams

Public Management Division: (16)
George McDonald (Division Head)
Luther Evans
Frank Jackson
Murray Long
Frederick Norton
Lee Thompson
Cooper Todd

Research & Development Division: (8)
Peter Dowell
Nelson Hobart
Ben Kimber
David Newlin
Chuck Ryder

* The number in parentheses indicates the number of individuals in the division who had served as team leader on a health-related project during the period 1966 through mid-1969.

Exhibit 2

SIGMA CONSULTANTS, INC. (A)

Major Health Care Projects, 1966–1969

1966	*Project description*	Team leader	Amount
Belvue.................	Merger of Oregon hospitals	Dowell	$ 20,000
L.A. College of Medicine..	Facilities development	Norton	60,000
Western Blue Cross.......	Organizational development	Williams	72,000
Eastex, Inc..............	Automated material delivery system design	Isaac	415,000
1967			
S.F. General Hospital.....	Administration, organization and operation of the radiology dept.	Dowell	67,000
W. Johnson Gen. Hospital..............	Establishment of a regional radiation therapy center	Long/ Norton	52,000
Medical Data Bureau, Chicago..............	Computer network	Young	59,500
City of Boston...........	Merger of two independent public health organizations	Todd	55,900
1968			
Public Health Service, North Carolina.........	Quantitative planning tools for national cancer program	Warren	236,084
Eastex, Inc..............	Pilot model of delivery system	Isaac	133,000
Regional Medical Program (HSMHA).....	Analysis of programs	Newlin	535,000
HSMHA (NCHSR&D)....	Financing of chronic leukemia treatment expense	Williams/ Satterlee	175,200
HEW..................	Systems analysis—artificial heart	Turner	290,000
1969			
New York Clinic.........	Computer applications	Warren	170,485
Department of Defense....	New military hospital system plan	Day	836,000
Univ. of Cal., Berkeley Medical Center.........	Medical center development	Dowell	220,000
NASA [proposal drafted]..............	Drug effects in space	Kimber	185,000

Exhibit 3

SIGMA CONSULTANTS, INC. (A)

Press Report on U.S. Health Care Situation

AILING HEALTH SYSTEM NEEDS MORE THAN MONEY

WASHINGTON—The Federal dollar looms large in American health care and is likely to loom larger, but the Government seems caught in the classic Alice-in-Wonderland predicament—the more money the Administration puts in, the more is needed. In short, as the Red Queen said to Alice: It takes all the running you can do to keep in the same place.

In large measure that was the central finding of the report made public last week from the task force on Medicaid and related problems. The task force, headed by Walter J. McNerney, president of the Blue Cross Association, was appointed a year ago by the Secretary of Health, Education and Welfare.

"It is a central conclusion of the task force that money is needed, but that money alone will not guarantee either capacity or effectiveness of the system," the report said. In that context, it was not discussing simply Medicaid, but the entire system of American health care.

Indeed, the clear implication of the report was that neither Medicaid nor any other major health program can be put in proper working order without making basic changes in the whole complex system by which Americans get health care when they need it.

The extent of the failure is apparent to the person with adequate income who nevertheless finds it hard to reach a doctor except by long waiting and who may go from specialist to specialist with little continuity of care. It is apparent to the doctor who may regularly work 60 to 80 hours a week and still may not have enough time for all he wants to do. It is probably less apparent, but more tragically real, to the poor and near-poor, many of whom get no care at all until it becomes a matter of life and death.

The report offered no concrete solution to the problem; indeed it said there is no simple solution. But it did suggest directions. These included less dependence on individual and isolated transactions between a doctor and a patient, more voice for the consumer, and more leadership by government to promote change. Since Medicare and Medicaid already exert a big influence on the system, they were cited as access points where the leadership can be applied.

Exert Leverage

Medicare, a Federal program of medical insurance for persons over 65 years of age, and Medicaid, a state-Federal medical welfare program designed to help the poor and the near-poor of all ages, exert great leverage on the whole health-care situation. In turn, they are powerfully affected by the changes they cause in the private sector.

Today health care in the United States is a roughly $64-billion enterprise, heavily hit by inflation. It is estimated that 26 cents of every health dollar comes from Federal sources. Medicare and Medicaid together form the main component of the Federal share. In size and proportion they have been increasing steadily in recent years and have been complicating the rest of the picture.

Neither program does the full job for which it was designed. Medicare helps virtually all Americans in the age group it covers, but, on the average, it pays only about half of their health bills; that still leaves a hardship for many of the elderly. Medicaid, at present, helps only about one-third of all the poor and near-poor for whom its benefits were intended.

Yet the cost of these programs is already large and growing. The one point on which there is hardly any disagreement among the experts is that the dollar growth cannot continue indefinitely without some other changes.

"If a benevolent and affluent government were to begin to pay for all the basic health care needed by all those who can't pay for it themselves, but no other changes were introduced into the existing system, the result would be a disastrous rise in the cost of services that are already scarce," the task force report said.

Community Affair

In its recommendations, the task force made it clear that health care must become a community affair where it has been an individual affair in the past. The Department of Health, Education and Welfare was singled out as the agency on which the greatest responsibility must rest for exerting leadership and achieving change.

Among the specific new directions that the group sees as desirable is greater emphasis on group practice of medicine and, in particular, on more extensive use of prepaid health plans that emphasize preventive care. Other study groups have come to much the same conclusions in the past; but it appears now that government is becoming more and more inclined to accept many of those conclusions and that the voice of organized medicine is less adamant and less powerful in opposition.

HAROLD M. SCHMECK Jr.

Exhibit 4

SIGMA CONSULTANTS, INC. (A)

Consultant's Report on Health Care Conference

MEMORANDUM

TO: (18 professionals)

FROM: Luther Evans

RE: Insurance Companies & Health Care

At the recent American Public Health Association meeting in Philadelphia a Mr. Howard Ennes, Vice President of Equitable, gave a talk on the insurance companies' role in health care.

Three hundred companies are covering 100 million people with "some type of health care insurance." These 300 companies account for 80% of the total health insurance business. In 1968 this amounted to 6.7 billion dollars.

There is a crisis in health care. $60 billion spent in 1968 with probably $100 billion a year within 5 years. If both President Nixon and Walter Reuther agree that there is a "health crisis," then *there is one.*

. . . . [Equitable] feel(s) that a complete revision of the present order of priorities is needed. Organized health care service will be the order of the day, and the GP will soon be out.

Systems of group practice such as Kaiser* should be carefully looked at. When they talk, as they do, about 2 beds per 1,000 population under group practice versus 4½ beds per 1,000 in communities, then we are talking of big money savings.

Action in the health care field is crucial for survival of insurance companies. Therefore, the conservative insurance companies are *now on the move.* If you are not part of the solution, you are part of the problem.

---

* Casewriter's note: The Kaiser Foundation medical care program conducted a prepaid comprehensive group practice health care program for more than 1.75 million persons on the West Coast through 18 hospital-based health centers and 45 out-patient facilities. (1968 data).

Exhibit 5

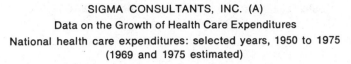

SIGMA CONSULTANTS, INC. (A)

Data on the Growth of Health Care Expenditures

National health care expenditures: selected years, 1950 to 1975
(1969 and 1975 estimated)

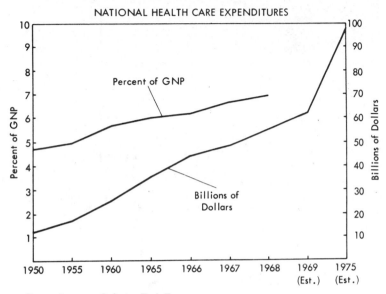

NATIONAL HEALTH CARE EXPENDITURES

Source: Insurance Industry Task Force.

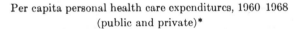

Per capita personal health care expenditures, 1960 1968
(public and private)*

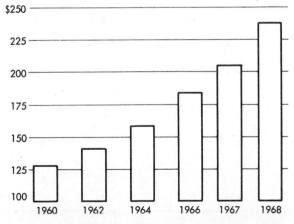

* Does not include expenses for prepayment; expenditures of private voluntary agencies for other health services; government public health activities and identifiable administrative expenses under public programs.

Sources: The Committee for National Health Insurance; data from the U.S. Department of Health, Education and Welfare.

Exhibit 5—Continued

Public and private expenditures for health and medical care
(1950–1969 fiscal year)

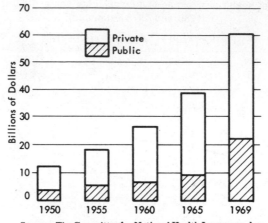

Sources: The Committee for National Health Insurance; data
from the U.S. Department of Health, Education and Welfare.

Exhibit 6

SIGMA CONSULTANTS, INC. (A)

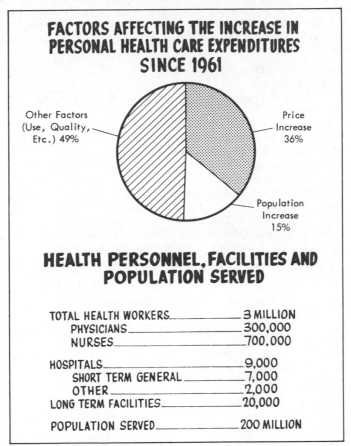

FACTORS AFFECTING THE INCREASE IN PERSONAL HEALTH CARE EXPENDITURES SINCE 1961

Other Factors (Use, Quality, Etc.) 49%

Price Increase 36%

Population Increase 15%

HEALTH PERSONNEL, FACILITIES AND POPULATION SERVED

TOTAL HEALTH WORKERS	3 MILLION
PHYSICIANS	300,000
NURSES	700,000
HOSPITALS	9,000
SHORT TERM GENERAL	7,000
OTHER	2,000
LONG TERM FACILITIES	20,000
POPULATION SERVED	200 MILLION

Source: Chart presented by Mr. Wilbur Cohen, Secretary Designate of HEW to Senate Subcommittee chaired by Senator Abraham Ribicoff, April 26, 1968. Reported in *Health Care in America: Hearings before the Subcommittee on Executive Reorganization of the Committee on Government Operations*, U.S. Senate, 90th Congress, 1968.

Exhibit 7

SIGMA CONSULTANTS, INC. (A)

Excerpts from F. Jackson Memorandum of August 18, 1969

Subject: HEALTH BUSINESS DEVELOPMENT

There appears to be little doubt that "Health" can be one of the significant growth areas for Sigma. The diversity of opportunities and the breadth of skills required demand the participation of all Divisions. It will also demand the broadening of skills as well as increasing depth in a number of areas.

Exhibit 7—Continued

The field of health is actually a number of categories for business development. While there is overlap between some, and while any one project might incorporate several, we think it useful to recognize a distinction for forming both an umbrella strategy and tactical steps for organizing business development activities.

1. Health Care—Overseas
2. Health Facilities
    (a) Hospital (community; teaching; medical centers)
    (b) Others
3. Community Health Projects
4. Bio-Medical Research
5. Medical/Health Economics and Financing
6. Industrial Health
7. Environmental Health
8. Bio-Medical Product Engineering
9. Epidemiology
10. Medical and Health Education
11. Policy and Evaluation Studies (federal, regional, etc.)
12. Pharmaceutical and Other Marketing for Health Care.

In order to develop Sigma's potential for each of these a centralized, organized development strategy is necessary and would include:

— determination of priority business development opportunities for the immediate future and three-year period
— establishment of a strategy for prospect *development* and *response*
— staff development
— staff recruitment, including consultants
— inquiry assignment, with evaluation of effectiveness
— publicity and public relations

The execution of this strategy must be a corporate effort, supported in significant part by corporate funds. The Corporation must sanction the effort, give it legitimacy, and make it accountable.

There seems to be much in the Sigma ethic to mitigate against strong, centralized direction. Certainly the strategy should not undercut Sigma's basic strengths stemming from its flexible mechanisms for response. However, our current flexible mechanism for business development is too dependent upon the interest and availability of individual staff members, or of loose coalitions among them, to likely lead a strong enough effort to make a relatively fast impact. The answer would seem to lie in an approach which allows the Sigma basic form of desired staff independence, while at the same time tightening and directing business development.

Five general models for organizational structures may be noted:

1. *Continued operations in the present form.* This is characterized by an essentially *ad hoc* response to opportunities which are brought to our attention.
2. *The appointment of one person,* well-qualified and generally knowledgeable about the entire health field, to have responsibility for directing all business development efforts.
3. *The establishment of a clearly identified Health Group* (Division, Subdivisional Department, or informal coalition) whose members devote their time almost exclusively to health.

Exhibit 7—Continued

4. *Expansion of the role of the present Client Inquiry Advisory Committee* to include responsibility for coordinating business development.
5. *Establishment of a new committee structure* to draw across Sigma Divisional lines. To be composed of people who would *commit* a certain part of their time to a business development effort. The committee would draw upon others in Sigma—organized informally or in some subcommittee structure—to carry out business development efforts with them.

None of those basic alternatives need be viewed as exclusive options. Indeed, the organizational structure which I pose below for discussion would include each of these components. This would include:

— A *Sigma Health Director,* appointed on the corporate level, who would function as a team leader for a Sigma project, "Health Business Development." The Director would orchestrate, and participate in, Sigma's business development thrusts. The Director would draw his legitimacy and backing from corporate management, through which he would relate to the Division V.P.'s. At this time no separate Health Department is envisioned, rather the Director would draw "staff" from the existing Sigma structure.
— *The Advisory Committee would continue* with its same charge and composition. However, rather than reporting to Contracting, it would report to the Director who would share project assignment responsibility with Contracting.
— A *rather elaborate Advisory Committee structure for business development* is called for to advise and assist in the task of initiating action (building project prospects, staff, and image). Working committees would be established for the major business development categories. These would be informal committees (composed of people with mutual interest for each area) and each chairman would work with the Director to articulate development opportunities and to involve people from the larger group.

   Throughout the initial years, it is not likely Sigma will have all the senior staff required to build our image and pursue our goals for a number of the business development areas. To overcome this, Sigma could retain the *exclusive consulting services of a cadre of senior people* of the calibre required. Such consultants would work with the Director and his business development groups as well as with project teams.

The structure outlined above would in part depend upon the strength and ability of the Director. However, to an even greater degree, its success would depend on the willingness of Sigma staff to cooperate and to commit at least part of their time to business development activities. Such commitment could be encouraged by the judicious use of the Health Business Development project funds to serve as an inducement: it would be understood that further funds would not be forthcoming if commitment was not carried out. Assignment of such funds, in all cases, should be expected to entail the same responsibility by staff as project work for clients.

As a first step, until a Director is appointed, or as an alternative to his appointment, a five-man committee might be established to play the coordinating, leadership role. The committee members should commit a required

Exhibit 7—Concluded

proportion of their time to the task—to be charged to project funds. It would be advisable to have one member of the corporate central staff sit as chairman of this group to strengthen its legitimacy and provide continuity of leadership. This group might well be built around the existing Client Inquiry Advisory Committee.

Exhibit 8

SIGMA CONSULTANTS, INC. (A)

Excerpts from P. Dowell Memorandum of August 18, 1969

Subject: ORGANIZING FOR BUSINESS DEVELOPMENT IN HEALTH CARE

At a recent meeting of corporate management and division heads, it was agreed that the company should put its chips on what looks like a winning area. Development activities financed from corporate funds might include things like:

1. increased contact with high-level health people in HEW, DOD, etc;
2. identification of people and skills Sigma should recruit;
3. coordinated public relations to get most mileage from our work;
4. identification of new areas to develop;
5. internal staff development;
6. articles;
7. time to coordinate health activities among divisions by keeping division heads and business managers up to date.

If corporate money is going to be available, there needs to be some organization through which to channel it and to be accountable for its use to Sigma management.

We have the Client Inquiry Steering Committee whose primary function is to recommend assignment of client inquiries to Contracting and suggest staffing resources to other people who would like to use the Committee. The Steering Committee operates primarily in a responsive mode. It sets the agenda for our large bi-monthly health care meetings. The Committee is becoming generally recognized throughout Sigma as a major organizational innovation in response to the problem of how to handle client inquiries in a large, diffuse, interdivisional field such as health.

The job now is to organize ourselves in a way that goes beyond the response function into the active area of business development. Corporate management recognizes the desirability of having the people who are involved professionally in health care work organize their own business development function, rather than having an organization imposed from top management.

We may be able to agree that the organization we evolve should possess certain characteristics and take into account certain organizational and interpersonal realities in Sigma. For example, the bulk of the people who have an interest in health care do not view it as their only or even their primary commitment. These people, as well as many we don't even know about yet, are and will be vital to the growth and development of health care consulting at Sigma. Any organization that we do develop should accommodate the fact of varying commitment. It should allow commitment and access to the health care projects to be as easy as possible.

The business development organizations should also be capable of change so that resources can be focused and refocused in a timely manner, to be re-

Exhibit 8—Continued

sponsive to market conditions and professional interests of particular people in Sigma. It should be able to operate across all of the existing divisions in a way that does not compete with them but rather uses those organizations, augments them, and draws strength from them. The organization should be capable of developing some reasonable focus or series of focuses to the health care field in a way that is believable, understandable and relevant to people who are professionally interested in health care as well as the management structure of the company. The business development organization should also be in close touch with what's going on in the health care field in Sigma and outside. Probably the best mechanism for doing the former is to have close touch with the Steering Committee.

We would like to suggest some alternative models.

Model #1

One person tapped by the group to head up our business development activities in health care.

This is a traditional way and it has the advantages of continuity and of having a single person accountable to top management. It provides an organizational nucleus with some stability around which people could cluster. It could provide recognition for a particular person. On the negative side, the notion of a czar might shut out a lot of people around Sigma. No one person completely embodies all of the interests of the health care people in Sigma, either with respect to particular functional areas (such as hospital administration, medical care financing, systems analysis, etc.) or with respect to basic philosophy of how to do consulting in the health care field. The person chosen to perform that business development function might find himself quickly out on the periphery or otherwise isolated from a substantial segment of the professionals interested or potentially interested in health care at Sigma.

Model #2

Having the Steering Committee take over the duties of business development as well as its existing functions.

In favor of this idea is the fact that the committee is an established body. It is continually energized by inquiries from the contracting office and others so that the members of the committee have to talk with one another frequently. Because it is in touch with the client inquiry assignment activity, it is also in touch with what is going on in health care generally in Sigma. On the negative side, business development is a basically different function from what the Steering Committee was originally set up to do. Also the combination of inquiry assignment and business development might be too heavy a burden on the members of the Steering Committee, even if it were funded by corporate money. Third, it would concentrate substantial power in the Steering Committee which might be viewed by some people as unwise. Fourth, the Steering Committee is only three people and probably should be kept to only three because of the need for rapid communication in the assignment function. Consequently it takes a long time to directly involve much of the professional staff.

Model #3

Form a separate business development committee consisting of three to four people operating parallel and similar to the Steering Committee.

On the positive side, it would be an additional organizational innovation

Exhibit 8—Concluded

patterned after one which has worked already. It would enable more people in the larger health care group to be involved in important aspects of our health care business. Because of the rotation feature, there would be built-in change and new ideas. But, there would also be built-in continuity. On the con side, there is probably feeling against the proliferation of committees. Decision making "by committee" is suspect to a greater or lesser degree by many people. Also unless this business development committee is activated in some way from the outside, it might do nothing. This perhaps could be overcome by requiring it to meet periodically with the Steering Committee to find out what is going on in the health care field, and also by making it accountable for a report to the larger health care group at the bi-monthly meeting of that group. Finally, it will be energized from time to time as it needs to consider potential health care applicants and bring these applicants to the attention of our personnel department, or various divisional people and staff members.

Model #4

Do not organize business development. We're doing pretty well as it is. Let it continue to evolve.

We hope that this memo can serve to stimulate some thoughts so that we can decide on our business development function in a way we can all live with and which can get the job done.

We would like to urge that we innovate, that we not be bound by past methods and ways of doing things. The organization should be made *primarily* responsible to the professional staff. We are not denying the responsibility and accountability needed to top management; but rather the constituency of the business development organization should be the professional staff.

Sigma Consultants, Inc. (B)

THE INFORMATION below describes practices and procedures at Sigma important to understanding Sigma Consultants (A).

THE GENERATION OF CLIENT ASSIGNMENTS

Prospective client assignments come into Sigma in a variety of ways according to one corporate officer:

> By and large business flows to Sigma; and much of it appears to be a result of previous projects. . . . you know—former clients, people who have heard of a project we did or who have been referred by former clients. There are also those that seem to come out of a general awareness of Sigma or the reputation or writings of one of our staff. I would say, therefore, that less than 25% of projects are developed purely on staff initiative.
>
> Some project possibilties start with a phone call to a Sigma office; some may be initiated by a general letter of inquiry or a government RFP (request for proposal); other inquiries come in the mail to individual professionals. One way and another, though, I would say 80%–90% of prospects come to us through members.
>
> Staff are encouraged to bring client inquiries along—to develop them —and then report them to management. The Contracting Office (which is responsible for registering prospects, reviewing contracts, and ensuring that the firm avoids conflicts of interest) can sometimes suggest relevant people for a project team. And in a case where there is doubt about whom an inquiry should go to, a management committee, which meets briefly every day, may be asked to decide. However, by the time they are reported to Contracting, three quarters of the prospects are being handled by the person who becomes project leader.

THE RECORD OF USAGE OF PROFESSIONAL TIME

As a research and management consulting firm, the largest single expense incurred by Sigma was the salary cost of the professional staff employed to conduct client assignments. The record of how consultants' time had been spent was built up from time reports submitted every Friday by each staff member on which every hour spent during the week was to be recorded. The basic workweek for accounting purposes was assumed to be 40 hours; all calculations of individual, group, division, and corporate activity were computed on this basis. The categories into which staff time was analyzed, with an indication of a typical breakdown for one division, are shown in the table below.

Table 1

TYPICAL DIVISIONAL USAGE OF DISTRIBUTABLE STAFF TIME

Administration—General	1.5%
Hiring	2.0
Prospect charges—Nontransferred commercial	2.7
Government	4.1
Business development	5.7
Professional activities	2.0
	18.0%
Chargeable time	82.0
Total	100.0%

The categories of "General Administration" and "Hiring" are self-explanatory. Other categories were used as follows:

Prospect charges. When a staff member got a promising project inquiry at Sigma, where the problem had been clearly identified and Sigma was sure that it wanted to write a proposal, the professional would usually request a "prospect number" or account. Any time that he spent pursuing this "prospect" such as making an initial study of the problems or writing a project proposal for the client would be charged to the prospect account number. Where a prospect turned into a firm project contract, in the case of commercial clients, it was Sigma's contract practice to charge the client the cost of developing the project (i.e., the time spent on writing the proposal, visiting the prospective client, etc.). The amount in Table 1 for commercial prospect charges, therefore, represents work charged to "prospect" accounts that has not resulted in a project contract. In the case of government projects, federal regulations did not permit firms to bill the government for time spent on a project in advance of a contract; hence this figure represented the total prospect cost for prospective government projects.

Business development. This was a very general category that covered business development and sales efforts that could not be identified with a particular serious prospect. For example, a campaign of formal calls on key organizations (e.g., federal and state agencies, professional, institutional and commercial organizations) would be charged to this category. Time spent on writing letters to prospective clients about matters of potential interest, inquiry follow-up (where it was necessary to investigate an inquiry to determine just what a client wanted Sigma to do), and possibly a visit to a trade convention might be charged to business development.

Professional activities.   This category might be used for time spent by staff on educational and professional society affairs, on writing a paper for a professional journal, or attending a national, annual professional meeting.

Chargeable Time.   This consisted essentially of time charged to clients for work on project assignments. As indicated earlier, this category also included transferred commercial prospect charges.

"The point of view taken by the professional staff to complete time cards," remarked one division business manager, "varies somewhat according to the individual. My particular hobby-horse though, is the time worked, over and above the basic 40 hours, which is not recorded." He continued:

> Occasionally some of this time may get on the record—but on the whole it doesn't. Many of the staff resist recording this time; they view it as "conscience time," time perhaps to bring a project or a report up to the quality that they will be happy with, but this can lead to unusual results. A little while ago, for example, we had a computer installation job and when the final time report came in I noticed that the project leader had finished the job and recorded charges which were billed to the client were about 5% under the original estimate. Yet I knew our men worked twelve hours a day for several weeks on that job—it's inevitable on a computer installation job—but the client didn't pay for the overtime!
>
> Of course, the way our business is set up, Sigma carries the risk on most jobs; you see we agree to bill the client only for the time recorded. So that, if it comes out less than the project budget, the client saves; but if it's over budget we carry the loss—unless we can, and wish to, negotiate an increase. But our firm policy is not to do so at the end of a project.
>
> In addition to ensuring quality, a project leader at Sigma is concerned to meet his project budget. What happens is that many leaders like to leave themselves a little cushion for the end of an assignment. Sometimes something can crop up at the last minute; so they like to have something available so that they won't go over their project budget. There's no particular credit to finishing under budget. But where nothing does crop up, however, one finishes up the project under budget—as happened in the computer case! As a result I'm experimenting in my division with methods of getting time over 40 hours a week recorded.

CORPORATE PROJECT DEVELOPMENT FUNDS

The net total of all the divisional profit margins represented the total Sigma "professional service margin." In preparing the annual budget two items were deducted from this total before arriving at the corporate income from operations: The first item was central service costs (e.g., corporate officers' salaries and expenses and general services like accounting, the computer lab, purchasing, etc.); the second was an amount for corporate funded development projects.

The amount of divisional new business development funds for Sigma as a whole totalled approximately $2.0 million at direct salary cost. At normal client billing rates (i.e., including overhead and profit markup) this represented say $6.0 million. In addition to these funds there was an amount of $600,000 (valued at billing rates) budgeted at the corporate level to fund what were termed "corporate projects." This amount was budgeted as a lump sum at the beginning of the year and was allocated during the year by Edward Robson, the executive vice president, to individual professional staff or small groups who approached him for support of activities they (and Mr. Robson) judged to be in the corporate interest. The median project size had tended to be about $15,000 and their nature was quite varied.

By valuing these funds at billing rates it was possible for a staff member to charge his time up to a corporate project without either him or his division suffering a drop in reported chargeable time levels or divisional profit. However, some staff members referred to corporate project money as "funny money" and, as one staff member observed, "Given a choice, a professional will always prefer to work on a client's assignment rather than a corporate or divisional project."

Federated Department Stores

In the spring of 1974, Federated Department Stores, the largest conventional department store company in the United States, announced record sales and profits for the fiscal year ending February 2, 1974. Known chiefly through the names of its divisions—Bloomingdale's, Bullock's, Filene's, Burdine's, Foley's, Ralphs, Gold Circle, etc.—Federated's 1973 sales were close to $3 billion and net income almost $114 million.[1]

The record performance, however, did not abate several disturbing trends in Federated's business. Profits as a percentage of sales had declined for the third time in the last five years and in recent years profit dollar growth had not matched Federated's performance of the early and mid-1960s largely due to rising expenses. In addition, the energy crisis had caused great concern and management wondered what effects an economy of scarcity would have on consumer shopping habits. Although it had not been necessary to reduce store hours during the energy-short 1973 Christmas period, extensive efforts were being made to reduce energy consumption at every Federated store.

Despite these problems, company executives felt that Federated's autonomous department store divisions would continue to be successful pursuing a strategy of "fashion merchandising." Harold Krensky, president of Federated and formerly chairman of Bloomingdale's and president of Filene's, described the strategy of the department store divisions:

> For a long time it was popular to say that a department store should be all things to all people. When John Wanamaker and Marshall Field started the first department stores, they were really bazaars and truly did sell all things to all people. Today we try to be most things to most people with several, not all, levels of fashion and price in each line of merchandise. It is this approach that creates *excitement* and when it's

---

[1] See Exhibit 1 for a complete listing of divisions and stores. Some names have been disguised.

done properly the department store becomes a three-ring circus under one tent.

You know, the market doesn't only change because of the passage of time and changing lifestyles. Good merchandising can add layers of excitement to a store and encourage change. A large percentage of the merchandise in Bloomingdale's is the same as in any other store. But much of the merchandise is different and is presented in a way that adds excitement to the store.

Of course, there are certain things that you can only do in Bloomingdale's and even some that Bloomingdale's can only do on 59th Street. But you can always do things to lend excitement to your store and this is exactly what we are doing in all of our department store divisions.

Since 1967, Federated had diversified into supermarkets, discount stores, and specialty discount stores. Ralph Lazarus, Federated's chairman, explained the role of these other retail activities in Federated's strategy:

If the regionalization program in our department store divisions works out as I anticipate that it will and if the quality of our management continues to improve the way it has over the past few years, then I think that we can make our goals with the department stores alone plus the specialty store spin-offs that the department stores will be developing throughout the rest of the 1970s. Beyond the 1970s, as the Gold Circle and Gold Triangle discount stores move into new markets, these businesses will have the potential to become national chains that will provide growth in the 1980s. We are trying to do more than just pursue growth. We are also trying to pursue a configuration of our divisions that will reflect the consumer's needs ten years from now.

In the spring of 1974, Ralph Lazarus and Harold Krensky faced a major decision about the future growth of the Gold Circle discount division. The decision involved Gold Circle's proposal to expand to either Washington, D.C., or Northern California. The size of the proposed capital expenditures for 1975 and 1976—$33 million in Washington or $42 million in California—underscored the importance of the decision.[2] The proposal had recommended expansion into the Northern California market, but since it would be Gold Circle's first venture outside the Ohio region, Mr. Lazarus and Mr. Krensky wanted to be sure the proposal was given a thorough examination.

THE RETAIL INDUSTRY

In 1974, almost 12 million people were employed in some form of retail trade in over a million establishments, accounting for 39 percent of the gross national product. From 1963 to 1973, retail sales grew from $244 billion to $503 billion, at an annual compounded rate of 7.5 percent. These aggregate figures, however, tend to disguise the tremendous variability in the performance of retail firms and the range of strategies

---

[2] During the past five years, Federated had invested about $100 million annually in new stores and store renovations.

Table 1

TYPES OF STORES

	1972 sales *($ billion)**
General merchandise stores:	
National chains........................	$ 17.2
Traditional department stores...........	20.4
Discount stores.......................	29.1
Variety stores........................	5.5
Specialty stores......................	n.a.
Miscellaneous........................	n.a.
	$231.1
Food Stores:	
Grocery chains.......................	56.4
Independents........................	56.7
Specialty stores.....................	7.0
	$120.1

Note: n.a.—not available.
* Sales figures are derived from company Annual Reports, *The Discount Merchandiser*, and *Progressive Grocer*.

adopted by these companies. Table 1 presents a breakdown of the types of firms in the retail industry. Exhibit 2 presents more detailed information on the performance of retail firms and some broad industry trends.

The major competitors for general merchandise sales were the national chains (Sears, Pennys, and Wards), the department stores, and the discount stores. Although there were differences between these types of stores, generally they all competed for the same customer. In fact, most consumers shopped in all of the types of stores listed in Table 1. The American consumer was also becoming more affluent as shown in Table 2, below. In terms of differences, the department store customer was predominantly female, and more affluent and socially mobile than the chain or discount customer.

Both the chains and the department stores usually located as "anchor stores" in large suburban shopping centers. Often several chain and department stores would compete in the same shopping center. The chain stores were located across the United States and thus had the advan-

Table 2

DISTRIBUTION OF FAMILIES INCOME CLASS

Income level (1971 dollars)	As a percent of total families		
	1970	1975 est.	1980 est.
In excess of $25,000..............	5.0%	10.0%	13.0%
$15,000–$25,000................	19.5	27.0	32.0
$10,000–$15,000................	27.5	26.0	23.0
Under $10,000..................	48.0	37.0	32.0
Total...................	100.0%	100.0%	100.0%

Source: Department of Commerce, The Conference Board, 1973.

tages of a national reputation, a national charge card, and national advertising. The department stores were local institutions and usually had more liberal delivery and return policies than the chains. The department stores began as downtown institutions and had to shift their source of sales to suburban areas. For example, from 1963 to 1972 the percentage of department store sales from suburban locations increased from 44 percent to 68 percent of total sales. In order to operate at lower margins, discount stores differed from both the chains and department stores by locating in less expensive strip shopping centers, by offering little sales assistance in the store, and by making less extensive use of credit sales. Most discount stores were built with adjoining grocery stores, which were usually leased to a regional grocery chain.

The major differences between the three types of stores, however, were in merchandising and the organization of their buying staffs. The chains did a larger portion of their business in hard goods and featured their own national brands of merchandise. In recent years, Sears' National Brand Program had made many of their own brands competitive with leading manufacturers' brands. As a group, the chains were becoming a major force in the appliance and the tire and battery industries. In contrast, department stores had emphasized soft goods, particularly those with fashion appeal. Table 3 shows the gross margins by major lines of merchandise that traditional department stores achieved in 1972. The higher gross margins tended to be in fashion merchandise and the department stores had been concentrating increasingly on these lines of goods. The national chains had also been trying to enlarge their fashion businesses. It is important to note that the chains achieved somewhat higher margins in the nonfashion departments than shown in Table 3 because of the lower costs on their branded merchandise. The discount stores sold both national and private brands of merchandise at prices below most of their competition. About 60 percent of sales were in hard goods and soft good merchandise tended to be in replenishment, rather than fashion items.

The differences between the general merchandise stores were typified in the organization of their buying staffs. National chains and discount stores had one buying staff for all their stores plus regional and store merchandising managers to plan individual store assortment. The department stores maintained a separate buying organization for each market in which they did business. Thus the chains and discount stores had a single buying staff regardless of the number of stores, while the department stores had buying staffs of about 100 professionals serving 10 to 15 stores. The conventional department stores claimed that their large buying staffs, close to the consumer, enabled them to anticipate and encourage the growing fashion orientation of such items as men's clothing and accessories, sheets, bedspreads, T-shirts, underwear, cookware, and planters.

Competitive trends

In 1974, several trends were evident in the competition between the chains, department stores, and discount stores. One trend was the increased emphasis on fashion merchandise which has been characterized by Professor Cort as "Focused Retailing."[3] Cort pointed out that "the retailer must develop a clearly focused concept of operations to attract some particular target customer group." Cort added that current trends point toward "specialty operations bent on attracting the consumer's discretionary dollar." Although the department stores seemed to have advantage in selling fashion merchandise, the national chains were intensifying their private brand and national advertising campaigns for fashion goods.

Table 3

GROSS MARGIN BY MAJOR CLASSIFICATIONS OF MERCHANDISE OF TRADITIONAL DEPARTMENT STORES, 1972

	Gross profit margin		*Gross profit margin*
Women's apparel	42.6%	Stationery, greeting cards	44.5%
Women's dresses	41.0	Grocery and delicatessen	33.6
Casual sportswear	45.0	Cosmetics and toiletries	37.9
		Drugs and health items	25.7
Women's accessories	45.9	Television	21.2
Corsets and bras	48.1	Toys	32.3
Sleepwear and robes	46.4	Books, reference, etc.	34.1
Costume jewelry	47.3	Photographic and optical	23.8
Women's hosiery	44.7	Luggage	44.2
Women's footwear	43.7	Sporting goods	28.4
		Furniture and bedding	41.7
Men's apparel	42.3	Floor coverings	34.7
Jackets and slacks	41.0	Chinaware and glassware	45.6
Men's furnishings	44.5	Major appliances	21.8
		Small appliances	25.2
Infants and Children's	42.4	Domestics	41.3
Infants and toddlers	43.4	Sewing materials	39.2
Girls' (school age)	42.5	Downstairs merchandise	39.7

Source: *Department and Specialty Store Merchandising and Operating Results of 1972*. Published by National Retail Merchants Association.

Among the discount stores sales growth had slowed from the rapid rates sustained in 1960s and by 1974 many industry observers commented that discounting had become "overstored." As more and more companies entered discounting (in 1972, 51 discount companies had sales over $100 million), competition in the industry became intensive. Many discount stores had been forced to close, but some companies, such as Kresge's K–Mart Stores, had seemingly been unaffected by the industry slowdown.

Grocery stores

In recent years the grocery store industry has been characterized by expanding sales, declining profit margins, and a decline in the number

---

[3] Stanton Cort, "Focused Retailing: A Strategy and Challenge for Success in Overstored Markets," Harvard Business School, 8–574–035.

of stores. Since the end of World War II, the large regional and national grocery chains have accounted for an increasing proportion of grocery sales. Although independent grocery stores outnumbered the chain stores by almost 4 to 1, sales of chain stores just about equaled those of the independents in 1973. During the same period, the average size of the chain supermarket grew larger. In 1973, an average new chain store contained 32,000 square feet.

The most serious problems facing the industry were bitter price competition and rapid inflation of food prices. In the early 1970s, price cutting became widespread, reducing the already narrow profit margins and forcing the closing of many marginal operations. The number of grocery stores in operation had declined 12 percent from 1968 to 1973. Rapid inflation in food prices put additional pressure on profit margins, caused customer criticism, and brought increasing scrutiny from congressional and consumer groups.

FEDERATED'S HISTORY

The holding company period (1929–1945)

Federated Department Stores was formed as a holding company in 1929 as a means of organizing family-owned department stores for the purpose of diversifying their risks and investments. The company consisted of Filene's of Boston, Abraham & Straus of Brooklyn, and Lazarus of Columbus, Ohio. In 1930, Bloomingdale's of New York joined the company. In addition Filene's and Lazarus each operated one department store subsidiary, R. H. White in Boston and Shillito's in Cincinnati. Management committee meetings were held once a month in New York, but Federated exerted little influence on the member stores.

The depression greatly limited Federated's growth and it was not until 1941 that sales volume surpassed 1929. Sales expanded during World War II, and after the war the role of Federated became an important issue to some members of management. Although he was 62 when World War II ended, Fred Lazarus, Jr. (his associates called him "Mr. Fred") was the member of management most concerned with this issue and was ready to change the philosophy and nature of Federated.

In 1941, Mr. Fred visited his son, Ralph, who was in the Air Force stationed in Texas. While traveling in Texas, Mr. Fred became convinced of the potential of the Southwest and thought that the acquisition of Foley Brothers Dry Goods Co. in Houston would be a good way of entering that region. In 1945, Mr. Fred proposed that Federated acquire Foley's and also submitted that:

1. Federated should become an operating company of wholly owned divisions.
2. He should become president of the company.
3. A corporate office should be established in Cincinnati.

4. The company should acquire and manage department stores in what he felt certain would be the rapidly growing parts of the country, the South and Southwest.
5. If the other members weren't willing to go along, he would withdraw Lazarus and Shillito's from Federated and proceed on his own.

Remarkably, Mr. Fred's proposals were accepted. At this time, Federated consisted of four divisions, sales were about $200 million, and net income was almost $5 million. By early 1974, the number of divisions had grown to 19. Sales had increased 15 fold to almost $3 billion and net income had increased to about $114 million, or 23 times higher than in 1945. (See Exhibits 3, 4, and 5 for additional financial information.)

Growth through acquisition (1945–1960)

Upon gaining control of Federated, Mr. Fred quickly moved to acquire Foley's and to shift the geographical mix of the Federated's business. The strategy was to expand from the East Coast to other parts of the country, particularly to the South and Southwest. Federated continued to acquire department stores from 1945 to 1964. All but one of the eight department store acquisitions were made for an exchange of stock.

Federated's strategy during this period included more than the acquisition of department stores. A total program was undertaken to improve the performance of all of the department stores. Federated was determined that each division have the best reputation for quality and the largest business in its trading area. In merchandising, each Federated division sought to become the "headquarters" store in its trading area. The approach was to develop each line of merchandise so that each department within the store had the best reputation (and did the most business) in its trading area. Great emphasis was also placed on the control of expenses. Armed with comparisons of expenses at all of the divisions, Mr. Fred would use his "on-the-wall" technique to put the expense performance of the best divisions "on-the-wall" and to challenge the weaker performers to improve. Ralph Lazarus, Chairman, explained the significance of expense control:

> Expense control was dad's expertise and twice a year dad, Herb Landsman, and I met with the divisions and used the on-the-wall technique. These meetings were quite effective. But having low expenses was not a viable long-term strategy, unless we could develop a merchandise base. By moving into the apparel areas, we developed a day-to-day, fashion-oriented, merchandising strategy.

During this period great emphasis was placed on developing each of Federated's downtown stores into the "headquarter's store" of the city. At a time when other retailers were already building suburban branches, Federated's suburban expansion was modest. Federated officials acknowledged the reluctance to build branches, but pointed out that it was the intensive development of the headquarter's downtown stores during the 1950s that led to the tremendous reputation of the Federated stores. When Federated began to move aggressively into branch stores this reputation was easily transferrable.

Within this framework, the divisions were autonomous with complete responsibility for their results. Particularly in merchandising, divisional control and autonomy was strictly upheld. Management felt it was important that the buying staff be close to its customers and be in a position to respond quickly to rapidly changing customer preferences. Each division maintained its own buying organization and in contrast to some other large department store companies Federated had avoided augmenting local buying with a central buying staff.

One attempt at centralized buying was the Fedway division, which Federated started in 1951. Fedway was to be a cross between a chain store and department store and a vehicle for entering the smaller towns in the Southwest (Albuquerque, Corpus Christi, Bakersfield, and so on). The idea was to develop a chain of smaller department stores that would be merchandised much like the chain stores, with a central buying office in New York. For a variety of reasons the Fedway division never fulfilled the expectations of management and the division was dissolved in 1971. Herbert Landsman, executive vice president, discussed Fedway:

> Fedway was an experiment conducted by Federated and it was not successful. In fact, it's the only failure that we've ever really had and for a long time it left its mark on the company by inhibiting innovation. As early as 1960, many of us thought we should get into discount retailing. The corporate office went so far as to draw up a proposal for a chain of discount stores and the proposal went all the way to the Executive Committee. They said that they weren't interested, but the real response was—remember Fedway!

In 1957, at the age of 74, Fred Lazarus, Jr. became chairman of the board of Federated and his son, Ralph, became president.

Suburban expansion, internal intensification, and diversification (1960–present)

In 1964, Federated acquired Bullock's—I. Magnin Co. of California. This acquisition remains the largest ever consummated in the department store industry. For Federated the acquisition meant entry into the rapidly growing Southern California market. The acquisition, however, was challenged by the Federal Trade Commission and to gain FTC approval of the acquisition Federated had to sign a consent decree agreeing not to acquire any more general merchandise stores over the following five years.

The FTC decision, however, seemed to have little impact on Federated's growth. By expanding the department stores to the suburbs and paying close attention to profitability, Federated continued to meet its goal of 10 percent annual increases in earnings per share and a return on equity of 13 percent to 15 percent.

In 1967, Federated diversified into another form of retailing with the acquisition of Ralphs Groceries, operator of 52 supermarkets in the Los Angeles area. Although Ralphs had a lower percentage return on sales than Federated had been earning, it was among the most profitable grocery companies and had substantial opportunity for expansion throughout California. Company officials added that since new supermarkets didn't take as long to plan, build, and bring to profitability, Ralphs had the ability to add profit dollars quickly.

In 1972, Federated acquired Lo-Rays Center, Inc., a small grocery chain located in San Francisco. Of the eight Lo-Rays' stores, one was closed and the remaining seven converted to Ralphs' style and quality and operated under the Ralphs' name and by Ralphs' management. By the spring of 1974, Ralphs had grown to include 76 supermarkets and was the largest division (in terms of sales volume) in Federated.

Fred Lazarus, Jr., retired from active management in 1967. Mr. Fred became chairman of the executive committee of the board, and was succeeded by his son, Ralph, as chairman. J. Paul Sticht, formerly executive vice president of Federated and before that a top executive at Campbell Soups, became president. Sticht served as president for five years and retired in 1972. The new president, Harold Krensky, had been with Federated for 30 years and had earned a national reputation as a leader in fashion merchandising while a principal officer at Filene's and Bloomingdale's. In May 1973, Fred Lazarus, Jr. died. Although he had retired from active management six years earlier, his legacy could still be felt in the hearts and minds of many company executives. The portrait of Mr. Fred in the board room stood as a remembrance of his leadership.

In recent years Federated had also developed three new discount store divisions—Gold Circle, Gold Triangle, and Gold Key. Gold Circle was a general merchandise discount store that opened its first store in Columbus in 1968 and had grown to include 17 Ohio discount stores by 1974. The Gold Triangle stores specialized in hard goods (TVs, stereos, appliances, sporting goods), and the Gold Key stores were warehouse showroom furniture stores. Company officials indicated that Gold Triangle and Gold Key were still in the experimental stages.

In April of 1974, Federated reported sales and earnings for the year ending February 2, 1974. Although sales were 11.1 percent higher than in the previous year, net income increased by only 4.8 percent and earnings per share were $2.57 versus $2.46 the previous year (see Exhibits 3, 4, and 5). Company officials indicated that the impact of inflation on the LIFO adjustment had reduced earnings by 19 cents per share compared to 3 cents in 1972.

Although management was uncertain as to long-range economic conditions, they set a goal of doubling earnings per share in constant dollars every ten years[4] and a return on equity of 13 percent to 15 percent. If economic conditions wouldn't permit this level of growth Federated wanted to "lead the pack among retail companies."

---

[4] During the 1960s this had meant a goal of 10 percent annual growth in earnings per share.

CURRENT ORGANIZATION AND OPERATIONS

Department stores

As shown in Table 4, the department and specialty store divisions accounted for the largest part of sales and an even larger proportion of earnings. These divisions also accounted for about 85 percent of average divisional investment.

Management credited the success and reputation of the department stores to setting high criteria of achievement, placing profit responsibility as close to the consumer as possible, and communicating each division's concept deep into the organization. In terms of developing fashion merchandise, management described the process as choosing what consumer group to serve and then becoming the "headquarter's store for the type of goods she buys."

One effect of the emphasis on fashion had been a steady increase in gross margins. Company executives pointed out that higher gross margins did not necessarily mean higher prices, but could also be achieved through changes in the "mix" of sales. Exhibit 6 summarizes some of the changes in the department stores' sales mix. It can be seen that the fashion areas—women's and men's clothing and decorative home furnishings—have been growing in importance. It was these fashion departments which not only had higher margins per se, but the greatest opportunity to increase margins as a result of fashion merchandising and merchandising excitement.

Exhibit 6 also shows that the increases in gross margin had not kept pace with expense increases. From 1964 to 1969, most of the expense increases had been in payroll as wages advanced rapidly. Since 1969, nonpayroll expenses such as state and property taxes, insurance, rent and EDP had risen the most rapidly. Although expense control was a divisional responsibility, some corporate executives were concerned that one way to combat expense increases—regional or centralized operations—ran counter to Federated's basic strategy.

In terms of organizational structure each division differed as to its exact approach, but there were many similarities among the department store divisions. Ralph Lazarus described Federated as an "upside down" organization and drew a chart (see Table 5) for the casewriter to illustrate the concept.

Federated had pioneered in the development of the Office of the Principals form of management in retailing. Here, the chairman and president of the division were equals in managing the division. Usually one man was responsible for merchandising and the other for operations, but it was common for them to work as a team on many aspects of the division's business.

All of Federated's divisions budgeted in six-month cycles, for the spring and fall seasons, where all aspects of store operations—merchandise performance by department and all expenses—were carefully planned. Analyses of actual performance compared to the budget were performed monthly by the corporate staff. In addition meetings were

Table 4

| | Department and specialty stores ($ in 000s) | | | | | Grocery and discount stores* (including Ohio Appliances, Inc.) ($ in 000s) | | | | | |
| | Sales | | Contribution | | | Sales | | Contribution | | |
Year ending	Amount	Percent of total	Amount	Percent to sales		Amount	Percent of total	Amount	Percent to sales
Feb. 1, 1969	$1,590,701	87.7%	$168,924	10.6%		$223,071	12.3%	$ 7,576	3.4%
Jan. 31, 1970	1,731,784	86.9	190,075	11.0		260,884	13.1	7,931	3.0
Jan. 30, 1971	1,792,240	85.7	176,555	9.9		299,275	14.3	5,577	1.9
Jan. 29, 1972	1,969,119	83.7	209,357	10.6		383,976	16.3	10,416	2.7
Feb. 3, 1973	2,157,391	80.9	232,721	10.8		507,757	19.1	15,294	3.0
Feb. 2, 1974	2,325,732	78.5	244,025	10.5		636,319	21.5	16,009	2.5
Compounded growth	7.9%		7.7%			23.3%		16.1%	

Notes:
1. Contribution is before federal, state and local income taxes, central office costs, interest expense (net of interest income) and the contribution of divisions not engaged in selling which aggregated $20,715,000, $21,303,000, $27,349,000, $28,982,000, and $35,302,000 for the five years ended February 2, 1974.
2. State and local income taxes previously included in costs and expenses which reduced the "contribution" (note [1] above) are currently included in "federal, state and local income taxes" so that they do not reduce the "contribution." Prior years have been restated on a comparable basis.
* Ralphs Groceries and Gold Circle comprised about 90 percent of this category.
Source: 10-K statement.

Table 5

UPSIDE DOWN ORGANIZATION
(simplified)

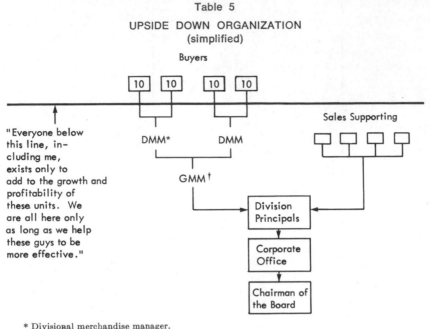

* Divisional merchandise manager.
† General merchandise manager.

also held throughout the year between top divisional and corporate management. Here Ralph Lazarus and Harold Krensky, armed with years of personal experience and extensive corporate staff reports on market characteristics and store performance, would meet with division management to help plot future plans. This would include issues such as what merchandise lines offered the best opportunities for development, new branch store opportunities, and expense control opportunities.

The development of branch department stores seemed to typify Federated's way of doing business. Ralph Lazarus commented that "I'd rather be late getting into these markets, but be right. Really, this is our whole philosophy of doing business." In building branches, Federated tried to enter very large regional shopping centers. Unlike most department store companies, Federated's branches were not "miniature downtown stores," but were smaller and included only the best departments. Federated preferred to open branches at a high level of sales productivity and then expand the store than have to wait for a store to mature. Ralph Lazarus commented:

> Admittedly this is more expensive from the point of view of construction costs, but it has enabled us to keep our expense rate down at the branch stores. By insisting that the productivity of the store be high from the beginning, we are able to keep our expenses as low as possible. Only when sales productivity reaches certain standards, will we add new space to a branch store.

Despite Federated's successful record of building branch stores, environmental trends as well as the sheer number of stores that a market could support were beginning to limit the number of opportunities for branch stores in several of Federated's cities. Herb Landsman commented:

> When we first started to aggressively build branch stores in the early 60s, the branches were sure successes. They were built in those areas with the highest population density and the highest income level. It was a case of bringing our downtown headquarter's concept to the suburbs. Well, now we've moved beyond the first ring of branches, to the second ring, and sometimes to the third ring. What happens is obvious. There isn't the population and income base to support full-line stores in many of these outlying regions. Although there are still opportunities in the better areas, sometimes the effect is to transfer substantial volume from our existing stores.

Exhibit 7 illustrates Landsman's point.

Future department store strategies

To succeed in the future, Federated's Department Store divisions had been developing many new strategies. In 1974, the department stores competed in 16 of the 25 largest "standard metropolitan statistical areas"[5] and several of the divisions were moving from city-based to regional or even national operations. For example, Bloomingdale's furniture department had long enjoyed a national reputation. To capitalize on this, a chain of Bloomingdale's Home Furnishings Stores had been developed—two in the New York area, one in Boston, and another in Philadelphia. Another store was being planned in the Washington, D.C., area. Cincinnati-based Shillito's had opened stores in Louisville and Lexington, Ky., and Miami-based Burdine's was aggressively entering the Orlando market. At Bullock's, operations had been extended well beyond Los Angeles and plans were being made for stores in San Diego and Phoenix. Also a new department store division, Bullock's North, was formed in 1971 to enter the northern California market. At Lazarus, stores had been opened in the central Ohio towns of Lima and Mansfield and in 1973 the first Lazarus store was opened in Indianapolis. Company officials indicated that these expansions hadn't diluted the overall profitability of the department stores.

Another approach was to build specialized stores within the division's trading area. Both Foley's and Lazarus had recently opened Home Stores in their traditional markets. Lazarus had opened smaller specialty-type stores (27,000 sq.ft.) in Columbus that carried high-quality women's, men's and children's clothing in budget price ranges. Federated officials expected that more of the department store divisions would develop specialty stores in the future.

---

[5] Population centers of greater than 50,000 people. Federated's representation in 3 of 16 SMSAs, San Diego, Philadelphia, and Chicago, consisted of one smaller specialty store in each market. Of the 261 SMSAs in the United States, Federated had department stores in 42.

Nondepartment store divisions

Although they comprised a much smaller portion of the company's business, the nondepartment store divisions were seen as having substantial opportunities for future growth. A basic difference between these divisions and the department stores was that they were organized to be like chain store operations. Individual stores were based on a basic prototype and didn't require as much lead time to construct as the average department store. Thus, the Gold Circle division had opened its first store in 1968 and by the end of 1973 had more stores than any of the department store divisions. Although Gold Key and Gold Triangle were still in the "testing stages," they also had this characteristic of being able to add new stores quickly.

By far the largest division was Ralphs Groceries, with 1973 sales around $450 million. Ralphs had a reputation for quality and since its acquisition in 1967 had continued to expand. In 1971, Ralphs perceived the trend toward discount pricing in the grocery industry and preempted much of its Los Angeles competition by adopting a low-pricing policy. It did not abandon its quality image in merchandise or store appearance. Ralphs operated its own meat processing warehouse, produce warehouse, creamery, and bakery in order to assure the high quality of its products. As the business continued to grow rapidly, extensive investments were made in enlarging these facilities. Federated's investment in Ralphs had increased by almost 50 percent since 1970. By the end of 1973, with expansion in the Los Angeles market and entry into the Northern California market, there were 76 Ralphs supermarkets. Ralph Lazarus commented on the role of Ralphs in Federated's development:

> We wanted Ralphs to help us learn the disciplines of a mass merchandise business. My exposure to Ralphs has taught me a great deal about what disciplines we need to be successful in mass merchandising and has helped us immeasurably as we have developed Gold Circle and Gold Triangle.
>
> When we bought Ralphs in 1967 it was third or fourth in the market. According to the *Los Angeles Times Survey* it is now first in that market. Since 1967, profit dollars have doubled despite a lower profit rate. The pretax ROI is also improving. A few years ago it was only about 3 percent, but this past year it was 7 percent and I foresee it going to as high as 15 percent. This is a large business with numerous opportunities to grow.

Gold Circle was described as a different type of discount store that "starts with the top end of K-Mart and moves into the heart of Penneys and Sears' business." By carrying a better quality assortment of soft goods merchandise, company executives felt that Gold Circle was offering something new to the discount industry.

Although Gold Triangle was considered to be more experimental than Gold Circle, management felt that it too had the potential of becoming a national chain. Gold Triangle was described as a do-it-yourself, leisure and recreation store. The stores featured top-of-the-line merchandise sold by well-trained salespeople at discount prices. Gold Triangle began with discount appliances, but by 1974 featured large selections of sporting goods such as tennis, fishing, and hunting equipment as well as a large number of hardware, hand tools, and do-it-yourself departments.

The first Gold Triangle stores were opened in the Miami area in 1970 and the company officials stated that 1973 was the first year that the division had operated in the black. In 1973, Gold Triangle also moved to central Florida by opening stores in Orlando and Tampa. Ralph Lazarus indicated that in time Gold Triangle could extend beyond the Florida region:

> If Gold Triangle continues to grow as it has, we will start banking property in some new markets. Once they reach a 6 percent pretax rate and a sales volume over $100 million, I think we can go into some of these markets.

CORPORATE SERVICES

Within Federated's decentralized framework, one of the main jobs of the corporate office was to provide specialized services which no single division would be likely to perform, but which could be provided economically by one central group. Thus the home office included such specialized functions as site location, real estate, insurance, warehouse planning, communications, and EDP.

Another important function of the home office was to provide policy recommendations and research that would enable the company to achieve better performance. Thus the controller's department set companywide accounting policies. Consumer and economic research provided important data on socioeconomic developments. Organization development tracked the progress of key executives. Finally, the operations research and corporate planning departments did extensive analyses of all aspects of the company's operations in order to identify any problems and new areas of opportunity.

Property development and site location

The development of new store locations exemplified the relationship between the autonomous divisions and the home office. In most cases the site location process began with a request from a division for a study of a particular area by Federated's Area Research Department. The request could be to examine a specific site or to study the overall market. Bob Richards, vice president for area research, commented on the nature of his department studies:

> No matter what the nature of the divisional request, we try to prepare as comprehensive a report and study as possible. Even if we're asked to look at one site, we like to take a broader view and explore that site plus some alternatives.

All reports of the Area Research Department were first reviewed by the divisional management. If necessary, changes were made and it was up to the division to release the report to corporate management. After the report was released, corporate management would review the findings with both Area Research and divisional management and if there was agreement on a recommendation, the division would draw up a capital expenditure request.

Although Federated had many years of experience with suburban stores, it was not until 1973 that Federated entered the development business with the formation of Federated Stores Realty, Inc. John Phelps, senior vice president for property development, felt that the development business was a natural extension of Federated's business:

> We now have the land for eight regional shopping centers and it has all been zoned favorably. Why should we sell this land to someone else when we can develop it ourselves or co-venture. Of course, in getting into this business I've had to convince our management that although development is a cash flow business and not a return on sales business, that it still makes sense for Federated.

Finance

Federated's financial activities were carried out by the Treasurer's Department in Cincinnati. Also the Finance Committee of the board of directors paid close attention to all financial flows and dealings. Frank Gibson, treasurer, described Federated's financial policies:

> Our approach to finance can be summed up in one word—conservative. Our balance sheet is extremely strong and our debt to capital ratio is low even for retail companies. Along with Sears, our bonds have the highest ratings of any retailer—AAA from Standard & Poors and AA from Moody's. We are very proud of this.

This conservative approach to finance was also reflected in a rather low usage of leases on new stores. Frank Gibson explained:

> With our financial strength we can get money cheaper than most of the leasing companies. We are doing more leasing and some sale leasebacks with our grocery stores now, but there is no great urgency in this.

Concerning the future, Gibson felt that expansion during the next five years could be financed through a combination of retained earnings and the use of Federated Acceptance Corporation, the company's captive finance subsidiary. Frank Gibson indicated that it was not necessary to compare the requests of the different divisions or types of businesses:

> You really can't compare the supermarkets, discount stores, and department stores in a meaningful way. Sure the supermarkets have a lower return, but you can close down and sell a bad supermarket. You can't do that with a department store and it's pretty hard to put these types of factors into any equations. Our growth is limited by people, not capital, and so far we haven't had to face a situation where capital was short.

Norman Lewis, chairman of the Finance Committee, expressed a similar opinion:

> You have to understand that retailing is not a capital intensive business. The important types of planning are people planning and market planning, not capital planning. If you approach this business from a capital point of view you are looking at the wrong variable.

Role in the community

Federated's divisions and executives had a long history of active involvement in their communities and the company was often cited as one of the most socially responsible in U.S. business. Federated's involvement in community affairs included such activities as working for urban transit, better housing, better schooling, and full employment. In some communities Federated had developed small parks adjacent to their downtown stores and had shared in the expense of developing day care centers.

Although Ralph Lazarus was reticent to talk about his own activities and felt that Federated's community involvement was just a part of good community and corporate citizenship, Lazarus had been a major spokesman for the Committee for Economic Development on a number of issues. In 1966, Lazarus was one of the first businessmen to speak out against the Vietnam War.[6] He had, as well, worked on the national level for greater federal aid to education and to urban areas.

CORPORATE MANAGEMENT

In the course of discussion on their jobs as president and chairman of Federated, Harold Krensky and Ralph Lazarus offered the following observations:

Harold Krensky

I view my work with the divisions as a field job. I spend three of four weeks in the field, seeing the stores and meeting the people. I work closely with the divisions on their seasonal plans. First we make an agreement on the profit goal. We care about profits first—sales are only a means to achieve profits. These goals are mutually agreed upon and are not dictated to the divisions.

In seasonal planning we try to develop our business. I try to work with the divisions in planning how to achieve their goals—how much margin they can get and where, what expense rate can be achieved.

Every president or top executive has his own style but I believe that the basic task of all managers is the same—to motivate people to get the highest return. If you are a major executive and you can't motivate, then you are not doing your job. People often talk of Mr. Fred's on-the-wall technique as his major management tool, but above all he was a tremendous motivator of people.

When I leave a store, no one should have the attitude of what the hell am I breaking my back for. Everyone is seeking approval and when I see that someone is doing a good job I tell them. Our Filene's Chestnut Hill store got rave reviews in the retail press when it recently opened. I phoned the store manager and assistant manager to congratulate them. But you can also motivate by criticism. If a person is having trouble they often don't know how to ask for help. A top executive must know how to sense this. If you can offer help in a constructive way, you can have a tremendous impact on your people.

---

[6] See, for example, David Halberstam, *The Best and the Brightest* (New York: Random House, Inc., 1972).

Ralph Lazarus

When I go to a store I ask an assistant buyer, the buyer, and the divisional merchandise manager what the three priorities of the department are. If the story isn't the same, I tell the principals that they have a problem. I like to tour a division with the DMMs. If all they tell me is how well they are doing, I'm suspicious. If they tell me their problems, and their plans to correct them, then I know that I have a good man.

I've moved from working on the seasonal plans to working on our longer range plans. Harold [Krensky] concentrates more on the seasonal plans. Of course, I check the figures monthly and call up and ask people what's wrong when we miss our plans. They know I'm alive.

The biggest part of my job over the past five years has been in building our organization. I'd estimate that I've spent 75 percent of my time on this. In the early 1960s a lot of our older management retired and we have had to build new management teams. Now we are just beginning to reap the benefits of these efforts. I have a good idea of what organizational depth has to be developed during the next five years. I plan on implementing that and then I'll let someone else worry about these things.

THE GOLD CIRCLE DECISION

In the spring of 1974, Federated's management faced a major decision on the future growth of the Gold Circle division. Gold Circle had requested funds to enter either the Northern California or Washington, D.C., markets. Since options on land would soon have to be taken, Ralph Lazarus and Harold Krensky were preparing to meet with Gold Circle's management and to make a decision on the proposal.

Formation of the Gold Circle division

The Gold Circle division was formed in 1967 and opened its first store in Columbus, Ohio, in April 1968. Federated's 1967 Annual Report described the reasons for expanding into discounting:

Since 1959, two seemingly contradictory trends have dominated the retail scene. Our department store divisions are unanimous in reporting that their customers have been "trading up" these last few years—expressing both their desire for better merchandise and service and their willingness to pay for them. At the same time, customers across the country have been turning in increasing numbers to the so-called "discount" stores. Sales through discount stores have grown from $3 billion in 1960 to an estimated $16 billion in 1967—convincing evidence that the discount formula (price appeal, convenient location, long hours, minimal service) has a basic attraction for huge numbers of families. In fact, it is probable that most families are discount customers for some kinds of goods, at some times, and under some circumstances. Discounting fills a real niche in the distribution chain.

This is why, after some years of study, your company, in 1967, decided to enter the discount field. We believe that discounting can provide real profit opportunities in the future. We are not vain enough to think that we are automatically assured of success in this new venture.

climatic similarities to Columbus, and the potential to penetrate the market. Largely because of the climatic similarities with Columbus, the merchandising function in Washington would be one of "modifying and coordinating the buying effort done at the Columbus office." The merchandising staff would include one manager and five coordinators. On the other hand, many of the merchandising functions in Northern California would have to be autonomous. Merchandising would be comprised of one manager, two divisional merchandise managers, six buyers, and three coordinators. Several people in Federated's home office commented that the independent merchandising organization would probably have a strong tendency to get much larger.

Others at the home office questioned the assumptions that land could be obtained at 10 percent below "asking prices" and that construction costs would increase by only 5 percent a year. The relatively low ROI of the Gold Circle plan also raised some questions as to what extent Federated's future potential lay in the development of discount stores.

In preparing for the meeting with Gold Circle, Ralph Lazarus and Harold Krensky reviewed the proposal as well as some staff reports. Both men agreed that Gold Circle's development to date had been "damn impressive" and both were pleased with the quality of Gold Circle's organization, its operations, and the appearance of the stores. In considering the proposal, Ralph Lazarus wondered if Ralphs Groceries couldn't operate the adjoining grocery stores if Gold Circle entered Northern California. Nevertheless, Lazarus did have some concerns:

> I want to make sure that these plans will not retard the overall year-to-year profit dollar growth of the division. I don't want to expand the division too rapidly. We must be careful to maintain the quality of the stores and of the management. Not doing this has been the problem of many discount stores.

Having been involved with Gold Circle since its inception, Hal Field reflected on the possibility of Gold Circle moving from a regional discount store towards the first step in becoming a national chain:

> I, more than anyone else in Federated or Gold Circle, have to take an interest in the long pull. One good year doesn't do me much good, because I'll still be around the next year and the year after that. What we have proven here is that a discount store called Gold Circle can go into a new city with certain concepts and organization and can make it. We have proven this in Columbus, in Dayton, in Cleveland, and in Cincinnati. Now we have to take a look at the long range and commit funds to develop a new market area and begin to think of our potential as a national chain. With our concept and organization there's no reason why we should not be successful.

Exhibit 1

DIVISIONS AND STORE LOCATIONS

ABRAHAM & STRAUS Established
   1865
   Acquired 1929
   *Brooklyn, N.Y. (1,593)
   Garden City, N.Y., 1950 (80)
   Hempstead, N.Y., 1952 (560)
   Babylon, N.Y., 1957 (257)
   Huntington, N.Y., 1962, 1974 ex-
   pansion (308)
   Manhasset, N.Y., 1965 (265)
   Smith Haven, N.Y., 1969 (236)
   Woodridge, N.J., 1971 (285)
   Rego Park, N.Y. 1973 (306)
   Paramus, N.J., Spring 1974 (300)

BLOOMINGDALE'S Established
   1872
   Acquired 1930
   *Manhattan, N.Y. (947)
   New Rochelle, N.Y., 1947 (110)
   Fresh Meadows, N.Y., 1949, 1974
   expansion (149)
   Stamford, Conn., 1954 (227)
   Bergen County, N.J., 1959 (240)
   Short Hills, N.J., 1967 (250)
   Garden City, N.Y., 1972 (260)
   Home Furnishings Specialty
   Stores:
   Manhasset, N.Y., 1971 (84)
   Scarsdale, N.Y., 1971 (26)
   Jenkintown, Pa., 1972 (110)
   Chestnut Hill, Mass., 1973 (85)

BOSTON STORE Established 1906
   Acquired 1948
   *Milwaukee, Wis. (516)
   Bay Shore, Glendale, Wis., 1958
   (141)
   Boston Village, Milwaukee, 1962
   (89)
   Brookfield, Wis., 1967 (179)
   Southridge, Greendale, Wis., 1969
   (179)
   Northridge, Milwaukee, 1972
   (128)

BULLOCK'S Established 1906
   Acquired 1964
   *Los Angeles, Cal. (804)
   Pasadena, Los Angeles, 1947
   (315)
   Westwood, Los Angeles, 1951
   (235)

Santa Ana, Los Angeles, 1958
   (336)
Sherman Oaks, Cal., 1962 (308)
Lakewood, Los Angeles, 1965
   (262)
Del Amo, Torrance, Cal., 1966
   (262)
La Habra, Los Angeles, 1968
   (272)
Northridge, Cal., 1971 (190)
South Coast Plaza, Costa Mesa,
   Cal., 1973 (186)
Specialty Stores:
Wilshire, Los Angeles, 1929 (231)
Palm Springs, Cal., 1930 (47)
Woodland Hills, Los Angeles,
   1973 (24)

BULLOCK'S NORTHERN CALIFOR-
   NIA Established 1971
   *Stanford, Palo Alto, Cal., 1972
   (154)
   Walnut Creek, Cal., 1973 (188)

BURDINE'S Established 1898
   Acquired 1955
   *Miami, Fla. (526)
   Ft. Lauderdale, Fla., 1947 (195)
   Miami Beach, Fla., 1953 (98)
   West Palm Beach, Fla., 1954
   (161)
   163rd Street, Miami, 1956 (256)
   Dadeland, Miami, 1962 (401)
   Westland, Hialeah, Fla., 1967
   (134)
   Pompano Beach, Fla., 1969 (152)
   Hollywood, Fla., 1970 (151)
   Colonial Fashion Square, Orlando,
   Fla., 1973 (206)

FILENE'S Established 1852
   Acquired 1929
   *Boston, Mass., 1973 reconstruc-
   tion (656)
   Wellesley, Mass., 1924 (37)
   Belmont, Mass., 1941 (47)
   Chestnut Hill, Mass., 1950, 1974
   replacement (135)
   North Shore, Peabody, Mass.,
   1957 (114)
   South Shore, Braintree, Mass.,
   1961 (126)
   Natick, Mass., 1965 (110)

EXHIBIT 1—Continued

Burlington, Mass., 1968 (119)
Hyannis, Mass., 1970 (43)
Warwick, Providence, R.I., 1970 (119)
Worcester, Mass., 1971 (106)
Chestnut Hill, Mass., Spring 1974 (140)

FOLEY'S Established 1900
Acquired 1945
*Houston, Texas (801)
Sharpstown, Houston, 1961 (321)
Pasadena, Houston, 1962 (127)
Almeda Mall, Houston, 1966 (210)
Northwest Mall, Houston, 1967 (313)
Home Furnishings Store, Houston, 1972 (65)
Memorial, Houston, Spring 1974 (135)

GOLD CIRCLE Established 1967
East, Columbus, Ohio, 1968 (118)
North, Columbus, 1968 (118)
Northwest, Columbus, 1969 (125)
East, Dayton, Ohio, 1969 (124)
Northwest, Dayton, 1969 (120)
Southeast, Dayton, 1969 (127)
West, Columbus, 1970 (135)
Elyria, Ohio, 1971 (103)
Middleburg Heights, Cleveland, Ohio, 1971 (103)
West, Cleveland, 1971 (134)
Willoughby Hills, Cleveland, 1971 (134)
East, Cincinnati, Ohio, 1973 (130)
North, Cincinnati, 1973 (130)
North Olmstead, Cleveland, 1973 (103)
West, Cincinnati, 1973 (133)
Mentor, Ohio, 1973 (104)
Springfield, Ohio, 1973 (135)
East, Akron, Ohio, Spring 1974 (130)
West, Akron, Spring 1974 (130)
Canton, Ohio, Fall 1974 (130)
Northwest, Cincinnati, Fall 1974 (130)
Bedford, Cleveland, Fall 1974 (130)

GOLD KEY Established 1971
Costa Mesa, Cal., 1972 (167)

San Jose, Cal., 1972 (158)
Van Nuys, Cal., 1973 (159)

GOLD TRIANGLE Established 1968
Skylake, Miami, Fla., 1970 (76)
Dadeland, Miami, Fla., 1970 (76)
Orlando, Fla., 1973 (86)
Tampa, Fla., 1973 (86)

GOLDSMITH'S Established 1870
Acquired 1959
*Memphis, Tenn. (496)
Oak Court, Memphis, 1961 (204)
Southland Mall, Memphis, 1966 (136)
Raleigh Springs, Memphis, 1971 (135)

I. MAGNIN & CO. Established 1876
Acquired 1964
*San Francisco, Cal. (253)
Oakland, Cal., 1931 (65)
Los Angeles, Cal., 1939 (141)
Beverly Hills, Cal., 1945 (99)
Santa Barbara, Cal., 1945 (24)
Pasadena, Cal., 1949 (41)
Sacramento, Cal., 1953 (7)
Seattle, Wash., 1954 (80)
La Jolla, Cal., 1954 (29)
Palo Alto, Cal., 1955 (100)
Fresno, Cal., 1955 (20)
Santa Ana, Cal., 1958 (42)
Carmel, Cal., 1960, 1974 expansion (19)
San Fernando Valley, Sherman Oaks, Cal., 1962 (28)
Portland, Ore., 1962 (32)
Phoenix, Ariz., 1963 (33)
Santa Clara, Cal., 1964 (32)
San Mateo, Cal., 1965 (29)
Del Amo, Torrance, Cal., 1967 (22)
Palm Springs, Cal., 1967 (21)
Walnut Creek, Cal., 1967 (32)
Chicago, Ill., 1971 (138)

LAZARUS Established 1851
Acquired 1929
*Columbus, Ohio (1,283)
Westland, Columbus, 1962, 1974 expansion (213)
Northland, Columbus, 1964 (271)
Eastland, Columbus, 1967 (195)
Richland, Mansfield, Ohio, 1969 (176)

EXHIBIT 1—Concluded

Kingsdale, Upper Arlington, Ohio 1970 (85)

Lima, Ohio, 1971 (166)

Home Store East, Columbus, 1972 (73)

Capri Shop, Columbus, 1973 (34)

Castleton, Indianapolis, Ind., 1973 (312)

Lafayette, Indianapolis, Ind., Spring 1974 (137)

LEVY'S Established 1903
Acquired 1960
*Tucson, Arizona (227)

RALPHS Established 1873
Acquired 1967
67 supermarkets in Greater Los Angeles totaling 2,099,000 square feet; five new markets, an additional 191,000 square feet, to open in 1974. Eight supermarkets in Greater San Francisco totaling 228,000 square feet; four new markets, an additional 130,000 square feet, to open in 1974.

RIKE'S Established 1853
Acquired 1959
*Dayton, Ohio (921)
Kettering, Ohio, 1961 (131)
Salem, Dayton, 1963 (128)
Dayton Mall, Dayton, 1969 (191)
Springfield, Ohio, 1971 (156)

SANGER-HARRIS Established 1857
Acquired 1951
*Dallas, Texas (460)
Highland Park, Dallas, 1949 (33)
Oak Cliff Harris Center, Dallas, 1955 (112)
Preston Center, Dallas, 1957 (212)
Big Town, Dallas, 1959 (113)
Plymouth Park, Irving, Texas 1963 (139)
Six Flags Mall, Arlington, Texas, 1970 (164)
Town East, Dallas, 1972 (168)
Valley View, Dallas, 1973 (200)

SHILLITO'S Established 1830
Acquired 1929
*Cincinnati, Ohio (850)
Tri-County, Cincinnati, 1960 (227)
Western Woods, Cincinnati, 1963 (178)
Kenwood Mall, Cincinnati, 1966 (207)
Beechmont Mall, Cincinnati, 1969 (114)
Oxmoor Center, Louisville, Ky., 1970 (188)
Fayette Mall, Lexington, Ky., 1971 (185)

* Indicates downtown location, ( ) indicates gross square footage.
Source: Annual Report.

Exhibit 2

INDUSTRY TRENDS AND PERFORMANCE OF SELECTED COMPANIES

	Sales ($ billion)			1973 net income		
	1964	*1973*	*Percent included*	*Percent sales*	*Percent equity*	*Percent included from 1964*
National chains						
J. C. Penney	$2.1	$ 6.2	200.3%	3.0%	14.1%	168.1%
Sears	5.7	12.3	114.4	5.5	13.6	107.3
Traditional department stores						
Allied Stores	0.9	1.6	78.9	2.1	9.8	90.3
Associated Dry Goods	0.5	1.2	170.6	3.7	14.1	178.0
Federated Department Stores	1.4	3.0	111.4	3.8	13.3	69.1
R. H. Macy	0.6	1.0	78.9	2.8	10.9	138.8

EXHIBIT 2—Continued

DISCOUNT INDUSTRY TRENDS

	1960	1965	1969	1970	1971	1972
Sales ($ billion)	2.0	13.2	22.2	24.4	26.6	29.0
No. of stores	1,329	3,216	4,655	5,058	5,481	5,928

DISCOUNT COMPANY PERFORMANCE

	Sales ($ million)		Percent included	Stores		EPS	
	1968	1972		1968	1972	1968	1972
Arlan's*	$ 337.0	$ 200.0	− 59%	90	73	2.27	def.
Kresge	1,201.0	3,288.0	+173	273	580	0.46	0.98
Zayre	525.0	939.7	+ 79	131	232	2.10	2.15

GROCERY INDUSTRY TRENDS

	Sales ($ billion)	Profit after tax percent of sales	Number of stores (000)
1966	67.9	1.2	227
1967	72.4	1.0	226
1968	75.9	1.0	227
1969	81.8	0.9	219
1970	88.4	0.9	208
1971	94.5	0.8	205
1972	101.7	0.5	201
1973	113.1	0.8	200

GROCERY COMPANY PERFORMANCE

	Sales ($ million)		Profit after tax percent of sales		EPS	
	1968	1973	1968	1973	1968	1973
National chains						
A&P	$5,436	$6,748	0.8	0.2	1.82	.49
Safeway	3,686	6,774	1.5	1.2	1.10	1.50
Krogers	3,161	4,205	1.1	0.7	2.64	2.22
Regional chains						
Albertsons	420	852	1.2	1.1	0.74	1.45
WinnDixie†	1,082	1,834	2.3	2.1	1.95	2.97

* In May 1973 Arlan's filed a petition for an arrangement under Chapter XI of the Bankruptcy Act.
† WinnDixie 1973 figures are for fiscal 1972.
Sources: Company Annual Reports, *Discount Merchandiser*, and *Progressive Grocer*.

Exhibit 3

FEDERATED DEPARTMENT STORES
Ten-Year Summary

	1973	1972	1971	1970	1969	1968	1967	1966	1965	1964
Operations (dollars in thousands)										
Net sales	$2,962,051	$2,665,148	$2,353,095	$2,091,515	$1,992,669	$1,813,771	$1,680,747	$1,560,663	$1,481,058	$1,401,642
Income before income taxes	224,732	219,033	192,424	160,829	177,291	169,169	162,170	149,684	141,638	134,098
Percent of sales	7.6%	8.2%	8.2%	7.7%	8.9%	9.3%	9.6%	9.6%	9.6%	9.6%
Federal, state, and local income taxes	111,000	110,460	96,218	78,660	91,349	88,899	78,916	73,043	68,186	66,839
Net income	113,732	108,573	96,206	82,169	85,942	80,270	83,254	76,641	73,452	67,259
Percent of sales	3.8%	4.1%	4.1%	3.9%	4.3%	4.4%	5.0%	4.9%	5.0%	4.8%
Dividends paid	47,786	45,997	43,790	43,547	42,430	40,203	35,965	35,423	32,840	31,015
Earnings retained	65,946	62,576	52,416	38,622	43,512	40,067	47,289	41,218	40,612	36,244
Capital expenditures	164,945	116,062	94,100	93,562	102,575	56,918	60,223	55,101	44,133	35,269
Depreciation and amortization	46,929	40,023	34,915	30,443	26,990	24,723	22,392	20,452	19,103	18,493
Taxes other than income taxes	61,781	52,901	45,451	41,386	38,414	34,018	31,000	28,208	26,457	24,516
Per Share of Common Stock										
Net income	$ 2.57	$ 2.46	$ 2.20	$ 1.89	$ 1.98	$ 1.85	$ 1.92	$ 1.77	$ 1.69	$ 1.55
Dividends	1.08	1.04	1.00	1.00	0.97½	0.92½	0.85	0.83¾	0.77½	0.72½
Shareholders' equity (book value)	20.11	18.67	17.18	15.89	15.03	14.08	13.21	12.13	11.24	10.35
Year-End Financial Position (dollars in thousands)										
Accounts receivable	$ 519,582	$ 467,692	$ 434,608	$ 403,176	$ 386,374	$ 345,902	$ 309,848	$ 304,373	$ 283,650	$ 263,679
Inventories	336,815	309,818	276,469	235,746	240,047	210,419	194,783	181,216	161,433	150,106
Cumulative effect of inflation on inventories	66,693	48,608	45,487	43,839	38,345	31,795	24,216	19,997	17,523	16,805
Working capital	377,602	419,568	415,692	395,829	357,103	375,405	362,642	342,972	336,751	297,159
Property and equipment—net	671,608	561,754	488,518	436,725	387,050	328,831	303,900	274,934	244,979	224,025
Long-term debt	116,505	117,623	113,937	112,065	69,531	70,793	72,317	75,657	82,026	62,432
Shareholders' equity	889,352	826,376	755,452	692,474	653,319	612,026	573,512	525,981	487,140	448,666
Return on shareholders' equity	13.3%	13.7%	13.3%	12.2%	13.6%	13.5%	15.1%	15.1%	15.7%	15.5%
Statistics										
Number of department stores at end of year	126	117	110	107	102	97	98	91	87	84
Number of square feet of department store space (in thousands)	27,384	25,592	24,461	23,459	22,595	21,078	20,528	19,369	18,203	17,300
Average number of shares outstanding (in thousands)	44,249	44,214	43,755	43,548	43,500	43,461	43,392	43,376	43,399	43,446

Exhibit 4

FEDERATED DEPARTMENT STORES
1973 Consolidated Statement of Income

	52 weeks ended February 2, 1974	*53 weeks ended February 3, 1973*
Net sales, including leased department sales.......	$2,962,050,636	$2,665,147,985
Rental revenues.............................	4,125,695	4,807,835
	$2,966,176,331	$2,669,955,820
Deduct:		
Cost of goods sold and expenses exclusive of items listed below.............	$2,551,242,781	$2,287,353,643
Taxes other than income taxes..............	61,780,794	52,901,374
Depreciation and amortization..............	46,928,975	40,023,142
Real estate rent expense...................	25,423,154	23,754,191
Maintenance and repairs..................	19,913,477	20,193,749
Retirement expense........................	20,209,265	16,565,384
Interest expense—net.....................	15,946,237	10,131,292
Total costs...........................	$2,741,444,683	$2,450,922,775
Income before income taxes....................	$ 224,731,648	$ 219,033,045
Federal, state, and local income taxes:		
Current................................	$ 103,389,000	$ 101,371,000
Deferred...............................	7,611,000	9,089,000
	$ 111,000,000	$ 110,460,000
Net income..................................	$ 113,731,648	$ 108,573,045
Earnings per share of common stock.............	$2.57	$2.46
Fully diluted earnings per share..............	2.50	2.39

Source: Annual Report.

Exhibit 5

FEDERATED DEPARTMENT STORES
1973 Consolidated Balance Sheet

ASSETS	*February 2, 1974*	*February 3, 1973*
Current assets		
Cash......................................	$ 34,618,142	$ 42,456,152
Accounts receivable.........................	431,944,893	425,702,375
Merchandise inventories......................	336,814,893	309,817,745
Supplies and prepaid expenses.................	12,971,247	11,459,138
Total current assets....................	$ 816,349,175	$ 789,435,410
Other assets		
Deferred tax charges........................	$ 79,963	$ 4,730,386
Property not used in operations—at		
cost, less accumulated depreciation...........	36,321,644	31,152,200
Investment in unconsolidated subsidiaries—		
at equity................................	16,262,744	15,090,722
Miscellaneous.............................	10,206,808	9,438,646
	$ 62,871,159	$ 60,411,954
Property and equipment—Net		
Land......................................	67,077,056	66,301,892
Buildings.................................	373,556,550	306,723,398
Property and equipment.....................	194,652,393	157,576,446
	$ 635,285,999	$ 530,601,736
	$1,514,506,333	$1,380,449,100

LIABILITIES AND SHAREHOLDERS' EQUITY	*February 2, 1974*	*February 3, 1973*
Current liabilities		
Notes payable and long-term debt due		
within one year...........................	$ 35,275,752	$ 20,249,792
Accounts payable and accrued liabilities........	294,229,978	242,343,936
Income taxes, current and deferred............	109,241,297	107,273,520
Total current liabilities.................	$ 438,747,027	$ 369,867,248
Deferred compensation........................	69,902,143	66,582,473
Long-term debt, due after one year..............	116,505,496	117,623,398
Shareholders' equity—44,230,745 and 44,272,471		
common shares outstanding...................	889,351,667	826,375,981
	$1,514,506,333	$1,380,449,100

Source: Annual Report

Exhibit 6

KEY DEPARTMENTS
(Change in percentage of total department store sales)

	*1964–1973**
Smallwares	(3.7%)
Fashion accessories	4.2
Women's ready-to-wear	7.2
Men's and boy's	13.2
Home furnishings	.9
Housewares and appliances	(.9)
Downstairs merchandise	(8.8)
All other departments	(12.1)

DEPARTMENT STORE PROFIT TRENDS
(Change in percentage of total sales)

	*1964–1973**
Gross margin	3.3%
Payroll expense	1.4
Nonpayroll expense	2.2
Pretax profits	(.3)

* Indicates percentage *point* change.
Note: Figures have been disguised, but reflect actual relationships.

Exhibit 7

SELECTED DEPARTMENT STORE BRANCH PRODUCTIVITY

Code number	Sales per sq. ft.
Branches built before 1960	
D7	173
F4	135
Z1	134
P2	124
N6	103
Branches built between 1960 and 1964	
D9	138
R1	158
T2	133
T3	118
X4	115
Branches built between 1965 and 1969	
F6	161
P5	106
V2	130
N8	104
N9	124
Branches built after 1970	
D13	72
F8	90
T7	91
V3	82
B11	105

Note: All figures are for 1972.
Source: Company records. Branch names and locations are disguised.

Exhibit 8

FEDERATED DIVISIONAL PERFORMANCE AND
INDUSTRY PERFORMANCE

Department Stores*

	Federated	Department store industry
Sales per square feet...............	$131	$86
Stock turnover (retail)...............	3.7	3.29
Gross margin‡......................	42.5%	40.5%
Payroll expense....................	17.7%	18.3%
Nonpayroll expense.................	14.8%	15.8%
Pretax income.....................	10.0%	6.4%

Discount Stores*

	Gold Circle	Discount industry
Average size.......................	100,000 sq.ft.	84,300 st.ft.
Sales per store.....................	$7,300,000	$6,700,000
Sales per square feet...............	73	80
Sales per employee.................	$66,124	$68,120
Gross margin......................	26.9%	25.45%
Total expense.....................	23.4%	23.8%
Pretax income.....................	3.5%	1.65%

Grocery Stores†

	Ralphs	Chain supermarkets
Average sales per store.............	$6,500,000	$1,400,000
Gross margin......................	20.4%	20.9%
Total expenses....................	18.4%	20.0%
Total payroll......................	8.3%	11.6%
Total nonpayroll...................	10.1%	8.4%
Profit before taxes.................	2.0%	0.9%
Stock turnover....................	23.1 times	12.7 times

* 1972
† 1973
‡ Gross margin percentage includes service charge (credit) income.
Note: All percents are the percentage of sales. All Federated figures have been disguised, but reflect key relationships.
Source: Company Records, *Progressive Grocer*, *Discount Merchandiser*, NRMA Reports.

Exhibit 9

GOLD CIRCLE ORGANIZATION

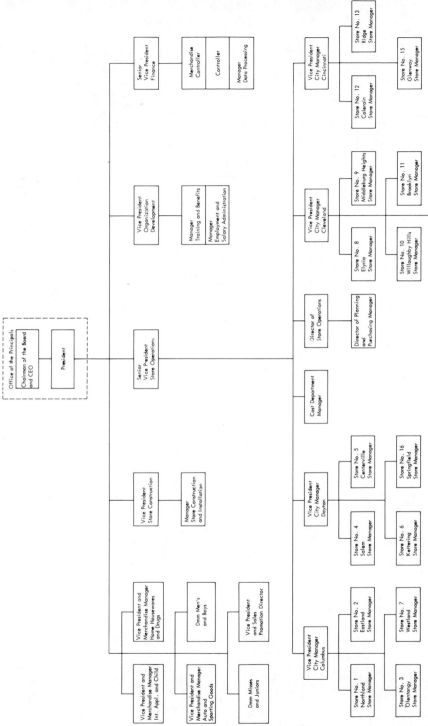

Exhibit 10
GOLD CIRCLE STORE LOCATIONS

GOLD CIRCLE
Established 1967
Hal W. Field, Chairman
Martin B. Clark, President

1   East, Columbus, Ohio, 1968 (118)
2   North, Columbus, 1968 (118)
3   Northwest, Columbus, 1969 (125)
4   East, Dayton, Ohio, 1969 (124)
5   Northwest, Dayton, Ohio, 1969 (120)
6   Southeast, Dayton, Ohio, 1969 (127)
7   West, Columbus, 1970 (135)
8   Elyria, Ohio, 1971 (103)
9   Middleburg Heights, Cleveland, Ohio, 1971 (103)
10 West, Cleveland, 1971 (134)
11 Willoughby Hills, Cleveland, 1971 (134)
12 East, Cincinnati, Ohio, Spring 1973 (130)
13 North, Cincinnati, Spring 1973 (130)
14 North Olmstead, Cleveland, Spring 1973 (130)
15 West, Cincinnati, Fall 1973 (130)
16 Mentor, Ohio, Fall 1973 (130)
17 Springfield, Ohio, Fall 1973 (130)

To Be Opened in 1974
18 East Akron
19 West Akron
20 Tri County (Cincinnati)
21 Bedford (Cleveland)
22 Canton
23 Columbus, Northeast

Exhibit 11

PROJECTED PROFIT AND LOSS STATEMENT, 1976–1980

	No. of stores	Sales ($000)	Pretax (percent sales)	Capital expenditures ($000)	Pretax ROI
Washington, D.C.					
1976...................	3	22,500	(7.8)	32,878*	—
1977...................	6	48,000	(2.3)		—
1978...................	6	53,500	(1.0)		—
1979...................	6	57,322	.4		0.5
1980...................	6	62,037	1.5		2.5
Northern California					
1976...................	4	33,300	(1.6)	41,897†	—
1977...................	11	96,400	(.1)		—
1978...................	11	106,100	0.7		—
1979...................	11	115,800	2.2		2.5
1980...................	11	126,500	3.4		5.5

* Includes $16.1 million incurred in 1975. Does not include $800,000 preopening expenses.
† Includes $14 million incurred in 1975. Does not include $1.2 million preopening expenses.
Note: All figures have been disguised.

Industrial Products, Inc.

ON APRIL 5, 1967, the finance committee of Industrial Products, Inc. approved its Equipment Division's capital request for $5.8 million to build a new plant for FIREGUARD, a line of fire protection equipment. However, in October 1967 Mr. Robert Kendall, Manager of the Chemical Process Department (see Exhibit 1), the department in which FIRE-GUARD was produced, was considering the possibility of killing the expansion project. Divisional pressure for improved departmental earnings and FIREGUARD's continued record of substantial operating losses argued for not using the appropriated capital funds. On the other hand, Kendall was well aware that many people in his department were committed to growing the FIREGUARD business and would be quite upset if the project were killed. The context in which Kendall had to make his decision was the following.

EQUIPMENT DIVISION, INDUSTRIAL PRODUCTS, INC.

Industrial Products, Inc. was founded in 1949 as a producer of refrigeration equipment. Since that time, the company had diversified its activities into areas such as material handling systems, machine tools, heavy industrial equipment, and laboratory instruments. In 1966, the company's sales were in excess of $350 million.

The Equipment Division was the largest of Industrial's divisions measured in terms of sales revenue. In 1966, the Equipment Division's sales were $135.4 million and its net income before taxes was $31.2 million on an investment of $96.5 million. FIREGUARD, the division's new fire protection line, contributed sales of $2.2 million but produced a net loss before taxes of $1.1 million in 1966. However, with forecasted potential sales in excess of $30 million per year and forecasted net income before taxes in excess of $6.0 million per year, FIREGUARD was considered one of the most promising new products in the Equipment Division.

FIREGUARD

In its continuing work on refrigerants, the Equipment Division's Refrigeration Department had developed a number of new plastic materials that exhibited superior fire extinguishing properties. At the same time, the division already produced some of the kind of equipment needed to extinguish fires. Because both the equipment and materials required were readily available in existing businesses, experimental and then commercial sales soon followed. The brand name under which the division developed this business was FIREGUARD.

The division management was highly optimistic concerning FIREGUARD's commercial prospects. Whereas all automatic fire extinction equipment required extensive piping to create a system, FIREGUARD was able to operate with a number of physically independent modules. Thus the size of a FIREGUARD system depended principally on the number of module units in the area to be protected.

The source of FIREGUARD's advantage lay in the chemical process used to extinguish fires. The Equipment Division's scientists had discovered a relatively inexpensive chemical substance they called NO-OX that expanded with explosive speed when exposed to air, reacting with the oxygen to free a heavy inert gas. The fire extinction properties of the gas were immediately recognized as superb.

The attack on the fire protection and extinguishing market called for early sales of single module equipment to the "traditional" market for portable extinguishers (local governments, schools, fire departments, industrial plants, commercial offices). Sales of automatic fire protection systems to the same users would follow. Finally, the strategy called for expanding primary demand by eventually introducing automatic residential systems. Exhibit 2 shows sales of the portable units from 1961 to 1966. The automatic systems market was entered for the first time during 1966.

The FIREGUARD business was the responsibility of Mr. Robert Kendall, Manager of the Equipment Division's Chemical Process Department (see the organization chart, Exhibit 1). The department manufactured and sold equipment for chemical manufacturing processes. In 1960, the division's General Manager, Mr. Lon Fischer, had become concerned with the quality of performance in the manufacturing and construction of chemical process equipment while it was part of the general refrigeration area and had reorganized the activity in a new department—chemical processes—so that "the chemical phase of the business could get separate attention." Because FIREGUARD was a "chemical" business, it was moved into the Chemical Process Department at the time of its formation.[1]

The Equipment Division's assessment of the market was described by George Kramer, Product Manager for FIREGUARD.

> When we went into FIREGUARD we thought we knew a great deal about the fire protection business. However, we discovered that we

---

[1] The NO-OX business remained in the Refrigeration Department. The Chemical Process Department "purchased" the chemical from the Refrigeration Department at a negotiated "market" price.

knew very little and our customers knew less. They couldn't have cared less about the product. They were protected because they had to be according to the law or the insurance company. So we have had to study the job for the customer. The result has been that we have had a big learning and education program.

Commenting on Mr. Kramer's description, Mr. Kendall observed:

We got into the FIREGUARD business because we knew how to build some equipment and we had superior extinguishing materials. In fact we know how to build the containers very well. We make them at our Akron, Ohio factory. But we're still learning how to put together the support equipment.

The difficulty in engineering has been to learn the requirements of different applications. We are marketing a system, not equipment, and not extinguishing material. Thus, most of our learning has to be in the field in a sequence of trial and error steps.

Out of the first 300 units, we had to take back 100 over time. Now it's 200 out of 3,000. The engineers are still worried: they can explain what happens after the fact but the problem of responding in a controlled way to undesired fires or explosions is still there.

The other aspect of FIREGUARD planning has been market definition. It has been going on for five or six years as we have tried to move from fire departments to industrial plants, to office building systems, to homeowners. Each area is a different problem in the field. Different costs can be cut, different customers have to be educated, and in some instances different parts of our division have to be educated.

For example, we have had an endless series of arguments with our automatic systems design group trying to define what fire protection was. When we finally got it settled, we found that we needed a larger container unit.

However, the decision to build a larger container posed an important facility problem for us. We knew we were going to have to expand because FIREGUARD was already using 250,000 out of 750,000 production man-hours available at Akron. By 1970, the forecasts indicated that FIREGUARD would require 650,000 man-hours. And our other lines were growing.

Add to this the problem of the large containers and it's clear we needed a new facility. We really weren't up to handle them in the existing facility. Therefore, I asked Steve Matthews, facilities planner for FIREGUARD, to study the Akron plant and make recommendations.

Steve Matthews' career at Industrial Products had begun at Akron. He left the company only to rejoin it later to work on a task force which introduced a new data processing system to the Cleveland facility. His performance on that job led to his assignment in February 1966, to head a team put together to study the organization and operation of the Equipment Division's activities at their Cleveland and Akron locations. This assignment was later expanded to cover a study in depth of the FIREGUARD facilities at Akron. Matthews commented on his approach to the study.

My problem was to get a feel for each of Akron's businesses out of marketing. I wanted a definition of the way we did business in each of these markets. It was not easy. For example, in FIREGUARD, George

Kramer's forecast was the greatest problem. It was absurdly conservative. I needed to know everything about the business, the way it was going to grow, the role of the parts business, the nature of customer service, and exactly how the business was going to be run so we could design a facility that would meet these needs.

We started the study on the assumption that the business would expand at Akron (location) because it appeared economic to do so. It seemed that the question of relocation costs, the problem of building a new building, and the location of the market indicated that we stay at Akron.

So we were evaluating existing facilities in the light of the markets of 1970 and beyond. If our product managers didn't give us the forecast, we interpolated as best we could. We wanted to build a facility which would enable us to do business the right way in 1970.

Matthews had found the major elements of his problems to be (1) Akron was poorly run, the data available were poor and the manpower available to gather data not always adequate; (2) problems at Akron resulted from the way in which the relationship between engineering and production were organized, an issue outside the scope of the study; (3) many of the study group's findings reflected unfavorably on Akron management and therefore raised political problems; and (4) the group came to feel that the need was for a "mass production" type activity although Akron was typically "job shop" oriented. As a result, the facility being planned looked as if it would be a radical departure from existing facilities both in terms of physical design and the mode of operation.

In fact, by November 1966, when Matthews was to meet with Kendall for a final review of the FIREGUARD project, he had been ready to recommend a new plant in the Carolinas.[2] It was Matthews' judgment that it would be easier to implement the critical nonfacility[3] part of the FIREGUARD expansion project in the new location. He had explained to Kendall that "failure to undertake and effectively implement nonfacility programs would negate the effects of the proposed physical facility plan."

The last part of the meeting with Kendall held November 15 had concerned the size of the capital investment and its timing. An excerpt from that conversation is reproduced below:

MATTHEWS: . . . And, I may be wrapping it up too soon, but we strongly recommend going to South Carolina. The existing manufacturing facilities are theoretically adequate to meet the FIREGUARD market demands through 1969. But, practically, we believe that conditions demand the acceleration of this project. Expanded production to meet 1967 and 1968 forecasts plus inventory build-up in anticipation of moving the production

---

[2] While Matthews formally reported to the Akron plant manager, he kept in close contact with Kendall throughout the FIREGUARD study. The Akron plant manager attended many of these meetings and was aware of Matthews' assessment of the Akron facility and its management. However, since the demand for Akron's other products was growing and their production caused less problems than FIREGUARD's, the Akron plant manager was not upset at the prospect of losing FIREGUARD.

[3] Accounting and information systems, inventory and production control systems, and material handling systems.

lines will be very difficult to achieve under the existing conditions. The new factory will be needed as soon as it can be constructed. We prefer to schedule the physical construction program to fit into the program for an orderly transfer of personnel, equipment and procedures. Systems and procedures are to be completely worked out before this move is made. Our schedule calls for completion of the plant in the late fall of 1968, assuming that authorization to proceed is obtained in the first quarter of 1967.

KENDALL: There is no way we can invest incrementally?

MATTHEWS: I don't really think so.

KENDALL: What are we going to do when they won't give us $5.8 million?

MATTHEWS: You either bet on a business or you don't. You either believe the forecasts or you don't.

KENDALL: What if you believe half a forecast?

MATTHEWS: You couldn't build half a plant. You save some, but not a lot. What's a half? What forecast are you going to hang your hat on?

KENDALL: Half: I'll commit myself for half but want to be able to make the whole thing. Can't you build one plant for 1971 and then another just like it for 1975? Or what about some added subcontracting? Why can't we do more subcontracting since our manufacturing process isn't that unique?

MATTHEWS: As for two plants, you put machines in for the product and you don't need more than one, even for peak volume. As for subcontracting, our make or buy analysis shows that if we realize forecasted sales, we can improve our return by manufacturing some parts that we now subcontract.

KENDALL: Well, yes, but if we really don't have a proprietary position in terms of knowledge and so on, why can't we subcontract our expansion in this area?

MATTHEWS: The trouble with subcontracting is that you never make your delivery promises. It's just impossible to get yourself organized so that you can produce the kind of customer service you need.

Bob, I know your problem. You're thinking about our original estimate of $1.9 million back in June. The original facility was just a factory. This is also a warehouse and a service center. And given the nonfacility expenditures for systems, the investment per unit of capacity is the same as the original proposal.

Kendall had accepted Matthews' argument and arranged to have the FIREGUARD project presented to a meeting of the Equipment Division's executive committee[4] on December 16. Matthews began that meeting by describing the basic strategic assumptions of the FIREGUARD business. He described it as "a business selling hardware at a profit, based on warehousing, service, and parts." He noted that at the rate the business was growing, by 1969, they would be handling five million parts. That meant, he argued, that FIREGUARD was a large-volume production-oriented operation rather than the traditional job shop kind of business typical of Akron.

Excerpts from the meeting included the exchange below:

BRIGGS (Gen Mgr.):   The rumor mill had it that the new facility at Akron was going to cost only $2 million. Why is it that your proposal is so expensive?

---

[4] The divisional executive committee consisted of the division's general manager, assistant general manager, department managers, and top functional managers.

KENDALL: The original facility the people were talking about was simply a plant for the large containers. This is a much larger operation with many more products.

MATTHEWS: Also, the original facility was just a factory. Not only are there more products but this is a warehouse and service center.

A substantial discussion of labor costs and related problems led to the question of systems.

HUGHES (Mgr. Eng.): What about systems, do you have any allowance for the cost of all these systems you are installing?

MATTHEWS: You have $175,000 project costs and $185,000 engineering and that ought to cover it.

HUGHES: That's not enough, how many programmers do you have?

MATTHEWS: Five, I think.

HUGHES: I think that is low. We had 10 programmers at East St. Louis [an earlier project] if I am not mistaken.

GOLDEN (Asst. Gen. Mgr.): How many accountants do you have?

Matthews looked the figure up in his back-up notebook. He explained that the nature of the FIREGUARD operation was such that it would produce for a full warehouse rather than on the basis of meeting customer demand. Therefore, the demand on accounting was different from traditional equipment businesses.

GOLDEN: I think traditionally we have had our overrun (spent more than budget) on systems and accounting.

MATTHEWS: I think I understand your point, Bill, and we will do our best to take care of it.

After this discussion, Matthews presented the project summary shown below.

	1967	1968	1969	1970	1975
			(millions of dollars)		
Sales.............................	$ 3.6	$ 9.0	$17.7	$24.5	$41.5
Net income before taxes...........	(1.1)*	(.4)*	.8*	3.9	7.5
ROI..............................	—	—	7.4	26.0	32.0
Fixed investment.................	1.0†	1.2†	4.3†	6.9†	8.0‡
Working capital..................	2.5	4.7	6.5	8.1	15.5
Total investment.................	3.5	5.9	10.8	15.0	23.5

* Includes $1.1 million for noncapital items associated with the move: i.e., costs of transfers, lay-offs, training, equipment moving, and project management.

† Will provide space to satisfy forecasted sales through 1975 and equipment to satisfy forecasted sales through 1970.

‡ $1.1 million additional equipment will be needed to satisfy 1975 forecasted sales.

On April 5, 1967, Briggs presented the FIREGUARD project to the corporate finance committee. While questions of subcontracting, poor current performance, and future ROI were raised, the general feeling of the group was that the project was a good one and the business very promising. Therefore, after a short discussion, the project was approved.

SECOND THOUGHTS

However, Kendall was still uneasy about the FIREGUARD project. Matthews argued that the future market for FIREGUARD products was large and lucrative. Yet the earnings record of FIREGUARD since its inception in 1961 had been poor. Moreover, as sales for the product grew, so did the losses.

· Kendall's concern was intensified when the review of his department's 1968 Business Plan was conducted in October 1967.[5] Divisional executives had expressed concern with the department's recent earnings record (see Exhibit 4). Moreover, Kendall was well aware that the corporation had specifically asked about the FIREGUARD business the previous fall. Since corporate requests for detailed information on an individual business were quite unusual, Kendall knew that FIREGUARD was in the limelight and that most likely there was pressure on the division officers to see that the business' performance improved.

In an effort to secure some guidance in this matter, Kendall asked Mike Richards, Corporate Director of Planning, to discuss FIREGUARD with him. While Richards reflected corporate thinking he did not represent it. Therefore, the meeting between Kendall and Richards was in the nature of "informal advice" rather than "formal corporate review."

The October 27 meeting began with Kendall expressing his concerns to Richards.

KENDALL: Mike, Briggs is putting pressure on me to raise the department's profits. But if FIREGUARD goes ahead with the approved expansion, earnings are not going to get much better. On the other hand, Matthews has some convincing arguments for FIREGUARD's market potential. To tell the truth, I'm perplexed.

RICHARDS: Well, . . . from my point of view, FIREGUARD doesn't fit with the rest of our products. We make machine tools, material handling systems, and refrigeration equipment. We enjoy a close relationship with our customers so that we can understand and help solve their technical problems.

On the other hand, FIREGUARD is a mass-produced, standard design product. Moreover, compared to our existing product line, FIREGUARD is mass marketed. That means problems of distribution and service that we haven't faced before.

KENDALL: OK, but FIREGUARD's got a fantastic future potential. Its sales in 1975 could easily exceed the total department's sales today.

RICHARDS: Look, I'm not arguing that you drop FIREGUARD completely. I'm merely saying that you don't really know how to market or produce the

---

[5] The Equipment Division's Business Plan attempted to answer the questions "What will happen to our products next year and the year after that?" and "What do we plan to do about it?". Departmental Plans were reviewed each fall by the division. (Performance against current plan was reviewed quarterly.) This plan review was a formal meeting in which departmental managers made presentations of their Business Plan to divisional officers. Officers were free to make comments and often did.

Plans were typically concerned with market size, market share, product volume, product price, and profit. Return on investment was sometimes used as a tool to measure the quality of a "business," but the business plans did not include specific investment planning. At most, a crude forecast of "capital requirement" was included.

product very well. If I were you, I would be inclined to concentrate on improving FIREGUARD's profits and then grow the business after you've learned how to run it profitably.

KENDALL: That's easier said than done. We've already asked for and received approval for a new plant. The division will not be too pleased if I now say that FIREGUARD should not be expanded for a while. Moreover, I'm sure Matthews will hit the roof.

RICHARDS: Mike, you asked for my opinion and I've given it to you. I think it's better to retrench now rather than sacrifice current earnings to a project that has yet to make a profit.

Following his conversation with Richards, Kendall decided to speak with Matthews about the FIREGUARD project. Kendall began the meeting by explaining his concern over FIREGUARD's past and current performance and expressing pessimism about its future performance. To support this view, Kendall used many of Richards' arguments. Matthews responded quickly.

MATTHEWS: First, it seems to me that the issue is closed since the corporation approved our request for capital funds. Moreover I think their decision was a wise one. It takes money to build the marketing and systems capabilities we need to take advantage of the FIREGUARD opportunity. If we don't spend money today, we'll surely fail in the years to come.

Anyway, we've carefully timed our expenditures for capital and noncapital items so that we can cut back if the assumed market doesn't develop. For example, by December we will have ordered about $1.1 million in equipment and spent about $160,000 on noncapital items. Yet since the penalty for cancelling the equipment order is only $290,000, our total exposure as of the beginning of 1968 will be $450,000. (Cancellation of equipment was not allowed after January 1, 1968.) Moreover, while the entire capital budget of $5.8 million will be irrevocably committed by the end of 1968, we will have spent only $650,000 of our $1.1 million noncapital budget by that time. In fact, we wouldn't spend our entire noncapital budget until September 1969.

Also, even if FIREGUARD doesn't make it, you've always got a new plant even though most of the machinery is specially designed for the FIREGUARD product line. (The plant represented 70% of the capital budget.)

But this isn't going to happen. FIREGUARD has an enormous business potential. Moreover, the division will make as much on the NO-OX as it does on the equipment. But we both know that FIREGUARD is a new kind of product for the Equipment Division. It depends on the sales and servicing of hardware. This coupled with distribution are major factors to cope with. It's just going to take time and money to develop the capabilities we need.

KENDALL: But we haven't done very well in the six years we've been trying to date.

MATTHEWS: That's because we've been producing at Akron. Our new plant in South Carolina will solve many of our problems. Bob, it takes time to develop a new business. The payoff doesn't come right away.

KENDALL: Steve, that all sounds very good but have you looked at Kramer's monthly reports for the first seven months of this year (see Exhibit 5)? After six years it still sounds as if we just began.

MATTHEWS: Even a great business can do poorly if it's mismanaged. We haven't been coordinating design with production. We haven't had a production line suitable for high volume manufacturing. We haven't had adequate part standardization. We haven't put nearly enough money into developing the needed management and production control systems. Bob, I could go on like this for 10 minutes, but you know these problems as well as I do. How do you expect to make money given this situation? And you certainly can't blame Kramer for a manufacturing problem.

KENDALL: You've got a point, but then where the hell does Kramer get his forecasts? Doesn't he take the production constraint into consideration?

MATTHEWS: OK, you've got a point. However, I don't think that should influence your view of the future of FIREGUARD. A lot of people[6] here have spent a lot of time on this project. We have finally got it out from under Akron and have the resources to make it. I don't see how you can even consider changing it at this late date.

---

[6] While Matthews and about a dozen other men had spent over a year and half on the project, the possibility of moving the operation to South Carolina had been kept highly confidential because of its potential impact on the Akron work force. Thus, in addition to the people planning the facility, only the top division and corporate officers were aware of the decision to move the FIREGUARD production operation.

However, while the construction of the new plant had not begun by the time of the Matthews-Kendall meeting, some equipment had been ordered and options had been taken on a piece of land. The cost of cancelling the equipment order and the land option would be $105,000. Moreover, $114,500 had already been spent for non-capital items.

Exhibit 1

INDUSTRIAL PRODUCTS, INC.

Equipment Division

Partial Organization Chart as of March 1966

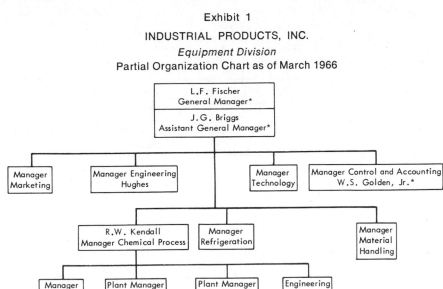

* After the promotion of Mr. Fischer to a position as a corporate officer, in July 1966, Mr. Briggs was made Division General Manager and Mr. Golden, Assistant General Manager.

Exhibit 2

INDUSTRIAL PRODUCTS, INC.

Sales of Portable FIREGUARD Units

1961–1966

(in number of units)

1961	400
1962	820
1963	1,450
1964	1,985
1965	3,775
1966	4,362

Exhibit 3

INDUSTRIAL PRODUCTS, INC.

Forecasted Sales for FIREGUARD
(millions of dollars)

Date of forecast	1964	1965	1966	1967	1968
September 1964................	$1.1	$2.5	$4.3		$13.3
July 1965....................		2.2	4.2	$8.1	
July 1966....................			3.4	4.8	9.2
April 1967...................				3.6	

Actual Sales and Earnings
for FIREGUARD
(millions of dollars)

Year	1961	1962	1963	1964	1965	1966
Sales........................	$ .20	$ .41	$ .73	$ 1.0	$ 1.9	$ 2.2
Net income before taxes						
Actual.....................	(.05)	(.15)	(.38)	(.45)	(.8)	(1.1)
Plan					(.3)	.1

Exhibit 4

INDUSTRIAL PRODUCTS, INC.

Chemical Process Department Sales and Income
(millions of dollars)

	1960	1961	1962	1963	1964	1965	1966
Sales........................	$ 12.4	$13.4	$15.1	$16.2	$17.8	$20.4	$23.2
Net income before taxes........	(.50)	.04	.75	1.72	2.3	3.0	3.1

Exhibit 5

INDUSTRIAL PRODUCTS, INC.

Product Manager's Written Comments on the Monthly
Progress Reports for FIREGUARD

January 1967: Equipment sales are 49% of plan because of large factory backlog ($790,000 on 1/31/66 from $439,000 on 12/31/65).

February 1967: Total equipment shipments are only 46% of plan. While Akron backlog has risen $500,000 this year, part of this is the customary seasonal build-up. It appears we may well be 20% below plan.

March 1967: Total shipments continue to lag with year-to-date sales at 50% of plan, up only 4% from February. We continue to have new equipment production difficulties as represented by a backlog of orders at Akron $850,000. Backlog as a result of shipments withheld due to production difficulties is $450,000 leaving sales to date substantially below plan as reflected by the latest yearly forecast.

April 1967: Sales continue to lag due to a continuing sales failure to penetrate the commercial market. Automatic systems sales have been delayed due to a lack of production of the new sensing device. Year-to-date total sales have improved 7% from March due to heavy overseas shipments. This foreign business is accomplished at significantly lower margins accounting for the continuing higher manufacturing cost versus sales.

May 1967: Sales continue to lag as reported in April with only slight improvement (0.4%). Equipment backlog is $725,000, about $300,000 above normal for sales to date. All costs to date are in line with the latest forecast except for development where there will be an overrun of $120,000 for 160% of plan due to automatic systems problems.

June 1967: The above listed low sales have been reflected in our 1968 Business Plan. Our entry into the industrial systems market has been set back at least one year for lack of satisfactory sensing equipment and is reflected in our 1968 Business Plan by a 94% reduction in plan sales in this area.

July 1967: The high manufacturing costs were due to accounting errors at Akron. One group of costs was cleared prior to sales clearing. Another group was cleared to cost of product when it should have been transferred to an inventory account. When these are corrected in August, the net effect will be to increase our August gross margin by about $75,000.

Strategy Revisited or Strategy with a Grain of Salt

PRESIDENT: Waiter, that takes care of the drinks; we'll wait a while before ordering dinner.

Now, look, professor, you have been working on us all day, and I think we at least begin to understand what you are talking about when you ask us about strategy. I think it is time we turned the tables a bit. I will be frank and say that I think the whole idea is just one big fat platitude. You guys at Harvard always think things to death. Aren't there any tough, hungry doers left? Look, we have got a guy in our industrial division who never got past high school and probably couldn't even read Andrews on corporate strategy—which I have, incidentally—and I don't think I'd want him to. He may not have a lot of smooth reasons for why he does what he does, but I do know he's got a lot of crust and a lot of gall which he uses to get in to see people that would not otherwise see him, and he sells a terrific lot of salt for us. Our problem is the same as everyone else has, and it shows up particularly when we deal with your graduates, if I may say so. That is, how do we get people off their dime and out doing something instead of sitting around worrying all the problems to death?

Another problem I have is that I think committing myself and the company to any such idea would completely tie my hands when it came to responding to new opportunities that are always coming up. Again, in our industrial division, we have got some specialists in salt dispensing. It's kind of a complicated history, but we have found ourselves as a result of this activity owning a patent on a new solenoid principle. Now when we got that patent, we began to be swamped with inquiries from all kinds of industries, because if the thing performed the way it is supposed to it would solve problems that a whole lot of people seem to have. Now, it seems to me that if I was wedded to some notion of strategy or image, we'd throw that opportunity away. It sure isn't "our business," whatever that means.

TREASURER: Let me take a couple of whacks too, because that solenoid example brings to mind a more general problem. We have been investigating quite intensively different capital budgeting systems. Of course, if we do anything with the solenoid, we have to make an appropriation, but of course it gets thrown into the hopper with all the other appropriations we might make. Now, as it is, we are a national and international company; we mine salt, we evaporate salt, and we sell it as a food product to consumers and to processors—canners, bakers, and the like—and we sell it on contract to chemical companies where it is the raw input in chlorine manufacture which in turn is the basic process for a major segment of the chemical industry, and we sell it on a bid basis to government agencies for ice control. The chemical business involves not only a real tough competitive situation, but the sales are negotiated on a long-term relationship basis, frequently involving the top officers of the companies. Of course, we are also selling to farmers and to a lot of other users. In short, we're already in about every kind of market you can think of.

Now, what I want to know is why we can't solve these so-called strategic problems simply by a good capital budgeting procedure. What does the idea offer that adds anything to a good hard look, project by project, at the different uses we might put our capital to?

ASSISTANT TO THE PRESIDENT: Well, why confine it to capital budgeting? There are a lot of other things going on which meet the same kind of purpose. This consensus-on-what-we're-trying-to-do and consistency-in-the-way-we-go-about-it idea seems to ignore a lot of things that have been happening. Take as one example the possibilities for information and control that a good size computer offers. I have been very interested in the hordes of articles about computers in the *Harvard Business Review*. Those authors say that with the computer you can simulate all the operations of a business, see all the interdependence of actions and decisions, get all the feedback you need, and keep everything going on a really integrated and efficient basis. Why couldn't you tie something like that in with a good capital budgeting procedure and solve most of your problems of consistent operating implementation of what you are trying to do?

Or, for that matter, there's been a lot of work in management science, and I am particularly interested in these sequential decision models where you plan a course of action which makes a series of small moves that gain information and then use the information in making the next move. Why isn't it better to recognize that you don't know what the future holds, that you can't really predict with accuracy, and work out a program like that? It seems to me that your strategy concept involves making a terrific commitment on pretty shaky information.

ADMINISTRATIVE VICE PRESIDENT: Well, believe it or not, I read those journals, too, but mathematics, computers, and that stuff I leave to these fellows. I do, however, pay quite a bit of attention to these management philosophers and that stuff which comes from the behavioral sciences, whatever they are. While you are answering these fellows who think that numbers and scientific method can do everything, I am going to be listening from that side.

It seems to me that our history indicates that this thing you call strategy only can come from the intuitive judgment of a strong leader. Don, here, [indicating the president], has had the imagination and foresight which has enabled us to go from a small company, specializing in consumer salt, strong only in one region and possessing only one mine, to where we are today. He did it, I think he will agree, by constant needling and pushing to get the rest of the organization to move. There wasn't any particular "we stuff," and I will be frank to say that if there had been, it would have been one of these pretty stagnant committee-type operations. So I guess I come back to what he said about that fellow in our sales force, only I would apply it to him. It was his insight and imagination, plus twenty years of constant needling, that got us where we are.

So, I guess my questions are these: How would a company that did not have such a concept develop and apply one? Also, what beneficial results would you expect to follow from a program to develop and implement a strategy, and finally, why do you think they would follow and what evidence have you got that they would be so beneficial? I guess that about sums up all our questions.

PROFESSOR: Waiter, another round please, and make mine a double!

Index of cases

This book has been set in 9 point and 8 point Primer, leaded 2 points. Part numbers, part titles, and chapter titles are set in 18 point Scotch Roman. The size of the type is 27 x 46½ picas.

tween 1970 and 1980. In assessing opportunities in the area, it was determined that the generally low-income area in the District of Columbia and the high-income area in Montgomery County would not be conducive to successful Gold Circle locations. Sewer and building moratoriums in many of the suburban areas restricted opportunities for store locations. In addition, Washington, D.C. was an extremely competitive area for discount stores. Between 1969 and 1974, total discount store square footage per capita had increased from 0.91 to 1.75. The same figure for the Northern California area was only 1.2. The high level of competitive activity, high land costs, and zoning problems limited Gold Circle's opportunities in the Washington area. Nevertheless, six sites had been identified as possible site locations for 1976 and 1977.

Exhibit 11 summarizes the basic financial dimensions of the Washington expansion. Total capital needs were estimated at over $32 million. Sales were projected to grow from $22.5 million in 1976 to $62 million by 1980. By the fifth year of operations, the pretax ROI of the Washington region was expected to be 2.3 percent.

Northern California

Gold Circle's plans for Northern California included locations in the San Jose, "East Bay," and Sacramento areas. The six counties in these areas were expected to grow by 20 percent, from 3.49 million to 4.19 million people, a slower rate than the Washington, D.C. area, but a larger population base. Competitive activity in the Northern California region was not as intense and good locations were more readily available. As a result, Area Research had identified 11 locations for Gold Circle stores to be built in 1976 and 1977.

Although the Northern California expansion called for almost twice as many stores as in Washington, total capital requirements were only 25 percent higher. The table below illustrates that this was mostly due to lower land costs. By 1980, the Northern California region was expected to produce sales of over $125 million and operate at a pretax return on investment of 5.5 percent (see Exhibit 11).

CAPITAL EXPENDITURES
($000)

	Number of stores	Land, building, parking lot*	Furniture, fixtures	Total
Washington, D.C.	6	29,157	3,721	32,878
Northern California	11	34,899	6,998	41,897

* Land costs are "asking prices" reduced by a 10 percent "negotiation factor." Construction costs are estimated to increase by 5 percent per year from 1973 levels.

Organization and evaluation

In evaluating new market opportunities, Gold Circle's management was concerned with the population base, the competitive situation, the

With six years of operating experience, management felt that Gold Circle had been thoroughly exposed to the discount business and had developed the organization and systems needed to be successful in the competitive discount field. In fact, 1973 had been Gold Circle's best year with sales 46 percent higher than in 1972 and pretax profits up almost 90 percent.

The 1973 pretax profit rate of 4.5 percent was high by industry standards and many company officials felt that the division would eventually operate at close to 5.5 percent return on sales. One reason for this expectation was that the Columbus stores were operating at profit rates about twice as high as in the other cities. It was believed that the other stores would soon match the Columbus performance. Other financial goals included five stock turns per year and a pretax return on investment of 15 percent.

Table 6 below, illustrates the growth of Gold Circle:

Table 6

	Sales ($000)	Pretax income from operations		Number of stores	Capital charges and pre-opening expenses ($000)	Divisional investment ($000)	Pretax ROI* percent
		($000)	Percent sales				
1973.........	$125,660	$5,654	4.5%	17	$2,648	$51,839	5.8%
1972.........	85,877	3,005	3.5	11	1,382	39,577	4.1
1971.........	65,100	1,627	2.5	11	1,530	32,436	0.3
1970.........	41,156	617	1.5	7	n.a.	20,384	—
1969.........	25,343	228	0.9	6	n.a.	13,336	—

* Pretax ROI was computed by subtracting capital charges and pre-opening expenses from pretax income from operations, and dividing by divisional investment.
Note: n.a.—not available.

PROPOSED EXPANSION

Since 1967, studies had been made periodically of opportunities for Gold Circle outside of the Ohio region. As performance continued to improve in 1972 and 1973, the studies began to attract serious consideration. In late 1972, Gold Circle asked Federated's Area Research Department to study the Chicago, Florida, Houston, San Francisco, and Washington markets. By September 1973, the choice had been narrowed down to Washington and San Francisco, Gold Circle commissioned in-depth analyses of these markets, and began to develop operations, merchandising, and organization plans for entering either market. By the spring of 1974, a formal proposal evaluating both markets and requesting expansion into the San Francisco market, was submitted to Federated's top management.

Washington, D.C.

The population of Washington, D.C. metropolitan area was expected to grow by 25.5 percent from 2.86 million to 3.58 million people, be-

Concept of Gold Circle

To compete successfully in the discount industry, Gold Circle built its business around several concepts. These are listed below with management's comments on their significance:

Organization

We have as good an organization as any regional discount operation anywhere and work hard to develop people at all levels. We pay our people better, and that's the basis for our ability to attract and keep good people.

Market penetration

We attempt to be important in a market. We have four stores in Columbus and we are building a fifth. In Cleveland there are six stores with a seventh coming on board. We do not want to further fragment the markets we enter, but to blanket them.

Merchandising

We merchandise a cut above K–Mart and the traditional discount stores in terms of fashion and quality. Our price points are generally a point above K–Mart. In terms of better fashion merchandise, we make every effort to have the right kinds of goods with the right looks.

Store operations

We try to create an appealing store environment and to run cleaner and better organized stores. Also, we make great efforts in the EDP and logistics areas. An efficient handling of goods is very important in a chain type of operation.

Organization

Hal Field, 44, and Martin Clark, 51, the division principals at Gold Circle, had M.B.A.s from the Harvard Business School. Clark joined Federated's Burdine's division (Miami) in 1957 as a divisional merchandise manager. He served next as general merchandise manager for all soft lines and finally as president from 1968 to 1972, the year he joined Gold Circle. Hal Field's background had been exclusively in operations. He had started with Lazarus in 1962 as assistant property manager, advancing to vice president for administration in charge of long-range planning, real estate, control, and finance.

Exhibit 9 is an organization chart of Gold Circle. Store operations were organized by city, with each store manager responsible for the profits of his store. The merchandising staff was centralized in Columbus with each buyer responsible for the gross margin and sales of his line of goods.

Operating results[7]

Since its opening in 1968, Gold Circle's sales had grown from $10 million to about $125 million in 1973. Stores were opened in Dayton, Ohio, in 1969 and Cleveland and Cincinnati in 1971 and 1973. Exhibit 10 summarizes the physical growth of the division.

---

[7] All data on Gold Circle in the remainder of the case have been disguised. Key relationships have been preserved.

At the same time, we have always felt that our stock-in-trade is knowledge of customers and how to serve them—and that kind of expertise should prove as useful in discounting as it has been in our traditional operations. In addition, we think we may be able to bring to the field a measure of the department store's fashion sophistication.

Hal Field had previously been vice president for administration at Federated's Lazarus department store division in Columbus. He was appointed project leader on the planning of Gold Circle's first store; in fact much of the early development of Gold Circle had been done under the auspices of Lazarus. When the discount division was formally established in late 1967, Field was named chairman and Ed Karp and Ken Harris left Lazarus to become the merchandising manager and head of operations at Gold Circle. The rest of the division's management was hired from other discount companies.

The discount industry

Gold Circle's management acknowledged that they had entered the discount industry at just about the time that total industry growth had begun to slow down. Nevertheless, they felt that the poor performance of their competitors offered opportunities for Gold Circle to gain at the expense of the industry's "weak sisters." Hal Field commented:

> Throughout the 1960s there were some phenomenal growth stories in this industry—Arlan's, Interstate, Zayre's, K–Mart, Woolco. It's amazing how few of these companies have been successful over the long pull. Arlan's is now reorganizing and Interstate is the largest Chapter 11 reorganization in retail history.

Gold Circle's management felt that the current problems in the discount industry were no different than they had been for several years. The following were cited as key industry problems:

1. An inability to increase sales in mature stores.
2. Inept management, particularly in store operations, logistics, and EDP.
3. An assumption that top management could improve results without first building an organization.
4. Poor market development and store expansion strategy.

Hal Field commented on the expansion strategy and general problems of other discounters:

> The discount stores have been so anxious to enter new markets that they haven't taken the time to develop market penetration. Columbus is an example of this. In the late 1950s Arlan's built a discount store here and it was a great success. They never built another store, though, and now they're no longer in business here. During the 1960s Zayre's and Topps also entered the market, but now they're leaving too.
>
> You know, since 1965 there has been tremendous uncertainty in the minds of consumers as to what they wanted a discount store to be. The successful stores have had to define an explicit concept from the point of view of the consumers.